# CHAPTER 12
# Psychological Disorders
# DSM-5 UPDATE

*Experience Psychology, 2e*

Laura A. King

# 12 Psychological Disorders

## *The Courage to Wake Up Every Morning*

B ill Garrett was a freshman scholarship recipient at Johns Hopkins University when he began to hear strange voices inside his head. Those voices told him profoundly disturbing things: that he was stupid and fat, that soap and shampoo were toxic, that his father had poisoned the family dog, and that his grandmother was putting human body parts in his food. Bill withdrew into this terrifying inner world. Eventually, he was diagnosed with schizophrenia, a disorder characterized by disturbed thought. Failing in his classes, this previously excellent student (and track and lacrosse star) was forced to return home.

Bill's mother understood her son's experience when she found herself at a support group for families of individuals with schizophrenia. At one point, surrounded by 10 people all speaking to her at once, she was overwhelmed by the confusing cacophony. Afterward she told her son, "You have to be the most courageous person. You wake up every morning" (M. Park, 2009). Bill had told her that sleep was his only escape from the ceaseless terror of hearing those voices.

At home, Bill was constantly faced with evidence of his previous successes. Looking at his trophies and awards, he said, "Mom, I was on top of the world. Now I'm in the gutter." His mother, however, has encouraged him to think of his disorder not as a sign of failure but as an opportunity to use the gifts he still possesses—symbolized by those past accomplishments—to fight for the rights and well-being of individuals who, like him, find their lives turned upside-down by psychological disorders.

This chapter explores the meaning of the word *abnormal* as it relates to psychology. We examine various theoretical approaches to understanding abnormal behavior and survey the main psychological disorders. We delve into how stigma plays a role in the lives of individuals struggling with psychological disorders, and we consider how even difficult, troubled lives remain valuable and meaningful.

# 1 Defining and Explaining Abnormal Behavior

What makes behavior "abnormal"? The American Psychiatric Association (2001, 2006, 2013) defines abnormal behavior in medical terms: a mental illness that affects or is manifested in a person's brain and can affect the way the individual thinks, behaves, and interacts with others. Abnormal behavior may also be defined by three criteria that distinguish it from normal behavior: **Abnormal behavior** is deviant, maladaptive, or personally distressful over a relatively long period of time. Only one of these criteria needs to be present for a behavior to be labeled "abnormal," but typically two or all three are present.

**abnormal behavior**
Behavior that is deviant, maladaptive, or personally distressful over a relatively long period of time.

**EXPERIENCE IT!**
Normal vs. Abnormal
Behavior

## Three Criteria of Abnormal Behavior

Let's take a close look at what each of the three characteristics of abnormal behavior entails:

- Abnormal behavior is *deviant*. Abnormal behavior is certainly atypical or statistically unusual. However, Alicia Keys, Hope Solo, and Mark Zuckerberg are atypical in many of their behaviors, and yet we do not categorize them as abnormal. We do often consider

*Accomplished individuals such as singer-songwriter Alicia Keys, champion soccer goalkeeper Hope Solo, and Facebook CEO Mark Zuckerberg are atypical but not abnormal. However, when atypical behavior deviates from cultural norms. it often is considered abnormal.*

atypical behavior abnormal, though, when it deviates from what is acceptable in a culture. A woman who washes her hands three or four times an hour and takes seven showers a day is abnormal because her behavior deviates from culturally acceptable norms.

■ Abnormal behavior is *maladaptive*. Maladaptive behavior interferes with one's ability to function effectively in the world. A man who believes that he can endanger others through his breathing may go to great lengths to isolate himself from people for what he believes is their own good. His belief negatively affects his everyday functioning; thus, his behavior is maladaptive. Behavior that presents a danger to the person or those around him or her is also considered maladaptive (and abnormal).

■ Abnormal behavior is *personally distressful* over a long period of time. The person engaging in the behavior finds it troubling. A woman who secretly makes herself vomit after every meal may never be seen by others as deviant (because they do not know about it), but this pattern of behavior may cause her to feel intense shame, guilt, and despair.

*Context matters! If the woman who washes her hands three or four times an hour and takes repeated showers works in a sterile lab with toxic chemicals or live viruses, her behavior might be quite adaptive.*

*Which of these three qualities—deviation from what is acceptable, maladaptiveness, and personal distress—do you think is most important to calling a behavior abnormal? Why?*

# Culture, Context, and the Meaning of Abnormal Behavior

*Consider, for instance, that a symptom of one of Sigmund Freud's most famous patients, Anna O., was that she was not interested in getting married.*

Because culture establishes the norms by which people evaluate their own and others' behaviors, culture is at the core of what it means to be normal or abnormal (Agorastos, Haasen, & Huber, 2012). In evaluating behavior as normal or abnormal, culture matters in complex ways (Sue & others, 2013). Cultural norms provide guidance about how people should behave and what behavior is healthy or unhealthy. Importantly, however, cultural norms can be mistaken. One only has to watch an episode of *Mad Men* to recognize that at one time cigarette smoking was not only judged to be an acceptable habit but also promoted as a healthy way to relax. The point is, definitions of *normal* change as society changes.

Significant, too, is the fact that cultural norms can be limiting, oppressive, and prejudicial (Potter, 2012). Individuals who fight to change the established social order sometimes face the possibility of being labeled deviant—and even mentally ill. In the late nineteenth and early twentieth centuries, for instance, women in Britain who demonstrated for women's right to vote were widely viewed to be mentally ill. When a person's or a group's behavior challenges social expectations, we must open our minds to the possibility that such actions are in fact an adaptive response to injustice. People may justifiably challenge what everyone thinks is true and may express ideas that seem strange. They should be able to make others feel uncomfortable without being labeled abnormal.

Further, as individuals move from one culture to another, interpretations and evaluations of their behavior must take into account the norms in their culture of origin (Bourque & others, 2012; John & others, 2012). Historically, people entering the United States from other countries were examined at Ellis Island, and many were judged to be mentally impaired simply because of differences in their language and customs.

Cultural variation in what it means to be normal or abnormal makes it very difficult to compare different psychological disorders across different cultures. Many of the diagnostic categories we trace in this chapter primarily reflect Western (and often U.S.) notions of normality, and applying these to other cultures can be misleading and even inappropriate (Agorastos, Haasen, & Huber, 2012). Throughout this chapter, we will see how culture influences the experience of psychological disorders.

## Do It!

Spend 15 to 20 minutes observing an area with a large number of people, such as a mall, a cafeteria, or a stadium during a game. Identify and make a list of behaviors you would classify as abnormal. How does your list of behaviors compare with the definition of *abnormal* provided above? What would you change in the list if you were in a different setting, such as a church, a bar, or a library? What does this exercise tell you about the meaning of *abnormal*?

# Theoretical Approaches
# to Psychological Disorders

What causes people to develop a psychological disorder, that is, to behave in deviant, maladaptive, and personally distressful ways? Theorists have suggested various approaches to this question.

**THE BIOLOGICAL APPROACH**    The *biological approach* attributes psychological disorders to organic, internal causes. This perspective primarily focuses on the brain, genetic factors, and neurotransmitter functioning as the sources of abnormality.

The biological approach is evident in the **medical model,** which describes psychological disorders as medical diseases with a biological origin. From the perspective of the medical model, abnormalities are called "mental illnesses," the afflicted individuals are "patients," and they are treated by "doctors."

**medical model**
The view that psychological disorders are medical diseases with a biological origin.

**THE PSYCHOLOGICAL APPROACH**    The *psychological approach* emphasizes the contributions of experiences, thoughts, emotions, and personality characteristics in explaining psychological disorders. Psychologists might focus, for example, on the influence of childhood experiences, personality traits, learning experiences, or cognitions in the development and course of psychological disorders.

**THE SOCIOCULTURAL APPROACH**    The *sociocultural approach* emphasizes the social contexts in which a person lives, including gender, ethnicity, socioeconomic status, family relationships, and culture. For instance, poverty is related to rates of psychological disorders (Jeon-Slaughter, 2012; Rosenthal & others, 2012).

The sociocultural perspective stresses the ways that cultures influence the understanding and treatment of psychological disorders. The frequency and intensity of psychological disorders vary and depend on social, economic, technological, and religious aspects of cultures (Matsumoto & Juang, 2013). Some disorders are culture-related, such as *windigo,* a disorder recognized by northern Algonquian Native American groups that involves fear of being bewitched and turned into a cannibal.

Importantly, different cultures may interpret the same pattern of behaviors in very different ways. When psychologists look for evidence of the occurrence of a particular disorder in different cultures, they must keep in mind that behaviors associated with a disorder might not be labeled as illness or dysfunction within a particular cultural context. Cultures might have their own interpretations of these behaviors, so researchers must probe whether locals ever observe these patterns of behavior, even if they are not considered illness (Draguns & Tanaka-Matsumi, 2003). For example, in one study researchers interviewed a variety of individuals in Uganda to see whether dissociative disorders, including dissociative identity disorder (which you might know as multiple personality disorder), existed in that culture (Van Duijl, Cardeña, & de Jong, 2011). They found that while most dissociative disorders were recognizable to Ugandans, the local healers consistently labeled what Westerners consider dissociative identity disorder as a spirit possession.

**THE BIOPSYCHOSOCIAL MODEL**    Abnormal behavior can be influenced by biological factors (such as genes), psychological factors (such as childhood experiences), and sociocultural factors (such as gender). These factors can operate alone, but they often act in combination with one another.

To appreciate how these factors work together, let's back up for a moment. Consider that not everyone with a genetic predisposition to schizophrenia develops the disorder. Similarly, not everyone who experiences childhood neglect develops depression. Moreover, even women who live in cultures that strongly discriminate against them do not always develop psychological disorders. Thus, to understand the development of psychological disorders, we must consider a variety of interacting factors from each of the domains of experience.

Sometimes this approach is called *biopsychosocial.* From the biopsychosocial perspective, none of the factors considered is necessarily viewed as more important than another; rather, biological, psychological, and social factors are all significant ingredients in producing both normal and abnormal behavior. Furthermore, these ingredients may combine in unique ways, so that one depressed person might differ from another in terms of the key factors associated with the development of the disorder.

# Classifying Abnormal Behavior

To understand, prevent, and treat abnormal behavior, psychiatrists and psychologists have devised systems classifying those behaviors into specific psychological disorders. Classifying psychological disorders provides a common basis for communicating. If one psychologist says that her client is experiencing depression, another psychologist understands that a particular pattern of abnormal behavior has led to this diagnosis. A classification system can also help clinicians predict how likely it is that a particular disorder will occur, which individuals are most susceptible to it, how the disorder progresses, and what the prognosis (or outcome) for treatment is (Birgegård, Norring, & Clinton; Skodol, 2012a, 2012b).

Further, a classification system may benefit the person suffering from psychological symptoms. Having a name for a problem can be a comfort and a signal that treatments are available. On the other hand, officially naming a problem can also have serious negative implications for the person because of the potential for creating *stigma,* a mark of shame that may cause others to avoid or to act negatively toward an individual. Being diagnosed with a psychological disorder can profoundly influence a person's life because of what the diagnosis means with respect to the person and his or her family and larger social world. We discuss stigma further at the end of this chapter.

**THE *DSM* CLASSIFICATION SYSTEM**　In 1952, the American Psychiatric Association (APA) published the first major classification of psychological disorders in the United States, the *Diagnostic and Statistical Manual of Mental Disorders.* Its current version, **DSM-5,** was approved in 2013. This edition of the *DSM* is the product of a 14-year revision process. *DSM-5* differs in many ways from its predecessors. Throughout the history of the *DSM,* the number of diagnosable disorders has increased dramatically. For example, *DSM-5* includes new diagnoses such as binge eating disorder and gambling addiction.

The *DSM* is not the only diagnostic system. The World Health Organization devised the *International Classification of Diseases and Related Problems (ICD-10),* which includes a chapter on mental and behavioral disorders. One of the goals of the authors of *DSM-5* was to bring diagnoses closer to the *ICD-10,* although the two manuals remain different in important ways.

**CRITIQUES OF THE DSM**　Even before it was published, the *DSM-5* was criticized on a number of bases (British Psychological Society, 2011; Skodol, 2012a, 2012b; Spiegel & others, 2013; Widiger & Craigo, 2013). A central criticism that applies to all versions of the *DSM* is that it treats psychological disorders as if they are medical illnesses, taking an overly biological view of disorders that may have their roots in social experience (Blashfield, 2014). Even as research has shed light on the complex interaction of genetic, neurobiological, cognitive, social, and environmental factors in psychological disorders, the *DSM-5* continues to reflect the medical

*DSM-5*
The *Diagnostic and Statistical Manual of Mental Disorders,* Fifth Edition; the major classification of psychological disorders in the United States.

model (British Psychological Society, 2011), neglecting factors such as poverty, unemployment, and trauma. Another general criticism of the *DSM* is that it focuses strictly on problems. Critics argue that emphasizing *strengths* as well as weaknesses might help to destigmatize psychological disorders. Identifying a person's strengths can be an important step toward maximizing his or her ability to contribute to society (Roten, 2007).

Other criticisms of the *DSM-5* include these:

▦ It relies too much on social norms and subjective judgments.

▦ Too many new categories of disorders have been added, some of which do not yet have consistent research support and whose inclusion will lead to a significant increase in the number of people being labeled as having a mental disorder.

▦ Loosened standards for some existing diagnoses will add to the already very high rates of these.

Figure 12.1 shows some of the changes that are part of the *DSM*'s newest formulation. In thinking about the critiques of these revisions, you might be wondering what all the fuss is about. One reason for these concerns is that U.S. insurance companies generally will reimburse patients only for treatments for diagnoses that appear in the *DSM-5*. Another reason for concern is that part of the medical model is the assumption that disorders optimally are treated through medical means. Generally, that means prescribing medications. With the loosening of diagnostic criteria, many more individuals might be given powerful psychoactive drugs, perhaps unnecessarily. Thus, it is imperative that the *DSM* gets it right, and many critics argue that it falls short in this high-stakes context (Andrews, 2014; Blashfield, 2014; Paris, 2013; Watson & others, 2013).

Concerns are about overdiagnosis and the proliferation of psychoactive drugs are well illustrated by the controversy surrounding **attention-deficit/hyperactivity disorder (ADHD).** To read more, see Challenge Your Thinking.

**attention-deficit/hyperactivity disorder (ADHD)**
One of the most common psychological disorders of childhood, in which individuals show one or more of the following: inattention, hyperactivity, and impulsivity.

| Disorder | Change | Sources of Concern |
|---|---|---|
| **Major Depressive Disorder** | In the past, those experiencing grief due to the loss of a loved one generally have not been considered depressed. This grief exclusion has been dropped. | This change may result in those experiencing normal grief to be labeled with depression. |
| **Attention-Deficit/Hyperactivity Disorder (ADHD)** | Some of the diagnostic requirements have been loosened, and the age of diagnosis has been changed. | Overdiagnosis of ADHD is already a concern, as is the proliferation of drugs used to treat the condition. |
| **Autism Spectrum Disorder** | The diagnosis of Asperger syndrome, which was given to high-functioning individuals with autistic characteristics, has been dropped. | Those who were previously diagnosed with Asperger's may not be diagnosed at all and may not receive treatment. |
| **Post-Traumatic Stress Disorder (PTSD)** | Previously, a person had to have experienced or witnessed a trauma. Now, PTSD can be diagnosed even for those who only hear about a trauma. | The change may lead to a huge increase in those with this disorder. |
| **Disruptive Mood Regulation Disorder** | This is a new diagnosis for children with wild mood swings. | Adding diagnoses targeting children is concerning. |
| **Mild Neurocognitive Impairment** | This new diagnosis is for adults experiencing cognitive decline. | Many adults experience mild cognitive decline with age, and this diagnosis may pathologize normal aging. |

**FIGURE 12.1** **New Features of *DSM-5*** *DSM-5* has dropped some diagnostic categories, added others, and changed the criteria for still others.

## Does *Everyone* Have ADHD?

Perhaps no diagnosis is more controversial these days than attention-deficit/hyperactivity disorder (ADHD), in which individuals, prior to the age of 7, show one or more of the following symptoms: inattention, hyperactivity, and impulsivity. Chances are you know someone who suffers from ADHD. You might even have it yourself.

ADHD is one of the most common psychological disorders of childhood, with diagnoses skyrocketing in recent years. In 1988 just 500,000 cases of ADHD were diagnosed, but by 2007, that number had jumped to 4 million per year (Bloom & Cohen, 2007). In 2010, 10.4 million children were diagnosed with ADHD (Garfield & others, 2012). Experts previously thought that most children "grow out of" ADHD. However, based on evidence showing that as many as 70 percent of adolescents (Sibley & others, 2012) and 66 percent of adults (Asherson & others 2010) diagnosed as children continue to experience ADHD symptoms, *DSM-5* recognizes ADHD in adults.

The sheer number of ADHD diagnoses has prompted speculation that psychiatrists, parents, and teachers are in fact labeling normal childhood behavior as psychopathology (Morrow & others, 2012). One reason for concern about overdiagnosing ADHD is that the form of treatment in well over 80 percent of cases is psychoactive drugs, including stimulants such as Ritalin and Adderall (Garfield & others, 2012). Animal research has shown that in the absence of ADHD, exposure to such stimulants can predispose individuals to later addiction problems (Leo, 2005). Those who question the diagnosis of ADHD in children find it equally problematic in adults (Marcus, Norris, & Coccaro, 2012). These scholars argue that the spread of ADHD is primarily a function of over-pathologizing normal behavior, confusing ADHD for other disorders, and aggressive marketing by pharmaceutical companies (Moncrieff & Timimi, 2010).

A recent study sheds some light on the controversy. Child psychologists, psychiatrists, and social workers were sent vignettes of cases of children in which symptoms were described (Brüchmiller, Margraf, & Schneider, 2012), and were asked to diagnose the children. Some of the descriptions fit the diagnostic criteria for ADHD, but others lacked key features of the disorder. In addition, in the case vignettes, the researchers varied whether the child was identified as male or female. The dependent variable was whether these professionals gave a diagnosis of ADHD to a case. The results showed that participants *overdiagnosed* ADHD, giving an ADHD diagnosis to cases that specifically lacked important aspects of the disorder about 17 percent of the time. Further, regardless of symptoms, boys were two times more likely than girls to receive such a diagnosis. An important lesson from this study is that professionals must be vigilant in their application of diagnostic criteria as they encounter different cases. The results also demonstrate how even professionals can fall prey to certain biases.

Certainly, individuals who experience ADHD have symptoms that make adjustment difficult, so it is critical that diagnosis of the disorder be accurate. Children diagnosed with ADHD are at heightened risk of dropping out of school, teen pregnancy, and antisocial behavior (Barkley & others, 2002; von Polier, Vloet, & Herpertz-Dahlmann, 2012). Adolescents and adults with ADHD symptoms are more likely to experience difficulties at work, while driving a car, and in interpersonal relationships; they are also more likely to have substance abuse problems (Chang, Lichtenstein, & Larsson, 2012; Kooij & others, 2010; Sibley & others, 2012).

ADHD is not the only controversial diagnosis; nor is this psychological disorder the only one given a great deal of attention by pharmaceutical companies (Mash & Wolfe, 2013). Drug companies commonly fund research that focuses on a disease model of psychological disorders. Clearly, psychological disorders are "real" in the sense that they lead to objectively negative outcomes in people's lives. The controversy over ADHD is a reminder of the important role of psychology research in clarifying and defining diagnostic categories. Indeed, the aim of the profession is to avoid inappropriately labeling, misdiagnosing, and mistreating people who are already suffering.

### What Do You Think?

- Would ADHD be as controversial if the treatment did not involve drugs? Why or why not?

- Do you think ADHD would be diagnosed as often as it is if drugs were not readily available for its treatment?

- If a teacher suggested that your child be tested for ADHD, what would you do?

Before we begin our survey of various psychological disorders, a word of caution. It is very common for individuals who are learning about psychological disorders to recognize the symptoms and behaviors of disorders in themselves or in people around them. Keep in mind that only trained professionals can diagnose a psychological disorder.

## self-quiz

1. All of the following are characteristics of abnormal behavior *except*
   A. it is typical.
   B. it causes distress.
   C. it is maladaptive.
   D. it is deviant.

2. The medical model interprets psychological disorders as medical diseases with a/an
   A. environmental origin.
   B. sociocultural origin.
   C. biological origin.
   D. biopsychosocial origin.

3. A central complaint about *DSM-5* is that it neglects factors such as
   A. inherited tendencies toward particular diseases.
   B. age.
   C. economic and employment status.
   D. All of the above.

**APPLY IT!** 4. Since she was a little girl, 19-year-old Francesca has believed that whenever she walks through a doorway, she must touch the doorframe 12 times and silently count to 12 or else her mother will die. She has never told anyone about this ritual, which she feels is harmless, similar to carrying a lucky charm. Which of the following is true of Francesca's behavior?
   A. Francesca's behavior is abnormal only because it is different from the norm. It is not maladaptive, nor does it cause her distress.
   B. Francesca's behavior fits all three characteristics of abnormal behavior.
   C. Francesca's behavior is maladaptive, but it is not abnormal because she does not feel personal distress over her ritual.
   D. Francesca's behavior does not fit any of the characteristics of abnormal behavior.

# 2 Anxiety and Anxiety-Related Disorders

Think about how you felt before a make-or-break exam or a big presentation—or perhaps as you noticed police lights flashing behind your speeding car. Did you feel jittery and nervous and experience tightness in your stomach? These are the feelings of normal anxiety, an unpleasant feeling of fear and dread.

In contrast, **anxiety disorders** involve fears that are uncontrollable, disproportionate to the actual danger the person might be in, and disruptive of ordinary life. They feature motor tension (jumpiness, trembling), hyperactivity (dizziness, a racing heart), and apprehensive expectations and thoughts. *DSM-5* recognizes 12 types of anxiety disorders. In this section, we survey four common anxiety disorders

**anxiety disorders**
Disabling (uncontrollable and disruptive) psychological disorders that feature motor tension, hyperactivity, and apprehensive expectations and thoughts.

- Generalized anxiety disorder
- Panic disorder
- Specific phobia
- Social anxiety disorder

as well as two disorders that are not classified as anxiety disorders but are related to the experience of anxiety:

- Obsessive-compulsive disorder (categorized under Obsessive-Compulsive and Related Disorders)
- Post-traumatic stress disorder (categorized under Trauma- and Stressor-Related Disorders)

## Generalized Anxiety Disorder

When you are worrying about getting a speeding ticket, you know why you are anxious; there is a specific cause. **Generalized anxiety disorder** is different from such everyday feelings of anxiety in that sufferers experience persistent anxiety for at least 6 months and are unable to specify the reasons for the anxiety (Freeman & Freeman, 2012). People with generalized anxiety disorder are nervous most of the time. They may worry

**generalized anxiety disorder**
Psychological disorder marked by persistent anxiety for at least 6 months, and in which the individual is unable to specify the reasons for the anxiety.

Recall from Chapter 2 that GABA is the neurotransmitter that inhibits neurons from firing—it's like the brain's brake pedal. Problems with GABA are often implicated in anxiety disorders.

about their work, relationships, or health. That worry can also take a physical toll and cause fatigue, muscle tension, stomach problems, and difficulty sleeping.

What is the etiology of generalized anxiety disorder? (*Etiology* means the causes or significant preceding conditions.) Among the biological factors are genetic predisposition, deficiency in the neurotransmitter GABA, and respiratory system abnormalities (Boschen, 2012). The psychological and sociocultural factors include having harsh (or even impossible) self-standards, overly strict and critical parents, automatic negative thoughts when feeling stressed, and a history of uncontrollable traumas or stressors (such as an abusive parent).

# Panic Disorder

Much like everyone else, you might sometimes have a specific experience that sends you into a panic. For example, you work all night on a paper, only to have your computer crash before you saved your last changes, or you are about to dash across a street just when you see a large truck coming right at you. Your heart races, your hands shake, and you might break into a sweat.

A panic attack can be a one-time occurrence. People with panic disorder have recurrent attacks that sometimes cause them to be afraid to even leave their homes, a condition called agoraphobia.

In a **panic disorder,** however, a person experiences recurrent, sudden onsets of intense terror, often without warning and with no specific cause. Panic attacks can produce severe palpitations, extreme shortness of breath, chest pains, trembling, sweating, dizziness, and a feeling of helplessness (Oral & others, 2012). People with panic disorder may feel that they are having a heart attack or going to die.

**panic disorder**
Anxiety disorder in which the individual experiences recurrent, sudden onsets of intense terror, often without warning and with no specific cause.

During a panic attack, the brain registers fear as areas of the fear network of the limbic system, including the amygdala and hippocampus, are activated (Holzschneider & Mulert, 2011). Charles Darwin, the scientist who proposed the theory of evolution, suffered from intense panic disorder (Barloon & Noyes, 1997). Former NFL running back Earl Campbell has dealt with this disorder.

What is the etiology of panic disorder? Theories of the origins of panic attack take into account biological, psychological, and sociocultural factors (Pilecki, Arentoft, & McKay, 2011). In terms of biological factors, individuals may have a genetic predisposition to the disorder (Bayoglu & others, 2012). Of particular interest to researchers are genes that direct the action of neurotransmitters such as norepinephrine (Buttenschøn & others, 2011) and GABA (Thoeringer & others, 2009). Another brain chemical, *lactate,* which plays a role in brain metabolism, has been found to be elevated in individuals with panic disorder (Maddock & others, 2009). Further, experimental research has shown that increasing lactate levels can produce panic attacks (Reiman & others 1989). Other research points to the involvement of a wider range of genes and bodily systems, implicating genes involved in hormone regulation (Wilson, Markie, & Fitches, 2012) and responses to stress (Esler & others, 2009).

*Many experts interpret Edvard Munch's painting* The Scream *as an expression of the terror brought on by a panic attack.*

With respect to psychological influences, learning processes, as described in Chapter 5, are one factor that has been considered in panic disorder. Classical conditioning research has shown that learned associations between bodily cues of respiration and fear can play a role in panic attacks (Acheson, Forsyth, & Moses, 2012). Interestingly, carbon dioxide ($CO_2$) has been found to be a very strong conditioned stimulus for fear, suggesting that humans may be *biologically prepared* to learn an association between high concentrations of $CO_2$ and fear (Acheson, Forsyth, & Moses, 2012; De Cort & others, 2012; Nardi & others, 2006; Schenberg, 2010). Thus, some learning researchers have suggested that at the heart of panic attacks are the learned associations between $CO_2$ and fear (De Cort & others, 2012).

In addition, the learning concept of *generalization* may apply to panic attack. Recall that in classical conditioning, generalization means showing a conditioned response (in this case, fear) to conditioned stimuli other than the particular one used in learning. Research shows that individuals who suffer from panic attacks are more likely to display overgeneralization of fear learning (Lissek & others, 2010). Why might those who suffer from panic attacks be more likely to show stronger and more generalized fear associations? One possibility is that the biological predispositions as well as early experiences with traumatic life events may play a role in setting the stage for such learning (Pilecki, Arentoft, & McKay, 2011).

In terms of sociocultural factors, in the United States, women are twice as likely as men to have panic attacks (Altemus, 2006). Possible reasons include biological differences in hormones and neurotransmitters (Altemus, 2006; Fodor & Epstein, 2002). Compared to men, women are more likely to complain of distressing respiratory experiences during panic attacks (Sheikh, Leskin, & Klein, 2002). Interestingly, a recent study showed that healthy women are more likely to experience panic-related emotions when exposed to air enriched with $CO_2$ (Nillni & others, 2012).

Research also suggests that women may cope with anxiety-provoking situations differently than men do, and these differences may explain the gender difference in panic disorder (Schmidt & Koselka, 2000; Viswanath & others, 2012). Panic attack has been observed in a variety of cultures, though there are some cultural differences in the experience of these attacks (Agorastos, Haasen, & Huber, 2012). For instance, in Korea, panic attacks are less likely to include a fear of dying than is the case in other societies (Weissman & others, 1995).

> An earlier explanation of panic attack was called the **suffocation false alarm theory**. Can you see why it was initially proposed?

> Whenever you encounter gender differences in this discussion, ask yourself whether men or women might be more likely to report having problems or to seek treatment. Research on psychological disorders is often based on individuals who have reported symptoms or sought help. If men are less likely to report symptoms or seek treatment, the data may underestimate the occurrence of psychological disorders in men.

## Specific Phobia

**specific phobia**
Psychological disorder in which an individual has an irrational, overwhelming, persistent fear of a particular object or situation.

Many people are afraid of spiders and snakes; indeed, thinking about letting a tarantula crawl over one's face is likely to give anyone the willies. It is not uncommon to be afraid of particular objects or specific environments such as extreme heights. For most of us, these fears do not interfere with daily life. A fear becomes a phobia when a situation is so dreaded that an individual goes to almost any length to avoid it. A snake phobia that keeps a city-dweller from leaving his apartment is clearly disproportionate to the actual chances of encountering a snake. **Specific phobia** is a psychological disorder in which an individual has an irrational, overwhelming, persistent fear of a particular object or situation. Specific phobias come in many forms, as shown in Figure 12.2.

Where do specific phobias come from? Approaches to answering this question typically first acknowledge that fear plays an important role in adaptive behavior. Fear tells us when we are in danger and need to take to action. The importance of this function

*"Stephen's fear of heights is particularly bad today."*
Used by permission of CartoonStock, www.CartoonStock.com.

| Acrophobia | Fear of high places | Arachnophobia | Fear of spiders | Mysophobia | Fear of dirt |
| Aerophobia | Fear of flying | Astrapophobia | Fear of lightning | Nyctophobia | Fear of darkness |
| Ailurophobia | Fear of cats | Cynophobia | Fear of dogs | Ophidiophobia | Fear of nonpoisonous snakes |
| Algophobia | Fear of pain | Gamophobia | Fear of marriage | | |
| Amaxophobia | Fear of vehicles, driving | Hydrophobia | Fear of water | Thanatophobia | Fear of death |
| | | Melissophobia | Fear of bees | Xenophobia | Fear of strangers |

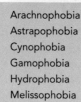

**FIGURE 12.2** **Specific Phobias** This figure features examples of specific phobias—anxiety disorders characterized by irrational and overwhelming fear of a particular object or situation.

suggests that fears should be relatively quickly learned, because learning to fear things that will harm us keeps us out of harm's way. Specific phobias, then, might be considered, an extreme and unfortunate variant on this adaptive process (Coelho & Purkis, 2009; Muris & Merckelbach, 2012).

Many explanations of specific phobias view these disorders as based on experiences, memories, and learned associations (Veale & others, 2013). For example, the individual with a fear of heights perhaps experienced a fall from a high place earlier in life and therefore associates heights with pain (a classical conditioning explanation). Alternatively, he or she may have heard about or watched others who demonstrated terror of high places (an observational learning explanation), as when a little girl develops a fear of heights after sitting next to her terrified mother and observing her clutch the handrails, white-knuckled, as the roller coaster creeps steeply uphill. Not all people who have a specific phobia can easily identify experiences that explain these, so other factors may also be at play (Coelho & Purkis, 2009). Each specific phobia may have its own neural correlates (Lueken, 2011), and some people may be especially prone to develop phobias (Burstein & others, 2012).

## Social Anxiety Disorder

Imagine how you might feel just before you first meet the parents of the person you hope to marry. You might feel fearful of committing some awful gaff, ruining the impression you hope to make on them. Or imagine getting ready to give a big speech before a crowd and suddenly realizing you have forgotten your notes. **Social anxiety disorder** (also called *social phobia*) is an intense fear of being humiliated or embarrassed in social situations like these (Lampe & Sutherland, 2013; Morrison & Heimberg, 2013). Singers Carly Simon and Barbra Streisand have dealt with social phobia.

Where does social anxiety disorder come from? Genes appear to play a role (Sakolsky, McCracken, & Nurmi, 2013), along with neural circuitry involving the thalamus, amygdala, and cerebral cortex (Damsa, Kosel, & Moussally, 2009). A number of neurotransmitters also may be involved, especially serotonin (Christensen & others, 2010). Social anxiety disorder may involve vulnerabilities, such as genetic characteristics or parenting styles that lay a foundation of risk, combined with learning experiences in a social context (Higa-McMillen & Besutani, 2011; Pejic & others, 2013).

**Social anxiety disorder (social phobia)** An intense fear of being humiliated or embarrassed in social situations.

In the *DSM-5,* generalized anxiety disorder, panic disorder, specific phobia, and social anxiety disorder are all classified as anxiety disorders (Andrews, 2014; Gallo & others, 2013). Our next two topics, obsessive-compulsive disorder and post-traumatic stress disorder, are not included under the umbrella of Anxiety Disorders. Instead, these disorders have their own separate categories. Nonetheless, anxiety is relevant to both of these disorders.

*"I gotta go—we're discussing my compulsive communications disorder."*

Used by permission of CartoonStock, www.CartoonStock.com.

## Obsessive-Compulsive Disorder

Just before leaving on a long road trip, you find yourself checking to be sure you locked the front door. As you pull away in your car, you are stricken with the thought that you forgot to turn off the coffeemaker. Going to bed the night before an early flight, you check your alarm clock a few times to be sure you will wake up on time. These are examples of normal checking behavior.

In contrast, the disorder known as **obsessive-compulsive disorder (OCD)** features anxiety-provoking thoughts that will not go away and/or urges to perform repetitive, ritualistic behaviors to prevent or produce some future situation. *Obsessions* are recurrent thoughts, and *compulsions* are recurrent behaviors. Individuals with OCD dwell on their doubts and repeat their routines sometimes hundreds of times a day (Yap, Mogan, & Kyrios, 2012). The most common compulsions are excessive checking, cleansing, and counting. Game show host Howie Mandel has coped with OCD, as have soccer star David Beckham, singer-actor Justin Timberlake, and actress Jessica Alba. Obsessive-compulsive symptoms have been found in many cultures, and culture plays a role in the content of obsessive thoughts or compulsive behaviors (Matsunaga & Seedat, 2011).

An individual with OCD might believe that she has to touch the doorway with her left hand whenever she enters a room and count her steps as she walks. If she does not complete this ritual, she may be overcome with a sense of fear that something terrible will happen (Victor & Bernstein, 2009).

What is the etiology of obsessive-compulsive disorder? In terms of biological factors, there seems to be a genetic component (Alonso & others, 2012; Angoa-Perez & others, 2012). Also, brain-imaging studies have suggested neurological links for OCD (Hou & others, 2012; Stern & others, 2012). One neuroscientific analysis is that the frontal cortex or basal ganglia are so active in OCD that numerous impulses reach the thalamus, generating obsessive thoughts or compulsive actions (Rotge & others, 2009).

In one study, fMRI was used to examine the brain activity of individuals with OCD before and after treatment (Nakao & others, 2005). Following effective treatment, a number of areas in the frontal cortex showed decreased activation. Interestingly, the amygdala, which is associated with the experience of anxiety, may be smaller in individuals with OCD compared to those who do not have the disorder (Atmaca & others, 2008). Low levels of the neurotransmitters serotonin and dopamine likely are involved in the brain pathways linked with OCD (Goljevscek & Carvalho, 2011; Soomro, 2012).

In terms of psychological factors, OCD sometimes occurs during a period of life stress such as that surrounding the birth of a child or a change in occupational or marital status (Uguz & others, 2007). According to the cognitive perspective, what differentiates individuals with OCD from those who do not have it is the ability to turn off negative, intrusive thoughts by ignoring or effectively dismissing them (Leahy, Holland, & McGinn, 2012; C. Williams, 2012).

**obsessive-compulsive disorder (OCD)** Anxiety disorder in which the individual has anxiety-provoking thoughts that will not go away and/or urges to perform repetitive, ritualistic behaviors to prevent or produce some future situation.

**EXPERIENCE IT!**
Obsessive-Compulsive Disorder

*As long as the person performs the ritual, she never finds out that the terrible outcome doesn't happen. The easing of the anxiety exemplifies* **negative reinforcement** *(having something bad taken away after performing a behavior).*

# OCD-Related Disorders

*DSM-5* expanded the disorders that are thought to be related to OCD (Abramowitz & Jacoby, 2014). All of these disorders involve repetitive behavior and often anxiety. Among the new additions are the following.

- *Hoarding disorder* involves compulsive collecting, poor organization skills, and difficulty discarding things, along with cognitive deficits in information processing speed, problems with decision making, and procrastination (Tolin, 2008). Individuals with hoarding disorder find it difficult to throw things away and are troubled by the feeling that they might need items like old newspapers at a later time (Dimauro & others, 2013).

- *Excoriation* (or skin picking) refers to the particular compulsion of picking at one's skin, sometimes to the point of injury. Skin picking is more common among women than men and is seen as a symptom of autism spectrum disorder.

- *Trichotillomania* (hair pulling) entails compulsively pulling at the hair from the scalp, eyebrows, and other body areas (Walther & others, 2013). Hair pulling from the scalp can lead to bald patches that the person can go to great lengths to disguise.

- *Body Dysmorphic Disorder* involves a distressing preoccupation with imagined or slight flaws in one's physical appearance (Kaplan & others, 2013). Individuals with this disorder cannot stop thinking about how they look and repeatedly compare their appearance to others, check themselves in the mirror, and so forth. Body dysmorphic disorder may include maladaptive behaviors such as compulsive exercise and body building and repeated cosmetic surgery and occurs about equally in men and women.

# Post-Traumatic Stress Disorder

**post-traumatic stress disorder (PTSD)**
Anxiety disorder that develops through exposure to a traumatic event, a severely oppressive situation, cruel abuse, or a natural or an unnatural disaster.

If you have ever been in even a minor car accident, you may have had a nightmare or two about it. You might have even found yourself reliving the experience for some time. This normal recovery process takes on a particularly devastating character in **post-traumatic stress disorder (PTSD),** develops through exposure to a traumatic event that overwhelms the person's abilities to cope (Beidel, Bulik, & Stanley, 2012). The *DSM-5* has expanded the kinds of experiences that might foster PTSD, recognizing that the disorder can occur not only in individuals who directly experience a trauma but also in those who witness it and those who only *hear* about it (APA, 2013). The symptoms of PTSD vary but include:

- Flashbacks in which the individual relives the event. A flashback can make the person lose touch with reality and reenact the event for seconds, hours, or, very rarely, days. A person having a flashback—which can come in the form of images, sounds, smells, and/or feelings—usually believes that the traumatic event is happening all over again (Brewin, 2012).

- Avoiding emotional experiences and avoiding talking about emotions with others.

- Reduced ability to feel emotions, often reported as feeling numb.

- Excessive arousal, resulting in an exaggerated startle response or an inability to sleep.

- Difficulties with memory and concentration.

- Impulsive behavior.

PTSD symptoms can follow a trauma immediately or after months or even years (Solomon & others, 2012). Most individuals who are exposed to a traumatic event experience some of the symptoms in the days and weeks following exposure (National Center for PTSD, 2012). However, not every individual exposed to the same event develops PTSD (Brewin & others, 2012; Nemeroff & others, 2006).

## The Psychological Wounds of War

**P**TSD has been a concern for soldiers who have served in Iraq and Afghanistan (Klemanski & others, 2012; Yoder & others, 2012). In an effort to prevent PTSD, the U.S. military gives troops stress-management training before deployment (Ritchie & others, 2006). Branches of the armed forces station mental health professionals in combat zones around the world to help prevent PTSD and to lessen the effects of the disorder (Rabasca, 2000). These measures appear to be paying off: Researchers have found that PTSD sufferers from the Iraq and Afghanistan wars are generally less likely to be unemployed or incarcerated and more likely to maintain strong social bonds following their term of service than veterans of earlier wars (Fontana & Rosenheck, 2008).

Historically, the stigma associated with psychological disorders has been especially strong within the military ranks, where struggling with a psychological problem is commonly viewed as a sign of weakness or incompetence (Warner & others, 2011). Yet individuals engaged in combat are at considerable risk of developing PTSD, and the disorder can profoundly affect their lives. A survey of almost 3,000 soldiers who had just returned from the Iraq War revealed that 17 percent met the criteria for PTSD (Hoge & others, 2007). This figure is likely an underestimate given the stigma linked to psychological disorders in the military.

In 2008, military psychologist John Fortunato suggested that veterans with PTSD ought to be eligible for the Purple Heart, the prestigious military decoration awarded to those who have been physically wounded or killed in combat (Schogol, 2009). Awarding PTSD sufferers the Purple Heart, Fortunato argued, would not only acknowledge their sacrifice but also reduce the stigma attached to psychological disorders. That year, the military did consider whether PTSD sufferers in its ranks ought to be awarded the Purple Heart. However, the Pentagon decided against awarding the Purple Heart to military personnel with PTSD on the grounds that the disorder is not limited to victims of physical trauma from enemy fire but also can affect eyewitnesses (Schogol, 2009). Still, the fact that the top brass considered the possibility suggests that the military is becoming more aware of the serious problems facing those who are traumatized while serving their country in combat.

Researchers have examined PTSD associated with various experiences (Harder & others, 2012). These include combat and war-related traumas (Khamis, 2012), sexual abuse and assault (S. Y. Kim & others, 2012), natural disasters such as hurricanes and earthquakes (Sezgin & Punamaki, 2012), and unnatural disasters such as plane crashes and terrorist attacks (Luft & others, 2012).

Clearly, one cause of PTSD is the traumatic event itself (Risbrough & Stein, 2012). However, because not everyone who experiences the same traumatic life event develops PTSD, other factors, aside from the event, must influence a person's vulnerability to the disorder (Gabert-Quillen & others, 2012). These include a history of previous traumatic events and conditions, such as abuse and psychological disorders

*Prior to deployment, U.S. troops receive stress-management training aimed at helping to prevent PTSD and other disorders that might be triggered by the high-stress conditions of war.*

(Canton-Cortes, Canton, & Cortes, 2012), cultural background as in the case of traumatized refugees (Hinton & others, 2012), and genetic predisposition (Mehta & Binder, 2012; Skelton & others, 2012).

1. Sudden episodes of extreme anxiety or terror that involve symptoms such as heart palpitations, trembling, sweating, and fear of losing control are characteristic of
   A. generalized anxiety disorder.
   B. post-traumatic stress disorder.
   C. obsessive-compulsive disorder.
   D. panic disorder.

2. Which of the following is true of post-traumatic stress disorder?
   A. It is caused by panic attacks.
   B. It is the natural outgrowth of experiencing trauma.

   C. It involves flashbacks.
   D. The symptoms always occur immediately following a trauma.

3. An irrational, overwhelming, persistent fear of a particular object or situation is a defining characteristic of
   A. post-traumatic stress disorder.
   B. specific phobia.
   C. panic disorder.
   D. generalized anxiety disorder.

APPLY IT! 4. Lately Tina has noticed that her mother appears to be overwhelmed with worry about everything. Her mother has told Tina that she is having trouble sleeping and experiencing racing thoughts of all the terrible things that might happen at any given moment. Tina's mother is showing signs of
   A. panic disorder.
   B. obsessive-compulsive disorder.
   C. generalized anxiety disorder.
   D. post-traumatic stress disorder.

# 3 Disorders Involving Emotion and Mood

Our emotions and moods tell us how we are doing in life. We feel good or bad depending on our progress on important goals, the quality of our relationships, and so on. For some individuals, however, the link between life experiences and emotions is off-kilter. They may feel sad for no reason or a sense of elation in the absence of any great accomplishment. Several psychological disorders involve this kind of dysregulation in a person's emotional life. In this section we examine the two such disorders—depressive disorders and bipolar disorders—and consider a tragic correlate of these disorders: suicide.

## Depressive Disorders

**depressive disorders**
Mood disorders in which the individual suffers from depression—an unrelenting lack of pleasure in life.

Everyone feels blue sometimes. A romantic breakup, the death of a loved one, or a personal failure can cast a dark cloud over life. Sometimes, however, a person might feel unhappy and not know why. **Depressive disorders** are disorders in which the individual suffers from *depression*, an unrelenting lack of pleasure in life. Depressive disorders are common. A representative U.S. survey including individuals aged 13 and up found that approximately 30 percent reported a depressive episode or diagnosis in the last 12 months (Kessler & others, 2012).

A variety of cultures have recognized depression, and studies have shown that across cultures depression is characterized as involving an absence of joy, low energy, and high levels of sadness (Dritschel & others, 2011; Kahn, 2012). Moreover, culture may influence the ways individuals describe their experience. For instance, people from Eastern cultures may be less likely to talk about their emotional states, and more likely to describe depressive symptoms in terms of bodily feelings and symptoms, than those from Western cultures (Draguns & Tanaka-Matsumi, 2003). Many successful individuals have been diagnosed with depression. They include musicians Sheryl Crow and Eric Clapton, actors Drew Barrymore, Halle Berry, and Jim Carrey, artist Pablo Picasso, astronaut Buzz Aldrin (the second moon walker), famed American architect Frank Lloyd Wright, and J. K. Rowling, the author of the *Harry Potter* series.

**major depressive disorder (MDD)** Psychological disorder involving a major depressive episode and depressed characteristics, such as lethargy and hopelessness, for at least two weeks.

**Major depressive disorder (MDD)** involves a significant depressive episode and depressed characteristics, such as lethargy and hopelessness, for at least two weeks. MDD impairs daily functioning, and the National Institute of Mental Health (NIMH) has called it the leading cause of disability in the United States (NIMH, 2008). The symptoms of major depressive disorder may include:

- Depressed mood most of the day
- Reduced interest or pleasure in activities that were once enjoyable
- Significant weight loss or gain or significant decrease or interest in appetite
- Trouble sleeping or sleeping too much
- Fatigue or loss of energy
- Feeling worthless or guilty in an excessive or inappropriate manner
- Problems in thinking, concentrating, or making decisions
- Recurrent thoughts of death and suicide
- No history of manic episodes (periods of euphoric mood)

*This painting by Vincent Van Gogh,* Portrait of Dr. Gachet, *reflects the extreme melancholy that characterizes the depressive disorders.*

Individuals who experience less-extreme depressive mood for more than two months may be diagnosed with *persistent depressive disorder.* This disorder includes symptoms such as hopelessness, lack of energy, poor concentration, and sleep problems.

What are the causes of depressive disorders? A variety of biological, psychological, and sociocultural factors have been implicated in their development.

**BIOLOGICAL FACTORS**   Genetic influences play a role in depression (Goenjian & others, 2012; Sabunciyan & others, 2012). In addition, specific brain structures are involved in depressive disorders. For example, depressed individuals show lower levels of brain activity in a section of the prefrontal cortex that is involved in generating actions (Duman & others, 2012) as well as in regions of the brain associated with the perception of rewards in the environment (Howland, 2012). A depressed person's brain may not recognize opportunities for pleasurable experiences.

Depression also likely involves problems in neurotransmitter regulation. Recall that neurotransmitters are chemicals that carry impulses from neuron to neuron. For smooth brain function, neurotransmitters must ebb and flow, often in harmony with one another. Individuals with major depressive disorder appear to have too few receptors for the neurotransmitters serotonin and norepinephrine (Houston & others, 2012; H. F. Li & others, 2012). Some research suggests that problems in regulating a neurotransmitter called *substance P* might be involved in depression (Munoz & Covenas, 2012). Substance P is thought to play an important role in the psychological experience of pain (Sacerdote & Levrini, 2012).

**PSYCHOLOGICAL FACTORS**   Psychological explanations of depression have drawn on behavioral learning theories and cognitive theories. One behavioral view of depression focuses on *learned helplessness,* which, as we saw in Chapter 5, involves an individual's feelings of powerlessness after exposure to aversive circumstances over which the person has no control. Martin Seligman (1975) proposed that learned helplessness is a reason that some people become depressed. When individuals cannot control their stress, they eventually feel helpless and stop trying to change their situations. This helplessness spirals into hopelessness (Becker-Weidman & others, 2009).

Cognitive explanations of depression focus on the thoughts and beliefs that contribute to this sense of hopelessness (Britton & others, 2012; Jarrett & others, 2012). Psychiatrist Aaron Beck (1967) proposed that negative thoughts reflect self-defeating beliefs that shape depressed individuals' experiences. These habitual negative thoughts magnify and expand depressed persons' negative experiences (Lam, 2012). For example, a depressed individual might overgeneralize about a minor occurrence—say, turning in a work assignment late—and think that he or she is worthless. A depressed person might view a minor setback such as getting a *D* on a paper as the end of the world. The accumulation of such cognitive distortions can lead to depression (T. W. Lee & others, 2011).

The way people think can also influence the course of depression. Depressed individuals may ruminate on negative experiences and negative feelings, playing them over and over again in their minds (Nolen-Hoeksema, 2011). This tendency to ruminate is associated with the development of depression as well as other psychological problems such as binge eating and substance abuse (Cowdrey & Park, 2012; Kuhn & others, 2012).

Another cognitive view of depression focuses on people's attributions—their attempts to explain what caused something to happen (Seidel & others, 2012). Depression is thought to be related to a *pessimistic* attributional style. In this style, individuals regularly explain negative events as having internal causes ("It is my fault I failed the exam"), stable causes ("I'm going to fail again and again"), and global causes ("Failing this exam shows that I won't do well in any of my courses"). Pessimistic attributional style means blaming oneself for negative events and expecting the negative events to recur (Abramson, Seligman, & Teasdale, 1978). This pessimistic style can be contrasted with an *optimistic* attributional style, which is essentially its opposite. Optimists make external attributions for bad things that happen ("I did badly on the test because it's hard to know what a professor wants on the first exam"). They also recognize that these causes can change ("I'll do better on the next one") and that they are specific ("It was only one test"). Optimistic attributional style

## PSYCHOLOGICAL INQUIRY

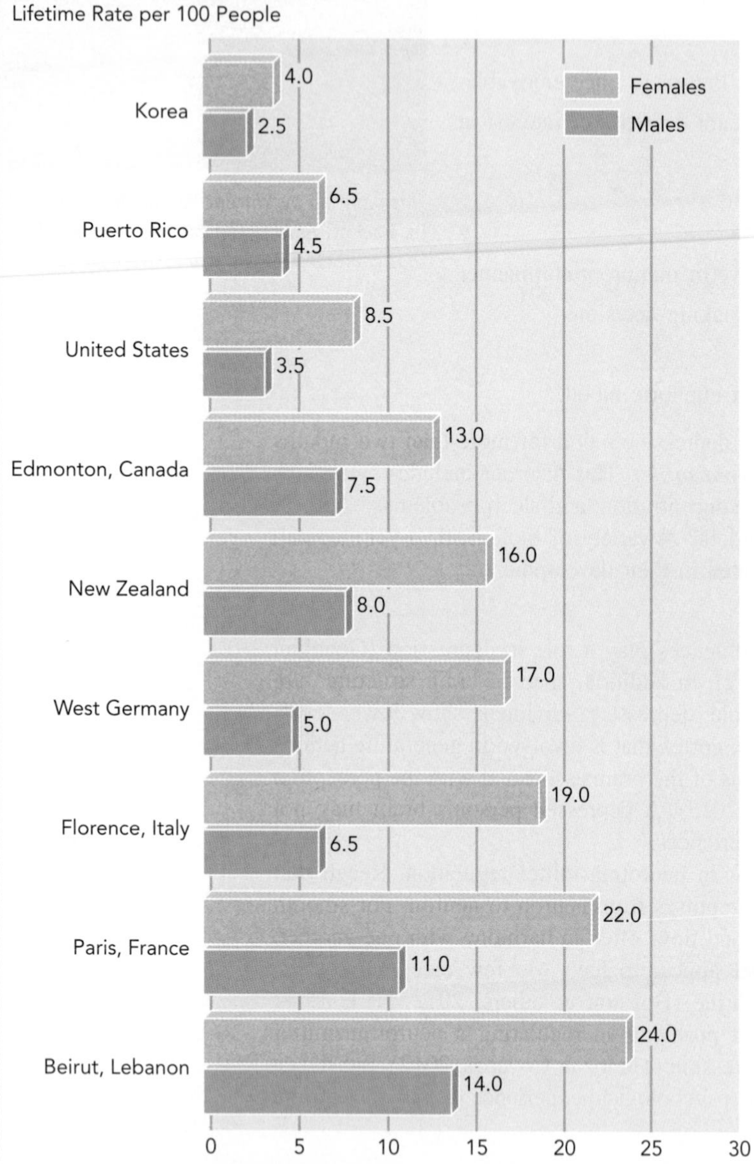

Lifetime Rate per 100 People

**FIGURE 12.3** **Gender Differences in Depression Across Cultures**
This graph shows the rates of depression for men and women in nine cultures (Weissman & Olfson, 1995). > *Which cultures have the highest and lowest rates of depression? What might account for these differences?* > *Which cultures have the largest gender difference in depression? What might account for these differences?* > *In order to be diagnosed with depression, a person has to seek treatment for the disorder. How might gender and culture influence a person's willingness to get treatment?*

has been related to lowered depression and decreased suicide risk in a variety of samples (Rasmussen & Wingate, 2012; Tindle & others, 2012).

Having a spouse, roommate, or friend who suffers from depression can increase the risk that an individual will also become depressed (Coyne, 1976; Joiner, Alfano, & Metalsky, 1992; Ruscher & Gotlib, 1988). Such effects are sometimes called *contagion* because they suggest that depression can spread from one person to another (Kiuru & others, 2012). Of course, the term *contagion* here is metaphorical. In fact, research suggests that whether depression and anxiety are contagious depends on the quality of interactions between people. To read more about this topic and its potential role in children's psychological health, see the Intersection.

**SOCIOCULTURAL FACTORS**  Individuals with a low socioeconomic status (SES), especially people living in poverty, are more likely to develop depression than their higher-SES counterparts (Boothroyd & others, 2006). A longitudinal study of adults revealed that depression increased as one's standard of living and employment circumstances worsened (Lorant & others, 2007). Studies have found very high rates of depression in Native American groups, among whom poverty, hopelessness, and alcoholism are widespread (Teesson & Vogl, 2006).

Women are nearly twice as likely as men to develop depression (Yuan & others, 2009). As Figure 12.3 shows, this gender difference occurs in many countries (Inaba & others, 2005). Incidence of depression is high, too, among single women who are the heads of households and among young married women who work at unsatisfying, dead-end jobs (Whiffen & Demidenko, 2006). Minority women also are a high-risk group for depression (Diefenbach & others, 2009).

*Another gender difference to consider: Why might men show lower levels of depression than women?*

# Bipolar Disorder

**bipolar disorder**
Mood disorder characterized by extreme mood swings that include one or more episodes of mania, an overexcited, unrealistically optimistic state.

Just as we all have down times, there are times when things seem to be going phenomenally well. For individuals with bipolar disorder, the ups and downs of life take on an extreme and often harmful tone. **Bipolar disorder** is a disorder characterized by extreme mood swings that include one or more episodes of *mania,* an overexcited, unrealistically optimistic state. A manic episode is like the flipside of a depressive episode (Goldney, 2012). The person who experiences mania feels on top of the world. She has tremendous energy and might sleep very little. A manic state also features an impulsivity that can get the individual in trouble. For example, the sufferer might spend his life savings on a foolish business venture.

Most bipolar individuals experience multiple cycles of depression interspersed with mania, usually separated by six months to a year. Unlike depressive disorders, which are more likely to occur in women, bipolar disorder is equally common in women and men. Bipolar disorder does not prevent a person from being successful. Award-winning actor Catherine Zeta-Jones, famed dancer and choreographer Alvin Ailey, and actor-writer Carrie Fisher (Princess Leia) have been diagnosed with bipolar disorder.

What factors play a role in the development of bipolar disorder? Genetic influences are stronger predictors of bipolar disorder than of depressive disorders (Pirooznia & others, 2012). An individual with an identical twin who has bipolar disorder has a 70 percent probability of also having the disorder, and a fraternal twin has a more than 10 percent probability (Figure 12.4). Researchers are zeroing in on the specific genetic location of bipolar disorder (Crisafulli & others, 2012; Pedroso & others, 2012).

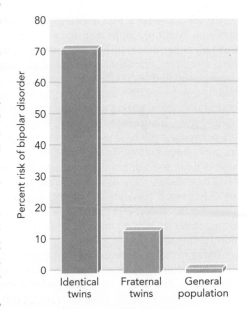

**FIGURE 12.4  Risk of Bipolar Disorder in Identical and Fraternal Twins If One Twin Has the Disorder, and in the General Population** Notice how much stronger the similarity of bipolar disorder is in identical twins as compared with fraternal twins and the general population. These statistics suggest a strong genetic role in the disorder.

## Clinical and Developmental Psychology: Can Kids "Catch" Depression and Anxiety?

The role of friendships in children's and adolescents' lives is increasingly of interest to developmental psychologists. Among youth, friends are important to self-esteem, well-being, and school adjustment (Mendel & others, 2012; Mora & Gil, 2012; Shany, Wiener, & Assido, 2012). Still, some friends may be better influences than others. A large body of evidence supports the conclusion that hanging around with friends who engage in problem behaviors such as delinquency and substance abuse increases the likelihood of youth involvement in such behavior (Giletta & others, 2012; Laursen & others, 2012). But what about associating closely with individuals who have psychological symptoms, like depression and anxiety, that are not as likely to be evident in behavior? Might such symptoms also "rub off" on friends?

Before addressing that question, let's clarify some terms. In children, symptoms of psychological disorders are often categorized as either externalizing or internalizing symptoms. *Externalizing symptoms,* commonly referred to as "acting out," include delinquency and aggression. *Internalizing symptoms* include feelings of depression and anxiety. While research supports the notion that externalizing symptoms are contagious (that is, they spread from one friend to another), only recently have researchers addressed the possibility that internalizing symptoms might be contagious as well. To put it concretely, can having a friend who is depressed or anxious increase the likelihood that a child or an adolescent will become depressed or anxious as well? Research suggests the answer is yes (Prinstein, 2007; Tompkins & others, 2011), and a recent study by Rebecca Schwartz-Mette and Amanda Rose (2012) provides an explanation for this effect.

These researchers proposed that depression and anxiety can pass from one friend to another through the conversations friends share. They examined a particular kind of social sharing called co-rumination (Rose, 2002; Rose & Smith, 2009). *Rumination* is a way of thinking that involves worrying about a topic without finding a resolution. When we ruminate, we might dwell on all the possible horrible consequences of some negative event or imagine everything that might go wrong in the future. *Co-rumination* is like that too, but it involves engaging in a conversation with someone and making a negative event that the person is going through seem even worse. When friends co-ruminate, they focus on problems, rehashing them repeatedly, speculating on possible future problems, and emphasizing negative emotions (Rose, 2002). Ironically, though co-rumination can make both members of a friendship feel pretty miserable, this kind of social sharing is also related to friendship quality and closeness (Rose, Carlson, & Waller, 2007). Perhaps because of this closeness, co-rumination is associated with strong feelings of *empathetic distress,* which occurs when one friend takes on the negative feelings of the other (Smith & Rose, 2011). If co-ruminating allows one to share deeply in the emotional life of another, it might well play a role in spreading depression or anxiety.

To explore this possibility, Schwartz-Mette and Rose (2012) examined whether symptoms of depression and anxiety in one youth predicted increases in these symptoms in that individual's friends and whether this contagion might be explained by the tendency to co-ruminate. They surveyed several hundred children (third- and fifth-graders) and adolescents (seventh- and ninth-graders) and their best friends and found that having a friend who was feeling depressed or anxious indeed predicted increases in feelings of depression or anxiety six months later in all but the youngest boys. Further, co-rumination was associated with contagion of anxiety for all but the youngest boys in the study. For depression, co-rumination was associated with the contagion of depression but only for adolescents. This work shows that peer relationships are a key factor to consider in psychological difficulties among youth.

Friends are a vital resource, and talking with friends is a primary channel by which we make sense of the world. Research is now showing that the quality of those conversations may be an important element in mental health.

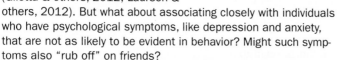

\\ **How do these results match your experiences of childhood friendship?**

\\ **Do some of your present-day friends co-ruminate over negative events?**

Other biological processes are also a factor. Like depression, bipolar disorder is associated with differences in brain activity. Figure 12.5 shows the metabolic activity in the cerebral cortex of an individual cycling through depressive and manic phases. Notice the decrease in metabolic activity in the brain during depression and the increase in metabolic activity during mania (Baxter & others, 1995). In addition to high levels of norepinephrine and low levels of serotonin, studies link high levels of the neurotransmitter glutamate to bipolar disorder (Singh & others, 2010; Sourial-Bassillious & others, 2009).

Psychologists and psychiatrists have recently noted cases of children who appear to suffer from bipolar disorder (Cosgrove, Roybal, & Chang, 2013; Defilippis & Wagner, 2013). A key dilemma in such cases is that treating bipolar disorder in adults involves administering psychoactive drugs that have not been approved for children's use. The side effects of these drugs could put children's health and development at risk. To address this issue, *DSM-5* includes a new diagnosis, *disruptive mood dysregulation disorder,* which is considered a depressive disorder in children who show persistent irritability and recurrent episodes of out-of-control behavior (APA, 2013). This decision is not without controversy. As we saw with ADHD, some children who are perceived to be prone to wild mood swings may be simply behaving like children.

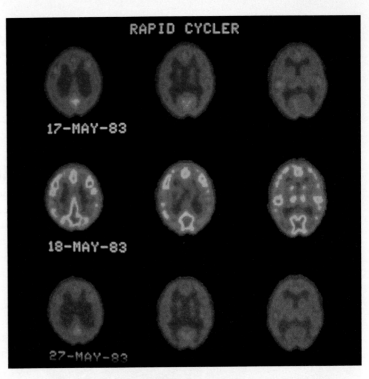

**FIGURE 12.5 Brain Metabolism in Mania and Depression** PET scans of an individual with bipolar disorder, who is described as a rapid-cycler because of how quickly severe mood changes occurred. (*Top and bottom*) The person's brain in a depressed state. (*Middle*) A manic state. The PET scans reveal how the brain's energy consumption falls in depression and rises in mania. The red areas in the middle row reflect rapid consumption of glucose.

# Suicide

Thinking about suicide is not necessarily abnormal. However, attempting or completing the act of suicide is abnormal. Approximately 90 percent of individuals who commit suicide are estimated to have a diagnosable mental disorder (NIMH, 2008), and the most common disorders among individuals who commit suicide are depression and anxiety (Blanco & others, 2012; Nauta & others, 2012). Depressed individuals are also likely to attempt suicide more than once (da Silva Cais & others, 2009). Sadly, many individuals who, to the outside eye, seem to be leading successful and fulfilling lives have ended their lives through suicide. Examples include poet Sylvia Plath, novelist Ernest Hemingway, and grunge icon Kurt Cobain (who committed suicide after lifelong battles with ADHD and bipolar disorder).

According to the Centers for Disease Control and Prevention (CDC), in 2010, 37,793 people in the United States committed suicide, and suicide was the 10th-highest cause of death in the country (CDC, 2012). There are twice as many suicides as homicides in the United States, and the suicide rate increased 13 percent from 1999 to 2010 (Schmitz & others, 2012). Research indicates that for every completed suicide, 8 to 25 attempted suicides occur (NIMH, 2008). Suicide is the third-leading cause (after automobile accidents and homicides) of death today among U.S. adolescents 13 through 19 years of age (Murphy, Xu, & Kochanek, 2012). Even more shocking, in the United States suicide is the third-leading cause of death among children 10 to 14 years of age (CDC, 2007).

## What to Do

1. Ask direct, straightforward questions in a calm manner. For example, "Are you thinking about hurting yourself?"

2. Be a good listener and be supportive. Emphasize that unbearable pain can be survived.

3. Take the suicide threat very seriously. Ask questions about the person's feelings, relationships, and thoughts about the type of method to be used. If a gun, pills, rope, or other means is mentioned and a specific plan has been developed, the situation is dangerous. Stay with the person until help arrives.

4. Encourage the person to get professional help and assist him or her in getting help. If the person is willing, take the person to a mental health facility or hospital.

## What Not to Do

1. Don't ignore the warning signs.

2. Don't refuse to talk about suicide if the person wants to talk about it.

3. Don't react with horror, disapproval, or repulsion.

4. Don't offer false reassurances ("Everything will be all right") or make judgments ("You should be thankful for . . .").

5. Don't abandon the person after the crisis seems to have passed or after professional counseling has begun.

**FIGURE 12.6  When Someone Is Threatening Suicide** Do not ignore the warning signs if you think someone you know is considering suicide. Talk to a counselor if you are reluctant to say anything to the person yourself.

*Note that people whose parents committed suicide may be more likely to consider suicide as an option. So, environment matters.*

Given these grim statistics, psychologists work with individuals to reduce the frequency and intensity of suicidal impulses. Figure 12.6 provides good advice on what to do and what not to do if you encounter someone who is threatening suicide.

What might prompt an individual to end his or her own life? Biological, psychological, and sociocultural circumstances can be contributing factors.

**BIOLOGICAL FACTORS**   Genetic factors appear to play a role in suicide, which tends to run in families (Althoff & others, 2012). The Hemingways are one famous family that has been plagued by suicide. Five Hemingways, spread across generations, committed suicide, including the writer Ernest Hemingway and his granddaughter Margaux, a model and actor. Similarly, in 2009, Nicholas Hughes—a successful marine biologist and the son of Sylvia Plath, a poet who had killed herself—tragically hanged himself.

Studies have linked suicide with low levels of the neurotransmitter serotonin (Lyddon & others, 2012). Individuals who attempt suicide and who have low serotonin levels are 10 times more likely to attempt suicide again than are attempters who have high serotonin levels (Courtet & others, 2004). Poor physical health, especially when it is chronic, is another risk factor for suicide (Webb & others, 2012).

**PSYCHOLOGICAL FACTORS**   Psychological factors that can contribute to suicide include mental disorders and traumas such as sexual abuse (Wanner & others, 2012). Struggling with the stress of a psychological disorder can leave a person feeling hopeless, and the disorder itself may tax the person's ability to cope with life's difficulties. Indeed, approximately 90 percent of individuals who commit suicide are estimated to have a diagnosable mental disorder (NIMH, 2008).

An immediate and highly stressful circumstance—such as the loss of a loved one or a job, flunking out of school, or an unwanted pregnancy—can lead people to threaten and/or to commit suicide (Videtic & others, 2009). In addition, substance abuse is linked with suicide more today than in the past (Conner & others, 2012).

In research focusing on suicide notes, Thomas Joiner and his colleagues have found that having a sense of belongingness or of being needed separates individuals who attempt suicide from those who complete it (Joiner, 2005; Joiner, Hollar, & Van Orden, 2006; Joiner & Ribeiro, 2011). Essentially, people who feel that someone will miss them or still need them are less likely than others to complete a suicide (A. R. Smith & others, 2012).

**SOCIOCULTURAL FACTORS**   Chronic economic hardship can be a factor in suicide (Ferretti & Coluccia, 2009; Rojas & Stenberg, 2010). Cultural and ethnic contexts also are related to suicide attempts. In the United States, adolescents' suicide attempts vary across ethnic groups. As Figure 12.7 illustrates, more than 20 percent of Native American/Alaska Native (NA/AN) female adolescents reported that they had attempted suicide in the previous year, and suicide accounts for almost 20 percent of NA/AN deaths in 15- to 19-year-olds (Goldston & others, 2008). As the figure also shows, African American and non-Latino White males reported the lowest incidence of suicide attempts. A major risk factor in the high rate of suicide attempts by NA/AN adolescents is their elevated rate of alcohol abuse.

Suicide rates vary worldwide; the lowest rates occur in countries with cultural and religious norms against ending one's own life. Among the nations with the highest suicide rates are several eastern European nations—including Belarus, Bulgaria, and Russia—along with Japan and South Korea. According to the World Health Organization (WHO), among the nations with the lowest rates are Haiti, Antigua and Barbuda, Egypt, and Iran (WHO, 2009). Of the 104 nations ranked by the WHO, the United States ranks 40th.

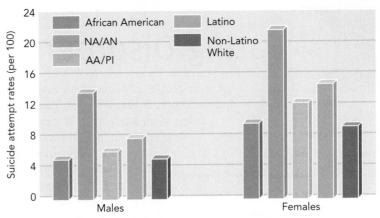

**FIGURE 12.7  Suicide Attempts by U.S. Adolescents from Different Ethnic Groups** Note that the data shown are for one-year rates of self-reported suicide attempts. NA/AN = Native Americans/Alaska Native; AA/PI = Asian American/Pacific Islander.

Research has also linked suicide to the culture of honor. Recall that in honor cultures, individuals are more likely to interpret insults as fighting words and to defend their personal honor with aggression. One set of studies examined suicide and depression in the United States, comparing geographic regions that are considered to have a culture of honor (that is, southern states) with other areas. Even accounting for a host of other factors, suicide rates were found to be higher in states with a culture of honor (Osterman & Brown, 2011). The researchers also examined how regions compared in terms of the use of prescription antidepressants and discovered that states with a culture of honor also had lower levels of use of these drugs. It may be that in a culture of honor, seeking treatment for depression is seen as a weakness or a mark of shame.

There are gender differences in suicide as well (Sarma & Kola, 2010). Women are three times more likely than men to attempt suicide. Men, however, are four times more likely than women to complete suicide (Kochanek & others, 2004). Men are also more likely than women to use a firearm in a suicide attempt (Maris, 1998). The highest suicide rate is among non-Latino White men ages 85 and older (NIMH, 2008).

*Men are less likely than women to report being depressed but are more likely to commit suicide. Clearly, depression in men might be underestimated.*

self-quiz

1. To be diagnosed with bipolar disorder, an individual must experience
   A. a manic episode.
   B. a depressive episode.
   C. a manic episode and a depressive episode.
   D. a suicidal episode.

2. All of the following are a symptom of major depressive disorder except
   A. fatigue.
   B. weight change.
   C. thoughts of death.
   D. substance use.

3. A true statement about suicide and gender is that
   A. women are more likely to attempt suicide than men.
   B. men are more likely to attempt suicide than women.
   C. men and women are equally likely to attempt suicide.
   D. men and women are equally likely to complete suicide.

**APPLY IT!** 4. During his first two college years, Barry has felt "down" most of the time. He has had trouble concentrating and difficulty making decisions. Sometimes he is so overwhelmed with deciding on his major and struggling to focus that he feels hopeless. He has problems with loss of appetite and sleeps a great deal of the time, and in general his energy level is low. Barry has found that things he used to love, like watching sports and playing video games are just no fun anymore. Which of the following is most likely to be true of Barry?
   A. Barry is suffering from major depressive disorder.
   B. Barry is entering the depressive phase of bipolar disorder.
   C. Barry has an anxiety disorder.
   D. Barry is experiencing the everyday blues that everyone gets from time to time.

Disorders Involving Emotion and Mood  //  **461**

# 4 Eating Disorders

For some people, concerns about weight and body image become a serious, debilitating disorder (Lock, 2012a; Wilson & Zandberg, 2012). For such individuals, the very act of eating is an arena where a variety of complex biological, psychological, and cultural issues are played out, often with tragic consequences.

A number of famous people have coped with eating disorders, including Princess Diana, Ashley Judd, Paula Abdul, Mary-Kate Olsen, and Kelly Clarkson. Eating disorders are characterized by extreme disturbances in eating behavior—from eating very, very little to eating a great deal. In this section we examine three eating disorders—anorexia nervosa, bulimia nervosa, and binge-eating disorder.

*Disorders of eating can vary across cultures. In Fiji, a disorder known as macake involves poor appetite and refusing to eat. Very high levels of social concern meet this refusal, and individuals with macake are strongly motivated to start eating and enjoying food again.*

## Anorexia Nervosa

**anorexia nervosa**
Eating disorder that involves the relentless pursuit of thinness through starvation.

**Anorexia nervosa** is an eating disorder that involves the relentless pursuit of thinness through starvation. Anorexia nervosa is much more common in girls and women than boys and men and affects between 0.5 and 3.7 percent of young women (NIMH, 2011). The American Psychiatric Association (2013) lists these main characteristics of anorexia nervosa:

- Weight less than 85 percent of what is considered normal for age and height, and refusal to maintain weight at a healthy level.

- An intense fear of gaining weight that does not decrease with weight loss.

- A distorted body image (Stewart & others, 2012). Even when individuals with anorexia nervosa are extremely thin, they never think they are thin enough.

Over time, anorexia nervosa can lead to physical changes, such as the growth of fine hair all over the body, thinning of bones and hair, severe constipation, and low blood pressure (NIMH, 2011). Dangerous and even life-threatening complications include damage to the heart and thyroid. Anorexia nervosa is said to have the highest mortality rate (about 5.6 percent of individuals with anorexia nervosa die within 10 years of diagnosis) of any psychological disorder (Hoek, 2006; NIMH, 2011).

*Individuals with anorexia nervosa lack personal distress over their symptoms. Recall that personal distress over one's behavior is just one aspect of the definition of abnormal.*

Anorexia nervosa typically begins in the teenage years, often following an episode of dieting and some type of life stress (Fitzpatrick, 2012). Most individuals with anorexia nervosa are non-Latino White female adolescents or young adults from well-educated middle- and upper-income families (Darcy, 2012; Dodge, 2012). They are often high-achieving perfectionists (Forbush, Heatherton, & Keel, 2007). Obsessive thinking about weight and compulsive exercise are also related to anorexia nervosa (Hildebrandt & others, 2012).

## Bulimia Nervosa

**bulimia nervosa**
Eating disorder in which an individual (typically a girl or woman) consistently follows a binge-and-purge eating pattern.

**Bulimia nervosa** is an eating disorder in which an individual (typically female) consistently follows a binge-and-purge eating pattern. The individual goes on an eating binge and then purges by self-induced vomiting or the use of laxatives. Most people with bulimia

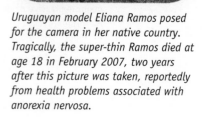

*Uruguayan model Eliana Ramos posed for the camera in her native country. Tragically, the super-thin Ramos died at age 18 in February 2007, two years after this picture was taken, reportedly from health problems associated with anorexia nervosa.*

nervosa are preoccupied with food, have a strong fear of becoming overweight, and are depressed or anxious (Birgegård, Norring, & Clinton, 2012). Because bulimia nervosa occurs within a normal weight range, the disorder is often difficult to detect. A person with bulimia nervosa usually keeps the disorder a secret and experiences a great deal of self-disgust and shame.

Bulimia nervosa can lead to complications such as a chronic sore throat, kidney problems, dehydration, and gastrointestinal disorders (NIMH, 2011). The disorder is also related to dental problems, as persistent exposure to the stomach acids in vomit can wear away tooth enamel.

*Dentists and dental hygienists are sometimes the first to recognize the signs of bulimia nervosa.*

Bulimia nervosa typically begins in late adolescence or early adulthood (Levine, 2002). The disorder affects between 1 and 4 percent of young women (NIMH, 2011). Like those with anorexia nervosa, many young women who develop bulimia nervosa are highly perfectionistic (Lampard & others, 2012). At the same time, they tend to have low levels of self-efficacy (Bardone-Cone & others, 2006). In other words, these are young women with very high standards but very low confidence that they can achieve their goals. Impulsivity, negative emotion, and obsessive-compulsive disorder are also related to bulimia (Roncero, Perpina, & Garcia-Soriano, 2011). Bulimia nervosa is associated, too, with a high incidence of sexual and physical abuse in childhood (Lo Sauro & others, 2008).

*Although much more common in women, bulimia can also affect men. Elton John has described his struggles with this eating disorder.*

## Anorexia Nervosa and Bulimia Nervosa: Causes and Treatments

What is the etiology (cause) of anorexia nervosa and bulimia nervosa? For many years researchers thought that sociocultural factors, such as media images of very thin women and family pressures, were the central determinants of these disorders (Le Grange & others, 2010). Media images that glorify extreme thinness can indeed influence women's body image, and emphasis on the thin ideal is related to anorexia nervosa and bulimia nervosa (Carr & Peebles, 2012). However, as powerful as these media messages might be, countless females are exposed to media images of unrealistically thin women, but relatively few develop eating disorders. Many young women embark on diets, but comparatively few of them develop eating disorders.

Eating disorders occur in cultures that do not emphasize the ideal of thinness, although the disorders may differ from Western descriptions. For instance, in Eastern cultures, individuals can show the symptoms of anorexia nervosa, but they lack the fear of getting fat that is common in North Americans with the disorder (Pike, Yamamiya, & Konishi, 2011).

Since the 1980s, researchers have increasingly probed the potential biological underpinnings of these disorders, examining in particular the interplay of social and biological factors. Genes play a substantial role in both anorexia nervosa and bulimia nervosa (Lock, 2012b). In fact, genes influence many psychological characteristics (for example, perfectionism, impulsivity, obsessive-compulsive tendencies, and thinness drive) and behaviors (restrained eating, binge eating, self-induced vomiting) that are associated with anorexia nervosa and bulimia nervosa (Mikolajczyk, Grzywacz, & Samochowiec, 2010; Schur, Heckbert, & Goldberg, 2010). These genes are also factors in the regulation of serotonin, and problems in regulating serotonin are related to both anorexia nervosa and bulimia nervosa (Capasso, Putrella, & Milano, 2009).

Even as biological factors play a role in the emergence of eating disorders, eating disorders themselves affect the body, including the brain. Most psychologists believe that while social factors and experiences may play a role in triggering dieting, the physical effects of dieting, bingeing, and purging may change the neural networks that then sustain the disordered pattern, in a kind of vicious cycle (Lock, 2012b).

Although anorexia and bulimia nervosa are serious disorders, recovery is possible (Fitzpatrick, 2012; Treasure, Claudino, & Zucker, 2010). Anorexia nervosa may require hospitalization. The first target of intervention is promoting weight gain, in extreme cases through the use of a feeding tube. A common obstacle in the treatment of anorexia nervosa is that individuals with the disorder deny that anything is wrong. They maintain their belief that thinness and restrictive dieting are correct and not a sign of mental illness (Wilson, Grilo, & Vitousek, 2007). Still, drug therapies and psychotherapy have been shown to be effective in treating anorexia nervosa, as well as bulimia nervosa (Hagman & Frank, 2012; Wilson & Zandberg, 2012).

## Binge-Eating Disorder

**binge-eating disorder (BED)**
Eating disorder characterized by recurrent episodes of eating large amounts of food during which the person feels a lack of control over eating.

**Binge-eating disorder (BED)** is characterized by recurrent episodes of consuming large amounts of food during which the person feels a lack of control over eating (APA, 2013). Unlike an individual with bulimia nervosa, someone with BED does not try to purge. Most individuals with BED are overweight or obese (Carrard, der Linden, & Golay, 2012).

Individuals with BED often eat quickly, eat a great deal when they are not hungry, and eat until they are uncomfortably full. They frequently eat alone because of embarrassment or guilt, and they feel ashamed and disgusted with themselves after overeating. BED is the most common of all eating disorders—affecting men, women, and ethnic groups within the United States more similarly than anorexia nervosa or bulimia nervosa (Azarbad & others, 2010). An estimated 2 to 5 percent of Americans will suffer from BED in their lifetime (NIMH, 2011).

BED is thought to characterize approximately 8 percent of individuals who are obese. Unlike obese individuals who do not suffer from BED, binge eaters are more likely to place great value on their physical appearance, weight, and body shape (Grilo, Masheb, & White, 2010). The complications of BED are those of obesity more generally, including diabetes, hypertension, and cardiovascular disease.

### Binge-Eating Disorder: Causes and Treatments

Researchers are examining the role of biological and psychological factors in BED. Genes play a role (Akkermann & others, 2012), as does dopamine, the neurotransmitter related to reward pathways in the brain (C. Davis & others, 2010). The fact that binge eating often occurs after stressful events suggests that binge eaters use food to regulate their emotions (Wilson, Grilo, & Vitousek, 2007). The areas of the brain and endocrine system that respond to stress are overactive in individuals with BED (Lo Sauro & others, 2008), and this overactivity leads to high levels of circulating cortisol, the hormone most associated with stress. Individuals with BED may be more likely to perceive events as stressful and then seek to manage that stress by binge eating.

Little research has examined the sociocultural factors in BED. One study examined whether exposure to U.S. culture might increase the risk of developing BED (Swanson & others, 2012). The results showed that Mexicans who immigrated to the United States and Mexican Americans were more likely to develop BED than were Mexicans who lived in Mexico, controlling for a variety of factors (Swanson & others, 2012).

*Unlike individuals with anorexia nervosa or bulimia nervosa, most people with binge eating disorder are overweight or obese.*

Just as treatment for anorexia nervosa first focuses on weight gain, some believe that treatment for BED should first target weight loss (DeAngelis, 2002). Others argue that individuals with BED must be treated for disordered eating per se, and they insist that if the underlying psychological issues are not addressed, weight loss will not be successful or permanent (de Zwaan & others, 2005; Hay & others, 2009).

# 5 Dissociative Disorders

Have you ever been on a long car ride and completely lost track of time, so that you could not even remember a stretch of miles along the road? Have you been so caught up in a daydream that you were unaware of the passage of time? These are examples of normal dissociation. *Dissociation* refers to psychological states in which the person feels disconnected from immediate experience.

**dissociative disorders**
Psychological disorders that involve a sudden loss of memory or change in identity due to the dissociation (separation) of the individual's conscious awareness from previous memories and thoughts.

At the extreme of dissociation are individuals who persistently feel a sense of disconnection. **Dissociative disorders** are psychological disorders that involve a sudden loss of memory or change in identity. Under extreme stress or shock, the individual's conscious awareness becomes dissociated (separated or split) from previous memories and thoughts (Espirito-Santo & Pio-Abreu, 2009). Individuals who develop dissociative disorders may have problems putting together different aspects of consciousness, so that experiences at different levels of awareness might be felt as if they are happening to someone else (Dell & O'Neil, 2007).

Psychologists believe that dissociation is a way of dealing with extreme stress (Brand & others, 2012). Through dissociation the individual mentally protects his or her conscious self from the traumatic event. Dissociative disorders often occur in individuals who also show signs of PTSD (Lanius & others, 2012). Both psychological disorders are thought to be rooted, in part, in extremely traumatic life events (Foote & others, 2006). The notion that dissociative disorders are related to problems in pulling together emotional memories is supported by findings showing lower volume in the hippocampus and amygdala in individuals with dissociative disorders (Vermetten & others, 2006). The hippocampus is especially involved in consolidating memory and organizing life experience into a coherent whole (Spiegel, 2006).

Dissociative disorders are perhaps the most controversial of all diagnostic categories, with some psychologists believing that they are often mistakenly diagnosed (Freeland & others, 1993) and others arguing that they are underdiagnosed (Sar, Akyuz, & Dogan, 2007; Spiegel, 2006). Three kinds of dissociative disorders are dissociative amnesia, dissociative fugue, and dissociative identity disorder.

 *In dissociative disorders, consciousness (see Chapter 4) is split off from experience—the "stream of consciousness" is disrupted. Hypnosis is often used to treat dissociative disorders.*

*The study on dissociative disorders in Uganda from earlier in this chapter found agreement among respondents that dissociative states are brought on by trauma.*

# Dissociative Amnesia

Recall from Chapter 6 that amnesia is the inability to recall important events (Markowitsch & Staniloiu, 2012). Amnesia can result from a blow to the head that produces trauma in the brain. **Dissociative amnesia** is a type of amnesia characterized by extreme memory loss that stems from extensive psychological stress. People experiencing dissociative amnesia remember everyday tasks like how to hail a cab and use a phone. They forget only aspects of their own identity and autobiographical experiences.

Sometimes individuals suffering from dissociative amnesia will also unexpectedly travel away from home, occasionally even assuming a new identity. For instance, on August 28, 2008, Hannah Upp, a 23-year-old middle school teacher in New York City, disappeared while out for a run (Marx & Didziulis, 2009). She had no wallet, no identification, no cell phone, and no money. Her family, friends, and roommates posted flyers around the city and messages on the Internet. As days went by, they became increasingly concerned that something terrible had happened. Finally, Hannah was found floating face down in the New York harbor on September 16, sunburned and dehydrated but alive. She remembered nothing of her experiences. To her, it felt like she had gone out for a run and 10 minutes later was being pulled from the harbor. To this day, she does not know what event might have led to her dissociative amnesia, nor does she remember how she survived during her two-week disappearance.

*At one point during her dissociative amnesia, Hannah was approached by someone who asked if she was the Hannah everyone was looking for, and she answered no.*

# Dissociative Identity Disorder

**Dissociative identity disorder (DID),** formerly called *multiple personality disorder,* is the most dramatic, least common, and most controversial dissociative disorder. Individuals with this disorder have two or more distinct personalities or identities (Belli & others, 2012). Each identity has its own memories, behaviors, and relationships. One identity dominates at one time, another takes over at another time. Individuals sometimes report that a wall of amnesia separates their different identities (Dale & others, 2009); however, research suggests that memory does transfer across these identities, even if the person believes it does not (Kong, Allen, & Glisky, 2008).

The shift between identities usually occurs under distress (Sar & others, 2007) but sometimes can also be controlled by the person (Kong, Allen, & Glisky, 2008).

A famous real-life example of dissociative identity disorder is the "three faces of Eve" case, based on the life of a woman named Chris Sizemore (Thigpen & Cleckley, 1957) (Figure 12.8). Eve White was the original dominant personality. She had no knowledge of her second personality, Eve Black, although Eve Black had been alternating with Eve White for a number of years. Eve White was bland, quiet, and serious. By contrast, Eve Black was carefree, mischievous, and uninhibited. Eve Black would emerge at the most inappropriate times, leaving Eve White with hangovers, bills, and a reputation in local bars that she could not explain. During treatment, a

**FIGURE 12.8** **The Three Faces of Eve** Chris Sizemore, the subject of the 1950s book and film *The Three Faces of Eve,* is shown here with a work she painted, titled *Three Faces in One.*

third personality emerged: Jane. More mature than the other two, Jane seems to have developed as a result of therapy. More recently, former Heisman Trophy winner and legendary NFL running back Herschel Walker (2008) revealed his experience with dissociative disorder in his book *Breaking Free: My Life with Dissociative Identity Disorder*.

Research on dissociative identity disorder links a high rate of extraordinarily severe sexual or physical abuse during early childhood to the condition (Ross & Ness, 2010). Some psychologists believe that a child can cope with intense trauma by dissociating from the experience and developing other alternate selves as protectors. Sexual abuse has occurred in as many as 70 percent or more of dissociative identity disorder cases (Foote & others, 2006); however, the majority of individuals who have been sexually abused do not develop dissociative identity disorder. The vast majority of individuals with dissociative identity disorder are women. A genetic predisposition might also exist, as the disorder tends to run in families (Dell & Eisenhower, 1990).

Until the 1980s, only about 300 cases of dissociative identity disorder had ever been reported (Suinn, 1984). In the past 30 years, hundreds more cases have been diagnosed. Social cognitive approaches point out that diagnoses have tended to increase whenever the popular media present a case, as in the miniseries *Sybil* and the Showtime drama *United States of Tara*. From this perspective, individuals develop multiple identities through social contagion. After exposure to these examples, people may be more likely to view multiple identities as a real condition. Some experts believe, in fact, that dissociative identity disorder is a *social construction*—that it represents a category some people adopt to make sense of their experiences (Spanos, 1996). Rather than being a single person with many conflicting feelings, wishes, and potentially awful experiences, the individual compartmentalizes different aspects of the self into independent identities. In some cases, therapists have been accused of creating alternate personalities. Encountering an individual who appears to have a fragmented sense of self, the therapist may begin to treat each fragment as its own "personality" (Spiegel, 2006).

*Therapists and patients are making attributions to understand abnormal behavior.*

Cross-cultural comparisons can shed light on whether dissociative identity disorder is primarily a response to traumatic events or the result of a social cognitive factor like social contagion. If dissociation is a response to trauma, individuals with similar levels of traumatic experience should show similar degrees of dissociation, regardless of their exposure to cultural messages about dissociation. In China, the popular media *do not* commonly portray individuals with dissociative disorder, and professional knowledge of the disorder is rare. One study comparing individuals from China and Canada (where dissociative identity disorder is a widely publicized condition) found reports of traumatic experience to be similar across groups and to relate to dissociative experiences similarly as well (Ross & others, 2008), casting some doubt on the notion that dissociative experiences are entirely a product of social contagion.

## self-quiz

1. Dissociative identity disorder is associated with unusually high rates of
   A. anxiety.
   B. abuse during early childhood.
   C. depression.
   D. divorce.

2. Someone who suffers memory loss after a psychological trauma is said to have
   A. dissociative identity disorder.
   B. dissociative recall disorder.
   C. dissociative amnesia.
   D. schizophrenia.

3. In cases of dissociative amnesia, the individual not only experiences amnesia but also
   A. has frequent thoughts of suicide.
   B. takes on multiple different identities.
   C. refuses to leave his or her home.
   D. travels away from home.

APPLY IT! 4. Eddie often loses track of time. He is sometimes late for appointments because he is so engrossed in whatever he is doing. While working on a term paper in the library, he gets so caught up in what he is reading that he is shocked when he looks up and sees that the sun has set and it is night. Which of the following best describes Eddie?
   A. Eddie is showing signs of dissociative identity disorder.
   B. Eddie is showing signs of dissociative memory disorder.
   C. Eddie is showing normal dissociative states.
   D. Eddie is at risk for dissociative amnesia.

# 6 Schizophrenia

Have you had the experience of watching a movie and suddenly noticing that the film bears an uncanny resemblance to your life? Have you ever listened to a radio talk show and realized that the host was saying exactly what you were just thinking? Do these moments mean something special about you, or are they coincidences? For individuals with severe psychological disorders, such random experiences feel not random but filled with meaning. **Psychosis** refers to a state in which a person's perceptions and thoughts are fundamentally removed from reality. *DSM-5* recognizes a class of disorders called Schizophrenia Spectrum and Other Psychotic Disorders. Within this group is one of the most debilitating psychological disorders (and our focus in this section), schizophrenia.

**psychosis**
A state in which a person's perceptions and thoughts are fundamentally removed from reality.

**Schizophrenia** is a severe psychological disorder that is characterized by highly disordered thought processes. These disordered thoughts are referred to as *psychotic* because they are far removed from reality. The world of the person with schizophrenia is deeply frightening and chaotic.

Schizophrenia is usually diagnosed in early adulthood, around age 18 for men and 25 for women. Individuals with schizophrenia may see things that are not there, hear voices inside their heads, and live in a strange world of twisted logic. They may say odd things, show inappropriate emotion, and move their bodies in peculiar ways. Often, they are socially withdrawn and isolated.

*Seeking treatment for schizophrenia takes courage. It requires that individuals accept that their perception of the world—their very sense of reality—is mistaken.*

It is difficult to imagine the ordeal of people living with schizophrenia, who comprise about half of the patients in psychiatric hospitals. The suicide risk for individuals with schizophrenia is eight times that for the general population (Pompili & others, 2007). For many with the disorder, controlling it means using powerful medications to combat symptoms. The most common cause of relapse is that individuals stop taking their medication. They might do so because they feel better and believe they no longer need the drugs, they do not realize that their thoughts are disordered, or the side effects of the medications are too unpleasant.

**schizophrenia**
Severe psychological disorder characterized by highly disordered thought processes; individuals suffering from schizophrenia may be referred to as psychotic because they are so far removed from reality.

## Symptoms of Schizophrenia

Psychologists generally classify the symptoms of schizophrenia as positive symptoms, negative symptoms, and cognitive deficits (NIMH, 2008).

**POSITIVE SYMPTOMS**  The positive symptoms of schizophrenia are marked by a distortion or an excess of normal function. They are "positive" because they reflect something added above and beyond normal behavior. Positive symptoms of schizophrenia include hallucinations, delusions, thought disorders, and disorders of movement.

**Hallucinations** are sensory experiences that occur in the absence of real stimuli. Hallucinations are usually auditory—the person might complain of hearing voices—or visual, and much less commonly they can be experienced as smells or tastes (Bhatia & others, 2009). Culture affects the form hallucinations take, as well as their content and sensory modality—that is, whether the hallucinations are visual, auditory, or manifest as smells or tastes (Bauer & others, 2011). Visual hallucinations involve seeing things that are not there, as in the case of Moe Armstrong. At the age of 21, while serving in Vietnam as a Marine medical corpsman, Armstrong experienced a psychotic break. Dead Vietcong soldiers appeared to talk to him and beg him for help and did not seem to realize that they were dead. Armstrong, now a successful businessman and a sought-after public speaker who holds two master's degrees, relies on medication to keep such experiences at bay (Bonfatti, 2005).

**Delusions** are false, unusual, and sometimes magical beliefs that are not part of an individual's culture. A delusional person might think that he is Jesus Christ or Muhammad;

**hallucinations**
Sensory experiences that occur in the absence of real stimuli.

**delusions**
False, unusual, and sometimes magical beliefs that are not part of an individual's culture.

another might imagine that her thoughts are being broadcast over the radio. It is crucial to distinguish delusions from cultural ideas such as the religious belief that a person can have divine visions or communicate personally with a deity. Generally, psychology and psychiatry do not treat these ideas as delusional.

For individuals with schizophrenia, delusional beliefs that might seem completely illogical to the outsider are experienced as all too real. At one point in his life, Bill Garrett (from the chapter-opening vignette) was convinced that a blister on his hand was a sign of gangrene. So strong was his belief that he tried to cut off his hand with a knife, before being stopped by his family (M. Park, 2009).

*Thought disorder* refers to the unusual, sometimes bizarre thought processes that are characteristic positive symptoms of schizophrenia. The thoughts of persons with schizophrenia can be disorganized and confused. Often individuals with schizophrenia do not make sense when they talk or write. For example, someone with schizophrenia might say, "Well, Rocky, babe, happening, but where, when, up, top, side, over, you know, out of the way, that's it. Sign off." These incoherent, loose word associations, called *word salad,* have no meaning for the listener. The individual might also make up new words (Kerns & others, 1999). In addition, a person with schizophrenia can show **referential thinking,** which means giving personal meaning to completely random events. For instance, the individual might believe that a traffic light has turned red because he or she is in a hurry.

A final type of positive symptom is *disorders of movement.* A person with schizophrenia may show unusual mannerisms, body movements, and facial expressions. The individual may repeat certain motions over and over or, in extreme cases, may become catatonic. **Catatonia** is a state of immobility and unresponsiveness that lasts for long periods of time (Figure 12.9).

**FIGURE 12.9  Disorders of Movement in Schizophrenia** Unusual motor behaviors are positive symptoms of schizophrenia. Individuals may cease to move altogether (a state called catatonia), sometimes holding bizarre postures.

**catatonia**
State of immobility and unresponsiveness lasting for long periods of time.

**flat affect**
The display of little or no emotion—a common negative symptom of schizophrenia.

**referential thinking**
Ascribing personal meaning to completely random events.

**NEGATIVE SYMPTOMS**  Whereas schizophrenia's positive symptoms are characterized by a distortion or an excess of normal functions, schizophrenia's negative symptoms reflect social withdrawal, behavioral deficits, and the loss or decrease of normal functions. One negative symptom is **flat affect,** which means the display of little or no emotion (LePage & others, 2011). Individuals with schizophrenia also may be lacking in the ability to read the emotions of others (Chambon, Baudouin, & Franck, 2006). They may experience a lack of positive emotional experience in daily life and show a deficient ability to plan, initiate, and engage in goal-directed behavior.

*Because negative symptoms are not as obviously part of a psychiatric illness, people with schizophrenia may be perceived as lazy and unwilling to better their lives.*

**COGNITIVE SYMPTOMS**  Cognitive symptoms of schizophrenia include difficulty sustaining attention, problems holding information in memory, and inability to interpret information and make decisions (Sitnikova, Goff, & Kuperberg, 2009; Torniainen & others, 2012). These symptoms may be subtle and are often detected only through neuropsychological tests. Researchers now recognize that to understand schizophrenia's cognitive symptoms fully, measures of these symptoms must be tailored to particular cultural contexts (Mehta & others, 2011).

# Causes of Schizophrenia

A great deal of research has investigated schizophrenia's causes, including biological, psychological, and sociocultural factors involved in the disorder.

**BIOLOGICAL FACTORS**     Research provides strong support for biological explanations of schizophrenia. Especially compelling is the evidence for a genetic predisposition (Tao & others, 2012). However, structural abnormalities and neurotransmitters also are linked to this severe psychological disorder (Perez-Costas & others, 2012; Sugranyes & others, 2012).

*Heredity*     Research supports the notion that schizophrenia is at least partially due to genetic factors (Vasco, Cardinale, & Polonia, 2012). As genetic similarity to a person with schizophrenia increases, so does a person's risk of developing schizophrenia, as Figure 12.10 shows (Cardno & Gottesman, 2000). Such data strongly suggest that genetic factors play a role in schizophrenia. Researchers are seeking to pinpoint the chromosomal location of genes involved in susceptibility to schizophrenia (Crowley & others, 2012; van Beveren & others, 2012).

*Structural Brain Abnormalities*     Studies have found structural brain abnormalities in people with schizophrenia. Imaging techniques such as MRI scans clearly show enlarged ventricles in the brain (Rais & others, 2012). Ventricles are fluid-filled spaces, and enlargement of the ventricles indicates the deterioration in other brain tissue. Individuals with schizophrenia also have a small frontal cortex (the area in which thinking, planning, and decision making take place) and show less activity in this area than individuals who do not have schizophrenia (Cotter & others, 2002).

Still, the differences between the brains of healthy individuals and those with schizophrenia are small (NIMH, 2008). Microscopic studies of brain tissue after death reveal small changes in the distribution or characteristics of brain cells in persons with schizophrenia. It appears that many of these changes occurred prenatally, because they are not accompanied by glial cells, which are always present when a brain injury occurs after

## PSYCHOLOGICAL INQUIRY

**FIGURE 12.10   Lifetime Risk of Developing Schizophrenia According to Genetic Relatedness**  As genetic relatedness to an individual with schizophrenia increases, so does the risk of developing schizophrenia. > *Which familial relationships have the lowest and highest level of genetic overlap?* > *What is the difference in genetic overlap between identical twins and non-twin siblings?* > *What is the difference in risk of schizophrenia between identical twins and non-twin siblings?*

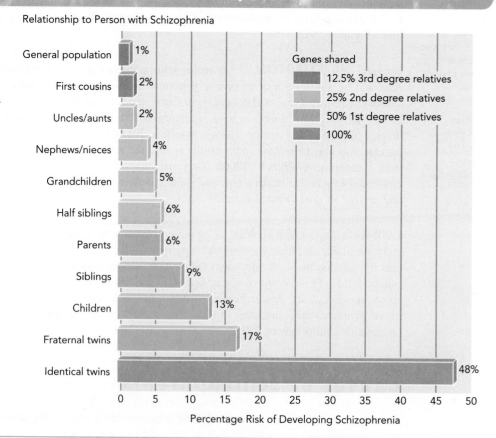

birth. It may be that problems in prenatal development such as infections (A. S. Brown, 2006) predispose a brain to developing schizophrenic symptoms during puberty and young adulthood (Fatemi & Folsom, 2009).

### Problems in Neurotransmitter Regulation

An early biological explanation for schizophrenia linked excess dopamine production to schizophrenia. The link between dopamine and psychotic symptoms was first noticed when the drug L-dopa (which increases dopamine levels) was given to individuals as a treatment for Parkinson disease. In addition to relieving their Parkinson symptoms, L-dopa caused some individuals to experience disturbed thoughts (Janowsky, Addario, & Risch, 1987). Furthermore, drugs that reduce psychotic symptoms often block dopamine (Kapur, 2003). Whether it is differences in the amount, the production, or the uptake of dopamine, there is good evidence that dopamine plays a role in schizophrenia (Brito-Melo & others, 2012; Howes & others, 2012).

As noted in the chapters about states of consciousness (Chapter 4) and learning (Chapter 5), dopamine is a "feel good" neurotransmitter that helps us recognize rewarding stimuli in the environment. As described in the chapter on personality (Chapter 10), dopamine is related to being outgoing and sociable. How can a neurotransmitter that is associated with good things play a crucial role in the most devastating psychological disorder?

*Excess dopamine basically tells the person that everything is important.*

One way to think about this puzzle is to view dopamine as a neurochemical messenger that in effect shouts out, "Hey! This is important!" whenever we encounter opportunities for reward. Imagine what it might be like to be bombarded with such messages about even the smallest details of life (Kapur, 2003). The person's own thoughts might take on such dramatic proportions that they sound like someone else's voice talking inside the person's head. Fleeting ideas such as "It's raining today because I didn't bring my umbrella to work" suddenly seem not silly but true. Shitij Kapur (2003) has suggested that hallucinations, delusions, and referential thinking may be expressions of the individual's attempts to make sense of such extraordinary feelings.

A problem with the dopamine explanation of schizophrenia is that antipsychotic drugs reduce dopamine levels very quickly, but delusional beliefs take much longer to disappear. Even after dopamine levels are balanced, a person might still cling to the bizarre belief that members of a powerful conspiracy are watching his every move. If dopamine causes these symptoms, why do the symptoms persist even after the dopamine is under control? According to Kapur, delusions serve as explanatory schemes that have helped the person make sense of the random and chaotic experiences caused by out-of-control dopamine. Bizarre beliefs might disappear only after experience demonstrates that such schemes no longer carry their explanatory power (Kapur, 2003). That is, with time, experience, and therapy, the person might come to realize that there is, in fact, no conspiracy.

**PSYCHOLOGICAL FACTORS** Psychologists used to explain schizophrenia as rooted in an individual's difficult childhood experiences with parents. Such explanations have mostly fallen by the wayside, but contemporary theorists do recognize that stress may contribute to the development of this disorder. The **diathesis-stress model** argues that a combination of biogenetic disposition and stress causes schizophrenia (Meehl, 1962). (*Diathesis* means "physical vulnerability or predisposition to a particular disorder.") For instance, genetic characteristics might produce schizophrenia only when (and if) the individual experiences extreme stress.

**diathesis-stress model**
View of schizophrenia emphasizing that a combination of biogenetic disposition and stress causes the disorder.

*Recall that Moe Armstrong experienced his first symptoms during the extremely stressful experience of the Vietnam War.*

**SOCIOCULTURAL FACTORS** A fascinating finding on sociocultural factors in schizophrenia is a consistent difference in the course of schizophrenia over time in developing versus developed nations. Specifically, individuals with schizophrenia in developing, nonindustrialized nations are more likely to show indications of recovery over time compared to those in developed, industrialized nations (Bhugra, 2006; Jablensky, 2000;

Myers, 2010). Whether measured in symptoms, disturbances in thought, or the ability to engage in productive work, individuals in less developed countries appear to do better than their counterparts in developed nations.

This difference is puzzling. Some experts argue that developing nations must be misdiagnosing more individuals or are better off than the label "developing" implies (Burns, 2009). Other commentators look to differences in cultural beliefs and practices to understand these effects. For instance, it might be that in more developed nations (such as the United States), there is not a very strong belief that individuals diagnosed with schizophrenia *can* recover (Luhrmann, 2007). In addition, cultures vary in terms of their beliefs about and responses to symptoms. In Chandigarh, India, for example, where some of the developing-nation data were collected, visual hallucinations were not viewed as very different from commonplace religious experiences (Luhrmann, 2007). Moreover, in developing nations, families remained involved in individuals' lives after diagnosis, and many families lived in close-knit communities where care of their loved one was not so burdensome (Hopper & Wanderling, 2000). The fact that culture matters to schizophrenia highlights the role of cultural context in psychological disorders. Consider that even if individuals with schizophrenia were found to share some common brain characteristics, these similar brains would have different experiences and different outcomes as a result of culture.

In developed nations, schizophrenia is strongly associated with poverty, but it is not clear if poverty increases the likelihood of experiencing the disorder (Luhrmann, 2007). Marriage, warm and supportive friends (Jablensky & others, 1992; Wiersma & others, 1998), and employment are related to better outcomes for people diagnosed with schizophrenia (Rosen & Garety, 2005). At the very least, this research suggests that some individuals with schizophrenia enjoy marriage, productive work, and friendships (Drake, Levine, & Laska, 2007; Fleischhaker & others, 2005; Marshall & Rathbone, 2006).

**Do It!**

If you have never met anyone with schizophrenia, why not get to know Moe Armstrong online? Search for clips of one of Moe's many speeches on YouTube.

## self-quiz

1. A negative symptom of schizophrenia is
   A. hallucinations.
   B. flat affect.
   C. delusions.
   D. catatonia.

2. Joel believes that he has superhuman powers. He is likely suffering from
   A. hallucinations.
   B. delusions.
   C. negative symptoms.
   D. referential thinking.

3. The biological causes of schizophrenia include

   A. problems with the body's regulation of dopamine.
   B. abnormalities in brain structure such as enlarged ventricles and a small frontal cortex.
   C. both A and B
   D. neither A nor B

**APPLY IT!** 4. During a psychiatric hospital internship, Tara approaches a young man sitting alone in a corner, and they have a short conversation. He asks her if she is with the government, and she tells him that she is not. She asks him a few

questions and walks away. She tells her advisor later that what disturbed her about the conversation was not so much what the young man said, but that she had this feeling that he just was not really there. Tara was noticing the _____ symptoms of schizophrenia.
   A. positive
   B. negative
   C. cognitive
   D. genetic

## 7 Personality Disorders

**personality disorders**
Chronic, maladaptive cognitive-behavioral patterns that are thoroughly integrated into an individual's personality.

Imagine that your personality—the very thing about you that makes you *you*—is the core of your life difficulties. That is what happens with **personality disorders,** which are chronic, maladaptive cognitive-behavioral patterns that are thoroughly integrated into an individual's personality. Personality disorders are relatively common. In one study of a representative U.S. sample, researchers found that 15 percent had a personality disorder (Grant & others, 2004).

With respect to *DSM-5,* the revisions for personality disorders were among the most highly anticipated. The biggest proposed change involved moving to an understanding of personality disorders within the context of the five-factor model of personality traits (see Chapter 10). Using the five factors to explain personality disorders is called the *dimensional approach*. From this perspective, personality disorders can be understood not as categories but as variants or extreme cases of the kinds of traits we see in healthy people. Many scholars looked forward to the integration of a dimensional approach to personality disorders (Krueger & Eaton, 2010; Miller & others, 2012; Trull, Carpenter, & Widiger, 2013; Widiger, 2011; Widiger & Costa, 2013). Some research supported the idea that approaching personality disorders from a trait perspective would lead to better diagnoses (Yalch, Thomas, & Hopwood, 2012). Other research, however, suggested that the change was unnecessary (Zimmerman & others, 2011; Morgan & others, 2013) and would be less useful to clinicians (Rottman & others, 2011). In the end, the proposed changes were not adopted. *DSM-5* lists the same 10 personality disorders as previous editions (see Figure 12.11).

In this section we survey the two personality disorders that have been the object of most study: antisocial personality disorder and borderline personality disorder. Both are associated with dire consequences. Specifically, antisocial personality disorder is linked to criminal activity and violence; borderline personality disorder, to self-harm and suicide.

# Antisocial Personality Disorder

**antisocial personality disorder (ASPD)** Psychological disorder characterized by guiltlessness, law-breaking, exploitation of others, irresponsibility, and deceit.

**Antisocial personality disorder (ASPD)** is a psychological disorder characterized by guiltlessness, law-breaking, exploitation of others, irresponsibility, and deceit. Although

| Personality Disorder | Description |
|---|---|
| Paranoid Personality Disorder | Paranoia, suspiciousness, and deep distrust of others. People with this disorder are always on the lookout for danger and the slightest social mistreatment. They may be socially isolated. |
| Schizoid Personality Disorder | Extreme lack of interest in interpersonal relationships. People with this disorder are emotionally cold and apathetic, and they are generally detached from interpersonal life. |
| Schizotypal Personality Disorder | Socially isolated and prone to odd thinking. People with this disorder often have elaborate and strange belief systems and attribute unusual meanings to life events and experiences. |
| Antisocial Personality Disorder | Manipulative, deceitful, and amoral. People with this disorder lack empathy for others, are egocentric, and are willing to use others for their own personal gain. |
| Borderline Personality Disorder | Emotionally volatile and unstable sense of self. These individuals are prone to mood swings, excessive self-criticism, extreme judgments of others, and are preoccupied with being abandoned. |
| Histrionic Personality Disorder | Attention-seeking, dramatic, lively, and flirtatious. These individuals are inappropriately seductive in their interactions with others. |
| Narcissistic Personality Disorder | Self-aggrandizing yet overly dependent on the evaluations of others. People with this disorder view themselves as entitled and better than others. They show deficits in empathy and in understanding the feelings of others. |
| Avoidant Personality Disorder | Socially inhibited and prone to feelings of inadequacy, anxiety, and shame. These individuals feel inadequate and hold back in social situations. They have unrealistic standards for their own behavior and avoid setting goals, taking personal risks, or pursuing new activities. |
| Dependent Personality Disorder | Dependent on others for emotional and physical needs. People with this disorder perceive others as powerful and competent and themselves as childlike and helpless. |
| Obsessive-Compulsive Personality Disorder | Conforming rigidly to rules. These individuals show an excessive attachment to moral codes and are excessively orderly in daily life. |

**FIGURE 12.11 The 10 Personality Disorders Included in *DSM-5*.** Diagnoses of these disorders require that the person be over the age of 18, and all involve pervasive aspects of the person that color cognition, emotion, and behavior. Note that some of the labels are potentially confusing. Schizoid and schizotypal personality disorders are not the same thing as schizophrenia (though schizotypal personality disorder may proceed to schizophrenia). Further, obsessive-compulsive personality disorder is not the same thing as obsessive-compulsive disorder.

they may be superficially charming, individuals with ASPD do not play by the rules, and they often lead a life of crime and violence. ASPD is far more common in men than in women and is related to criminal behavior, vandalism, substance abuse, and alcoholism (Cale & Lilienfeld, 2002).

ASPD is characterized by:

- Failure to conform to social norms or obey the law
- Deceitfulness, lying, using aliases, or conning others for personal profit or pleasure
- Impulsivity
- Irritability and aggressiveness; getting into physical fights or perpetrating assaults
- Reckless disregard for the safety of self or others
- Consistent irresponsibility, inconsistent work behavior; not paying bills
- Lack of remorse, indifference to the pain of others, or rationalizing; hurting or mistreating another person

Generally, ASPD is not diagnosed unless a person has shown persistent antisocial behavior before the age of 15.

Although ASPD is associated with criminal behavior, not all individuals with ASPD engage in crime, and not all criminals suffer from ASPD. Some individuals with ASPD can have successful careers. There are antisocial physicians, clergy members, lawyers, and just about any other occupation. Still, such individuals tend to be exploitative of others, and they break the rules, even if they are never caught.

What is the etiology of ASPD? Biological factors include genetic, brain, and autonomic nervous system differences. We consider these in turn.

ASPD is genetically heritable (Nordstrom & others, 2012). Certain genetic characteristics associated with ASPD may interact with testosterone (the hormone most associated with aggressive behavior) to promote antisocial behavior (Sjoberg & others, 2008). Although the experience of childhood abuse may be implicated in ASPD, there is evidence that genetic differences may distinguish abused children who go on to commit violent acts themselves from those who do not (Caspi & others, 2002).

*Lack of autonomic nervous system activity suggests why individuals with ASPD might be able to fool a polygraph (lie detector).*

In terms of the brain, research has linked ASPD to low levels of activation in the prefrontal cortex and has related these brain differences to poor decision making and problems in learning (Raine & others, 2000). With regard to the autonomic nervous system, researchers have found that individuals with ASPD are less stressed than others by aversive circumstances, including punishment (Fung & others, 2005), and that they have the ability to keep their cool while engaging in deception (Verschuere & others, 2005). The underaroused autonomic nervous system may be a key difference between adolescents who become antisocial adults and those whose behavior improves during adulthood (Raine, Venables, & Williams, 1990).

The term *psychopath* is sometimes used to refer to a subgroup of individuals with ASPD (Pham, 2012). Psychopaths are remorseless predators who engage in violence to get what they want. Examples of psychopaths include serial killers John Wayne Gacy, who murdered 33 boys and young men, and Ted Bundy, who confessed to murdering at least 30 young women. Psychopaths tend to show less prefrontal activation than normal individuals and to have structural abnormalities in the amygdala, as well as the hippocampus, the brain structure most closely associated with

*John Wayne Gacy* (top) *and Ted Bundy* (bottom) *exemplify the subgroup of people with ASPD who are also psychopathic.*

memory (Weber & others, 2008). Importantly, these brain differences are most pronounced in "unsuccessful psychopaths"—individuals who have been arrested for their behaviors (Yang & others, 2005). In contrast, "successful psychopaths"—individuals who have engaged in antisocial behavior but have not gotten caught—are more similar to healthy controls in terms of brain structure and function. However, in their behavior, successful psychopaths demonstrate a lack of empathy and a willingness to act immorally; they victimize others to enrich their own lives. Psychopaths show deficiencies in learning about fear and have difficulty processing information related to the distress of others, such as sad or fearful faces (Dolan & Fullam, 2006).

*Their functioning frontal lobes might help successful psychopaths avoid getting caught.*

A key challenge in treating individuals with ASPD, including psychopaths, is their ability to con even sophisticated mental health professionals. Many never seek therapy, and others end up in prison, where treatment is rarely an option.

## Borderline Personality Disorder

**Borderline personality disorder (BPD)** is a pervasive pattern of instability in interpersonal relationships, self-image, and emotions, and of marked impulsivity beginning by early adulthood and present in various contexts. Individuals with BPD are insecure, impulsive, and emotional (Hooley, Cole, & Gironde, 2012). BPD is related to self-harming behaviors such as *cutting* (injuring oneself with a sharp object but without suicidal intent) and also to suicide (Soloff & others, 1994).

**borderline personality disorder (BPD)** Psychological disorder characterized by a pervasive pattern of instability in interpersonal relationships, self-image, and emotions, and of marked impulsivity beginning by early adulthood and present in a variety of contexts.

At the very core of BPD is profound instability in mood, in sense of self, and in relationships. BPD is characterized by four essential features (Trull & Brown, 2013):

- Unstable affect
- Unstable sense of self and identity, including self-destructive impulsive behavior and chronic feelings of emptiness
- Negative interpersonal relationships that are unstable, intense, and characterized by extreme shifts between idealization and devaluation
- Self-harm, including recurrent suicidal behavior, gestures, or threats or self-mutilating behavior.

**EXPERIENCE IT!**
Borderline Personality Disorder

Individuals with BPD are prone to wild mood swings and very sensitive to how others treat them. They often feel as if they are riding a nonstop emotional rollercoaster (Selby & others, 2009), and their loved ones may have to work hard to avoid upsetting them. Individuals with BPD tend to see the world in black-and-white terms, a thinking style called *splitting*. For example, they typically view other people as either hated enemies with no positive qualities or as beloved, idealized friends who can do no wrong.

Borderline personality disorder is far more common in women than men. Women make up 75 percent of those with the disorder (Korzekwa & others, 2008; Oltmanns & Powers, 2012).

*Movie depictions of BPD include Fatal Attraction, Single White Female, and Obsessed. Where these films get it wrong is that they show BPD as leading to more harm to others than to the self.*

The potential causes of BPD are likely complex and include biological factors as well as childhood experiences. The role of genes in BPD has been demonstrated in a variety of studies and across cultures (Mulder, 2012). The heritability of BPD is about 40 percent (Distel & others, 2008).

Many individuals with borderline personality disorder report experiences of childhood sexual abuse, as well as physical abuse and neglect (Al-Alem & Omar, 2008; De Fruyt & De Clercq, 2012). It is not clear, however, whether abuse is a primary cause of the disorder (Trull & Widiger, 2003). Childhood abuse experiences may combine with genetic factors in promoting BPD.

Cognitive factors associated with BPD include a tendency to hold a set of irrational beliefs (Leahy & McGinn, 2012). These include thinking that one

*This would be a diathesis-stress model explanation for BPD.*

is powerless and innately unacceptable and that other people are dangerous and hostile (Arntz, 2005). Individuals with BPD also display *hypervigilance:* the tendency to be constantly on the alert, looking for threatening information in the environment (Sieswerda & others, 2007).

Up until 20 years ago, experts thought that BPD was untreatable. More recent evidence, however, suggests that many individuals with BPD show improvement over time—as many as 50 percent within two years of starting treatment (Gunderson, 2008). One key aspect of successful treatment appears to be a reduction in social stress, such as that due to leaving an abusive romantic partner or establishing a sense of trust in a therapist (Gunderson & others, 2003).

*To recognize the severe toll of BPD on those suffering from it (and on their families and friends), in 2008 the U.S. House of Representatives declared May to be National Borderline Personality Disorder Awareness Month.*

## self-quiz

1. Individuals with ASPD
   A. are incapable of having successful careers.
   B. are typically women.
   C. are typically men.
   D. rarely engage in criminal behavior.

2. People with BPD
   A. pay little attention to how others treat them.
   B. rarely have problems with anger or strong emotion.
   C. tend to have suicidal thoughts or engage in self-harming actions.
   D. tend to have a balanced viewpoint of people and things rather than to see them as all black or all white.

3. All of the following are true of BPD except
   A. BPD can be caused by a combination of nature and nurture—genetic inheritance and childhood experience.
   B. Recent research has shown that people with BPD respond positively to treatment.
   C. A common symptom of BPD is impulsive behavior such as binge eating and reckless driving.
   D. BPD is far more common in men than women.

APPLY IT! 4. Your new friend Maureen tells you that she was diagnosed with borderline personality disorder at the age of 23. She feels hopeless when she considers that her mood swings and unstable self-esteem are part of her very personality. Despairing, she asks, "How will I ever change?" Which of the following statements about Maureen's condition is accurate?
   A. Maureen should seek therapy and strive to improve her relationships with others, as BPD is treatable.
   B. Maureen's concerns are realistic, because a personality disorder like BPD is unlikely to change.
   C. Maureen should seek treatment for BPD because there is a high likelihood that she will end up committing a criminal act.
   D. Maureen is right to be concerned, because BPD is most often caused by genetic factors.

## 8 Combatting Stigma

Putting a label on a person with a psychological disorder can make the disorder seem like something that happens only to other people (Baumann, 2007). The truth is that psychological disorders are not just about other people; they are about people, period. Over 26 percent of Americans ages 18 and older suffer from a diagnosable psychological disorder in a given year—an estimated 57.7 million U.S. adults (Kessler & others, 2005; NIMH, 2008). Chances are that you or someone you know will experience a psychological disorder. Figure 12.12 shows how common many psychological disorders are in the United States.

A classic and controversial study illustrates that labels of psychological disorder can be "sticky"—hard to remove once they are applied to a person. David Rosenhan (1973) recruited eight adults (including a stay-at-home mother, a psychology graduate student, a pediatrician, and some psychiatrists), none with a psychological disorder, to see a psychiatrist at various hospitals. These "pseudo-patients" were instructed to act normally except to complain about hearing voices that said things like "empty" and "thud." All eight expressed an interest in leaving the hospital and behaved cooperatively. Nevertheless, all eight were labeled with schizophrenia and kept in the hospital from 3 to 52 days. None of the mental health professionals they encountered ever questioned the diagnosis that was given to these individuals, and all were discharged with the label "schizophrenia in remission." The label "schizophrenia" had stuck to the pseudo-patients and caused the professionals around them to interpret their quite normal behavior as abnormal. Clearly, once a person has been labeled with a psychological disorder, that label colors how others perceive everything else he or she does.

Labels of psychological disorder carry with them a wide array of implications for the individual. Is the person still able to be a good friend? A good parent? A competent worker? A significant concern for individuals with psychological disorders is the negative attitudes that others might have about people struggling with mental illness (Phelan & Basow, 2007). Stigma can be a barrier for individuals coping with a psychological disorder, as well as for their families and loved ones (Corrigan, 2007; Hinshaw, 2007). Negative attitudes about individuals with psychological disorders are common in many cultures, and cultural norms and values influence these attitudes (Abdullah & Brown, 2011). Fear of stigma can prevent individuals from seeking treatment and from talking about their problems with family and friends.

| | Number of U.S. Adults in a Given Year (Millions) | Percentage of U.S. Adults |
|---|---|---|
| **Anxiety Disorders** | | |
| General anxiety disorder | 6.8 | 3.1% |
| Panic disorder | 6.0 | 2.7% |
| Specific phobia | 19.2 | 8.7% |
| PTSD | 7.7 | 3.5% |
| **Major Depressive Disorder** | 14.8 | 6.7% |
| **Bipolar Disorder** | 5.7 | 2.6% |
| **Schizophrenia** | 2.4 | 1.1% |

**FIGURE 12.12  The 12-Month Prevalence of the Most Common Psychological Disorders** If you add up the numbers in this figure, you will see that the totals are higher than the numbers given in the text. The explanation is that people are frequently diagnosed with more than one psychological disorder. An individual who has both a depressive and an anxiety disorder would be counted in both of those categories.

# Consequences of Stigma

The stigma attached to psychological disorders can provoke prejudice and discrimination toward individuals who are struggling with these problems, thus complicating an already difficult situation. Having a disorder and experiencing the stigma associated with it can also negatively affect the physical health of such individuals.

**PREJUDICE AND DISCRIMINATION**   Labels of psychological disorders can be damaging because they may lead to negative stereotypes, which play a role in prejudice. For example, the label "schizophrenic" often has negative connotations such as "frightening" and "dangerous."

Vivid cases of extremely harmful behavior by individuals with psychological disorders can perpetuate the stereotype that people with such disorders are violent. For example, Cho Seung-Hui, a 23-year-old college student, murdered 32 students and faculty at Virginia Tech University in April 2007 before killing himself. The widely reported fact that Cho had struggled with psychological disorders throughout his life may have reinforced the notion that individuals with disorders are dangerous. In fact, however, people with psychological disorders (especially those in treatment) are no more likely to commit violent acts than the general population. Cho was no more representative of people with psychological disorders than he was representative of students at Virginia Tech.

Individuals with psychological disorders are often aware of the negative stigma attached to these conditions and may themselves have previously held such negative attitudes. Seeking the assistance they need may involve accepting a stigmatized identity (Thornicroft & others, 2009; Yen & others, 2009). Even mental health professionals can fall prey to prejudicial attitudes toward those who are coping with psychological disorders (Nordt, Rossler, & Lauber, 2006). Improved knowledge about the neurobiological and genetic processes involved in many psychological disorders appears to be a promising direction for interventions to reduce such prejudice. Research shows that information about the role of genes in these disorders reduces prejudicial attitudes (WonPat-Borja & others, 2012).

Among the most feared aspects of stigma is discrimination, or acting prejudicially toward a person who is a member of a stigmatized group. In the workplace, discrimination against a person with a psychological disorder violates the law. The Americans with

Disabilities Act (ADA) of 1990 made it illegal to refuse employment or a promotion to someone with a psychological disorder when the person's condition does not prevent performance of the job's essential functions (Cleveland, Barnes-Farrell, & Ratz, 1997). A person's appearance or behavior may be unusual or irritating, but as long as that individual is able to complete the duties required of a position, employment or promotion cannot be denied.

**PHYSICAL HEALTH**    Individuals with psychological disorders are more likely to be physically ill and two times more likely to die than their psychologically healthy counterparts (Gittelman, 2008; Kumar, 2004). They are also more likely to be obese, to smoke, to drink excessively, and to lead sedentary lives (Kim & others, 2007; Lindwall & others, 2007; Mykletun & others, 2007; Osborn, Nazareth, & King, 2006).

You might be thinking that these physical health issues are the least of their worries. If people struggling with schizophrenia want to smoke, why not let them? This type of thinking sells short the capacity of psychological and psychiatric treatments to help those with psychological disorders. Research has shown that health-promotion programs can work well for individuals with a severe psychological disorder (Addington & others, 1998; Chafetz & others, 2008). When we disregard the potential of physical health interventions for people with psychological disorders to make positive life changes, we reveal our biases.

# Overcoming Stigma

How can we combat the stigma of psychological disorders? One obstacle to changing people's attitudes toward individuals with psychological disorders is that mental illness is often "invisible." That is, sometimes a person we know can have a disorder without our being aware. We may be unaware of *many* good lives around us that are being lived under a cloud of psychological disorder, because worries about being stigmatized keep the affected individuals from "coming out." Thus, stigma leads to a catch-22: Positive examples of individuals coping with psychological disorders are often missing from our experience because those who are doing well shun public disclosure of their disorders (Jensen & Wadkins, 2007).

A critical step toward eliminating stigma is to resist thinking of people with disorders as limited by their condition. Instead, it is vital to recognize their strengths—both in confronting their disorder and in carrying on despite their problems—and their achievements. By creating a positive environment for people with disorders, we encourage more of them to become confidently "visible" and empower them to be positive role models.

When Milton Greek arrived at Ohio University in the 1980s as a young undergraduate, he had an ambitious goal: "to discover a psychological code that people should live by, to create world peace" (Carey, 2011a). He became known as a person with very strange ideas. By his senior year, Milt was in a failing marriage and was convinced that he had met God one day on the street and Jesus a few days later. Although he was a lifelong atheist, his delusions took on a distinctive religious character. He believed the Rapture would occur at any moment and that he himself was the anti-Christ. He heard voices no one else did and saw things that were not there. Eventually diagnosed with schizophrenia, Milt began taking medication and started to put his life back together. While in graduate school, he stopped taking his medications when things seemed to be going well, only to have a close friend give him a reality check. "When she used the word 'hallucination' I knew it was true," he said (Carey, 2011a).

Today Milt is a 49-year-old, happily married computer programmer. He takes medications to control his symptoms and seems again to have found a mission in life. This time it is about making a difference in the lives of others by sharing his story as a man with schizophrenia. Along with a small group of other people with serious psychiatric disorders, Milt has "come out" and related his experiences to combat stigma, providing hope for others who are suffering with psychological disorders and helping psychologists who are interested in experiences like his.

After reading this chapter, you know that many admired individuals have dealt with psychological disorders. Their diagnoses do not detract from their accomplishments. To the contrary, their accomplishments are all the more remarkable in the context of the challenges they have faced.

## self-quiz

1. The percentage of Americans 18 years of age and older who suffer from a diagnosable psychological disorder in a given year is closest to
   A. 15 percent.
   B. 26 percent.
   C. 40 percent.
   D. 46 percent.

2. The stigma attached to psychological disorders can have implications for
   A. the physical health of an individual with such a disorder.
   B. the psychological well-being of an individual with such a disorder.
   C. other people's attitudes and behaviors toward the individual with such a disorder.
   D. all of the above.

3. Labeling psychological disorders can lead to damaging
   A. stereotyping.
   B. discrimination.
   C. prejudice.
   D. all of the above.

APPLY IT! 4. Liliana has applied for a job after graduation doing data entry for a polling firm. During her second interview, Liliana asks the human resources manager whether the job's health benefits include prescription drug coverage, as she is on anti-anxiety medication for generalized anxiety disorder. Which of the following statements is most applicable, legally and otherwise, in light of Liliana's request?
   A. The human resources manager should tell the hiring committee to avoid hiring Liliana because she has a psychological disorder.
   B. It is illegal for the firm to deny Liliana employment simply because she has a psychological disorder.
   C. Liliana should not have asked that question, because she will not be hired.
   D. Liliana must be given the job, or the firm could face a lawsuit.

## SUMMARY

### ① Defining and Explaining Abnormal Behavior

Abnormal behavior is deviant, maladaptive, or personally distressful. Theoretical perspectives on the causes of psychological disorders include biological, psychological, sociocultural, and biopsychosocial approaches.

Biological approaches to disorders describe psychological disorders as diseases with origins in structural, biochemical, and genetic factors. Psychological approaches include the behavioral, social cognitive, and trait perspectives. Sociocultural approaches place emphasis on the larger social context in which a person lives, including marriage, socioeconomic status, ethnicity, gender, and culture. Biopsychosocial approaches view the interactions among biological, psychological, and social factors as significant forces in producing both normal and abnormal behavior.

The classification of disorders provides a shorthand for communication, allows clinicians to make predictions about disorders, and helps them to decide on appropriate treatment. The *Diagnostic and Statistical Manual of Mental Disorders (DSM)* is the classification system clinicians use to diagnose psychological disorders. Some psychologists contend that the *DSM* perpetuates the medical model of psychological disorders, labels everyday problems as psychological disorders, and fails to address strengths.

### ② Anxiety and Anxiety-Related Disorders

Anxiety disorders are characterized by unrealistic and debilitatingly high levels of anxiety. Generalized anxiety disorder involves a high level of anxiety with no specific reason for the anxiety. Panic disorder involves attacks marked by the sudden onset of intense terror.

Specific phobias entail an irrational, overwhelming fear of a particular object, such as snakes, or a situation, such as flying. Social anxiety disorder refers to the intense fear that one will do something embarrassing or humiliating in public. Obsessive-compulsive disorder involves anxiety-provoking thoughts that will not go away (obsession) and/or urges to perform repetitive, ritualistic behaviors to prevent or produce some future situation (compulsion). Post-traumatic stress disorder (PTSD) is a disorder that develops through exposure to traumatic events. Symptoms include flashbacks, emotional avoidance, emotional numbing, and excessive arousal. A variety of experiential, psychological, and genetic factors have been shown to relate to these disorders.

### ③ Disorders Involving Emotion and Mood

In depressive disorders, the individual experiences a serious depressive episode and depressed characteristics such as lethargy and hopelessness. Biological explanations of depressive disorders focus on heredity, neurophysiological abnormalities, and neurotransmitter deregulation. Psychological explanations include behavioral and cognitive perspectives. Sociocultural explanations emphasize socioeconomic and ethnic factors, as well as gender.

Bipolar disorder is characterized by extreme mood swings that include one or more episodes of mania (an overexcited, unrealistic, optimistic state). Most individuals with bipolar disorder go through multiple cycles of depression interspersed with mania. Genetic influences are stronger predictors of bipolar disorder than depressive disorder, and biological processes are also a factor in bipolar disorder.

Severe depression and other psychological disorders can cause individuals to want to end their lives. Theorists have proposed biological, psychological, and sociocultural explanations of suicide.

 ## Eating Disorders

Anorexia nervosa is characterized by extreme underweight and starvation. The disorder is related to perfectionism and obsessive-compulsive tendencies. Bulimia nervosa involves a pattern of binge eating followed by purging through self-induced vomiting. In contrast, binge eating disorder involves binge eating without purging.

Anorexia nervosa and bulimia nervosa are much more common in women than men, but there is no gender difference in binge-eating disorder. Although sociocultural factors were once primary in explaining eating disorders, newer evidence points to the role of biological factors.

 ## Dissociative Disorders

Dissociative amnesia involves memory loss caused by extensive psychological stress. In dissociative identity disorder, formerly called multiple personality disorder, two or more distinct personalities are present in the same individual; this disorder is rare.

 ## Schizophrenia

Schizophrenia is a severe psychological disorder characterized by highly disordered thought processes. Positive symptoms of schizophrenia are behaviors and experiences that are present in individuals with schizophrenia but absent in healthy people; they include hallucinations, delusions, thought disorder, and disorders of movement. Negative symptoms of schizophrenia are behaviors and experiences that are part of healthy human life that are absent for those with this disorder; they include flat affect and an inability to plan or engage in goal-directed behavior.

Biological factors (heredity, structural brain abnormalities, and problems in neurotransmitter regulation, especially dopamine), psychological

factors (diathesis-stress model), and sociocultural factors may be involved in schizophrenia. Psychological and sociocultural factors are not viewed as stand-alone causes of schizophrenia, but they are related to the course of the disorder.

 ## Personality Disorders

Personality disorders are chronic, maladaptive cognitive-behavioral patterns that are thoroughly integrated into an individual's personality. Two common types are antisocial personality disorder (ASPD) and borderline personality disorder (BPD).

Antisocial personality disorder is characterized by guiltlessness, law-breaking, exploitation of others, irresponsibility, and deceit. Individuals with this disorder often lead a life of crime and violence. Psychopaths—remorseless predators who engage in violence to get what they want—are a subgroup of individuals with ASPD.

Borderline personality disorder is a pervasive pattern of instability in interpersonal relationships, self-image, and emotions. This disorder is related to self-harming behaviors such as cutting and suicide.

Biological factors for ASPD include genetic, brain, and autonomic nervous system differences. The potential causes of BPD are complex and include biological and cognitive factors as well as childhood experiences.

 ## Combatting Stigma

Stigma can create a significant barrier for people coping with a psychological disorder, as well as for their loved ones. Fear of being labeled can prevent individuals with a disorder from getting treatment and from talking about their problems with family and friends. In addition, the stigma attached to psychological disorders can lead to prejudice and discrimination toward individuals who are struggling with these problems. Having a disorder and experiencing the stigma associated with it can also negatively affect the physical health of such individuals. We can help to combat stigma by acknowledging the strengths and the achievements of individuals coping with psychological disorders.

## KEY TERMS

abnormal behavior, p. 441
medical model, p. 443
*DSM-5,* p. 444
attention deficit hyperactivity disorder (ADHD), p. 445
anxiety disorders, p. 447
generalized anxiety disorder, p. 447
panic disorder, p. 448
specific phobia, p. 449

social anxiety disorder, p. 450
obsessive-compulsive disorder (OCD), p. 451
post-traumatic stress disorder (PTSD), p. 452
depressive disorders, p. 454
major depressive disorder (MDD), p. 455
bipolar disorder, p. 457
anorexia nervosa, p. 462

bulimia nervosa, p. 462
binge-eating disorder (BED), p. 464
dissociative disorders, p. 465
dissociative amnesia, p. 466
dissociative identity disorder (DID), p. 466
psychosis, p. 468
schizophrenia, p. 468
hallucinations, p. 468
delusions, p. 468

referential thinking, p. 469
catatonia, p. 469
flat affect, p. 469
diathesis-stress model, p. 471
personality disorders, p. 472
antisocial personality disorder (ASPD), p. 473
borderline personality disorder (BPD), p. 475

## Multiple Choice

1. The name for a mark of shame that may cause people to avoid, or act negatively toward, an individual is
   A. disfigurement.
   B. mortification.
   C. stigma.
   D. prejudice.

2. Feeling an overwhelming sense of dread and worry without a specific cause is known as
   A. obsessive-compulsive disorder.
   B. generalized anxiety disorder.
   C. social anxiety disorder.
   D. panic disorder.

3. A characteristic of post-traumatic stress disorder is
   A. panic attacks.
   B. an exaggerated startle response.
   C. persistent nervousness about a variety of things.
   D. extreme fear of an object or place.

4. All of the following are disorders involving emotion or mood *except*
   A. generalized anxiety disorder.
   B. disruptive mood dysregulation disorder.
   C. major depressive disorder.
   D. bipolar disorder.

5. The diagnostic criteria for major depressive disorder include the standard that a depressive episode must last at least
   A. one week.
   B. two weeks.
   C. two months.
   D. two years.

6. Insistently focusing on being depressed is characteristic of
   A. catastrophic thinking.
   B. a ruminative coping style.
   C. bipolar disorder.
   D. learned helplessness.

7. The eating disorder that involves binge eating followed by purging through self-induced vomiting is
   A. binge eating disorder.
   B. bulimia nervosa.
   C. anorexia nervosa.
   D. compulsive eating disorder.

8. A dissociative disorder sometimes accompanied by unexpected sudden travel is
   A. dissociate disorder.
   B. dissociative personality disorder.
   C. dissociative identity disorder.
   D. dissociative amnesia.

9. _____ symptoms of schizophrenia reflect a loss of normal functioning, while _____ symptoms reflect the addition of abnormal functioning.
   A. Cognitive; behavioral
   B. Behavioral; cognitive
   C. Positive; negative
   D. Negative; positive

10. Antisocial personality disorder is characterized by _____, whereas borderline personality disorder is characterized by

    _____.
    A. avoidance of impulsive behavior; avoidance of physical aggression
    B. avoidance of physical aggression; avoidance of impulsive behavior
    C. a tendency to harm oneself; violence toward others
    D. violence toward others; a tendency to harm oneself

## Apply It!

11. What is the diathesis-stress model? In the text this model was applied to schizophrenia. Apply it to one eating disorder and one anxiety disorder.

ISBN 978-1-259-12139-5
MHID 1-259-12139-9

www.mhhe.com

# personally, critically, actively

## An Emphasis on Critical Thinking

Challenge Your Thinking features involve you in debates over findings from psychological research. Thought-provoking questions encourage you to examine the evidence on both sides. See, for example, p. 132.

## Do It!

Write down a memory that you feel has been especially important in making you who you are. What are some characteristics of this self-defining memory? What do you think the memory says about you? How does it relate to your current goals and aspirations? Do you think of the memory often? You might find that this part of your life story can be inspiring when things are going poorly or when you are feeling down.

## Challenge YOUR THINKING

### Why Do We Have Conscious Awareness?

In what ways are human beings better adapted to the environment than lower animals because they have private awareness? Why is it adaptive for human beings, unlike other animals, not only to sense and perceive the world but also to privately feel ourselves doing so? Psychologists and philosophers have long puzzled over these questions. To address them, let's first consider some of the purposes of consciousness.

Perhaps the most obvious function of awareness is to override automatic and unconscious processes when these are likely to produce errors (Evans, 2010; Geary, 2004). Consider all the times you have made a mistake and realized, "I just wasn't thinking." Conscious awareness allows us to harness our mental abilities to think our way past our ordinary routine. The human social world is highly complex and variable. Some have suggested that this complex social world requires awareness (Geary, 2004; Mercier & Sperber, 2011) and lays the foundation for the emergence of culture (Baumeister & Masicampo, 2010).

Without consciousness, moreover, we could not engage in mental time travel. John Bargh (2004) described unconscious, automatic processes as tied to the present moment—a kind of "minding the store" mode—while conscious thought ventures into the realm of future (and past) states. The abilities to think into the future, to plan, and to imagine have often been recognized as essential features of consciousness (Baumeister & Masicampo, 2010; Heidegger, 1927/1962). Certainly, the ability to think back into the past to seek ways to correct prior mistakes is enormously important, as is the ability to plan for imagined futures.

Consciousness also allows us to reason and use logic, the basis of scientific knowledge (Evans, 2002, 2010). Consciousness

empowers us to ask why and to know the reasons behind our knowledge about the world. Thus, awareness is crucial to critical thinking. Further, the conscious organism has the capacity to ask questions not only about what is happening in the world or even about internal thoughts and feelings, but also about existence itself: Why am I here? What purpose do I serve? Thus, consciousness brings the issue of personal significance to the fore.

In grappling with the purpose of consciousness, Nicholas Humphrey (2000, 2006) suggested the provocative possibility that it is the very mysteriousness of consciousness that explains its adaptive significance. For Humphrey, awareness imbues human life with a vital survival need, raising the self beyond the natural world to something larger and potentially better. Private awareness is the foundation for ideas like the soul, promoting the feeling of a self that is not limited by space or time. Because we know that others possess a private self, we are motivated to treat them with respect and kindness—in other words, to behave ethically (Tamburrini & Mattia, 2011). Consciousness, then, makes human life matter to us in ways that influence our capacity to survive and to promote the survival of other members of our species. In answer to the question "Why does consciousness matter?" Humphrey (2006, p. 131) replied, "Consciousness matters because *it is its function to matter.*"

#### What Do You Think?

- Why are you better off because you have awareness?
- What would your life be like without awareness?

## An Emphasis on Active Engagement

Do It! is a brief, recurring activity that gives you an opportunity to test your assumptions and learn through hands-on exploration and discovery. Such exercises provide you with a more active experience of psychology. See, for example, p. 223.

### EXPERIENCE IT!

Experience It! allows students to easily access related videos and Concept Clips by using a QR code scanner app on a mobile device (free QR code scanner apps are available on most app stores). This content is also available in McGraw-Hill's Connect Psychology.

# experience psychology

### Second Edition

## Laura A. King

*University of Missouri, Columbia*

# For Sam

EXPERIENCE PSYCHOLOGY, SECOND EDITION
Published by McGraw-Hill, a business unit of The McGraw-Hill Companies, Inc., 1221 Avenue of the Americas, New York, NY, 10020. Copyright © 2013 by The McGraw-Hill Companies, Inc. All rights reserved. Printed in the United States of America. Previous edition © 2010. No part of this publication may be reproduced or distributed in any form or by any means, or stored in a database or retrieval system, without the prior written consent of The McGraw-Hill Companies, Inc., including, but not limited to, in any network or other electronic storage or transmission, or broadcast for distance learning.

Some ancillaries, including electronic and print components, may not be available to customers outside the United States.

This book is printed on acid-free paper.

3 4 5 6 7 8 9 0 DOW/DOW 1 0 9 8 7 6 5 4 3

ISBN    978-0-07-803534-0
MHID    0-07-803534-1

Senior Vice President, Products & Markets:
  Kurt L. Strand
Vice President, General Manager: *Michael Ryan*
Vice President, Content Production & Technology
  Services: *Kimberly Meriwether David*
Directors: *Mike Sugarman and Krista Bettino*
Senior Brand Manager: *Nancy Welcher*
Director of Development: *Dawn Groundwater*
Content Development Editor: *Sylvia Mallory*
Editorial Coordinator: *Kevin Fitzpatrick*
Digital Development Editor: *Sarah Colwell*
Digital Product Analyst: *Neil Kahn*
Marketing Managers: *Ann Helgerson, AJ Laferrera*
Director, Content Production: *Terri Schiesl*

Senior Production Editor: *Catherine Morris*
Senior Buyer: *Carol Bielski*
Design Manager and Cover Designer:
  *Preston Thomas*
Interior Designer: *Linda Beaupré*
Cover Image: *Chris Collins © Corbis*
Senior Content Licensing Specialist: *John Leland*
Photo Researcher: *David Tietz/Editorial Image, LLC*
Connect Media Project Manager:
  *Katie Klochan*
OLC Media Project Manager: *Jennifer Barrick*
Typeface: *10/12 Times Roman*
Compositor: *Aptara®, Inc.*
Printer: *R.R. Donnelley & Sons*

All credits appearing on page or at the end of the book are considered to be an extension of the copyright page.

### Library of Congress Cataloging-in-Publication Data

King, Laura A. (Laura Ann)
  Experience psychology / Laura A. King.—SECOND EDITION.
    pages cm
  ISBN 978-0-07-803534-0 (alk. paper)
  ISBN 0-07-803534-1 (alk. paper)
   1. Psychology—Textbooks.   I. Title.
  BF121.K536 2012
  150—dc23
                                                    2012032473

The Internet addresses listed in the text were accurate at the time of publication. The inclusion of a website does not indicate an endorsement by the authors or McGraw-Hill, and McGraw-Hill does not guarantee the accuracy of the information presented at these sites.

www.mhhe.com

# Laura A. King

Laura King did her undergraduate work at Kenyon College, where, an English major, she declared a second major in psychology during the second semester of her junior year. She completed her A.B. in English with high honors and distinction and in psychology with distinction in 1986. Laura then did graduate work at Michigan State University and the University of California, Davis, receiving her Ph.D. in personality psychology in 1991.

Laura began her career at Southern Methodist University in Dallas, moving to the University of Missouri in 2001, where she now holds the Frederick A. Middlebush chair in psychology. In addition to seminars in the development of character, social psychology, and personality psychology, she has taught undergraduate lecture courses in introductory psychology, introduction to personality psychology, and social psychology. At SMU, she received six different teaching awards, including the "M" award for "sustained excellence" in 1999. At the University of Missouri, she received the Chancellor's Award for Outstanding Research and Creative Activity in 2004.

Her research, which has been funded by the National Institute of Mental Health and the National Science Foundation, has focused on a variety of topics relevant to the question of what it is that makes for a good life. She has studied goals, life stories, happiness, well-being, and meaning in life. In general, her work reflects an enduring interest in studying what is good and healthy in people. In 2001, her research accomplishments were recognized by a Templeton Prize in positive psychology. In 2011, she received the Ed and Carol Diener Award for Distinguished Contributions to Personality Psychology. Laura's research (often in collaboration with undergraduate and graduate students) has appeared in many publications, including *American Psychologist, Journal of Personality and Social Psychology, Personality and Social Psychology Bulletin,* and *Psychological Science.*

Currently the editor of the *Journal of Personality and Social Psychology: Personality and Individual Differences,* Laura has also served as editor of the *Journal of Research in Personality;* as associate editor of *Personality and Social Psychology Bulletin,* the *Journal of Personality and Social Psychology,* and *Social and Personality Psychology Compass;* and on numerous grant panels. She has edited or coedited special sections of the *Journal of Personality* and *American Psychologist.*

In "real life," Laura is an accomplished cook and enjoys listening to music (mostly jazz vocalists and singer-songwriters), running with her faithful dog Bill, and swimming and roller-skating with Sam, her 8-year-old son.

# brief contents

**CHAPTER 1**   The Science of Psychology   1

**CHAPTER 2**   The Brain and Behavior   42

**CHAPTER 3**   Sensation and Perception   84

**CHAPTER 4**   States of Consciousness   125

**CHAPTER 5**   Learning   166

**CHAPTER 6**   Memory   201

**CHAPTER 7**   Thinking, Intelligence, and Language   242

**CHAPTER 8**   Human Development   278

**CHAPTER 9**   Motivation and Emotion   324

**CHAPTER 10**   Personality   361

**CHAPTER 11**   Social Psychology   400

**CHAPTER 12**   Psychological Disorders   440

**CHAPTER 13**   Therapies   482

**CHAPTER 14**   Health Psychology   513

Answers to Self-Quizzes and Self-Tests   A-1

Glossary   G-1

References   R-1

Credits   C-1

Name Index   NI-1

Subject Index   SI-1

# contents

PREFACE xiii

## 1 The Science of Psychology  1

1  **Defining Psychology and Exploring Its Roots**  2
The Psychological Frame of Mind  3
Psychology as the Science of All Human Behavior  4
Psychology in Historical Perspective  6

2  **Contemporary Approaches to Psychology**  8
The Biological Approach  8
The Behavioral Approach  9
The Psychodynamic Approach  9
The Humanistic Approach  10
The Cognitive Approach  10
The Evolutionary Approach  10
The Sociocultural Approach  11
Summing up the Seven Contemporary Approaches  11

3  **Psychology's Scientific Method**  13

4  **Types of Psychological Research**  17
Descriptive Research  17
Correlational Research  20
Experimental Research  23
Applications of the Three Types of Research  27
INTERSECTION: *Social Psychology and Cross-Cultural Psychology: How Does Culture Influence the Meaning of Success?*  28

5  **Research Samples and Settings**  29
The Research Sample  29
The Research Setting  30
PSYCHOLOGY IN OUR WORLD: *The Global Science of Happiness*  31

6  **Conducting Ethical Research**  33
Ethics Guidelines  33
CHALLENGE YOUR THINKING: *Is It Ethical to Use Deception in Research?*  34
The Ethics of Research with Animals  36
The Place of Values in Psychological Research  36

7  **Learning About Psychology Means Learning About You**  37
Encountering Psychology in Everyday Life  37
Appreciating Psychology as the Science of You  39

SUMMARY  40
KEY TERMS  40
SELF-TEST  41

## 2 The Brain and Behavior  42

1  **The Nervous System**  43
Characteristics of the Nervous System  43
Pathways in the Nervous System  44
Divisions of the Nervous System  45

2  **Neurons**  47
Specialized Cell Structure  47
CHALLENGE YOUR THINKING: *Do Mirror Neurons Hold the Key to Social Understanding?*  48
The Neural Impulse  50
Synapses and Neurotransmitters  51
Neural Networks  55

3  **Structures of the Brain and Their Functions**  56
How Researchers Study the Brain and Nervous System  56
INTERSECTION: *Neuroscience and Personality: Are Some Brains Nicer Than Others?*  58
How the Brain Is Organized  59
The Cerebral Cortex  64
The Cerebral Hemispheres and Split-Brain Research  67
Integration of Function in the Brain  70

TOURING THE NERVOUS SYSTEM AND THE BRAIN

4  **The Endocrine System**  71

5  **Brain Damage, Plasticity, and Repair**  73
The Brain's Plasticity and Capacity for Repair  73
PSYCHOLOGY IN OUR WORLD: *Protecting the Athlete's Brain*  74
Brain Tissue Implants  75

6  **Genetics and Behavior**  76
Chromosomes, Genes, and DNA  76
The Study of Genetics  77
Genes and the Environment  79

SUMMARY  81
KEY TERMS  82
SELF-TEST  83

# 3 Sensation and Perception 84

1 **How We Sense and Perceive the World** 85
The Processes and Purposes of Sensation and Perception 85
Sensory Receptors and the Brain 87
Thresholds 89
**CHALLENGE YOUR THINKING:** *Can We Feel the Future?* 90
Perceiving Sensory Stimuli 93
Sensory Adaptation 95

2 **The Visual System** 96
The Visual Stimulus and the Eye 96
Visual Processing in the Brain 100
Color Vision 102
Perceiving Shape, Depth, Motion, and Constancy 103

3 **The Auditory System** 109
The Nature of Sound and How We Experience It 109
Structures and Functions of the Ear 109
Theories of Hearing 112
Auditory Processing in the Brain 113
Localizing Sound 113

4 **Other Senses** 114
The Skin Senses 114
**INTERSECTION:** *Social Psychology and Perception: The Social Glow of Feeling Warm* 116
The Chemical Senses 117
**PSYCHOLOGY IN OUR WORLD:** *Why Salt Is the Salt of the Earth* 119
The Kinesthetic and Vestibular Senses 120

SUMMARY 122
KEY TERMS 123
SELF-TEST 124

# 4 States of Consciousness 125

1 **The Nature of Consciousness** 126
Defining Consciousness 126
Consciousness and the Brain 127
Theory of Mind 127
Levels of Awareness 128
**INTERSECTION:** *Consciousness and Cross-Cultural and Developmental Psychology: How Does Culture Shape Theory of Mind Development?* 129
**CHALLENGE YOUR THINKING:** *Why Do We Have Conscious Awareness?* 132

2 **Sleep and Dreams** 133
Biological Rhythms and Sleep 133
Why Do We Need Sleep? 135
Stages of Wakefulness and Sleep 136

Sleep Throughout the Life Span 139
Sleep and Disease 141
Sleep Disorders 141
Dreams 143

3 **Psychoactive Drugs** 146
Uses of Psychoactive Drugs 146
Types of Psychoactive Drugs 147

4 **Hypnosis** 157
The Nature of Hypnosis 157
Explaining Hypnosis 158
Uses of Hypnosis 159

5 **Meditation** 160
Mindfulness Meditation 160
The Meditative State of Mind 161
**PSYCHOLOGY IN OUR WORLD:** *Meditation at Work* 162
Getting Started with Meditation 162

SUMMARY 163
KEY TERMS 164
SELF-TEST 164

# 5 Learning 166

1 **Types of Learning** 167

2 **Classical Conditioning** 169
Pavlov's Studies 169
Classical Conditioning in Humans 173
**PSYCHOLOGY IN OUR WORLD:** *Marketing Between the Lines* 176

3 **Operant Conditioning** 177
Defining Operant Conditioning 178
Thorndike's Law of Effect 178
Skinner's Approach to Operant Conditioning 179
Shaping 180
Principles of Reinforcement 180
Applied Behavior Analysis 187

4 **Observational Learning** 188

5 **Cognitive Factors in Learning** 190
Purposive Behavior 190
Insight Learning 191
**INTERSECTION:** *Educational and Cross-Cultural Psychology: How Does Cultural Diversity Affect Learning?* 193

6 **Biological, Cultural, and Psychological Factors in Learning** 194
Biological Constraints 194
Cultural Influences 196
Psychological Constraints 196
**CHALLENGE YOUR THINKING:** *Do Learning Styles Matter to Learning?* 197

SUMMARY 199
KEY TERMS 200
SELF-TEST 200

# 6 Memory 201

1 **The Nature of Memory** 202

2 **Memory Encoding** 203
Attention 203
Levels of Processing 204
Elaboration 204
Imagery 205

3 **Memory Storage** 207
Sensory Memory 207
Short-Term Memory 208
Long-Term Memory 211
INTERSECTION: *Cognitive and Cultural Psychology: How Does Culture Influence Episodic Memory?* 214

4 **Memory Retrieval** 220
Serial Position Effect 220
Retrieval Cues and the Retrieval Task 221
Special Cases of Retrieval 223
CHALLENGE YOUR THINKING: *Can Children Be Reliable Eyewitnesses to Their Own Abuse?* 226
PSYCHOLOGY IN OUR WORLD: *Using Psychological Research to Improve Police Lineups* 229

5 **Forgetting** 230
Encoding Failure 231
Retrieval Failure 232

6 **Tips from the Science of Memory—for Studying and for Life** 235
Organizing, Encoding, Rehearsing, and Retrieving Course Content 235
Autobiographical Memory and the Life Story 237
Keeping Memory Sharp 237

SUMMARY 239
KEY TERMS 240
SELF-TEST 240

# 7 Thinking, Intelligence, and Language 242

1 **The Cognitive Revolution in Psychology** 243

2 **Thinking** 245
Concepts 245
Problem Solving 246
Reasoning and Decision Making 249
Thinking Critically and Creatively 253
PSYCHOLOGY IN OUR WORLD: *Help Wanted: Critical and Creative Thinkers* 255

3 **Intelligence** 255
Measuring Intelligence 256
Genetic and Environmental Influences on Intelligence 259
Extremes of Intelligence 261
CHALLENGE YOUR THINKING: *Is Intelligence Related to Prejudice and Political Beliefs?* 262
Theories of Multiple Intelligences 264

4 **Language** 266
The Basic Properties of Language 266
Language and Cognition 267
INTERSECTION: *Language, Culture, and Cognition: How Does Language Shape Answers to the Question "Where"?* 269
Biological and Environmental Influences on Language 270
Language Development over the Life Span 272

SUMMARY 275
KEY TERMS 276
SELF-TEST 277

# 8 Human Development 278

1 **Exploring Human Development** 279
Research Methods in Developmental Psychology 279
Do Early Experiences Rule Us for Life? 280
How Do Nature and Nurture Influence Development? 280
CHALLENGE YOUR THINKING: *Genes or Superparents: Which Matters More to Kids?* 281
Nature, Nurture, and You 282
Three Domains of Development 282

2 **Physical Development** 284
Prenatal Physical Development 284
Physical Development in Infancy and Childhood 286
Physical Development in Adolescence 289
Physical Development in Adulthood 290

3 **Cognitive Development** 294
Cognitive Development from Childhood into Adulthood 294
PSYCHOLOGY IN OUR WORLD: *The Joy of the Toy* 298
Cognitive Processes in Adulthood 300

4 **Socioemotional Development** 302
Socioemotional Development in Infancy 302
Erikson's Theory of Socioemotional Development 305

5 **Gender Development** 312
Biology and Gender Development 312
Cognitive Aspects of Gender Development 313
Socioemotional Experience and Gender Development 313
Nature and Nurture Revisited: The John/Joan Case 314

6 **Moral Development** 315
Kohlberg's Theory 315
Critics of Kohlberg 316
Moral Development in a Socioemotional Context 316
INTERSECTION: *Developmental and Social Psychology: Attachment and Honesty* 317

**7 Death, Dying, and Grieving 318**
   Terror Management Theory: A Cultural Shield Against
     Mortality 318
   Kübler-Ross's Stages of Dying 319
   Bonanno's Theory of Grieving 320
   Carving Meaning Out of the Reality of Death 320

**8 Active Development as a Lifelong Process 321**

SUMMARY 322
KEY TERMS 323
SELF-TEST 323

# 9 Motivation and Emotion 324

**1 Theories of Motivation 325**
   The Evolutionary Approach 325
   Drive Reduction Theory 326
   Optimum Arousal Theory 326

**2 Hunger and Sex 327**
   The Biology of Hunger 328
   Obesity 329
   The Biology of Sex 330
   Cognitive and Sensory/Perceptual Factors in Sexuality 332
   Cultural Factors in Sexuality 332
   Sexual Behavior and Orientation 333
   CHALLENGE YOUR THINKING: *How Different Are Men and
     Women When It Comes to Sex?* 337

**3 Beyond Hunger and Sex: Motivation
in Everyday Life 340**
   Maslow's Hierarchy of Human Needs 340
   INTERSECTION: *Motivation and Social Psychology: What
     Motivates Suicide Bombers?* 341
   Self-Determination Theory 342
   Intrinsic Versus Extrinsic Motivation 343
   Self-Regulation: The Successful Pursuit of Goals 344

**4 Emotion 345**
   Biological Factors in Emotion 345
   Cognitive Factors in Emotion 349
   Behavioral Factors in Emotion 350
   Sociocultural Factors in Emotion 351
   PSYCHOLOGY IN OUR WORLD: *Expressing Ourselves Online:
     The Psychology of Emoticons* 353
   Classifying Emotions 354
   Adaptive Functions of Emotions 355

**5 Motivation and Emotion: The Pursuit
of Happiness 356**
   Biological Factors in Happiness 356
   Obstacles in the Pursuit of Happiness 357
   Happiness Activities and Goal Striving 357

SUMMARY 358
KEY TERMS 359
SELF-TEST 360

# 10 Personality 361

**1 Psychodynamic Perspectives 362**
   Freud's Psychoanalytic Theory 362
   PSYCHOLOGY IN OUR WORLD: *Defense Mechanisms and the
     Psychology of Hypocrisy* 365
   Psychodynamic Critics and Revisionists 367
   Evaluating the Psychodynamic Perspectives 369

**2 Humanistic Perspectives 370**
   Maslow's Approach 370
   Rogers's Approach 371
   Evaluating the Humanistic Perspectives 372

**3 Trait Perspectives 373**
   Trait Theories 373
   The Five-Factor Model of Personality 374
   Evaluating the Trait Perspectives 378
   INTERSECTION: *Personality Psychology and Health Psychology:
     Are Traits Linked to Obesity?* 379

**4 Personological and Life Story Perspectives 380**
   Murray's Personological Approach 380
   The Life Story Approach to Identity 381
   Evaluating the Life Story Approach and Similar Perspectives 382

**5 Social Cognitive Perspectives 383**
   Bandura's Social Cognitive Theory 383
   Mischel's Contributions 384
   Evaluating the Social Cognitive Perspectives 387

**6 Biological Perspectives 387**
   Personality and the Brain 388
   Personality and Behavioral Genetics 390
   Evaluating the Biological Perspectives 391

**7 Personality Assessment 391**
   Self-Report Tests 392
   Projective Tests 393
   CHALLENGE YOUR THINKING: *Are Personality Judgments
     Accurate?* 394
   Other Assessment Methods 397

SUMMARY 397
KEY TERMS 399
SELF-TEST 399

# 11

## Social Psychology   400

**1   Social Cognition**   401
Person Perception   401
Attribution   403
The Self as a Social Object   404
Attitudes   406

**2   Social Behavior**   409
Altruism   410
Aggression   412
CHALLENGE YOUR THINKING: *Do Video Games Influence Social Behavior?*   417

**3   Social Influence**   418
Conformity and Obedience   418
PSYCHOLOGY IN OUR WORLD: *Conformity and the American Strip Mall*   420
INTERSECTION: *Social Psychology and Cross-Cultural Psychology: Why Are Some Nations More Conforming Than Others?*   421
Group Influence   425

**4   Intergroup Relations**   428
Group Identity: Us Versus Them   428
Prejudice   430
Ways to Improve Intergroup Relations   432

**5   Close Relationships**   434
Attraction   434
Attachment   435
Love   436
Models of Close Relationships   436

SUMMARY   437
KEY TERMS   438
SELF-TEST   439

# 12

## Psychological Disorders   440

**1   Defining and Explaining Abnormal Behavior**   441
Three Criteria of Abnormal Behavior   441
Culture, Context, and the Meaning of Abnormal Behavior   442
Theoretical Approaches to Psychological Disorders   443
Classifying Abnormal Behavior   444
CHALLENGE YOUR THINKING: *Does Everyone Have ADHD?*   447

**2   Anxiety Disorders**   448
Generalized Anxiety Disorder   448
Panic Disorder   449
Phobic Disorder   450

Obsessive-Compulsive Disorder   451
Post-Traumatic Stress Disorder   452
PSYCHOLOGY IN OUR WORLD: *The Psychological Wounds of War*   453

**3   Mood Disorders**   454
Depressive Disorders   454
Bipolar Disorder   457
INTERSECTION: *Clinical and Developmental Psychology: Can Kids "Catch" Depression and Anxiety?*   458
Suicide   459

**4   Eating Disorders**   462
Anorexia Nervosa   462
Bulimia Nervosa   463
Anorexia Nervosa and Bulimia Nervosa: Causes and Treatments   463
Binge Eating Disorder   464
Binge Eating Disorder: Causes and Treatments   464

**5   Dissociative Disorders**   465
Dissociative Amnesia and Dissociative Fugue   466
Dissociative Identity Disorder   466

**6   Schizophrenia**   468
Symptoms of Schizophrenia   468
Causes of Schizophrenia   470

**7   Personality Disorders**   473
Antisocial Personality Disorder   473
Borderline Personality Disorder   475

**8   Combatting Stigma**   476
Consequences of Stigma   477
Overcoming Stigma   478

SUMMARY   479
KEY TERMS   480
SELF-TEST   481

# 13

## Therapies   482

**1   Biological Therapy**   483
Drug Therapy   483
CHALLENGE YOUR THINKING: *Do Antidepressants Increase Suicide Risk in Youth?*   486
Electroconvulsive Therapy   487
Psychosurgery   488

**2   Psychotherapy**   490
Psychodynamic Therapies   491
Humanistic Therapies   493
Behavior Therapies   494
Cognitive Therapies   495
PSYCHOLOGY IN OUR WORLD: *Seeking Therapy? There Might Be an App for That*   497
Therapy Integrations   500

**3   Sociocultural Approaches and Issues in Treatment   501**
Group Therapy   501
Family and Couples Therapy   502
Self-Help Support Groups   503
Community Mental Health   504
Cultural Perspectives   504
INTERSECTION: *Clinical and Cultural Psychology:*
*How Can Cognitive-Behavior Therapy Work Across*
*Different Belief Systems?*   505

**4   The Effectiveness of Psychotherapy   506**
Research on the Effectiveness of Psychotherapy   507
Health and Wellness Benefits of Psychotherapy   508
Common Themes in Effective Psychotherapy   509

SUMMARY   510
KEY TERMS   511
SELF-TEST   511

# 14 Health Psychology   513

**1   Health Psychology and Behavioral Medicine   514**
The Biopsychosocial Model   514
Connections Between Mind and Body   515

**2   Making Positive Life Changes   515**
Theoretical Models of Change   516
The Stages of Change Model   516

**3   Resources for Effective Life Change   519**
Motivation   520
Social Relationships   520
INTERSECTION: *Health and Cross-Cultural Psychology: How*
*Does Culture Influence the Meaning of Social Support?*   522
Religious Faith   523
Personality Characteristics   523
CHALLENGE YOUR THINKING: *How Powerful Is the Power*
*of Positive Thinking?*   524

**4   Toward a Healthier Mind (and Body):**
**Controlling Stress   526**
Stress and Its Stages   526
Stress and the Immune System   527
Stress and Cardiovascular Disease   529
Stress and Cancer   530
Cognitive Appraisal and Coping with Stress   530
Strategies for Successful Coping   531
Stress Management Programs   532

**5   Toward a Healthier Body (and Mind):**
**Behaving as If Your Life Depends upon It   533**
Becoming Physically Active   534
Eating Right   535
PSYCHOLOGY IN OUR WORLD: *Environments That Support*
*Active Lifestyles*   536
Quitting Smoking   538
Practicing Safe Sex   539

**6   Psychology and Your Good Life   540**

SUMMARY   541
KEY TERMS   542
SELF-TEST   543

■ Answers to Self-Quizzes and Self-Tests A-1

■ Glossary G-1

■ References R-1

■ Credits C-1

■ Name Index NI-1

■ Subject Index SI-1

# Experience Psychology

## Some people take introductory psychology; others experience it.

*Experience Psychology*, Second Edition, is an integrated learning system that empowers students to personally, critically, and actively experience the impact of psychology in daily life and master even the most difficult course topics. *Experience Psychology*, Second Edition, is about, well, experience—our own behaviors; our relationships at home and in our communities, in school, and at work; and our interactions in different learning environments. Grounded in meaningful real-world contexts, *Experience Psychology*, Second Edition's contemporary examples, personalized author notes, and applied exercises speak directly to students, allowing them to engage with psychology and to learn verbally, visually, and experientially—by reading, seeing, and doing. The new edition continues the first edition's precedent of introducing function before dysfunction, building student understanding by looking first at typical, everyday behavior before delving into the less common—and likely less personally experienced—rare and abnormal behavior. *Experience Psychology*, Second Edition, places the science of psychology, and the research that helps students see the academic foundations of the discipline, at the forefront of the course.

With the learning system of *Experience Psychology*, Second Edition, students do not just "take" psychology but actively *experience* it.

## Experience a Personalized Approach

How many students *think* they know everything about introductory psychology but struggle on the first exam? LearnSmart, McGraw-Hill's adaptive learning system, pinpoints students' metacognitive abilities and limitations, identifying what they know—and, more importantly, what they don't know. Using Bloom's taxonomy and a highly sophisticated "smart" algorithm, LearnSmart creates a personalized, customized study plan that is unique to each student's demonstrated needs. With virtually no administrative overhead, instructors using LearnSmart are reporting an increase in student performance by a letter grade or more.

LearnSmart is part of McGraw-Hill's Connect Psychology, a wealth of interactive course materials for both instructors and students. Videos, interactive assessments, and simulations invite engagement and add real-world perspective to the introductory psychology course. Detailed reporting helps students and instructors gauge comprehension and retention—*without adding administrative load.*

*Experience Psychology*, Second Edition, emphasizes a personal approach as well, with an abundance of personal pedagogical "asides" communicated directly by author Laura King to students to guide their understanding and stimulate their interest as they read. Some of these helpful notes highlight important terms and concepts; others prompt students to think critically about the complexities of the issues; still others encourage students to apply what they have learned to their prior reading or to a new situation. These mini-conversations between the author and the reader help develop students' analytical skills for them to carry and apply well beyond their course.

*Notice that these first two studies involve examining two different cultures, while the last one focuses on a culture within a culture. These studies exemplify the sociocultural approach.*

# —Personally, Critically, and Actively

## Experience an Emphasis on Critical Thinking

*Experience Psychology,* Second Edition, stimulates critical reflection and analysis. The **Challenge Your Thinking** sidebars involve students in debates relevant to findings from contemporary psychological research. Thought-provoking questions encourage examination of the evidence on both sides of a debate or issue. For example, the Chapter 7 selection asks students to reflect on whether intelligence is related to prejudicial thinking, while Chapter 11's "Challenge" prompts them to consider whether playing violent video games leads to violence in real life.

The text's **Intersection** features are also designed to spark critical thought. Showcasing studies in different areas of psychological research that focus on the same topic, the Intersections shed light on the links between, and the reciprocal influences of, this exciting work, and they raise provocative questions for student reflection and class discussion. For example, the Chapter 9 Intersection, "Motivation and Social Psychology: What Motivates Suicide Bombers?" prompts students to think about whether researchers can clarify the motives of suicide attackers as a step toward preventing their horrific actions, as well as to consider the implications of this research for incidents such as the inadvertent burning of religious texts.

In addition, the new **Psychological Inquiry** feature draws students into analyzing and interpreting figures and photos by embedding a range of critical thinking questions in selected captions.

To help students master challenging concepts, *Experience Psychology,* Second Edition, also includes a special section, "Touring the Nervous System and the Brain," featuring detailed, full-color transparency overlays of important figures. Conceived and developed with the input of an expert in each specific area, the overlays offer students hands-on practice to help them grasp key biological structures and processes that are essential to success in the course. The **Apply It to Our World** feature links the subject matter of the transparency overlays to common real-life situations, such as the fear of spiders. On-page assessment questions and answers, as well as critical thinking questions, accompany each figure.

## Experience an Emphasis on Active Engagement

**EXPERIENCE IT!**
Three Stages of Memory

With the new **Experience It!** feature, students can use their mobile devices to practice and master key concepts wherever and whenever they choose. By snapping easily located QR codes, students gain access to videos and Concept Clips for a highly portable, rich, and immersive experience that powerfully reinforces the chapter reading.

Through **Do It!,** a series of brief, recurring sidebar activities linked to the text reading, students get an opportunity to test their assumptions and learn through hands-on exploration and discovery. Reinforcing that the science of psychology requires active participation, Do It! selections include, for example, an exercise on conducting an informal survey to observe and classify behaviors in a public setting, as well as an activity guiding students on how to research a "happiness gene." Such exercises provide vibrant and involving experiences that get students thinking as psychologists do.

Created by a team of instructional designers, **Concept Clips** help students comprehend some of the most difficult ideas in introductory psychology. Colorful graphics and stimulating animations describe core concepts in a step-by-step manner, engaging students and aiding in retention. Powered by McGraw-Hill's Connect Psychology, Concept Clips can be used as a presentational tool for the classroom or for student assessment.

In the next few days, look through several newspapers, magazines, and your favorite online news sources for reports about psychological research. Apply the guidelines for being a wise consumer of information about psychology to these media reports.

Through the connection of psychology to students' own lives, concepts become more relevant and understandable. Powered by McGraw-Hill's Connect Psychology, **Newsflash** exercises tie current news stories to key psychological principles and learning objectives. After interacting with a contemporary news story, students are assessed on their ability to make the link between real life and research findings. Many cases are revisited across chapters, encouraging students to consider multiple perspectives. In Chapter 2, students consider the case of Congresswoman Gabrielle Giffords, who suffered a brain injury in a 2011 shooting. The case is revisited in Chapter 7, "Thinking, Intelligence, and Language."

McGraw-Hill's new **PsychInteractive** provides students with the opportunity to experience the scientific method as they actively learn to observe data, formulate and test a hypothesis, communicate their findings, and apply their understanding of psychology to the world. PsychInteractive is available through McGraw-Hill's Connect Psychology.

# Chapter-by-Chapter Changes

*Experience Psychology*, Second Edition, includes important new material while stream-lining where possible; each chapter is up-to-date to capture the latest trends and findings in the field. The key content changes, chapter by chapter, include but are not limited to the following:

## CHAPTER 1: THE SCIENCE OF PSYCHOLOGY
- Revised and expanded discussion of the nature of scientific research.
- New discussion of the frequency of counterintuitive results in research.
- New material on falsifiability.
- Detailed new discussion of within-participant and quasi-experimental research designs.
- New tips for critically evaluating psychological research that is available online.
- New Challenge Your Thinking selection: "Is It Ethical to Use Deception in Research?"
- New Intersection box: "Social Psychology and Cross-Cultural Psychology: How Does Culture Influence the Meaning of Success?"
- New Psychology in Our World feature: "The Global Science of Happiness."

## CHAPTER 2: THE BRAIN AND BEHAVIOR
- New discussion of the use of transcranial magnetic stimulation in the study of brain functioning.
- Updated treatment of hemispheric differences in brain functioning.
- New discussion of recent research identifying the multiple factors involved in children's capacity for recovery after a traumatic brain injury.
- Expanded and updated treatment of neurogenesis.
- Discussion of the growing volume of research concerned with gene × environment (g × e) interaction.
- New Challenge Your Thinking selection: "Do Mirror Neurons Hold the Key to Social Understanding?"
- New Intersection box: "Neuroscience and Personality: Are Some Brains Nicer Than Others?"
- New Psychology in Our World feature: "Protecting the Athlete's Brain."

## CHAPTER 3: SENSATION AND PERCEPTION
- Updated discussion of subliminal perception.
- Added coverage of signal detection theory.
- Discussion of recent research on inattentional blindness suggesting the dangers of multitasking when one of the tasks is driving.
- New information regarding research on binding and its role in visual perception.
- New section on culture, attention, and perception, looking at how culture influences which stimuli individuals attend to as they perceive the world.
- New information analyzing research on the role of differences in biological sex and cultural expectations in the experience and reporting of pain.
- New Challenge Your Thinking selection: "Can We Feel the Future?"
- New Intersection box: "Social Psychology and Perception: The Social Glow of Feeling Warm."
- New Psychology in Our World feature: "Why Salt Is the Salt of the Earth."

## CHAPTER 4: STATES OF CONSCIOUSNESS
- Updated treatments of theories about why humans need sleep and the role of sleep throughout the human life span.
- Revised discussion of various sleep disorders and problems, including sleepwalking, sleep talking, narcolepsy, sleep apnea, and SIDS.

- Updated data and discussion on drug use among U.S. teenagers.
- Thoroughly updated treatment of alcohol—its effects and abuse.
- New data on U.S. and global use of tobacco products.
- Updated treatment of hypnosis and its applications.
- New Challenge Your Thinking selection: "Why Do We Have Conscious Awareness?"
- New Intersection box: "Consciousness and Cross-Cultural and Developmental Psychology: How Does Culture Shape Theory of Mind Development?"

## CHAPTER 5: LEARNING
- New and extended discussion and analysis of applications of classical conditioning, including treatments of research findings on breaking habits, the placebo effect, taste aversion learning, and drug habituation.
- Updated discussion of avoidance learning.
- Revised, expanded account of insight learning.
- New Challenge Your Thinking selection: "Do Learning Styles Matter to Learning?"
- New Intersection box: "Educational and Cross-Cultural Psychology: How Does Cultural Diversity Affect Learning?"
- Updated Psychology in Our World feature: "Marketing Between the Lines."

## CHAPTER 6: MEMORY
- Revised account of the role of attention in memory encoding.
- Updated treatment of the use of mental imagery to make memories distinctive.
- Up-to-date approach to working memory, including examination of its use as a framework for addressing practical real-world problems.
- Consideration of how the ready availability of information on the Internet has influenced memory.
- Fresh analysis of flashbulb memory.
- Updated discussion of the retrieval of autobiographical memories.
- New discussion of discovered memories.
- Examination of new research findings on how modern conveniences like GPS devices can be counterproductive to the goal of keeping the brain active.
- New Challenge Your Thinking selection: "Can Children Be Reliable Eyewitnesses to Their Own Abuse?"
- New Intersection box: "Cognitive and Cross-Cultural Psychology: How Does Culture Influence Episodic Memory?"
- New Psychology in Our World feature: "Using Psychological Research to Improve Police Lineups."

## CHAPTER 7: THINKING, INTELLIGENCE, AND LANGUAGE
- Updated treatment of reasoning and decision making, integrating recent research.
- Fresh look at various biases and heuristics that affect decision making.
- New information on Spearman's *g*.
- New details on genetic and environmental influences on intelligence, featuring recent research results.
- Revised, expanded discussion of intellectual disability.
- New Challenge Your Thinking selection: "Is Intelligence Related to Prejudice and Political Beliefs?"
- New Intersection box: "Language, Culture, and Cognition: How Does Language Shape Answers to the Question 'Where?'"

## CHAPTER 8: HUMAN DEVELOPMENT

- Reorganization of the chapter content by developmental domain—physical, cognitive, and socioemotional—rather than by chronological developmental periods, providing an integrated account that gives students a solid grounding in the seminal developmental theories and allows them to grasp the content more easily because it is presented as a coherent whole.
- Expanded survey of gender development in a new main section integrating biological, cognitive, and socioemotional aspects.
- All-new main section on death, dying, and grieving featuring the work of Kübler-Ross and Bonanno and including analysis of terror management theory.
- New coverage of infants' motor and perceptual skills development.
- Updated, extended treatment of physical development in adulthood, including new research findings on menopause.
- Updated discussion of cognitive processes in adulthood.
- New section on the cultural context of parenting.
- Extensively revised treatment of socioemotional development in late adulthood, including examination of Carstensen's socioemotional selectivity theory.
- Updated Challenge Your Thinking selection: "Genes or Superparents: Which Matters More to Kids?"
- New Intersection box: "Developmental and Social Psychology: Attachment and Honesty."

## CHAPTER 9: MOTIVATION AND EMOTION

- Updated discussion of the problem of obesity.
- New sections on sex education in theory and in practice.
- Up-to-date information on recent research on sexual behavior, including new details on trends in sexual practices in the United States.
- Updated discussion of factors determining sexual orientation.
- New global and U.S. data on numbers of gays, lesbians, and bisexuals.
- New Challenge Your Thinking selection: "How Different Are Men and Women When It Comes to Sex?"
- New Intersection box: "Motivation and Social Psychology: What Motivates Suicide Bombers?"

## CHAPTER 10: PERSONALITY

- Incorporation of new research findings related to the big five factors of personality.
- Updated analysis of Mischel's CAPS theory.
- Expanded treatment of the role of neurotransmitters in personality.
- New Challenge Your Thinking selection: "Are Personality Judgments Accurate?"
- New Intersection box: "Personality Psychology and Health Psychology: Are Traits Linked to Obesity?"
- New Psychology in Our World feature: "Defense Mechanisms and the Psychology of Hypocrisy."

## CHAPTER 11: SOCIAL PSYCHOLOGY

- New section on cultural differences in conformity.
- All-new section examining the Stanford prison experiment.
- New discussion of Facebook as a venue for social comparison.
- Updated treatment of sex differences in aggression, including new information on relational aggression.
- New section on adult attachment within the larger treatment of close relationships.
- Updated discussion of models of close relationships.

- New Intersection box: "Social Psychology and Cross-Cultural Psychology: Why Are Some Nations More Conforming Than Others?"
- New Psychology in Our World feature: "Conformity and the American Strip Mall."

## CHAPTER 12: PSYCHOLOGICAL DISORDERS

- Extensive new discussion of culture, context, and the meaning of abnormal behavior.
- New analysis looking at how different cultures may interpret the same pattern of behaviors in different ways.
- All-new preview of anticipated significant revisions in the *DSM-V* (2013) and of emerging criticisms of them.
- Updated discussion of critiques of the *DSM-IV*.
- Revised and expanded treatment of the etiology of panic disorder.
- New discussion of cultural influences in phobias and depression.
- Up-to-date data on U.S. suicides, plus extensively updated treatment of sociocultural factors in suicide.
- New details on findings from cross-cultural comparisons looking at the reasons for dissociative identity disorder.
- New information on cultural influences on symptoms of schizophrenia.
- All-new discussion and analysis of research on differences in the course of schizophrenia over time in developing versus developed nations.
- New material on proposed changes to the personality disorders categories for the *DSM-V*.
- New Challenge Your Thinking selection: "Does *Everyone* Have ADHD?"
- New Intersection box: "Clinical and Developmental Psychology: Can Kids 'Catch' Depression and Anxiety?"

## CHAPTER 13: THERAPIES

- New discussion of the complex ways in which culture can influence the psychotherapeutic process.
- New discussion of tetracyclic antidepressants.
- Updated examination of trends in the prescription of antidepressants.
- New material on deep brain stimulation as a treatment for depression and other disorders.
- New discussion of the pros and cons of online support groups.
- New material exploring the idea that specific therapeutic techniques can work best for particular disorders, and analysis of the related development of evidence-based practice.
- New Intersection box: "Clinical and Cultural Psychology: How Can Cognitive-Behavior Therapy Work Across Different Belief Systems?"
- New Psychology in Our World feature: "Seeking Therapy? There Might Be an App for That."

## CHAPTER 14: HEALTH PSYCHOLOGY

- Exploration of new research on the power of optimism in promoting positive functioning.
- New material on the Type D behavior pattern and its effects.
- Updated information on the links between regular physical activity and various positive personal outcomes.
- Up-to-date data on the growing problems of overweight and obesity.
- Streamlined, refocused section on practicing safe sex.
- Updated data on U.S. and global rates of HIV/AIDS infection.
- New Challenge Your Thinking selection: "How Powerful Is the Power of Positive Thinking?"
- New Intersection box: "Health and Cross-Cultural Psychology: How Does Culture Influence the Meaning of Social Support?"
- New Psychology in Our World feature: "Environments That Support Active Lifestyles."

# Experience the Course You Want to Teach

## McGraw-Hill/BB/Do More

Through McGraw-Hill's partnership with Blackboard, *Experience Psychology*, Second Edition, offers an ideal integration of content and tools:

- Seamless gradebook between Blackboard and McGraw-Hill's Connect Psychology
- Single sign-on providing seamless integration between McGraw-Hill content and Blackboard
- Simplicity in assigning and engaging your students with course materials

**Mc Graw Hill create**

Craft your teaching resources to match the way you teach. With McGraw-Hill **Create, www.mcgrawhillcreate.com,** you can easily rearrange chapters, combine material from other content sources, and quickly upload content you have written, such as your course syllabus or teaching notes. Find the content you need in Create by searching through thousands of leading McGraw-Hill textbooks. Arrange your book to fit your teaching style. Create even allows you to personalize your book's appearance by selecting the cover and adding your name, school, and course information. Order a Create book and you'll receive a complimentary print review copy in 3 to 5 business days or a complimentary electronic review copy (eComp) via e-mail in about an hour. Go to **www.mcgrawhillcreate.com** today and register. Experience how McGraw-Hill Create empowers you to teach *your* students *your* way.

## Tegrity Campus

**Tegrity Campus** is a service that makes class time available all the time by automatically capturing every lecture in a searchable format for students to review when they study and complete assignments. With a simple one-click start-and-stop process, users capture all computer screens and corresponding audio. Students replay any part of any class with easy-to-use browser-based viewing on a PC or Mac. Educators know that the more students can see, hear, and experience class resources, the better they learn. With Tegrity Campus, students quickly recall key moments by using its unique search feature. This search helps students efficiently find what they need, when they need it, across an entire semester of class recordings. Help turn all your students' study time into learning moments immediately supported by your lectures.

## CourseSmart

This text is available as an e-textbook at **www.CourseSmart.com.** At **CourseSmart** your students can take advantage of significant savings off the cost of a print textbook, reduce their impact on the environment, and gain access to powerful web tools for learning. CourseSmart e-textbooks can be viewed online or downloaded to a computer. The e-textbooks allow students to do full-text searches, add highlighting and notes, and share comments with classmates. CourseSmart has the largest selection of e-textbooks available anywhere. Visit **www.CourseSmart.com** to learn more and to try a sample chapter.

# Instructor Resources

All of the instructor resources described below can be found on the password-protected instructor's side of the **Online Learning Center** for *Experience Psychology,* Second Edition. Contact your local McGraw-Hill publishing representative for log-in information: **www.mhhe.com/kingep2e.**

***Testing Program***   In the previous edition of this text, Laura King raised the bar for student assessment. For this edition, we are raising the bar even higher. We've enlisted ANSR, a dedicated educational supplements development company, to update all of our instructor resources for this edition. This edition's Test Bank has gone through the extensive reviews of accuracy, clarity, effectiveness, and accessibility. We've also annotated questions' difficulty level and Bloom's taxonomy, in line with the previous edition. The Test Bank is compatible with McGraw-Hill's computerized testing program, EZ Test, and most course management systems.

***Instructor's Manual***   The Instructor's Manual provides a variety of tools and resources for enhancing your course, including learning objectives, lecture ideas, and handouts. The Instructor's Manual also includes discussion ideas for starting in-class discussions on relevant topics in psychology.

***PowerPoint Presentations***   Our PowerPoint presentations cover the key points of each chapter and include graphs and charts taken directly from the text. These presentations serve as an organizational and navigational tool, and they are integrated with examples and activities. The PowerPoint slides can be used as-is or modified to meet the individual needs of an instructor.

***Image Gallery***   The Image Gallery features the complete set of figures and tables from the text. These images are available for download and can be easily embedded into instructors' PowerPoint slides.

# acknowledgments

*The quality of Experience Psychology, Second Edition, is a testament to the skills and abilities of so many people, and I am tremendously grateful to the following individuals for their insightful contributions during the project's development.*

## Second Edition Contributors

Jackie Adamson, *Del Mar College*
William Addison, *Eastern Illinois University*
Brien K. Ashdown, *Hobart and William Smith Colleges*
Patricia A. Badt, *Ivy Technical Community College of Indiana*
Thomas J. Baker, *Indiana University–Bloomington*
Lena Barber, *Lee University*
Carolyn Brodnicki, *College of Lake County*
Gidget Brogdon, *California State University–Northridge*
Sharon Calhoon, *Indiana University–Kokomo*
Bernice L. Carson, *Virginia State University*
Michael R. Cassens, *Irvine Valley College*
Diane Catanzaro, *Christopher Newport University*
Michelle Caya, *Trident Technical College*
Stanley Christopher, *Winston-Salem State University*
Wanda Clark, *South Plains College*
Tametryce Collins, *Hillsborough Community College–Brandon*
Carol L. Cooper, *Davenport University*
Satoris S. Culbertson, *Kansas State University*
Mark Davis, *University of West Alabama*
Neeru Deep, *Northwestern State University of Louisiana*
Hadassah DeJack, *Delaware Technical and Community College*
Stephanie B. Ding, *Del Mar College*
Jewel Dirks, *Central Wyoming College*
Mary Dolan, *California State University–San Bernardino*
Sheri Dunlavy, *Ivy Technical Community College of Indiana–Fort Wayne*
Linda Emerson, *College of the Desert*
Sarah Estow, *Guilford College*
Robert W. Fisher, *Lee University*

Murray Fortner, *Tarrant County College–Northeast*
Laurie Fowler, *Weber State University*
Rhonda Frazelle, *State Fair Community College*
Anne Garcia, *Washtenaw Community College*
Ericka Hamilton, *Moraine Valley Community College*
Moira Hanna, *Greenville Technical College*
Cassidy Hawf, *Iowa Central Community College*
Brett Heintz, *Delgado Community College*
Carmon Weaver Hicks, *Ivy Technical Community College of Indiana–Indianapolis*
Brooke Hindman, *Greenville Technical College*
Linda Hoke-Sinex, *Indiana University–Bloomington*
Carol Holding, *Illinois Central College*
Deborah Horn, *Blinn College*
Rick Howe, *College of the Canyons*
Alycia Hund, *Illinois State University*
Darren Iwamoto, *Chaminade University*
Robin Joynes, *Kent State University*
Inna Glaz Kanevsky, *San Diego Mesa College*
David Kreiner, *University of Central Missouri*
Cynthia Kreutzer, *Georgia Perimeter College*
David Kurz, *Del Mar College*
Martha Low, *Winston-Salem University*
Claire Mann, *Coastline Community College*
Karen Marsh, *University of Minnesota–Duluth*
Randy Martinez, *Cypress College*
Gabriela Martorell, *Virginia Wesleyan College*
Kirsten Matthews, *Harper College*
William McCracken, *Delaware Technical and Community College*
Colleen McDonough, *Neumann University*
Douglas McHugh, *Indiana University–Bloomington*
Bruce L. Merrick, *Clear Creek Baptist Bible College*
Andrew Mienaltowski, *Western Kentucky University*
Dara Musher-Eizenman, *Bowling Green State University*
Ian Norris, *Murray State University*

Karen Osterholm, *Blinn College*
Cynthia Porter Rickert, *Ivy Technical Community College of Indiana–Indianapolis*
Rebecca Rahschulte, *Ivy Technical Community College of Indiana–Lawrenceburg*
Gail Robertson, *Idaho State University*
Erin Rogers, *Florida State College–South*
Margherita Rossi, *Broome County Community College*
Traci Sachteleben, *Southwestern Illinois College*
Edie Sample, *Metropolitan Community College*
James E. Schork, *Kentucky Community and Technical College System–Elizabethtown*
Valerie B. Scott, *Indiana University Southeast*
Christopher Stanley, *Winston-Salem State University*
Deborah Stipp, *Ivy Technical Community College of Indiana*
Jutta Street, *Campbell University*
Donna Stuber, *Friends University*
Shawn Talbot, *Kellogg Community College*
Sean Taylor, *Des Moines Area Community College–Boone*
William Travis Suits, *Seminole State College of Florida*
Elizabeth Tuckwiller, *Florida State College–South*
James A. Villarreal, *Delaware Technical and Community College*
Kacy Welsh, *University of Georgia*
Brandy Young, *Cypress College*

## Adaptive Learning Consultants

Ted Barker, *Northwest Florida State*
Michelle Caya, *Trident Tech Community College*
Lisa Fozio-Thielk, *Waubonsee Community College*

Brett Marroquín, *Yale University*
Rebecca Peral, *Yale University*
Anthony Yankowski, *Bergen County Community College*

# Introductory Psychology Symposia Participants

Every year, McGraw-Hill conducts several introductory psychology symposia that are attended by instructors from across the country. These events are an opportunity for McGraw-Hill staff to gather information about the needs and challenges of instructors teaching the course. The symposia also offer a forum for the attendees to exchange ideas and experiences with colleagues whom they might not otherwise have met. The feedback we have received has been invaluable and has contributed, directly and indirectly, to the development of *Experience Psychology*, Second Edition.

Melissa Acevedo, *Westchester Community College*
Terry Scott Adcock, *Parkland College*
Mark Alicke, *Ohio University*
Cheryl Almeida, *Johnson & Wales University*
Carol Anderson, *Bellevue College*
Jeff Anderson, *Oklahoma City Community College*
Susan A. Anderson, *University of South Alabama*
Clarissa Arms-Chavez, *Auburn University*
Diane Davis Ashe, *Valencia Community College*
Erskine Ausbrooks, *Dyersburg State Community College*
Michael Babcock, *Montana State University*
Thomas C. Bailey, *University of Maryland–University College*
Marina Baratian, *Brevard Community College–Melbourne*
Ted Barker, *Northwest Florida State College*
Steven Barnhart, *Middlesex County College*
David E. Baskind, *Delta College*
Shirley Bass-Wright, *St. Philip's College*
Scott C. Bates, *Utah State University*
Holly Beard, *Midlands Technical College*
Jennifer Beck, *Austin Community College*
Karen Beck, *Rio Hondo College*
James L. Becker, *Pulaski Technical College*
Aileen M. Behan-Collins, *Chemeketa Community College*
Dan Bellack, *Trident Technical College*
Andrew Berns, *Milwaukee Area Technical College–Milwaukee*

Joy L. Berrenberg, *University of Colorado–Denver*
Jennifer Bizon, *Texas A&M University*
Ginette Blackhart, *East Tennessee State University*
Kathryn Becker Blease, *Oregon State University*
Stephen Blessing, *University of Tampa*
Jeffrey Blum, *Los Angeles City College*
Susan Boatright, *University of Rhode Island*
Thomas Brandon, *University of South Florida–Tampa*
Deborah Briihl, *Valdosta State University*
William Brinnier, *Central Piedmont Community College*
Gidget Brogdon, *California State University–Northridge*
Tamara Brown, *University of Kentucky*
Brad Brubaker, *Indiana State University*
Amy Buckingham, *Red Rocks Community College*
Aimee Callender, *Auburn University*
Carrie Canales, *West Los Angeles College*
Jessica Carpenter, *Elgin Community College*
Lorelei A. Carvajal, *Triton Community College*
Michelle Caya, *Trident Technical College*
Karen Christoff, *University of Mississippi*
Jack Chuang, *San Jacinto College–Central*
Douglas L. Chute, *Drexel University*
Diana Ciesko, *Valencia Community College–East*
Marsha G. Clarkson, *Georgia State University*
Alexis Collier, *Ohio State University*
Tametryce Collins, *Hillsborough Community College*
Doreen Collins-McHugh, *Seminole State College of Florida*
Barbara Corbisier, *Blinn College*
Brent Costleigh, *Brookdale Community College*
Laurie L. Couch, *Morehead State University*
Layton Curl, *Metropolitan State College of Denver*
Christopher L. Curtis, *Delta College*
Michaela DeCataldo, *Johnson & Wales University*
Neeru Deep, *Northwestern State University of Louisiana*
Deanna Degidio, *Northern Virginia Community College–Annandale*
Suzanne Delaney, *University of Arizona*
Bonnie Dennis, *Virginia Western Community College*
Penny Devine, *Florida State College–Jacksonville*
Jaime Diaz-Granados, *Baylor University*
Tom DiLorenzo, *University of Delaware*
Peggy Dombrowski, *Harrisburg Area Community College*
Carol Donnelly, *Northwestern University and Purdue University*
Anne Marie Donohue, *Montgomery County Community College*

Joan Doolittle, *Anne Arundel Community College*
Dale Doty, *Monroe Community College*
Katherine Dowdell, *Des Moines Area Community College*
Kimberley J. Duff, *Cerritos College*
Robert Dunkle, *Ivy Technical Community College of Indiana–Indianapolis*
Shari Dunlavy, *Ivy Technical Community College of Indiana–Ft. Wayne*
Laura Duvall, *Heartland Community College*
David Echevarria, *University of Southern Mississippi*
Penny S. Edwards, *Tri-County Technical College*
Joelle Elicker, *University of Akron*
Jay Brophy Ellison, *University of Central Florida*
Andrea Ericksen, *San Juan College*
Lena Ericksen, *Western Washington University*
Michael Erickson, *University of California–Riverside*
Barbara Etzel, *Finger Lakes Community College*
Dan Fawaz, *Georgia Perimeter College*
Greg J. Feist, *San Jose State University*
Kay Fernandes, *Trident Technical College*
Dave Filak, *Joliet Junior College*
Barbara Defilippo, *Lane Community College*
Beth Finders, *St. Charles Community College*
Tom Fischer, *Wayne State University*
Raymond Fleming, *University of Wisconsin–Milwaukee*
Don Forsyth, *Virginia Commonwealth University*
Murray Fortner, *Tarrant County College–Northeast*
Eric Fox, *Western Michigan University–Kalamazoo*
Paul A. Fox, *Appalachian State University*
Debra L. Frame, *University of Cincinnati–Raymond Walters College*
Paula Frioli, *Truckee Meadows Community College*
Dale Fryxell, *Chaminade University*
Ellen Furlong, *Ohio State University*
Lynne Gabriel, *Lakeland Community College*
John Gambon, *Ozarks Technical and Community College*
Anne Garcia, *Washtenaw Community College*
Travis Gibbs, *Riverside Community College–Moreno Valley*
Charles W. Ginn, *University of Cincinnati*
Diana Glynn, *Brookdale Community College*
Robert L. Gordon, *Wright State University–Dayton*
Sam Gosling, *University of Texas–Austin*
Bonnie Gray, *Scottsdale College*
Jeff Green, *Virginia Commonwealth University*
Jerry Green, *Tarrant County College*

Daine Grey, *Middlesex Community College*
Mark Griffin, *Georgia Perimeter College*
Sara Grison, *University of Illinois–Champaign*
Paul Grocoff, *Scottsdale College*
Regan Gurung, *University of Wisconsin–Green Bay*
Robert Guttentag, *University of North Carolina–Greensboro*
Mike Hackett, *Westchester Community College*
Robin Hailstorks, *Prince George Community College*
David T. Hall, *Baton Rouge Community College*
Ericka Hamilton, *Moraine Valley Community College*
Erin Hardin, *Texas Tech University*
Lora Harpster, *Salt Lake Community College*
Gregory Eugene Harris, *Polk Community College–Winter Haven*
Leslie Hathorn, *Metropolitan State College of Denver*
Rose Hattoh, *Austin Community College*
B. Sarah Haynes, *St. Petersburg College*
Traci Haynes, *Columbus State Community College*
Bert Hayslip, Jr., *University of North Texas*
Brett Heintz, *Delgado Community College*
Jeffrey Henriques, *University of Wisconsin–Madison*
Carmon Weaver Hicks, *Ivy Technical Community College of Indiana*
Debra Hollister, *Valencia Community College*
Theresa T. Holt, *Middlesex County College*
Natalie Hopson, *Salisbury University*
Susan Hornstein, *Southern Methodist University*
Vahan Hovsepian, *Butte College*
Mark Hoyert, *Indiana University–Northwest*
John Huber, *Texas State University–San Marcos*
Danae Hudson, *Missouri State University–Springfield*
Ray Huebschmann, *Georgia Perimeter College*
Charlie Huffman, *James Madison University*
Rachel Hull, *Texas A&M University*
Mark W. Hurd, *College of Charleston*
Mayte Insua-Auais, *Miami Dade College–North*
Linda A. Jackson, *Michigan State University*
Nita Jackson, *Butler Community College*
Michael James, *Ivy Technical Community College of Indiana–Bloomington*
Margaret Jenkins, *Seminole State College of Florida*
Heather Jennings, *Mercer County Community College*
Sean P. Jennings, *Valencia Community College*
Joan Batelle Jenson, *Central Piedmont Community College*

Susan T. Johnson, *Cypress College*
Charles H. Jones, *Wayne County Community College*
Linda Jones, *Blinn College*
Diana Joy, *Community College of Denver*
Robin Joynes, *Kent State University*
Nicole Judice-Campbell, *University of Oklahoma*
Barbara Kabat, *Sinclair Community College*
Kiesa Getz Kelly, *Tennessee State University*
Barbara Kennedy, *Brevard Community College*
Shelia Kennison, *Oklahoma State University*
Shirin Khosropour, *Austin Community College–Pinnacle*
Yuthika Kim, *Oklahoma City Community College*
Kevin King, *University of Washington*
Christina Knox, *College of the Sequoias*
Dana Kuehn, *Florida Community College–Deerwood Center*
Eric Landrum, *Boise State University*
Mark Laumakis, *San Diego State University*
Cindy Lausberg, *University of Pittsburgh*
Natalie Kerr Lawrence, *James Madison University*
Phil Lehman, *Virginia Tech*
Tera Letzring, *Idaho State University*
Dawn Lewis, *Prince George's Community College*
Ladonna Lewis, *Glendale Community College*
Mary Lewis, *Oakland University*
Deborah Licht, *Pikes Peak Community College*
Mark Licht, *Florida State University*
Irv Lichtman, *Houston Community College–Northeast College*
Paul Livingstone, *Midlands Technical College*
Shayn Lloyd, *Tallahassee Community College*
Maria Lopez, *Mt. San Jacinto College–San Jacinto*
Sonya L. Lott-Harrison, *Community College of Philadelphia*
Jeff Love, *Penn State University*
Lea Ann Lucas, *Sinclair Community College*
Mark Ludor, *Stephen Austin State University*
Wade Lueck, *Mesa Community College*
Ken Luke, *Tyler Junior College*
Janet Lumpkin, *Trinity Valley Community College*
Lynda Mae, *Arizona State University*
Clem Magner, *Milwaukee Area Technical College–West*
Mike Majors, *Delgado Community College*
Brian Malley, *University of Michigan–Ann Arbor*
Mike Mangan, *University of New Hampshire–Durham*
Karen Marsh, *University of Minnesota–Duluth*
Diane Martichuski, *University of Colorado–Boulder*
Randall Martinez, *Cypress College*

Krista Mazza, *Georgia Highlands College*
Wanda C. McCarthy, *University of Cincinnati–Clermont College*
Jason McCoy, *Cape Fear Community College–Downtown*
Sean Meegan, *University of Utah*
Sheila Mehta, *Auburn University*
Charlene Melrose, *Orange Coast College*
Kathleen Mentink, *Chippewa Valley Technical College*
Steven P. Mewaldt, *Marshall University*
Shawn Mikulay, *Elgin Community College*
Michelle D. Miller, *Northern Arizona University*
Joel Morgovsky, *Brookdale Community College*
Kristie L. Morris, *SUNY Rockland Community College*
Kathy Morrow, *Wayne County Community College*
Glenn Musgrove, *Broward Community College*
Patricia Nation, *Bluegrass Community and Technical College*
Dana Narter, *University of Arizona–Tucson*
Bethany Neal-Beliveau, *Indiana University-Purdue University–Indianapolis*
Jeff Neubauer, *Pima Community College–Northwest and West*
John Nezlek, *College of William and Mary*
Binh Nguyen, *Santa Rosa Junior College*
Glenda Nichols, *Tarrant County College–South*
Jane Noll, *University of Southern Florida*
Annette Nolte, *Tarrant County College–Northwest*
Eileen O'Brien, *University of Maryland–Baltimore County*
Brian Oppy, *California State University–Chico*
Donald Orso, *Anne Arundel Community College*
Randall Osborne, *Texas State University–San Marcos*
Amy Osmon, *Daytona State College*
Jack A. Palmer, *University of Louisiana–Monroe*
Debra Parish, *Lone Star College–Tomball*
Jeff Parsons, *CUNY–Hunter College*
Jeffrey J. Pedroza, *Santa Ana College*
John Pellew, *Greenville Tech College*
Jennifer Peluso, *Florida Atlantic University*
Julie A. Penley, *El Paso Community College*
Suzanna Penningroth, *University of Wyoming–Laramie*
Elaine Perea, *Daytona State College*
Lori Perez, *Anne Arundel Community College*
David Perkins, *University of Louisiana–Lafayette*
Deb Podwika, *Kankakee Community College*
Susan Pollock, *Mesa Community College*
Bryan Porter, *Old Dominion University*
Elisabeth Post, *University of California–Davis*

Frank Provenzano, *Greenville Technical College*
Liz Purcell, *Greenville Technical College*
Alida Quick, *Wayne County Community College–Downtown*
Reginald Rackley, *Southern University*
Chris Randall, *Kennesaw State University*
Cynthia K. S. Reed, *Tarrant County College*
Diane Reddy, *University of Wisconsin, Milwaukee*
Laura Reichel, *Front Range Community College*
Joe Reish, *Tidewater Community College*
Tanya Renner, *Kapi'olani Community College*
Lisa Renzi, *University of Georgia*
Tonja Ringgold, *Baltimore City Community College*
Vicki Ritts, *St. Louis Community College–Meramec*
Alan Roberts, *Indiana University*
Caton F. Roberts, *University of Wisconsin–Madison*
Edna Ross, *University of Louisville–Louisville*
Steven Ross, *Owens Community College*
Debra Rowe, *Oakland Community College*
Larry Rudiger, *University of Vermont*
Phyllis Rundhaug, *San Jacinto College*
Traci Sachteleben, *Southwestern Illinois College*
Sharleen Sakai, *Michigan State University*
Edie Sample, *Metropolitan Community College*
Dave Schroeder, *University of Arkansas*
Donna Love Seagle, *Chattanooga State Technical Community College*
Steve Seidel, *Texas A&M University*
James Shannon, *Citrus College*
Wayne Shebilske, *Wright State University*
Randi Shedlosky, *York College of Pennsylvania*
Elizabeth Sheehan, *Georgia State University*
Elisabeth Sherwin, *University of Arkansas–Little Rock*
Robert Short, *Arizona State University–Tempe*
Maria Shpurik, *Florida International University*
Harvey Shulman, *Ohio State University*

Jennifer Siciliani, *University of Missouri–St. Louis*
Barry Silber, *Hillsborough Community College*
Pam Simon, *Baker College–Flint*
Nancy Simpson, *Trident Technical College*
Brian Sims, *North Carolina A&T State University*
Peggy Skinner, *South Plains College*
Christopher L. Smith, *Tyler Junior College*
Jamie Smith, *Ohio State University*
Jeff Smith, *Northern Kentucky University*
Lilliette Johnson Smith, *Southwest Tennessee Community College*
Randi Smith, *Metropolitan State College of Denver*
Vivian Smith, *Lakeland Community College*
Karina R. Sokol, *Glendale Community College*
Wayne S. Stein, *Brevard Community College–Melbourne*
Genevieve Stevens, *Houston Community College–Central*
Rick Stevens, *University of Louisiana–Monroe*
Mark Stewart, *American River College*
Pamela E. Stewart, *Northern Virginia Community College*
Claire St. Peter Pipkin, *West Virginia University–Morgantown*
Catherine Strathern, *University of Cincinnati*
Richard Suplita, *University of Georgia*
Eva Szeli, *Arizona State University–Tempe*
Shawn Talbot, *Kellogg Community College*
Nina Tarner, *Sacred Heart University*
Helen Taylor, *Bellevue College*
Sheila E. Ten Eyck, *Pittsburgh Technical Institute*
Rachelle Tennenbaum, *Anne Arundel Community College–Arnold*
Felicia Friendly Thomas, *California State Polytechnic University–Pomona*
Lisa Thomassen, *Indiana University–Bloomington*
Clarissa A. Thompson, *University of Oklahoma*
Pat Tinken, *Joliet Junior College*
Karen Tinker, *Northwest Arkansas Community College*

Connie Toffle, *West Virginia University*
Annette Towler, *Depaul University*
Stephen Tracy, *Community College of Southern Nevada*
Isabel A. Trombetti, *Community College of Rhode Island–Warwick*
Margot Underwood, *Joliet Junior College*
Suzanne Valentine-French, *College of Lake County*
Lisa Valentino, *Seminole Community College–Sanford*
Donna Vandergrift, *Burlington County College*
Tom Vandermolen, *Allan Hancock College*
Barbara Van Horn, *Indian River State College–Central*
Lori Van Wallendael, *University of North Carolina–Charlotte*
Tom Vasile, *Bakersfield College*
Anre Venter, *University of Notre Dame*
Ruth Wallace, *Butler Community College*
Andrew Walters, *Northern Arizona University*
Berta Ward, *Pellissippi State Community College*
Kacy Welsh, *University of Georgia*
Fred Whitford, *Montana State University–Bozeman*
Gordon Whitman, *Tidewater Community College*
Beth Wiediger, *Lincoln Land Community College*
Catina Williams, *Southwestern Illinois College*
Gordon C. Williams, *Eastern Washington University*
Keith Williams, *Oakland University*
William Winter, *Kingsborough Community College*
Steve Withrow, *Guilford Technical Community College–Jamestown*
Martin Wolfger, *Ivy Technical Community College of Indiana–Bloomington*
Andrew Woster, *South Dakota State University*
John W. Wright, *Washington State University*
Matt Yeazel, *Anne Arundel Community College*
Jill Yee, *City College of San Francisco*
Mona Yektaparast, *Central Piedmont Community College*

# Personal Acknowledgments

Returning to *Experience Psychology* for this second edition has been an amazing experience, in no small part because of the enthusiasm, encouragement, and innovation of so many people at McGraw-Hill. I want to say thanks to all those who have brought their energies to bear on the goal of making this second edition such a unique and exciting introduction to psychology.

As always, I am thankful beyond words to Sylvia Mallory, whose amazing work is evident in every line of the text. Thanks as well to Mike Sugarman, Dawn Groundwater, Sheryl Adams, Beth Mejia, and Mark Georgiev, who supported and contributed to the innovative features of the second edition. So much of what students and instructors will love about the second edition is due to the inspiring contributions made to this book by those in production, especially Catherine Morris and Preston Thomas. The second edition of *Experience Psychology* is so beautiful and so downright tempting because of their creativity and resourcefulness. A big shout-out as well to Jennifer Gordon, whose copyediting was painstaking and enormously helpful. Thanks also to the McGraw-Hill sales representatives who inspire me every day with their energy and commitment. I hope you guys love the second edition as much as I do. A special thanks to Julia Flohr, who has done so much to connect me with the reps and with the instructors and students who have found *Experience Psychology* so effective. Finally, my gratitude goes to Kim Nentwig for her constant encouragement and for occasionally "talking me down" when needed!

Thanks to my colleagues at the University of Missouri, for their enthusiasm, advice, patience, and support. I owe a special debt of gratitude to Samantha Heintzelman and Jason Trent, my graduate students, who have patiently endured having an advisor who is not only a journal editor but also an author and teacher, while generating their own very exciting scholarship. Thanks to the students and instructors across the country whom I have visited over the last year—especially the folks at Middlesex Community College and Anne Arundel Community College. Those visits happened just as I was toiling over this second edition, and meeting the faculty and students at these institutions was a rejuvenating and stimulating experience. It meant so much to me to have students come up and chat and say, "You sound just like you do in the book!" That's what *Experience Psychology* is all about, and nothing could be more gratifying.

Finally, a heartfelt thank-you goes to my family and friends who have supported and inspired me, especially Lisa and Sam.

# 1 The Science of Psychology

## Reality TV and Reality: What Are People Really Like?

Are you suspicious that reality TV is pretty, well, *un*realistic? Consider shows like *The Bachelor, The Bachelorette,* and *Keeping Up with the Kardashians.* Viewers are treated to romances and (sometimes) lavish weddings. Those marriages, however, last months at best. In 2011, for example, over 4 million people tuned in to Kim Kardashian's wedding (Ng, 2011), a union that lasted all of 72 days. In fact, the average couple is engaged for 17 months before tying the knot (Fairchild Bridal Group, 2005), and the average marriage lasts 7 years (OECD Family Database, 2010).

On shows like *Real Housewives,* interpersonal conflict is standard fare. One study found that on *The Apprentice,* acts of interpersonal aggression (insults, arguments, an occasional punch) occurred nearly 85 times *per hour* (Coyne, Robinson, & Nelson, 2010). That study also determined that just over half of all aggressive encounters on reality TV programs were engineered by the producers. So, what's the truth? According to research that tracks conflict among friends using daily diary reports, friends generally report *less than one* conflict interaction *per week* (Burk & others, 2009).

Reality TV viewing might be a guilty pleasure or voyeurism (Baruh, 2010), and many of us hesitate to admit that we watch (Nabi & others, 2006). But a lot of us *are* tuning in, eager for a taste of others' "real behavior." We get an opportunity to compare their lives to our own, to learn about how people interact, and to see what they do in unlikely situations. To borrow *Bravo*'s catchphrase, we "watch what happens" out of an undeniable curiosity: the need to know what other people are like.

We have many other ways to feed this curiosity. Twitter claims more than 175 million users. Tracking someone else's life, even in 140-character bites, is just plain interesting to many of us. Through *Facebook*, blogs, and YouTube clips, we get a chance to see and try to understand what is arguably the most fascinating aspect of our lives: our interactions with others. Understanding people is also a key goal of the science of psychology.

Psychologists are scientists who are interested in "watching what happens," but in very different ways from what we see on reality TV. Psychologists bring a disciplined curiosity to explaining human behavior, relying on the methods of science. Like a fan following a celebrity's Twitter feed, psychologists are passionate about what they study—and what they study is people of all kinds. There is not a single thing about people that is not fascinating to some psychologist somewhere.

preview

This chapter begins by defining psychology and reviewing the history of the field. Next we survey seven broad approaches that characterize psychological science today. Then, in sequence, we examine the elements of the scientific method, review the different kinds of research psychologists do, and consider the importance of conducting psychological research according to ethical guidelines. We conclude with a look at applications of psychology to daily life—a central focus of this book.

# 1 Defining Psychology and Exploring Its Roots

*What is your definition of psychology? When you think of the word psychology, what first comes to mind?*

Formally defined, **psychology** is the scientific study of behavior and mental processes. Let's consider the three key terms in this definition: *science, behavior,* and *mental processes*.

As a **science,** psychology uses systematic methods to observe human behavior and draw conclusions. The goals of psychological science are to describe, predict, and explain behavior. In addition, psychologists are often interested in controlling or changing behavior, and they use scientific methods to examine interventions that might help, for example, reduce violence or promote happiness.

Researchers might be interested in knowing whether individuals will help a stranger who has fallen down. The researchers could devise a study in which they observe people walking past a person who needs help. Through many observations, the researchers could come to *describe* helping behavior by counting how many times it occurs in particular circumstances. They might also try to *predict* who will help, and when, by examining characteristics of the individuals studied. Are happy people more likely to help? Are women or men more likely to help? After the psychologists have analyzed their data, they also will want to *explain* why helping behavior occurred when it did. Finally, they might be interested in changing helping behavior, such as by devising strategies to increase helping.

**Behavior** is everything we do that can be directly observed—two people kissing, a baby crying, a college student riding a motorcycle to campus. **Mental processes** are the thoughts, feelings, and motives that each of us experiences privately but that cannot be observed directly. Although we cannot directly see thoughts and feelings, they are nonetheless real. They include *thinking* about kissing someone, a baby's *feelings* when its mother leaves the room, and a student's *memory* of a motorcycle trip.

**psychology**
The scientific study of behavior and mental processes.

**science**
The use of systematic methods to observe the natural world, including human behavior, and to draw conclusions.

**behavior**
Everything we do that can be directly observed.

*Behavior includes the observable act of two people kissing; mental processes include their unobservable thoughts about kissing.*

**mental processes**
The thoughts, feelings, and motives that people experience privately but that cannot be observed directly.

# The Psychological Frame of Mind

What makes for a good job, a good marriage, or a good life? Psychologists approach these big life questions as scientists. Psychology is a rigorous discipline that tests assumptions, bringing scientific data to bear on the questions of central interest to human beings (Gravetter & Forzano, 2012; Stanovich, 2010). Psychologists conduct research and rely on that research to provide evidence for their conclusions. They examine the available evidence about some aspect of mind and behavior, evaluate how strongly the data (information) support their hunches, analyze disconfirming evidence, and carefully consider whether they have explored all possible factors and explanations (Leary, 2012). At the core of this scientific approach are four attitudes: *critical thinking, curiosity, skepticism,* and *objectivity.*

Like all scientists, psychologists are *critical thinkers.* **Critical thinking** is the process of thinking deeply and actively, asking questions, and evaluating the evidence (Bonney & Sternberg, 2011). Critical thinkers question and test what some people say are facts. They examine research to see how soundly it supports an idea (Jackson, 2012). Critical thinking reduces the likelihood that conclusions will be based on unreliable personal beliefs, opinions, and emotions. Critical thinking also comes into play when scientists consider the conclusions they draw from research. As critical thinkers who are open to new information, scientists must tolerate uncertainty, knowing that even long-held views are subject to revision.

**critical thinking**
The process of thinking deeply and actively, asking questions, and evaluating the evidence.

Critical thinking is very important as you are reading this book. Some of what you read might fit with your existing beliefs, and some might challenge you to reconsider your assumptions. Actively engaging in critical thinking is vital to making the most of psychology. As you study the field, think about how what you are learning relates to your life experiences and your assumptions about people.

Scientists are also *curious.* The scientist notices things in the world (a star in the sky, an insect, a happy person) and wants to know what it is and why it is that way. Science involves asking questions, even very big questions such as where did the earth come from, and how does love between two people endure for 50 years? Thinking like a psychologist means opening your mind and imagination to wondering why things are the way they are.

In addition, scientists are *skeptical* (Stanovich, 2010). Skeptical people challenge whether a supposed fact is really true. Being skeptical can mean questioning what "everybody knows." There was a time when "everybody knew" that women were morally inferior to men, that race could influence a person's IQ, and that the earth was flat. Psychologists, like all scientists, look at assumptions in new and questioning ways. Psychology is different from common sense because psychologists are skeptical of commonsensical answers.

Psychological research often turns up the unexpected in human behavior. Such results are called *counterintuitive* because they contradict our intuitive impressions of how the world works. Consider the following study, which demonstrates how a little dose of negative information can actually make consumers feel more positive about a product (Ein-Gar, Shiv, & Tormala, 2012). Students who were on their way to an exam were approached by an experimenter offering to sell them chocolate bars. All of the participants were told that the chocolate bars were a favorite among consumers, that they were nicely chilled (the study was conducted on a hot day in California), and that they were being offered at a special discount of only 50 cents. However, half of the participants received one more piece of information: The chocolate bars were just a little broken. The experimenter showed them an example of a bar with minor breakage. Participants who were given this mild negative information ended up purchasing more chocolate bars than those who heard only the positive information. Why?

The experimenters reasoned that when we have encountered positive information about something, a little bit of negative information causes us to stop and reconsider that positive information. We think about it more and eventually come to evaluate a mildly "blemished" product as actually really good. Note that these results were limited to students who were preoccupied by a test. Other students who were not thinking about a test bought

*You might be wondering about the names and dates in parentheses. They are research citations that identify the authors of particular studies and the year each study was published. If you see an especially interesting study, you might look it up in the References at the back of this book and check it out online or in your school's library.*

less chocolate when it was presented as broken. The researchers' explanation is that when we do not have time or energy to think things through, a minor blemish can enhance evaluations of a product.

Last, practicing science also means being *objective*. Being objective involves trying to see things as they really are, not just as the observer would like them to be. Scientific knowledge ultimately is based on objective evidence.

**empirical method**
Gaining knowledge through the observation of events, the collection of data, and logical reasoning.

To gather objective evidence, scientists rely on empirical methods. An **empirical method** involves gaining knowledge through the observation of events, the collection of data, and logical reasoning. For scientists, objectivity means waiting to see what the evidence tells them rather than going with their hunches. Does the latest herbal dietary supplement really help relieve depression? A scientist would say, "That's an empirical question," meaning that hard evidence is required to answer it. An objective thinker insists on sound evidence before drawing conclusions. Like critical thinking, relying on evidence to provide the foundation for conclusions means being open to uncertainty. Empirical evidence provides the best answers to questions at any given moment.

*This is why researchers often say that a study "supports" a particular prediction, but rarely if ever say that it "proves" anything.*

Once you start to think like a psychologist, you might notice that the world starts to look like a different place. Easy answers and simple assumptions will not do. As you can probably imagine, psychologists, as a group, are people with many different opinions about many different things. If a number of these critical thinkers were to gather around a table, it is a safe bet that they would have a lively conversation.

Indeed, as you will see throughout this book, there are many things about which psychologists disagree, and psychology (like any science) is filled with debate and controversy. For example, one controversy in psychology concerns the emergence of so-called Generation Me (Twenge, 2006). Jean Twenge and her colleagues (Twenge, 2006; Twenge & Campbell, 2010) argue that Americans born since the 1980s are different from previous generations in that they are unusually self-confident, self-assertive, and self-centered. Based on her research examining scores on questionnaires concerning *narcissism* (a condition of intense, unhealthy self-love) over many years, Twenge (2006) refers to these individuals as Generation Me. She suggests that we are in the midst of an epidemic of narcissism. Other psychologists, however, sharply challenge this claim. In doing so, they present data showing no changes in narcissism over the last three decades (Trzesniewski & Donnellan, 2010).

So, debate and controversy are a natural part of thinking like a psychologist. Psychology has advanced as a field because psychologists do not always agree with one another about why mind and behavior work the way they do. Psychologists have reached a more accurate understanding of human behavior because psychology fosters controversies and because psychologists think deeply and reflectively and examine the evidence on all sides. A good place to try out your critical thinking skills is by revisiting the definition of psychology.

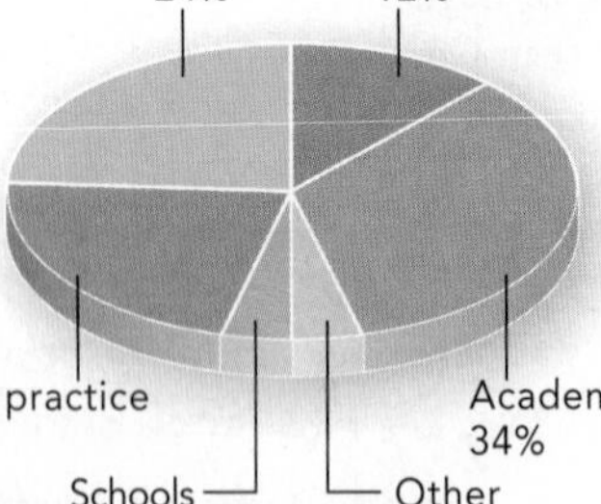

**FIGURE 1.1 Settings in Which Psychologists Work** More psychologists work in academic settings (34 percent), such as colleges and universities, than any other setting. However, clinical (24 percent) and private practice (22 percent) settings—both of which are contexts in which many psychologists in the mental health professions work—together make up almost half of the total settings.

Clinical 24%
Industrial 12%
Private practice 22%
Academic 34%
Schools 4%
Other 4%

# Psychology as the Science of All Human Behavior

As you consider the general definition of psychology as the science of human behavior, you might be thinking, okay, where's the couch? Where's the mental illness? Psychology certainly includes the study of therapy and psychological disorders. Clinical psychologists in particular are psychologists who specialize in studying and treating psychological disorders. By definition, though, psychology is a much more general science (Shiraev, 2011), practiced in several environments in addition to clinical settings (Figure 1.1). How did we end up with the idea that psychology is only about mental illness? Surely, psychological disorders are very interesting, and the media often portray psychologists as therapists. Yet the view of psychology as the science of what is wrong with people started long before TV was even invented.

When they think of psychology, many people think of Sigmund Freud (1856–1939). Freud believed that most of human behavior is caused by dark, unpleasant, unconscious impulses pressing for expression. For Freud, even the average person on the street is a mysterious well of unconscious desires. Certainly, Freud has had a lasting impact on psychology and on society. Consider, though, that Freud based his ideas about human nature on the patients that he saw in his clinical practice—individuals who were struggling with psychological problems. His experiences with these patients, as well as his analysis of himself, colored his outlook on all of humanity. Freud once wrote, "I have found little that is 'good' about human beings on the whole. In my experience most of them are trash" (1918/1996).

*You have probably heard of a "Freudian slip." Freud's name has become part of our everyday language.*

Freud's view of human nature has crept into general perceptions of what psychology is all about. Imagine, for example, that you are seated on a plane, having a pleasant conversation with the woman (a stranger) sitting next to you. At some point you ask your seatmate what she does for a living, and she informs you she is a psychologist. You might think to yourself, "Uh oh. What have I already told this person? What secrets does she know about me that I don't know about myself? Has she been analyzing me this whole time?" Would you be surprised to discover that this psychologist studies happiness? Or intelligence? Or the processes related to the experience of vision? The study of psychological disorders is a very important aspect of psychology, but it represents only one part of the science of psychology.

Psychology seeks to understand the truths of human life in *all* its dimensions, including people's best and worst experiences. Psychologists acknowledge the existence of long, satisfying marital unions, as well as unmitigated disasters like Kim Kardashian's short-lived marriage. Research on the human capacity for forgiveness demonstrates this point (Balliet, Li, & Joireman, 2011; McCullough, Kurzban, & Tabak, 2011; McCullough & others, 2010). Forgiveness is the act of letting go of anger and resentment toward someone who has done something harmful to us. Through forgiveness we cease seeking revenge or avoiding the person who did us harm, and we might even wish that person well.

In October 2006, after Charles Carl Roberts took 10 young Amish girls hostage in a one-room schoolhouse in Pennsylvania, eventually killing 5 of them and wounding 5 others before killing himself, the grief-stricken Amish community focused not on hatred and revenge but on forgiveness. As funds were being set up for the victims' families, the Amish insisted on establishing one for the murderer's family. They prepared simple funerals for the dead girls, and the community invited the killer's wife to attend. The science of psychology has much to offer to our understanding not only of the violent acts of the perpetrator but also of the forgiveness of the victims.

The willingness of these Amish people to forgive this horrible crime is both remarkable and puzzling. Can we scientifically understand the human ability to forgive even what might seem to be unforgivable? A number of psychologists have taken up the topic of forgiveness in research and clinical practice (Jacinto & Edwards, 2011; Worthington & others, 2011). Michael McCullough and his colleagues (McCullough & others, 2010) have shown that the capacity to forgive is an unfolding process that often takes time. For the Amish, their deep religious faith led them to embrace forgiveness, while many others might have been motivated to seek revenge and retribution. Researchers also have explored the relationship between religious commitment and forgiveness (McCullough, Bono, & Root, 2007), the cognitive skills required for forgiveness (Pronk & others, 2010), and even the potential dark side of forgiveness, which might emerge, for example, when forgiveness leads an abusive spouse to feel free to continue a harmful behavior (McNulty, 2011).

*The murder in 2006 of five Amish schoolgirls evoked feelings in the community not of hatred and revenge but of forgiveness.*

Some psychologists argue that the field has focused too much on the negative aspects of humanity and neglected topics that reflect the best of human life (Seligman & Csikszentmihalyi, 2000; Snyder,

Lopez, & Pedrotti, 2010). Others insist that human weaknesses are the most important aspects of life to study (Lazarus, 2003). The fact is that to be a truly general science of human behavior, psychology must address all sides of human experience. Surely, controversy is a part of any science. Healthy debate characterizes the field of psychology, and a new psychological perspective sometimes arises when one scientist questions the views of another. Such ongoing debate is a sign of a lively discipline. Indeed, the very birth of the field was marked by debate. Great minds do not always think alike, especially when they are thinking about psychology.

## Psychology in Historical Perspective

Psychology seeks to answer questions that people have been asking for thousands of years—for example:

- How do we learn?
- What is memory?
- Why does one person grow and flourish while another struggles?

The notion that such questions might be answered through scientific inquiry is relatively new. From the time human language included the word *why* and became rich enough to let people talk about the past, we have been creating myths to explain why things are the way they are. Ancient myths attributed most important events to the pleasure or displeasure of the gods: When a volcano erupted, the gods were angry; if two people fell in love, they had been struck by Cupid's arrows. Gradually, myths gave way to *philosophy*—the rational investigation of the underlying principles of being and knowledge. People attempted to explain events in terms of natural rather than supernatural causes.

Western philosophy came of age in ancient Greece in the fourth and fifth centuries B.C.E. Socrates, Plato, Aristotle, and others debated the nature of thought and behavior, including the possible link between the mind and the body. Later philosophers, especially René Descartes, argued that the mind and body were completely separate, and they focused their attention on the mind. Psychology grew out of this tradition of thinking about the mind and body. The influence of philosophy on contemporary psychology persists today, as researchers who study emotion still talk about Descartes, and scientists who study happiness often refer to Aristotle (McMahan & Estes, 2011).

In addition to philosophy, psychology also has roots in the natural sciences of biology and physiology (Schultz & Schultz, 2012). Indeed, it was Wilhelm Wundt (1832–1920), a German philosopher-physician, who put the pieces of the philosophy–natural science puzzle together to create the academic discipline of psychology. Some historians like to say that modern psychology was born in December 1879 at the University of Leipzig, when Wundt and his students (most notably E. B. Titchener) performed an experiment to measure the time lag between the instant a person heard a sound and when that person pressed a telegraph key to signal that he had heard it.

What was so special about this experiment? Wundt's study was about the workings of the brain: He was trying to measure the time it took the human brain and nervous system to translate information into action. At the heart of this experiment was the idea that mental processes could be measured. This focus ushered in the new science of psychology.

Wundt and his collaborators concentrated on discovering the basic elements, or "structures," of mental processes. Their approach was called **structuralism** because of its focus on identifying the structures of the human mind. The method they used in the study of mental structures was *introspection* (literally, "looking inside"). For this type of research, a person was placed in a laboratory setting and was asked to think (to introspect) about what was going on mentally as various events took place. For example, the

**Wilhelm Wundt (1832–1920)**
*Wundt founded the first psychology laboratory (with his two co-workers) in 1879 at the University of Leipzig in Germany.*

**structuralism**
Wundt's approach to discovering the basic elements, or structures, of mental processes.

individual might be subjected to a sharp, repetitive clicking sound and then might be asked to report whatever conscious feelings the clicking produced. What made this method scientific was the systematic, detailed self-reports required of the person in the controlled laboratory setting.

Although Wundt is most often regarded as the founding father of modern psychology, it was psychologist and philosopher William James (1842–1910), perhaps more than anyone else, who gave the field an American stamp. From James's perspective, the key question for psychology is not so much what the mind is (that is, its structures) as what it is for (its purpose or function). James's view was eventually named *functionalism*.

**functionalism**
James's approach to mental processes, emphasizing the functions and purposes of the mind and behavior in the individual's adaptation to the environment.

In contrast to structuralism, which emphasized the components of the mind, **functionalism** probed the functions and purposes of the mind and behavior in the individual's adaptation to the environment. Whereas structuralists were looking inside the mind and searching for its structures, functionalists focused on what was going on in human interactions with the outside world and trying to understand the purpose of thoughts. If structuralism is about the "what" of the mind, functionalism is about the "why."

A central question in functionalism is, why is human thought *adaptive?* When we talk about whether a characteristic is adaptive, we are concerned with how it makes an organism better able to survive. So, the functionalist asks, why are people better off because they can think than they would be otherwise? Unlike Wundt, James did not believe in the existence of rigid structures of the mind. Instead, James saw the mind as flexible and fluid, characterized by constant change in response to a continuous flow of information from the world. Not surprisingly, James called the natural flow of thought a "stream of consciousness."

**natural selection**
Darwin's principle of an evolutionary process in which organisms that are best adapted to their environment will survive and produce offspring.

Functionalism fit well with the theory of evolution through natural selection proposed by British naturalist Charles Darwin (1809–1882). In 1859, Darwin published his ideas in *On the Origin of Species.* He proposed the principle of **natural selection,** an evolutionary process in which organisms that are best adapted to their environment will survive and, importantly, produce offspring. Darwin noted that members of any species are often locked in competition for scarce resources such as food and shelter. Natural selection is the process by which the environment determines who wins that competition. Darwin asserted that organisms with biological features that led to survival and reproduction would be better represented in subsequent generations. Over many generations, organisms with these characteristics would constitute a larger percentage of the population. Eventually this process could change an entire species. If environmental conditions changed, however, other characteristics might become favored by natural selection, moving the process in a different direction.

If you are unfamiliar with Darwin's theory of evolution, it might be helpful to consider the simple question, why do giraffes have long necks? An early explanation might have been that giraffes live in places where the trees are very tall, and so the creatures must stretch their necks to get their food—leaves. Lots of stretching might lead to adult giraffes that have longer necks. This explanation does not tell us, though, why giraffes are *born* with long necks. A characteristic cannot be passed from one generation to the next unless it is recorded in the *genes,* those collections of molecules that are responsible for heredity.

According to evolutionary theory, species change through random genetic mutation. That means that essentially by accident, some members of a species are born with genetic characteristics that make them different from other members (for instance, some lucky giraffes being born with unusually long necks). If these changes are adaptive (for example, if they help those giraffes compete for food, survive, and reproduce), they become more common in members of the species. So, presumably long, long ago, some giraffes were genetically predisposed to have longer necks, and some giraffes were genetically predisposed to have shorter necks. Only those with the long necks

**William James (1842–1910)**
*James's approach became known as functionalism.*

survived to reproduce, giving us the giraffes we see today. The survival of the giraffes with long necks is a product of natural selection. Evolutionary theory implies that the way we are, at least partially, is the way that is best suited to survival in our environment (Buss, 2012).

Darwin's theory continues to influence psychologists today because it is strongly supported by observation. We can make such observations every day. Right now, for example, in your kitchen sink, various bacteria are locked in competition for scarce resources in the form of those tempting food particles from your last meal. When you use an antibacterial cleaner, you are playing a role in natural selection, because you are effectively killing off the bacteria that cannot survive the cleaning agents. However, you are also letting the bacteria that are genetically adapted to survive that cleaner to take over the sink. The same principle applies to taking an antibiotic medication at the first sign of a sore throat or an earache. By killing off the bacteria that may be causing the illness, you are creating an environment where their competitors (so-called antibiotic-resistant bacteria) may flourish. These observations powerfully demonstrate Darwinian selection in action.

If structuralism won the battle to be the birthplace of psychology, functionalism won the war. To this day, psychologists continue to talk about the adaptive nature of human characteristics. Indeed, from these beginnings, psychologists have branched out to study more aspects of human behavior than Wundt or James might have imagined. We now examine various contemporary approaches to the science of psychology.

## self-quiz

1. The one *correct* statement among the following is
   A. there are many controversies in the field of psychology.
   B. psychologists on the whole agree among themselves on most aspects of the field.
   C. psychologists do not engage in critical thinking.
   D. there are few controversies in the field of psychology.

2. Of the following, the characteristic that is *not* at the heart of the scientific approach is
   A. skepticism.
   B. critical thinking.

C. prejudging.
D. curiosity.

3. Charles Darwin's work is relevant to psychology because
   A. Darwin's research demonstrated that there are few differences between humans and animals.
   B. Darwin's principle of natural selection suggests that human behavior is partially a result of efforts to survive.
   C. Darwin stated that humans descended from apes, a principle that allows psychologists to understand human behavior.
   D. Darwin created functionalism.

APPLY IT! 4. Two psychologists, Clayton and Sam, are interested in studying emotional expressions. Clayton wants to determine whether emotional expression is healthy and if it has an influence on well-being. Sam is interested in describing the types of emotions people express and building a catalog of all the emotions and emotional expressions that exist. In this example, Clayton is most like _____ and Sam is most like _____.
A. Wilhelm Wundt; William James
B. William James; Wilhelm Wundt
C. Wilhelm Wundt; Sigmund Freud
D. Sigmund Freud; Wilhelm Wundt

# 2 Contemporary Approaches to Psychology

In this section we survey seven different approaches—biological, behavioral, psychodynamic, humanistic, cognitive, evolutionary, and sociocultural—that represent the intellectual backdrop of psychological science.

## The Biological Approach

**biological approach**
An approach to psychology focusing on the body, especially the brain and nervous system.

Some psychologists examine behavior and mental processes through the **biological approach,** which is a focus on the body, especially the brain and nervous system. For example, researchers might investigate the way your heart races when you are afraid or how your hands sweat when you tell a lie. Although a number of physiological systems may be involved in thoughts and feelings, perhaps the largest contribution to physiological psychology has come through the emergence of neuroscience (Bavelier & others, 2012; Koch, 2011).

**Neuroscience** is the scientific study of the structure, function, development, genetics, and biochemistry of the nervous system. Neuroscience emphasizes that the brain and nervous system are central to understanding behavior, thought, and emotion. Neuroscientists believe that thoughts and emotions have a physical basis in the brain. Electrical impulses zoom throughout the brain's cells, releasing chemical substances that enable us to think, feel, and behave. Our remarkable human capabilities would not be possible without the brain and nervous system, which constitute the most complex, intricate, and elegant system imaginable. Although biological approaches might sometimes seem to reduce complex human experience to simple physical structures, developments in neuroscience have allowed psychologists to understand the brain as an amazingly complex organ, perhaps just as complex as the psychological processes linked to its functioning.

*Richard J. Davidson of the University of Wisconsin, Madison, shown with the Dalai Lama, is a leading researcher in behavioral neuroscience.*

## The Behavioral Approach

The **behavioral approach** emphasizes the scientific study of observable behavioral responses and their environmental determinants. It focuses on an organism's visible interactions with the environment—that is, behaviors, not thoughts or feelings. The principles of the behavioral approach have been widely applied to help people change their behavior for the better (Miltenberger, 2012). The psychologists who adopt this approach are called *behaviorists*. Under the intellectual leadership of John B. Watson (1878–1958) and B. F. Skinner (1904–1990), behaviorism dominated psychological research during the first half of the twentieth century.

Skinner (1938) emphasized that psychology should be about what people do—their actions and behaviors—and should not concern itself with things that cannot be seen, such as thoughts, feelings, and goals. He believed that rewards and punishments determine our behavior. For example, a child might behave in a well-mannered fashion because her parents have rewarded this behavior. We do the things we do, say behaviorists, because of the environmental conditions we have experienced and continue to experience.

Contemporary behaviorists still emphasize the importance of observing behavior to understand an individual, and they use rigorous methods advocated by Watson and Skinner (Rehfeldt, 2011). They also continue to stress the importance of environmental determinants of behavior (Martin & Pear, 2011). However, not every behaviorist today accepts the earlier behaviorists' rejection of thought processes, which are often called *cognition* (Bandura, 2011).

## The Psychodynamic Approach

The **psychodynamic approach** emphasizes unconscious thought, the conflict between biological drives (such as the drive for sex) and society's demands, and early childhood family experiences. Practitioners of this approach believe that sexual and aggressive impulses buried deep within the unconscious mind influence the way people think, feel, and behave.

Sigmund Freud, the founding father of the psychodynamic approach, theorized that early relationships with parents shape an individual's personality. Freud's theory (1917) was the basis for the therapeutic technique that he called *psychoanalysis,* which involves an analyst's unlocking a person's unconscious conflicts by talking with the individual about his or her childhood memories, dreams, thoughts, and feelings. Certainly, Freud's views have been controversial, but they remain a part of contemporary psychology. Today's psychodynamic theories tend to place less emphasis on sexual drives and more on cultural or social experiences as determinants of behavior (Borden & Clark, 2012).

**Sigmund Freud (1856–1939)**
*Freud was the founding father of the psychodynamic approach.*

## The Humanistic Approach

The **humanistic approach** emphasizes a person's positive qualities, the capacity for positive growth, and the freedom to choose one's destiny. Humanistic psychologists stress that people have the ability to control their lives and are not simply controlled by the environment (Maslow, 1971; Rogers, 1961). They theorize that rather than being driven by unconscious impulses (as the psychodynamic approach dictates) or by external rewards (as the behavioral approach emphasizes), people can choose to live by higher human values such as *altruism*—unselfish concern for other people's well-being—and free will. Many aspects of this optimistic approach appear in research on motivation, emotion, and personality psychology (Sheldon, Cheng, & Hilpert, 2011; Sheldon & Schüler, 2011).

**humanistic approach**
An approach to psychology emphasizing a person's positive qualities, the capacity for positive growth, and the freedom to choose one's destiny.

## The Cognitive Approach

According to cognitive psychologists, your brain houses a "mind" whose mental processes allow you to remember, make decisions, plan, set goals, and be creative (Friedenberg & Silverman, 2012; Sternberg, 2012a, 2012b). The **cognitive approach,** then, emphasizes the mental processes involved in knowing: how we direct our attention, perceive, remember, think, and solve problems. For example, cognitive psychologists want to know how we solve math problems, why we remember some things for only a short time but others for a lifetime, and how we can use our imaginations to plan for the future.

**cognitive approach**
An approach to psychology emphasizing the mental processes involved in knowing: how we direct our attention, perceive, remember, think, and solve problems.

Cognitive psychologists view the mind as an active and aware problem-solving system. This view contrasts with the behavioral outlook, which portrays behavior as controlled by external environmental forces. In the cognitive perspective, an individual's mental processes are in control of behavior through memories, perceptions, images, and thinking.

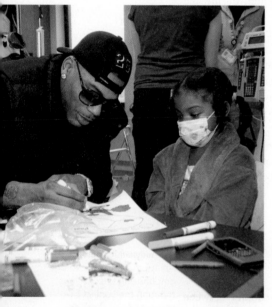

*According to humanistic psychologists, warm, supportive behavior toward others helps us to realize our tremendous capacity for self-understanding.*

## The Evolutionary Approach

Although arguably all of psychology emerges out of evolutionary theory, some psychologists emphasize an **evolutionary approach** that uses evolutionary ideas such as adaptation, reproduction, and natural selection as the basis for explaining specific human behaviors. David Buss (2012) argues that just as evolution molds our physical features, such as body shape, it also influences our decision making, level of aggressiveness, fears, and mating patterns. Thus, evolutionary psychologists say, the way we are is traceable to problems early humans faced in adapting to their environments (Cosmides, 2011).

**evolutionary approach**
An approach to psychology centered on evolutionary ideas such as adaptation, reproduction, and natural selection as the basis for explaining specific human behaviors.

Evolutionary psychologists believe that their approach provides an umbrella that unifies the diverse fields of psychology (Bjorklund, 2012). Not all psychologists agree with this conclusion, however. For example, some critics stress that the evolutionary approach provides an inaccurate explanation of why men and women have different social roles, and it does not adequately account for cultural diversity and experiences (Matlin, 2012; Wood & Eagly, 2010). Yet keep in mind that even psychologists who disagree with the application of the evolutionary approach to psychological characteristics still agree with the general principles of evolutionary theory.

*Human beings originally evolved long ago in a very different environment than we occupy today. The survivors were those who were most able to endure extremely difficult circumstances, struggling to find food, avoid predators, and create social groups. What do you think were the most adaptive traits for these early people? To what specific environments are humans adapting even now?*

## The Sociocultural Approach

**sociocultural approach**
An approach to psychology that examines the influences of social and cultural environments on behavior.

The **sociocultural approach** examines the influences of social and cultural environments on behavior. Socioculturalists argue that understanding a person's behavior requires knowing about the cultural context in which the behavior occurs (Matsumoto & Juang, 2013; Matthews & Gallo, 2011). (*Culture* refers to the shared knowledge, practices, and attitudes of groups of people and can include language, customs, and beliefs about what behavior is appropriate and inappropriate.) The sociocultural approach often includes *cross-cultural* research, meaning research that compares individuals in various cultures to see how they differ on important psychological attributes. Cross-cultural research is important for testing the assumption that findings for one culture also generalize to other cultural contexts, and as such it allows psychologists to test for the possibility that some characteristics are universal (Cai & others, 2011).

The sociocultural approach focuses not only on comparisons of behavior across countries but also on the behavior of individuals from different ethnic and cultural groups within a country (Cheah & Leung, 2011). In light of rising cultural diversity in the United States in recent years, there has been increasing interest in the behavior of African Americans, Latinos, and Asian Americans, especially in terms of the factors that have restricted or enhanced their ability to adapt and cope with living in a predominantly non-Latino White society (Aguayo & others, 2011; Banks, 2010). The influence of culture on behavior has led to important findings about psychological processes and especially about the role of culture in the psychological experience of our own sense of self (Wan & others, 2011).

## Summing up the Seven Contemporary Approaches

These seven approaches to studying psychology provide different views of behavior, and therefore each may contribute uniquely valuable insights. Think about the simple experience of seeing a cute puppy. Looking at that puppy involves physical processes in the eyes, nervous system, and brain—the focus of the biological approach to psychology. The moment you spot that puppy, though, you might smile without thinking and reach down to pet the little guy. That reaction might be a learned response based on your past learning with your own dog (behavioral perspective), or unconscious memories of a childhood dog (psychodynamic perspective), or conscious memories that you especially like this breed of dogs (cognitive perspective), or even evolutionary processes that promoted cuteness to help offspring survive (evolutionary approach). You might find yourself striking up a conversation with the puppy's owner, based on your shared love of dogs (humanistic perspective). Further, sociocultural factors might play a role in your decision about whether to ask the owner if holding the puppy would be okay, whether to share those warm feelings about the puppy with others, and even whether (as in some cultures) to view that puppy as food.

These broad approaches are reflected in the variety of specialties within which psychologists work (Figure 1.2). Many of these specialties are represented by chapters in

| Specialization and Relevant Chapters in This Book | Focus of Specialists |
|---|---|
| **Behavioral Neuroscience** (Chapter 2) | Behavioral neuroscience focuses on biological processes, especially the brain's role in behavior. |
| **Sensation and Perception** (Chapter 3) | Sensation and perception researchers focus on the physical systems and psychological processes of vision, hearing, touch, and smell that allow us to experience the world. |
| **Learning** (Chapter 5) | Learning specialists study the complex process by which behavior changes to adapt to shifting circumstances. |
| **Cognitive** (Chapters 4, 6, & 7) | Cognitive psychology examines attention, consciousness, information processing, and memory. Cognitive psychologists are also interested in cognitive skills and abilities such as problem solving, decision making, expertise, and intelligence. |
| **Developmental** (Chapter 8) | Developmental psychology examines how people become who they are, from conception to death, concentrating on biological and environmental factors. |
| **Motivation and Emotion** (Chapter 9) | Researchers from a variety of specializations are interested in these two aspects of experience. Motivation researchers examine questions such as how individuals attain difficult goals. Emotion researchers study the physiological and brain processes that underlie emotional experience, the role of emotional expression in health, and the possibility that emotions are universal. |
| **Personality** (Chapter 10) | Personality psychology focuses on the relatively enduring characteristics of individuals, including traits, goals, motives, genetics, and personality development. |
| **Social** (Chapter 11) | Social psychology studies how social contexts influence perceptions, social cognition, and attitudes. Social psychologists study how groups influence attitudes and behavior. |
| **Clinical and Counseling** (Chapters 12 & 13) | Clinical and counseling psychology, the most widely practiced specialization, involves diagnosing and treating people with psychological problems. |
| **Health** (Chapter 14) | Health psychology emphasizes psychological factors, lifestyle, and behavior that influence physical health. |
| **Industrial and Organizational (I/O)** | I/O psychology applies findings in all areas of psychology to the workplace. |
| **Community** | Community psychology is concerned with providing accessible care for people with psychological problems. Community-based mental health centers are one means of delivering such services as outreach programs. |
| **School and Educational** | School and educational psychology centrally concerns children's learning and adjustment in school. School psychologists in elementary and secondary school systems test children and make recommendations about educational placement, and work on educational planning teams. |
| **Environmental** | Environmental psychologists explore the effects of physical settings in most major areas of psychology, including perception, cognition, learning, and others. An environmental psychologist might study how different room arrangements influence behavior or what strategies might be used to reduce human behavior that harms the environment. |
| **Psychology of Women** | Psychology of women stresses the importance of integrating information about women with current psychological knowledge and applying that information to society and its institutions. |
| **Forensic** | Forensic psychology applies psychology to the legal system. Forensic psychologists might help with jury selection or provide expert testimony in trials. |
| **Sport** | Sport psychology applies psychology to improving sport performance and enjoyment of sport participation. |
| **Cross-Cultural** | Cross-cultural psychology studies culture's role in understanding behavior, thought, and emotion, with a special interest in whether psychological phenomena are universal or culture-specific. |

**FIGURE 1.2   Areas of Specialization in Psychology** Psychology has many overlapping subfields.

this book. As you read the text, keep in mind that psychology is a science in which psychologists work together collaboratively to examine a wide range of research questions. Indeed, many times scholars from different specialties within psychology join forces to understand some aspect of human behavior. It is the purpose of this book's Intersection feature to review research that represents a collaboration among scientists from different specialties to answer the same question.

## self-quiz

1. The approach to psychology that is most interested in early childhood relationships is
   A. evolutionary psychology.
   B. cognitive psychology.
   C. psychodynamic psychology.
   D. behavioral psychology.

2. The approach to psychology that views psychological distress as a result of persistent negative thoughts is
   A. the humanistic approach.
   B. the behavioral approach.
   C. the sociocultural approach.
   D. the cognitive approach.

3. The approach to psychology that focuses on self-fulfillment, altruism, and personal growth is
   A. the cognitive approach.
   B. the behavioral approach.
   C. the psychodynamic approach.
   D. the humanistic approach.

**APPLY IT!** 4. In 2007 a father posted a video clip of his young sons on YouTube. Widely known as "Charlie Bit My Finger," the clip, which quickly went viral, shows a British baby laughing hysterically as he bites his crying brother's finger. The clip is the most viewed nonprofessional music video on YouTube. If you haven't seen it, take a look: http://www.youtube.com/watch?v=he5fpsmH_2g. What explains the clip's enduring appeal? Each of the contemporary approaches we have reviewed might offer an explanation. Which of the following is most like what a *psychodynamic* thinker might say?
   A. Human beings have been *rewarded* for watching children bite each other.
   B. Adorable children are *universally* loved.
   C. Human beings have an *unconscious* desire to harm their siblings, which is disguised by the humor of the clip.
   D. This clip demonstrates that cuteness is an important *adaptation*. Cute kids are more likely to survive and reproduce.

# 3 Psychology's Scientific Method

Science is not defined by *what* it investigates but by *how* it investigates. Whether you study photosynthesis, butterflies, Saturn's moons, or happiness, the *way* you study your question of interest determines whether your approach is scientific. The scientific method is how psychologists gain knowledge about mind and behavior. A key theme in the scientific method is that knowledge comes from empirical research.

It is the use of the scientific method that makes psychology a science (Ray, 2012). Indeed, most of the studies psychologists publish in research journals follow the scientific method, which may be summarized in these five steps (Figure 1.3):

**1.** Observing some phenomenon

**2.** Formulating hypotheses and predictions

**3.** Testing through empirical research

**4.** Drawing conclusions

**5.** Evaluating conclusions

**1. OBSERVING SOME PHENOMENON** The first step in conducting a scientific inquiry involves observing some phenomenon in the world. The critical-thinking, curious psychologist sees something and wants to know why or how it is the way it is. Inspiration for scientific inquiry can come from contemporary social problems, current events, personal experiences, and more. The phenomena that scientists study are called variables, a word related to the verb *to vary*. A **variable** is anything that can change.

For example, one variable that interests psychologists is happiness. Some people seem to be happier than others. What might account for these

**variable**
Anything that can change.

*Science is defined not by what it studies but by how it investigates. Photosynthesis, butterflies, and relationships among people all can be studied in a scientific manner.*

spend on yourself

spend on someone else

### 1
**Observing Some Phenomenon**

We feel good when we give someone a gift. However, do we genuinely feel better giving something away than we might feel if we could keep it? Elizabeth Dunn, Lara Aknin, and Michael Norton (2008) decided to test this question.

### 2
**Formulating Hypotheses and Predictions**

These researchers hypothesized that spending money on other people would lead to greater happiness than spending money on oneself.

### 3
**Testing Through Empirical Research**

In an experiment designed to examine this prediction, the researchers randomly assigned undergraduate participants to receive money ($5 or $20) that they had to spend either on themselves or on someone else by 5 P.M. that day. Those who spent the money on *someone else* reported greater happiness that night.

### 4
**Drawing Conclusions**

The experiment supported the hypothesis that spending money on others can be a strong predictor of happiness. Money might not buy happiness, the researchers concluded, but spending money in a particular way, that is, on other people, may enhance happiness.

### 5
**Evaluating Conclusions**

The experimental results were published in the prestigious journal *Science*. Now that the findings are public, other researchers might investigate related topics and questions inspired by this work, and their experiments might shed further light on the original conclusions.

**FIGURE 1.3** **Steps in the Scientific Method: Is It Better to Give Than to Receive?** This figure shows how the steps in the scientific method were applied in a research experiment examining how spending money on ourselves or others can influence happiness (Dunn, Aknin, & Norton, 2008). The researchers theorized that although money does not typically buy happiness, the way we spend it might well predict happy feelings. **> *For each step in the process, what decisions did the researchers make, and how did those decisions influence the research?* > *Are the findings counterintuitive or not?* > *This study was inspired by the saying "It is better to give than to receive." Does the study do a good job of evaluating that cliché? How else might a researcher have addressed this question?***

---

differences? As scientists consider answers to such questions, they often develop theories. A **theory** is a broad idea or set of closely related ideas that attempts to explain observations. Theories seek to explain why certain things are as they are or why they have happened, and they can be used to make predictions about future observations. For instance, some psychologists theorize that the most important human need is the need to belong to a social group (Leary & Guadagno, 2011). This theory would seek to explain human behaviors through the need to belong.

A key characteristic of a scientific theory is that it must be *falsifiable*, meaning that even a scientist who believes that a theory is true must be able to generate ideas about research that would prove the theory wrong and test those ideas. This is what separates scientific theories from beliefs and opinions.

*A scientist must be able to anticipate being wrong and remain open to that possibility.*

**EXPERIENCE IT!**
Scientific Method

**theory**
A broad idea or set of closely related ideas that attempts to explain observations and to make predictions about future observations.

## 2. FORMULATING HYPOTHESES AND PREDICTIONS
The second step in the scientific method is stating a hypothesis. A **hypothesis** is a testable prediction that derives logically from a theory. A theory can generate many hypotheses. If more and more hypotheses related to a theory turn out to be true, the theory gains in credibility. So, a researcher who believes that social belonging is the most important aspect of human

**hypothesis**
A testable prediction that derives logically from a theory.

functioning might predict that people who belong to social groups will be happier than others, or might hypothesize that individuals who are excluded by a social group will be more aggressive. Each of these hypotheses would lead to specific predictions within a particular empirical study.

### 3. TESTING THROUGH EMPIRICAL RESEARCH

The next step in the scientific method is to test the hypotheses by conducting empirical research—that is, by collecting and analyzing data. At this point, it is time for the researcher to design a study that will test his or her predictions. We will review the specifics of various research methods for testing predictions later in this chapter. Whatever the method used to test a prediction, the first thing a researcher needs in order to conduct a study is a concrete way to measure the variables of interest.

Try operationally defining the following variables: generosity, love, aggression, liberal, conservative, exhaustion, stress, attractiveness. What are some things that you find interesting that you think a psychologist should study? How might you operationally define these variables?

An **operational definition** provides an objective description of how a variable is going to be measured and observed in a particular study. Such a definition eliminates the fuzziness that might creep into thinking about a problem. Imagine, for example, that your psychology class is asked to observe a group of children and to keep track of kind behaviors. Do you think that everyone will define "kind behaviors" in the same way? An operational definition allows the class to be sure that everyone agrees on what a variable means. To measure personal happiness, for example, prominent psychologist Ed Diener and his students (Diener & others, 1985) devised a self-report questionnaire that measures how satisfied a person is with his or her life, called the Satisfaction with Life Scale. You will get a chance to complete the questionnaire later in this chapter. Scores on this scale are then used as measures of happiness. Research using this scale and others like it has shown that certain specific factors are strongly related to being happy: marriage, religious faith, purpose in life, and good health (Diener, 1999; Diener & Chan, 2011; Pavot & Diener, 2008).

**operational definition**
A definition that provides an objective description of how a variable is going to be measured and observed in a particular study.

Importantly, there is not just one operational definition for any variable. For example, in a study that examined happiness as a predictor of important life outcomes, Lee Anne Harker and Dacher Keltner (2001) looked at the yearbook pictures of college women who had graduated three decades earlier. They coded the pictures for the appearance of *Duchenne smiling*—that is, genuine smiling, the kind that creates little wrinkles around the outer corner of the eyes. Duchenne smiling has been shown to be a sign of genuine happiness. (If you want to see whether someone in a photograph is smiling genuinely, cover the bottom of the person's face. Can you still tell that he or she is smiling? A genuine smile can be seen in the eyes, not just the mouth.) So, while Diener and colleagues operationally defined happiness as a score on a questionnaire, Harker and Keltner operationally defined happiness as Duchenne smiling. Harker and Keltner found that happiness, as displayed in these yearbook pictures, predicted positive life outcomes, such as successful marriages and satisfying lives, some 30 years later.

*Researchers have identified Duchenne smiling (notice the wrinkles) as a sign of genuine happiness.*

Coming up with operational definitions for the variables in a study is a crucial step in designing psychological research. To study anything, we must have a way to see it or measure it. Clearly, to devise an operational definition for any variable, we first must agree on what it is that we are trying to measure. If we think of happiness as something that people know about themselves, then a questionnaire score might be a good operational definition of the variable. If we think that people might not be aware of how happy they are (or are not), then facial expression might be a better operational definition. In other words, our definition of a variable must be set out clearly before we operationally define it.

Because operational definitions allow researchers to measure variables, they have a lot of numbers to deal with once they have conducted a study. A key aspect of the process of testing hypotheses is *data analysis*. *Data* refers to all the information (all those numbers) researchers collect in a study—say, the questionnaire scores or the behaviors observed. Data analysis means "crunching" those numbers mathematically to see if they support predictions. In other words, data analysis involves applying mathematical procedures to understand what the numerical information means (Howell, 2013). Many psychology students are surprised to learn that much of psychologists' work relies heavily on sophisticated *statistics,* numbers that help them describe what the data have to tell them.

Let's pause and examine an example that demonstrates the first three steps in the scientific method. One theory of well-being is *self-determination theory* (Ryan, Huta, & Deci, 2008; Ryan & Deci, 2011). This theory states that people are likely to feel fulfilled when their lives meet three important needs: relatedness (warm relations with others), autonomy (independence), and competence (mastering new skills).

One hypothesis that follows logically from this theory is that people who value money, material possessions, prestige, and physical appearance (that is, extrinsic rewards) over the needs of relatedness, autonomy, and competence (intrinsic rewards) should be less fulfilled, less happy, and less well adjusted. In a series of studies entitled "The Dark Side of the American Dream," researchers Timothy Kasser and Richard Ryan asked participants to complete self-report measures of values and of psychological and physical functioning (Kasser & Ryan, 1993, 1996; Kasser & others, 2004). Thus, the operational definitions of values and psychological functioning were questionnaire scores. The researchers found that individuals who value material rewards over intrinsic rewards do indeed tend to suffer as predicted, and similar findings have emerged in nations throughout the world (Kasser, 2011).

**4. DRAWING CONCLUSIONS**   Based on the results of the data analyses, scientists then draw conclusions from their research. If the results of a study (or a series of studies) support predictions, then a theory may gain credibility. A theory, however, is always open to revision. Before a theory is accepted or changed, the scientific community must establish that the research can be replicated, or repeated, by other scientists using different methods. If a particular research finding is demonstrated again and again across different researchers and different methods, it is considered *reliable*—in other words, it is a dependable result.

**5. EVALUATING CONCLUSIONS**   The final step in the scientific method, evaluating conclusions, is one that never ends. Researchers submit their work for publication, and it undergoes rigorous review. Afterward, the published studies are there for all to see, read, and evaluate continually.

*Because scientists are skeptical and critical thinkers, published studies often lead to alternative theories and hypotheses that are themselves tested.*

Although the published research literature represents the current state of scientific knowledge about various topics and areas, the research community maintains an active conversation about this knowledge and constantly questions conclusions. Inspired by published studies, a scientist might come up with a new idea to be tested, one that will eventually change the thinking on some topic. Steps 3, 4, and 5 in the scientific method are thus part of an ongoing process. That is, researchers go back and do more research, revise their theories, hone their methods, and draw and evaluate their new conclusions.

1. Any changeable phenomenon that a scientist studies is called a
   A. differential.
   B. predictor.
   C. variation.
   D. variable.

2. The statement "I believe this research will demonstrate that students who study in groups will get better grades than those who study alone" is an example of
   A. a theory.
   B. an observation.
   C. a conclusion.
   D. a hypothesis.

3. The last step in the scientific method, and one that never ends, is
   A. drawing conclusions.
   B. evaluating conclusions.
   C. testing through empirical research.
   D. running a statistical analysis.

APPLY IT! 4. Paul believes that physically attractive people are selfish. He conducts a study to see if he is right. He goes up to five people he thinks are good-looking and asks them for spare change. They all turn him down. Paul concludes, "Aha! I knew it all along." The operational definition of selfish in Paul's study is
   A. physical attractiveness.
   B. whether people gave Paul spare change.
   C. whether Paul thought the person was attractive.
   D. asking for spare change.

BONUS: As you practice thinking like a scientist and learn about research design, give further thought to Paul's study. Can you spot at least four big problems with it?

# 4 Types of Psychological Research

The five steps of the scientific method are reflected differently in three types of research commonly used in psychology. *Descriptive research* involves finding out about the basic dimensions of some variable (for example, what is the average level of happiness of men in the United States?). *Correlational research* is interested in discovering relationships between variables (for instance, are married men happier than single men?). *Experimental research* concerns establishing causal relationships between variables (if we make men smile, do women perceive them as more attractive?). Let's examine each of these types of research.

## Descriptive Research

Just as its name suggests, descriptive research is about describing some phenomenon—determining its basic dimensions and defining what this thing is, how often it occurs, and so on. By itself, descriptive research cannot prove what causes some phenomenon, but it can reveal important information about people's behaviors and attitudes (Salkind, 2012). Descriptive research methods include observation, surveys and interviews, and case studies.

**OBSERVATION** Imagine that you are going to conduct a study on how children who are playing a game resolve conflicts that arise during the game. The data that are of interest to you concern conflict resolution. As a first step, you might go to a playground and simply observe what the children do—how often you see conflict resolution occur and how it unfolds. You would likely keep careful notes of what you observe.

This type of scientific observation requires an important set of skills (Smith & Davis, 2010). Unless you are a trained observer and practice your skills regularly, you might not know what to look for, you might not remember what you saw, you might not realize that what you are looking for is changing from one moment to the next, and you might not communicate your observations effectively. Furthermore, it might be important to have one or more others do the observations as well, to develop a sense of how accurate your observations are. For observations to be effective, they must be systematic. You must know

Public opinion polls are a type of descriptive research.

Psychologists carefully noted the pets' response to the broken water dish.

Used by permission of CartoonStock, www. CartoonStock.com.

Maa, averaged a 5.4 on the life satisfaction scale (Biswas-Diener, Vitterso, & Diener, 2005).

Finally, the Old Order Amish of the midwestern and northeastern United States belong to a strict religious sect that explicitly rejects modern aspects of life. The Amish separate themselves from mainstream society and travel by horse and buggy. The women wear bonnets, and the men sport beards, dark clothes, and dark brimmed hats. The Amish farm without modern machinery and dedicate their lives to simplicity—without radios, TVs, CDs, DVDs, iPods, smartphones, washing machines, and cars. Still, the Amish are relatively happy, averaging 4.4 on the 7-point happiness scale (Biswas-Diener, Vitterso, & Diener, 2005).

Like a host of other studies in industrialized nations, these results indicate that most individuals are pretty happy. Such descriptive findings provide researchers on well-being a foundation for further examining the processes that lead to feelings of happiness in different cultural settings. If a researcher wanted to examine, for example, what predicts happiness within these different groups, he or she would use a correlational design.

*How does your score compare with the score of the Inughuits, the Masai, and the Old Order Amish? Is the Satisfaction with Life Scale a good measure of happiness? Why or why not?*

# Correlational Research

We have seen that descriptive research tells us about the basic dimensions of a variable. In contrast, **correlational research** tells us about the relationships between variables, and its purpose is to examine whether and how two variables *change together*. That is, correlational research looks at a co-relationship. For instance, if one of the variables increases, what happens to the other one? When two variables change together, we can predict one from the other, and we say that the variables are correlated.

Correlational research is so named because of the statistical technique, *correlation*, that is typically used to analyze this type of data. The key feature of a correlational study is that the variables of interest are measured or observed to see how they relate. If we wanted to know whether shy people are happy, we might give the same people two questionnaires, one that measures shyness and another that measures happiness. For each person we would have two scores, and we would then see whether shyness and happiness relate to each other in a systematic way.

The degree of relationship between two variables is expressed as a numerical value called a *correlational coefficient*, which is most commonly represented by the letter $r$. The correlation coefficient is a statistic that tells us two things about the relationship between two variables—its strength and its direction. The value of a correlation always falls between $-1.00$ and $+1.00$. The number or magnitude of the correlation tells us about the *strength* of the relationship. The closer the number is to $\pm 1.00$, the stronger the relationship. The sign ($+$ or $-$) tells us about the *direction* of the relationship between the variables. A positive sign means that as one variable increases, the other also increases. A negative sign means that as one variable increases, the other decreases. A zero correlation means that there is no systematic relationship between the variables. Examples of *scatter plots* (a type of graph that plots scores on the two variables) showing positive and negative correlations appear in Figure 1.4. Note that every dot in this figure represents both scores for one person.

**correlational research**
Research that examines the relationships between variables, whose purpose is to examine whether and how two variables change together.

**EXPERIENCE IT!**
Correlation

**CORRELATION IS *NOT* CAUSATION**   Look at the terms in bold type in the following news headlines:

Researchers **Link** Coffee Consumption to Happiness in Women

Scientists Find **Connection** Between Ear Hair and Heart Attacks

Psychologists Discover **Relationship** Between Marital Status and Health

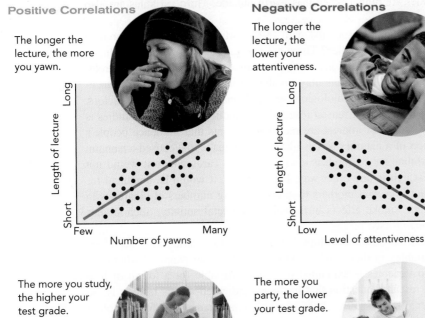

**Positive Correlations**

The longer the lecture, the more you yawn.

*[Scatter plot: Length of lecture (Short to Long) vs. Number of yawns (Few to Many), positive correlation]*

The more you study, the higher your test grade.

*[Scatter plot: Hours of studying (Few to Many) vs. Test grade (Low to High), positive correlation]*

**Negative Correlations**

The longer the lecture, the lower your attentiveness.

*[Scatter plot: Length of lecture (Short to Long) vs. Level of attentiveness (Low to High), negative correlation]*

The more you party, the lower your test grade.

*[Scatter plot: Number of parties (Few to Many) vs. Test grade (Low to High), negative correlation]*

**FIGURE 1.4** **Scatter Plots Showing Positive and Negative Correlations** A positive correlation is a relationship in which two factors vary in the same direction, as shown in the two scatter plots on the left. A negative correlation is a relationship in which two factors vary in opposite directions, as shown in the two scatter plots on the right. Note that each dot on these graphs represents one person's (or one class's) score on the two variables of interest. For each graph, consider these questions. >*How might one of these variables cause the other? Can you imagine a way that the causal direction could be reversed?* >*What is a possible third variable that might account for these relationships?* >*Identify two variables that you think are positively correlated and two that are negatively correlated.* >*What would the graphs look like if the two variables were not systematically related?*

From these headlines a reader might conclude that coffee causes pancreatic cancer, ear hair causes heart attacks, and so on. The words in bold type are synonymous only with correlation, however, not with causality. *Correlation does not equal causation.* Remember, correlation means only that two variables change together. Being able to predict one event based on the occurrence of another event does not necessarily tell us anything about the cause of either event (Heiman, 2011; Pagano, 2013). Sometimes some other variable that has not been measured accounts for the relationship between two others. Researchers refer to this circumstance as the **third variable problem.** Third variables are also known as confounds.

To understand the third variable problem, consider the following example. A researcher measures two variables: the number of ice cream cones sold in a town and the number of violent crimes that occur in that town throughout the year. The researcher finds that ice cream cone sales and violent crimes are positively correlated, to the magnitude of +.50. This high positive correlation would indicate that as ice cream sales increase, so does violent crime. Would it be reasonable for the local paper to run the headline "Ice Cream Consumption Leads to Violence"? Should concerned citizens gather outside the local Frosty Freeze to stop the madness? Probably not. Perhaps you have already thought of the third variable that might explain this correlation—heat. Research

**third variable problem**
The circumstance where a variable that has not been measured accounts for the relationship between two other variables. Third variables are also known as confounds.

*Crime, then, is probably also "linked" to air conditioning sales and repair profits, as well as swimsuit sales.*

has shown that crime goes up when the temperature rises (Anderson & others, 2000; Bushman, Wang, & Anderson, 2005), and, as any ice cream shop manager will tell you, ice cream sales are higher when it is warm outside. Third variables are also called *confounds*.

Given the potential problems with third variables, why do researchers conduct correlational studies? There are several very good reasons. One is that some important questions can be investigated only by using a correlational design. Such questions may involve variables that can only be measured or observed, such as biological sex, personality traits, genetic factors, and ethnic background. Another reason researchers conduct correlational studies is that sometimes the variables of interest are real-world events that influence people's lives, such as the effects of a natural disaster like the earthquake that caused a tsunami in Japan in 2011. Correlational research is also valuable in cases where it would not be ethical to do the research in any other way. For example, it would be unethical for an experimenter to direct expectant mothers to smoke varying numbers of cigarettes in order to see how cigarette smoke affects birth weight and fetal activity. Such studies are called *quasi-experimental* (see p. 25).

Although we have focused on relationships between just two variables, researchers often measure many variables in their studies. This way, they can examine whether a relationship between two variables is explained by a third variable (or a fourth or fifth variable). An interesting research question that has been addressed in this fashion is, do happy people live longer? In one study, 2000 Mexican Americans aged 65 and older were interviewed twice over the course of two years (Ostir & others, 2000). In the first assessment, participants completed measures of happiness but also reported about potential third variables such as diet, physical health, smoking, marital status, and distress. Two years later, the researchers contacted the participants again to see who was still alive. Even with these many potential third variables taken into account, happiness predicted who was still living two years later.

Correlational studies are useful, too, when researchers are interested in everyday experience. For example, some correlational researchers use the *experience sampling method (ESM)* to study people in their natural settings. This approach involves having people report on their daily experiences in a diary a few times a day or to complete measures of their mood and behavior whenever they are beeped by an electronic organizer or smartphone.

## LONGITUDINAL DESIGNS
One way that correlational researchers can deal with the issue of causation is to employ a special kind of systematic observation called a **longitudinal design.** Longitudinal research involves observing and measuring the same variables periodically over time. Longitudinal research can suggest potential causal relationships because if one variable is thought to cause changes in another, it should at least come before that variable in time.

**longitudinal design**
A special kind of systematic observation, used by correlational researchers, that involves obtaining measures of the variables of interest in multiple waves over time.

One intriguing longitudinal study is the Nun Study, conducted by David Snowdon and his colleagues (Mortimer, Snowdon, & Markesbery, 2009; Santacruz & others, 2011; Snowdon, 2003; Tyas & others, 2007). The study began in 1986 and has followed a sample of 678 School Sisters of Notre Dame ever since. The nuns ranged in age from 75 to 103 when the study began. These women complete a variety of psychological and physical measures annually. This sample is unique in many respects. However, some characteristics render the participants an excellent group for correlational research. For one thing, many potential extraneous third variables are relatively identical for all the women in the group. Their gender, living conditions, diet, activity levels, marital status, and religious participation are essentially held constant, providing little chance that differences in these variables can explain results.

Researchers recently examined the relationship between happiness and longevity using this rich dataset. All of the nuns had been asked to write a spiritual autobiography when they entered the convent (for some, as many as 80 years before). Deborah Danner and her colleagues (2001) were given access to these documents and used them as indicators of happiness earlier in life by counting the number of positive emotions expressed in the autobiographies (note that here we have yet another operational definition of happiness). Higher levels of positive emotion expressed in autobiographies written at an average age of 22 were associated with a 2.5-fold difference in risk of mortality when the nuns were in their 80s and 90s. That is, women who included positive emotion in their autobiographies when they were in their early 20s were two-and-a-half times more likely to survive some 60 years later.

Longitudinal designs provide ways by which correlational researchers may attempt to demonstrate causal relations among variables. Still, it is important to be aware that even in longitudinal studies, causal relationships are not completely clear. For example, the nuns who wrote happier autobiographies may have had happier childhood experiences that might be influencing their longevity, or a particular genetic factor might explain both their happiness and their survival. As you read about numerous correlational research studies throughout this book, do so critically, and with some skepticism, and consider that even the brightest scientist may not have thought of all of the potential third variables that might have explained his or her results. Keep in mind how easy it is to assume causality when two events or characteristics are merely correlated. Think about those innocent ice cream cones and critically evaluate conclusions that may be drawn from simple observation.

## Experimental Research

To determine whether a causal relationship exists between variables, researchers must use experimental methods (Myers & Hansen, 2012). An **experiment** is a carefully regulated procedure in which the researcher manipulates one or more variables that are believed to influence some other variable. Imagine that a researcher notices that people who listen to classical music seem to be of above-average intelligence. A correlational study on this question would not tell us if listening to classical music *causes* increases in intelligence. In order to demonstrate causation, the researcher would manipulate whether or not people listen to classical music. He or she might create two groups: one that listens to classical music and one that listens to pop music. To test for differences in intelligence, the researcher would then measure intelligence.

**experiment**
A carefully regulated procedure in which the researcher manipulates one or more variables that are believed to influence some other variable.

If that manipulation led to differences between the two groups on intelligence, we could say that the manipulated variable *caused* those differences. In other words, the experiment has demonstrated cause and effect. This notion that experiments can demonstrate causation is based on the idea that if participants are randomly assigned to groups, the only systematic difference between them must be the manipulated variable. **Random assignment** means that researchers assign participants to groups by chance. This technique reduces the likelihood that the experiment's results will be due to any preexisting differences between groups (Eimes, Kantowitz, & Roediger, 2012).

**random assignment**
Researchers' assignment of participants to groups by chance, to reduce the likelihood that an experiment's results will be due to preexisting differences between groups.

To get a sense of what experimental studies, as compared to correlational studies, can tell us, consider the following example. Psychologists have long assumed that experiencing one's life as meaningful is an important aspect of psychological well-being (Frankl, 1963/1984; Steger & Frazier, 2005). Because surveys that measure meaning in life and well-being correlate positively (that is, the more meaningful your life, the happier you are), the assumption has been that experiencing meaning in life causes greater happiness. Because the studies involved in exploring this relationship have been correlational, however, the causal pathway is unknown. Meaning in life may lead people to be happier, but the reverse might also be true: Happiness might make people feel that their lives are more meaningful.

To address this issue, Laura King and her colleagues (2006; King & Hicks, 2012) conducted a series of laboratory experiments. The researchers had some people listen to

*"This GPS eliminates all the guesswork"*

Used by permission of CartoonStock, www.CartoonStock.com.

influence the outcome of the research. No one designs an experiment without wanting meaningful results. Consequently, experimenters can sometimes subtly communicate to participants what they want the participants to do. **Demand characteristics** are any aspects of a study that communicate to the participants how the experimenter wants them to behave. The influence of experimenter expectations can be very difficult to avoid.

**demand characteristics**
Any aspects of a study that communicate to the participants how the experimenter wants them to behave.

In a classic study, Robert Rosenthal (1966) turned college students into experimenters. He randomly assigned the participants rats from the same litter. Half of the students were told that their rats were "maze bright," whereas the other half were told that their rats were "maze dull." The students then conducted experiments to test their rats' ability to navigate mazes. The results were stunning. The so-called maze-bright rats were more successful than the maze-dull rats at running the mazes. The only explanation for the results is that the college students' expectations affected the rats' performance.

Often the participants in psychological studies are not rats but people. Imagine that you are an experimenter and you know that a participant is going to be exposed to disgusting pictures in a study. Is it possible that you might treat the person differently than you would if you were about to show him photos of cute kittens? The reason experimenter bias is important is that it introduces systematic differences between the experimental and control groups, so that we cannot know if those who looked at disgusting pictures were more, say, upset because of the pictures or because of different treatment by the experimenter. Like third variables in correlational research, these systematic biases are called *confounds*. In experimental research, confounds are factors that "ride along" with the experimental manipulation, systematically and undesirably influencing the dependent variable. Experimenter bias, demand characteristics, and confounds may all lead to differences between groups on the dependent variable that bias results.

### Research Participant Bias and the Placebo Effect

Like the experimenters, research participants may have expectations about what they are supposed to do and how they should behave, and these expectations may affect the results of experiments (Bonds-Raache & Raache, 2012). **Research participant bias** occurs when the behavior of research participants during the experiment is influenced by how they think they are supposed to behave or their expectations about what is happening to them.

**research participant bias**
In an experiment, the influence of participants' expectations, and of their thoughts about how they should behave, on their behavior.

One example of the power of participant expectations is the placebo effect. The **placebo effect** occurs when participants' expectations, rather than the experimental treatment, produce an outcome. Participants in a drug study might be assigned to an experimental group that receives a pill containing an actual painkiller or to a control group that receives a placebo pill. A **placebo** is a harmless substance that has no physiological effect. This placebo is given to participants in a control group so that they are treated identically to the experimental group except for the active agent—in this case, the painkiller. Giving individuals in the control group a placebo pill allows researchers to determine whether changes in the experimental group are due to the active drug agent and not simply to participants' expectations.

**placebo effect**
The situation where participants' expectations, rather than the experimental treatment, produce an experimental outcome.

**placebo**
In a drug study, a harmless substance that has no physiological effect, given to participants in a control group so that they are treated identically to the experimental group except for the active agent.

Another way to ensure that neither the experimenter's nor the participants' expectations affect the outcome is to design a **double-blind experiment.** In this design, neither the experimenter administering the treatment nor the participants are aware of which participants are in the experimental group and which are in the control group until the results are calculated. This setup ensures that the experimenter cannot, for example, make subtle gestures signaling who is receiving a drug and who is not. A double-blind

**double-blind experiment**
An experimental design in which neither the experimenter nor the participants are aware of which participants are in the experimental group and which are in the control group until the results are calculated.

study allows researchers to identify the specific effects of the independent variable from the possible effects of the experimenter's and the participants' expectations about it.

*Volunteering for a double-blind drug study might seem risky. Would you do it? How might differences in willingness to volunteer to participate in this research influence its external validity?*

# Applications of the Three Types of Research

All three types of research that we have considered—descriptive, correlational, and experimental—can be used to address the same research topic (Figure 1.5). For instance, researchers have been interested in examining the role of intensely positive experiences in human functioning. Abraham Maslow (1971) believed that the healthiest, happiest people in the world were capable of having intense moments of awe, and he used the descriptive case study approach to examine the role of such "peak experiences" in the lives of individuals who seemed to exemplify the best in human life. Through correlational research, Dan McAdams (2001) probed individuals' descriptions of the most intensely positive experiences of their lives. He found that people who were motivated toward warm interpersonal experiences tended to mention such experiences as the best memories of their lives. Experimental researchers have also investigated this question. In their work, people who were randomly assigned to write about their most intensely positive experiences for a few minutes each day for two or three days experienced enhanced positive mood as well as fewer physical illnesses two months later, compared to individuals in control groups who wrote about unemotional topics (Burton & King, 2004, 2008). Experimental and correlational methods are often combined as psychologists grapple with the intriguing question of the role of culture in psychological processes, as we explore in the Intersection.

| | Descriptive Research | | | Correlational Research | Experimental Research |
|---|---|---|---|---|---|
| **Goal** | To determine the basic dimensions of a phenomenon. | | | To determine how variables change together. | To determine whether a causal relationship exists between two variables. |
| **Sample Research Questions** | **Observation**<br><br>How much time are individuals spending each day on Facebook and similar sites?<br><br>How many people use different kinds of social media? | **Interviews/Surveys**<br><br>How do people describe their use of social media? Are they accurate?<br><br>Do people view the social media they use positively or negatively? | **Case studies**<br><br>Does the social media page of a particular person (for instance, someone who has committed suicide) reveal important information about the individual? | What is the relationship between the number of hours spent on social media and face-to-face interactions?<br><br>How does personal page content relate to personality characteristics? | How does going "cold turkey" on social media influence stress levels?<br><br>If we randomly assign a smiling picture to a personal page, does it produce more friend requests than the identical page with a frowning picture? |
| **Strengths and Weaknesses** | The findings would lay the groundwork for future research by establishing the types of questions that ought to be addressed. This work would not tell us, however, about the processes involved or provide generalizable conclusions. | | | This research would give us information about how variables change together. However, it would not allow us to make causal conclusions. | This research would permit causal conclusions. The potential artificiality of the manipulations might raise concerns about external validity. |

**FIGURE 1.5** **Psychology's Research Methods Applied to Studying Social Media Use** Psychologists can apply different methods to study the same phenomenon. The popularity of social media has opened up a host of new research questions for psychologists.

*Whoa. A random sample is not the same thing as random assignment. A random sample is about selecting participants from a population so that the sample is representative of that population, and random assignment is about making sure experimental and control groups are equivalent. In neither case does the word random mean that these aspects of setting up a study are haphazard.*

to which the investigator wants to generalize his or her results. That is, the researcher might study only 100 gifted adolescents, but he or she wants to apply these results to all gifted and talented adolescents.

To mirror the population as closely as possible, the researcher uses a **random sample,** a sample that gives every member of the population an equal chance of being selected. A representative sample would reflect population factors such as age, socioeconomic status, ethnic origin, marital status, geographic location, and religion. A random sample provides much better grounds for generalizing the results to a population than a nonrandom sample, because random selection improves the chances that the sample is representative of the population.

In selecting a sample, researchers must strive to minimize bias, including gender bias. Because psychology is the scientific study of human behavior, it should pertain to *all* humans, and so the participants in psychological studies ought to be representative of humanity as a whole. Early research in the field often included just the male experience—not only because the researchers themselves were often male, but also because the participants too were typically male (Matlin, 2012). For a long time, the human experience studied by psychologists was primarily the male experience.

There also has been a growing realization that psychological research needs to include more people from diverse ethnic groups (Nieto & Bode, 2012). Because a great deal of psychological research involves college student participants, individuals from groups that have not had as many educational opportunities have not been strongly represented in that research. Given the fact that individuals from diverse ethnic groups were excluded from psychological research for so long, we might reasonably conclude that people's real lives are more varied than past research data have indicated.

These issues are important because scientists want to be able to predict *human* behavior, not just non-Latino White male college student behavior. Imagine if policymakers planned their initiatives for a broad range of Americans based on research derived from only a small group of individuals from a particular background. What might the results be? Recent research on the science of happiness around the world has caught the eye of public policymakers, as evidenced in the Psychology in Our World feature.

**random sample**
A sample that gives every member of the population an equal chance of being selected.

# The Research Setting

All three types of research we examined in the preceding section can take place in different settings. The setting of the research does not determine the type of research it is. Common settings include the research laboratory and natural settings.

Because psychological researchers often want to control as many aspects of the situation as possible, they conduct much of their research in a laboratory, a controlled setting with many of the complex factors of the real world, including potential confounds, removed (Tucker-Drob, 2011). Although laboratory research provides a great deal of control, doing research in the laboratory has drawbacks. First, it is almost impossible to conduct research in the lab without the participants knowing they are being studied. Second, the laboratory setting is not the real world and therefore can cause the participants to behave unnaturally. A third drawback of laboratory research is that people who are willing to go to a university laboratory may not be representative of groups from diverse cultural backgrounds. Individuals who are unfamiliar with university settings and with the idea of "helping science" may be intimidated by the setting. Fourth, some aspects of the mind and behavior are difficult if not impossible to examine in the laboratory.

## The Global Science of Happiness

**B**etween 2005 and 2006, the Gallup Organization collected the first-ever representative sample of Planet Earth, called the Gallup World Poll (GWP) (Diener & others, 2010). GWP data were collected from 132 nations (accounting for 96 percent of the world's population). Within each country, a representative sample of all adults was collected; the total sample was 136,839 people. Economic prosperity was measured through items about income, buying power, and ownership of modern conveniences. Social prosperity was measured by asking whether respondents had felt respected, had other people they could count on, had a chance to do what they were good at, and felt in control of their life, in the previous day. Finally, respondents indicated their life satisfaction and gave feedback on whether they had had positive emotional experiences (enjoyment, smiling, or laughter) and negative emotional events (worry, sadness, depression, and anger) in the preceding

day. These data allowed for an examination of the intriguing question, what factors contribute to happiness levels around the globe?

Psychologist Ed Diener and his colleagues (2010; Tay & Diener, 2011) reported the first results of the GWP. They found that although economic factors predicted greater life satisfaction across nations, positive feelings (and low levels of negative feelings) were more strongly predicted by social prosperity—factors such as feeling respected and having people to count on (Diener & others, 2010).

From the full sample, 89 nations were ranked according to their standing on the different variables collected in the survey. Comparing the ranks of different nations provides interesting clues about the pathways to national happiness. The United States ranked first in income levels but was 26th in positive feelings and 49th in terms of low levels of negative feelings. *Read:* Despite their relative wealth, Americans are not that happy. In contrast, the happiest nation was New Zealand, which ranked 22nd on economic factors. Clearly the wealth of a nation is no guarantee of happiness among its citizens. Costa Rica ranked 4th in positive feelings and 6th in social prosperity but was 41st in economic prosperity. Thus, high levels of positive feelings can exist even in the face of relatively low wealth.

Diener and his colleagues concluded that if nations are interested in fostering well-being among their citizens, focusing on economic variables will not suffice. Attention to variables that represent the social prosperity of citizens will be required to make the world a happier place.

Policymakers have taken notice. In July 2011, the United Nations General Assembly passed a resolution emphasizing the enhancement of the experience of happiness around the world (United Nations, 2011). The resolution stated that:

- The pursuit of happiness is a fundamental and universal human goal.
- The gross domestic product of a nation does not adequately reflect the happiness and well-being of its citizens.
- Nations should develop measures of happiness and well-being and use them to guide their national policies.

The authors of the Declaration of Independence recognized the pursuit of happiness as an unalienable human right. In short, the United States' very founders believed that all people are born with the right to seek out and enjoy happiness. Today, the global science of happiness is dedicated to identifying the routes by which nations can help their citizens achieve this goal.

## Is It Ethical to Use Deception in Research?

Imagine that you have signed up to participate in an experiment for which you will receive $3. The experimenter tells you that the study concerns decision making and timing. Your task is to solve a list of word jumbles. For each jumble you solve correctly, you and a randomly selected participant from another study will both receive $1. The experimenter cautions that you must solve the jumbles *in the order presented*. If you fail to solve an early jumble, you will not receive payment for any subsequent jumbles in the list.

The experimenter then leaves you alone with a list of nine scrambled words to solve. Skimming the list, you see that the first two words are a cinch, but the third one is tricky: UNAAGT. The rest of the words look pretty easy too, except the last one: YOMSEELVD. When the experimenter returns, he gives you another copy of the list and asks you to check off which jumbles you got correct, but he *does not ask you for the actual answers*.

After you complete a few other measures, the experimenter tells you that this study was actually not about decision making

- ✔ APLEP
- ✔ LACSIO
- ✔ UNAAGT
- ✔ ECOFEF
- ✔ PACUSM
- ✔ RINGPAK
- ✔ ZAZIP
- ✔ LATEB
- ✔ YOMSEELVD

and timing at all. Instead, it was about *lying*. This experiment, which was in fact conducted in real life by Scott Wiltermuth (2011), tested the prediction that people will be more likely to lie if doing so benefits not only themselves but another person as well, as in the condition described above. Wiltermuth found that participants were more likely to lie and to say they solved the seemingly impossible jumbles if doing so was advantageous not just for themselves but for another person as well. (By the way, those impossible jumbles have solutions: The *taguan* is a large nocturnal flying squirrel, and *semovedly* is a little-used synonym for *separately*.)

Certainly, this interesting study has implications for understanding ethical behaviors. Many real-world situations involve unethical behaviors that benefit not only the person engaging in the behavior but others too. Think of athletes in team sports who take steroids to benefit their teammates as well as themselves, and accountants who cheat on their clients' taxes to benefit those clients. Even Wall Street broker Bernie Madoff's infamous Ponzi scheme paid off (temporarily) not only for Bernie but also for some of his investors. These are important human behaviors for scientists to probe.

Association (APA) has developed ethics guidelines for its members. The APA code of ethics instructs psychologists to protect their participants from mental and physical harm. The participants' best interests need to be kept foremost in the researcher's mind (Christensen, Johnson, & Turner, 2011). APA's guidelines address four important issues:

- *Informed consent:* All participants must know what their participation will involve and what risks might develop. For example, participants in a study on dating should be told beforehand that a questionnaire might stimulate thoughts about issues in their relationships that they have not considered. Participants also should be informed that in some instances a discussion of the issues might improve their relationships but that in others it might worsen the relationships and possibly end them. Even after informed consent is given, participants must retain the right to withdraw from the study at any time and for any reason.

- *Confidentiality:* Researchers are responsible for keeping all of the data they gather on individuals completely confidential and, when possible, completely anonymous. Confidential data are not the same as anonymous. When data are confidential, it is possible to link a participant's identity to his or her data.

- *Debriefing:* After the study has been completed, the researchers should inform the participants of its purpose and the methods they used. In most cases, the experimenters also can inform participants in a general manner beforehand about the purpose of the research without leading the participants to behave in a way that they think that

Yet consider the irony implicit in a study such as Wiltermuth's. A study about *lying*, an unethical behavior, employed *deception*. A study on lying involved lying to participants. Is that really okay?

Deception in psychological research can range from deception by omission to active deception. *Deception by omission* means not telling participants what a study is really about. *Active deception* means misleading participants about what is going on in a study. Active deception might include, for example, giving participants false feedback about their performance on a task or leading them to believe that a confederate is just another participant in the study.

The use of deception in research has been criticized on a variety of grounds (Hertwig & Ortmann, 2008; Kimmel, 2012). For one thing, religions and cultures view lying as morally wrong. Exceptions are made, of course, in situations that call for "little white lies." Are psychological studies also an exception to this rule? For another thing, deception is criticized because of its influence on the availability of naive participants. Once a person has been deceived in a study, he or she may be less likely to believe researchers in later studies, even when no deception is involved. Thus, deception in one study may create suspicion among participants in general and might influence the validity of future studies (Hertwig & Ortmann, 2008). Such a possibility has led to a general prohibition against deception in experiments in economics (Ariely & Norton, 2007). Finally, studies using deception may erode public trust in the science of psychology generally (Kimmel, 2012). If people believe that psychological researchers engage in unethical behavior, why should they believe anything these scholars have to say?

Another issue is that a study that uses deception inherently violates the principle of informed consent. Even in the case of deception by omission, the participants cannot be fully informed prior to giving consent. This is why participants in studies involving deception should have the option of withdrawing consent after they find out what the study is actually about.

As a student of psychology, you will encounter many studies that employ deception. That deception can be as profound as leading people to believe that they are administering harmful electrical shocks to another person (in classic and controversial research by Stanley Milgram that we will explore in Chapter 11). Researchers who employ deception in their studies must be able to justify lying to participants, because doing so is vital to the scientific merit of their work (Benham, 2008). Psychological researchers take deception seriously and employ it only when no other options would allow them to ask the questions they seek to answer.

### What Do You Think?

- How do you feel about the use of deception in psychological research?

- If you participated in a study and found out that it involved deception, would that experience change your perspective on future studies? Why or why not?

the experimenters are expecting. When preliminary information about the study is likely to affect the results, participants can at least be debriefed after the study's completion.

- *Deception:* This is an ethical issue that psychologists debate extensively. In some circumstances, telling the participants beforehand what the research study is about substantially alters the participants' behavior and invalidates the researcher's data. For example, suppose a psychologist wants to know whether bystanders will report a theft. A mock theft is staged, and the psychologist observes which bystanders report it. Had the psychologist informed the participants beforehand that the study intended to discover the percentage of bystanders who will report a theft, the whole study would have been ruined. Thus, the researcher deceives participants about the purpose of the study, perhaps leading them to believe that it has some other purpose. In all cases of deception, however, the psychologist must ensure that the deception will not harm the participants and that the participants will be told the true nature of the study (will be debriefed) as soon as possible after the study is completed. To read more about the issues involved in the use of deception in research, see Challenge Your Thinking.

The federal government also takes a role in ensuring that research involving human participants is conducted ethically. The Federal Office for Protection from Research Risks is devoted to safeguarding the well-being of participants in research studies. Over the years, the office has dealt with many challenging and controversial issues—among them, informed consent rules for research on psychological disorders, regulations governing research on pregnant women and fetuses, and ethical issues regarding AIDS vaccine research.

Of considerable concern is the ways that the principles of ethical research apply when studies involve *vulnerable populations,* which include children, individuals with psychological disorders, incarcerated individuals, and others who may be especially susceptible to coercion. For example, when children participate in research, parental consent is essential. Children may be asked to agree to participate as well. When prisoners or individuals who are on parole participate in research, it must be clear that their treatment and decisions about their future release or parole will not be influenced by their willingness to participate.

## The Ethics of Research with Animals

For generations, psychologists have used animals in some research. Animal studies have provided a better understanding of and solutions for many human problems (Pinel, 2009). Neal Miller (1985), who has made important discoveries about the effects of biofeedback on health, listed the following areas in which animal research has benefited humans:

- Psychotherapy techniques and behavioral medicine
- Rehabilitation of neuromuscular disorders
- Alleviation of the effects of stress and pain
- Drugs to treat anxiety and severe mental illness
- Methods for avoiding drug addiction and relapse
- Treatments to help premature infants gain weight so they can leave the hospital sooner
- Methods used to alleviate memory deficits in old age

Only about 5 percent of APA members use animals in their research. Rats and mice account for 90 percent of all psychological research with animals. It is true that researchers sometimes use procedures with animals that would be unethical with humans, but they are guided by a set of standards for housing, feeding, and maintaining the psychological and physical well-being of their animal subjects. Researchers are required to weigh potential benefits of the research against possible harm to the animal and to avoid inflicting unnecessary pain. Animal abuse is not as common as animal activist groups charge. In short, researchers must follow stringent ethical guidelines, whether animals or humans are the subjects in their studies.

## The Place of Values in Psychological Research

Questions are asked not only about the ethics of psychology but also about its values and its standards for judging what is worthwhile and desirable. Some psychologists argue that psychology should be value-free and morally neutral. From their perspective, the psychologist's role as a scientist is to present facts as objectively as possible. Others believe that because psychologists are human, they cannot possibly be value-free. Indeed, some people go so far as to argue that psychologists should take stands on certain issues. For example, psychological research shows that children reared by gay male and lesbian parents are no more likely to be gay than other children and that the children of homosexual partners tend to demonstrate levels of psychological health that are equal to or higher than those of children reared by heterosexual parents (Patterson, 2012; Patterson & Farr, 2012; Patterson & Wainright, 2010). To the extent that some have argued against the rights of gay individuals to adopt children or to retain custody of their biological children, psychologists may have a role to play in the debate about these issues.

self-quiz

1. Providing research participants with information about the purpose of a study at the study's conclusion is called
   A. informed consent.
   B. deception.
   C. debriefing.
   D. confidentiality.

2. The organization that provides ethical guidelines for psychologists is the
   A. American Psychiatric Association.
   B. Institutional Review Board.
   C. American Medical Association.
   D. American Psychological Association.

3. A study could possibly put participants at risk of harm, but the participants are not told about that risk. The ethical standard that has been violated is
   A. debriefing.
   B. informed consent.
   C. deception.
   D. confidentiality.

**APPLY IT!** 4. Amanda is participating in a psychological study as part of her Intro Psychology course. While filling out items on a questionnaire, Amanda finds that some of them embarrass her, and she decides to skip them. As she leaves the study, the experimenter notices these blank questions and asks Amanda to complete them because the research will be ruined without complete data from all participants. Which of the following accurately assesses the ethics of this situation?
   A. Amanda should really complete those questions. What's the big deal?
   B. Amanda is within her rights to leave any question blank if she chooses, and the experimenter has definitely "crossed a line."
   C. Amanda is ethically wrong because she agreed to be in the study, and so she must see it through.
   D. If Amanda read and signed the consent form, she is obligated to do as the experimenter says.

# 7 Learning About Psychology Means Learning About You

Throughout your life you have been exposed to a good deal of information about psychological research. In this book and your introductory psychology class, you will also learn about a multitude of research findings. In this last section, we consider the ways that learning about psychological studies can help you learn about yourself. We start by looking at some guidelines for evaluating psychological research findings that you might encounter in your everyday life.

## Encountering Psychology in Everyday Life

Not all psychological information that is presented for public consumption comes from professionals with excellent credentials and reputations at colleges or universities or in applied mental health settings (Stanovich, 2010). Because journalists, television reporters, and other media personnel are not usually trained in psychological research, they often have trouble sorting through the widely varying material they find and making sound decisions about the best information to present to the public. In addition, the media often focus on sensationalistic and dramatic psychological findings to capture public attention. They tend to go beyond what actual research articles and clinical findings really say.

Even when the media present the results of excellent research, they have trouble accurately informing people about the findings and their implications for people's lives. This entire book is dedicated to carefully introducing, defining, and elaborating on key concepts and issues, research, and clinical findings. The media, however, do not have the luxury of so much time and space to detail and specify the limitations and qualifications of research. In the end, you have to take responsibility for evaluating media reports on psychological research. To put it another way, you have to consume psychological information critically and wisely. Five guidelines follow.

### AVOID OVERGENERALIZING BASED ON LITTLE INFORMATION

Media reports of psychological information often leave out details about the nature of the sample used in a given study. Without information about sample characteristics—such as the number of participants, how many were male or female, or their ethnic representation—it is wise to take research results with a grain of salt.

### DISTINGUISH BETWEEN GROUP RESULTS AND INDIVIDUAL NEEDS

Just as we cannot generalize from a small group to all people, we also cannot apply conclusions from a group to an individual. When you learn about psychological research through the media, you might be disposed to apply the results to your life. It is important to keep in mind that statistics about a group do not necessarily represent each individual in the group equally well. Imagine, for example, taking a test in a class and being told that the class average was 75 percent, but you got 98 percent. It is unlikely that you would want the instructor to apply the group average to your score.

Sometimes consumers of psychological research can get the wrong idea about whether their experience is "normal" if it does not match group statistics. New parents face this issue all the time. They read about developmental milestones that supposedly characterize an entire age group of children; one such milestone might be that most 2-year-olds are conversing with their parents. However, this group information does not necessarily characterize all children who are developing normally. Albert Einstein did not start talking until he was the ripe old age of 3.

### LOOK FOR ANSWERS BEYOND A SINGLE STUDY

The media might identify an interesting piece of research and claim that it is something phenomenal with far-reaching implications. Although such pivotal studies do occur, they are rare. It is safer to assume that no single study will provide conclusive answers to an important question, especially answers that apply to all people. In fact, in most psychological domains that prompt many investigations, conflicting results are common. Answers to questions in research usually emerge after many scientists have conducted similar investigations that yield similar conclusions. Remember that you should not take one research study as the absolute, final answer to a problem, no matter how compelling the findings.

### AVOID ATTRIBUTING CAUSES WHERE NONE HAVE BEEN FOUND

Drawing causal conclusions from correlational studies is one of the most common mistakes the media make. When a true experiment has not been conducted—that is, when participants have not been randomly assigned to treatments or experiences—two variables might have only a non-causal relationship to each other. Remember from the discussion of correlation earlier in the chapter that causal interpretations cannot be made when two or more factors are simply correlated. We cannot say that one causes the other. When you hear about correlational studies, be skeptical of words indicating causation until you know more about the particular research.

### CONSIDER THE SOURCE OF PSYCHOLOGICAL INFORMATION

Studies conducted by psychologists are not automatically accepted by the rest of the research community. The researchers usually must submit their findings to a journal for review by their colleagues, who make a decision about whether to publish the paper, depending on its scientific merit. This process, called *peer review*, means that research that is published in scholarly journals has survived the scrutiny of experts in a particular area. Although the quality of research and findings is not uniform among all psychology journals, in most cases journals submit the findings to far greater scrutiny than the popular media do (Stanovich, 2010).

Within the media, though, you can usually draw a distinction. The reports of psychological research in respected newspapers such as the *New York Times* and the *Washington Post,* as well as in credible magazines such as *Time* and *Newsweek,* are more trustworthy than reports in tabloids such as the *National Enquirer* and *Star.*

Finally, it is not unusual to read about psychological research online, where bloggers and others might comment on the validity of researchers' findings. When you encounter research-related information on the web, see if you can find the actual study and read it. As helpful as a Google search, a blog, or a Wikipedia entry might be, reading the actual science is crucial to evaluating the conclusions drawn. Whatever the source—serious publication, tabloid, blog, online news outlet, or even academic journal—you are responsible for reading the details behind the reported findings and for analyzing the study's credibility.

*Do It!*

In the next few days, look through several newspapers, magazines, and your favorite online news sources for reports about psychological research. Apply the guidelines for being a wise consumer of information about psychology to these media reports.

## Appreciating Psychology as the Science of You

In taking introductory psychology, you have an amazing opportunity. You will learn a great deal about human beings, especially one particular human being: you. Whether the psychological research presented is about emotions and motivation or the structures of the nervous system, it is still essentially about you.

When you think of psychology, you might think first and foremost about the mind and its complex mental processes such as those involved in love, gratitude, hate, and anger. However, psychology has come to recognize more and more that the mind and its operations are intricately connected to the body. As you will see when we examine neuroscience in Chapter 2, observations of the brain at work reveal that when mental processes change, so do physical processes. This mind–body link has fascinated philosophers for centuries. Psychology occupies the very spot where the mind and the body meet.

It might be helpful to think concretely about the ways the mind and body can relate to each other even as they are united in the physical reality of a person. Let's say you experience a mental event such as watching an episode of *The Biggest Loser*. You decide to embark on a workout regimen for six-pack abdominals. Dedication, goal setting, and self-discipline will be the kinds of mental processes necessary to transform your body. The mind can work on the body, prompting changes to its shape and size.

Similarly, the body can dramatically influence the mind. Consider how fuzzy your thinking is after you stay out too late and how much easier it is to solve life's problems after a good night's sleep. Also think about your outlook on the first day of true recovery from a nagging cold: Everything seems better. Your mood and your work improve. Clearly, physical states such as illness and health influence how we think.

The relationship between the body and mind is illustrated in a major dilemma that countless psychologists have faced: the impact of nature versus nurture. Essentially, psychologists have wondered and debated which of the two is more important to a person—nature (that is, genetic heritage) or nurture (social experiences). The influence of genetics on a variety of psychological characteristics, and the ways that genetic influence can itself be altered by experience, will be addressed in many of the main topics in this book, from development (Chapter 8) to personality traits (Chapter 10) to psychological disorders (Chapter 12). You will see that at every turn, your physical and mental self are intertwined in ways you may have never considered.

Throughout this book, we investigate the ways that all of the various approaches to psychology matter to your life. Psychology is crucially about you, essential to your understanding of your life, your goals, and the ways that you can use the insights of thousands of scientists to make your life healthier and happier.

## SUMMARY

### 1 Defining Psychology and Exploring Its Roots

Psychology is the scientific study of human behavior and mental processes. Psychologists approach human behavior as scientists who think critically and who are curious, skeptical, and objective. Psychology emerged as a science from philosophy and physiology. Two founders of the science of psychology are Wilhelm Wundt and William James.

### 2 Contemporary Approaches to Psychology

Approaches to psychology include biological, behavioral, psychodynamic, humanistic, cognitive, evolutionary, and sociocultural. All of these perspectives consider important questions about human behavior from different but complementary vantage points.

### 3 Psychology's Scientific Method

Psychologists use the scientific method to address research questions. This method involves starting with a theory and then making observations, formulating hypotheses, testing these through empirical research, drawing conclusions, and evaluating these conclusions. The science of psychology is an ongoing conversation among scholars.

### 4 Types of Psychological Research

Three types of research commonly used in psychology are descriptive research (finding out about the basic dimensions of some variable), correlational research (finding out if and how two variables change together), and experimental research (determining the causal relationship between variables). In an experiment, the independent variable is manipulated to see if it produces changes in the dependent variable. Experiments involve comparing two groups: the experimental group (the one that receives the treatment or manipulation of the independent variable)

and the control group (the comparison group or baseline that is equal to the experimental group in every way except for the independent variable). Experimental research relies on random assignment to ensure that the groups are roughly equivalent before the manipulation of the independent variable.

### 5 Research Samples and Settings

Two important decisions that must be made for psychological research are whom to study and where to study them. A sample is the group that participates in a study; the population is the group to which the researcher wishes to generalize the results. A random sample is the best way of ensuring that the sample reflects the population. Research settings include the laboratory as well as real-world, naturalistic contexts. The laboratory allows a great deal of control, but naturalistic settings may give a truer sense of natural behavior.

### 6 Conducting Ethical Research

For all kinds of research, ethical treatment of participants is very important. Participants should leave a psychological study no worse off than they were when they entered. Guiding principles for ethical research in psychology include informed consent, confidentiality, debriefing (participants should be fully informed about the purpose of a study once it is over), and explaining fully the use of deception in a study.

### 7 Learning About Psychology Means Learning About You

In your everyday life and in introductory psychology, you will be exposed to psychological research findings. In encountering psychological research in the media, you should adopt the attitude of a scientist and critically evaluate the research as presented. In introductory psychology, you should make the most of the experience by applying it to your life. Psychology is, after all, the scientific study of you—your behavior, thoughts, goals, and well-being.

## KEY TERMS

psychology, p. 2
science, p. 2
behavior, p. 2
mental processes, p. 2
critical thinking, p. 3

empirical method, p. 4
structuralism, p. 6
functionalism, p. 7
natural selection, p. 7
biological approach, p. 8

neuroscience, p. 9
behavioral approach, p. 9
psychodynamic approach, p. 9
humanistic approach, p. 10
cognitive approach, p. 10

evolutionary approach, p. 10
sociocultural approach, p. 11
variable, p. 13
theory, p. 14
hypothesis, p. 14

operational definition, p. 15
case study, p. 18
correlational research, p. 20
third variable problem, p. 21
longitudinal design, p. 22
experiment, p. 23
random assignment, p. 23

independent variable, p. 24
confederate, p. 24
dependent variable, p. 24
experimental group, p. 24
control group, p. 24
validity, p. 25
external validity, p. 25

internal validity, p. 25
experimenter bias, p. 25
demand characteristics, p. 26
research participant bias, p. 26
placebo effect, p. 26
placebo, p. 26
double-blind experiment, p. 26

population, p. 29
sample, p. 29
random sample, p. 30
naturalistic observation, p. 32

## SELF-TEST

### Multiple Choice

1. The beginning of psychology as a science began in the discipline of
   A. philosophy.
   B. physics.
   C. sociology.
   D. biology.

2. Of the following experimental situations that a structuralist might conduct, the one that reflects the method of introspection is
   A. documenting subjects' descriptions of an experience.
   B. asking subjects to remember a list of words.
   C. testing rats in a maze to see how fast they learn.
   D. rewarding subjects for solving problems.

3. Structuralism focuses on _____, and functionalism focuses on _____.
   A. thoughts; behaviors
   B. the components of the mind; the purposes of the mind
   C. pragmatism; idealism
   D. natural selection; environment

4. The individual most closely associated with behaviorism is
   A. B. F. Skinner.
   B. Charles Darwin.
   C. Wilhelm Wundt.
   D. William James.

5. Of the following, the topic that would be of most interest to a psychodynamic psychologist is
   A. altruism.
   B. unconscious drives.
   C. the adaptiveness of behaviors.
   D. people's thought processes.

6. The type of research design that allows a researcher to test for causation is
   A. correlational design.
   B. longitudinal design.
   C. case study design.
   D. experimental design.

7. A researcher finds that as scores on optimism go up, scores on depression go down. Moreover, she finds a strong relationship between optimism and depression. Which of the following correlation coefficients would be most consistent with her findings?
   A. .38
   B. .79
   C. 2.11
   D. 2.68

8. An experimenter told a research participant that the purpose of the study was to examine people's reaction to media violence. In reality, the purpose was to examine group dynamics. A potential ethical problem for this study would be
   A. debriefing.
   B. confidentiality.
   C. informed consent.
   D. deception.

9. Alfonso is in a study testing the effectiveness of a new type of medication. He is given a pill that contains no actual medicine (a sugar pill). After taking the pill, he reports significantly fewer symptoms. Which of the following is at play?
   A. experimenter bias
   B. placebo effect
   C. external validity
   D. internal validity

10. An example of selecting a random sample is
    A. randomly choosing a group of 50 students from a roster of all students in a school.
    B. randomly choosing a classroom from all classrooms in a school.
    C. randomly choosing students who attended a soccer game.
    D. choosing each 50th student who enters the building's front entrance.

### Apply It!

11. Georgia believes that people are more likely to behave kindly toward others if they are in a good mood. She randomly assigns participants (who are psychology students participating for research credit) to one of two groups. In one group, participants are told to write for 10 minutes about the happiest moment of their life. In the other group, participants write for 10 minutes about a typical day in their life.
    A. Why did Georgia assign participants to groups *randomly*?
    B. In Georgia's study, what are the *independent variable* and the *dependent variable*, and how is each of these operationally defined?
    C. Identify the *experimental group* and the *control group* in Georgia's study.

# 2 The Brain and Behavior

## *Extraordinary Engine: The Human Brain*

In August 2007, Adam Lepak was a first-year community college student who had spent the previous summer touring with his high school friends as a "straight edge" rock band. Late to class one morning, he sped along on his motorcycle. As he swerved to miss a car that had stopped in his lane, he lost control and crashed into the pavement.

After lying unconscious in a hospital bed for six months, Adam began to regain awareness. As he did, the world was eerily different to him. Adam was convinced that his family and friends—who had waited patiently by his bedside, coaxing him to wake up—were impostors who did not seem to recognize that they were fakes. Adam's accident had damaged the regions of his brain responsible for the warm glow of familiarity that comes from recognizing others. His brain no longer detected the feeling of "home." Not only did Adam question the identities of his loved ones, but he also struggled to recognize that the young man looking back at him in the mirror was himself (Carey, 2009).

Today Adam continues his difficult recovery. He has relearned how to walk and talk but has struggled to regain the feeling of familiarity that provides humans with a sense of self. He has to be reminded—and to remind himself repeatedly—that he had a motorcycle accident and that the "impostors" around him are in truth his family and friends.

Adam's case illuminates the brain's role in the precious human experiences of having an identity and of feeling warmth toward others. His experience demonstrates that the brain can potentially repair itself but that such healing requires hard work and active effort.

The brain is extraordinarily complex. Imagine: This intricate organ that you are reading about is the engine that is doing the work of learning this material. The brain is also the organ responsible for the research presented here. In other words, the brain is at once the object of study and the reason we are able to study it.

In this chapter, our focus is the nervous system and its command center—the brain. We will study the essentials of what the brain has come to know about itself, including the biological foundations of human behavior and the brain's extraordinary capacity for adaptation and repair. The chapter concludes with a look at how genetic processes influence who we are as individuals and how we behave.

# 1 The Nervous System

The **nervous system** is the body's electrochemical communication circuitry. The field that studies the nervous system is called *neuroscience,* and the people who study it are *neuroscientists.*

The human nervous system is made up of billions of communicating cells, and it is likely the most intricately organized aggregate of matter on the planet. A single cubic centimeter of the human brain consists of well over 50 million nerve cells, each of which communicates with many other nerve cells in information-processing networks that make the most elaborate computer seem primitive.

**nervous system**
The body's electrochemical communication circuitry.

 *One cubic centimeter of brain = 50 million nerve cells. That's about the size of a snack cube of cheese.*

## Characteristics of the Nervous System

The brain and nervous system guide our interactions with the world, moving the body and directing our adaptation to our environment. Several extraordinary characteristics allow the nervous system to direct our behavior: complexity, integration, adaptability, and electrochemical transmission.

**COMPLEXITY**   The human brain and nervous system are enormously complex. The orchestration of all the billions of nerve cells in the brain—to allow you to sing, dance, write, talk, and think—is an awe-inspiring achievement. As you are reading, your brain is carrying out a multitude of tasks, including seeing, reading, learning, and breathing. Extensive assemblies of nerve cells participate in each of these activities, all at once.

**INTEGRATION**   Neuroscientist Steven Hyman (2001) calls the brain the "great integrator," meaning that the brain does a wonderful job of pulling information together. Sounds, sights, touch, taste, smells, hearing—the brain integrates all of these as we function in the world.

The brain and the nervous system have different levels and many different parts. Brain activity is integrated across these levels through countless interconnections of brain cells and extensive pathways that link different parts of the brain. Each nerve cell communicates, on average, with 10,000 others, making an astronomical number of connections (Bloom, Nelson, & Lazerson, 2001). The evidence for these connections is observable, for example, when a loved one takes your hand. How does your brain know, and tell you, what has happened? Bundles of interconnected nerve cells relay information about the sensation in your hand through the nervous system in very orderly fashion, all the way to the areas of the brain involved in recognizing that someone you love is holding your hand. Then the brain might send a reply back and prompt your hand to give him or her a little squeeze.

**ADAPTABILITY** The world around us is constantly changing. To survive, we must adapt to new conditions. Our brain and nervous system together serve as our agent in adapting to the world. Although nerve cells reside in certain brain regions, they are not fixed, unchanging structures. They have a hereditary, biological foundation, but they are constantly adapting to changes in the body and the environment.

*Adaptation, adaptability, and adapt: Psychologists use these terms when referring to the ability to function in a changing world.*

The term **plasticity** denotes the brain's special capacity for change. You might believe that thinking is a mental process, not a physical one. Yet thinking *is* a physical event, because your every thought is reflected in physical activity in the brain. Moreover, the brain can be changed by experience. London cab drivers who have developed a familiarity with the city show increases in the size of the brain area thought to be responsible for reading maps (Maguire & others, 2000). Think about that: When you change the way you think, you are literally changing the brain's physical processes and even its shape. Your daily experiences contribute to the wiring or rewiring of the brain (Nelson, 2011), just as the experiences of those London cab drivers did (Bavelier & others, 2012).

**plasticity**
The brain's special capacity for change.

**ELECTROCHEMICAL TRANSMISSION** The brain and the nervous system function essentially as an information-processing system, powered by electrical impulses and chemical messengers (Emes & Grant, 2012). When an impulse travels down a nerve cell, or *neuron,* it does so electrically. When that impulse gets to the end of the line, it communicates with the next neuron using chemicals, as we will consider in detail later in this chapter.

*Afferent and efferent are hard to keep straight. It might be helpful to remember that a̲fferent nerves a̲rrive at the brain and spinal cord, while e̲fferent nerves e̲xit the brain and spinal cord—a for afferent and arrive, and e for efferent and exit.*

## Pathways in the Nervous System

As we interact with and adapt to the world, the brain and the nervous system receive and transmit sensory input (like sounds, smells, and flavors), integrate the information received from the environment, and direct the body's motor activities. Information flows into the brain through input from our senses, and the brain makes sense of that information, pulling it together and giving it meaning. In turn, information moves out of the brain to the rest of the body, directing all of the physical things we do (Alstermark & Isa, 2012).

The nervous system possesses specialized pathways that are adapted for different functions. These pathways are made up of afferent nerves, efferent nerves, and neural networks. **Afferent nerves,** or sensory nerves, carry information to the brain and spinal cord. These sensory pathways communicate information about the external environment (for example, seeing a sunrise) and internal body processes (for example, feeling tired or hungry) from sensory receptors to the brain and spinal cord. **Efferent nerves,** or motor nerves, carry information out of the brain and spinal cord—that is, they carry the nervous system's output. These motor pathways communicate information from the brain and spinal cord to other areas of the body, including muscles and glands, telling them to get busy.

Most information processing occurs when information moves through **neural networks.** These networks of nerve cells integrate sensory input and motor output (Marchiori & Warglien, 2011; Wickersham & Feinberg, 2011). For example, as you read your class notes, the input from your eyes is transmitted to your brain and then passed through many neural networks, which translate the characters on the page into neural codes for letters, words, associations, and meanings. Some of the information is stored in the neural networks, and, if you read aloud, some is passed on as messages to your lips

**afferent nerves**
Also called sensory nerves; nerves that carry information about the external environment to the brain and spinal cord via sensory receptors.

**efferent nerves**
Also called motor nerves; nerves that carry information *out of* the brain and spinal cord to other areas of the body.

**neural networks**
Networks of nerve cells that integrate sensory input and motor output.

*When we touch or gaze at an object, electrical charges and chemical messages pulse through our brain, knitting the cells together into pathways and networks for processing the information.*

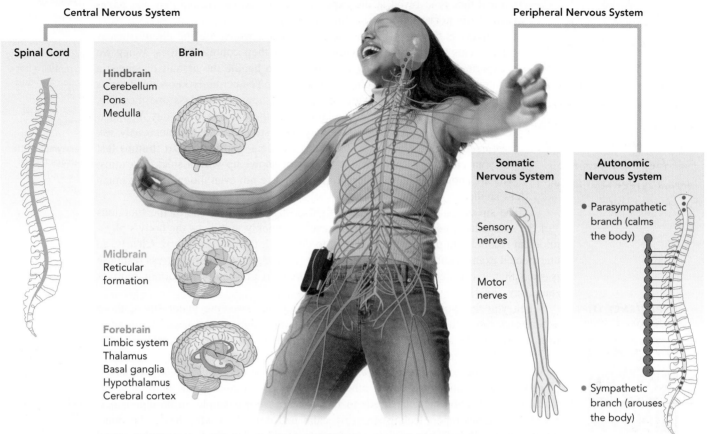

**Central Nervous System**

**Spinal Cord**

**Brain**

**Hindbrain**
Cerebellum
Pons
Medulla

**Midbrain**
Reticular
formation

**Forebrain**
Limbic system
Thalamus
Basal ganglia
Hypothalamus
Cerebral cortex

**Peripheral Nervous System**

**Somatic Nervous System**

Sensory
nerves

Motor
nerves

**Autonomic Nervous System**

• Parasympathetic
  branch (calms
  the body)

• Sympathetic
  branch (arouses
  the body)

**FIGURE 2.1    Major Divisions of the Human Nervous System** The nervous system has two main divisions. One is the *central nervous system* (*left*), which comprises the brain and the spinal cord. The nervous system's other main division is the *peripheral nervous system* (*right*), which itself has two parts—the *somatic nervous system,* which controls sensory and motor neurons, and the *autonomic nervous system,* which monitors processes such as breathing, heart rate, and digestion. These complex systems work together to help us successfully navigate the world.

and tongue. Neural networks make up most of the brain. Working in networks amplifies the brain's computing power.

# Divisions of the Nervous System

This truly elegant system is highly ordered and organized for effective function. Figure 2.1 shows the two primary divisions of the human nervous system: the central nervous system and the peripheral nervous system.

The **central nervous system (CNS)** is made up of the brain and spinal cord. More than 99 percent of all our nerve cells are located in the CNS. The **peripheral nervous system (PNS)** is the network of nerves that connects the brain and spinal cord to other parts of the body. The functions of the peripheral nervous system are to bring information to and from the brain and spinal cord and to carry out the commands of the CNS to execute various muscular and glandular activities.

The peripheral nervous system has two major divisions: the somatic nervous system and the autonomic nervous system. The **somatic nervous system** consists of *sensory nerves,* whose function is to convey information from the skin and muscles to the CNS about conditions such as pain and temperature, and *motor nerves,* whose function is to tell muscles what to do. The function of the **autonomic nervous system** is to take messages to and from the body's internal organs, monitoring such processes as breathing, heart rate, and digestion. The autonomic nervous system also is divided into two parts.

**central nervous system (CNS)**
The brain and spinal cord.

**peripheral nervous system (PNS)**
The network of nerves that connects the brain and spinal cord to other parts of the body.

**somatic nervous system**
The body system consisting of the sensory nerves, whose function is to convey information from the skin and muscles to the CNS about conditions such as pain and temperature, and the motor nerves, whose function is to tell muscles what to do.

**autonomic nervous system**
The body system that takes messages to and from the body's internal organs, monitoring such processes as breathing, heart rate, and digestion.

Sympathetic, parasympathetic—how to distinguish these? Remember that the sympathetic nervous system feels "sympathy" for you when you're stressed out, and prompts you to take action to reduce the stressor, and that the parasympathetic nervous system helps you to "rest and digest."

**EXPERIENCE IT!**
The Nervous System

The first part, the **sympathetic nervous system,** arouses the body to mobilize it for action and thus is involved in the experience of stress; the second part, the **parasympathetic nervous system,** calms the body.

**Stress** is the body's response to **stressors,** which are the circumstances and events that threaten individuals and tax their coping abilities. When we experience stress, our body readies itself to handle the assault of stress; a number of physiological changes take place. You certainly know what stress feels like. Imagine, for example, that you show up for class one morning, and it looks as if everyone else knows that there is a test that day. You hear others talking about how much they have studied, and you nervously ask yourself: "Test? What test?" You start to sweat, and your heart thumps fast in your chest. Sure enough, the instructor shows up with a stack of exams. You are about to be tested on material you have not even thought about, much less studied.

The stress response begins with a fight-or-flight reaction, one of the functions of the sympathetic nervous system. This reaction quickly mobilizes the body's physiological resources to prepare the organism to deal with threats to survival. Clearly, an unexpected exam is not literally a threat to your survival, but the human stress response is such that it can occur in reaction to any threat to personally important motives (Sapolsky, 2004).

When you feel your heart pounding and your hands sweating under stress, those experiences reveal the sympathetic nervous system in action. If you need to run away from a stressor, the sympathetic nervous system sends blood out to your extremities to get you ready to take off.

When we undergo stress, we also experience the release of *corticosteroids,* which are powerful stress hormones (Smith & others, 2011). Corticosteroids in the brain allow us to focus our attention on what needs to be done *now.* For example, in an emergency, people sometimes report feeling strangely calm and doing just what has to be done, whether it is calling 911 or applying pressure to a serious cut. Such experiences reveal the benefits of corticosteroids for humans in times of emergency (Holsboer & Ising, 2010). *Acute stress* is the momentary stress that occurs in response to life experiences. When the stressful situation ends, so does acute stress.

However, we are not in a live-or-die situation most of the time when we experience stress. Indeed, we can even "stress ourselves out" just by thinking. *Chronic stress*—that is, stress that goes on continuously—may lead to persistent autonomic nervous system arousal (Rohleder, 2012). While the sympathetic nervous system is working to meet the demands of whatever is stressing us out, the parasympathetic nervous system is not getting a chance to do its job of maintenance and repair, of digesting food, or of keeping our organs in good working order. Thus, over time, chronic autonomic nervous system activity can break down the immune system (Pervanidou & Chrousos, 2012). Chronic stress is clearly best avoided, although this objective is easier said than done.

Yet the brain, an organ that is itself powerfully affected by chronic stress, can be our ally in preventing such continuous stress. Consider that when you face a challenging situation, you can exploit the brain's abilities and interpret the experience in a less stressful way. For example, you might approach an upcoming exam or an audition for a play not so much as a stressor but as an opportunity to shine. Many cognitive therapists believe that changing the way people think about their life opportunities and experiences can help them live less stressfully (Clark & Beck, 2011; Nay, 2012).

At the beginning of this chapter, you learned how changing the way you think can produce physical changes in the brain. In light of this remarkable capacity, it is reasonable to conclude that you can use your brain's powers to change how you look at life experiences—and maybe even deploy the brain as a defense against stress.

**sympathetic nervous system**
The part of the autonomic nervous system that arouses the body to mobilize it for action and thus is involved in the experience of stress.

**parasympathetic nervous system**
The part of the autonomic nervous system that calms the body.

**stress**
The response of individuals to environmental stressors.

**stressors**
Circumstances and events that threaten individuals and tax their coping abilities and that cause physiological changes to ready the body to handle the assault of stress.

"It was the classic fight or flight response.
Next time, try flight."

Used by permission of CartoonStock, www.CartoonStock.com.

1. The characteristics that allow the nervous system to direct behavior are its complexity, integration, electrochemical transmission, and
   A. constancy.
   B. adaptability.
   C. sensitivity.
   D. fight-or-flight response.

2. Neural networks are networks of nerve cells that integrate sensory input and
   A. the fight-or-flight response.
   B. electrochemical transmission.
   C. bodily processes such as heart rate and digestion.
   D. motor output.

3. When you are in danger, the part of the nervous system that is responsible for an increase in your heart rate is the
   A. central nervous system.
   B. peripheral nervous system.
   C. sympathetic nervous system.
   D. parasympathetic nervous system.

**APPLY IT!** 4. Shannon and Terrell are two college students. Shannon is in a constant state of low-level stress. She spends a lot of time worrying about what might happen, and she gets herself worked up about imagined catastrophes. Terrell is more easy-going, but on his way to class one day he is in a near-miss traffic accident—at the moment he sees the truck coming at him, his body tenses up, his heart races, and he experiences extreme panic. Which answer most accurately identifies the individual who is most likely to catch the cold that is going around their dorm this semester?
A. Shannon, who is experiencing chronic stress
B. Terrell, who is experiencing acute stress
C. Shannon, who is experiencing acute stress
D. Terrell, who is experiencing chronic stress

# 2 Neurons

Within each division of the nervous system, much is happening at the cellular level. Nerve cells, chemicals, and electrical impulses work together to transmit information at speeds of up to 330 miles per hour. As a result, information can travel from your brain to your hands (or vice versa) in just milliseconds (Zoupi, Savvaki, & Karagogeos, 2011).

There are two types of cells in the nervous system: neurons and glial cells. **Neurons** are the nerve cells that handle the information-processing function. The human brain contains about 100 billion neurons. The average neuron is a complex structure with as many as 10,000 physical connections with other cells. Recently, researchers have been especially interested in a special type of neuron called *mirror neurons*. Mirror neurons seem to play a role in imitation and are activated (in primates and humans) when we perform an action but also when we watch someone else perform that same task (Fontana & others, 2011). In addition to imitation, these neurons may play a role in empathy and in our understanding of others, although their function in this regard is a matter of controversy. To read more about these mysterious neurons, see Challenge Your Thinking.

**Glial cells** provide support, nutritional benefits, and other functions in the nervous system (Cooper, Jones, & Comer, 2011; Selvaraj & others, 2012). Glial cells keep neurons running smoothly. These cells are not specialized to process information in the way that neurons are, and there are many more of them in the nervous system than there are neurons. In fact, for every neuron there are about 10 glial cells.

**neurons**
One of two types of cells in the nervous system; neurons are the nerve cells that handle the information-processing function.

**glial cells**
The second of two types of cells in the nervous system; glial cells (also called glia) provide support, nutritional benefits, and other functions and keep neurons running smoothly.

*That's fast! Most of us will never experience driving a car that fast. The supersonic rocket car that holds the world record can drive over 700 miles per hour. Its British developers are shooting for over 1,000 miles per hour. Now, the wisdom of driving a car faster than we can think is another story . . .*

*You might think of glial cells as the pit crew of the nervous system.*

## Specialized Cell Structure

Not all neurons are alike, as they are specialized to handle different information-processing functions. However, all neurons do have some common characteristics. Most neurons are created very early in life, but their shape, size, and connections can change throughout the life span. The way neurons' function reflects the major characteristic of the nervous system described at the beginning of the chapter: plasticity. Neurons can and do change.

**EXPERIENCE IT!**
Mirror Neurons

## Do Mirror Neurons Hold the Key to Social Understanding?

**M**irror neurons are active while we enact a behavior *and* when we passively observe another person performing that behavior (Glenberg, 2011a). That's a big deal, because neurons are specialized: Motor neurons do not respond to sensory information, and sensory neurons do not respond to motor information. Yet mirror neurons appear to respond to *both* kinds of information, doing and seeing (Gallese & others, 2011). This responsiveness to two different kinds of input makes mirror neurons pretty fascinating.

Not fascinated yet? What if you thought that mirror neurons represented a kind of mental telepathy? Cognitive psychologist Cecilia Heyes (2010) describes scientists as "mesmerized" by the way mirror neurons suggest communication without talking. For example, if I see you performing an action, my mirror neurons put my brain in the very same state you are in, even if you do not speak a word. Even if I am not intending to imitate your behavior, mirror neurons in my body will fire. My brain somehow seems to "know" what you are doing—and mentally starts doing it too. In this way, mirror neurons suggest a direct connection between an observer's brain and the person being observed. Such a direct link between individuals—occurring without language, explanation, or effort—is exciting to scientists who are interested in understanding human behavior.

The discovery of mirror neurons has led to provocative predictions about the role of these neurons in imitation, social cognition (that is, thinking about oneself and others), empathy, understanding behavior (Iacoboni, 2009), and even autism, a disorder of neural development characterized by impaired communication and social interaction (Ramachandran & Oberman, 2006). These predictions have met with great controversy. Although some scholars hail mirror neurons as a promising new direction in understanding the origins of human sociability (Ramachandran, 2008), others charge that such claims far overstep the evidence (Gernsbacher, Stevenson, & Schweigart, 2012; Hickok, 2009).

We know that mirror neurons are active when we observe someone perform an action, but does that indicate understanding for the action? The answer depends on what we mean by understanding. Of course, mirror neurons, like other neurons, do not "understand." The idea, rather, is that because of mirror neurons, the human brain is prepared to imitate. Imitation is an especially important behavior in a highly social species such as human beings, and some scholars argue that mirror neurons are a fundamental factor in imitation (Gallese & others, 2011).

Experience plays a role in mirror neuron activation. Mirror neuron activity is higher for behaviors for which we have expertise and lower for behaviors we have never performed. Trained musicians and dancers have different mirror neuron systems than others, and their mirror neurons fire differently while watching another expert perform (Calvo-Merino & others, 2006; D'Ausilio & others, 2006). Mirror neurons do not respond when we observe a behavior that is not part of our typical repertoire; for instance, human mirror neurons do not activate while we watch a dog bark (Rizzolatti & Fabbri-Destro, 2010).

These findings suggest that if mirror neurons are involved in understanding action, they do not cover the full range of behaviors we comprehend. If you watch someone play a violin, having never played one yourself, you still understand what the person is doing (Hickok, 2009; Hickok & Hauser, 2010). So, we can understand behavior even without the involvement of mirror neurons. Some researchers question whether mirror neurons play a central role in *understanding* behavior at all (Brass & others, 2007; Hickok, 2009; Kilner & Frith, 2008). While acknowledging that there are many ways to gain an understanding of another person's action, others argue that mirror neurons provide a unique route—from the inside out (Rizzolatti & Sinigaglia, 2010).

The potential role of mirror neurons in autism is especially controversial (Glenberg, 2011b). Researchers who champion mirror neurons as an important evolutionary adaptation suggest that these neurons may hold the key to illuminating what makes us human (Ramachandran, 2008). They assert that "broken mirror neurons" may help to explain the deficits seen in individuals with autism (Ramachandran & Oberman, 2006). Other researchers strongly criticize this theory, contending that we know far too little about mirror neurons to claim a central role for them in autism; they point to mixed results in research linking mirror neuron function to autism (Gallese & others, 2011).

Mirror neurons have powerfully captured neuroscientists' attention. This fascination perhaps reveals an important truth: that the mystery of human social behavior is an immensely compelling area of scientific inquiry. The notion that the key to this mystery might lie in a set of specialized neurons is, well, simply mesmerizing.

### What Do You Think?

- Why has the discovery of mirror neurons led to such excitement and controversy?

- What characteristics make human beings different from other animals? How would you study those characteristics?

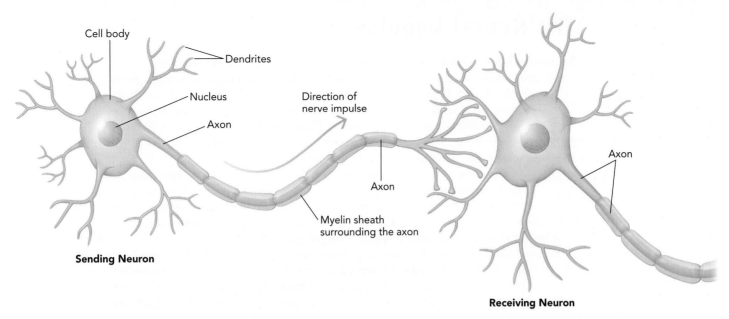

Cell body

Dendrites

Nucleus

Direction of
nerve impulse

Axon

Axon

Myelin sheath
surrounding the axon

Axon

**Sending Neuron**

**Receiving Neuron**

**FIGURE 2.2** **The Neuron** The drawing shows the parts of a neuron and the connection between one neuron and another. Note the cell body, the branching of dendrites, and the axon with a myelin sheath.

**cell body**
The part of the neuron that contains the nucleus, which directs the manufacture of substances that the neuron needs for growth and maintenance.

Every neuron has a cell body, dendrites, and an axon (Figure 2.2). The **cell body** contains the nucleus, which directs the manufacture of substances that the neuron needs for growth and maintenance. **Dendrites,** treelike fibers projecting from a neuron, receive information and orient it toward the neuron's cell body. Most nerve cells have numerous dendrites, which increase their surface area, allowing each neuron to receive input from many other neurons. The **axon** is the part of the neuron that carries information away from the cell body toward other cells. Although extremely thin (1/10,000th of an inch—a human hair by comparison is 1/1,000 of an inch), axons can be very long, with many branches. Some extend more than 3 feet—from the top of the brain to the base of the spinal cord.

**dendrites**
Treelike fibers projecting from a neuron, which receive information and orient it toward the neuron's cell body.

**axon**
The part of the neuron that carries information away from the cell body toward other cells.

Covering all surfaces of neurons, including the dendrites and axons, are very thin cellular membranes that are much like the surface of a balloon. The neuronal membranes are semipermeable, meaning that they contain tiny holes, or channels, that allow only certain substances to pass into and out of the neurons.

**myelin sheath**
A layer of fat cells that encases and insulates most axons.

A **myelin sheath,** consisting of a layer of cells containing fat, encases and insulates most axons. By insulating axons, myelin sheaths speed up transmission of nerve impulses (Lu & others, 2011). Numerous disorders are associated with problems in either the creation or the maintenance of this vital insulation. One of them is multiple sclerosis (MS), a degenerative disease of the nervous system in which myelin hardens, disrupting the flow of information through the neurons. Symptoms of MS include blurry and double vision, tingling sensations throughout the body, and general weakness.

The myelin sheath developed as the nervous system evolved. As brain size increased, it became necessary for information to travel over longer distances in the nervous system. Axons without myelin sheaths are not very good conductors of electricity. With the insulation of myelin sheaths, axons transmit electrical impulses and convey information much more rapidly (Aggarwal & others, 2011). We can compare the myelin sheath's development to the evolution of interstate highways as cities grew. Highways keep fast-moving, long-distance traffic from getting snarled by slow local traffic.

# The Neural Impulse

*The rate of the blips determines the intensity of the impulse. So, if you are dying of suspense while reading about neural impulses (and who isn't?), the blips are happening faster as you rush to turn each page.*

To transmit information to other neurons, a neuron sends brief electrical impulses (let's call them "blips") through its axon to the next neuron. As you reach to turn this page, hundreds of such impulses will stream down the axons in your arm to tell your muscles when to flex and how quickly. By changing the rate of the signals, or blips, the neuron can vary its message. Those impulses traveling down the axon are electrical. How does a neuron—a living cell—generate electricity? To answer this question, we need to examine the axon.

The axon is a tube encased in a membrane. The membrane has hundreds and thousands of tiny gates in it. These gates are generally closed, but they can open. We call the membrane *semipermeable* because fluids can sometimes flow in and out of these gates. Indeed, there are fluids both inside and outside the axon. Floating in those fluids are electrically charged particles called *ions*.

Some of these ions, notably sodium and potassium, carry positive charges. Negatively charged ions of chlorine and other elements also are present. The membrane surrounding the axon prevents negative and positive ions from randomly flowing into or out of the cell. The neuron creates electrical signals by moving positive and negative ions back and forth through its outer membrane. How does the movement of ions across the membrane occur? Those tiny gates mentioned above, called *ion channels,* open and close to let the ions pass into and out of the cell. Normally when the neuron is *resting,* or not transmitting information, the ion channels are closed, and a slight negative charge is present along the inside of the cell membrane. On the outside of the cell membrane, the charge is positive. Because of the difference in charge, the membrane of the resting neuron is said to be *polarized,* with most negatively charged ions on the inside of the cell and most positively charged ions on the outside. This polarization creates a voltage between the inside and the outside of the axon wall (Figure 2.3). That voltage, called the neuron's **resting potential,** is between −60 and −75 millivolts. (A millivolt is 1/1000 of a volt.)

**resting potential**
The stable, negative charge of an inactive neuron.

For ions, it is true that opposites attract. The negatively charged ions inside the membrane and the positively charged ions outside the membrane will rush to each other if given the chance. Impulses that travel down the neuron do so by opening and closing ion channels, allowing the ions to flow in and out.

A neuron becomes activated when an incoming impulse—a reaction to, say, a pinprick or the sight of someone's face—raises the neuron's voltage, and the sodium gates at the base of the axon open briefly. This action allows positively charged sodium ions to flow

**FIGURE 2.3  The Resting Potential** An oscilloscope measures the difference in electrical potential between two electrodes. When one electrode is placed inside an axon at rest and one is placed outside, the electrical potential inside the cell is −70 millivolts (mV) relative to the outside. This potential difference is due to the separation of positive (+) and negative (−) charges along the membrane.

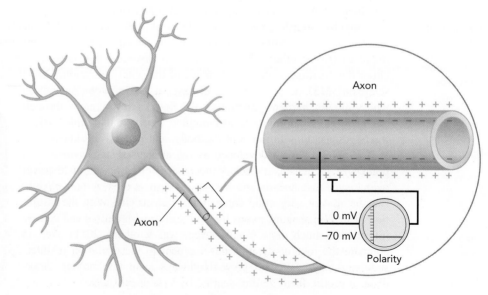

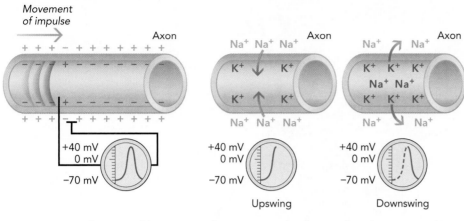

**FIGURE 2.4 The Action Potential**
An action potential is a brief wave of positive electrical charge that sweeps down the axon as the sodium channels in the axon membrane open and close. (a) The action potential causes a change in electrical potential as it moves along the axon. (b) The movements of sodium ions (Na$^+$) and potassium ions (K$^+$) into and out of the axon cause the electrical changes.

(a) Action potential generated by an impulse within a neuron

(b) Movement of sodium (Na$^+$) and potassium (K$^+$) ions responsible for the action potential

into the neuron, creating a more positively charged neuron and *depolarizing* the membrane by decreasing the charge difference between the fluids inside and outside the neuron. Then potassium channels open, and positively charged potassium ions move out through the neuron's semipermeable membrane. This outflow returns the neuron to a negative charge. Then the same process occurs as the next group of channels flips open briefly. So it goes all the way down the axon, like a long row of cabinet doors opening and closing in sequence. It is hard to imagine, but this simple system of opening and closing tiny doors is responsible for the fluid movements of a ballet dancer and the flying fingers of a pianist playing a concerto.

The term **action potential** describes the brief wave of positive electrical charge that sweeps down the axon (Figure 2.4). An action potential lasts only about 1/1000 of a second, because the sodium channels can stay open for only a very brief time. They quickly close again and become reset for the next action potential. When a neuron sends an action potential, it is commonly said to be "firing."

The action potential abides by the **all-or-nothing principle:** Once the electrical impulse reaches a certain level of intensity, called its *threshold,* it fires and moves all the way down the axon without losing any of its intensity. The impulse traveling down an axon can be compared to the burning fuse of a firecracker. Whether you use a match or blowtorch to light the fuse, once the fuse has been lit, the spark travels quickly and with the same intensity down the fuse.

**action potential**
The brief wave of positive electrical charge that sweeps down the axon.

**all-or-nothing principle**
The principle that once the electrical impulse reaches a certain level of intensity (its threshold), it fires and moves all the way down the axon without losing any intensity.

## Synapses and Neurotransmitters

The movement of an impulse down an axon may be compared to a crowd's "wave" motion in a stadium. With the wave, there is a problem, however—the aisles. How does the wave get across the aisle? Similarly, neurons do not touch each other directly, and electricity cannot travel over the space between them. Yet somehow neurons manage to communicate. This is where the chemical part of electrochemical transmission comes in. Neurons communicate with each other through chemicals that carry messages across the space. This connection between one neuron and another is one of the most intriguing and highly researched areas of contemporary neuroscience (Emes & Grant, 2012). Figure 2.5 gives an overview of how this connection between neurons takes place.

**SYNAPTIC TRANSMISSION** **Synapses** are tiny spaces between neurons; the gap between neurons is referred to as a *synaptic gap.* Most synapses lie between the axon of one neuron and the dendrites or cell body of another neuron (Turrigiano, 2011).

**synapses**
Tiny spaces between neurons; the gaps between neurons are referred to as *synaptic gaps.*

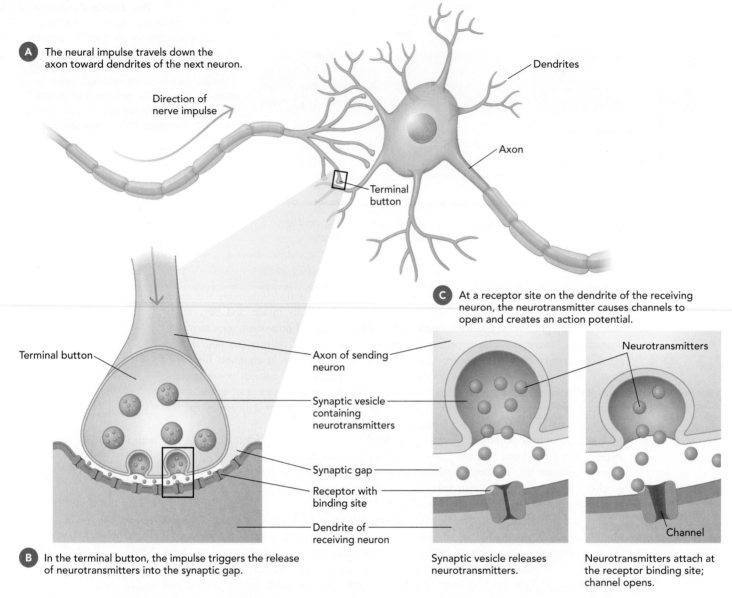

**A** The neural impulse travels down the axon toward dendrites of the next neuron.

Dendrites

Direction of nerve impulse

Axon

Terminal button

**C** At a receptor site on the dendrite of the receiving neuron, the neurotransmitter causes channels to open and creates an action potential.

Terminal button

Axon of sending neuron

Synaptic vesicle containing neurotransmitters

Neurotransmitters

Synaptic gap

Receptor with binding site

Dendrite of receiving neuron

Channel

**B** In the terminal button, the impulse triggers the release of neurotransmitters into the synaptic gap.

Synaptic vesicle releases neurotransmitters.

Neurotransmitters attach at the receptor binding site; channel opens.

**FIGURE 2.5** **How Synapses and Neurotransmitters Work** (*A*) The axon of the *presynaptic* (sending) neuron meets dendrites of the *postsynaptic* (receiving) neuron. (*B*) This is an enlargement of one synapse, showing the synaptic gap between the two neurons, the terminal button, and the synaptic vesicles containing a neurotransmitter. (*C*) This is an enlargement of the receptor site. Note how the neurotransmitter opens the channel on the receptor site, triggering the neuron to fire.

Before an impulse can cross the synaptic gap, it must be converted into a chemical signal.

Each axon branches out into numerous fibers that end in structures called *terminal buttons*. Stored in very tiny synaptic vesicles (sacs) within the terminal buttons are chemical substances called **neurotransmitters.** As their name suggests, neurotransmitters transmit, or carry, information across the synaptic gap to the next neuron. When a nerve impulse reaches the terminal button, it triggers the release of neurotransmitter molecules from the synaptic vesicles (Liu & others, 2011). The neurotransmitter molecules flood the synaptic gap. Their movements are random, but some of them bump into receptor sites in the next neuron.

The neurotransmitters are like pieces of a puzzle, and the receptor sites on the next neuron are differently shaped spaces. If the shape of the receptor site corresponds to the shape of the neurotransmitter molecule, the neurotransmitter acts like a key to open the

**neurotransmitters**
Chemical substances that are stored in very tiny sacs within the terminal buttons and involved in transmitting information across a synaptic gap to the next neuron.

receptor site, so that the neuron can receive the signals coming from the previous neuron. After delivering its message, some of the neurotransmitter is used up in the production of energy, and some of it is reabsorbed by the axon that released it to await the next neural impulse. This reabsorption is termed *reuptake*. Essentially, a message in the brain is delivered across the synapse by a neurotransmitter, which pours out of the terminal button just as the message approaches the synapse.

The neurotransmitter-like venom of the black widow spider does its harm by disturbing neurotransmission.

**NEUROCHEMICAL MESSENGERS**   There are many different neurotransmitters. Each plays a specific role and functions in a specific pathway. Whereas some neurotransmitters stimulate or excite neurons to fire, others can inhibit neurons from firing (Ellender & others, 2011). Some neurotransmitters are both excitatory *and* inhibitory.

As the neurotransmitter moves across the synaptic gap to the receiving neuron, its molecules might spread out, or they might be confined to a small space. The molecules might come in rapid sequence or might be spaced out. The receiving neuron integrates this information before reacting to it.

Neurotransmitters fit into the receptor sites like keys in keyholes. Other substances, such as drugs, can sometimes fit into those receptor sites as well, producing a variety of effects. Similarly, many animal venoms, such as that of the black widow spider, are neurotransmitter-like substances that act by disturbing neurotransmission.

Most neurons secrete only one type of neurotransmitter, but often many different neurons are simultaneously secreting different neurotransmitters into the synaptic gaps of a single neuron. At any given time, a neuron is receiving a mixture of messages from the neurotransmitters. At its receptor sites, the chemical molecules bind to the membrane and either excite the neuron, bringing it closer to the threshold at which it will fire, or inhibit the neuron from firing. Usually the binding of an excitatory neurotransmitter from one neuron will not be enough to trigger an action potential in the receiving neuron. Triggering an action potential often takes a number of neurons sending excitatory messages simultaneously or fewer neurons sending rapid-fire excitatory messages.

Researchers have identified more than 100 neurotransmitters in the brain alone, each with a unique chemical makeup. The rapidly growing list is likely to increase beyond 100 (G. B. Johnson, 2012). In organisms ranging from snails to whales, neuroscientists have found the same neurotransmitter molecules that our own brains use. To get a better sense of what neurotransmitters do, let's consider seven that have major effects on behavior.

*Botox injections contain botulin, a poison that, by destroying ACh, blocks the recipient's facial muscles from moving. Wrinkles, as well as many genuine facial expressions, are thereby prevented.*

*Acetylcholine*   Acetylcholine (ACh) usually stimulates the firing of neurons and is involved in the action of muscles, learning, and memory (Kalmbach, Hedrick, & Waters, 2012). ACh is found throughout the central and peripheral nervous systems. The venom of the black widow spider causes ACh to gush out of the synapses between the spinal cord and skeletal muscles, producing violent spasms.

Individuals with Alzheimer disease, a degenerative brain disorder that involves a decline in memory, have an acetylcholine deficiency (Griguoli & Cherubini, 2012). Some of the drugs that alleviate the symptoms of Alzheimer disease do so by compensating for the loss of the brain's supply of acetylcholine.

*GABA*   GABA (gamma aminobutyric acid) is found throughout the central nervous system. It is believed to be the neurotransmitter in as many as one-third of the brain's synapses. GABA is important in the brain because it keeps many neurons from firing (Richter & others, 2012). In this way, it helps to control the precision of the signal being carried from one neuron to the next. Low levels of

*You can think of GABA as the brain's brake pedal.*

GABA are linked with anxiety. Antianxiety drugs increase the inhibiting effects of GABA.

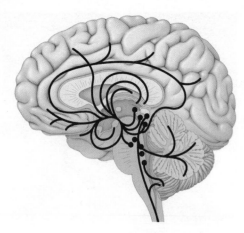

**FIGURE 2.6  Serotonin Pathways**
Each of the neurotransmitters in the brain has specific pathways in which it functions. Shown here are the pathways for serotonin.

*Norepinephrine*  *Norepinephrine* inhibits the firing of neurons in the central nervous system, but it excites the heart muscle, intestines, and urogenital tract. Stress stimulates the release of norepinephrine (Wong & others, 2012). This neurotransmitter also helps to control alertness. Too little norepinephrine is associated with depression, and too much triggers agitated, manic states. For example, amphetamines and cocaine cause hyperactive, manic states of behavior by rapidly increasing brain levels of norepinephrine (Janak, Bowers, & Corbit, 2012).

Recall from the beginning of the chapter that one of the most important characteristics of the brain and nervous system is integration. In the case of neurotransmitters, they may work in teams of two or more. For example, norepinephrine works with acetylcholine to regulate states of sleep and wakefulness.

*Dopamine*  *Dopamine* helps to control voluntary movement and affects sleep, mood, attention, learning, and the ability to recognize rewards in the environment (Meyer, 2012). Dopamine is related to the personality trait of extraversion (being outgoing and gregarious), as we will see in Chapter 10. Stimulant drugs such as cocaine and amphetamines produce excitement, alertness, elevated mood, decreased fatigue, and sometimes increased motor activity mainly by activating dopamine receptors (Perez-Costas, Melendez-Ferro, & Roberts, 2010).

Low levels of dopamine are associated with Parkinson disease, in which physical movements deteriorate (Berthet & others, 2012). High levels of dopamine are associated with schizophrenia (Eriksen, Jorgensen, & Gether, 2010), a severe psychological disorder that we will examine in Chapter 12.

*Serotonin*  *Serotonin* is involved in the regulation of sleep, mood, attention, and learning. In regulating states of sleep and wakefulness, it teams with acetylcholine and norepinephrine. Lowered levels of serotonin are associated with depression (Karg & Sen, 2012). The antidepressant drug Prozac works by slowing down the reuptake of serotonin into terminal buttons, thereby increasing brain levels of serotonin (Little, Zhang, & Cook, 2006). Figure 2.6 shows the brain pathways for serotonin. There are 15 known types of serotonin receptors in the brain (Hoyer, Hannon, & Martin, 2002), and each type of antidepressant drug has its effects on different receptors.

*Endorphins*  *Endorphins* are natural opiates that mainly stimulate the firing of neurons. Endorphins shield the body from pain and elevate feelings of pleasure. A long-distance runner, a woman giving birth, and a person in shock after a car wreck all have elevated levels of endorphins (Mahler & others, 2009).

As early as the fourth century B.C.E., the Greeks used wild poppies to induce euphoria. More than 2,000 years later, the magical formula behind opium's addictive action was finally discovered. In the early 1970s, scientists found that opium plugs into a sophisticated system of natural opiates that lie deep within the brain's pathways (Pert, 1999; Pert & Snyder, 1973). Morphine (the most important narcotic of opium) mimics the action of endorphins by stimulating receptors in the brain involved with pleasure and pain (Vetter & others, 2006).

*Research has linked the hormone oxytocin to bonding between parents and their newborn.*

*Oxytocin*  *Oxytocin* is a hormone and neurotransmitter that plays an important role in the experience of love and social bonding. A powerful surge of oxytocin is released in mothers who have just given birth, and oxytocin is related to the onset of lactation and breast feeding (Vrachnis & others, 2012). Oxytocin, however, is not only involved in a mother's ability to provide nourishment for her baby (Carter & others, 2007). It is also a factor in the experience of parents who find themselves "in love at first sight" with their newborn (Young, 2009).

Oxytocin is released as part of the sexual orgasm and is thought to play a role in the human tendency to feel pleasure during orgasm and to form emotional bonds with romantic partners (Magon & Kaira, 2011). Provocative research has related oxytocin to the way that women respond to stress. According to Shelley Taylor (2001, 2007, 2011a, 2011b), women under stress do not experience the classic fight-or-flight response—rather, the influx of oxytocin suggests that women may seek bonds with others when under stress. Taylor refers to this response as "tend and befriend."

**DRUGS AND NEUROTRANSMITTERS**   Most drugs that influence behavior do so mainly by interfering with the work of neurotransmitters (Hart, Ksir, & Ray, 2011). Drugs can mimic or increase the effects of a neurotransmitter, or they can block those effects. An **agonist** is a drug that mimics or increases a neurotransmitter's effects. For example, the drug morphine mimics the actions of endorphins by stimulating receptors in the brain and spinal cord associated with pleasure and pain. An **antagonist** is a drug that blocks a neurotransmitter's effects. For example, drugs used to treat schizophrenia interfere with the activity of dopamine.

**antagonist**
A drug that blocks a neurotransmitter's effects.

**agonist**
A drug that mimics or increases a neurotransmitter's effects.

# Neural Networks

So far, we have focused mainly on how a single neuron functions and on how a nerve impulse travels from one neuron to another. Now let's look at how large numbers of neurons work together to integrate incoming information and coordinate outgoing information. Figure 2.7 shows a simplified drawing of a neural network, or pathway. This diagram gives you an idea of how the activity of one neuron is linked with that of many others.

Some neurons have short axons and communicate with other, nearby neurons. Other neurons have long axons and communicate with circuits of neurons some distance away. These neural networks are not static (Fietta & Fietta, 2011). They can be altered through changes in the strength of synaptic connections. Any piece of information, such as a name, might be embedded in hundreds or even thousands of connections between neurons (Wickersham & Feinberg, 2012). In this way, human activities such as being attentive, memorizing, and thinking are distributed over a wide range of connected neurons. The strength of these connected neurons determines how well you remember the information (Goldman, 2009).

*There's a big hint here for how to study successfully. When your goal is to remember something, the best way is to build a neural network. That means making connections between the material and other things in your life—experiences, family, everyday habits. Actively engaging with the material will create neural networks to help you remember.*

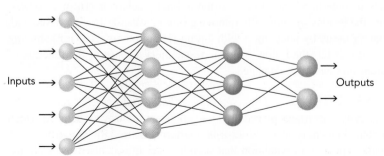

**FIGURE 2.7   An Example of a Neural Network** Inputs (information from the environment and from sensory receptors, such as the details of a person's face) become embedded in extensive connections between neurons in the brain. This embedding process leads to outputs such as remembering the person's face.

Inputs →

Outputs

1. The part of the neuron that carries information away from the cell body toward other cells is the
   A. dendrite.
   B. synapse.
   C. nucleus.
   D. axon.

2. The law stating that once the electrical impulse reaches its threshold, it fires and moves down the axon without losing intensity is called
   A. neurotransmission.
   B. the action potential.
   C. the neural impulse.
   D. the all-or-nothing principle.

3. The chemical substances that carry information across the synaptic gap to the next neuron are called
   A. neurotransmitters.
   B. synapses.
   C. endorphins.
   D. hormones.

APPLY IT! 4. Many years ago some researchers found that when people were experiencing stressful, threatening circumstances—in this case, getting a painful electrical shock—they did not "fight" and they did not "flee." Instead, they asked for a friend to sit by them during the shocks. Which of the following helps to explain this "misery loves company" effect?
A. The participants were all men.
B. The participants were all women.
C. The participants had faulty autonomic nervous systems.
D. The participants had serious psychological disorders.

# 3 Structures of the Brain and Their Functions

Of course, the human body's extensive networks of neurons are not visible to the naked eye. Fortunately technology is available to help neuroscientists form pictures of the structure and organization of neurons and the larger structures they make up without harming the organism being studied. This section explores techniques that scientists use in brain research and discusses what these tools reveal about the brain's structures and functions. We pay special attention to the cerebral cortex, the region of the brain that is most relevant to the topics in this book.

## How Researchers Study the Brain and Nervous System

Early knowledge of the human brain came mostly from studies of individuals who had suffered brain damage from injury or disease or who had brain surgery to relieve another condition. Modern discoveries have relied largely on technology that enables researchers to "look inside" the brain while it is at work. Let's examine some of these innovative techniques.

**BRAIN LESIONING** *Brain lesioning* is an abnormal disruption in the tissue of the brain resulting from injury or disease. In a lab setting, neuroscientists produce lesions in laboratory animals to determine the effects on the animal's behavior (Hosp & others, 2011). They create the lesions by surgically removing brain tissue, destroying tissue with a laser, or eliminating tissue by injecting it with a drug (Ho & others, 2011). Examining the person or animal that has the lesion gives the researchers a sense of the function of the part of the brain that has been damaged.

**ELECTRICAL RECORDING** The *electroencephalograph (EEG)* records the brain's electrical activity. Electrodes placed on the scalp detect brain-wave activity, which is recorded on a chart known as an *electroencephalogram* (Figure 2.8). This device can assess brain damage, epilepsy (a condition that produces seizures, caused by abnormal electrical surges in the brain), and other problems (Rosenthal, 2012). Paul Ekman,

Richard Davidson, and Wallace Friesen (1990) measured EEG activity during emotional experiences provoked by film clips. Individuals in this study watched amusing film clips (such as a puppy playing with flowers, and monkeys taking a bath) as well as clips likely to provoke fear or disgust (a leg amputation and a third-degree burn victim). How does the brain respond to such stimuli? The researchers found that while watching the amusing clips, people tended to exhibit more left than right prefrontal activity, as shown in EEGs. In contrast, when the participants viewed the fear-provoking films, the right prefrontal area was generally more active than the left.

Do these differences generalize to overall differences in feelings of happiness? They just might. Heather Urry and her colleagues (2004) found that individuals who have relatively more left than right prefrontal activity (what is called *prefrontal asymmetry*) tend to rate themselves higher on a number of measures of well-being, including self-acceptance, positive relations with others, purpose in life, and life satisfaction.

Not every recording of brain activity is made with surface electrodes that are attached to the scalp. In *single-unit recording*, which provides information about a single neuron's electrical activity, a thin probe is inserted in or near an individual neuron. The probe transmits the neuron's electrical activity to an amplifier so that researchers can "see" the activity.

**BRAIN IMAGING** For years, medical practitioners have used X rays to reveal damage inside and outside the body, both in the brain and in other locations. A single X ray of the brain is hard to interpret, however, because it shows a two-dimensional image of the three-dimensional interior of the brain. An improved technique, *computerized axial tomography* (CAT scan or CT scan), produces a three-dimensional image obtained from X rays of the head that are assembled into a composite image by a computer. The CT scan provides valuable information about the location and extent of damage involving stroke, language disorder, or loss of memory (Pasi, Poggesi, & Pantoni, 2011).

*Positron-emission tomography* (PET scan) is based on metabolic changes in the brain related to activity. PET measures the amount of glucose in various areas of the brain and then sends this information to a computer for analysis. Neurons use glucose for energy, so glucose levels vary with the levels of activity throughout the brain. Tracing the amounts of glucose generates a picture of activity levels throughout the brain.

An interesting application of the PET technique is the work of Stephen Kosslyn and colleagues (1996) on mental imagery, the brain's ability to create perceptual states in the absence of external stimuli. For instance, if you were to think of your favorite song right now, you could "hear" it in your mind's ear; or if you reflected on your mother's face, you could probably "see" it in your mind's eye. Research using PET scans has shown that often the same area of the brain—a location called Area 17—is activated when we think of seeing something as when we are actually seeing it. However, Area 17 is not always activated for all of us when we imagine a visual image. Kosslyn and his colleagues asked their participants to visualize a letter in the alphabet and then asked those individuals to answer some yes or no questions about the letter. For instance, a person might be thinking of the letter C and have to answer the question "Does it have curvy lines?" The answer would be yes. If the person was thinking of *F*, the answer would be no. The fascinating result of this work was that individuals who showed brain activation on the PET scan in Area 17 while engaged in the visualization task answered the questions faster than those who were not using Area 17.

Another technique, *magnetic resonance imaging (MRI)*, involves creating a magnetic field around a person's body and using radio waves to construct images of the person's tissues and biochemical activities. The magnetic field of the magnet used to create an

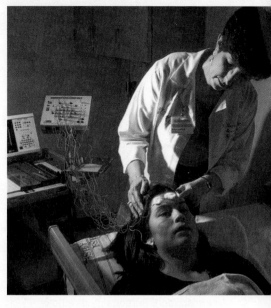

**FIGURE 2.8   An EEG Recording**
The electroencephalograph (EEG) is widely used in sleep research. It has led to some major breakthroughs in understanding sleep by showing how the brain's electrical activity changes during sleep. Do you know anyone who has experienced a stroke or brain-damaging head injury? These experiences create lesioned areas in the brain.

So, although human brains are similar to one another in some ways, in other ways, all brains are unique.

# INTERSECTION

## Neuroscience and Personality: Are Some Brains Nicer Than Others?

Upon meeting someone for the first time, probably one of the things you notice is whether the person is kind, warm, and genuine (think of the nicest person you know) or hostile, cold, mean, and antagonistic (think of Simon Cowell from *The X Factor* and *American Idol*). Personality psychologists refer to "niceness" as *agreeableness,* a trait that reflects the tendency to be kind, altruistic, and compassionate. Agreeable people are cooperative rather than competitive, and polite rather than rude. When measured using questionnaire items such as "I try to be courteous to everyone I meet" and "Most people I know like me," agreeableness is associated with many positive personal qualities, including altruism, honesty, and kindness (Graziano & Tobin, 2009; Hall & others, 2010; MacDonald, Bore, & Munro, 2008). Might particular brain differences be associated with agreeableness?

Colin DeYoung and his colleagues (2010) investigated this question. They asked 116 adults to complete questionnaires measuring aspects of their personalities, including agreeable-

ness, and then used MRI scans to examine whether personality characteristics were related to structural differences in the brain. In this study, the researchers specifically looked at the correlation between personality traits and volume in various brain areas. They found that agreeableness was associated with greater volume in the *fusiform face area,* a dime-size location on the right hemisphere (just above the ear) that is believed to play a role in face recognition (Wiese & others, 2012). Agreeableness was also related to greater volume in the *posterior cingulate cortex,* a brain area associated with empathy and understanding other people's beliefs (Saxe & Powell, 2006).

What does this research tell us about personality and brain? Does a person's brain structure make that individual nicer? Remember that the brain is influenced by experience. Just as cab drivers developed different connections in their brains after learning London's map, agreeable people might be creating nicer brains by behaving kindly.

\\ **What kind of brain are you creating in your typical behavior?**

MRI image is over 50,000 times more powerful than the earth's magnetic field (Parry & Matthews, 2002). MRI generates very clear pictures of the brain's interior, does not require injecting the brain with a substance, and (unlike X rays) does not pose a problem of radiation overexposure (Nyberg, 2004). Getting an MRI scan involves lying still in a large metal barrel-like tunnel. MRI scans provide an excellent picture of the architecture of the brain and allow us to see if and how experience affects brain structure. In one MRI study, Katrin Amunts and colleagues (1997) documented a link between the number of years a person has practiced musical skills (playing the piano, for example) and the size of the brain region that is responsible for controlling hand movements.

Recently, MRI has been applied to the emerging neuroscience of personality. Personality psychology (see Chapter 10) focuses on the ways individuals differ from one another on dimensions such as extraversion and emotional stability. To read about work in this area, check out the Intersection.

Although MRI reveals considerable information about brain structure, it cannot portray brain function. Other techniques, however, can serve as a window on the brain in action (Sperling, 2011). The newest such method, *functional magnetic resonance imaging,* or *fMRI,* allows scientists literally to see what is happening in the brain while it is working (Figure 2.9). Like the PET scan, fMRI rests on the idea that mental activity is associated with changes in the brain. While PET is about the use of glucose as fuel for thinking, fMRI exploits changes in blood oxygen that occur in association with brain activity. When part of the brain is working, oxygenated blood rushes into the area. This oxygen, however, is more than is needed. In a sense, fMRI is based on the fact that thinking is like running sprints. When you run the 100-yard dash, blood rushes to the muscles in your legs, carrying oxygen. Right after you stop, you might feel a tightness in your leg, because the oxygen has not all been used. Similarly, if an area of the brain is hard at work—for example, solving a math problem—the increased activity leads to a surplus of oxygenated blood. This "extra" oxygen allows the brain activity to be imaged.

Getting an fMRI involves reclining in the same large metal barrel as does an MRI, but in the case of fMRI, the person is active—listening to audio signals sent by the researcher through headphones or watching visual images that are presented on a screen mounted overhead. Pictures of the brain are taken, both while the brain is at rest and while it is engaging in an activity such as listening to music, looking at a picture, or making a decision. By comparing the at-rest picture to the active picture, fMRI reveals what specific brain activity is associated with the mental experience being studied. fMRI technology is one of the most exciting methodological advances to hit psychology in a long time.

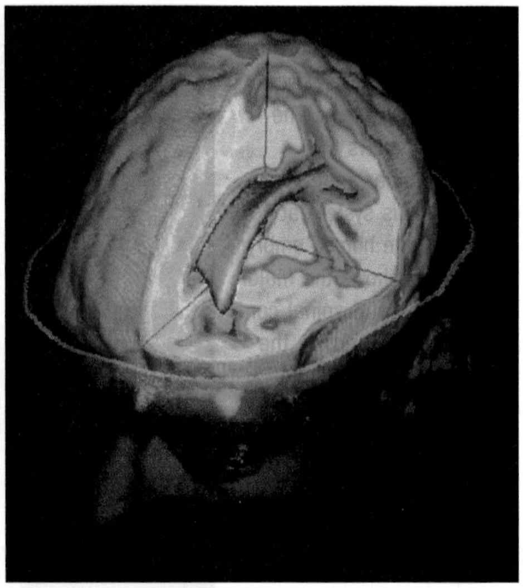

FIGURE 2.9 **Functional Magnetic Resonance Imaging (fMRI)** Through fMRI, scientists can literally see what areas of the brain are active during a task by monitoring oxygenated blood levels.

Note that saying that fMRI tells us about the brain activity *associated* with a mental experience is a *correlational* statement. As we saw in Chapter 1, correlations point to the association between variables, not to the potential causal link between them. Although, for example, identifying a picture as a cat may relate to activation in a particular brain area, we do not know if recognizing the cat *caused* the brain activity (Dien, 2009).

An additional method for studying brain functioning, and one that *does* allow for causal inferences, is *transcranial magnetic stimulation (TMS)* (Lepage & Theoret, 2010). First introduced in 1985 (Barker, Jalinous, & Freeston, 1985), TMS is often combined with brain-imaging techniques to establish causal links between brain activity and behavior, to examine neuronal functioning following brain-injuring events such as accidents and strokes, and even to treat some neurological and psychological disorders.

*Sorry, lefties! Most fMRI studies include only right handed people. As we will see later, handedness can influence brain structure.*

In the TMS procedure, magnetic coils are placed over the person's head and directed at a particular brain area. TMS uses a rapidly changing magnetic field to induce brief electric current pulses in the brain, and these pulses trigger action potentials in neurons (Siebner & others, 2009). Immediately following this burst of action potentials, activity in the targeted brain area is inhibited, causing what is known as a *virtual lesion*. Completely painless, this technique, when used with brain imaging, allows scientists to examine the role of various brain regions. If a brain region is *associated* with a behavior, as demonstrated using fMRI or PET, then the temporary disruption of processing in that area should disrupt that behavior as well. So, for instance, if researchers were doing a study involving the cat recognition example described above, they might use TMS to disrupt the brain area that was associated with cat recognition and see whether the study's participants are temporarily unable to identify a picture of the feline.

*It sounds kinda scary, huh? But it's not. TMS is also used to treat some psychological disorders.*

## How the Brain Is Organized

As a human embryo develops inside its mother's womb, the nervous system begins forming as a long, hollow tube on the embryo's back. At 3 weeks or so after conception, cells making up the tube differentiate into a mass of neurons, most of which then develop into three major regions of the brain: the hindbrain, which is adjacent to the top part of the spinal cord; the midbrain, which rises above the hindbrain; and the forebrain, which is the uppermost region of the brain (Figure 2.10).

■ The right hemisphere also may be more involved than the left hemisphere in processing information about emotions, both when we express emotions ourselves and when we recognize others' emotions (Carmona, Holland, & Harrison, 2009). People are more likely to remember emotion words if they hear them in the left ear. Much of our sense of humor resides in the right hemisphere (Marinkovic & others, 2011). In fact, if you want to be sure that someone laughs at your joke, tell it to the person's left ear.

■ The right hemisphere is also adept at interpreting story meanings and voice intonations. Further, the right hemisphere excels at picking up a song melody. Importantly, though, it is difficult to learn exactly what the right hemisphere can do, because it cannot just tell us. We have to come up with a way for the right hemisphere to communicate what it knows. The right hemisphere certainly has some verbal abilities, for instance, because people with split brains can draw (with their left hand) pictures of words that have been spoken to them (in the left ear).

*The right hemisphere is expert at recognizing faces. Researchers have asked people to watch images on a computer screen and to press a button when they see a face. Even right-handed people are much faster at this task when they use their left hand because the information goes directly from the right hemisphere to the hand that hemisphere controls.*

Because differences in the functioning of the brain's two hemispheres are known to exist, people commonly use the phrases *left-brained* (meaning logical and rational) and *right-brained* (meaning creative or artistic) as a way of categorizing themselves and others. Such generalizations have little scientific basis, and that is a good thing. We have both hemispheres because we use them both. Regardless of how much fun it might be to label ourselves "right-brained" or "left-brained," we are fortunate to be whole-brained, period. The reality is that most day-to-day activities involve a complex interplay between the brain's two hemispheres (Abbassi & others, 2012; Ibrahim & Eviatar, 2012).

*Could this be why women, even right-handed women (but not men), automatically carry a baby in the left hand?*

# Integration of Function in the Brain

How do all of the regions of the brain cooperate to produce the wondrous complexity of thought and behavior that characterizes humans? Neuroscience still does not have answers to questions such as how the brain solves a murder mystery or composes a poem or an essay. Even so, we can get a sense of integrative brain function by using a real-world scenario, such as the act of escaping from a burning building.

Imagine that you are sitting at your computer, writing an e-mail, when a fire breaks out behind you. The sound of crackling flames is relayed from your ear through the thalamus, to the auditory cortex, and on to the auditory association cortex. At each stage, the stimulus is processed to extract information, and at some stage, probably at the association cortex level, the sounds are finally matched with something like a neural memory representing sounds of fires you have heard previously. The association "fire" sets new machinery in motion. Your attention (guided in part by the reticular formation) shifts to the auditory signal being held in your association cortex and on to your auditory association cortex, and simultaneously (again guided by reticular systems) your head turns toward the noise. Now your visual association cortex reports in: "Objects matching flames are present." In other regions of the association cortex, the visual and auditory reports are synthesized ("We have things that look and sound like fire"), and neural associations representing potential actions ("flee") are activated. However, firing the neurons that code the plan to flee will not get you out of the chair. The basal ganglia must become engaged, and from there the commands will arise to set the brain stem, motor cortex, and cerebellum to the task of transporting you out of the room. All of this happens in mere seconds.

Which part of your brain did you use to escape? Virtually all systems had a role. By the way, you would probably remember this event because your limbic circuitry would

# Touring the Nervous System and the Brain

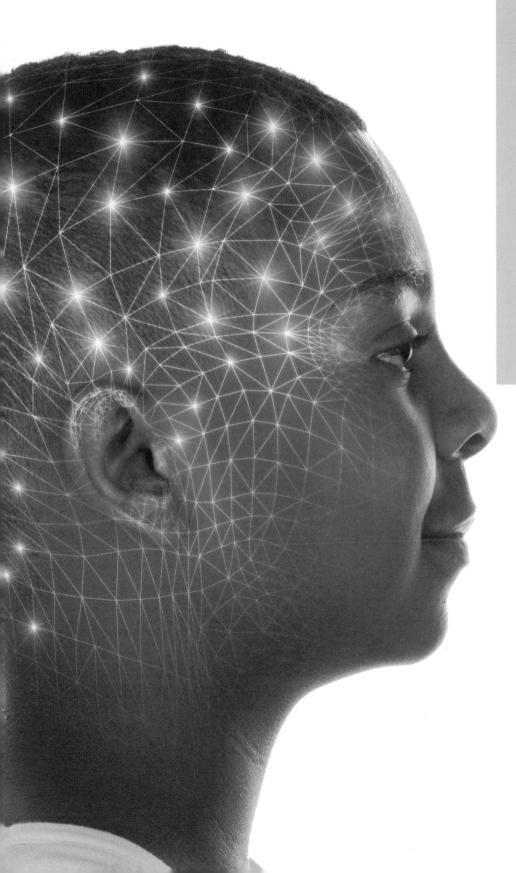

1. The Neuron and the Synapse

2. Structures and Functions of the Human Brain

3. Cerebral Cortex Lobes and Association Areas

4. Central and Peripheral Nervous Systems

5. Sympathetic and Parasympathetic Nervous Systems

# 1 The Neuron and the Synapse

Identify parts of the neuron and synapse and describe how they communicate information.

The **neuron** consists of a **cell body, dendrites,** and an **axon.** Dendrites are branches of the neuron that receive information from other neurons. The axon is a single process that sends information to other cells. Some axons are surrounded by a **myelin sheath** (fatty layer) that speeds up the transmission of the neural impulse down the axon. When a neuron "fires" it sends an electrical impulse down the axon, called an **action potential.** The arrival of the impulse at the axon terminal buttons causes the release of **neurotransmitter** molecules into the **synapse** (the gap junction between two neurons). Neurons communicate with each other by means of chemical signals provided by neurotransmitters. A neurotransmitter can cause a change in the membrane properties of the receiving neuron, allowing certain electrically charged particles (ions) to enter or leave the neuron. The entry of a positively charged ion, like sodium (Na+), will cause a change in the electrical charge (potential) of the receiving neuron making it more likely to fire (generate its own action potential).

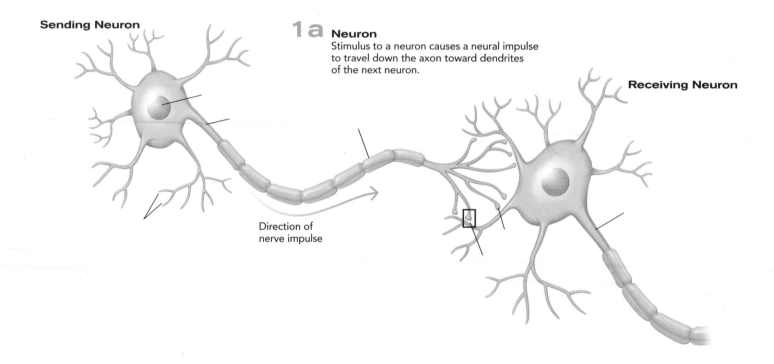

**Sending Neuron**

**1a** **Neuron**
Stimulus to a neuron causes a neural impulse to travel down the axon toward dendrites of the next neuron.

**Receiving Neuron**

Direction of nerve impulse

# Structures and Functions of the Human Brain

## 2

### Identify the brain's key structures and functions.

**Brainstem structures** are within the core of the brain and provide a number of vital functions for survival. *Medulla:* life-sustaining reflexes including breathing, coughing, vomiting, and heart rate. *Pons:* sleep and arousal. *Cerebellum:* motor coordination and balance; attention to visual and auditory stimuli. *Reticular formation:* arousal, attention, and sleep patterns; also involved in stereotyped patterns such as posture and locomotion. *Thalamus:* relays auditory, visual, and somatosensory (bodily senses) information to the cerebral cortex.

**Limbic system** comprises a number of structures involved in motivation, emotion, and memory. *Hypothalamus:* controls the autonomic nervous system and endocrine system; involved in eating, drinking, sexual behavior, and the expression of emotions. *Hippocampus:* special role in learning and memory. *Amygdala:* fear and anxiety; involved in discrimination of objects necessary for survival.

**Cerebral cortex** is the outer layer of the brain; it is involved in higher-order brain functions including thinking, consciousness, learning, memory, perception, and language.

## 2a Brain Stem Structures

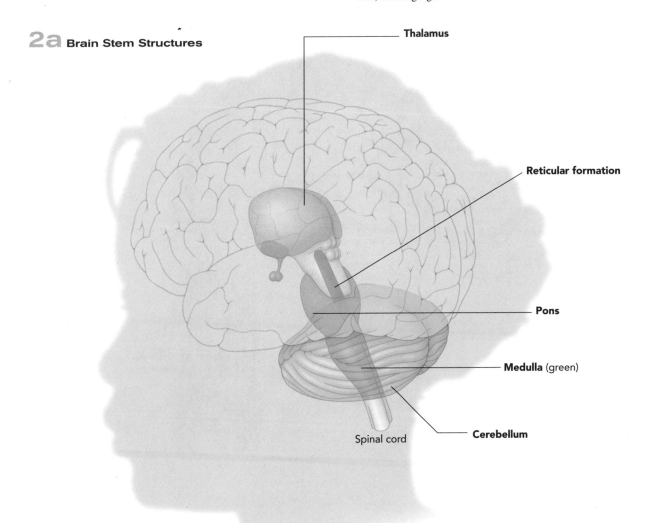

Thalamus

Reticular formation

Pons

Medulla (green)

Cerebellum

Spinal cord

# Cerebral Cortex Lobes and Association Areas

**Identify the location of the four cerebral cortex lobes and describe their primary functions.**

The **cerebral cortex** is divided into four lobes. The *occipital lobe* is located in the back region of the cortex and is involved in *vision.* The *parietal lobe* is involved in *bodily senses* and lies between the occipital lobe and the *central sulcus.* The area just behind the central sulcus is called the *somatosensory cortex* because it is the primary target for the *touch senses* of the body. The *temporal lobe* is involved in *hearing* and lies behind the frontal lobe and below the lateral fissure. The *frontal lobe* extends forward from the central sulcus. The region of the frontal lobe immediately adjacent to the central sulcus is called the *motor cortex* because it controls *voluntary movements.* The *prefrontal cortex* (forehead region) is involved in higher functions including *cognition, memory,* the *planning of movement,* and aspects of *emotion.*

**Association areas** are not primarily sensory or motor; rather, they associate various sensory and motor inputs that give rise to higher mental functions, such as perception, learning, remembering, thinking, and speaking.

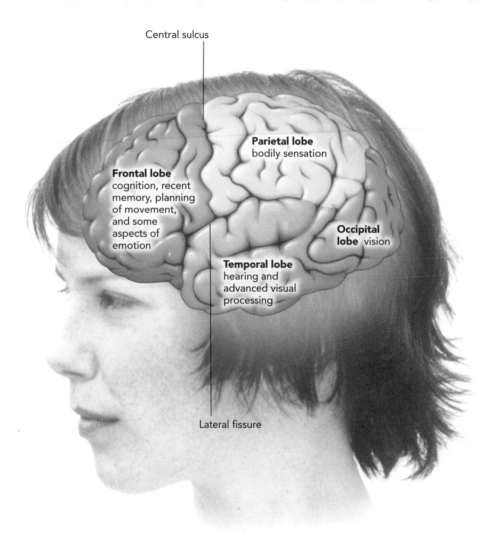

Central sulcus

**Parietal lobe**
bodily sensation

**Frontal lobe**
cognition, recent
memory, planning
of movement,
and some
aspects of
emotion

**Occipital
lobe** vision

**Temporal lobe**
hearing and
advanced visual
processing

Lateral fissure

# 4 Central and Peripheral Nervous Systems

**Identify the bodily changes that occur when the sympathetic branch or the parasympathetic branch of the autonomic nervous system is activated.**

The **central nervous system** is comprised of the brain and the spinal cord. The **peripheral nervous system** consists of all nerves outside the brain and spinal cord. The peripheral nervous system is made up of two major divisions: the *somatic division* and the *autonomic division.* The somatic division consists of nerve fibers that convey information from the brain and spinal cord to skeletal muscles to control movement and send information back to the brain via the spinal cord from sensory receptors. The autonomic division controls the glands and muscles of the internal organs such as the heart, digestive system, lungs, salivary glands, and so on. The autonomic division consists of two branches: the *sympathetic branch* and the *parasympathetic branch.* The sympathetic branch is involved in arousing the body and mobilizing its energy during physical exercise and in stressful situations. It also activates the adrenal glands to release epinephrine into the bloodstream. The parasympathetic branch calms the body and is involved in the conservation and replenishment of energy.

## 5a The Central Nervous System

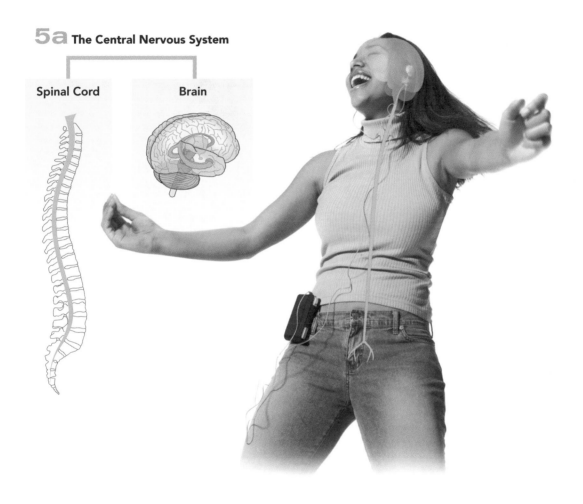

Spinal Cord          Brain

# 5 Sympathetic and Parasympathetic Nervous Systems

Identify the parts of the sympathetic and parasympathetic nervous systems and describe their role in arousing and calming the body.

**Sympathetic branch:** general increase in arousal and excitation accompanied by an increase in heart rate, breathing rate, dilation of the pupils, release of epinephrine from the adrenal glands, and a halt in digestion.

**Parasympathetic branch:** relaxation and energy conservation accompanied by a reduction in heart rate, breathing rate, constriction of the pupils, and stimulation of digestion.

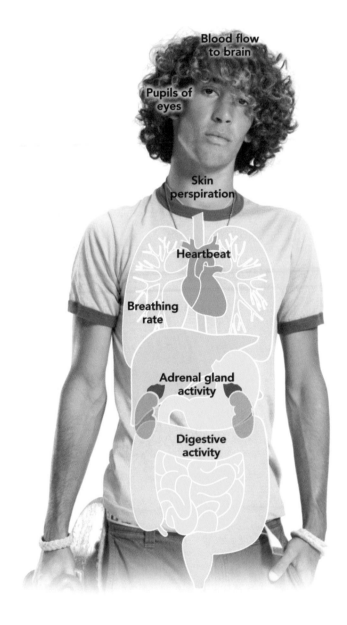

Blood flow to brain

Pupils of eyes

Skin perspiration

Heartbeat

Breathing rate

Adrenal gland activity

Digestive activity

likely have started memory formation when the association "fire" was triggered. The next time the sounds of crackling flames reach your auditory association cortex, the associations triggered would include this most recent escape. In sum, considerable integration of function takes place in the brain (Rissman & Wagner, 2012; Squire & Wixted, 2011). All of the parts of the nervous system work together as a team to keep you safe and sound.

self-quiz

1. Four ways that researchers study the brain and the nervous system are electrical recording, imaging, staining, and
   A. biopsy.
   B. lesioning.
   C. lobotomy.
   D. neurosurgery.

2. The brain's three major regions are the hindbrain, the midbrain, and the
   A. brain stem.
   B. reticular formation.
   C. forebrain.
   D. temporal lobes.

3. The most recently developed level of the human brain is the
   A. midbrain.
   B. forebrain.
   C. reticular formation.
   D. brain stem.

APPLY IT! 4. Because Miles suffers from extreme seizures, a surgeon severs his corpus callosum. Using a special technique, researchers present a picture of a flower to Miles's right brain and a picture of a bumblebee to Miles's left brain. When Miles is asked to say out loud what he sees, he is likely to answer
   A. "A flower."
   B. "I don't know."
   C. "A bee."
   D. There is no way to know.

# 4  The Endocrine System

**glands**
Organs or tissues in the body that create chemicals that control many of our bodily functions.

The **endocrine system** consists of a set of glands that regulate the activities of certain organs by releasing their chemical products into the bloodstream. **Glands** are organs or tissues in the body that create chemicals that control many bodily functions. Neuroscientists have discovered that the nervous system and endocrine system are intricately interconnected. They know that the brain's hypothalamus connects the nervous system and the endocrine system and that the two systems work together to control the body's activities. Yet the endocrine system differs significantly from the nervous system in a variety of ways. For one thing, the parts of the endocrine system are not all connected in the way that the parts of the nervous system are. For another thing, the endocrine system works more slowly than the nervous system, because the chemicals released by the endocrine glands are transported through the circulatory system, in the blood. The heart does a mind-boggling job of pumping blood through the body, but blood moves far more slowly than neural impulses do.

**endocrine system**
The body system consisting of a set of glands that regulate the activities of certain organs by releasing their chemical products into the bloodstream.

**hormones**
Chemical messengers that are produced by the endocrine glands and carried by the bloodstream to all parts of the body.

The chemical messengers produced by the endocrine glands are called **hormones.** The bloodstream carries hormones to all parts of the body, and the membrane of every cell has receptors for one or more hormones.

The endocrine glands consist of the pituitary gland, the thyroid and parathyroid glands, the adrenal glands, the pancreas, the ovaries in women, and the testes in men (Figure 2.20). In much the same way that the brain's control of muscular activity is constantly monitored and altered to suit the information received by the nervous system, the action of the endocrine glands is continuously monitored and changed by nervous, hormonal, and chemical signals (Enger, Ross, & Bailey, 2012). Recall from earlier in the chapter that the autonomic nervous system regulates processes such as respiration, heart rate, and digestion. The autonomic nervous system acts on the endocrine glands

FIGURE 2.20 **The Major Endocrine Glands** The pituitary gland releases hormones that regulate the hormone secretions of the other glands. The pituitary gland is regulated by the hypothalamus.

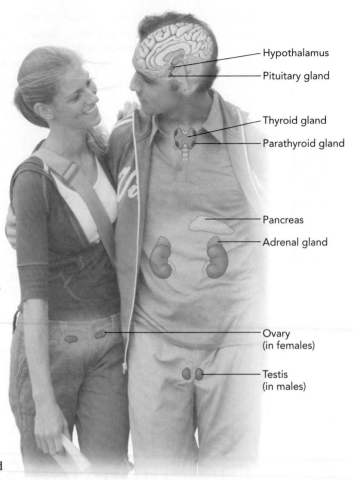

- Hypothalamus
- Pituitary gland
- Thyroid gland
- Parathyroid gland
- Pancreas
- Adrenal gland
- Ovary (in females)
- Testis (in males)

**pituitary gland**
A pea-sized gland just beneath the hypothalamus that controls growth and regulates other glands.

**adrenal glands**
Glands at the top of each kidney that are responsible for regulating moods, energy level, and the ability to cope with stress.

to produce a number of important physiological reactions to strong emotions, such as rage and fear.

The **pituitary gland,** a pea-sized gland just beneath the hypothalamus, controls growth and regulates other glands (Figure 2.21). The anterior (front) part of the pituitary is known as the *master gland* because almost all of its hormones direct the activity of target glands elsewhere. In turn, the anterior pituitary gland is controlled by the hypothalamus.

The **adrenal glands,** located at the top of each kidney, regulate mood, energy level, and the ability to cope with stress. Each adrenal gland secretes epinephrine (also called *adrenaline*) and norepinephrine (also called *noradrenaline*). Unlike most hormones, epinephrine and norepinephrine act quickly. Epinephrine helps a person get ready for an emergency by acting on smooth muscles, the heart, stomach, intestines, and sweat glands. In addition, epinephrine stimulates the reticular formation, which in turn arouses the sympathetic nervous system, and this system subsequently excites the adrenal glands to produce more epinephrine. Norepinephrine also alerts the individual to emergency situations by interacting with the pituitary gland and the liver. You may remember that norepinephrine functions as a neurotransmitter when it is released by neurons. In the adrenal glands, norepinephrine is released as a hormone. In both instances, norepinephrine conveys information—in the first case, to neurons; in the second case, to glands (G. B. Johnson, 2012).

The **pancreas,** located under the stomach, is a dual-purpose gland that performs both digestive and endocrine functions. The part of the pancreas that serves endocrine functions produces a number of hormones, including insulin. This part of the pancreas, the islets of Langerhans, turns out hormones like a little factory. Insulin is an essential hormone that controls glucose (blood sugar) levels in the body and is related to metabolism, body weight, and obesity.

The **ovaries,** located in the pelvis on either sides of the uterus in women, and **testes,** located in the scrotum in men, are the sex-related endocrine glands that produce hormones related to sexual development and reproduction. These glands and the hormones they produce play important roles in developing sexual characteristics such as breasts in women and a beard in men. They are also involved in other characteristics and behaviors, as we will see throughout this book.

FIGURE 2.21 **The Pituitary Gland** The pituitary gland, which hangs by a short stalk from the hypothalamus, regulates the hormone production of many of the body's endocrine glands. Here it is enlarged 30 times.

**pancreas**
A dual-purpose gland under the stomach that performs both digestive and endocrine functions.

**ovaries**
Sex-related endocrine glands that produce hormones involved in women's sexual development and reproduction.

**testes**
Sex-related endocrine glands in the scrotum that produce hormones involved in men's sexual development and reproduction.

1. The endocrine glands produce chemicals called
   A. hormones.
   B. neurotransmitters.
   C. endocrine secretions.
   D. bile.

2. The endocrine glands include all of the following *except* the
   A. pituitary.
   B. pancreas.
   C. liver.
   D. thyroid.

3. The adrenal glands regulate energy level, the ability to deal with stress, and
   A. appetite.
   B. digestion.
   C. motor coordination.
   D. mood.

**APPLY IT!** 4. Diabetes, a common disorder worldwide, involves problems in the body's regulation of glucose, or blood sugar. This disorder is often treated by diet, but sometimes individuals with diabetes must inject themselves with insulin. The endocrine system gland that is involved in diabetes is the
   A. pituitary.
   B. ovaries.
   C. pancreas.
   D. adrenal.

# 5 Brain Damage, Plasticity, and Repair

Recall from earlier in this chapter that plasticity is an example of the brain's remarkable adaptability. Neuroscientists have studied plasticity, especially following brain damage, and have charted the brain's ability to repair itself (Rossignol & Frigon, 2011). Brain damage can produce horrific effects, including paralysis, sensory loss, memory loss, and personality deterioration. When such damage occurs, can the brain recover some or all of its functions? Recovery from brain damage varies considerably, depending on the age of the individual and the extent of the damage (Anderson, Spencer-Smith, & Wood, 2011).

## The Brain's Plasticity and Capacity for Repair

For much of the twentieth century, it was generally concluded that the younger children are, the better their recovery will be from a traumatic brain injury. However, recently researchers have found that age alone is often not a good indicator of the brain's ability to recover from a traumatic injury (Maxwell, 2012). Although the young child's brain has more plasticity than an older child's, because of its immaturity it also is more vulnerable to insults (Anderson & others, 2009). Thus, assessing outcomes of brain insults based on age alone can be misleading. A recent research review concluded that children's outcomes following injury to their brain depend on factors related to the injury (nature, severity, and timing of insult), physical factors (age, cognitive capacity, and genetic makeup), and environmental influences (intervention and quality of rehabilitation, family functioning, and social status) (Anderson, Spencer-Smith, & Wood, 2011). Regarding age, researchers have found that in general, a more severe insult is more damaging to the young child's brain than the older child's brain (Anderson & others, 2005).

A significant factor in recovery is whether some or all of the neurons in an affected area are just damaged or are completely destroyed (Huang & Chang, 2009). If the neurons have not been destroyed, brain function often becomes restored over time.

There are three ways in which repair of the damaged brain might take place:

- *Collateral sprouting,* in which the axons of some healthy neurons adjacent to damaged cells grow new branches (Onifer, Smith, & Fouad, 2011).

- *Substitution of function,* in which the damaged region's function is taken over by another area or areas of the brain.

## Protecting the Athlete's Brain

During a 2011 matchup between heated NFL rivals the Cleveland Browns and the Pittsburgh Steelers, Browns quarterback Colt McCoy took a brutal helmet-to-helmet hit from linebacker James Harrison. Moments later, McCoy was back leading the Cleveland offense. The Browns' sideline personnel failed to notice what was evident in postgame interviews (Battista, 2011): McCoy showed a number of symptoms of *concussion,* or *mild traumatic brain injury (MBTI),* including sensitivity to bright light, emotional funk, and difficulty answering questions.

MBTIs are head injuries that lead to temporary loss of brain function (Khurana & Kaye, 2012). In addition to those suffered by McCoy, symptoms include headache, dizziness, nausea, unequal pupil size, and lack of memory for events surrounding the trauma. Importantly, these symptoms may not be immediately apparent and, contrary to common belief, concussions do not necessarily lead to a lack of consciousness.

MBTIs are an increasing concern among health professionals who work with athletes at every level. Among high school athletes, MBTIs are thought to make up at least 15 percent of sports

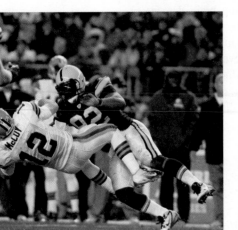

injuries (Meehan & others, 2011). Although concussions can occur in any sport, head injuries are a special concern for youth football players, because of the risk of tackles (Centers for Disease Control and Prevention, 2011). One review of deaths among youth football players, spanning 1945 to 1999, found that 69 percent of fatalities on the field resulted from brain injuries, and most were the result of tackling (Cantu, 2003).

Treatment for concussion involves rest and careful monitoring (Doolan & others, 2012). The brain requires time to recover from injury. The dangers of repeated brain injury are great. A longitudinal study of NFL players found that those who experienced repeated head injuries were more likely to suffer from depression, suicide, and cognitive deficits (American Association of Neurological Surgeons, 2003). *Second impact syndrome* is a particularly deadly outcome of repeated head injury. When the brain has not had time to recover from a concussion, a second injury can cause rapid swelling of the brain, leading to brain stem failure and eventual coma or death (Cobb & Battin, 2004).

For a concussion to be treated properly, someone must first notice that it has occurred and then must respond appropriately. This responsibility ought not to fall on the injured athlete. Indeed, an individual suffering from a concussion may not recognize his or her own injury, because the trauma has damaged the very organ that would provide the person with insight on the injury. For high school athletes, the Centers for Disease Control and Prevention (CDC) recommends that coaches have players evaluated by a trained medical professional in cases where any suspected brain injury has occurred (2011).

Psychologists know that motivation can influence perception (Balcetis & Dunning, 2010). Our motives can shape what we see and how we interpret that evidence. Teams, individual players, and their fans want to win, and having star players on the field is seen as crucial to victory. In this context, a coach might reason that an injured player is well enough to return to the field because he or she "seems" normal. And the player, even if suffering from a powerful headache, might choose not to complain because he or she is so motivated to win, to show team loyalty, and to avoid appearing weak.

Policymakers must do their part to protect this crucial organ from sports injuries. In response to the injury to McCoy, the NFL instituted a policy of appointing an independent observer to each game to monitor potential head injuries (Battista & Sandomir, 2011). Clearly, player health may require just such a separation of the motivation to win from the recognition and evaluation of potential brain injuries.

■ *Neurogenesis,* the process by which new neurons are generated. Until the 1990s, scientists believed that virtually no neurons, only increased connections between neurons, could be formed following infancy. However, it is now accepted that neurogenesis can occur in human adults (Curtis, Kam, & Faull, 2011; Snyder & Cameron, 2011). But researchers have documented neurogenesis in only two brain regions: the hippocampus, which is involved in memory, and the olfactory bulb, which is involved in smell (Couillard-Despres, Iglseder, & Aigner, 2011; Ming & Song, 2011). It also is not known what functions these new brain cells perform, and at this point they have been found to last for only several weeks. Researchers currently are probing factors that might inhibit and promote neurogenesis, including various drugs, stress, and exercise (Gil-Mohapel & others, 2010; van Praag, 2009). A recent study revealed that coping with stress stimulated hippocampal neurogenesis in adult monkeys (Lyons & others, 2010).

Researchers also recently have discovered that if rats are cognitively challenged to learn something, new brain cells survive longer (Shors, 2009). They are examining as well how the grafting of neural stem cells to various regions of the brain, such as the hippocampus, might increase neurogenesis (Taupin, 2011). Interest also is developing the possible role neurogenesis might play in neurogenerative diseases, such as Alzheimer disease, Parkinson disease, and Huntington disease (Gil-Mohapel & others, 2011; Mu & Gage, 2012).

## Brain Tissue Implants

The brain naturally recovers some functions that are lost following damage, but not all. Recent research has generated excitement about *brain grafts*—implants of healthy tissue into damaged brains (Fagerlund & others, 2012; Wijeyekoon & Barker, 2012). The potential success of brain grafts is much better when brain tissue from the fetal stage (an early stage in prenatal development) is used (Gallina & others, 2011). The neurons of the fetus are still growing and have a much higher probability of making connections with other neurons than do the neurons of adults. In a number of studies, researchers have damaged part of an adult rat's brain, waited until the animal recovered as much as possible by itself, and assessed its behavioral deficits. Then they take the corresponding area of a fetal rat's brain and transplant it into the damaged brain of the adult rat. In these studies, the rats that receive the brain transplants demonstrate considerable behavioral recovery (Shetty, Rao, & Hattiangady, 2008).

Might such brain grafts be successful with humans suffering from brain damage? Research suggests that they might, but finding donors is a problem (Glaw & others, 2009). Aborted fetuses are a possibility, but using them as a source of graft tissue raises ethical issues. Another type of treatment has been attempted with individuals who have Parkinson disease, a neurological disorder that affects about a million people in the United States (D. H. Park & others, 2009). Parkinson disease impairs coordinated movement to the point that just walking across a room can be a major ordeal. Fetal dopamine cells are transplanted into the basal ganglia of the individual with Parkinson disease in an effort to improve motor performance. A recent study found that this type of brain grafting did make motor performance better (Freed, Zhou, & Breeze, 2011).

Perhaps one of the most heated debates in recent years has concerned the use of human embryonic stem cells in research and treatment (Nicoleau & others, 2011; Wu & others, 2011). The human body contains more than 220 different types of cells, but **stem cells** are unique because they are primitive cells that have the capacity to develop into most types of human cells. Stem cells were first harvested from embryos by researchers at the University of Wisconsin, Madison, and Johns Hopkins University, in 1998. Because of their amazing plasticity, stem cells might potentially replace damaged cells in the human body, including cells involved in spinal cord injury and brain damage.

**stem cells**
Unique primitive cells that have the capacity to develop into most types of human cells.

Typically, researchers have harvested the stem cells from frozen embryos left over from in vitro fertilization procedures. In these procedures, a number of eggs, or ova, are collected from a woman's ovaries in order to be fertilized in a lab (rather than in the woman's body). In successful in vitro fertilization, the ova are brought together with sperm, producing human embryos. Because the procedure is difficult and delicate, doctors typically fertilize a large number of eggs with the hope that some will survive when implanted in the woman's uterus. In the typical procedure, there are leftover embryos. These embryos are in the *blastocyst* stage, which occurs five days after conception. At this stage the embryo has not yet attached to the uterus. The blastocyst has no brain, no central nervous system, and no mouth—it is an undifferentiated ball of cells.

*Do you support or oppose stem cell research? Why?*

Some supporters of stem cell technology (among them the late actor Christopher Reeve, 2000) emphasize that using these cells for research and treatment might relieve a great deal of human suffering. Opponents of abortion disapprove of the use of stem cells in research or treatment on the grounds that the embryos die when the stem cells are removed. (In fact, leftover embryos are likely to be destroyed in any case.) In 2009, President Barack Obama removed restrictions on stem cell research.

## self-quiz

1. Repair of the damaged brain might take place by all of the following *except*
   A. substitution of function.
   B. psychotherapy.
   C. collateral sprouting.
   D. neurogenesis.

2. The process by which the axons of healthy neurons adjacent to damaged cells grow new branches is called
   A. substitution of function.
   B. neurogenesis.
   C. collateral sprouting.
   D. dendritic branching.

3. The primitive cells that have the capacity to develop into most types of human cells are called
   A. stem cells.
   B. blastocysts.
   C. collateral cells.
   D. neurogenetic cells.

APPLY IT! 4. Taylor is injured in a serious car accident, suffering head injuries. After the accident, Taylor, who used to be talkative, seems to be unable to speak. Which of the following would best predict that Taylor is likely to regain the ability to talk?
   A. Taylor is male.
   B. Taylor is under 5 years old.
   C. Taylor is over the age of 21.
   D. Taylor is female.

## 6 Genetics and Behavior

In addition to the brain and nervous system, other aspects of our physiology also have consequences for psychological processes. Genes are one important contributor to these processes. As noted in Chapter 1, the particular influences of nature (genetic endowment) and of nurture (experience) on psychological characteristics have long fascinated psychologists. Here we begin by examining the central agent of nature: our genetic heritage.

**chromosomes**
In the human cell, threadlike structures that come in 23 pairs, one member of each pair originating from each parent, and that contain DNA.

### Chromosomes, Genes, and DNA

Within the human body are literally trillions of cells. The nucleus of each human cell contains 46 **chromosomes,** threadlike structures that come in 23 pairs, one member of each pair originating from each parent. Chromosomes contain the remarkable substance **deoxyribonucleic acid (DNA),** a complex molecule that carries genetic information.

**deoxyribonucleic acid (DNA)**
A complex molecule in the cell's chromosomes that carries genetic information.

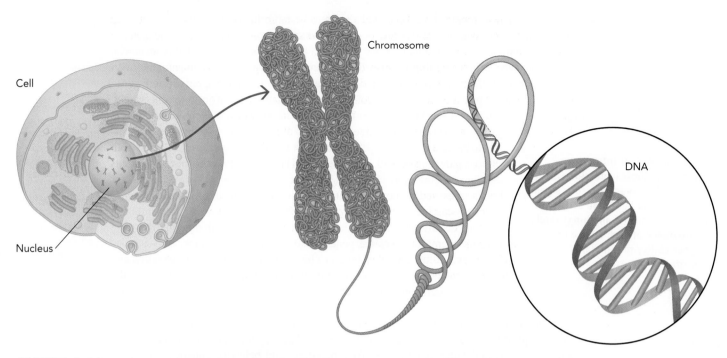

**FIGURE 2.22  Cells, Chromosomes, Genes, and DNA** (*Left*) The body contains trillions of cells, which are the basic structural units of life. Each cell contains a central structure, the nucleus. (*Middle*) Chromosomes and genes are located in the nucleus of the cell. Chromosomes are made up of threadlike structures composed mainly of DNA molecules. (*Right*) A gene is a segment of DNA that contains the hereditary code. The structure of DNA resembles a spiral ladder.

**genes**
The units of hereditary information, consisting of short segments of chromosomes composed of DNA.

**Genes,** the units of hereditary information, are short segments of chromosomes composed of DNA. Genes enable cells to reproduce and manufacture the proteins that are necessary for maintaining life.

It is not the case that each gene is translated into one and only one protein; moreover, a gene does not act independently (Diamond, Casey, & Munakata, 2011). Indeed, rather than being a group of independent genes, the human genome (*genome* refers to an organism's complete genetic material) consists of many genes that collaborate both with one another and with nongenetic factors inside and outside the body. The cellular machinery mixes, matches, and links small pieces of DNA to reproduce the genes, and that machinery is influenced by what is going on around it. Figure 2.22 illustrates the relationship among cells, chromosomes, genes, and DNA.

An international research program called the Human Genome Project is dedicated to documenting the human genome. Human beings have approximately 20,500 genes (Ensembl Human, 2008). When these 20,500 genes from one parent combine at conception with the same number of genes from the other parent, the number of possibilities is staggering. Although scientists are still a long way from unraveling all the mysteries of the way genes work, some aspects of this process are well understood, starting with the fact that multiple genes interact to give rise to observable characteristics.

## The Study of Genetics

Historically speaking, genetics is a relatively young science. Its origins go back to the mid-nineteenth century, when an Austrian monk named Gregor Mendel studied heredity in generations of pea plants. By cross-breeding plants with different characteristics and noting the characteristics of the offspring, Mendel discovered predictable patterns of heredity and laid the foundation for modern genetics.

**Do It!**

Search the web for information about a happiness gene. How would you evaluate research on such a gene given what you have read so far in this book? What (if anything) would the existence of such a gene mean for your ability to find happiness in your life?

Mendel noticed that some genes seem to be more likely than others to show up in the physical characteristics of an organism. In some gene pairs, one gene is dominant over the other. If one gene of a pair is dominant and one is recessive, according to the **dominant-recessive genes principle,** the dominant gene overrides the recessive gene. A recessive gene exerts its influence only if both genes of a pair are recessive. If you inherit a recessive gene from only one parent, you may never know you carry the gene. In the world of dominant-recessive genes, brown eyes, farsightedness, and dimples rule over blue eyes, nearsightedness, and freckles. If you inherit a recessive gene for a trait from both of your parents, you will show the trait. That is why two brown-eyed parents can have a blue-eyed child: Each parent would have a dominant gene for brown eyes and a recessive gene for blue eyes. Because dominant genes override recessive genes, the parents have brown eyes. However, the child can inherit a recessive gene for blue eyes from each parent. With no dominant gene to override them, the recessive genes make the child's eyes blue.

Unlike eye color, complex human characteristics such as personality and intelligence are likely influenced by many different genes. Scientists use the term *polygenic inheritance* to describe the influences of multiple genes on behavior.

Today researchers continue to apply Mendel's methods, as well as modern technology, in their quest to expand knowledge about genetics. This section discusses three ways to study genetics: molecular genetics, selective breeding, and behavior genetics.

### MOLECULAR GENETICS

The field of *molecular genetics* involves the manipulation of genes using technology to determine their effect on behavior. There is currently a great deal of enthusiasm about the use of molecular genetics to discover the specific locations on genes that determine an individual's susceptibility to many diseases and other aspects of health and well-being (Brooker, 2012; Cowan, 2013).

### SELECTIVE BREEDING

*Selective breeding* is a genetic method in which organisms are chosen for reproduction based on how much of a particular trait they display. Mendel developed this technique in his studies of pea plants. A more recent example involving behavior is the classic selective breeding study conducted by Robert Tryon (1940). He chose to study maze-running ability in rats. After he trained a large number of rats to run a complex maze, he then mated the rats that were the best at maze running ("maze bright") with each other and the ones that were the worst ("maze dull") with each other. He continued this process with 21 generations of rats. After several generations, the maze-bright rats significantly outperformed the maze-dull rats.

Selective breeding studies have demonstrated that genes are an important influence on behavior, but that does not mean that experience is unimportant. For example, in another study, maze-bright and maze-dull rats were reared in one of two environments: (1) an impoverished environment that consisted of a barren wire-mesh group cage or (2) an enriched environment that contained tunnels, ramps, visual displays, and other stimulating objects (Cooper & Zubek, 1958). When they reached maturity, only the maze-dull rats that had been reared in an impoverished environment made more maze-learning errors than the maze-bright rats.

### BEHAVIOR GENETICS

*Behavior genetics* is the study of the degree and nature of heredity's influence on behavior. Behavior genetics is less invasive than molecular genetics and selective breeding. Using methods such as the *twin study,* behavior geneticists examine the extent to which individuals are shaped by their heredity and their environmental experiences (Gregory, Ball, & Button, 2011).

In the most common type of twin study, researchers compare the behavioral similarity of identical twins with the behavioral similarity of fraternal twins (Cardno & others, 2012). Identical twins develop from a single fertilized egg that splits into two genetically identical embryos, each of which becomes a person. Fraternal twins develop from

**dominant-recessive genes principle**
The principle that if one gene of a pair is dominant and one is recessive, the dominant gene overrides the recessive gene. A recessive gene exerts its influence only if both genes of a pair are recessive.

*You might recall Rosenthal's study with maze-bright, maze-dull rats in Chapter 1. Psychologists have learned a lot from studying rats in mazes.*

separate eggs and separate sperm, and so they are genetically no more similar than non-twin siblings. They may even be of different sexes.

By comparing groups of identical and fraternal twins, behavior geneticists capitalize on the fact that identical twins are more similar genetically than are fraternal twins. In one twin study, researchers compared 7,000 pairs of Finnish identical and fraternal twins with respect to the personality traits of extraversion (which, as we have seen, means being outgoing) and neuroticism (being psychologically unstable) (Rose & others, 1988). The identical twins were much more alike than the fraternal twins on both of these personality traits, and this result suggests that genes influence both traits.

One problem with twin studies is that adults might stress the similarities of identical twin children more than those of fraternal twins, and identical twins might perceive themselves as a "set" and play together more than fraternal twins do. If so, observed similarities in identical twins might be more strongly influenced by environmental factors than usually thought.

In another type of twin study, researchers evaluate identical twins who have been reared in separate environments. If their behavior is similar, the assumption is that heredity has

*The Jim twins: Springer* (right) *and Lewis were unaware of each other for 39 years. The similarities between the two Jims seem pretty amazing. Let's take a closer look.* **> Imagine that you did not see the photo of the two Jims and were simply asked how similar two men of the same ethnicity, age, and first name might be. In what ways might such men be similar? > How many dogs might be named Toy, how many women of the same age might be named Betty, and how many men the same age as the Jims might own Chevrolets? > Which similarities between the Jims may not be so surprising after all? > What does this Psychological Inquiry tell you about the power of vivid and unusual cases in the conclusions we reach?**

played an important role in shaping their behavior. This strategy is the basis for the Minnesota Study of Twins Reared Apart, directed by Thomas Bouchard and his colleagues (1996). They bring identical twins who have been reared apart to Minneapolis from all over the world to study their behavior. They ask thousands of questions about their family, childhood, interests, and values. Detailed medical histories are obtained, including information about diet, smoking, and exercise habits.

One pair of twins in the Minnesota study, Jim Springer and Jim Lewis, were separated at 4 weeks of age and did not see each other again until they were 39 years old. They had an uncanny number of similarities, even though they had lived apart for decades. For example, they both worked as part-time deputy sheriffs, had vacationed in Florida, had owned Chevrolets, had dogs named Toy, and had married and divorced women named Betty. Both liked math but not spelling. Both were good at mechanical drawing. Both put on 10 pounds at about the same time in their lives, and both started suffering headaches at 18 years of age. They did have a few differences. For example, one expressed himself better orally, and the other was more proficient at writing. One parted his hair over his forehead; the other wore his hair slicked back with sideburns.

Critics argue that some of the separated twins in the Minnesota study had been together several months prior to their adoption, that some had been reunited prior to testing (in certain cases, for a number of years), that adoption agencies often put identical twins in similar homes, and that even strangers are likely to have some coincidental similarities (Joseph, 2006).

## Genes and the Environment

So far, we have talked a lot about genes, and you are probably getting the picture that genes are a powerful force in an organism. The role of genetics in some characteristics may seem obvious; for instance, how tall you are depends to a large degree on how tall your parents

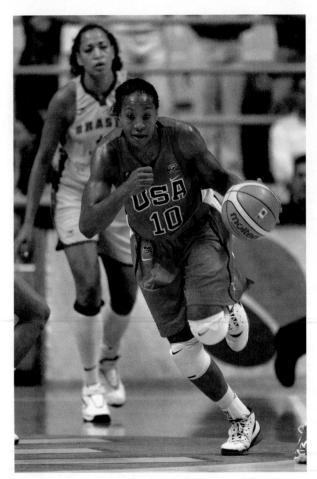

Our height depends significantly on the genes we inherit. However, even if we have genes that call for the stature of a basketball center, we may not reach that genetically programmed height if we lack good nutrition, adequate shelter, and medical care.

are. However, imagine a person growing up in a severely impoverished environment—with poor nutrition, inadequate shelter, little or no medical care, and a mother who had received no prenatal care. This individual may have genes that call for the height of an NBA or a WNBA center, but without environmental support for this genetic capacity, he or she may never reach that genetically programmed height. Thus, the relationship between an individual's genes and the actual person we see before us is not a perfect one-to-one correspondence. Even for a characteristic such as height, genes do not fully determine where a person will stand on this variable. We need to account for the role of nurture, or environmental factors, in the actual characteristics we see in the fully grown person.

If the environment matters for an apparently simple characteristic such as height, imagine the role it might play in complex characteristics such as being outgoing or intelligent. For these psychological characteristics, genes are, again, not directly reflected in the characteristics of the person. Indeed, genes cannot tell us exactly what a person will be like. Genes are simply related to some of the characteristics we see in a person.

To account for this gap between genes and actual observable characteristics, scientists distinguish between a genotype and a phenotype. A **genotype** is a person's genetic heritage, his or her actual genetic material. A **phenotype** is the individual's observable characteristics. The relationship between a genotype and phenotype is not always obvious. Recall that some genetic characteristics are dominant and others are recessive. Seeing that a person has brown eyes (his or her phenotype) tells us nothing about whether the person might also have a gene for blue eyes (his or her genotype) hiding out as well. The phenotype is influenced by the genotype but also by environmental factors.

**genotype**
A person's genetic heritage; his or her actual genetic material.

**phenotype**
An individual's observable characteristics.

The term *phenotype* applies to both physical and psychological characteristics. Consider a trait such as extraversion, the tendency to be outgoing and sociable. Even if we knew the exact genetic recipe for extraversion, we still could not perfectly predict a person's level of (phenotypic) extraversion from his or her genes, because at least some of this trait comes from the person's experience. We will revisit the concepts of genotype and phenotype throughout this book, including in Chapter 7 when we look at intelligence, Chapter 8 when we explore development, and Chapter 10 when we examine personality.

*Environmental influences can affect things like hair color. Just because Mom is blonde doesn't mean she's genetically blonde! Only her hairdresser knows for sure.*

Whether a gene is "turned on"—working to assemble proteins—is also a matter of collaboration. The activity of genes *(genetic expression)* is affected by their environment (Gottlieb, 2007). For example, hormones that circulate in the blood make their way into the cell where they can turn genes on and off. The flow of hormones, too, can be affected by environmental conditions, such as light, day length, nutrition, and behavior. Numerous studies have shown that external events outside of the original cell and the person, as well as events inside the cell, can excite or inhibit gene expression (Gottlieb, 2007). One study revealed that an increase in the concentration of stress hormones such as cortisol produced a fivefold increase in DNA damage (Flint & others, 2007).

Studies are exploring how interactions between heredity and environment influence development, including interactions that involve specific DNA sequences (Caspi & others, 2011; Rutter & Dodge, 2011). These studies are concerned with how individuals with the same genetic characteristics can, because of environmental factors, differ from one another in significant ways. For instance, research has found that variations in dopamine-related genes interact with supportive or unsupportive rearing environments to influence children's aggressive behavior (Bakersmans-Kranenburg & van IJzendoorn, 2011). Children with a particular genetic characteristic were more likely to behave aggressively if their parents were harsh and insensitive. This type of research concerns **gene × environment (g × e) interaction**—the interaction of a specific measured variation in DNA and a specific measured aspect of the environment (Karg & Sen, 2012; Lahey & others, 2011).

The biological foundations of psychology are in evidence across the entire nervous system, including the brain, the intricately working neurotransmitters, the endocrine system, and the genes. These physical realities of the body work in amazing concert to produce behaviors, thoughts, and feelings. The activities you do each day, from large to small, are all signs of the spectacular success of this physical system. Your mastery of the material in this chapter is but one reflection of the extraordinary capabilities of this biological feat.

**gene × environment (g × e) interaction**
The interaction of a specific measured variation in DNA and a specific measured aspect of the environment.

## self-quiz

1. The threadlike structures that are present in the cell nucleus and contain genes and DNA are called
   A. genomes.
   B. polygenic markers.
   C. chromosomes.
   D. stem cells.

2. Researchers study genetics through all of the following methods *except*
   A. twin studies.
   B. selective breeding.
   C. environmental impact studies.
   D. molecular genetics.

3. The individual's *observable* characteristics, influenced by both genetic and environmental factors, are called the
   A. genome.
   B. genotype.
   C. phenotype.
   D. prototype.

APPLY IT! 4. Sarah and Jack both have brown hair. When their son Trent is born, he has bright red hair. Family and friends start making jokes about any male friends of Sarah's who have red hair. Should Jack be worried that he is not Trent's father?

A. Jack should not be worried because brown hair color is part of the phenotype, not necessarily Sarah's and Jack's genotypes.

B. Jack should not be worried because Trent's hair color is part of his genotype, not necessarily his phenotype.

C. Jack should be worried because there is no way for two brunettes to have a baby with red hair. Sarah's been up to no good.

D. Jack should be worried because Trent's phenotype should match his parents' exactly.

## SUMMARY

## ① The Nervous System

The nervous system is the body's electrochemical communication circuitry. Four important characteristics of the brain and nervous system are complexity, integration, adaptability, and electrochemical transmission. The brain's special ability to adapt and change is called plasticity.

Decision making in the nervous system occurs in specialized pathways of nerve cells. Three of these pathways involve sensory input, motor output, and neural networks.

The nervous system is divided into two main parts: central (CNS) and peripheral (PNS). The CNS consists of the brain and spinal cord. The PNS has two major divisions: somatic and autonomic. The autonomic nervous system consists of two main divisions: sympathetic and parasympathetic. In particular, the sympathetic nervous system is involved in the experience of stress.

## ② Neurons

Neurons are cells that specialize in processing information. They make up the communication network of the nervous system. The three main parts of the neuron are the cell body, dendrite (receiving part), and axon (sending part). A myelin sheath encases and insulates most axons and speeds up transmission of neural impulses.

A neuron sends information along its axon in the form of brief electric impulses. Resting potential is the stable, slightly negative charge of an inactive neuron. The brief wave of electrical charge that sweeps down the axon, called the action potential, is an all-or-nothing response. The synapse is the space between neurons. At the synapse, neurotransmitters are released from the sending neuron, and some of these attach to receptor sites on the receiving neuron, where they stimulate another electrical impulse. Neurotransmitters include acetylcholine, GABA, norepinephrine, dopamine, serotonin, and endorphins. Neural networks are clusters of neurons that are interconnected to process information.

## ③ Structures of the Brain and Their Functions

Techniques used to study the brain include brain lesioning, electrical recording, and brain imaging. These methods have revealed much about the brain's major divisions—hindbrain, midbrain, and forebrain.

The cerebral cortex makes up most of the outer layer of the brain, and it is here that higher mental functions such as thinking and planning take place. The wrinkled surface of the cerebral cortex is divided into hemispheres, each with four lobes: occipital, temporal, frontal, and parietal. There is considerable integration and connection among the brain's lobes.

The brain has two hemispheres. Two areas in the left hemisphere that involve specific language functions are Broca's area (speech) and Wernicke's area (language comprehension). The corpus callosum is a large bundle of fibers that connects the two hemispheres. Research suggests that the left brain is more dominant in processing verbal information (such as language) and the right brain in processing nonverbal information (such as spatial perception, visual recognition, faces, and emotion). Nonetheless, in a person whose corpus callosum is intact, both hemispheres of the cerebral cortex are involved in most complex human functioning.

## ④ The Endocrine System

The endocrine glands release hormones directly into the bloodstream for distribution throughout the body. The pituitary gland is the master endocrine gland. The adrenal glands play important roles in mood, energy level, and ability to cope with stress. Other parts of the endocrine system include the pancreas, which produces insulin, and the ovaries and testes, which produce sex hormones.

## ⑤ Brain Damage, Plasticity, and Repair

The human brain has considerable plasticity, although this plasticity is greater in young children than later in development. Three ways in which a damaged brain might repair itself are collateral sprouting, substitution of function, and neurogenesis. Brain grafts are implants of healthy tissue into damaged brains. Brain grafts are more successful when fetal tissue is used. Stem cell research may allow for new treatments for damaged nervous systems.

## ⑥ Genetics and Behavior

Chromosomes are threadlike structures that occur in 23 pairs, with one member of each pair coming from each parent. Chromosomes contain the genetic substance deoxyribonucleic acid (DNA). Genes, the units of hereditary information, are short segments of chromosomes composed of DNA. According to the dominant-recessive genes principle, if one gene of a pair is dominant and one is recessive, the dominant gene overrides the recessive gene.

Two important concepts in the study of genetics are the genotype and phenotype. The genotype is an individual's actual genetic material. The phenotype is the observable characteristics—both physical and psychological—of the person.

Three methods of studying heredity's influence are molecular genetics, selective breeding, and behavior genetics. Two methods used by behavior geneticists are twin studies and adoption studies. Both genes and environment play a role in determining the phenotype of an individual. Even for characteristics in which genes play a large role (such as height and eye color), the environment also is a factor.

## KEY TERMS

nervous system, p. 43
plasticity, p. 44
afferent nerves, p. 44
efferent nerves, p. 44
neural networks, p. 44
central nervous system (CNS), p. 45
peripheral nervous system (PNS), p. 45
somatic nervous system, p. 45
autonomic nervous system, p. 45
sympathetic nervous system, p. 46
parasympathetic nervous system, p. 46
stress, p. 46
stressors, p. 46
neurons, p. 47
glial cells, p. 47
cell body, p. 49

dendrites, p. 49
axon, p. 49
myelin sheath, p. 49
resting potential, p. 50
action potential, p. 51
all-or-nothing principle, p. 51
synapses, p. 51
neurotransmitters, p. 52
agonist, p. 55
antagonist, p. 55
hindbrain, p. 60
brain stem, p. 61
midbrain, p. 61
reticular formation, p. 61
forebrain, p. 61
limbic system, p. 61
amygdala, p. 61
hippocampus, p. 62

thalamus, p. 62
basal ganglia, p. 62
hypothalamus, p. 63
cerebral cortex, p. 64
neocortex, p. 64
occipital lobes, p. 64
temporal lobes, p. 65
frontal lobes, p. 65
prefrontal cortex, p. 65
parietal lobes, p. 65
somatosensory cortex, p. 65
motor cortex, p. 65
association cortex, p. 67
corpus callosum, p. 68
endocrine system, p. 71
glands, p. 71
hormones, p. 71
pituitary gland, p. 72

adrenal glands, p. 72
pancreas, p. 72
ovaries, p. 72
testes, p. 72
stem cells, p. 75
chromosomes, p. 76
deoxyribonucleic acid (DNA), p. 76
genes, p. 77
dominant-recessive genes principle, p. 78
genotype, p. 80
phenotype, p. 80
gene × environment (g × e) interaction, p. 81

## Multiple Choice

1. Nerves that carry information from other parts of the body to the brain are called
   A. neural networks.
   B. afferent nerves.
   C. efferent nerves.
   D. neurotransmitters.

2. The purpose of myelin is to
   A. promote the release of presynaptic neurotransmitters.
   B. insulate axons to increase the speed of electrical impulses.
   C. open and close channels.
   D. create GABA.

3. When a neuron is resting, the inside of the cell membrane is _____, and the outside of the cell membrane is _____.
   A. positive; negative
   B. negative; positive
   C. negative; negative
   D. positive; positive

4. The structures at the end of the axon are called
   A. dendrites.
   B. terminal buttons.
   C. cell bodies.
   D. synaptic gaps.

5. The neurotransmitter most associated with love and bonding is
   A. serotonin.
   B. oxytocin.
   C. endorphins.
   D. norepinephrine.

6. The lobe of the cerebral cortex that responds to visual stimuli is the
   A. occipital lobe.
   B. parietal lobe.
   C. temporal lobe.
   D. frontal lobe.

7. The lobe of the cerebral cortex associated with personality is the
   A. occipital lobe.
   B. parietal lobe.
   C. temporal lobe.
   D. frontal lobe.

8. The part of the brain that acts as a central relay station is the
   A. reticular formation.
   B. limbic system.
   C. hippocampus.
   D. thalamus.

9. Broca's area plays an important role in _____, while Wernicke's area plays a key role in _____.
   A. motor function; sensation
   B. sensation; motor function
   C. speech production; speech comprehension
   D. speech comprehension; speech production

10. The corpus callosum is responsible for
    A. verbal processing.
    B. relaying information between the right and left hemispheres.
    C. speech production.
    D. sleep.

## Apply It!

11. After reading about the right brain and the left brain, Carl announces that it makes no sense to wear a helmet while skateboarding, because we all have an extra brain to spare. He announces, "I am cool as long as I have my left brain, since that's the one that does the talking!" Explain to Carl what life might be like with no right hemisphere.

# 3 Sensation and Perception

## *Pain: An Essential Sensation*

Plagued by a nagging headache, or smarting over a stubbed toe, you might curse your feeling of pain. A pain-free existence might sound nice, but in fact pain is an important sensation. Consider the situation of Ashlyn Blocker, age 12. She was born without the ability to sense pain. Ashlyn was a baby who did not cry, even when stinging eye drops were put in her eyes, even when she had a terrible diaper rash.

Researchers have studied Ashlyn to understand not only the cause of her condition but also the nature of pain itself (Staud & others, 2011). It turns out that Ashlyn has two genetic mutations that short-circuit the pain signals in her brain. Without pain, she has missed some of life's "warning signals," suffering severe burns as well as two broken ankles in her short life. She has had to remind herself that the sight of blood coming from a cut means that something is wrong. According to her mother, Ashlyn's inability to experience pain has caused a lack of empathy for the suffering of others: She cannot understand, for example, why a child would cry after falling off a swing (Chun, 2010).

The feeling of pain provides us with information about what is happening to us. This feeling, like all of our other senses, connects us to the external world. We see a beloved friend's face, feel a comforting hand on our shoulder, or hear our name called from across a room. Our abilities to sense and to perceive are what allow us to reach out into that world in the many ways we do every day.

preview

This chapter explores sensation and perception, the processes by which we engage with the external world. We first examine vision and then probe hearing, the skin senses, taste, smell, and the kinesthetic and vestibular senses. Without the senses, we would be isolated from the world around us; we would live in dark silence—and in a tasteless, colorless, feelingless void.

# How We Sense and Perceive the World

Sensation and perception researchers represent a broad range of specialties, including *ophthalmology,* the study of the eye's structure, function, and diseases; *audiology,* the science concerned with hearing; *neurology,* the scientific study of the nervous system; and many others. Understanding sensation and perception requires comprehending the physical properties of the objects of our perception—light, sound, the texture of material things, and so on. The psychological approach to these processes involves understanding the physical structures and functions of the sense organs, as well as the brain's conversion of the information from these organs into experience.

## The Processes and Purposes of Sensation and Perception

Our world is alive with stimuli—all the objects and events that surround us. Sensation and perception are the processes that allow us to detect and understand these various stimuli. We do not actually experience these stimuli directly; rather, our senses allow us to get information about aspects of our environment, and we then take that information and form a perception of the world. **Sensation** is the process of receiving stimulus energies from the external environment and transforming those energies into neural energy. Physical energy such as light, sound, and heat is detected by specialized receptor cells in the sense organs—eyes, ears, skin, nose, and tongue. When the receptor cells register a stimulus, the energy is converted into an electrochemical impulse or action potential that relays information about the stimulus through the nervous system to the brain (Harris & Attwell, 2012). Recall from Chapter 2 that an action potential is the brief wave of electrical charge that sweeps down the axon of a neuron for possible transmission to another neuron. When it reaches the brain, the information travels to the appropriate area of the cerebral cortex (Swaminathan & Freedman, 2012).

The brain gives meaning to sensation through perception. **Perception** is the process of organizing and interpreting sensory

**sensation**
The process of receiving stimulus energies from the external environment and transforming those energies into neural energy.

**perception**
The process of organizing and interpreting sensory information so that it makes sense.

*Through sensation we take in information from the world; through perception we identify meaningful patterns in that information. Thus sensation and perception work hand in hand when we enjoy a hug and the sweet fragrance of a flower.*

information so that it makes sense. Receptor cells in our eyes record—that is, sense—a sleek silver object in the sky, but they do not "see" a jet plane. So, sensation is about the biological processing that occurs between our sensory systems and the environment, while perception is our experience of those processes in action.

**BOTTOM-UP AND TOP-DOWN PROCESSING**   Psychologists distinguish between bottom-up and top-down processing in sensation and perception. In **bottom-up processing,** sensory receptors register information about the external environment and send it up to the brain for interpretation. Bottom-up processing means taking in information and trying to make sense of it (McMains & Kastner, 2011). An example of bottom-up processing might be the way you experience a song the first time you hear it: You listen carefully to get a "feel" for it. In contrast, **top-down processing** starts with cognitive processing at the higher levels of the brain; in top-down processing we begin with some sense of what is happening and apply that framework to information from the world (van Gaal & Lamme, 2011). You can experience top-down processing by "listening" to your favorite song in your head right now. As you "hear" the song in your mind's ear, you are engaged in perceptual experience produced by top-down processing.

Bottom-up and top-down processing work together in sensation and perception to allow us to function accurately and efficiently (Meyer, 2011). By themselves our ears provide only incoming information about sound in the environment. Only when we consider both what the ears hear (bottom-up processing) and what the brain interprets (top-down processing) can we fully understand how we perceive sounds in our world. In everyday life, the two processes of sensation and perception are essentially inseparable. For this reason, most psychologists refer to sensation and perception as a unified information-processing system (Goldstein, 2010).

**THE PURPOSES OF SENSATION AND PERCEPTION**   Why do we perceive the world? From an evolutionary perspective, the purpose of sensation and perception is adaptation that improves a species' chances for survival (Mader & Windelspecht, 2012). An organism must be able to sense and respond quickly and accurately to events in the immediate environment, such as the approach of a predator, the presence of prey, and the appearance of a potential mate. Not surprisingly, therefore, most animals—from goldfish to gorillas to humans—have eyes and ears, as well as sensitivities to touch and chemicals (smell and taste). Furthermore, a close comparison of sensory systems in animals

*If you've ever begged someone to try your favorite food only to have the person give you a shrug and "meh," that's the difference between sensation and perception. Both tongues had the same experience. But perception is subjective.*

*Eating strawberries, cherries, and red popsicles, little kids often get the idea that red = sweet . . . then they get a taste of red beets! It's always a fun moment when bottom-up experience collides with top-down expectations.*

*Dogs can smell better than humans. But that's because dogs need to and humans don't.*

**bottom-up processing**
The operation in sensation and perception in which sensory receptors register information about the external environment and send it up to the brain for interpretation.

**top-down processing**
The operation in sensation and perception, launched by cognitive processing at the brain's higher levels, that allows the organism to sense what is happening and to apply that framework to information from the world.

*Most predatory animals have eyes at the front of the face; most animals that are prey have eyes on the side of their head. Through these adaptations, predators perceive their prey accurately, and prey gain a measure of safety from their panoramic view of their environment.*

reveals that each species is exquisitely adapted to the habitat in which it evolved (Hoefnagels, 2012). Animals that are primarily predators generally have their eyes at the front of their faces so that they can perceive their prey accurately. In contrast, animals that are more likely to be someone else's lunch have their eyes on either side of their heads, giving them a wide view of their surroundings at all times.

## Sensory Receptors and the Brain

**sensory receptors**
Specialized cells that detect stimulus information and transmit it to sensory (afferent) nerves and the brain.

All sensation begins with sensory receptors. **Sensory receptors** are specialized cells that detect stimulus information and transmit it to sensory (afferent) nerves and the brain. Sensory receptors are the openings through which the brain and nervous system experience the world. Figure 3.1 shows the human sensory receptors for vision, hearing, touch, smell, and taste.

Figure 3.2 depicts the flow of information from the environment to the brain. Sensory receptors take in information from the environment, creating local electrical currents. These currents are graded; that means they are sensitive to the intensity of stimulation, such as the difference between a dim and a bright light. These receptors trigger action potentials in sensory neurons, which carry that information to the central nervous system. Because sensory neurons (like all neurons) follow the all-or-nothing principle, described in Chapter 2, the intensity of the stimulus cannot be communicated to the brain by changing the strength of the action potential. Instead, the receptor varies the *frequency* of action potentials sent to the brain. So, if a stimulus is very intense, like the bright sun on a hot day, the neuron will fire more frequently (but with the same strength) to let the brain know that the light is indeed very, very bright.

Other than frequency, the action potentials of all sensory nerves are alike. This sameness raises an intriguing question: How can an animal distinguish among sight, sound, odor, taste, and touch? The answer is that sensory receptors are selective and have different neural pathways. They are specialized to absorb a particular type of energy—light energy, sound vibrations, or chemical energy, for example—and convert it into an action potential.

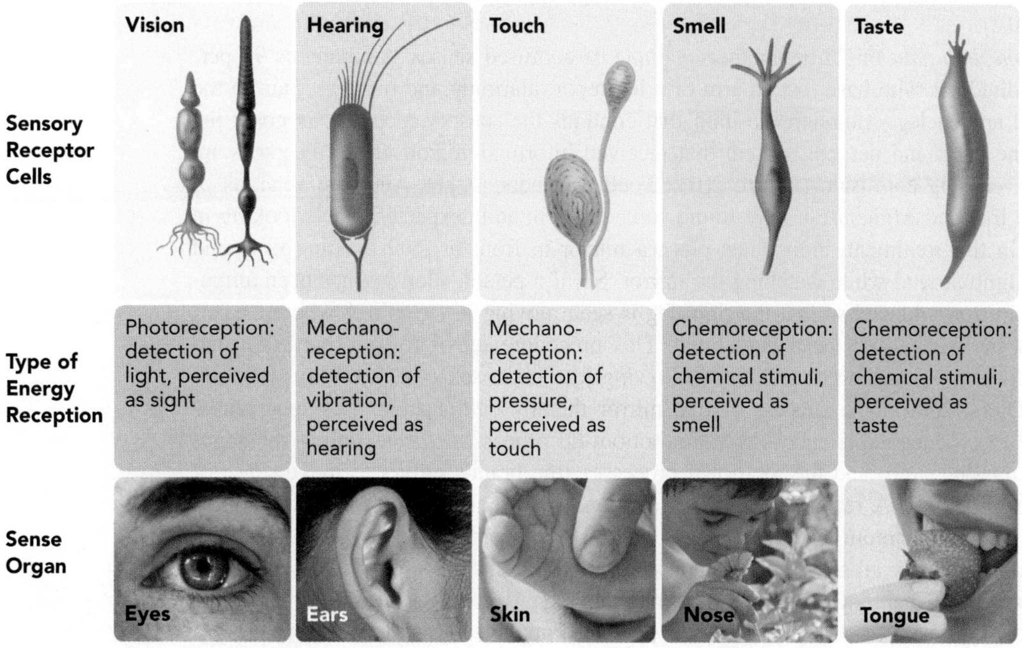

*There is that word again, afferent. Remember that afferent = arrives at the brain.*

**FIGURE 3.1 Human Senses: Organs, Energy Stimuli, and Sensory Receptors** The receptor cells for each sense are specialized to receive particular types of energy stimuli.

|  | Vision | Hearing | Touch | Smell | Taste |
|---|---|---|---|---|---|
| **Sensory Receptor Cells** | | | | | |
| **Type of Energy Reception** | Photoreception: detection of light, perceived as sight | Mechanoreception: detection of vibration, perceived as hearing | Mechanoreception: detection of pressure, perceived as touch | Chemoreception: detection of chemical stimuli, perceived as smell | Chemoreception: detection of chemical stimuli, perceived as taste |
| **Sense Organ** | Eyes | Ears | Skin | Nose | Tongue |

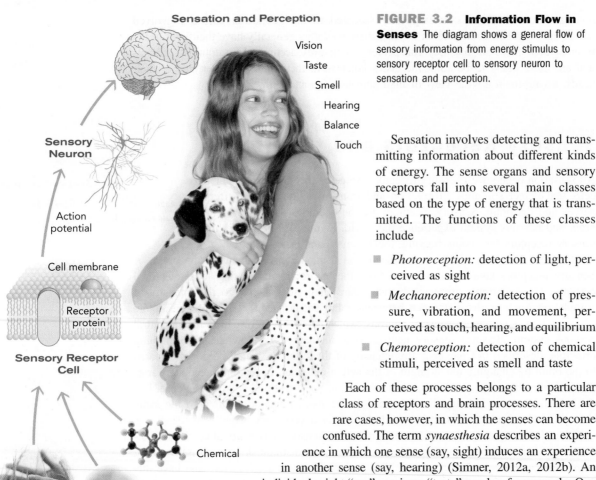

Sensation and Perception

Vision
Taste
Smell
Hearing
Balance
Touch

Sensory Neuron

Action potential

Cell membrane

Receptor protein

Sensory Receptor Cell

Chemical

Mechanical

Light

Energy Stimulus

**FIGURE 3.2** **Information Flow in Senses** The diagram shows a general flow of sensory information from energy stimulus to sensory receptor cell to sensory neuron to sensation and perception.

Sensation involves detecting and transmitting information about different kinds of energy. The sense organs and sensory receptors fall into several main classes based on the type of energy that is transmitted. The functions of these classes include

- *Photoreception:* detection of light, perceived as sight

- *Mechanoreception:* detection of pressure, vibration, and movement, perceived as touch, hearing, and equilibrium

- *Chemoreception:* detection of chemical stimuli, perceived as smell and taste

Each of these processes belongs to a particular class of receptors and brain processes. There are rare cases, however, in which the senses can become confused. The term *synaesthesia* describes an experience in which one sense (say, sight) induces an experience in another sense (say, hearing) (Simner, 2012a, 2012b). An individual might "see" music or "taste" a color, for example. One woman was able to taste sounds, so that a piece of music might taste like tuna fish (Beeli, Esslen, & Jancke, 2005). Neuroscientists are exploring the neurological bases of synaesthesia, especially in the connections between the various sensory regions of the cerebral cortex. For example, a recent fMRI study identified the parietal cortex as the key auditory-visual location in the brain for individuals with synaesthesia who experienced music as color (Neufeld & others, 2012).

*Phantom limb pain* might be another example of confused senses. As many as 95 percent of individuals who have lost an arm or a leg report alarming and puzzling pain in the amputated arm or leg. Although the limb that contains the sensory receptors is gone, the areas of the brain and nervous system that received information from those receptors are still there, causing confusion (Elbert, 2012; Foell & others, 2011). Amputee veterans of combat in Iraq and Afghanistan have found some relief in an unexpected place: looking in a mirror. In this treatment, individuals place a mirror in front of their existing limb and move the limb around while watching the mirror. So, if a person's left leg has been amputated, the mirror is placed so that the right leg is seen moving in the mirror where the left leg would be if it had not been amputated. This procedure seems to trick the brain into perceiving the missing limb as still there, allowing it to make sense of incoming sensation (Flor & Diers, 2009). The success of this mirror therapy demonstrates how our senses cooperate to produce experience—how the bottom-up processes (the incoming messages from the missing limb) and the top-down processes (the brain's efforts to make sense of these) work together. A recent research review concluded that mirror therapy has mixed results in treating phantom leg syndrome (Subedi & Grossberg, 2011).

In the brain, nearly all sensory signals pass through the thalamus, the brain's relay station, described in Chapter 2. From the thalamus, the signals go to the sensory areas of the cerebral cortex, where they are modified and spread throughout a vast network of neurons.

Recall from Chapter 2 that certain areas of the cerebral cortex are specialized to handle different sensory functions. Visual information is processed mainly in the occipital lobes; hearing, in the temporal lobes; and pain, touch, and temperature, in the parietal lobes. Keep in mind, however, that the interactions and pathways of sensory information are complex, and the brain often must coordinate extensive information and interpret it.

An important part of perception is interpreting the sensory messages. Many top-down factors determine this meaning, including signals from different parts of the brain, prior learning, the person's goals, and his or her degree of arousal. Moving in the opposite direction, bottom-up signals from a sensory area may help other parts of the brain maintain arousal, form an image of where the body is in space, or regulate movement.

The principles we have surveyed so far apply to all of the senses. We've seen that the senses are about detecting different energies and that all have specialized receptor cells and areas of the brain that serve their functions. You have probably heard about a "sixth sense"—*extrasensory perception*, or *ESP*. ESP means that a person can detect information from the world without receiving concrete sensory input. Examples of ESP include *telepathy* (the ability to read another person's mind) and *precognition* (the ability to sense future events). To read about how psychologists view these apparent phenomena, see Challenge Your Thinking.

*In case you don't remember: occipital = the back of the brain; temporal = on the sides; parietal = on the top. (You're welcome!)*

**EXPERIENCE IT!**
Thresholds

# Thresholds

Any sensory system must be able to detect varying degrees of energy. This energy can take the form of light, sound, chemical, or mechanical stimulation. How much of a stimulus is necessary for you to see, hear, taste, smell, or feel something? What is the lowest possible amount of stimulation that will still be detected?

**ABSOLUTE THRESHOLD**   One way to think about the lowest limits of perception is to assume that there is an **absolute threshold,** or minimum amount of stimulus energy that a person can detect. When the energy of a stimulus falls below this absolute threshold, we cannot detect its presence; when the energy of the stimulus rises above the absolute threshold, we can detect the stimulus (Lim, Kyung, & Kwon, 2012). As an example, find a clock that ticks; put it on a table and walk far enough away that you no longer hear it. Then gradually move toward the clock. At some point, you will begin to hear it ticking. Hold your position and notice that occasionally the ticking fades, and you may have to move forward to reach the threshold; at other times, it may become loud, and you can move backward.

In this experiment, if you measure your absolute threshold several times, you likely will record several different distances for detecting the stimulus. For example, the first time you try it, you might hear the ticking at 25 feet from the clock. However, you probably will not hear it every time at 25 feet. Maybe you hear it only 38 percent of the time at this distance, but you hear it 50 percent of the time at 20 feet away and 65 percent of the time at 15 feet. People have different thresholds. Some have better hearing than others, and some have better vision. Figure 3.3 shows one person's

**absolute threshold**
The minimum amount of stimulus energy that a person can detect.

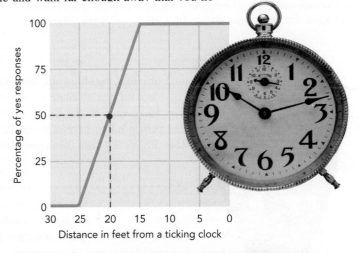

**FIGURE 3.3   Measuring Absolute Threshold** Absolute threshold is the minimum amount of energy we can detect. To measure absolute threshold, psychologists have arbitrarily decided to use the criterion of detecting the stimulus 50 percent of the time. In this graph, the person's absolute threshold for detecting the ticking clock is at a distance of 20 feet.

## Can We Feel the Future?

People have experiences that seem to involve precognition—for instance, "just knowing" that a friend is in trouble and later finding out that he was in a car accident. Such experiences can be fascinating and even spooky, but do they reflect the existence of ESP? Or is simple coincidence at work?

There are many reasons to question the existence of ESP. Think about precognition in the ways we have considered sensation and perception. Sensation involves detecting energy from the environment. If ESP exists, consider: Which afferent neurons send psychic messages from the future to the brain, and what sort of energy conveys these messages? In truth, the notion that human beings can sense future events challenges the basic principle that cause precedes effect (and not the other way around). Proof of the existence of precognition would require a revision of not only psychology but also biology and physics (Rouder & Morey, 2011).

Paraphrasing French mathematician Pierre-Simon Laplace, the late American astrophysicist Carl Sagan famously observed, "Extraordinary claims require extraordinary evidence." The assertion that ESP exists is an extraordinary claim. Is the evidence for this claim equally extraordinary? For most psychologists, the answer is a definite no (French, 2010; Hyman, 2010; Wiseman & Watt, 2006).

Distinguished social psychologist Daryl Bem (2011) rekindled the ESP debate, publishing nine studies testing for the existence of precognition. In eight of those studies, Bem claimed to show that future events could influence present behavior. For example, in one study, participants were shown 48 common words for 3 seconds each. After seeing the words, they were asked to recall all of the words they could. *After* the memory test, the computer randomly assigned the participants to study half of the words. A staunch believer in ESP, Bem hypothesized that participants would do a better job of remembering the words that they later *were going to* study. Results showed that participants remembered the words that they would later study about 2 percent better than the words they would not study. Bem concluded that the future act of studying had "in fact reach[ed] back in time and facilitate[d]" word recall.

In another study, participants saw two pictures of curtains on a computer screen. They were told that one curtain had a picture behind it and the other did not. Their task was to select the curtain with a picture. Some of the pictures contained erotic images; others showed positive, negative, or neutral images. The computer randomly placed the pictures behind the curtains *after* participants had made their guesses. Bem predicted that participants would select the curtain that would eventually show the erotic images at rates greater than chance—and the results did reveal that they had selected that curtain 53.1 percent of the time (higher than the chance rate of 50 percent).

Bem's findings and their publication in the most prestigious journal in social psychology caused an uproar, inspiring articles in the *New York Times* (Carey, 2011) and *Science* (Miller, 2011); a flurry of activity in the blogosphere; and an appearance by Bem on the *Colbert Report*. Critics of Bem's work pointed to inconsistencies across the studies (LeBel & Peters, 2011; Wagenmakers & others, 2011). For instance, in some studies precognition was shown for erotic (but not negative) images, in others for negative (but not erotic) images; in other studies women (but not men) showed precognition; and in other cases only extraverts did.

measured absolute threshold for detecting a clock's ticking sound. Psychologists have arbitrarily decided that absolute threshold is the point at which the individual detects the stimulus 50 percent of the time—in this case, 20 feet away. Using the same clock, another person might have a measured absolute threshold of 26 feet, and yet another, 18 feet. Figure 3.4 lists the approximate absolute thresholds of five senses.

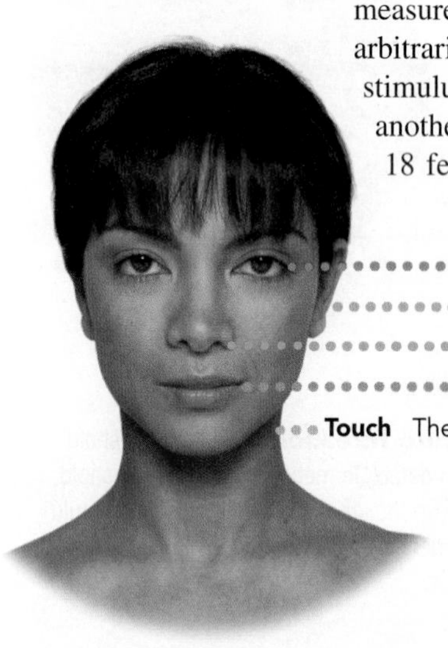

**Vision** A candle flame at 30 miles on a dark, clear night

**Hearing** A ticking clock at 20 feet under quiet conditions

**Smell** One drop of perfume diffused throughout three rooms

**Taste** A teaspoon of sugar in 2 gallons of water

**Touch** The wing of a fly falling on your neck from a distance of 1 centimeter

**FIGURE 3.4  Approximate Absolute Thresholds for Five Senses**
These thresholds show the amazing power of our senses to detect even very slight variations in the environment.

The statistical tests Bem used are at the heart of the controversy. To understand this issue, reconsider the questions posed above: Do Bem's results reflect ESP—or simple coincidence? Psychologists typically use statistics to determine whether an effect is real or a matter of chance (or coincidence). In the results just described, participants were 3.1 percent more likely than chance to select the curtain with the erotic image. Is this difference extraordinary evidence for an extraordinary claim? Before answering, consider the following situation. Imagine that you are offered $1 million if you can accurately assess whether a coin is rigged (that is, biased to produce more heads than tails). If you flip that coin 100 times and it comes up heads 53 times, should you conclude the coin is biased? How sure are you of your conclusion? How many times will you need to repeat your test to be sure? The probability of Bem's obtaining his result completely by chance was 1 in 100. But is 1 in 100 convincing enough to support the existence of a phenomenon that challenges the very nature of cause and effect? Many critics answered that question with a resounding no (Hyman, 2010; Kruschke, 2011; LeBel & Peters, 2011; Miller, 2011; Rouder & Morey, 2011; Wagenmakers & others, 2011; Wetzels & others, 2011).

E. J. Wagenmakers and his colleagues (2011) analyzed the data from each of Bem's studies using a different statistical technique and concluded that the results did not provide strong evidence for ESP. Jeffrey Rouder and Richard Morey (2011) applied yet another statistical tool to the entire package of studies and concluded that although there might be some evidence in Bem's data for the existence of precognition, it was too slight to overcome the appropriate level of skepticism that scholars should have for ESP.

Clearly, although an important tool, statistics are not a direct pathway to truth. Statistics are not a substitute for a sound rationale for predictions and conclusions. Raymond Hyman (2010), a longtime critic of research on ESP, argues that in the absence of a theory about why or how precognition exists, along with indepen-

dently repeatable methods, any evidence for the phenomenon is suspect.

Statistically speaking, Bem's findings were not terribly different from the findings in other published psychological studies (Wetzels & others, 2011). Most researchers consider a finding "real" if it is likely to occur fewer than 5 times in 100 by chance. Some have concluded that the lesson from Bem's work is not so much that ESP exists as that psychologists need to rethink how they test their hypotheses (LeBel & Peters, 2011; Wagenmakers & others, 2011). Still, some scholars continue to argue for the existence of ESP and defend research like Bem's (Bem, Utts, & Johnson, 2011; Dossey, 2011; Radin, 2006; Storm, Tressoldi, & Di Risio, 2010).

The controversy over Bem's paper highlights a tension within science between openness and enthusiasm for ideas (no matter how strange or counterintuitive they might seem) and a deep and intense skepticism. Recognizing this difficult tension between wonder and skepticism, Carl Sagan concluded, "This is how deep truths are winnowed from deep nonsense."

### What Do You Think?

- Do you believe in the phenomenon of ESP? Why or why not?

- What kind of evidence would be necessary for you to change your belief?

- Should research on ESP be held to a higher standard than other research? Explain.

Under ideal circumstances, our senses have very low absolute thresholds, so we can be remarkably good at detecting small amounts of stimulus energy. You might be surprised to learn that the human eye can see a candle flame at 30 miles on a dark, clear night. However, our environment seldom gives us ideal conditions with which to detect stimuli. If the night were cloudy or the air smoky, for example, you would have to be much closer to see the candle flame. In addition, other lights on the horizon—car or house lights—would hinder your ability to detect the candle's flicker. **Noise** is the term given to irrelevant and competing stimuli—not just sounds but any distracting stimuli for our senses (Ikeda, Sekiguchi, & Hayashi, 2010).

**noise**
Irrelevant and competing stimuli—not only sounds but also any distracting stimuli for the senses.

**DIFFERENCE THRESHOLD**   In addition to studying how much energy is required for a stimulus to be detected, psychologists investigate the degree of difference that must exist between two stimuli before the difference is detected. This is the **difference threshold,** or just noticeable difference. An artist might detect the difference between two similar shades of color. A fashion designer might notice a difference in the texture of two fabrics. How different must the colors and textures be for someone to say, "These are different"? Like the absolute threshold, the difference threshold is the smallest difference in stimulation required to discriminate one stimulus from another 50 percent of the time.

**difference threshold**
The degree of difference that must exist between two stimuli before the difference is detected.

Difference thresholds increase as a stimulus becomes stronger. That means that at very low levels of stimulation, small changes can be detected, but at very high levels, small changes are less noticeable. When music is playing softly, you may notice when your roommate increases the volume by even a small amount. If, however, he or she turns the volume up an equal amount when the music is playing very loudly, you may not notice. **Weber's law** (discovered by German physiologist E. H. Weber more than 150 years ago) is the principle that two stimuli must differ by a constant proportion to be perceived as different. For example, we add 1 candle to 20 candles and notice a difference in the brightness of the candles; we add 1 candle to 120 candles and do not notice a difference, but we would notice the difference if we added 6 candles to 120 candles. Weber's law generally holds true (Gao & Vasconcelos, 2009; Mohring, Libertus, & Bertin, 2012).

*Note that 1:20 = 6:120.*

**SUBLIMINAL PERCEPTION** Can sensations that occur below our absolute threshold affect us without our being aware of them? **Subliminal perception** refers to the detection of information below the level of conscious awareness. In 1957, James Vicary, an advertising executive, announced that he was able to increase popcorn and soft drink sales by secretly flashing the words "EAT POPCORN" and "DRINK COKE" on a movie screen in a local theater (Weir, 1984). Vicary's claims were a hoax, but people have continued to wonder whether behavior can be influenced by stimuli that are presented so quickly that we cannot perceive them.

*This was an experiment. The participants who saw "thirsty words" were the experimental group, and the other participants were the control group. Now, why were they randomly assigned to the conditions?*

Studies have shown that the brain responds to information that is presented below the conscious threshold, and such information can also influence behavior (Dupoux, de Gardelle, & Kouider, 2008; Radel, Sarrazin, & Pelletier, 2009). In one study, researchers randomly assigned participants to observe either words related to being thirsty or control words of the same length being flashed on a computer screen for 16 milliseconds while they performed an unrelated task (Strahan, Spencer, & Zanna, 2002). All of the participants thought they were participating in a taste test study, and all were thirsty. None of the participants reported seeing the flashed words, but when given a chance to drink a beverage afterward, those who had seen thirst-related words drank more. Research has also supported the notion that people's performance on learning tasks is affected by stimuli that are too faint to be recognized at a conscious level (Cleeremans & Sarrazin, 2007). You will read further about these effects in Chapter 6's discussion of priming.

The notion that stimuli we do not consciously perceive can influence our behavior challenges the usefulness of the idea of thresholds (Rouder & Morey, 2009). If stimuli that fall below the threshold can have an impact on us, you may be wondering, what do thresholds really tell us? Further, you might have noticed that the definition of absolute threshold is not that absolute. It refers to the intensity of stimulation detected *50 percent of the time.* How can something absolute change from one trial to the next?

If, for example, you tried the ticking clock experiment described earlier, you might have found yourself making judgment calls. Sometimes you felt very sure you could hear the clock, but other times you were uncertain and probably took a guess. Sometimes you guessed right, and other times you were mistaken. Now, imagine that someone offered to pay you $50 for every correct answer you gave—would the presence of that incentive change your judgments? Alternatively, what if you were charged $50 for every time you said you heard the clock and it was not ticking? In fact, perception is often about making such judgment calls.

An alternative approach to the question of whether a stimulus is detected would emphasize that saying (or not saying) "Yes, I hear that ticking" is actually a *decision*. This approach is called signal detection theory. **Signal detection theory** focuses on decision making about stimuli under conditions of uncertainty. In signal detection theory, detection of sensory stimuli depends on a variety of factors besides the physical intensity of the stimulus and the sensory abilities of the observer (Haase & Fisk, 2011; Olma & others, 2011). These factors include individual and

**Weber's law**
The principle that two stimuli must differ by a con-stant minimum percentage (rather than a constant amount) to be perceived as different.

**subliminal perception**
The detection of information below the level of conscious awareness.

**signal detection theory**
An approach to perception that focuses on decision making about stimuli under conditions of uncertainty.

contextual variations, such as fatigue, expectations, and the urgency of the moment. Figure 3.5 shows how signal detection works.

# Perceiving Sensory Stimuli

As we just saw, the perception of stimuli is influenced by more than the characteristics of the environmental stimuli themselves. Two important factors in perceiving sensory stimuli are attention and perceptual set.

|  | "Yes, I see the signal." | "No, I don't see the signal." |
|---|---|---|
| **Signal Present** | Hit (correct) | Miss (mistake) |
| **Signal Absent** | False alarm (mistake) | Correct rejection (correct) |

**FIGURE 3.5** **Four Outcomes in Signal Detection** Signal detection research helps to explain when and how perceptual judgments are correct or mistaken.

**ATTENTION**   The world holds a lot of information to perceive. At this moment you are perceiving the letters and words that make up this sentence. Now gaze around you and fix your eyes on something other than this book. Afterward, curl up the toes on your right foot. In each of these circumstances, you engaged in **selective attention,** which involves focusing on a specific aspect of experience while ignoring others (Reed & Hicks, 2012). A familiar example of selective attention is the ability to focus on one voice among many in a crowded airline terminal or noisy restaurant. Psychologists call this common occurrence the *cocktail party effect* (Kuyper, 1972).

Not only is attention selective, but it also is shiftable. For example, you might be paying close attention to your instructor's lecture, but if the person next to you starts texting a friend, you might look to see what is going on over there. The fact that we can attend selectively to one stimulus and shift readily to another indicates that we must be monitoring many things at once.

Certain features of stimuli cause people to attend to them. Novel stimuli (those that are new, different, or unusual) often attract our attention. If a Ferrari convertible whizzes by, you are more likely to notice it than you would a Ford. Size, color, and movement also influence our attention. Objects that are large, vividly colored, or moving are more likely to grab our attention than objects that are small, dull-colored, or stationary.

Sometimes even very interesting stimuli can be missed if our attention is otherwise occupied. *Inattentional blindness* refers to the failure to detect unexpected events when attention is engaged by a task (Chabris & Simons, 2010). When we are working intently on something, such as finding a seat in a packed movie theater, we might not even see an unusual stimulus, such as a friend waving to us in the crowd. Research conducted by Daniel Simons and Christopher Chabris (1999) provides a remarkable example of inattentional blindness. In that study, participants were asked to watch a video of two teams playing basketball. The participants were instructed to closely count the number of passes thrown by each team. During the video, a small woman dressed in a gorilla suit walked through the action, clearly visible for 5 seconds. Surprisingly, over half of the participants (who were apparently deeply engaged in the counting task) never noticed the gorilla. Inattentional blindness is more likely to occur when a task is difficult (Macdonald & Lavie, 2008) and when the distracting stimulus is very different from stimuli that are relevant to the task at hand (White & Aimola Davies, 2008; Wiemer, Gerdes, & Pauli, 2012).

Research on inattentional blindness suggests the dangers of multitasking when one of the tasks is driving. Engaging in a task such as talking on a cell phone or sending text messages can so occupy attention that little is left over for the important task of piloting a motor vehicle. Research revealed that

**selective attention**
The act of focusing on a specific aspect of experience while ignoring others.

*EXPERIENCE IT!*
Inattentional Blindness

*"Now that I have your attention, dear . . ."*

Used by permission of CartoonStock, www.CartoonStock.com.

individuals who text-message while they drive face 23 times the risk of a crash or near-crash compared to non-distracted drivers (Blanco & others, 2009; Hanowski & others, 2009). In this research, cameras continuously observed drivers for more than 6 million miles of driving. Texting drew the drivers' eyes away from the road long enough for the vehicle to travel the length of a football field at 55 miles an hour.

**CULTURE, ATTENTION, AND PERCEPTION**   Research shows that culture influences which stimuli we attend to as we perceive the world. Individuals from Western cultures are more likely to attend to objects in the foreground of scenes (or *focal objects*), while East Asians looking at the same scenes are more likely to notice aspects of the context. For example, in one study (Masuda & Nisbett, 2001), American and Japanese participants were shown video clips of underwater scenes. When asked to describe what they had seen, the Americans were more likely to talk about the colorful fish swimming around, and Japanese participants were more likely to talk about the locations of objects and aspects of the setting. Such differences have led psychologists to conclude that Westerners take a more analytical orientation, while Asians are more likely to see the big picture. Culture also influences the kinds of stimuli that are missed in inattentional blindness. Research on *change blindness* (the tendency to miss changes that have occurred in a scene) shows that when objects in the foreground change, Americans are more likely to notice, while Japanese are more likely to notice when changes occur in the context (Masuda & Nisbett, 2006).

What might explain these cultural differences in attention? One possibility may be differences in the environments that individuals in these cultures typically encounter. In a series of studies, Yuri Miyamoto and her colleagues (Miyamoto, Nisbett, & Masuda, 2006) found through photographic comparisons that Japanese hotels and schools had more detail and were more complex than American hotels and schools. Japanese individuals, then, may develop the tendency to look at the whole picture because navigating their world requires such attention. Interestingly, in another study, Miyamoto and her colleagues had American and Japanese participants watch brief video clips of American or Japanese scenes (Miyamoto, Nisbett, & Masuda, 2006). They found that American and Japanese participants alike noticed changes in focal objects in American scenes but noticed changes in the context in Japanese scenes. This research suggests that while the mechanics of sensation are the same for human beings, the experience of perception can be shaped by the physical environment in which each person lives.

**PERCEPTUAL SET**   Place your hand over the playing cards on the right in the illustration and look at the playing cards on the left. As quickly as you can, count how many aces of spades you see. Then place your hand over the cards on the left and count the number of aces of spades among the cards on the right.

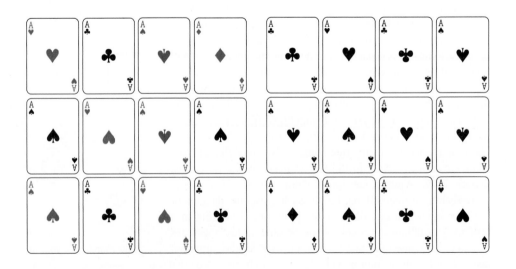

Most people report that they see two or three aces of spades in the set of cards on the left. However, if you look closely, you will see that there are five. Two of the aces of spades are black and three are red. When people look at the set of cards on the right, they are more likely to count five aces of spades. Why do we perceive the two sets of cards differently? We expect the ace of spades to be black because it is always black in a regular deck of cards. We do not expect red spades, so we skip right over the red ones: Expectations influence perceptions.

Psychologists refer to a predisposition or readiness to perceive something in a particular way as a **perceptual set.** Perceptual sets act as "psychological" filters in processing information about the environment (Fei-Fei & others, 2007). Perceptual sets reflect top-down influences on perception. Interestingly, young children are more accurate at the task involving the ace of spades than adults are. Why? Because they have not built up the perceptual set that the ace of spades is black.

**perceptual set**
A predisposition or readiness to perceive something in a particular way.

## Sensory Adaptation

**sensory adaptation**
A change in the responsiveness of the sensory system based on the average level of surrounding stimulation.

Turning out the lights in your bedroom at night, you stumble across the room to your bed, blind to the objects around you. Gradually the objects reappear and become clearer. The ability of the visual system to adjust to a darkened room is an example of **sensory adaptation**—a change in the responsiveness of the sensory system based on the average level of surrounding stimulation (Iglesias, 2012; Elliott & others, 2009).

You have experienced sensory adaptation countless times in your life. You adjust to the water in an initially "freezing" swimming pool. You turn on your windshield wipers while driving, and shortly you are unaware of their rhythmic sweeping back and forth. When you first enter a room, you might be bothered by the hum of the air conditioner, but after a while you get used to it. All of these experiences represent sensory adaptation.

In the example of adapting to the dark, when you turn out the lights, everything is black. Conversely, when you step out into the bright sunshine after spending time in a dark basement, light floods your eyes and everything appears light. These momentary blips in sensation arise because adaptation takes time.

*EXPERIENCE IT!*
Sensory Adaptation

## self-quiz

1. Every day, you see, hear, smell, taste, and feel stimuli from the outside world. Collecting data about that world is the function of _____, and interpreting the data collected is the function of _____.
   A. the brain; the spinal cord
   B. the spinal cord; the brain
   C. sensation; perception
   D. perception; sensation

2. The main classes into which the sense organs and sensory receptors fall include all of the following *except*
   A. chemoreception.
   B. electroreception.
   C. photoreception.
   D. mechanoreception.

3. An architect is designing apartments and wants them to be soundproof. She asks a psychologist what the smallest amount of sound is that can be heard. Her question is most related to
   A. the absolute threshold.
   B. the difference threshold.
   C. Weber's law.
   D. the sensory receptors.

**APPLY IT!** 4. Trina, a first-year college student, goes home at Thanksgiving break after being away from home (for the first time) for three months. She feels as if she has changed a lot, but her parents still treat her like a kid in high school. At Thanksgiving dinner she confronts them, bursting out, "Stop top-down processing me!" Her parents think Trina has lost her mind. Which of the following explains her outburst?
   A. Trina feels that her parents are judging her sophisticated college ways too harshly.
   B. Trina probably ate too much turkey.
   C. Trina feels that her parents have spent too much time analyzing her behavior.
   D. Trina believes that her parents are letting their preconceived ideas of who she is prevent them from seeing her as the person she has become.

# 2 The Visual System

When Michael May of Davis, California, was 3 years old, an accident left him visually impaired, with only the ability to perceive the difference between night and day. He lived a rich, full life, marrying and having children, founding a successful company, and becoming an expert skier. Twenty-five years passed before doctors transplanted stem cells into May's right eye, a new procedure that gave him partial sight (Kurson, 2007). May can now see; his right eye is functional and allows him to detect color and negotiate the world without the use of a cane or reliance on his seeing-eye dog. His visual experience remains unusual, however: He sees the world as if it is an abstract painting. He can catch a ball thrown to him by his sons, but he cannot recognize his wife's face. His brain has to work at interpreting the new information that his right eye is providing. May's experience highlights the intimate connection between the brain and the sense organs in producing perception. Vision is a remarkable process that involves the brain's interpretation of the visual information sent from the eyes. We now explore the physical foundations of the visual system and the processes involved in the perception of visual stimuli.

## The Visual Stimulus and the Eye

Our ability to detect visual stimuli depends on the sensitivity of our eyes to differences in light.

**LIGHT**   *Light* is a form of electromagnetic energy that can be described in terms of wavelengths. Light travels through space in waves. The *wavelength* of light is the distance from the peak of one wave to the peak of the next. Wavelengths of visible light range from about 400 to 700 nanometers (a nanometer is 1 billionth of a meter and is abbreviated nm). The wavelength of light that is reflected from a stimulus determines its hue or color.

Outside the range of visible light are longer radio and infrared radiation waves and shorter ultraviolet and X rays (Figure 3.6). These other forms of electromagnetic energy continually bombard us, but we do not see them.

We can also describe waves of light in terms of their height, or *amplitude,* which determines the brightness of the stimulus. Finally, the *purity* of the wavelengths—whether they are all the same or a mix of waves—determines the perceived *saturation,* or richness, of a visual stimulus (Figure 3.7). The color tree shown in Figure 3.8 can help you to understand saturation. White light is a combination of color wavelengths that is perceived as colorless, like sunlight. Very pure colors have no white light in them. They are located on the outside of the color tree. Notice how, the closer we get to the center of the color tree, the more white light has been added to the single wavelength of a particular color. In other words, the deep colors at the edge fade into pastel colors toward the center.

**THE STRUCTURE OF THE EYE**   The eye, like a camera, is constructed to get the best possible picture of the world. An accurate picture is in focus, is not too dark or too light, and has good contrast between the dark and light parts. Each of several structures in the eye plays an important role in this process.

If you look closely at your eyes in the mirror, you will notice three parts—the sclera, iris, and pupil (Figure 3.9). The *sclera* is the white, outer part of the eye that helps to maintain the shape of the eye and to protect it from injury. The *iris* is the colored part of the eye, which might be light blue in one individual and dark brown in another. The

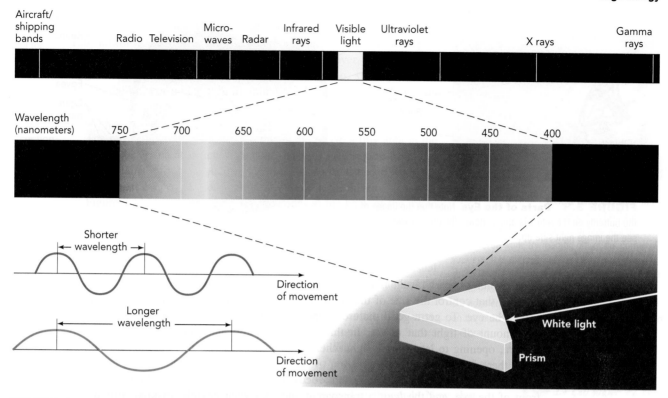

Aircraft/ shipping bands | Radio | Television | Micro- waves | Radar | Infrared rays | Visible light | Ultraviolet rays | X rays | Gamma rays

Wavelength (nanometers)  750  700  650  600  550  500  450  400

Shorter wavelength

Direction of movement

Longer wavelength

Direction of movement

White light

Prism

**FIGURE 3.6** **The Electromagnetic Spectrum and Visible Light** (*Top*) Visible light is only a narrow band in the electromagnetic spectrum. Visible light wavelengths range from about 400 to 700 nanometers. X rays are much shorter, radio waves much longer. (*Bottom*) The two graphs show how waves vary in length between successive peaks. Shorter wavelengths are higher in frequency, as reflected in blue colors; longer wavelengths are lower in frequency, as reflected in red colors.

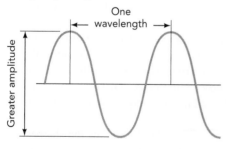

Light waves of greater amplitude make up brighter light.

One wavelength

Greater amplitude

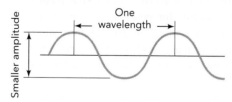

Light waves of smaller amplitude make up dimmer light.

One wavelength

Smaller amplitude

**FIGURE 3.7** **Light Waves of Varying Amplitude** The top graph might suggest a spotlight on a concert stage; the bottom, a candlelit dinner.

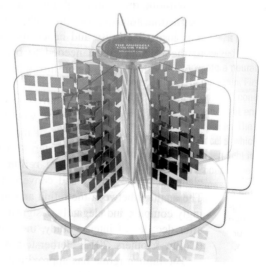

**FIGURE 3.8** **A Color Tree Showing Color's Three Dimensions: Hue, Saturation, and Brightness** Hue is represented around the color tree— saturation horizontally and brightness vertically.

# Color Vision

Imagine how dull the world would be without color. Art museums are filled with paintings that are remarkable for their use of color, and flowers would lose much of their beauty if we could not see their rich hues. The process of color perception starts in the retina, the eyes' film. Interestingly, theories about how the retina processes color were developed long before methods existed to study the anatomical and neurophysiological bases of color perception. Instead, psychologists made some extraordinarily accurate guesses about how color vision occurs in the retina by observing how people see. The two main theories proposed were the trichromatic theory and opponent-process theory. Both turned out to be correct.

**trichromatic theory**
Theory stating that color perception is produced by three types of cone receptors in the retina that are particularly sensitive to different but overlapping ranges of wavelengths.

The **trichromatic theory,** proposed by Thomas Young in 1802 and extended by Hermann von Helmholtz in 1852, states that color perception is produced by three types of cone receptors in the retina that are particularly sensitive to different but overlapping ranges of wavelengths. The theory is based on experiments showing that a person with normal vision can match any color in the spectrum by combining three other wavelengths. Young and Helmholtz reasoned that if the combination of any three wavelengths of different intensities is indistinguishable from any single pure wavelength, the visual system must base its perception of color on the relative responses of three receptor systems—cones sensitive to red, blue, and green.

The study of defective color vision, or *color blindness* (Figure 3.15), provides further support for the trichromatic theory. Complete color blindness is rare; most color-blind people, the vast majority of whom are men, can see some colors but not others. The nature of color blindness depends on which of the three kinds of cones is inoperative (Machado, Oliveira, & Fernandes, 2009). The three cone systems are green, red, and blue. In the most common form of color blindness, the green cone system malfunctions in some way, rendering green indistinguishable from certain combinations of blue and red.

In 1878, the German physiologist Ewald Hering observed that some colors cannot exist together, whereas others can. For example, it is easy to imagine a greenish blue but nearly impossible to imagine a reddish green. Hering also noticed that trichromatic theory could not adequately explain *afterimages,* sensations that remain after a stimulus is removed (Figure 3.16 gives you a chance to experience an afterimage). Color afterimages are common and involve particular pairs of colors. If you look at red long enough, eventually a green afterimage will appear. If you look at yellow long enough, eventually a blue afterimage will appear.

**opponent-process theory**
Theory stating that cells in the visual system respond to complementary pairs of red-green and blue-yellow colors; a given cell might be excited by red and inhibited by green, whereas another cell might be excited by yellow and inhibited by blue.

Hering's observations led him to propose that there were not three types of color receptor cones (as proposed by trichromatic theory) but four, organized into complementary pairs: red-green and blue-yellow. Hering's view, **opponent-process theory,** states that cells in the visual system respond to red-green and blue-yellow colors; a given cell

**FIGURE 3.15  Examples of Stimuli Used to Test for Color Blindness** People with normal vision see the number 16 in the left circle and the number 8 in the right circle. People with red-green color blindness may see just the 16, just the 8, or neither. A complete color-blindness assessment involves the use of 15 stimuli.

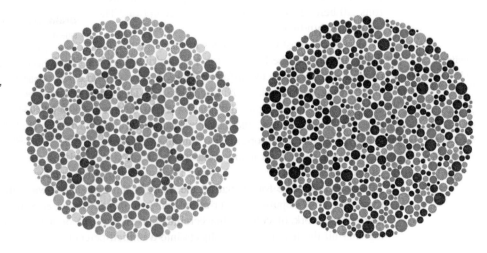

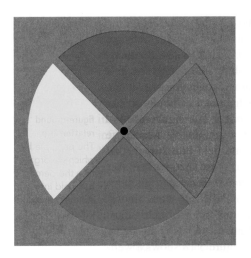

**FIGURE 3.16** **Negative Afterimage—Complementary Colors** If you gaze steadily at the dot in the colored panel on the left for a few moments, then shift your gaze to the gray box on the right, you will see the original hues' complementary colors. The blue appears as yellow, the red as green, the green as red, and the yellow as blue. This pairing of colors has to do with the fact that color receptors in the eye are apparently sensitive as pairs: When one color is turned off (when you stop staring at the panel), the other color in the receptor is briefly turned on. The afterimage effect is especially noticeable with bright colors.

might be excited by red and inhibited by green, whereas another cell might be excited by yellow and inhibited by blue. Researchers have found that opponent-process theory does indeed explain afterimages (Jameson & Hurvich, 1989). If you stare at red, for instance, your red-green system seems to "tire," and when you look away, it rebounds and gives you a green afterimage.

If the trichromatic theory of color perception is valid and we do in fact have three kinds of cone receptors like those predicted by Young and Helmholtz, then how can the opponent-process theory also be accurate? The answer is that the red, blue, and green cones in the retina are connected to retinal ganglion cells in such a way that the three-color code is immediately translated into the opponent-process code (Figure 3.17). For example, a green cone might inhibit and a red cone might excite a particular ganglion cell. Thus, both the trichromatic and opponent-process theories are correct—the eye and the brain use both methods to code colors.

## Perceiving Shape, Depth, Motion, and Constancy

Perceiving visual stimuli means organizing and interpreting the fragments of information that the eye sends to the visual cortex. Information about the dimensions of what we are seeing is critical to this process. Among these dimensions are shape, depth, motion, and constancy.

**SHAPE**  Think about the visible world and its shapes—buildings against the sky, boats on the horizon, the letters on this page. We see these shapes because they are

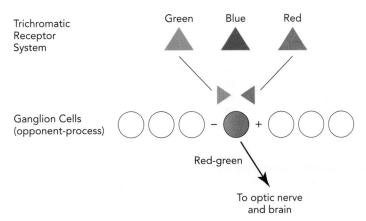

**FIGURE 3.17** **Trichromatic and Opponent-Process Theories: Transmission of Color Information in the Retina** Cones responsive to green, blue, or red light form a trichromatic receptor system in the retina. As information is transmitted to the retina's ganglion cells, opponent-process cells are activated. As shown here, a retinal ganglion cell is inhibited by a green cone (−) and excited by a red cone (+), producing red-green color information.

**FIGURE 3.21** **Texture Gradient** The gradients of texture create an impression of depth on a flat surface.

4. *Overlap:* We perceive an object that partially conceals or overlaps another object as closer.

5. *Shading:* This cue involves changes in perception due to the position of the light and the position of the viewer. Consider an egg under a desk lamp. If you walk around the desk, you will see different shading patterns on the egg.

6. *Texture gradient:* Texture becomes denser and finer the farther away it is from the viewer (Figure 3.21).

Depth perception is a remarkably complex adaptation. Individuals with only one functioning eye cannot see depth in the way that those with two eyes can. Other disorders of the eye can also lead to a lack of depth perception. Oliver Sacks (2006) described the case of Susan Barry, who had been born with crossed eyes. The operation to correct her eyes left her cosmetically normal, but she was unable to perceive depth throughout her life. As an adult, she became determined to see depth. With a doctor's aid, she found special glasses and performed eye muscle exercises to improve her chances of perceiving in three dimensions. It was a difficult and long process, but one day she noticed things starting to "stick out" at her—as you might when watching a film in 3-D. Although Barry had successfully adapted to life in a flat visual world, she had come to realize that relying on monocular cues was not the same as experiencing the rich visual world of binocular vision. She described flowers as suddenly appearing "inflated." She noted how "ordinary things looked extraordinary" as she saw the leaves of a tree, an empty chair, and her office door projecting out from the background. For the first time, she had a sense of being inside the world she was viewing.

**MOTION PERCEPTION**    Motion perception plays an important role in the lives of many species (Boeddeker & Hemmi, 2010). Indeed, for some animals, motion perception is critical for survival. Both predators and their prey depend on being able to detect motion quickly (Borst, Haag, & Reiff, 2010). Frogs and some other simple vertebrates may not even see an object unless it is moving. For example, if a dead fly is dangled motionlessly in front of a frog, the frog cannot sense its winged meal. The bug-detecting cells in the frog's retinas are wired only to sense movement.

Whereas the retinas of frogs can detect movement, the retinas of humans and other primates cannot. According to one neuroscientist, "The dumber the animal, the 'smarter' the retina" (Baylor, 2001). In humans the brain takes over the job of analyzing motion through highly specialized pathways (Lee & Lee, 2012).

How do humans perceive movement? First, we have neurons that are specialized to detect motion. Second, feedback from our body tells us whether we are moving or whether someone or some object is moving; for example, you move your eye muscles as you watch a ball coming toward you. Third, the environment we see is rich in cues that give us information about movement (Badler & Heinen, 2006). For example, when we run, our surroundings appear to be moving.

Psychologists are interested in both real movement and **apparent movement,** which occurs when we perceive a stationary object as moving. You can experience apparent movement at IMAX movie theaters. In watching a film of a climb of Mount Everest, you may find yourself feeling breathless as your visual field floods with startling images. In theaters without seats, viewers of these films are often warned to hold the handrail because perceived movement is so realistic that they might fall.

**apparent movement**
The perception that a stationary object is moving.

**PERCEPTUAL CONSTANCY**    Retinal images change constantly. Yet even though the stimuli that fall on our retinas change as we move closer to or farther away from objects, or as we look at objects from different orientations and in light or dark settings, our perception of them remains stable. **Perceptual constancy** is the recognition that objects are constant and unchanging even though sensory input about them is changing.

We experience three types of perceptual constancy—size constancy, shape constancy, and color constancy—as follows:

- *Size constancy* is the recognition that an object remains the same size even though the retinal image of the object changes (Figure 3.22). Experience is important to size perception: No matter how far away you are from your car, you know how large it is.

- *Shape constancy* is the recognition that an object retains the same shape even though its orientation to you changes. Look around. You probably see objects of various shapes—chairs and tables, for example. If you walk around the room, you will view these objects from different sides and angles. Even though the retinal image of the object changes as you walk, you still perceive the objects as having the same shape (Figure 3.23).

- *Color constancy* is the recognition that an object retains the same color even though different amounts of light fall on it. For example, if you are reaching for a green Granny Smith apple, it looks green to you whether you are having it for lunch, in the bright noon sun, or as an evening snack in the pale pink of sunset.

**FIGURE 3.22** **Size Constancy** Even though our retinal images of the hot air balloons vary, we still realize the balloons are approximately the same size. This illustrates the principle of size constancy.

Perceptual constancy tells us about the crucial role of interpretation in perception: We interpret sensation. That is, we perceive objects as having particular characteristics regardless of the retinal image detected by our eyes. Images may flow across the retina, but experiences are made sensible through perception. The many cues we use to visually perceive the real world can lead to optical illusions when they are taken out of that real-world context, as you can experience for yourself in Figure 3.24.

As you look over these illusions, consider that culture can influence the extent to which people experience these illusions. In cultures where two-dimensional images, such as drawings on a piece of paper, are not typically used, geometrical illusions are less likely to lead to errors (Segall, Campbell, & Herskovits, 1966).

**FIGURE 3.23** **Shape Constancy** The various projected images from an opening door are quite different, yet you perceive a rectangular door.

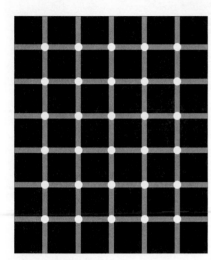

**Rotational Illusion**
The two rings appear to rotate in different directions when we approach or move away from this figure while fixing our eyes on the center.

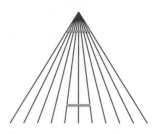

**Ponzo Illusion**
The top line looks much longer than the bottom, but they are the same length.

**Blinking Effect Illusion**
Stare at the white circles and notice the intermittent blinking effect. Your eyes make the static figure seem dynamic, attempting to fill in the white circle intersections with the black of the background.

**Pattern Recognition**
Although the diagram contains no actual triangles, your brain "sees" two overlapping triangles. The explanation is that the notched circles and angled lines merely suggest gaps in which complete objects should be. The brain fills in the missing information.

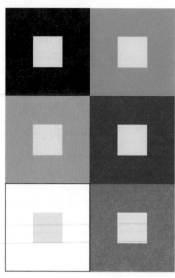

**Induction Illusion**
The yellow patches are identical, but they look different and seem to take on the characteristics of their surroundings when they appear against different-color backgrounds.

**FIGURE 3.24** **Perceptual Illusions** These illusions show how adaptive perceptual cues can lead to errors when taken out of context. They are definitely fun, but keep in mind that these illusions are based on processes that are quite adaptive in real life. Remember, not everyone sees these illusions. In cultures where exposure to two-dimensional representations is not common, individuals are less fooled by geometric illusions.

## self-quiz

1. When we refer to the hue of a light wave, we are referring to what we perceive as
   A. intensity.
   B. radiation.
   C. brightness.
   D. color.

2. To read this question, you are looking at it. After the light passes into your eyes, the incoming light waves are recorded by receptor cells located in the
   A. retina.
   B. cornea.
   C. blind spot.
   D. optic chiasm.

3. If you are in a well-lighted room, your rods are being used _____ and cones are being used _____.
   A. infrequently; frequently
   B. infrequently; infrequently
   C. frequently; infrequently
   D. frequently; frequently

**APPLY IT!** 4. Sondra was driving in the country one afternoon. There was not much traffic on the long, straight road, though Sondra noticed a man walking along the roadside some distance away. Suddenly, as she approached the person, he drifted toward the middle of the road, and Sondra, with screeching brakes, was shocked to realize she had nearly hit a child. Fortunately, the child was not harmed. It had become clear to Sondra that what had seemed like a man some distance away was actually a child who was much closer than she realized. What explains this situation?
A. Sondra's occipital lobe must be damaged.
B. Because objects that are smaller on the retina are typically farther away, Sondra was fooled by relative size.
C. Because objects in the mirror are closer than they appear, Sondra was not able to detect the just-noticeable difference.
D. Because objects that are smaller on the retina are typically closer than they appear, Sondra was fooled by shape constancy.

# 3 The Auditory System

Just as light provides us with information about the environment, so does sound. Sounds tell us about the presence of a person behind us, the approach of an oncoming car, the force of the wind, and the mischief of a 2-year-old. Perhaps most important, sounds allow us to communicate through language and song.

## The Nature of Sound and How We Experience It

At a fireworks display, you may feel the loud boom of the explosion in your chest. At a concert, you might have sensed that the air around you was vibrating. Bass instruments are especially effective at creating mechanical pulsations, even causing the floor to vibrate. When the bass is played loudly, we can sense air molecules being pushed forward in waves from the speaker. How does sound generate these sensations?

Sound waves are vibrations in the air that are processed by the *auditory* (hearing) system. Remember that light waves are much like the waves in the ocean moving toward the beach. Sound waves are similar. Sound waves also vary in length. Wavelength determines the sound wave's *frequency,* that is, the number of cycles (full wavelengths) that pass through a point in a given time interval. *Pitch* is the perceptual interpretation of the frequency of a sound. We perceive high-frequency sounds as having a high pitch, and low-frequency sounds as having a low pitch. A soprano voice sounds high-pitched; a bass voice has a low pitch. As with the wavelengths of light, human sensitivity is limited to a range of sound frequencies. It is common knowledge that dogs, for example, can hear higher frequencies than humans can.

Sound waves vary not only in frequency but also, like light waves, in amplitude (see Figure 3.7). A sound wave's *amplitude,* measured in decibels (dB), is the amount of pressure the sound wave produces relative to a standard. The typical standard, 0 decibels, is the weakest sound the human ear can detect. *Loudness* is the perception of the sound wave's amplitude. In general, the higher the amplitude of the sound wave, or the higher the decibel level, the louder we perceive the sound to be. Thus, in terms of amplitude, the air is pressing more forcibly against you and your ears during loud sounds and more gently during quiet sounds.

So far we have been describing a single sound wave with just one frequency. A single sound wave is similar to the single wavelength of pure colored light, discussed in the context of color matching. Most sounds, including those of speech and music, are complex sounds, those in which numerous frequencies of sound blend together. *Timbre* is the tone saturation, or the perceptual quality, of a sound. Timbre is responsible for the perceptual difference between a trumpet and a trombone playing the same note and for the quality differences we hear in human voices. Figure 3.25 illustrates the physical differences in sound waves that produce the various qualities of sounds.

## Structures and Functions of the Ear

What happens to sound waves once they reach your ear? How do various structures of the ear transform sound waves into signals that the brain will recognize as sound? Functionally the ear is analogous to the

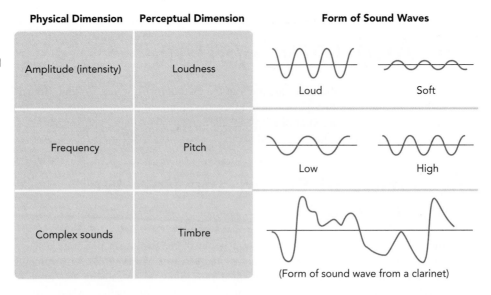

| Physical Dimension | Perceptual Dimension | Form of Sound Waves | |
| --- | --- | --- | --- |
| Amplitude (intensity) | Loudness | Loud | Soft |
| Frequency | Pitch | Low | High |
| Complex sounds | Timbre | (Form of sound wave from a clarinet) | |

eye. The ear serves the purpose of transmitting a high-fidelity version of sounds in the world to the brain for analysis and interpretation. Just as an image needs to be in focus and sufficiently bright for the brain to interpret it, a sound needs to be transmitted in a way that preserves information about its location, its frequency (which helps us distinguish the voice of a child from that of an adult), and its timbre (which allows us to identify the voice of a friend on the telephone). The ear is divided into three parts: outer ear, middle ear, and inner ear (Figure 3.26).

**OUTER EAR**   The **outer ear** consists of the pinna and the external auditory canal. The funnel-shaped *pinna* (plural, *pinnae*) is the outer, visible part of the ear. (Elephants have very large pinnae.) The pinna collects sounds and channels them into the interior of the ear. The pinnae of many animals, such as cats, are movable and serve a more important role in sound localization than do the pinnae of humans. Cats turn their ears in the direction of a faint and interesting sound.

**outer ear**
The outermost part of the ear, consisting of the pinna and the external auditory canal.

**FIGURE 3.26   The Outer, Middle, and Inner Ear** On entering the outer ear, sound waves travel through the auditory canal, where they generate vibrations in the eardrum. These vibrations are transferred via the hammer, anvil, and stirrup to the fluid-filled cochlea in the inner ear. There the mechanical vibrations are converted into an electrochemical signal that the brain will recognize as sound.

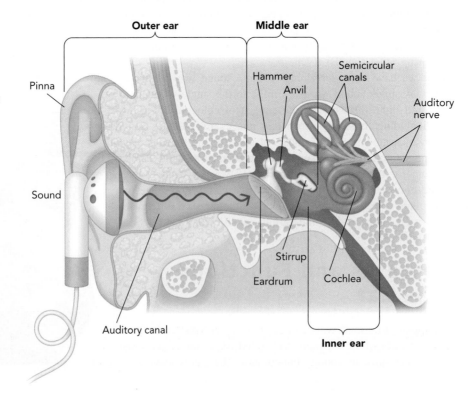

**MIDDLE EAR**  After passing the pinna, sound waves move through the auditory canal to the middle ear. The **middle ear** channels the sound through the eardrum, hammer, anvil, and stirrup to the inner ear. The *eardrum,* or *tympanic membrane,* separates the outer ear from the middle ear and vibrates in response to sound. It is the first structure that sound touches in the middle ear. The *hammer, anvil,* and *stirrup* are an intricately connected chain of very small bones. When they vibrate, they transmit sound waves to the fluid-filled inner ear (Stenfelt, 2006). The muscles that operate these tiny bones take the vibration of the eardrum and transmit it to the *oval window,* the opening of the inner ear.

If you are a swimmer, you know that sound travels far more easily in air than in water. Sound waves entering the ear travel in air until they reach the inner ear. At the border between the middle and the inner ear—which, as we will see below, is a border between air and fluid—sound meets the same kind of resistance as do shouts directed at an underwater swimmer when the shouts hit the surface of the water. To compensate, the muscles of the middle ear can maneuver the hammer, anvil, and stirrup to amplify the sound waves. Importantly, these muscles, if necessary, can also work to decrease the intensity of sound waves, to protect the inner ear.

**INNER EAR**  The function of the **inner ear,** which includes the oval window, cochlea, and basilar membrane, is to convert sound waves into neural impulses and send them on to the brain (Gregan, Nelson, & Oxenham, 2011). The stirrup is connected to the membranous *oval window,* which transmits sound waves to the cochlea. The *cochlea* is a tubular, fluid-filled structure that is coiled up like a snail (Figure 3.27). The *basilar*

**middle ear**
The part of the ear that channels sound through the eardrum, hammer, anvil, and stirrup to the inner ear.

*The hammer, anvil, and stirrup are also called the ossicles. These are the tiniest bones in the human body.*

**inner ear**
The part of the ear that includes the oval window, cochlea, and basilar membrane and whose function is to convert sound waves into neural impulses and send them to the brain.

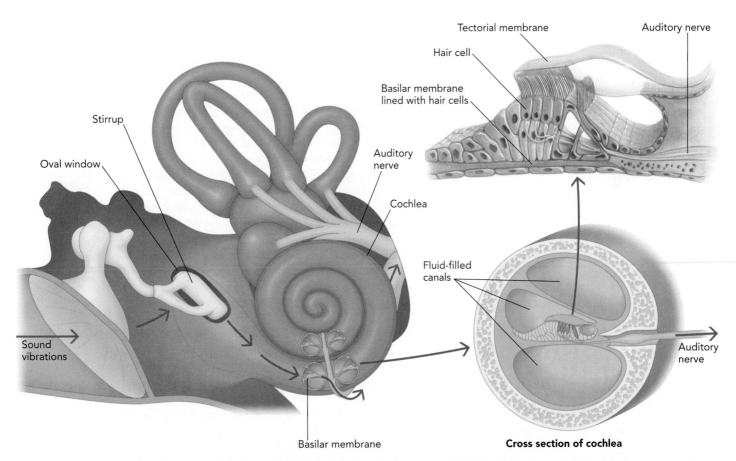

**FIGURE 3.27**  **The Cochlea**  The cochlea is a spiral structure consisting of fluid-filled canals. When the stirrup vibrates against the oval window, the fluid in the canals vibrates. Vibrations along portions of the basilar membrane correspond to different sound frequencies. The vibrations exert pressure on the hair cells (between the basilar and tectorial membranes); the hair cells in turn push against the tectorial membrane, and this pressure bends the hairs. This triggers an action potential in the auditory nerve.

*membrane* lines the inner wall of the cochlea and runs its entire length. It is narrow and rigid at the base of the cochlea but widens and becomes more flexible at the top. The variation in width and flexibility allows different areas of the basilar membrane to vibrate more intensely when exposed to different sound frequencies (Wojtczak & Oxenham, 2009). For example, the high-pitched tinkle of a little bell stimulates the narrow region of the basilar membrane at the base of the cochlea, whereas the low-pitched tones of a tugboat whistle stimulate the wide end.

In humans and other mammals, hair cells line the basilar membrane (see Figure 3.27). These *hair cells* are the sensory receptors of the ear. They are called hair cells because of the tufts of fine bristles, or *cilia,* that sprout from the top of them. The movement of the hair cells against the *tectorial membrane,* a jellylike flap above them, generates resulting impulses that the brain interprets as sound (Nowatny & Gummer, 2011). Hair cells are so delicate that exposure to loud noise can destroy them, leading to deafness or difficulties in hearing. Once lost, hair cells cannot regenerate.

Cochlear implants are devices that were specifically developed to replace damaged hair cells. A *cochlear implant*—a small electronic device that is surgically implanted in the ear and head—allows deaf or profoundly hard-of-hearing individuals to detect sound (Sparreboom, Snik, & Mylanus, 2012). The implant works by using electronic impulses to directly stimulate whatever working auditory nerves the recipient has in his or her cochlea (Zhou, Xu, & Pfingst, 2012). In the United States, approximately 41,500 adults and 25,500 children have had cochlear implants (U.S. Food and Drug Administration, 2009).

# Theories of Hearing

One of the auditory system's mysteries is how the inner ear registers the frequency of sound. Two theories aim to explain this mystery: place theory and frequency theory.

**Place theory** states that each frequency produces vibrations at a particular place on the basilar membrane. Georg von Békésy (1960) studied the effects of vibration applied at the oval window on the basilar membrane of human cadavers. Through a microscope, he saw that this stimulation produced a traveling wave on the basilar membrane. A traveling wave is like the ripples that appear in a pond when you throw in a stone. However, because the cochlea is a long tube, the ripples can travel in only one direction, from the oval window at one end of the cochlea to the far tip of the cochlea. High-frequency vibrations create traveling waves that maximally displace, or move, the area of the basilar membrane next to the oval window; low-frequency vibrations maximally displace areas of the membrane closer to the tip of the cochlea.

*Békésy won a Nobel Prize in 1961 for his research on the basilar membrane.*

**place theory**
Theory on how the inner ear registers the frequency of sound, stating that each frequency produces vibrations at a particular place on the basilar membrane.

Place theory adequately explains high-frequency sounds but not low-frequency sounds. A high-frequency sound, like the screech of a referee's whistle or the piercing high note of an opera diva, stimulates a precise area on the basilar membrane, just as the theory suggests. However, a low-frequency sound, like the tone of a tuba or the croak of a bullfrog, causes a large part of the basilar membrane to be displaced, making it hard to identify an exact location that is associated with hearing this kind of sound. Looking only at the movement of the basilar membrane, you would get the impression that humans are probably not very good at hearing low-frequency sounds, and yet we are. Therefore, some other factors must be at play in low-frequency hearing.

**frequency theory**
Theory on how the inner ear registers the frequency of sound, stating that the perception of a sound's frequency depends on how often the auditory nerve fires.

**Frequency theory** gets at these other influences by stating that the perception of a sound's frequency depends on how often the auditory nerve fires. Higher-frequency sounds cause the auditory nerve to fire more often than do lower-frequency sounds. One limitation of frequency theory, however, is that a single neuron has a maximum firing rate of about 1,000 times per second. Therefore, frequency theory does not apply to tones with frequencies that would require a neuron to fire more rapidly.

To deal with this limitation of frequency theory, researchers developed the **volley principle,** which states that a cluster of nerve cells can fire neural impulses in rapid succession, producing a volley of impulses. Individual neurons cannot fire faster than 1,000 times per second, but if the neurons team up and alternate their neural firing, they can attain a combined frequency above that rate. To get a sense for how the volley principle works, imagine a troop of soldiers who are all armed with guns that can fire only one round at a time and that take time to reload. If all the soldiers fire at the same time, the frequency of firing is limited and cannot go any faster than it takes to reload those guns. If, however, the soldiers are coordinated as a group and fire at different times, some of them can fire while others are reloading, leading to a greater frequency of firing. Frequency theory better explains the perception of sounds below 1,000 times per second, whereas a combination of frequency theory and place theory is needed to account for sounds above 1,000 times per second.

*Phew! Two theories and a principle just to explain how we hear.*

## Auditory Processing in the Brain

As we considered in the discussion of the visual system, once our receptors pick up energy from the environment, that energy must be transmitted to the brain for processing and interpretation. We saw that in the retina, the responses of the rod and cone receptors feed into ganglion cells and leave the eye via the optic nerve. In the auditory system, information about sound moves from the hair cells of the inner ear to the **auditory nerve,** which carries neural impulses to the brain's auditory areas. Remember that it is the movement of the hair cells that transforms the physical stimulation of sound waves into the action potential of neural impulses.

Auditory information moves up the auditory pathway via electrochemical transmission in a more complex manner than does visual information in the visual pathway. Many synapses occur in the ascending auditory pathway, with most fibers crossing over the midline between the hemispheres of the cerebral cortex, although some proceed directly to the hemisphere on the same side as the ear of reception (Lewald & Getzmann, 2011). This means that most of the auditory information from the left ear goes to the right side of the brain, but some also goes to the left side of the brain. The auditory nerve extends from the cochlea to the brain stem, with some fibers crossing over the midline. The cortical destination of most of these fibers is the temporal lobes of the brain (beneath the temples of the head). As in the case of visual information, researchers have found that features are extracted from auditory information and transmitted along parallel pathways in the brain (Recanzone & Sutter, 2008).

## Localizing Sound

Do It!

When we hear a fire engine's siren or a dog's bark, how do we know where the sound is coming from? The basilar membrane gives us information about the frequency, pitch, and complexity of a sound, but it does not tell us where a sound is located.

Earlier in the chapter we saw that because our two eyes see slightly different images, we can determine how near or far away an object is. Similarly, having two ears helps us to localize a sound because each receives somewhat different stimuli from the sound source. A sound coming from the left has to travel different distances to the two ears, so if a barking dog is to your left, your left ear receives the sound sooner than your right ear. Also, your left ear will receive a slightly more intense sound than your right ear in this case. The sound reaching one ear is more intense than the sound reaching the other ear for two reasons: (1) It has traveled less distance, and (2) the other ear is in what is called the *sound shadow* of the listener's head, which

**Imagine hearing impossible sounds, nonexistent words, or three voices where only two exist. Welcome to the world of auditory illusions. In Figure 3.24 you tried out some visual illusions. Did you know that there are auditory illusions as well? Search the web for "auditory illusions" and try some out. They can be truly amazing and baffling! Keep in mind, just as you did when looking at the optical illusions, that these illusions emerge as a function of capacities that work very well in the "real world."**

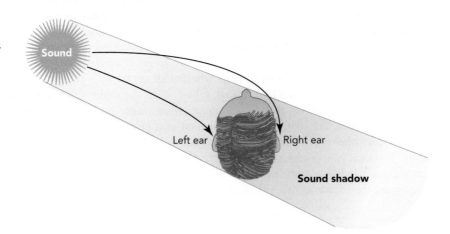

**FIGURE 3.28  The Sound Shadow** The sound shadow is caused by the listener's head, which forms a barrier that reduces the sound's intensity. Here the sound is to the person's left, so the sound shadow will reduce the intensity of the sound that reaches the right ear.

Sound

Left ear    Right ear

**Sound shadow**

provides a barrier that reduces the sound's intensity (Figure 3.28). Blind individuals use the sound shadow to orient themselves.

Thus, differences in both the *timing* of the sound and the *intensity* of the sound help you to localize a sound (Salminen & others, 2010). You often have difficulty localizing a sound that is coming from a source directly in front of you because it reaches both ears simultaneously. The same is true for sounds directly above your head or directly behind you, because the disparities that provide information about location are not present.

**self-quiz**

1. Your mother's and sister's voices have the same pitch and loudness, but you can tell them apart on the telephone. This is due to the perceptual quality, or _____, of their voices.
   A. timbre
   B. wavelength
   C. frequency
   D. amplitude

2. The major function of the hammer, anvil, and stirrup of the middle ear is
   A. to soften the tone of incoming stimuli for appropriate processing.
   B. to stir cochlear fluid so that bone conduction hearing can occur.
   C. to amplify vibrations and pass them on to the inner ear.
   D. to clean the external auditory canal of any potential wax buildup.

3. The bones of the middle ear are set into motion by vibrations of the
   A. cochlea.
   B. eardrum.
   C. saccule.
   D. basilar membrane.

**APPLY IT!** 4. Conservative radio personality Rush Limbaugh experienced sudden hearing loss in 2001, after which he received a cochlear implant. He has described his ability to listen to music as dependent on what he heard before becoming deaf. If he had heard a song prior to becoming deaf, he could hear it, but if it was a new song, he could not make sense of it. Which of the following explains Limbaugh's experience?
   A. He is no longer able to listen to music from a top-down perspective.
   B. He is able to engage in top-down listening, but not bottom-up listening.
   C. He is likely to have experienced damage to the temporal lobes.
   D. He is not able to experience any auditory sensation.

# 4 Other Senses

Beyond vision and hearing, the body has other sensory systems. These include the skin senses and the chemical senses (smell and taste), as well as the kinesthetic and vestibular senses (systems that allow us to stay upright and to coordinate our movements).

## The Skin Senses

You know when a friend has a fever by putting your hand to her head; you know how to find your way to the light switch in a darkened room by groping along the wall; and you know whether a pair of shoes is too tight by the way the shoes touch different parts of your feet when you walk. Many of us think of our skin as a canvas rather than a sense. We color it with cosmetics, dyes, and tattoos. In fact, the skin is our largest sensory system, draped over the body with receptors for touch, temperature, and pain. These three kinds of receptors form the *cutaneous senses*.

**TOUCH**   Touch is one of the senses that we most often take for granted, yet our ability to respond to touch is astounding. What do we detect when we feel "touch"? What kind of energy does our sense of touch pick up from our external environment? In vision we detect light energy. In hearing we detect the vibrations of air or sound waves pressing against our eardrums. In touch we detect mechanical energy, or pressure against the skin. The lifting of a single hair causes pressure on the skin around the hair shaft. This tiny bit of mechanical pressure at the base of the hair is sufficient for us to feel the touch of a pencil point. More commonly we detect the mechanical energy of the pressure of a car seat against our buttocks or of a pencil in our hand. Is this energy so different from the kind of energy we detect in vision or hearing? Sometimes the only difference is one of intensity—the sound of a rock band playing softly is an auditory stimulus, but at the high volumes that make a concert hall reverberate, this auditory stimulus is also felt as mechanical energy pressing against our skin.

> *Your ability to find a nickel in your pocket without looking is a truly amazing feat of touch. Not even the most sophisticated robot can do it.*

How does information about touch travel from the skin through the nervous system? Sensory fibers arising from receptors in the skin enter the spinal cord. From there the information travels to the brain stem, where most fibers from each side of the body cross over to the opposite side of the brain. Next the information about touch moves on to the thalamus, which serves as a relay station. The thalamus then projects the map of the body's surface onto the somatosensory areas of the parietal lobes in the cerebral cortex (Hirata & Castro-Alamancos, 2010).

Just as the visual system is more sensitive to images on the fovea than to images in the peripheral retina, our sensitivity to touch is not equally good across all areas of the skin. Human toolmakers need excellent touch discrimination in their hands, but they require much less touch discrimination in other parts of the body, such as the torso and legs. The brain devotes more space to analyzing touch signals coming from the hands than from the legs.

**TEMPERATURE**   We not only can feel the warmth of a comforting hand on our hand, we also can feel the warmth or coolness of a room. We must be able to detect temperature in order to maintain our body temperature. **Thermoreceptors,** sensory nerve endings under the skin, respond to temperature changes at or near the skin and provide input to keep the body's temperature at 98.6 degrees Fahrenheit. There are two types of thermoreceptors: warm and cold. Warm thermoreceptors respond to the warming of the skin, and cold thermoreceptors respond to the cooling of the skin. When warm and cold receptors that are close to each other in the skin are stimulated simultaneously, we experience the sensation of hotness. Figure 3.29 illustrates this "hot" experience. To read about fascinating research on the social significance of the feeling of temperature and other tactile experiences, see the Intersection.

**thermoreceptors**
Sensory nerve endings under the skin that respond to changes in temperature at or near the skin and provide input to keep the body's temperature at 98.6 degrees Fahrenheit.

**pain**
The sensation that warns an individual of damage to the body.

**PAIN**   **Pain** is the sensation that warns us of damage to our bodies. When contact with the skin takes the form of a sharp pinch, our sensation of mechanical pressure changes from touch to pain. When a pot handle is so hot that it burns our hand, our sensation of temperature becomes one of pain. Intense stimulation of any one of the senses can produce pain—too much light, very loud sounds, or too many habanero peppers, for example. Our ability to sense pain is vital for our survival as a species. It functions as a quick-acting messenger that tells the brain's motor systems that they must act fast to minimize or eliminate damage.

Pain receptors are dispersed widely throughout the body—in the skin, in the sheath tissue surrounding muscles, in internal organs, and in the membranes around bone.

Warm water      Cold water

**FIGURE 3.29**
**A "Hot" Experience**
When two pipes, one containing cold water and the other warm water, are braided together, a person touching the pipes feels a sensation of "hot." The perceived heat coming from the pipes is so intense that the individual cannot touch them for longer than a couple of seconds.

The brain pathways for the vestibular sense begin in the auditory nerve, which contains both the cochlear nerve (with information about sound) and the vestibular nerve (which has information about balance and movement). Most of the axons of the vestibular nerve connect with the medulla, although some go directly to the cerebellum. There also appear to be vestibular projections to the temporal cortex, but research has not fully charted their specific pathways.

Information from the sense of vision supplements the combination of kinesthetic and vestibular senses. This principle causes a motorist to slam on the brakes in his tiny sports car when the big truck next to him starts to move forward. When everything in our visual field appears to be moving, it is generally because we are moving.

Throughout this chapter we have viewed sensation and perception as our connections to the world. Sensation builds a bridge between the objects in our environment and the creative interpreter that is our brain. Through perception our sensations become meaningful and our mental life engages with the environment. Sensation and perception allow us to survive in that environment but also to experience the world in all its vibrancy. Sue Berry, a woman who achieved the ability to perceive depth only after a long, arduous effort, described her encounter with nature on a snowy day. "I felt myself within the snow fall, among the snowflakes. . . . I was overcome with a sense of joy. A snow fall can be quite beautiful—especially when you see it for the first time" (quoted in Sacks, 2006, p. 73). Also, recall Michael May, who was able to see after 25 years of blindness. One night, with his seeing-eye dog Josh at his side, he decided to go look at the sky. Lying on the grass in a field, he opened his eyes. He thought he was "seeing stars"—in the metaphorical sense. He thought that the thousands of white lights in the sky could not really be real, but they were. As he remarked in his vision diary: "How sweet it is" (May, 2003; Stein, 2003).

**Do It!**

If you have a few minutes and a strong stomach, give your vestibular system a workout. Spin around quickly and repeatedly for a minute. You can do it in a swivel chair or standing in the center of a room (be careful of sharp edges). When you stop, you will feel dizzy. Here's what's happening. The fluid in the semicircular canals moves rather slowly and changes direction very slowly. When we spin for a while, the fluid eventually catches up with our rate of motion and starts moving in the same direction. When we stop moving, however, the slow-moving fluid keeps on moving. It tells the hair cells in the vestibular canals (which in turn tell the brain) "We are still spinning"—and we feel as if we are.

## self-quiz

1. Taste buds are bunched together in
   A. taste cells.
   B. the papillae.
   C. salivary glands.
   D. the olfactory epithelium.

2. _____ is/are involved in the sense of smell.
   A. The papillae
   B. The olfactory epithelium
   C. The thalamus
   D. The pinnae

3. The inner-ear structures that contain the sensory receptors that detect head motion, as when we move our head and/or body, are the
   A. stirrups.
   B. semicircular canals.
   C. hammer.
   D. cochlea.

**APPLY IT!** 4. Sean loves anchovy, mushroom, and double-cheese pizza on a whole-wheat crust from his hometown pizzeria. He brings a pie back from home to give his roommate Danny a chance to taste it. Sean is stunned by Danny's reaction to the pizza: "Dude! Epic Fail" (in other words, he hates it). What does this example demonstrate?
   A. Danny may not have the taste receptors for umami.
   B. Although Sean and Danny have similar tongue anatomy, perception is still a subjective process. Sean is apparently a big umami fan, but Danny is not.
   C. Danny may have a disorder of the olfactory epithelium.
   D. Danny is engaged in top-down processing.

## SUMMARY

### 1 How We Sense and Perceive the World

Sensation is the process of receiving stimulus energies from the environment. Perception is the process of organizing and interpreting sensory information to give it meaning. Perceiving the world involves both bottom-up and top-down processing. All sensation begins with sensory receptors, specialized cells that detect and transmit information about a stimulus to sensory neurons and the brain. Sensory receptors are selective and have different neural pathways.

Psychologists have explored the limits of our abilities to detect stimuli. Absolute threshold refers to the minimum amount of energy that people can detect. The difference threshold, or just noticeable difference, is the smallest difference in stimulation required to discriminate one stimulus from another 50 percent of the time.

Perception is influenced by attention, beliefs, and expectations. Sensory adaptation is a change in the responsiveness of the sensory system based on the average level of surrounding stimulation, essentially the ways that our senses start to ignore a particular stimulus once it is around long enough.

## ② The Visual System

Light is the stimulus that is sensed by the visual system. Light can be described in terms of wavelengths. Three characteristics of light waves determine our experience: wavelength (hue), amplitude (brightness), and purity (saturation).

In sensation, light passes through the cornea and lens to the retina, the light-sensitive surface in the back of the eye that houses light receptors called rods (which function in low illumination) and cones (which react to color). The fovea of the retina contains only cones and sharpens detail in an image. The optic nerve transmits neural impulses to the brain. There it diverges at the optic chiasm, so that what we see in the left visual field is registered in the right side of the brain and vice versa. In the occipital lobes of the cerebral cortex, the information is integrated.

The trichromatic theory of color perception holds that three types of color receptors in the retina allow us to perceive three colors (green, red, and blue). The opponent-process theory states that cells in the visual system respond to red-green and blue-yellow colors. Both theories are probably correct—the eye and the brain use both methods to code colors.

Shape perception is the ability to distinguish objects from their background. Depth perception is the ability to perceive objects three-dimensionally and depends on binocular (two-eyes) cues and monocular (one-eye) cues. Motion perception by humans depends on specialized neurons, feedback from the body, and environmental cues. Perceptual constancy is the recognition that objects are stable despite changes in the way we see them.

## ③ The Auditory System

Sounds, or sound waves, are vibrations in the air that are processed by the auditory system. These waves vary in important ways that influence what we hear. Pitch (how high or low in tone a sound is) is the perceptual interpretation of wavelength frequency. Amplitude of wavelengths, measured in decibels, is perceived as loudness. Complex sounds involve a blending of frequencies. Timbre is the tone saturation, or perceptual quality, of a sound.

The outer ear consists of the pinna and external auditory canal and acts to funnel sound to the middle ear. In the middle ear, the eardrum, hammer, anvil, and stirrup vibrate in response to sound and transfer the vibrations to the inner ear. Important parts of the fluid-filled inner ear are the oval window, cochlea, and basilar membrane. The movement of hair cells between the basilar membrane and the tectorial membrane generates nerve impulses.

Place theory states that each frequency produces vibrations at a particular spot on the basilar membrane. Place theory adequately explains high-frequency sounds but not low-frequency sounds. Frequency theory holds that the perception of a sound's frequency depends on how often the auditory nerve fires. The volley principle states that a cluster of neurons can fire impulses in rapid succession, producing a volley of impulses.

Information about sound moves from the hair cells to the auditory nerve, which carries information to the brain's auditory areas. The cortical destination of most fibers is the temporal lobes of the cerebral cortex. Localizing sound involves both the timing of the sound and the intensity of the sound arriving at each ear.

## ④ Other Senses

The skin senses include touch, temperature, and pain. Touch is the detection of mechanical energy, or pressure, against the skin. Touch information travels through the spinal cord, brain stem, and thalamus and on to the somatosensory areas of the parietal lobes. Thermoreceptors under the skin respond to increases and decreases in temperature. Pain is the sensation that warns us about damage to our bodies.

The chemical senses of taste and smell enable us to detect and process chemicals in the environment. Papillae are bumps on the tongue that contain taste buds, the receptors for taste. The olfactory epithelium contains a sheet of receptor cells for smell in the roof of the nose.

The kinesthetic senses provide information about movement, posture, and orientation. The vestibular sense gives us information about balance and movement. Receptors for the kinesthetic senses are embedded in muscle fibers and joints. The semicircular canals in the inner ear contain the sensory receptors that detect head motion.

## KEY TERMS

sensation, p. 85
perception, p. 85
bottom-up processing, p. 86
top-down processing, p. 86
sensory receptors, p. 87
absolute threshold, p. 89
noise, p. 91
difference threshold, p. 91
Weber's law, p. 92
subliminal perception, p. 92
signal detection theory, p. 92
selective attention, p. 93

perceptual set, p. 95
sensory adaptation, p. 95
retina, p. 98
rods, p. 99
cones, p. 99
optic nerve, p. 99
visual cortex, p. 100
feature detectors, p. 100
parallel processing, p. 101
binding, p. 101
trichromatic theory, p. 102
opponent-process theory, p. 102

figure-ground relationship, p. 104
gestalt psychology, p. 104
depth perception, p. 104
binocular cues, p. 104
convergence, p. 105
monocular cues, p. 105
apparent movement, p. 106
perceptual constancy, p. 107
outer ear, p. 110
middle ear, p. 111
inner ear, p. 111
place theory, p. 112

frequency theory, p. 112
volley principle, p. 113
auditory nerve, p. 113
thermoreceptors, p. 115
pain, p. 115
papillae, p. 118
olfactory epithelium, p. 119
kinesthetic senses, p. 121
vestibular sense, p. 121
semicircular canals, p. 121

## THE EFFECTS OF CHRONIC SLEEP DEPRIVATION

We do our best when we sleep more than 8 hours a night (Habeck & others, 2004). Lack of sleep is stressful and has an impact on the body and the brain (Koenis & others, 2011; Monk, 2012). When deprived of sleep, people have trouble paying attention to tasks and solving problems (Jackson & others, 2011). Studies have shown that sleep deprivation decreased brain activity in the thalamus and the prefrontal cortex (Libedinsky & others, 2011) and reduced the complexity of brain activity (Jeong & others, 2001). The tired brain must compensate by using different pathways or alternative neural networks when thinking (Koenis & others, 2011). Sleep deprivation can even influence moral judgment. Following 53 hours of wakefulness, participants in a recent study had more difficulty making moral decisions and were more likely to agree with decisions that violated their personal standards (Killgore & others, 2007).

Although sleep is unquestionably key to optimal physical and mental performance, many of us do not get sufficient sleep. In a recent national survey of more than 1,500 U.S. adults conducted by the National Sleep Foundation (2011), 43 percent of 19- to 64-year-olds reported that they rarely or ever get a good night's sleep on weeknights. Sixty percent said that they experience a sleep problem every night or almost every night, such as waking during the night, waking too early, or feeling tired when they wake up in the morning. A majority stated that they get slightly less than 7 hours of sleep a night on weeknights, and 15 percent indicated that they sleep less than 6 hours a night.

Why do Americans get too little sleep? Pressures at work and school, family responsibilities, and social obligations often lead to long hours of wakefulness and irregular sleep/wake schedules (Artazcoz & others, 2009). Not having enough hours to do all that we want or need to do in a day, we cheat on our sleep. As a result we may suffer from a "sleep debt," an accumulated level of exhaustion.

Sleep researchers record Randy Gardner's behavior (he's the person doing pushups) during his 264-hour period of sleep deprivation. Most people who try to stay up even one night have difficulty remaining awake from 3 A.M. to 6 A.M.

# Stages of Wakefulness and Sleep

Have you ever been awakened from your sleep and been totally disoriented? Have you ever awakened in the middle of a dream and suddenly gone right back into the dream as if it were a movie running just under the surface of your consciousness? These two circumstances reflect two distinct stages in the sleep cycle.

Stages of sleep correspond to massive electrophysiological changes that occur throughout the brain as the fast, irregular, and low-amplitude electrical activity of wakefulness is replaced by the slow, regular, high-amplitude waves of deep sleep. Using the electroencephalograph (EEG) to monitor the brain's electrical activity, scientists have identified two stages of wakefulness and five stages of sleep.

**WAKEFULNESS STAGES** When people are awake, their EEG patterns exhibit two types of waves: beta and alpha. *Beta waves* reflect concentration and alertness. These waves are

FWOMP!

7-29

McPherson

Sensing that he was about to doze off, the air bag on Wayne's computer rapidly deployed.

Used by permission of CartoonStock, www.CartoonStock.com.

the highest in frequency and lowest in amplitude. This means that the waves go up and down a great deal, but they do not have very high peaks or very low ebbs. They also are more *desynchronous* than other waves, meaning they do not form a very consistent pattern. Inconsistent patterning makes sense given the extensive variation in sensory input and activities we experience when we are awake.

When we are relaxed but still awake, our brain waves slow down, increase in amplitude, and become more *synchronous,* or regular. These waves, associated with relaxation or drowsiness, are called *alpha waves.*

The five stages of sleep also are differentiated by the types of wave patterns detected with an EEG, and the depth of sleep varies from one stage to another, as we now consider.

**SLEEP STAGES 1–4**    *Stage 1 sleep* is characterized by drowsy sleep. In this stage, the person may experience sudden muscle movements called *myoclonic jerks.* EEGs of individuals in this stage are characterized by *theta waves,* which are even slower in frequency and greater in amplitude than alpha waves. The difference between just being relaxed and stage 1 sleep is gradual. Figure 4.4 shows the EEG pattern of stage 1 sleep, along with the EEG patterns for the other four sleep stages and beta and alpha waves.

*Watch people in your classes fight to stay awake—you'll see their heads jerk up. This first stage of sleep often involves the feeling of falling.*

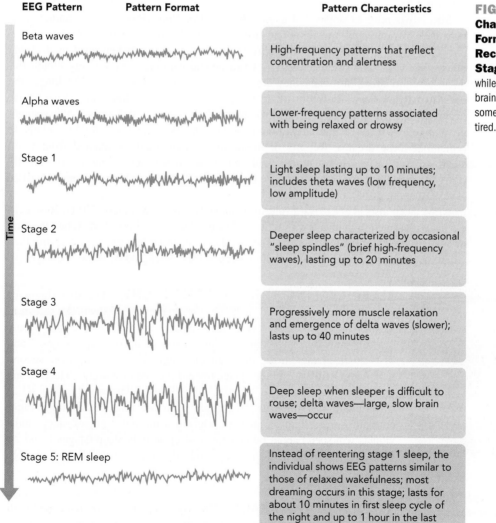

| EEG Pattern | Pattern Format | Pattern Characteristics |
|---|---|---|
| Beta waves | | High-frequency patterns that reflect concentration and alertness |
| Alpha waves | | Lower-frequency patterns associated with being relaxed or drowsy |
| Stage 1 | | Light sleep lasting up to 10 minutes; includes theta waves (low frequency, low amplitude) |
| Stage 2 | | Deeper sleep characterized by occasional "sleep spindles" (brief high-frequency waves), lasting up to 20 minutes |
| Stage 3 | | Progressively more muscle relaxation and emergence of delta waves (slower); lasts up to 40 minutes |
| Stage 4 | | Deep sleep when sleeper is difficult to rouse; delta waves—large, slow brain waves—occur |
| Stage 5: REM sleep | | Instead of reentering stage 1 sleep, the individual shows EEG patterns similar to those of relaxed wakefulness; most dreaming occurs in this stage; lasts for about 10 minutes in first sleep cycle of the night and up to 1 hour in the last |

**FIGURE 4.4**

**Characteristics and Formats of EEG Recordings During Stages of Sleep** Even while you are sleeping, your brain is busy. No wonder you sometimes wake up feeling tired.

In *stage 2 sleep,* muscle activity decreases, and the person is no longer consciously aware of the environment. Theta waves continue but are interspersed with a defining characteristic of stage 2 sleep: *sleep spindles.* These involve a sudden increase in wave frequency (Andrillon & others, 2011). Stages 1 and 2 are both relatively light stages of sleep, and if people awaken during one of these stages, they often report not having been asleep at all.

*Stage 3 sleep* and *stage 4 sleep* are characterized by *delta waves,* the slowest and highest-amplitude brain waves during sleep. These two stages are often referred to as *delta sleep.* Distinguishing between stage 3 and stage 4 is difficult, although typically stage 3 is characterized by delta waves occurring less than 50 percent of the time and stage 4 by delta waves occurring more than 50 percent of the time. Delta sleep is our deepest sleep, the time when our brain waves are least like waking brain waves. It is during delta sleep that it is the most difficult to wake sleepers. This is also the stage when bedwetting (in children), sleepwalking, and sleep talking occur. When awakened during this stage, people usually are confused and disoriented.

**REM sleep**

An active stage of sleep during which dreaming occurs.

**REM SLEEP**    After going through stages 1–4, sleepers drift up through the sleep stages toward wakefulness. Instead of reentering stage 1, however, they enter *stage 5 sleep,* a different form of sleep called REM (rapid eye movement) sleep (Colrain & Baker, 2012). **REM sleep** is an active stage of sleep during which dreaming occurs. The EEG pattern for REM sleep shows fast waves similar to those of relaxed wakefulness, and the sleeper's eyeballs move up and down and from left to right (Figure 4.5).

Specialists refer to stages 1–4 as *non-REM sleep.* Non-REM sleep is characterized by a lack of rapid eye movement and little dreaming. A person who is awakened during REM sleep is more likely to report having dreamed than when awakened at any other stage (Marzano & others, 2011). Even people who claim they rarely dream frequently report dreaming when they are awakened during REM sleep. The longer the period of REM sleep, the more likely the person will report dreaming. Dreams also occur during slow-wave or non-REM sleep, but the frequency of dreams in these stages is relatively low (McNamara, McLaren, & Durso, 2007), and we are less likely to remember these dreams. Reports of dreaming by individuals awakened from REM sleep are typically longer, more vivid, more physically active, more emotionally charged, and less related to waking life than reports by those awakened from non-REM sleep (Hobson, 2004).

REM sleep also likely plays a role in memory (Blagrove & others, 2011). Researchers have presented individuals with unique phrases before they go to bed. When they are awakened just before they begin REM sleep, they remember less the next morning than when they are awakened during the other sleep stages (Stickgold & Walker, 2005).

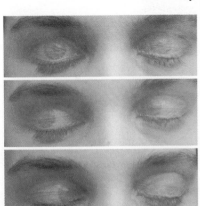

**FIGURE 4.5    REM Sleep** During REM sleep, your eyes move rapidly, as if following the images moving in your dreams.

**SLEEP CYCLING THROUGH THE NIGHT**    The five stages of sleep we have considered make up a normal cycle of sleep. As shown in Figure 4.6, one of these cycles lasts about 90 to 100 minutes and recurs several times during the night. The amount of deep sleep (stages 3 and 4) is much greater in the first half of a night's sleep than in the second half. Most REM sleep takes place toward the end of a night's sleep, when the REM stage becomes progressively longer. The night's first REM stage might last for only 10 minutes, but the final REM stage might continue for as long as an hour. During a normal night of sleep, individuals will spend about 60 percent of sleep in light sleep (stages 1 and 2), 20 percent in delta or deep sleep, and 20 percent in REM sleep (Webb, 2000).

**SLEEP AND THE BRAIN**    The five sleep stages are associated with distinct patterns of neurotransmitter activity initiated in the reticular formation, the core of the brain stem (Peigneux, Urbain, & Schmitz, 2012). In all vertebrates, the reticular formation plays a crucial role in sleep and arousal (see Figure 4.2). As previously noted, damage to the reticular formation can result in coma and death.

Three important neurotransmitters involved in sleep are serotonin, norepinephrine, and acetylcholine (Koziorynska & Rodriquez, 2011). As sleep begins, the levels of neurotransmitters sent to the forebrain from the reticular formation start dropping, and they continue to fall until they reach their lowest levels during the deepest sleep stage—stage 4. REM sleep (stage 5) is initiated by a rise in acetylcholine, which activates the cerebral cortex while the rest of the brain remains relatively inactive. REM sleep ends when there is a rise in serotonin and norepinephrine, which increase the level of forebrain activity nearly to the awakened state (Miller & O'Callaghan, 2006). You are most likely to wake up just after a REM period. If you do not wake up then, the level of the neurotransmitters falls again, and you enter another sleep cycle.

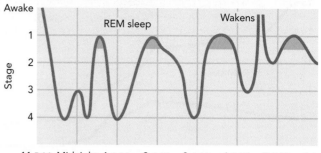

**FIGURE 4.6** **Cycling Through a Night's Sleep** During a night's sleep, we go through several cycles. Depth of sleep decreases, and REM sleep (shown in green) increases as the night progresses. In this graph, the person is depicted as awakening at about 5 A.M. and then going back to sleep for another hour. > *How many sleep cycles are presented?* > *How many times does the sleeper wake up?* > *Trace the rise and fall of the neurotransmitters acetylcholine, serotonin, and norepinephrine in the sleep cycle depicted. Has this sleeper achieved a good night's rest? Why or why not?*

# Sleep Throughout the Life Span

Getting sufficient sleep is important at every period in human life (Lee & Rosen, 2012). Figure 4.7 shows how total sleep time and time spent in each type of sleep vary over the human life span.

Sleep may benefit physical growth and brain development in infants and children. For example, deep sleep coincides with the release of growth hormone in children. Children are more likely to sleep well when they avoid caffeine, experience a regular bedtime routine, are read to before going to bed, and do not have a television in their bedroom (Mindell & others, 2009).

As children age, their sleep patterns change. Many adolescents stay up later at night and sleep longer in the morning than they did when they were children, and these shifting sleep patterns may influence their academic work. During adolescence, the brain, especially the cerebral cortex, is continuing to develop, and the adolescent's need for sleep may be linked to this brain development (Colrain & Baker, 2011).

Mary Carskadon and her colleagues have conducted a number of studies on adolescent sleep patterns (Carskadon, 2006, 2011a, 2011b; Crowley & Carskadon, 2010; Tarokh & Carskadon, 2010). They found that when given the opportunity, adolescents will sleep an average of 9 hours and 25 minutes a night. Most, however, get considerably less than 9 hours of sleep, especially during the week. This shortfall creates a sleep debt that adolescents often attempt to make up on the weekend.

The researchers also found that older adolescents tend to be sleepier during the day than younger adolescents. They theorized that this sleepiness was not due to academic work or social pressures. Rather, their research suggests that adolescents' biological clocks undergo a shift as they get older, delaying their period of wakefulness by about an hour. A delay in the nightly release of the sleep-inducing hormone melatonin seems to underlie this shift. Melatonin is secreted at about 9:30 P.M. in younger adolescents and approximately an hour later in older adolescents. Based on her research, Carskadon has

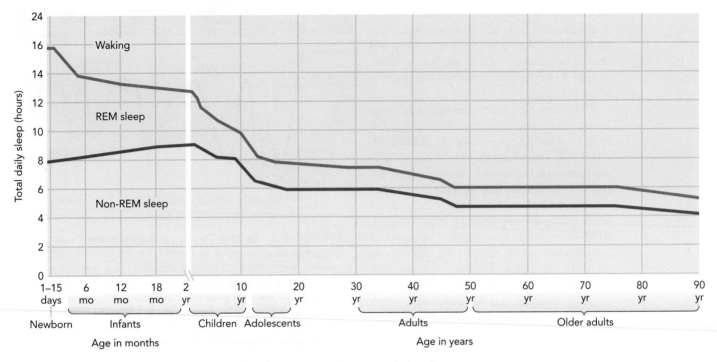

**FIGURE 4.7** **Sleep Across the Human Life Span** With age, humans require less sleep.

suggested that early school starting times may cause grogginess, inattention in class, and poor performance on tests. One study revealed that just a 30-minute delay in school start time was linked to improvements in adolescents' sleep, alertness, mood, and health (Owens, Belon, & Moss, 2010).

Do sleep patterns change in emerging adulthood (18–25 years of age)? Research indicates that they do (Galambos, Howard, & Maggs, 2011). In a recent study, the weekday bedtimes and rise times of first-year college students were approximately 1 hour 15 minutes later than those of high school seniors (Lund & others, 2010). However, the first-year college students had later bedtimes and rise times than third- and fourth-year college students, indicating that at about 20–22 years of age, a reverse in the timing of bedtimes and rise times occurs.

Sleep patterns also change as people age through the middle-adult (40s and 50s) and late-adult (60s and older) years (Malhotra & Desai, 2010; Nakamura & others, 2011; Olbrich & Dittmer, 2011). Many adults in these age spans go to bed earlier at night and wake up earlier in the morning than they did in their younger years. As well, beginning in the 40s, individuals report that they are less likely to sleep through the entire night than when they were younger. Middle-aged adults also spend less time in deep sleep than they did before their middle years.

A recent study found that changes in sleep duration across five years in middle age were linked to cognitive abilities such as problem solving and memory (Ferrie & others, 2011). In this study, a decrease from 6, 7, or 8 hours of sleep and an increase from 7 or 8 hours were related to lower scores on most cognitive assessments. In late adulthood, approximately 50 percent of older adults complain of having difficulty sleeping (Neikrug & Ancoli-Israel, 2010). Poor sleep can result in earlier death and is linked to a lower level of cognitive functioning (Naismith, Lewis, & Rogers, 2011; Tuckman & others, 2011).

# Sleep and Disease

Sleep plays a role in a large number of health problems, diseases, and disorders (Fontana & Wohlgemuth, 2010; Patel & others, 2012). For example, stroke and asthma attacks are more common during the night and in the early morning, probably because of changes in hormones, heart rate, and other characteristics associated with sleep (Teodorescu & others, 2006). Sleeplessness is also associated with obesity and heart disease (Sabanayagam & Shankar, 2010).

Neurons that control sleep interact closely with the immune system (Imeri & Opp, 2009). As anyone who has had the flu knows, infectious diseases make us sleepy. The probable reason is that chemicals called cytokines, produced by the body's cells while we are fighting an infection, are powerfully sleep-inducing (Besedovsky, Lange, & Born, 2012). Sleep may help the body conserve energy and other resources it needs to overcome infection (Irwin & others, 2006).

Sleep problems afflict most people who have psychological disorders, including those with depression (Eidelman & others, 2012; Hidaka, 2012). Individuals with depression often awaken in the early hours of the morning and cannot get back to sleep, and they often spend less time in delta wave or deep sleep than do non-depressed individuals.

Sleep problems are common in many other disorders as well, including Alzheimer disease, stroke, and cancer (Banthia & others, 2009; Fleming & Davidson, 2012; Gaig & Iranzo, 2012). In some cases, however, these problems may be due not to the disease itself but to the drugs used to treat the disease.

# Sleep Disorders

Many individuals suffer from undiagnosed and untreated sleep disorders that leave them struggling through the day, feeling unmotivated and exhausted (Edinger & Morin, 2012; Rajaratnam & others, 2011). Some of the major sleep problems are insomnia, sleepwalking and sleep talking, nightmares and night terrors, narcolepsy, and sleep apnea.

**INSOMNIA**    A common sleep problem is *insomnia,* the inability to sleep. Insomnia can involve a problem in falling asleep, waking up during the night, or waking up too early (Gehrman, Findley, & Perlis, 2012). In the United States, as many as one in five adults has insomnia (Pearson, Johnson, & Nahin, 2006). Insomnia is more common among women and older adults, as well as individuals who are thin, stressed, or depressed (National Sleep Foundation, 2007).

For short-term insomnia, most physicians prescribe sleeping pills. However, most sleeping pills stop working after several weeks of nightly use, and their long-term use can interfere with good sleep. Mild insomnia often can be reduced by simply practicing good sleep habits, such as always going to bed at the same time, even on weekends, and sleeping in a dark, quiet place. In more serious cases, researchers are experimenting with light therapy, melatonin supplements, and other ways to alter circadian cycles (Cardinali & others, 2011; Lichstein, Vander Wal, & Dillon, 2012; Zeitzer, Friedman, & Yesavage, 2011). Behavioral changes (such as avoiding naps and setting an alarm in the morning) can help insomniacs increase their sleep time and awaken less frequently in the night (Jernelov & others, 2012).

**SLEEPWALKING AND SLEEP TALKING**    *Somnambulism* is the formal term for sleepwalking, which occurs during the deepest stages of sleep (Umanath, Sarezky, & Finger, 2011). For many years, experts believed that somnambulists were acting out their dreams. However, somnambulism takes place during stages 3 and 4, usually early in the night, when a person is unlikely to be dreaming (Zadra & Pilon, 2012).

The specific causes of sleepwalking have not been identified, but it is more likely to occur when individuals are sleep deprived or have been drinking alcohol. There is nothing abnormal about sleepwalking, and despite superstition, it is safe to awaken sleepwalkers. In fact, they probably should be awakened, as they may harm themselves wandering around in the dark (Swanson, 1999).

Another quirky night behavior is sleep talking, or *somniloquy*. If you interrogate sleep talkers, can you find out what they did, for instance, last Thursday night? Probably not. Although sleep talkers will converse with you and make fairly coherent statements, they are soundly asleep. Thus, even if a sleep talker mumbles a response to your question, do not count on its accuracy.

Recently, a few cases of an even rarer sleep behavior have come to light—sleep eating. Ambien is a widely prescribed sleep medication for insomnia. Some Ambien users began to notice odd things upon waking up from a much-needed good night's sleep, such as candy wrappers strewn around the room, crumbs in the bed, and food missing from the refrigerator. One woman gained 100 pounds without changing her awake eating or exercise habits. How could this be? Dr. Mark Mahowald, the medical director of the Minnesota Regional Sleep Disorders Center in Minneapolis, has confirmed that sleep eating may be a side effect of using Ambien (McNamara, 2009).

The phenomenon of sleep eating illustrates that even when we feel fast asleep, we may be "half-awake"—and capable of putting together some unusual late-night snacks, including buttered cigarettes, salt sandwiches, and raw bacon. The maker of Ambien has noted this unusual side effect on the label of the drug. Even more alarming than sleep eating is sleep driving (Saul, 2006). Sleep experts agree that sleep driving while taking Ambien is rare and extreme but plausible.

For individuals who are battling persistent insomnia, a drug that provides a good night's rest may be worth the risk of these unusual side effects. Furthermore, no one should abruptly stop taking any medication without consulting a physician.

**NIGHTMARES AND NIGHT TERRORS** A *nightmare* is a frightening dream that awakens a dreamer from REM sleep (Germain, 2012). The nightmare's content invariably involves danger—the dreamer is chased, robbed, or thrown off a cliff. Nightmares are common. Most of us have had them, especially as young children. Nightmares peak at 3 to 6 years of age and then decline, although the average college student experiences four to eight nightmares a year (Hartmann, 1993). Reported increases in nightmares or worsening nightmares are often associated with an increase in life stressors such as the loss of a relative or a job and conflicts with others.

LAST NIGHT I DREAMED THAT I HAD SIX-PACK ABS... THEN I WOKE UP SCREAMING.

© Steve Moore/Distributed by Universal Uclick via CartoonStock.com

A *night terror* features sudden arousal from sleep and intense fear. Night terrors are accompanied by a number of physiological reactions, such as rapid heart rate and breathing, loud screams, heavy perspiration, and movement (Zadra & Pilon, 2012). Night terrors, which peak at 5 to 7 years of age, are less common than nightmares, and unlike nightmares, they occur during slow-wave, non-REM sleep.

**NARCOLEPSY** The disorder *narcolepsy* involves the sudden, overpowering urge to sleep. The urge is so uncontrollable that the person may fall asleep while talking or standing up. Narcoleptics immediately enter REM sleep rather than progressing through the first four sleep stages (Siegel, 2011). Individuals with narcolepsy are often very tired during the day. Narcolepsy can be triggered by extreme emotional reactions, such as surprise, laughter, excitement, and anger. The disorder appears to involve problems with the hypothalamus and amygdala (Brabec & others, 2011). Although narcolepsy usually emerges in adulthood, signs of the problem may be evident in childhood (Nevsimalova, 2009).

**SLEEP APNEA**  *Sleep apnea* is a sleep disorder in which individuals stop breathing because the windpipe fails to open or because brain processes involved in respiration fail to work properly. People with sleep apnea experience numerous brief awakenings during the night so that they can breathe better, although they usually are not aware of their awakened state. During the day, these people may feel sleepy because they were deprived of sleep at night. A common sign of sleep apnea is loud snoring, punctuated by silence (the apnea).

Sleep apnea affects approximately 18 million Americans (Ho & Brass, 2011). The disorder is most common among infants and adults over the age of 65. Sleep apnea also occurs more frequently among obese individuals, men, and individuals with large necks and recessed chins (Kotsis & others, 2010). Untreated sleep apnea can cause high blood pressure, stroke, and sexual dysfunction (Ho & Brass, 2011; Parati, Lombardi, & Narkiewicz, 2007). In addition, the daytime sleepiness caused by sleep apnea can result in accidents, lost productivity, and relationship problems (Hartenbaum & others, 2006). Sleep apnea is commonly treated by weight-loss programs, side sleeping, propping the head on a pillow, or wearing a device (called a CPAP, for *continuous positive airway pressure*) that sends pressurized air through a mask that prevents the airway from collapsing.

Sleep apnea may also be a factor in *sudden infant death syndrome (SIDS)*, the unexpected sleep-related death of an infant less than one year old. SIDS is typically confirmed with an autopsy that reveals no specific cause of death (Byard & Krous, 2004; Fifer & Myers, 2002). It is common for infants to have short pauses in their breathing during sleep, but for some infants frequent sleep apnea may be a sign of problems in regulating arousal (Kato & others, 2003). There is evidence that infants who die of SIDS in fact experience multiple episodes of sleep apnea in the days before the fatal event (Kahn & others, 1992). One possible explanation for SIDS is an abnormality in the brain stem areas responsible for arousal (Kinney, 2009). Such an abnormality may lead to sleep apnea, which in turn might worsen the brain stem damage, ultimately leading to death.

**Do It!**

Keep a sleep journal for several nights. Compare your sleep patterns with those described in the text. Do you have a sleep debt? If so, which stages of sleep are you most likely missing? Does a good night's sleep affect your behavior? Keep a record of your mood and energy levels after a short night's sleep and then after you have had at least 8 hours of sleep in one night. What changes do you notice, and how do they compare with the changes predicted by research on sleep deprivation described in the chapter?

# Dreams

Have you ever dreamed that you left your long-term romantic partner for a former lover? If so, did you tell your partner about that dream? Probably not. However, you would have likely wondered about the dream's meaning, and if so you would not be alone. Since the dawn of language, human beings have attributed great meaning to dreams. As early as 5000 B.C.E., Babylonians recorded and interpreted their dreams on clay tablets. Egyptians built temples in honor of Serapis, the god of dreams. Dreams are described at length in more than 70 passages in the Bible. Psychologists have also examined this fascinating topic.

Sigmund Freud put great stock in dreams as a key to our unconscious minds. He believed that dreams (even nightmares) symbolize unconscious wishes and that analysis of dream symbols could uncover our hidden desires. Freud distinguished between a dream's manifest content and its latent content. **Manifest content** is the dream's surface content, which contains dream symbols that disguise the dream's true meaning; **latent content** is the dream's hidden content, its unconscious—and true—meaning. For example, if a person had a dream about riding on a train and talking with a friend, the train ride would be the dream's manifest content. Freud thought that this manifest content expresses a wish in disguised form. To get to the latent or true meaning of the dream, the person would have to analyze the dream images. In our example, the dreamer would be asked to think of all the things that come to mind when the person thinks of a train, the friend, and so forth. By following these associations to the objects in the manifest content, the latent content of the dream could be brought to light. Artists have sometimes

**latent content**
According to Freud, a dream's hidden content; its unconscious and true meaning.

**manifest content**
According to Freud, the surface content of a dream, containing dream symbols that disguise the dream's true meaning.

**FIGURE 4.8** **Artist's Portrayal of a Dream** Marc Chagall (1887–1985) painted a world of dreams in *I and the Village* (1911).

incorporated the symbolic world of dreaming in their work (Figure 4.8).

More recently, psychologists have approached dreams not as expressions of unconscious wishes but as mental events that come from various sources. Research has revealed a great deal about the nature of dreams (De Koninck, 2012). A common misconception is that dreams are typically bizarre or strange, but many studies of thousands of dreams, collected from individuals in sleep labs and sleeping at home, have shown that dreams generally are not especially strange. Instead, research shows that dreams are often very similar to waking life (Domhoff, 2007; Schredl, 2009; Schwartz, 2010).

Although some aspects of dreams are unusual, dreams often are no more bizarre than a typical fairy tale, TV show episode, or movie plot. Dreams do generally contain more negative emotion than everyday life; and certainly some unlikely characters, including dead people, sometimes show up in dreams.

There is also no evidence that dreams provide opportunities for problem solving or advice on handling life's difficulties. We may dream about a problem we are dealing with, but we typically find the solution while we are awake and thinking about the dream, not during the dream itself (Domhoff, 2007). There is also no evidence that people who remember their dreams are better off than those who do not (Blagrove & Akehurst, 2000).

So, if the typical dream involves doing ordinary things, what are dreams? The most prominent theories that attempt to explain dreams are cognitive theory and activation-synthesis theory.

*Why might we believe dreams are stranger than they really are? Which type of dreams are we more likely to remember? Why?*

**COGNITIVE THEORY OF DREAMING** The **cognitive theory of dreaming** proposes that we can understand dreaming by applying the same cognitive concepts we use in studying the waking mind. The theory rests on the idea that dreams are essentially subconscious cognitive processing. Dreaming involves information processing and memory. Indeed, thinking during dreams appears to be very similar to thinking in waking life (Domhoff, 2011).

In the cognitive theory of dreaming, there is little or no search for the hidden, symbolic content of dreams that Freud sought. Instead, dreams are viewed as dramatizations of general life concerns that are similar to relaxed daydreams. Even very unusual aspects of dreams, such as odd activities, strange images, and sudden scene shifts, can be understood as metaphorically related to a person's preoccupations while awake (Domhoff, 2007, 2011; Zadra & Domhoff, 2010). The cognitive theory also ties the brain activity that occurs during dreams to the activity that occurs during waking life. The term *default network* refers to a collection of neurons that are active during mind wandering and daydreaming, essentially whenever we are not focused on a task.

**cognitive theory of dreaming** Theory proposing that we can understand dreaming by applying the same cognitive concepts we use in studying the waking mind.

Research suggests that dreaming during sleep may also emerge from the activity of this network (Domhoff, 2011).

The cognitive theory of dreaming strongly argues that dreams should be viewed as a kind of mental simulation that is very similar in content to our everyday waking thoughts. The same themes that occupy us in our waking life occupy our dreams. This perspective on dreams contrasts with activation-synthesis theory of dreams.

### ACTIVATION-SYNTHESIS THEORY

According to **activation-synthesis theory,** dreaming occurs when the cerebral cortex synthesizes neural signals generated from activity in the lower part of the brain. Dreams result from the brain's attempts to find logic in random brain activity that occurs during sleep (J. A. Hobson, 1999; A. Hobson & Voss, 2011).

When we are awake and alert, our conscious experience tends to be driven by *external* stimuli, all those things we see, hear, and respond to. During sleep, according to activation-synthesis theory, conscious experience is driven by internally generated stimuli that have no apparent behavioral consequence. A key source of such internal stimulation is spontaneous neural activity in the brain stem (J. A. Hobson, 2000). Some of the neural activity that produces dreams comes from external sensory experiences. If a fire truck with sirens blaring drives past your house, you might find yourself dreaming about an emergency. Many of us have had the experience of incorporating the sound of our alarm clock going off in an early morning dream.

Supporters of activation-synthesis theory have suggested that neural networks in other areas of the forebrain play a significant role in dreaming (J. A. Hobson, Pace-Schott, & Stickgold, 2000). Specifically, they believe that the same regions of the forebrain that are involved in certain waking behaviors also function in particular aspects of dreaming (Lu & others, 2006). As levels of neurotransmitters rise and fall during the stages of sleep, some neural networks are activated and others shut down. Random neural firing in various areas of the brain leads to dreams that are the brain's attempts to make sense of the activity. So, firing in the primary motor and sensory areas of the forebrain might be reflected in a dream of running and feeling wind on your face. From the activation-synthesis perspective, our nervous system is cycling through various activities, and our consciousness is simply along for the ride (J. A. Hobson, 2000, 2004). Dreams are merely a flashy sideshow, not the main event (Hooper & Teresi, 1993). Indeed, one activation-synthesis theorist has referred to dreams as so much "cognitive trash" (J. A. Hobson, 2002, p. 23).

Like all dream theories, activation-synthesis theory has its critics. A key criticism is that damage to the brain stem does not necessarily reduce dreaming, suggesting that this area of the brain is not the only starting point for dreaming. Furthermore, life experiences stimulate and shape dreaming more than activation-synthesis theory acknowledges (Domhoff, 2007; Malcolm-Smith & others, 2008).

**activation-synthesis theory**
Theory that dreaming occurs when the cerebral cortex synthesizes neural signals generated from activity in the lower brain and that dreams result from the brain's attempts to find logic in random brain activity that occurs during sleep.

*You may have noticed how internal states influence your dreams if you have ever been very thirsty while sleeping, and you dream that you get a glass of water.*

*self-quiz*

1. The brain structure that is responsible for the synchronization of circadian rhythm is the
   A. cerebral cortex.
   B. hypothalamus.
   C. reticular formation.
   D. suprachiasmatic nucleus.

2. Immediately entering REM sleep is a symptom of
   A. sleep apnea.
   B. narcolepsy.
   C. night terrors.
   D. somnambulism.

3. The brain waves that are active when we are awake and focused are
   A. alpha waves.
   B. beta waves.
   C. delta waves.
   D. theta waves.

**APPLY IT!** 4. Bobby and Jill have a friendly competition going in their psychology class. Both have spent several hours studying for the final exam over the last few weeks of school. The night before the final, Bobby declares that he is going to pull an all-nighter, adding 12 full hours to his study time compared to Jill. Altogether, Jill studies 23 hours for the exam, while Bobby studies 35 hours. All other things being equal, who is likely to do better on the exam and why?
A. Bobby will do better because he studied much more than Jill did.
B. Jill will do better because she studied a great deal and has the benefit of a good night's sleep, allowing her memory for course material to consolidate.
C. Bobby will do better because even though he missed some hours of sleep, his memories will be fresher than Jill's.
D. Jill will do better because Bobby is probably overprepared—35 hours is too long to study anything.

# 3 Psychoactive Drugs

One way that people seek to alter their own consciousness is through the use of psycho-active drugs. In fact, illicit drug use is a global problem. According to the United Nations Office on Drugs and Crime (UNODC), more than 200 million people worldwide use drugs each year (UNODC, 2011). Among those, approximately 27 million individuals are characterized as problem drug users—individuals whose drug habit interferes with their ability to engage in work and social relationships (UNODC, 2011).

Drug consumption among youth is a special concern because of its links to problems such as unsafe sex, sexually transmitted infections, unplanned pregnancy, depression, and school-related difficulties (Eaton & others, 2008; UNODC, 2011). The use of drugs among U.S. secondary school students declined in the 1980s but began to increase in the early 1990s (Johnston & others, 2012). Then in the late 1990s and early 2000s, the proportion of secondary school students reporting the use of any illicit drug again declined (Johnston & others, 2012).

Drug use by U.S. high school seniors since 1975 and by U.S. eighth- and tenth-graders since 1991 has been tracked in a national survey called *Monitoring the Future* (Johnston & others, 2012). Figure 4.9 shows the trends for these groups in these periods (Johnston & others, 2012). The most notable declines in adolescent drug use in the twenty-first century have occurred for marijuana, LSD, Ecstasy, steroids, and cigarettes. However, marijuana use by adolescents increased from 2007 to 2010. The United States still has the highest rate of adolescent drug use of any industrialized nation (Johnston & others, 2012).

## Uses of Psychoactive Drugs

**psychoactive drugs**
Drugs that act on the nervous system to alter consciousness, modify perceptions, and change moods.

**Psychoactive drugs** act on the nervous system to alter consciousness, modify perceptions, and change moods. Some people use psychoactive drugs as a way to deal with life's difficulties. Drinking, smoking, and taking drugs reduce tension, relieve boredom and fatigue, and help people to escape from the harsh realities of life. Some people use drugs because they are curious about their effects.

The use of psychoactive drugs, whether it is to cope with problems or just for fun, can carry a high price tag. These include losing track of one's responsibilities, problems

## PSYCHOLOGICAL INQUIRY

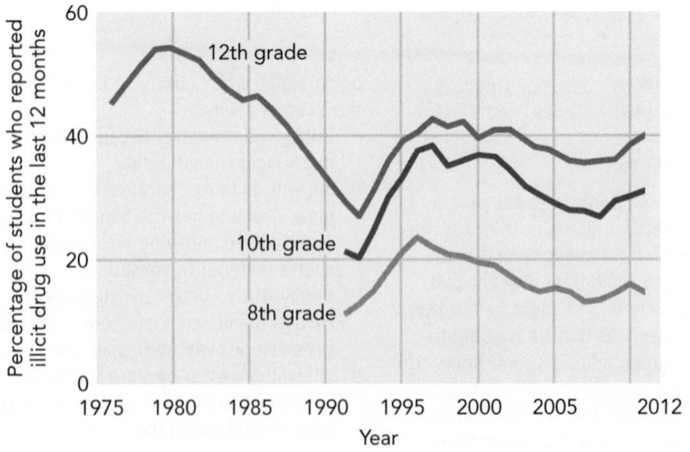

**FIGURE 4.9  Trends in Drug Use by U.S. Eighth-, Tenth-, and Twelfth-Grade Students** This graph shows the percentage of U.S. eighth-, tenth-, and twelfth-grade students who reported having taken an illicit drug in the last 12 months from 1991 to 2012 (for eighth- and tenth-graders) and from 1975 to 2012 (for twelfth-graders) (Johnston & others, 2012). > *Note that data were not collected from eighth- and tenth-graders until 1991. Why do you think these groups were added?* > *After the mid-1990s, all age groups show a similar pattern of decline in drug use. Why might this pattern have occurred in all three groups?* > *What are the implications of using self-reports from children and adolescents in this research? Do you think each group would be similarly likely to be honest, to over-report, or to under-report their drug use?*

in the workplace and in relationships, drug dependence, and increased risk for serious, sometimes fatal diseases (Fields, 2013; Zilney, 2011). For example, drinking alcohol may initially help people relax and forget about their worries. If, however, they turn more and more to alcohol to escape reality, they may develop a dependence that can destroy relationships, careers, and their bodies.

Continued use of psychoactive drugs leads to **tolerance,** the need to take increasing amounts of a drug to get the same effect (Goldberg, 2010). For example, the first time someone takes 5 milligrams of the tranquilizer Valium, the person feels very relaxed. However, after taking the pill every day for six months, the individual may need to consume twice as much to achieve the same calming effect.

Continuing drug use can also result in **physical dependence,** the physiological need for a drug that causes unpleasant withdrawal symptoms such as physical pain and a craving for the drug when it is discontinued. **Psychological dependence** is the strong desire to repeat the use of a drug for emotional reasons, such as a feeling of well-being and reduction of stress. Experts on drug abuse use the term **addiction** to describe either a physical or psychological dependence, or both, on the drug (Hales, 2011).

How does the brain become addicted? Psychoactive drugs increase dopamine levels in the brain's reward pathways (De Biasi & Dani, 2011). This reward pathway is located in the ventral tegmental area (VTA) and nucleus accumbens (NAc) (Figure 4.10). Only the limbic and prefrontal areas of the brain are directly activated by dopamine, which comes from the VTA (Koob, 2006). Although different drugs have different mechanisms of action, each drug increases the activity of the reward pathway by increasing dopamine transmission. As we will see throughout this book, the neurotransmitter dopamine plays a vital role in the experience of rewards.

**tolerance**
The need to take increasing amounts of a drug to get the same effect.

**physical dependence**
The physiological need for a drug that causes unpleasant withdrawal symptoms such as physical pain and a craving for the drug when it is discontinued.

**psychological dependence**
The strong desire to repeat the use of a drug for emotional reasons, such as a feeling of well-being and reduction of stress.

**addiction**
Either a physical or a psychological dependence, or both, on a drug.

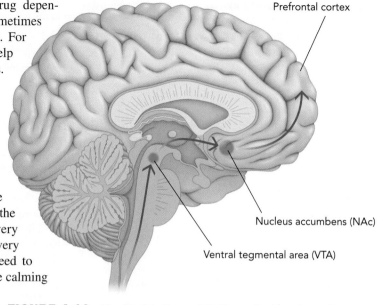

**FIGURE 4.10** **The Brain's Reward Pathway for Psychoactive Drugs** The ventral tegmental area (VTA) and nucleus accumbens (NAc) are important locations in the reward pathway for psychoactive drugs. Information travels from the VTA to the NAc and then up to the prefrontal cortex. The VTA is located in the midbrain just above the pons, and the NAc is located in the forebrain just beneath the prefrontal cortex.

*Ventral tegmental area and nucleus accumbens are mouthfuls, but these areas of the brain are vital to the experience of pleasure. Remember these structures; they will come up again and again.*

## Types of Psychoactive Drugs

Three main categories of psychoactive drugs are depressants, stimulants, and hallucinogens. All have the potential to cause health or behavior problems or both. To evaluate whether you abuse drugs, see Figure 4.11.

**DEPRESSANTS**  **Depressants** are psychoactive drugs that slow down mental and physical activity. Among the most widely used depressants are alcohol, barbiturates, tranquilizers, and opiates.

*Alcohol*  Alcohol is a powerful drug. It acts on the body primarily as a depressant and slows down the brain's activities (Hales, 2011). This effect might seem surprising, as people who tend to be inhibited may begin to talk, dance, and socialize after a few drinks. However, people "loosen up" after a few drinks because the brain areas involved in inhibition and judgment

**depressants**
Psychoactive drugs that slow down mental and physical activity.

**FIGURE 4.11 Do You Abuse Drugs?** Take this short quiz to see if your use of drugs and alcohol might be a cause for concern.

Respond yes or no to the following items:

| Yes | No | |
|-----|-----|---|
| ☐ | ☐ | I have gotten into problems because of using drugs. |
| ☐ | ☐ | Using alcohol or other drugs has made my college life unhappy at times. |
| ☐ | ☐ | Drinking alcohol or taking other drugs has been a factor in my losing a job. |
| ☐ | ☐ | Drinking alcohol or taking other drugs has interfered with my studying for exams. |
| ☐ | ☐ | Drinking alcohol or taking drugs has jeopardized my academic performance. |
| ☐ | ☐ | My ambition is not as strong since I've been drinking a lot or taking drugs. |
| ☐ | ☐ | Drinking or taking drugs has caused me to have difficulty sleeping. |
| ☐ | ☐ | I have felt remorse after drinking or taking drugs. |
| ☐ | ☐ | I crave a drink or other drugs at a definite time of the day. |
| ☐ | ☐ | I want a drink or other drug in the morning. |
| ☐ | ☐ | I have had a complete or partial loss of memory as a result of drinking or using other drugs. |
| ☐ | ☐ | Drinking or using other drugs is affecting my reputation. |
| ☐ | ☐ | I have been in the hospital or another institution because of my drinking or taking drugs. |

College students who responded yes to items similar to these on the Rutgers Collegiate Abuse Screening Test were more likely to be substance abusers than those who answered no. If you responded yes to just 1 of the 13 items on this screening test, consider going to your college health or counseling center for further screening.

*Sometimes friends think someone who is dangerously drunk just needs to "sleep it off." Drinking to the point of passing out is a symptom of alcohol poisoning. Call 911.*

slow down. As people drink more, their inhibitions decrease even further, and their judgment becomes increasingly impaired. Activities that require intellectual functioning and motor skills, such as driving, become harder to perform. Eventually the drinker falls asleep. With extreme intoxication, the person may lapse into a coma and die. Figure 4.12 illustrates alcohol's main effects on the body.

The effects of alcohol vary from person to person. Factors in this variation are body weight, the amount of alcohol consumed, individual differences in the way body metabolizes alcohol, and the presence or absence of tolerance (Sparling & Redican, 2012). Men and women differ in terms of the intoxicating effects of alcohol. Because of differences in body fat as well as stomach enzymes, women are likely to be more strongly affected by alcohol than men.

How does alcohol affect the brain? Like other psychoactive drugs, alcohol goes to the VTA and the NAc (Hopf & others, 2010). Alcohol also increases the concentration of the neurotransmitter gamma aminobutyric acid (GABA), which is widely distributed in many brain areas, including the cerebral cortex, cerebellum, hippocampus, amygdala, and nucleus accumbens (Tateno & Robinson, 2011).

*This explains how getting the next drink can become more important than anything else in the person's life.*

Researchers believe that the frontal cortex holds a memory of the pleasure involved in prior alcohol use and contributes to continued drinking. Alcohol consumption also may affect the areas of the frontal cortex involved in judgment and impulse control (Bouchard, Brown, & Nadeau, 2012). It is further believed that the basal ganglia, which are involved in compulsive behaviors, may lead to a greater demand for alcohol, regardless of reason and consequences (Brink, 2001).

After caffeine, alcohol is the most widely used drug in the United States. As many as two-thirds of U.S. adults drink beer, wine, or liquor at least occasionally, and in one survey approximately 30 percent reported drinking more than five drinks at one sitting

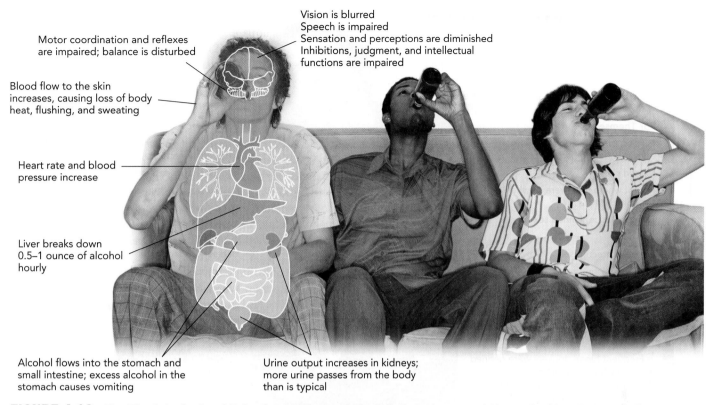

Motor coordination and reflexes are impaired; balance is disturbed

Vision is blurred
Speech is impaired
Sensation and perceptions are diminished
Inhibitions, judgment, and intellectual functions are impaired

Blood flow to the skin increases, causing loss of body heat, flushing, and sweating

Heart rate and blood pressure increase

Liver breaks down 0.5–1 ounce of alcohol hourly

Alcohol flows into the stomach and small intestine; excess alcohol in the stomach causes vomiting

Urine output increases in kidneys; more urine passes from the body than is typical

**FIGURE 4.12** **The Physiological and Behavioral Effects of Alcohol** Alcohol has a powerful impact throughout the body. Its effects touch everything from the operation of the nervous, circulatory, and digestive systems to sensation, perception, motor coordination, and intellectual functioning.

at least once in the last year (National Center for Health Statistics, 2005). The common use of alcohol is related to other serious problems, including death and injury from driving while drinking (Levinthal, 2010; National Highway Traffic Safety Administration, 2007). Research has also found a link between alcohol and violence and aggression (Gallagher & Parrott, 2010). More than 60 percent of homicides involve alcohol use by the offender or the victim, and 65 percent of aggressive sexual acts against women are associated with alcohol consumption by the offender.

A special concern is the high rate of alcohol use by U.S. secondary school and college students (Chen & Jacobson, 2012; Chung & others, 2012). In the Monitoring the Future survey, 40 percent of high school seniors surveyed reported consuming alcohol in the last 30 days in 2011 (Johnston & others, 2012). The good news: That percentage (40) represents a decline from 54 percent in 1991. In the most recent survey, 25 percent of the high school seniors surveyed had engaged in *binge drinking* (having five or more drinks in a row) at least once during the previous month, down from 34 percent in 1997.

Binge drinking often increases during the first two years of college, and, as Figure 4.13 shows, it can take its toll on students (Littlefield & Sher, 2010). In a Monitoring the Future survey of college students, 41 percent reported engaging in binge drinking in the last two weeks (49 percent of males, 33 percent of females) (Johnston & others, 2008). In a national survey of drinking patterns on college campuses, almost half of the binge drinkers reported problems such as missed classes, injuries, trouble with police, and unprotected sex (Wechsler & others, 2000, 2002). Binge-drinking college students were 11 times more likely to fall behind in school, 10 times more likely to drive after drinking, and twice as likely to have unprotected sex as college students who did not binge drink. Many emerging adults, however, decrease their alcohol use as they assume

*EXPERIENCE IT!*
Binge Drinking and the Adolescent Brain

similar to other states of consciousness. For example, individuals in a hypnotic state, when monitored by an EEG, display a predominance of alpha and beta waves, characteristic of persons in a relaxed waking state (Williams & Gruzelier, 2001). In a brain-imaging study, widespread areas of the cerebral cortex—including the occipital lobes, parietal lobes, sensorimotor cortex, and prefrontal cortex—were activated when individuals were in a hypnotic state (Faymonville, Boly, & Laureys, 2006). A similar activation pattern is found in individuals in a non-hypnotic waking state who are engaging in mental imagery. How does the hypnotist lead people into this state of relaxation and imagery?

### THE FOUR STEPS IN HYPNOSIS
Hypnosis involves four steps. The hypnotist

1. Minimizes distractions and makes the person to be hypnotized comfortable.

2. Tells the person to concentrate on something specific, such as an imagined scene or the ticking of a watch.

3. Informs the person what to expect in the hypnotic state, such as relaxation or a pleasant floating sensation.

4. Suggests certain events or feelings he or she knows will occur or observes occurring, such as "Your eyes are getting tired." When the suggested effects occur, the person interprets them as being caused by the hypnotist's suggestions and accepts them as an indication that something is happening. This increase in the person's expectations that the hypnotist will make things happen in the future makes the person even more suggestible.

### INDIVIDUAL VARIATIONS IN HYPNOSIS
Some people are more easily hypnotized than others, and some are more strongly influenced by hypnotic suggestions. *Hypnotizability* refers to the extent to which a person's responses *are changed* when he or she is hypnotized (Milling & others, 2010; Raz & others, 2010). There is no easy way to know if a person is hypnotizable without first trying to hypnotize the individual. If you have the capacity to immerse yourself deeply in an imaginative activity—listening to a favorite piece of music or reading a novel, for example—you might be a likely candidate (Spiegel, 2010). Still, the relationship between the ability to become completely absorbed in an experience and hypnotizability is weak (Nash, 2001).

## Explaining Hypnosis

How does hypnosis have its effects? Contemporary theorists disagree as to whether hypnosis is a divided state of consciousness or simply a learned social behavior.

**divided consciousness view of hypnosis**
Hilgard's view that hypnosis involves a splitting of consciousness into two separate components, one of which follows the hypnotist's commands and the other of which acts as a "hidden observer."

### A DIVIDED STATE OF CONSCIOUSNESS
Ernest Hilgard (1977, 1992), in his **divided consciousness view of hypnosis,** proposed that hypnosis involves a special state of consciousness in which consciousness is split into separate components. One component follows the hypnotist's commands, while another component acts as a "hidden observer."

Hilgard placed one hand of hypnotized individuals in a bucket of ice-cold water and told them that they would not feel pain but that a part of their mind—a hidden part that would be aware of what was going on—could signal any true pain by pressing a key with the hand that was not submerged (Figure 4.18). The individuals under hypnosis reported afterward that they had not experienced any pain; yet while their hand had been submerged in the ice-cold water, they had pressed the key with their non-submerged hand, and they had pressed it more frequently the longer their hand was in the cold water. Hilgard thus concluded that in hypnosis, consciousness has a hidden part that stays in contact with reality and feels pain while another part of consciousness feels no pain.

Critics of Hilgard's view suggest that the hidden observer simply demonstrates that the hypnotized person is not in an altered state of consciousness at all. From this perspective, the hidden observer is simply the person himself or herself, having been given permission to admit to the pain that he or she was always feeling (Green & others, 2005). This argument is part of the social cognitive behavior view of hypnosis.

### SOCIAL COGNITIVE BEHAVIOR

Some experts are skeptical that hypnosis is an altered state of consciousness (Chaves, 2000; Lynn & Green, 2011). In the **social cognitive behavior view of hypnosis,** hypnosis is a normal state in which the hypnotized person behaves the way he or she believes that a hypnotized person should behave. The social cognitive perspective frames the important questions about hypnosis around cognitive factors—the attitudes, expectations, and beliefs of good hypnotic participants—and around the powerful social context in which hypnosis occurs (Lynn and Green, 2011). Individuals being hypnotized surrender their responsibility to the hypnotist and follow the hypnotist's suggestions; and they have expectations about what hypnosis is supposed to be like.

Experts have continued to debate whether hypnosis is indeed an altered state of consciousness (Kihlstrom, 2005) or simply a reaction to a special social situation (Lynn & Green, 2011). Although there may be no consensus about what hypnosis is, health professionals have begun to apply this powerful technique to a number of problems.

**social cognitive behavior view of hypnosis**
The perspective that hypnosis is a normal state in which the hypnotized person behaves the way he or she believes that a hypnotized person should behave.

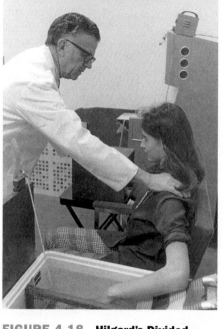

**FIGURE 4.18   Hilgard's Divided Consciousness Experiment** Ernest Hilgard tests a participant in the study in which he had individuals place one arm in ice-cold water.

## Uses of Hypnosis

As psychologists' interest in studying consciousness has grown, hypnosis has emerged as a useful tool (Nash & others, 2009). Some researchers employ hypnosis in a way similar to transcranial magnetic stimulation (described in Chapter 3), to dampen brain processes experimentally (Cox & Bryant, 2008). Combining hypnosis with brain imaging allows researchers to understand both the effects of hypnosis itself and the brain's functioning (Oakley & Halligan, 2011).

Beyond its role in basic research, hypnosis has been applied to a variety of problems. In the United States, practitioners of hypnosis use the technique to treat alcoholism, somnambulism, depression, suicidal tendencies, post-traumatic stress disorder (see Chapter 12), migraines, overeating, diabetes, and smoking (Hammond, 2010; Lynn & others, 2010). Whether hypnosis actually works for these diverse problems remains debatable (D. Brown, 2007). Individuals in hypnosis-based treatment programs rarely achieve dramatic results unless they are already motivated to change. Hypnosis is most effective when combined with psychotherapy (Rossi, 2009).

A long history of research and practice has clearly demonstrated that hypnosis can reduce the experience of pain (Gottsegen, 2011; Jensen, 2009; Lew & others, 2011). A fascinating study examined the pain perceptions of hypnotized individuals, with the goal of changing their pain threshold. In this study, the brain of each participant was monitored while each received painful electrical shocks (rated 8 or higher on a 1 to 10 pain scale) (Schulz-Stubner & others, 2004). Those who were hypnotized to find the shocks less painful did rate them as lower in pain (giving them a 3 or less). Furthermore, the brain-scanning results were most interesting: The subcortical brain areas (the brain stem and midbrain) of the hypnotized patients responded the same as those of the patients who were not hypnotized, a finding suggesting that these brain structures recognized the painful stimulation. However, the sensory cortex was not activated in the hypnotized patients, an indication that although they sensed pain on some level, they were never conscious of it. In essence, the "ouch" signal never made it to awareness.

In summary, although the nature of hypnosis remains a mystery, evidence is increasing that hypnosis can play a role in a variety of health contexts, and it can influence the brain in fascinating ways (Raz, 2011). For psychologists, part of the ambiguity about the definition of hypnosis arises from the fact that it has been studied in specific social contexts, involving a hypnotist. It is also possible, however, to experience altered states of consciousness without these special circumstances, as we next consider.

1. The type of brain waves that hypnotized people display include
   A. alpha waves.
   B. delta waves.
   C. gamma waves.
   D. theta waves.

2. The divided consciousness theory of hypnosis receives support from evidence that
   A. hypnosis can block sensory input.
   B. hypnosis can affect voluntary, but not involuntary, behaviors.
   C. hypnotized people often seem to play the role of "good hypnotic subjects."
   D. hypnotized people can be aware of pain sensation without experiencing emotional distress.

3. Hypnosis treatments tend to work best when they are accompanied by

A. daily meditation.
B. physical exercise.
C. yoga.
D. psychotherapy.

**APPLY IT!** 4. Ryan and his friends attend a show by the Great Chorizo, a hypnotist. Chorizo asks for volunteers to be hypnotized, and he picks the first five people who raise their hands. He puts the five people into a trance, and within minutes he has them lying on stage sizzling like slices of bacon in a frying pan. When it is all over, one of Ryan's friends remarks that Chorizo must have amazing powers: "That guy could make a person do anything!" Ryan, who has been working on his critical thinking and the psychology of hypnosis, wisely notes which of the following about Chorizo's act?

A. As long as Chorizo followed the steps of hypnosis described in this text, he probably does have amazing powers of suggestion.
B. Ryan would need to see Chorizo's training and qualifications prior to rendering judgment.
C. Chorizo selected the first five volunteers, and these individuals may have been especially motivated, suggestible, and likely to believe in the effects of hypnosis. There is no way to gauge whether Chorizo could have influence over anyone else.
D. Hypnotizability is similar for all people, so if Chorizo was able to get five people to act like frying bacon, he could probably do just about anything.

# 5 Meditation

**meditation**
The attainment of a peaceful state of mind in which thoughts are not occupied by worry; the meditator is mindfully present to his or her thoughts and feelings but is not consumed by them.

Hypnosis involves a powerful social context, but harnessing the power of consciousness is also possible without the aid of a hypnotist—through meditation. **Meditation** involves attaining a peaceful state of mind in which thoughts are not occupied by worry; the meditator is mindfully present to his or her thoughts and feelings but is not consumed by them. Let's look at how meditation can enhance well-being and examine more closely what it is.

## Mindfulness Meditation

Melissa Munroe, a Canadian woman diagnosed with Hodgkin lymphoma (a cancer of the immune system), was tormented by excruciating pain. Seeking ways to cope with the agony, Munroe enrolled in a meditation program. She was skeptical at first. "What I didn't realize," she said, "is that if people have ever found themselves taking a walk in the countryside or in the forest or on a nice pleasant autumn day . . . and find themselves in a contemplative state, that's a form of meditation." Munroe worked hard to use meditation to control her pain. Interestingly, the way she harnessed the power of her mind to overcome pain was by concentrating her thoughts on the pain—not trying to avoid it.

Using *mindfulness meditation,* a technique practiced by yoga enthusiasts and Buddhist monks, Munroe focused on her pain. By doing so, she was able to isolate the pain from her emotional response to it and to her cancer diagnosis. She grew to see her physical discomfort as bearable. Munroe's success shows that contrary to what a non-meditator might think, meditation is not about avoiding one's thoughts. Indeed, the effort involved in avoidance steers the person away from the contemplative state. Munroe described her thoughts as like people striding by her on the street, walking in the other direction; she explained, "They come closer and closer, then they pass you by."

Jon Kabat-Zinn (2006, 2009) has pioneered using meditation techniques in medical settings. Research by Kabat-Zinn and colleagues has demonstrated the beneficial effects of mindfulness meditation for a variety of conditions, including depression, panic attacks, and anxiety (Miller, Fletcher, & Kabat-Zinn, 1995), chronic pain (Kabat-Zinn, Lipworth, & Burney, 1985), and stress and the skin condition psoriasis (Kabat-Zinn & others, 1998). Many of these effects have also been shown to be long-lasting.

As noted in Chapter 2, Richard Davidson and colleagues (including Jon Kabat-Zinn) have studied the brain and immune system changes that might underlie the health and wellness effects of meditation (Davidson & others, 2003; Kabat-Zinn & Davidson, 2012). They performed MRIs on the brains of individuals who were in a standard eight-week meditation-training program. After the training program and as compared to a control group, those in the meditation program reported reduced anxiety and fewer negative emotions. Furthermore, brain scans revealed that these individuals showed increased activation in the left hemisphere. As noted in Chapter 2, such activation is associated with happiness. In addition, the meditators had a better immune system response to a flu vaccine (Davidson & others, 2003). These results suggest that our conscious minds may have a role to play in enhancing our psychological and physical health (Davidson & Begley, 2012; Kabat-Zinn & Davidson, 2012).

*Among those practicing meditation are Zen monks who explore the Buddha-nature at the center of their being.*

## The Meditative State of Mind

What actually is the meditative state of mind? As a physiological state, meditation shows qualities of sleep and wakefulness yet is distinct from both. You may have experienced a state called *hypnagogic reverie*—an overwhelming feeling of wellness right before you fall asleep, the sense that everything is going to work out. Meditation has been compared to this relaxed sense that all is well (Friedman, Myers, & Benson, 1998).

In a study of Zen meditators, researchers examined what happens when people switch from their normal waking state to a meditative state (Ritskes & others, 2003). Using fMRI, the experimenters got images of the brain before and after the participants entered the meditative state. They found that the switch to meditation involved initial increases in activation in the basal ganglia and prefrontal cortex (the now familiar area that is often activated during consciousness). However, and interestingly, they also found that these initial activations led to decreases in the anterior cingulate, a brain area that is thought to be associated with acts of will. These results provide a picture of the physical events

## Meditation at Work

**M**ore and more companies are discovering the benefits of giving their staff a chance to learn about meditation. Apple, Yahoo, and Google, along with more traditional organizations such as Deutsche Bank and McKinsey, have pioneered in making meditation a staple of their wellness programs. Trainers work with employees to reduce stress, sharpen mental focus, clarify thinking, boost productivity, improve communication, and help them balance work responsibilities with family life and outside interests.

Health and well-being can improve significantly for employees who take part in such programs. The corporation benefits, too. Andy Puddicombe, a former Buddhist monk with over 20 years of practical meditation experience, writes, "These benefits make for a handsome return on investment, with a sharp decline in absenteeism and health costs accompanied by a significant increase in productivity and staff retention. The bottom line—it pays to meditate" (Puddicombe, 2008).

of the brain that are connected with the somewhat paradoxical state of meditation—controlling one's thoughts in order to let go of the need to control.

# Getting Started with Meditation

Would you like to experience the meditative state? If so, you can probably reach that state by following some simple instructions:

- Find a quiet place and a comfortable chair.
- Sit upright in the chair, rest your chin comfortably on your chest, and place your arms in your lap. Close your eyes.
- Now focus on your breathing. Every time you inhale and every time you exhale, pay attention to the sensations of air flowing through your body, the feeling of your lungs filling and emptying.
- After you have focused on several breaths, begin to repeat silently to yourself a single word every time you breathe out. You can make a word up, use the word *one,* or try a word associated with an emotion you want to produce, such as *trust, love, patience,* or *happy.* Experiment with several different words to see which one works for you.
- If you find that thoughts are intruding and you are no longer attending to your breathing, refocus on your breathing and say your chosen word each time you exhale.

After you have practiced this exercise for 10 to 15 minutes, twice a day, every day for two weeks, you will be ready for a shortened version. If you notice that you are experiencing stressful thoughts or circumstances, simply meditate, on the spot, for several minutes. If you are in public, you do not have to close your eyes; just fix your gaze on a nearby object, attend to your breathing, and say your word silently every time you exhale.

Meditation is an age-old practice. Without explicitly mentioning meditation, some religions advocate related practices such as daily prayer and peaceful introspection.

Whether the practice involves praying over rosary beads, chanting before a Buddhist shrine, or taking a moment to commune with nature, a contemplative state clearly has broad appeal and conveys many benefits (Kabat-Zinn & Davidson, 2012; Sharma, Gupta, & Bijiani, 2008). Current research on the contemplative state suggests that there are good reasons why human beings have been harnessing its beneficial powers for centuries.

# SUMMARY

## 1 The Nature of Consciousness

Consciousness is the awareness of external events and internal sensations, including awareness of the self and thoughts about experiences. Most experts agree that consciousness is likely distributed across the brain. The association areas and prefrontal lobes are believed to play important roles in consciousness.

William James described the mind as a stream of consciousness. Consciousness occurs at different levels of awareness that include higher-level awareness (controlled processes and selective attention), lower-level awareness (automatic processes and daydreaming), altered states of consciousness (produced by drugs, trauma, fatigue, and other factors), subconscious awareness (waking subconscious awareness, sleep, and dreams), and no awareness (unconscious thought).

## 2 Sleep and Dreams

Sleep is a natural state of rest for the body and mind that involves the reversible loss of consciousness. The biological rhythm that regulates the daily sleep/wake cycle is the circadian rhythm. The part of the brain that keeps our biological clocks synchronized is the suprachiasmatic nucleus, a small structure in the hypothalamus that registers light. Such things as jet travel and work shifts can desynchronize biological clocks. Some strategies are available for resetting the biological clock.

We need sleep for physical restoration, adaptation, growth, and memory. Research studies increasingly reveal that people do not function optimally when they are sleep-deprived.

Stages of sleep correspond to massive electrophysiological changes that occur in the brain and that can be assessed by an EEG. Humans go through four stages of non-REM sleep and one stage of REM sleep, or rapid eye movement sleep. Most dreaming occurs during REM sleep. A sleep cycle of five stages lasts about 90 to 100 minutes and recurs several times during the night. The REM stage lasts longer toward the end of a night's sleep.

The sleep stages are associated with distinct patterns of neurotransmitter activity. Levels of the neurotransmitters serotonin, norepinephrine, and acetylcholine decrease as the sleep cycle progresses from stage 1 through stage 4. Stage 5, REM sleep, begins when the reticular formation raises the level of acetylcholine.

Sleep plays a role in a large number of diseases and disorders. Neurons that control sleep interact closely with the immune system, and when our bodies are fighting infection our cells produce a substance that makes us sleepy. Individuals with depression often have sleep problems.

Many people in the United States suffer from chronic, long-term sleep disorders that can impair normal daily functioning. These include insomnia, sleepwalking and sleep talking, nightmares and night terrors, narcolepsy, and sleep apnea.

Contrary to popular belief, most dreams are not bizarre or strange. Freud thought that dreams express unconscious wishes in disguise. The cognitive theory of dreaming attempts to explain dreaming in terms of the same cognitive concepts that are used in studying the waking mind. According to activation-synthesis theory, dreaming occurs when the cerebral cortex synthesizes neural signals emanating from activity in the lower part of the brain. In this view, the rising level of acetylcholine during REM sleep plays a role in neural activity in the brain stem that the cerebral cortex tries to make sense of.

## Psychoactive Drugs

Psychoactive drugs act on the nervous system to alter states of consciousness, modify perceptions, and change moods. Humans are attracted to these types of drugs because they ease adaptation to change.

Addictive drugs activate the brain's reward system by increasing dopamine concentration. The reward pathway involves the ventral tegmental area (VTA) and nucleus accumbens (NAc). The abuse of psychoactive drugs can lead to tolerance, psychological and physical dependence, and addiction—a pattern of behavior characterized by a preoccupation with using a drug and securing its supply.

Depressants slow down mental and physical activity. Among the most widely used depressants are alcohol, barbiturates, tranquilizers, and opiates.

After caffeine, alcohol is the most widely used drug in the United States. The high rate of alcohol abuse by high school and college students is especially alarming. Alcoholism is a disorder that involves long-term, repeated, uncontrolled, compulsive, and excessive use of alcoholic beverages that impairs the drinker's health and work and social relationships.

Stimulants increase the central nervous system's activity and include caffeine, nicotine, amphetamines, cocaine, and MDMA (Ecstasy). Hallucinogens modify a person's perceptual experiences and produce visual images that are not real. Marijuana has a mild hallucinogenic effect; LSD has a strong one.

 ## Hypnosis

Hypnosis is a psychological state or possibly altered attention and awareness in which the individual is unusually receptive to suggestions.

The hypnotic state is different from a sleep state, as confirmed by EEG recordings. Inducing hypnosis involves four basic steps, beginning with minimizing distractions and making the person feel comfortable and ending with the hypnotist's suggesting certain events or feelings that he or she knows will occur or observes occurring.

There are substantial individual variations in people's susceptibility to hypnosis. People in a hypnotic state are unlikely to do anything that violates their morals or that involves a real danger.

Two theories have been proposed to explain hypnosis. In Hilgard's divided consciousness view, hypnosis involves a divided state of consciousness, a splitting of consciousness into separate components. One component follows the hypnotist's commands; the other acts as a hidden observer. In the social cognitive behavior view, hypnotized individuals behave the way they believe hypnotized individuals are expected to behave.

## Meditation

Meditation refers to a state of quiet reflection. Meditation has benefits for a wide range of psychological and physical illnesses. Meditation can also benefit the body's immune system. Research using fMRI suggests that meditation allows an individual to control his or her thoughts in order to "let go" of the need to control.

Mindfulness meditation is a powerful tool for managing life's problems. How we think about our lives and experiences plays a role in determining whether we feel stressed and worried or challenged and excited about life. Seeking times of quiet contemplation can have a positive impact on our abilities to cope with life's ups and downs.

## KEY TERMS

stream of consciousness, p. 126
consciousness, p. 126
theory of mind, p. 127
controlled processes, p. 128
automatic processes, p. 130
unconscious thought, p. 131
sleep, p. 133
biological rhythms, p. 133
circadian rhythms, p. 133

suprachiasmatic nucleus
  (SCN), p. 133
REM sleep, p. 138
manifest content, p. 143
latent content, p. 143
cognitive theory of
  dreaming, p. 144
activation-synthesis
  theory, p. 145

psychoactive drugs, p. 146
tolerance, p. 147
physical dependence, p. 147
psychological dependence, p. 147
addiction, p. 147
depressants, p. 147
alcoholism, p. 150
barbiturates, p. 151
tranquilizers, p. 151

opiates, p. 151
stimulants, p. 151
hallucinogens, p. 154
hypnosis, p. 157
divided consciousness view of
  hypnosis, p. 158
social cognitive behavior view of
  hypnosis, p. 159
meditation, p. 160

## SELF-TEST

### Multiple Choice

1. You are aware of the thoughts running through your mind and the emotions triggered by those thoughts. You are also aware of sounds, things you see outside the window, and the smell of coffee. You are in a state of
   A. consciousness.
   B. transcendence.
   C. divided perception.
   D. heightened sensation.

2. Jordan has decided to go to sleep early. Although her eyes are closed and she is very relaxed, she has not yet fallen asleep. An EEG is most likely to indicate the presence of
   A. delta waves.
   B. alpha waves.

C. sleep spindles.

D. rapid eye movements.

3. Which of the following best characterizes a night's sleep?
   A. We begin the night in light sleep and end in deep sleep.
   B. We pass from light sleep to dream sleep to deep sleep.
   C. Our depth of sleep alternates up and down many times.
   D. We alternate from the waking state to dream sleep about six times.

4. Dreams occurring during _____ sleep are briefer, less fragmented, and less likely to involve visual images compared to _____ sleep.
   A. REM; non-REM
   B. non-REM; REM
   C. stage 2; REM
   D. stage 2; non-REM

5. The hormone _____ is a key factor in regulating a person's level of sleepiness.
   A. testosterone
   B. melatonin

C. estrogen

D. glutamate

6. Jane says she smokes marijuana because it makes her feel indescribably happy. This effect is indicative of
   A. transcendent experiences.
   B. psychological withdrawal.
   C. physical dependence.
   D. an altered state of consciousness.

7. Your friend reported feeling greater energy and a sense of well-being after taking a drug. Medical tests reveal increased activity of her central nervous system. The drug she took is most likely some type of
   A. depressant.
   B. tranquilizer.
   C. hallucinogen.
   D. stimulant.

8. Amphetamines are classified as a _____ and _____ in the same class as nicotine and caffeine.
   A. depressant; are not
   B. stimulant; are not

C. depressant; are

D. stimulant; are

9. In terms of states of consciousness, hypnosis involves a
   A. high degree of controlled processing.
   B. strong defense against suggestibility.
   C. sense of deep relaxation and altered body awareness.
   D. dependence on a belief in supernatural powers.

10. Meditation results in an altered state of consciousness by
    A. reducing the activity level.
    B. lowering the heart rate.
    C. decreasing the use of oxygen.
    D. refocusing attention.

## Apply It!

11. Review the steps in hypnosis on page 158. Apply the social cognitive behavior view to each step. When and how, specifically, do social and cognitive factors play a role in hypnosis?

# 5 Learning

## Sniffer Dogs on Call: Putting Learning to Work in Japan

On March 11, 2011, a magnitude 9.0 undersea earthquake rocked the eastern coast of Japan. The Tohoku earthquake was the most powerful ever to hit the island nation, causing 133-foot tsunami waves that led to the meltdown of the Fukushima nuclear power plant. The quake's damage killed over 15,000 people and left at least 300,000 homeless. In the temblor's aftermath, humanitarian aid poured in. In addition to the throngs of people who rushed to help, battalions of rescue dogs were dispatched from around the world. Elite teams of humans and dogs from the United Kingdom, Australia, New Zealand, the United States, South Korea, Russia, Mexico, Switzerland, and many other nations reported for duty.

The "sniffer" dogs in these teams rely not only on their amazing canine olfactory abilities but also on the months and years of laborious training they receive, geared toward locating survivors trapped under rubble. Indeed, rescue dogs (some of which are themselves "rescued dogs"—that is, adopted from shelters) are rigorously trained animals that have passed a set of strict criteria to earn a place on the special teams. In the United States, the Federal Emergency Management Administration (FEMA) has established strict guidelines for the training of rescue dogs (FEMA, 2003). The dogs must demonstrate mastery of a set of difficult skills, including walking off-leash with a trainer on a crowded city street, without getting distracted, and performing search-and-rescue tasks without immediate practice and without their regular trainer. They must demonstrate their abilities without food rewards (although a toy reward placed on rubble is allowed). Further, these hardworking canines must be recertified every two years to ensure that their skills remain at peak level. In the invaluable work they performed in Japan, the dogs not only helped with rescue efforts but also raised everyone's spirits with their tirelessness and persistence.

Truly, rescue dogs are nothing less than highly skilled professionals. You might well wonder *how* the dogs are trained to perform these complex acts. It's simple—through the principles that psychologists have uncovered in studying learning, our focus in this chapter.

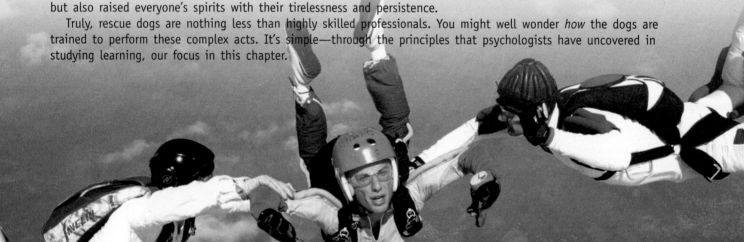

This chapter begins by defining learning and sketching out its main types—associative learning and observational learning. We then turn to two types of associative learning—classical conditioning and operant conditioning—followed by a close look at observational learning. We next probe into the role of cognitive processes in learning, before finally considering biological, cultural, and psychological constraints on learning. As you read, ask yourself about your own beliefs concerning learning. If a dog can learn to rescue earthquake victims, surely the human potential for learning has barely been tapped.

# 1  Types of Learning

Learning anything new involves change. Once you learned the alphabet, it did not leave you; it became part of a "new you" who had been changed through the process of learning. Similarly, once you learn how to drive a car, you do not have to go through the process again at a later time. If you ever try out for the X-Games, you may break a few bones along the way, but at some point you probably will learn a trick or two through the experience, changing from a novice to an enthusiast who can at least stay on top of a skateboard.

*Learning is RELATIVELY permanent—sometimes we forget what we've learned. Also, learning involves EXPERIENCE. Changes in behavior that result from physical maturation would not be considered learning.*

By way of experience, too, you may have learned that you have to study to do well on a test, that there usually is an opening act at a rock concert, and that a field goal in U.S. football adds 3 points to the score. Putting these pieces together, we arrive at a definition of **learning:** a systematic, relatively permanent change in behavior that occurs through experience.

**learning**
A systematic, relatively permanent change in behavior that occurs through experience.

If someone were to ask you what you learned in class today, you might mention new ideas you heard about, lists you memorized, or concepts you mastered. However, how would you define learning if you could not refer to unobservable mental processes? You might follow the lead of behavioral psychologists. **Behaviorism** is a theory of learning that focuses on observable behaviors. From the behaviorist perspective, understanding the causes of behavior requires looking at the environmental factors that produce them. Behaviorists view internal states like thinking, wishing, and hoping as behaviors that are caused by external factors as well. Psychologists who examine learning from a behavioral perspective define learning as relatively stable, observable changes in behavior. The behavioral approach has emphasized general laws that guide behavior change and make sense of some of the puzzling aspects of human life (Miltenberger, 2012).

**behaviorism**
A theory of learning that focuses solely on observable behaviors, discounting the importance of such mental activity as thinking, wishing, and hoping.

Behaviorism maintains that the principles of learning are the same whether we are talking about animals or humans. Because of the influence of behaviorism, psychologists' understanding of learning started with studies of rats, cats, pigeons, and even raccoons. A century of research on learning in animals and in humans suggests that many of the principles generated initially in research on animals also apply to humans (Domjan, 2010).

**associative learning**
Learning that occurs when an organism makes a connection, or an association, between two events.

In this chapter we look at two types of learning: associative learning and observational learning. **Associative learning** occurs when we make a connection, or an association, between two events. *Conditioning* is the process of learning these associations (Klein, 2009). There are two types of conditioning: classical and operant, both of which have been studied by behaviorists.

*"I didn't actually catch anything, but I do feel I gained some valuable experience."*

Used by permission of CartoonStock, www.CartoonStock.com.

*This is going to sound very abstract right now. Hang on—once we get to the details, it will make sense.*

**observational learning**
Learning that occurs through observing and imitating another's behavior.

*Have you ever noticed that humans' eyes differ from other animals' eyes because the "whites" can be seen? It might be that this characteristic allows humans to model one another closely—because we can see what the model is looking at.*

In *classical conditioning,* organisms learn the association between two stimuli. As a result of this association, organisms learn to anticipate events. For example, lightning is associated with thunder and regularly precedes it. Thus, when we see lightning, we anticipate that we will hear thunder soon afterward. Fans of horror films know the power of classical conditioning. Watching one of the *Friday the 13th* movies, we find the tension building whenever we hear that familiar "Ch-ch-ch—ch-ha-ha-ha-ha" that signals Jason's arrival.

In *operant conditioning,* organisms learn the association between a behavior and a consequence, such as a reward. As a result of this association, organisms learn to increase behaviors that are followed by rewards and to decrease behaviors that are followed by punishment. For example, children are likely to repeat their good manners if their parents reward them with candy after they have shown good manners. Also, if children's bad manners are followed by scolding words and harsh glances by parents, the children are less likely to repeat the bad manners. Figure 5.1 compares classical and operant conditioning.

Much of learning, however, is not a result of direct consequences but rather of exposure to models performing a behavior or skill. For instance, as you watch someone shoot baskets, you get a sense of how it is done. The learning that takes place when a person observes and imitates another's behavior is called **observational learning.** Observational learning is a common way that people learn in educational and other settings. Observational learning is different from the associative learning described by behaviorism because it relies on mental processes: The learner has to pay attention, remember, and reproduce what the model did. Observational learning is especially important to human beings. In fact, watching other people is another way in which human infants acquire skills.

Human infants differ from baby monkeys in their strong reliance on imitation (Bandura, 2010). After watching an adult model perform a task, a baby monkey will figure out its own way to do it, but a human infant will do exactly what the model did. Imitation may be the human baby's way to solve the huge problem it faces: to learn the vast amount of cultural knowledge that is part of human life. Many of our behaviors are rather arbitrary. Why do we clap to show approval or wave "hello" or "bye-bye"? The human infant has a lot to learn and may be well served to follow the old adage "When in Rome, do as the Romans do."

Learning applies to many areas of acquiring new behaviors, skills, and knowledge (Bjork, Dunlosky, & Kornell, 2013; Mayer, 2011). Our focus in this chapter is on the two types of associative learning—classical conditioning and operant conditioning—and on observational learning.

**Classical Conditioning**

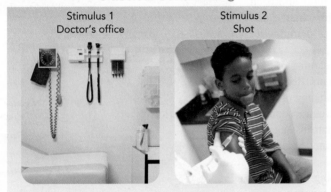

Stimulus 1
Doctor's office

Stimulus 2
Shot

**Operant Conditioning**

Behavior

Consequences

**FIGURE 5.1** **Associative Learning: Comparing Classical and Operant Conditioning** (*Left*) In this example of classical conditioning, a child associates a doctor's office (stimulus 1) with getting a painful injection (stimulus 2). (*Right*) In this example of operant conditioning, performing well in a swimming competition (behavior) becomes associated with getting awards (consequences).

1. Any situation that involves learning
   A. requires some relatively permanent change to occur.
   B. requires a great deal of effort.
   C. involves conscious determination.
   D. is relatively automatic.

2. A cat that associates the sound of a can opener with being fed has learned through
   A. behaviorism.
   B. operant conditioning.
   C. classical conditioning.
   D. observational learning.

3. Which one of the following statements is *true* about learning?

   A. Learning can be accomplished only by higher-level species, such as mammals.
   B. Learning is not permanent.
   C. Learning occurs through experience.
   D. Learning processes in humans are distinct from learning processes in animals.

**APPLY IT!** 4. After seeing dogs catching Frisbees in the park, Lionel decides that he wants to teach his dog Ivan to do it too. He takes Ivan to the park and sits with him, making sure that he watches the other dogs successfully catching Frisbees. What technique is Lionel using on Ivan, and what are the chances for success?

   A. He is using associative learning, and his chances for success are very good, because dogs and humans both learn this way.
   B. He is using operant conditioning, and his chances for success are very good, because dogs and humans both learn this way.
   C. He is using observational learning, and his chances for success are pretty bad, because dogs are not as likely as people to learn in this way.
   D. He is using classical conditioning, and his chances for success are pretty bad, because dogs are much less likely than people to learn in this way.

# 2 Classical Conditioning

Early one morning, Bob is in the shower. While he showers, his wife enters the bathroom and flushes the toilet. Scalding hot water bursts down on Bob, causing him to yell in pain. The next day, Bob is back for his morning shower, and once again his wife enters the bathroom and flushes the toilet. Panicked by the sound of the toilet flushing, Bob yelps in fear and jumps out of the shower stream. Bob's panic at the sound of the toilet illustrates the learning process of **classical conditioning,** in which a neutral stimulus (the sound of a toilet flushing) becomes associated with a meaningful stimulus (the pain of scalding hot water) and acquires the capacity to elicit a similar response (panic).

**classical conditioning**
Learning process in which a neutral stimulus becomes associated with an innately meaningful stimulus and acquires the capacity to elicit a similar response.

## Pavlov's Studies

Even before beginning this course, you might have heard about Pavlov's dogs. The Russian physiologist Ivan Pavlov's work is very well known. Still, it is easy to take its true significance for granted. Importantly, Pavlov demonstrated that neutral aspects of the environment can attain the capacity to evoke responses through pairing with other stimuli and that bodily processes can be influenced by environmental cues.

In the early 1900s, Pavlov was interested in the way the body digests food. In his experiments, he routinely placed meat powder in a dog's mouth, causing the dog to salivate. By accident, Pavlov noticed that the meat powder was not the only stimulus that caused the dog to salivate. The dog salivated in response to a number of stimuli associated with the food, such as the sight of the food dish, the sight of the individual who brought the food into the room, and the sound of the door closing when the food arrived. Pavlov recognized that the dog's association of these sights and sounds with the food was an important type of learning, which came to be called *classical conditioning.*

Pavlov wanted to know why the dog salivated in reaction to various sights and sounds before eating the meat powder. He observed that the dog's behavior included both unlearned and learned components. The unlearned part of classical conditioning is based on the fact that some stimuli automatically produce certain responses apart from any prior learning; in other words, they are innate (inborn). *Reflexes* are such automatic stimulus–response connections. They include salivation in response to food, nausea in response to spoiled food, shivering in response to low temperature, coughing in response to throat congestion, pupil constriction in response to light, and withdrawal in response

**EXPERIENCE IT!**
Classical Conditioning

*Pavlov (the white-bearded gentleman in the center) is shown demonstrating the nature of classical conditioning to students at the Military Medical Academy in Russia.*

**unconditioned response (UR)**
An unlearned reaction that is automatically elicited by the unconditioned stimulus.

**conditioned stimulus (CS)**
A previously neutral stimulus that eventually elicits a conditioned response after being paired with the unconditioned stimulus.

*Note that the association between food and salivating is natural (unlearned), while the association between a bell and salivating is learned.*

*Awesome addition to any résumé: Cockroach Saliva Technician.*

**acquisition**
The initial learning of the connection between the unconditioned stimulus and the conditioned stimulus when these two stimuli are paired.

to pain. An **unconditioned stimulus (US)** is a stimulus that produces a response without prior learning; food was the US in Pavlov's experiments. An **unconditioned response (UR)** is an unlearned reaction that is automatically elicited by the US. Unconditioned responses are involuntary; they happen in response to a stimulus without conscious effort. In Pavlov's experiment, salivating in response to food was the UR.

In classical conditioning, a **conditioned stimulus (CS)** is a previously neutral stimulus that eventually elicits a conditioned response after being paired with the unconditioned stimulus. The **conditioned response (CR)** is the learned response to the conditioned stimulus that occurs after CS–US pairing (Pavlov, 1927). Sometimes conditioned responses are quite similar to unconditioned responses, but typically they are not as strong.

In studying a dog's response to various stimuli associated with meat powder, Pavlov rang a bell before giving meat powder to the dog. Until then, ringing the bell did not have a particular effect on the dog, except perhaps to wake the dog from a nap. The bell was a neutral stimulus. However, the dog began to associate the sound of the bell with the food and salivated when it heard the bell. The bell had become a conditioned (learned) stimulus (CS), and salivation was now a conditioned response (CR). In the case of Bob's interrupted shower, the sound of the toilet flushing was the CS, and panicking was the CR after the scalding water (US) and the flushing sound (CS) were paired. Figure 5.2 summarizes how classical conditioning works.

Research has shown that salivation can be used as a conditioned response not only in dogs and humans but also in, of all things, cockroaches. In one study, researchers paired the smell of peppermint (the CS, which was applied to the cockroaches' antennae) with sugary water (the US) (Watanabe & Mizunami, 2007). Cockroaches naturally salivate (the UR) in response to sugary foods, and after repeated pairings between the peppermint smell and sugary water, the cockroaches salivated in response to the peppermint scent (the CR). Collecting and measuring the cockroach saliva, the researchers found that the cockroaches had slobbered over that scent for two minutes.

**ACQUISITION**  Whether it is human beings, dogs, or cockroaches, the first part of classical conditioning is called acquisition. **Acquisition** is the initial learning of the

**unconditioned stimulus (US)**
A stimulus that produces a response without prior learning.

**conditioned response (CR)**
The learned response to the conditioned stimulus that occurs after conditioned stimulus–unconditioned stimulus pairing.

**Before Conditioning**

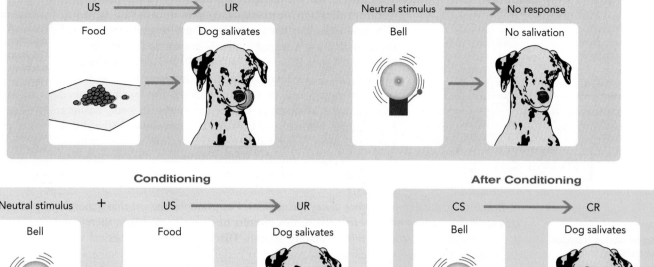

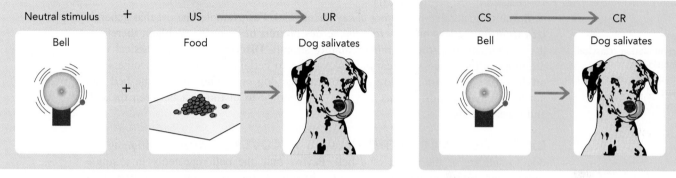

**FIGURE 5.2** **Pavlov's Classical Conditioning** In one experiment, Pavlov presented a neutral stimulus (bell) just before an unconditioned stimulus (food). The neutral stimulus became a conditioned stimulus by being paired with the unconditioned stimulus. Subsequently, the conditioned stimulus (bell) by itself was able to elicit the dog's salivation.

connection between the US and CS when these two stimuli are paired (as with the peppermint scent and the sugary water). During acquisition, the CS is repeatedly presented followed by the US. Eventually, the CS will produce a response. Note that classical conditioning is a type of learning that occurs without awareness or effort, based on the presentation of two stimuli together. For this pairing to work, however, two important factors must be present: contiguity and contingency.

*Contiguity* simply means that the CS and US are presented very close together in time—even a mere fraction of a second (Wheeler & Miller, 2008). In Pavlov's work, if the bell had rung 20 minutes before the presentation of the food, the dog probably would not have associated the bell with the food. However, pairing the CS and US close together in time is not all that is needed for conditioning to occur.

*Contingency* means that the CS must not only precede the US closely in time, it must also serve as a reliable indicator that the US is on its way (Rescorla, 1966, 1988, 2009). To get a sense of the importance of contingency, imagine that the dog in Pavlov's experiment is exposed to a ringing bell at random times all day long. Whenever the dog receives food, the delivery of the food always immediately follows a bell ring. However, in this situation, the dog will not associate the bell with the food, because the bell is not a reliable signal that food is coming: It rings a lot when no food is on the way. Whereas contiguity refers to the fact that the CS and US occur close together in time, contingency refers to the information value of the CS relative to the US. When contingency is present, the CS provides a systematic signal that the US is on its way.

**GENERALIZATION AND DISCRIMINATION**  Pavlov found that the dog salivated in response not only to the bell tone but also to other sounds, such as a whistle. These sounds had not been paired with the unconditioned stimulus of the food. Pavlov

PAVLOV'S CAT

DREAM ON, BUDDY.

Used by permission of CartoonStock, www.CartoonStock.com.

discovered that the more similar the noise was to the original sound of the bell, the stronger was the dog's salivary flow.

**Generalization** in classical conditioning is the tendency of a new stimulus that is similar to the original conditioned stimulus to elicit a response that is similar to the conditioned response (April, Bruce, & Galizio, 2011; Harris, Andrew, & Livesey, 2012). Generalization has value in preventing learning from being tied to specific stimuli. For example, once you learn the association between a given CS (say, flashing police lights behind your car) and a particular US (the dread associated with being pulled over), you do not have to learn it all over again when a similar stimulus presents itself (a police car with its siren moaning as it cruises directly behind your car).

Stimulus generalization is not always beneficial. For example, the cat that generalizes from a harmless minnow to a dangerous piranha has a major problem; therefore, it is important to also discriminate among stimuli. **Discrimination** in classical conditioning is the process of learning to respond to certain stimuli and not others. To produce discrimination, Pavlov gave food to the dog only after ringing the bell and not after other sounds. In this way, the dog learned to distinguish between the bell and other sounds.

### EXTINCTION AND SPONTANEOUS RECOVERY

After conditioning the dog to salivate at the sound of a bell, Pavlov rang the bell repeatedly in a single session and did not give the dog any food. Eventually the dog stopped salivating. This result is **extinction,** which in classical conditioning is the weakening of the conditioned response when the unconditioned stimulus is absent (Joscelyne & Kehoe, 2007). Without continued association with the US, the CS loses its power to produce the CR.

Extinction is not always the end of a conditioned response (Urcelay, Wheeler, & Miller, 2009). The day after Pavlov extinguished the conditioned salivation to the sound of a bell, he took the dog to the laboratory and rang the bell but still did not give the dog any meat powder. The dog salivated, indicating that an extinguished response can spontaneously recur. **Spontaneous recovery** is the process in classical conditioning by which a conditioned response can recur after a time delay, without further conditioning (Gershman, Blei, & Niv, 2010). Consider an example of spontaneous recovery you may have experienced: You thought that you had forgotten about (extinguished) an ex-girlfriend or boyfriend, but then you found yourself in a particular context (perhaps the restaurant where you always dined together), and you suddenly got a mental image of your ex, accompanied by an emotional reaction to him or her from the past (spontaneous recovery).

Figure 5.3 shows the sequence of acquisition, extinction, and spontaneous recovery. Spontaneous recovery can occur several times, but as long as the conditioned stimulus is

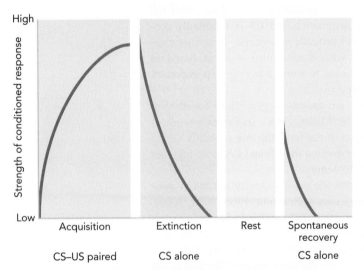

**FIGURE 5.3 The Strength of a Classically Conditioned Response During Acquisition, Extinction, and Spontaneous Recovery** During acquisition, the conditioned stimulus and unconditioned stimulus are associated. As the graph shows, when this association occurs, the strength of the conditioned response increases. During extinction, the conditioned stimulus is presented alone, and, as can be seen, the result is a decrease in the conditioned response. After a rest period, spontaneous recovery appears, although the strength of the conditioned response is not nearly as great at this point as it was after a number of CS–US pairings. When the CS is presented alone again, after spontaneous recovery, the response is extinguished rapidly.

presented alone (that is, without the unconditioned stimulus), spontaneous recovery becomes weaker and eventually ceases.

## Classical Conditioning in Humans

Classical conditioning has a great deal of survival value for human beings (Powell & Honey, 2013). Here we review examples of classical conditioning at work in human life.

**EXPLAINING FEARS**   Classical conditioning provides an explanation of fears (Amano & others, 2011; Hawkins-Gilligan, Dygdon, & Conger, 2011). John B. Watson (who coined the term *behaviorism*) and Rosalie Rayner (1920) demonstrated classical conditioning's role in the development of fears with an infant named Albert. They showed Albert a white laboratory rat to see whether he was afraid of it. He was not (so the rat was a neutral stimulus or CS). As Albert played with the rat, the researchers sounded a loud noise behind his head (the noise was then the US). The noise caused little Albert to cry (the UR). After only seven pairings of the loud noise with the white rat, Albert began to fear the rat even when the noise was not sounded (the CR). Albert's fear was generalized to a rabbit, a dog, and a sealskin coat.

*Watson and Rayner conditioned 11-month-old Albert to fear a white rat by pairing the rat with a loud noise. When little Albert was later presented with other stimuli similar to the rat, such as the rabbit shown here with Albert, he was afraid of them too. This study illustrates stimulus generalization in classical conditioning.*

Today, Watson and Rayner's (1920) study would violate the ethical guidelines of the American Psychological Association (see Chapter 1). In any case, Watson correctly concluded that we learn many of our fears through classical conditioning. We might develop fear of the dentist because of a painful experience, fear of driving after having been in a car crash, and fear of dogs after having been bitten by one.

If we can learn fears through classical conditioning, we also can possibly unlearn them through that process (Tronson & others, 2012; Vetere & others, 2011). In Chapter 13, for example, we will examine the application of classical conditioning to therapies for treating phobias.

**BREAKING HABITS**   Psychologists have applied classical conditioning to helping individuals unlearn certain feelings and behaviors. For example, **counterconditioning** is a classical conditioning procedure for changing the relationship between a conditioned stimulus and its conditioned response. Therapists have used counterconditioning to break the association between certain stimuli and positive feelings (Kerkhof & others, 2011).

**counterconditioning**
A classical conditioning procedure for changing the relationship between a conditioned stimulus and its conditioned response.

**aversive conditioning**
A form of treatment that consists of repeated pairings of a stimulus with a very unpleasant stimulus.

**Aversive conditioning** is a form of treatment that involves repeated pairings of a stimulus with a very unpleasant stimulus. Electric shocks and nausea-inducing substances are examples of noxious stimuli that are used in aversive conditioning (A. R. Brown & others, 2011). In a treatment to reduce drinking, for example, every time a person drinks an alcoholic beverage, he or she also consumes a mixture that induces nausea. In classical conditioning terminology, the alcoholic beverage is the conditioned stimulus and the nausea-inducing agent is the unconditioned stimulus. Through a repeated pairing of alcohol with the nausea-inducing agent, alcohol becomes the conditioned stimulus that elicits nausea, the conditioned response. As a consequence, alcohol no longer is associated with something pleasant but rather something highly unpleasant. Antabuse, a drug treatment for alcoholism since the late 1940s, is based on this association (Ullman, 1952). When someone takes this drug, ingesting even the smallest amount of alcohol will make the person quite ill, even if the exposure to the alcohol is through mouthwash or cologne. Antabuse continues to be used in the treatment of alcoholism today (Baser & others, 2011).

**CLASSICAL CONDITIONING AND THE PLACEBO EFFECT**   Chapter 1 defined the *placebo effect* as the effect of a substance (such as a pill taken orally) or procedure (such as using a syringe to inject a fluid) that researchers use as a control to

improve performance in settings such as a workplace and a classroom. Advocates of applied behavior analysis believe that many emotional and behavioral problems stem from inadequate or inappropriate consequences (Alberto & Troutman, 2009).

Applied behavior analysis has been effective in a wide range of situations. Practitioners have used it, for example, to train autistic individuals (Frazier, 2012), children and adolescents with psychological problems (Miltenberger, 2012), and residents of mental health facilities (Phillips & Mudford, 2008); to instruct individuals in effective parenting (Phaneuf & McIntyre, 2007); to enhance environmentally conscious behaviors such as recycling and not littering (Geller, 2002); to get people to wear seatbelts (Streff & Geller, 1986); and to promote workplace safety (Geller, 2006). Applied behavior analysis can help people improve their self-control in many aspects of mental and physical health (Spiegler & Guevremont, 2010).

self-quiz

1. A mother takes away her son's favorite toy when he misbehaves. Her action is an example of
   A. positive reinforcement.
   B. negative reinforcement.
   C. positive punishment.
   D. negative punishment.

2. The schedule of reinforcement that results in the greatest increase in behavior is
   A. fixed ratio.
   B. variable ratio.
   C. fixed interval.
   D. variable interval.

3. Kelley is scolded each time she teases her little brother. Her mother notices that the frequency of teasing has decreased. Scolding Kelley is an effective
   A. negative reinforcer.
   B. negative punisher.
   C. conditioner.
   D. positive punisher.

APPLY IT! 4. Kevin's girlfriend is very moody, and he never knows what to expect from her. When she is in a good mood, he feels as if he is in heaven, but when she is in a bad mood, she makes him crazy. His friends all think that he should dump her, but Kevin finds that he just cannot break it off. Kevin's girlfriend has him on a _____ schedule of reinforcement.
   A. variable
   B. fixed
   C. continuous
   D. nonexistent

# 4 Observational Learning

Would it make sense to teach a 15-year-old boy how to drive with either classical conditioning or operant conditioning procedures? Driving a car is a voluntary behavior, so classical conditioning would not apply. In terms of operant conditioning, we could ask him to try to drive down the road and then reward his positive behaviors. Not many of us would want to be on the road, though, when he makes mistakes. Albert Bandura (2007b, 2008, 2010) believes that if we learned only in such a trial-and-error fashion, learning would be exceedingly tedious and at times hazardous. Instead, he says, many complex behaviors are the result of exposure to competent models. By observing other people, we can acquire knowledge, skills, rules, strategies, beliefs, and attitudes (Schunk, 2011).

Bandura's *observational learning,* also called *imitation* or *modeling,* is learning that occurs when a person observes and imitates behavior. The capacity to learn by observation eliminates trial-and-error learning. Often observational learning takes less time than operant conditioning. Bandura (1986) described four main processes that are involved in observational learning: attention, retention, motor reproduction, and reinforcement.

In observational learning, the first process that must occur is *attention* (which we initially considered in Chapter 3 due to its crucial role in perception). To reproduce a model's actions, you must attend to what the model is saying or doing. You might not hear what a friend says if the stereo is blaring, and you might miss your instructor's analysis of a problem if you are admiring someone sitting in the next row. As a further example, imagine that you decide to take a class to improve your drawing skills. To succeed, you need to attend to the instructor's words and hand movements. Characteristics of the model can influence attention to the model. Warm, powerful, atypical people, for example, command more attention than do cold, weak, typical people.

*Retention* is the second process required for observational learning to occur. To reproduce a model's actions, you must encode the information and keep it in memory so that you can retrieve it. A simple verbal description, or a vivid image of what the model did, assists retention. (Memory is such an important cognitive process that Chapter 6 is devoted exclusively to it.) In the example of taking a class to sharpen your drawing ability, you will need to remember what the instructor said and did in modeling good drawing skills.

*Motor reproduction,* a third element of observational learning, is the process of imitating the model's actions. People might pay attention to a model and encode what they have seen, but limitations in motor development might make it difficult for them to reproduce the model's action. Thirteen-year-olds might see a professional basketball player do a reverse two-handed dunk but be unable to reproduce the pro's play. Similarly, in your drawing class, if you lack fine motor reproduction skills, you might be unable to follow the instructor's example.

*Reinforcement* is a final component of observational learning. In this case, the question is whether the model's behavior is followed by a consequence. Seeing a model attain a reward for an activity increases the chances that an observer will repeat the behavior—a process called *vicarious reinforcement*. On the other hand, seeing the model punished makes the observer less likely to repeat the behavior—a process called *vicarious punishment*. Unfortunately, vicarious reinforcement and vicarious punishment are often absent in, for example, media portrayals of violence and aggression.

Observational learning has been studied in a variety of contexts. Researchers have explored observational learning, for example, as a means by which gorillas learn from one another about motor skills (Byrne, Hobaiter, & Klailova, 2011). They have also studied it as a process by which people learn whether stimuli are likely to be painful (Helsen, & others, 2011) and as a tool individuals use to make economic decisions (Feri & others, 2011). Researchers are also interested in comparing learning from experience with learning through observation (Nicolle, Symmonds, & Dolan, 2011).

Observational learning can be an important factor in the functioning of role models in inspiring people and changing their perceptions. Whether a model is similar to us can influence that model's effectiveness in modifying our behavior. The shortage of role models for women and minorities in science and engineering has often been suggested as a reason for the lack of women and minorities in these fields. After the election of Barack Obama as president of the United States, many commentators noted that for the first time, African American children could see concretely that they might also attain the nation's highest office someday. You may have seen the photo of 5-year-old Jacob Philadelphia feeling President Obama's hair, to see if it was just like his (Calmes, 2012).

Figure 5.12 summarizes Bandura's model of observational learning.

Observational learning occurs when a person observes and imitates someone else's behavior. A famous example of observational learning is the Bobo doll study (Bandura, Ross, & Ross, 1961), in which children who had watched an aggressive adult model were more likely to behave aggressively when left alone than were children who had observed a non-aggressive model.

Having positive role models and mentors you can observe can be a significant factor in your learning and success. Make a list of your most important role models and mentors. Next to each, briefly describe how they have influenced you. What would your *ideal* role model or mentor be like?

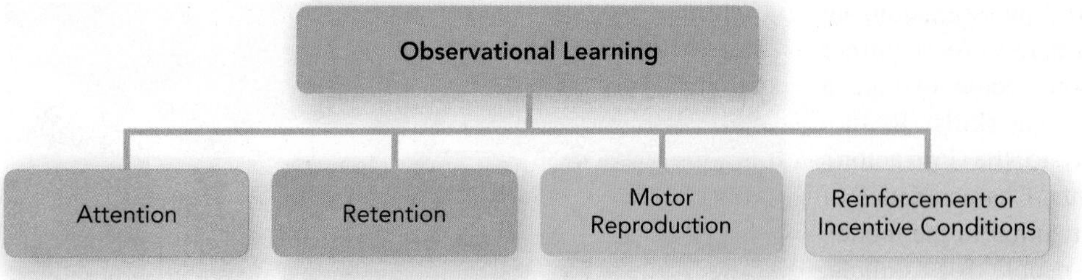

FIGURE 5.12 **Bandura's Model of Observational Learning** In terms of Bandura's model, if you are learning to ski, you need to attend to the instructor's words and demonstrations. You need to remember what the instructor did and his or her tips for avoiding disasters. You also need the motor abilities to reproduce what the instructor has shown you. Praise from the instructor after you have completed a few moves on the slopes should improve your motivation to continue skiing.

## self-quiz

1. Another name for observational learning is
   A. replication.
   B. modeling.
   C. trial-and-error learning.
   D. visualization.

2. According to Bandura, _____ occurs first in observational learning.
   A. motor reproduction
   B. retention
   C. attention
   D. reinforcement

3. A friend shows you how to do a card trick. However, you forget the second step in the trick and are thus unable to replicate the card trick. There has been a failure in
   A. motor reproduction.
   B. retention.
   C. attention.
   D. reinforcement.

**APPLY IT!** 4. Shawna is a 15-year-old high school girl whose mother is a highly paid accountant. Shawna's mom works long hours, often complains about her workplace and how much she hates her boss, and seems tired most of the time. When she is asked what she might do when she grows up, Shawna says she does not think she wants to pursue a career in accounting. Her mother is shocked and cannot understand why Shawna would not want to follow in her footsteps. Which of the following is the most likely explanation for this situation?
   A. Shawna has not observed her mother being reinforced for her behavior. She has only experienced vicarious punishment.
   B. Shawna is not aware that her mother is an accountant.
   C. Shawna is too different from her mother for her mother to be an effective role model.
   D. Shawna has not been paying attention to her mother.

# 5 Cognitive Factors in Learning

In learning about learning, we have looked at cognitive processes only as they apply in observational learning. Skinner's operant conditioning and Pavlov's classical conditioning focus on the environment and observable behavior, not what is going on in the head of the learner. Many contemporary psychologists, including some behaviorists, recognize the importance of cognition and believe that learning involves more than environment–behavior connections (Bandura, 2011; Bjork, Dunlosky, & Kornell, 2013; Schunk, 2011). A good starting place for considering cognitive influences in learning is the work of E. C. Tolman.

## Purposive Behavior

E. C. Tolman (1932) emphasized the *purposiveness* of behavior—the idea that much of behavior is goal-directed. Tolman believed that it is necessary to study entire behavioral sequences in order to understand why people engage in particular actions. For example, high school students whose goal is to attend a leading college or university study hard in their classes. If we focused only on their studying, we would miss the purpose of their behavior. The students do not always study hard because they have been reinforced for studying in the past. Rather, studying is a means to intermediate goals (learning, high grades) that in turn improve their likelihood of getting into the college or university of their choice (Schunk, 2011).

We can see Tolman's legacy today in the extensive interest in the role of goal setting in human behavior (Petri & Govern, 2013). Researchers are especially curious about how people self-regulate and self-monitor their behavior to reach a goal (Bjork, Dunlosky, & Kornell, 2013; Matthews & Moran, 2011).

**EXPECTANCY LEARNING AND INFORMATION** In studying the purposiveness of behavior, Tolman went beyond the stimuli and responses of Pavlov and Skinner to focus on cognitive mechanisms. Tolman said that when classical conditioning and operant conditioning occur, the organism acquires certain expectations. In classical conditioning, the young boy fears the rabbit because he expects it will hurt him. In operant conditioning, a woman works hard all week because she expects a paycheck on Friday. Expectancies are acquired from people's experiences with their environment. Expectancies influence a variety of human experiences. We set the goals we do because we believe that we can reach them.

Expectancies also play a role in the placebo effect. Many painkillers have been shown to be more effective in reducing pain when patients can see the intravenous injection sites than when they cannot (Price, Finniss, & Benedetti, 2008). If patients can see that they are getting a drug, they can harness their own expectations for pain reduction.

Tolman (1932) emphasized that the information value of the conditioned stimulus is important as a signal or an expectation that an unconditioned stimulus will follow. Anticipating contemporary thinking, Tolman believed that the information that the CS provides is the key to understanding classical conditioning. One contemporary view of classical conditioning describes an organism as an information seeker, using logical and perceptual relations among events, along with preconceptions, to form a representation of the world (Rescorla, 2003, 2005, 2009).

A classic experiment conducted by Leon Kamin (1968) illustrates the importance of an organism's history and the information provided by a conditioned stimulus in classical conditioning. Kamin conditioned a rat by repeatedly pairing a tone (CS) and a shock (US) until the tone alone produced fear (conditioned response). Then he continued to pair the tone with the shock, but he turned on a light (a second CS) each time the tone sounded. Even though he repeatedly paired the light (CS) and the shock (US), the rat showed no conditioning to the light (the light by itself produced no CR). Conditioning to the light was blocked, almost as if the rat had not paid attention. The rat apparently used the tone as a signal to predict that a shock would be coming; information about the light's pairing with the shock was redundant with the information already learned about the tone's pairing with the shock. In this experiment, conditioning was governed not by the contiguity of the CS and US but instead by the rat's history and the information it received. Contemporary classical conditioning researchers are further exploring the role of information in an organism's learning (Kluge & others, 2011; Knight, Lewis, & Wood, 2011; Rescorla & Wagner, 2009).

**LATENT LEARNING**    Experiments on latent learning provide other evidence to support the role of cognition in learning. **Latent learning** (or *implicit learning*) is unreinforced learning that is not immediately reflected in behavior. In one study, researchers put two groups of hungry rats in a maze and required them to find their way from a starting point to an end point (Tolman & Honzik, 1930). The first group found food (a reinforcer) at the end point; the second group found nothing there. In the operant conditioning view, the first group should learn the maze better than the second group, which is exactly what happened. However, when the researchers subsequently took some of the rats from the non-reinforced group and gave them food at the end point of the maze, they quickly began to run the maze as effectively as the reinforced group. The non-reinforced rats apparently had learned a great deal about the maze as they roamed around and explored it. However, their learning was latent, stored cognitively in their memories but not yet expressed behaviorally. When these rats were given a good reason (reinforcement with food) to run the maze speedily, they called on their latent learning to help them reach the end of the maze more quickly.

Outside a laboratory, latent learning is evident when you walk around a new setting to get "the lay of the land." The first time you visited your college campus, you may have wandered about without a specific destination in mind. Exploring the environment made you better prepared when the time came to find that 8 A.M. class.

## Insight Learning

Like E. C. Tolman, the German gestalt psychologist Wolfgang Köhler believed that cognitive factors play a significant role in learning. Köhler spent four months in the Canary Islands during World War I observing the behavior of apes. There he conducted two fascinating experiments—the stick problem and the box problem. Although these

**latent learning (implicit learning)** Unreinforced learning that is not immediately reflected in behavior.

two experiments are basically the same, the solutions to the problems are different. In both situations, the ape discovers that it cannot reach an alluring piece of fruit, either because the fruit is too high or because it is outside of the ape's cage and beyond reach. To solve the stick problem, the ape has to insert a small stick inside a larger stick to reach the fruit. To master the box problem, the ape must stack several boxes to reach the fruit (Figure 5.13).

According to Köhler (1925), solving these problems does not involve trial and error or simple connections between stimuli and responses. Rather, when the ape realizes that its customary actions are not going to help it get the fruit, it often sits for a period of time and appears to ponder how to solve the problem. Then it quickly rises, as if it has had a flash of insight, piles the boxes on top of one another, and gets the fruit. **Insight learning** is a form of problem solving in which the organism develops a sudden insight into or understanding of a problem's solution.

The idea that insight learning is essentially different from learning through trial and error or through conditioning has always been controversial (Spence, 1938). Insight learning appears to entail both gradual and sudden processes, and understanding how these lead to problem solving continues to fascinate psychologists (Chu & MacGregor, 2011). In one study, researchers observed orangutans trying to figure out a way to get a tempting peanut out of a clear plastic tube (Mendes, Hanus, & Call, 2007). The primates wandered about their enclosures, experimenting with various strategies. Typically, they paused for a moment before finally landing on a solution: Little by little they filled the tube with water that they transferred by mouth from their water dishes to the tube. Once the peanut floated to the top, the clever orangutans had their snack. More recent research shows that chimps can solve the floating peanut task through observational learning (Tennie, Call, & Tomasello, 2010).

Insight learning requires thinking "outside the box," setting aside previous expectations and assumptions. One way that insight learning can be enhanced in human beings is through multicultural experiences (Leung & others, 2008). Correlational studies have shown that time spent living abroad is associated with higher insight learning performance among MBA students (Maddux & Galinsky, 2007). Furthermore, experimental studies have demonstrated that exposure to other cultures can influence insight learning. In one study, U.S. college students were randomly assigned to view one of two slide shows—one about Chinese and U.S. culture and the other about a control topic. Those who saw the multicultural slide show scored higher on measures of creativity and insight, and these changes persisted for a week (Leung & others, 2008). Being exposed to other cultures and other ways of thinking can be a key way to enhance insight and creativity, and a person does not have to travel to enjoy the learning benefits of multicultural experience. For more on this topic, see the Intersection.

**insight learning**
A form of problem solving in which the organism develops a sudden insight into or understanding of a problem's solution.

What makes insight learning unique is that "Aha!" moment— but that moment often comes after some trial and error during which many of the "wrong" answers have been thoroughly dismissed.

**FIGURE 5.13** **Insight Learning** Sultan, one of Wolfgang Köhler's brightest chimps, is faced with the problem of reaching a cluster of bananas overhead. He solves the problem by stacking boxes on top of one another to reach the bananas. Köhler called this type of problem solving "insight learning."

# INTERSECTION

## Educational and Cross-Cultural Psychology: How Does Cultural Diversity Affect Learning?

One of the most dramatic changes in U.S. higher education is the shift to a more diverse student body. The table below summarizes changes in the social landscape of four-year colleges and universities from 1976 to 2011 (U.S. Department of Education, 2011), as well as the projected changes by 2019 (Chronicle of Higher Education, 2011).

| Groups | Percentage of Students 1976 | Percentage of Students 2011 | Projected Percentage *Increase* 2011–2019 |
|---|---|---|---|
| Women | 41 | 57 | +18 |
| Non-Latino White/European American | 83 | 62 | +5 |
| African American | 9.4 | 14 | +24 |
| Latino | 3.5 | 12 | +37 |
| Asian American | 1.8 | 7 | +23 |

Research has shown that diversity is beneficial to student learning. For instance, in a study of over 53,000 undergraduates at 124 colleges and universities, students' reported interactions with individuals from other racial and ethnic backgrounds predicted a variety of positive outcomes, including academic achievement, intellectual growth, and social competence (Hu & Kuh, 2003). Many universities recognize that as U.S. society becomes more multiculturally diverse, students must be prepared to interact in a diverse

community as they enter the job market. Participation in diversity courses in college is related to cognitive development (Bowman, 2010) and civic involvement (Gurin & others, 2002), with outcomes especially positive for non-Latino White students (Hu & Kuh, 2003).

How does exposure to diversity influence the learning of ethnic minority members? In this case, the link between diversity and academic performance is more complicated. For one thing, due to societal attitudes about their ethnic group, minority students may worry about taking learning risks and offering ideas. For another, these students may be influenced by their concerns about how others perceive them and their ethnic group. These feelings can take a toll on academic efforts (Ely, Thomas, & Padavic, 2007; Guillaume, Brodbeck, & Riketta, 2012). However, diversity may have benefits for these individuals as well, especially as the university setting becomes increasingly diverse.

A recent study examined diversity and individual learning in a group context at an international business school in Great Britain (Brodbeck, Guillaume, & Lee, 2011). Students represented a variety of ethnic backgrounds. The British students included White/Anglo students and ethnically Indian and Pakistani students. In addition, some students were Black Caribbean, Black African, Chinese, and Arab, and some were from other European countries. Students were assigned to workgroups for a course that involved running a car company in a computer simulation game. In groups of typically five, the students met weekly, developed a business plan, made decisions together, and tracked their company's progress. Each student also wrote an individual essay that was part of the course grade. The groups varied in terms of ethnic diversity. The results of the study showed that ethnic minority students who were in groups with low diversity tended to perform relatively poorly, but their performance increased as group diversity did. Especially important, though, was the inclusion of one other person from the student's same ethnic group. The researchers estimated that for an ethnic minority student, being in a diverse group that included at least one other member from his or her own group was associated with the difference between a C+ and an A grade. The highest level of learning among ethnic minorities occurred in groups in which the ethnic minorities made up the majority of the group. And White/Anglo students performed very well in groups in which they were the only member of their ethnic group.

There is no question that the undergraduate student population continues to change dramatically. This development would appear to be a very good thing for learning. Diverse groups provide broader knowledge and more varied perspectives than do homogeneous groups, to the positive benefit of all group members. As university communities become more diverse, they offer students an ever-greater opportunity to share and to benefit from those differences.

\\ **How diverse is your learning environment?**

\\ **How do you benefit from the diversity at your school?**

1. E. C. Tolman emphasized the *purposiveness* of behavior—the idea that much of behavior is oriented toward the achievement of
   A. immortality.
   B. altruism.
   C. goals.
   D. self-esteem.

2. When the answer to a problem just pops into your head, you have experienced
   A. latent learning.
   B. insight learning.
   C. implicit learning.
   D. expectancy learning.

3. A type of learning that does *not* involve trial and error is
   A. insight learning.
   B. latent learning.
   C. expectancy learning.
   D. implicit learning.

**APPLY IT!** 4. Derek is rehearsing his lines and songs for an upcoming production of *Grease*. He is playing the lead role of Danny Zucco. His friend Maria helps him practice his lines and learn the words to his songs. Maria is not in the play and wouldn't even think of appearing onstage. On open-

ing night, Maria is in the audience, and halfway through "Summer Lovin'" people sitting around her are complaining because she is singing along. She also has been saying all of Danny's lines under her breath. What is the explanation?
A. Maria is demonstrating the power of latent learning.
B. Maria is demonstrating insight learning.
C. Maria is showing purposive behavior.
D. Maria secretly dreams of playing Danny Zucco in an all-female version of *Grease* someday.

# 6 Biological, Cultural, and Psychological Factors in Learning

Albert Einstein had many special talents. He combined enormous creativity with keen analytic ability to develop some of the twentieth century's most important insights into the nature of matter and the universe. Genes obviously endowed Einstein with extraordinary intellectual skills that enabled him to think and reason on a very high plane, but cultural factors also contributed to his genius. Einstein received an excellent, rigorous European education, and later in the United States he experienced the freedom and support believed to be important in creative exploration. Would Einstein have been able to develop his skills fully and to make such brilliant insights if he had grown up in a less advantageous environment? It is unlikely. Clearly, both biological and cultural factors contribute to learning.

## Biological Constraints

Humans cannot breathe under water, fish cannot ski, and cows cannot solve math problems. The structure of an organism's body permits certain kinds of learning and inhibits others (Chance, 2009). For example, chimpanzees cannot learn to speak English because they lack the necessary vocal equipment.

Service dogs also illustrate the limits of learning principles. One type of service dog, the seizure-alert dog, warns individuals with epilepsy of an oncoming attack minutes or even hours before the seizure takes place. These dogs may whine, bark, or paw their owners prior to a seizure. No one knows how these canines sense an oncoming seizure, though learning principles of reward are used in their training. Dogs that show sensitivity to seizures receive treats when they successfully anticipate a seizure. Using rewards, trainers also teach the dogs to stay with their human companions after a seizure and to press a button to call 911. However, as one trainer noted, "I can train a dog to sit . . . and fetch, but I can't teach a dog to alert" (Mott, 2004). That is, if the dog does not have a natural sensitivity to seizures, no amount of training will produce it.

**INSTINCTIVE DRIFT** Keller and Marion Breland (1961), students of B. F. Skinner, used operant conditioning to train animals to perform at fairs and conventions and in television advertisements. They applied Skinner's techniques to teach pigs to cart large wooden nickels to a piggy bank and deposit them. They also trained raccoons to pick up a coin and place it in a metal tray. Although the pigs and raccoons, as well as chickens and other animals, performed most of the tasks well (raccoons became adept basketball players, for example—see Figure 5.14), some of the animals began acting strangely. Instead of picking up the large wooden nickels and carrying them to the piggy bank, the pigs dropped the nickels on the ground, shoved them with their snouts, tossed them in the air, and then repeated these actions. The raccoons began to hold on to their coins rather than dropping them into the metal tray. When two coins were introduced, the raccoons rubbed them together in a miserly fashion. Somehow these behaviors overwhelmed the strength of the reinforcement. This example of biological influences on learning illustrates **instinctive drift,** the tendency of animals to revert to instinctive behavior that interferes with learning.

Why were the pigs and the raccoons misbehaving? The pigs were rooting, an instinct that is used to uncover edible roots. The raccoons were engaging in an instinctive food-washing response. Their instinctive drift interfered with learning.

**FIGURE 5.14** **Instinctive Drift** This raccoon's skill in using its hands made it an excellent basketball player, but because of instinctive drift, the raccoon had a much more difficult time dropping coins in a tray.

**instinctive drift**
The tendency of animals to revert to instinctive behavior that interferes with learning.

**preparedness**
The species-specific biological predisposition to learn in certain ways but not others.

**PREPAREDNESS**   Some animals learn readily in one situation but have difficulty learning in slightly different circumstances (Garcia & Koelling, 1966, 2009). The difficulty might result not from some aspect of the learning situation but from the organism's biological predisposition (Seligman, 1970). **Preparedness** is the species-specific biological predisposition to learn in certain ways but not others.

Much of the evidence for preparedness comes from research on taste aversion (Garcia, 1989; Garcia & Koelling, 2009). Recall that taste aversion involves a single trial of learning the association between a particular taste and nausea. Rats that experience low levels of radiation after eating show a strong aversion to the food they were eating when the radiation made them ill. This aversion can last for as long as 32 days. Such long-term effects cannot be accounted for by classical conditioning, which would argue that a single pairing of the conditioned and unconditioned stimuli would not last that long (Garcia, Ervin, & Koelling, 1966). Taste aversion learning occurs in animals, including humans, that choose their food based on taste and smell. Other species are prepared to learn rapid associations between, for instance, colors of foods and illness.

Another example of preparedness comes from research on conditioning humans and monkeys to associate snakes with fear. Susan Mineka and Arne Ohman (2002; Ohman & Mineka, 2003) have investigated the fascinating natural power of snakes to evoke fear in many mammals. Many monkeys and humans fear snakes, and both monkeys and humans are very quick to learn the association between snakes and fear. In classical conditioning studies, when pictures of snakes (CS) are paired with electrical shocks (US), the snakes are likely to quickly and strongly evoke fear (the CR). Interestingly, pairing pictures of, say, flowers (CS) with electrical shocks produces much weaker associations (Mineka & Ohman, 2002; Ohman & Soares, 1998). Even more significantly, pictures of snakes can serve as conditioned stimuli for fearful responses, even when the pictures are presented so rapidly that they cannot be consciously perceived (Ohman & Mineka, 2001).

The link between snakes and fear has been demonstrated not only in classical conditioning paradigms. Monkeys that have been raised in the lab and that have never seen a snake rapidly learn to fear snakes, even entirely by observational learning. Lab monkeys that see a video of a monkey expressing fear toward a snake learn to be afraid of snakes faster than monkeys seeing the same fear video spliced so that the feared object is a rabbit, a flower, or a mushroom (Ohman & Mineka, 2003).

Mineka and Ohman (2002) suggest that these results demonstrate preparedness among mammals to associate snakes with fear and aversive stimuli. They suggest that this association is related to the amygdala (the part of the limbic system that is linked to emotion) and is difficult to modify. These researchers suggest that this preparedness for fear of snakes has emerged out of the threat that reptiles likely posed to our evolutionary ancestors.

# Cultural Influences

On the Indonesian island of Bali, young children learn traditional dances, whereas in Norway children commonly learn to ski early in life. As cultures vary, so does the content of learning. **> Think of some activities you learned at an early age; how are they related to the culture in which you grew up? > What sorts of basic knowledge did these experiences allow you to acquire? > How might such early experiences relate to your current learning? > How did the adults in your life respond to success or failure, and how has that shaped your experience of learning?**

Traditionally, interest in the cultural context of human learning has been limited, partly because the organisms in those contexts typically were animals. The question arises, how might culture influence human learning? Most psychologists agree that the principles of classical conditioning, operant conditioning, and observational learning are universal and are powerful learning processes in every culture. However, culture can influence the degree to which these learning processes are used (Matsumoto & Juang, 2013). For example, Mexican American students may learn more through observational learning, while non-Latino White students may be more accustomed to learn through direct instruction (Mejia-Arauz, Rogoff, & Paradise, 2005).

In addition, culture can determine the content of learning (Shiraev, 2011). We cannot learn about something we do not experience. The 4-year-old who grows up among the Bushmen of the Kalahari Desert is unlikely to learn about taking baths and eating with a knife and fork. Similarly, a child growing up in Chicago is unlikely to be skilled at tracking animals and finding water-bearing roots in the desert. Learning often requires practice, and certain behaviors are practiced more often in some cultures than in others. In Bali, many children are skilled dancers by the age of 6, whereas Norwegian children are much more likely to be good skiers and skaters by that age.

# Psychological Constraints

Are there psychological constraints on learning? For animals, the answer is probably no. For humans, the answer may well be yes. This section opened with the claim that fish cannot ski. The truth of this statement is clear. Biological circumstances make it impossible. If we put biological considerations aside, we might ask ourselves about times in our lives when we feel like a fish trying to ski—when we feel that we just do not have what it takes to learn a skill or master a task. Some people believe that humans have particular learning styles that make it easier for them to learn in some ways but not others. To read about this possibility, see Challenge Your Thinking.

Carol Dweck (2006, 2012) uses the term *mindset* to describe the way our beliefs about ability dictate what goals we set for ourselves, what we think we *can* learn, and ultimately what we *do* learn. Individuals have one of two mindsets: a *fixed mindset,* in which

## Do Learning Styles Matter to Learning?

Learning styles refers to the idea that people differ in terms of the method of instruction that will be most effective for them. You may have heard, for example, that someone can be a *visual learner* (he or she learns by seeing), an *aural learner* (the person learns by listening), or a *kinesthetic learner* (the individual learns through hands-on experience).

The notion that people have different learning styles is extremely popular. Educational psychology textbooks, as well as many school districts, instruct teachers to take such differences into account in the classroom. The argument that teachers should tailor their methods to fit students' learning styles suggests a specific scientific hypothesis: that individuals will *learn better* when instructions are targeted to their particular learning style. What is the evidence for the prediction that tailoring instruction to students' learning styles improves learning?

In 2008, the Association for Psychological Science commissioned a panel of specialists to answer this question. Led by psychologist Harold Pashler, a human learning expert, the panel found that while children and adults report consistent preferences for particular learning styles, there is *no evidence* that tailoring instructional methods to "visual," "aural," or "kinesthetic" learners produces better learning (Pashler & others, 2008). Let's consider some of the evidence that led to this controversial conclusion.

In one study, researchers first measured whether participants were verbal or visual learners and then had them study a list of words presented verbally or visually. This study period was followed by a memory test. Results showed that all participants did better in the visual condition, and there was no relationship between preferred learning styles and memory for the material (Constantinidou & Baker, 2002). In another series of studies, participants who identified themselves as visual or verbal learners were given the option to use visual or verbal help materials as they completed a computer-based learning unit. Although learning styles predicted the kind of materials participants preferred, the match between a person's learning style and the mode of instruction was unrelated to learning (Massa & Mayer, 2006). The investigators concluded that there was no evidence that different instructional methods should be used for different

*"And this year's 'Inquisitive Learner Award' goes to…"*
Used by permission of CartoonStock, www.CartoonStock.com.

learners (Massa & Mayer, 2006). Based on these and other studies, Pashler and his colleagues judged that the disconnect between the popularity of the learning styles approach within education and the lack of credible evidence for its usefulness was both "striking and disturbing" (2008, p. 117).

The notion of learning styles is appealing at least in part because it reflects something we know to be true: People learn differently. However, the different ways humans learn do not seem to be well captured by learning styles (Willingham, 2011). The effectiveness of particular methods of teaching may depend more on the material to be covered, a student's prior knowledge, motivation, and other factors. Coming at any topic from many different angles may improve student learning. Teachers may reach more students more effectively when they try different ways of approaching material—for instance, coming up with a hands-on tool to demonstrate a problem—but that is just good instruction, not instruction that is tailored to particular styles. As we saw in Chapter 3, our senses work together to connect us to the external world. The brain and our sensory organs are not specialized to learn in specific ways.

Is there any harm in our trying to find out our preferred learning style? Perhaps, if the outcome constrains learning—if we assume, for example, that our personal learning style tells us what we cannot do or should not try. Sometimes the most meaningful learning experiences are those that push us outside our comfort zone. Teachers and topics that challenge us to put in extra effort, to see the world and ourselves in different ways, may be the key to meaningful learning. Sometimes the easiest path is not the one most likely to lead to life-changing learning.

### What Do You Think?

- Do you think that you have a particular learning style? If so, how does it influence your learning?

- Even if evidence supported the effectiveness of tailoring teaching methods to specific types of learning styles, how would we implement a program based on these ideas?

they believe that their qualities are carved in stone and cannot change; or a *growth mindset,* in which they believe their qualities can change and improve through their effort. These two mindsets have implications for the meaning of failure. From a fixed mindset, failure means lack of ability. From a growth mindset, however, failure tells the person what he or she still needs to learn. Your mindset influences whether you will be optimistic or pessimistic, what your goals will be, how hard you will strive to reach those goals, and how successful you are in college and after.

Dweck (2006) studied first-year pre-med majors taking their first chemistry class in college. Students with a growth mindset got higher grades than those with a fixed mindset. Even when they did not do well on a test, the growth-mindset students bounced back on the next test. Fixed-mindset students typically read and re-read the text and class notes or tried to memorize everything verbatim. The fixed-mindset students who did poorly on tests concluded that chemistry and maybe pre-med were not for them. By contrast, growth-mindset students took charge of their motivation and learning, searching for themes and principles in the course and going over mistakes until they understood why they made them. In Dweck's analysis, "They were studying to learn, not just ace the test. And, actually, this is why they got higher grades—not because they were smarter or had a better background in science" (2006, p. 61),

Following are some effective strategies for developing a growth mindset (Dweck, 2006):

- *Understand that your intelligence and thinking skills are not fixed but can change.* Even if you are extremely bright, with effort you can increase your intelligence.

- *Become passionate about learning and stretch your mind in challenging situations.* It is easy to withdraw into a fixed mindset when the going gets tough; but as you bump up against obstacles, keep growing, work harder, stay the course, and improve your strategies; you will become a more successful person.

- *Think about the growth mindsets of people you admire.* Possibly you have a hero, someone who has achieved something extraordinary. You may have thought his or her accomplishments came easy because the person is so talented. However, find out more about this person and how he or she works and thinks. You likely will discover that much hard work and effort over a long period of time were responsible for this individual's achievements.

- *Begin now.* If you have a fixed mindset, commit to changing now. Think about when, where, and how you will begin using your new growth mindset.

Dweck's work challenges us to consider the limits we place on our own learning. When we think of the relative absence of women and minorities in math and science professions, we might consider the messages these groups have received about whether they have what it takes to succeed in these domains. Our beliefs about ability profoundly influence what we try to learn. As any 7-year-old with a growth mindset would tell you, you never know what you can do until you try.

1. When a pig's rooting behavior interferes with its learning, the phenomenon is an example of
   A. preparedness.
   B. learned helplessness.
   C. a taste aversion.
   D. instinctive drift.

2. Mineka and Ohman suggest that humans' preparedness for fear of snakes emerged because of
   A. cultural myths.
   B. the religious symbolism of snakes.
   C. the danger that snakes and other reptiles posed to earlier humans.
   D. the limitations of human learning.

3. Believing that studying hard will result in a good grade in a course is an example of
   A. a growth insight.
   B. a growth mindset.
   C. preparedness.
   D. a fixed mindset.

APPLY IT! 4. Frances is a dog person who has just adopted her first-ever cat. Given her experience in housebreaking her pet dogs, Frances is shocked that her new kitty, Tolman, uses the litter box the very first day and never has an accident in the house. Frances thinks that Tolman must be a genius cat. Tolman's amazing ability demonstrates
A. psychological constraints on learning.
B. biological preparedness.
C. cultural constraints on learning.
D. that dog people are not very bright.

# ① Types of Learning

Learning is a systematic, relatively permanent change in behavior that occurs through experience. Associative learning involves learning by making a connection between two events. Observational learning is learning by watching what other people do.

Conditioning is the process by which associative learning occurs. In classical conditioning, organisms learn the association between two stimuli. In operant conditioning, they learn the association between behavior and a consequence.

# ② Classical Conditioning

Classical conditioning occurs when a neutral stimulus becomes associated with a meaningful stimulus and comes to elicit a similar response. Pavlov discovered that an organism learns the association between an unconditioned stimulus (US) and a conditioned stimulus (CS). The US automatically produces the unconditioned response (UR). After conditioning (CS–US pairing), the CS elicits the conditioned response (CR) by itself. Acquisition in classical conditioning is the initial linking of stimuli and responses, which involves a neutral stimulus being associated with the US so that the CS comes to elicit the CR. Two important aspects of acquisition are contiguity and contingency.

Generalization in classical conditioning is the tendency of a new stimulus that is similar to the original conditioned stimulus to elicit a response that is similar to the conditioned response. Discrimination is the process of learning to respond to certain stimuli and not to others. Extinction is the weakening of the CR in the absence of the US. Spontaneous recovery is the recurrence of a CR after a time delay without further conditioning.

In humans, classical conditioning has been applied to explaining and eliminating fears, breaking habits, combating taste aversion, and understanding such different experiences as pleasant emotions and drug habituation.

# ③ Operant Conditioning

Operant conditioning is a form of learning in which the consequences of behavior produce changes in the probability of the behavior's occurrence. Skinner described the behavior of the organism as operant: The behavior operates on the environment, and the environment in turn operates on the organism. Whereas classical conditioning involves respondent behavior, operant conditioning involves operant behavior. In most instances, operant conditioning is better at explaining voluntary behavior than is classical conditioning.

Thorndike's law of effect states that behaviors followed by positive outcomes are strengthened, whereas behaviors followed by negative outcomes are weakened. Skinner built on this idea to develop the notion of operant conditioning.

Shaping is the process of rewarding approximations of desired behavior in order to shorten the learning process. Principles of reinforcement include the distinction between positive reinforcement (the frequency of a behavior increases because it is followed by a rewarding stimulus) and negative reinforcement (the frequency of behavior increases because it is followed by the removal of an aversive stimulus). Positive reinforcement can be classified as primary reinforcement (using

reinforcers that are innately satisfying) and secondary reinforcement (using reinforcers that acquire positive value through experience). Reinforcement can also be continuous (a behavior is reinforced every time) or partial (a behavior is reinforced only a portion of the time). Schedules of reinforcement—fixed ratio, variable ratio, fixed interval, and variable interval—determine when a behavior will be reinforced.

Operant conditioning involves generalization (giving the same response to similar stimuli), discrimination (responding to stimuli that signal that a behavior will or will not be reinforced), and extinction (a decreasing tendency to perform a previously reinforced behavior when reinforcement is stopped).

Punishment is a consequence that decreases the likelihood that a behavior will occur. In positive punishment, a behavior decreases when it is followed by a (typically unpleasant) stimulus. In negative punishment, a behavior decreases when a positive stimulus is removed from it.

Applied behavior analysis involves the application of operant conditioning principles to a variety of real-life behaviors.

# ④ Observational Learning

Observational learning occurs when a person observes and imitates someone else's behavior. Bandura identified four main processes in observational learning: attention, retention, motor reproduction, and reinforcement.

# ⑤ Cognitive Factors in Learning

Tolman emphasized the purposiveness of behavior. Purposiveness refers to Tolman's belief that much of behavior is goal-directed. In studying purposiveness, Tolman went beyond stimuli and responses to discuss cognitive mechanisms. Tolman believed that expectancies, acquired through experiences with the environment, are an important cognitive mechanism in learning.

Köhler developed the concept of insight learning, a form of problem solving in which the organism develops a sudden insight into or understanding of a problem's solution.

# ⑥ Biological, Cultural, and Psychological Factors in Learning

Biological constraints restrict what an organism can learn from experience. These constraints include instinctive drift (the tendency of animals to revert to instinctive behavior that interferes with learned behavior), preparedness (the species-specific biological predisposition to learn in certain ways but not in others), and taste aversion (the biological predisposition to avoid foods that have caused sickness in the past).

Although most psychologists agree that the principles of classical conditioning, operant conditioning, and observational learning are universal, cultural customs can influence the degree to which these learning processes are used. Culture also often determines the content of learning.

In addition, what we learn is determined in part by what we believe we can learn. Dweck emphasizes that individuals benefit enormously from having a growth mindset rather than a fixed mindset.

learning, p. 167

behaviorism, p. 167

associative learning, p. 167

observational learning, p. 168

classical conditioning, p. 169

unconditioned stimulus (US), p. 170

unconditioned response (UR), p. 170

conditioned stimulus (CS), p. 170

conditioned response (CR), p. 170

acquisition, p. 170

generalization (classical conditioning), p. 172

discrimination (classical conditioning), p.172

extinction (classical conditioning), p. 172

spontaneous recovery, p. 172

counterconditioning, p. 173

aversive conditioning, p. 173

habituation, p. 175

operant conditioning (instrumental conditioning), p. 178

law of effect, p. 178

shaping, p. 180

reinforcement, p. 180

positive reinforcement, p. 181

negative reinforcement, p. 181

avoidance learning, p. 182

learned helplessness, p. 182

primary reinforcer, p. 182

secondary reinforcer, p. 182

generalization (operant conditioning), p. 182

discrimination (operant conditioning), p. 183

extinction (operant conditioning), p. 183

schedules of reinforcement, p. 183

punishment, p. 185

positive punishment, p. 185

negative punishment, p. 185

applied behavior analysis (behavior modification), p. 187

latent learning (implicit learning), p. 191

insight learning, p. 192

instinctive drift, p. 195

preparedness, p. 195

# SELF-TEST

## Multiple Choice

1. Salivation in response to food, shivering from exposure to a low temperature, and coughing in reaction to throat congestion are examples of automatic stimulus–response connections, or
   A. contractions.
   B. reflexes.
   C. associations.
   D. acquisitions.

2. Researchers found that raccoons that were trained to deposit coins in a tray began to rub the coins together instead of dropping them in the tray. Why?
   A. extinction
   B. spontaneous recovery
   C. instinctive drift
   D. counterconditioning

3. When a child hears a loud noise, he cries. The loud noise is
   A. the unconditioned stimulus.
   B. the conditioned stimulus.
   C. the unconditioned response.
   D. the conditioned response.

4. Which of the following is consistent with the law of effect?
   A. A child who is rewarded for getting good grades begins to do poorly in school.
   B. A dog that is punished for barking barks more.
   C. A cat that is yelled at when it scratches the sofa stops scratching the sofa.

   D. An adult who is fired from his job for being late is late at his next job.

5. Meghan is scared of flying. When she goes on vacation with her husband, he helps her to relax by holding her hand, having her breathe deeply, and imagining herself on a sandy beach. After several flights with her husband, Meghan is no longer afraid of flying. Which of the following processes occurred?
   A. counterconditioning
   B. extinction
   C. discrimination
   D. spontaneous recovery

6. Every sixth time Miguel cleans his room, his mother takes him to dinner as a reward. On what type of reinforcement schedule is Miguel?
   A. variable-ratio schedule
   B. variable-interval schedule
   C. fixed-ratio schedule
   D. fixed-interval schedule

7. The schedule of reinforcement that is most resistant to extinction is the
   A. variable-ratio schedule.
   B. variable-interval schedule.
   C. fixed-ratio schedule.
   D. fixed-interval schedule.

8. Putting a child who misbehaves in time-out is an example of
   A. a negative reinforcer.
   B. negative punishment.

   C. a positive reinforcer.
   D. positive punishment.

9. Sally witnesses her friend get arrested for drug possession. As a result, Sally avoids drugs. Sally has experienced what type of learning?
   A. negative reinforcement
   B. classical conditioning
   C. operant learning
   D. observational learning

10. _____ accounts for the finding that taste aversions develop more quickly than other types of learning.
    A. Instinctive drift
    B. Preparedness
    C. Insight learning
    D. Contingency

## Apply It!

11. Imagine that you are about to begin an internship in an organization that you would like to join someday as a professional. Use the processes of observational learning to describe your strategy for making the most of your intern experience. Recall that learning is relatively permanent, which means that we can sometimes forget things we have learned. Also, learning involves experience—so changes in behavior that occur because of physical maturation are typically not considered learning.

# 6

# Memory

## *Photographs, Souvenirs, and Mementos: Memory and Meaning*

On May 20, 2011, Joplin, Missouri, was struck by a tornado that killed 160 people and leveled a third of the city. Within days of the storm, residents of Arkansas, Kansas, Oklahoma, Tennessee, and across Missouri started finding photos from Joplin in unexpected places. Carried by the tornado's 200 mph winds, these treasured mementos turned up in trees, barns, yards, and barbed wire fences.

Oklahoman Angela Walters set up a Facebook page as a clearinghouse for people from Joplin to claim their lost photos. Eventually the page featured 27,000 images. Walters observed, "When a disaster happens, as soon as you hear a family is safe, the next thing you always think about is photos. They're irreplaceable. . . . They're the record of our lives" (Cohen, 2011). A woman who lost her home in the storm found comfort in a photo of her now 8-year-old son taken when he was 2, mugging for the camera and pretending to shave. "It's a day and a memory and a piece of time. . . . All this other stuff is just stuff," she said. "It's the memories that count—and the photos" (Cohen, 2011).

Human beings naturally collect concrete evidence to support their memories. When something important happens, we take a picture. Visiting an unusual place, we might pick up a T-shirt, a coffee mug, or a postcard. The preciousness of this material evidence of where we have been, with whom, and what we did tells us two important truths about memory: There are some things we want to remember forever, and we are not sure that memory itself will suffice. Certainly, memory provides crucial support for many mundane activities—for example, it allows us to know what we were looking for when we opened the fridge, where we left our running shoes, and when we need to mail a birthday card. But our memories are also precious because they represent a lasting imprint of our experiences, moments from the past that give our lives meaning.

I WAS A DRUM MAJOR FOR JUSTICE, PEACE AND RIGHTEOUSNESS

There are few moments when your life is not steeped in memory. Memory is at work with each step you take, each thought you think, and each word you speak. Through memory, you weave the past into the present. In this chapter, we explore the key processes of memory, including how information gets into memory and how it is stored, retrieved, and sometimes forgotten. We also probe what the science of memory reveals about the best way to study and retain course material, as well as how memory processes can enrich our lives.

# 1 The Nature of Memory

The stars are shining and the moon is full. A beautiful evening is coming to a close. You look at your significant other and think, "I'll never forget this night." How is it possible that in fact you never will forget it? Years from now, you might tell your children about that one special night so many years ago, even if you had not thought about it in the years since. How does one perfect night become a part of your enduring life memories?

**memory**
The retention of information or experience over time as the result of three key processes: encoding, storage, and retrieval.

Psychologists define **memory** as the retention of information or experience over time. Memory occurs through three important processes: encoding, storage, and retrieval. Memory requires taking in information (encoding the sights and sounds of that night), storing it or representing it (retaining it in some mental storehouse), and then retrieving it for a later purpose (recalling it when someone asks, "So, how did you two end up together?"). In the next three sections, we focus on these phases of memory: encoding, storage, and retrieval (Figure 6.1).

Except for the annoying moments when your memory fails or the upsetting situation where someone you know experiences memory loss, you most likely do not consider how much everything you do and say depends on the smooth operation of your memory systems (Schacter, 2001, 2007). Think about asking someone for his or her phone number when you have no pencil, paper, or cell phone handy. You must attend to what the person tells you and rehearse the digits in your head until you can store them someplace permanently. Then, when the time comes to record the numbers, say, in your phone, you have to retrieve the identity of the person and the reason you got that phone number to begin with. Was it to ask the person out or to borrow notes for your psychology class? Human memory systems are truly remarkable considering how much information we put into memory and how much we must retrieve to perform life's activities (Kahana, 2012; Lieberman, 2012).

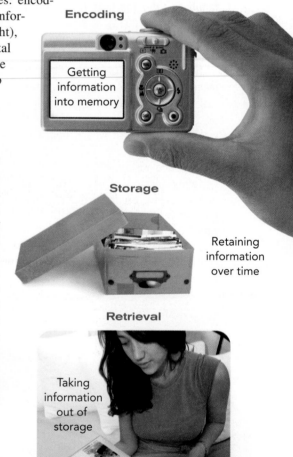

**Encoding**
Getting information into memory

**Storage**
Retaining information over time

**Retrieval**
Taking information out of storage

**FIGURE 6.1 Processing Information in Memory** As you read about the many aspects of memory in this chapter, think about the organization of memory in terms of these three main activities.

1. Memory is the _____ of information or experience over a period of time.
   A. rehearsal
   B. intake
   C. association
   D. retention

2. When we take in information in the course of daily life, such as the words and diagrams presented during a lecture, we are using the memory process of
   A. retention.
   B. encoding.
   C. retrieval.
   D. fixation.

3. The three processes of memory are encoding, _____, and retrieval.
   A. storage
   B. rehearsal
   C. recollection
   D. fixation

**APPLY IT!** 4. James and Adam are very good friends and often sit next to each other in Intro Psych. James spends a lot of time in class working on homework for his biology lab, while Adam listens to the lecture and takes lots of notes. Before the first exam, James asks to borrow Adam's notebook from Intro and studies those notes very carefully. In fact, both James and Adam study for 10 hours for the test. After the exam, James finds out he got a C, while Adam got an A. James cannot understand how they could have studied the same notes yet gotten such different grades. The most likely, most accurate explanation is that

A. James and Adam encoded the information differently.
B. Adam simply has a better memory than James.
C. James is taking too many hard courses and could not retrieve the information as well as Adam because of stress.
D. Adam probably gave James fake notes to torpedo his work.

# 2 Memory Encoding

The first step in memory is **encoding,** the process by which information gets into memory storage. When you are listening to a lecture, watching a play, reading a book, or talking with a friend, you are encoding information into memory. Some information gets into memory virtually automatically, whereas encoding other information takes effort. Let's examine some of the encoding processes that require effort. These include attention, deep processing, elaboration, and the use of mental imagery.

**encoding**
The first step in memory; the process by which information gets into memory storage.

## Attention

To begin the process of memory encoding, we have to pay attention to information (Chun, Turk-Browne, & Golomb, 2011; Flom & Bahrick, 2010). Recall from Chapter 3 that *selective attention* involves focusing on a specific aspect of experience while ignoring others. Attention is selective because the brain's resources are limited—they cannot attend to everything. These limitations mean that we have to attend selectively to some things in our environment and ignore others (Matzel & Kolata, 2010). So, on that special night with your romantic partner, you never noticed the bus that roared by or the people whom you passed as you strolled along the street. Those details did not make it into your enduring memory.

In addition to selective attention, psychologists have described two other ways that attention may be allocated: divided attention and sustained attention (Robinson-Riegler & Robinson-Riegler, 2012). **Divided attention** involves concentrating on more than one activity at the same time. If you are listening to music or the television while you are reading this chapter, you are dividing your attention. **Sustained attention** (also called *vigilance*) is the ability to maintain attention to a selected stimulus for a prolonged period of time. For example, paying close attention to your notes while studying for an exam is a good application of sustained attention.

Divided attention can be especially detrimental to encoding. *Multitasking,* which in some cases involves dividing attention not just between two activities but among three or more (Lin, 2009), may be the ultimate in divided attention. It is not unusual for

**divided attention**
Concentrating on more than one activity at the same time.

**sustained attention**
The ability to maintain attention to a selected stimulus for a prolonged period of time.

*How many times a day do you find yourself multitasking like this individual?*

high school and college students simultaneously to divide their attention among homework, instant messaging, web surfing, and looking at an iTunes playlist. Multitaskers are often very confident in their multitasking skills (Pattillo, 2010). However, a recent study revealed that heavy media multitaskers performed worse on a test of task-switching ability, apparently because of their decreased ability to filter out interference from the irrelevant task (Ophir, Nass, & Wagner, 2009). Such research indicates that trying to listen to a lecture in class while texting or playing a game on your cell phone is likely to impede your ability to pay adequate attention to the lecture (Glenn, 2010).

## Levels of Processing

**levels of processing**
A continuum of memory processing from shallow to intermediate to deep, with deeper processing producing better memory.

Another factor that influences memory is whether we engage with information superficially or really get into it. Fergus Craik and Robert Lockhart (1972) first suggested that encoding can be influenced by levels of processing. The term **levels of processing** refers to a continuum from shallow to intermediate to deep, with deeper processing producing better memory.

Imagine that you are asked to memorize a list of words, including the word *mom*. Shallow processing includes noting the physical features of a stimulus, such as the shapes of the letters in the word *mom*. Intermediate processing involves giving the stimulus a label, as in reading the word *mom*. The deepest level of processing entails thinking about the meaning of a stimulus—for instance, thinking about the meaning of the word *mom* and about your own mother, her face, and her special qualities.

The more deeply we process, the better the memory (Howes, 2006; Rose & Craik, 2012). For example, researchers have found that if we encode something meaningful about a face and make associations with it, we are more likely to remember the face (Harris & Kay, 1995). The restaurant server who strives to remember the face of the customer and to imagine her eating the food she has ordered is using deep processing (Figure 6.2).

## Elaboration

**elaboration**
The formation of a number of different connections around a stimulus at any given level of memory encoding.

Effective encoding of a memory depends on more than just depth of processing. Within deep processing, the more extensive the processing, the better the memory (Terry, 2009). **Elaboration** refers to the formation of a number of different connections around a stimulus at any given level of memory encoding. Elaboration is like creating a huge spider web of links between some new information and everything one already knows,

**FIGURE 6.2 Depth of Processing** According to the levels of processing principle, deeper processing of stimuli produces better memory of them.

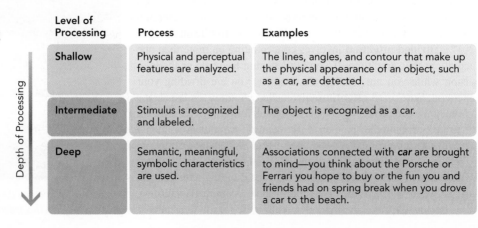

| Level of Processing | Process | Examples |
|---|---|---|
| **Shallow** | Physical and perceptual features are analyzed. | The lines, angles, and contour that make up the physical appearance of an object, such as a car, are detected. |
| **Intermediate** | Stimulus is recognized and labeled. | The object is recognized as a car. |
| **Deep** | Semantic, meaningful, symbolic characteristics are used. | Associations connected with *car* are brought to mind—you think about the Porsche or Ferrari you hope to buy or the fun you and friends had on spring break when you drove a car to the beach. |

Depth of Processing

and it can occur at any level of processing. In the case of the word *mom,* a person can elaborate on mom even at a shallow level—for example, by thinking of the shapes of the letters and how they relate to the shapes of other letters, say, how an *m* looks like two *n*'s. At a deep level of processing, a person might focus on what a mother is or might think about various mothers he or she knows, images of mothers in art, and portrayals of mothers on television and in film. Generally speaking, the more elaborate the processing, the better memory will be. Deep, elaborate processing is a powerful way to remember.

For example, rather than trying to memorize the definition of memory, you would do better to weave a complex spider web around the concept of memory by coming up with a real-world example of how information enters your mind, how it is stored, and how you can retrieve it. Thinking of concrete examples of a concept is a good way to understand it. *Self-reference*—relating material to your own experience—is another effective way to elaborate on information, drawing mental links between aspects of your own life and new information (Hunt & Ellis, 2004) (Figure 6.3).

The process of elaboration is evident in the physical activity of the brain. Neuroscience research has shown a link between elaboration during encoding and brain activity (Han & others, 2012; Holland, Addis, & Kensinger, 2011). In one study, researchers placed individuals in magnetic resonance imaging (MRI) machines (see Chapter 2) and flashed one word every 2 seconds on a screen inside (Wagner & others, 1998). Initially, the individuals simply noted whether the words were in uppercase or lowercase letters. As the study progressed, they were asked to determine whether each word meant something concrete, such as chair or book, or abstract, such as love or democracy. The participants showed more neural activity in the left frontal lobe of the brain during the concrete/abstract task than they did when they were asked merely to state whether the words were in uppercase or lowercase letters. Further, they demonstrated better memory in the concrete/abstract task. The researchers concluded that greater elaboration of information is linked with neural activity, especially in the brain's left frontal lobe, and with improved memory.

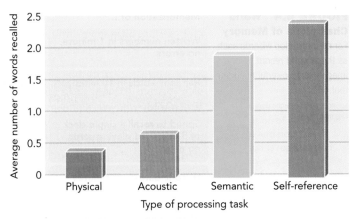

**FIGURE 6.3  Memory Improves When Self-Reference Is Used** In one study, researchers asked participants to remember lists of words according to the words' physical, acoustic (sound), semantic (meaning), or self-referent characteristics. As the figure illustrates, when individuals generated self-references for the words, they remembered them better.

## Imagery

One of the most powerful ways to make memories distinctive is to use mental imagery (Keogh & Pearson, 2011; Scholl, 2013). Mental imagery entails visualizing material that we want to remember in ways that create a lasting portrait. Imagery functions as a powerful encoding tool for all of us, certainly including the world champions of memory listed in Figure 6.4. Consider, for instance, Akira Haraguchi, who in 2005 recited the digits of pi to the first 83,431 decimal places (BBC News, 2005). Think about memorizing a list of over 80,000 numbers. How would you go about it? One way would be to use mental imagery to create a kind of visual mental walk through the digits. To memorize the first 8 digits of pi (3.1415926), one might say, "3 is a chubby fellow who walks with a cane (1), up to a take-out window (4), and orders 15 hamburgers. The cook (9), who has very large biceps (2), slips on his way to deliver the burgers (6)."

The Guinness Book of World Records has not recognized this feat just yet. The current record holder is Chao Lu, who recited pi to 67,890 digits. No small potatoes. Lu used mental imagery to complete the task.

7,500 people in the United States are arrested for and wrongly convicted of serious crimes (Huff, 2002).

Faulty memory is not just about accusing the wrong person. For example, faulty memories were evident in descriptions of the suspects' vehicle in the sniper attacks that killed 10 people in the Washington, DC, area in 2002. Witnesses reported seeing a white truck or van fleeing several of the crime scenes. It appears that a white van may have been near one of the first shootings and that media repetition of this information contaminated the memories of witnesses to later attacks, making them more likely to remember a white truck or van. When caught, the sniper suspects were driving a blue car.

Before police even arrive at a crime scene, witnesses talk among themselves, and this dialogue can contaminate memories. This is why, during the DC sniper attacks in 2002, law enforcement officials advised any persons who might witness the next attack to immediately write down what they had seen—even on their hands if they did not have a piece of paper.

*More recently, researchers have suggested that eyewitness accounts can be more accurate if the witness closes his or her eyes. Why might that help?*

self quiz

1. The tendency to remember the items at the beginning and end of a list more easily than the items in the middle is the
   A. bookends effect.
   B. serial cues effect.
   C. serial position effect.
   D. endpoints effect.

2. Carrie prides herself on "never forgetting a face," although she frequently cannot put the correct name with a specific face. Carrie is really saying that she
   A. is better at recognition than at recall.
   B. is better at recall than at recognition.
   C. is better at memory retrieval than at memory reconstruction.
   D. is better at memory reconstruction than at memory recall.

3. Faulty memory can occur due to
   A. bias.
   B. receipt of new information.
   C. distortion.
   D. all of the above

APPLY IT! 4. Andrew is getting ready for a group interview for a job he really wants. The group session will take place at the beginning of the day, followed by individual interviews. When the manager who is conducting the interviews calls Andrew, he tells him that because he has not talked to any of the other candidates yet, Andrew can decide when he would like his individual interview to be. There are five candidates. Which position should Andrew take?
   A. Andrew should go third because that way he will be right in the middle, and the interviewer will not be too nervous or too tired.
   B. Andrew should go either first or last, to be the candidate most likely to be remembered.
   C. Andrew should probably go second so that he will not be sitting around feeling nervous for too long—and besides, asking to go first might seem pushy.
   D. It will not matter, so Andrew should just pick a spot randomly.

# 5 Forgetting

Human memory has its imperfections, as we have all experienced. It is not unusual for two people to argue about whether something did or did not happen, each supremely confident that his or her memory is accurate and the other person's is faulty. We all have had the frustrating experience of trying to remember the name of some person or some place but not quite being able to retrieve it. Missed appointments, misplaced keys, the failure to recall the name of a familiar face, and inability to recall your password for Internet access are everyday examples of forgetting. Why do we forget?

One of psychology's pioneers, Hermann Ebbinghaus (1850–1909), was the first person to conduct scientific research on forgetting. In 1885, he made up and memorized a list of 13 nonsense syllables and then assessed how many of them he could remember as time passed. (Nonsense syllables are meaningless combinations of letters that are unlikely to have been learned already, such as *zeq, xid, lek,* and *riy.*) Even just an hour later, Ebbinghaus could recall only a few of the nonsense syllables he had memorized. Figure 6.16 shows Ebbinghaus's learning curve for nonsense syllables. Based on his research, Ebbinghaus concluded that most forgetting takes place soon after we learn something.

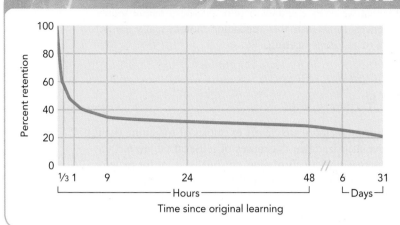

**FIGURE 6.16** **Ebbinghaus's Forgetting Curve**
This figure illustrates Ebbinghaus's conclusion about forgetting.
> *When is information most likely to be forgotten?* > *What might explain differences in the slope of this curve for different individuals and different material?* > *Based on this graph, when is the best time to study new material to prevent it from being forgotten?*

If we forget so quickly, why put effort into learning something? Fortunately, researchers have demonstrated that forgetting is not as extensive as Ebbinghaus envisioned (Hsieh & others, 2009). Ebbinghaus studied meaningless nonsense syllables. When we memorize more meaningful material—such as poetry, history, or the content of this text—forgetting is neither so rapid nor so extensive. Following are some of the factors that influence how well we can retrieve information from long-term memory.

## Encoding Failure

Sometimes when people say they have forgotten something, they have not really forgotten it; rather, they never encoded the information in the first place. Encoding failure occurs when the information was never entered into long-term memory.

As an example of encoding failure, think about what the U.S. penny looks like. In one study, researchers showed 15 versions of the penny to participants and asked them which one was correct (Nickerson & Adams, 1979). Look at the pennies in Figure 6.17 (but do not read the caption yet) and see whether you can tell which is the real penny. Most people do not do well on this task. Unless you are a coin collector, you probably have not encoded a lot of specific details about pennies. You may have encoded just enough information to distinguish them from other coins

**Hermann Ebbinghaus (1850–1909)**
*Ebbinghaus was the first psychologist to conduct scientific research on forgetting.*

(a)    (b)    (c)    (d)

(e)    (f)    (g)

**FIGURE 6.17** **Which Is a Real U.S. Penny?**
In the original experiment, participants viewed 15 versions of pennies; only one version was an actual U.S. penny. This figure shows only 7 of the 15 versions, and as you likely can tell, the task is still very difficult. Why? By the way, the actual U.S. penny is (c).

(pennies are copper-colored; dimes and nickels are silver-colored; pennies fall between the sizes of dimes and quarters).

The penny exercise illustrates that we encode and enter into long-term memory only a small portion of our life experiences. In a sense, then, encoding failures really are not cases of forgetting; they are cases of not remembering.

# Retrieval Failure

Problems in retrieving information from memory are clearly examples of forgetting (Law & others, 2011). Psychologists have theorized that the causes of retrieval failure include problems with the information in storage, the effects of time, personal reasons for remembering or forgetting, and the condition of the brain (Barrouillet, De Paepe, & Langerock, 2012; Oztekin & Badre, 2011).

**interference theory**
The theory that people forget not because memories are lost from storage but because other information gets in the way of what they want to remember.

**INTERFERENCE** *Interference* is one reason that people forget (Malmberg & others, 2012). According to **interference theory,** people forget not because memories are lost from storage but because other information gets in the way of what they want to remember.

There are two kinds of interference: proactive and retroactive. **Proactive interference** occurs when material that was learned earlier disrupts the recall of material learned later (Yi & Friedman, 2011). Remember that *pro-* means "forward in time." For example, suppose you had a good friend 10 years ago named Prudence and that last night you met someone named Patience. You might find yourself calling your new friend Prudence because the old information (Prudence) interferes with retrieval of new information (Patience). **Retroactive interference** occurs when material learned later disrupts the retrieval of information learned earlier (Solesio-Jofre & others, 2011). Remember that *retro-* means "backward in time." Suppose you have lately become friends with Ralph. In sending a note to your old friend Raul, you might mistakenly address it to Ralph because the new information (Ralph) interferes with the old information (Raul). Figure 6.18 depicts another example of proactive and retroactive interference.

**proactive interference**
Situation in which material that was learned earlier disrupts the recall of material that was learned later.

**retroactive interference**
Situation in which material that was learned later disrupts the retrieval of information that was learned earlier.

Proactive and retroactive interference might both be explained as problems with retrieval cues. The reason the name Prudence interferes with the name Patience and the name Ralph interferes with the name Raul might be that the cue you are using to remember the one name does not distinguish between the two memories. For example, if the cue you are using is "my good friend," it might evoke both names. The result might be

**FIGURE 6.18**
**Proactive and Retro-active Interference**
*Pro-* means "forward"; in proactive interference, old information has a forward influence by getting in the way of new material learned. *Retro-* means "backward"; in retroactive interference, new information has a backward influence by getting in the way of material learned earlier.

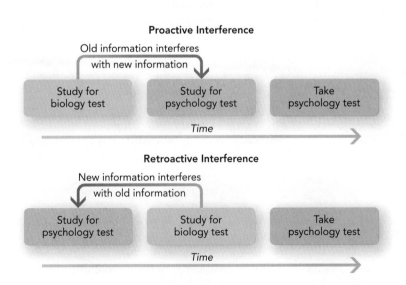

retrieval of the wrong name or a kind of blocking in which each name interferes with the other and neither comes to mind. Retrieval cues (such as "friend" in our example) can become overloaded, and when that happens we are likely to forget or to retrieve incorrectly.

**DECAY**    Another possible reason for forgetting is the passage of time (Barrouillet, De Paepe, & Langerock, 2012). According to **decay theory,** when we learn something new, a neurochemical memory trace forms, but over time this trace disintegrates. Decay theory suggests that the passage of time always increases forgetting.

Memories often do fade with the passage of time, but decay alone cannot explain forgetting. For example, under the right retrieval conditions, we can recover memories that we seem to have forgotten. You might have forgotten the face or name of someone in your high school class, for instance, but when you return to the setting where you knew the person, you might remember. Similarly, you may not have thought about someone from your past for a very long time, but when the person friends you on Facebook, you may remember a lot of prior experiences with him or her.

*"Of course I forgot what I learned last year. I have to make room in my brain for the new stuff."*

Used by permission of CartoonStock, www.CartoonStock.com.

*Many things we think we have forgotten are just waiting for the right cues to pop into our lives.*

**TIP-OF-THE-TONGUE PHENOMENON**    We are all familiar with the retrieval glitch called **tip-of-the-tongue (TOT) phenomenon**—a type of "effortful retrieval" that occurs when we are confident that we know something but cannot quite pull it out of memory (Schwartz, 2011). In a TOT state we usually can successfully retrieve characteristics of the word, such as the first letter and the number of syllables, but not the word itself. The TOT phenomenon arises when we can retrieve some of the desired information but not all of it (Hanley, 2011; Schwartz & Metcalfe, 2011).

The TOT phenomenon demonstrates that we do not store all of the information about a particular topic or experience in one way. If you have ever struggled to think of a specific word, you probably came up with various words that mean the same thing as the word you were looking for, but you still had a nagging feeling that none was quite right. Sometimes you might find the solution in an unexpected way. For example, imagine that you are doing a crossword puzzle with the clue "Colorful scarf" for a seven-letter word. You have a feeling you know this word. If you have not thought of the answer yet, say the following word aloud: *bandage.* If you were experiencing the TOT phenomenon when doing the crossword, thinking of *bandage* might have helped you come up with the correct answer, *bandana.* Although the meaning of *bandage* is unrelated to that of *bandana,* the fact that these words start with the same sounds (and therefore are linked in verbal memory) can lead you to the word *bandana* (Abrams & Rodriguez, 2005).

**PROSPECTIVE MEMORY: REMEMBERING (OR FORGETTING) WHEN TO DO SOMETHING**    The main focus of this chapter has been on **retrospective memory,** which is remembering the past. **Prospective memory** involves remembering information about doing something in the future; it includes memory for intentions (Costa, Carlesimo, & Caltagirone, 2012; Delprado & others, 2012). Prospective memory includes both timing (when we have to do something) and content (what we have to do).

We can make a distinction between time-based and event-based prospective memory. *Time-based prospective memory* is our intention to engage in a given behavior after a specified amount of time has gone by, such as an intention to make a phone call to someone in one hour. In *event-based prospective memory,* we engage in the intended

**decay theory**
Theory stating that when an individual learns something new, a neurochemical memory trace forms, but over time this trace disintegrates; suggests that the passage of time always increases forgetting.

**tip-of-the-tongue (TOT) phenomenon**
A type of effortful retrieval associated with a person's feeling that he or she knows something (say, a word or a name) but cannot quite pull it out of memory.

**retrospective memory**
Remembering information from the past.

**prospective memory**
Remembering information about doing something in the future; includes memory for intentions.

others experiencing less supportive contexts), genetic characteristics may be less predictive of differences in intelligence in that group, relative to environmental factors.

Even if the heritability of a characteristic is very high, the environment still matters. Take height, for example. More than 90 percent of the variation in height is explained by genetic variation. Humans continue to get taller and taller, however, and this trend demonstrates that environmental factors such as nutrition have an impact. Similarly, in the case of intelligence, researchers widely agree that for most people, modifications in environment can change their IQ scores considerably (Esposito, Grigorenko, & Sternberg, 2012; Nisbett & others, 2012). Enriching an environment can improve children's achievement in school and support their development of crucial workplace skills. Children from impoverished socioeconomic backgrounds who are adopted into more economically advantaged families often have IQs that are higher than those of their biological parents (Sternberg, Grigorenko, & Kidd, 2005). A recent research review by leading experts on intelligence concluded that the importance of environmental influences has been established by the 12- to 18-point increase in IQ that is observed when children from low-income backgrounds are adopted by parents from middle-income backgrounds (Nisbett & others, 2012). Although heredity influences intellectual ability, environmental factors and opportunities also make a difference.

Researchers are increasingly interested in manipulating the early environment of children who are at risk for impoverished intelligence (Phillips & Lowenstein, 2011). Programs that educate parents to be more sensitive caregivers and that train them to be better teachers can make a difference in a child's intellectual development, as can support services such as high-quality child-care programs (Morrison, 2012).

One effect of education on intelligence is evident in rapidly increasing IQ test scores around the world, a phenomenon called the *Flynn effect* (Flynn, 1999, 2006, 2011). Scores on these tests have been rising so fast that a high percentage of people regarded as having average intelligence at the turn of the twentieth century would be regarded as having below average intelligence today (Figure 7.11). Because the increase has taken place in a relatively short period of time, it cannot be due to heredity but rather may be due to rising levels of education attained by a much greater percentage of the world's population or to other environmental factors, such as the explosion of information to which people are now exposed.

## PSYCHOLOGICAL INQUIRY

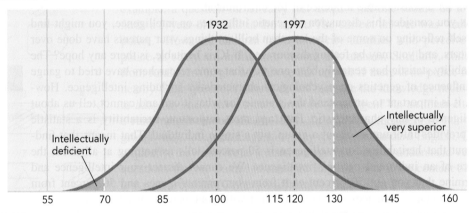

**FIGURE 7.11  The Increase in IQ Scores from 1932 to 1997** As measured by the Stanford-Binet intelligence test, American children seem to be getting smarter. Scores of a group tested in 1932 fell along a bell-shaped curve, with half below 100 and half above. Note that if children's scores from 1997 were plotted on this same scale, the average would be 120. ➤ *How would average children from 1932 compare to children from the more recent sample? Would they still be "average"?* ➤ *Note the far ends (or tails) of the 1932 curve. How would these children be considered by the standards of the more recent scores?* ➤ *What do you think is responsible for the Flynn effect?*

Environmental influences are complex (Grusec, 2011; Wright & others, 2012). Growing up with all the advantages does not guarantee success. Children from wealthy families may have easy access to excellent schools, books, tutors, and travel, but they may take such opportunities for granted and not be motivated to learn and to achieve. Alternatively, poor or disadvantaged children may be highly motivated and successful. Caregivers who themselves lacked educational opportunities may instill a strong sense of the value of learning and achievement in their children. Oprah Winfrey, the offspring of an unwed teenage couple, was reared in the inner city by her grandmother, who instilled in her a love of reading and a strong belief that she had the ability to do great things.

Let's return to the idea that the word *intelligent* describes not only people but also behaviors. Mastering skills, thinking about life actively, and making life decisions thoughtfully are intelligent behaviors that people can engage in regardless of the numerical intelligence quotient on their permanent record. Intelligent behavior is always an option, no matter one's IQ score. As we saw in Chapter 5, our beliefs about cognitive ability, specifically whether it is fixed or changeable, have important implications for the goals we set for learning new skills (Dweck, 2006, 2012). We never know what we might accomplish if we try, and no one is doomed because of a number, no matter how powerful that number may seem.

Cognitive abilities are clearly important to academic accomplishments, but they are also involved in the mastery of social and interpersonal skills. Cognitive abilities, such as abstract reasoning, are fundamental to skills such as taking another person's perspective and understanding the behaviors and intentions of others (Murphy & Hall, 2011). Recent research has found a provocative connection between intelligence and the social problem of prejudice. To read about this controversial research, see Challenge Your Thinking.

## Do It!

Many different intelligence tests are available online, such as at www.iqtest.com/. Give this one a try and then do a web search for intelligence tests and see if you get the same results when you take a different test. Do the websites tell you how reliable the tests are? Do they provide information on standardization or validity? If your scores on the two tests are very different, what might account for this variation?

## Extremes of Intelligence

Intelligence, then, appears to emerge from a combination of genetic heritage and environmental factors. As we have seen, scores on IQ tests generally conform to the bell-shaped normal curve. We now examine the implications of falling on either tail of that curve.

**gifted**
Possessing high intelligence (an IQ of 130 or higher) and/or superior talent in a particular area.

**GIFTEDNESS** There are people whose abilities and accomplishments outshine those of others—the *A*+ student, the star athlete, the natural musician. People who are **gifted** have high intelligence (an IQ of 130 or higher) and/or superior talent in a particular area. Lewis Terman (1925) conducted a study of 1,500 children whose Stanford-Binet IQs averaged 150, a score that placed them in the top 1 percent. A popular myth is that gifted children are maladjusted, but Terman found that his participants (the "Termites") were not only academically gifted but also socially well adjusted. Many of them later became successful doctors, lawyers, professors, and scientists. Do gifted children grow into gifted and highly creative adults? In Terman's research, gifted children typically did become experts in a well-established domain, such as medicine, law, or business; but the Termites did not become major creators or innovators (Winner, 2000, 2006).

In light of the sweeping social and economic changes of the digital age, are today's gifted children perhaps better

*Olympic speed-skating gold medalist Joey Cheek well illustrates giftedness. Beyond his accomplishments on the ice, he is studying economics and Chinese at Princeton University and is cofounder of Team Darfur, an organization dedicated to raising awareness of human rights abuses in Sudan.*

# Challenge

## Is Intelligence Related to Prejudice and Political Beliefs?

An important aspect of our interpersonal world is our attitudes toward individuals who are different from us. *Prejudice,* which we will examine in Chapter 11, means having a negative attitude about someone based on the person's membership in a particular group. A specific type of prejudice is *racism,* a negative attitude toward members of a particular racial group. Most research on racism has focused on the motivational or emotional side of this problematic attitude (Jost & others, 2003). From this perspective, prejudice can be understood as emerging from competition for resources between different groups or as arising from the need to feel good about one's own group memberships.

Researchers have explored the link between cognitive ability and prejudicial attitudes. This work has generally shown that intelligence is negatively correlated with prejudice (Piber-Dabrowska, Sedek, & Kofta, 2010). In other words, the more intelligent people are, the less likely they are to be prejudiced, and vice versa.

For example, in a recent study, Gordon Hodson and Michael Busseri (2012) examined two large representative samples in the United Kingdom that included nearly 16,000 people. Intelligence was measured when the participants were 10 or 11 years old, and racial attitudes were assessed when they were in their early 30s. Prejudicial attitudes were assessed with items like "I wouldn't mind working with people from other races" (for such an item, a high rating would indicate low racism). Results for both samples showed that lower intelligence in childhood predicted greater racism in adulthood. The negative relationship between intelligence and prejudice remained even when differences in education levels and socioeconomic status were taken into account. These results suggest the not terribly controversial conclusion that holding prejudicial attitudes is not especially intelligent.

The researchers then boldly took these questions one step further. Beyond measuring intelligence and racism, Hodson and Busseri measured intelligence and social conservatism. They assessed social conservatism by asking individuals about their positions on such matters as valuing traditional roles for men and women and supporting harsh sentences for criminals. The results

able than the Termites to use their gifts in innovative and important ways in adulthood? The results from a longitudinal study of profoundly gifted children begun by Julian Stanley at Johns Hopkins University in 1971 seem to indicate just that. The Study of Mathematically Precocious Youth includes 320 participants whom researchers recruited before age 13 based on IQ scores, with the group's average IQ estimated at 180. This group is said to represent the top 1 in 10,000 IQ scores (Lubinski & others, 2001). Following up on these individuals in their 20s, David Lubinski and his colleagues (2006) found that these strikingly gifted young people were doing remarkable things. At age 23, they were pursuing doctoral degrees at a rate 50 times higher than the average. Some reported achievements such as receiving creative writing awards, creating original art and music, publishing in scholarly journals, and developing commercially viable software and video games. Thus, unlike the Termites, this group has been extraordinarily creative and innovative (Wai, Lubinski, & Benbow, 2005).

Like intelligence itself, giftedness is likely a product of both heredity and environment. Experts who study giftedness point out that gifted individuals recall showing signs of high ability in a particular area at a very young age, prior to or at the beginning of formal training (Howe & others, 1995). This result suggests the importance of innate ability in giftedness. However, researchers also have found that the individuals who enjoy world-class status in the arts, mathematics, science, and sports all report strong family support and years of training and practice (Bloom, 1985). Deliberate practice is an important characteristic of individuals who become experts in a particular domain (Grigorenko & others, 2009).

An increasing number of experts argue that typical U.S. classrooms often do not meet the educational needs of gifted children (Reis & Renzulli, 2011; Sternberg, 2012d). Some

indicated that individuals who were lower in cognitive ability were more likely to endorse traditional views on these matters. The researchers argued that this endorsement explained the respondents' tendency to report more prejudicial attitudes.

When these results spread across the Internet, blog headlines clearly revealed the biases of bloggers in responding to the controversial findings. "Conservatives scientifically proven as stupid and racist" declared a liberal blog. "Low IQ and liberal beliefs linked to poor research?" posed a conservative blog. As observed by social psychologist Brian Nosek, who was not involved in the study, Hodson and Busseri "pulled off the trifecta of controversial topics. When one selects intelligence, political ideology, and racism and looks at any of the relationships between those three variables, it's bound to upset somebody" (quoted in Pappas, 2012).

Before trying to sort out what these controversial findings can—and cannot—tell us about potential associations between cognitive ability, prejudice, and political orientation, let's consider the research methods used in the study. First, the researchers' measure of political orientation was very limited: Social conservatism was defined in *narrow terms,* using items that omitted many aspects of this factor. Further, economic conservatism or political conservatism was not addressed more generally. Second, the measure of racism relied on *self-reports.* Consider that possibly brighter individuals know better than to admit to any undesirable negative attitudes. Third, this research was *correlational,* meaning that

causation cannot be assumed between the factors studied (for example, we cannot conclude that being less intelligent caused individuals to be more socially conservative). Fourth, group-level results *cannot be generalized* to specific individuals. As Hodson and Busseri themselves noted, there are certainly very intelligent conservatives in the world, and not-so-bright liberals as well. Further, all social conservatives are not prejudiced, and all prejudiced individuals are not social conservatives.

Holding either extreme right-wing or extreme left-wing views may be a way for those with lower cognitive ability to find easy answers in a difficult world. Thinking critically and mindfully about the social world may be a more difficult but worthwhile alternative. Thinking critically and mindfully about provocative research is similarly worthwhile.

### What Do You Think?

■ According to the Flynn effect (see p. 260), intelligence has been rising around the world. This increase in intelligence should mean, based on the research about which you just read, that prejudice is likely decreasing. Do you think that is the case? Explain.

■ The researchers assessed the intelligence of children when they were 11 years old in an effort to predict prejudice in adulthood. What other childhood factors might likely be stronger predictors of prejudice in adulthood than intelligence?

educators conclude that the problem of inadequate education of gifted adolescents has been compounded by the federal government's No Child Left Behind policy, which seeks to raise the achievement level of students who are not doing well in school at the expense of enriching the education of gifted children (Clark, 2008; Cloud, 2008). Ellen Winner (1996, 2006) recommends that when children and adolescents are underchallenged, they be allowed to attend advanced classes in their domain of exceptional ability, as did Bill Gates, Microsoft's founder, who took college math classes at 13, and famed cellist Yo-Yo Ma, who graduated from high school at 15 and then attended the Juilliard School of Music.

*A serious public policy question in the United States is, should resources be dedicated to enhancing the experience of gifted students—or to bringing everyone up to a standard? What's your opinion? How much money would you be willing to pay in taxes to accomplish both goals?*

### INTELLECTUAL DISABILITY

**intellectual disability**
A condition of limited mental ability in which an individual has a low IQ, usually below 70 on a traditional intelligence test, and has difficulty adapting to everyday life.

Just as some individuals are at the high extreme of intelligence, others are at the lower end. **Intellectual disability** (formerly termed *mental retardation*) is a condition of limited mental ability in which an individual has a low IQ, usually below 70 on a traditional intelligence test, and has difficulty adapting to everyday life; he or she would have exhibited these characteristics by age 18. In the United States, about 5 million people fit this definition of intellectual disability. Note that for a person to be described as intellectually disabled, low IQ and low adaptiveness are evident in childhood. We do not usually think of a college student who suffers massive brain damage in a car accident, resulting in an IQ of 60, as intellectually disabled.

Intellectual disability may have an organic cause, or it may be cultural and social in origin (Hallahan, Kauffman, & Pullen, 2012). *Organic intellectual disability* is caused by a genetic disorder or brain damage; *organic* refers to the tissues or organs of the body,

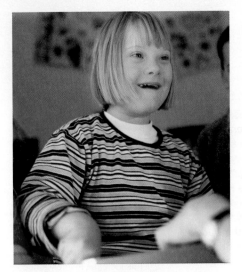

*Individuals with Down syndrome may excel in sensitivity toward others. The possibility that other strengths or intelligences coexist with cognitive ability (or disability) has led some psychologists to propose the need for expanding the concept of intelligence.*

so there is some physical damage in organic retardation. Down syndrome, one form of organic intellectual disability, occurs when an extra chromosome is present in the individual's genetic makeup. Most people who suffer from organic retardation have an IQ between 0 and 50.

*Cultural-familial intellectual disability* is a mental deficit with no evidence of organic brain damage. Individuals with this type of disability have an IQ between 55 and 70. Psychologists suspect that such mental deficits result at least in part from growing up in a below-average intellectual environment. As children, individuals with this disability can be identified in school, where they often fail, need tangible rewards (candy rather than grades, for example), and are highly sensitive to what peers and adults expect of them (Vaughn, Bos, & Schumm, 2003). As adults, however, these individuals usually go unnoticed, perhaps because adult settings do not tax their cognitive skills as much. It may also be that the intelligence of such individuals increases as they move toward adulthood.

There are several classifications of intellectual disability (Hodapp & others, 2011). In one classification system, disability ranges from mild, to moderate, to severe or profound, according to the person's IQ (Heward, 2013). The large majority of individuals diagnosed with intellectual disability fall in the mild category. Most school systems still use this system. However, these categories, based on IQ ranges, are not perfect predictors of functioning. Indeed, it is not unusual to find clear *functional* differences between two people who have the same low IQ. For example, looking at two individuals with a similarly low IQ, we might find that one of them is married, employed, and involved in the community while the other requires constant supervision in an institution. Such differences in social competence have led psychologists to include deficits in adaptive behavior in their definition of intellectual disability (Turnbull & others, 2013).

The American Association on Intellectual and Developmental Disabilities (2010) has developed an assessment that examines a person's level of adaptive behavior in three life domains:

- *Conceptual skills:* For example, literacy and understanding of numbers, money, and time.
- *Social skills:* For example, interpersonal skills, responsibility, self-esteem, and ability to follow rules and obey.
- *Practical skills:* For example, activities of daily living such as personal care, occupational skills, health care, travel/transportation, and use of the telephone.

Assessment of capacities in these areas can be used to determine the amount of care the person requires for daily living, not as a function of IQ but of the person's ability to negotiate life's challenges.

Individuals with Down syndrome may never accomplish the academic feats of those who are gifted. However, they may be capable of building close, warm relations with others; inspiring loved ones; and bringing smiles into an otherwise gloomy day (Van Riper, 2007). Individuals with Down syndrome moreover might possess different kinds of intelligence, even if they are low on general cognitive ability. The possibility that other intelligences exist alongside cognitive ability (or disability) has inspired some psychologists to suggest that we need more than one concept of intelligence.

## Theories of Multiple Intelligences

Is it more appropriate to think of an individual's intelligence as a general ability or, rather, as a number of specific abilities? Traditionally, most psychologists have viewed intelligence as a general, all-purpose problem-solving ability that, as we have seen, is sometimes referred to as *g*, Others have proposed that we think about different kinds of intelligence, such as *emotional intelligence,* the ability to perceive emotions in ourselves and others accurately (Brackett, Rivers, & Salovey, 2011; Mayer & others, 2011). Robert Sternberg and Howard Gardner have developed influential theories presenting the viewpoint that there are *multiple intelligences.*

### STERNBERG'S TRIARCHIC THEORY AND GARDNER'S MULTIPLE INTELLIGENCES
Robert J. Sternberg (1986, 2004, 2008, 2011, 2012a, 2012b) developed the **triarchic theory of intelligence,** which says that intelligence comes in multiple (specifically, three) forms:

**triarchic theory of intelligence** Sternberg's theory that intelligence comes in three forms: analytical, creative, and practical.

*Analytical intelligence:* The ability to analyze, judge, evaluate, compare, and contrast.

*Creative intelligence:* The ability to create, design, invent, originate, and imagine.

*Practical intelligence:* The ability to use, apply, implement, and put ideas into practice.

Howard Gardner (1983, 1993, 2002) suggests there are nine types of intelligence, or "frames of mind." These are described here, with examples of the types of vocations in which they are reflected as strengths (Campbell, Campbell, & Dickinson, 2004):

*Verbal:* The ability to think in words and use language to express meaning. Occupations: author, journalist, speaker.

*Mathematical:* The ability to carry out mathematical operations. Occupations: scientist, engineer, accountant.

*Spatial:* The ability to think three-dimensionally. Occupations: architect, artist, sailor.

*Bodily-kinesthetic:* The ability to manipulate objects and to be physically adept. Occupations: surgeon, craftsperson, dancer, athlete.

*Musical:* The ability to be sensitive to pitch, melody, rhythm, and tone. Occupations: composer, musician.

*Interpersonal:* The ability to understand and interact effectively with others. Occupations: teacher, mental health professional.

*Intrapersonal:* The ability to understand oneself. Occupations: theologian, psychologist.

*Naturalist:* The ability to observe patterns in nature and understand natural and human-made systems. Occupations: farmer, botanist, ecologist, landscaper.

*Existentialist:* The ability to grapple with the big questions of human existence, such as the meaning of life and death, with special sensitivity to issues of spirituality. Gardner has not identified an occupation for existential intelligence, but one career path would likely be philosopher.

*Do you know people some might call "book smart" and others who are "people smart"? What kinds of intelligence do they show?*

According to Gardner, everyone has all of these intelligences to varying degrees. As a result, we prefer to learn and process information in different ways. We learn best when we can do so in a way that uses our stronger intelligences.

### EVALUATING THE APPROACHES OF MULTIPLE INTELLIGENCES
Sternberg's and Gardner's approaches have stimulated teachers to think broadly about what makes up children's competencies. They have motivated educators to develop programs that instruct students in multiple domains. These theories have also contributed to interest in assessing intelligence and classroom learning in innovative ways, such as by evaluating student portfolios (Woolfolk, 2013).

Doubts about multiple intelligences persist, however. A number of psychologists think that the proponents of multiple intelligences have taken the concept of specific intelligences too far (Reeve & Charles, 2008). Some critics argue that a research base to support the three intelligences of Sternberg or the nine intelligences of Gardner has not yet emerged. One expert on intelligence, Nathan Brody (2007), observes that people who excel at one type of intellectual task are likely to excel in others. Thus, individuals who do well at memorizing lists of digits are also likely to be good at solving verbal problems and spatial layout problems. Other critics ask, if musical skill, for example, reflects a distinct type of intelligence, why not also label the skills of outstanding chess players, prizefighters, painters, and poets as types of intelligence? In sum, controversy still characterizes whether it is more accurate to conceptualize intelligence as a general ability, specific abilities, or both (Brody, 2007; Nisbett & others, 2012; Sternberg, 2012a, 2012b).

Our examination of cognitive abilities has highlighted how individuals differ in the quality of their thinking and how thoughts may differ from one another. Some thoughts reflect critical thinking, creativity, or intelligence. Other thoughts are perhaps less inspired. One thing thoughts have in common is that they often involve language. Even when we talk to ourselves, we do so with words. The central role of language in cognitive activity is the topic to which we now turn.

## self-quiz

1. The reproducibility of a test's result is known as
   A. criterion validity.
   B. validity.
   C. standardization.
   D. reliability.

2. A 10-year-old child has a mental age of 8. The child's IQ is
   A. 60.
   B. 80.
   C. 100.
   D. 125.

3. The heritability index for intelligence is approximately
   A. 35 percent.
   B. 50 percent.
   C. 75 percent.
   D. 90 percent.

**APPLY IT!** 4. Shortly after Joshua's birth, his parents found that he had a genetic condition that causes mental retardation. They worried about their son's future. Which of the following most accurately relates to Joshua's future?
A. Genes are not the sole cause of intelligence, and providing Joshua with a rich and stimulating environment will make the most of his genetic endowment. Furthermore, although Joshua may never excel in cognitive ability, there are likely other realms of life in which he can be successful.
B. Because intelligence is strongly heritable, providing a rich environment to Joshua is unlikely to have any impact on his eventual intelligence and ability.
C. Genes cause 75 percent of Joshua's intelligence, so environmental factors can influence only 25 percent of his cognitive abilities.
D. Genes have nothing to do with intelligence, so Joshua's parents have no need to worry.

# 4 Language

**Language** is a form of communication, whether spoken, written, or signed, that is based on a system of symbols. We need language to speak with others, listen to others, read, and write (Berko Gleason, 2009). Language is not just how we speak to others but how we talk to ourselves. Consider an occasion, for example, when you have experienced the feeling of a guilty conscience, of having done something you should not have. The little voice in your head that clamors, "You shouldn't have done that! Why did you do it?" speaks to you in your mother tongue. In this section we first examine the fundamental characteristics of language and then trace the links between language and cognition.

**language**
A form of communication—whether spoken, written, or signed—that is based on a system of symbols.

## The Basic Properties of Language

**infinite generativity**
The ability of language to produce an endless number of meaningful sentences.

All human languages have **infinite generativity,** the ability to produce an endless number of meaningful sentences. This superb flexibility comes from five basic rule systems:

■ **Phonology:** a language's sound system. Language is made up of basic sounds, or *phonemes.* Phonological rules ensure that certain sound sequences occur (for example, *sp, ba,* and *ar*) and others do not (for example, *zx* and *qp*) (Menn & Stoel-Gammon,

**phonology**
A language's sound system.

2009). A good example of a phoneme in the English language is /k/, the sound represented by the letter *k* in the word *ski* and by the letter *c* in the word *cat*. Although the /k/ sound is slightly different in these two words, the /k/ sound is described as a single phoneme in English.

- **Morphology:** a language's rules for word formation. Every word in the English language is made up of one or more morphemes. A *morpheme* is the smallest unit of language that carries meaning. Some words consist of a single morpheme—for example, *help*. Others are made up of more than one; for example, *helper* has two morphemes, *help* + *er*. The morpheme *-er* means "one who"—in this case, "one who helps." As you can see, not all morphemes are words; for example, *pre-*, *-tion*, and *-ing* are morphemes. Just as the rules that govern phonemes ensure that certain sound sequences occur, the rules that govern morphemes ensure that certain strings of sounds occur in particular sequences (Croft, 2012).

- **Syntax:** a language's rules for combining words to form acceptable phrases and sentences (Dixon, 2012). If someone says, "John kissed Emily" or "Emily was kissed by John," you know who did the kissing and who was kissed in each case because you share that person's understanding of sentence structure. You also understand that the sentence "You didn't stay, did you?" is a grammatical sentence but that "You didn't stay, didn't you?" is unacceptable.

- **Semantics:** the meaning of words and sentences in a particular language. Every word has a unique set of semantic features (Pan & Uccelli, 2009). *Girl* and *woman,* for example, share many semantic features (for instance, both signify female human beings), but they differ semantically in regard to age. Words have semantic restrictions on how they can be used in sentences. The sentence "The bicycle talked the boy into buying a candy bar" is syntactically correct but semantically incorrect. The sentence violates our semantic knowledge that bicycles do not talk.

- **Pragmatics:** the useful character of language and the ability of language to communicate even more meaning than is said (Al-Wer, 2012). The pragmatic aspect of language allows us to use words to get the things we want. If you ever find yourself in a country in which you know only a little of the language, you will certainly take advantage of pragmatics. Wandering the streets of, say, Madrid, you might approach a stranger and ask, simply, "Autobus?" (the Spanish word for *bus*). You know that given your inflection and perhaps your desperate facial expression, the person will understand that you are looking for the bus stop.

With this basic understanding of language in place, we can examine the connections between language and cognition.

## Language and Cognition

Language is a vast system of symbols capable of expressing most thoughts. Language is the vehicle for communicating most of our thoughts to one another. Although we do not always think in words, our thinking would be greatly impoverished without words.

The connection between language and thought has been of considerable interest to psychologists. Some have even argued that we cannot think without language. This proposition has produced heated controversy. Is thought dependent on language, or is language dependent on thought?

### THE ROLE OF LANGUAGE IN COGNITION
Recall from Chapter 6 that memory is stored not only in the form of sounds and images but also in words. Language helps us think, make inferences, tackle difficult decisions, and solve problems (Gleitman & Papafragou, 2012; Goldin-Meadow & Cook, 2012). Language is a tool for representing ideas (Kovacs, 2009).

**morphology**
A language's rules for word formation.

**syntax**
A language's rules for combining words to form acceptable phrases and sentences.

**semantics**
The meaning of words and sentences in a particular language.

**pragmatics**
The useful character of language and the ability of language to communicate even more meaning than is verbalized.

*Whorf's view is that our cultural experiences with a particular concept shape a catalog of names that can be either rich or poor. Consider how rich your mental library of names for a camel might be if you had extensive experience with camels in a desert world, and how poor your mental library of names for snow might be if you lived in a tropical world of palm trees and parrots. Despite its intriguing appeal, Whorf's view is controversial, and many psychologists do not believe it plays a pivotal role in shaping thought.*

Today, most psychologists would accept these points. However, linguist Benjamin Whorf (1956) went a step further: He argued that language determines the way we think, a view that has been called the *linguistic relativity hypothesis*. Whorf and his student Edward Sapir were specialists in Native American languages, and they were fascinated by the possibility that people might perceive the world differently as the result of the different languages they speak. The Inuit people in Alaska, for instance, have a dozen or more words to describe the various textures, colors, and physical states of snow. In contrast, English has relatively few words to describe snow, and thus, according to Whorf's view, English speakers cannot see the different kinds of snow because they have no words for them.

*Think of all the words we have for coffee drinks. What might this say about our society?*

Whorf's bold claim appealed to many scholars. Some even tried to apply Whorf's view to sex differences in color perception. Asked to describe the colors of two sweaters, a woman might say, "One is mauve and the other is magenta," while a man might say, "They're both pink." Whorf's view of the influence of language on perceptual ability might suggest that women are able to see more colors than men simply because they have a richer color vocabulary (Hepting & Solle, 1973). It turns out, however, that men can learn to discriminate among the various hues that women use, and this outcome suggests that Whorf's view is not quite accurate.

Indeed, critics of Whorf's ideas say that words merely reflect, rather than cause, the way we think. The Inuits' adaptability and livelihood in Alaska depend on their capacity to recognize various conditions of snow and ice. A skier or snowboarder who is not Inuit might also know numerous words for snow, far more than the average person, and a person who does not know the words for the different types of snow might still be able to perceive these differences.

Interestingly, research has shown that Whorf might have been accurate for information that is presented to the left hemisphere of the brain. That is, when colors were presented in the right visual field (and therefore went to the left brain), having names for the colors enhanced perception of and discrimination between those colors (Gilbert & others, 2006).

Language is a key feature of culture, and one of the ways that psychologists study the link between language and cognition is by comparing cognitive reasoning across differing cultures. To read about this research, see the Intersection.

## Language, Culture, and Cognition: How Does Language Shape Answers to the Question "Where"?

Imagine the following scenario. Sitting at breakfast with friends, you ask, "Where's the salt?" One of your companions answers, "It's to the west of the eggs." Where would you look? (You might be tempted to pull out the compass app on your smartphone to locate your desired seasoning on the table.) Although it may be surprising, in many languages, spatial relationships between objects are described in just such terms.

How we think about spatial relationships is one aspect of cognitive reasoning. This kind of reasoning is at work when we note that a book is on top of a desk, the dog is under the table, and the salt is just to your left. Spatial reasoning influences our judgments as well. While driving, for instance, we gauge the timing and amount of pressure we should apply to the brake to stop our car to avoid hitting the vehicle in front of us. And when playing a video game, spatial reasoning allows us to shoot a moving target accurately.

An interesting question is, does the way we talk about spatial relationships influence our capacities for spatial reasoning? A recent series of studies by Daniel Haun and colleagues (2011) examined this question using schoolchildren from the Netherlands and Namibia. Like other European languages (including English), Dutch includes *relativistic* terms to describe spatial relationships. This means that the self serves as a landmark in spatial statements, so that a person might say, "The salt is to the left of your plate (from my perspective)." Namibians speak a language called ≠, Akhoe Hai‖om (Hai‖om, for short) which relies on *absolute* or *geocentric* terms to describe spatial relations. This means that the placement of objects *in the world* is the key, not where those objects are relative to the self. In Hai‖om, then, someone might well say, "The salt is to the west (literally, where the sun sets) of your plate." Most European languages reserve geocentric terms for geographic contexts ("The lake is on the east side of town") and never use them for other objects.

Children in the studies were asked to memorize the arrangement of a set of animal toys—for instance, a cow, a sheep, and a pig—lined up on a table. At this first table, children stood looking at the objects from the south end. Then they were asked to re-create the arrangement on another table, while standing at the west end of the table (requiring a 90-degree rotation of the objects). The researchers found that all children were generally very good at rearranging the toys to re-create the previous pattern, but they did so in different ways. The Dutch children placed the toys so that they remained in the same positions *from their perspective.* The Namibian children, on the other hand, rearranged the toys so that the animals conformed to their placement *in geocentric terms.* Confronted with more complex tasks, the children showed these same differences—and when they were instructed to use the other way of thinking, they were not successful. Specifically, when Dutch children were told to remember which toy was on the western side of the table, and when Hai‖om children were told to remember which toy was on the right, they both had difficulty (even though both languages have terms for these locations). The researchers concluded that spatial reasoning preferences are strongly related to linguistic conventions, even by the age of 8.

Clearly, the human brain can handle both relativistic and geocentric spatial descriptions, but cultures and languages vary in terms of how much they use these and for what contexts. The way we talk can influence the way we think in ways we might never notice. Many of us are confounded if our GPS tells us to "head east," but small children in Namibia would find that a lot easier than trying to remember what "turn right" means.

\\ **How might these differences affect individuals moving from one culture to another?**

\\ **What might using the self as a landmark in spatial reasoning say about the Western sense of self?**

Although the strongest form of Whorf's hypothesis—that language determines perception—seems doubtful, research has continued to demonstrate the influence of language on how we think, even about something as fundamental as our own personalities. For example, in a series of studies, researchers interviewed bilingual individuals (that is, people who fluently speak two languages, in this case Spanish and English)

(Ramirez-Esparza & others, 2006). Each person rated his or her own personality characteristics, once in Spanish and once in English. Across all studies, and regardless of whether the individuals lived in a Spanish-speaking or an English-speaking country, respondents reported themselves as more outgoing, nicer, and more responsible when responding to the survey in English.

*Consider how this research connects to theory of mind, described in Chapter 4. Why would infants point to a place where an object used to be if they didn't know that something was going on in the head of a person with them? Why would we talk to one another at all if we didn't know that other people have a subjective awareness?*

**THE ROLE OF COGNITION IN LANGUAGE**   Clearly, then, language can influence cognition (Siegel & Surian, 2012). Researchers also study the possibility that cognition is an important foundation for language (Jackendoff, 2012).

One feature of human language that separates it from animal communication is the capacity to talk about objects that are not currently present (Hockett, 1960). A study comparing 12-month-old infants (who had not yet begun to talk) to chimpanzees suggests that this cognitive skill may underlie eventual language (Liszkowski & others, 2009). In this study, infants were more likely to communicate their desire for a toy by pointing to the place where the toy *used to be*. For many infants, this was the first thing they did to get their point across to another person who was present. In contrast, chimpanzees rarely pointed to where their desired object (food) had been, except as they desperately started pointing all over the place. So, even before they can talk, humans are communicating with others about what they want. Sometimes that communication demonstrates an appreciation of shared knowledge even about objects that are no longer present.

If language is a reflection of cognition in general, we would expect to find a close link between language ability and general intellectual ability. In particular, we would expect to find that problems in cognition are paralleled by problems in language. We would anticipate, for example, that general intellectual disability is accompanied by lowered language abilities. It is often but not always the case that individuals with intellectual disability have reduced language proficiency. For instance, individuals with Williams syndrome, a genetic disorder that affects about 1 in 20,000 births, tend to show extraordinary verbal, social, and musical abilities while having an extremely low IQ and difficulty with motor tasks and numbers. Williams syndrome demonstrates that intellectual disability is not always accompanied by poor language skills.

In summary, although thought influences language and language influences thought, there is increasing evidence that language and thought are not part of a single system. Instead, they seem to have evolved as separate but related components of the mind.

# Biological and Environmental Influences on Language

Everyone who uses language in some way "knows" its rules and has the ability to create an infinite number of words and sentences. Is this knowledge the product of biology, or is language learned and influenced by experiences in the environment?

**BIOLOGICAL INFLUENCES**   Scientists believe that humans acquired language about 100,000 years ago. In evolutionary time, then, language is a very recent human ability. However, a number of experts believe that biological evolution that occurred long before language emerged undeniably shaped humans into linguistic creatures (Chomsky, 1975). The brain, nervous system, and vocal apparatus of our predecessors changed over hundreds of thousands of years. Physically equipped to do so, *Homo sapiens* went beyond grunting and shrieking to develop abstract speech. This sophisticated language ability gave humans an enormous edge over other animals and increased their chances of survival (Pinker, 1994).

Used by permission of CartoonStock, www.CartoonStock.com.

*Language Universals*    American linguist Noam Chomsky (1975) has argued that humans come into the world biologically prewired to learn language at a certain time and in a certain way. According to Chomsky and many other language experts, the strongest evidence for language's biological basis is the fact that children all over the world reach language milestones at about the same time and in about the same order, despite vast variations in the language input they receive from their environments. For example, in some cultures adults never talk to infants under 1 year of age, yet these infants still acquire language.

In Chomsky's view, children cannot possibly learn the full rules and structure of languages by only imitating what they hear. Rather, nature must provide children with a biological, prewired, universal grammar, allowing them to understand the basic rules of all languages and to apply these rules to the speech they hear. They learn language without an awareness of its underlying logic. Think about it: The terms we used above to define the characteristics of language—*phonology, morphology, semantics,* and so forth—may be new to you, but on some level you have mastered these principles. This mastery is demonstrated by your reading of this book, writing a paper for class, and talking with a friend. Like all other humans, you are engaged in the use of a rule-based language system even without knowing that you know those rules.

**Noam Chomsky (b. 1928)**
*MIT linguist Noam Chomsky was one of the early architects of the view that children's language development cannot be explained by environmental input. In Chomsky's view, language has strong biological underpinnings, with children biologically prewired to learn language at a certain time and in a certain way.*

*Language and the Brain*    There is strong evidence to back up experts who believe language has a biological foundation. Neuroscience research has shown that the brain contains particular regions that are predisposed to language use (Tremblay, Monetta, & Joanette, 2009). As we saw in Chapter 2, accumulating evidence suggests that language processing, such as speech and grammar, mainly occurs in the brain's left hemisphere (Harpaz, Levkovitz, & Lavidor, 2009; Hornickel, Skoe, & Kraus, 2009). Recall the importance of Broca's area, which contributes to speech production, and Wernicke's area, which is involved in language comprehension. Using brain-imaging techniques such as PET scans, researchers have found that when an infant is about 9 months old, the part of the brain that stores and indexes many kinds of memory becomes fully functional (Bauer, 2009). This is also the time at which infants appear to be able to attach meaning to words, for instance to look at the ball if someone says "ball"—a development suggesting links among language, cognition, and the development of the brain.

**ENVIRONMENTAL INFLUENCES**    Decades ago, behaviorists opposed Chomsky's hypothesis and argued that language represents nothing more than chains of responses acquired through reinforcement (Skinner, 1957). A baby happens to babble "ma-ma"; mama rewards the baby with hugs and smiles; the baby says "mama" more and more. Bit by bit, said the behaviorists, the baby's language is built up. According to behaviorists, language is a complex learned skill, much like playing the piano or dancing.

Such a view of language development is simply not tenable, however, given the rapid way children learn language, as well as the lack of evidence that social environments carefully reinforce language skills (R. Brown, 1973). This is not to say the environment has no role in language development. Many language experts argue that a child's experiences, the particular language to be learned, and the context in which learning takes place can strongly influence language acquisition (Berko Gleason, 2009).

Cases of children who have lacked exposure to language provide evidence for the important role of the environment in language development. In 1970, a California social worker made a routine visit to the home of a partially blind woman who had applied for public assistance. The social worker discovered that the woman and her husband had kept their 13-year-old daughter, Genie, locked away in almost total isolation during her childhood. Genie could not speak or stand erect. She had spent every day bound naked

to a child's potty seat. She could move only her hands and feet. At night, she had been placed in a kind of straightjacket and caged in a crib with wire mesh sides and a cover. Whenever Genie had made a noise, her father had beaten her. He had never communicated with her in words; he had growled and barked at her instead (Rymer, 1993).

After she was rescued from her parents, Genie spent a number of years in extensive rehabilitation programs, including speech and physical therapy (Curtiss, 1977). She eventually learned to walk, although with a jerky motion, and to use the toilet. Genie also learned to recognize many words and to speak in rudimentary sentences. Gradually, she was able to string together two-word combinations such as "Big teeth," "Little marble," and "Two hand" and then three-word combinations such as "Small two cup." As far as we know, unlike normal children, Genie did not learn to ask questions and did not develop a language system that allowed her to understand English grammar. As an adult, she speaks in short, mangled sentences such as "Father hit leg," "Big wood," and "Genie hurt."

**FIGURE 7.12** **The Power of Smile and Touch** Research has shown that when mothers immediately smiled and touched their 8-month-old infants after they had babbled, the infants subsequently made more complex speechlike sounds than when mothers responded randomly to their infants.

Children who, like Genie, are abused and lack exposure to language for many years rarely speak normally. Some language experts have argued that these cases support the idea that there is a "critical period" for language development, a special time in a child's life (usually the preschool years) during which language must develop or it never will. Because these children also suffer severe emotional trauma and possible neurological deficits, however, the issue is still far from clear. Whether or not these cases suggest such a critical period, they certainly support the idea that the environment is crucial for the development of language.

Clearly, most humans do not learn language in a social vacuum. Most children are bathed in language from a very early age (Berko Gleason, 2009). The support and involvement of caregivers and teachers greatly facilitate a child's language learning (Goldfield & Snow, 2009; Pan & Uccelli, 2009). For example, one study showed that when mothers immediately smiled and touched their 8-month-old infants after they had babbled, the infants subsequently made more complex speechlike sounds than when mothers responded to their infants in a random manner (Goldstein, King, & West, 2003) (Figure 7.12).

Research findings about environmental influences on language learning complicate the understanding of its foundations. In the real world of language learning, children appear to be neither exclusively biologically programmed linguists nor exclusively socially driven language experts (Ratner, 1993). We have to look at how biology and environment interact when children learn language. That is, children are biologically prepared to learn language but benefit enormously from being immersed in a competent language environment from an early age (Goldfield & Snow, 2009).

# Language Development over the Life Span

Most individuals develop a clear understanding of their language's structure, as well as a large vocabulary, during childhood. Most adults in the United States have acquired a vocabulary of nearly 50,000 words. Researchers have taken a great interest in the process by which these aspects of language develop (Pan, 2011). Their many studies have provided an understanding of the milestones of language development (Figure 7.13).

| 0–6 Months | Cooing<br>Discrimination of vowels<br>Babbling present by 6 months |
|---|---|
| 6–12 Months | Babbling expands to include sounds of spoken language<br>Gestures used to communicate about objects<br>First words spoken 10–13 months |
| 12–18 Months | Understands 50+ words on average |
| 18–24 Months | Vocabulary increases to an average of 200 words<br>Two-word combinations |
| 2 Years | Vocabulary rapidly increases<br>Correct use of plurals<br>Use of past tense<br>Use of some prepositions |
| 3–4 Years | Mean length of utterances increases to 3–4 morphemes<br>   in a sentence<br>Use of yes and no questions, wh- questions<br>Use of negatives and imperatives<br>Increased awareness of pragmatics |
| 5–6 Years | Vocabulary reaches an average of about 10,000 words<br>Coordination of simple sentences |
| 6–8 Years | Vocabulary continues to increase rapidly<br>More skilled use of syntactical rules<br>Conversational skills improve |
| 9–11 Years | Word definitions include synonyms<br>Conversational strategies continue to improve |
| 11–14 Years | Vocabulary increases with addition of more abstract words<br>Understanding of complex grammar forms<br>Increased understanding of function a word plays in a<br>   sentence<br>Understands metaphor and satire |
| 15–20 Years | Understands adult literary works |

*Note:* This list is meant not to be exhaustive but rather to highlight some of the main language milestones. Also keep in mind that there is a great deal of variation in the ages at which children can reach these milestones and still be considered within the normal range of language development.

**FIGURE 7.13** **Language Milestones** All children are different and acquire language at varying rates, but these milestones provide a general sense of how language emerges in human life.

**FIGURE 7.14** **From Universal Linguist to Language-Specific Listener** A baby is shown in Patricia Kuhl's research laboratory. In this research, babies listen to recorded voices that repeat syllables. When the sounds of the syllables change, the babies quickly learn to look at the bear. Using this technique, Kuhl has demonstrated that babies are universal linguists until about 6 months of age but in the next 6 months become language-specific listeners.

Language researchers are fascinated by babies' speech even before the little ones say their first words (Cartmill, Demir, & Goldin-Meadow, 2011). *Babbling*—endlessly repeating sounds and syllables, such as *bababa* and *dadada*—begins at the age of about 4 to 6 months and is determined by biological readiness, not by the amount of reinforcement or the ability to hear (Menn & Stoel-Gammon, 2009). Even deaf babies babble for a time (Lenneberg, Rebelsky, & Nichols, 1965). Babbling probably allows babies to exercise their vocal cords and helps develop the ability to articulate different sounds.

Patricia Kuhl's research reveals that long before they begin to learn words, infants can sort through a number of spoken sounds in search of the ones that have meaning (1993, 2000, 2007, 2009, 2011a, 2011b). Kuhl argues that from birth to about 6 months of age, children are "universal linguists" who are capable of distinguishing each of the sounds that make up human speech. By about 6 months of age, they have started to specialize in the speech sounds (or phonology) of their native language (Figure 7.14).

Around the world, young children learn to speak in two-word utterances at 18 to 24 months of age.

A child's first words, uttered at the age of 10 to 13 months, name important people ("dada"), familiar animals ("kitty"), vehicles ("car"), toys ("ball"), food ("milk"), body parts ("eye"), clothes ("hat"), household items ("clock"), and greetings ("bye"). These were babies' first words a century ago, and they are babies' first words still (Bloom, 2004).

By the time children reach the age of 18 to 24 months, they usually utter two-word statements. They quickly grasp the importance of expressing concepts and the role that language plays in communicating with others (Sachs, 2009). To convey meaning in two-word statements, the child relies heavily on gesture, tone, and context. Although these two-word sentences omit many parts of speech, they are remarkably effective in conveying many messages. When a toddler demands, "Pet doggie!" parents know he means, "May I please pet the doggie?" Very young children learn that language is a good way to get what they want, suggesting that they grasp another aspect of language—its pragmatics.

Although childhood is an important time for language learning, we continue to learn language (new words, new skills) throughout life (Obler, 2009). For many years, it was claimed that if individuals did not learn a second language prior to puberty, they would never reach native-language learners' levels in the second language (Johnson & Newport, 1991). However, recent research indicates a more complex conclusion: Sensitive periods likely vary across different language systems (Thomas & Johnson, 2008). Thus, for late second-language learners, such as adolescents and adults, new vocabulary is easier to learn than new sounds and new grammar (Neville, 2006). For example, children's ability to pronounce words with a native-like accent in a second language typically decreases with age, with an especially sharp drop occurring after about 10 to 12 years of age.

For adults, learning a new language requires a special kind of cognitive exercise. As we have seen, a great deal of language learning in infancy and childhood involves recognizing the sounds that are part of one's native tongue. This process also entails learning to ignore sounds that are not important to one's first language. For instance, in Japanese, the phonemes /l/ and /r/ are not distinguished from each other, so that, for a Japanese adult, the word *lion* is not distinguishable from the name *Ryan*. Research suggests that mastering a new language in adulthood may involve overriding such learned habits and learning to listen to sounds that one previously ignored. Indeed, adults can learn to hear and discriminate sounds that are part of a new language, and this learning can contribute to speech fluency and language skill (Evans & Iverson, 2007).

Thus, learning a new language in adulthood involves cognitively stretching ourselves away from our assumptions. Such a process might play a role in enhancing not only our language skills but also our cognitive ability generally. Susanne Jaeggi and colleagues (2008) found that undertaking complex memory tasks led to enhanced reasoning ability.

*This study is an experiment, so we know that playing the memory game CAUSED changes in reasoning ability.*

In this work, the participants engaged in a complicated memory game similar to the card game Concentration, in which all the cards are placed face down and players have to remember where each one is in order to find matches. After training for a half hour a day for several days, participants increased their scores on reasoning ability, compared to a control group who did not complete the training. The more the participants trained, the smarter they got. One aspect of the study is especially interesting. The researchers designed the memory game so that as participants mastered it, it became harder and harder. In short, getting smarter is not just a matter of mastering a skill and then resting on our laurels. Reasoning ability can increase, but for that to happen, we have to keep challenging ourselves to think about things in increasingly new, and sometimes difficult, ways.

**The Candle Problem**

The solution requires a unique perception of the function of the box in which the matches came. It can become a candleholder when tacked to the wall.

**The Nine-Dot Problem**

Most people have difficulty with this problem because they try to draw the lines within the boundaries of the dots. Notice that by extending the lines beyond the dots, the problem can be solved.

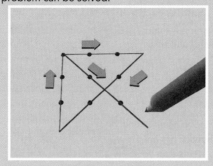

**The Six-Matchstick Problem**

Nothing in the instructions said that the solution had to be two-dimensional.

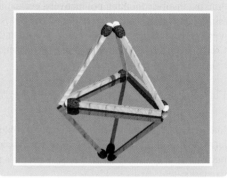

*Solutions to problems from Figure 7.4.*

# SUMMARY

## ❶ The Cognitive Revolution in Psychology

Cognition is the way in which information is processed and manipulated in remembering, thinking, and knowing. The advent of the computer in the mid-twentieth century spurred a cognitive revolution in which psychologists took on the challenge of understanding human information processing. Artificial intelligence (AI), the science of creating machines capable of performing activities that require intelligence when they are done by people, is a byproduct of the cognitive revolution.

## ❷ Thinking

Concepts are mental categories used to group objects, events, and characteristics. Concepts help us to generalize; they improve our memories; and they keep us from having to learn new things with every new instance or example of a concept. The prototype model suggests that members of a concept vary in terms of their similarity to the most typical item.

Problem solving is an attempt to find a way to attain a goal when the goal is not readily available. The four steps in problem solving are to (1) find and frame the problem, (2) develop good problem-solving strategies, (3) evaluate solutions, and (4) rethink and redefine problems and solutions over time. Among effective strategies for solving problems are subgoaling (the setting of intermediate goals that put you in a better position to reach your goal), algorithms (strategies that guarantee a solution), and heuristics (shortcuts that suggest, but do not guarantee, a solution to a problem).

Reasoning is the mental activity of transforming information to reach conclusions. Inductive reasoning is reasoning from the specific to the general. Deductive reasoning is reasoning from the general to the specific. Decision making involves evaluating alternatives and making choices among them. Biases and heuristics that may lead to problematic decision making include confirmation bias, hindsight bias, the availability heuristic, and the representativeness heuristic.

Critical thinking and creativity improve problem solving. Critical thinking involves thinking productively, evaluating the evidence, being mindful, and keeping an open mind. Creativity is the ability to think in novel and unusual ways and to come up with unconventional solutions. Creative thinkers are flexible and playful, self-motivated, willing to face risk, and objective in evaluating their work.

##  Intelligence

Intelligence consists of the ability to solve problems and to adapt to and learn from everyday experiences. Traditionally, intelligence has been measured by tests designed to compare people's performance on cognitive tasks.

A good test of intelligence meets three criteria: validity, reliability, and standardization. Validity is the extent to which a test measures what it is intended to measure. Reliability is how consistently an individual performs on a test. Standardization focuses on uniform procedures for administering and scoring a test and establishing norms.

Binet developed the first intelligence test. Individuals from age 2 through adulthood take the current Stanford-Binet test (so called because the revisions were completed at Stanford University). Some intelligence tests are unfair to individuals from different cultures. Culture-fair tests are intelligence tests that are intended to be culturally unbiased.

Genes are clearly involved in intelligence. The proportion of differences in intelligence that is explained by genetic variation (or heritability) is substantial. Environmental influences on intelligence have also been demonstrated. The fact that intelligence test scores have risen considerably around the world in recent decades—called the Flynn effect—supports the role of environment in intelligence.

At the extreme ends of intelligence are giftedness and intellectual disability. People who are gifted have high intelligence (IQ of 130 or higher) and/or superior talent for a particular domain. Research has shown that individuals who are gifted are likely to make important and creative contributions. Intellectual disability is a condition of limited mental ability in which the individual has a low IQ, usually below 70; has difficulty adapting to everyday life; and has an onset of these characteristics during childhood. Intellectual disability can have an organic cause (called organic intellectual disability) or can be social and cultural in origin (called cultural-familial intellectual disability).

Instead of focusing on intelligence as a single, broad cognitive ability, some psychologists have broken intelligence up into a variety of areas of life skills. Sternberg's triarchic theory states there are three main types of intelligence: analytical, creative, and practical. Gardner identifies nine types of intelligence, involving skills that are verbal, mathematical, spatial, bodily-kinesthetic, musical, interpersonal, intrapersonal, naturalist, and existential. The multiple-intelligences approaches have broadened the definition of intelligence and motivated educators to develop programs that instruct students in different domains. Critics maintain that multiple-intelligences theories include factors that really are not part of intelligence, such as musical skills. Critics also say that there is not enough research to support the concept of multiple intelligences.

## ④ Language

Language is a form of communication that is based on a system of symbols. All human languages have common aspects, including infinite generativity and organizational rules about structure. Any language has five characteristics: phonology, the sound system of a language; morphology, the rules for combining morphemes, which are meaningful strings of sounds that contain no smaller meaningful parts; syntax, the ways words are combined to form acceptable phrases and sentences; semantics, the meaning of words and sentences; and pragmatics, the uses of language.

Although language and thought influence each other, there is increasing evidence that they evolved as separate, modular, biologically prepared components of the mind. Evolution shaped humans into linguistic creatures. Chomsky said that humans are biologically prewired to learn language at a certain time and in a certain way. In addition, there is strong evidence that particular regions in the left hemisphere of the brain are predisposed to be used for language. Experience is also crucial to language development. It is important for children to interact with language-skilled people. Children are biologically prepared to learn language but benefit enormously from being in a competent language environment from early in development.

Although we often think of language, thinking, and intelligence as fixed when we are adults, research shows that we can continue to master skills and even increase intelligence by engaging in challenging mental tasks.

## KEY TERMS

cognition, p. 243
artificial intelligence (AI), p. 244
thinking, p. 245
concept, p. 245
prototype model, p. 246
problem solving, p. 246
subgoaling, p. 247
algorithms, p. 247
heuristics, p. 247
fixation, p. 248
functional fixedness, p. 248

reasoning, p. 249
inductive reasoning, p. 249
deductive reasoning, p. 249
decision making, p. 250
confirmation bias, p. 252
hindsight bias, p. 252
availability heuristic, p. 252
base rate fallacy, p. 252
representativeness heuristic, p. 252
mindfulness, p. 253
open-mindedness, p. 254
creativity, p. 254

divergent thinking, p. 254
convergent thinking, p. 254
intelligence, p. 256
validity, p. 256
reliability, p. 257
standardization, p. 257
mental age (MA), p. 257
intelligence quotient (IQ), p. 257
normal distribution, p. 257
culture-fair tests, p. 258
heritability, p. 259

gifted, p. 261
intellectual disability, p. 263
triarchic theory of intelligence, p. 265
language, p. 266
infinite generativity, p. 266
phonology, p. 267
morphology, p. 267
syntax, p. 267
semantics, p. 267
pragmatics, p. 267

## Multiple Choice

1. Cognitive psychology was considered a revolutionary development in psychology because
   A. it was a radical departure from behaviorism.
   B. it was a radical departure from psychoanalysis.
   C. it was a radical departure from the study of mental processes.
   D. John von Neumann used basic cognitive principles to develop the first modern computer.

2. Shantae, a sales representative, uses MapQuest to get driving directions to her clients' offices. Shantae is using a(n) _____ to reach her destinations.
   A. algorithm
   B. heuristic
   C. prototype
   D. category

3. Categories by which the mind groups things, events, and characteristics are called
   A. algorithms.
   B. cognitions.
   C. concepts.
   D. heuristics.

4. Someone who has difficulty exploring more than one possible solution to a problem is demonstrating
   A. functional fixedness.
   B. deductive reasoning.
   C. inductive reasoning.
   D. subgoaling.

5. Looking for available information that is consistent with our viewpoint is an example of
   A. the availability heuristic.
   B. hindsight bias.
   C. functional fixedness.
   D. confirmation bias.

6. The relationship between reliability and validity is that
   A. a reliable test is valid.
   B. a valid test is reliable.
   C. a reliable test is not valid.
   D. a valid test is not reliable.

7. The common criterion for determining mental retardation is
   A. an IQ below 100.
   B. an IQ below 85.
   C. an IQ below 70.
   D. an IQ below 55.

8. The sentence "the book ate the yellow house" is problematic because
   A. it has incorrect syntax.
   B. it has incorrect semantics.
   C. it has incorrect phonology.
   D. it has incorrect morphology.

9. Children begin saying words at the age of
   A. 4 to 6 months.
   B. 10 to 13 months.
   C. 18 to 24 months.
   D. 24 to 30 months.

10. Infinite generativity refers to the ability of languages
    A. to produce an unlimited number of meaningful sentences.
    B. to produce an unlimited number of sounds.
    C. to keep adding new words.
    D. to keep changing over time.

## Apply It!

11. Jeremy's Uncle Ted, who is 70 years old, is taking a course in French for the first time. Jeremy tells you, "I don't know why he's bothering—you can't learn a language at that age." Respond to Jeremy's assertion using material from the text. Can Uncle Ted learn French? What challenges is he likely to face?

# 8 Human Development

## *The Time Machine of Human Development*

Have you ever fantasized about traveling in a time machine to the distant past to see live dinosaurs or into a future featuring flying cars and moving sidewalks? These are fantastic ideas, but in a way every human being's development is like a trip in a time machine. From the moment life begins, we are on a developmental journey into the future. Generally speaking, that personal journey through time is lengthening as the human life span increases.

Consider the long life of U.S. pediatrician Leila Denmark. Dr. Denmark (1898–2012) lived to age 114. In her lifetime, the United States changed from a nation in which women could not vote or own property to one where women are CEOs, mayors, governors, senators, and candidates for the highest office in the land. She had the mind-boggling experiences of seeing the first cars ever manufactured *and* the first moon walk, both World Wars, and the wars in Vietnam, Iraq, and Afghanistan, plus the Great Depression of the 1930s and the global recession at the start of the twenty-first century. The only woman in her medical school graduating class in 1928, Dr. Denmark dedicated herself to serving the needs of impoverished children until she retired—at age *103*.

An astonishing variety of events and experiences can be part of one human life span. Someone born in the early 1990s has on average over 50 years to fill with experiences. Imagine if such an individual rode this time machine of life well into the twenty-first century. What would be the path of that person's development as a human being—a path in some ways unique but in many ways in common with the development of all people? In this chapter, you step into the time machine of human development, looking back on your own development and seeing yourself as an infant, a child, and an adolescent—and getting new perspective on your present plus a glimpse into your future.

Developmental psychologists are interested in all the ways a person grows and changes throughout the time travel that is life, from its beginning to its inevitable end. We start by defining human development and examining central issues in developmental psychology. In the heart of the chapter, we look at the processes and outcomes of development in three broad domains of life: physical, cognitive, and socioemotional. We then explore the links among these developmental areas by probing gender development, followed by a survey of moral development and death, dying, and grieving. The chapter closes with a look at the positive ways individuals can shape their development in adulthood. Throughout, we consider how the active developer—the time traveler himself or herself—can influence the journey of life and its meaning.

# 1  Exploring Human Development

**Development** refers to the pattern of continuity and change in human capabilities that occurs throughout the course of life. Most development involves growth, although it also includes decline (for example, physical abilities may decline with age). Let's begin our consideration of human development by addressing several key questions and issues that are especially relevant to understanding how human beings grow and change through the life span.

**development**
The pattern of continuity and change in human capabilities that occurs throughout life, involving both growth and decline.

## Research Methods in Developmental Psychology

Human development is about the changes that occur with age. To know what age-related differences mean, however, we must consider the kind of research presented.

In studies with a **cross-sectional design,** a number of people are assessed at one point in time. Age differences can then be noted. By examining how the ages of these individuals relate to the characteristics measured, researchers can find out whether younger individuals differ from older ones. Age differences, however, are not the same as developmental change.

**cross-sectional design**
A research design in which a group of people are assessed on a psychological variable at one point in time.

One problem in cross-sectional studies is cohort effects. *Cohort effects* are differences between individuals that stem not necessarily from their ages but from the historical and social time period in which they were born and developed (Schaie, 2009). For instance, individuals who were born in the 1940s might be less likely to have attended college than those born in the 1990s. Differences observed between these groups might be due not to their age but rather to these differing experiences. Consider your own cohort. How might experiences that are unique to your age group lead you and your peers to be different from other generations?

In contrast to a cross-sectional study, a longitudinal study, as described in Chapter 1, assesses the same participants multiple times over a lengthy period. A longitudinal study can find out not only whether age groups differ but also whether the same individuals change with respect to a particular characteristic as they age. Strong statements about developmental changes in psychological characteristics require longitudinal designs. Using these and other methods, human development researchers have grappled with big questions that are relevant to all of psychology, as we consider next.

# How Do Nature and Nurture Influence Development?

**nature**
An individual's biological inheritance, especially his or her genes.

Developmental psychologists are interested in understanding how nature and nurture contribute to development. **Nature** refers to a person's biological inheritance, especially his or her genes. **Nurture** refers to the individual's environmental and social experiences. Understanding development requires that we take into account the contributions of both genes (nature) and the environment (nurture).

**nurture**
An individual's environmental and social experiences.

In Chapter 2, we considered the concept of a *genotype* (the individual's genetic heritage—the actual genetic material). We also examined the idea of a *phenotype* (the person's observable characteristics). The phenotype shows the contributions of both nature (genetic heritage) and nurture (environment). Whether and how the genotype is expressed in the phenotype may depend on the environment. For example, a person might be born with the genes to be the next Michael Phelps; but in the absence of environmental factors such as good nutrition, sound medical care, access to a swimming pool, and superb coaching, that potential might never be reached.

*What factors in your childhood environment influenced your expression of your gifts and abilities?*

One example of the role of environmental influences on genetic expression is a genetic condition called *phenylketonuria* (PKU). Caused by two recessive genes, PKU results in an inability to metabolize the amino acid phenylalanine. Decades ago, it was thought that the genotype for PKU led to a specific phenotype, namely, irreversible brain damage, intellectual disability, and seizures. However, experts now know that as long as individuals with the genotype for PKU stick to a diet that is very low in phenylalanine, these characteristics in the phenotype can be avoided (Cotugno & others, 2011). These environmental precautions can change the phenotype associated with this genotype.

The PKU example tells us that a person's observable characteristics (phenotype) might not reflect his or her genetic heritage (genotype) very precisely because of the particular experiences the person has had. Instead, for each genotype, a *range* of phenotypes may be expressed, depending on environmental experiences. The person whom we see before us emerges out of an interplay of genetic and environmental experiences. Development is the product of nature, nurture, and the complex interaction of the two (Beaver & Belsky, 2012; Cicchetti & Rogosch, 2012; Dick, 2011).

*Phenylalanine is a major component of the artificial sweetener aspartame (check the side of a diet soda can...). In most developed nations, infants are tested for PKU shortly after birth.*

One crucial source of nurture is our parents, and recently some parents have been taking a very active role in their children's lives. To read about how parenting fits into the nature-versus-nurture question, check out Challenge Your Thinking.

Although it might be easy to think of genes as the blueprint for a person, development is not a process that follows a genetic master plan (Turkheimer, 2011). In fact, it is difficult to tell a simple story about how development occurs. One way that scientists and philosophers think about complex processes such as development is through the concept of emergent properties. An *emergent property* is a big entity (like a person) that is a consequence of the interaction of multiple lower-level factors (Gottlieb, 2007). Development is about the complex interactions of genes and experience that build the whole person.

*A flock of birds flying in formation illustrates an emergent property. The birds may appear to be following a leader, but they aren't. Instead, each individual bird is following its own local rules. What you see as a flock of birds is in fact a collection of individual birds, each one "doing its own thing" but creating the formation (the emergent property) you recognize as a flock.*

## Do Early Experiences Rule Us for Life?

The PKU example above suggests the power of early experience (nurture) in human development. A key question in developmental psychology is the extent to which childhood experiences determine aspects of later life. Some research shows that unless infants experience warm, nurturing caregiving in the first year or so of life, they will not develop to their full potential (Phillips & Lowenstein, 2011; Sroufe, Coffino, & Carlson, 2010). Other studies demonstrate the power of later experience in influencing development in adulthood (Stanley & Isaacowitz, 2011). Life-span

# Challenge

## YOUR THINKING

## Genes or Superparents: Which Matters More to Kids?

Compared to past generations, today's parents are more likely to be preoccupied with their children's lives and behaviors. Whereas decades ago parents might have worried about getting their children into the right college, today some parents obsess over enrolling their little ones in the right preschool and kindergarten. Is this obsession necessary to ensure healthy development? Some experts would give that question a definite no.

Judith Harris (1998), author of the book *The Nurture Assumption*, argues that what parents do makes no difference in children's behavior. Spank them. Hug them. Read to them. Ignore them. It will not influence how they turn out, because genes and peers are far more important than parents in children's development, Harris maintains. Similarly, developmental researcher Sandra Scarr (1992, 2000) suggests that "superparenting" is unnecessary. She asserts that the genotype is so strong that it makes most environmental experiences irrelevant. Scarr suggests that the only parenting that has a negative effect on a child is parenting that is far outside the normal range—for example, chronic physical abuse. Apart from such extremes, Scarr asserts, genes are the primary determinant of developmental outcomes. So, can parents take a breather? Not necessarily.

Claims such as those of Harris and Scarr have met with a firestorm of criticism. Diana Baumrind (1993) countered that "good enough" parenting *is not* good enough, and she cited evidence that highly demanding and highly responsive parents are more likely to have high-achieving and socially well-adjusted children. A longitudinal study by W. Andrew Collins and his colleagues (2000) supported Baumrind's claims; it showed that even with genetic influences taken into account, parenting practices made a difference in children's lives. Baumrind also expressed concern that Scarr's opinion might lead parents to give up the important responsibility of childrearing or to conclude that their efforts on behalf of their children are not worthwhile.

So, in the view of those in the Baumrind and Collins camp, although a person's genetic heritage certainly has a role to play in development, we cannot cuddle our genes, be scolded by them, laugh with them, or look to them for advice. For those important aspects of experience we need parents— super or otherwise (Sandler, Wolchik, & Schoenfelder, 2011). Despite the strong criticism of her views, Harris (2009) published a revised and updated edition of her earlier book, restating her claim that parents matter far less than most people think.

### What Do You Think?

- What is your position in this debate? Why?
- Why might today's parents be more likely than parents in the past to try to be superparents?

developmentalists stress that experiences throughout life contribute to development (Lüdtke & others, 2011; Specht, Egloff, & Schmukle, 2011). Both early and later experience make significant contributions to development, so no one is doomed to be a total prisoner of his or her childhood.

A key concept in understanding the role of negative early experiences in later development is resilience. **Resilience** refers to a person's ability to recover from or adapt to difficult times. Resilience means that despite encountering adversity, a person shows signs of positive functioning (DiCorcia & Tronick, 2011). Resilience can involve factors that compensate for difficulties, buffering the individual from the effects of these hardships. Moderate difficulties early in life can be strengthening experiences that lay the groundwork for future coping (Seery, Holman, & Silver, 2010). Although often studied as an aspect of childhood (Masten, 2009) and adolescence (Montgomery, 2010), resilience can also characterize development in adulthood (Gooding & others, 2012; McFadden & Basting, 2010).

**resilience**
A person's ability to recover from or adapt to difficult times.

 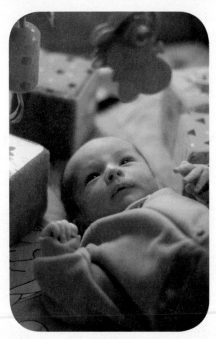 

*Human development is complex because it is the product of several processes. The hormonal changes of puberty, a baby's observation of a mobile, and an older couple's embrace reflect physical, cognitive, and socioemotional processes, respectively.*

## Nature, Nurture, and You

Because you cannot pick your genes or your parents, it would seem as if you are stuck with the genes and environment you got at birth. However, the truth is that you have a vital role to play throughout development. As an active developer, you take the raw ingredients of nature and nurture and make them into the person you are (Turkheimer, 2011).

Indeed, some psychologists believe that people can develop beyond what their genetic inheritance and environment give them. They argue that a key aspect of development involves seeking optimal experiences in life (Armor, Massey, & Sackett, 2008). History is filled with examples of people who go beyond what life has given them to achieve extraordinary things. Such individuals author a unique developmental path, sometimes transforming apparent weaknesses into real strengths.

*A person does not have to be famous to take an active role in shaping his or her development.*

In individuals' efforts to experience life in optimal ways, they develop *life themes* that involve activities, social relationships, and life goals (Frensch, Pratt, & Norris, 2007; Rathunde, 2010). Some people are more successful at constructing optimal life experiences than others. Among the public figures who have succeeded are Martin Luther King, Jr., Mother Teresa, Nelson Mandela, Bill and Melinda Gates, and Oprah Winfrey. These individuals looked for and found meaningful life themes as they developed. Their lives were not restricted to biological survival or to settling for their particular life situations.

## Three Domains of Development

The pattern of development is complex because it is the product of several processes in three domains of life—physical, cognitive, and socioemotional:

- *Physical processes* involve changes in an individual's biological nature. Genes inherited from parents, the hormonal changes of puberty and menopause, and changes throughout life in the brain, height and weight, and motor skills all reflect the developmental role of biological processes.

- *Cognitive processes* involve changes in an individual's thought, intelligence, and language. Observing a colorful mobile as it swings above a crib, constructing a sentence about the future, imagining oneself as a contestant on *The X Factor* or as president of the United States, memorizing a new telephone number—these activities reflect the role of cognitive processes in development.

- *Socioemotional processes* involve changes in an individual's relationships with other people, changes in emotions, and changes in personality. An infant's smile in response to her mother's touch, a girl's development of assertiveness, an adolescent's joy at the senior prom, a young man's aggressiveness in sport, and an older couple's affection for each other all reflect the role of socioemotional processes.

Throughout this chapter we will trace these developmental processes along the broad periods of the life span, namely:

- *Childhood,* the period from infancy (birth to 24 months) through childhood (up to about age 10).

- *Adolescence,* the period beginning around ages 10 to 12 and spanning the transition from childhood to adulthood.

- *Adulthood,* the period that is generally separated into early (the 20s and 30s), middle (the 40s and 50s), and late (age 60 and beyond).

After tracing changes in physical, cognitive, and socioemotional development across the life span, we will turn to topics that demonstrate how strongly intertwined these processes are, including gender and moral development as well as death and dying. Think of Hannah, an infant whose parents place a teddy bear in her crib. As an infant she might simply look at the teddy bear when her parents jiggle it in front of her. Over time, she not only can see the teddy bear but also can reach for it. She might even remember that the teddy bear exists and might cry for it when it is not with her. As a toddler, when she carries it around, she is demonstrating her physical abilities to do so, as well as her capacity to use the teddy bear as a source of comfort. As an adolescent, Hannah might no longer sleep with her teddy, but she might give him a place of honor on a shelf. As you read this chapter's separate sections on physical, cognitive, and socioemotional development, remember that you are studying the development of an integrated human being in whom body, mind, emotion, and social relationships are interdependent.

## self-quiz

1. The late Diana, Princess of Wales, devoted a considerable effort to eliminating land mines. Her work illustrates
   A. a life theme.
   B. a genotype.
   C. a socioemotional process.
   D. a phenotype.

2. Development can be best described as
   A. due entirely to nature.
   B. due entirely to nurture.
   C. the product of the interaction of nature and nurture.
   D. none of the above

3. An example of an optimal experience is
   A. cooking food to eat.
   B. getting a great buy on those boots you wanted.
   C. volunteering time to teach adults to read.
   D. competing with others.

**APPLY IT!** 4. Sonja and Pete are engineers who met during college. They share a love of mathematics and science and have successful engineering careers. When their daughter Gabriella is born, they decorate her room with numbers and spend a great deal of time counting objects and talking about math with her. In her school years, Gabriella is particularly gifted in mathematics. Gabriella does not become an engineer, but she does have a career as a terrific math teacher. Which statement is most accurate in describing Gabriella?

A. Her math ability is a direct result of her genetic heritage.
B. Her math ability is a direct result of her environmental experiences.
C. The fact that she became a teacher instead of an engineer shows that neither genetics nor environment matters that much to development.
D. Gabriella's development shows the influence of genetics, environment, their interaction, and Gabriella's capacity to forge a life theme that is meaningful to her.

# 2 Physical Development

In exploring human development in this section, we first trace the ways that individuals grow and change *physically,* starting with *prenatal* ("before birth") physical development. Then we consider the physical changes associated with childhood, adolescence, and the phases of adulthood. Throughout, we consider the ways the brain changes in each developmental period.

## Prenatal Physical Development

Prenatal development is a time of astonishing change, beginning with conception. Conception occurs when a single sperm cell from the male merges with the female's ovum (egg) to produce a zygote, a single cell with 23 chromosomes from the mother and 23 from the father.

**THE COURSE OF PRENATAL DEVELOPMENT**  Development from zygote to fetus is divided into three periods:

- *Germinal period—weeks 1 and 2:* The germinal period begins with conception. After 1 week and many cell divisions, the zygote is made up of 100 to 150 cells. By the end of 2 weeks, the mass of cells has attached to the uterine wall.

- *Embryonic period—weeks 3 through 8:* The rate of cell differentiation intensifies, support systems for the cells develop, and the beginnings of organs appear (Figure 8.1a). In the third week, the neural tube, which eventually becomes the spinal cord, starts to take shape. Within the first 28 days after conception, the neural tube is formed and closes, encased inside the embryo. Problems in neural tube development can lead to

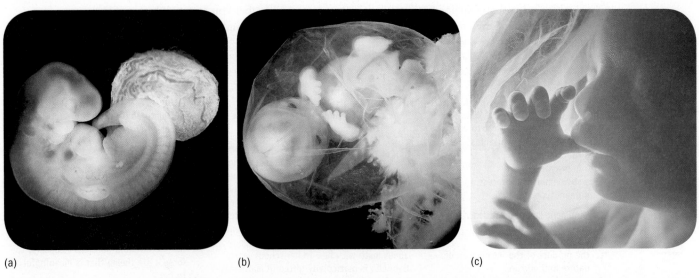

(a)                                    (b)                                    (c)

**FIGURE 8.1**  **From Embryo to Fetus** (a) At about 4 weeks, an embryo is about 0.2 inch (less than 1 centimeter) long. The head, eyes, and ears begin to show; the head and neck are half the length of the body; the shoulders will be located where the whitish arm buds are attached. (b) At 8 weeks, the developing individual is about 1.6 inches (4 centimeters) long and has reached the end of its embryonic phase. It has become a fetus. Everything that will be found in the fully developed human being has now begun to form. The fetal stage is a period of growth and perfection of detail. The heart has been beating for a month, and the muscles have just begun their first exercises. (c) At 4½ months, the fetus is just over 7 inches (about 18 centimeters) long. When the thumb comes close to the mouth, the head may turn, and the lips and tongue begin their sucking motions—a reflex for survival.

birth defects such as spina bifida, in which the spinal cord is not completely enclosed by the spinal column, or severe underdevelopment of the brain. Folic acid, a B vitamin found in orange juice and leafy green vegetables, greatly reduces the chances of neural tube defects. By the end of the embryonic period, the heart begins to beat, the arms and legs become more differentiated, the face starts to form, and the intestinal tract appears (Figure 8.1b).

*Note that 28 days is before most women even know they are pregnant. That's why doctors recommend that all women who might become pregnant take folic acid supplements (about 400 micrograms a day) to prevent neural tube defects.*

- *Fetal period—months 2 through 9:* At 2 months, the fetus is the size of a kidney bean and has already started to move around. At 4 months, the fetus is 5 inches long and weighs about 5 ounces (Figure 8.1c). At 6 months, the fetus has grown to a pound and a half. The last three months of pregnancy are the time when organ functioning increases, and the fetus puts on considerable weight and size, adding baby fat. The average newborn is about 19 inches long and weighs about 7 pounds.

Until about 60 years ago, mothers and their doctors were unaware of the role that maternal diet and behavior might play for the developing fetus. Although it floats in a comfortable, well-protected womb, the fetus is not immune to the larger environment surrounding the mother (Dunkel Schetter, 2011). Indeed, sometimes prenatal development is disrupted by environmental insults.

**THREATS TO THE FETUS**   A *teratogen* is any agent that causes a birth defect. Teratogens include chemical substances ingested by the mother (such as nicotine, if the mother smokes) and certain illnesses (such as rubella, or German measles). Substances that are ingested by the mother can lead to serious birth defects (Holmes & Westgate, 2011). Heroin is an example of a teratogen. Babies born to heroin users are at risk for many problems, including premature birth, low birth weight, physical defects, breathing problems, and death.

*A reality check for pregnant women who continue to smoke to alleviate stress: Imagine a baby puffing on a lit cigarette. A pregnant woman who smokes is smoking for two.*

*Fetal alcohol spectrum disorders (FASD)* are a cluster of abnormalities and problems that appear in the offspring of mothers who drink alcohol heavily during pregnancy (Yang & others, 2012). These abnormalities include a small head; facial characteristics such as wide-spaced eyes, a flattened nose, and an underdeveloped upper lip; defects in the limbs and heart; and below-average intelligence. Heavy drinking is linked to FASD, but even moderate drinking can lead to serious problems (Cannon & others, 2012). The best advice for a woman who is pregnant or thinking of becoming pregnant is to avoid alcohol.

The effects of chemical teratogens depend on the timing of exposure (May & Gossage, 2011). The body part or organ system that is developing when the fetus encounters the teratogen is most vulnerable. Genetic characteristics may buffer or worsen the effects of a teratogen. Perhaps most importantly, the environment the child encounters *after birth* can influence the ultimate effects of prenatal insults.

Sexually transmitted infections (STIs) also threaten the fetus. Some STIs, such as gonorrhea, can be transferred to the baby during delivery. Others, including syphilis and AIDS, can also infect the fetus while it is in the womb. Because the human immunodeficiency virus (HIV) that causes AIDS leads to an incurable infection, antiviral medications are given to HIV-positive mothers to reduce the chances that they will pass the virus to their fetus. Besides transmission of infections to the fetus and newborns, STI exposure enhances the risk of stillbirth, as well as a number of other problems, such as eye infections and blindness (in the case of gonorrhea). Many STIs also increase the risk of preterm birth.

A *preterm infant,* one who is born prior to 37 weeks after conception, may be at risk for developmental difficulties. Whether a preterm infant will have developmental problems is a complex issue, however. Postnatal experience plays a crucial role in determining the ultimate effects of preterm birth. For example, research has shown that massage can improve developmental outcomes for premature infants (Field, Diego, & Hernandez-Rief, 2010, 2011).

# Physical Development in Infancy and Childhood

Human infants are among the world's most helpless neonates. One reason for that helplessness is that we are born not quite finished. From an evolutionary perspective, what sets humans apart from other animals is our enormous brain. Getting that big brain out of the relatively small birth canal is a challenge that nature has met by sending human babies out of the womb before the brain has fully developed. The first months and years of life allow the developing human (and his or her environment) to put the finishing touches on that important organ.

**REFLEXES**   Newborns come into the world equipped with several genetically wired reflexes that are crucial for survival. Babies are born with the ability to suck and swallow. If they are dropped in water, they will naturally hold their breath, contract their throats to keep water out, and move their arms and legs to stay afloat at least briefly. Some reflexes persist throughout life—coughing, blinking, and yawning, for example. Others, such as automatically grasping something that touches the fingers, disappear in the months following birth as higher brain functions mature and infants develop voluntary control over many behaviors. Figure 8.2 shows some examples of infant reflexes.

**MOTOR AND PERCEPTUAL SKILLS**   Relative to the rest of the body, a newborn's head is gigantic, and it flops around uncontrollably. Within 12 months, the infant becomes capable of sitting upright, standing, stooping, climbing, and often walking. During the second year, growth decelerates, but rapid gains occur in such activities as running and climbing.

   Motor skills and perceptual skills are coupled and depend on each other. To reach for something, the infant must be able to see it. Babies are continually coordinating their movements with information they perceive through their senses to learn how to maintain their balance, reach for objects in space, and move across various surfaces and terrains (Adolph & others, 2008; Clearfield, 2011). Consider what happens when a baby sees a fun toy across the room. Because she can see it, she is motivated to get it. She must

**Rooting**

*What provokes the response?*
Stroking of the infant's cheek

*What the infant does* Head turns in the direction of the touch, and the infant opens his or her mouth for feeding.

**Gripping**

*What provokes the response?*
Something that is placed in the infant's hand

*What the infant does* The infant grasps the item and can hold on very well—almost enough to support his or her own weight.

**Toe Curling**

*What provokes the response?*
Stroking of the inner or outer sole of the infant's foot

*What the infant does* If the inner sole is stroked, the infant curls his or her toes. If the outer sole is stroked, the toes spread out.

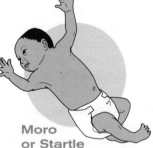

**Moro or Startle**

*What provokes the response?*
Sudden noise or movement

*What the infant does* The infant throws his or her head back and arms and legs out (and then cries).

**Galant**

*What provokes the response?*
Stroking of the infant's lower back, next to the spinal cord

*What the infant does* The infant curves toward the side that was stroked—and looks like a fencer when doing so.

**FIGURE 8.2   Some Infant Reflexes** Infants are born with a number of reflexes to get them through life, and they are incredibly cute when they perform them. These reflexes disappear as infants mature.

perceive the current state of her body and learn how to use her limbs to get to the goal. Action in turn educates perception. For example, watching an object while holding and touching it helps infants to learn about its texture, size, and hardness. Moving from place to place in the environment teaches babies how objects and people look from different perspectives and whether surfaces will support their weight.

Infants are energetic developers. When infants are motivated to do something, they may create a new motor behavior, such as reaching out to grab a new toy or mommy's earrings. That new behavior is the result of many converging factors: the developing nervous system, the body's physical properties and its movement possibilities, the goal the infant is motivated to reach, and environmental support for the skill (van Hof, van der Kamp, & Savelsbergh, 2008).

Researchers used to think that motor milestones (such as sitting up, crawling, and walking) unfolded as part of a genetic plan. Psychologists now recognize that motor development is not the consequence of nature or nurture alone (Keen, 2011).

Environmental experiences play a role in motor development. In one study, 3-month-old infants participated in play sessions wearing "sticky mittens"—mittens with palms that stick to the edges of toys and allow the infants to pick up the toys (Needham, Barrett, & Peterman, 2002, p. 279) (Figure 8.3). Infants who participated in sessions with the mittens grasped and manipulated objects earlier in their development than a control group of infants who did not receive the "mitten" experience. The experienced infants looked at the objects longer, swatted at them, and were more likely to put the objects in their mouths.

Psychologists face a daunting challenge in studying infant perception. Infants cannot talk, so how can scientists learn whether they can see or hear certain things? Psychologists who study infants rely on what infants can do to understand what they know (Hollich, 2006). One thing infants can do is look. The **preferential looking** technique involves giving an infant a choice of what object to look at. If an infant shows a reliable preference for one stimulus (say, a picture of a face) over another (a scrambled picture of a face) when these are repeatedly presented in differing locations, we can infer that the infant can tell the two images apart.

Using this technique, researchers have found that as early as 7 days old, infants are already engaged in organized perception of faces and are able to put together sights and sounds. If presented with two faces with mouths moving, infants will watch the face whose mouth matches the sounds they are hearing (Lewkowicz, 2010; Lewkowicz & Hansen-Tift, 2012; Pascalls & Kelly, 2008). At 3 months, infants prefer real faces to scrambled faces, and their mother's face to a stranger's (Barrera & Maurer, 1981). Research using brain imaging suggests that infants may know more than even this clever strategy can tell us.

**THE BRAIN**   As an infant plays, crawls, shakes a rattle, smiles, and frowns, his or her brain is changing dramatically. At birth and in early infancy, the brain's 100 billion neurons have only minimal connections. The infant brain literally is ready and waiting for the experiences that will create these connections. During the first 2 years of life, the dendrites of the neurons branch out, and the neurons become far more interconnected (Figure 8.4). Myelination, the process of encasing axons with fat cells (the myelin sheath

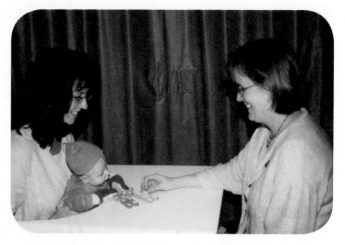

**FIGURE 8.3   Infants' Use of "Sticky Mittens" to Explore Objects**   Amy Needham and her colleagues (2002) found that "sticky mittens" enhance young infants' object exploration skills.

*Infants' motor skills are limited by gravity. Infants can sometimes do a lot more when weightless. Holding a baby up in a kiddie pool, we can see how the infant can stand and even take some steps quite deftly, without body weight getting in the way.*

*The brain's plasticity makes it different from any other bodily organ. It comes into the world ready for whatever world it might encounter, and the features of that world influence its very structure. Other organs physically grow as we do. But the brain's very essence is attached to the world in which it lives.*

**preferential looking**
A research technique that involves giving an infant a choice of what object to look at.

## FIGURE 8.4
**Dendritic Spreading**
Note the increase in connections among neurons over the course of the first 2 years of life.

Reprinted by permission of the publisher from *The Postnatal Development of the Human Cerebral Cortex, Vols. I–VIII* by Jesse Leroy Conel, Cambridge, Mass.: Harvard University Press, Copyright © 1939, 1975 by the President and Fellows of Harvard College.

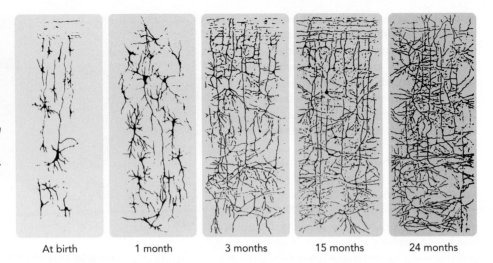

| At birth | 1 month | 3 months | 15 months | 24 months |

described in Chapter 2), begins prenatally and continues after birth well into adolescence and adulthood (Abrahám & others, 2011).

During childhood, *synaptic connections* increase dramatically. Recall from Chapter 2 that a synapse is a gap between neurons that is bridged by chemical neurotransmitters. Nearly twice as many synapses are available as will ever be used (Huttenlocher, 1999). The connections that are made become stronger and will survive; the unused ones will be replaced by other neural pathways or disappear. In the language of neuroscience, these unused connections will be "pruned." Figure 8.5 illustrates the steep growth and later pruning of synapses during infancy in specific areas of the brain.

Brain-imaging studies show that children's brains also undergo amazing anatomical changes. Repeated brain scans of the same children for up to four years show that the amount of brain material in some areas can nearly double within as little as a year, followed by a drastic loss of tissue as unneeded cells are purged and the brain continues to reorganize itself. The overall size of the brain does not change very much, but local patterns within the brain change tremendously. From 3 to 6 years of age, the most rapid

## FIGURE 8.5
**Synaptic Density in the Human Brain from Infancy to Adulthood**
The graph shows the dramatic increase and then pruning in synaptic density in three regions of the brain: visual cortex, auditory cortex, and prefrontal cortex. Synaptic density is believed to be an important indication of the extent of connectivity between neurons.

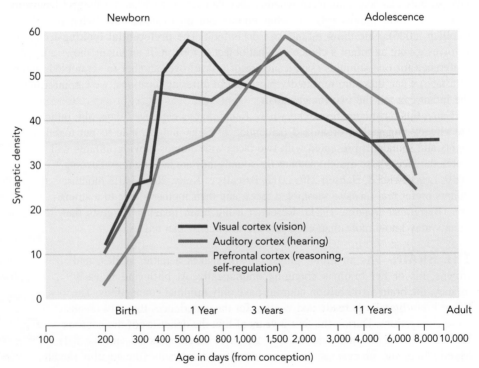

growth takes place in the frontal lobe areas, which are involved in planning and organizing new actions and in maintaining attention to tasks. These brain changes are not simply the result of nature; new experiences in the world also promote brain development (Levine & others, 2012; Sullivan & others, 2006; Trainor, Lee, & Bosnyak, 2011). Thus, as in other areas of development, nature and nurture operate together.

# Physical Development in Adolescence

*Adolescence* refers to the developmental period spanning the transition from childhood to adulthood, beginning around 10 to 12 years of age and ending at 18 to 21 years of age. Dramatic physical changes characterize adolescence, especially early adolescence. Among the major physical changes of adolescence are those involving puberty and the brain.

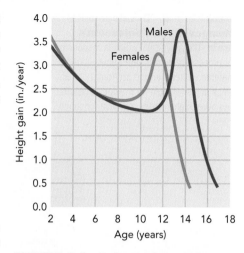

**FIGURE 8.6  Pubertal Growth Spurt**
On average, the pubertal growth spurt begins and peaks about two years earlier for girls (starts at 9, peaks at 11½) than for boys (starts at 11½, peaks at 13½).

From J. M. Tanner et al., in *Archives of Diseases in Childhood* 41, 1966. Reproduced with permission from the BMJ Publishing Group.

**puberty**
A period of rapid skeletal and sexual maturation that occurs mainly in early adolescence.

**PUBERTY**  The signature physical change in adolescence is **puberty,** a period of rapid skeletal and sexual maturation that occurs mainly in early adolescence. In general, we know when an individual is going through puberty, but we have a hard time pinpointing its beginning and its end. Except for *menarche* (girls' first menstrual cycle), no single marker defines it. For boys the first whisker or first nocturnal ejaculation (or wet dream) could mark its appearance, but both may go unnoticed.

The jump in height and weight that characterizes pubertal change occurs about two years earlier for girls than for boys (Figure 8.6). In the United States today, the average beginning of the growth spurt is 9 years of age for girls and 11 years for boys. The peak of pubertal change occurs at an average age of 11½ for girls and 13½ for boys.

Hormonal changes lie at the core of pubertal development. The concentrations of certain hormones increase dramatically during puberty (Dorn & Biro, 2011). *Testosterone,* an androgen, is associated in boys with the development of genitals, an increase in height, and voice change. *Estradiol,* an estrogen, is associated in girls with breast, uterine, and skeletal development. Developmental psychologists believe that hormonal changes account for at least some of the emotional ups and downs of adolescence, but hormones are not alone responsible for adolescent behavior (Negriff, Susman, & Trickett, 2011).

From our discussion earlier in this chapter, recall that physical and socioemotional development are intertwined. This link is demonstrated in the implications of timing of puberty for socioemotional outcomes. Boys who mature earlier than their peers tend to show more positive socioemotional outcomes, such as being popular with their peers and having higher self-esteem (Graber, Brooks-Gunn, & Warren, 2006). In one study, boys who matured early in adolescence were more successful and less likely to drink alcohol or smoke cigarettes than late-maturing boys some 39 years later (Taga, Markey, & Friedman, 2006). In contrast, girls who are early bloomers tend to be less outgoing and less popular, and they are more likely to smoke, use drugs, become sexually active, and engage less in academic pursuits (Dorn & Biro, 2011).

*Recently, experts have noted that children seem to be entering puberty earlier than in previous times. What factors might explain this change?*

**THE ADOLESCENT BRAIN**  Brain-imaging studies show important changes in the brain during adolescence (Raznahan & others, 2011). These changes focus on the earlier development of the amygdala, which involves emotion, and the later development of the prefrontal cortex, which is concerned with reasoning and decision making (Figure 8.7). These changes in the brain may help to explain why adolescents often display very strong emotions but may not successfully control these passions. Because of the relatively

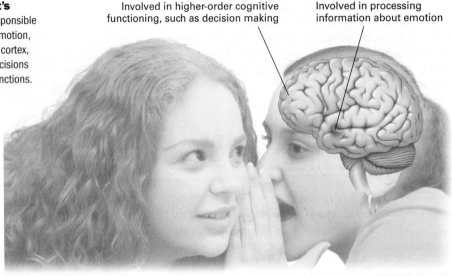

**FIGURE 8.7 Developmental Changes in the Adolescent's Brain** The amygdala, which is responsible for processing information about emotion, matures earlier than the prefrontal cortex, which is responsible for making decisions and other higher-order cognitive functions.

**Prefrontal Cortex**
Involved in higher-order cognitive functioning, such as decision making

**Amygdala**
Involved in processing information about emotion

slow development of the prefrontal cortex, which continues to mature into early adulthood, adolescents may lack the cognitive skills to control their impulses effectively. This developmental disjunction may account for increased risk taking and other problems in adolescence (Casey, Jones, & Somerville, 2011).

A major question is which comes first—biological changes in the brain or experiences that stimulate these changes? Consider a study in which the prefrontal cortex thickened and more brain connections formed when adolescents resisted peer pressure (Paus & others, 2008). Were the results due to biology or to experience? This correlational study cannot answer that question, and once again we encounter the fascinating truth about the brain: It shapes and is shaped by experience.

# Physical Development in Adulthood

As in other developmental periods, our bodies change during adulthood. Most of the changes that occur after adolescence involve declines in physical and perceptual abilities, as we now consider.

**PHYSICAL CHANGES IN EARLY ADULTHOOD** Most adults reach their peak physical development during their 20s and are the healthiest then. Early adulthood, however, is also the time when many physical skills begin to decline. The downward trend in strength and speed often is noticeable in the 30s. Another realm in which physical changes occur with age is in the ability to perceive the world. Hearing loss is very common with age. In fact, starting at about age 18, hearing begins a gradual decline.

**PHYSICAL CHANGES IN MIDDLE AND LATE ADULTHOOD** Many physical changes in the 40s or 50s involve changes in appearance. The skin has begun to wrinkle and sag because of the loss of fat and collagen in underlying tissues. Small, localized areas of skin pigmentation produce age spots, especially in areas exposed to sunlight such as the hands and face. Hair becomes

GLASBERGEN

*"After all these years, I'm finally comfortable in my own skin. Maybe it's because my skin is a lot bigger than it used to be!"*

Reprinted by permission of Randy Glasbergen. www.glasbergen.com

thinner and grayer due to a lower replacement rate and a decline in melanin production. Individuals lose height in middle age as a result of bone loss in the vertebrae, and many gain weight (Onwudiwe & others, 2011). Once individuals reach their 40s, age-related changes to their vision usually become apparent, especially difficulty in seeing things up close. The sense of taste can also be affected by age, as taste buds (described in Chapter 3) are less likely to be replaced.

For women, entering middle age means that menopause will soon occur. Usually in the late 40s or early 50s, a woman's menstrual periods cease. With menopause comes a dramatic drop in the ovaries' production of estrogen. Estrogen decline produces uncomfortable symptoms in some menopausal women, such as *hot flashes* (sudden, brief flushing of the skin and a feeling of elevated body temperature), nausea, fatigue, and rapid heartbeat. However, menopause overall is not the negative experience for most women it was once thought to be (Henderson, 2011; Judd, Hickey, & Bryant, 2011).

With age, for both men and women, a variety of bodily systems are likely to show the effects of wear and tear as the body becomes less and less able to repair damage and regenerate itself (Lamoureux & others, 2010). Physical strength declines and motor speed slows; bones may become more brittle (especially for women). Nearly every bodily system changes with age. Significantly, however, even as age is associated with some inevitable decline, important aspects of successful aging are within the person's control. For instance, a healthy diet and regular exercise can help to prevent or slow these effects. Regular physical activity can have wide-reaching benefits not only for physical health but for cognitive functioning as well (Kraft, 2012; Snowden & others, 2011). A recent study of older adults, for example, revealed that exercise increased the size of the hippocampus and improved memory (Erickson & others, 2011).

*How is your current behavior building a foundation for a healthy late adulthood? If your future self could time-travel to visit you, would he or she say "Thanks!"—or instead "What were you thinking?"*

One way older adults navigate the physical changes associated with age is through a process of changing their goals and developing new ways to engage in desired activities. Psychologists refer to this process as *selective optimization with compensation,* which means that older adults match their goals with their current abilities and compensate for declines by finding other ways to do the things they enjoy (Riediger & Freund, 2006). A 75-year-old who can no longer drive because of cataracts might become an expert on her city's train and bus system, for example.

On the island of Okinawa (part of Japan), individuals live longer than anywhere else in the world, and Okinawa has the world's highest prevalence of *centenarians*—people who live to 100 years or beyond. Examination of Okinawans' lives provides insights into their longevity. Specific factors are diet (they eat nutritious foods such as grains, fish, and vegetables); lifestyle (they are easygoing and experience low stress); community (Okinawans look out for one another and do not isolate or ignore older adults); activity (they lead active lifestyles, and many older adults continue to work); and spirituality (they find a sense of purpose in spiritual matters) (Willcox & others, 2008). Just as physical changes are interwoven with socioemotional processes in childhood and adolescence, so they are as human beings enter the later stages of life.

### Biological Theories of Aging

Of the many proposed biological theories of aging, three especially merit attention: cellular-clock theory, free-radical theory, and hormonal stress theory.

The *cellular-clock theory* is Leonard Hayflick's (1977) view that cells can divide a maximum of about 100 times and that, as we age, our cells become less capable of dividing. Hayflick found that cells extracted from adults in their 50s to 70s had divided fewer than 100 times. The total number of cell divisions was roughly related to the individual's age. Based on the way cells divide, Hayflick places the upper limit of the human life span at about 120 years.

**Do It!**

Have you ever thought about how long you are likely to live? Might you be able to live to be 100 years old? Type in the following on your Internet browser: The Living to Be 100 Life Expectancy Calculator. That will give you access to Dr. Thomas Perl's website (www.livingtobe100. com), where in only about 10 minutes you can answer questions about different aspects of your life that will provide a number indicating how long you are likely to live. A special benefit is that you also will get feedback about how to improve your number. Dr. Perl is currently conducting one of the largest studies of *centenarians* (those who live to be 100), and his life expectancy calculator is based on research that has been conducted on the factors that predict longevity.

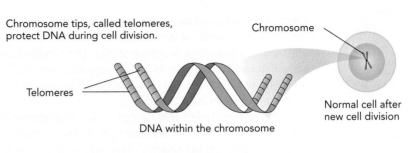

① Chromosome tips, called telomeres, protect DNA during cell division.

Chromosome

Telomeres

DNA within the chromosome

Normal cell after new cell division

② Telomeres shorten as cell undergoes many cell divisions.

Dividing cell

③ Ultimately, telomeres become too short, exposing DNA, which becomes damaged, and the cell dies. This is the normal life and death cycle of a cell.

Cell death

**FIGURE 8.8** **Telomeres and Aging** The photograph shows telomeres lighting up the tips of chromosomes. The figure illustrates how the telomeres shorten every time a cell divides. Eventually, after about 100 divisions, the telomeres are greatly reduced in length. As a result, the cell can no longer reproduce and it dies.

*People often say life's too short. But imagine living to be 120 years old. At age 70 you would still have 50 years to fill with life.*

*Participants paid over $3,000 to take part in this unusual study!*

Recently, scientists have been examining why cells lose their ability to divide. The answer may lie at the tips of chromosomes (Mather & others, 2011). Each time a cell divides, the *telomeres* protecting the ends of chromosomes shorten (Figure 8.8). After about 100 replications, the telomeres are dramatically reduced, and the cell no longer can reproduce (Prescott & others, 2011). There is considerable interest in discovering ways to maintain high levels of the telomere-extending enzyme—telomerase—through genetic manipulation of chemical telomerase activators. Meditation, described in Chapter 4, might also help to enhance telomerase activity. A recent study found that individuals who participated in a three-month meditation retreat (which included meditating for 6 hours a day) showed greater telomerase activity relative to a control group (Jacobs & others, 2011).

The *free-radical theory* of aging states that people age because unstable oxygen molecules known as *free radicals* are produced inside their cells. These molecules damage DNA and other cellular structures (Harman, 1956; Kregel & Zhang, 2006). The damage done by free radicals may lead to a range of disorders, including cancer and arthritis (Eckert, Schmitt, & Gotz, 2011).

*Hormonal stress theory* argues that aging in the body's hormonal system can lower resistance to stress and increase the likelihood of disease. As individuals age, the hormones stimulated by stress stay in the bloodstream longer than is the case for younger people. Prolonged, elevated levels of stress hormones are linked to increased risks for many diseases, including cardiovascular disease, cancer, and diabetes (Hefner, 2011). Recently, the hormonal stress theory of aging has focused on the role of chronic stress in diminishing the functioning of the immune system (Mahbub, Brubaker, & Kovacs, 2011).

***Aging and the Brain*** Just as the aging body has a greater capacity for renewal than previously thought, so does the aging brain. For decades, scientists believed that no new brain cells are generated past early childhood. However, researchers have recently discovered that adults can grow new brain cells throughout life (Curtis, Kam, & Faull,

2011), although evidence is limited to two areas of the brain: the hippocampus and the olfactory bulb (Ming & Song, 2011).

Even in late adulthood, the brain has remarkable repair capability (Couillard-Despres, Iglsseder, & Aigner, 2011; Gil-Mohapel & others, 2011; Zeng & others, 2011). Stanley Rapaport (1994) compared the brains of younger and older adults when they were engaged in the same tasks. The older adults' brains literally rewired themselves to compensate for losses. If one neuron was not up to the job, neighboring neurons helped to pick up the slack. Rapaport concluded that as brains age, they can shift responsibilities for a given task from one region to another.

Changes in lateralization may provide one type of adaptation in aging adults. *Lateralization* is the specialization of function in one hemisphere of the brain or the other. Using neuroimaging techniques, researchers have found that brain activity in the prefrontal cortex is lateralized less in older adults than in younger adults when they are engaging in cognitive tasks (Cabeza, 2002; Raw & others, 2012). For example, when younger adults are given the task of recognizing words they have previously seen, they process the information primarily in the right hemisphere, whereas older adults are more likely to use both hemispheres (Madden & others, 1999). The decrease in lateralization in older adults might play a compensatory role in the aging brain (Angel & others, 2011). That is, using both hemispheres may improve the cognitive functioning of older adults.

Research from the Nun Study (described in Chapter 1) supports the role of experience in maintaining brain function. Recall that this study involves nearly 700 nuns in a convent in Mankato, Minnesota (Snowdon, 2003, 2007) (Figure 8.9). By examining the nuns' donated brains as well as others, neuroscientists have documented the aging brain's ability to grow and change. Even the oldest Mankato nuns lead intellectually challenging lives, and neuroscientists believe that stimulating mental activities increase dendritic branching. Keeping the brain actively engaged in challenging activities can help to slow the effects of age, as we noted in Chapter 6.

In sum, in the physical domain across the life span, we see a dramatic pattern of growth and change in infancy, childhood, and adolescence followed by leveling off and decline in adulthood. How might this progression influence (and be influenced by) the way the developing person thinks about himself or herself and the world? To examine this question, we turn to the cognitive domain of human development.

**FIGURE 8.9  The Brains of the Mankato Nuns** At 95 years old, Nun Study participant Sister Nicolette Welter remains an active contributing member of her community of sisters. (*Inset*) A neuroscientist holds a brain donated by one of the Mankato Nun Study participants.

## self-quiz

1. The first two weeks after conception are referred to as the
   A. fetal period.
   B. germinal period.
   C. embryonic period.
   D. zygotic period.

2. Puberty is generally characterized by all of the following *except*
   A. a decrease in concentrations of certain hormones.
   B. a dramatic increase in height and weight.
   C. an increase in idealistic and abstract thinking.
   D. the development of thought.

3. The hormone associated with girls' breast, uterine, and skeletal development during puberty is
   A. testosterone.
   B. estradiol.
   C. androgen.
   D. norepinephrine.

**APPLY IT!** 4. Gabriel's grandfather has always been a fitness nut. Even at age 83, he continues to work out, lifting weights, swimming, and taking pride in his physique. After his grandfather beats him in a swimming race, Gabriel rolls his eyes and comments that all this work makes no sense at this point in his grandfather's life. Aside from calling him on his sour grapes, what would you say about Gabriel's viewpoint?
   A. Gabriel is right. All that working out is probably inappropriate and even unhealthy for someone in his 80s.
   B. Gabriel is wrong, because if his grandfather stays active, he can completely avoid all of the physical changes associated with age.
   C. Gabriel is wrong. His grandfather's hard work might be paying off in a variety of ways, including his physical health and his cognitive and emotional functioning generally.
   D. Gabriel is right, and his grandfather seems to be in denial about the effects of age on physical development.

# 3 Cognitive Development

*Cognitive development* refers to how thought, intelligence, and language processes change as people mature. *Cognition* refers to the operation of thinking and also to our cognitive skills and abilities. In this section, you will encounter one of the biggest names in all of psychology, Jean Piaget, who presented a theory of cognitive development that has had lasting impact on the field. We examine Piaget's contributions and also consider more recent research on the relationship between cognitive abilities and age.

## Cognitive Development from Childhood into Adulthood

The Swiss developmental psychologist Jean Piaget (1896–1980) traced cognitive development through childhood into adulthood. Let's begin by reviewing Piaget's approach.

**Jean Piaget (1896–1980)**
*Piaget, the famous Swiss psychologist, changed the way we think about the development of children's minds.*

**PIAGET'S THEORY OF COGNITIVE DEVELOPMENT**   In Piaget's view, human beings use schemas to make sense of their experience. As we considered in Chapter 6, a *schema* is a mental concept or framework that organizes information and provides a structure for interpreting it. Schemas are expressed as various behaviors and skills that the child can exercise in relation to objects or situations. For example, sucking is an early, simple schema. Later and more complex schemas include licking, blowing, crawling, and hiding. In adulthood, schemas may represent more complex expectations and beliefs about the world.

Piaget (1952) described two processes responsible for how people use and adapt their schemas:

**assimilation**
An individual's incorporation of new information into existing knowledge.

- **Assimilation** occurs when individuals incorporate new information into existing knowledge. As a result of assimilation, the person, when faced with a new experience, applies old ways of doing things. For infants, this might involve applying the schema of sucking to whatever new object they encounter. For an adolescent, it might mean using the skills learned while playing video games to drive a car. For an adult, it might mean solving a conflict with a spouse using ways that worked in the past with friends or previous romantic partners.

**accommodation**
An individual's adjustment of his or her schemas to new information.

- **Accommodation** occurs when individuals adjust their schemas to new information. Accommodation means that rather than using one's old ways of doing things, a new experience promotes new ways of dealing with experience. Existing schemas can be changed and new schemas can be developed in response to new experiences. For example, after several months of experience, the infant who has been sticking everything in her mouth might begin to accommodate the sucking schema by being more selective with it. The adolescent who has typically gone with the flow of social pressure might develop a new way of dealing with peer pressure by standing up for his or her beliefs. For an adult, accommodation may mean rethinking old strategies for problem solving when a new challenge, such as the loss of a job or the onset of illness, presents itself.

*So, we assimilate experiences into schemas and accommodate schemas to experience.*

**PIAGET'S STAGES OF COGNITIVE DEVELOPMENT**   According to Piaget, we go through four stages in understanding the world (Figure 8.10). Each stage involves a qualitatively different way of making sense of the world than the one before it.

| **Sensorimotor Stage** | **Preoperational Stage** | **Concrete Operational Stage** | **Formal Operational Stage** |
|---|---|---|---|
| The infant constructs an understanding of the world by coordinating sensory experiences with physical actions. An infant progresses from reflexive, instinctual action at birth to the beginning of symbolic thought toward the end of the stage. | The child begins to represent the world with words and images. These words and images reflect increased symbolic thinking and go beyond the connection of sensory information and physical action. | The child can now reason logically about concrete events and classify objects into different sets. | The adolescent reasons in more abstract, idealistic, and logical ways. |
| **Birth to 2 Years of Age** | **2 to 7 Years of Age** | **7 to 11 Years of Age** | **11 Years of Age Through Adulthood** |

**FIGURE 8.10** **Piaget's Four Stages of Cognitive Development** Jean Piaget described how human beings, through development, become ever more sophisticated thinkers about the world.

*Sensorimotor Stage*    Piaget's first stage, the **sensorimotor stage,** lasts from birth to about 2 years of age. In this stage, infants construct an understanding of the world by coordinating sensory experiences (such as seeing and hearing) with motor (physical) actions—hence the term *sensorimotor*. As newborns they have little more than reflexive patterns with which to work. By the end of this stage, 2-year-olds show complex sensorimotor patterns and are beginning to use symbols or words in their thinking.

**Object permanence** is Piaget's term for the crucial accomplishment of understanding that objects continue to exist even when they cannot directly be seen, heard, or touched. Piaget believed that "out of sight" literally was "out of mind" for very young infants. Piaget studied object permanence by showing an infant an interesting toy and then covering the toy with a blanket. Piaget reasoned that if infants understood that the toy still existed, they would try to uncover it (Figure 8.11). Piaget thought the development of object permanence continues throughout the sensorimotor period.

*Preoperational Stage*    Piaget's second stage of cognitive development, the **preoperational stage,** lasts from approximately 2 to 7 years of age. Preoperational thought is more symbolic than sensorimotor thought. In preschool years, children begin to represent their world with words, images, and drawings. Thus, their thoughts begin to exceed simple connections of sensorimotor information and physical action.

The type of symbolic thinking that children are able to accomplish during this stage is limited. They still cannot perform what Piaget called *operations,* by which he meant mental representations that are "reversible." Preoperational children have difficulty understanding that reversing an action may restore the original conditions from which the action began.

A well-known test of whether a child can think "operationally" is to present a child with two identical beakers, A and B, filled with liquid to the same height

**sensorimotor stage**
Piaget's first stage of cognitive development, lasting from birth to about 2 years of age, during which infants construct an understanding of the world by coordinating sensory experiences with motor (physical) actions.

**object permanence**
Piaget's term for the crucial accomplishment of understanding that objects and events continue to exist even when they cannot directly be seen, heard, or touched.

**preoperational stage**
Piaget's second stage of cognitive development, lasting from about 2 to 7 years of age, during which thought is more symbolic than sensorimotor thought.

*With object permanence, the infant starts thinking about future events, as in "When will I see Mommy again?" The child can take comfort in the knowledge that Mommy will be back. Object permanence also means getting a first taste of the human capacity for longing—for missing someone who is not there.*

**FIGURE 8.11** **Object Permanence** Piaget regarded object permanence as one of infancy's landmark cognitive accomplishments. For this 5-month-old boy, out of sight is literally out of mind. The infant looks at the toy dog (*left*), but when his view of the toy is blocked (*right*), he does not search for it. > *If this boy fails to try to find the toy dog, Piaget assumed that meant he does not know it still exists. What other factors might explain his lack of looking for the toy?* > *What motor skills are necessary for the little boy to perform this behavior?* > *What kinds of goals are required for him to seek out the toy?*

(Figure 8.12). Next to them is a third beaker (C). Beaker C is tall and thin, whereas beakers A and B are short and wide. The liquid is poured from B into C, and the child is asked whether the amounts in A and C are the same. The 4-year-old child invariably says that the amount of liquid in the tall, thin beaker (C) is greater than that in the short, wide beaker (A). The 8-year-old child consistently says the amounts are the same. The 4-year-old child, a preoperational thinker, cannot mentally reverse the pouring action; that is, she cannot imagine the liquid going back from container C to container B. Piaget said that such a child has not grasped the concept of *conservation,* a belief in the permanence of certain attributes of objects despite superficial changes.

The child's thought in the preoperational stage is egocentric. This does not mean that the child is self-centered or arrogant but that preoperational children cannot put

**FIGURE 8.12** **Piaget's Conservation Task** The beaker test determines whether a child can think operationally—that is, can mentally reverse action and understand conservation of the substance. (*a*) Two identical beakers are presented to the child, each containing the same amount of liquid. As the child watches, the experimenter pours the liquid from B into C, which is taller and thinner than A and B. (*b*) The experimenter then asks the child whether beakers A and C have the same amount of liquid. The preoperational child says no. When asked to point to the beaker that has more liquid, the child points to the tall, thin one.

themselves in someone else's shoes. They cannot take another person's mental states into account.

Preoperational thinking is also intuitive. This means that preoperational children make judgments based on gut feelings rather than logic. In reaching a basic level of operational understanding, the child progresses to the third of Piaget's cognitive stages.

### Concrete Operational Stage

**concrete operational stage**
Piaget's third stage of cognitive development, lasting from about 7 to 11 years of age, during which the individual uses operations and replaces intuitive reasoning with logical reasoning in concrete situations.

Piaget's **concrete operational stage** (7 to 11 years of age) involves using operations and replacing intuitive reasoning with logical reasoning in concrete situations. Children in the concrete operational stage can successfully complete the beaker task described above. They are able to mentally imagine the operation of reversing the pouring of the liquid back into the wide beaker. Many of the concrete operations identified by Piaget are related to the properties of objects. For instance, when playing with Play-doh, the child in the concrete operational stage realizes that *the amount of Play-doh is not changed by changing its shape*. One important skill at this stage of reasoning is the ability to classify or divide things into different sets or subsets and to consider their interrelations. (You might remember learning the childhood song that goes, "One of these things is not like the others," which effectively aimed to coax you into concrete operations.)

Concrete operational thought involves operational thinking, classification skills, and logical reasoning in concrete but not hypothetical contexts. According to Piaget, this kind of abstract, logical reasoning occurs in the fourth, and final, cognitive stage.

### Formal Operational Stage

Individuals enter the **formal operational stage** of cognitive development at 11 to 15 years of age. This stage continues through the adult years. Formal operational thought is more abstract and logical than concrete operational thought. Most importantly, formal operational thinking includes thinking about things that are not concrete, making predictions, and using logic to come up with hypotheses about the future.

**formal operational stage**
Piaget's fourth stage of cognitive development, which begins at age 11 to 15 and continues through adulthood; it features thinking about things that are not concrete, making predictions, and using logic to come up with hypotheses about the future.

Unlike elementary schoolchildren, adolescents can conceive of hypothetical, purely abstract possibilities. This type of thinking is called *idealistic* because it involves comparing how things are to how they might be. Adolescents also think more logically. They begin to think more as a scientist thinks, devising plans to solve problems and systematically testing solutions. Piaget called this type of problem solving *hypothetical-deductive reasoning*. The phrase denotes adolescents' ability to develop hypotheses, or best hunches, about ways to solve a problem such as an algebraic equation. It also denotes their ability to systematically deduce, or come to a conclusion about, the best path for solving the problem. In contrast, before adolescence, children are more likely to solve problems by trial and error.

In summary, over the course of Piaget's four developmental stages, a person progresses from sensorimotor cognition to abstract, idealistic, and logical thought. Piaget based his stages on careful observation of children's behavior, but there is always room to evaluate theory and research. Let's consider the current thinking about Piaget's theory of cognitive development.

### EVALUATING AND EXPANDING ON PIAGET'S THEORY

Piaget opened up a new way of looking at how children's minds develop. We owe him for a long list of masterful concepts that have enduring power and fascination. These include the concepts of schemas, assimilation, accommodation, cognitive stages, object permanence, egocentrism, and conservation. We owe Piaget, for example, for the currently accepted vision of children as active, constructive thinkers who play a role in their own development. Nevertheless, just as other psychological theories have been criticized and amended, so have Piaget's.

### Baillargeon: An Alternative View of Object Permanence

As methods have improved for testing infants and children, researchers have found that many cognitive

## The Joy of the Toy

When kids are playing, they are often playing with toys. Toys have been around for a very long time. Archaeologists have dated the first toy, an ancient Egyptian doll made of paper, cloth, and string, to 2000 B.C.E. Today, toys are a huge U.S. industry. From 2004 to 2010, Americans spent nearly *$22 billion* on toys every year (NPD Group, 2011), and nearly half of Americans have toys on their holiday shopping lists (Harris Interactive, 2011).

Toy manufacturers are well aware of the importance of understanding developmental psychology when designing toys. As noted by toy designer Barry Kudrowitz (quoted in Benson, 2006), "Before brainstorming, the designer should know what types of behaviors are typical for that age group; . . . the social, mental, and physical abilities of the age group, and what types of play are most common." Developmental psychology courses are required in the toy design degree program at the Fashion Institute of Technology in New York City, where the first U.S. toy design program was founded in the 1980s.

Toy manufacturers conduct a great deal of research examining toys and children's cognitive and perceptual abilities. Outside the toy industry, psychologists have investigated such topics as the effects of advertising on toy preferences and the influence of toys on children's body images. They have found, for example, that boys are more susceptible than girls to gender in ads (Pike & Jennings, 2005) and that exposure to Barbie can predict lowered body image among girls (Dittmar, Halliwell, & Ive, 2006).

The value of a toy lies in its capacity to capture a child's imagination. How many parents have stood by in shock as their child tossed aside an expensive new toy and played for hours with the box it came in? In that box, the child may have discovered a house, a cave, a car, or a spaceship. In 2011, *the blanket* was inducted into the Toy Hall of Fame. Every kid knows that if you have a blanket, you've got a tent, a superhero cape, and a magic carpet—not to mention a great cover for reading by flashlight when you are supposed to be sleeping.

abilities emerge earlier in children than Piaget thought (Sloane, Baillargeon, & Premack, 2012). Piaget's object permanence task, for example, has been criticized for not giving infants a chance to show their stuff. Rather than indicating that small children do not have a sense of object permanence, such a task might be demonstrating that these children simply are not able to enact the plan of getting the toy back.

Indeed, Renee Baillargeon has documented that infants as young as 3 months of age know that objects continue to exist even when hidden, and that even these very young infants have expectations about objects in the world that seem quite a bit more sophisticated than Piaget imagined (Baillargeon, Scott, & He, 2010; Baillargeon & others, 2012; Luo, Kaufman, & Baillargeon, 2009).

*These researchers also monitored infant facial expressions. Three-month-old jaws dropping in shock? Too cute.*

In one study, researchers showed 3-month-old infants a puppet show of Minnie Mouse (Luo & Baillargeon, 2005). In the center of the stage was a flat cardboard cutout of a castle, with an open door in the middle. Minnie entered stage right and proceeded toward the castle, disappearing behind. When Minnie went behind the castle walls from one side, the infants looked for her to come out on the other side. Furthermore, if, as she made her way behind the castle walls, Minnie did not appear in the open doorway, infants as young as 3 months were surprised. Not only did they realize that Minnie still existed, but they also had expectations about where she was heading, and they believed that she certainly should appear in the door as she passed behind the castle. Also, memory and other forms of symbolic activity occur much earlier than Piaget thought possible (Sloane, Baillargeon, & Premack, 2012).

### *Vygotsky: Cognitive Development in Cultural Context*

Piaget did not think that culture and education play important roles in children's cognitive development. For Piaget, the child's active interaction with the physical world was all that was needed to go through these stages. The Russian psychologist Lev Vygotsky (1962) took a different approach, recognizing that cognitive development is an interpersonal process that happens in a cultural context.

Vygotsky thought of children as apprentice thinkers who develop as they interact in dialogue with more knowledgeable others, such as parents and teachers. Vygotsky believed that these expert thinkers spur cognitive development by interacting with a child in a way that is just above the level of sophistication the child has mastered. In effect, these interactions provide *scaffolding* that allows the child's cognitive abilities to be built higher and higher.

Teachers and parents, in other words, provide a framework for thinking that is always just at a level the child can strive to attain. Furthermore, in Vygotsky's view, the goal of cognitive development is to learn the skills that will allow the individual to be competent in his or her particular culture. These expert thinkers are not simply guiding a child into a level of cognitive sophistication, but also, along the way, sharing with the child important aspects of culture, such as language and customs. For Vygotsky, a child is not simply learning to think about the world—he or she is learning to think about *his or her own world*.

> *Scaffolding is a way of learning that we use throughout life. Whenever we interact with someone who has more expertise, we have a new scaffold to climb.*

### *Revisionist Views of Adolescent and Adult Cognition*

Researchers have also expanded on Piaget's view of adolescent cognition. In addition to advancing into Piaget's stage of formal operational thinking, another characteristic of adolescent thinking, especially in early adolescence, is egocentrism. Although egocentrism has been noted as an aspect of children's cognition, adolescent egocentrism involves the belief that others are as preoccupied with the adolescent as he or she is, that one is unique, and that one is invincible (meaning unable to be harmed) (Albert & Steinberg, 2011). Egocentrism at this developmental stage is revealed, for example, when an adolescent perceives others to be noticing and watching her or him more than is the case. Think of the teenage girl who says, "My mother has no idea about how much pain I'm going through. She has never been hurt like me! Why did he break up with me?"

> *At every age we put our own special stamp on egocentrism. Have you ever noticed that each of your instructors seems to think that his or her class is the only one you're taking?*

The sense of invincibility is the most dangerous aspect of adolescent egocentrism. This belief may lead to behaviors such as drag racing, drug use, and unsafe sex. In one study of sixth- through twelfth-graders, feeling invincible was linked to risky behaviors such as smoking cigarettes, drinking alcohol, and delinquency (Aalsma, Lapsley, & Flannery, 2006).

Just as Piaget may have underestimated infant cognition, he may have overestimated some of adolescents' and adults' cognitive achievements. Formal operational thought does not emerge as consistently and universally in early adolescence as Piaget envisioned (Kuhn, 2008), and many adolescents and adults do not reason as logically as Piaget proposed. It may be that even in adulthood, we do not use logical reasoning to make decisions but rather to justify decisions that are the product of the intuitive hunches that characterize cognition in childhood (Mercier & Sperber, 2011).

Finally, developmental psychologists interested in cognition have noted that cognitive changes can occur *after* Piaget's formal operations stage. For Piaget, formal operational thought is the highest level of thinking, and he argued that no new qualitative changes in cognition take place in adulthood. Developmental psychologists, however, in expanding their focus to the entire life span, have tracked the ways that cognitive skills might change throughout adulthood.

# Cognitive Processes in Adulthood

Although Piaget did not recognize changes in cognitive processes in adulthood, researchers have examined how these processes might change throughout adult life. When, during your life journey, do you think your cognitive skills are likely to peak?

**COGNITION IN EARLY ADULTHOOD** Between the ages of 20 and 30, perceptual speed is at its peak. Individuals in early adulthood have quick reflexes and are better able to respond to sensory input than at any other time in adulthood (Schaie, 2009). Some cognitive abilities increase between the ages of 20 and 30, as adults accrue greater capacities for reasoning and verbal memory (Schaie, 2009). Cognitive abilities in early adulthood may serve as a kind of reserve that promotes positive development throughout adulthood (Bielak & others, 2012). Longitudinal research shows that cognitive abilities in early adulthood predict better physical (Phillips & others, 2011) and psychological (Gale & others, 2008) outcomes in later life. How can people in early adulthood maximize their cognitive resources? Recall from Chapter 7 that by engaging in challenging tasks, by thinking outside the box, and by exposure to different cultures we can optimize our cognitive skills.

**COGNITION IN MIDDLE ADULTHOOD** What happens to cognitive skills in middle adulthood? The answer depends on the methods researchers use to address this question. We have seen that in cross-sectional studies, a number of people of different ages are assessed at one point in time. By examining how the ages of these individuals relate to the cognitive abilities measured, researchers can find out whether younger people differ from older people. Research using cross-sectional designs has compared individuals in early and middle adulthood on two forms of cognitive abilities: *crystallized intelligence,* an individual's accumulated information and verbal skills, and *fluid intelligence,* the ability to reason abstractly. The results show that crystallized intelligence is higher in middle adulthood compared to early adulthood, but fluid intelligence is higher in early adulthood compared to middle adulthood (Horn & Cattell, 1967).

Recall that in contrast to cross-sectional research, a longitudinal study assesses the same participants repeatedly over a lengthy period. A longitudinal study of intelligence in middle adulthood might consist of giving the same intelligence test to the same individuals over a 20-year time span, when they are 40, 50, and 60 years of age. Whether data on intelligence are collected cross-sectionally or longitudinally can make a difference in the conclusions we draw about cognitive ability in middle adulthood (Schaie, 2009).

K. Warner Schaie is conducting an extensive longitudinal study of intellectual abilities in adulthood. Five hundred individuals were tested initially in 1956 and have been tested repeatedly over the years (Schaie, 1994, 2007). New waves of participants are added periodically. Schaie (2006) has measured a host of different cognitive abilities, and the results of his studies are shown in Figure 8.13. Schaie found middle adulthood to be a time of peak performance for aspects of both crystallized intelligence (vocabulary) and fluid intelligence (spatial orientation and inductive reasoning). Based on the longitudinal data he has collected so far, Schaie (2006, 2007) concludes that *middle* adulthood, not early adulthood, is the developmental time frame when many people reach their peak for a range of intellectual skills.

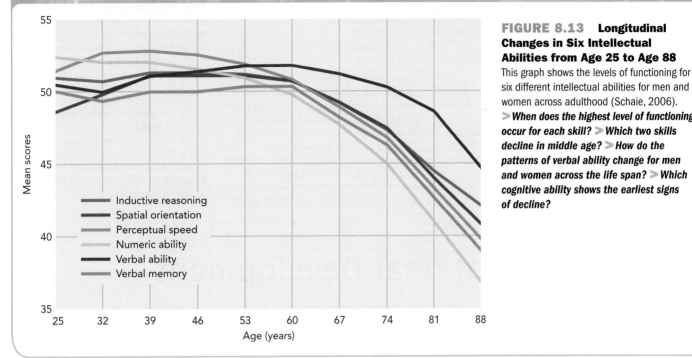

**FIGURE 8.13** **Longitudinal Changes in Six Intellectual Abilities from Age 25 to Age 88** This graph shows the levels of functioning for six different intellectual abilities for men and women across adulthood (Schaie, 2006). *> When does the highest level of functioning occur for each skill? > Which two skills decline in middle age? > How do the patterns of verbal ability change for men and women across the life span? > Which cognitive ability shows the earliest signs of decline?*

## COGNITION IN LATE ADULTHOOD

Many contemporary psychologists conclude that a number of dimensions of intelligence decline in late adulthood but that some are maintained or may even increase (see Figure 8.13). A consistent finding is that when the speed of processing information is involved, older adults do not perform as well as their younger counterparts. Decline in the speed of processing is apparent in middle-aged adults and becomes more pronounced in older adults (Salthouse, 2012).

Older adults also tend to not do as well as younger adults in most aspects of memory (Salthouse, 2012). In the area of memory involving knowledge of the world (for instance, the capital of Peru or the chemical formula for water), older adults usually take longer than younger adults to remember the information, but they often are able to retrieve it (Singh-Manoux & others, 2012). Further, in the important area of memory in which individuals manipulate and assemble information to solve problems and make decisions, decline occurs in older adults.

Some aspects of cognition might improve with age. One such area is **wisdom,** expert knowledge about the practical aspects of life (Taylor, Bates, & Webster, 2011). Wisdom may increase with age because of the buildup of life experiences, but individual variations characterize people throughout their lives (Staudinger & Gluck, 2011). Thus, not every older person has wisdom, and some young people are wise beyond their years.

Even for those aspects of cognitive aging that decline, older adults can improve their cognitive skills with training (Schaie, 2006; Willis & Schaie, 2005). Physical activity can help to ward off cognitive declines. One study showed that residents of a retirement community who rode a stationary bike as part of a video game and virtual reality tour showed less cognitive decline than those who engaged in traditional exercise or none at all (Anderson-Hanley & others, 2012). Still, many experts conclude that older adults are less able to adapt than younger adults and thus are limited with respect to how much they can improve their cognitive skills (Salthouse, 2012; Stanford Center for Longevity, 2012).

**wisdom**
Expert knowledge about the practical aspects of life.

*In younger individuals wisdom may come at a cost. They might gain wisdom from living through difficult life experiences.*

1. Of the following activities, the one that uses crystallized intelligence is
   A. reciting facts about the Civil War.
   B. solving a jigsaw puzzle.
   C. using a mathematical formula to solve a problem.
   D. visualizing the way an object would look if rotated.

2. Most cognitive skills reach their peak during _____, and most show decline during _____
   A. early adulthood; middle adulthood.
   B. middle adulthood; late adulthood.
   C. adolescence; early adulthood.
   D. adolescence; middle adulthood.

3. Vygotsky stressed that cognitive development is an interpersonal process that happens in a _____ context.
   A. historical
   B. physical
   C. cultural
   D. positive

APPLY IT! 4. Tyrone is babysitting his younger cousins, who are ages 3, 4, and 9. For lunch, each child will be drinking apple juice, which they all love. Tyrone has only three serving cups—one that is short and wide, and two that are tall and thin. Although Tyrone pours the same amount of juice into all the cups, the younger kids fuss and fight over who gets stuck with the short, wide cup. The 9-year-old shrugs and takes the wide cup. Tyrone later proclaims, "Those other two kids are really spoiled brats! Thank goodness the oldest is not so selfish." Which of the following best applies to Tyrone's conclusion?
   A. Tyrone is right—young kids are more likely to be spoiled and whiny.
   B. Tyrone does not understand that the younger kids do not recognize that the amount of juice in the cups is the same. The 9-year-old is not being unselfish; he or she knows the amounts are the same.
   C. The 9-year-old probably does not understand that the wider cup contains the same amount of juice as the other two.
   D. Tyrone probably got an *A* in Developmental Psychology.

# 4 Socioemotional Development

So far we have examined the developmental course of physical and cognitive changes. How do our social and emotional lives change through childhood and adulthood? Recall that *socioemotional processes* involve changes in an individual's social relationships, emotional life, and personal qualities.

## Socioemotional Development in Infancy

Emotionally speaking, an infant does not enter the world as a blank slate. When we observe the newborns behind the window of a hospital nursery, one thing is clear: Humans differ from one another in terms of their emotional demeanor from the very beginnings of life. Some are easygoing, and some are prone to distress. Furthermore, in the earliest days of life, infants encounter a social network that will play an important role as they develop their sense of self and the world. To begin exploring the socioemotional aspects of development, we focus first on these ingredients of emotional and social processes that are present very early in life—infant temperament and attachment.

**temperament**
An individual's behavioral style and characteristic ways of responding.

**TEMPERAMENT**  **Temperament** refers to an individual's behavioral style and characteristic ways of responding. For infants, temperament centers on their emotionality and ways of reacting to stimuli in the environment. Does the infant look with interest at a new toy, or shy away? Is he or she easily soothed after an upset? Answers to these questions provide information about infant temperament.

There are a number of ways to think about infant temperament. For example, psychiatrists Alexander Chess and Stella Thomas (1977) identified three basic types of temperament in children:

> *Culture can influence the meaning of a difficult child. In cultures where women are expected to spend all of their time and energy catering to their children, a "difficult" child might be just the ticket.*

- The *easy child* generally is in a positive mood, quickly establishes regular routines in infancy, and easily adapts to new experiences.

- The *difficult child* tends to be fussy and to cry frequently and engages in irregular daily routines.

- The *slow-to-warm-up child* has a low activity level, tends to withdraw from new situations, and is very cautious in the face of new experiences.

Other researchers have suggested that we should think about infants as being high or low on different dimensions, such as *effortful control* or *self-regulation* (controlling arousal and not being easily agitated), *inhibition* (being shy and showing distress in an

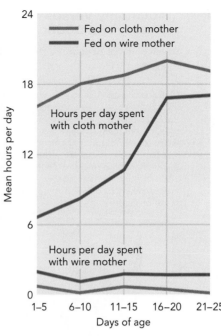

FIGURE 8.14
**Contact Time with Wire and Cloth Surrogate Mothers** Regardless of whether the infant monkeys were fed by a wire or a cloth mother, they overwhelmingly preferred to spend contact time with the cloth mother.

unfamiliar situation), and *negative affectivity* (tending to be frustrated or sad) (Kagan, 2008). Thus, psychologists have not reached agreement about the core dimensions of temperament (Evans & Rothbart, 2009). The emotional characteristics that a child brings into the world serve as a foundation for later personality (Casalin & others, 2012; Komsi & others, 2006), and the child's earliest social bonds might set the stage for later social relationships.

**ATTACHMENT**   Just as infants require nutrition and shelter, they need warm social interaction to survive and develop. A classic study by Harry Harlow (1958) demonstrates the essential importance of warm contact. Harlow separated infant monkeys from their mothers at birth and placed them in cages in which they had access to two artificial "mothers." One of the mothers was a physically cold wire mother; the other was a warm, fuzzy cloth mother (the "contact comfort" mother). Each mother could be outfitted with a feeding mechanism. Half of the infant monkeys were fed by the wire mother, half by the cloth mother. The infant monkeys nestled close to the cloth mother and spent little time on the wire one, even if it was the wire mother that gave them milk (Figure 8.14). When afraid, the infant monkeys ran to the comfy mom. This study clearly demonstrates that what the researchers described as "contact comfort," not feeding, is crucial to the attachment of an infant to its caregiver.

*As skeptical scientists, psychologists needed Harlow to demonstrate that even if the warm, snuggly mother didn't provide food, she was still a source of comfort.*

**Infant attachment** is the close emotional bond between an infant and his or her caregiver. British psychiatrist John Bowlby (1969, 1989) theorized that the infant and the mother instinctively form an attachment. In Bowlby's view, the newborn comes into the world equipped to stimulate the caregiver to respond; it cries, clings, smiles, and coos. Bowlby thought that our early relationships with our caregiver are internalized so that they serve as our schemas for our sense of self and the social world. Many developmental psychologists concur that attachment during the first year provides an important foundation for later development (Sroufe, Coffino, & Carlson, 2010).

Mary Ainsworth devised a way to study differences in children's attachment, called the *strange situation test* (Ainsworth, 1979; Ainsworth & others, 1978). In this procedure, caregivers leave infants alone with a stranger and then return. Reponses of children to this situation are used to classify their attachment style. Ainsworth used the term **secure attachment**

**infant attachment**
The close emotional bond between an infant and its caregiver.

**secure attachment**
The ways that infants use their caregiver, usually their mother, as a secure base from which to explore the environment.

| **Trust Versus Mistrust** | **Autonomy Versus Shame and Doubt** | **Initiative Versus Guilt** | **Industry Versus Inferiority** |
|---|---|---|---|
| **Developmental period:** Infancy (Birth to 1½ years) | **Developmental period:** Toddlerhood (1½ to 3 years) | **Developmental period:** Early childhood (preschool years, ages 3–5) | **Developmental period:** Middle and late childhood (elementary school years, 6 years–puberty) |
| **Characteristics:** A sense of trust requires a feeling of physical comfort and minimal amount of fear about the future. Infants' basic needs are met by responsive, sensitive caregivers. | **Characteristics:** After gaining trust in their caregivers, infants start to discover that they have a will of their own. They assert their sense of autonomy, or independence. They realize their will. If infants are restrained too much or punished too harshly, they are likely to develop a sense of shame and doubt. | **Characteristics:** As preschool children encounter a widening social world, they are challenged more and need to develop more purposeful behavior to cope with these challenges. Children are now asked to assume more responsibility. Uncomfortable guilt feelings may arise, though, if the children are irresponsible and are made to feel too anxious. | **Characteristics:** At no other time are children more enthusiastic than at the end of early childhood's period of expansive imagination. As children move into the elementary school years, they direct their energy toward mastering knowledge and intellectual skills. The danger at this stage involves feeling incompetent and unproductive. |

**FIGURE 8.15**

**Erikson's Eight Stages of Psychosocial Development** Erikson changed the way psychologists think about development by tracing the process of growth over the entire life span.

*EXPERIENCE IT!*
Attachment

to describe how infants use the caregiver, usually the mother, as a secure base from which to explore the environment. In the strange situation, the secure infant is upset when the mother leaves, but calms down and appears happy to see her when she returns. Infants who are securely attached are more likely to have mothers who are responsive and accepting and who express affection toward them than are infants who are insecurely attached (Behrens, Parker, & Haltigan, 2011). The securely attached infant moves freely away from the mother but also keeps tabs on her by periodically glancing at her. An insecurely attached infant, in contrast, avoids the mother or is ambivalent toward her. In the strange situation, such an infant might not even notice the mother has gone (sometimes called *avoidant* or *dismissive attachment style*), or conversely might respond with intense distress, only to rage at the mother when she returns (sometimes called *anxious* or *preoccupied attachment style*).

One criticism of attachment theory is that it does not adequately account for cultural variations (van IJzendoorn & Bakermans-Kranenburg, 2010). For example, in some cultures infants show strong attachment to many people, not just to their primary caregiver (Rothbaum & others, 2000, 2007). Infants in agricultural societies tend to form attachments to older siblings who are assigned a major responsibility for younger siblings' care.

Another critique of attachment theory is that it may not account for temperamental differences among infants that might color the attachment relationship. In addition, caregivers and infants likely share genetic characteristics, and it might be that the attachment relationship is really a product of these shared genes. Despite such criticisms there is ample evidence that secure attachment is important to development (Sroufe, Coffino, & Carlson, 2010).

Equipped with the key basic ingredients of temperament and attachment, how does a human being develop in the socioemotional domain? This question was addressed by Erik Erikson, who devised a theory of what he called psychosocial development. Erikson's

| Identity Versus Identity Confusion | Intimacy Versus Isolation | Generativity Versus Stagnation | Integrity Versus Despair |
|---|---|---|---|
| **Developmental period:** Adolescence (10–20 years) | **Developmental period:** Eary adulthood (20s, 30s) | **Developmental period:** Middle adulthood (40s, 50s) | **Developmental period:** Late adulthood (60s– ) |
| **Characteristics:** Individuals are faced with finding out who they are, what they are all about, and where they are going in life. An important dimension is the exploration of alternative solutions to roles. Career exploration is important. | **Characteristics:** Individuals face the developmental task of forming intimate relationships with others. Erikson described intimacy as finding oneself yet losing oneself in another person. | **Characteristics:** A chief concern is to assist the younger generation in developing and leading useful lives. | **Characteristics:** Individuals look back and evaluate what they have done with their lives. The retrospective glances can be either positive (integrity) or negative (despair). |

theory has powerfully guided thinking about how human beings' social and emotional capacities develop throughout the entire life span.

# Erikson's Theory of Socioemotional Development

The life-span development theory of the influential psychologist Erik Erikson (1902–1994), who trained as a psychoanalyst under Sigmund Freud, proposed eight psychosocial stages of development from infancy through late adulthood. In calling the stages *psychosocial*, Erikson meant to emphasize how a person's psychological life is embedded in and shaped by social relationships and challenges faced by the developing person. Figure 8.15 illustrates all of Erikson's stages.

From Erikson's (1968) perspective, each stage represents the developmental task that the individual must master at a particular place in the life span. According to Erikson, these developmental tasks are represented by two possible outcomes, such as trust versus mistrust (Erikson's first stage). If an infant's physical and emotional needs are well taken care of, he or she will experience an enduring sense of trust in others. If, however, these needs are frustrated, the person might carry concerns about trust throughout life, with bits of this unfinished business being reflected in the rest of the stages. For Erikson, each stage is a turning point with two opposing possible outcomes—one, greater personal competence; the other, greater weakness and vulnerability. Using Erikson's stages as a guide, let's consider the various ways that human beings develop in terms of their capacities for interpersonal relationships and emotional well-being.

**Erik Erikson (1902–1994)**
*Erikson generated one of the most important developmental theories of the twentieth century.*

## SOCIOEMOTIONAL DEVELOPMENT IN CHILDHOOD: FROM TRUST TO INDUSTRY

Erikson's first four stages apply to childhood. Each stage is intimately linked with the kinds of activities associated with human life at each age:

- *Trust versus mistrust:* Infancy (birth to 1½ years) is concerned with establishing trust in the social world. At this stage, the helpless infant depends on caregivers to establish a sense that the world is a predictable and friendly place. Once trust is established, toddlers begin to see themselves as independent agents in the world.

- *Autonomy versus shame and guilt:* During toddlerhood (1½ to 3 years), children, many of whom are going through toilet training, experience the beginnings of self-control. When these young children have the opportunity to experience control over their own behaviors, they develop the capacity for independence and confidence.

- *Initiative versus guilt:* In early childhood (ages 3 to 5), preschoolers experience what it is like to forge their own interests and friendships and to take on responsibilities. If you have ever spent time with a 3-year-old, you know how often the child wants to help with whatever an adult is doing. When they experience a sense of taking on responsibility, preschoolers develop initiative. Otherwise, according to Erikson, they may feel guilty or anxious.

- *Industry versus inferiority:* During middle and late childhood (6 years to puberty), children enter school and gain competence in academic skills. Just as the label *industry* would suggest, children find that this is the time to get to work, learn, achieve, and learn to enjoy learning.

From Erikson's perspective, then, children should grow toward greater levels of autonomy and self-confidence as they progress from infancy to school age and beyond. Is there a particular parenting style that is most likely to lead to these sorts of outcomes? Let's find out.

### *Parenting and Childhood Socioemotional Development*

Researchers have tried to identify styles of parenting associated with positive developmental outcomes. Diana Baumrind (1991, 1993) described four basic styles of interaction between parents and their children:

**authoritarian parenting**
A restrictive, punitive style in which the parent exhorts the child to follow the parent's directions.

- **Authoritarian parenting** is a strict punitive style. The authoritarian parent firmly limits and controls the child with little verbal exchange. In a difference of opinion about how to do something, for example, the authoritarian parent might say, "You do it my way or else." Children of authoritarian parents sometimes lack social skills, show poor initiative, and compare themselves with others.

**authoritative parenting**
A parenting style that encourages the child to be independent but that still places limits and controls on behavior.

- **Authoritative parenting** encourages the child to be independent but still places limits and controls on behavior. This parenting style is more collaborative. Extensive verbal give-and-take is allowed, and parents are warm and nurturing toward the child. An authoritative father might put his arm around the child in a comforting way and say, "You know you should not have done that; let's talk about how you can handle the situation better next time." Children of authoritative parents tend to be socially competent, self-reliant, and socially responsible.

**neglectful parenting**
A parenting style characterized by a lack of parental involvement in the child's life.

- **Neglectful parenting** is distinguished by a lack of parental involvement in the child's life. Children of neglectful parents might develop a sense that other aspects of the parents' lives are more important than they are. Children whose parents are neglectful tend to be less competent socially, to handle independence poorly, and (especially) to show poor self-control.

**permissive parenting**
A parenting style characterized by the placement of few limits on the child's behavior.

- **Permissive parenting** places few limits on the child's behavior. A permissive parent lets the child do what he or she wants. Some parents deliberately rear their children this way because they believe that the combination of warm involvement and few limits will produce a creative, confident child. However, children with very permissive parents typically rate poorly in social competence. They often fail to learn respect for others, expect to get their own way, and have difficulty controlling their behavior.

Recall that socioemotional development means becoming increasingly adept at controlling and regulating one's emotions and behaviors. Children may require structure from their caregivers to acquire these skills.

**The Cultural Context of Parenting**  Culture influences the effects of parenting on children, especially authoritarian parenting. In one study, mothers from four collectivistic cultures (Iran, India, Egypt, and Pakistan) described themselves as authoritarian but did not express negative attitudes about their children, and the children did not show negative outcomes (Rudy & Grusec, 2006). For Latino families, some psychologists have suggested that authoritarian parenting may express culturally valued childrearing goals such as family, respect, and education and that this parenting style must be understood in the context of these cultural ideals (Halgunseth, Ispa, & Rudy, 2006). On the basis of her research, Ruth Chao (2001, 2007; Chao & Otsuki-Clutter, 2011) has argued that many Asian American mothers and fathers function as "training parents" who focus exclusively on directing and guiding their children to high academic achievement.

*"Relax, Ted, it's only a phase."*

Used by permission of CartoonStock, www.CartoonStock.com.

## SOCIOEMOTIONAL DEVELOPMENT IN ADOLESCENCE: THE EMERGENCE OF IDENTITY

Erikson (1968) viewed the key challenge of adolescence as identity versus identity confusion. In seeking an *identity,* adolescents must find out who they are, what they are all about, and where they are going in life. Adolescents are confronted with many new roles and adult statuses—from the vocational to the romantic. If they do not adequately explore their identities during this stage, they emerge confused about who they are. Adolescents who spend this time in their lives exploring alternatives can reach some resolution of the identity crisis and emerge with a new sense of self. Those who do not successfully resolve the crisis become confused, suffering what Erikson calls *identity confusion.* This confusion is expressed in one of two ways: Either individuals withdraw, isolating themselves from peers and family, or they lose themselves in the crowd.

**Marcia's Theory of Identity Status**  Building on Erikson's ideas, James Marcia proposed the concept of *identity status* to describe an adolescent's position in the development of an identity (Kroger, Martinussen, & Marcia, 2010; Marcia, 1980, 2002). In Marcia's view, two dimensions of identity, exploration and commitment, are important. *Exploration* refers to a person's investigating various options for a career and for personal values. *Commitment* involves deciding which identity path to follow and personally investing in attaining that identity. Various combinations of exploration and commitment give rise to one of four identity statuses, according to Marcia (Figure 8.16):

- *Identity diffusion:* The adolescent has neither explored nor committed to an identity. Adolescents experiencing identity diffusion may describe themselves as not caring about much in the world. They have not confronted the crisis of identity or are so overwhelmed by the challenge of answering the question "Who am I?" that they have withdrawn. These individuals may find themselves in crisis. Eventually, as they engage in life, these adolescents will begin the process of thinking about what matters (and what does not) and enter into the stage of exploration called *moratorium.*

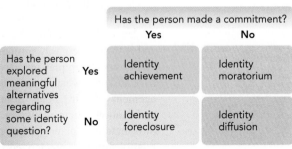

|  |  | Has the person made a commitment? | |
|  |  | Yes | No |
| Has the person explored meaningful alternatives regarding some identity question? | Yes | Identity achievement | Identity moratorium |
|  | No | Identity foreclosure | Identity diffusion |

**FIGURE 8.16  Marcia's Four Statuses of Identity**
Who are you? When you think of how you have come to identify yourself, which of these four statuses does your answer best represent?

- *Identity moratorium:* The adolescent is actively exploring and trying on new roles but has not committed to a particular identity. For example, consider an adolescent who passionately throws himself into a variety of internship opportunities to see what different jobs might be like, or the first-year college student who takes a range of different classes to explore potential careers.

- *Identity foreclosure:* The adolescent has committed to a particular identity but has done so without actually exploring his or her options. An example is a girl who decides to pursue accounting as a major in college because everyone in her family is an accountant.

- *Identity achievement:* After exploring the options and committing to an identity, the adolescent emerges with a sense of his or her own values and principles, a sense of the kind of person he or she wishes to be, and goal commitments that provide his or her life with a feeling of purpose.

Marcia therefore views identity as an active construction, an outcome of a process of thinking about and trying on different identities (Klimstra & others, 2009, 2010). Some of the things we associate with adolescence, then—such as rebelling against one's parents, asserting one's own sense of style, and developing one's own interests and relationships—are part of the active developer's assertion of himself or herself in the service of identity.

### Ethnic Identity Within a Larger Culture

Developing an identity in adolescence can be especially challenging for individuals from ethnic minority groups (Syed, 2010; Syed, Azmitia, & Cooper, 2011). As they mature cognitively, many adolescents become acutely aware of the evaluation of their ethnic group by the majority culture. In addition, an increasing number of minority adolescents face the challenge of *biculturalism*— identifying in some ways with their ethnic minority group and in other ways with the majority culture (Marks, Patton, & Coll, 2011).

Research has shown that for ethnic minority youth, feeling both a positive attachment to their minority group and an attachment to the larger culture is related to more positive academic and emotional outcomes (Umaña-Taylor, Updegraff, & Gonzales-Bracken, 2011). Although it might seem that being a member of an ethnic minority would make life more stressful, studies have indicated that having a strong ethnic identity can buffer adolescents from the effects of discrimination (Iturbide, Raffaelli, & Carlo, 2009). For both minority and majority adolescents, developing a positive identity is an important life theme (Kort-Butler & Hagewen, 2011; Oyserman & others, 2003; Umaña-Taylor, Gonzales-Backen, & Guimond, 2009). In addition to ethnic identity, adolescence can be a time when other aspects of one's identity come to the fore, such as sexual orientation or gender roles. We will examine the latter later in this chapter.

### Parents and Peers

Parents and peers can help the adolescent answer the central questions of identity, "Who am I, and who do I hope to become?" To help adolescents reach their full potential, a key parental role is to be an effective manager—one who locates information, makes contacts, helps to structure offsprings' choices, and provides guidance. By assuming this managerial role, parents help adolescents to avoid pitfalls and to work their way through the decisions they face (Simpkins & others, 2009).

For parents to play an active role in the development of their sons and daughters, they have to know what is going on in their adolescent's life. Research on adolescents' management of their parents' access to information, especially disclosing or concealing strategies about their activities, shows that adolescents are more willing to disclose information to parents when parents ask teenagers questions and when the parent–child relationship is characterized by a high level of trust, acceptance, and quality (Smetana & others, 2010; Tasopoulos-Chan, Smetana, & Yau, 2009).

During adolescence, individuals spend more time with peers than they did in childhood. These peer influences can be positive or negative. A significant aspect of positive peer relations is having one or more close friends. Adolescents can learn to be skilled and sensitive partners in intimate relationships by forging close friendships with selected peers. However, some peers and friends can negatively impact adolescents' development. Researchers have found that hanging out with delinquent peers in adolescence can be a strong predictor of substance abuse, delinquent behavior, and depression (Laursen & others, 2012).

*If you could travel back in time and visit your adolescent self, what would you tell him or her?*

For Erikson, once the issues of identity have been resolved, the young adult turns to the important domain of intimate relationships. However, recently, scholars have noted that during the life stage after adolescence, many young people seem to be putting off the kinds of commitments to marriage, family, and career that we associate with adult life. Jeffrey Arnett (2004, 2007, 2010) introduced the concept of emerging adulthood to describe this transitional period that is partly an extended adolescence and partly a phase of experimenting with adult roles. If you are a traditional-age college student, you are at this point in the life span. Let's briefly examine socioemotional development typical to this life stage.

## SOCIOEMOTIONAL DEVELOPMENT IN EMERGING ADULTHOOD

**emerging adulthood**
The transitional period from adolescence to adulthood, spanning approximately 18 to 25 years of age.

**Emerging adulthood** is the transitional period from adolescence to adulthood (Arnett, 2004, 2006, 2007). The age range for emerging adulthood is approximately 18 to 25 years of age. Experimentation and exploration characterize the emerging adult. At this point in their development, many individuals are still investigating their career path, their identity, and the kinds of close relationships they will have.

Jeffrey Arnett (2006, 2010) identified five main features of emerging adulthood:

*Some people enter adulthood earlier than others. Some marry, start a family, and take up full-time employment right out of high school. Do you think these individuals experience "emerging adulthood"?*

- *Identity exploration, especially in love and work:* Emerging adulthood is the time of significant changes in identity for many individuals.

- *Instability:* Residential changes peak during emerging adulthood, a time during which there also is often instability in love, work, and education.

- *Self-focus:* Emerging adults "are self-focused in the sense that they have little in the way of social obligations, little in the way of duties and commitments to others, which leaves them with a great deal of autonomy in running their own lives" (Arnett, 2006, p. 10).

- *Feeling "in between":* Many emerging adults consider themselves neither adolescents nor full-fledged adults.

- *The age of possibilities, a time when individuals have an opportunity to transform their lives:* Arnett (2006) describes two ways in which emerging adulthood is the age of possibilities: (1) Many emerging adults are optimistic about their future, and (2) for emerging adults who have experienced difficult times while growing up, emerging adulthood presents an opportunity to guide their lives in a more positive direction.

Emerging adults have more choices—and more control over those choices—in their daily life. The choices emerging adults make with regard to their life goals have implications for their later well-being. A longitudinal study spanning 17 years showed that the changes emerging adults made in their goals predicted their levels of well-being as adults (Hill & others, 2011), suggesting that this time of life sets the stage for later development. Eventually, though perhaps later than previous generations, emerging adults adopt the mantle of adulthood. According to Erikson, the early part of adulthood is occupied with the experience of loving, intimate relationships.

## SOCIOEMOTIONAL DEVELOPMENT IN EARLY ADULTHOOD: INTIMACY VERSUS ISOLATION

Erikson's (1968) sixth stage, *intimacy versus isolation,* refers to the challenge of forming intimate relationships with others or becoming socially isolated. Erikson describes intimacy as both finding oneself and losing oneself in another. If the young adult develops healthy friendships and an intimate relationship with a partner, intimacy will likely be achieved. One key way that young adults achieve intimacy is through long-term relationships with a romantic partner, often including marriage.

***Marriage***   Just as the notion of emerging adulthood would indicate, in the last two decades or so, men and women are waiting longer to marry. For example, in 2010, the average age for a first marriage in the United States climbed to just over 28 years for men and 26 years for women (Copen & others, 2012). This may be good news for marital stability. Women who marry before age 20 are three times more likely to divorce within five years than those who marry after age 20 (Copen & others, 2012).

What makes for a successful marriage? John Gottman has been studying married couples' lives since the early 1970s. He interviews couples, films them interacting with each other, and even measures their heart rate and blood pressure during their interactions (Gottman, Swanson, & Swanson, 2002; Madhyastha, Hamaker, & Gottman, 2011). He also checks back with the couples every year to see how their marriages are faring. He and his colleagues continue to follow married couples, as well as same-sex partners, to try to understand what makes relationships successful. A key issue, according to Gottman (2006), is getting past the notion that love is magical. From his perspective, love is a decision and a responsibility, and we have control over extramarital temptations.

Gottman (2006) has found these four principles at work in successful marriages:

■ *Nurturing fondness and admiration:* Partners sing each other's praises. When couples put a positive spin on their talk with and about each other, the marriage tends to work.

■ *Turning toward each other as friends:* Partners see each other as friends and turn toward each other for support in times of stress and difficulty.

■ *Giving up some power:* Bad marriages often involve one partner who is a powermonger. This is more common in husbands, but some wives have the problem as well.

■ *Solving conflicts together:* Couples work to solve problems, regulate their emotion during times of conflict, and compromise to accommodate each other.

### SOCIOEMOTIONAL DEVELOPMENT IN MIDDLE ADULTHOOD: GENERATIVITY VERSUS STAGNATION

Erikson's seventh stage, *generativity versus stagnation,* occurs in middle adulthood. Generativity means creating something of value that will benefit future generations. A generative person feels that he or she has left a lasting legacy and helped the next generation in important ways. This feeling that one has made a lasting and memorable contribution to the world is related to higher levels of psychological well-being (Busch & Hofer, 2012; Cox & others, 2010). The feeling of having done nothing of value for future generations is stagnation.

Erikson did not think that simply having children was sufficient to make a lasting contribution to the future. Rather, generativity might be expressed in engaged parenting, work accomplishments, mentoring, or teaching or through volunteer activities.

### SOCIOEMOTIONAL DEVELOPMENT AND AGING: INTEGRITY VERSUS DESPAIR

From Erikson's perspective, the person who has entered life's later years is engaged in looking back—evaluating his or her life, seeking meaning, and coming to terms with death. Erikson called this final stage *integrity versus despair*. If the individual has a well-established sense of integrity, experiencing life as a

*"Can you believe we got married, raised a family and retired, all without the help of a hand-held computer?"*

Used by permission of CartoonStock, www.CartoonStock.com.

meaningful and coherent whole, he or she faces the later years with a strong sense of meaning and low fear of death. In the absence of integrity, the older adult is filled with despair and fear. Current research on socioemotional development and aging reveals that Erikson was correct in his view that meaning is a central concern for older adults. However, he may have overlooked that this meaning derives not necessarily just from the past but also from the present.

In terms of social relationships, older adults may become more selective about their social networks. This observation was first made decades ago, and it was interpreted as indicating that older adults, in preparation for death, were disengaging from social life (Cumming & Henry, 1961). Late adulthood, according to the view of those earlier times, was characterized not as a stage of enjoying life, hobbies, and one's children and grandchildren but as a lonely period of disengagement from society and waiting to leave the earth. This older view stands in contrast to the perspectives that have emerged from various recent studies demonstrating that older adults report higher levels of happiness than their younger counterparts (Carstensen & others, 2011; Mroczek & Spiro, 2005; Realo & Dobewall, 2011; Stanley & Isaacowitz, 2011).

Laura Carstensen developed *socioemotional selectivity theory* to address the narrowing of social contacts and the increase in positive emotion that occur with age (Carstensen, 2006; Carstensen & others, 2011). The theory states that because they recognize their limited time on earth, older adults tend to be selective in their social interactions, striving to maximize positive and meaningful experiences. Although younger adults may gain a sense of meaning in life from long-term goals and hopes for the future, older adults achieve meaning by focusing on satisfying relationships and activities in the *present*. For older adults, a sense of purpose in life emerges from emotion regulation in the present, maximizing positive experiences and not sweating the negative. Unlike younger adults, who may be preoccupied with the future, older adults may embrace the present moment with increasing vitality (Hicks & others, 2012; Kotter-Grühn & Smith, 2011; Lachman & others, 2008).

The capacity to regulate emotions, and to thereby maximize positive experiences, appears to be a central feature of aging (Sullivan, Mikels, & Carstensen, 2010). Researchers have found that across diverse samples—Norwegians, Catholic nuns, African Americans, Chinese Americans, and non-Latino White Americans—older adults report better control of their emotions than younger adults (Charles & Carstensen, 2010).

Just as physical changes can influence socioemotional experience, socioemotional factors can influence physical health. One longitudinal study demonstrated that over time, women who avoided their problems (rather than confronting them) and who experienced low levels of positive emotion were more likely to show physical changes associated with diabetes (Tsenkova & others, 2008). Further, in one study, adults who had expressed positive attitudes about aging some 20 years previously, lived, on average, 7.5 years longer than those with more negative attitudes about aging (Levy, Slade, & Kasl, 2002). An important factor in the link between attitudes and longevity was a person's belief that life is full, hopeful, and worthwhile.

### EVALUATING ERIKSON'S THEORY

Using the framework of Erikson's socioemotional development theory, we have followed the active developer from the early accomplishment of trust in the social world through to his or her capacity to experience a strong sense of meaning in a life well lived. But like Piaget's theory, Erikson's conclusions have had their critics. Erikson mainly practiced case study research, which some reject as the sole research foundation for his approach. Critics also argue that Erikson's attempt to capture each stage with a single concept leaves out other important developmental tasks. For example, Erikson said that the main task for young adults is to resolve the conflict between intimacy and isolation. However, another significant developmental task in early adulthood involves careers and work. Despite these criticisms, Erikson, like Piaget, is a giant in developmental psychology.

**EXPERIENCE IT!**
Widows Enjoy Life

*Note that these effects are not thought to be about age but about the experience of limited time. If you were about to take a yearlong trip, how, and with whom, would you choose to spend your last 2 weeks at home?*

1. All of the following are examples of generativity *except*
   A. teaching the English language to recent U.S. immigrants.
   B. successfully investing one's earnings and enjoying a satisfying retirement.
   C. volunteering at a homeless shelter.
   D. acting as a scout leader.

2. Recent studies on socioemotional development and aging indicate that
   A. older adults put a great deal of stock in life's meaning.
   B. older adults may be more selective in their social interactions than younger adults.
   C. older adults are happier than their younger counterparts.
   D. all of the above

3. With regard to ethnic identity, psychological research indicates that
   A. adolescents who downplay the importance of their ethnic identity do better in school.
   B. adolescents use their ethnic identity to avoid developmental tasks.
   C. adolescents who have a strong ethnic identity are better able to cope with stress.
   D. adolescents from different racial groups face the same challenges to their ethnic identity.

**APPLY IT!** 4. Rosemary's Grandpa Jack is 80 years old and wears a hearing aid and glasses, and he has always been very active. He and Rosemary's grandmother spend a great deal of time with their children and grandchildren, and both laugh a lot and seem genuinely to enjoy life. Grandpa Jack recently resigned his position as a member of the local senior citizen's council. He tells Rosemary that the council had become a hassle. Rosemary wonders whether this decision is normal and reasonable or whether her granddad is feeling depressed.

Based on your reading of this example and this chapter, should Rosemary be worried?
A. Rosemary should be worried because it appears that Grandpa Jack is withdrawing from opportunities for generativity.
B. Rosemary should be worried because Grandpa Jack should stay involved in community activities given that such involvement is related to being happier and healthier.
C. Rosemary should probably not be worried. Grandpa Jack just sounds as if he is going through what most people do when they are faced with limited time: maximizing meaningful social contacts.
D. Rosemary should not be worried because Grandpa Jack has completed Erikson's stages, and it makes sense that he is probably preparing for death by withdrawing from the world.

# 5 Gender Development

So far, we have explored development across the human life span in the physical, cognitive, and socioemotional domains. In this section, we examine an important aspect of the human experience—gender development—that illustrates the links across the various domains of development. Understanding the development of gender requires attention to all three life domains—physical (or biological), cognitive, and socioemotional.

**Gender** refers to the broad set of characteristics of people as males and females. Although checking off "male" or "female" on a questionnaire may seem simple, the development of gender is a complex process that includes biological, cognitive, and socioemotional factors (Halpern & others, 2007). Gender comprises not only biological sex but also the individual's understanding of the meaning of gender in his or her life.

**gender**
The social and psychological aspects of being male or female.

## Biology and Gender Development

Humans normally have 46 chromosomes arranged in pairs. The 23rd pair may have two X-shaped chromosomes, which produces a female, or it may have both an X-shaped and an (upside-down) Y-shaped chromosome, which produces a male.

In the first few weeks after conception, male and female embryos look alike. When the Y chromosome in the male embryo triggers the secretion of *androgens,* the main class of male sex hormones, male sex organs start to differentiate from female sex organs. Low androgen levels in a female embryo allow for the normal development of female sex organs.

Research on very young infants suggests the roles of genes and prenatal hormones in producing differences between the sexes. For example, one study examined 1-day-old male and female infants. The infants were shown two stimuli: a human face and a mobile

*This is why males are more likely to show characteristics like color blindness that are linked to the X chromosome. Females have a backup X chromosome.*

made from a picture of that face (Connellan & others, 2000). The researchers found that the baby girls spent more time looking at the human face, while the baby boys were more interested in the mobile (Connellan & others, 2000). Research on infants from 3 to 8 months of age found that males spent more time looking at typical boy toys, including trucks and machines, and females spent more time looking at typical girl toys, such as dolls (Alexander, Wilcox, & Woods, 2009). Such differences are thought to be biologically, not socially, based because very young children have not yet had social experiences that might influence gender development. These physical differences, though, do not tell the whole story of gender development.

## Cognitive Aspects of Gender Development

Recall from Piaget's theory that a schema is a mental framework that organizes and guides an individual's thoughts. A *gender schema* is a mental framework for understanding what it means to be male or female in one's culture (Martin & Ruble, 2010). Through experience, children learn that gender is an important organizing principle in social life, and they come to recognize that boys and girls, and men and women, are different in ways that matter. This gender schema then serves as a cognitive framework by which children interpret further experiences related to gender.

How do gender schemas develop? Theorists suggest that children acquire these schemas through learning in the social world (Bandura & Bussey, 2004). Such learning occurs through processes we examined in Chapter 5, including reinforcement and punishment, observational learning, and modeling (Bandura & Bussey, 2004).

In subtle ways, children may be rewarded (or punished) for behavior depending on whether the behavior conforms to expectations for their sex. The child's social environment responds to behaviors in various ways, coloring his or her perception of their appropriateness. A girl might learn that pretending to be a professional football player is not a way to please her parents. A boy might pick up on his mother's subtle frown when he announces that he wants to try on her high-heeled shoes.

According to Albert Bandura (1986), modeling is an especially potent mechanism for transmitting values. Children gain information about gender from models of each sex. Who goes to work every day? Who does the housekeeping? When children see their parents and other adults engaging in gender-related behavior (and as they observe whether and how these behaviors are reinforced), they learn about how men and women behave.

> Because of where they are in cognitive development, very young children may believe that a person's sex can change depending on superficial features. They may reason that girls have long hair, and so if that hair is cut short, a girl becomes a boy.

## Socioemotional Experience and Gender Development

Social experiences clearly influence gender development. After all, behaviors are rewarded or punished by other people in the child's world. In addition to parents, peers also play an important role in gender development. Especially between the ages of 6 and 11, peer groups often segregate into boy groups and girl groups (Maccoby, 2002). Peers are stricter than most parents in rewarding behavior that conforms to gender rules and in punishing behavior that violates those rules. For example, children can be punitive toward boys who engage in behaviors that are not typically boyish (Wallien & others, 2010). As children grow up, they adopt **gender roles,** which involve expectations for how females and males should think, act,

**gender roles**
Roles that reflect the individual's expectations for how females and males should think, act, and feel.

*Children learn about gender differences through experience—by observing the activities and behavior of others.*

*Again we see how cognitive development matters. At this age, kids are in Piaget's concrete operations stage, associated with putting things (and people) in categories.*

and feel (Eagly, 2009). These gender roles represent beliefs about appropriate behavior for the sexes.

Culture plays a vital role in the content of gender roles (Eagly & Wood, 2011, 2012; Koenig & others, 2011). Some cultures emphasize that children should be reared to adopt traditional gender roles. Parents in these cultures bring up boys to be "masculine" (say, powerful, aggressive, and independent) and girls to be "feminine" (sensitive to others, good at relationships, and less assertive). Other cultures emphasize rearing boys and girls to be more similar—raising boys to be just as caring toward others as girls and raising girls to be just as assertive as boys. Iran and China are two countries in which traditional gender roles continue to dominate, but the United States has moved toward more diversity in gender roles.

While acknowledging biological differences between males and females, many psychologists believe that social and cultural factors have a much stronger influence on eventual gender identity (Bandura & Bussey, 2004; Eagly & Wood, 2011, 2012). From this perspective, differences in men's and women's career and life choices can be explained by differences in the availability of role models and beliefs about self-efficacy and personal control in these roles. Janet Shibley Hyde (2005), an expert on the psychology of gender, reviewed studies of gender differences in a wide range of characteristics. She found that where differences did emerge, they were quite small. Overall, Hyde found strong support for what she came to call the **gender similarities hypothesis**—the idea that men and women (and boys and girls) are much more similar than they are different (Hyde, 2005, 2006, 2007).

*In Iran, legal and cultural beliefs about women's and men's respective roles in the family and society have roots in religious tradition. Despite some change, traditional gender roles widely persist in the Islamic republic.*

**gender similarities hypothesis** Hyde's proposition that men and women (and boys and girls) are much more similar than they are different.

*The gender differences we see in terms of pursuing math and science careers do not seem to be about differences in ability. Rather, they appear to be about the kinds of beliefs, expectations, and role models males and females have about these careers.*

# Nature and Nurture Revisited: The John/Joan Case

Although it seems clear that gender emerges as a function of a variety of intermingling processes, some have debated whether one of these processes is more important than the others.

John Money, a well-known sex researcher, believed strongly that socialization was the main determinant of gender. In the 1960s, a case presented itself that gave Money the opportunity to test this theory. In 1965 twin boys were born, and a few months after birth, one twin's penis was destroyed during circumcision. Money persuaded the boy's parents to allow him to surgically transform the injured male genitals into female genitals and to agree to treat the child as a girl. The former boy was reared as a girl and, according to Money, essentially became a girl (Money & Tucker, 1975). The John/Joan case became famous as an example of nurture's triumph over nature. For many years, this case was used as evidence for the amazing flexibility of gender.

*Though David's story seems to indicate that biological factors powerfully guide gender development, remember that it is difficult to make generalizations based on a single case study. Other similar cases have had more positive outcomes.*

Milton Diamond, a biologist and strong critic of Money's theory, followed up on Money's most famous case (Diamond & Sigmundson, 1997). Diamond found that over time, "Joan" became less and less interested in being a girl and eventually refused to continue the process of feminization that Money had devised. We now know that "Joan" was really David Reimer, whose biography, *As Nature Made Him,* written by John Colapinto (2000), revealed the difficulties of his life as a boy, then a girl, then a boy, and finally a man. David struggled with traumatic gender-related life experiences and depression, eventually committing suicide in 2004. The John/Joan case of gender development illuminates the complex ways in which the physical, cognitive, and socioemotional domains of development intersect and influence one another.

1. Among other factors, the development of gender involves
   A. personality factors.
   B. cognitive factors.
   C. sensory factors.
   D. all of the above

2. The term for a cognitive framework for understanding what it means to be male or female in a given culture is
   A. gender role.
   B. gender identity.
   C. gender diversity.
   D. gender schema.

3. Childhood peer groups
   A. are not concerned with rewarding and punishing gender-related behavior in members of the group.
   B. play a key role in a person's gender development.
   C. typically are mixed, including both males and females.
   D. none of the above

**APPLY IT!** 4. When Jerry announces he's planning to major in mechanical engineering, his proud parents are not surprised. They tell their friends, "We *knew* he was destined to be interested in mechanical things. Even as a tiny infant he loved mechanical toys and never gave his stuffed animals a second look! He's always been our little engineer." What does research on the psychology of gender development have to say about Jerry's parents' conclusion?

A. Jerry may have always been their little engineer, but their comments to friends suggest that Jerry was not very different from most baby boys.
B. Jerry's parents' observations are supported by research showing that very early interest in mechanical toys predicts later career decisions in both males and females.
C. Jerry's parents' observations cannot be true, because very young infants cannot tell the difference between mechanical toys and stuffed animals.
D. Jerry's parents are probably biased by cultural beliefs, and so they remember his behavior in infancy fitting their preexisting beliefs about gender roles.

# 6 Moral Development

Moral development involves changes that occur with age in people's thoughts, feelings, and behaviors regarding the principles and values that guide them. Much research on moral reasoning and thinking has revolved around Lawrence Kohlberg's theory of moral development and reactions to it.

## Kohlberg's Theory

Kohlberg (1958) began his study of moral thinking by asking children, adolescents, and adults questions about a series of stories. One of the stories goes something like this. A man, Heinz, whose wife is dying of cancer, knows about a drug that might save her life. He approaches the pharmacist who has the drug, but the pharmacist refuses to give it to him without being paid a very high price. Heinz is unable to scrape together the money and decides to steal the drug.

After reading the story, the interviewee was asked questions about the moral dilemma. Should Heinz have stolen the drug? Kohlberg was less interested in the answer to this question than he was to the response to the next one: Why? Based on the reasons people gave for their answers, Kohlberg (1986) evaluated their level of moral development. Kohlberg's stages of moral development consisted of three broad levels, which include:

1. *Preconventional:* The individual's moral reasoning is based primarily on the consequences of a behavior and on punishments and rewards from the external world. Reasoning is guided by not wanting Heinz to go to jail or by concern for the pharmacist's profits.

2. *Conventional:* The individual abides by standards learned from parents or society's laws. At this level the person might reason that Heinz should act in accord with expectations or his role as a good husband or should follow the law no matter what.

3. *Postconventional:* The individual recognizes alternative moral courses, explores the options, and then develops an increasingly personal moral code. At this level, the person might reason that Heinz's wife's life is more important than a law.

**Lawrence Kohlberg (1927–1987)**
*Kohlberg created a provocative theory of moral development. In his view, "Moral development consists of a sequence of qualitative changes in the way an individual thinks."*

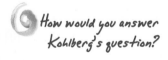

How would you answer Kohlberg's question?

Kohlberg linked moral development strongly to cognitive development. In addition to developments in cognition, he thought that advances in moral development occur through opportunities for role taking, as well as through the chance to discuss moral issues with a person who reasons at a stage just above one's own. For Kohlberg, a sense of justice was at the heart of moral reasoning, which he believed laid the foundation for moral behavior.

## Critics of Kohlberg

A criticism of Kohlberg is that his view does not adequately reflect concern for other people and social bonds (Hardy & Carlo, 2011). Kohlberg's theory is called a *justice perspective* because it emphasizes the rights of the individual as the key to sound moral reasoning. In contrast, the *care perspective*, which is at the core of Carol Gilligan's (1982) approach to moral development, views people in terms of their connectedness with others and stresses interpersonal communication, relationships, and concern for others. From Gilligan's perspective this weakness in Kohlberg's approach explains why, using his measures, women generally score lower than men on moral development.

More recently, psychologists interested in moral development have emphasized that Kohlberg neglected the influence of culture morality. Because of its central role in how we relate to each other, culture influences the ways individuals navigate moral dilemmas (C. S. Johnson, 2011). Current research on moral judgment shows that moral decisions are influenced by many different cultural values; it is not limited to care versus justice (Graham & others, 2011; Rai & Fiske, 2011).

You might have noticed a particular limitation of Kohlberg's emphasis on cognitive reasoning—that a person can know the right thing to do and yet might act in an immoral way (Hardy & Carlo, 2011). More recent research on moral development has focused on behavior that reflects moral goodness and on the socioemotional factors associated with this behavior.

One potentially important factor in moral behavior is attachment. Recall that Bowlby thought that our early attachments formed the basis of the sense of self we carry throughout life. By this way of thinking, attachment is important as adults experience relationships with their parents, friends, and romantic partners.

Research in social psychology has examined the ways that adults' attachment styles, whether secure or insecure, relate to many aspects of their life, including close romantic relationships (Simpson & Rholes, 2010). In adult relationships, secure attachment means having trust in relationship partners, feeling comfortable with being close to them, and not worrying excessively about being abandoned. Can secure attachment provide a basis for being more honest about who you really are? To read about work addressing this intriguing question, see the Intersection.

## Moral Development in a Socioemotional Context

Researchers interested in moral development have increasingly focused on the factors that predict **prosocial behavior,** behavior that is intended to benefit other people (Eisenberg & others, 2005). For example, researchers are probing the influences of parents (Farrant & others, 2012), peers (Eivers & others, 2012), school programs (Schonert-Reichl & others, 2012), and culture (Carlo & others, 2011) and whether children engage in

**Carol Gilligan (b. 1936)**
*Gilligan argues that Kohlberg's approach does not give adequate attention to relationships. In Gilligan's view, "Many girls seem to fear, most of all, being alone—without friends, family and relationships."*

**prosocial behavior**
Behavior that is intended to benefit other people.

# INTERSECTION

## Developmental and Social Psychology: Attachment and Honesty

Although we often hear that honesty is the best policy, it is sometimes a challenge to be honest. Daily life is filled with opportunities to lie to get ahead—perhaps presenting ourselves as a little better than we know we really are as we meet a potential romantic partner, or cheating just a little on a test to get a better grade. How do we avoid the temptation to bend our moral rules?

In recent research, Omri Gillath and his colleagues (2010) showed that secure attachment in adulthood could provide a basis for honest behavior. They found that adults who described themselves as being in a secure relationship were also more likely to provide honest reports about their own failings and embarrassing experiences. In experiments, the researchers discovered that after being reminded of warm interpersonal relationships, participants were less likely to say that they would be willing to lie, compared with participants who were reminded of going to the grocery store (the control group).

In a fascinating final study, Gillath and his colleagues (2010) examined the influence of reminders of warm attachment on a specific dishonest behavior: cheating on a test. The researchers first primed participants with either words related to attachment

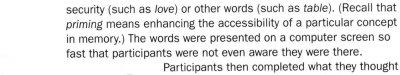

security (such as *love*) or other words (such as *table*). (Recall that *priming* means enhancing the accessibility of a particular concept in memory.) The words were presented on a computer screen so fast that participants were not even aware they were there.

Participants then completed what they thought was an IQ test. The test in fact included some unsolvable items, such as "What theory is Plastoconus famous for?" Before leaving the participants alone to complete the test, the experimenter placed the answer key on the desk, telling participants that they could check their answers once they had finished (but not before). The dependent variable in this study was the number of unsolvable questions that participants answered "correctly." If participants got these questions right, the researchers knew that they had cheated. Results showed that those who had been reminded of secure attachment were less likely to cheat than the others.

Being who we genuinely are and living honestly are guiding principles in a moral life. As the ancient Greeks liked to say, "To thine own self be true." The research reviewed here tells us that the ability to live our lives honestly and to do the right thing is supported by the warm social relationships we experience.

\\ **Who provides you with your most secure sense of attachment?**

\\ **Are you more authentic or less authentic with this person than with others?**

everyday acts of kindness toward others. Research has also examined how cognitive abilities (Eggum & others, 2011; Han & others, 2012) and personality characteristics (Caprara, Alessandri, & Eisenberg, 2012) influence acts of kindness in children and adults. Warm, empathic parenting is associated with children's prosocial behavior (Michalik & others, 2007), while rejecting and harsh parenting is linked to lower prosocial behavior and moral disengagement (Hyde, Shaw, & Moilanen, 2010). Childhood characteristics are important because longitudinal research shows that kind, moral children are more likely to be kind, moral adults (Eisenberg & others, 2002, 2005).

Other recent work has focused on when a child first shows signs of possessing a conscience (Kochanska & others, 2008). Having a conscience means hearing that voice in our head that tells us that something is morally good or bad. Deborah Laible and Ross Thompson (2000, 2002) have examined the conversations between mothers and toddlers at times when the child did something well or got into trouble. They have found that by 3 years of age, children show signs of early conscience development. Clear and elaborate parent–child interactions that are rich with emotional content and that include shared positive emotion foster conscience development.

1. In Kohlberg's preconventional stage, moral reasoning centers on
   A. parental standards and established laws.
   B. personal moral standards.
   C. a behavior's consequences, as well as rewards and punishments from the external world.
   D. loyalty to other people.

2. Moral behavior is influenced by all of the following *except*
   A. early attachments.
   B. culture.
   C. parenting.
   D. the senses.

3. Efforts that are geared to helping others are referred to as

A. the care perspective.
B. prosocial behavior.
C. the justice perspective.
D. socioemotional behavior.

**APPLY IT!** 4. Chris and Amanda are parents to 3-year-old Emma, who is always getting into trouble in preschool. She says mean things, snatches toys from other children, and engages in a lot of mischief. Her parents want to instill a strong sense of conscience in their little troublemaker. Which of the following strategies is best supported by the research you read about above?
A. The parents should punish Emma for her mischief swiftly and without a word of discussion. Trying to reason with a 3-year-old is a mistake.

B. The parents should reward Emma consistently for good behavior and ignore her misdeeds. She is probably just trying to get attention.
C. The parents should engage Emma in conversations about her behaviors, praising her for her good deeds and talking about the feelings that others might have when she gets in trouble. They should try to be clear and not focus only on the bad things she does.
D. The parents should do nothing. Age 3 is too young to worry about these issues, and Emma will not understand what they are talking about until she is much older.

# 7 Death, Dying, and Grieving

Everything that lives will eventually die. This is, and always has been, the reality for living organisms. Because human beings possess the capacity for consciousness (as explored in Chapter 4), we are aware of our own mortality. Our ability to time-travel mentally, to imagine ourselves in the future, makes the reality of our own eventual demise inescapable. Researchers from a variety of perspectives have examined the ways that the awareness of death influences our thoughts, feelings, and behaviors.

## Terror Management Theory: A Cultural Shield Against Mortality

*Fireworks displays are thrilling rituals that make us feel like valued and invested participants in the larger culture.*

In the 1970s anthropologist Ernest Becker (1971) drew together theory and research from the social sciences to devise a grand theory of human life and culture. According to Becker, the human capacity for awareness that we will someday die creates the potential for overwhelming terror. Yet somehow we go about life without being preoccupied by the terrifying reality of death. Why is this so?

Becker proposed that as our capacity for self-awareness evolved, so did the human ability to create and invest in culture. Culture provides the customary beliefs, practices, religious rules, and social order for humans living together. Becker asserted that being part of a larger culture shields us from the terror of our own mortality. He maintained that by investing in our cultural worldview (our beliefs, routine practices, and standards for conduct), we are able to enjoy a sense of immortality.

Culture provides both religious ideas about life after death and a context for accomplishments that will outlive us. As long as we feel that we are valued members of a culture, this status will buffer us against our fears of personal death.

Social psychologists Jeffrey Greenberg, Sheldon Solomon, and Tom Pyszczynski applied Becker's ideas in empirical research. They named their approach *terror management theory (TMT)* (Solomon, Greenberg, & Pyszczynski, 1991). A multitude of studies have explored terror management theory (Burke, Martens, & Faucher, 2010). This research shows that when reminded of their own death, people will endorse cultural beliefs more strongly (Kashima, 2010), reject individuals who violate those beliefs (Greenberg & Kosloff, 2008), and seek to maintain or enhance their self-esteem (Pyszczynski & others, 2004). Terror management studies support Becker's idea that cultural beliefs act as a buffer against the ultimate reality of our inevitable demise. Recent studies on the theory suggest that reminders of death can serve not only to promote defensive processes but also to spur people's creativity and motivation toward personal growth (Vail & others, 2012). Interestingly, research shows that compared to younger adults, older adults are less likely to strongly defend their cultural worldview after contemplating their own death (Maxfield & others, 2012), perhaps because they have come to accept that death is a fact of life.

Although terror management research tells us a great deal about how individuals cope with the reality of death in the abstract, it has yet to explore the process of dying itself. Even if one invests in a culture and in so doing establishes a sense of symbolic immortality, the reality of death remains. For aged or gravely ill persons, that reality can be experienced with particular vividness. How do individuals react when their own death is near?

## Kübler-Ross's Stages of Dying

Elisabeth Kübler-Ross pioneered psychology's interest in the process of dying in her seminal book *On Death and Dying* (1969). Focusing on terminally ill individuals, Kübler-Ross identified five progressive stages of coping with death:

1. *Denial:* The person rejects the reality of impending death. He or she may express thoughts such as "I feel fine—this cannot be true."

2. *Anger:* Once the reality of death sets in, the individual feels angry and asks, "Why me?" The unfairness of the situation may be especially upsetting.

3. *Bargaining:* The individual may bargain with God, with doctors, or within his or her own head: "If I can just have a little more time, I'll do anything."

4. *Depression:* The person feels profound sadness and may begin to give up on life: "What's the point of doing anything?"

5. *Acceptance:* The person comes to terms with the difficult reality of his or her own death. A realization sets in that "it will be okay."

Kübler-Ross eventually applied her stages of dying to a variety of life experiences, such as grieving for a loved one or mourning the loss of a job or relationship. Her book was important because it called on psychologists to confront the difficult problem of death. Still, her work has been criticized, and recent research has called into question a number of her ideas, such as the notion that everyone goes through these stages in the order she envisioned. One danger in the presentation of stages of dying is that it seems to represent a "right" way to die or the "best" way to grieve. Clearly, just as infants differ from one another from birth, so do individuals who face the end of life.

# Bonanno's Theory of Grieving

Losing a loved one is certainly likely to be stressful. Research by George Bonanno and his colleagues has tracked individuals who have experienced bereavement, such as the loss of a spouse, over time (Bonanno, 2004, 2005; Bonanno, Westphal, & Mancini, 2011; Mancini & Bonanno, 2009; Ong, Fuller-Rowell, & Bonanno, 2010). That research has identified four different patterns of grief:

*You might think that resilient individuals represent the lucky few. But Bonanno has found that resilience is actually the most common pattern.*

■ *Resilience:* Resilient individuals experience immediate grief over their loss but only for a brief time and return quickly to their previous levels of functioning. Such individuals do not experience a profound disruption of life, despite having gone through a staggering loss.

■ *Recovery:* In the recovery pattern, the individual experiences profound sadness and grief that dissipates more slowly. The individual will ultimately return to previous levels of functioning, but as a much slower and more gradual unfolding over time.

■ *Chronic dysfunction:* In this case, a traumatic grief experience leads to a long-term disruption of functioning in important life domains. Chronically dysfunctional individuals may ultimately be at risk for psychological disorders such as depression, which we will consider in Chapter 12.

■ *Delayed grief or trauma:* Some individuals do not experience the sadness or distress evoked by a loss immediately following that loss. Instead, these intense feelings may come over the person weeks or even months later.

# Carving Meaning Out of the Reality of Death

Death is a difficult concept to contemplate. Consider, though, that the reality of death is one of the things that makes life so precious. Research has shown that reminders of death can increase individuals' perception that life is meaningful and satisfying (King, Hicks, & Abdelkhalik, 2009). Furthermore, knowing that our loved ones will eventually die makes our commitments to our social relationships all the more heroic.

Indeed, the reality of death makes our commitment to life more meaningful. Let's revisit that commitment, an important factor in development itself.

## self-quiz

1. Studies on terror management theory indicate that when reminded of their own death, people
   A. lose interest in maintaining or building their self-esteem.
   B. endorse cultural beliefs more strongly.
   C. become less creative.
   D. reject the mainstream thinking of their culture.

2. Kübler-Ross's proposed stages of coping with death include all of the following *except*
   A. feeling angry.
   B. making amends to others.
   C. denying that death will come.
   D. accepting death.

3. In Bonanno's theory of grieving, the pattern in which the individual grieves for only a brief time and quickly resumes normal functioning is called
   A. recovery.
   B. rehabilitation.
   C. resilience.
   D. resolution.

**APPLY IT!** 4. When Lionel, Tawnya's beloved husband of 20 years, dies of a sudden heart attack, Tawnya is grief stricken. But just a few weeks later, she returns to work and is back to her routine, caring for her teenage sons. Considering her loss, she seems to be doing surprisingly well. Tawnya starts to wonder if there is something wrong with her. She loved Lionel deeply and remembers how, when her own father died, her mother seemed to be devastated for a long time. Tawnya confesses her feelings to a friend. According to research on grieving, which of the following would be the friend's best response?
   A. "Just work through your grief, and maybe join a support group so you can open up more. You need to get in touch with your feelings!"
   B. "So maybe your relationship with Lionel wasn't so great after all."
   C. "There are lots of ways to grieve. Your experience isn't unusual. Maybe it's your way of bouncing back. Talk about your loss if you wish, but don't assume there's something wrong."
   D. "You're holding in your emotions. You're going to get an ulcer or cancer if you keep this up. Let your feelings out!"

# Active Development as a Lifelong Process

When you think about developmental psychology, child development may still be the first thing that pops into mind. However, development is in fact a lifelong process: You remain on this very day in the midst of your development, wherever you are in the adult life span. Further, as an active developer, you blaze your own developmental trail. Where will you carve that path as you go through life? How might you "grow yourself"?

One way that adults develop is through coping with life's difficulties. Psychologist Carolyn Aldwin and her colleagues have suggested that stress and coping play a role in development (Boeninger & others, 2009). To understand how, let's revisit Piaget's ideas of assimilation and accommodation in childhood cognitive development and see how they apply to adult development (Block, 1982).

Recall that in assimilation, existing cognitive structures are used to make sense out of the current environment. Assimilation allows a person to enjoy a feeling of meaning because current experiences fit into his or her preexisting schemas (King & Hicks, 2007). However, life does not always conform to one's expectations. When experience conflicts with existing schemas, it is necessary to modify current ways of thinking. Accommodation is the process whereby existing schemas are modified or new structures are developed. Accommodation helps individuals to change so that they can make sense of life's previously incomprehensible events. For example, when people encounter a negative life circumstance such as an illness or a loss, they have the opportunity to change—to develop and to mature (Bauer, Schwab, & McAdams, 2011; Caserta & others, 2009; Gunty & others, 2011; LoSavio & others, 2011). Indeed, research suggests that those who are faced with difficulties in life are more likely to come to a rich, complex view of themselves and the world when they are able to acknowledge, with mindfulness, the ways these experiences have changed them (King & Hicks, 2007).

*All of us have experiences that we might regret. But even these experiences can have meaning to the extent that they contribute to who we are now.*

In Chapter 1, you had the opportunity to complete the Satisfaction with Life Scale. An item on that scale was, "If I could live my life over I would change almost nothing." One way to think about maturity is to revisit that item and consider the experiences you have had in your trip in the time machine of development. The mature person, dedicated to life while also acknowledging potentially negative experiences, may be the person who is able to give that item a high rating, valuing his or her life "warts and all" (King & Hicks, 2007).

Development involves change, so development in adulthood may mean maintaining an openness to changing and to being changed by experience. Consider someone who has spent much of his or her early adult life pursuing wealth and career success but then turns to more selfless pursuits in middle age. To contribute to the well-being of the next generation, the individual devotes energy and resources to helping others—say, by volunteering for a charity or working with young people.

These motivations are demonstrated by numerous individuals who are using their successes for the world's betterment. Actor George Clooney, for example, has dedicated himself to a variety of

*George Clooney has turned his celebrity and energies to addressing some urgent world problems.*

humanitarian causes. Clooney cofounded the organization Not On Our Watch to end the genocide in Sudan as well as to stop atrocities elsewhere. Among other charitable work, Clooney also organized a telethon to raise funds to aid victims of the 2010 earthquake in Haiti and has donated generously to homeless people elsewhere.

Development, then, is an ongoing process we experience throughout life as we encounter opportunities to grow, change, and make a mark in the world, however grandly or humbly. Indeed, the amazing time machine of our developmental life leads us continuously to new possibilities.

# SUMMARY

##  Exploring Human Development

Development is the pattern of change in human capabilities that begins at birth and continues throughout the life span. Both nature (biological inheritance) and nurture (environmental experience) influence development extensively. However, people are not at the mercy of either their genes or their environment when they actively construct optimal experiences. Resilience refers to the capacity of individuals to thrive during difficulties at every stage of development. Development is characterized along three interrelated levels—physical, cognitive, and socioemotional aspects of experience.

##  Physical Development

Prenatal development progresses through the germinal, embryonic, and fetal periods. Certain drugs, such as alcohol, can have an adverse effect on the fetus. Preterm birth is another potential problem, but its effects may depend on experiences after birth. The infant's physical development is dramatic in the first year, and a number of motor milestones are reached in infancy. Extensive changes in the brain, including denser connections between synapses, take place in infancy and childhood.

Puberty is a period of rapid skeletal and sexual maturation that occurs mainly in early adolescence. Hormonal changes lie at the core of pubertal development. Most adults reach their peak physical performance during their 20s and are healthiest then. However, physical skills begin to decline during the 30s. Even in late adulthood, the brain has remarkable repair capacity and plasticity.

##  Cognitive Development

Jean Piaget introduced a theory of cognitive development. From his view, children use schemas to actively construct their world, either assimilating new information into existing schemas or adjusting schemas to accommodate it. Piaget identified four stages of cognitive development: the sensorimotor stage, the preoperational stage, the concrete operational stage, and the formal operational stage. According to Piaget, cognitive development in adolescence is characterized by the appearance of formal operational thought, the final stage in his theory. This stage involves abstract, idealistic, and logical thought.

Piaget argued that no new cognitive changes occur in adulthood. However, some psychologists have proposed that the idealistic thinking of adolescents is replaced by the more realistic, pragmatic thinking of young adults. Longitudinal research on intelligence shows that many cognitive skills peak in middle age. Overall, older adults do not do as well on memory and other cognitive tasks and are slower to process information than younger adults. However, older adults may have greater wisdom than younger adults.

##  Socioemotional Development

In infancy, among the key basic ingredients of socioemotional development are temperament—the child's overall emotional demeanor—and attachment. Erik Erikson proposed an influential theory of eight psychosocial stages that characterize socioemotional development from infancy to late adulthood. In each stage, the individual seeks to resolve a particular socioemotional conflict. The childhood stages involve a movement from trust to industry. Adolescents experience Erikson's fifth stage, identity versus identity confusion.

Marcia proposed four statuses of identity based on crisis and commitment. Psychologists refer to the period between adolescence and adulthood as emerging adulthood. This period is characterized by the exploration of identity through work and relationships, instability, and self-focus.

Erikson's three stages of socioemotional development in adulthood are intimacy versus isolation (early adulthood), generativity versus stagnation (middle adulthood), and integrity versus despair (late adulthood). Researchers have found that remaining active increases the likelihood that older adults will be happier and healthier. They also have found that older adults often reduce their general social affiliations. Older adults are motivated to spend more time with close friends and family members.

##  Gender Development

Gender development involves physical (biological), cognitive, and socioemotional processes. Biological factors in gender development include sex chromosomes and hormones. Cognitive factors include gender schemas and gender roles, with the latter being strongly influenced by culture. Socioemotional aspects of gender include parental and peer responses to gender-related behavior. With regard to gender differences, research indicates that men and women are more similar than different.

## 6 Moral Development

Moral development encompasses both cognitive and socioemotional processes. Kohlberg proposed a cognitive-developmental theory of moral development with three levels (preconventional, conventional, and postconventional). More recent research has focused on the development of prosocial behavior and the influence of socioemotional factors in putting moral reasoning into action.

resilience, recovery, chronic dysfunction, and delayed grief. Awareness of death can render life more meaningful and satisfying.

 ## Death, Dying, and Grieving

Understanding the physical reality of death requires consideration of its socioemotional features. Terror management theory research has shown that awareness of death leads to investment in cultural worldviews. Elisabeth Kübler-Ross proposed a stage model of confronting death, in which the dying individual progresses from denial to acceptance. George Bonanno has shown that grief unfolds in four patterns—

 ## Active Development as a Lifelong Process

Development is an ongoing process that is influenced by the active developer at every point in the life span. In adulthood, development can be especially shaped by the ways individuals confront significant life events. Coping with stressful experiences and being open to change can be catalysts for adult development.

## KEY TERMS

development, p. 279
cross-sectional design, p. 279
nature, p. 280
nurture, p. 280
resilience, p. 281
preferential looking, p. 287
puberty, p. 289

assimilation, p. 294
accommodation, p. 294
sensorimotor stage, p. 295
object permanence, p. 295
preoperational stage, p. 295
concrete operational stage, p. 297
formal operational stage, p. 297

wisdom, p. 301
temperament, p. 302
infant attachment, p. 303
secure attachment, p. 303
authoritarian parenting, p. 306
authoritative parenting, p. 306
neglectful parenting, p. 306

permissive parenting, p. 306
emerging adulthood, p. 309
gender, p. 312
gender roles, p. 313
gender similarities
  hypothesis, p. 314
prosocial behavior, p. 316

## SELF-TEST

### Multiple Choice

1. The phrase "out of sight, out of mind" is true of children's cognitive processing in the _____ of development.
   A. sensorimotor stage
   B. preoperational stage
   C. concrete operational stage
   D. formal operational stage

2. The period of prenatal development that occurs just before birth is the
   A. embryonic period.
   B. zygotic period.
   C. fetal period.
   D. germinal period.

3. Of the following, the activity that is consistent with the concept of a life theme is
   A. competing against others.
   B. making a great deal of money.
   C. procreating.
   D. being altruistic.

4. A baby who is shown an image of a lion and an image of a tractor gazes at the tractor more. This finding is an example of
   A. preferential looking.
   B. visual development.

C. assimilation.
D. object permanence.

5. During the course of successful prenatal development, a human organism begins as a(n)
   A. zygote and finally develops into an embryo.
   B. embryo and finally develops into a fetus.
   C. zygote and finally develops into a fetus.
   D. fetus and finally develops into an embryo.

6. A developmental stage characteristic of early childhood (3 to 5 years) is
   A. identity versus identity confusion.
   B. trust versus mistrust.
   C. intimacy versus isolation.
   D. initiative versus guilt.

7. The theory of aging that focuses on the division of cells is the
   A. telomere theory.
   B. life expectancy theory.
   C. cellular-clock theory.
   D. free-radical theory.

8. The ability to think abstractly is known as
   A. fluid intelligence.
   B. cohort effects.

C. crystallized intelligence.
D. accommodation.

9. A newly pregnant woman is warned by a doctor about teratogens. She does not know what these are and asks you to explain. You tell her that the teratogens named in your psychology text include
   A. testosterone.
   B. serotonin.
   C. dopamine.
   D. alcohol.

10. A person who does not do something because he or she is fearful of getting in trouble is at the level of moral reasoning called
   A. preconventional.
   B. conventional.
   C. postconventional.
   D. formal operational.

### Apply It!

11. Based on this chapter's definition of wisdom, what are three wise decisions you have made? Why do you think they qualify as wise?

Indeed, it would hardly seem adaptive for humans to have a fixed action pattern that is invariably set in motion by a particular signal in the environment. To understand human behavior, psychologists have developed a variety of other approaches, as we now consider.

## Drive Reduction Theory

Another way to think about motivation is through the constructs of drive and need. A **drive** is an aroused state that occurs because of a physiological need. You can think of a drive as a psychological itch that requires scratching. A **need** is a deprivation that energizes the drive to eliminate or reduce the deprivation. Generally, psychologists think of needs as underlying our drives. You may have a need for water; the drive that accompanies that need is your feeling of being thirsty. Usually but not always, needs and drives are closely associated. For example, when your body needs food, your hunger drive will probably be aroused. An hour after you have eaten a hamburger, your body might still need essential nutrients (thus you need food), but your hunger drive might have subsided.

The following example should reinforce that drive pertains to a psychological state whereas need involves a physiological state, and that drives do not always follow from needs. If you are deprived of oxygen because of a gas leak, you may feel light-headed but may not realize that your condition is the result of a gas leak that is creating a need for air. Because you do not perceive it, your need for air fails to create a drive for oxygen that might lead you to open a window. Moreover, drives sometimes seem to come out of nowhere. Imagine, for instance, having eaten a fine meal and feeling full to the point of not wanting another single bite—until the waiter wheels over the dessert cart. Suddenly you feel ready to tackle the double chocolate oblivion, despite your lack of hunger.

*Drive reduction theory* explains that as a drive becomes stronger, we are motivated to reduce it. The goal of drive reduction is **homeostasis,** the body's tendency to maintain an equilibrium, or steady state. Literally hundreds of biological states in our bodies must be maintained within a certain range: temperature, blood sugar level, potassium and sodium levels, oxygenation, and so on. When you dive into an icy swimming pool, your body uses energy to maintain its normal temperature. When you walk out of an air-conditioned room into the heat of a summer day, your body releases excess heat by sweating. These physiological changes occur automatically to keep your body in an optimal state of functioning.

Most psychologists believe that drive reduction theory does not provide a comprehensive framework for understanding motivation because people often behave in ways that increase rather than reduce a drive. For example, when dieting, you might choose to skip meals, but this tactic can increase your hunger drive rather than reduce it. Similarly, many other things that you might opt to do involve increasing (not decreasing) tensions—for example, taking a challenging course in school, raising a family, and working at a difficult job.

## Optimum Arousal Theory

When psychologists talk about arousal, they are generally referring to a person's feelings of being alert and engaged. When we are very excited, our arousal levels are high. When we are bored, they are low. You have probably noticed that motivation influences

*Human newborns display behavioral reflexes such as holding on to a rope so that they can be lifted. In our evolutionary past, this gripping reflex appeared in primates, allowing an infant to cling to its mother's hair while she moved about.*

**drive**
An aroused state that occurs because of a physiological need.

**need**
A deprivation that energizes the drive to eliminate or reduce the deprivation.

**homeostasis**
The body's tendency to maintain an equilibrium, or steady state.

arousal levels. Sometimes you can want something (for example, to do well on a test) so much that you feel "overmotivated" and anxious. On the other hand, you might be so unmotivated for a task (such as doing dishes) that you can hardly force yourself to complete it.

Early in the twentieth century, two psychologists described how arousal can influence performance. According to their formulation, now known as the **Yerkes-Dodson law,** performance is best under conditions of moderate arousal rather than either low or high arousal. At the low end of arousal, you may be too lethargic to perform tasks well; at the high end, you may not be able to concentrate. Think about how aroused you were the last time you took a test. If your arousal was too high, you might have felt too nervous to concentrate, and your performance likely suffered. If it was too low, you may not have worked fast enough to finish the test. Also think about performance in sports. Being too aroused usually harms athletes' performance; a thumping heart and rapid breathing have accompanied many golfers' missed putts. However, if athletes' arousal is too low, they may not concentrate well on the task at hand.

The relationship between arousal and performance is one reason that individuals who have to perform well under stressful conditions (such as EMTs and lifeguards) are trained to *overlearn* important procedures so that they do not require much thought. With this extra learning, when these individuals are under conditions of high arousal, they can rely on automatic pilot to do what needs to be done.

**Yerkes-Dodson law**
The psychological principle stating that performance is best under conditions of moderate arousal rather than either low or high arousal.

*Overlearning is a crucial part of the training regimen by which the elite Navy SEALS prepare for missions, such as the 2011 raid on Osama bin Laden's compound in Pakistan and the al Qaeda leader's eventual death.*

## self-quiz

1. The force that moves people to behave, think, and feel the way they do is
   A. emotion.
   B. instinct.
   C. need.
   D. motivation.

2. Natalie will be taking an exam today. According to the Yerkes-Dodson law, the condition that will allow Natalie to score highest on the exam is
   A. no anxiety.
   B. moderate anxiety.
   C. high anxiety.
   D. high relaxation.

3. Which of the following statements is correct?

   A. Instincts have little to do with animal behavior.
   B. Instincts are learned patterns of behavior.
   C. Instincts direct most aspects of human behavior.
   D. Instincts are innate and biological.

**APPLY IT!** 4. Jared is a star basketball player on his school's team. In a crucial game, the score is tied with just a few seconds left on the clock, and Jared finds himself at the free-throw line preparing to shoot the winning baskets. The opponents' coach calls a time-out to "ice" Jared's nerves. Finally, as Jared steps up to the line, the rival team's students scream and jump around in an attempt to psych Jared out. His heart racing, Jared sinks both baskets, and his team wins. Which of the following is most likely true of this situation?

A. The opposing team's coach and student fans know that low arousal leads to poor performance.
B. Jared has practiced free throws so many times that he can land them even when he is highly aroused.
C. Jared is showing the effects of very high arousal on performance.
D. Jared is generally a sluggish person, and his performance is helped by his low levels of arousal.

## 2 Hunger and Sex

Some of the influence of motivation in our lives is tied to physiological needs. Two behaviors that are central to the survival of our species are eating and sex. In this section we examine the motivational processes underlying these behaviors.

# The Biology of Hunger

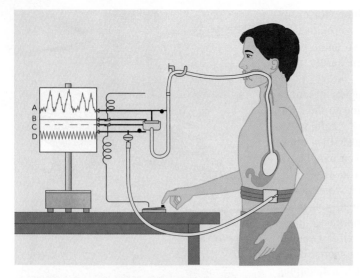

**FIGURE 9.1** **Cannon and Washburn's Classic Experiment on Hunger** In this experiment, the researchers demonstrated that stomach contractions, which were detected by the stomach balloon, accompany a person's hunger feelings, which were indicated by pressing the key. Line A in the chart records increases and decreases in the volume of the balloon in the participant's stomach. Line B records the passage of time. Line C records the participant's manual signals of feelings of hunger. Line D records a reading from the belt around the participant's waist to detect movements of the abdominal wall and ensure that such movements are not the cause of changes in stomach volume.

You know you are hungry when your stomach growls and you feel those familiar hunger pangs. What role do such signals play in hunger?

**GASTRIC SIGNALS** In 1912, Walter Cannon and A. L. Washburn conducted an experiment that revealed a close association between stomach contractions and hunger (Figure 9.1). As part of the procedure, a partially inflated balloon was passed through a tube inserted in Washburn's mouth and pushed down into his stomach. A machine that measures air pressure was connected to the balloon to monitor Washburn's stomach contractions. Every time Washburn reported hunger pangs, his stomach was also contracting. Sure enough, a growling stomach needs food. The stomach tells the brain not only how full it is but also how much nutrient is present, which is why rich food stops hunger faster than the same amount of water. The hormone cholecystokinin (CCK) helps start the digestion of food, travels to the brain through the bloodstream, and signals us to stop eating (Moss & others, 2012). Hunger involves a lot more than an empty stomach, however.

*EXPERIENCE IT!*
Hunger and Nutrients

**BLOOD CHEMISTRY** Three key chemical substances play a role in hunger, eating, and satiety (the state of feeling full): glucose, insulin, and leptin.

*Glucose* (blood sugar) is an important factor in hunger, probably because the brain critically depends on sugar for energy. One set of sugar receptors, located in the brain itself, triggers hunger when sugar levels fall too low. Another set of sugar receptors is in the liver, which stores excess sugar and releases it into the blood when needed. The sugar receptors in the liver signal the brain when its sugar supply falls, and this signal also can make you hungry.

The hormone *insulin* also plays a role in glucose control (Hansen & others, 2012). When we eat complex carbohydrates such as bread and pasta, insulin levels go up and fall off gradually. When we consume simple sugars such as candy, insulin levels rise and then fall sharply—the all-too-familiar "sugar low" (Rodin, 1984). Blood glucose levels are affected by complex carbohydrates and simple sugars in similar ways, so we are more likely to eat within the next several hours after eating simple sugars than after eating complex carbohydrates.

The chemical substance *leptin* (from the Greek word *leptos,* meaning "thin"), released by fat cells, decreases food intake and increases energy expenditure or metabolism (Mantzoros & others, 2011). Leptin's functions were discovered in a strain of genetically obese mice, called *ob mice* (Pelleymounter & others, 1995). Because of a genetic mutation, the fat cells of ob mice cannot produce leptin. The ob mouse has a low metabolism, overeats, and gets extremely fat. Leptin appears to act as an anti-obesity hormone (Procaccini, Jirillo, & Matarese, 2012; Vong & others, 2011). If ob mice are given daily injections of leptin, their metabolic rate increases, and they become more active, eat less, and lose weight. Figure 9.2 shows an untreated ob mouse and an ob mouse that has received injections of leptin.

In humans, leptin concentrations have been linked with weight, body fat, and weight loss in response to dieting (Lee & Bishop, 2011; Lopez & Knudson, 2012). Scientists continue to explore the possibility that disorders in the production and uptake of leptin may explain human obesity (Carnell & others, 2012; Kissileff & others, 2012).

**BRAIN PROCESSES** Chapter 2 described the central role of the hypothalamus in regulating important body functions, including hunger. More specifically, activity in two areas of the hypothalamus contributes to our understanding of hunger. The *lateral hypothalamus* is involved in stimulating eating. When an electrical current is passed through this area in a well-fed animal, the animal begins to eat. If this part of the hypothalamus is destroyed, even a starving animal will show no interest in food. The *ventromedial hypothalamus* is involved in reducing hunger and restricting eating.

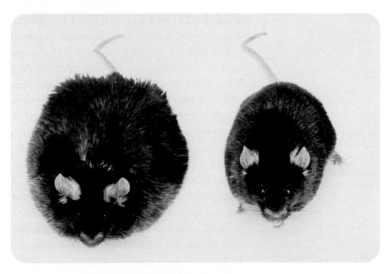

**FIGURE 9.2   Leptin and Obesity** The ob mouse on the left is untreated; the one on the right has been given injections of leptin.

When this area of an animal's brain is stimulated, the animal stops eating. When the area is destroyed, the animal eats profusely and quickly becomes obese.

Although the lateral and ventromedial hypothalamuses both influence hunger, there is much more to the brain's role in determining hunger than these on/off centers in the hypothalamus. Neurotransmitters (the chemical messengers that convey information from neuron to neuron) and neural circuits (clusters of neurons that often involve different parts of the brain) also function in hunger (Marston & others, 2011). Leptin influences eating by inhibiting the production of a neurotransmitter in the hypothalamus that induces eating. The neurotransmitter serotonin is partly responsible for the satiating effect of CCK, and serotonin antagonists have been used to treat obesity in humans (Halford & others, 2011; Zhao, Goldberg, & Vaccarino, 2012).

*The World Health Organization has used the term globesity to refer to the worldwide problem of obesity.*

# Obesity

Given that the brain and body are elegantly wired to regulate eating behavior, why do so many people in the United States overeat and suffer the effects of overeating? Sixty percent of Americans are overweight, and one-third are considered obese (dangerously overweight) (Centers for Disease Control & Prevention, 2009). The National Health and Nutrition Examination Survey (NHANES) projected that 86 percent of Americans will be overweight or obese by 2030 if current weight trends continue (Beydoun & Wang, 2009). A recent international comparison of 33 developed countries revealed that the United States had the highest percentage of obese adults (OECD, 2010).

Being obese or overweight raises one's risk for a variety of health problems, including cardiovascular disease and type 2 diabetes (Grundy, 2012; Roos, Quax, & Jukema, 2012). Currently, the number of people considered overweight around the world is 20 percent higher than the number suffering from hunger. Overweight and obesity are global health problems.

Why so many people overeat to the point of obesity is a motivational puzzle, because it involves eating when one is not in need of nutrition. As is the case with much behavior, in eating, biological, cognitive, and sociocultural factors interact in diverse ways in different individuals, making it difficult to point to a specific cause (Adler & Stewart, 2009).

"I've got a complaint. This laptop doesn't fit my lap!"

FRY.

**THE BIOLOGY OF OBESITY**    Obesity clearly has a genetic component. After the discovery of the ob gene in mice, researchers found a similar gene in humans. Some individuals do inherit a tendency to be overweight (Almen & others, 2012). Only 10 percent of children who do not have obese parents become obese themselves, whereas 40 percent of children who have one obese parent become obese, and 70 percent of children who have two obese parents become obese. Identical human twins have similar weights, even when they are reared apart (Maes, Neal, & Eaves, 1997).

Another factor in weight is **set point,** the weight maintained when the individual makes no effort to gain or lose weight. Set point is determined in part by the amount of stored fat in the body (Speakman & others, 2011). Fat is stored in *adipose cells,* or fat cells. When these cells are filled, you do not get hungry. When people gain weight—because of genetic predisposition, childhood eating patterns, or adult overeating—their fat-cell number increases, and they might not be able to get rid of extra ones. A normal-weight individual has 10 to 20 billion fat cells. An obese individual can have up to 100 billion fat cells (Fried, 2008). Consequently, an obese individual has to eat more to feel satisfied.

**PSYCHOLOGICAL FACTORS IN HUNGER AND OBESITY**    Psychologists used to think that obesity stemmed from factors such as unhappiness and external food cues. These ideas make some sense; drowning one's sorrows in chocolate or eating some cookies just because they are there seems common enough to explain overeating. However, a number of factors are more important than emotional state and external stimuli (Rodin, 1984).

Time and place affect our eating (Jaeger & others, 2011). Learned associations of food with a particular place and time are characteristic of many organisms (Fiese, Foley, & Spagnola, 2006). If it is noon, we are likely to feel hungry even if we ate a big breakfast. We also associate eating with certain places. Many people link watching television with eating and feel uncomfortable if they are not eating something while watching TV. From an evolutionary framework, human taste preferences developed at a time when reliable food sources were scarce. Our earliest ancestors probably developed a preference for sweets and fatty foods because ripe fruit, a concentrated source of sugar (and calories), was accessible and because high-fat foods carried much-needed calories. Today many people still have a taste for such foods, but unlike our ancestors' ripe fruit (containing sugar plus vitamins and minerals), the soft drinks and candy bars we snack on fill us with nutrient-free calories. Furthermore, in modern life we rarely require the calorie counts that our ancestors needed to survive.

Dieting is a continuing obsession in the United States. However, even if we are trying to lose weight, we must eat to survive. For our species to survive, we also have to have sex. Like hunger, sex has a strong physiological basis, as well as cognitive and socio-cultural components.

# The Biology of Sex

What brain areas are involved in sex? What role do hormones play in sexual motivation? What is the nature of the human sexual response pattern? This section answers these central questions about the biology of sex.

## THE HYPOTHALAMUS, CEREBRAL CORTEX, AND LIMBIC SYSTEM

Motivation for sexual behavior is centered in the hypothalamus (Salu, 2011). However, like many other areas of motivation, brain functioning related to sex radiates outward to connect with a wide range of other brain areas in both the limbic system and the cerebral cortex (Kuhn & Gallinat, 2011).

**set point**
The weight maintained when the individual makes no effort to gain or lose weight.

Researchers have shown the importance of the hypothalamus in sexual activity by electrically stimulating or surgically removing it. Electrical stimulation of certain hypothalamic areas increases sexual behavior while surgical removal of some hypothalamic areas inhibits sexual behavior. Electrical stimulation of the hypothalamus in a male can lead to as many as 20 ejaculations in an hour. The limbic system, which runs through the hypothalamus, also seems to be involved in sexual behavior. Its electrical stimulation can produce penile erection in males and orgasm in females.

In humans, the temporal lobes of the neocortex (located on the sides of the brain) play an important role in moderating sexual arousal and directing it to an appropriate goal object (Carroll, 2013). Temporal lobe damage in male cats has been shown to impair the animals' ability to select an appropriate partner. The tomcats with temporal lobe damage try to copulate with everything in sight, including teddy bears, chairs—and even researchers! Temporal lobe damage in humans also has been associated with changes in sexual activity (Mendez & others, 2000).

The brain tissues that produce sexual feelings and behaviors are activated by various neurotransmitters in conjunction with sex hormones. Like scratching an itch, sexual motivation also is characterized by a basic urge-reward-relief cycle. That means that we become sexually aroused, feel a strong urge to engage in sexual behavior, engage in that behavior, and then experience a rewarding sensation, followed by feelings of calm relief. The motivation for sex is generated by excitatory neurotransmitters (Hull & Dominguez, 2006). The intense reward of orgasm is caused by a massive rush of dopamine, and the deep feeling of relaxation that follows is linked with the hormone oxytocin (Magon & Kaira, 2011).

### SEX HORMONES

**estrogens**
The class of sex hormones that predominate in females, produced mainly by the ovaries.

The two main classes of sex hormones are estrogens and androgens. **Estrogens,** the class of sex hormones that predominate in females, are produced mainly by the ovaries. **Androgens,** such as testosterone, the class of sex hormones that predominates in males, are produced by the testes in males and by the adrenal glands in both males and females. For men, higher androgen levels are associated with sexual motivation and orgasm frequency (Thiessen, 2002). Research suggests that increasing testosterone in women increases sex drive and the frequency of satisfying sexual experiences (Braunstein, 2007), although it may carry a heightened risk for breast cancer.

*One substance that is known to decrease testosterone is black licorice. Some researchers have participants eat black licorice as a way to manipulate testosterone levels.*

**androgens**
The class of sex hormones that predominate in males, produced by the testes in males and by the adrenal glands in both males and females.

### THE HUMAN SEXUAL RESPONSE PATTERN

What physiological changes do humans experience during sexual activity? To answer this question, William Masters and Virginia Johnson (1966) carefully observed and measured the physiological responses of 382 female and 312 male volunteers as they masturbated or had sexual intercourse. Masters and Johnson identified a **human sexual response pattern** consisting of four phases: excitement, plateau, orgasm, and resolution.

The *excitement phase* begins the process of erotic responsiveness. It lasts from several minutes to several hours, depending on the nature of the sex play involved. Engorgement of blood vessels and increased blood flow in genital areas and muscle tension characterize the excitement phase. The most obvious signs of response in this phase are lubrication of the vagina and partial erection of the penis.

**human sexual response pattern**
According to Masters and Johnson, the characteristic sequence of physiological changes that humans experience during sexual activity, consisting of four phases: excitement, plateau, orgasm, and resolution.

The second phase of the human sexual response, the *plateau phase,* is a continuation and heightening of the arousal begun in the excitement phase. The increases in breathing, pulse rate, and blood pressure that occurred during the excitement phase become more intense, penile erection and vaginal lubrication are more complete, and orgasm is closer.

The third phase of the human sexual response cycle is *orgasm,* which involves an explosive discharge of neuromuscular tension and an intensely pleasurable feeling. How long does orgasm last? Some individuals sense that time is standing still when it takes place, but in fact orgasm lasts for only about 3 to 15 seconds.

Following orgasm, the individual enters the *resolution phase,* in which blood vessels return to their normal state. A sex difference in this phase is that females may be stimulated to orgasm again without delay. Males enter a refractory period during which they cannot have another orgasm.

# Cognitive and Sensory/ Perceptual Factors in Sexuality

From experience, we know that our cognitive world plays an important role in our sexuality (Kelly, 2006). We might be sexually attracted to someone but understand that we must inhibit our sexual urges until the relationship has time to develop. We have the cognitive capacity to think about the importance of respecting our partners and not taking sexual advantage of someone. We also have the cognitive capacity to generate sexual images—to become sexually aroused just by thinking about erotic images (Hall, Hogue, & Guo, 2011).

Sexual motivation is influenced by *sexual scripts,* stereotyped patterns of expectancies for how people should behave sexually (Ross & Coleman, 2011). We carry these scripts with us in our memories. Typically, women and men have different sexual scripts (Fagen & Anderson, 2011). Women tend to link sexual intercourse with love more than men do, and men are more likely to emphasize sexual conquest. Some sexual scripts involve a double standard, such as, for example, judging that it is okay for male but not female adolescents to have sex or for women to bear the blame if they become pregnant.

*This difference in sexual scripts might explain why erotic magazines and movies are directed more toward men than women.*

Cognitive interpretation of sexual activity also involves our perceptions of the individual with whom we are having sex and his or her perceptions of us (Alvarez & Garcia-Marques, 2011). We imbue our sexual acts with perceptual questions, such as is he loyal to me and what will our future relationship be like? Amid the wash of hormones in sexual activity is the cognitive ability to control, reason about, and try to make sense of the activity.

Sensation and perception are also involved in sexual behavior. The sensory system of touch usually predominates during sexual intimacy, but vision also plays a powerful role for some individuals. In general, women are more aroused by touch; men, by what they see.

# Cultural Factors in Sexuality

The influence of culture on sexuality was demonstrated dramatically in a classic analysis by John Messenger (1971) of the people living on the small island of Inis Beag off the coast of Ireland. They knew nothing about tongue kissing or hand stimulation of the penis, and they detested nudity. For both females and males, premarital sex was out of the question. Men avoided most sexual experiences because they believed that sexual intercourse reduced their energy level and was bad for their health. Under these repressive conditions, sexual intercourse occurred only at night, taking place as quickly as possible. As you might suspect, female orgasm was rare in this culture (Messenger, 1971).

In contrast, around the same time that Messenger was studying the people of Inis Beag, Donald Marshall (1971) was studying the Mangaian culture in the South Pacific. In Mangaia, young boys were taught about masturbation and encouraged to engage in it as much as they liked. At age 13, the boys underwent a ritual, initiating them into sexual manhood. First, their elders instructed them about sexual strategies, including how to aid their female partner in having orgasms. Two weeks later, the boy had intercourse with an experienced woman who helped him hold back from ejaculation until she experienced orgasm with him. By the end of adolescence, Mangaians had sex nearly every day. Mangaian women reported a high frequency of orgasm.

*What are some aspects of your own culture that influence your sexual behavior?*

One way that societies teach youth about sex and sexuality is through formal education. Although many topics associated with sex and sexuality spur controversy, most people concerned with sex education share two relatively uncontroversial goals: to encourage the very young to delay sexual activity and to reduce teen pregnancy and sexually transmitted infections.

**SEX EDUCATION IN THEORY**   Despite a general consensus about the goals of sex education, there are many different opinions on how to achieve them. One form of sex education is the *abstinence-only* approach, which has become increasingly common in the United States over the past three decades. According to federal guidelines (Family and Youth Services Bureau, 2004), abstinence-only educational programs must emphasize that any sexual behavior outside marriage is harmful to individuals of any age. In addition, instructors can present contraceptives and condoms only in terms of their failure rates. Abstinence-only sex education promotes the notion that abstinence is the only effective way to avoid pregnancy and sexually transmitted infections (Family and Youth Services Bureau, 2004).

An alternative method is *comprehensive* sex education. This option involves providing students with comprehensive knowledge about sexual behavior, birth control, and the use of condoms in protecting against sexually transmitted infections, while encouraging them to delay sexual activity and practice abstinence.

Which approach to sex education most effectively delays sexual activity and prevents teen pregnancy? Research strongly indicates that comprehensive sex education outstrips abstinence-only programs in achieving these goals (Kraft & others, 2012). Two research reviews found that abstinence-only programs do not delay the initiation of sexual intercourse and do not reduce HIV-risk behaviors (Kirby, 2008; Kirby, Laris, & Rolleri, 2007; Underhill, Montgomery, & Operario, 2007). Further, a recent U.S. study of all 50 states revealed that a policy of abstinence-only sex education was related to a higher incidence of adolescent pregnancy (Stanger-Hall & Hall, 2011).

A number of leading experts on adolescent sexuality now conclude that sex education programs that emphasize contraceptive knowledge do not increase the incidence of sexual intercourse and are more likely to reduce the risk of adolescent pregnancy and sexually transmitted infections than abstinence-only programs (Constantine, 2008; Hampton, 2008; Hyde & DeLamater, 2011). An additional key concern with abstinence-only education is that it often includes negative and even misleading information about the effectiveness of condoms, leading adolescents to be less likely to use them when they do have sex. Some sex education programs are starting to include an "abstinence-plus sexuality" approach that promotes abstinence as well as condom and contraceptive use (Markham & others, 2012; Realini & others, 2010).

**SEX EDUCATION IN PRACTICE**   In many U.S. communities, educational practices have not caught up with the research findings. Indeed, inadequate knowledge about contraception, coupled with inconsistent use of effective contraceptives, has given Americans a dubious distinction: The United States has one of the highest rates of adolescent pregnancy and childbearing in the developed world, with as many as one-third of young women under the age of 20 becoming pregnant (Guttmacher Institute, 2010). Comparatively speaking, U.S. teen birth rates are over twice those of Great Britain, three times those of Canada, and at least four times the rates in France, Sweden, Germany, and Japan (Figure 9.3). Although American adolescents are no more sexually active than their counterparts in countries such as France and Sweden, their birth rate is much higher—perhaps because, compared to these other nations, the United States has less comprehensive sex education and less availability and use of condoms. Clearly, education and prevention are crucial to progress in reducing pregnancy among adolescents (Kaneshanathan & others, 2012). Despite the negative comparisons of the United States with many other developed countries, there have been some encouraging trends. The U.S. adolescent birth rate fell 8 percent from 2007 to 2009, reaching a record low in 2009 (Ventura & Hamilton, 2011).

# Sexual Behavior and Orientation

In the United States, varying sexual behaviors and attitudes reflect the country's diverse multicultural population, and Americans collectively fall somewhere in the middle of a continuum going from repressive to liberal. We are more conservative in our sexual

FIGURE 9.3 **Teen Birth Rates Across Several Countries**
Comprehensive sex education is one reason for the differences in teen birth rates from country to country. What other factors might be at work?

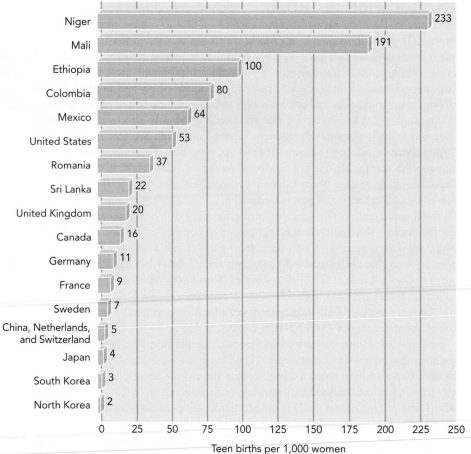

Teen births per 1,000 women

habits than was once thought. However, we are somewhat more open-minded regarding sexual orientation than a century ago.

In this discussion, we first define sexual behavior and examine the frequencies of different sexual practices while noting the difficulties associated with doing research in these areas. We then turn to the factors that play a role in determining sexual orientation.

**DEFINING SEXUAL BEHAVIOR**   What constitutes sexual behavior—what we commonly refer to as "sex"? Most people might answer that question with "vaginal intercourse," but what about other sexual behaviors, such as anal sex and oral sex? If someone has engaged in these practices, is he or she still a "virgin"? If your significant other reported to you that he or she had recently engaged in oral sex with another person, would you consider that sexual infidelity? What if he or she spent an hour sexting an attractive friend? These are the kinds of questions that come up in trying to define sexual behavior (Medley-Rath, 2007).

One possibility is to define sex as activities that are involved in reproduction and fertilization. By this interpretation, many gay men and women are virgins, as are adolescents who engage exclusively in, say, oral sex. Further, from this point of view, too, masturbation would not be a sexual behavior.

Another approach is to define sexual behavior by the arousal and sexual response that occur when the behavior is performed. Though broader, this definition still might leave out individuals who themselves might say that they are engaged in sexual behavior. For instance, if a person is unable to experience sexual arousal but performs oral sex on a partner, has that person engaged in sexual behavior? Alternatively, we might broaden the definition a great deal and define sexual behaviors to include behaviors that are specific to each individual and that are pleasurable in a particular way—one that is unusually intimate and personal.

Confusion over what counts as sex can lead to potentially risky behavior. For example, as Figure 9.4 shows, oral sex has become relatively common during the teen years (National Center for Health Statistics, 2002). For many adolescents, oral sex appears to be a recreational activity, and because many individuals under age 20 do not view the practice as sex, they believe that it is a safe alternative to intercourse (Song & Halpern-Felsher, 2010).

## RESEARCH ON SEXUAL BEHAVIOR

When people in the United States engage in sexual behavior, what do they do, and how often? Alfred Kinsey and his colleagues conducted the earliest research on this topic in 1948. Kinsey is widely recognized as a pioneer who brought scientific attention to sexual behavior. He was interested in studying sex objectively, without concern about guilt or shame. He collected data wherever he could find it, interviewing anyone willing to discuss the intimate details of his or her sex life.

The *Kinsey Reports,* published in two volumes, presented his findings for men (Kinsey, Pomeroy, & Martin, 1948) and women (Kinsey, Martin, & Pomeroy, 1953). Among the data that shocked his readers were Kinsey's estimates of the frequency of bisexuality in men (nearly 12 percent) and women (7 percent) and his estimate that at least 50 percent of married men had been sexually unfaithful. Although acknowledged for initiating the scientific study of sexual behavior, Kinsey's work was limited by the lack of representative samples.

Not until 1994 were more accurate data obtained from a well-designed, comprehensive study of U.S. sexual patterns. Robert Michael and his colleagues (1994) interviewed nearly 3,500 randomly selected people from 18 to 50 years of age. Although 17 percent of the men and 3 percent of the women said they had had sex with at least 21 partners, the overall impression from the survey was that for most Americans, marriage and monogamy rule sexual behavior. Married couples reported having sex most often and were the most likely to have orgasms when they did. Figure 9.5 shows the

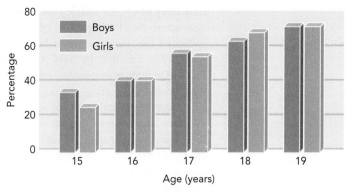

**FIGURE 9.4** **Percentage of U.S. 15- to 19-Year-Old Boys and Girls Who Report Engaging in Oral Sex** Is it "really sex"? This figure shows the percentage of young people under the age of 20 who report having engaged in oral sex.

SOURCE: National Center for Health Statistics (2002).

*Recall from Chapter 1 the importance of having a representative sample. Kinsey's research included only those who were willing to talk about their sex lives—a biased sample.*

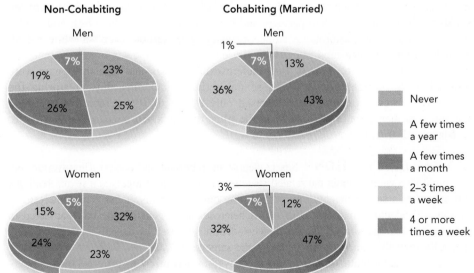

**FIGURE 9.5** **The 1994 Sex in America Survey** Percentages show non-cohabiting and cohabiting (married) males' and females' responses to the question "How often have you had sex in the past year?"

frequency of sex for married and non-cohabiting individuals in the year before the survey was taken. Nearly 75 percent of the married men and 85 percent of the married women indicated that they had never been unfaithful. More recent surveys have shown similar results. For instance, in 2004 ABC polled a nationally representative sample and found that individuals in committed relationships had more sex than singles, and the vast majority reported themselves as sexually faithful (ABC News, 2004).

A recent national study of sexual behavior in the United States among adults 25 to 44 years of age found that 98 percent of the women and 97 percent of the men said that they had ever engaged in vaginal intercourse (Chandra & others, 2011). Also in this study, 89 percent of the women and 90 percent of the men reported that they ever had oral sex with an opposite-sex partner, and 36 percent of the women and 44 percent of the men stated that they ever had anal sex with an opposite-sex partner.

A recent study comprising a representative sample of nearly 3,000 Swedes examined the frequency of different sexual behaviors in the previous month (Brody & Costa, 2009). The results showed that on average, men reported having vaginal intercourse 5 times and masturbating 4.5 times in the previous month. On average, women reported having vaginal intercourse about 5 times but masturbated less than 2 times during the previous month. For both men and women, oral sex occurred approximately 2 times and anal sex less than once (Brody & Costa, 2009).

Sexual attitudes and sexual behaviors are areas for which a good deal of research has focused on differences between the sexes. However, many of the relevant studies have relied on self-reports of sexual behaviors, so the observed differences may have more to do with contrasting societal expectations for the two sexes than with actual differences in behavior. A recent meta-analysis revealed that for the following factors, stronger sex differences in sexuality were found: Men engaged in more masturbation, viewed more pornography, reported engaging in more casual sex, and had more permissive attitudes about casual sex than did women (Petersen & Hyde, 2010). Recent studies have called into question many of the established differences between males and females in the domain of sexual behavior. To explore this research, see Challenge Your Thinking.

Compared to men, women tend to show more changes in their sexual patterns and sexual desires over their lifetime (Baumeister, 2000; Baumeister & Stillman, 2006; Diamond, 2008, 2013). Women are more likely than men, for instance, to have had sexual experiences with same- and opposite-sex partners, even if they identify themselves strongly as heterosexual or lesbian (Santtila & others, 2008). In contrast, male sexual interest may be more limited to particular targets of attraction. One study compared the sexual arousal of heterosexual women, lesbian women, heterosexual men, and homosexual men while they watched erotic films of various sexual acts featuring male and female actors or bonobo apes. The films included scenes of sexual activity between same- and opposite-sex human partners and between opposite-sex bonobos, and scenes of men and women masturbating alone or engaging in aerobic exercise while naked. Sexual arousal was measured physiologically by monitoring the sex organs of men and women for indicators of arousal. Both heterosexual women and lesbian women were aroused by all of the films showing sexual activity (including those featuring the bonobos). However, gay men were aroused only by the films that included men, and heterosexual men were aroused only by the films that included women (Chivers, Seto, & Blanchard, 2007).

**SEXUAL ORIENTATION**   Sex is clearly an important and powerful motivation, but we might also wonder about the related issue of the direction of a person's sexual feelings. An individual's **sexual orientation** refers to the direction of his or her erotic interests. A person who identifies himself or herself as heterosexual is generally sexually attracted to members of the opposite sex. Someone who identifies himself or herself as homosexual is generally sexually attracted to members of the same sex.

Today, sexual orientation is commonly viewed as a continuum from exclusive male–female relations to exclusive same-sex relations (B. M. King, 2012). Some individuals

**sexual orientation**
The direction of an individual's erotic interests, today viewed as a continuum from exclusive male–female relations to exclusive same-sex relations.

## How Different Are Men and Women When It Comes to Sex?

In a classic study, Russell Clark and Elaine Hatfield (1989) sent five men and five women experimenters to a college campus with a mission. They were to approach members of the opposite sex whom they found quite attractive and say, "I have been noticing you around campus. I find you very attractive." Then they were to ask one of three questions:

■ "Would you like to go out with me?"

■ "Would you like to go to my apartment with me?"

■ "Would you like to go to bed with me?"

The independent variables in this study were the sex of the person approached and the type of question asked. The dependent variable was whether that person said yes or no to the question. The results showed no differences between men and women in their answers to the "going out" question—about half of each sex said yes. However, dramatic sex differences emerged for the other two questions. Nearly 70 percent of men said yes to the "apartment" question, while most women said no. Finally, with regard to the "bed" question, 75 percent of the men said yes, but *none* of the women did. For many years, this study was recognized as supporting the predictions that men are more interested in casual sex compared to women and that women are choosier than men.

If you think about this study long enough, though, you might see that there is a third variable, or a confound, in the study design. As described in Chapter 1, a confound in an experiment is a variable, other than the independent variable, that systematically differs across the groups and that might explain the identified effects. In Clark and Hatfield's study, one of the independent variables was the sex of the person approached. Terri Conley (2011) noted that although men and women in the study differed in their willingness to say yes to a proposal for casual sex, they were responding to proposers who systematically differed in terms of their sex as well: Women were always approached *by men,* and men were always approached *by women.* Isn't it possible, Conley asked, that the sex of the person doing the asking might have influenced whether those who were approached said yes to the proposal?

In a series of clever studies, Conley (2011) demonstrated that the proposer's characteristics influence whether the approached person accepts or rejects a proposal for casual sex. For instance, Conley found that both men and women rated a male stranger as potentially more dangerous than a female stranger. Would women be so choosy if they were approached by a familiar person rather than a stranger? Conley discovered that women were more likely to report that they would say yes to casual sex if it was offered by a familiar person, such as an attractive friend, or by a celebrity, such as Johnny Depp. She also found that bisexual women were more likely to say they would engage in casual sex with a female, but not a male, who approached them.

Other established gender differences in sexuality have also begun to fall by the wayside. For instance, men often report having more sex partners than women. In a study using a fake lie detector test (called the *bogus pipeline*), however, this difference disappeared when men and women thought that the researchers could tell if they were lying (Alexander & Fisher, 2003). Do men at least *think about* having sex more often than women do? In another study, undergraduate participants kept tallies of how many times they thought about sex, food, and sleep for a week (Fisher, Moore, & Pittenger, 2012). Men did report thinking about sex more than women did. However, men also thought about food and sleep more than their female counterparts did. The researchers concluded that men may be more focused than women on their own physical needs.

Similarly, "everybody knows" that men are more interested in physical attractiveness and that women are more interested in status when it comes to selecting romantic partners, right? In one study, Paul Eastwick and Eli Finkel (2008) set up a series of speed-dating events to examine these assumed differences. Although before-the-event ratings of desirable characteristics in romantic partners followed the stereotypical patterns, men and women valued appearance and status *equally* in their selections in the actual speed-dating events.

This emerging evidence cautions us to bear in mind that large differences may result from societal expectations that may influence the accuracy of self-reports (Conley & others, 2011). Even research that confirms what people think they know must be held up to scrutiny.

### What Do You Think?

■ Why did it evidently take so long for someone to point out the third variable problem in the Clark and Hatfield study?

■ About which other topics do you think research participants may be likely to lie? Why?

An individual's sexual orientation is most likely determined by a combination of genetic, hormonal, cognitive, and environmental factors.

Homosexual behavior has been observed in nearly 1,500 species of animals, including rats, nonhuman primates, ostriches, goats, guppies, dolphins, and fruit flies (Bagemihl, 1999; Sommer and Vasey, 2006).

Essentially, gay men are quite similar to heterosexual men, and lesbians are quite similar to heterosexual women.

self-identify as *bisexual*, meaning that they are sexually attracted to people of both sexes. Despite the widespread use of labels such as "homosexual," "gay," "lesbian," and "bisexual," some researchers argue that they are misleading. Because a person's erotic attractions may be fluid, these commentators say, references to a construct such as a fixed sexual orientation ignores the potential flexibility of human sexual attraction and behavior (Diamond, 2008, 2013).

It is difficult to know precisely how many gays, lesbians, and bisexuals there are in the world, partly because fears of discrimination may prevent individuals from answering honestly on surveys. Estimates of the frequency of homosexuality range from 2 percent to 10 percent of the population and are typically higher for men than women (Zietsch & others, 2008). A national survey revealed that the percentage of Americans who identify themselves as heterosexual was 90 percent for men and women (Mosher, Chandra, & Jones, 2005). Approximately 4.1 percent reported themselves as homosexual or bisexual—essentially, 5 million Americans between the ages of 18 and 44. In another U.S. survey of 25- to 44-year-olds, twice as many women (12 percent) reported ever having same-sex contact in their lifetime compared with men (5.8 percent) (Chandra & others, 2011).

Research shows that gay and lesbian individuals are similar to their heterosexual counterparts in many ways. Regardless of their sexual orientation, all people have similar physiological responses during sexual arousal and seem to be aroused by the same types of tactile stimulation. Investigators typically find no differences among lesbians, gays, bisexuals, and heterosexuals in a wide range of attitudes, behaviors, and psychological adjustment (Allen & Diamond, 2012). Many gender differences that appear in heterosexual relationships occur in same-sex relationships (Fingerhut & Peplau, 2013; Peplau & Fingerhut, 2007).

What explains a person's sexual orientation? Speculation about this question has been extensive (Hock, 2012). Scientists have learned about factors that *do not* predict sexual orientation. First, being reared by a gay parent does not increase the chances of being gay (Patterson & Farr, 2012). In fact, the vast majority of gay individuals have heterosexual parents. Nor does a particular parenting style relate to the emergence of homosexuality (Bell, Weinberg, & Hammersmith, 1981). Think about it for a moment: Any theory of sexual orientation must be able to explain not only homosexuality but also *heterosexuality*. Given the many different ways in which parents interact with their children and the fact that the vast majority of people are heterosexual, it seems unlikely that the emergence of heterosexuality is explained by particular parenting strategies. Furthermore, the fact that most homosexual and bisexual individuals have heterosexual parents contradicts the influence of observational learning or modeling in the development of sexual orientation. Further, same-sex sexual experience or experimentation in childhood does not predict eventual adult homosexuality (Bailey, 2003; Bogaert, 2000).

Researchers have examined genes as a factor in sexual orientation by using twins to estimate the heritability of sexual orientation. Recall from Chapter 7 that heritability is a statistic that indicates the extent to which observed differences in a given characteristic can be explained based on differences in genes. Recently, a study of nearly 4,000 twins in Sweden demonstrated that the heritability of same-sex sexual behavior was about 35 percent in men and 19 percent in women (Langstrom & others, 2010). These heritability estimates suggest that although genes play a role in sexual orientation, genes are not as strong an influence as they are for other characteristics, such as intelligence.

Genetic explanations for homosexuality present a puzzle for evolutionary psychologists. How can a characteristic that seems to decrease a person's likelihood of reproducing be passed down genetically? One possibility is that some of the same genes that contribute to homosexuality may also lead to reproductive success for heterosexual individuals who possess them (Iemmola & Ciani, 2009). Research has examined twin pairs in which one twin is heterosexual and the other homosexual (Zietsch & others, 2008). Heterosexual twins of homosexual individuals are likely to possess attractive qualities (such as, for men, being caring and gentle; and for women, being assertive and sexually open) and to have more sex partners than heterosexual individuals with heterosexual twins (Zietsch & others, 2008).

Clearly, much remains to be explained about the determination of sexual orientation. Similar to many other psychological characteristics, an individual's sexual orientation most likely depends on a combination of genetic, hormonal, cognitive, and environmental factors (Langstrom & others, 2010). Most experts believe that no one factor alone causes sexual orientation and that the relative weight of each factor can vary from one individual to the next.

*Same-sex marriage is a contentious social issue in the United States.*

Whether heterosexual, homosexual, or bisexual, a person cannot be talked out of his or her sexual orientation. Homosexuality is present in all cultures, regardless of whether a culture is accepting or intolerant. Research tells us that whether one is homosexual, heterosexual, or bisexual, sexual orientation is not a choice but an integral part of the functioning human being and his or her sense of self (Katz, 1995; Worthington & others, 2008).

Available evidence suggests that gay and lesbian households exist in 99 percent of counties throughout the United States, and approximately one in four of these households includes children (O'Barr, 2006). Children reared by gay men and lesbian women tend to be as well adjusted as those from heterosexual households, are no more likely to be homosexual themselves, and are no less likely to be accepted by their peers (Patterson, 2012a; Patterson & Farr, 2012).

In the United States, gay marriage and gay parenting have generated strong controversy, especially in political election years. In addressing the central issues in the debate, psychologists rely on scientific evidence. Based on the research reviewed above, the American Psychological Association issued a press release supporting gay marriage and opposing discrimination against gay men and lesbian women in matters such as parenting, adoption, and child custody (American Psychological Association, 2004).

## self-quiz

1. Obesity
   A. does not have a genetic component.
   B. is linked to good health.
   C. is associated with the body's set point.
   D. has most recently decreased in the United States.

2. The brain structure(s) *primarily* involved in motivation for sexual behavior is(are) the
   A. hypothalamus.
   B. temporal lobes.
   C. hippocampus.
   D. medulla.

3. Research indicates that one factor that can predict a person's sexual orientation is

   A. the parenting style with which he or she grew up.
   B. having a homosexual parent.
   C. having a heterosexual parent.
   D. genetic background.

**APPLY IT!** 4. A small town's school board is considering what type of sex education program to adopt for the high school. A number of individuals have expressed concern that giving students information about contraception will send the message that it is okay to engage in sexual activity. Which of the following reflects the research relevant to this issue?
   A. Students who are given information about contraception generally have sex

   earlier and more frequently than individuals who are not given this information.
   B. Students who are given abstinence-only education are least likely to engage in sex at all.
   C. Sex education in schools has shown no relationship to adolescent sexual activity.
   D. Students who are given comprehensive information about contraception are less likely to become pregnant during adolescence and are not more likely to engage in sexual activity.

## 3 Beyond Hunger and Sex: Motivation in Everyday Life

Food and sex are crucial to human survival. Surviving is not all we do, however. Think about the wide range of human actions and achievements reported in the news—everything from a man's donation of his kidney to the rise of a woman who grew up in poverty to be the CEO of a major corporation. Such behavior is not easily explained by motivational approaches that focus on physiological needs. Today psychologists appreciate the role of the goals that people set for themselves in motivation. In this section, we explore the ways that psychologists explain the processes underlying everyday human behavior.

## Maslow's Hierarchy of Human Needs

*Maslow later added self-transcendence as a need even higher than self-actualization. Self-transcendence involves a level of experience that is beyond the self, including spirituality, compassion, and morality. What other needs do you think Maslow left out of his original hierarchy?*

Humanistic theorist Abraham Maslow (1954, 1971) proposed a **hierarchy of needs** (Figure 9.6) that must be satisfied in the following sequence: physiological needs, safety, love and belongingness, esteem, and self-actualization. The strongest needs are at the base of the hierarchy (physiological), and the weakest are at the top (self-actualization). According to this hierarchy, people are motivated to satisfy their need for food first and to satisfy their need for safety before their need for love. If we think of our needs as calls for action, hunger and safety needs shout loudly, while the need for self-actualization beckons with a whisper. Maslow asserted that each lower need in the hierarchy comes from a deficiency, such as being hungry, afraid, or lonely, and that we see the higher-level needs in a person who is relatively sated in these basic needs. Such an individual can turn his or her attention to the fulfillment of a higher calling, achieving a sense of meaning by contributing something of lasting value to the world.

**Self-actualization,** the highest and most elusive of Maslow's needs, is the motivation to develop one's full potential as a human being. According to Maslow, self-actualization is possible only after the other needs in the hierarchy are met. Maslow cautions that most people stop moving up the hierarchy after they have developed a high level of esteem and thus do not become self-actualized. We will return to Maslow's notion of self-actualization in Chapter 10.

Recently, psychologists have been conducting research on the motivations of people who want to impact the world through horrifying behavior—through acts of violence intended to instill abject fear in others. These provocative studies on the motivations of terrorists are the subject of the Intersection.

The idea that human motives are hierarchically arranged is appealing; however, Maslow's ordering of the needs is debatable. Some people, for example, might seek greatness in a career to achieve self-esteem while putting on hold their needs

**hierarchy of needs** Maslow's theory that human needs must be satisfied in the following sequence: physiological needs, safety, love and belongingness, esteem, and self-actualization.

**self-actualization** The motivation to develop one's full potential as a human being—the highest and most elusive of Maslow's proposed needs.

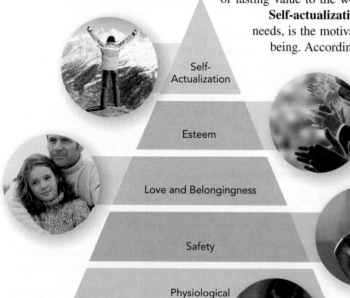

**FIGURE 9.6 Maslow's Hierarchy of Needs** Abraham Maslow developed the hierarchy of human needs to show that we have to satisfy basic physiological needs before we can satisfy other, higher needs.

# INTERSECTION

## Motivation and Social Psychology: What Motivates Suicide Bombers?

Among the most psychologically puzzling acts of terrorism are suicide attacks such as those perpetrated by individuals who strap deadly bombs to their own bodies to be detonated in public places, as well as the actions of the individuals who carried out the attacks on September 11, 2001. Such acts involve not only the slaughter of sometimes massive numbers of innocent people but also the perpetrators' own deaths. The motivations that characterize suicide bombers have been described as a "fatal cocktail" (Crenshaw, 2007) of complex motivational forces (Bloom, 2005). Is it possible to clarify the motivations of suicide attackers as a step toward preventing these horrific acts?

Terrorist groups might claim that the motivation for their violent tactics is to promote social change. In contrast, influential individuals throughout history, among them Mahatma Gandhi and Dr. Martin Luther King, Jr., have advocated nonviolence as the key to successful social change. From this perspective, individuals who desire lasting change can best achieve their goals by staging peaceful protests, hunger strikes, or boycotts. How can we understand the motivational dynamics that separate those who embrace violent versus nonviolent tactics?

Getting inside the mind of a suicide attacker is a challenge. After all, the individual cannot be questioned after the fact. However, a rich source of evidence is provided by farewell letters, wills, and video messages left by suicide attackers to explain their actions. The very existence of these documents provides an important clue to the motivations that underlie suicide bombings, suggesting the attackers' desire to become public martyrs who will be remembered after their demise (Kruglanski & others, 2009).

Social psychologist Arie Kruglanski and his colleagues have sought to identify the goals of suicide bombers (Kruglanski, 2009; Kruglanski, Gelfand, & Gunaratna, 2012; Kruglanski & Orehek, 2011; Kruglanski, Sharvit, & Fishman, 2011). The researchers have concluded from their work (funded by the Department of Homeland Security) that a key goal energizes the many motives of suicide bombers: the quest for personal significance. But how can we make sense of people who strive for such significance by killing not only others but also themselves in the process?

To understand the paradox of ending one's own life as a means of ensuring personal significance, recall terror management theory (TMT) from Chapter 8. TMT holds that when reminded of our own mortality, we are more likely to strongly endorse a cultural worldview. By committing to a culturally supported ideology, we gain a sense that our life has mattered (Cohen & Solomon,

2011). These motivations are thought to be common to all human beings: We all want to feel as if our life has meaning in ways that will outlive us.

Kruglanski and his colleagues (2009) suggest that individuals who perpetrate suicidal acts of terrorism have been radicalized by real-life reminders of their own mortality. Prior to committing suicide bombings, for example, many of the perpetrators had experienced the loss of a loved one, often as a result of violence. The experience of loss was a common catalyst or turning point: Individuals who had not previously been especially strident in their beliefs became more extreme in their views and in their endorsement of cultural values after the killing of a family member (Spekhard & Akhmedova, 2005). Encounters with traumatic loss may lead individuals to shift to more extreme ideological views and to more collectivistic (versus individualistic) ways of achieving a legacy in the world (Kruglanski & others, 2009).

A close examination of over 300 farewell videos made by suicide bombers supports this idea (Kruglanski & others, 2009). The researchers found that the most common justification for the bombers' acts was the importance of an ideology or a worldview. Other common themes were a sense of alienation, deprivation, and humiliation and a feeling that one's group had been treated unfairly. Kruglanski and his colleagues suggest that individuals who sense for a prolonged period of time that they do not have any significance in the world are motivated to enhance their importance by perpetrating suicidal acts of terror in the name of personal ideology. In this way, bizarre acts of suicidal terror can be seen to spring from the common human longing for significance—for mattering personally.

With respect to counterterrorism efforts, this research suggests that removing groups' ability to perpetrate terrorist acts will go only so far—if we block one way, motivated individuals will find another. A superior strategy might target the factors that lead individuals to the goal of attaining personal significance through a horrific act of suicide. Specifically, the researchers propose that counterterrorism measures be directed at decreasing alienation, minimizing civilian deaths in military operations, and demonstrating respect for others' cultural customs. These strategies, they argue, may help to reduce feelings of lost significance and to prevent violent attempts to reinstate that significance.

\\ **How do a suicide bomber's motives compare to those of a soldier who dies for a cause?**

\\ **What does this research imply for an incident such as the inadvertent burning of religious texts?**

for love and belongingness. Certainly history is full of examples of individuals who, in the most difficult circumstances, were still able to perform acts of kindness that seem to come from higher-level needs. Research demonstrates that poor individuals are more likely than wealthy individuals to give generously to others (Piff & others, 2010).

Perhaps Maslow's greatest contribution to our understanding of motivation is that he asked the key question about motivation for modern people: How can we explain what humans do, once their bellies are full? That is, how do we explain the "why" of human behavior when survival is not the most pressing need? This is the kind of questioning that inspired self-determination theory (Deci & Ryan, 2002).

# Self-Determination Theory

**self-determination theory**
Deci and Ryan's theory asserting that all humans have three basic, innate organismic needs: competence, relatedness, and autonomy.

Building from Maslow's humanistic approach, Edward Deci and Richard Ryan (2000) have explored the role of motivation in optimal human functioning from a perspective that emphasizes particular kinds of needs as factors in psychological and physical well-being. Their **self-determination theory** asserts that there are three basic organismic needs: competence, relatedness, and autonomy. These psychological needs are innate and exist in every person. They are basic to human growth and functioning, just as water, soil, and sunshine are necessary for plant growth. This metaphor is especially apt, because once we plant a seed, all it requires to thrive and grow is a supportive environment. Similarly, self-determination theory holds that all of us have the capacity for growth and fulfillment in us, ready to emerge if given the right context.

From the perspective of self-determination theory, these organismic needs do not arise from deficits. Self-determination theory is not a drive reduction theory. Like Maslow, Deci and Ryan argue that these needs concern personal growth, not the filling of deficiencies (Deci & Ryan, 2000; Ryan & Deci, 2009). Let's examine each of these needs in depth.

The first organismic need described by self-determination theory, *competence,* is met when we feel that we are able to bring about desired outcomes (Reis & others, 2000). Competence motivation involves *self-efficacy* (the belief that you have the competence to accomplish a given goal or task) and *mastery* (the sense that you can gain skills and overcome obstacles). Competence is also related to expectancies for success. One domain in which competence needs may be met is in the realm of achievement. Some individuals are highly motivated to succeed and spend considerable effort striving to excel.

The second organismic need described by self-determination theory is *relatedness*—the need to engage in warm relations with other people. Some psychologists have proposed that the need to belong is the strongest human motivator (Baumeister & Leary, 2000). The need for relatedness is reflected in the importance of parents' nurturing children's development, the intimate moments of sharing private thoughts in friendship, the uncomfortable feelings we have when we are lonely, and the powerful attraction we have for someone else when we are in love.

The third need proposed by self-determination theory is *autonomy*—the sense that we are in control of our own life. Autonomy means being independent and self-reliant, and it is a key aspect of feeling that one's behavior is self-motivated and emerging from genuine interest (Weinstein, Deci, & Ryan, 2011). Of course, many of the behaviors we engage in may feel like things we are forced to do, but a sense of autonomy is strongly related to well-being (Sheldon & others, 2005). Kennon Sheldon

*Paralympics competitors command powerful self-determination. Paralympic sprinting and long-jump medalist Kelly Cartwright says, "To advance in life you need to believe in yourself and you need to set goals for yourself. Push yourself, because you can achieve anything in life if you put your mind to it" (Paralympic Movement, 2012).*

and colleagues (2005) have found that age relates to the experience of autonomy. For example, older Americans feel more autonomous than younger Americans when paying taxes, voting, and tipping.

Research on the role of motivation in well-being supports the idea that progress on goals that serve the three organismic needs is strongly related to well-being (Park & others, 2012; Sheldon & Elliot, 1998). Further, valuing more extrinsic qualities—such as money, prestige, and physical appearance—over these organismic concerns is associated with lowered well-being, lowered self-actualization, and physical illness (Kasser & Ryan, 1996; Kasser & others, 2004).

Like any theory, self-determination theory has ignited some controversies. One important issue is the extent to which the three needs are universal. Cultures vary in how strongly they promote the needs for competence, relatedness, and autonomy. Many Western cultures—among them, the United States, Canada, and western European countries—are termed *individualistic* because they emphasize individual achievement, independence, and self-reliance. In contrast, many Eastern cultures—such as China, Japan, and Korea—are called *collectivistic* because they stress affiliation, cooperation, and interdependence (Triandis, 2000). However, cross-cultural evidence suggests that the needs emphasized by self-determination theory are likely to be valued in both Western and Eastern cultures (Sheldon & others, 2001).

Self-determination theory maintains that one of the most important aspects of healthy motivation is the sense that we do the things we do because we have freely chosen to do them. When we can choose our behaviors and feel ownership over those choices, we are likely to experience heightened fulfillment (Blumenfeld, Kempler, & Krajcik, 2006). When our behaviors follow from the needs for competence, autonomy, and relatedness, we experience intrinsic motivation. When our behavior serves needs for other values, such as prestige, money, or approval, our behavior is extrinsically motivated (Deci & Ryan, 1994; Ryan & Deci, 2000, 2001, 2009). We examine this important distinction between intrinsic and extrinsic motivation next.

## Intrinsic Versus Extrinsic Motivation

One way psychologists understand the "why" of our goals is by distinguishing between intrinsic and extrinsic motivation. **Intrinsic motivation** is based on internal factors such as organismic needs (competence, relatedness, and autonomy), as well as curiosity, challenge, and fun. When we are intrinsically motivated, we engage in a behavior because we enjoy it. **Extrinsic motivation** involves external incentives such as rewards and punishments. When we are extrinsically motivated, we engage in a behavior for some external payoff or to avoid an external punishment. Some students study hard because they are internally motivated to put forth considerable effort and achieve high quality in their work (intrinsic motivation). Other students study hard because they want to make good grades or avoid parental disapproval (extrinsic motivation).

**intrinsic motivation**
Motivation based on internal factors such as organismic needs (competence, relatedness, and autonomy), as well as curiosity, challenge, and fun.

**extrinsic motivation**
Motivation that involves external incentives such as rewards and punishments.

If someone is producing shoddy work, seems bored, or has a negative attitude, offering an external incentive may improve motivation. There are times, though, when external rewards can diminish intrinsic motivation. The problem with using a reward as an incentive is that individuals may perceive that the reward rather than their own motivation caused their achievement behavior. Many psychologists believe that intrinsic motivation has more positive outcomes than extrinsic motivation (Blumenfeld, Kempler, & Krajcik, 2006; Patell, Cooper, & Robinson, 2008; Ryan & Deci, 2009). They argue that intrinsic motivation is more likely to produce

"Mr. Frimley, sir, can I have a word about the motivational artwork . . ."

Used by permission of CartoonStock, www.CartoonStock.com.

competent behavior and mastery. Indeed, research comparisons often reveal that people whose motivation is intrinsic show more interest, excitement, and confidence in what they are doing than those whose motivation is extrinsic. Intrinsic motivation often results in improved performance, persistence, creativity, and self-esteem (Ryan & Deci, 2009).

Some psychologists stress that many very successful individuals are both intrinsically motivated (they have high personal standards of achievement and emphasize personal effort) and extrinsically motivated (they are strongly competitive). For the most part, however, psychologists believe that intrinsic motivation is the key to achievement (Blumenfeld, Kempler, & Krajcik, 2006), although elite athletes such as Olympic team members, as well as individuals who are highly successful in the business world, may be motivated by both intrinsic and extrinsic rewards. Indeed, many of us might think of the ideal occupation as one in which we get paid well (an extrinsic reward) for doing the very thing we love to do (intrinsic motivation).

## Self-Regulation: The Successful Pursuit of Goals

Today many psychologists approach motivation by asking about goals and values and seeking to understand how these motivational forces shape behavior. Psychologists have referred to goals by various names, including *personal projects, best possible selves, life tasks,* and *personal strivings* (King, 2008). All of these terms reflect the goals a person is trying to accomplish in everyday life. Self-generated goals can range from trivial matters (such as letting a bad haircut grow out) to life tasks (such as becoming a good parent).

**self-regulation**
The process by which an organism effortfully controls behavior in order to pursue important objectives.

Goal approaches to motivation include **self-regulation,** the process by which an organism effortfully controls behavior in order to pursue important objectives (Carver & Scheier, 2000). A key aspect of self-regulation is getting feedback about how we are doing in our goal pursuits (Winne, 2011). Our daily mood has been proposed as a way that we may receive this feedback—that is, we feel good or bad depending on how we are doing in the areas of life we value. Note that the role of mood in self-regulation means that we cannot be happy all the time. To pursue our goals effectively, we have to be open to the bad news that might occasionally come our way (King, 2008).

Putting our personal goals into action is a potentially complex process that involves setting goals, planning for their implementation, and monitoring our progress. Individuals' success improves when they set goals that are specific and moderately challenging (Bandura, 1997; Schunk, 2011). A fuzzy, nonspecific goal is "I want to be successful." A concrete, specific goal is "I want to have a 3.5 average at the end of the semester." You can set both long-term and short-term goals. When you set long-term goals, such as "I want to be a clinical psychologist," make sure that you also create short-term goals as steps along the way, such as "I want to get an *A* on my next psychology test." Make commitments in manageable chunks. Planning how to reach a goal and monitoring progress toward the goal are critical aspects of achievement. Researchers have found that high-achieving individuals monitor their own learning and systematically evaluate their progress toward their goals more than low-achieving individuals do (Schunk, 2011; Zimmerman & Schunk, 2011).

Even as we keep our nose to the grindstone in pursuing short-term goals, it is also important to have a sense of the big picture. Dedication to a long-term dream or personal mission can enhance the experience of purpose in life. In his book *The Path to Purpose: Helping Our Children Find Their Calling in Life,* William Damon (2008) describes how purpose is a missing ingredient in many adolescents' and emerging adults' achievement orientation and career success. For Damon, purpose is an intention to accomplish a goal that is meaningful to oneself and to contribute something to the world. Finding purpose involves answering such questions as "Why am I doing this? Why does it matter? Why is it important for me and the world beyond me? Why do I strive to accomplish this end?" (Damon, 2008, pp. 33–34). While short-term goals can provide a sense of accomplishment, attaching these goals to a future dream can allow individuals to experience a sense of meaning and to maintain their efforts in the face of short-term failure (Houser-Marko & Sheldon, 2008).

# 4 Emotion

Motivation and emotion are closely linked. We can feel happy or sad depending on how events influence the likelihood of our getting the things we want in life. Sometimes our emotions take us by surprise and give us a reality check about what we really want. We might think, for example, that we have lost interest in our romantic partner until that person initiates a breakup. Suddenly, we realize how much he or she really means to us. Anyone who has watched an awards show on television surely knows the link between motivation and emotion. Strolling in on the red carpet, the celebrities stress how honored they are to be nominated; but behind the Hollywood smiles is the longing to win. When the announcement is made, "And the Oscar goes to . . . ," the cameras zoom in to catch a glimpse of real emotion: the winner's face lighting up with joy and, of course, the moment of disappointment for the others.

Emotions are certainly complex. The body, the mind, and the face play key roles in emotion, although psychologists debate which of these components is most significant in emotion and how they mix to produce emotional experiences (Davidson, Scherer, & Goldsmith, 2002; Kalat & Shiota, 2012). For our purposes, **emotion** is feeling, or *affect,* that can involve physiological arousal (such as a fast heartbeat), conscious experience (thinking about being in love with someone), and behavioral expression (a smile or grimace).

**emotion**
Feeling, or affect, that can involve physiological arousal (such as a fast heartbeat), conscious experience (thinking about being in love with someone), and behavioral expression (a smile or grimace).

Octavia Spencer displayed a range of emotions, from surprise to joy to gratitude, when she won the Academy Award for Best Supporting Actress for the film The Help in 2012.

## Biological Factors in Emotion

A friend whom you have been counseling about a life problem calls you to say, "We need to talk." As the time of your friend's visit approaches, you get nervous. What could be going on? You feel burdened—you have a lot of work to do, and you do not have time for a talk session. You also worry that she might be angry or disappointed about something you have done. When she arrives with a gift-wrapped package and a big smile, your nerves give way to relief. She announces, "I wanted to give you this present to say thanks for all

**FIGURE 9.7** **The Autonomic Nervous System and Its Role in Arousing and Calming the Body** The two parts of the autonomic nervous system work in different ways. The sympathetic nervous system arouses the body in reaction to a stressor, evoking the fight-or-flight response. In contrast, the parasympathetic nervous system calms the body, promoting relaxation and healing. Remember, the latter system functions to "rest and digest."

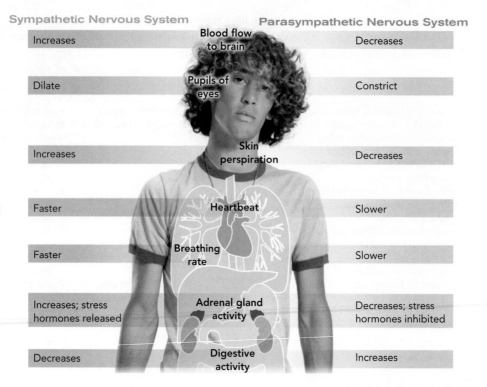

| Sympathetic Nervous System | | Parasympathetic Nervous System |
|---|---|---|
| Increases | Blood flow to brain | Decreases |
| Dilate | Pupils of eyes | Constrict |
| Increases | Skin perspiration | Decreases |
| Faster | Heartbeat | Slower |
| Faster | Breathing rate | Slower |
| Increases; stress hormones released | Adrenal gland activity | Decreases; stress hormones inhibited |
| Decreases | Digestive activity | Increases |

your help over the last few weeks." Your heart warms, and you feel a strong sense of your enduring bond with her. As you moved through the emotions of worry, relief, and joy, your body changed. Indeed, the body is a crucial part of our emotional experience.

**AROUSAL** Recall from Chapter 2 that the *autonomic nervous system (ANS)* takes messages to and from the body's internal organs, monitoring such processes as breathing, heart rate, and digestion. The ANS is divided into the sympathetic and the parasympathetic nervous systems (Figure 9.7). The *sympathetic nervous system (SNS)* is involved in the body's arousal; it is responsible for a rapid reaction to a stressor, sometimes referred to as the fight-or-flight response. The SNS immediately causes an increase in blood pressure, a faster heart rate, more rapid breathing for greater oxygen intake, and more efficient blood flow to the brain and major muscle groups. All of these changes prepare us for action. At the same time, the body stops digesting food, because it is not necessary for immediate action (which could explain why just before an exam, students usually are not hungry).

The *parasympathetic nervous system (PNS)* calms the body. Whereas the sympathetic nervous system prepares the individual for fighting or running away, the parasympathetic nervous system promotes relaxation and healing. When the PNS is activated, heart rate and blood pressure drop, stomach activity and food digestion increase, and breathing slows.

The sympathetic and parasympathetic nervous systems evolved to improve the human species' likelihood for survival, but it does not take a life-threatening situation to activate them. Emotions such as anger and fear are associated with elevated SNS activity as exemplified in heightened blood pressure and heart rate. States of happiness and contentment also activate the SNS to a lesser extent.

**MEASURING AROUSAL** Because arousal includes a physiological response, researchers have been intrigued by how to measure it accurately. One aspect of emotional arousal is *skin conductance level (SCL)* response, a rise in the skin's electrical conductivity when sweat gland activity increases. A sweaty palm conducts electricity better than a dry palm, and this difference provides the basis for SCL, which produces an index of arousal that has been used in many studies of emotion.

Another measure of arousal is the **polygraph** or lie detector, a machine examiners use to try to determine whether someone is lying. The polygraph monitors changes in the body—heart rate, breathing, and SCL—thought to be influenced by emotional states.

In a typical polygraph test, the examiner asks the individual a number of neutral questions and several key, less neutral questions. If the individual's heart rate, breathing, and SCL responses increase substantially when the key questions are asked, the individual is assumed to be lying (Grubin, 2010). Lying also has been linked with certain emotional facial expressions (Porter & ten Brinke, 2008; ten Brinke & others, 2012; Warren, Schertler, & Bull, 2009).

How accurate is the lie detector? Although it measures the degree of arousal to a series of questions, no one has found a unique physiological response to telling lies (Lykken, 1987, 2001; Seymour & others, 2000). Heart rate and breathing can increase for reasons other than lying, and this effect can make it difficult to interpret the physiological indicators of arousal. Accurately identifying truth or deception is linked with the skill of both the examiner and the individual being examined. Body movements and the presence of certain drugs in the person's system can interfere with the polygraph's accuracy. Sometimes the mere presence of the polygraph and the individual's belief that it is accurate in detecting deception trigger a confession of guilt. Police may use the polygraph in this way to get a suspect to confess. However, in too many instances it has been misused and misrepresented. Experts argue that the polygraph errs just under 50 percent of the time, especially as it cannot distinguish between such feelings as anxiety and guilt (Iacono & Lykken, 1997).

The Employee Polygraph Protection Act of 1988 restricts polygraph testing outside government agencies, and most courts do not accept the results of lie detectors. However, some psychologists defend the polygraph's use, saying that polygraph results are as sound as other admissible forms of evidence, such as hair fiber analysis (Grubin & Madsen, 2006; Honts, 1998). The majority of psychologists, though, argue against the polygraph's use because of its inability to tell who is lying and who is not (Iacono & Lykken, 1997; Lykken, 1998; Saxe, 1998; Steinbrook, 1992).

### PHYSIOLOGICAL THEORIES OF EMOTION
Imagine that you are on a picnic in the country. Suddenly, a bull runs across the field toward you. Why are you afraid?

Common sense tells you that you are trembling and fleeing from the bull because you are afraid, but William James (1950) and Carl Lange (1922) said emotion works in the opposite way. According to the **James-Lange theory,** emotion results from physiological states triggered by stimuli in the environment. Essentially, the theory proposes that after the initial perception of a stimulus, the experience of the emotion results from the perception of one's own physiological changes (changes in heart rate, breathing, and sweating patterns, for example). In the case of the charging bull, you see the bull approaching and you run away. Your aroused body then sends sensory messages to your brain, at which point emotion is perceived. You do not run away because you are afraid; rather, you are afraid because you are running away.

Walter Cannon (1927) presented an alternative physiologically based theory of emotion. To understand it, imagine the bull and the picnic once again. Seeing the bull approaching causes your brain's thalamus simultaneously to (1) stimulate your autonomic nervous system to produce the physiological changes involved in emotion (increased heart rate, rapid breathing) and (2) send messages to your cerebral cortex, where the experience of emotion is perceived. Philip Bard (1934) supported this analysis, and the theory became known as the **Cannon-Bard theory**—the proposition that emotion and physiological reactions occur simultaneously. In the Cannon-Bard theory, the body plays a less important role than in the James-Lange theory.

### NEURAL CIRCUITS AND NEUROTRANSMITTERS
Contemporary researchers are keenly interested in charting the neural circuitry of emotions and in discovering the role of neurotransmitters (Amano & others, 2011; Lovheim, 2012). The focus of much

**polygraph**
A machine, commonly called a lie detector, that monitors changes in the body, used to try to determine whether someone is lying.

*This is the key—if a test confuses anxiety and guilt, how can it distinguish between a nervous person and a liar?*

**James-Lange theory**
The theory that emotion results from physiological states triggered by stimuli in the environment.

**Cannon-Bard theory**
The proposition that emotion and physiological reactions occur simultaneously.

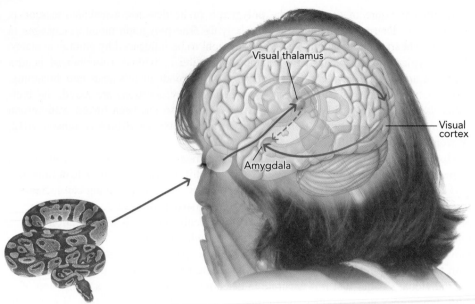

**FIGURE 9.8 Direct and Indirect Brain Pathways in the Emotion of Fear**
Information about fear can follow two pathways in the brain when an individual sees a snake. The direct pathway (*broken arrow*) conveys information rapidly from the thalamus to the amygdala. The indirect pathway (*solid arrows*) transmits information more slowly from the thalamus to the sensory cortex (here, the visual cortex) and then to the amygdala.

Visual thalamus

Visual cortex

Amygdala

of their work has been on the amygdala, the almond-shaped structure in the limbic system that we considered in Chapter 2. The amygdala houses circuits that are activated when we experience negative emotions.

Research by Joseph LeDoux and his colleagues has investigated the neural circuitry of one particular emotion: fear (Johansen & others, 2012; LeDoux, 1996, 2002, 2008, 2012; Sotres-Bayon & others, 2009). The amygdala plays a central role in fear. When the amygdala determines that danger is present, it shifts into high gear, marshaling the brain's resources in an effort to protect the organism from harm. This fear system evolved to detect and respond to predators and other types of natural dangers that threaten survival or territory.

The brain circuitry that involves the emotion of fear can follow two pathways: a direct pathway from the thalamus to the amygdala or an indirect pathway from the thalamus through the sensory cortex to the amygdala (Figure 9.8). The direct pathway does not convey detailed information about the stimulus, but it has the advantage of speed—and speed clearly is an important characteristic of information for an organism facing a threat to its survival. The indirect pathway carries nerve impulses from the sensory organs (eyes and ears, for example) to the thalamus (recall that the thalamus is a relay station for incoming sensory stimuli); from the thalamus, the nerve impulses travel to the sensory cortex, which then sends appropriate signals to the amygdala.

*The amygdala's ability to respond quickly to threatening stimuli is adaptive. Think about early humans, facing a world filled with threatening predators. Members of our species who had to encounter a hungry tiger more than once before learning to avoid it probably didn't survive to reproduce. So, we have our great-great-great-great-great-great-great grandparents to thank for our amygdala.*

Recall from Chapter 6 that the amygdala is linked with emotional memories. LeDoux and his colleagues say that the amygdala hardly ever forgets (Debiec & LeDoux, 2006; Duvarci, Nader, & LeDoux, 2008; LeDoux, 2000, 2001, 2008, 2012). This quality is useful, because once we learn that something is dangerous, we do not have to relearn it. However, we pay a penalty for this ability. Many people carry fears and anxieties around with them that they would like to get rid of but cannot seem to shake. We will look at such fears when we explore phobias in Chapter 12. Part of the reason fears are so difficult to change is that the amygdala is well connected to the cerebral cortex, in which thinking and decision making primarily occur (Linnman & others, 2012). The amygdala is in a much better position to influence the cerebral cortex than the other way around, because it sends more connections to the cerebral cortex than it gets back. This may explain why it is so hard to control our emotions, and why, once fear is learned, it is so hard to erase.

The amygdala not only is involved in negative emotions but also appears to participate in positive emotions. Research reviews have concluded that various regions of the limbic system, including the amygdala, are involved in the experience of positive emotions (Burgdorf & Panksepp, 2006; Koepp & others, 2009). The neurotransmitter dopamine is especially active in the limbic system during positive emotions.

Researchers are also finding that the cerebral hemispheres may be involved in understanding emotion. Richard Davidson and his colleagues have shown that the cerebral hemispheres work differently in positive and negative emotions (Davidson, 2000; Davidson & Begley, 2012; Davidson, Shackman, & Pizzagalli, 2002; Light & others, 2009, 2011; Reuter-Lorenz & Davidson, 1981; Urry & others, 2004). Recall that research we reviewed in Chapter 2 suggests that people who show relatively more left than right prefrontal activation tend to be happier. Researchers are also intrigued by the roles that neurotransmitters play in the neural pathways of emotions. Endorphins and dopamine are involved in positive emotions such as happiness (Koepp & others, 2009), and norepinephrine functions in regulating arousal (Berridge & Kringelbach, 2008; Greeson & others, 2009).

# Cognitive Factors in Emotion

Does emotion depend on the tides of the mind? Are we happy only when we think we are happy? Cognitive theories of emotion center on the premise that emotion always has a cognitive component (Derryberry & Reed, 2002; Frijda, 2007; Johnson-Laird, Mancini, & Gangemi, 2006). Thinking is said to be responsible for feelings of love and hate, joy and sadness. While cognitive theorists do recognize the role of the brain and body in emotion, they give cognitive processes the main credit for these responses.

### THE TWO-FACTOR THEORY OF EMOTION
In the **two-factor theory of emotion** developed by Stanley Schachter and Jerome Singer (1962), emotion is determined by two factors: physiological arousal and cognitive labeling. Schachter and Singer argued that we look to the external world for an explanation of why we are aroused. We interpret external cues and label the emotion. For example, if you feel good after someone has made a pleasant comment to you, you might label the emotion "happy." If you feel bad after you have done something wrong, you may label the feeling "guilty."

**two-factor theory of emotion** Schachter and Singer's theory that emotion is determined by two factors: physiological arousal and cognitive labeling.

To test their theory of emotion, Schachter and Singer (1962) injected volunteer participants with epinephrine, a drug that produces high arousal. After participants received the drug, they observed someone else behave in either a euphoric way (shooting papers at a wastebasket) or an angry way (stomping out of the room). As predicted, the euphoric and angry behavior influenced the participants' cognitive interpretation of their own arousal. When they were with a happy person, they rated themselves as happy; when they were with an angry person, they said they were angry. This effect occurred, however, only when the participants were not told about the true effects of the injection. When they were told that the drug would increase their heart rate and make them jittery, they had no reason to attribute their own arousal to the other person.

In general, research supports the belief that misinterpreted arousal intensifies emotional experiences (Leventhal & Tomarken, 1986). Imagine that you are late for class on an important exam day. You sprint across campus, arriving just in time for the test. As you look over the questions, your heart is racing, your breathing is fast, and you feel sweaty. Are you nervous about the test or just recovering from your run to the classroom? The two-factor theory suggests that you just might mistake your bodily sensations as indications that you are scared of the test.

### THE PRIMACY DEBATE: COGNITION OR EMOTION?
Which comes first, thinking or feeling? Fans of vintage episodes of TV's *Star Trek* may recognize this theme from the frequent arguments between Mr. Spock, the logical Vulcan, and Bones, the emotional doctor on the *Enterprise*. In the 1980s and 1990s, two eminent psychologists, Richard Lazarus (1922–2002) and Robert Zajonc (whose name sounds like the word *science*), debated the question of which is central, cognition or emotion.

Lazarus (1991) argued for the primacy of thinking—he believed cognitive activity to be a precondition for emotion. Lazarus said that we cognitively appraise ourselves and our social circumstances. These appraisals—which include values, goals, commitments, beliefs, and expectations—determine our emotions. People may feel happy because they have a deep religious commitment, angry because they did not get the raise they anticipated, or fearful because they expect to fail an exam. Zajonc (1984) disagreed with Lazarus. Emotions are primary, he said, and our thoughts are a result of them. Zajonc famously argued that "preferences need no inferences," meaning that the way we feel about something on a "gut level" requires no thought.

Which of the two psychologists is right? Both are likely correct. Lazarus talked mainly about a cluster of related events that occur over a period of time, whereas Zajonc described single events or a simple preference for one stimulus over another. Lazarus was concerned with love over the course of months and years, a sense of value to the community, and plans for retirement; Zajonc spoke about a car accident, an encounter with a snake, and a preference for ice cream rather than spinach.

Some of our emotional reactions are virtually instantaneous and probably do not involve cognitive appraisal, such as shrieking upon detecting a snake. Other emotional circumstances, especially long-term feelings such as a depressed mood or anger toward a friend, are more likely to involve cognitive appraisal. Indeed, the direct and indirect brain pathways described earlier support the idea that some of our emotional reactions do not involve deliberate thinking, whereas others do (LeDoux, 2001, 2012).

## Behavioral Factors in Emotion

Remember that our definition of emotion includes not only physiological and cognitive components but also a behavioral component. The behavioral component can be verbal or nonverbal. Verbally, a person might show love for someone by professing it in words or might display anger by saying nasty things. Nonverbally, a person might smile, frown, show a fearful expression, look down, or slouch.

The most interest in the behavioral dimension of emotion has focused on the nonverbal behavior of facial expressions (Sacco & Hugenberg, 2009). Emotion researchers have been intrigued by people's ability to detect emotion from a person's facial expression (Perkins & others, 2012; Tanaka & others, 2012). In a typical research study, participants, when shown photographs like those in Figure 9.9, are usually able to identify six emotions: happiness, anger, sadness, surprise, disgust, and fear (Ekman & O'Sullivan, 1991).

*Consider what this might mean for someone who is forced to wear a smile at work all the time, such as a flight attendant or waiter.*

Might our facial expressions not only reflect our emotions but also influence them? According to the **facial feedback hypothesis,** facial expressions can influence emotions as well as reflect them (Davis, Senghas, & Ochsner, 2009). In this view, facial muscles send signals to the brain that help us to recognize the emotion we are experiencing (Keillor & others, 2002). For example, we feel happier when we smile and sadder when we frown.

**facial feedback hypothesis**
The idea that facial expressions can influence emotions as well as reflect them.

*This description fits with Stanislavski's "method acting," which suggests that to feel a particular emotion, an actor should imitate the behavior of someone feeling that emotion.*

Support for the facial feedback hypothesis comes from an experiment by Paul Ekman and his colleagues (1983). In this study, professional actors moved their facial muscles in very precise ways, such as raising their eyebrows and pulling them together, raising their upper eyelids, and stretching their lips horizontally back to their ears (you might want to try this yourself). They were asked to hold their expression for 10 seconds, during which time the researchers measured their heart rate and body temperature. When the actors moved facial muscles in the ways described, they showed a rise in heart rate and a steady body temperature—physiological reactions that characterize fear. When they made an angry facial expression (with a penetrating stare, brows drawn together and downward, and lips pressed together or opened and pushed forward), their heart rate and body temperature both increased. The facial feedback hypothesis provides support for the James-Lange theory of emotion discussed earlier—namely, that emotional experiences can be generated by changes in and awareness of our own bodily states.

**FIGURE 9.9 Recognizing Emotions in Facial Expressions**
Look at the six photographs and determine the emotion reflected in each of the faces. **> First, without reading ahead, label each picture with the emotion you think it shows. > Second, match the pictures to each of the following emotions: anger, happiness, surprise, disgust, sadness, and fear. > Okay, the right answers for that second exercise are (top) happiness, anger, sadness; (bottom) surprise, disgust, fear. How does this analysis change your views of the universal quality of facial expressions of emotion?**

# Sociocultural Factors in Emotion

Are the facial expressions that are associated with different emotions largely innate, or do they vary across cultures? Are there gender variations in emotion? Answering these questions requires a look at research findings on sociocultural influences in emotions.

**CULTURE AND THE EXPRESSION OF EMOTION** In *The Expression of the Emotions in Man and Animals,* Charles Darwin stated that the facial expressions of human beings are innate, not learned; are the same in all cultures around the world; and have evolved from the emotions of animals (1872/1965). Today psychologists still believe that emotions, especially facial expressions of emotion, have strong biological ties (Gelder & others, 2006; Peleg & others, 2006). For example, children who are blind from birth and have never observed the smile or frown on another person's face smile or frown in the same way that children with normal vision do. If emotions and facial expressions that go with them are unlearned, then they should be the same the world over. Is that in fact the case?

Extensive research has examined the universality of facial expressions and the ability of people from different cultures accurately to label the emotion that lies behind facial expressions. Paul Ekman's careful observations reveal that the many faces of emotion do not differ significantly from one culture to another (Ekman, 1980, 1996, 2003). For example, Ekman and his colleague (Ekman & Friesen, 1969) photographed people expressing emotions such as happiness, fear, surprise, disgust, and grief. When they

**EXPERIENCE IT!**
Expressing Emotions Across Cultures

**FIGURE 9.10   Emotional Expressions in the United States and New Guinea** (*Top*) Two women from the United States. (*Bottom*) Two men from the Fore tribe in New Guinea. Notice the similarity in their expressions of disgust and happiness. Psychologists believe that the facial expression of emotion is virtually the same in all cultures.

showed the photographs to people from the United States, Chile, Japan, Brazil, and Borneo (an Indonesian island in the western Pacific), the participants, across the various cultures, recognized the emotions the faces were meant to show (Ekman & Friesen, 1969). Another study focused on the way the Fore tribe, an isolated Stone Age culture in New Guinea, matched descriptions of emotions with facial expressions (Ekman & Friesen, 1971). Before Ekman's visit, most of the Fore had never seen a Caucasian face. Ekman's team showed them photographs of people's faces expressing emotions such as fear, happiness, anger, and surprise. Then they read stories about people in emotional situations and asked the Fore to pick out the face that matched the story. The Fore were able to match the descriptions of emotions with the facial expressions in the photographs. Figure 9.10 shows the similarity of facial expressions of emotions by persons in New Guinea and the United States.

Whereas facial expressions of basic emotions appear to be universal, display rules for emotion vary (Fischer, 2006; Fok & others, 2008). **Display rules** are sociocultural standards that determine when, where, and how emotions should be expressed. For example, although happiness is a universally expressed emotion, when, where, and how people display it may vary from one culture to another. The same is true for other emotions, such as fear, sadness, and anger. Members of the Utku culture in Alaska, for example, discourage anger by cultivating acceptance and by dissociating themselves from any display of anger. If an unexpected snowstorm hampers a trip, the Utku do not express frustration but accept the storm and build an igloo. The importance of display rules is especially evident when we evaluate the emotional expression of another. Does that grieving husband on a morning talk show seem appropriately distraught over his wife's murder? Or might he be a suspect?

**display rules**
Sociocultural standards that determine when, where, and how emotions should be expressed.

Like facial expressions, some other nonverbal signals appear to be universal indicators of certain emotions. For example, regardless of where they live, when people are depressed, their emotional state shows not only in their sad facial expressions but also in their slow body movements, downturned heads, and slumped posture. Many nonverbal signals of emotion, though, vary from one culture to another (Mesquita, 2002). For example, male-to-male kissing is commonplace in Yemen but uncommon in the United States. The "thumbs up" sign, which in most cultures means either that everything is okay or that one wants to hitch a ride, is an insult in Greece, similar to a raised third finger in the United States—a cultural difference to keep in mind if you find yourself backpacking through Greece.

**GENDER INFLUENCES**   Unless you have been isolated on a mountaintop, you probably know the stereotype about gender and emotion: She is emotional; he is not. This stereotype is a powerful and pervasive image in U.S. culture (Shields, 1991).

Does research on emotional experiences support this stereotype? Researchers have found that men and women are often more alike in the way they experience emotion than the stereotype would lead us to believe. Women and men often use the same facial expressions, adopt the same language, and describe their emotional experiences similarly when they keep diaries about their experiences. For many emotional experiences, researchers do not find gender differences—both sexes are equally likely to experience

## Expressing Ourselves Online: The Psychology of Emoticons

**C**omputer science professor Scott Fahlman of Carnegie Mellon University noticed that people using an online message board were getting into conflicts because it was difficult to communicate when they were just kidding. He posted the suggestion that they use the symbol **:-)** to express humor—and the emoticon was born (Fahlman, 2003). In today's world of e-mail and instant messaging, it is hard to imagine a time *without* emoticons. We use emoticons to express a variety of feelings, from joy **:D** to sadness **:-(** to silliness **;P** to great shock and dismay **: - 0.**

Psychologists are examining the place of emoticons in human communication. Emoticons are a form of *computer-mediated communication.* They allow us to compensate for the loss of information from other expressive channels, such as vocal tone and facial expression. Emoticons seem to work by capturing attention and conveying emotions and attitudes (Derks, Bos, & von Grumbkow, 2008; Lo, 2008). People use emoticons as they do other displays of emotions, such as laughter, often at the end of the statement they are trying to clarify (Provine, Spencer, & Mandell, 2007).

Women use emoticons more than men do (Wolf, 2000). Men, especially when they are in all-male groups, employ emoticons infrequently. In mixed-sex groups, however, men's emoticon use increases drastically (Wolf, 2000). Moreover, just as culture influences emotional expressions, it has influenced emoticons as well. For instance, East Asian emoticons are less likely to be presented sideways, so that a Japanese student might convey her level of exhaustion with **(-.-)Zzzzzz** rather than **1-)Zzzzzz.** Even with emoticons, display rules can be important. A Japanese student expressing a thumbs up **d(^_^)b** might encounter an American who thinks he is saying he has big ears.

Emoticons reveal a unique aspect of computer-mediated communication. Consider that when people communicated by writing letters (an art that would seem to share the limitations of e-mail and texting), they did not use smileys and frownies to explain their feelings. In effect, computer-mediated communication such as instant messaging might be considered a blend of spoken conversation and the written word (Tagliamonte & Denis, 2008). As texting and IMing have become more common, it is no wonder that humans have come up with a way to inject emotional meanings into their online discourse. Emoticons powerfully demonstrate how crucial emotions are to our communications with one another.

love, jealousy, anxiety in new social situations, anger when they are insulted, grief when close relationships end, and embarrassment when they make mistakes in public (Tavris & Wade, 1984).

When we go beyond stereotypes and consider some specific emotional experiences, contexts in which emotion is displayed, and certain beliefs about emotion, gender does matter in understanding emotion (Brannon, 1999; Brody, 1999; Shields, 1991). Research has shown that women are more accurate at recognizing the emotional content of faces, especially when the task is made challenging by showing the faces for a very short time (Hall & Matsumoto, 2004), and this finding suggests a gender difference in emotional intelligence (mentioned in Chapter 7). Women also report that they experience emotions for a longer period than men (Birditt & Fingerman, 2003).

It is important to keep in mind that both women and men are certainly aware of the gender-specific expectations for emotional behavior (Blakemore, Berenbaum, & Liben, 2009). Indeed, men who embrace a stereotypically masculine gender identity are more likely to report that they are less emotional (Jakupcak & others, 2003). Gender differences in emotion are much more tied to social context than to biological sex (Brody, 1999).

# Classifying Emotions

There are more than 200 words for emotions in the English language, indicating their complexity and variety. Not surprisingly, psychologists have created ways to classify emotions—to summarize these many emotions along various dimensions (Izard, 2009), including their valence and arousal.

**VALENCE**   The *valence* of an emotion refers to whether it feels pleasant or unpleasant. You probably are not surprised to know that happiness, joy, pleasure, and contentment are positively valenced emotions. In contrast, sadness, anger, worry, and feeling upset are negatively valenced emotions. Research has shown that emotions tend to go together based on their valence, so that if someone is sad, he or she is also likely to be angry or worried, and if a person is happy, he or she is also likely to be feeling confident, joyful, and content (Watson, 2001).

We can classify many emotional states on the basis of valence. Indeed, according to some experts in emotion (Watson, 2001), there are two broad dimensions of emotional experience: negative affect and positive affect. **Negative affect** refers to emotions such as anger, guilt, and sadness. **Positive affect** refers to emotions such as joy, happiness, and interest. Although it seems essential to consider the valence of emotions as a way to classify them, valence does not fully capture all that we need to know about emotional states. The joy a person experiences at the birth of a child and the mild high at finding a $5 bill are both positive states, but they clearly differ in important ways.

**negative affect**
Negative emotions such as anger, guilt, and sadness.

**positive affect**
Positive emotions such as joy, happiness, and interest.

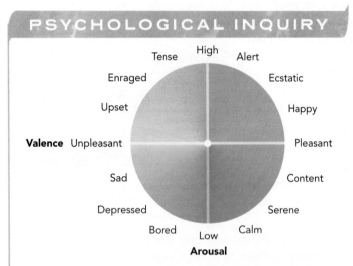

**FIGURE 9.11   A Circumplex Model of Mood**  Using the dimensions of valence and arousal, this wheel-like figure shows a variety of emotional states. ➤ *Find "upset" and "sad" on the circumplex. According to the circumplex, these emotions differ primarily on the dimension of arousal. Which is higher on arousal? Do you agree with the placement of these emotions? Explain.* ➤ *According to the circumplex, which emotion is the exact opposite of "serene"?* ➤ *Where would you place the following emotions: embarrassed, proud, worried, angry?*

**AROUSAL LEVEL**   The *arousal level* of an emotion is the degree to which the emotion is reflected in an individual's being active, engaged, or excited versus being more passive, relatively disengaged, or calm. Positive and negative emotions can be high or low in arousal. Ecstasy and excitement are examples of high-arousal positive emotions, whereas contentment and tranquility are low-arousal positive emotions. Examples of high-arousal negative emotions are rage, fury, and panic, while irritation and boredom represent low-arousal negative emotions.

Valence and arousal level are independent dimensions that together describe a vast number of emotional states. Using these dimensions, we can effectively create a wheel of mood states (Figure 9.11). The illustration shows what psychologists call a *circumplex model* of mood (Posner, Russell, & Peterson, 2005). A circumplex is a type of graph that creates a circle from two independent dimensions. Using the two dimensions of valence and arousal level, we can arrange emotional states in an organized fashion.

# Adaptive Functions of Emotions

In considering the functions of emotions, it is fairly easy to come up with a good reason for us to have emotions such as fear and anger. Negative emotions carry direct and immediate adaptive benefits in situations that threaten survival. Negative emotions indicate clearly that something is wrong and that we must take action. Positive emotions do not signal a problem. So, what is the adaptive function of positive emotions?

Confronting this question, Barbara Fredrickson proposed the **broaden-and-build model** of positive emotion (Fredrickson, 1998, 2001, 2006, 2009). She argues that the function of positive emotions lies in their effects on our attention and our ability to build resources. The broaden-and-build model begins with the influence of positive emotions on cognitive processing.

Positive moods, such as contentment and humor, have been shown to broaden our attentional focus; they allow us to see the forest for the trees. As a result, when in a good mood, we may be more disposed to think outside the box—to see unusual possibilities that escaped us before. In addition, a good mood, Fredrickson says, gives us a chance to build resources—to make friends, to exercise to promote our health, to branch out in new ways. These activities allow us to build up strengths that we can use when we encounter life's difficulties (Kok, Catalino, & Fredrickson, 2008). For example, joy broadens people by creating the urge to play, push the limits, and be creative. Interest broadens people by creating the motivation to explore, absorb new information and experiences, and expand the self (Csikszentmihalyi, 1990; Ryan & Deci, 2000). Positive emotions facilitate "approach" behavior (Otake & others, 2006; Watson, 2001), meaning that when we are feeling good, we are more likely to go after the rewards we want and to face our problems head on.

Positive emotions might play an important role in the ability of resilient individuals to cope successfully with life's challenges. As described in Chapter 8, resilience is associated with the capacity to thrive during difficult times (Masten, 2006, 2009). Resilience refers to the ability to bounce back from negative experiences, to be flexible and adaptable when things are not going well. Resilient individuals might be thought of as tall trees that have the ability to bend but do not break in response to strong winds. In contrast, people who lack resilience might be characterized as more brittle—more likely to snap or break in the face of adversity (Block & Kremen, 1996).

Resilient individuals are zestful, optimistic, and energetic in their approach to life (Block & Kremen, 1996). They cultivate positive emotion through the use of humor (Segerstrom, 2006). Michelle Tugade, Barbara Fredrickson, and Lisa Feldman Barrett (2004) found that the superior coping of resilient individuals came from their ability to use positive emotions to spring back from negative emotional experiences. Using measures of cardiovascular activity, the researchers discovered that resilient individuals were better able to regulate their responses to stressful situations (for instance, being told they were about to give an important speech) by strategically experiencing positive emotion.

Resilient individuals seem to show a kind of emotional wisdom; they capitalize on the power of positive emotions to reverse the stress of negative feelings. This skill has been demonstrated in response to a specific stressful event: the terrorist attacks of September 11, 2001. In one study, resilient individuals were found to be less likely to fall prey to depression after 9/11, and this capacity to flourish in the face of the crisis was a result of their attention to positive emotions (Fredrickson & others, 2003).

**broaden-and-build model**
Fredrickson's model of positive emotion, stating that the function of positive emotions lies in their effects on an individual's attention and ability to build resources.

**Do It!**

Recall from Chapter 7 that some psychologists believe that the ability to identify and regulate one's emotions is a kind of intelligence. Emotionally intelligent people are also thought to be better at reading the emotional expressions of others. Do a web search for *emotional intelligence tests* and take some online quizzes, or just try this one at http://greatergood.berkeley.edu/ei_quiz/. Do you think you are emotionally intelligent? Does your performance on the test seem to reflect your actual experience? What is your opinion of the test you tried? Is there information on the site for its validity and reliability?

1. The James-Lange theory of emotion states that
   A. emotion happens first, followed by physiological reactions.
   B. physiological reactions happen first, followed by emotion.
   C. physiological reactions and emotion happen simultaneously.
   D. the body plays a minimal role in emotion.

2. In the case of fearful stimuli, *indirect* neural pathways go first to the thalamus and
   A. then to the hypothalamus, followed by the amygdala.
   B. then to the sensory cortex, followed by the amygdala.
   C. then to the hippocampus.
   D. then to the hypothalamus, followed by the sensory cortex, and finally the hippocampus.

3. The facial feedback hypothesis is consistent with the theory of emotion known as
   A. the James-Lange theory.
   B. the Cannon-Bard theory.
   C. direct theory.
   D. indirect theory.

**APPLY IT!** 4. Seymour is talking to his friend about his sadness over his recent breakup with his girlfriend. His girlfriend cheated on him, but Seymour was willing to forgive her. She was not interested, though, and broke things off. As Seymour talks, his friend notices that Seymour is clenching his teeth, making fists, and generally getting angry. The friend says, "You know, you sound more angry than sad." Why might Seymour have confused anger and sadness?
   A. Sadness and anger are similar in terms of their arousal level.
   B. Seymour's friend is probably wrong given that sadness produces the same facial expression as anger.
   C. Because he is a man, Seymour probably does not understand emotion very well.
   D. Sadness and anger have the same valence, so someone who is feeling sad is likely to also feel angry. Seymour is probably feeling both of these negative emotions.

## 5 Motivation and Emotion: The Pursuit of Happiness

Motivation is about what people want, and a quick scan of the best-seller list or the self-help section of any bookstore would seem to indicate that one thing people want very much is to be happy or happier. Can people get happier? Let's consider the evidence.

## Biological Factors in Happiness

As we have seen, the brain is certainly at work in the experience of positive emotions. Genes also play a role. For instance, research on the heritability of well-being has tended to show that a substantial proportion of well-being differences among people can be explained by genetic differences. The heritability estimates for happiness range from 50 to 80 percent (Lykken, 1999). Remember from Chapter 7 that heritability is a statistic that describes characteristics of a group, that heritability estimates can vary across groups and over time, and that even highly heritable characteristics can be influenced by experience. Thus, a person is not necessarily doomed to an unhappy life, even if the person knows that he or she has particularly miserable parents.

Recall the concept of *set point* in our discussion of weight. There may also be a happiness set point, a person's general level of happiness when the individual is not trying to increase happiness (Sheldon & Lyubomirsky, 2007, 2012). Like our weight, our happiness levels may fluctuate around this set point. In trying to increase happiness, we must consider the role of this powerful starting spot that is likely the result of genetic factors and personal dispositions.

Given these potential biological limitations, other factors also complicate the pursuit of happiness, including the hedonic treadmill and the dangers of striving for happiness itself.

# Obstacles in the Pursuit of Happiness

The first key challenge individuals encounter in trying to increase their happiness is the hedonic (meaning "related to pleasure") treadmill (Brickman & Campbell, 1971; Fredrick & Loewenstein, 1999). The term *hedonic treadmill* captures the idea that any aspect of life that enhances one's positive feelings is likely to do so for only a short time, because individuals generally adapt rapidly to any life change that would presumably influence their happiness. Winning the lottery, moving into a dream home, or falling in love may lead to temporary gains in the experience of joy, but eventually people go back to their baseline (Schkade & Kahneman, 1998). That is, what is first experienced as a life-changing improvement fades to a routine. How can individuals increase their happiness if such pleasure enhancers quickly lose their power? Clearly, happiness is not about shopping at the right stores, because new possessions will likely lead to only a momentary burst of pleasure, gradually giving way to the set point.

A second obstacle in the goal of enhancing happiness is that pursuing happiness for its own sake is rarely a good way to get happy or happier. When happiness is the goal, the pursuit is likely to backfire (Schooler, Ariely, & Loewenstein, 2003). Indeed, those who explicitly link the pursuit of their everyday goals to happiness fare quite poorly (McIntosh, Harlow, & Martin, 1995).

In light of this difficult path, how can we enhance our happiness without having any new capacity for joy become ho-hum? How might we achieve happiness without pursuing it in and of itself?

# Happiness Activities and Goal Striving

Sonja Lyubomirsky and her colleagues have proposed a promising approach to enhancing happiness (Lyubomirsky, 2008, 2011, 2013; Sheldon & Lyubomirsky, 2007; Sin & Lyubomirsky, 2009). They suggest that intentional activities like being physically active, expressing kindness, showing gratitude, being optimistic, dwelling less on negative experiences, and engaging in positive self-reflection all enhance positive affect (Lyubomirsky & others, 2011a, 2011b; Sheldon & Lyubomirsky, 2007). Behaving altruistically—habitually helping others, especially through acts of service—is another powerful happiness booster, according to Lyubomirsky (2008, 2013).

One technique for practicing positive self-reflection is to keep a gratitude journal. Studies by Robert Emmons and Michael McCullough (2004) have demonstrated the ways that being grateful can enhance happiness and psychological well-being. In one study, individuals kept a diary in which they counted their blessings every day. Those who did so were better off than others on various measures of well-being. Although some individuals seem to be naturally more grateful than others, experimental evidence indicates that even people who are not naturally grateful can benefit from counting their blessings (Emmons & McCullough, 2003; McCullough, Emmons, & Tsang, 2002).

Another potentially useful approach to amplifying happiness is to commit to the pursuit of personally meaningful goals. Pause and write down the things you are trying to accomplish in your everyday behavior. You might identify goals such as "to get better grades" and "to be a good friend (or partner or parent)." Working toward such everyday goals relates strongly to subjective well-being (Brunstein, 1993; Sheldon, 2002). Goal pursuit provides the glue that meaningfully relates a chain of life events, endowing life with beginnings, middles, and ends (King, 2008).

The scientific literature on goal investment offers a variety of ideas about the types of goals that are likely to enhance happiness. To optimize the happiness payoffs of goal pursuit, one ought to set goals that are important and personally valuable and that reflect the intrinsic needs of relatedness, competence, and autonomy (Sheldon, 2002). These goals also should be moderately challenging and should share an instrumental relationship with each other so that the pursuit of one goal facilitates the accomplishment of another (Emmons & King, 1988).

With regard to the hedonic treadmill, goal pursuit has a tremendous advantage over many other ways of trying to enhance happiness. Goals change and are changed by life experience. As a result, goal pursuit may be less susceptible to the hedonic treadmill over time. Goals accentuate the positive but do not necessarily eliminate the negative. When we fail to reach our goals, we may experience momentary increases in unhappiness (Pomerantz, Saxon, & Oishi, 2000), which can be a very good thing. Because goals can make us happy and unhappy, they keep life emotionally interesting, and their influence on happiness does not wear off over time.

Overall, goal pursuit may lead to a happier life. Goals keep the positive possible and interesting. The conclusion to be drawn from the evidence, assuming that you want to enhance your happiness, is to strive mightily for the goals that you value. You may fail now and then, but missing the mark will only make your successes all the sweeter. As pleasant as happiness is, even the very happiest people in the world are unhappy sometimes (Diener & Seligman, 2002). Even in the pursuit of happiness, it is important to keep in mind that positive and negative emotions are both adaptive and that the best life is one that is emotionally rich.

**self-quiz**

1. Studies have demonstrated that variance in well-being is
   A. quite heritable.
   B. surprisingly unpredictable.
   C. extreme.
   D. dependent on the cultural context.

2. Similarly to our body weight, our personal happiness levels may fluctuate around
   A. our popularity.
   B. our stress levels.
   C. a set point.
   D. the seasons of the year.

3. Researchers have discovered that one way for individuals to engage in positive self-reflection and experience meaning in life is to
   A. write down what they are thankful for in a diary.
   B. pursue the hedonic treadmill.
   C. practice transience.
   D. refresh their coping skills.

**APPLY IT!** 4. Bonita works at a small advertising agency. She is committed to her work goals and always gives her all when she has a task to perform. She is deeply disappointed when a potential client decides to go with another firm after Bonita put a whole week into her presentation. A coworker notices Bonita's distress and says, "You know, you only feel so bad because you care too much. You should be like me. I don't care about anything, and I'm never disappointed."

What does the psychology of happiness tell us about this situation?
   A. Although Bonita feels disappointed now, her overall approach will likely lead to greater happiness in the long term.
   B. Bonita's colleague is right on. Bonita should disengage from her goals, and then she will never be disappointed.
   C. Bonita's colleague will probably be happier than Bonita in the long term and will likely have a greater sense of purpose in life.
   D. Bonita's happiness depends more on her genetic makeup than on any particular life experience.

---

## SUMMARY

### ① Theories of Motivation

Motivated behavior is energized, directed, and sustained. Early evolutionary theorists considered motivation to be based on instinct—the innate biological pattern of behavior.

A drive is an aroused state that occurs because of a physiological need or deprivation. Drive reduction theory was proposed as an explanation of motivation, with the goal of drive reduction being homeostasis: the body's tendency to maintain equilibrium.

Optimum arousal theory focuses on the Yerkes-Dodson law, which states that performance is best under conditions of moderate rather than low or high arousal. Moderate arousal often serves us best, but there are times when low or high arousal is linked with better performance.

### ② Hunger and Sex

Stomach signals are one factor in hunger. Glucose (blood sugar) and insulin both play an important role in hunger. Glucose is needed for the brain to function, and low levels of glucose increase hunger. Insulin can cause a rise in hunger.

Leptin, a protein secreted by fat cells, decreases food intake and increases energy expenditure. The hypothalamus plays an important role in regulating hunger. The lateral hypothalamus is involved in stimulating eating; the ventromedial hypothalamus, in restricting eating.

Obesity is a serious problem in the United States. Heredity, basal metabolism, set point, and fat cells are biological factors involved in obesity. Time and place affect eating. Our early ancestors ate fruits to satisfy nutritional needs, but today we fill up on the empty calories in sweets.

Motivation for sexual behavior involves the hypothalamus. The role of sex hormones in human sexual behavior, especially in women, is not clear. Masters and Johnson mapped out the human sexual response pattern, which consists of four physiological phases: excitement, plateau, orgasm, and resolution.

Thoughts and images are central in the sexual lives of humans. Sexual scripts influence sexual behavior, as do sensory/perceptual factors. Females tend to be more sexually aroused by touch; males, by visual stimulation.

Sexual values vary across cultures. These values influence sexual behavior.

Describing sexual practices in the United States has been challenging due to the difficulty of surveying a representative sample of the population. In general, research shows that people are less sexually active and less likely to cheat than popular beliefs may suggest. Sex education has sometimes been a controversial issue, but research shows that nations with comprehensive sex education have far lower rates of teen pregnancy and sexually transmitted infections than does the United States.

Sexual orientation refers to the direction of a person's erotic attraction. Sexual orientation—heterosexual, homosexual, or bisexual—is most likely determined by a combination of genetic, hormonal, cognitive, and environmental factors. Based on scientific evidence, the APA recently supported gay marriage and argued against discriminating against gay men and lesbians in parenting, custody, and adoption.

## ③ Beyond Hunger and Sex: Motivation in Everyday Life

According to Maslow's hierarchy of needs, our main needs are satisfied in this sequence: physiological needs, safety, love and belongingness, esteem, and self-actualization. Maslow gave the most attention to self-actualization: the motivation to develop to one's full potential.

Self-determination theory states that intrinsic motivation occurs when individuals are engaged in the pursuit of organismic needs that are innate and universal. These needs include competence, relatedness, and autonomy. Intrinsic motivation is based on internal factors. Extrinsic motivation is based on external factors, such as rewards and punishments.

Self-regulation involves setting goals, monitoring progress, and making adjustments in behavior to attain desired outcomes. Research suggests that setting subgoals to reach a long-term goal is a good strategy.

## ④ Emotion

Emotion is feeling, or affect, that has three components: physiological arousal, conscious experience, and behavioral expression. The biology of emotion focuses on physiological arousal involving the autonomic nervous system and its two subsystems. Skin conductance level and the polygraph have been used to measure emotional arousal.

The James-Lange theory states that emotion results from physiological states triggered by environmental stimuli: Emotion follows physiological reactions. The Cannon-Bard theory states that emotion and physiological reactions occur simultaneously. Contemporary biological views of emotion increasingly highlight neural circuitry and neurotransmitters. LeDoux has charted the neural circuitry of fear, which focuses on the amygdala and consists of two pathways, one direct and the other indirect. It is likely that positive and negative emotions use different neural circuitry and neurotransmitters.

Schachter and Singer's two-factor theory states that emotion is the result of both physiological arousal and cognitive labeling. Lazarus believed that cognition always directs emotion, but Zajonc has argued that emotion directs cognition. Both probably are right.

Research on the behavioral component of emotion focuses on facial expressions. The facial feedback hypothesis states that facial expressions can influence emotions, as well as reflect them.

Most psychologists believe that facial expressions of basic emotions are the same across cultures. However, display rules, which involve nonverbal signals of body movement, posture, and gesture, vary across cultures.

Emotions can be classified based on valence (pleasant or unpleasant) and arousal (high or low). Using the dimensions of valence and arousal, emotions can be arranged in a circle, or circumplex model.

Positive emotions likely play an important role in well-being by broadening our focus and allowing us to build resources. Resilience is an individual's capacity to thrive even during difficult times. Research has shown that one way resilient individuals thrive is by experiencing positive emotions.

## ⑤ Motivation and Emotion: The Pursuit of Happiness

Happiness is highly heritable, and there is reason to consider each person as having a happiness set point. Still, many people would like to increase their level of happiness. One obstacle to changing happiness is the hedonic treadmill: the idea that we quickly adapt to changes that might enhance happiness. Another obstacle is that pursuing happiness for its own sake often backfires.

Ways to enhance happiness include engaging in physical activity, helping others, positively self-reflecting, and experiencing meaning (such as by keeping a gratitude journal). Another way to enhance happiness is to pursue personally valued goals passionately.

## KEY TERMS

motivation, p. 325
instinct, p. 325
drive, p. 326
need, p. 326

homeostasis, p. 326
Yerkes-Dodson law, p. 327
set point, p. 330
estrogens, p. 331

androgens, p. 331
human sexual response pattern, p. 331
sexual orientation, p. 336

hierarchy of needs, p. 340
self-actualization, p. 340
self-determination theory, p. 342
intrinsic motivation, p. 343

In this chapter, we survey classic theories of personality from the major psychological perspectives. We also review contemporary research on personality. The chapter concludes with a look at personality assessment.

# 1 Psychodynamic Perspectives

**Personality** is a pattern of enduring, distinctive thoughts, emotions, and behaviors that characterize the way an individual adapts to the world. Psychologists have approached these enduring characteristics in a variety of ways, focusing on different aspects of the person.

**Psychodynamic perspectives** on personality emphasize that personality is primarily unconscious (that is, beyond awareness). According to this viewpoint, those enduring patterns that make up personality are largely unavailable to our conscious awareness, and they powerfully shape our behaviors in ways that we cannot consciously comprehend. Psychodynamic theorists use the word *unconscious* differently from how other psychologists might use the term. From the psychodynamic perspective, aspects of our personality are unconscious because they must be; this lack of awareness is motivated. These mysterious, unconscious forces are simply too frightening to be part of our conscious awareness.

Psychodynamic theorists believe that behavior is only a surface characteristic and that to truly understand someone's personality, we have to explore the symbolic meanings of that behavior and the deep inner workings of the mind (C. Levin, 2010). Psychodynamic theorists also stress the role of early childhood experience in adult personality. From this vantage point, the adult is a reflection of those childhood experiences that shape our earliest conceptions of ourselves and others. These characteristics were sketched by the architect of psychoanalytic theory, Sigmund Freud.

> *If we knew the dark truth of our existence, we might do something as desperate as the tragic Greek hero Oedipus, who unwittingly murdered his father and married his mother—and then gouged out his own eyes.*

**personality**
A pattern of enduring, distinctive thoughts, emotions, and behaviors that characterize the way an individual adapts to the world.

**psychodynamic perspectives**
Theoretical views emphasizing that personality is primarily unconscious (beyond awareness).

## Freud's Psychoanalytic Theory

Sigmund Freud, one of the most influential thinkers of the twentieth century, was born in Freiberg, Moravia (today part of the Czech Republic), in 1856 and died in London at the age of 83. Freud spent most of his life in Vienna, but he left the city near the end of his career to escape the Holocaust.

For Freud, the sexual drive was the most important motivator of all human activity. As we will see, Freud thought that the human sexual drive was the main determinant of personality development, and he felt that psychological disorders, dreams, and all human behavior represent the conflict between this unconscious sexual drive and the demands of civilized human society.

Freud developed *psychoanalysis,* his approach to personality, through his work with patients suffering from hysteria.

> *So, if you hear someone describe the joys of eating a decadent dessert like double-chocolate fudge cake as "better than sex," remember that in Freud's view, eating that cake is sex.*

**Sigmund Freud (1856–1939)**
*Freud's theories have strongly influenced how people in Western cultures view themselves and the world.*

*Hysteria* refers to physical symptoms that have no physical cause. For instance, a person might be unable to see, even with perfectly healthy eyes, or unable to walk, despite having no physical injury.

In Freud's day (the Victorian era, a time marked by strict rules regarding sexual relations), many young women suffered from physical problems that could not be explained by actual physical illness. In his practice, Freud spent many long hours listening to these women talk about their symptoms. Freud came to understand that the hysterical symptoms stemmed from unconscious psychological conflicts. These conflicts centered on experiences in which the person's drive for pleasure was thwarted by the social pressures of Victorian society. Furthermore, the particular symptoms were symbolically related to these underlying conflicts. One of Freud's patients, Fraulein Elisabeth Von R., suffered from horrible leg pains that prevented her from standing or walking. The fact that Fraulein Elisabeth could not walk was no accident. Through analysis, Freud discovered that Fraulein Elisabeth had had a number of experiences in which she wanted nothing more than to take a walk but had been prevented from doing so by her duty to her ill father.

TV and movie portrayals of hysterical symptoms typically culminate in a psychologist's unlocking of the unconscious secret of the person's problem. For example, a young soap opera heroine's problems may be solved in one climactic episode revealing that she is hysterically blind because she has witnessed her father cheating on her mother. Importantly, however, Freud believed that hysterical symptoms were *overdetermined*—that is, they had *many* causes in the unconscious. Thus, although unlocking one unconscious traumatic memory might work for Hollywood, it does not accurately represent Freud's view. Eventually, Freud came to use hysterical symptoms as his metaphor for understanding dreams, slips of the tongue, and all human behavior. Everything we do, he said, has a multitude of unconscious causes.

Drawing from his work in analyzing patients (as well as himself), Freud developed his model of the human personality. He described personality as like an iceberg, existing mostly below the level of awareness, just as the massive part of an iceberg lies beneath the surface of the water. Figure 10.1 illustrates this analogy and depicts the extensiveness of the unconscious part of our mind, in Freud's view.

*Today, we call hysterical symptoms* **somatoform** *disorders—physical symptoms with no physical cause.*

*We call it a* **Freudian slip** *when someone makes a mistake in speech or action that seems to express unconscious wishes—such as a typo spelling "Freud" as "Fraud."*

## STRUCTURES OF PERSONALITY

The three parts of the iceberg in Figure 10.1 reflect the three structures of personality that Freud described. Freud (1917) called these structures the id, the ego, and the superego. You can get a better feel for these Latin labels by considering their English translations: The id is literally the "it," the ego is the "I," and the superego is the "above-I."

The **id** consists of unconscious drives and is the individual's reservoir of sexual energy. This "it" is a pool of amoral and often vile urges pressing for expression. In Freud's view, the id has no contact with reality. The id works according to the *pleasure principle*, the Freudian concept that the id always seeks pleasure.

The world would be dangerous and scary, however, if personalities were all id.

*One of Freud's most famous essays, "The Ego and the Id," was titled "Das Ich und Das Ess" in German, meaning "The I and the It."*

**id**
The part of the person that Freud called the "it," consisting of unconscious drives; the individual's reservoir of sexual energy.

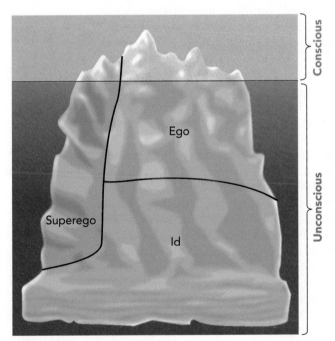

**FIGURE 10.1** **The Conscious and Unconscious Mind: The Iceberg Analogy** The iceberg analogy illustrates how much of the mind is unconscious in Freud's theory. The conscious mind is the part of the iceberg above water; the unconscious mind, the part below water. Notice that the id is totally unconscious, whereas the ego and the superego can operate at either the conscious or the unconscious level.

**superego**
The Freudian structure of personality that serves as the harsh internal judge of our behavior; what we often call conscience.

**defense mechanisms**
Tactics the ego uses to reduce anxiety by unconsciously distorting reality.

As young children mature, they learn that they cannot slug other children in the face, that they have to use the toilet instead of diapers, and that they must negotiate with others to get the things they want. As children experience the constraints of reality, a new element of personality is formed—the **ego,** the Freudian structure of personality that deals with the demands of reality. Indeed, according to Freud, the ego abides by the *reality principle.* That is, it tries to bring the individual pleasure within the norms of society. The ego helps us to test reality, to see how far we can go without getting into trouble and hurting ourselves. Whereas the id is completely unconscious, the ego is partly conscious. It houses our higher mental functions—reasoning, problem solving, and decision making, for example.

The id and ego do not consider whether something is right or wrong. Rather, the **superego** is the harsh internal judge of our behavior. The superego is reflected in what we often call conscience and evaluates the morality of our behavior. Like the id, the superego does not consider reality; it considers only whether the id's impulses can be satisfied in acceptable moral terms.

The ego acts as a mediator between the conflicting demands of the id and the superego, as well as the real world. Your ego might say, for example, "I will have sex only in a committed relationship and always practice safe sex." Your id, however, screams, "Sex! Now!" and your superego commands, "Sex? Don't even think about it."

**ego**
The Freudian structure of personality that deals with the demands of reality.

## DEFENSE MECHANISMS

The conflicts that erupt among the demands of the id, the superego, and reality create a great deal of anxiety for the ego. The ego has strategies for dealing with this anxiety, called defense mechanisms. **Defense mechanisms** are tactics the ego uses to reduce anxiety by unconsciously distorting reality. Freud's daughter Anna introduced and developed many different kinds of defense mechanisms.

The most primitive defense mechanism is *denial,* in which the ego simply refuses to acknowledge anxiety-producing realities. In denial, for instance, a man might refuse to accept his diagnosis of cancer. Other defense mechanisms are more complex. For example, imagine that Jason's id is demanding to express an unconscious desire to have sex with his mother. Clearly, acting on this impulse would not please the superego or society at large. If he became aware of this impulse, Jason might recoil in horror. Instead, Jason's ego might use the defense mechanism of displacement, and he might develop a relationship with a girlfriend who looks and acts like his mother. *Displacement* means directing unacceptable impulses at a less threatening target. Through displacement, the ego allows Jason to express his id impulse in a way that will not land him in trouble. Of course, Jason's friends might chuckle at the resemblance between his mother and his girlfriend, but you can bet that Jason will never notice.

Displacement provides the foundation for another defense mechanism, sublimation. *Sublimation* is a special form of displacement in which the person expresses an unconscious wish in a socially valued way, such as a boxer who sublimates his aggressive drive in the ring. Another defense mechanism is *projection,* in which we see in others those impulses that we most fear or despise in ourselves. For instance, our negative attitudes toward individuals who are different from us may express our unconscious beliefs about ourselves.

*Repression* is the most powerful and pervasive defense mechanism. Repression pushes unacceptable id impulses back into the unconscious mind. Repression is the foundation for all of the psychological defense mechanisms, whose goal is to repress threatening impulses, that is, to push them out of awareness. Freud said, for example, that our early childhood experiences, many of which he believed were sexually laden, are too threatening for us to deal with consciously, so we reduce the anxiety of childhood conflict through repression.

Two final points about defense mechanisms are important. First, defense mechanisms are unconscious; we are not aware that we are calling on them.

**Anna Freud (1895–1982)**
*The youngest of Sigmund Freud's six children, Anna Freud not only did influential work on defense mechanisms but also pioneered in the theory and practice of child psychoanalysis.*

# PSYCHOLOGY IN OUR WORLD

## Defense Mechanisms and the Psychology of Hypocrisy

**H**ave you noticed that sex scandals frequently seem to erupt around people who have been staunch advocates of traditional sexual mores? Consider, for example, the case of minister Ted Haggard, who outspokenly opposed gay rights and then was himself revealed to be engaging in a secret homosexual relationship with a male prostitute. Why would a person who experiences same-sex attraction be such a vocal opponent of gay rights?

One way psychologists understand the psychological processes that give rise to such apparent hypocrisy is through the concept of reaction formation. *Reaction formation* is a defense mechanism in which a person's conscious experience is the exact opposite of his or her unconscious feelings. In reaction formation, unconscious attraction to members of the same sex is experienced instead as *homophobia* (prejudice against homosexual people). The idea that conscious negative feelings toward gay people are related to unconscious feelings of same-sex attraction was initially supported in a study showing that men who expressed a strong homophobic bias against gay men also showed higher sexual arousal to same-sex erotic material (Adams, Wright, & Lohr, 1996).

A more recent series of studies by Netta Weinstein and colleagues (2012) explored the relationship between unconscious same-sex feelings and homophobia. The researchers measured sexual orientation in two ways. One measure was thought to tap unconscious (or *implicit*) feelings, and the other assessed conscious (or *explicit*) feelings. Note that a participant's implicit and explicit sexual orientation could match up—or not. In a variety of studies that included participants in the United States and Germany, subjects whose implicit and explicit sexual orientations matched reported lower homophobia compared to those whose implicit sexual orientation revealed homosexual feelings while their self-report did not.

A key factor in these studies was the participants' perceived autonomy support by parents. *Autonomy support* means allowing a person the freedom to explore and identify his or her own needs, feelings, wishes, and desires. Individuals who reported high levels of parental autonomy support showed a stronger match between implicit and explicit sexual orientation, as well as less homophobia. Conversely, participants who reported lower parental autonomy support were more likely to show a discrepancy between their implicit and explicit sexual orientation, plus high levels of homophobia.

The researchers concluded that individuals who experience same-sex attraction may shut out this aspect of themselves due to the stigma associated with being gay and their deep fears of parental rejection. Strident negative attitudes may be a way for such individuals to protect a fragile sense of self. The fragility of that sense of self is evidenced in scandals like the one that surrounded Ted Haggard.

---

Second, when used in moderation or on a temporary basis, defense mechanisms are not necessarily unhealthy (Cramer, 2008b). For example, the defense mechanism of *denial* can help a person cope upon first getting the news that his or her death is impending, and the defense mechanism of *sublimation* involves transforming unconscious impulses into activities that benefit society. Note that the defense mechanism of sublimation means that even the very best things that human beings accomplish—a beautiful work of art, an amazing act of kindness—are still explained by unconscious sexual drives and defenses.

## PSYCHOSEXUAL STAGES OF PERSONALITY DEVELOPMENT

Freud believed that human beings go through universal stages of personality development and that at each developmental stage we experience sexual pleasure in one part of the body more than in others. Each stage is named for the location of sexual pleasure at that stage. *Erogenous zones* are parts of the body that have especially strong pleasure-giving qualities at particular stages of development. Freud thought that our adult personality is determined by the way we resolve conflicts between these early sources of pleasure—the mouth, the anus, and then the genitals—and the demands of reality.

■ *Oral stage (first 18 months):* The infant's pleasure centers on the mouth. Chewing, sucking, and biting are the chief sources of pleasure that reduce tension in the infant.

■ *Anal stage (18 to 36 months):* During a time when most children are experiencing toilet training, the child's greatest pleasure involves the anus and urethra and their functions. Freud recognized that there is pleasure in "going" and "holding it" as well as in the experience of control over one's parents in deciding when to do either.

■ *Phallic stage (3 to 6 years):* The name of Freud's third stage comes from the Latin word *phallus,* which means "penis." Pleasure focuses on the genitals as the child discovers that self-stimulation is enjoyable.

In Freud's view, the phallic stage has a special importance in personality development because it triggers the Oedipus complex. This name comes from the Greek tragedy, mentioned earlier, in which Oedipus kills his father and marries his mother. The **Oedipus complex** is the boy's intense desire to replace his father and enjoy the affections of his mother. Eventually, the boy recognizes that his father might punish him for these incestuous wishes, specifically by cutting off the boy's penis. *Castration anxiety* refers to the boy's intense fear of being mutilated by his father. To reduce this conflict, the boy identifies with his father, adopting the male gender role. The intense castration anxiety is repressed into the unconscious and serves as the foundation for the development of the superego.

Freud recognized that there were differences between boys and girls in the phallic stage. Because a girl does not have a penis, she cannot experience castration anxiety, Freud reasoned. Instead, she compares herself to boys and realizes that she is missing something—a penis. Without experiencing the powerful force of castration anxiety, a girl cannot develop a superego in the same sense that boys do. Given this inability, Freud concluded, women were morally inferior to men, and this inferiority explained their place as second-class citizens in Victorian society. Freud believed that girls experience "castration completed," resulting in *penis envy—* the intense desire to obtain a penis by eventually marrying and bearing a son.

While noting that his views ran counter to the early feminist thinkers of his time, Freud stood firm that the sexes are not equal in every way. He considered women to be somewhat childlike in their development and thought it was good that fathers, and eventually husbands, should guide them through life. He asserted that the only hope for women's moral development was education.

■ *Latency period (6 years to puberty):* This phase is not a developmental stage but rather a kind of psychic time-out. After the drama of the phallic stage, the child sets aside all interest in sexuality. Although we now consider these years extremely important to development, Freud felt that this was a time in which no psychosexual development occurred.

■ *Genital stage (adolescence and adulthood):* The genital stage is the time of sexual reawakening, a point when the source of sexual pleasure shifts to someone outside the family. Freud believed that in adulthood the individual becomes capable of the two hallmarks of maturity: love and work. However, Freud felt that human beings are inevitably subject to intense conflict, reasoning that everyone, no matter how healthy or well adjusted, still has an id pressing for expression. Adulthood, even in the best of circumstances, still involves reliving the unconscious conflicts of childhood.

*The superego wields a lot of power—it is essentially the internalized castrating father.*

*In Freud's view, anatomy is destiny. By this he meant that anatomy (whether a person has a penis or not) determines whether he or she will develop a superego.*

**Oedipus complex**
According to Freud, a boy's intense desire to replace his father and enjoy the affections of his mother.

| Stage | Adult Extensions (Fixations) | Sublimations | Reaction Formations |
|-------|------------------------------|--------------|---------------------|
| Oral | Smoking, eating, kissing, oral hygiene, drinking, chewing gum | Seeking knowledge, humor, wit, sarcasm, being a food or wine expert | Speech purist, food faddist, prohibitionist, dislike of milk |
| Anal | Notable interest in one's bowel movements, love of bathroom humor, extreme messiness | Interest in painting or sculpture, being overly giving, great interest in statistics | Extreme disgust with feces, fear of dirt, prudishness, irritability |
| Phallic | Heavy reliance on masturbation, flirtatiousness, expressions of virility | Interest in poetry, love of love, interest in acting, striving for success | Puritanical attitude toward sex, excessive modesty |

**FIGURE 10.2** **Defense Mechanisms and Freudian Stages** If a person is fixated at a psychosexual stage, the fixation can color his or her personality in many ways, including the defense mechanisms the person might use to cope with anxiety.

Freud argued that the individual may become stuck in any of these developmental stages if he or she is underindulged or overindulged at a given stage. For example, a parent might wean a child too early, be too strict in toilet training, punish the child for masturbating, or smother the child with too much attention. *Fixation* occurs when a particular psychosexual stage colors an individual's adult personality. For instance, an *anal retentive* person (someone who is obsessively neat and organized) is fixated at the anal stage. The construct of fixation thus explains how, according to Freud's view, childhood experiences can have an enormous impact on adult personality. Figure 10.2 illustrates possible links between adult personality characteristics and fixation at the oral, anal, and phallic stages.

## Psychodynamic Critics and Revisionists

Because Freud was among the first theorists to explore personality, some of his ideas have needed updating and revision over time, while others have been tossed out altogether (Blass, 2012; Burston, 2012). In particular, Freud's critics have said that his ideas about sexuality, early experience, social factors, and the unconscious mind were misguided (Adler, 1927; Erikson, 1968; Fromm, 1947; Horney, 1945; Jung, 1917; Kohut, 1977; Rapaport, 1967; Sullivan, 1953). They stress the following points:

■ Sexuality is not the pervasive force behind personality that Freud believed it to be. Furthermore, the Oedipus complex is not as universal as Freud maintained. Freud's concepts were heavily influenced by the setting in which he lived and worked—turn-of-the-century Vienna, a society that, compared with contemporary society, was sexually repressed and male-dominated.

■ The first five years of life are not as powerful in shaping adult personality as Freud thought. Later experiences deserve more attention.

■ The ego and conscious thought processes play a more dominant role in our personality than Freud believed; he claimed that we are forever captive to the instinctual, unconscious clutches of the id. In addition, the ego has a separate line of development from the id, so achievement, thinking, and reasoning are not always tied to sexual impulses.

■ Sociocultural factors are much more important than Freud believed. In stressing the id's dominance, Freud placed more emphasis on the biological basis of personality. More contemporary psychodynamic scholars have especially emphasized the interpersonal setting of the family and the role of early social relationships in personality development (A. E. Harris, 2011; Holmes, 2011).

A number of dissenters and revisionists to Freud's theory have been influential in the development of psychodynamic theories. Erik Erikson, whose psychosocial stages we

**Karen Horney (1885–1952)**
*Horney developed the first feminist criticism of Freud's theory. Horney's view emphasizes women's positive qualities and self-evaluation.*

examined in Chapter 8, is among these. Here we consider three other thinkers—Karen Horney, Carl Jung, and Alfred Adler—who made notable revisions to Freud's approach.

**HORNEY'S SOCIOCULTURAL APPROACH**  Karen Horney (1885–1952) rejected the classical psychoanalytic concept that anatomy is destiny and cautioned that some of Freud's most popular ideas were only hypotheses. She insisted that these hypotheses be supported with observable data before being accepted as fact. She also argued that sociocultural influences on personality development should be considered (Schultz & Schultz, 2012).

Consider Freud's concept of penis envy, which attributed some of the behavior of his female patients to their repressed desire to have a penis. Horney pointed out that women might envy the penis not because of some neurotic tendencies but because of the status that society bestows on those who have one. Further, she suggested that both sexes envy the attributes of the other, with men coveting women's reproductive capacities (Horney, 1967).

Horney also believed that the need for security, not for sex, is the prime motive in human existence. Horney reasoned that an individual whose needs for security are met should be able to develop his or her capacities to the fullest extent. She viewed psychological health as allowing the person to express his or her talents and abilities freely and spontaneously.

**JUNG'S ANALYTICAL THEORY**  Freud's contemporary Carl Jung (1875–1961) shared Freud's interest in the unconscious, but he believed that Freud underplayed the unconscious mind's role in personality. In fact, Jung believed that the roots of personality go back to the dawn of human existence. The **collective unconscious** is Jung's name for the impersonal, deepest layer of the unconscious mind, shared by all human beings because of their common ancestral past. In Jung's theory, the experiences of a common past have made a deep, permanent impression on the human mind (Hunt, 2012).

**collective unconscious**
Jung's name for the impersonal, deepest layer of the unconscious mind, shared by all human beings because of their common ancestral past.

Jung posited that the collective unconscious contains **archetypes,** emotionally laden ideas and images that have rich and symbolic meaning for all people. Jung concluded that these archetypes emerge in art, literature, religion, and dreams (Dourley, 2011; Morgan, 2012). He used archetypes to help people understand themselves (Meredith-Owen, 2011). Archetypes are essentially predispositions to respond to the environment in particular ways.

**archetypes**
Jung's term for emotionally laden ideas and images in the collective unconscious that have rich and symbolic meaning for all people.

Jung used the terms *anima* and *animus* to identify two common archetypes. He believed each of us has a passive feminine side—the anima—and an assertive masculine side—the animus. Another archetype, the *persona,* represents the public mask that we all wear during social interactions. Jung believed that the persona is an essential archetype because it allows us always to keep some secret part of ourselves hidden from others.

**ADLER'S INDIVIDUAL PSYCHOLOGY**  Alfred Adler (1870–1937) was one of Freud's earliest followers, but his approach to personality was drastically different from Freud's. In Adler's **individual psychology,** people are motivated by purposes and goals—thus, perfection, not pleasure, is their key motivator. Adler argued that people have the ability to take their genetic inheritance and their environmental experiences and act upon them creatively to become the person they want to be.

**individual psychology**
Adler's view that people are motivated by purposes and goals and that perfection, not pleasure, is thus the key motivator in human life.

Adler thought that everyone strives for superiority by seeking to adapt, improve, and master the environment (Del Corso, Rehfuss, & Galvin, 2011). Striving for superiority is our response to the uncomfortable feelings of inferiority that we experience as infants and young children when we interact with bigger, more powerful people. *Compensation* is Adler's term for the individual's attempt to overcome imagined or real inferiorities or weaknesses

**Carl Jung (1875–1961)**
*Swiss psychoanalytic theorist Carl Jung developed the concepts of the collective unconscious and archetypes.*

by developing one's own abilities. Adler believed that compensation is normal, and he said that we often make up for a weakness in one ability by excelling in a different ability. For example, a person of small stature and limited physical abilities (like Adler himself) might compensate by excelling in academics.

Adler believed that birth order could influence how successfully a person would strive for superiority (Khodarahimi & Ogletree, 2011). He viewed firstborn children to be particularly vulnerable given that they begin life as the center of attention but then are knocked off their pedestal by their siblings. Adler in fact believed that the firstborn are more likely to suffer from psychological disorders and to engage in criminal behavior. Youngest children, however, also are potentially in trouble because they are most likely to be spoiled. The healthiest birth order? According to Adler, those (including Adler himself) who are middle-born are in an especially advantageous situation because they have older siblings as built-in inspiration for superiority striving. Importantly, though, Adler did not believe that anyone was doomed by birth order. Rather, sensitive parents could help children in any position in the family to negotiate their needs for superiority.

# Evaluating the Psychodynamic Perspectives

Although psychodynamic theories have diverged from Freud's original psychoanalytic version, they share some core principles:

- Personality is determined both by current experiences and, as the original psychoanalytic theory proposed, by early life experiences.

- Personality can be better understood by examining it developmentally—as a series of stages that unfold with the individual's physical, cognitive, and socioemotional development.

- We mentally transform our experiences, giving them meaning that shapes our personality.

- The mind is not all consciousness; unconscious motives lie behind some of our puzzling behavior.

- The individual's inner world often conflicts with the outer demands of reality, creating anxiety that is not easy to resolve.

- Personality and adjustment—not just the experimental laboratory topics of sensation, perception, and learning—are rightful and important topics of psychological inquiry.

Psychodynamic perspectives have come under fire for a variety of reasons. Some critics say that psychodynamic theorists overemphasize the influence of early family experiences on personality and do not acknowledge that people retain the capacity for change and adaptation throughout life. Some psychologists believe moreover that Freud and Jung put too much faith in the unconscious mind's ability to control behavior. Others object that Freud placed too much importance on sexuality in explaining personality.

Some have argued, too, that psychoanalysis is not a theory that researchers can test through empirical studies. However, numerous empirical studies on concepts such as defense mechanisms and the unconscious have proved this criticism to be unfounded (Cramer, 2009; Weinstein & others, 2012). At the same time, another version of this argument may be accurate. Although it is certainly possible to test hypotheses derived from psychoanalytic theory through research, the question remains whether psychoanalytically oriented individuals who believe strongly in Freud's ideas would be open to research results that call for serious changes in the theory. For example, a recent meta-analysis found that evidence for the effectiveness of long-term psychoanalytic psychotherapy was limited and conflicting (Smit & others, 2012).

In light of these criticisms, it may be hard to appreciate why Freud continues to have an impact on psychology (Mendes, 2011). It is useful to keep in mind that Freud made a number of important contributions, including being the first to propose that childhood is crucial to later functioning, that development might be understood in terms of stages, and that unconscious processes might play a significant role in human life.

self quiz

1. According to Freud, our conscience is a reflection of the
   A. ego.
   B. collective unconscious.
   C. id.
   D. superego.

2. All of the following are examples of defense mechanisms *except*
   A. sublimation.
   B. repression.
   C. latency.
   D. displacement.

3. A theorist who focused on archetypes is
   A. Karen Horney.
   B. Sigmund Freud.
   C. Alfred Adler.
   D. Carl Jung.

APPLY IT! 4. Simone and her older sister have an intense sibling rivalry. Simone has tried to best her sister in schoolwork, fashion sense, and sporting achievements. Simone's sister complains that Simone needs to get a life of her own. What would Alfred Adler say about Simone's behavior?

A. Simone is engaging in the defense mechanism of displacement, striving to conquer her sister when it is really her mother she wishes to defeat.

B. Simone is expressing her animus archetype by engaging in masculine-style competition.

C. Simone is expressing superiority striving by trying to overcome her sister—a healthy way for middle children to pursue superiority.

D. Simone lacks a sense of basic trust in the world, and her parents must have been neglectful of her.

# 2 Humanistic Perspectives

**Humanistic perspectives** stress a person's capacity for personal growth and positive human qualities. Humanistic psychologists believe that we all have the ability to control our lives and to achieve what we desire (Schultz & Schultz, 2012).

Humanistic perspectives contrast with both psychodynamic perspectives and behaviorism, discussed in Chapter 5. Humanistic theorists sought to move beyond Freudian psychoanalysis and behaviorism to a theory that might capture the rich and potentially positive aspects of human nature.

**humanistic perspectives** Theoretical views stressing a person's capacity for personal growth and positive human qualities.

## Maslow's Approach

A leading architect of the humanistic movement was Abraham Maslow (1908–1970), whose hierarchy of needs we considered in Chapter 9. Maslow believed that we can learn the most about human personality by focusing on the very best examples of human beings—self-actualizers.

Recall that at the top of Maslow's (1954, 1971) hierarchy was the need for self-actualization. Self-actualization is the motivation to develop one's full potential as a human being. Maslow described self-actualizers as spontaneous, creative, and possessing a childlike capacity for awe. According to Maslow, a person at this optimal level of existence would be tolerant of others, have a gentle sense of humor, and be likely to pursue the greater good. Self-actualizers also maintain a capacity for "peak experiences," or breathtaking moments of spiritual insight. As examples of self-actualized individuals, Maslow included Pablo Casals (cellist), Albert Einstein (physicist), Ralph Waldo Emerson (writer), William James (psychologist), Thomas Jefferson (politician), Eleanor Roosevelt (humanitarian, diplomat), and Albert Schweitzer (humanitarian).

Created more than 40 years ago, Maslow's list of self-actualizers is clearly biased. Maslow focused on highly successful individuals who he thought represented the best of the human species. Because Maslow concentrated on people who were successful in a particular historical context, his self-actualizers were limited to those who had opportunities for success in that context. Maslow thus named considerably more men than women, and most of the individuals were from Western cultures and of European ancestry. Today, we might add to Maslow's list individuals such as Nobel Peace Prize winners the Dalai Lama (Tenzin Gyatso), Tibetan spiritual and political leader; and Ellen Johnson Sirleaf, Leymah Gbowee, and Tawakkol Karman, three women who received the coveted 2011 prize "for their nonviolent struggle for the safety of women and for women's rights to full participation in peace-building work."

## Rogers's Approach

The other key figure in the development of humanistic psychology, Carl Rogers (1902–1987), began his career as a psychotherapist struggling to understand the unhappiness of the individuals he encountered in therapy. Rogers's groundbreaking work established the foundations for more contemporary studies of personal growth and self-determination.

**Carl Rogers (1902–1987)**
*Rogers was a pioneer in the development of the humanistic perspective.*

**unconditional positive regard**
Rogers's construct referring to the individual's need to be accepted, valued, and treated positively regardless of his or her behavior.

**conditions of worth**
The standards that the individual must live up to in order to receive positive regard from others.

In the knotted, anxious verbal stream of his clients, Rogers (1961) noted the things that seemed to be keeping them from reaching their full potential. Based on his clinical observations, Rogers devised his own approach to personality. Rogers believed that we are all born with the raw ingredients of a fulfilling life. We simply need the right conditions to thrive. Just as a sunflower seed, once planted in rich soil and given water and sunshine, will grow into a strong and healthy flower, all humans will flourish in the appropriate environment.

This analogy is particularly apt and reveals the differences between Rogers's view of human nature and Freud's. A sunflower seed does not have to be shaped away from its dark natural tendencies by social constraints, nor does it have to reach a difficult compromise between its vile true impulses and reality. Instead, given the appropriate environment, it will grow into a beautiful flower. Rogers believed that, similarly, each person is born with natural capacities for growth and fulfillment. We are also endowed with an innate sense—a gut feeling—that allows us to evaluate whether an experience is good or bad for us. Finally, we are all born with a need for positive regard from others. We need to be loved, liked, or accepted by people around us. As children interacting with our parents, we learn early on to value the feeling that they value us, and we gain a sense of valuing ourselves.

**EXPLAINING UNHAPPINESS**  If we have innate tendencies toward growth and fulfillment, why are so many people so unhappy? The problem arises when our need for positive regard from others is not met *unconditionally*. **Unconditional positive regard** is Rogers's term for being accepted, valued, and treated positively regardless of one's behavior. Unfortunately, others often value us only when we behave in particular ways that meet what Rogers called conditions of worth. **Conditions of worth** are the standards we must live up to in order to receive positive regard from others. For instance, parents might give their son positive regard only when he achieves in school, succeeds on the soccer field, or chooses a profession that they themselves value. According to Rogers, as we grow up, people who are central to our lives condition us to move away from our genuine feelings, to earn their love by pursuing those goals that they value, even if those goals do not reflect our deepest wishes.

Rogers's theory includes the idea that we develop a *self-concept,* our conscious representation of who we are and who we wish to become, during childhood. Optimally, this self-concept reflects our genuine, innate desires, but it also can be influenced by conditions of worth. Conditions of worth can become part of who we think we ought to be. As a result, we can become alienated from our genuine feelings and strive to actualize a self that is not who we were meant to be. A person who dedicates himself or herself to such goals might be very successful by outward appearances but might feel utterly unfulfilled. Such an individual might be able to check off all the important boxes in life's to-do lists, and to do all that he or she is "supposed to do," but never feel truly happy.

**PROMOTING OPTIMAL FUNCTIONING**   To remedy this situation, Rogers believed that the person must reconnect with his or her true feelings and desires. He proposed that to achieve this reconnection, the individual must experience a relationship that includes three essential qualities: unconditional positive regard, as defined above; empathy; and genuineness.

First, Rogers said that regardless of what they do, people need unconditional positive regard. Although an individual might lack unconditional positive regard in childhood, he or she can experience this unconditional acceptance from others later, in friendships and/or romantic relationships or during sessions with a therapist. Even when a person's behavior is inappropriate, obnoxious, or unacceptable, he or she still needs the respect, comfort, and love of others (Ryckman, 2013).

Second, Rogers said that individuals can become more fulfilled by interacting with people who are empathic toward them. Empathy involves being a sensitive listener and understanding another's true feelings.

Genuineness is a third requirement in the individual's path to becoming fully functioning. Being genuine means being open with one's feelings and dropping all pretenses and facades. The importance that Rogers placed on the therapist's acting genuinely in the therapeutic relationship demonstrates his strong belief in the positive character of human nature. For Rogers, we can help others simply by being present for them as the authentic individuals we are.

## Evaluating the Humanistic Perspectives

The humanistic perspectives emphasize that the way we perceive ourselves and the world is an essential element of personality. Humanistic psychologists also stress that we need to consider the whole person and the positive bent of human nature (Schultz & Schultz, 2012). Their emphasis on conscious experience has given us the view that personality contains a well of potential that can be developed to its fullest.

Some critics believe that humanistic psychologists are too optimistic about human nature and that they overestimate people's freedom and rationality. Others say that the humanists may promote excessive self-love and narcissism by encouraging people to think so positively about themselves. Still others argue that humanistic approaches do not hold individuals accountable for their behaviors, if all negative human behavior is seen as emerging out of negative situations.

Self-determination theory, which we considered in Chapter 9, demonstrates the way that psychologists have tested humanistic ideas that might appear too abstract and difficult to test (Kusurkar & others, 2012; Standage & others, 2012). Their work bears witness to the enduring impact of humanistic perspectives on contemporary personality psychology.

self-quiz

1. In Maslow's theory, the motivation to develop one's full potential as a human being is called
   A. self-satisfaction.
   B. self-actualization.
   C. self-sufficiency.
   D. self-determination.

2. Rogers proposed that in order to become fulfilled, the individual requires all of the following *except*
   A. unconditional positive regard.
   B. genuineness.
   C. self-actualization.
   D. empathy.

3. A child who consistently strives for an *A* in math and science in order to secure the affection of her parents is trying to establish
   A. unconditional positive regard.
   B. conditions of worth.
   C. self-actualization.
   D. empathy.

**APPLY IT!** 4. Phoebe and Joey, parents to little Jennifer, believe that because so many things in life involve hard work, it is important for Jennifer to earn the good things that happen to her. They make it clear to Jennifer that one of the things she must earn is their approval, and they tell her that they love her only when she does well in school and behaves according to their standards. They are certain that this training will instill in Jennifer the importance of working hard and valuing the good things she gets in life. What would Carl Rogers say about Phoebe and Joey's parenting style?
   A. They are on the right track, as all children need strict limits and must learn discipline.
   B. What they are doing is fine but will have little influence on Jennifer, because genes matter most to personality.
   C. They are likely to be creating a fixation in Jennifer, and she will spend a lifetime working out her unconscious conflicts.
   D. They are setting Jennifer up to value herself only when she meets certain standards and would be better advised to love her unconditionally.

# 3 Trait Perspectives

If you are setting up a friend on a blind date, you are likely to describe the person in terms of his or her traits, or lasting personality characteristics. Trait perspectives on personality have been the dominant approach for the past three decades.

## Trait Theories

According to **trait theories,** personality consists of broad, enduring dispositions (traits) that tend to lead to characteristic responses. In other words, we can describe people in terms of the ways they behave, such as whether they are outgoing, friendly, private, or hostile. People who have a strong tendency to behave in certain ways are referred to as "high" on the traits; those with a weak tendency to behave in these ways are "low" on the traits. Although trait theorists differ about which traits make up personality, they agree that traits are the fundamental building blocks of personality (McCrae & Sutin, 2009; Miserandino, 2012).

**trait theories**
Theoretical views stressing that personality consists of broad, enduring dispositions (traits) that tend to lead to characteristic responses.

Gordon Allport (1897–1967), sometimes referred to as the father of American personality psychology, was particularly bothered by the negative view of humanity that psychoanalysis portrayed. He rejected the notion that the unconscious was central to an understanding of personality. He further believed that to understand healthy people, we must focus on their lives in the present, not on their childhood experiences.

Allport believed that personality psychology should be concerned with understanding healthy, well-adjusted individuals. He described such persons as showing a positive but objective sense of self and others, interest in issues beyond their own experience, a sense of humor, common sense, and a unifying philosophy of life—typically but not always provided by religious faith (Allport, 1961). Allport dedicated himself to the idea that psychology should have relevance to social issues facing contemporary society, and his scholarship has influenced not only personality psychology but also the psychology of religion and prejudice.

In defining personality, Allport (1961) stressed each person's uniqueness and capacity to adapt to the environment. For Allport, the crucial unit for understanding personality is the trait. He defined traits as mental structures that make different situations the same for the person. For Allport, traits are structures inside a person that cause behavior to be similar even in different situations. For instance, if Carly is sociable, she is likely to behave in an outgoing, happy fashion whether she is at a party or in a group study session. Allport's definition implies that behavior should be consistent across different situations.

We get a sense of the down-to-earth quality of Allport's approach to personality by looking at his study of traits. In the late 1930s, Allport and his colleague H. S. Odbert (1936) sat down with two big unabridged dictionaries and pulled out all the words that could be used to describe a person—a method called the *lexical approach*. This approach reflects the idea that if a trait is important to people in real life, it ought to be represented in the natural language people use to talk about one another. Furthermore, the more important a trait is, the more likely it is that it should be represented by a single word. Allport and Odbert started with 18,000 words and gradually pared down that list to 4,500.

*It's called "lexical" because a lexicon is a dictionary or vocabulary. These researchers are generally starting with the words we use to describe other people.*

As you can appreciate, 4,500 traits make for a very long questionnaire. Imagine that you are asked to rate a person, Ignacio, on some traits. You use a scale from 1 to 5, with 1 meaning "not at all" and 5 meaning "very much." If you give Ignacio a 5 on "outgoing," what do you think you might give him on "shy"? Clearly, we may not need 4,500 traits to summarize the way we describe personality. Still, how might we whittle down these descriptors further without losing something important?

With advances in statistical methods and the advent of computers, the lexical approach became considerably less unwieldy, as researchers began to analyze the words to look for underlying structures that might account for their overlap. Specifically, a statistical procedure called *factor analysis* allowed researchers to identify which traits go together in terms of how they are rated. Factor analysis essentially tells us what items on a scale people are responding to as if they mean the same thing. For example, if Ignacio got a 5 on "outgoing," he probably would get a 5 on "talkative" and a 1 or 2 on "shy." One important characteristic of factor analysis is that it relies on the scientist to interpret the meaning of the factors, and the researcher must make some decisions about how many factors are enough to explain the data (Goldberg & Digman, 1994).

In 1963, W. T. Norman reanalyzed the Allport and Odbert traits and concluded that only five factors were needed to summarize these traits. Norman's research set the stage for the dominant approach in personality psychology today: the five-factor model (Digman, 1990).

## The Five-Factor Model of Personality

*Neuroticism is sometimes identified by its opposite, emotional stability.*

Pick a friend and jot down 10 of that person's most notable personality traits. Did you perhaps list "reserved" or "a good leader"? "Responsible" or "unreliable"? "Sweet," "kind," or "friendly"? Maybe even "creative"? Researchers in personality psychology have found that there are essentially five broad personality dimensions that are represented in the natural language; these dimensions also summarize the various ways psychologists have studied traits (Costa & McCrae, 2006; Crede & others, 2012; Hogan, 2006).

The **big five factors of personality**—the broad traits that are thought to describe the main dimensions of personality—are neuroticism (which refers to the tendency to worry and experience negative emotions), extraversion, openness to experience, agreeableness, and conscientiousness. Although personality psychologists typically refer to the traits

**big five factors of personality**
The five broad traits that are thought to describe the main dimensions of personality: openness to experience, conscientiousness, extraversion, agreeableness, and neuroticism (emotional instability).

| **O**penness | **C**onscientiousness | **E**xtraversion | **A**greeableness | **N**euroticism (emotional stability) |
|---|---|---|---|---|
| • Imaginative or practical | • Organized or disorganized | • Sociable or retiring | • Softhearted or ruthless | • Calm or anxious |
| • Interested in variety or routine | • Careful or careless | • Fun-loving or somber | • Trusting or suspicious | • Secure or insecure |
| • Independent or conforming | • Disciplined or impulsive | • Affectionate or reserved | • Helpful or uncooperative | • Self-satisfied or self-pitying |

**FIGURE 10.3** **The Big Five Factors of Personality** Each of the broad supertraits encompasses more narrow traits and characteristics. Use the acronym *OCEAN* to remember the big five personality factors (openness, conscientiousness, extraversion, agreeableness, and neuroticism).

as N, E, O, A, and C on the basis of the order in which they emerge in a factor analysis, if you create an anagram from these first letters of the trait names, you get the word *OCEAN*. Figure 10.3 more fully defines the big five traits.

Each of the big five traits has been the topic of extensive research (Karsten & others, 2012; McCrae & Sutin, 2007). The following sampling of research findings on each trait sheds light on the interesting work that the five-factor model has inspired:

*Take a good look at Figure 10.3 so that you understand each of the traits. Openness to experience is often the trickiest.*

- *Neuroticism* is related to feeling negative emotion more often than positive emotion in one's daily life and to experiencing more lingering negative states (Widiger, 2009). Neuroticism has been shown as well to relate to more health complaints (Carver & Connor-Smith, 2010) and is linked to coronary heart disease risk (Koelsch, Enge, & Jentschke, 2012). In a longitudinal study, individuals were tracked for nearly seven years. Neuroticism was associated with dying during the study (Fry & Debats, 2009). In general, neurotic individuals appear to suffer in silence: Acquaintances and observers have difficulty detecting how neurotic another person is (Vazire, 2010).

- Individuals high in *extraversion* are more likely than others to engage in social activities (Emmons & Diener, 1986), experience gratitude (McCullough, Emmons, & Tsang, 2002), and show a strong sense of meaning in life (King & others, 2006). In addition, extraverts are more forgiving (Thompson & others, 2005). People rate extraverts as smiling and standing energetically and as dressing stylishly (Naumann & others, 2009), and observers know an extravert when they see one (Vazire, 2010). One study found that extraverted salespeople sold more cars, especially if they were also good at picking up interpersonal cues (Blickle, Wendel, & Ferris, 2010).

- *Openness to experience* is related to liberal values, open-mindedness, tolerance (McCrae & Sutin, 2009), and creativity (Silvia & others, 2009). Openness is also associated with superior cognitive functioning and IQ across the life span (Sharp & others, 2010). Individuals who rate themselves as open to experience are more likely to dress distinctively (Naumann & others, 2009), to pursue entrepreneurial goals (for instance, starting their own business), and to experience success in those pursuits (Zhao, Seibert, & Lumpkin, 2010). Individuals high on openness to experience are also more likely to interact with others on Internet websites and to use social media (Correa, Hinsley, & de Zuniga, 2010). Moreover, a recent meta-analysis found that higher levels of openness to experience were linked to living longer (Ferguson & Bibby, 2012).

- *Agreeableness* is related to generosity and altruism (Caprara & others, 2010), to reports of religious faith (Haber, Koenig, & Jacob, 2011), and to more satisfying romantic relationships (Donnellan, Larsen-Rife, & Conger, 2005). There are also links between agreeableness and viewing

Do It!

You are probably getting curious to know where you stand on the big five factors of personality. This website will give you a chance to find out: www.learnmyself.com/.

other people positively (Wood, Harms, & Vazire, 2010). In online dating profiles, agreeable individuals are less likely than people who score low on this trait to lie about themselves (J. A. Hall & others, 2010).

■ *Conscientiousness* is a key factor in a variety of life domains. Researchers have found that conscientiousness is positively related to high school and college students' grade point averages (Noftle & Robins, 2007). Conscientiousness is also linked to better-quality friendships (Jensen-Campbell & Malcolm, 2007), higher levels of religious faith (Saroglou, 2010), and a forgiving attitude (Balliet, 2010). Conscientiousness is associated as well with dressing neatly, especially in the case of men (Naumann & others, 2009), and, like openness, is related to entrepreneurial success (Zhao, Seibert, & Lumpkin, 2010). Low levels of conscientiousness are linked to higher levels of criminal behavior (Wiebe, 2004), substance abuse (Walton & Roberts, 2004), and pathological gambling (Hwang & others, 2012), while high levels are linked to better health and lower stress levels (Gartland, O'Connor, & Lawton, 2012; Takahashi, Roberts, & Hoshino, 2012). A recent study revealed that more conscientious adolescents were less likely to experience stress in a number of aspects of their lives, including school and interpersonal relationships (Murphy, Miller, & Wrosch, 2012).

*Keep in mind that because the five factors are theoretically independent of one another, a person can be any combination of them. Do you know a neurotic extravert or an agreeable introvert?*

Some psychologists have described the optimal personality as a combination of high extraversion, conscientiousness, agreeableness, and openness to experience on the one hand, and low neuroticism on the other (Rushton & Irwing, 2009; van der Linden, te Nijenhuis, & Bakker, 2010). The observed variation in traits suggests that the existence of people who differ from one another in these different dimensions is adaptive for human beings (Buss, 2009; Nettle, 2006). Further, the value that is placed on different traits varies depending on culture (Fulmer & others, 2010).

In many ways, the role of personality traits in our life depends on the situations in which we find ourselves. Personality traits can be strengths or weaknesses, depending on the types of situations we encounter and the kinds of situations we seek out for ourselves (Block, 2010; King & Trent, 2012). Even a trait like agreeableness may be a liability when the situation calls for confrontational behavior. For instance, a woman whose marriage is breaking up might wish for a divorce lawyer who treats her kindly but might prefer one who is less than agreeable at the bargaining table. Eminent psychologist Lee Cronbach (1957, p. 679) once said, "If for each environment there is a best organism, for every organism there must be a best environment." If our personalities are not particularly well suited to a situation, we can change that situation or create one that fits better (King & Trent, 2012).

*Seeking out opportunities to turn our traits into strengths is one of the challenges of life.*

### CROSS-CULTURAL STUDIES ON THE BIG FIVE
Some research on the big five factors addresses the extent to which the factors appear in personality profiles in different cultures (Lingjaerde, Foreland, & Engvik, 2001; Miacic & Goldberg, 2007; Pukrop, Sass, & Steinmeyer, 2000). The question is, do the big five show up in the assessment of personality in cultures around the world? Some research suggests that they do: A version of the five factors appears in people in countries as diverse as Canada, Finland, Poland, China, and Japan (Paunonen & others, 1992; X. Zhou & others, 2009a). Among the big five, the factors most likely to emerge across cultures and languages are extraversion, agreeableness, and conscientiousness, with neuroticism and openness to experience being more likely to emerge only in English-speaking samples (De Raad & others, 2010).

### ANIMAL STUDIES ON THE BIG FIVE
Researchers have found evidence for at least some of the big five personality traits in animals, including domestic dogs (Gosling, 2008b; Gosling, Kwan, & John, 2003) and hyenas (Gosling & John, 1999). In addition, studies have turned up evidence for general personality traits (such as overall outgoingness) in orangutans, geese, lizards, fish, cockatiels, and squid (Fox & Millam, 2010; McGhee & Travis, 2010; Sinn, Gosling, & Moltschaniwskyj, 2008; Weinstein, Capitanio, & Gosling,

2008; Wilson & Godin, 2010), though some researchers have found that squid "personality" may be more a function of environmental factors than stable individual differences (Sinn & others, 2010).

## NEUROTICISM, EXTRAVERSION, AND WELL-BEING

A great deal of research in personality psychology has examined the links between personality traits and a person's level of happiness, or what psychologists call subjective well-being (Diener, Kesebir, & Tov, 2009; Oerlemans, Bakker, & Veenhoven, 2011), which we will explore further below. You have probably noticed that some people seem to go through life having fun, while others appear to feel distress at even the slightest problem. You might think that most happiness can be explained by the events that happen to us—of course, you reason, a person is going to be happy if she is doing well in school and has a loving romantic partner, but unhappy if she is doing poorly and has just experienced a painful breakup. In fact, research has shown that life events explain relatively little about a person's overall well-being.

On average, some people appear to be happier than others. Among the most consistent findings in personality research is the strong relationship between personality traits and well-being. Specifically, extraversion is related to higher levels of well-being, and neuroticism is strongly related to lower levels of well-being (Ni Mhaolain & others, 2012; Otonari & others, 2012; Wilt & Revelle, 2009). These links between extraversion and higher levels of well-being, and between neuroticism and lower levels of well-being, are consistent and have even been found in orangutans (Weiss, King, & Perkins, 2006). What explains these connections?

**subjective well-being**
A person's assessment of his or her own level of positive affect relative to negative affect, and the individual's evaluation of his or her life in general.

*Traits, Mood, and Subjective Well-Being*    To begin, let's define subjective well-being as psychologists do. **Subjective well-being** is a person's assessment of his or her own level of positive affect relative to negative affect, and the individual's evaluation of his or her life in general (Diener, 2000). When psychologists measure subjective well-being, they often focus on a person's positive and negative moods and life satisfaction.

*Remember you completed the Satisfaction with Life Scale in Chapter 1.*

This definition of subjective well-being provides a clue as to why the traits of neuroticism and extraversion might be so strongly related to one's level of well-being. Neuroticism is the tendency to worry, to feel distressed, and to experience negative emotion. Neurotic individuals experience more negative mood than others, and their moods are more changeable. David Watson, a personality and clinical psychologist who specializes in the study of mood, has suggested that negative emotion is at the core of the trait of neuroticism, while positive emotion is at the core of the trait of extraversion (Watson & Clark, 1997). To the extent that neurotic individuals are more prone to negative emotion, it would seem that this trait might take a toll on overall well-being. Interestingly, however, research has shown that neurotics can be happy—especially if they are also extraverted (Hotard & others, 1989). That is, for neurotic individuals, extraversion is especially strongly related to well-being. Extraversion is strongly related to well-being, even for those high on neuroticism. Why might this be the case?

An early theory about the relationship between extraversion and high levels of well-being was that extraverts engage in behaviors that are themselves related to higher well-being and positive mood, such as socializing with others. Thus, the thinking went, maybe extraverts are happier because they choose to spend more time with other people. Despite the logic of this explanation, research has shown that extraverts are happier than introverts even when they are alone (Lucas & Baird, 2004). Personality psychologists continue to puzzle over the explanation for this powerful link (Smillie & others, 2012).

In fact, research has supported the conclusion that extraverts are simply happier regardless of what they are doing or with whom they are doing it. Richard Lucas and Brendan Baird (2004) conducted a series of studies to examine the relationship between extraversion and positive mood. They exposed students who differed on the trait of extraversion to a variety of positive or neutral stimuli. The positive mood conditions included writing about a dream vacation or winning the lottery, viewing pleasant film clips about gardening or a Bill Cosby comedy routine, or reading jokes and cartoons. The neutral mood conditions included writing about taking a drive or going grocery shopping or watching a financial news report from PBS. In all of the studies, the strong relationship between extraversion and positive affect was found even in the neutral conditions. In other words, the extraverts were happier than the introverts regardless of whether the researchers had tried to put them in a pleasant mood. Even when they had just read a financial news report, the extraverts were happier.

***Traits and States*** If you are neurotic or an introvert—or even a neurotic introvert—you may be feeling your mood deflating like a helium-filled balloon in a heat wave. If personality is stable, what good is it to find out that your personality might make you miserable?

One way to think about these issues is to focus on the difference between *traits* and *states* (Marine & others, 2006). As we have seen, traits are enduring characteristics—they represent the way you generally are. In contrast, states (such as positive and negative moods) are briefer experiences. Having a trait, such as neuroticism, that predisposes you to feelings of worry (a state) does not mean that your overall well-being must suffer. Instead, recognizing that you tend to be neurotic may be an important step in noting when your negative moods are potentially being fed by traits and are not necessarily the result of objective events. Finding out that you have a personality style associated with lowered levels of happiness should not lead you to conclude that you are doomed. Rather, this information can allow you to take steps to improve your life, to foster good habits, and to make the most of your unique qualities.

In addition to happiness, researchers have examined the influence of the big five traits on body weight (van Reedt Dortland & others, 2012). To read about how personality relates to overweight and obesity, see the Intersection.

# Evaluating the Trait Perspectives

Studying people in terms of their personality traits has practical value. Identifying a person's traits allows us to know that individual better. Using traits, psychologists have learned a great deal about the connections between personality and our health, ways of thinking, career success, and relations with others (George, Helson, & John, 2011; Leary & Hoyle, 2009a; Turiano & others, 2012).

The trait approach has been faulted, however, for missing the importance of situational factors in personality and behavior (Kammrath & Scholer, 2012; Leary & Hoyle, 2009b). For example, a person might say that she is introverted when meeting new people but very outgoing when with family and friends. Further, some have criticized the trait perspective for painting an individual's personality with very broad strokes. Traits can tell us much about someone whom we have never met but reveal little about the nuances of each individual's personality.

## Personality Psychology and Health Psychology: Are Traits Linked to Obesity?

Obesity is a major worldwide health crisis (Hahn, Payne, & Lucas, 2013; Thompson & Manore, 2013). Overweight and obesity are second only to smoking in terms of controllable causes of death (Mokdad & others, 2004). Controllable means that these unhealthy conditions of body composition can be influenced by behavior, specifically by eating patterns and physical activity levels. If personality traits predict typical patterns of behavior, might they provide a way to understand preferences in eating and activity? Do personality traits predict weight gain and obesity?

A recent longitudinal study that followed nearly 2,000 people over the course of 50 years examined this question. Conducted by Angelina Sutin and her colleagues (2011), the study involved collecting measures of personality traits, including the big five, as well as weighing participants at each testing occasion. Looking at the data cross-sectionally, the researchers found that neuroticism and extraversion were positively related to body weight. In contrast, conscientiousness was negatively related to body weight. These relationships were most strongly explained by *impulsivity,* a trait that involves acting without planning. Impulsivity has been conceptualized as a dimension of neuroticism and extraversion, and it is negatively related to conscientiousness. How strongly was impulsivity related to weight? On average, those scoring in the top 10 percent on impulsivity weighed *24 pounds more* than those scoring in the bottom 10 percent.

Examining the sample over time, the researchers found that although in general people gained weight gradually over the 50-year span, certain traits related to how quickly they gained over time. While conscientiousness was strongly negatively related to rate of weight gain, neuroticism was associated with gaining weight more quickly.

Although this study might suggest that personality can make a person fat (depressing news for those low on conscientiousness!),

several facts are important to keep in mind. First, even in a longitudinal study, third variables, such as genetics, cannot be ruled out as an explanation—in this case, an explanation for the link between personality and body weight. Second, personality does not directly add inches to one's waistline; rather, it is proposed to do so through *behavior.* So, Sutin and her colleagues suggest that information about personality traits might be useful in tailoring interventions to help individuals control their weight. Consider that personality traits relate to one's typical behavior patterns. If losing weight means stepping outside those patterns, interventions can perhaps pinpoint behavioral strategies that a person might not otherwise use. Individuals high on impulsivity (or low on conscientiousness) might benefit, for example, by engaging in active planning of meals and exercise routines. For extraverts, support groups might work best, while for introverts self-directed programs or one-on-one interventions might be most successful in bringing about weight loss.

The researchers also noted that their study could not address the potential influence on personality of intentional efforts to lose weight over time. A provocative question arises: Could engaging in healthy behavior lead to a healthier personality? This intriguing possibility is supported by a recent longitudinal study on smoking and personality. In that study, college students who reduced their smoking behavior were more likely to show decreases in both neuroticism and impulsivity, and these changes were especially strong between the ages of 18 and 25 (Littlefield & Sher, 2012).

These results highlight the remarkable and complex links between mind and body. They also remind us that healthy behavior can have benefits for our entire being.

\\ **How do your personality traits relate to your health behaviors?**

\\ **Could changing your health behaviors improve your personality?**

1. All of the following are among the big five factors of personality *except*
   A. openness to experience.
   B. altruism.
   C. conscientiousness.
   D. extraversion.

2. Researchers have found that some version of the big five factors appears in
   A. people in diverse countries around the world.
   B. domestic dogs.
   C. lizards.
   D. all of the above

3. The personality factor that is most linked with a higher IQ is

A. neuroticism.
B. conscientiousness.
C. agreeableness.
D. openness to experience.

**APPLY IT!** 4. Sigmund, a high-achieving psychoanalyst, always sees his patients in a timely manner and completes his written work ahead of the deadline. A brilliant public speaker, he is often surrounded by enthusiastic admirers, and he enjoys being the center of attention. He has some pretty wild, abstract ideas and has developed a complex theory to explain all of human behavior. He is an unconventional thinker, to say the least. He does not respond well

to criticism and reacts poorly to even slight disapproval. Which of the following best describes Sigmund's personality?
A. low conscientiousness, high extraversion, low neuroticism, high openness to experience
B. high conscientiousness, high extraversion, high openness to experience, high neuroticism
C. high conscientiousness, low extraversion, low openness to experience, low neuroticism
D. low conscientiousness, high extraversion, low openness to experience, high neuroticism

# 4 Personological and Life Story Perspectives

Imagine giving 1,000 people a questionnaire measuring them on each of the big five traits. In looking at their scores, you might conclude that individuals are not all unique, like snowflakes, but more like Chips Ahoy cookies: They differ in small ways, but there are plenty who share very similar traits.

If two people have the same levels of the big five traits, do they essentially have the same personality? Researchers who approach personality from the personological and life story perspectives do not think so (McAdams & Olson, 2010). **Personological and life story perspectives** stress that the way to understand the person is to focus on his or her life history and life story—aspects that distinguish the individual from everyone else.

**personological and life story perspectives**
Theoretical views stressing that the way to understand the person is to focus on his or her life history and life story.

## Murray's Personological Approach

Henry Murray (1893–1988) was a young biochemistry graduate student when he became interested in the psychology of personality after meeting Carl Jung and reading his work.

Henry Murray's psychological profile of Adolf Hitler, developed in 1943 during World War II, serves as a model for criminal profiling today.

Murray went on to become the director of the Psychological Clinic at Harvard at the same time that Gordon Allport was on the faculty there. Murray and Allport saw personality very differently. Whereas Allport was most comfortable focusing on conscious experience and traits, Murray embraced the psychodynamic notion of unconscious motivation.

Murray coined the word *personology* to refer to the study of the whole person. He famously stated that "the history of the organism is the organism," meaning that in order to understand a person, we have to understand that person's history, including all aspects of the person's life.

Murray applied his insights into personality during World War II, when he was called upon by the Office of Strategic Services (or OSS, a precursor to the CIA) to develop a psychological profile of Adolf Hitler. That document, produced in 1943, accurately predicted that Hitler would commit suicide rather than be taken alive by the Allies. Murray's analysis of Hitler was the first "offender profile," and it has served as a model for modern criminal profiling.

The aspect of Murray's research that has had the most impact on contemporary personality psychology is his approach to motivation. Murray believed that our motives are largely unknown to us, so that measures of motivation must be developed that do not just ask people to say what it is they want. Thus, along with Christiana Morgan, Murray developed the Thematic Apperception Test (or TAT), to which we return later in this chapter (Morgan & Murray, 1935).

Moreover, a variety of scoring procedures have been devised for analyzing the unconscious motives that are revealed in imaginative stories (C. P. Smith, 1992). These scoring procedures involve *content analysis,* a procedure in which a psychologist takes the person's story and codes it for different images, words, and so forth. Murray posited 22 different unconscious needs to explain behavior. The three needs that have been the focus of most current research are the need for achievement (an enduring concern for attaining excellence and overcoming obstacles), for affiliation (an enduring concern for establishing and maintaining interpersonal connections), and for power (an enduring concern for having impact on the social world).

David Winter (2005) analyzed the motives revealed in inaugural addresses of U.S. presidents. He found that certain needs evidenced in these speeches corresponded to later events during the person's presidency. For instance, presidents who scored high on need for achievement (such as Jimmy Carter) were less successful during their terms. Note that the need for achievement is about striving for personal excellence and may have little to do with playing politics, negotiating interpersonal relationships, or delegating responsibility. Presidents who scored high on need for power tended to be judged as more successful (John F. Kennedy, Ronald Reagan), and presidents whose addresses included a great deal of warm, interpersonal imagery (suggesting a high need for affiliation) tended to experience scandal during their presidencies (Richard M. Nixon).

*Motivation is a central part of personality psychology. Personality psychologists consider motivation an enduring part of the person and examine how individuals vary in their levels of different motives.*

## The Life Story Approach to Identity

Following in the Murray tradition, Dan McAdams (2001, 2006, 2011a, 2012) developed the *life story approach* to identity. His work centers on the idea that each of us has a unique life story, full of ups and downs. These stories represent our memories of what makes us who we are. McAdams found that the life story is a constantly changing narrative that provides our lives with a sense of coherence. Just as Murray said that the history of the organism is the organism, McAdams suggests that our life stories are our identities.

McAdams has conducted research using large samples of individuals who have undergone "life story interviews." Interview responses are coded for themes that are relevant to differing life stages and transitions. For example, McAdams and his colleagues found that kindergarten teachers (who are assumed to be high in generativity, which we considered in Chapter 8) are more likely to tell life stories characterized by a redemption pattern, with things going from bad to good.

McAdams (1989) also introduced the concept of intimacy motivation. The *intimacy motive* is an enduring concern for warm interpersonal encounters for their own sake. Intimacy motivation is revealed in the warm, positive interpersonal imagery in the stories people tell. Intimacy motive has been shown to relate to positive outcomes. For instance, college men who were high on intimacy motivation showed heightened levels of happiness and lowered work strain some 30 years later (McAdams & Bryant, 1987). A study of the coming-out stories of gay men and lesbians demonstrated that intimacy-related imagery (for example, experiencing falling in love or warm acceptance from others) was associated with both measures of well-being and personality development (King & Smith, 2005).

**Do It!**

Pick a potentially negative experience from your life and write the story of that experience. Is the ending happy or sad? In reading your story, what might a personality psychologist learn about you?

Other personality psychologists have relied on narrative accounts of life experiences as a means of understanding how individuals create meaning in life events (King & others, 2000). In one study, parents of children with Down syndrome wrote the story of how they found out about their child's diagnosis. Parents whose stories ended happily scored higher on measures of happiness, life meaning, and personal growth than others (King & others, 2000). By using narratives, personal documents (such as diaries), and even letters and speeches, personality psychologists look for the deeper meaning that cannot be revealed through tests that ask people directly about whether specific items capture their personality traits.

Finally, some personality psychologists take very seriously Murray's commitment to understanding the whole person, by focusing on just one case. *Psychobiography* is a means of inquiry in which the personality psychologist attempts to apply a personality theory to a single person's life (Runyon, 2007; Schultz, 2005). Freud himself wrote the first psychobiography in his analysis of Michelangelo. However, some problems with his interpretations of Michelangelo's life have caused his work to become a road map for what a psychobiographer ought *not* to do (Elms, 2005).

*Scholars have written psychobiographies about a wide variety of individuals, including Jesus Christ (Capps, 2004), Elvis Presley (Elms and Heller, 2005), and Osama bin Laden (Dennis, 2005), as well as Sigmund Freud (Elms, 2005), Carl Rogers (J. W. Anderson, 2005), and Gordon Allport (Berenbaum, 2005).*

## Evaluating the Life Story Approach and Similar Perspectives

Studying individuals through narratives and personal interviews provides an extraordinarily rich opportunity for the researcher. Imagine having the choice of reading someone's diary versus seeing that person's scores on a questionnaire measuring traits. Not many would pass up the chance to read the diary.

However, life story studies are difficult and time-consuming. Personologist Robert W. White (1992) referred to the study of narratives as exploring personality "the long way." Collecting interviews and narratives is often just the first step. In order for these personal stories to become scientific data, they must be transformed into numbers, a process involving extensive coding and content analysis. Further, for narrative studies to be worthwhile, they must tell us something we could not have found out in a much easier way (King, 2003). Psychobiographical inquiries moreover are prone to the biases of the scholars who conduct them and may not serve the scientific goal of generalizability.

*Recall that generalizability refers to whether a particular finding is true of all people or just a narrow sample of even a single person.*

self quiz

1. Murray's personological approach is consistent with the
   A. humanistic perspective.
   B. psychodynamic perspective.
   C. trait perspective.
   D. lexical perspective.

2. Personology focuses primarily on
   A. objective tests.
   B. genetic factors.
   C. traits.
   D. unconscious motivations.

3. McAdams suggests that our identities are dependent on our
   A. heredity.
   B. cultural context.
   C. life stories.
   D. social networks.

**APPLY IT!** 4. Larry takes a test that involves looking at a series of pictures and telling stories about them. Based on his stories, he receives feedback that he is very high on need for power, and that means that he might be a good leader. Larry is shocked at this information, as he has never been put in charge before, and he cannot believe the score. According to the personological approach to motivation, what likely explains Larry's experience?
   A. Need for power is unconscious, and so Larry is not aware that he is high on this motive.
   B. The measure used to assess need for power is probably not appropriate.
   C. Larry is likely low on need for power. It is very unlikely that a personality measure would tell you something you do not already know about yourself.
   D. Larry is probably a neurotic introvert.

# 5 Social Cognitive Perspectives

**Social cognitive perspectives** on personality emphasize conscious awareness, beliefs, expectations, and goals. While incorporating principles from behaviorism (see Chapter 5), social cognitive psychologists explore the person's ability to reason; to think about the past, present, and future; and to reflect on the self. They emphasize the person's individual interpretation of situations and thus focus on the uniqueness of each person by examining how behavior is tailored to the diversity of situations in which people find themselves.

**social cognitive perspectives**
Theoretical views emphasizing conscious awareness, beliefs, expectations, and goals.

Social cognitive theorists are not interested in broad traits. Rather, they investigate how more specific factors, such as beliefs, relate to behavior and performance. In this section we consider the two major social cognitive approaches, developed respectively by Albert Bandura and Walter Mischel.

**Albert Bandura (b. 1925)**
*Bandura's practical, problem-solving social cognitive approach has made a lasting mark on personality theory and therapy.*

## Bandura's Social Cognitive Theory

B. F. Skinner, whose work we examined in Chapter 5, believed that there is no such thing as "personality"; rather, he emphasized behavior and felt that internal mental states were irrelevant to psychology. Albert Bandura (1986, 2001, 2007b, 2011a, 2011b) found Skinner's approach to be far too simplistic for understanding human functioning. Bandura took the basic tenets of behaviorism and added recognition of the role of mental processes in determining behavior. While Skinner saw behavior as caused by the situation, Bandura pointed out that the person can cause situations, and sometimes the very definition of the situation itself depends on the person's beliefs about it. For example, is that upcoming exam an opportunity to show your stuff or a threat to your ability to achieve your goals? The test is the same either way, but your unique take on it can influence a host of behaviors (studying hard, worrying, and so on).

Bandura's social cognitive theory states that behavior, environment, and person/cognitive factors are all important in understanding personality. Bandura coined the term *reciprocal determinism* to describe the way behavior, environment, and person/cognitive factors interact to create personality (Figure 10.4). The environment can determine a person's behavior, and the person can act to change the environment. Similarly, person/cognitive factors can both influence behavior and be influenced by behavior. From Bandura's perspective, then, behavior is a product of a variety of forces, some of which come from the situation and some of which the person brings to the

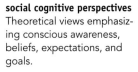

## PSYCHOLOGICAL INQUIRY

Behavior

Person/
Cognitive
Factors

Environment

**FIGURE 10.4  Bandura's Social Cognitive Theory**
Bandura's social cognitive theory emphasizes the reciprocal influences of behavior, environment, and person/cognitive factors. Notice that from Bandura's perspective, all of those arrows are double-headed, meaning that causation goes in both directions. Consider the following events and experiences. Describe how factors from each of the three points on the triangle spur changes in the other two and how those influences might come back again. ➤*A Behavior: You study hard and get an A on your Intro Psych exam.* ➤*An Environment: Your Intro Psych instructor provides lecture notes online and does a thorough review for each exam.* ➤*A Person/Cognitive Factor: You feel very confident about your ability to do well in Intro Psych.*

situation. We now review the important processes and variables Bandura used to understand personality.

**OBSERVATIONAL LEARNING**   Recall from Chapter 5 Bandura's belief that observational learning is a key aspect of how we learn. Through observational learning, we form ideas about the behavior of others and then possibly adopt this behavior ourselves. For example, a young boy might observe his father's aggressive outbursts and hostile exchanges with other people; when the boy is with his peers, he might interact in a highly aggressive way, showing the same characteristics as his father's behavior. Social cognitive theorists believe that we acquire a wide range of behaviors, thoughts, and feelings through observing others' behavior and that these observations strongly shape our personalities (Bandura, 2010a).

**PERSONAL CONTROL**   Social cognitive theorists emphasize that we can regulate and control our own behavior despite our changing environment (Bandura, 2011b; Mischel & others, 2011). For example, a young executive who observes her boss behave in an overbearing and sarcastic manner toward his subordinates may find the behavior distasteful and go out of her way to encourage and support her own staff. Psychologists commonly describe a sense of behavioral control as coming from inside the person (an *internal locus of control*) or outside the person (an *external locus of control*). When we feel that we ourselves are controlling our choices and behaviors, the locus of control is internal, but when other influences are controlling them, the locus of control is external.

Consider the question of whether you will perform well on your next test. With an internal locus of control, you believe that you are in command of your choices and behaviors, and your answer will depend on what you can realistically do (for example, study hard or attend a special review session). From the perspective of an external locus of control, however, you might say that you cannot predict how things will go because so many factors influence performance, such as whether the test is difficult and if the exam room is too hot or too cold.

Feeling a strong sense of personal control is vital to many aspects of performance, well-being, and physical health (Bandura, 2011b; Frazier & others, 2011; Morrison, Ponitz, & McClelland, 2010; Tigani & others, 2012). Self-efficacy is an important aspect of the experience of control, as we next consider.

**SELF-EFFICACY**   **Self-efficacy** is the belief that one has the competence to accomplish a given goal or task. Bandura and others have shown that self-efficacy is related to a number of positive developments in people's lives, including solving problems, becoming more sociable, initiating and maintaining a diet or an exercise program, and quitting smoking (Bandura, 2011b; Schunk, 2011). Self-efficacy influences whether people even try to develop healthy habits, as well as how much effort they expend in coping with stress, how long they persist in the face of obstacles, and how much stress and pain they experience (Becker, Kang, & Stuifbergen, 2012; Sawatzky & others, 2012; Schaubroeck & others, 2011). Self-efficacy is also related to whether people initiate psychotherapy to deal with their problems and whether it succeeds (Longo, Lent, & Brown, 1992). In addition, researchers have found that self-efficacy is linked with successful job interviewing, job performance, and achievement in a creative profession (Beeftink & others, 2012; Tay, Ang, & Van Dyne, 2006). We will return to the topics of personal control and self-efficacy in Chapter 14, in the context of making healthy changes in behavior.

**self-efficacy**
The belief that one can accomplish a given goal or task and produce positive change.

*Self-efficacy means having a can-do attitude.*

## Mischel's Contributions

Like Bandura, Walter Mischel is a social cognitive psychologist who has explored how personality influences behavior. Mischel has left his mark on the field of personality in two notable ways. First, his critique of the idea of consistency in behavior ignited a flurry of controversy. Second, he has proposed the CAPS model, a new way of thinking about personality.

**MISCHEL'S CRITIQUE OF CONSISTENCY**   Whether we are talking about unconscious sexual conflicts, traits, or motives, all of the approaches we have considered so far maintain that these various personality characteristics are an enduring influence on behavior. This shared assumption was attacked in 1968 with the publication of Walter Mischel's *Personality and Assessment,* a book that nearly ended the psychological study of personality.

To understand Mischel's argument, recall Gordon Allport's definition of a trait as a characteristic that ought to make different situations equivalent for a given person. This quality of traits suggests that a person should behave consistently in different situations— in other words, the individual should exhibit *cross-situational consistency.* For example, an outgoing person should act highly sociably whether she is at a party or in the library. However, Mischel looked at the research compiled on trait prediction of behavior and found it to be lacking. He concluded that there was no evidence for cross-situational consistency in behavior—and thus no evidence for the existence of personality as it had been previously assumed to exist.

Rather than understanding personality as consisting of broad, internal traits that make for consistent behavior across situations, Mischel said that personality often changes according to a given situation. Mischel asserted that behavior is discriminative—that is, a person looks at each situation and responds accordingly. Mischel's view is called *situationism,* the idea that personality and behavior often vary considerably from one context to another.

Personality psychologists responded to Mischel's situationist attack in a variety of ways (Donnellan, Lucas, & Fleeson, 2009; Funder, 2009; Hogan, 2009). Researchers showed that it is not a matter of *whether* personality predicts behavior, but *when and how* it does so, often in combination with situational factors. The research findings were that

- The narrower and more limited a trait is, the more likely it will predict behavior.

- Some people are consistent on some traits, and other people are consistent on other traits.

- Personality traits exert a stronger influence on an individual's behavior when situational influences are less powerful. A very powerful situation is one that contains many clear cues about how a person is supposed to behave. For example, even a highly talkative person typically sits quietly during a class lecture. In weaker situations, however, such as during his or her leisure time, the person may spend most of the time talking.

Moreover, individuals select the situations they are in. This means that even if situations determine behavior, traits play a role in determining which situations people choose— such as going to a party or staying home to study (Emmons & Diener, 1986).

Let's pause and consider what it means to be consistent. You might believe that being consistent is part of being a genuine, honest person and that tailoring behavior to different situations means being fake. On the other hand, consider that someone who never changes his or her behavior to fit a situation might be unpleasant—a "drag" to have around. Think for example about someone who cannot put aside his competitive drive even when playing checkers with a 4-year-old. Clearly, adaptive behavior might involve sometimes being consistent and sometimes tailoring behavior to the situation.

Over time, Mischel (2004, 2009) has developed an approach to personality that he feels is better suited to capturing the nuances of the relationship between the individual and situations in producing behavior. Imagine trying to study personality without using traits or broad motives. What would you focus on? Mischel's answer to this dilemma is his CAPS theory.

**CAPS THEORY**   Mischel's theory of personality is centered in his work on *delay of gratification*—putting off a pleasurable experience in the interest of some larger but later reward. Mischel and his colleagues examined how children managed to delay gratification (Mischel, Cantor, & Feldman, 1996; Mischel & Moore, 1980; Mischel & others, 2011). They placed children in a specific difficult situation—being alone in a room with a tempting cookie in their reach. The children were told that if they wanted to at any time, they could ring a bell and eat the cookie. Otherwise, they could wait until the experimenter returned, and then they would get two cookies. The children were then left alone to face this self-control dilemma. In truth, the experimenter was not coming back. The researchers were interested in measuring how long the children could wait before giving in to temptation and eating the cookie.

The children responded in various ways. Some kids sat dead still, focused on the tempting cookie. Some smelled the cookie. Others turned away, sang songs, picked their noses, or did anything but pay attention to the cookie. How did the children who were able to resist temptation do it? Mischel and colleagues found that the kids who distracted themselves from the cookie by focusing on "cool thoughts" (non-cookie-related things) were better able to delay gratification. In contrast, children who remained focused on the cookie and all its delightful qualities—what Mischel called "hot thoughts"—ate the cookie sooner (Metcalfe & Mischel, 1999). This work demonstrates that avoiding these hot issues might be a good way to see a long-term plan through to completion.

How does this work relate to personality? Mischel and his colleagues continued to study those children for many years. They found that the amount of time the children were able to delay gratification predicted their academic performance in high school and college (Mischel, 2004) and even their self-regulation skills in their 40s (Casey & others, 2011). These results indicate remarkable stability in personality over time.

*Mischel focused on coherence, or whether behaviors make sense across different situations—not whether they are the very same behavior.*

Mischel's revised approach to personality is concerned with just such stability (or *coherence*) in the pattern of behavior over time, not with consistency across differing situations. That is, Mischel and his colleagues have studied how behaviors in very different situations have a coherent pattern, such as a child's waiting to eat the cookie versus that same individual's (as a grown college student) deciding to stay home and study instead of going out to party.

**cognitive affective processing systems (CAPS)** Mischel's theoretical model for describing that individuals' thoughts and emotions about themselves and the world affect their behavior and become linked in ways that matter to that behavior.

In keeping with the social cognitive emphasis on the person's cognitive abilities and mental states, Mischel conceptualizes personality as a set of interconnected **cognitive affective processing systems (CAPS)** (Kross, Mischel, & Shoda, 2010; Mischel, 2004, 2009; Mischel & Ayduk, 2011; Mischel & Shoda, 1999; Orom & Cervone, 2009). According to CAPS theory, our thoughts and emotions about ourselves and the world affect our behavior and become linked in ways that matter to behavior. Personal control and self-efficacy are connections of sorts that a person has made among situations, beliefs, and behaviors. Imagine someone—let's call him Raoul—who is excited by the challenge of a new assignment given by his boss. Raoul may think about all the possible strategies to complete the project and get down to work immediately. Yet this go-getter may respond differently to other challenges, depending on who gives the assignment, what it is, or whether he feels he can do a good job.

CAPS is concerned with how personality works, not with what it is (Mischel & Ayduk, 2011; Shoda & Mischel, 2006). From the CAPS perspective, it makes no sense to ask a person "How extraverted are you?" because the answer is always, "It depends." A person may be outgoing in one situation (on the first day of class) and not another (right before an exam), and this unique pattern of flexibility is what personality is all about.

Not surprisingly, CAPS theory focuses on how people behave in different situations and how they uniquely interpret situational features. From this perspective, knowing that Crystal is an extravert tells us little about how she will behave in a group discussion in her psychology class. We need to know about Crystal's beliefs and goals in the discussion. For example, does she want to impress the instructor? Is she a psychology major? Are several members of the class good friends of hers? We also need to

*Is your own behavior mostly consistent across different situations?*

know about her personal understanding of the situation itself: Is this an opportunity to shine, or is she thinking about her test for the next class? Research using the CAPS approach generally involves observing individuals behaving in a variety of contexts in order to identify the patterns of associations that exist among beliefs, emotions, and behavior for each individual person across different situations.

## Evaluating the Social Cognitive Perspectives

Social cognitive theory focuses on the interactions of individuals with their environments. The social cognitive approach has fostered a scientific climate for understanding personality that highlights the observation of behavior. Social cognitive theory emphasizes the influence of cognitive processes in explaining personality and suggests that people have the ability to control their environment.

Critics of the social cognitive perspective on personality take issue with one or more aspects of the theory. For example, they charge that

- The social cognitive approach is too concerned with change and situational influences on personality. It does not pay adequate tribute to the enduring qualities of personality.

- Social cognitive theory ignores the role biology plays in personality.

- In its attempt to incorporate both the situation and the person into its view of personality, social cognitive psychology tends to lead to very specific predictions for each person in any given situation, making generalizations impossible.

self-quiz

1. The following are components of Bandura's social cognitive theory *except*
   A. self-efficacy.
   B. unconscious motivations.
   C. personal control.
   D. observational learning.

2. According to Mischel's 1968 book, behavior is determined by
   A. traits.
   B. biology.
   C. situations and the person's perceptions of them.
   D. unconscious motives.

3. The cognitive affective processing systems (CAPS) approach is centrally concerned with
   A. how personality works in different situations.
   B. how genetic inheritance affects personality.
   C. what biological factors influence personality.
   D. what personality is.

**APPLY IT!** 4. Omri thinks of himself as an extravert, but he rarely speaks up in his classes. He is especially quiet when he meets new people, especially authority figures such as a new boss. What would Walter Mischel say about Omri's behavior?
   A. Omri is not really an extravert at all; he just does not understand that.
   B. Omri is being discriminative in his behavior. He is probably extraverted in some situations and introverted in others, and that should not be surprising.
   C. Omri is probably fixated at the phallic stage of development.
   D. Omri was not given enough unconditional positive regard in his childhood.

## 6 Biological Perspectives

The notion that physiological processes influence personality has been around since ancient times. Around 400 B.C.E., Hippocrates, the father of medicine, described human beings as having one of four basic personalities based on levels of particular bodily fluids (called *humours*). For Hippocrates, a "sanguine" personality was a happy, optimistic individual who happened to have an abundance of blood. A "choleric" person was quick-tempered with too much yellow bile. A "phlegmatic" personality referred to a placid, sluggish individual with too much phlegm (mucus), and a "melancholic" pessimist had too much black bile.

Although Hippocrates' ideas about bodily fluids have fallen by the wayside, personality psychologists have long acknowledged that personality involves the brain and biological processes, although they often have assumed the processes to exist rather than actually studying them. Freud's psychosexual stages bear witness to his strong belief in the connection between the mind (personality) and the body. Allport defined traits as "neuropsychic" structures and personality as a "psychophysical" system. Murray once declared, "No brain, no personality." More recently, advances in method and theory have led to fascinating research on the role of biological processes in personality.

# Personality and the Brain

The brain is clearly important in personality, as in other psychological phenomena. Recall the case of Phineas Gage, described in Chapter 2. One of the key effects of Gage's horrific accident was that it changed his personality. He went from being gentle, kind, and reliable to being angry, hostile, and untrustworthy.

A great deal of research is addressing the ways in which brain activity is associated with various personality traits (Adelstein & others, 2011; DeYoung, 2010; Xu & Potenza, 2012). For example, research has shown an extraverted person's left frontal cortex is more responsive to positive stimuli and that the same area in neurotic individuals is more responsive to negative stimuli (Canli, 2008a, 2008b; Haas & others, 2007; Schmidtke & Heller, 2004). Extraverts' amygdalae are more responsive to seeing happy faces than are introverts' amygdalae (Canli & others, 2002). Two theoretical approaches to the biology of personality, by Hans Eysenck and Jeffrey Gray, have garnered the most interest.

**EYSENCK'S RETICULAR ACTIVATION SYSTEM THEORY** British psychologist Hans Eysenck (1967) was among the first to describe the role of a particular brain system in personality. He developed an approach to extraversion/introversion based on the *reticular activation system* (RAS).

Recall from Chapters 2 and 4 that the reticular formation is located in the brain stem and plays a role in wakefulness or arousal. The RAS is the name given to the reticular formation and its connections. Eysenck posited that all of us share an optimal arousal level, a level at which we feel comfortably engaged with the world. However, Eysenck proposed, the RAS of extraverts and introverts differs with respect to the baseline level of arousal. You know that an extravert tends to be outgoing, sociable, and dominant and that an introvert is quieter and more reserved and passive. According to Eysenck, these outward differences in behavior reflect different arousal regulation strategies (Figure 10.5). Extraverts wake up in the morning under-aroused, *below* the optimal level, whereas introverts start out *above* the optimal level.

If *you* were feeling under-engaged with life, what might you do? You might listen to loud music or hang out with friends—in other words, behave like an extravert. If, on the

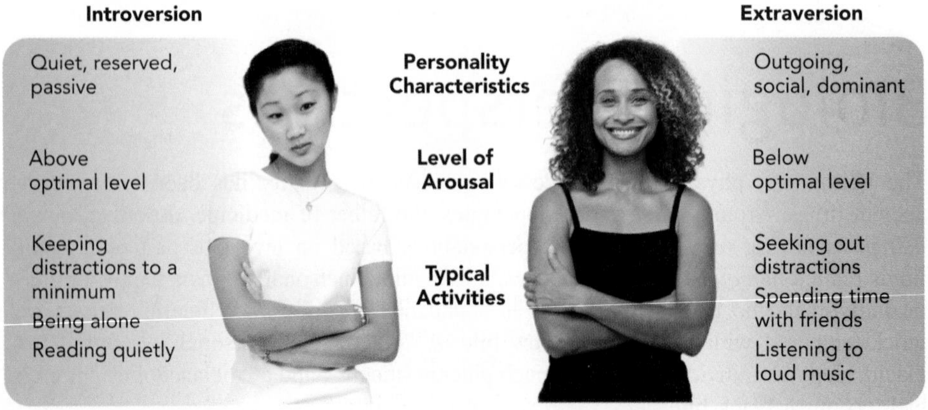

**FIGURE 10.5**
**Eysenck's Reticular Activation System Theory** Eysenck viewed introversion and extraversion as characteristic behavioral patterns that aim to regulate arousal around the individual's baseline level.

Introversion

Personality Characteristics

Extraversion

Quiet, reserved, passive

Outgoing, social, dominant

Above optimal level

Level of Arousal

Below optimal level

Keeping distractions to a minimum

Typical Activities

Seeking out distractions

Being alone

Spending time with friends

Reading quietly

Listening to loud music

other hand, you were feeling over-aroused or too stimulated, what would you do? You might spend time alone, keep distractions to a minimum, maybe sit quietly and read a book—in other words, you might act like an introvert.

Thus, from Eysenck's perspective, we can understand the traits of extraversion/introversion as characteristic patterns of behavior that aim to regulate arousal around our baseline. Research has not shown that extraverts and introverts differ in terms of baseline arousal but, rather, that introverts may be more sensitive to arousing stimuli.

**GRAY'S REINFORCEMENT SENSITIVITY THEORY**  Building from Eysenck's work, Jeffrey Gray proposed a neuropsychology of personality, called *reinforcement sensitivity theory,* that has been the subject of much research (Gray, 1987; Gray & McNaughton, 2000; Smillie & others, 2012). On the basis of animal learning principles, Gray posited that two neurological systems—the *behavioral activation system (BAS)* and the *behavioral inhibition system (BIS)*—could be viewed as underlying personality, as Figure 10.6 shows.

According to Gray, these systems explain differences in an organism's attention to rewards and punishers in the environment. An organism sensitive to rewards is more likely to learn associations between behaviors and rewards and therefore to show a characteristic pattern of seeking out rewarding opportunities. In contrast, an organism with a heightened sensitivity to punishers in the environment is more likely to learn associations between behaviors and negative consequences. Such an organism shows a characteristic pattern of avoiding such consequences.

In Gray's theory, the BAS is sensitive to rewards in the environment, predisposes one to feelings of positive emotion, and underlies the trait of extraversion. In contrast, the BIS is sensitive to punishments and is involved in avoidance learning; it predisposes the individual to feelings of fear and underlies the trait of neuroticism (Berkman, Lieberman, & Gable, 2009; Corr, 2008; Gray & McNaughton, 2000). Psychologists often measure the BAS and BIS in humans by using questionnaires that assess a person's attention to rewarding or punishing outcomes (Schmeichel, Harmon-Jones, & Harmon-Jones, 2010).

Gray's conceptual model of reinforcement sensitivity proposed interacting brain systems as primarily responsible for the behavioral manifestations of the BAS and BIS. Research has provided some evidence for the biological underpinnings of these systems. The amygdala, the prefrontal cortex, and the anterior cingulated cortex appear to serve together as a system for affective style (Davidson, 2005; McNaughton & Corr, 2008) and are especially implicated in the BAS or extraversion (Pickering & Smillie, 2008; Smillie & others, 2012).

**BAS**
**Behavioral Approach System**

**Sensitive to**
Environmental reward

**Behavior**
Seek positive consequences/rewards

**Character of Emotion**
Positive

**Personality Trait**
Extraversion

**BIS**
**Behavioral Inhibition System**

**Sensitive to**
Environmental punishment

**Behavior**
Avoid negative consequences/punishments

**Character of Emotion**
Negative

**Personality Trait**
Neuroticism

**FIGURE 10.6  Gray's Reinforcement Sensitivity Theory**  Gray theorized that two neurological systems, the BAS and the BIS, explain differences in an organism's attention to environmental rewards and punishments, and in this way shape personality.

**THE ROLE OF NEUROTRANSMITTERS**  Neurotransmitters have also been implicated in personality in ways that fit Gray's model. Recall from Chapter 4 that dopamine is a "feel good" neurotransmitter vital to learning that certain behaviors are rewarding and to sending the message "Do it again!" Research has shown that dopamine is also a factor in BAS or extraversion (Munafo & others, 2008; Wacker & others, 2012). Studies have suggested that early encounters with warm caregivers and positive life experiences can promote the growth of dopamine-producing cells and receptors. These early experiences can make the brain especially sensitive to rewards, setting the neurochemical stage for extraversion (Depue & Collins, 1999).

Perhaps even stronger than the link between dopamine and extraversion is the link between the neurotransmitter serotonin and the trait of neuroticism (Brummett & others, 2008; Middeldorp & others, 2007). Neuroticism is especially related to a certain serotonin transporter gene and to the binding of serotonin in the thalamus (Gonda & others, 2009; Harro & others, 2009; Vinberg & others, 2010). Individuals who have less circulating serotonin are prone to negative mood; giving them drugs that inhibit the reuptake of serotonin tends to decrease negative mood and enhance feelings of sociability (Hart, Kisr, & Ray, 2011). Serotonin is also implicated in aggressive behavior (Yanowitch & Coccaro, 2011), as well as in depression (Rocha & others, 2012), as we will consider in Chapters 11 and 12, respectively.

Finding associations between brain activity or neurotransmitters and personality does not tell us, however, about the potential *causal pathways* between these variables. Consider that behavior and experience can influence brain processes and therefore determine brain activity. The link between neuroticism and serotonin provides a telling example. Although neuroticism has been related to the serotonin transporter gene, research demonstrates that individuals with this genetic marker are not inevitably likely to be worriers. For such individuals, the levels of well-being or distress they experience may depend mostly on their environment. For example, if a person has this gene and experiences a warm, supportive environment, he or she is at *lower* risk for depression and distress (Eley & others, 2004; Vinberg & others, 2010; Way & Gurbaxani, 2008). In short, biological processes take place within a larger social context, and how these processes express themselves may depend on that social world.

# Personality and Behavioral Genetics

**Behavioral genetics** is the study of the inherited underpinnings of behavioral characteristics. A great deal of research in behavioral genetics has involved twin studies, and the hub of this work is, appropriately, the University of Minnesota, Twin Cities.

*It might surprise you that well-being, like many psychological characteristics—including intelligence, religiosity, and political attitudes—is influenced by genes.*

Twin study findings demonstrate that genetic factors explain a substantial amount of the observed differences in each of the big five traits. Heritability estimates for the five factors are about 50 percent (Bouchard & Loehlin, 2001; Jang, Livesley, & Vernon, 1996; South & Krueger, 2008). Remember that to do these studies, researchers compare identical twins, who share 100 percent of their genes, with fraternal twins, who share just 50 percent. All of the participants complete questionnaires measuring their traits. Then the researchers see if the identical twins are more similar to each other than the fraternal twins. One potential explanation for the strong relationship between personality characteristics and well-being is that the same genetic factors may play a role in traits such as extraversion, neuroticism, and well-being (Carprara & others, 2009; Weiss, Bates, & Luciano, 2008).

Even aspects of personality that are not traits reveal some genetic influence. For example, research has shown that autobiographical memories about one's childhood and early family experiences (the kind of data a personologist might find interesting) are influenced by genetics. Robert Krueger and his colleagues (Krueger, Markon, & Bouchard, 2003) examined retrospective reports on the quality of family environments in a sample of twins who were reared apart. Participants rated their adoptive families on a variety of characteristics such as parental warmth, feelings of being wanted, and the strictness of their parents. These twins, though obviously sharing genetics, were reared by different families, so they were describing different experiences. Yet their recollections of their early family experiences were similar, and the heritability estimate for family cohesion ranged from 40 to 60 percent.

*Consider how genes might influence the processes of autobiographical memory—encoding, retention, and recall. In which memory process would genes matter most?*

As we saw in Chapter 7's discussion of intelligence and Chapter 9's examination of happiness, the heritability statistic describes a group, not an individual, and heritability does not mean that traits are set in stone. Understanding the role of genetic factors in personality is enormously complex. Research on non-twin samples often suggests much lower heritability, for reasons that are not well understood (South & Krueger,

2008). Furthermore, because genes and environment are often intertwined, it is very difficult to tease apart whether, and how, genes or experience explains enduring patterns of behavior. For instance, a child who is genetically predisposed to disruptive behavior may often end up in a time-out or involved in arguments with parents or teachers. When that child emerges as an adult with a "fighting spirit" or lots of "spunk," are those adult traits the product of genes, experiences, or both? Finally, most traits are probably influenced by multiple genes (Costa & others, 2010; Wacker & others, 2012), making the task of identifying specific molecular links very challenging.

## Evaluating the Biological Perspectives

Research that explores the biological aspects of personality is likely to remain a key avenue of research. This work ties the field of personality to animal learning models, advances in brain imaging, and evolutionary theory (Revelle, 2008). However, a few cautions are necessary in thinking about biological variables and their place in personality.

As we considered above, biology can be the effect, not the cause, of personality. To be sure that you grasp this idea, first remember that personality is the individual's characteristic pattern of behavior, thoughts, and feelings. Then recall from previous chapters that behavior, thoughts, and feelings are physical events in the body and brain. If traits predispose individuals to particular, consistent behaviors, thoughts, and emotional responses, traits may play a role in forging particular habitually used pathways in the brain. Recall, too, from Chapter 6 that memory may be thought of as patterns of activation among neurons. The autobiographical memories that interest personologists, then, might be viewed as well-worn patterns of activation. To the extent that personality represents a person's characteristic pattern of thought or the accumulation of memories over the life span, personality may not only be influenced by the brain—it may also play a role in the brain's very structure and functions.

1. Eysenck suggested that introversion and extraversion are influenced by the brain's
   A. amygdala.
   B. reticular activation system.
   C. thalamus.
   D. prefrontal cortex.

2. Gray's reward sensitivity theory of personality suggests that extraversion and neuroticism can be understood as two neurological systems linked to _____ in the individual's environment.
   A. stability and consistency
   B. stability and change

C. rewards and punishments
D. opportunities for growth

3. A technique commonly used by researchers in the specialized field known as behavioral genetics is
   A. life story interviews.
   B. naturalistic observation.
   C. case studies.
   D. twin studies.

APPLY IT! 4. Dorian's parents are both very outgoing, while Dorian is quiet and reserved. Her parents often embarrass her in public with their loud voices and crazy an-

tics. When Dorian learns that extraversion is 50 percent heritable, she starts to wonder if she will eventually become as irritating as her parents. What is your advice for Dorian?
A. She should start getting used to the idea of being an extravert—she's doomed.
B. She has nothing to worry about, because heritability is only about twins.
C. She should remember that heritability is a statistic that applies only to a group, not to a single case.
D. She should be glad, because as an extravert she is likely to be happier.

# 7 Personality Assessment

One of the great contributions of personality psychology to the science of psychology is its development of rigorous methods for measuring mental processes. Psychologists use a number of scientifically developed methods to evaluate personality. They assess personality for different reasons, from clinical evaluation to career counseling and job selection (Lowmaster & Morey, 2012; Makransky, Mortensen, & Glas, 2012).

OK CLASS, THESE CAREER PATH SUGGESTIONS ARE BASED ON THE PERSONALITY ASSESSMENTS YOU ALL TOOK LAST WEEK...

©Scott Hilburn/Distributed by Universal Uclick via CartoonStock.com

Used by permission of CartoonStock, www.CartoonStock.com.

# Self-Report Tests

The most commonly used method of measuring personality characteristics is the **self-report test,** which directly asks people whether specific items describe their personality traits. Self-report personality tests include items such as

I am easily embarrassed.

I love to go to parties.

I like to watch cartoons on TV.

Respondents choose from a limited number of answers (yes or no, true or false, agree or disagree).

One problem with self-report tests is a factor called *social desirability.* To grasp the idea of social desirability, imagine answering the item "I am lazy at times." This statement is probably true for everyone, but would you feel comfortable admitting it? When motivated by social desirability, individuals say what they think the researcher wants to hear or what they think will make them look better. One way to measure the influence of social desirability is to give individuals a questionnaire that is designed to tap into this tendency. Such a scale typically contains many universally true but threatening items ("I like to gossip at times," "I have never said anything intentionally to hurt someone's feelings"). If scores on a trait measure correlate with this measure of social desirability, we know that the test takers were probably not being straightforward with respect to the trait measure. That is, if a person answers one questionnaire in a socially desirable fashion, he or she is probably answering all the questionnaires that way.

Another way to get around social desirability is to design scales so that it is virtually impossible for the respondent to know what the researcher is trying to measure. One means of accomplishing this goal is to use an **empirically keyed test,** a type of self-report test that is created by first identifying two groups that are known to be different.

The researcher would give these two groups a large number of questionnaire items and then see which items show the biggest differences between the groups. Those items would then become part of the scale to measure the group difference. For instance, a researcher might want to develop a test that distinguishes between individuals with a history of substance abuse and those with no such history. The researcher might generate a long list of true/false items that ask about a variety of different topics but that do not even mention substance abuse. These numerous questions are presented to the members of the two groups, and on the basis of the responses, the researcher can then select the items that best discriminate between the members of the differing groups (Segal & Coolidge, 2004).

Note that an empirically keyed test avoids the issue of social desirability because the items that distinguish between the two groups are not related in any obvious way to the actual purpose of the test. For instance, those without a substance abuse history might typically respond "true" to the item "I enjoy taking long walks," while those with a history of substance abuse might respond "false"; but this item does not mention substance use, and there is no clear reason why it should distinguish between these groups.

Indeed, an important consideration with respect to empirically keyed tests is that researchers often do not know why a given test item distinguishes between two groups. Imagine, for example, that an empirically keyed test of achievement motivation includes an item such as "I prefer to watch sports on TV instead of romantic movies." A researcher might find that this item does a good job of distinguishing between higher-paid versus lower-paid managers in a work setting. However, does an item such as this example measure achievement motivation or, instead, simply the respondents' gender?

**self-report test**
Also called an objective test or an inventory, a method of measuring personality characteristics that directly asks people whether specific items describe their personality traits.

**empirically keyed test**
A type of self-report test that presents many questionnaire items to two groups that are known to be different in some central way.

An empirically keyed test can have items that seem to have nothing to do with the variable of interest.

**Minnesota Multiphasic Personality Inventory (MMPI)**
The most widely used and researched empirically keyed self-report personality test.

**MMPI**     The **Minnesota Multiphasic Personality Inventory (MMPI)** is the most widely used and researched empirically keyed self-report personality test. The MMPI was initially constructed in the 1940s to assess "abnormal" personality tendencies. The current version of the inventory, the MMPI-2, is the most extensively used measure in the United States and around the world to assess personality and predict outcomes (Butcher, 2010; Butcher & others, 2011; Graham, 2012). The scale features 567 items and provides information on a variety of personality characteristics. The MMPI also includes a variety of items meant to assess whether the respondent is lying or trying to make a good impression.

*Some of the MMPI-2 scales measure characteristics associated with psychological disorders, such as depression and schizophrenia, which we will examine in Chapter 12. Other scales include masculinity/femininity and introversion.*

The MMPI is not only used by clinical psychologists to assess mental health (Greene, 2011). It is also a tool for hiring decisions (Caillouet & others, 2010), and in forensic settings it is used for assessing criminal risk (Bow, Flens, & Gould, 2010).

### ASSESSMENT OF THE BIG FIVE FACTORS

Paul Costa and Robert McCrae (1992) constructed the *Neuroticism Extraversion Openness Personality Inventory— Revised* (or *NEO-PI-R,* for short), a self-report test geared to assessing the five-factor model: openness, conscientiousness, extraversion, agreeableness, and neuroticism (emotional instability). The test also evaluates six subdimensions that make up the five main factors (McCrae, Harwood, & Kelly, 2011). Other measures of the big five traits have relied on the lexical approach and offer the advantage of being available without a fee.

**face validity**
The extent to which a test item appears to fit the particular trait it is measuring.

Unlike empirically keyed tests, measures of the big five generally contain items that are straightforward; for instance, the trait "talkative" might show up on an extraversion scale. These items have what psychologists call **face validity.** A test item has face validity if it seems on the surface to fit the trait in question. Measures of the big five typically involve items that are obvious in terms of what they measure, but not all self-report assessments have this quality.

*For example, an item measuring neuroticism that is very face valid would be "I am a worrier."*

A key challenge for researchers who use self-report tests is ensuring the accuracy of participants' responses (Griffith & Converse, 2011; Ziegler, MacCann, & Roberts, 2011). One way that researchers gauge the truthfulness or accuracy of responses in self-reports is by having an individual who knows the test taker well provide ratings of that person (Anusic & others, 2009). If the test taker's and the acquaintance's ratings agree, the researchers might put more faith in the self-reports than they otherwise would. However, the situation is more complex than meets the eye. Addressing the question of whether individuals' personality judgments are accurate is a flourishing area of research in personality psychology (Holden & Book, 2011). To read about this work, see Challenge Your Thinking.

It is likely that you would be able to give a reasonably good assessment of your own levels of traits such as neuroticism and extraversion. What about the more mysterious aspects of yourself and others? If you are like most people, you view psychological assessments as tools to find out things you do not already know about yourself. For that objective, psychologists might turn to projective tests.

## Projective Tests

A **projective test** presents individuals with an ambiguous stimulus and asks them to describe it or to tell a story about it—to project their own meaning onto the stimulus. This method assumes that the ambiguity of the stimulus allows individuals to interpret it based on their feelings, desires, needs, and attitudes. The test is especially designed to elicit the individual's unconscious feelings and conflicts, providing an assessment that goes deeper than the surface of personality (Sahly & others, 2011). Projective tests attempt to get inside the mind to discover how the test taker really feels and thinks; they aim to go beyond the way the individual overtly presents himself or herself. Projective

**projective test**
A personality assessment test that presents individuals with an ambiguous stimulus and asks them to describe it or tell a story about it—to project their own meaning onto the stimulus.

# Challenge

## Are Personality Judgments Accurate?

How well do we need to know someone to judge his or her personality accurately? A large body of evidence suggests that an observer's ratings of another person's personality agree remarkably well with the individual's ratings in self-reports, even in cases where the two people are only slightly acquainted. For example, in one study, participants watched video clips of a group of target individuals for varying amounts of time. Then they rated the targets on various traits. After just 5 seconds, those trait ratings related very well to the targets' self-reports for extraversion, conscientiousness, and intelligence. Neuroticism, openness to experience, and agreeableness took a little longer, but within *1 minute,* judges were reasonably good at producing ratings that agreed with the targets' self-ratings (Carney, Colvin, & Hall, 2007).

Such studies suggest that people are surprisingly accurate at detecting what a person would say about his or her own personality, even with very limited information. But these results raise some interesting questions: Is agreement between an observer's and a person's own ratings the same thing as accuracy?

What if self-ratings themselves are not particularly accurate reflections of a person's behavior? Further, might there be times when observer ratings are more accurate than a person's self-ratings? The accuracy of personality judgments depends on several factors, including the meaning of accuracy, the traits being considered, and the qualities of the person being judged.

Simine Vazire (2010) proposed a model to predict the accuracy of personality ratings made by a person about himself or herself and by observers of that person. From Vazire's perspective, accuracy means the extent to which a trait's rating predicts behavior relevant to that trait. In formulating her approach, Vazire focused on two questions about traits:

- Can we see the trait in action?
- Is the trait socially valued?

With regard to the first question, Vazire posited that when traits are highly visible, that is, when they have observable behavioral expressions, both the person and others should be good at

**FIGURE 10.7 Type of Stimulus Used in the Rorschach Inkblot Test** What do you see in this figure? Do you see two green seahorses? Or a pair of blue spiders? A psychologist who relies on the Rorschach test would examine your responses to find out who you are.

tests are theoretically aligned with the psychodynamic perspectives on personality, which give more weight to the unconscious than do other perspectives. Projective techniques also require content analysis. The examiner must code the responses for the underlying motivations revealed in the story.

A famous projective test is the **Rorschach inkblot test,** developed in 1921 by the Swiss psychiatrist Hermann Rorschach. The test consists of 10 cards, half in black-and-white and half in color, which the individual views one at a time (Figure 10.7). The test taker is asked to describe what he or she sees in each of the inkblots. The individual may say, for example, "I see two fairies having a tea party" or "This is a picture of the female reproductive organs." These responses are scored based on indications of various underlying psychological characteristics (Bornstein, 2012).

From a scientific perspective, researchers are skeptical about the Rorschach (Garb & others, 2001; Hunsley & Bailey, 2001; Weiner, 2004). They have criticized the test's reliability and validity. If the Rorschach were reliable, two different scorers would agree on the personality characteristics of the individual being tested. If the Rorschach

**Rorschach inkblot test**
A famous projective test that uses an individual's perception of inkblots to determine his or her personality.

rating these traits accurately. So, for a trait like extraversion, the self and others should agree, and these ratings should predict outgoing social behavior. For other traits, like neuroticism, that do not have an obvious behavioral dimension (most worrying occurs in the quiet of our own heads), the self has unique access to the thoughts and feelings provoked by these. For such traits, the person should be more accurate than an observer.

For the second question, Vazire noted that when traits are socially valued, as in the case of intelligence, self-ratings might be less accurate because people might be tempted to "fudge" their ratings, either to look especially good or to appear humble. In this case, then, Vazire predicted that an outsider should be more accurate than the person in judging highly desirable traits.

To test her hypotheses, Vazire had college students rate themselves on various personality characteristics. All of these individuals were also rated by four friends and four strangers. Participants then took part in various activities at different stations. For example, at one station, participants gave a 2-minute impromptu speech on the topic "What I like and don't like about my body" while being video-recorded by a stern-looking experimenter. At other stations, they completed an IQ test, as well as a test of creativity, and engaged in a leaderless group discussion.

Consistent with predictions, Vazire found that self-ratings and observer ratings of traits like extraversion were equally good at predicting behavior during the activities. In contrast, for less visible traits, such as neuroticism, the person's own ratings were the best predictors of behavior (such as showing nerves during the speech). With regard to intelligence, friends' ratings most strongly predicted actual IQ performance.

Additional intriguing work on this question has focused on whether some people are easier to judge than others. Lauren Human and Jeremy Biesanz (2011) found that individuals who are well adjusted (low on depression and high on psychological well-being) are easier to judge than those who are not. Judges' ratings of their personalities tend to match their own responses in self-reports closely, because well-adjusted individuals tend to share more of their private traits with others.

Sometimes, of course, we try to control the impression we make on others. A study by Human and her colleagues (2012) examined how putting one's best foot forward influences the agreement between targets and judges. In this study, participants answered questions about themselves while being recorded on a webcam. Participants were randomly assigned two different instructions. The experimental group was encouraged to make the best impression possible. The control group was told that the researchers were not concerned with their actual responses but wanted to see how people felt about the webcam experience. Judges then rated the participants' personalities based on the recordings. How did trying to make a good impression influence the agreement between self-ratings and judges' ratings? Judges' ratings were *more accurate* for those who put their best foot forward compared to those in the control condition. Sometimes our best self is a good way to reveal our true self.

**What Do You Think?**

■ Are you a good judge of others' personality? Explain.

■ Are you an easy person to judge? Why or why not?

■ Do you have friends who know you better than you know yourself? If so, what might explain their ability in this regard?

were valid, it would predict behavior outside of the testing situation; it would predict, for example, whether an individual will attempt suicide, become severely depressed, cope successfully with stress, or get along well with others. Conclusions based on research evidence suggest that the Rorschach does not meet these criteria of reliability and validity (Lilienfeld, Wood, & Garb, 2000). Thus, many psychologists have serious reservations about the Rorschach's use in diagnosis and clinical practice.

Although still administered in clinical circles (Hibbard & others, 2010; Krishnamurthy, Archer, & Groth-Marnat, 2011), the Rorschach is not commonly used in personality research. However, the projective method itself remains a tool for studying personality, especially in the form of the Thematic Apperception Test (TAT).

The **Thematic Apperception Test (TAT),** developed by Henry Murray and Christiana Morgan in the 1930s, is designed to elicit stories that reveal something about an individual's personality. The TAT consists of a series of pictures like the one in Figure 10.8, each on an individual card or slide. The TAT test taker is asked to tell a story about each of the pictures, including events leading up to the situation described, the characters' thoughts and feelings, and the way the situation turns out. The tester assumes that the person projects his or her own unconscious feelings and thoughts into the story (Hibbard & others, 2010). In addition to being administered as a projective test in clinical practice, the TAT is used in research on people's need for achievement, affiliation, power, intimacy,

**Thematic Apperception Test (TAT)**
A projective test that is designed to elicit stories that reveal something about an individual's personality.

**FIGURE 10.8** **Picture from the Thematic Apperception Test (TAT)** What are this man and woman thinking and feeling? How did they come to this situation, and what will happen next? A psychologist who uses the TAT would analyze your story to find out your unconscious motives.

Reprinted by permission of the publishers from *Thematic Apperception Test* by Henry A. Murray, Card 12F, Cambridge, Mass.: Harvard University Press. Copyright © 1943 by the President and the Fellows of Harvard College. Copyright © 1971 by Henry A. Murray.

## PSYCHOLOGICAL INQUIRY

| Approach | Summary | Assumptions | Typical Methods | Sample Research Question |
|---|---|---|---|---|
| **Psychodynamic** | Personality is characterized by unconscious processes. Childhood experiences are of great importance to adult personality. | The most important aspects of personality are unconscious. | Case studies, projective techniques. | How do unconscious conflicts lead to dysfunctional behavior? |
| **Humanistic** | Personality evolves out of the person's innate, organismic motives to grow and actualize the self. These healthy tendencies can be undermined by social pressure. | Human nature is basically good. By getting in touch with who we are and what we really want, we can lead happier, healthier lives. | Questionnaires, interviews, observation. | Can situations be changed to support individuals' organismic values and enhance their well-being? |
| **Social Cognitive** | Personality is the pattern of coherence that characterizes a person's interactions with the situations he or she encounters in life. The individual's beliefs and expectations, rather than global traits, are the central variables of interest. | Behavior is best understood as changing across situations. To understand personality, we must understand what each situation means for a given person. | Multiple observations over different situations; video-recorded behaviors rated by coders; questionnaires. | When and why do individuals respond to challenging tasks with fear versus excitement? |
| **Trait** | Personality is characterized by five general traits that are represented in the natural language that people use to describe themselves and others. | Traits are relatively stable over time. Traits predict behavior. | Questionnaires, observer reports. | Are the five factors universal across cultures? |
| **Personology and Life Story** | To understand personality, we must understand the whole person. We all have unique life experiences, and the stories we tell about those experiences make up our identities. | The life story provides a unique opportunity to examine the personality processes associated with behavior, development, and well-being. | Written narratives, TAT stories, autobiographical memories, interviews, and psychobiography. | How do narrative accounts of life experiences relate to happiness? |
| **Biological** | Personality characteristics reflect underlying biological processes such as those carried out by the brain, neurotransmitters, and genes. Differences in behaviors, thoughts, and feelings depend on these processes. | Biological differences among individuals can explain differences in their personalities. | Brain imagining, twin studies, molecular genetic studies. | Do genes explain individual differences in extraversion? |

**FIGURE 10.9** **Approaches to Personality Psychology** This figure summarizes the broad approaches to personality described in this chapter. Many researchers in personality do not stick with just one approach but apply the various theories and methods that are most relevant to their research questions. > *What is one question you have that is relevant to personality psychology? How would each approach address that question?* > *Which approach do you think is most likely to have an impact on the future of personality psychology?* > *How might the popularity of social media and access to online studies influence the various approaches to personality?*

and a variety of other needs (Brunstein & Maier, 2005; Schultheiss & Brunstein, 2005; C. P. Smith, 1992); unconscious defense mechanisms (Cramer, 2008a; Cramer & Jones, 2007); and cognitive styles (Woike, 2008). In contrast to the Rorschach, TAT measures have shown high inter-rater reliability and validity (Woike, 2001).

# Other Assessment Methods

Self-report questionnaires and projective techniques are just two of the multitude of assessment methods developed and used by personality psychologists. Personality psychologists might also measure behavior directly, by observing a person either live or in a video (Kelly & Agnew, 2012). In addition, cognitive assessments have become more common in personality psychology, as researchers probe such topics as the relationship between personality and processes of attention and memory. Many personality psychologists incorporate friend or peer ratings of individuals' traits or other characteristics. Personality psychologists also employ a host of psychophysiological measures, such as heart rate and skin conductance. Increasingly, personality psychologists are incorporating brain imaging as well.

Whether personality assessments are being used by clinical psychologists, psychological researchers, or other practitioners, the choice of assessment instrument depends on the researcher's theoretical perspective. Figure 10.9 lists which methods are associated with each perspective, summarizes each approach and its major assumptions, and gives a sample research question for each. Personality psychology is a diverse field, unified by a shared interest in understanding people—all of us.

## self-quiz

1. An empirically keyed test is one that
   A. has right and wrong answers.
   B. discriminates between different groups.
   C. has face validity.
   D. has both easy and difficult questions.

2. A problem with self-report tests, and one that researchers try to overcome, is the issue of
   A. social desirability.
   B. memory lapse.
   C. participant bias.
   D. scorer bias.

3. The assessment technique that asks participants to tell a story about the stimuli they see is the

   A. Rorschach inkblot test.
   B. Minnesota Multiphasic Personality Inventory (MMPI).
   C. NEO-P-I.
   D. Thematic Apperception Test (TAT).

   **APPLY IT!** 4. Hank applies for a job as a ticket taker at a movie theater. After his interview, he is asked to complete a set of questionnaires. That night, he brags to friends, "They had me answer all these questions about whether I would ever steal from work, gossip about people, or sneak into a movie without paying. I just lied about everything! They'll never know. The job is mine." One of Hank's friends has taken Intro Psych and has news for Hank.

   Which of the following best captures what he will say?
   A. Good job, Hank. They have no way of knowing you lied. Good luck with the job!
   B. Hank, if you lied on all the questions to make yourself look good, they will be able to detect it. It's called social desirability, and you fell for it.
   C. Hank, unless the measures involved telling stories, your lies will never be revealed.
   D. Hank, you will probably get the job, but your future employer sounds naive. Didn't they know you could just lie on those tests?

## SUMMARY

### ① Psychodynamic Perspectives

Freud developed psychoanalysis through his work with patients suffering from hysterical symptoms (physical symptoms with no physical cause). Freud viewed these symptoms as representing conflicts between sexual drive and duty. Freud believed that most personality—which, in his theory, includes components he called the id, ego, and superego—is

unconscious. The ego uses various defense mechanisms, Freud said, to reduce anxiety.

A number of theorists criticized and revised Freud's approach. Horney said that the need for security, not sex or aggression, is our most important need. Jung developed the concept of the collective unconscious, a storehouse of archetypes. Adler's individual psychology stresses that people are striving toward perfection.

Weaknesses of the psychodynamic perspectives include overreliance on reports from the past and overemphasis of the unconscious mind. Strengths of psychodynamic approaches include recognizing the importance of childhood, conceptualizing development through stages, and calling attention to the role of unconscious processes in behavior.

## ② Humanistic Perspectives

Humanistic perspectives stress a person's capacity for personal growth and positive human qualities. Maslow developed the concept of a hierarchy of needs, with self-actualization being the highest human need. In Rogers's approach, each of us is born with a tendency toward growth, a sense of what is good and bad for us, and a need for unconditional positive regard. Because we are often denied unconditional positive regard, we may become alienated from our innate growth tendencies. In order to reconnect with these innate tendencies, Rogers felt, a person required a relationship that included unconditional positive regard, empathy, and genuineness.

The humanistic perspectives promote the positive capacities of human beings. The weaknesses of the approach are a tendency to be too optimistic and an inclination to downplay personal responsibility.

## ③ Trait Perspectives

Trait theories emphasize that personality consists of traits—broad, enduring dispositions that lead to characteristic responses. Allport stated that traits should produce consistent behavior in different situations, and he used the lexical approach to personality traits, which involves using all the words in the natural language that could describe a person as a basis for understanding the traits of personality.

The current dominant perspective in personality psychology is the five-factor model. The big five traits include openness, conscientiousness, extraversion, agreeableness, and neuroticism. Extraversion is related to enhanced well-being, and neuroticism is linked to lowered well-being.

Studying people in terms of their traits has value. However, trait approaches are criticized for focusing on broad dimensions and not attending to each person's uniqueness.

## ④ Personological and Life Story Perspectives

Murray described personology as the study of the whole person. Contemporary followers of Murray study personality through narrative accounts and interviews. McAdams introduced the life story approach to identity, which views identity as a constantly changing story with a beginning, a middle, and an end. Psychobiography is a form of personological investigation that applies personality theory to one person's life.

Life story approaches to personality reveal the richness of each person's unique life story. However, this work can be very difficult to carry out.

## ⑤ Social Cognitive Perspectives

Social cognitive theory states that behavior, environment, and person/cognitive factors are important in understanding personality. In Bandura's view, these factors reciprocally interact.

Two key concepts in social cognitive theory are self-efficacy and personal control. Self-efficacy is the belief that one can master a situation and produce positive outcomes. Personal control refers to individuals' beliefs about whether the outcomes of their actions depend on their own internal acts or on external events.

In 1968, Mischel's controversial book *Personality and Assessment* stressed that people do not behave consistently across different situations but rather tailor their behavior to suit particular situations. Personality psychologists countered that personality does predict behavior for some people some of the time. Very specific personality characteristics predict behavior better than very general ones, and personality characteristics are more likely to predict behavior in weak versus strong situations.

Mischel developed a revised approach to personality centered on a cognitive affective processing system (CAPS). According to CAPS, personality is best understood as a person's habitual emotional and cognitive reactions to specific situations.

A particular strength of social cognitive theory is its focus on cognitive processes. However, social cognitive approaches have not given adequate attention to enduring individual differences, to biological factors, and to personality as a whole.

## ⑥ Biological Perspectives

Eysenck suggested that the brain's reticular activation system (RAS) plays a role in introversion/extraversion. He thought of these traits as the outward manifestations of arousal regulation. Gray developed a reward sensitivity theory of personality, suggesting that extraversion and neuroticism can be understood as two neurological systems that respond to rewards (the behavioral approach system, or BAS) and punishments (the behavioral inhibition system, or BIS) in the environment.

Dopamine is associated with behavioral approach (extraversion), and serotonin with behavioral avoidance (neuroticism). Behavioral genetics studies have shown that the heritability of personality traits is about 50 percent. Studies of biological processes in personality are valuable but can overestimate the causal role of biological factors.

## ⑦ Personality Assessment

Self-report tests assess personality by asking participants about their preferences and behaviors. One problem in self-report research is the tendency for individuals to respond in socially desirable ways. Empirically keyed tests avoid social desirability problems by using items that distinguish between groups even if we do not know why the items do so.

The most popular test for assessing the big five traits is the NEO-PI-R, which uses self-report items to measure each of the traits. The Minnesota Multiphasic Personality Inventory (MMPI) is the most widely used empirically keyed personality test.

Projective tests, designed to assess unconscious aspects of personality, present individuals with an ambiguous stimulus, such as an inkblot or a picture, and ask them to tell a story about it. Projective tests are based on the assumption that individuals will project their personalities onto these stimuli. The Thematic Apperception Test (TAT) is a projective test that has been used in personality research. Other assessment methods include behavioral observation, obtaining peer reports, and psychophysiological and neuropsychological measures.

personality, p. 362

psychodynamic perspectives, p. 362

id, p. 363

ego, p. 364

superego, p. 364

defense mechanisms, p. 364

Oedipus complex, p. 366

collective unconscious, p. 368

archetypes, p. 368

individual psychology, p. 368

humanistic perspectives, p. 370

unconditional positive regard, p. 371

conditions of worth, p. 371

trait theories, p. 373

big five factors of personality, p. 374

subjective well-being, p. 377

personological and life story perspectives, p. 380

social cognitive perspectives, p. 383

self-efficacy, p. 384

cognitive affective processing systems (CAPS), p. 386

behavioral genetics, p. 390

self-report test, p. 392

empirically keyed test, p. 392

Minnesota Multiphasic Personality Inventory (MMPI), p. 393

face validity, p. 393

projective test, p. 393

Rorschach inkblot test, p. 394

Thematic Apperception Test (TAT), p. 395

## SELF-TEST

## Multiple Choice

1. Psychologists who study personality investigate
   A. the distinctive thoughts, emotions, and behavior that individuals demonstrate over time.
   B. relatively permanent changes in behavior due to experience.
   C. the organization of sensation into a meaningful interpretation.
   D. the pleasantness or sociability of an individual.

2. The strongest proponents of the role of the unconscious mind in personality are
   A. humanists.
   B. psychodynamic theorists.
   C. behaviorists.
   D. trait theorists.

3. According to Freud, the personality structure that negotiates the pull between a person's baser needs and higher conscience is the
   A. superego.
   B. alter ego.
   C. ego.
   D. id.

4. The theorist who emphasized unconditional positive regard was
   A. Carl Jung.
   B. Karen Horney.
   C. Henry Murray.
   D. Carl Rogers.

5. Broad, enduring dispositions that produce characteristic responses are called
   A. attitudes.
   B. traits.
   C. schemas.
   D. archetypes.

6. Jaime is punctual, hardworking, shy, and conservative. Jaime is likely to be
   A. high in agreeableness, low in extraversion, and high in openness to experience.
   B. low in extraversion, high in conscientiousness, and low in openness to experience.
   C. high in conscientiousness, low in neuroticism, and high in extraversion.
   D. low in conscientiousness, low in openness to experience, and high in extraversion.

7. The perspective on understanding personality that focuses on situational factors is the
   A. psychodynamic approach.
   B. trait approach.
   C. personological approach.
   D. social cognitive approach.

8. Gray's reinforcement sensitivity theory is based on an organism's attention and sensitivity to
   A. cues and feedback from others.
   B. rewards and punishments in the organism's environment.

   C. stressors in the organism's environment.
   D. the impact of experiences early in the life span.

9. The Thematic Apperception Test (TAT) is consistent with
   A. personology.
   B. the humanistic approach to personality.
   C. the social cognitive approach to personality.
   D. trait perspectives.

10. The Minnesota Multiphasic Personality Inventory (MMPI) is a
    A. projective test.
    B. reliable but not valid test.
    C. face-valid test.
    D. self-report test.

## Apply It!

11. Personality psychologists often consider the role of childhood experience in adult personality. Choose something about your childhood (a particularly vivid memory or pattern of experiences) and describe how it is reflected in your current personality, drawing on the work of Freud, Adler, and Rogers.

# Social Psychology

# 11

## *The Power of Social Movements*

Social progress in the United States is shaped by social movements. Groups of people can do more than any individual acting alone. Rosa Parks (1913–2005) became a heroine of the civil rights movement when, on December 1, 1955, in Montgomery, Alabama, she refused to give up her seat on a bus to a White man. From a broader perspective, Ms. Parks was part of a larger social movement that pushed for—and, over time, effected—urgently needed civil rights reforms.

Groups of people today, aided by social media, are having a major impact across the globe. Consider some of the recent headline-grabbing events. December 2010 saw the birth of the Arab Spring. In this surge of civil activism, countries in the Middle East and northern Africa erupted in protests, rallies, marches, strikes, and demonstrations in the name of social progress, leading to the ouster of leaders in Tunisia, Egypt, Libya, and Yemen and to unrest elsewhere. In the United States, bold, new social activism—including the Tea Party and the Occupy movement—has drawn much attention.

Whether for critically needed policymaking or leadership change, or simply for saving a favorite TV show from cancellation, groups of people who share a common interest band together to make a difference. The power and workings of such social groups are a major area of interest in social psychology, our focus in this chapter.

The chapter begins by examining humans' social cognitive nature and then explores social behavior, zeroing in on its extreme forms: altruism and aggression. We next look at the two-way street of social influence: how we influence others and how they influence us. Then we consider how the groups to which we belong shape our interactions with other groups. The discussion concludes with a look at close relationships, including attraction and love.

# 1 Social Cognition

**Social psychology** is the study of how people think about, influence, and relate to other people. There are probably few issues reported in the news today that social psychologists have not studied. Social psychologists take many of the topics we have covered so far—including perception, cognition, emotion, and personality—and examine them in a social context.

*Social cognition* is the area of social psychology that explores how people select, interpret, remember, and use social information (Forgas, Fiedler, & Sedikides, 2012). Essentially, it is the way in which individuals think in social situations (Eiser, 2012; Koerner, 2012).

**social psychology**
The study of how people think, influence, and relate to other people.

 *We've looked at cognition in previous chapters. Some experts have argued that social cognition—thinking about other people—is more fundamental than thinking about anything else.*

## Person Perception

*Person perception* refers to the processes by which we use social stimuli to form impressions of others (Semin & Garrido, 2012). One important social cue is the face (Waenke, Samochowiecz, & Landwehr, 2012). The power of the face is demonstrated in research by Alexander Todorov and his colleagues (2005), who examined the ways that perceptions of faces can influence political elections. These researchers asked people to rate the competence of individuals from photographs of their faces. The faces were of candidates in the 2000, 2002, and 2004 U.S. House and Senate elections. Respondents' ratings accurately predicted the outcome for about *70 percent* of the elections. Those faces gave away information about the candidates that was meaningful to the perceivers, including how competent the perceivers felt each office-seeker would be (Mattes & others, 2010). Other aspects of faces can also have important implications for social perception, as we now consider.

### PHYSICAL ATTRACTIVENESS AND OTHER PERCEPTUAL CUES
Physical attractiveness has been recognized as a powerful social cue (Harter, 2012). Judith Langlois and her colleagues found that even infants as young as 3 to 6 months of age showed a preference for looking at attractive faces versus unattractive faces, as rated by adults (Hoss & Langlois, 2003; Ramsey & others, 2004). Attractive individuals are generally assumed to have a variety of other positive characteristics, including being better adjusted, socially skilled, friendly, likable, extraverted, and apt to achieve superior job performance (Langlois & others, 2000). These positive expectations for physically attractive individuals have been referred to as the "beautiful is good" stereotype.

*The face is a powerful social cue.*

A **stereotype** is a generalization about a group's characteristics that does not consider any variations from one individual to another. Stereotypes are a natural extension of the limits on human cognitive processing and our reliance on concepts in cognitive processing (Gaines, 2012).

We simplify the task of understanding people by classifying them as members of groups or categories with which we are familiar. It takes more mental effort to consider a person's individual characteristics than it does to label him or her as a member of a particular group or category. Thus, when we categorize an individual, the categorization is often based on stereotypes.

Is there any truth to the "beautiful is good" stereotype? Research has shown that attractive people may indeed possess a number of positive characteristics (Langlois & others, 2000). Does that mean that attractiveness is naturally related to, for example, better social skills? Not necessarily.

One way that stereotypes can influence individuals is through the phenomenon of *self-fulfilling prophecy*. In a self-fulfilling prophecy, expectations cause individuals to act in ways that serve to make the expectations come true. Robert Rosenthal and Lenore Jacobsen conducted the classic self-fulfilling prophecy study in 1968. The researchers told grade-school teachers that five students were likely to be "late bloomers"—that these students had high levels of ability that would likely emerge over time. In reality, the students had been randomly selected by the researchers. Nonetheless, a year later, the researchers found that teachers' expectations for the late bloomers were reflected in student performance—the academic performance of the late bloomers was beyond that of other students. Self-fulfilling prophecy effects show the potential power of stereotypes and other sources of expectations on human behavior.

*Recall from Chapter 7 how we use concepts to simplify the world. However, when we use concepts to understand groups of people, we are stereotyping.*

*How do you think the teachers influenced the late bloomers? What kind of behaviors led to the kids' enhanced performance?*

How might self-fulfilling prophecy effects apply when people interact with physically attractive versus unattractive individuals? Consider that attractive people may receive differential treatment from others throughout their life. This special treatment increases the likelihood that the attractive individuals might well develop enhanced social skills and be more self-confident than others.

Another relevant question is, what makes a face attractive? *People* magazine's "Most Beautiful People" issue might lead you to conclude that attractiveness is about being exceptional in some way: Think of Jennifer Lopez's sensuous lips and Zac Efron's unusual blue eyes. Research has examined what specifically makes a face attractive, with surprising results. Using computer technology that allowed them to average together digitized photographs of a large group of individuals of varying attractiveness, Langlois and her colleagues (1994) created composite faces. A large sample of college students then rated the individual faces and the composites. The results showed that individual faces were less attractive than faces that were created by averaging 8, 16, or 32 other faces. The researchers concluded that attractive faces are actually "just average." Although "averageness" is not the only predictor of attractiveness, Langlois and her colleagues suggest that being average is an essential component (along with variables such as symmetry and youthfulness) of facial attractiveness.

**Do It!**

Check out this website to see how the averaging of faces works: www.faceresearch.org/demos/average. Pick some faces you consider unattractive. What happens when you average them together? If you have a digital photograph of yourself and some friends, see what happens when you average those faces. Do you agree that average faces are more attractive than any single face?

**FIRST IMPRESSIONS** When we first meet someone, typically the new acquaintance quickly makes an impression. That first impression can have lasting effects (North & Fiske, 2012). Recall the primacy effect from Chapter 6—people's tendency to attend to and remember what they learned first (N. H. Anderson, 1965). The power of first impressions is likely due to just such an effect. How quickly do we make these initial impressions of others? In one study, judgments made after just a 100-millisecond exposure time to unfamiliar faces was sufficient for individuals to form an impression (Willis & Todorov, 2006).

Of course, once you become acquainted with someone, you have a lot more information with which to form an opinion of the person. The process by which we come to understand the causes of others' behavior and form an impression of them as individuals is called *attribution*.

"She's late with her report because she can't concentrate on her own responsibilities."

# Attribution

Trying to understand why people do the things they do is a puzzle that fascinates all of us. We can observe people's behavior and listen to what they say, but to determine the underlying cause of their behavior, we often have to make inferences from these observations. Making inferences means taking the information we have and coming up with a good guess about who someone is and what the person is likely to do in the future (Manusov, 2012; Todorov, 2013).

**Attribution theory** views people as motivated to discover the underlying causes of behavior as part of their effort to make sense of the behavior (Heider, 1958; Kelley, 1973; Weiner, 2006). Attributions vary along three dimensions (Jones, 1998):

**Actor** Tends to give external, situational explanations of own behavior

"I'm late with my report because other people keep asking me to help them with their projects."

**attribution theory** The view that people are motivated to discover the underlying causes of behavior as part of their effort to make sense of the behavior.

- *Internal/external causes:* Internal attributions include causes inside and specific to the person, such as his or her traits and abilities. External attributions include causes outside the person, such as social pressure, aspects of the social situation, and the weather. Did Beth get an *A* on the test because she is smart or because the test was easy?

- *Stable/unstable causes:* Is the cause relatively enduring and permanent, or is it temporary? Did Aaron blow up at his girlfriend because he is a hostile guy or because he was in a bad mood that day?

- *Controllable/uncontrollable causes:* We perceive that we have power over some causes (for instance, by preparing delicious food for a picnic) but not others (rain on picnic day).

**FIGURE 11.1 The Fundamental Attribution Error** In this situation, the supervisor is the observer, and the employee is the actor.

**ATTRIBUTIONAL ERRORS AND BIASES** In attribution theory, the person who produces the behavior to be explained is called the *actor*. The person who offers a causal explanation of the actor's behavior is called the *observer*. Actors often explain their own behavior in terms of external causes. In contrast, observers frequently explain the actor's behavior in terms of internal causes. Susannah might explain that she honked her car horn at someone who was slow to move when the light turned green because she was in a hurry to get to the hospital to see her ill father, but the driver she honked at might think she was rude.

In committing the **fundamental attribution error,** observers overestimate the importance of internal traits and underestimate the importance of external situations when they seek explanations of another person's behavior (Gilbert & Malone, 1995; Jones & Harris, 1967) (Figure 11.1). For example, news coverage of Hurricane Katrina, which devastated New Orleans and other Gulf Coast locales in 2005, conveyed grim images of individuals who had not evacuated and were left homeless and helpless in the storm's aftermath. An observer might have concluded, "They were foolish not to get out in time." In fact, situational factors, including lacking financial resources and a means of transportation, may have prevented them from leaving.

Some have wondered just how fundamental the fundamental attribution error is. Cross-cultural studies indicate that although Westerners tend to attribute causes of behavior to the person, those from more collectivistic cultures are more likely to look to the situation to explain the behavior of others (Imada, 2012; Morris & Peng, 1994; Rips, 2011). Indeed, recent research has shown that even among people in the United States, attributions can vary as a function of religion. A recent series of studies showed that Protestants were more likely than Catholics to attribute behavior to the person rather than the situation (Li & others, 2012).

**fundamental attribution error** Observers' overestimation of the importance of internal traits and underestimation of the importance of external situations when they seek explanations of another person's behavior.

*It's challenging to remember how much the situation can influence behavior. Try avoiding this attributional error for just one day: When you see someone do something, think about the situational factors that might cause their behavior.*

*The investigators suggest that this difference was due to the ways Protestants and Catholics conceive of the soul. What do you think?*

**HEURISTICS IN SOCIAL INFORMATION PROCESSING** Heuristics, as described in Chapter 7, are cognitive shortcuts that allow us to make decisions rapidly. Heuristics can be useful in processing social information (Gigerenzer & Gaissmaier, 2011; McDonald & others, 2011). Indeed, they are sometimes helpful tools for navigating the complex social landscape, although they can lead to mistakes (Weaver & others, 2007).

Stereotypes can be considered a type of heuristic in that they allow us to make quick judgments using very little information. Relying on stereotypes can lead to serious errors in social information processing. For example, having never encountered an Asian American point guard, many college basketball coaches failed to appreciate the skills of Jeremy Lin. Lin simply did not fit the stereotype of a great point guard, and stereotypes of Asian Americans did not suggest that his abilities would be well suited to success on the court. Could an Asian American fulfill the leadership role of point guard on an elite basketball team? Lin had a stellar career at Harvard University; but it was not until 2012 that he captured the attention of NBA fans everywhere during his streak of amazing games for the New York Knicks, shattering stereotypes along the way.

Another common heuristic is the false consensus effect. Ask yourself: "How many students at my school support the death penalty?" Your answer is likely to depend on whether you support the death penalty. The **false consensus effect** is the overestimation of the degree to which everybody else thinks or acts the way we do. False consensus effects can be important in social interactions. Imagine for example that someone in a group to which you belong makes a racially insensitive remark. According to the false consensus effect, that person is likely to interpret silence on the part of others in the group as agreement.

**false consensus effect**
Observers' overestimation of the degree to which everybody else thinks or acts the way they do.

The fundamental attribution error and the false consensus effect are related to the special significance of our personal thoughts and circumstances as we process social information. We have ready access to our own thoughts and feelings. Both effects reflect the vast amount of information we have about ourselves relative to the more limited information we have about others, and they suggest the special place of the self in social information processing.

# The Self as a Social Object

*Recall from Chapter 4 how important consciousness is to our sense of self.*

*Some have argued that self-esteem is a bad thing. Typically such arguments focus on unrealistically high or unstable self-esteem.*

Each of us carries around mental representations of ourselves. We can think of the self as our schema for who we are, what we are like, and how we feel about these perceptions. The self is different from other social objects because we know so much more about ourselves than we do about others. Although we are more likely to think that behavior is very important to understanding who other people really are, we are also more likely to think that our private thoughts and feelings are most indicative of our true self (Johnson, Robinson, & Mitchell, 2004).

The self is special not only because we have direct access to these private experiences but also because we value ourselves. One of the most important self-related variables is *self-esteem,* the degree to which we have positive or negative feelings about ourselves (Harter, 2012). In general, research has shown that it is good to feel good about oneself (Bosson & Swann, 2009).

Individuals with high self-esteem often possess a variety of **positive illusions**—rosy views of themselves that are not necessarily rooted in reality (Hansen & Pronin, 2012). Constantine Sedikides and his colleagues have shown that many of us think of ourselves as above average on a number of valued characteristics, including how trustworthy and attractive we are (Gregg & Sedikides, 2010; Hepper & Sedikides, 2010; Sedikides, 2007, 2009; Sedikides, Gaertner, & Vevea, 2005; Sedikides & Gregg, 2008; Sedikides & Skowronski, 2009, 2012). Of course, the very definition of *average* indicates that not all of us can be "above average."

**positive illusions**
Favorable views of the self that are not necessarily rooted in reality.

Shelley Taylor and her colleagues have demonstrated that having positive illusions about the self is often related to heightened well-being (Taylor, 2011c; Taylor & Sherman, 2008; Taylor & others, 2003a, 2003b, 2007). Individuals who tend to have positive illusions about themselves are psychologically healthier and more likely to be judged positively by others. Self-esteem also affects our attributions about our own behavior. Individuals with high self-esteem, for instance, tend to give themselves breaks when it comes to judging their own behavior.

**Self-serving bias** refers to the tendency to take credit for one's own successes and to deny responsibility for one's own failures (Helzer & Dunning, 2012). Think about taking a psychology exam. If you do well, you are likely to take credit for that success ("I'm smart" or "I knew that stuff")—that is, to make internal attributions. If you do poorly, however, you are more likely to blame situational factors ("The test was too hard")—that is, to make external attributions.

**self-serving bias**
The tendency to take credit for one's own successes and to deny responsibility for one's own failures.

## STEREOTYPE THREAT
Stereotypes not only influence our views of others but also sometimes influence the feelings and performance of individuals in stereotyped groups (Burgess & others, 2012; Stahl, Van Laar, & Ellemers, 2012). **Stereotype threat** is an individual's fast-acting, self-fulfilling fear of being judged based on a negative stereotype about his or her group. A person who experiences stereotype threat is well aware of stereotypical expectations for him or her as a member of the group. In stereotype-relevant situations, the individual experiences anxiety about living "down" to expectations and consequently underperforms (Kerger, Martin, & Brunner, 2011; Weger & others, 2012). Claude Steele and Eliot Aronson (1995, 2004) have shown that when a test is presented to African American and non-Latino White American students who have first simply checked a box indicating their ethnicity, African Americans do not perform as well. In situations where ethnicity was not made salient, no differences in performance emerged.

**stereotype threat**
An individual's fast-acting, self-fulfilling fear of being judged based on a negative stereotype about his or her group.

Research has also demonstrated that stereotype threat affects performance on math tests by women compared to men, even when both groups have equally strong math training (Spencer, Steele, & Quinn, 1999). Non-Latino White men, too, can fall prey to stereotype threat; in a study of golf ability, non-Latino White American men did not perform as well as African American men when they were told the test measured "natural athletic ability" (Stone, 2002). Asian women performed better on a math test if asked first for their ethnicity, but not as well if asked first about their sex (Shih & others, 2007).

*What might happen to scores if standardized tests did not ask questions about sex and ethnicity until the end of the test?*

Researchers have begun to identify factors that may help prevent the consequences of stereotype threat (Stahl, Van Laar, & Ellemers, 2012). For example, in one study, African American schoolchildren who were asked their race prior to a math test did not perform as well unless the test was presented to them as a challenge, not as a threat (Alter & others, 2010). Some research suggests that self-esteem may help buffer the effects of stereotype threat in women, especially if women are reminded of another aspect of the self (for instance, "college student") that is positively associated with math performance (Rydell & Boucher, 2010).

## SOCIAL COMPARISON
Have you ever felt a sense of accomplishment about getting a *B* on a test, only to feel deflated when you found out that your friend in the class got an *A*? You gain self-knowledge from your own behavior, of course, but you also acquire it from others through **social comparison,** the process by which individuals evaluate their thoughts, feelings, behaviors, and abilities in relation to others. Social comparison helps individuals to evaluate themselves, to identify their distinctive characteristics, to build an identity.

**social comparison**
The process by which individuals evaluate their thoughts, feelings, behaviors, and abilities in relation to others.

Nearly 60 years ago, Leon Festinger (1954) proposed a theory of social comparison positing that when individuals lack objective means to evaluate their opinions and abilities, they compare themselves with others. Furthermore, to get an accurate self-appraisal, people are most likely to compare themselves with others who are similar to themselves. Extended and modified over the years, Festinger's social comparison theory continues to

*Beyond being places to connect and keep up with others, social media sites like Facebook and Twitter are forums for comparing how we measure up to other people.*

provide an important rationale for how individuals come to know themselves (Brakel, Dijkstra, & Buunk, 2012; Carrieri, 2012).

Festinger concentrated on comparisons between similar people, but other researchers have focused on downward social comparisons, that is, individuals' comparisons with people whom they consider inferior to themselves. People under threat (from negative feedback or low self-esteem, for example) try to feel better by comparing themselves with others who are less fortunate (Caricati, 2012).

Facebook provides a venue for social comparison. Facebook lets users present their best selves. Think about the photos you see on Facebook—most of them show people smiling and having a great time. A recent study of college students found that those who spent more time each week on Facebook agreed that other people have better lives than they do and are happier than they are (Chou & Edge, 2012).

# Attitudes

**attitudes**
An individual's opinions and beliefs about people, objects, and ideas—how the person feels about the world.

**Attitudes** are our feelings or opinions about people, objects, and ideas. We have attitudes about all sorts of things. Social psychologists are interested in how attitudes relate to behavior and in whether and how attitudes can change (Arpan, Rhodes, & Roskos-Ewoldsen, 2012; Brinol & Petty, 2012).

**CAN ATTITUDES PREDICT BEHAVIOR?**   People sometimes say one thing but do another. You might report positive attitudes about recycling on a survey but still pitch an aluminum soda can in the trash. Studies over the past half-century indicate some of the conditions under which attitudes guide actions (Brinol & Petty, 2012; Schomerus, Matschinger, & Angermeyer, 2009):

- *When the person's attitudes are strong* (Ajzen, 2001): For example, senators whose attitudes toward the president are "highly favorable" are more likely to vote for the president's policies than are senators who have only "moderately favorable" attitudes toward the chief executive.

- *When the person shows a strong awareness of his or her attitudes and when the person rehearses and practices them* (Fazio & Olsen, 2007; Fazio & others, 1982): For example, a person who has been asked to give a speech about the benefits of recycling is more likely to recycle than is an individual with the same attitude about recycling who has not put the idea into words or defined it in public.

- *When the person has a vested interest:* People are more likely to act on attitudes when the issue at stake will affect them personally. For example, a classic study examined whether students would show up for a rally protesting a change that would raise the legal drinking age from 18 to 21 (Sivacek & Crano, 1982). Although students in general were against the change, those in the critical age group (from 18 to 20) were more likely to turn out to protest.

*What are your attitudes about social issues such as the death penalty, gun ownership, and climate change? How do these views influence your behavior?*

**CAN BEHAVIOR PREDICT ATTITUDES?**   Just as attitudes guide behavior, ample evidence also exists that changes in behavior sometimes precede changes in attitudes. Social psychologists offer two main explanations of why behavior influences attitudes: cognitive dissonance theory and self-perception theory.

***Cognitive Dissonance Theory***   **Cognitive dissonance,** a concept developed by Festinger (1957), is an individual's psychological discomfort (*dissonance*) caused by two inconsistent thoughts. According to the theory, we feel uneasy when we notice an inconsistency between what we believe and what we do (Fotuhi & others, 2012). Cognitive

**cognitive dissonance**
An individual's psychological discomfort (dissonance) caused by two inconsistent thoughts.

dissonance is at the root of that uncomfortable feeling of being a hypocrite (McConnell & Brown, 2010).

In a classic study of cognitive dissonance, Festinger and J. Merrill Carlsmith (1959) asked college students to engage in very boring tasks such as sorting spools into trays and turning wooden pegs. The participants were later asked to persuade another student (who was in fact a confederate) to participate in the study by telling him that the task was interesting and enjoyable. Half of the participants were randomly assigned to be paid $1 for telling this white lie, and the other half were randomly assigned to receive $20. Afterward, all of the participants rated how interesting and enjoyable the task was.

Interestingly, those who were paid only $1 to tell the lie rated the task as significantly more enjoyable than those who were paid $20. Festinger and Carlsmith reasoned that those paid $20 to tell the lie could attribute their behavior to the high value of the money they received. On the other hand, those who were paid $1 experienced cognitive dissonance. The inconsistency between *what they did* (tell a lie) and *what they were paid for it* (just $1) moved these individuals to change their attitudes about the task ("I wouldn't lie for just $1. If I said I liked the task, I must have really liked it").

We can reduce cognitive dissonance in one of two ways: change our behavior to fit our attitudes or change our attitudes to fit our behavior. In the classic study above, participants changed their attitudes about the task to match their behavior. Thus, when our attitudes and behavior are at odds, our behavior can influence our attitudes. After you have pitched that soda can, for example, you might feel guilty and relieve that guilt by deciding, "Recycling is not really that important."

*Effort justification,* one type of dissonance reduction, means rationalizing the amount of effort we put into something. Effort justification explains strong feelings of loyalty toward a group based on the effort it takes to gain admission into that group. Working hard to get into an organization (such as a Greek society or the Marines) or a profession (such as medicine or law) can change our attitudes about it. According to cognitive dissonance theory, individuals in these situations are likely to think, "If it's this tough to get into, it must be worth it."

*Remember, random assignment is used to make sure that groups are equal in every way except for the independent variable—which in this study was how much the participants were paid for the lie. The rating of enjoyment was the dependent variable.*

**EXPERIENCE IT!**
Cognitive Dissonance
Theory

*If you have ever played devil's advocate in an argument (arguing a point just for the sake of argument), you might have found yourself realizing that maybe you do hold the views you have pretended to advocate. That's self-perception theory at work.*

### *Self-Perception Theory*

**self-perception theory**
Bem's theory on how behaviors influence attitudes, stating that individuals make inferences about their attitudes by perceiving their behavior.

**Self-perception theory** is Daryl Bem's (1967) explanation of how behaviors influence attitudes. According to this theory, individuals make inferences about their attitudes by perceiving their behavior. That is, behaviors can cause attitudes because when we are questioned about our attitudes, we think back on our behaviors for information. When asked about your attitude toward exercise, for instance, you might think, "Well, I run every morning, so I must like it." From Bem's perspective, your behavior has led you to recognize something about yourself that you had not noticed before. Bem believes that we are especially likely to look to our own behavior to determine our attitudes when those attitudes are not completely clear, and research has supported this assertion (Olson & Stone, 2005).

Figure 11.2 compares cognitive dissonance theory and self-perception theory. Both theories have merit in explaining the connection between attitudes and behavior, and these opposing views bring to light the complexity that may exist in this connection. Another route to attitude change is persuasion.

### PERSUASION

Persuasion involves trying to change someone's attitude—and often his or her behavior as well (Brinol & Petty, 2012; Prislin & Crano, 2012). There are two central questions with respect to persuasion: What makes an individual decide to give

*Barack Obama called on his powers of persuasion when he ran for presidential reelection in 2012, as well as when, in previous years, he served as a U.S. senator representing the state of Illinois.*

up an original attitude and adopt a new one, and what makes a person decide to act on an attitude that he or she has not acted on before? Teachers, lawyers, and sales representatives study techniques that will help them sway their audiences (children, juries, and buyers). Presidential candidates have arsenals of speechwriters and image consultants to help ensure that their words are persuasive. Perhaps the most skilled persuaders of all are advertisers, who combine a full array of techniques to sell everything from cornflakes to carpets to cars.

Carl Hovland and his colleagues originally identified the elements of persuasion as follows (Hovland, Janis, & Kelley, 1953; Janis & Hovland, 1959):

| Festinger Cognitive Dissonance Theory | Bem Self-Perception Theory |
| --- | --- |
| We are motivated toward consistency between attitudes and behavior and away from inconsistency. | We make inferences about our attitudes by perceiving and examining our behavior and the context in which it occurs, which might involve inducements to behave in certain ways. |
| *Example: "I hate my job. I need to develop a better attitude toward it or else quit."* | *Example: "I am spending all of my time thinking about how much I hate my job. I really must not like it."* |

**FIGURE 11.2  Two Theories of the Connections Between Attitudes and Behavior** Although we often think of attitudes as causing behavior, behavior can change attitudes, through either dissonance reduction or self-perception.

■ *The communicator (source):* Suppose you are running for student body president. You tell your fellow students that you are going to make life at your college better. Will they believe you? Most likely, that will depend on your characteristics as a communicator. Whether they believe you will depend in large part on your credibility—that is, how much the other students trust what you say. Trustworthiness and expertise are credibility characteristics that help a communicator change people's attitudes or convince them to act. Other source factors include power, attractiveness, and likability.

■ *The medium:* Another persuasion factor is the medium or the technology used to get the message across. Consider the difference between watching a presidential debate live on television or over the Internet and reading about it in the newspaper. Because they present live images, digital media are generally more powerful than print sources for changing attitudes.

■ *The target (audience):* Age and attitude strength are two characteristics of the audience that determine whether a message will be effective. Younger people are more likely to change their attitudes than older individuals. Weaker attitudes on the part of the audience make attitude change more likely than do deeply held attitudes.

■ *The message:* What kind of message is persuasive? Some messages involve strong logical arguments, and others focus on exciting emotions such as fear and anger in the audience. Which is more likely to work and when? The elaboration likelihood model addresses this question.

The **elaboration likelihood model** identifies two ways to persuade: a central route and a peripheral route (Brinol & Petty, 2012; DeMarree & Petty, 2007; Petty & Brinol, 2008; Petty & Cacioppo, 1986). The central route to persuasion works by engaging someone thoughtfully with a sound, logical argument. The peripheral route involves non-message factors such as the source's credibility and attractiveness or emotional appeals. The peripheral route is effective when people are not paying close attention or do not have the time or energy to think about what the communicator is saying (Brewer, Barnes, & Sauer, 2011). As you might guess, television advertisers often use the peripheral route to persuasion on the assumption that during the commercials you are probably not paying full attention to the screen. However, the central route is more persuasive when people have the ability and the motivation to pay attention to the facts (Sparks & Areni, 2008).

**elaboration likelihood model** Theory identifying two ways to persuade: a central route and a peripheral route.

*Attitudes that are changed using the central route are more likely to persist than attitudes that are changed using the peripheral route.*

***Successful Persuasion*** Sooner or later, nearly everyone will be in a position of selling someone something. Social psychologists have studied a variety of ways in which social psychological principles influence whether a salesperson makes that sale (Cialdini, 1993).

One strategy for making a sale is called the *foot-in-the-door* technique (Freedman & Fraser, 1966), which involves making a smaller request ("Would you be interested in a three-month trial subscription to a magazine?") at the beginning and saving the biggest demand ("How about a full year?") for last. The foot-in-the-door approach relies on the notion that in agreeing to the smaller offer, the customer has created a relationship with the seller, expressing some level of trust.

Robert Cialdini and his colleagues introduced a different strategy, called the *door-in-the-face* technique (Cialdini & others, 1975), that involves making the biggest pitch at the beginning ("Would you be interested in a full-year subscription?"), which the customer probably will reject, and then making a smaller, "concessionary" demand ("Okay, then, how about a three-month trial?"). The door-in-the-face technique relies on the fact that the customer feels a sense of reciprocity and obligation: Because you let him off the hook with that big request, maybe he should be nice and take that smaller offer.

*Cognitive dissonance can also be a powerful sales tool. Sometimes the harder we work to buy something, the more we want it. After all, did you buy that strange lamp on eBay— or did you win it?*

***Resisting Persuasion*** Advertisers and salespeople work their hardest to persuade us to buy their products. How do we resist their appeals? According to William McGuire, one way to resist persuasion is through *inoculation* (McGuire, 2003; McGuire & Papageorgis, 1961). McGuire proposed that just as administering a vaccine inoculates individuals from a virus by introducing a weakened or dead version of that virus to the immune system, giving people a weak version of a persuasive message and allowing them time to argue against it can help individuals avoid persuasion.

Research has shown that such "inoculation" helps college students resist plagiarism (Compton & Pfau, 2008) as well as credit card marketing appeals (Compton & Pfau, 2004). When individuals are warned that they are going to be hit with persuasive appeals and are given arguments to help them resist these pitches, they are able to do so.

*Consider yourself inoculated! Credit card companies often prey on college students.*

self quiz

1. Stereotype threat refers to
   A. the damage potentially caused by stereotyping others.
   B. the strategy of changing someone's behavior by threatening to use a stereotype.
   C. humans' tendency to categorize people using broad generalizations.
   D. an individual's self-fulfilling fear of being judged based on a negative stereotype about his or her group.

2. In committing the fundamental attribution error, we overemphasize _____ and underemphasize _____ when making attributions about others' behavior.

A. internal factors; external factors
B. external factors; internal factors
C. controllability; stability
D. stability; controllability

3. Which of the following statements about positive illusions is *true*?
   A. Positive illusions are more common in people with low self-esteem.
   B. Positive illusions are accurate.
   C. Positive illusions have been linked to better well-being.
   D. Positive illusions are focused on actors rather than observers.

APPLY IT! 4. Thomas has spent long hours working to get his candidate elected

president of the student body. When he talks to his mother on election night, Thomas is overjoyed to report that his candidate won by a landslide. His mom points out that Thomas never cared about campus politics before, and she asks him about his sudden interest. Thomas admits that she is right, but notes that he now cares deeply about campus issues and is likely to continue to be involved in politics. What theory best explains Thomas's change?
   A. social comparison theory
   B. self-perception theory
   C. stereotype threat
   D. the elaboration likelihood model

# 2 Social Behavior

We do not just think socially; we also behave in social ways. Two particular behaviors that have interested psychologists represent the extremes of human social activity: altruism and aggression.

# Altruism

In 2009, Rick Hohl, a Florida man, heard about a sheriff's deputy in dire need of a kidney transplant. Hohl made an on-the-spot decision to be tested, and he eventually donated his kidney to Johnnie Briggs, a complete stranger (Farris, 2009). Asked why he did it, Hohl replied, in tears, "I'm a Christian." He added, "And I just want to make a difference."

Such a selfless act of kindness is a part of our social experience, as are the huge relief efforts that have followed disasters such as the massive earthquake and tsunami in Japan in 2011. In everyday life, we witness and perform random acts of kindness—maybe adding a quarter to someone's expired parking meter or giving up our seat on a bus to someone in need. We may volunteer for the Special Olympics or serve as a literacy tutor. What all of these acts have in common is **altruism,** an unselfish interest in helping another person (Burks & Kobus, 2012).

**altruism**
Unselfish interest in helping another person.

In examining potentially altruistic behavior (or *prosocial behavior*), psychologists have questioned how genuinely selfless it is. Some psychologists even argue that true altruism has never been demonstrated (Cialdini, 1991; Maner & others, 2002). True altruism means giving to another person with the ultimate goal of benefiting that person. In contrast to altruism is **egoism,** which involves giving to another person to gain self-esteem; to present oneself as powerful, competent, or caring; or to avoid censure, both from oneself and from society, for failing to live up to expectations. Egoism may also entail helping another person because we want to increase the chances that the person will return the favor someday—that is, we may be kind to another person to ensure *reciprocity*.

**egoism**
Giving to another person to ensure reciprocity; to gain self-esteem; to present oneself as powerful, competent, or caring; or to avoid social and self-censure for failing to live up to society's expectations.

*Do you think altruism is a puzzle to be solved—or a natural expression of human nature? Why?*

The principle of reciprocity encourages us to do unto others as we would have them do unto us. Reciprocity lies at the heart of the Golden Rule. Reciprocity involves an expression of trust for another person, as well as feelings of obligation and guilt. The principle of reciprocity means that we behave kindly, as kidney donor Rick Hohl did, under the assumption that someone will show us the same kindness someday.

An example of animal altruism—a baboon plucking bugs from another baboon. Most acts of animal altruism involve kin.

**EVOLUTIONARY VIEWS OF ALTRUISM**    Altruism has presented a puzzle for evolutionary psychologists (Andre & Morin, 2011; Van Doorn & Taborsky, 2012). How can a behavior that rewards others, and not oneself, be adaptive? Interestingly, kindness is not exclusive to humans. Ethologists studying nonhuman primates have shown that altruistic acts of kindness also occur in other species (de Waal, Leimgruber, & Greenberg, 2008; Horner & others, 2011). Perhaps kindness is not a mystery but an important adaptation.

Evolutionary theorists note that helping is especially likely to occur among family members, because helping a relative also means promoting the survival of the family's genes (Buss, 2012; Leigh, 2010). Evolutionary theorists believe that reciprocity in relationships with nonfamily members is essentially the mistaken application of a heuristic that made sense in human evolutionary history—to engage in selfless acts of kindness to one's own family members (Nowak, Page, & Sigmund, 2000).

Dale Miller (1999, 2001) suggested that altruism may be an expression of true human nature. From Miller's perspective, although human beings are socialized to believe that the human species is naturally selfish, a great deal of research indicates that humans are not necessarily self-centered and do not engage in selfish acts as a natural response (Holmes, Miller, & Lerner, 2002).

## PSYCHOLOGICAL FACTORS IN ALTRUISM

In addition to *reciprocity,* psychological factors involved in altruism include mood and empathy. A strong conclusion from the research literature is that happy people are more likely to help (Snyder, Lopez, & Pedrotti, 2010). Does it then follow that when they are in a bad mood, people are less likely to help? Not necessarily, because adults (especially) generally understand that doing good for another person can be a mood booster. Thus, when in a bad mood, they might be likely to help if they think that doing so will improve their mood. Furthermore, sometimes those who have experienced distressing traumatic events find helping others to be an effective and meaningful way of coping (Staub & Vollhardt, 2008).

*What was the last altruistic act you committed? What led to your behavior?*

A key social emotion involved in altruism is empathy (Burks & Kobus, 2012). **Empathy** is a person's feeling of oneness with the emotional state of another. Daniel Batson has spent the better part of his career searching for proof that truly altruistic behavior does exist (Batson, 2002, 2006, 2012; Batson & others, 2007). The key to such altruism is the extent to which we can put ourselves in another's shoes. Empathy for someone else's plight moves us to action—not to make ourselves feel better but out of genuine concern for the other person. Empathy can produce altruistic behavior even toward members of rival groups and even when we believe no one will ever hear about our kind act (Fultz & others, 1986).

**empathy**
A feeling of oneness with the emotional state of another person.

## SOCIOCULTURAL FACTORS IN ALTRUISM

Sociocultural research has examined the characteristics of cultures that are associated with the emergence of altruism and with the belief that everyone deserves fair treatment. A study comparing 15 different cultures examined two particular factors: market economies and investment in established religion (Henrich & others, 2010).

A *market economy* is a decentralized system featuring the free exchange of products and services between producers and consumers. Market economies, such as the U.S. economy, require individuals to extend the principle of reciprocity to strangers, because the normal flow of business requires a certain degree of trust. For example, when you order a book online, you assume a great deal on the part of the strangers who are selling you that book. You give them your credit card information, confident that they will not use it to purchase things and will not share it with someone else. Even though you have no personal knowledge of these sellers, you assume that they will not take advantage of you.

Another important factor in prosocial behavior across cultures is established religions. World religions tend to share an emphasis on the Golden Rule and on treating others fairly. A series of studies conducted with participants in places as varied as Papua New Guinea, Samburu in Kenya, and the U.S. state of Missouri demonstrated that prosocial behaviors were more common in communities characterized by market economies and by investment in established religion (Henrich & others, 2010).

In addition to these two broad cultural factors, social psychologists have examined other sociocultural variables as predictors of altruism and helping, including gender, the influence of bystanders, and the media.

### *Altruism and Gender*

Given the role of empathy in helping, we might think that women should be more likely to help than men. After all, stereotypes tell us that women are by nature more empathic than men. However, as in most domains, it is useful to think about gender in context (Biernat & Deaux, 2012). Researchers have found that women are more likely than men to help when the context involves existing interpersonal relationships or nurturing, such as volunteering time to help a child with a personal problem (Eagly, 2009). Men, on the other hand, are more likely to help in situations in

*The Samburu people of Kenya are very spiritual, believing in and praying daily to the god Ngai. The presence of established religions within a culture is related to prosocial behaviors.*

which a perceived danger is present (for instance, picking up a hitchhiker) and in which they feel competent to help (as in assisting someone with a flat tire) (Eagly & Crowley, 1986). Interestingly, men and women were equally heroic in helping Jews escape the Nazi Holocaust during World War II (Becker & Eagly, 2004).

***The Bystander Effect***   Nearly 50 years ago, a young woman named Kitty Genovese was brutally murdered in New York City. She was attacked at about 3 A.M. in a courtyard surrounded by apartment buildings. It took the slayer approximately 30 minutes to kill Genovese. Thirty-eight neighbors watched the gory scene from their windows and heard Genovese's screams. No one helped or called the police.

*The bystander effect is still in evidence. In October 2009, a 15-year-old California girl was raped and beaten by as many as 10 people outside a high school dance (Martinez, 2009). More than 20 people watched—and no one called for help.*

Inspired by the Genovese case, social psychologists John Darley and Bibb Latané (1968) conducted a number of studies on the **bystander effect,** the tendency of an individual who observes an emergency to help less when other people are present than when the observer is alone. Most bystander studies show that when alone, a person will help 75 percent of the time, but when another bystander is present, the figure drops to 50 percent. Apparently the difference is due to diffusion of responsibility among witnesses and the tendency to look to the behavior of others for cues about what to do. We may think that someone else will call the police or that, because no one else is helping, possibly the person does not need help.

**bystander effect** The tendency for an individual who observes an emergency to help less when other people are present than when the observer is alone.

***Media Influences***   Psychologists have long considered media influences to be a factor in aggressive behavior. Researchers are also investigating whether media can elicit prosocial behavior as well. Studies suggest that the answer is yes. For example, listening to music with prosocial lyrics can promote kindness (Greitemeyer, 2009), and watching television shows with positive content has been associated with prosocial behavior (Hearold, 1986). Thus, exposure to prosocial media may be an important way to spread kindness.

This discussion of altruism highlights the capacity of human beings to help one another, whether through a simple gesture like holding a door open for another person or a selfless act such as donating an organ. This ability to engage in kindness coincides with other capacities, such as the capacity to cause others harm. Some evolutionary scientists have suggested that altruism, especially when it is directed at the members of one's own group, may coexist with hostile feelings and actions toward other groups (Arrow, 2007; Choi & Bowles, 2007; Glasford & Calcagno, 2012). Indeed, research shows that oxytocin, the hormone and neurotransmitter associated with social bonding, is related not only to stronger allegiance to a social group but also to greater hatred for individuals in other groups (De Dreu & others, 2010). A soldier may perform selfless, heroic acts of altruism for his or her country, but for a person on the other side of the combat, that behavior is harmful and potentially deadly. Thus, altruism within a group may be linked to aggression.

# Aggression

**Aggression** refers to social behavior whose objective is to harm someone, either physically or verbally. Aggression is common in contemporary society. Perhaps the greatest puzzle of aggression is that a species capable of incredible acts of kindness can also perpetrate horrifying acts of violence.

**aggression** Social behavior whose objective is to harm someone, either physically or verbally.

## BIOLOGICAL INFLUENCES   There is nothing new about human aggression. The primate ancestors of human beings and the earliest humans are thought to have committed aggressive acts against others of their own kind. Researchers who approach aggression from a biological viewpoint examine the influence of evolutionary tendencies, genetics, and neurobiological factors (Kenrick & Cohen, 2012).

***Evolutionary Views***   Ethologists say that certain stimuli release innate aggressive responses (Lorenz, 1965; Tinbergen, 1969). For example, a male robin will attack another male bird when it sees the red patch on the other bird's breast. When the patch is removed, no attack takes place. However, in the animal kingdom, most hostile encounters do not escalate to killing or even severe harm. Much of the fighting is ritualistic and involves threat displays—for example, a cat arching its back, baring its teeth, and hissing or a chimpanzee staring, stomping on the ground, and screaming.

Evolutionary theorists believe that human beings are not much different from other animals. A basic theme of their theory is the survival of the fittest (Wrangham & Glowacki, 2012). Thus, they conclude that early in human evolution the survivors were probably aggressive individuals.

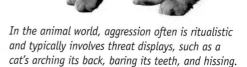

### Genetic Basis

Genes are important in explaining the biological basis of aggression (Butovskaya & others, 2012). The selective breeding of animals provides evidence for genetic influences in aggression. After a number of breedings among only aggressive animals and among only docile animals, vicious and timid strains of animals emerge. The vicious strains attack nearly anything in sight; the timid strains rarely fight, even when attacked.

*In the animal world, aggression often is ritualistic and typically involves threat displays, such as a cat's arching its back, baring its teeth, and hissing.*

The genetic basis for aggression is more difficult to demonstrate in humans than animals and may depend on the type of aggression studied (Brendgen & others, 2008). Specifically, twin studies have shown that physical aggression that is proactive in nature may be more influenced by genes, but more reactive aggression and social aggression (for instance, starting rumors about someone) may be more susceptible to environmental effects. Also, genetic influences may be stronger for males than for females (Baker & others, 2008).

### Neurobiological Factors

In 1966, Charles Whitman climbed to the top of the campus tower at the University of Texas at Austin and killed 15 people below with a high-powered rifle before he was felled by police bullets. Shortly before the rampage, he had murdered his wife and mother in their homes. An autopsy revealed a tumor in the limbic system of Whitman's brain, an area associated with emotion. Although humans do not appear to have a specific aggression center in the brain, aggressive behavior often results when areas such as the limbic system are stimulated by electric currents (Herbert, 1988; Wood & Liossi, 2006).

The frontal lobes of the brain—the areas most involved in executive functions such as planning and self-control—have also been implicated in aggression. Research by Adriane Raine and his colleagues has examined the brains of individuals who have committed the ultimate act of violence: murder (Nordstrom & others, 2011; Raine, 2008; Yang, Glen, & Raine, 2008). The results indicate that murderers may differ from others in deficits in the functioning of these areas of the brain.

Neurotransmitters—particularly, lower levels of serotonin—have been linked to aggressive behavior (Neumann, Veenema, & Beiderbeck, 2010; Rosell & others, 2010). In one study, young men whose serotonin levels were low relative to those of other men their age were far more likely to have committed a violent crime (Moffitt & others, 1998). Similarly, aggressive children have lower levels of serotonin than do children who display low rates of aggression (Blader, 2006; Nevels & others, 2010).

Hormones are another biological factor that may play a role in aggression. The hormone that is typically implicated in aggressive behavior is testosterone. Research on rats and other animals has shown that testosterone relates to aggression (Cunningham & McGinnis, 2007). However, results with humans have been less consistent (van Bokhoven & others, 2006).

*Remember that behavior can influence hormone levels. So, higher testosterone may be an effect of aggressive behavior, not its cause.*

A fascinating study examined how testosterone is influenced by experience and how experience and testosterone together might help explain aggression (Klinesmith, Kasser, & McAndrew, 2006). In this study, college men interacted with either a gun or a child's toy. Testosterone was measured before and after this phase of the study. Men who interacted with the gun showed greater increases in testosterone, compared to the control group. Furthermore, later in the study, the men who had interacted with the gun were more aggressive (they put more hot sauce in a cup of water they thought someone else was going to drink). The role of testosterone in this increase in aggression suggests that testosterone changes may shed light on why some people respond more aggressively to violent cues than do others (Klinesmith, Kasser, & McAndrew, 2006).

*This controversy over the operational definitions of aggression reflects concern over the external validity of this work.*

It is worth noting that many of the studies of aggression that have been conducted in social psychology laboratories rely on a variety of behaviors that may be considered aggressive even if they do not involve, for example, actually punching someone in the face. In studies on aggression, participants might have an opportunity to "aggress" against another, for instance, by subjecting the individual to a blast of loud noise, dispensing a mild electrical shock, or even, as in the study described above, administering a large dose of hot sauce to swallow. Whether these operational definitions of aggression are applicable to real-life violence is a matter of much debate (Savage & Yancey, 2008).

**PSYCHOLOGICAL FACTORS**    Numerous psychological factors appear to be involved in aggression. They include individuals' responses to circumstances, as well as cognitive and learning factors.

*Frustrating and Aversive Circumstances*    Many years ago, John Dollard and his colleagues (1939) proposed the *frustration-aggression hypothesis,* which states that *frustration*—the blocking of an individual's attempts to reach a goal—always leads to aggression. However, psychologists subsequently found that aggression is not the only possible response to frustration: Some individuals who experience frustration become passive, for example (N. E. Miller, 1941).

Psychologists later recognized that besides frustration, a broad range of aversive experiences can cause aggression. They include physical pain, personal insults, crowding, and unpleasant events. Aversive circumstances also include factors in the physical environment, such as the weather. Murder, rape, and assault increase when temperatures are the highest, as well as in the hottest years and the hottest cities (Anderson & Bushman, 2002).

*Cognitive Determinants*    Aspects of the environment may prime us to behave aggressively (Englander, 2006). Recall from Chapter 6 that priming can involve making something salient to a person, even subliminally or without the person's awareness. Leonard Berkowitz (1993; Berkowitz & LePage, 1996) has shown how the mere presence of a weapon (such as a gun) may prime hostile thoughts and produce aggression (Anderson, Benjamin, & Bartholow, 1998). Indeed, in accordance with Berkowitz's ideas, a famous study found that individuals who lived in a household with a gun were 2.7 times more likely to be murdered than those dwelling in a household without a gun (Kellerman & others, 1993).

*This is a correlational study. What are some third variables that might explain the association between gun ownership and murder?*

A variety of other cognitive factors determine whether an individual responds aggressively to aversive situations (Baumeister, 1999; Berkowitz, 1990; DeWall & others, 2009). For instance, if a person perceives that another's actions are unfair or intentionally hurtful, aggression is more likely to occur. Indeed, in the workplace, individuals who perceive that they have been treated unfairly are more likely to aggress, verbally and physically, against supervisors (Dupre & Barling, 2006).

*Observational Learning*    Social cognitive theorists believe that aggression is learned through reinforcement and observational learning (Englander, 2006). Aggression can be learned by watching others engage in aggressive actions. Perhaps the most famous example of observational learning is the Bobo doll study (Bandura, Ross, & Ross, 1961). Albert Bandura and his colleagues randomly assigned some children to watch an adult model aggressive behavior and other children to watch an adult behaving non-aggressively. In the experimental condition, children saw the model hit an inflated Bobo doll with a mallet, kick it in the air, punch it, and throw it, all the while hollering aggressive phrases such as "Hit him!" "Punch him in the nose!" and "Pow!" In the control condition, the model played with Tinkertoys and ignored the Bobo doll. Children who watched the aggressive model were much more likely to engage in aggressive behavior when left alone with Bobo (Bandura, Ross, & Ross, 1961). One of the most frequent opportunities people have to observe aggression in our culture is to watch violence on television (see related discussion below on media violence).

**SOCIOCULTURAL FACTORS** Aggression involves not only biological and cognitive factors but also factors in the wider social world. Among the sociocultural factors in aggression are variations in economic inequity, the "culture of honor," and the extent to which people watch violence in the media.

Used by permission of CartoonStock, www.CartoonStock.com.

### *Cultural Variations and the Culture of Honor*
Aggression and violence are more common in some cultures than others (Kitayama & Cohen, 2007). Dov Cohen has examined the ways in which some cultural norms about masculine pride and family honor may foster aggressive behavior (Cohen, 2001; Vandello & Cohen, 2004). In a *culture of honor*, a man's reputation is thought to be an essential aspect of his economic survival. Such a culture sees insults to a man's honor as diminishing his reputation and views violence as a way to compensate for that loss. Cultures of honor are obvious in countries where family pride might lead to so-called honor killings—in which, for example, a female rape victim is slain by her male family members so that they are not "contaminated" by the rape. In April 2009, a Jordanian man confessed to stabbing his pregnant sister with a meat cleaver because she had left her husband and he believed she was seeing other men. He felt that he had to kill her to protect his family honor (Gavlak, 2009).

*Cognitive dissonance could lead to even greater valuing of one's personal honor. That honor would have to be really important for a person to harm someone else physically or to kill his own sister.*

Cohen has examined how, in the United States, southerners are more likely than northerners to be aggressive when honor is at stake. In one study, Cohen and his colleagues (1996) had White men who were from either the North or the South take part in an experiment that required them to walk down a hallway. A confederate passed all the men, bumping against them and quietly calling them a derogatory name. The southerners were more likely than the northerners to think that their masculine reputation was threatened, to become physiologically aroused by the insult, and to engage in actual aggressive or dominant acts. In contrast, the northerners were less likely to perceive a random insult as "fightin' words."

### *Media Violence*
Images of violence pervade the U.S. popular media. Moreover, television shows, movies, video games, and song lyrics usually portray violence unrealistically and without showing its lasting effects. It is easy to get the message that aggression and violence are the norm.

Although some critics have disputed the conclusion that TV violence causes aggression (Savage & Yancey, 2008), many scholars insist that television violence can prompt aggressive or antisocial behavior in children (P. Brown & Tierney, 2011; Bushman & Huesman, 2012; Comstock, 2012). Of course, television violence is not the only cause of aggression in children or adults. Aggression, like all other social behaviors, has multiple determinants (Matos, Ferreira, & Haase, 2012). The link between TV violence and aggression in children is influenced by children's aggressive tendencies, by their attitudes toward violence, and by the monitoring of children's exposure to it. Perhaps the strongest predictor of aggression is witnessing aggression in one's own family (Ferguson & others, 2008).

Another type of media violence that has interested social psychologists is violent pornography—films, videos, websites, and magazines portraying the degradation of women in a sexual context. Do such media foster violence toward women? Based on several meta-analyses and research of their own, Neil Malamuth and his colleagues concluded that pornography consumption does have a small effect on male sexual aggression and is related to more accepting attitudes about violence toward women (Hald, Malamuth, & Yuen, 2010; Malamuth, Addison, & Koss, 2000). Yet Malamuth and his colleagues caution that pornography is only one of a number of factors that may lead to sexual violence against women (Hald, Malamuth, & Yuen, 2010; Vega & Malamuth, 2007). The most problematic materials are those that depict women enjoying being the victims of male sexual violence (Hald, Malamuth, & Yuen, 2010). Such violent pornography reinforces the *rape myth*—the false belief that women desire coercive sex.

As explored in Challenge Your Thinking, researchers have also examined the influence of video games on social behavior. These games provide an especially powerful experience in which players perpetrate a wide range of social behaviors while engrossed in the action.

### AGGRESSION AND GENDER

Are men or women more aggressive? The answer depends on the particular *type* of aggression we are talking about.

**Overt aggression** refers to physically or verbally harming another person directly. Males tend to be higher in overt aggression than females. As children, boys are more likely than girls to get in fights in which they are physically aggressive toward one another (Underwood, 2011). As adolescents, males are more likely to join gangs and to commit violent acts. Children and adolescents who are diagnosed with *conduct disorder*—a pattern of offensive behavior that violates the basic rights of others—are three times more likely to be boys than girls (Kjelsberg, 2005). Of the murders committed in 2010, 90 percent of these were committed by men (FBI, 2012).

*Men were also the victims of these crimes, 70 percent of the time.*

**overt aggression**
Physical or verbal behavior that directly harms another person.

Women's smaller physical size may be one reason they are less likely to engage in overt aggression. In probing aggressive tendencies in girls and women, researchers have focused instead on **relational aggression,** behavior that is meant to harm the social standing of another person through activities such as gossiping and spreading rumors (Underwood, 2011). Relational aggression differs from overt aggression in that it requires that the aggressor have a considerable level of social and cognitive skill. To be relationally aggressive, an individual must have a strong understanding of the social environment and must be able to plant rumors that are most likely to damage the intended party. Relational aggression is subtler than overt aggression, and the relationally aggressive individual may not seem to be aggressive to others, as the aggressive acts typically are committed secretly. Research conclusions are mixed on whether girls show more relational aggression than boys, but one consistency in the findings is that relational aggression composes a greater percentage of girls' overall aggression than is the case for boys (Underwood, 2011). A recent research review revealed that girls engage in more relational aggression than boys in adolescence but not in childhood (Smith, Rose, & Schwartz-Mette, 2010).

**relational aggression**
Behavior that is meant to harm the social standing of another person.

Generally, both overt aggression and relational aggression are related to reduced peer acceptance (Underwood, 2011). Relational aggression in girls is associated in particular with less acceptance by other girls; in contrast, relationally aggressive adolescent girls are more likely to enjoy acceptance by boys. This pattern suggests that girls who relationally aggress toward other girls may do so to improve their standing with boys (Smith, Rose, & Schwartz-Mette, 2010).

Although relational aggression may not lead to the physical injury that is often the result of overt aggression, it can be extremely painful nevertheless. In 2010, Phoebe Prince, a 15-year-old who had recently moved from Ireland to the United States with her family, became the target of unrelenting rumors and harassment from a group of popular girls at her high school after she had a brief relationship with a popular senior boy. Prince became so distraught that she hanged herself after school one day. Even after her suicide, the girls who had harassed her posted rumors about her on the Facebook page that was set up as a memorial (Cullen, 2010).

# Challenge

## Do Video Games Influence Social Behavior?

Video games are an extremely potent medium. One of the most hotly contested issues in social psychology is the potential role of violent video games in promoting aggressive behavior. It has been suggested that violent video games engage children and adolescents so intensely that they experience an altered state of consciousness in which "rational thought is suspended and highly arousing aggressive scripts are increasingly likely to be learned" (Roberts, Henriksen, & Foehr, 2009,

p. 328). Unlike other media, such as TV shows, video games allow the individual to play an active role in perpetrating violence. A recent meta-analysis concluded that children and adolescents who play violent video games extensively are more aggressive, less sensitive to real-life violence, more likely to engage in delinquent acts, and more likely to get lower grades in school than counterparts who spend less time playing the games or do not play them at all (C. A. Anderson & others, 2010).

Social psychologist Craig Anderson has been a vocal spokesperson against media violence, especially violent video games (Anderson, 2003; Anderson, Gentile, & Dill, 2012; Anderson & Huesmann, 2007; Anderson & Prot, 2011; Bushman & Anderson, 2007; Saleem & Anderson, 2012). Critics of the work of Anderson and his colleagues, however, have pointed out that acts of aggression studied in the laboratory (for instance, blasting someone with loud noise) are not generalizable to real-world criminal violence (Ritter & Elsea, 2005; Savage, 2008; Savage & Yancey, 2008). Furthermore, they stress that many studies have not measured important third variables, such as family violence, in predicting both video game use and aggression (Ferguson & others, 2008; Ferguson & Kilburn, 2010). Others have argued that action games can instill more noble motives, among them civic duty (Ferguson & Garza, 2011).

If video games exert a powerful force on social behavior, might they be used to foster kindness rather than aggression? Although research on this intriguing question is much less common than research on aggression, the results of relevant studies might surprise you. For example, a series of studies examined the effects of playing prosocial video games on behavior. In these studies, participants who had played a video game such as Lemmings, in which the player tries to save the hapless creatures from a variety of disasters, were more likely than those who had played either a neutral or a violent game to help an experimenter pick up a cup of spilled pencils (Greitemeyer & Osswald, 2010). In another study, participants who played a prosocial video game were more likely to intervene when a confederate posing as the female experimenter's ex-boyfriend came in and began to harass her (Greitemeyer & Osswald, 2010). Prosocial video games foster prosocial thoughts (Greitemeyer & Osswald, 2011) and lead individuals to donate more money to a partner (Whitaker & Bushman, 2012).

When we think about the influence of video games on human behavior, it may seem natural to focus immediately on the negative effects. But by comprehensively investigating and understanding this powerful medium, we might gain valuable perspective on many human social behaviors, not just aggression.

### What Do You Think?

- Would you allow your child to play violent video games? Why or why not?

- A friend with a child comments, "I never let my son play video games—they will make him violent." Using the research discussed above, how would you respond?

**REDUCING AGGRESSION**   Social cognitive theorists believe that people who act aggressively often are rewarded for their aggression and that individuals learn to be aggressive by watching others behave aggressively. Research has supported this view (Bandura, 1997). Thus, promising strategies for reducing aggression are to decrease rewards for aggression and to lessen exposure to it. Parents have been especially targeted to help children to reduce aggression (Leaper & Friedman, 2007).

Recommended parenting strategies include encouraging young children to develop empathy toward others and closely monitoring adolescents' activities (Dick & others, 2011; Furlong & McGilloway, 2012).

**self-quiz**

1. Egoism is in evidence when
   A. a mother physically protects her children from the ravages of a tornado at risk to her own life.
   B. a person donates bone marrow to a complete stranger.
   C. a coffee shop customer pays for the latte of the stranger in line behind him.
   D. a speaker compliments his staff's achievements in order to make himself look good.

2. The following are ways to reduce aggression *except*
   A. minimizing the amount of violence witnessed.
   B. increasing empathy.

   C. rewarding aggressive actions.
   D. not modeling aggressive behaviors at home.

3. With respect to male and female aggression,
   A. males engage in more overt aggression than females.
   B. females engage in more overt aggression than males.
   C. males engage in more relational aggression than females.
   D. both sexes engage about equally in overt and relational aggression.

**APPLY IT!** 4. While driving, Nate sees an elderly man struggling to change a flat tire. Nate stops and helps the man and then

continues to his girlfriend's house. When Nate tells his girlfriend about his act of kindness, she says, "I would never have done that." Nate suggests that he just must be nicer than she is. Considering the social psychology of helping, is Nate right?
   A. Nate is right because men are generally more helpful then women.
   B. Nate is right because he engaged in a selfless act of altruism.
   C. Nate is not right because his girlfriend may not have felt safe stopping to help someone on a country road at night.
   D. Nate is not right because he probably got a lot of praise from his girlfriend, rendering his act selfish.

# 3 Social Influence

Another topic of interest to social psychologists is how our behavior is influenced by other individuals and groups (Levine & Moreland, 2012; Reis, 2012). This section explores key aspects of social influence: conformity, obedience, and group influence.

## Conformity and Obedience

Research on conformity and obedience started in earnest after World War II. Psychologists sought answers to the disturbing question of how ordinary people could be influenced to commit the sort of atrocities inflicted on Jews, Gypsies, and other minorities during the Holocaust. A central question is, how extensively will people change their behavior to coincide with what others are doing or dictating?

**conformity**
A change in a person's behavior to coincide more closely with a group standard.

**CONFORMITY** **Conformity** is a change in a person's behavior to coincide more closely with a group standard. Conformity takes many forms and affects many aspects of people's lives, in negative and positive ways. Conformity is at work, for example, when a person comes to college and starts to drink alcohol heavily at parties, even though he or she might have never been a drinker before. Conformity is also involved when we obey the rules and regulations that allow society to run smoothly. Consider how chaotic it would be if people did not conform to social norms such as stopping at a red light and not punching others in the face. Conformity can also be a powerful way to increase group cohesion. Even something as simple as marching in step together or singing a song with a group can lead to enhanced cooperation among group members (Wiltermuth & Heath, 2009).

**EXPERIENCE IT!**
Asch's Conformity
Experiment

*Asch's Experiment* Put yourself in this situation: You are taken into a room where you see five other people seated along a table. A person in a white lab coat enters the room and announces that you are about to participate in an experiment on perceptual accuracy. The group is shown two cards—the first having only a single vertical line on it and the second having three vertical lines of vary-ing length. You are told that the task is to determine which of the three lines on the second card is the same length as the line on the first card. You look at the cards and think, "What a snap. It's so obvious which is the same" (Figure 11.3).

What you do not know is that the other people in the room are confederates working with the experi-menter. On the first several trials, everyone agrees about which line matches the standard. Then on the fourth trial, each of the others picks the same incor-rect line. As the last person to make a choice, you have the dilemma of responding as your eyes tell you or conforming to what the others before you said. How would you answer?

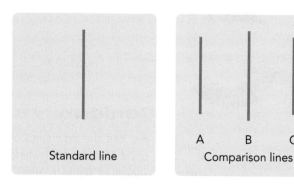

**FIGURE 11.3** **Asch's Conformity Experiment** The figures show the stimulus materials for the Asch conformity experiment on group influence.

Solomon Asch conducted this classic experiment on conformity in 1951. Asch instructed the confederates to give incorrect responses on 12 of 18 trials. To his surprise, Asch (1951) found that the volunteer participants conformed to the incorrect answers 35 percent of the time. Subsequent research has supported the notion that the pressure to conform is strong (Fein & others, 1993; Pines & Maslach, 2002)—but why do people go along with the group even when faced with clear-cut information such as the lines in the Asch experiment?

### *Going Along to Be Right and Going Along to Be Liked*   Two main factors have been identified as contributing to conformity: informational social influence and normative social influence.

**informational social influence** The influence other people have on us be-cause we want to be right.

**Informational social influence** refers to the influence other people have on us because we want to be right. The social group can provide us with information that we did not know, or may help us see things in ways that had not occurred to us. As a result, we may conform because we have come to agree with the group. The tendency to conform based on informational social influence depends especially on two factors: how confident we are in our own independent judg-ment and how well informed we perceive the group to be. For example, if you know little about computers and three of your acquaintances who are IT geeks tell you not to buy a particular brand of computer, you are likely to conform to their recommendation.

*To feel the pressure of conformity, the next time you get on an elevator with other people, do not turn around to face the door.*

In contrast, **normative social influence** is the influence others have on us because we want them to like us. Whether the group is an inner-city gang or members of a profes-sion such as medicine or law, if a particular group is important to us, we might adopt a clothing style that people in the group wear or use the same slang words, and we might assume a certain set of attitudes that characterizes the group's members (Hewlin, 2009).

**normative social influence** The influence other people have on us because we want them to like us.

### *Conformity and the Brain*   Conformity is a powerful social force, but why is it so important to us to fit in with a group? Recent research in social psychology and neuroscience has provided an interesting answer. Just as the brain is involved in all human behavior, it is involved in conformity. Researchers have gained intriguing insights into the ways the brain responds to moments when we do not fit in with a group. The findings suggest that our brain may actually "feel better" when we fit in.

In a study using fMRI, Vasily Klucharev and his colleagues examined what happens in the brain when people find out that their opinions conflict with those of others (Klucharev & others, 2009). Women were asked to rate a variety of female faces for attractiveness, and their brains were scanned while they received feedback about whether their ratings agreed with those of the other group members. When participants were told that their ratings differed from the group's ratings, they showed enhanced activation in the brain area typically associated with monitoring for errors. In other words, the brain responded to judgments that differed from the group judgments as if they were *mistakes*. Furthermore,

# PSYCHOLOGY IN OUR WORLD

## Conformity and the American Strip Mall

Have you had the experience of driving along an unfamiliar U.S. highway and feeling that you could be almost anywhere? Perhaps it's because virtually identical clusters of commercial landmarks, including Walmart, Home Depot, the Gap, and Best Buy, have cropped up everywhere. And whether it is a suburb of Houston or Boston or Minneapolis, the housing developments look essentially the same. There's no escaping that Americans construct look-alike landscapes. This architectural conformity is puzzling in a nation known for its devotion to individuality. Why would a culture so invested in uniqueness again and again reproduce an architectural landscape that is the same? Social psychologist Shigehiro Oishi and his colleagues (2012) suggest that the answer may lie in Americans' freedom of movement.

Compared to people in other parts of the world, Americans are endowed with a high level of freedom to live wherever they wish. Moreover, unlike individuals in other nations, Americans can move without learning a new language. Relative to people in those other countries, Americans move a great deal. Oishi and his colleagues suggest that this residential mobility plays a role in the uniformity of constructed landscapes across the United States. The researchers propose that the stress of moving from one place to another may prompt individuals to seek out the familiar. They have examined this prediction in varied studies.

First, Oishi and his colleagues showed that across the 50 states, the degree of population mobility is strongly related to the number of chain stores—that is, the more chain stores, the higher the degree of mobility in a state. Second, they found that college students who had a history of moves during their lifetime were more likely to have positive attitudes about chain stores and more likely to prefer them over local stores. Although people generally prefer familiar things, this tendency was especially true for individuals who had moved a great deal. Experimental studies showed that even thinking about moving made participants like familiar faces more. These results indicate that one reason why U.S. constructed landscapes look so similar is that in strip malls and suburbs that scream conformity, the mobile American population feels a tiny sense of home.

when the women's ratings were different from the group's ratings, women experienced less activation in the nucleus accumbens and the ventral tegmental area, the brain's reward centers. The greater the degree to which women's brains responded to being different as an error and as not rewarding, the more they tended to conform when given a chance to re-rate the faces at the end of the study. Klucharev and colleagues suggest that their findings demonstrate that humans *learn* that conformity is rewarding.

In a second study, the researchers found that these effects were specific to social conformity. In that study, the women were given feedback about a *computer's* ratings of the faces. Results showed that the brain did not mind being different from a computer nearly as much as being different from a group of other humans.

*Do you think the brain could learn to like being different?*

***Conformity and Culture*** We have seen elsewhere in this book that cultures often differ as to whether they are individualistic or collectivistic in nature. Individualistic cultures value individuals and individual accomplishments and emphasize differences and uniqueness. Collectivistic cultures value the group, emphasize group harmony, and believe that accomplishments depend on individuals' carrying out their roles in the larger social network. It is not surprising, then, that collectivism has been associated with greater levels of conformity. One research review, summarizing 133

## Social Psychology and Cross-Cultural Psychology: Why Are Some Nations More Conforming Than Others?

Recently, researchers have sought to identify the origins of cultural differences in conformity in an unusual place: germs. That's right: Scholars have suggested that one factor that might influence cultural characteristics and help explain the origins of cultural differences is the prevalence of *pathogens*—agents, such as viruses and bacteria, that cause infectious disease—in particular locales. Geographic locations with relatively more pathogens floating around should have certain characteristics associated with adapting to these disease-causing agents, researchers say.

Unique cooking traditions are often used to distinguish among cultures. In particular, some cultures are known for their fiery cuisine, while others feature blander foods. Why might these variations exist? To get at the answer, you might first consider that some spices can be natural antibiotics. Thus, Damian Murray and Mark Schaller (2010) proposed that cultures favoring spicier foods would also be those that emerged in places with relatively more pathogens, a prediction they supported in a large-scale cross-cultural examination (Murray & Schaller, 2010). Consider, too, that surviving in a world in which infectious agents are an ever-present threat might also mean curtailing those social behaviors through which diseases are more likely to spread. Interestingly, extraversion—a trait associated with outgoing sociable behavior—is lower in nations in which pathogen prevalence is high (Mortensen & others, 2010).

If pathogen presence impacts social behaviors, might pathogen prevalence help to explain the origins of cultural differences in conformity? Murray and Schaller suggest that establishing strong cultural norms for conformity might be a way that groups control the spread of infectious diseases. Although valuing conformity may exact a cost in terms of innovation and novel ideas,

conforming to social norms may be worth this risk if it prevents an epidemic.

In a provocative study, Murray and his colleagues examined how pathogen prevalence in a host of nations related to four indicators of conformity (Murray, Trudeau, & Schaller, 2011). Among these conformity indicators were (1) the findings from 133 Asch-style conformity studies conducted in various nations (Bond & Smith, 1996); (2) the percentage of people in each nation who prioritized the value of obedience in a world survey; and (3) the scope of personality differences observed in the countries in a worldwide study of personality traits in various nations. The fourth indicator of conformity was the percentage of adults reporting themselves as left-handed. To this day in some countries, children who show a preference for left-handedness are trained away from this inclination, sometimes being forced to use their right hand while learning to write and perform other tasks. Murray and his colleagues predicted that nations with a low tolerance for nonconformists would be more likely to pressure lefties to conform to the dominant right-handed way of doing things. Interestingly, the study results indicated that pathogen prevalence was positively related to higher levels of conformity in laboratory settings and to endorsement of the value of obedience, and negatively related to the percentage of left-handers in the adult population.

Many factors beyond pathogens play a role in the emergence of cultural traditions, of course. But probing the connections between these traditions and the natural world is a promising step toward understanding the kinds of problems that culture solves, as well as the functions that cultural norms serve in survival.

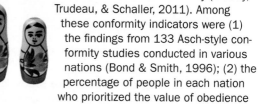

\\ **What other cultural norms might be related to germs?**

\\ **How do you think the prevalence of pathogens influences your own behavior?**

experiments following Asch's design, found that individualism within cultures was negatively correlated with conformity (Bond & Smith, 1996).

An intriguing question, however, is *why* people who live in different geographic locations have developed and preserved different cultural traditions. One important set of factors is characteristics of the natural environment in which cultures exist, such as the terrain, the weather, and whether the environment facilitates farming or hunting (Kitayama & Bowman, 2010; Murray & Schaller, 2010; Van de Vliert, 2009). These aspects of the natural world determine what a group must do to survive. Cultural norms provide clues about how groups of human beings have managed to adapt to life together in that environment. To read about how another aspect of the natural environment helps to explain cultural differences in conformity, check out the Intersection.

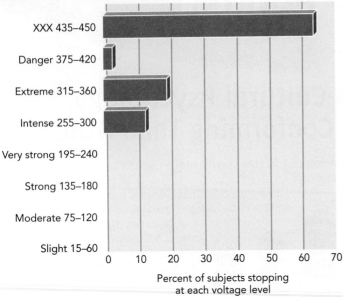

Voltage range (amps) and description

XXX 435–450

Danger 375–420

Extreme 315–360

Intense 255–300

Very strong 195–240

Strong 135–180

Moderate 75–120

Slight 15–60

Percent of subjects stopping
at each voltage level

**FIGURE 11.4** **Milgram's Obedience Study** In Milgram's experiments, the "learner" was strapped into a chair. The experimenter made it look as if a shock generator was being connected to the learner's body through several electrodes. The chart shows the percentage of "teachers" who stopped shocking the learner at each voltage level.

**EXPERIENCE IT!**
Milgram's Obedience
Experiment

*Milgram's studies became the subject of a 1970s TV movie called* **The Tenth Level.** *The film starred William Shatner as Stephen Turner—a character based on Stanley Milgram.*

**OBEDIENCE** **Obedience** is behavior that complies with the explicit demands of the individual in authority. We are obedient when an authority figure demands that we do something, and we then do it. Note that in conformity, people change their thinking or behavior so that it will be more like that of others, while in obedience, there is an explicit demand to comply (Blass, 2007).

Obedient behavior, such as that involved in the Nazi crimes against Jews and others during World War II, can sometimes be distressingly cruel. More recent examples include the obedience of radical Muslims instructed to participate in suicide attacks against Israelis and Westerners (McCauley & Segal, 2009), as well as the behavior of U.S. military personnel at Abu Ghraib prison in Iraq, who justified their horrendous abuse of detainees by asserting that they were "just following orders" (A. G. Miller, 2004).

*Milgram's Obedience Experiments* A classic series of experiments by Stanley Milgram (1965, 1974) provides insight into such obedience. Imagine that as part of an experiment, you are asked to deliver a series of painful electric shocks to another person. You are told that the purpose of the study is to determine the effects of punishment on memory. Your role is to be the "teacher" and to punish the mistakes made by the "learner." Each time the learner makes a mistake, you are to increase the intensity of the shock.

You are introduced to the learner, a nice 50-year-old man who mumbles something about having a heart condition. He is strapped to a chair in the next room; he communicates with you through an intercom. The apparatus in front of you has 30 switches, ranging from 15 volts (light shock) to 450 volts (marked as "severe shock XXX").

As the trials proceed, the learner runs into trouble and is unable to give the correct answers. Should you shock him? As you increase the intensity of the shock, the learner says that he is in pain. At 150 volts, he demands to have the experiment stopped. At 180 volts, he cries out that he cannot stand it anymore. At 300 volts, he yells about his heart condition and pleads to be released. If you hesitate in shocking the learner, however, the experimenter tells you that you have no choice; the experiment must continue. Eventually the learner stops responding altogether, and the experimenter tells you that not responding is the same as a wrong answer. At this point, the learner appears to be injured or even dead. Would you keep going?

Prior to doing the study, Milgram asked 40 psychiatrists how they thought individuals would respond to this situation. The psychiatrists predicted that most teachers would go no farther than 150 volts, that fewer than 1 in 25 would go as far as 300 volts, and that only 1 in 1,000 would deliver the full 450 volts. The psychiatrists were way off. As shown in Figure 11.4, the majority of the teachers obeyed the experimenter: Almost two-thirds delivered the full 450 volts.

By the way, the 50-year-old man was a confederate in the experiment. In Milgram's study, the learner was not being shocked at all. Of course, the teachers were unaware that the learner was only pretending to be shocked.

At very strong voltage levels, the learner quit responding. When the teacher asked the experimenter what to do, the experimenter simply replied, "You must go on. The experiment requires that you continue." Imagine that with those simple statements, the experimenter was able to command people calmly to (as far

**obedience**
Behavior that complies with the explicit demands of the individual in authority.

as they knew) shock a man to unconsciousness and possibly death. Such is the power of obedience to authority.

In variations of the experiment, Milgram discovered that more people would disobey in certain circumstances. Specifically, disobedience was more common when participants could see others disobey, when the authority figure was not perceived to be legitimate and was not close by, and when the victim was made to seem more human.

The ethics of Milgram's studies has been a subject of controversy since he began them. The teachers in the experiment clearly felt anguish; some were very disturbed about "harming" another individual. Milgram had deceived all of the participants as part of the study. Even though they found out that they had not actually shocked or harmed anyone, was the anguish imposed on them ethical? Milgram's studies certainly revealed a great deal about human nature, and none of the volunteers expressed regret that they had taken part.

Under today's ethical guidelines, it is unlikely that these experiments would have been approved. Nonetheless, we are still learning from Milgram's data. A recent meta-analysis of Milgram's experiments suggested that the critical decision was at the 150-volt level, when the learner first requested that the experiment be halted. At that point, 80 percent of those who were going to stop did so (Packer, 2008). Apparently, individuals who were going to disobey were those who responded not to the later anguished cries of pain but to the learner's first request to be set free.

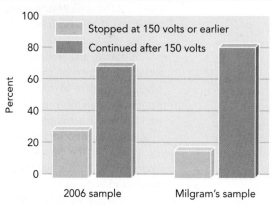

Adapted from Burger, 2009.

**FIGURE 11.5** **Obedience Now and Then** This figure shows, side by side, the results of Burger's (2009) study and the results of one of Milgram's studies. The vertical, or Y, axis shows the percent of individuals who stopped or continued after the learner's first expression of a desire to end the study. > *Comparing the two sets of results, does the similarity surprise you? Why or why not?* > *If you had been a "teacher" in either of these studies, what would you have done? How does learning about Milgram's study influence your response?*

Jerry Burger (2009) recently re-created Milgram's study at Santa Clara University in California. Burger's study was similar to Milgram's except that in Burger's experiment the participants were never allowed to go higher than 150 volts. At 150 volts, the confederate asked to conclude the study, and immediately after participants decided whether to continue, the experiment was ended. Burger's participants were only slightly less likely to obey than Milgram's had been (Figure 11.5). In a diverse sample of individuals in the California study, 70 percent of participants chose to continue even when the confederate asked to be released from the study. Notably, Burger's study employed safeguards to protect his participants.

*Burger had to exclude participants who had heard of Milgram's studies. In effect, people who had learned the lessons of Milgram's work were not given a chance to show their stuff.*

### The Stanford Prison Experiment

Another controversial demonstration of the power of obedience is provided by the famous Stanford prison experiment, conducted by Philip Zimbardo in 1971. This research illustrates the potentially horrific effects of obedience, not only on those who obey but on those who wield authority. The U.S. military funded the study to help understand conflicts between military prisoners and guards.

Zimbardo and his students created a simulated prison in the basement of a Stanford University building (Haney, Banks, &

*A guard keeps a stern and watchful eye on a prisoner during the Stanford prison experiment.*

Zimbardo, 1973; Zimbardo, 1972, 1973, 2007). Newspaper ads recruited men for a two-week study of prison life for which participants would be paid $15 per day (about $85 today). After undergoing screening to ensure they were psychologically healthy, 24 men began the study. Each was assigned to the role of either prisoner or guard.

The prisoners were "arrested" at their homes, booked and fingerprinted at the local police station, and brought to the prison, where they were strip-searched and given uncomfortable uniforms of smocks and stocking caps. Prisoners were assigned three to a cell, where they were to spend most of their time, night and day, for the entire study. The guards wore uniforms and mirrored sunglasses (to prevent eye contact with prisoners) and wielded wooden batons. They could leave the prison between their eight-hour shifts.

Zimbardo, who served as the prison superintendent, told the guards that they had all the power in the prison and the prisoners would have none (Zimbardo, 1989). He informed the guards that they would be taking away each prisoner's individuality. Guards were to refer to the prisoners only by their uniforms' identification numbers.

The course of this study surprised even Zimbardo (2007). Things got ugly very quickly. Within the first 36 hours, a prisoner had to be released when he started screaming, cursing, and raging uncontrollably. On the second day, a group of prisoners blockaded themselves in their cells. Additional guards were brought in to control the uprising. Some guards attacked prisoners with fire extinguishers while not being watched by the research staff. One-third of the guards behaved in extremely sadistic ways, humiliating and harassing prisoners, forcing them to stand naked in their cells, or allowing them to urinate and defecate only in a bucket in their cells. A prisoner who went on a hunger strike was locked in "solitary confinement," essentially a dark closet. The study was cut short after just six days, prompted by a graduate student's concern for participant safety (Zimbardo, Maslach, & Haney, 2000).

Zimbardo (2007) concluded that situational factors powerfully affect human behavior. To explain why prisoners did not quit the study, he argued that they had internalized their roles. To explain the guards' cruelty, Zimbardo reasoned that when an authority figure removes personal responsibility, when other people are dehumanized, and when norms support otherwise horrifying behavior, true evil can emerge. The conclusions drawn from this work are similar to those of the Milgram obedience studies: Anyone would do these vile things if put in the same situation, and good people will do evil things to other good people if the situation supports those deeds (Zimbardo, Maslach, & Haney, 2000).

Like Milgram's studies, the Stanford prison experiment has been criticized on ethical grounds (De Vos, 2010; Fromm, 1973; Savin, 1973). As was the case with Milgram's participants, those in the prison experiment did not express regret and felt the study was worthwhile (Zimbardo, 2007). Perhaps you can see how cognitive dissonance might explain such responses.

Scholars have questioned whether the study provides evidence for Zimbardo's portrayal of human nature as open to shocking acts in situations that invite evil deeds (Haslam & Reicher, 2003). One study suggests that Zimbardo's participants may not have been representative of people in general. Recall that Zimbardo recruited participants with an ad that mentioned "prison life." Thomas Carnahan and Sam McFarland (2007) placed two ads in a newspaper, one that mentioned prison life and one that did not. They found that individuals who answered the first ad differed from those who answered the second: They were higher on characteristics such as aggression and exploitativeness and lower in altruism and empathy, suggesting that the volunteers for Zimbardo's study may have differed from the general public in important ways.

Still, the Stanford prison experiment is an influential study in social psychology. It continues to inform our understanding of human behavior in prison contexts (Zimbardo, 1971), including the abuses of prisoners at Abu Ghraib (Zimbardo, 2007), and to inspire controversy (McAdams, 2007).

**EXERTING PERSONAL CONTROL**  It is safe to say that as we go through life, we are both conformists and nonconformists. Sometimes we go with the flow, and other times we stand up and stand out. Our relationship to the social world is reciprocal. Individuals may try to control us, but we can exert personal control over our actions and influence others in turn (Bandura, 2007b; Knowles, Nolan, & Riner, 2007). Although it may not be easy to resist authority, living with the knowledge that you compromised your own moral integrity may be more difficult in the long run.

*Can you think of a time when you resisted conformity or obedience? Would you have obeyed in Milgram's and/or Zimbardo's experiments?*

## Group Influence

On November 19, 2011, a frantic 911 call reported that a member of Florida A&M University's famous Marching 100 ("the marchingest, playingest band in the land") had lost consciousness in the band's bus. The injured man, 26-year-old drum major Robert Champion, died that day as a result of an alleged hazing. To gain membership in an elite percussion group in the band, Champion had walked down the aisle of the charter bus that had taken the band to an away game. That passageway had become a gauntlet of punches from bandmates that Champion's body could not withstand. None of the band members disliked Champion. Certainly, none would have ever hit him or behaved aggressively toward him in any way in their daily interactions. Yet in the context of that bus on that fateful day, members of the group to which Champion, by all accounts, was wholly devoted, had beaten him to death. Why do individuals who would never perform destructive, even murderous, acts when alone perpetrate them when in a group? This central question has driven research in the social psychology of group influence.

**DEINDIVIDUATION**   One process that sheds light on the behavior of individuals in groups is **deindividuation,** which occurs when being part of a group reduces personal identity and erodes the sense of personal responsibility (Levine, Cassidy, & Jentzsch, 2010). The effects of deindividuation are visible in the wild street revelry that erupts after a team's victory in the World Series or Super Bowl, as well as in mass civic observances such as big-city Fourth of July celebrations. Deindividuation is apparent not just in the behavior of mobs. The Stanford prison experiment described earlier provides a dramatic example of how social situations and the roles we take on in life can influence deindividuation.

**deindividuation**
The reduction in personal identity and erosion of the sense of personal responsibility when one is part of a group.

One explanation for the effects of deindividuation is that groups give us anonymity. When we are part of a group, we may act in an uninhibited way because we believe that no one will be able to identify us.

**social contagion**
Imitative behavior involving the spread of behavior, emotions, and ideas.

**SOCIAL CONTAGION**   Have you ever noticed that a movie you watched in a crowded theater seemed funnier than it did when you watched the DVD alone at home? People laugh more when others are laughing. Babies cry when other babies are crying. The effects of others on our behavior can take the form of **social contagion,** imitative behavior involving the spread of behavior, emotions, and ideas (Kiuru & others, 2012; Poirier & Cobb, 2012). Social contagion effects can be observed in such varied phenomena as social fads, the popularity of dog breeds (Herzog, 2006), the spread of unhealthy behaviors such as smoking and drinking among adolescents (Rodgers, 2007), and symptoms of eating disorders among young women (Crandall, 2004; Forman-Hoffman & Cunningham, 2008).

One way to observe social contagion is to sit in a quiet but crowded library and start coughing. You will soon notice others coughing. Similarly, imagine that you are walking down the sidewalk, and you come upon a group of people who are all looking up. How likely is it that you can avoid the temptation of looking up to see what is so interesting to them?

**GROUP PERFORMANCE**   Are two or three heads better than one? Some studies reveal that we do better in groups; others show that

*The Ku Klux Klan demonstrates a variety of ways that human beings can deindividuate: turning out in groups, acting under cover of darkness, and wearing white hoods to conceal identity.*

we are more productive when we work alone (Paulus, 1989). We can make sense out of these contradictory findings by looking closely at the circumstances in which performance is being analyzed (Nijstad, 2009).

### Social Facilitation

If you have ever given a presentation in a class, you might have noticed that you did a much better job standing in front of your classmates than during any of your practice runs. **Social facilitation** occurs when an individual's performance improves because of the presence of others (Mendes, 2007). Robert Zajonc (1965) argued that the presence of other individuals arouses us. The arousal produces energy and facilitates our performance in groups. If our arousal is too high, however, we are unable to learn new or difficult tasks efficiently. Social facilitation, then, improves our performance on well-learned tasks. For new or difficult tasks, we might be best advised to work things out on our own before trying them in a group.

### Social Loafing

Another factor in group performance is the degree to which one's behavior is monitored. **Social loafing** refers to each person's tendency to exert less effort in a group because of reduced accountability for individual effort. The effect of social loafing is lowered group performance (Latané, 1981). The larger the group, the more likely it is that an individual can loaf without detection.

Social loafing commonly occurs when a group of students is assigned a class project, and it is one reason that some students intensely dislike group assignments. These same individuals will not be surprised to learn that under certain conditions, working with others can increase individual effort (J. M. Levine, 2000). For example, a person who views the group's task as important (say, a student who strongly wants an *A* on the project) and who does not expect other group members to contribute adequately is likely to work harder than usual—and perhaps to do most of the work himself or herself.

Researchers have identified ways to decrease social loafing. They include making individuals' contributions more identifiable and unique, simplifying the evaluation of these contributions, and making the group's task more attractive (Karau & Williams, 1993).

## GROUP DECISION MAKING

Many social decisions take place in groups—juries, teams, families, clubs, school boards, and the U.S. Senate, for example (Nunez, McCrea, & Culhane, 2011; Sueur, Deneubourg, & Petit, 2012). What happens when people put their minds to the task of making a group decision? How do they decide whether a criminal is guilty, whether one country should attack another country, whether a family should stay home or go on vacation, or whether sex education should be part of a school curriculum? Three aspects of group decision making bear special mention: risky shift and group polarization; groupthink; and majority and minority influence.

### Risky Shift and Group Polarization

Imagine that you have a friend, Lisa, who works as an accountant. All her life Lisa has longed to be a writer. In fact, she believes that she has the next great American novel in her head and that she just needs time and energy to devote to writing it. Would you advise Lisa to quit her job and go for it? What if you knew beforehand that her chances of success were 50-50? How about 60-40? How much risk would you advise her to take?

In one investigation, researchers asked participants to consider fictitious dilemmas like this one and asked them how much risk the characters in the dilemmas should take (Stoner, 1961). When the individuals discussed the dilemmas as a group, they were more willing to endorse riskier decisions than when they were queried alone. The so-called

**risky shift** is the tendency for a group decision to be riskier than the average decision made by the individual group members. Many studies have been conducted on this topic with similar results (Goethals & Demorest, 1995).

We do not always make riskier decisions in a group than when alone, however; hundreds of research studies show that being in a group moves us more strongly in the direction of the position we initially held (Moscovici, 1985). The **group polarization effect** is the solidification and further strengthening of an individual's position as a consequence of a group discussion or interaction. Initially held views often become more

A groupthink mentality may have caused people around Jerry Sandusky to ignore warning signs that he was abusing children.

polarized because of group discussion. Group polarization may occur because, during the discussion, people hear new, more persuasive arguments that strengthen their original position. Group polarization also might arise because of social comparison. We may find that our opinion is not as extreme as others' opinions, and we might be influenced to take a stand at least as strong as the most extreme advocate's position.

### Groupthink: Getting Along but Being Very Wrong

**Groupthink** refers to the impaired group decision making that occurs when making the right decision is less important than maintaining group harmony. Instead of engaging in an open discussion of all the available information, in groupthink, members of a group place the highest value on conformity and unanimity. Members are encouraged to "get with the program," and dissent meets with very strong disapproval.

Groupthink can result in disastrous decisions. Irving Janis (1972) introduced the concept of groupthink to explain a number of enormous decision-making errors throughout history. Such errors include the lack of U.S. preparation for the Japanese bombing of Pearl Harbor during World War II, the escalation of the Vietnam War in the 1960s, the Watergate coverup in 1974, and the *Challenger* space shuttle disaster in 1986. After the terrorist attacks of September 11, 2001, some suggested that groupthink had interfered with the proper implementation of intelligence. Whistleblower Colleen Rowley, a special agent in the Federal Bureau of Investigation (FBI), revealed that the FBI power hierarchy had been unresponsive to information that might have helped prevent the attacks. Similarly, many people criticized President George W. Bush and his cabinet for not listening to dissenting voices in the days leading up to the Iraq War.

Leaders who engage in groupthink can be at risk. Groupthink may have been the reason Hosni Mubarak, the former president of Egypt, ignored dissenting voices and did not appreciate the depth of the Egyptian people's unrest. Groupthink might also help explain the unresponsiveness of officials to allegations that former assistant football coach Jerry Sandusky of Penn State University engaged in many acts of child abuse.

Symptoms of groupthink include overestimating the power and morality of one's group, lack of willingness to hear all sides of an argument, and pressure for uniformity (Post & Panis, 2011). Groupthink can occur whenever groups value conformity over accuracy (Degnin, 2009). However, groupthink can be prevented if groups avoid isolation, allow the airing of all sides of an argument, have an impartial leader, and include outside experts in the debate; it is also critical that members who are strongly identified with the group speak out in dissent (Packer, 2009).

### Majority and Minority Influence

Most groups make decisions by voting, and, even in the absence of groupthink, the majority usually wins. The majority impacts group decision making through both informational influence (they have greater opportunity to share their views) and normative influence (they set group norms). Those who do not go along may be ignored or even given the boot.

Even so, minority opinion holders can make a difference. Because it is outnumbered, the minority cannot win through normative pressure; instead, it must apply informational pressure. If the minority presents its views consistently and confidently, then the majority is more likely to listen to the minority's perspectives. A powerful way that minority opinion holders can exert influence is by winning over former majority members to their points of view.

**groupthink**
The impaired group decision making that occurs when making the right decision is less important than maintaining group harmony.

The decision in 2011 for the Navy SEALS to conduct a raid on Osama bin Laden's compound and to assassinate him involved an open discussion. Although most of President Obama's advisors hedged their bets, Vice President Biden specifically advised against the raid, while then-CIA Director Leon Panetta explicitly recommended going in (Landler, 2012).

In crowdsourcing, individuals provide ideas to solve problems, usually through Internet sites. This way of collecting ideas is thought to reduce the kinds of group biases that exist in face-to-face groups. Are online groups more or less likely to exhibit groupthink or minority influence?

1. All of the following are related to deindividuation *except*
   A. doing something as part of a large group.
   B. hearing someone explicitly call your name and express recognition of you.
   C. losing your sense of personal responsibility while taking part in a group activity.
   D. wearing a disguise while taking part in a group activity.

2. A difference between conformity and obedience is that
   A. conformity has a stronger influence on behavior than obedience.
   B. conformity does not involve an explicit command from others.
   C. conformity happens in small groups, whereas obedience happens in large groups.
   D. conformity is based on wanting to be right; obedience is based on wanting to be liked.

3. Social contagion is
   A. the tendency of people to perform worse when in the presence of others.
   B. the rapid spread of bad ideas among the members of a group.
   C. behavior that imitates others' actions, thoughts, or emotions.
   D. the influence of minority groups on the majority group.

**APPLY IT!** 4. Serena is serving on a jury in a driving-under-the-influence case. When she first enters the jury room with the other jurors, she is pretty sure the suspect is not guilty. During deliberations, one juror points out that in his testimony, the suspect made inconsistent remarks, first saying that he'd had only one beer and later mentioning that he'd drunk whiskey that night. Serena had completely missed those details. When the jury votes, Serena finds the suspect guilty. What explains Serena's change of heart?
   A. risky shift
   B. normative social influence
   C. informational social influence
   D. groupthink

# 4 Intergroup Relations

Conflicts between groups, especially ethnic and cultural groups, are rampant around the world (Dovidio, Newheiser, & Leyens, 2012; Gelfand & others, 2012; Mambou, 2011). The Islamic terrorist organization al Qaeda attacks countries that its members perceive to be too secular and materialistic. The wronged nations retaliate. Israelis and Palestinians fight over territory in the Middle East, each claiming religious and historical rights to the disputed land. Across Africa, tribal chiefs try to establish new social orders favorable to their own rule. A variety of social psychological concepts can help us understand the intensity of such cultural and ethnic conflicts and can provide insights into how to reduce them (Maoz, 2012; Reynolds, Haslam, & Turner, 2012).

## Group Identity: Us Versus Them

Think about the groups of which you are a member—religious and social organizations, your ethnic group, your nationality. When someone asks you to identify yourself, how often do you respond by mentioning these group memberships? How much does it matter to you whether the people you associate with are members of the same groups as you?

**SOCIAL IDENTITY** Social identity refers to the way individuals define themselves in terms of their group membership. In contrast to personal identity, which can be highly individualized, social identity assumes some

**social identity**
The way individuals define themselves in terms of their group membership.

Group conflict such as that between Israelis and Palestinians in the Middle East is rampant in the world today.

| Ethnicity & Religion | Relationships | Vocations & Avocations | Political Affiliation | Stigmatized Identities |
|---|---|---|---|---|

Jewish
Asian American
Southern Baptist
West Indian

Parent
Mother
Son
Widow

Artist
Athlete
Psychologist
Military veteran

Environmentalist
Feminist
Republican

Overweight person
Person with AIDS
Homeless person
Alcoholic

**FIGURE 11.6** **Types of Social Identity** When we identify ourselves, we draw on a host of different characteristics associated with the various social groups to which we belong.

commonalities with others (Biernat & Deaux, 2012; Haslam, Reicher, & Reynolds, 2012). A person's social identity might include identifying with a religious group, a country, a social organization, a political party, and many other groups (M. Becker & others, 2012; Fleischmann, Phalet, & Klein, 2011). These diverse forms of social identity reflect the numerous ways people connect to groups and social categories (Hogg, 2012; Jaspal & Cinnirella, 2012). Social psychologist Kay Deaux (2001) identified five distinct types of social identity: ethnicity and religion, political affiliation, vocations and avocations, personal relationships, and stigmatized groups (Figure 11.6).

Ethnic identity and religious identity are central to many individuals' social identity (King, Ramos, & Clardy, 2012; Rivas-Drake, 2012). Ethnic identity can be a source of pride for individuals. In the United States, special events celebrate the rich cultural contributions of many different groups to the society. Such experiences may provide individuals with an important resource in coping with biases they may encounter in life (Crocker, Major, & Steele, 1998). Feeling connected to one's ethnic group may buffer individuals from the stressful effects of injustice (Torres, Yznaga, & Moore, 2011; Tynes & others, 2012).

Social psychologist Henry Tajfel (1978), a Holocaust survivor, wanted to explain the extreme violence and prejudice that his religious group (Jews) experienced. Tajfel's **social identity theory** states that social identity is a crucial part of self-image and a valuable source of positive feelings about oneself. To feel good about ourselves, we need to feel good about the groups to which we belong. For this reason, we invariably think of the group to which we belong as an *in-group,* a group that has special value in comparison with other groups, called *out-groups.* To improve our self-image, we continually compare our in-groups with out-groups (Parks, 2007). In the process, we often focus more on the differences between the two groups than on their similarities.

Research by Tajfel (1978), along with that by many others who have used his theory, showed how easy it is to lead people to think in terms of "us" and "them." In one experiment, Tajfel had participants look at a screen featuring a huge number of dots and estimate how many dots were displayed. He then assigned the participants to groups based on whether they overestimated or underestimated the number of dots. Once assigned to one of the two groups, the participants were asked to award money to other participants. Invariably, individuals awarded money only to members of their own group. If we favor the members of a group that was formed on such trivial bases, it is no wonder that we show intense in-group favoritism when differences are not so trivial.

**ETHNOCENTRISM** The tendency to favor one's own ethnic group over other groups is called **ethnocentrism.** Ethnocentrism does not simply mean taking pride in one's group; it also involves asserting the group's superiority over other groups. As such, ethnocentrism encourages in-group/out-group, we/they thinking (Dovidio & others, 2012). Consequently, ethnocentrism implies that ethnic out-groups are not simply different; they are worse than one's group. Hence, ethnocentrism may underlie prejudice.

**social identity theory**
The view that social identity is a crucial part of self-image and a valuable source of positive feelings about oneself.

**ethnocentrism**
The tendency to favor one's own ethnic group over other groups.

*Such groups are referred to as minimal groups because group assignment is arbitrary and meaningless.*

*As noted in the description of altruism, there may be a thin line between positive feelings and behaviors toward one's own group and hostile feelings and behaviors toward out-groups.*

# Prejudice

**prejudice**
An unjustified negative attitude toward an individual based on the individual's membership in a group.

**Prejudice** is an unjustified negative attitude toward an individual based on the individual's membership in a group. The group can be made up of people of a particular ethnicity, sex, age, religion—essentially, people who are different in some way from a prejudiced person (Billig, 2012). Prejudice can be seen in many eruptions of hatred in human history. In the Balkan Peninsula of eastern Europe, Serbs were so prejudiced against Bosnians that they pursued a policy of "ethnic cleansing." Hutus in Rwanda were so prejudiced against Tutsis that they went on a murderous rampage, hacking off their arms and legs with machetes.

A powerful example of destructive prejudice within U.S. society is racial prejudice against African Americans. When Africans were brought to colonial America as slaves, they were considered property and treated inhumanely. In the first half of the twentieth century, most African Americans still lived in the South and remained largely segregated from White society by law.

Despite progress in racial equality over the years, a much higher percentage of African Americans than non-Latino Whites still live in impoverished neighborhoods and lack access to good schools, jobs, and healthcare, even decades after the abolition of legal segregation. Research continues to demonstrate the influence of race in U.S. life. In one study, Marianne Bertrand and Sendhil Mullainathan (2004) sent out 5,000 résumés in response to 1,200 job ads placed in newspapers in Chicago and Boston. They constructed résumés so that applicants were identical in qualifications but differed in how stereotypically White or Black their names sounded. "White" names included Meredith, Emily, Brad, and Greg. "Black" names included Tamika, Lakisha, Darnell, and Kareem. The researchers found that even with identical qualifications, the applicants with White-sounding names were 50 percent more likely to be called for an interview.

**RECENT STUDIES ON RACIAL PREJUDICE**    In a recent study, Jean Braucher, Dov Cohen, and Robert Lawless (2012) examined the way race influenced the advice attorneys gave clients filing for bankruptcy. During the recent financial crisis, many Americans have turned to filing bankruptcy to handle their financial problems. Declaring bankruptcy means that a person is admitting that he or she is unable to repay debts. This legal claim can allow individuals to start the long process of regaining financial solvency. The two ways of declaring bankruptcy are Chapter 7 and Chapter 13. Chapter 7 bankruptcy is less expensive and often less burdensome than Chapter 13. Chapter 13 may allow a person to retain ownership of some possessions (such as a home), but it can involve years of abiding by a very difficult schedule of repayment.

In an analysis of bankruptcy cases across the United States, Braucher, Cohen, and Lawless found that African Americans were more likely than non-Latino Whites to file Chapter 13 rather than Chapter 7 bankruptcy. Why would individuals choose a more difficult and expensive form of bankruptcy? Could attorneys be steering African Americans toward this more burdensome path? To address this question, the researchers conducted an experiment involving a random sample of bankruptcy lawyers. Participants read scenarios in which potential clients were identified as either "Reggie and Latisha" or "Todd and Alison." Even when all other aspects of the cases were identical, lawyers were more likely to recommend that Todd and Alison declare Chapter 7 and that Reggie and Latisha pursue Chapter 13. The researchers suggest that these differences might not reflect intentional biases but instead subtle and potentially unconscious racial biases. The potentially unconscious nature of racism in modern life is a challenge for researchers interested in understanding and reducing prejudice.

Want to participate in a social psychological experiment? You can do so online. Hundreds of studies are available at www.socialpsychology.org.

Because racial prejudice is socially unacceptable, few people today would readily admit to racist or prejudicial views. In a CNN poll (2006), 88 percent of individuals answered no to the question "Are you racist?" It is not clear whether such results reflect genuine feelings or simply the recognition of this shifting social standard. Today, prejudiced individuals are more likely than before to appear unprejudiced on the surface while nevertheless holding racist views at a deeper level (Sears, 2008; Sears & Henry, 2007). As in the study by Braucher and others, individuals may not be consciously aware of their own racial biases, or of their gender or age biases for that matter.

To confront this problem, social psychologists examine prejudicial attitudes on two levels—explicit or overt racism and implicit or covert racism. *Explicit racism* is a person's conscious and openly shared racist attitudes, which might be measured using a questionnaire. *Implicit racism* refers to racial attitudes that exist on a deeper, hidden level. Implicit attitudes require measures that do not rely on awareness, such as the Implicit Associations Test (IAT), a computerized survey that assesses the ease with which respondents can associate a Black or a White person with good things (for example, flowers) or bad things (for example, misery) (Greenwald & others, 2009; Nosek & Banaji, 2007; Sriram & Greenwald, 2009). The IAT assumes that preexisting biases make it easier to associate some social stimuli with positive rather than negative items. Although the IAT is widely used, some scholars have raised concerns about its validity (Blanton & others, 2009).

In one study, a sample of non-Latino White college students completed measures of explicit and implicit attitudes toward African Americans using an implicit measure similar to the IAT (Dovidio, Kawakami, & Gaertner, 2002). The students then interacted with a Black partner. Explicit prejudice predicted what people said to a person of a different race—that is, students who said they were not prejudiced were unlikely to say overtly racist things and how friendly the students felt they had behaved toward their Black partner. However, implicit prejudice related to nonverbal aspects of the interaction, such as how close the students sat to their partners, as well as their facial expressions.

**FACTORS IN PREJUDICE** Social psychologists have explored why people develop prejudice. Competition between groups, especially when resources are scarce, can contribute to prejudice. For example, competition between immigrants and established low-income members of a society for jobs

*What are your attitudes toward individuals of an ethnic background different from your own? How do these attitudes compare with those of your parents?*

can lead to prejudice. Cultural learning is also clearly involved. Children can adopt the prejudicial attitudes of their families and friends before they even meet a person from an out-group. In addition, when people feel bad about themselves, they might bolster their self-esteem by demeaning out-group members.

A final factor that might underlie prejudice comes from the limits on our information-processing abilities. Human beings are limited in their capacity for effortful thought, but they face a complex social environment. To simplify the challenge of understanding others' behavior, people use categories or stereotypes. Stereotypes can be a powerful force in developing and maintaining prejudicial attitudes.

**STEREOTYPING AND PREJUDICE**   Recall that stereotypes are generalizations about a group that deny variations within the group. Researchers have found that we are less likely to detect variations among individuals who belong to "other" groups than among individuals who belong to "our" group. So, we might see the people in our in-group as varied, unique individuals while viewing the members of out-groups as all the same. Thinking that "they all look alike" can be a particular concern in the context of eyewitness identification (Brigham, 1986). At the root of prejudice is a particular kind of stereotype: a generalization about a group that contains negative information that is applied to all members of that group (Wetherell, 2012).

**discrimination**
An unjustified negative or harmful action toward a member of a group simply because the person belongs to that group.

**DISCRIMINATION**   **Discrimination** refers to an unjustified negative or harmful action toward a member of a group simply because the person belongs to that group. Discrimination results when negative emotional reactions combine with prejudicial beliefs and are translated into behavior (Bergman & others, 2012; D. R. Williams & others, 2012). Many forms of discrimination are illegal in the U.S. workplace. Since the Civil Rights Act of 1964 (revised in 1991), it has been unlawful to deny someone employment on the basis of gender or ethnicity (Parker, 2006).

**sexual harassment**
Unwelcome behavior or conduct of a sexual nature that offends, humiliates, or intimidates another person.

A particular form of discrimination is **sexual harassment,** unwelcome behavior or conduct of a sexual nature that offends, humiliates, or intimidates another person. In the workplace and schools, sexual harassment includes unwanted sexual advances, requests for sexual favors, and other verbal or physical conduct of a sexual nature against an employee's, a teacher's, or a peer's wishes (Glick & Fiske, 2012; Nielsen & Einarsen, 2012). In the United States, sexual harassment is an illegal form of sexual discrimination. Victims include not only the person harassed but also anyone affected by the offensive conduct. For example, a man who works in a setting in which women are routinely demeaned may experience the environment as a toxic place to work.

# Ways to Improve Intergroup Relations

*Although legal segregation is no longer permitted, voluntary segregation continues. Look around your classrooms and dining halls. Do you see students separating themselves by ethnic categories? How does this convention impede intergroup relations, and how might it be broken?*

Martin Luther King, Jr., said, "I have a dream that my four little children will one day live in a nation where they will not be judged by the color of their skin but by the content of their character." How might we attain the world that King envisioned?

One way might be for people to come to know one another better so that they can get along. However, in daily life many people interact with individuals from other ethnic groups, and this contact does not necessarily lead to tolerance or warm relations. Indeed, researchers have consistently found that contact by itself—attending the same school or working in the same company—does not necessarily improve relations among people of different ethnic backgrounds. So, rather than focusing on contact per se, researchers have examined how *various features* of a contact situation may be optimal for reducing prejudice and promoting intergroup harmony (Stott, Drury, & Reicher, 2012; Vezzali & others, 2012).

Studies have shown that contact is more effective if the people involved think that they are of equal status, feel that an authority figure sanctions their positive relationships, and believe that friendship might emerge from the interaction (Pettigrew & Tropp, 2006). Another important feature of optimal intergroup contact is *task-oriented cooperation*—working together on a shared goal.

An example of the power of task-oriented cooperation is Muzafer Sherif's Robbers Cave Study. It may be hard to imagine in our post-*Survivor* era, but even before Jeff Probst started handing out color-coded "buffs" on the TV show *Survivor,* Sherif and his colleagues (1961) had the idea of exploring group processes by assigning 11-year-old boys to two competitive groups (the "Rattlers" and the "Eagles") in a summer camp called Robbers Cave. Sherif, disguised as a janitor so that he could unobtrusively observe the Rattlers and the Eagles, arranged for the two groups to compete in baseball, touch football, and tug-of-war. If you have watched reality television, you have some idea how this experiment went. In short order, relations between the groups got down-right ugly. Members of each group expressed negative opinions of members of the other group, and the Rattlers and Eagles became battling factions. What would bring these clashing groups together? Sherif created tasks that required the joint efforts of both groups, such as working together to repair the camp's only water supply and pooling their money to rent a movie. When the groups were required to work cooperatively to solve problems, the Rattlers and Eagles developed more positive relationships. Figure 11.7 shows how competitive and cooperative activities changed perceptions of the out-group.

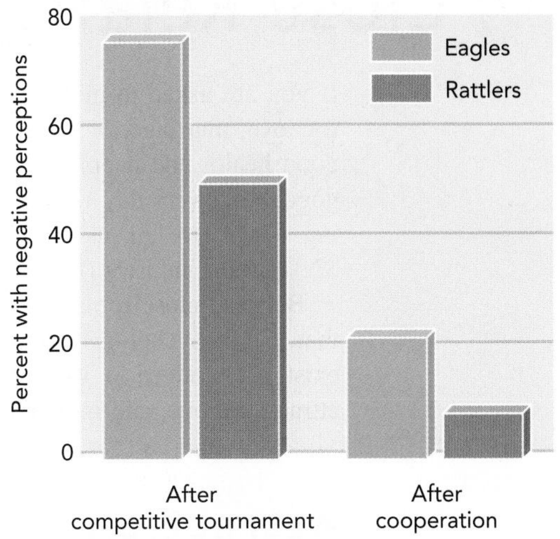

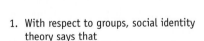

**FIGURE 11.7** **Attitudes Toward the Out-Group Following Competitive and Cooperative Activities** This graph shows the negative feelings expressed by members of the Eagles and Rattlers toward the other group after a competitive tournament and cooperative activity. > *When did hostility between the groups peak? When did it drop?* > *In your own life, what examples are there of holding particular attitudes toward a group different from your own? How have your attitudes changed, and what events preceded those changes?* > *What is up with the Eagles? What are some reasons why they might be more negative about the Rattlers?*

1. With respect to groups, social identity theory says that
   A. groups naturally cooperate with one another.
   B. members of the in-group feel positively about members of the out-group.
   C. groups tend to highlight the differences rather than the similarities between themselves.
   D. group membership has little to do with our sense of self.

2. All of the following statements are true about ethnocentrism *except*
   A. ethnocentrism involves asserting one group's superiority over other groups.
   B. ethnocentrism leads to we-versus-they thinking.

   C. ethnocentrism is unrelated to prejudice.
   D. ethnocentrism is related to group pride.

3. A White woman says she is not racist but avoids sitting near Black individuals. She has
   A. high explicit racism, low implicit racism.
   B. high explicit racism, high implicit racism.
   C. low explicit racism, low implicit racism.
   D. low explicit racism, high implicit racism.

APPLY IT! 4. Will is bothered by the way students segregate themselves in the campus commons, with all the African American

students generally eating in one area, the Latinos in another, the Asians in another, and the non-Latino Whites in another. Bill starts the Students Together program to get students to interact more and to promote interethnic harmony. Which of the following strategies is most likely to work, based on the social psychological evidence?
   A. Assign seats in the lunchroom so that students have to sit with members of other ethnic groups.
   B. Identify problems of common interest to students of all groups and initiate ethnically diverse discussion groups aimed at solving those problems.
   C. Post signs in the commons that encourage interethnic contact.
   D. None of the above, because nothing will work.

# 5 Close Relationships

If you are asked to make three wishes for anything at all, chances are that one will be for love, marriage, or a partner to share your life (King & Broyles, 1997). Along with good health and happiness, close relationships figure prominently in most notions of a good life. Every day we see commercials lauding the ability of this or that Internet dating service to link us up with the love of our life. Online dating services represent a $2.1 billion industry (DatingSitesReviews.com, 2012).

Because close romantic relationships are so crucial for most of us, it is no wonder that social psychologists should be interested in studying this fascinating aspect of human existence. Indeed, a vast literature has accumulated in social psychology, examining attraction, love, and intimacy.

## Attraction

At the beginning of this chapter, we considered one key factor in interpersonal attraction, namely, physical attractiveness. Research on interpersonal attraction has illuminated a variety of other factors that play a role in the process of becoming attracted to someone.

### PROXIMITY, ACQUAINTANCE, AND SIMILARITY

Even in the age of Internet dating, it is very unlikely that you are going to become attracted to someone without meeting the person. *Proximity,* or physical closeness, is a strong predictor of attraction. You are more likely to become attracted to an individual you pass in the hall every day than someone you rarely see. One potential mechanism for the role of proximity in attraction is the mere exposure effect (Zajonc, 1968, 2001). The **mere exposure effect** means that the more we encounter someone or something (a person, a word, an image), the more likely we are to start liking the person or thing even if we do not realize we have seen it before.

We are not only more likely to be attracted to people whom we have seen before, but also more likely to like someone if we are led to believe we will be meeting that person. Let's say you are sitting in a room and an experimenter tells you there are two strangers next door, one of whom you will be meeting and the other not. Research shows that you are likely to begin to like the first person, in anticipation of your interaction (Insko & Wilson, 1977). In addition, if you find out that someone whom you do not yet know already likes you, that is a sure sign that you will find yourself attracted to that person.

Similarity also plays an important role in attraction (Qian, 2009). We have all heard that opposites attract, but what is true of magnets is not typically true of human beings. We like to associate with people who are similar to us (Berscheid, 2000). Our friends and lovers are much more like us than unlike us: We share with them similar attitudes, behavior patterns, taste in clothes, intelligence, personality, other friends, values, lifestyle, and physical attractiveness.

The concept of *consensual validation* explains why people are attracted to others who are similar to them. Our own attitudes and behavior are supported when someone else's attitudes and behavior are similar to ours—their attitudes and behavior validate ours. Another reason that similarity matters is that we tend to shy away from the unknown. Similarity implies that we will enjoy doing things with another person who has similar tastes and attitudes.

*Potential matchmakers, take note: If you want to pair up two friends in a romantic relationship, tell each of them how much the other liked his or her Facebook page.*

**mere exposure effect**
The phenomenon that the more individuals encounter someone or something, the more probable it is that they will start liking the person or thing even if they do not realize they have seen it before.

*"When I said in my on-line profile that I was athletic, I meant that I like **watching** sports!"*

Used by permission of CartoonStock, www.CartoonStock.com.

**EVOLUTIONARY APPROACHES TO ATTRACTION** Evolutionary psychologists focus on gender differences in the variables that account for attraction (Buss, 2012). Evolutionary psychologists argue that women and men have faced different pressures in the course of human evolution (Geary, 2006). They stress that the sexes' different statuses in reproduction are the key to understanding how this evolution took place (Buss, 2012).

From the perspective of evolutionary psychology, the goal for both men and women is to procreate—to produce children. For men, this evolutionary task is complicated by the fact that in the human species, paternity is somewhat more mysterious than motherhood. To be sure that a woman is not already pregnant with another man's child, evolutionary psychologists say, men should be more strongly attracted to younger women. Youth is also likely to indicate a woman's fertility. For women, the task of producing offspring is an innately difficult one. Although a man might focus on quantity of sexual partners, a woman must focus on quality and search for a mate who will invest his resources in her and her offspring (Caporeal, 2007).

Personal ads show evidence of these evolutionary differences. When men place ads seeking women, they typically look for youth and beauty (a potential proxy for health and fertility) and offer tangible resources—for example, by describing themselves as a "professional homeowner" (Buss, 2012). When women place ads seeking men, they are more likely to offer youth and beauty and to seek resources. The personal ads of gay men and lesbians offer an intriguing context for consideration. In general, research has shown that gay men seek youth and beauty, whereas lesbians seek personal qualities such as stability and a sense of humor. Evolutionary thinkers suggest that such results provide evidence for strong sex-linked adaptive patterns.

Critics of evolutionary psychology theory argue that humans have the decision-making ability to change their gender behavior and thus are not locked into their evolutionary past. They cite extensive cross-cultural variation in gender behavior and mate preference as proof that social experience affects gender behavior (Matlin, 2012). For example, Alice Eagly's (2010, 2012) *social role view of gender* asserts that social, not evolutionary, experiences have led to differences in gender behavior. The social role approach acknowledges the biological differences between men and women but stresses the ways these differences are played out in a range of cultures and societal contexts. Indeed, in cultures that view the sexes more equally, women appear to be less likely to prefer mates with economic resources (Kasser & Sharma, 1999).

# Attachment

Romantic partners fulfill some of the same needs for adults as parents do for their children (Nosko & others, 2011; Shaver & Mikulincer, 2013). Recall from Chapter 8 that *securely attached* infants are defined as those who use the caregiver as a secure base from which to explore the environment. Similarly, adults may count on their romantic partners to be a secure base to which they can return and obtain comfort and security in stressful times.

Adults' attachment is categorized as secure, avoidant, or anxious:

- **Secure attachment style:** Securely attached adults have positive views of relationships, find it easy to get close to others, and are not overly concerned with or stressed out about their romantic relationships. These adults tend to enjoy sexuality in the context of a committed relationship and are less likely than others to have one-night stands.
- **Avoidant attachment style:** Avoidant individuals are hesitant about getting involved in romantic relationships and once in a relationship tend to distance themselves from their partner.
- **Anxious attachment style:** These individuals demand closeness, are less trusting, and are more emotional, jealous, and possessive.

The majority of adults (about 60 to 80 percent) describe themselves as securely attached, and not surprisingly adults prefer having a securely attached partner (Zeifman & Hazan, 2008).

**anxious attachment style**
An attachment style that describes adults who demand closeness, are less trusting, and are more emotional, jealous, and possessive.

**secure attachment style**
An attachment style that describes adults who have positive views of relationships, find it easy to get close to others, and are not overly concerned or stressed out about their romantic relationships.

**avoidant attachment style**
An attachment style that describes adults who are hesitant about getting involved in romantic relationships and once in a relationship tend to distance themselves from their partner.

The following recent studies confirmed the importance of attachment in adults' lives:

■ Securely attached individuals had more positive romantic relationships (Holland & Roisman, 2010).

■ Anxiously attached individuals showed strong ambivalence toward a romantic partner (Mikulincer & others, 2010) and were more ambivalent about relationship commitment than their securely attached counterparts (Joel, MacDonald, & Shimotomai, 2011).

■ A national survey indicated that insecurely attached (avoidant and anxious) adults were more likely to develop diseases and chronic illnesses, especially cardiovascular problems such as high blood pressure, heart attack, and stroke (McWilliams & Bailey, 2010).

Attachment categories are somewhat stable in adulthood, but adults do have the capacity to change their attachment thinking and behavior. Although attachment insecurities are linked to relationship problems, attachment style is only one of various factors that contribute to relationship functioning, satisfaction, and success (Shaver & Mikulincer, 2013).

## Love

Some relationships never progress much beyond the attraction stage. Others deepen to include attachment to friends and lovers (Berscheid, 2010). Here we consider two types of love: romantic and affectionate.

Poets, playwrights, and songwriters through the ages have celebrated the fiery passion of romantic love—and lamented the searing pain when it fails. Think about songs and books that hit the top of the charts. Chances are, they are about romantic love.

**romantic love**
Love with strong components of sexuality and infatuation, often predominant in the early part of a love relationship; also called passionate love.

**Romantic love,** also called *passionate love,* is love with strong components of sexuality and infatuation, and it often predominates in the early part of a love relationship (Berscheid, 2010). Ellen Berscheid (1988) says that it is romantic love we mean when we say that we are "in love" with someone. It is romantic love that she believes we need to understand if we are to learn what love is all about. Berscheid judges sexual desire to be the most important ingredient of romantic love. Although we often think of romantic love as a "chick thing," men, not women, are the ones who fall in love more quickly and easily (Dion & Dion, 2001; Harrison & Shortall, 2011).

Love is more than just passion, however. **Affectionate love,** also called *companionate love,* is the type of love that occurs when an individual has a deep, caring affection for another person and desires to have that person near. There is a growing belief that the early stages of love have more romantic ingredients and that as love matures, passion tends to give way to affection (Berscheid & Regan, 2005).

**affectionate love**
Love that occurs when an individual has a deep, caring affection for another person and desires to have that person near; also called companionate love.

## Models of Close Relationships

*As love matures, romantic love tends to evolve into affectionate love.*

Once people are in a relationship, what predicts whether they are happy and stay together or ultimately separate? Social psychologists have approached this question in various ways. Here we review two of these theories: social exchange theory and the investment model.

**SOCIAL EXCHANGE THEORY** The social exchange approach to close relationships focuses on the costs and benefits of one's romantic partner. **Social exchange theory** is based on the idea of social relationships as involving an exchange of goods, the objective of which is to minimize costs and maximize benefits. From this

**social exchange theory**
The view of social relationships as involving an exchange of goods, the objective of which is to minimize costs and maximize benefits.

perspective, the most important predictor of relationship success is *equity*—that is, having both partners feel that each is doing his or her "fair share." Essentially, social exchange theory asserts that we keep a mental balance sheet, tallying the pluses and minuses associated with our romantic partner—what we put in ("I paid for our last date") and what we get out ("He brought me flowers").

As relationships progress, however, equity may no longer apply. Happily married couples are less likely to keep track of "what I get versus what I give," and they avoid thinking about the costs and benefits of their relationships (Buunk & Van Yperen, 1991; Clark & Chrisman, 1994).

**THE INVESTMENT MODEL**    Another way to think about long-term romantic relationships is to focus on the underlying factors that characterize stable, happy relationships compared to others. The **investment model** examines the ways that commitment, investment, and the availability of attractive alternative partners predict satisfaction and stability in relationships (Rusbult, Agnew, & Arriaga, 2012). From this perspective, long-term relationships are likely to continue when both partners are committed to, and have invested a great deal in, the relationship and when there are few tempting alternatives—other attractive partners—around.

Commitment to the relationship is especially important and predicts a willingness to sacrifice for a romantic partner. In one study, individuals were given a chance to climb up and down a short staircase, over and over, so that their partner would not have to do so. Those who were more committed to their partner worked harder to climb up and down repeatedly, to spare their loved one the burden (Van Lange & others, 1997).

A loving intimate relationship is surely a part of most notions of a fulfilling life. In every couple, two individuals come together. In turn, each couple is embedded in a social network, including their families, friends, and the social groups and societies to which they belong. Social psychologists are dedicated to understanding these many and varied social forces and their influence on people's lives and behavior.

**investment model** A model of long-term relationships that examines the ways that commitment, investment, and the availability of attractive alternative partners predict satisfaction and stability in relationships.

*Think of long-term couples you know in which one partner remains committed even when the benefits are hard to see, as when a person's romantic partner is gravely ill for a long time.*

**self-quiz**

1. With regard to happy relationships, social exchange theory tells us that
   A. we are happiest when we are giving in a relationship.
   B. we are happiest when we are receiving in a relationship.
   C. we are happiest when there is a balance between giving and receiving in a relationship.
   D. equity is important to happiness only in long-lasting relationships.

2. Consensual validation would predict
   A. that opposites attract.
   B. that relationships with more give and take are best.
   C. that we are attracted to people who are similar to us.
   D. that romantic love is more important than affectionate love.

3. Affectionate love is more common _____, whereas romantic love is more common _____.
   A. in men; in women
   B. in women; in men
   C. early in a relationship; later in a relationship
   D. later in a relationship; early in a relationship

**APPLY IT!** 4. Daniel and Alexa have been dating for two years. Alexa meets a new guy during spring break and cheats on Daniel. When she tells Daniel about it, he is crushed but forgives her. He reasons that because the two of them have worked together on their relationship for two years, it makes no sense to throw it all away based on one mistake. Which theory would predict that Daniel is likely to cheat on Alexa in the future?
   A. the investment model
   B. social exchange theory
   C. evolutionary theory
   D. theory of affectionate love

## SUMMARY

### ① Social Cognition

The face conveys information to social perceivers, including attractiveness. Self-fulfilling prophecy means that our expectations of others can have a powerful impact on their behavior.

Attributions are our thoughts about why people behave as they do and about who or what is responsible for the outcome of events. Attribution

theory views people as motivated to discover the causes of behavior as part of their effort to make sense of it. The dimensions used to make sense of the causes of human behavior include internal/external, stable/unstable, and controllable/uncontrollable.

The fundamental attribution error is observers' tendency to overestimate traits and to underestimate situations when they explain an actor's behavior. Self-serving bias means attributing our successes to internal causes and blaming our failures on external causes. Heuristics are used as shortcuts in social information processing. One such heuristic is a stereotype—a generalization about a group's characteristics that does not consider any variations among individuals in the group.

The self is our mental representation of our own characteristics. Self-esteem is important and is related to holding unrealistically positive views of ourselves. Stereotype threat is an individual's fast-acting, self-fulfilling fear of being judged based on a negative stereotype about his or her group. To understand ourselves better, we might engage in social comparison, evaluating ourselves by comparison with others.

Attitudes are our feelings about people, objects, and ideas. We are better able to predict behavior on the basis of attitudes when an individual's attitudes are strong, when the person is aware of his or her attitudes and expresses them often, and when the attitudes are specifically relevant to the behavior. Sometimes changes in behavior precede changes in attitude.

According to cognitive dissonance theory, our strong need for cognitive consistency causes us to change our behavior to fit our attitudes or to change our attitudes to fit our behavior. Self-perception theory stresses the importance of making inferences about attitudes by observing our own behavior, especially when our attitudes are not clear.

## ② Social Behavior

Altruism is an unselfish interest in helping someone else. Reciprocity often is involved in altruism. Individuals who are in a good mood are more helpful. Empathy is also linked to helping. The bystander effect means that individuals who observe an emergency help less when someone else is present than when they are alone.

Women are more likely to help in situations that are not dangerous and involve caregiving. Men are more likely to help in situations that involve danger or in which they feel competent.

One view of the biological basis of aggression is that early in human evolution, the most aggressive individuals were likely to be the survivors. Neurobiological factors involved in aggressive behavior include the neurotransmitter serotonin and the hormone testosterone. Psychological factors in aggression include frustrating and aversive circumstances. Sociocultural factors include cross-cultural variations, the culture of honor, and violence in the media. The question of whether men or women are more aggressive depends on the particular *type* of aggression that is involved.

## ③ Social Influence

Conformity involves a change in behavior to coincide with a group standard. Factors that influence conformity include informational social influence (going along to be right) and normative social influence (going along to be liked).

Obedience is behavior that complies with the explicit demands of an authority. Milgram's classic experiment demonstrated the power of obedience. Another such demonstration is the Stanford prison experiment,

illustrating the potential effects of obedience not only on individuals who obey but also on those who exercise authority.

People often change their behaviors when they are in a group. Deindividuation refers to the lack of inhibition and diffusion of responsibility that can occur in groups. Social contagion refers to imitative behaviors involving the spread of behavior, emotions, and ideas. Our performance in groups can be improved through social facilitation and lowered because of social loafing.

Risky shift refers to the tendency for a group decision to be riskier than the average decision made by the individual group members. The group polarization effect is the solidification and further strengthening of a position as a consequence of group discussion or interaction. Groupthink involves impaired decision making and avoidance of realistic appraisal to maintain harmony in the group.

## ④ Intergroup Relations

Social identity is our definition of ourselves in terms of our group memberships. Social identity theory states that when individuals are assigned to a group, they invariably think of it as the in-group. Identifying with the group allows the person to have a positive self-image. Ethnocentrism is the tendency to favor one's own ethnic group over others.

Prejudice is an unjustified negative attitude toward an individual based on membership in a group. The underlying reasons for prejudice include the presence of competition between groups over scarce resources, a person's motivation to enhance his or her self-esteem, cognitive processes that tend to categorize and stereotype others, and cultural learning. Prejudice is also based on stereotypes. The cognitive process of stereotyping can lead to discrimination, an unjustified negative or harmful action toward a member of a group simply because he or she belongs to that group. Discrimination results when negative emotional reactions combine with prejudicial beliefs and are translated into behavior.

An effective strategy for enhancing the effects of intergroup contact is to set up task-oriented cooperation among individuals from different groups.

## ⑤ Close Relationships

We tend to be attracted to people whom we see often, whom we are likely to meet, and who are similar to us. Romantic love (passionate love) includes feelings of infatuation and sexual attraction. Affectionate love (companionate love) is more akin to friendship and includes deep, caring feelings for another. Adult attachments are categorized as secure, avoidant, or anxious. A secure attachment style is linked with positive aspects of relationships.

Social exchange theory states that a relationship is likely to be successful if individuals feel that they get out of the relationship what they put in. The investment model focuses on commitment, investment, and the availability of attractive alternatives in predicting relationship success.

---

### KEY TERMS

social psychology, p. 401
stereotype, p. 402
attribution theory, p. 403

fundamental attribution error, p. 403
false consensus effect, p. 404

positive illusions, p. 404
self-serving bias, p. 405
stereotype threat, p. 405

social comparison, p. 405
attitudes, p. 406
cognitive dissonance, p. 406

self-perception theory, p. 407
elaboration likelihood
    model, p. 408
altruism, p. 410
egoism, p. 410
empathy, p. 411
bystander effect, p. 412
aggression, p. 412
overt aggression, p. 416

relational aggression, p. 416
conformity, p. 418
informational social
    influence, p. 419
normative social influence, p. 419
obedience, p. 422
deindividuation, p. 425
social contagion, p. 425
social facilitation, p. 426

social loafing, p. 426
risky shift, p. 426
group polarization effect, p. 426
groupthink, p. 427
social identity, p. 428
social identity theory, p. 429
ethnocentrism, p. 429
prejudice, p. 430
discrimination, p. 432

sexual harassment, p. 432
mere exposure effect, p. 434
secure attachment style, p. 435
avoidant attachment style, p. 435
anxious attachment style, p. 435
romantic love, p. 436
affectionate love, p. 436
social exchange theory, p. 436
investment model, p. 437

# SELF-TEST

## Multiple Choice

1. Which of the following is *true* about stereotypes?
   A. Stereotypes take mental effort.
   B. Stereotypes are accurate.
   C. Stereotypes do not account for individual variation.
   D. Stereotypes are always negative.

2. Believing that everyone shares the same view as you is known as
   A. the availability heuristic.
   B. the false consensus effect.
   C. a stereotype.
   D. stereotype threat.

3. If 10 people are competing as one team in a tug-of-war contest, their combined effort level is likely to be
   A. more than the sum of their individual abilities.
   B. less than the sum of their individual abilities.
   C. the same as the sum of their individual abilities.
   D. the same as the sum of their individual abilities for men, but less than the sum of their individual abilities for women.

4. Despite evidence to the contrary, Denise thinks she is smarter than most others in her class. Denise's unfounded attitude about herself is an example of
   A. a positive illusion.
   B. a self-serving bias.
   C. a negative illusion.
   D. a self-fulfilling prophecy.

5. "Am I as popular as Cathy?" This question is an example of gaining self-knowledge through the process of
   A. peer review.
   B. peripheral attribute.
   C. wishful thinking.
   D. social comparison.

6. Marilyn smokes; however, she is well aware of the negative health consequences of smoking. As a result, Marilyn feels guilty about smoking. Marilyn is most likely experiencing
   A. effort justification.
   B. a negative illusion.
   C. a fundamental attribution error.
   D. cognitive dissonance.

7. Having negative views of an out-group is
   A. explicit bias.
   B. implicit bias.
   C. prejudice.
   D. discrimination.

8. A defining characteristic of groupthink is
   A. accurate decision making.
   B. decisions that are more extreme than normal.
   C. the discouragement of minority viewpoints.
   D. group discord.

9. The results of the Milgram study are disturbing because
   A. the majority of participants who went all the way to 450 volts did so quite happily.
   B. Milgram violated the ethical principles of his time.
   C. the experimenter had no real power to force the subjects to comply.
   D. the subjects volunteered to be the "teacher" rather than the "learner."

10. Conclusions about human nature drawn from the Stanford prison experiment have been called into question because
    A. the ad recruiting participants may have led to a biased sample.
    B. the prisoners admitted later that they were only faking.
    C. the study was unethical.
    D. participants were assigned to roles of prisoner or guard based on psychological characteristics.

## Apply It!

11. Organizations are using the Internet as a way to put many heads together to solve problems. This technique, called *crowdsourcing,* involves posting problems to the Internet and having huge numbers of individuals post their solutions to the problems. Evaluate the possible effectiveness of crowdsourcing. Is it more likely or less likely to demonstrate processes such as social loafing, social facilitation, group polarization, and groupthink than face-to-face group interactions? Why?

atypical behavior abnormal, though, when it deviates from what is acceptable in a culture. A woman who washes her hands three or four times an hour and takes seven showers a day is abnormal because her behavior deviates from culturally acceptable norms.

- Abnormal behavior is *maladaptive*. Maladaptive behavior interferes with one's ability to function effectively in the world. A man who believes that he can endanger others through his breathing may go to great lengths to isolate himself from people for what he believes is their own good. His belief negatively affects his everyday functioning; thus, his behavior is maladaptive. Behavior that presents a danger to the person or those around him or her is also considered maladaptive (and abnormal).

- Abnormal behavior is *personally distressful* over a long period of time. The person engaging in the behavior finds it troubling. A woman who secretly makes herself vomit after every meal may never be seen by others as deviant (because they do not know about it), but this pattern of behavior may cause her to feel intense shame, guilt, and despair.

*Context matters! If the woman who washes her hands three or four times an hour and takes repeated showers works in a sterile lab with toxic chemicals or live viruses, her behavior might be quite adaptive.*

*Which of these three qualities—deviation from what is acceptable, maladaptiveness, and personal distress—do you think is most important to calling a behavior abnormal? Why?*

# Culture, Context, and the Meaning of Abnormal Behavior

*Consider, for instance, that a symptom of one of Sigmund Freud's most famous patients, Anna O., was that she was not interested in getting married.*

Because culture establishes the norms by which people evaluate their own and others' behaviors, culture is at the core of what it means to be normal or abnormal (Ago-rastos, Haasen, & Huber, 2012). In evaluating behavior as normal or abnormal, culture matters in complex ways (Sue & others, 2013). Cultural norms provide guidance about how people should behave and what behavior is healthy or unhealthy. Importantly, however, cultural norms can be mistaken. One only has to watch an episode of *Mad Men* to recognize that at one time cigarette smoking was not only judged to be an acceptable habit but also promoted as a healthy way to relax. The point is, definitions of *normal* change as society changes.

Significant, too, is the fact that cultural norms can be limiting, oppressive, and preju-dicial (Potter, 2012). Individuals who fight to change the established social order some-times face the possibility of being labeled deviant—and even mentally ill. In the late nineteenth and early twentieth centuries, for instance, women in Britain who dem-onstrated for women's right to vote were widely viewed to be mentally ill. When a person's or a group's behavior challenges social expectations, we must open our minds to the possibility that such actions are in fact an adaptive response to injustice. People may justifiably challenge what everyone thinks is true and may express ideas that seem strange. They should be able to make others feel uncomfortable without being labeled abnormal.

Further, as individuals move from one culture to another, interpretations and evaluations of their behavior must take into account the norms in their culture of origin (Bourque & others, 2012; John & others, 2012). His-torically, people entering the United States from other countries were examined at Ellis Island, and many were judged to be mentally impaired simply because of differences in their language and customs.

Cultural variation in what it means to be normal or abnormal makes it very difficult to compare different psychological disorders across different cultures. Many of the diagnostic categories we trace in this chapter primar-ily reflect Western (and often U.S.) notions of normality, and applying these to other cultures can be misleading and even inappropriate (Agorastos, Haasen, & Huber, 2012). Throughout this chapter, we will see how culture influences the experience of psychological disorders.

## Do It!

Spend 15 to 20 minutes observing an area with a large number of people, such as a mall, a cafeteria, or a stadium during a game. Identify and make a list of behaviors you would classify as abnormal. How does your list of behaviors compare with the definition of *abnormal* provided above? What would you change in the list if you were in a different setting, such as a church, a bar, or a library? What does this exercise tell you about the meaning of *abnormal*?

# Theoretical Approaches to Psychological Disorders

What causes people to develop a psychological disorder, that is, to behave in deviant, maladaptive, and personally distressful ways? Theorists have suggested various approaches to this question.

**THE BIOLOGICAL APPROACH**  The *biological approach* attributes psychological disorders to organic, internal causes. This perspective primarily focuses on the brain, genetic factors, and neurotransmitter functioning as the sources of abnormality.

The biological approach is evident in the **medical model,** which describes psychological disorders as medical diseases with a biological origin. From the perspective of the medical model, abnormalities are called "mental illnesses," the afflicted individuals are "patients," and they are treated by "doctors."

**medical model**
The view that psychological disorders are medical diseases with a biological origin.

**THE PSYCHOLOGICAL APPROACH**  The *psychological approach* emphasizes the contributions of experiences, thoughts, emotions, and personality characteristics in explaining psychological disorders. Psychologists might focus, for example, on the influence of childhood experiences, personality traits, learning experiences, or cognitions in the development and course of psychological disorders.

**THE SOCIOCULTURAL APPROACH**  The *sociocultural approach* emphasizes the social contexts in which a person lives, including gender, ethnicity, socioeconomic status, family relationships, and culture. For instance, poverty is related to rates of psychological disorders (Jeon-Slaughter, 2012; Rosenthal & others, 2012).

The sociocultural perspective stresses the ways that cultures influence the understanding and treatment of psychological disorders. The frequency and intensity of psychological disorders vary and depend on social, economic, technological, and religious aspects of cultures (Matsumoto & Juang, 2013). Some disorders are culture-related, such as *windigo,* a disorder recognized by northern Algonquian Native American groups that involves fear of being bewitched and turned into a cannibal.

Importantly, different cultures may interpret the same pattern of behaviors in very different ways. When psychologists look for evidence of the occurrence of a particular disorder in different cultures, they must keep in mind that behaviors associated with a disorder might not be labeled as illness or dysfunction within a particular cultural context. Cultures might have their own interpretations of these behaviors, so researchers must probe whether locals ever observe these patterns of behavior, even if they are not considered illness (Draguns & Tanaka-Matsumi, 2003). For example, in one study researchers interviewed a variety of individuals in Uganda to see whether dissociative disorders, including dissociative identity disorder (which you might know as multiple personality disorder), existed in that culture (Van Duijl, Cardeña, & de Jong, 2011). They found that while most dissociative disorders were recognizable to Ugandans, the local healers consistently labeled what Westerners consider dissociative identity disorder as a spirit possession.

**THE BIOPSYCHOSOCIAL MODEL**  Abnormal behavior can be influenced by biological factors (such as genes), psychological factors (such as childhood experiences), and sociocultural factors (such as gender). These factors can operate alone, but they often act in combination with one another.

To appreciate how these factors work together, let's back up for a moment. Consider that not everyone with a genetic predisposition to schizophrenia develops the disorder. Similarly, not everyone who experiences childhood neglect develops depression. Moreover, even women who live in cultures that strongly discriminate against them do not always develop psychological disorders. Thus, to understand the development of psychological disorders, we must consider a variety of interacting factors from each of the domains of experience.

Sometimes this approach is called *biopsychosocial.* From the biopsychosocial perspective, none of the factors considered is necessarily viewed as more important than another; rather, biological, psychological, and social factors are all significant ingredients in producing both normal and abnormal behavior. Furthermore, these ingredients may combine in unique ways, so that one depressed person might differ from another in terms of the key factors associated with the development of the disorder.

## Classifying Abnormal Behavior

To understand, prevent, and treat abnormal behavior, psychiatrists and psychologists have devised systems classifying those behaviors into specific psychological disorders. Classifying psychological disorders provides a common basis for communicating. If one psychologist says that her client is experiencing depression, another psychologist understands that a particular pattern of abnormal behavior has led to this diagnosis. A classification system can also help clinicians predict how likely it is that a particular disorder will occur, which individuals are most susceptible to it, how the disorder progresses, and what the prognosis (or outcome) for treatment is (Birgegård, Norring, & Clinton; Skodol, 2012a, 2012b).

Further, a classification system may benefit the person suffering from psychological symptoms. Having a name for a problem can be a comfort and a signal that treatments are available. On the other hand, officially naming a problem can also have serious negative implications for the person because of the potential for creating *stigma,* a mark of shame that may cause others to avoid or to act negatively toward an individual. Being diagnosed with a psychological disorder can profoundly influence a person's life because of what the diagnosis means with respect to the person and his or her family and larger social world. We discuss stigma further at the end of this chapter.

**THE *DSM-IV* CLASSIFICATION SYSTEM**   In 1952, the American Psychiatric Association (APA) published the first major classification of psychological disorders in the United States, the *Diagnostic and Statistical Manual of Mental Disorders.* Its current version, the ***DSM-IV*** (APA, 1994), was introduced in 1994 and revised in 2000, producing the *DSM-IV-TR* (text revision) (APA, 2000). *DSM-V* is due in 2013.

*The DSM-IV was the work of more than 200 mental health professionals, including more women, ethnic minorities, and non-psychiatrists than any previous version.*

Throughout the development of the *DSM,* the number of diagnosable disorders has increased dramatically. The first *DSM* listed 112 disorders; the *DSM-IV-TR* includes 374.

The *DSM-IV* classifies individuals on the basis of five dimensions, or *axes,* that take into account the individual's history and highest level of functioning in the previous year. The system's creators meant to ensure that the individual is not merely assigned to a psychological disorder category but instead is characterized in terms of a number of factors. The five axes of *DSM-IV* are:

*Axis I:* All diagnostic categories except personality disorders and mental retardation

*Axis II:* Personality disorders and mental retardation

*Axis III:* General medical conditions

*Axis IV:* Psychosocial and environmental problems

*Axis V:* Current level of functioning

Axes I and II are concerned with the classification of psychological disorders. Figure 12.1 describes the major categories of these disorders. Axes III through V may not be needed to diagnose a psychological disorder, but they are included so that the person's overall

***DSM-IV***
The *Diagnostic and Statistical Manual of Mental Disorders,* Fourth Edition; the major classification of psychological disorders in the United States.

| Major Categories of Psychological Disorders | Description |
|---|---|
| **Axis I Disorders** | |
| Disorders usually first diagnosed in infancy, childhood, or adolescence and communication disorders | Include disorders that appear before adolescence, such as attention deficit hyperactivity disorder, autism, and learning disorders (stuttering, for example). |
| Anxiety disorders | Characterized by motor tension, hyperactivity, and apprehensive expectations/thoughts. Include generalized anxiety disorder, panic disorder, phobic disorder, obsessive-compulsive disorder, and post-traumatic stress disorder. |
| Somatoform disorders | Occur when psychological symptoms take a physical form even though no physical causes can be found. Include hypochondriasis and conversion disorder. |
| Factitious disorders | Characterized by the individual's deliberate fabrication of a medical or mental disorder, but not for external gain (such as a disability claim). |
| Dissociative disorders | Involve a sudden loss of memory or change of identity. Include the disorders of dissociative amnesia, dissociative fugue, and dissociative identity disorder. |
| Delirium, dementia, amnesia, and other cognitive disorders | Consist of mental disorders involving problems in consciousness and cognition, such as substance-induced delirium or dementia related to Alzheimer disease. |
| Mood disorders | Disorders in which there is a primary disturbance in mood; include depressive disorders and bipolar disorder (which involves wide mood swings from deep depression to extreme euphoria and agitation). |
| Schizophrenia and other psychotic disorders | Disorders characterized by distorted thoughts and perceptions, odd communication, inappropriate emotion, and other unusual behaviors. |
| Substance-related disorders | Include alcohol-related disorders, cocaine-related disorders, hallucinogen-related disorders, and other drug-related disorders. |
| Sexual and gender identity disorders | Consist of three main types of disorders: gender-identity disorders (person is not comfortable with identity as a female or male), paraphilias (person has a preference for unusual sexual acts to stimulate sexual arousal), and sexual dysfunctions (impairments in sexual functioning). |
| Eating disorders | Include anorexia nervosa, bulimia nervosa, and binge eating disorder. |
| Sleep disorders | Consist of primary sleep disorders, such as insomnia and narcolepsy (see Chapter 4), and sleep disorders due to a general medical condition. |
| Impulse control disorders not elsewhere classified | Include kleptomania, pyromania, and compulsive gambling. |
| Adjustment disorders | Characterized by distressing emotional or behavioral symptoms in response to an identifiable stressor. |
| **Axis II Disorders** | |
| Mental retardation | Low intellectual functioning and an inability to adapt to everyday life (see Chapter 7). |
| Personality disorders | Develop when personality traits become inflexible and maladaptive. Include antisocial personality disorder and borderline personality disorder. |
| Other conditions that may be a focus of clinical attention | Include relational problems (with a partner, sibling, and so on), problems related to abuse or neglect (physical abuse of a child, for example), or additional conditions (such as bereavement, academic problems, religious or spiritual problems). |

**FIGURE 12.1** **Main Categories of Psychological Disorders in the *DSM-IV*** The *DSM-IV* provides a way for mental health professionals and researchers to communicate with one another about these well-defined psychological disorders.

life situation is considered. Axis III information helps to clarify whether symptoms may be rooted in physical illness. On Axis V, the clinician evaluates the highest level of adaptive functioning the person has attained in the preceding year in social, occupational, or school activities.

**CRITIQUES OF THE *DSM-IV*** A number of criticisms of the *DSM-IV* have been voiced (Frances & Widiger, 2012; Robbins & others, 2012; Trull & others, 2012). Most controversial is the fact that the manual classifies individuals based on their symptoms, using medical terminology in the psychiatric tradition of thinking about mental disorders in terms of disease (Oltmanns & Emery, 2013). This emphasis implies that the abnormalities have an internal cause that is relatively independent of environmental factors (Kring & others, 2007). So, even though researchers have begun to shed light on the complex interaction of genetic, neurobiological, cognitive, and environmental factors in psychological disorders, the *DSM-IV* continues to reflect the medical model (APA, 2006). That said, some biological factors, such as brain processes and pathways, also are not adequately reflected in *DSM-IV* categories (Robbins & others, 2012).

Another criticism is that the *DSM-IV* focuses strictly on pathology and problems. Critics argue that emphasizing *strengths* as well as weaknesses might help to destigmatize labels such as "schizophrenic." Indeed, professionals avoid such labels, using what is called *people-first language*. Bill Garrett, whom you met in the chapter-opening vignette, is a "person with schizophrenia," not a "schizophrenic." Identifying a person's strengths can be an important step toward maximizing his or her ability to contribute to society (Compton & Hoffman, 2013; Roten, 2007).

Among the proposed changes for the *DSM-V,* expected in May 2013, are (APA, 2012):

- A new category, *behavioral addictions,* with one main disorder: gambling
- A new category, *binge eating disorder,* and improved diagnostic criteria for anorexia nervosa and bulimia nervosa
- A new category, *mood dysregulation,* among mood disorders
- Improved diagnostic criteria for identifying adolescents and adults most at risk for suicide
- A new category, *risk syndromes,* to help mental health professionals make earlier diagnoses of some disorders, such as dementias and psychoses
- A change in the terminology: *mental retardation* to *intellectual disability*
- Elimination of 4 or 5 of the 10 categories of personality disorders

**attention deficit hyperactivity disorder (ADHD)**
One of the most common psychological disorders of childhood, in which individuals show one or more of the following: inattention, hyperactivity, and impulsivity.

Some of these proposed revisions have come under fire (Skodol, 2012a, 2012b). The criticisms include (Frances & Widiger, 2012):

- Diagnostic inflation, with too many new categories that do not yet have consistent research support and would lead to a significant increase in the number of people being labeled as having a mental disorder
- Concern that some of the proposed new categories, such as mood dysregulation, will increase what is already an overuse of antipsychotic drugs in treating children
- Lower thresholds for some existing categories—such as attention deficit hyperactivity disorder (ADHD), generalized anxiety disorder, and post-traumatic stress disorder—that would add to the already very high rates of such disorders

However, labels such as those described by the *DSM-IV* and those proposed for the *DSM-V* are based on the idea that psychological disorders are real and often medically treatable. Some individuals have questioned this very assumption. Over 50 years ago, in his book *The Myth of Mental Illness,* psychiatrist Thomas Szasz argued that psychological disorders are not illnesses and are better labeled "problems of living." Szasz said that it makes no sense to refer to a person's problems of living as "mental illness" and to treat him or her through a medical model. To consider these issues in the context of an increasingly common psychological disorder, see Challenge Your Thinking.

# Challenge

## Does *Everyone* Have ADHD?

Perhaps no diagnosis is more controversial these days than **attention deficit hyperactivity disorder (ADHD)**, in which individuals, prior to the age of 7, show one or more of the following symptoms: inattention, hyperactivity, and impulsivity. Chances are you know someone who suffers from ADHD. You might even have it yourself.

ADHD is one of the most common psychological disorders of childhood, with diagnoses skyrocketing in recent years. In 1988 just 500,000 cases of ADHD were diagnosed, but by 2007, that number had jumped to 4 million per year (Bloom & Cohen, 2007). In 2010, 10.4 million children were diagnosed with ADHD (Garfield & others, 2012). Although experts previously thought that most children "grow out" of ADHD, more recent evidence suggests that as many as 70 percent of adolescents (Sibley & others, 2012) and 66 percent of adults (Asherson & others, 2010) who were diagnosed as children continue to experience ADHD symptoms. Many professionals believe that adult ADHD should be recognized as a psychological disorder in its own right (Kooij & others, 2010), and changing the age for diagnosis with ADHD is one of the proposed revisions for the *DSM-V*.

The sheer number of ADHD diagnoses has prompted speculation that psychiatrists, parents, and teachers are in fact labeling normal childhood behavior as psychopathology (Morrow & others, 2012). One reason for concern about overdiagnosing ADHD is that the form of treatment in well over 80 percent of cases is psychoactive drugs, including stimulants such as Ritalin and Adderall (Garfield & others, 2012). Animal research has shown that in the absence of ADHD, exposure to such stimulants can predispose individuals to later addiction problems (Leo, 2005). Those who question the diagnosis of ADHD in children find it equally problematic in adults (Marcus, Norris, & Coccaro, 2012). These scholars argue that the spread of ADHD is primarily a function of over-pathologizing normal behavior, confusing ADHD for other disorders, and aggressive marketing by pharmaceutical companies (Moncrieff & Timimi, 2010).

A recent study sheds some light on the controversy. Child psychologists, psychiatrists, and social workers were sent vignettes of cases of children in which symptoms were described (Brüchmiller, Margraf, & Schneider, 2012), and were asked to diagnose the children. Some of the descriptions fit the diagnostic criteria for ADHD, but others lacked key features of the disorder. In addition, in the case vignettes, the researchers varied whether the child

was identified as male or female. The dependent variable was whether these professionals gave a diagnosis of ADHD to a case. The results showed that participants *overdiagnosed* ADHD, giving an ADHD diagnosis to cases that specifically lacked important aspects of the disorder about 17 percent of the time. Further, regardless of symptoms, boys were two times more likely than girls to receive such a diagnosis. An important lesson from this study is that professionals must be vigilant in their application of diagnostic criteria as they encounter different cases. The results also demonstrate how even professionals can fall prey to certain biases.

Certainly, individuals who experience ADHD have symptoms that make adjustment difficult, so it is critical that diagnosis of the disorder be accurate. Children diagnosed with ADHD are at heightened risk of dropping out of school, teen pregnancy, and antisocial behavior (Barkley & others, 2002; von Polier, Vloet, & Herpertz-Dahlmann, 2012). Adolescents and adults with ADHD symptoms are more likely to experience difficulties at work, while driving a car, and in interpersonal relationships; they are also more likely to have substance abuse problems (Chang, Lichtenstein, & Larsson, 2012; Kooij & others, 2010; Sibley & others, 2012).

ADHD is not the only controversial diagnosis; nor is this psychological disorder the only one given a great deal of attention by pharmaceutical companies (Mash & Wolfe, 2013). Drug companies commonly fund research that focuses on a disease model of psychological disorders. Clearly, psychological disorders are "real" in the sense that they lead to objectively negative outcomes in people's lives. The controversy over ADHD is a reminder of the important role of psychology research in clarifying and defining diagnostic categories. Indeed, the aim of the profession is to avoid inappropriately labeling, misdiagnosing, and mistreating people who are already suffering.

### What Do You Think?

■ Would ADHD be as controversial if the treatment did not involve drugs? Why or why not?

■ Do you think ADHD would be diagnosed as often as it is if drugs were not readily available for its treatment?

■ If a teacher suggested that your child be tested for ADHD, what would you do?

Before we begin our survey of various psychological disorders, a word of caution. It is very common for individuals who are learning about psychological disorders to recognize the symptoms and behaviors of disorders in themselves or in people around them. Keep in mind that only trained professionals can diagnose a psychological disorder.

self quiz

1. All of the following are characteristics of abnormal behavior *except*
   A. it is typical.
   B. it causes distress.
   C. it is maladaptive.
   D. it is deviant.

2. The medical model interprets psychological disorders as medical diseases with a/an
   A. environmental origin.
   B. sociocultural origin.
   C. biological origin.
   D. biopsychosocial origin.

3. Mental retardation is classified on _____ of the *DSM-IV.*
   A. Axis I
   B. Axis II
   C. Axis III
   D. Axis IV

**APPLY IT!** 4. Since she was a little girl, 19-year-old Francesca has believed that whenever she walks through a doorway, she must touch the doorframe 12 times and silently count to 12 or else her mother will die. She has never told anyone about this ritual, which she feels is harmless, similar to carrying a lucky charm. Which of the following is true of Francesca's behavior?
   A. Francesca's behavior is abnormal only because it is different from the norm. It is not maladaptive, nor does it cause her distress.
   B. Francesca's behavior fits all three characteristics of abnormal behavior.
   C. Francesca's behavior is maladaptive, but it is not abnormal because she does not feel personal distress over her ritual.
   D. Francesca's behavior does not fit any of the characteristics of abnormal behavior.

# 2 Anxiety Disorders

Think about how you felt before a make-or-break exam or a big presentation—or perhaps as you noticed police lights flashing behind your speeding car. Did you feel jittery and nervous and experience tightness in your stomach? These are the feelings of normal anxiety, an unpleasant feeling of fear and dread.

**anxiety disorders**
Disabling (uncontrollable and disruptive) psychological disorders that feature motor tension, hyperactivity, and apprehensive expectations and thoughts.

In contrast, **anxiety disorders** involve fears that are uncontrollable, disproportionate to the actual danger the person might be in, and disruptive of ordinary life. They feature motor tension (jumpiness, trembling), hyperactivity (dizziness, a racing heart), and apprehensive expectations and thoughts. In this section we examine five types of anxiety disorders:

- Generalized anxiety disorder
- Panic disorder
- Phobic disorder
- Obsessive-compulsive disorder
- Post-traumatic stress disorder

## Generalized Anxiety Disorder

**generalized anxiety disorder**
Psychological disorder marked by persistent anxiety for at least 6 months, and in which the individual is unable to specify the reasons for the anxiety.

When you are worrying about getting a speeding ticket, you know why you are anxious; there is a specific cause. **Generalized anxiety disorder** is different from such everyday feelings of anxiety in that sufferers experience persistent anxiety for at least 6 months and are unable to specify the reasons for the anxiety (Freeman & Freeman, 2012). People with generalized anxiety disorder are nervous most of the time. They may worry about their work, relationships, or health. That worry can also take a physical toll and cause fatigue, muscle tension, stomach problems, and difficulty sleeping.

What is the etiology of generalized anxiety disorder? (*Etiology* means the causes or significant preceding conditions.) Among the biological factors are genetic predisposition, deficiency in the neurotransmitter GABA, and respiratory system abnormalities

(Boschen, 2012). The psychological and sociocultural factors include having harsh (or even impossible) self-standards, overly strict and critical parents, automatic negative thoughts when feeling stressed, and a history of uncontrollable traumas or stressors (such as an abusive parent).

*Recall from Chapter 2 that GABA is the neurotransmitter that inhibits neurons from firing—it's like the brain's brake pedal. Problems with GABA are often implicated in anxiety disorders.*

## Panic Disorder

Much like everyone else, you might sometimes have a specific experience that sends you into a panic. For example, you work all night on a paper, only to have your computer crash before you saved your last changes, or you are about to dash across a street just when you see a large truck coming right at you. Your heart races, your hands shake, and you might break into a sweat.

**panic disorder**
Anxiety disorder in which the individual experiences recurrent, sudden onsets of intense terror, often without warning and with no specific cause.

In a **panic disorder,** however, a person experiences recurrent, sudden onsets of intense terror, often without warning and with no specific cause. Panic attacks can produce severe palpitations, extreme shortness of breath, chest pains, trembling, sweating, dizziness, and a feeling of helplessness (Oral & others, 2012). People with panic disorder may feel that they are having a heart attack or going to die.

During a panic attack, the brain registers fear as areas of the fear network of the limbic system, including the amygdala and hippocampus, are activated (Holzschneider & Mulert, 2011). Charles Darwin, the scientist who proposed the theory of evolution, suffered from intense panic disorder (Barloon & Noyes, 1997). Southern cooking icon Paula Deen and former NFL running back Earl Campbell also have dealt with this disorder.

*A panic attack can be a one-time occurrence. People with panic disorder have recurrent attacks that sometimes cause them to be afraid to even leave their homes, a condition called agoraphobia.*

What is the etiology of panic disorder? Theories of the origins of panic attack take into account biological, psychological, and sociocultural factors (Pilecki, Arentoft, & McKay, 2011). In terms of biological factors, individuals may have a genetic predisposition to the disorder (Bayoglu & others, 2012). Of particular interest to researchers are genes that direct the action of neurotransmitters such as norepinephrine (Buttenschøn & others, 2011) and GABA (Thoeringer & others, 2009). Another brain chemical, *lactate,* which plays a role in brain metabolism, has been found to be elevated in individuals with panic disorder (Maddock & others, 2009). Further, experimental research has shown that increasing lactate levels can produce panic attacks (Reiman & others 1989). Other research points to the involvement of a wider range of genes and bodily systems, implicating genes involved in hormone regulation (Wilson, Markie, & Fitches, 2012) and responses to stress (Esler & others, 2009).

With respect to psychological influences, learning processes, as described in Chapter 5, are one factor that has been considered in panic disorder. Classical conditioning research has shown that learned associations between bodily cues of respiration and fear can play a role in panic attacks (Acheson, Forsyth, & Moses, 2012). Interestingly, carbon dioxide ($CO_2$) has been found to be a very strong conditioned

*Many experts interpret Edvard Munch's painting* The Scream *as an expression of the terror brought on by a panic attack.*

*An earlier explanation of panic attack was called the* **suffocation false alarm theory.** *Can you see why it was initially proposed?*

stimulus for fear, suggesting that humans may be *biologically prepared* to learn an association between high concentrations of $CO_2$ and fear (Acheson, Forsyth, & Moses, 2012; De Cort & others, 2012; Nardi & others, 2006; Schenberg, 2010). Thus, some learning researchers have suggested that at the heart of panic attacks are the learned associations between $CO_2$ and fear (De Cort & others, 2012).

In addition, the learning concept of *generalization* may apply to panic attack. Recall that in classical conditioning, generalization means showing a conditioned response (in this case, fear) to conditioned stimuli other than the particular one used in learning. Research shows that individuals who suffer from panic attacks are more likely to display overgeneralization of fear learning (Lissek & others, 2010). Why might those who suffer from panic attacks be more likely to show stronger and more generalized fear associations? One possibility is that the biological predispositions as well as early experiences with traumatic life events may play a role in setting the stage for such learning (Pilecki, Arentoft, & McKay, 2011).

*Whenever you encounter gender differences in this discussion, ask yourself whether men or women might be more likely* **to report** *having problems or* **to seek treatment.** *Research on psychological disorders is often based on individuals who have reported symptoms or sought help. If men are less likely to report symptoms or seek treatment, the data may underestimate the occurrence of psychological disorders in men.*

In terms of sociocultural factors, in the United States, women are twice as likely as men to have panic attacks (Altemus, 2006). Possible reasons include biological differences in hormones and neurotransmitters (Altemus, 2006; Fodor & Epstein, 2002). Compared to men, women are more likely to complain of distressing respiratory experiences during panic attacks (Sheikh, Leskin, & Klein, 2002). Interestingly, a recent study showed that healthy women are more likely to experience panic-related emotions when exposed to air enriched with $CO_2$ (Nillni & others, 2012).

Research also suggests that women may cope with anxiety-provoking situations differently than men do, and these differences may explain the gender difference in panic disorder (Schmidt & Koselka, 2000; Viswanath & others, 2012). Panic attack has been observed in a variety of cultures, though there are some cultural differences in the experience of these attacks (Agorastos, Haasen, & Huber, 2012). For instance, in Korea, panic attacks are less likely to include a fear of dying than is the case in other societies (Weissman & others, 1995).

# Phobic Disorder

*"Stephen's fear of heights is particularly bad today."*

Used by permission of CartoonStock, www.CartoonStock.com.

Many people are afraid of spiders and snakes; indeed, thinking about letting a tarantula crawl over one's face is likely to give anyone the willies. It is not uncommon to be afraid of particular objects or specific environments such as extreme heights. For most of us, these fears do not interfere with daily life. Some of us, however, have an irrational, overwhelming, persistent fear of a particular object or situation—an anxiety disorder called a **phobic disorder (phobia).** Whereas individuals with generalized anxiety disorder cannot pinpoint the cause of their nervous feelings, individuals with phobias can.

A fear becomes a phobia when a situation is so dreaded that an individual goes to almost any length to avoid it. As with any anxiety disorder, phobias are fears that are uncontrollable, disproportionate, and disruptive. A snake phobia that keeps a city-dweller from leaving his apartment is clearly disproportionate to the actual chances of encountering a snake. John Madden— former NFL coach, recently retired football commentator, and successful video game consultant—has a famous fear of flying that led him to take a bus to the games that he broadcast.

Anxiety is a universal emotion, and phobias have been found in many cultures. Culture, though, may play a role in the object of

**phobic disorder (phobia)**
Anxiety disorder characterized by an irrational, overwhelming, persistent fear of a particular object or situation.

| Acrophobia | Fear of high places | Arachnophobia | Fear of spiders | Mysophobia | Fear of dirt |
| Aerophobia | Fear of flying | Astrapophobia | Fear of lightning | Nyctophobia | Fear of darkness |
| Ailurophobia | Fear of cats | Cynophobia | Fear of dogs | Ophidiophobia | Fear of nonpoisonous snakes |
| Algophobia | Fear of pain | Gamophobia | Fear of marriage | | |
| Amaxophobia | Fear of vehicles, driving | Hydrophobia | Fear of water | Thanatophobia | Fear of death |
| | | Melissophobia | Fear of bees | Xenophobia | Fear of strangers |

**FIGURE 12.2** **Phobias** This figure features examples of phobic disorder—an anxiety disorder characterized by irrational and overwhelming fear of a particular object or situation.

a particular phobia. For example, *koro* is a phobia that is found in Malaysia and Indonesia, and some forms also appear in South China and parts of Africa. This phobia involves abject terror among men that their genitals are shrinking into their bodies (Agorastos, Haasen, & Huber, 2012). Koro is often accompanied by a strong terror that one is going to die.

Another phobic disorder, *social phobia,* is an intense fear of being humiliated or embarrassed in social situations (Pull, 2012). Singers Carly Simon and Barbra Streisand have dealt with social phobia. Social phobia is recognized in many cultures, but it appears in a different form in collectivistic cultures. In Japan and Korea, for instance, social phobia often involves being afraid not of doing something embarrassing but of insulting or harming another person (Agorastos, Haasen, & Huber, 2012). Researchers have found that East Asians are more likely to have social anxiety than North Americans (Hsu & others, 2012).

Phobias usually begin in childhood (National Institute of Mental Health, 2008) and come in many forms. Figure 12.2 labels and describes a number of phobias.

What is the etiology of phobic disorder? Genes appear to play a role in social phobia (Reich, 2009). Researchers have proposed that there is a neural circuit for social phobia that includes the thalamus, amygdala, and cerebral cortex (Damsa, Kosel, & Moussally, 2009). Also, a number of neurotransmitters may be involved in social phobia, especially serotonin (Nash & Nutt, 2005).

With regard to psychological factors, learning theorists consider phobias learned fears (Vriends & others, 2012). Perhaps, for example, the individual with the fear of falling off a building experienced a fall from a high place earlier in life and therefore associates heights with pain (a classical conditioning explanation). Alternatively, he or she may have heard about or watched others who demonstrated terror of high places (an observational learning explanation), as when a little girl develops a fear of heights after sitting next to her terrified mother and observing her clutch the handrails, white-knuckled, as the roller coaster creeps steeply uphill.

*Systematic desensitization, described in Chapter 13, involves the application of learning principles to the unlearning of phobias.*

## Obsessive-Compulsive Disorder

Just before leaving on a long road trip, you find yourself checking to be sure you locked the front door. As you pull away in your car, you are stricken with the thought that you

*"I gotta go—we're discussing my compulsive communications disorder."*

Used by permission of CartoonStock, www.CartoonStock.com.

**EXPERIENCE IT!**
Obsessive-Compulsive
Disorder

*As long as the person performs the ritual, she never finds out that the terrible outcome doesn't happen. The easing of the anxiety exemplifies* **negative reinforcement** *(having something bad taken away after performing a behavior).*

forgot to turn off the coffeemaker. Going to bed the night before an early flight, you check your alarm clock a few times to be sure you will wake up on time. These are examples of normal checking behavior.

In contrast, the anxiety disorder known as **obsessive-compulsive disorder (OCD)** features anxiety-provoking thoughts that will not go away and/or urges to perform repetitive, ritualistic behaviors to prevent or produce some future situation. *Obsessions* are recurrent thoughts, and *compulsions* are recurrent behaviors. Individuals with OCD dwell on their doubts and repeat their routines sometimes hundreds of times a day (Yap, Mogan, & Kyrios, 2012). The most common compulsions are excessive checking, cleansing, and counting. Game show host Howie Mandel has coped with OCD, as have soccer star David Beckham, singer-actor Justin Timberlake, and actress Jessica Alba. Obsessive-compulsive symptoms have been found in many cultures, and culture plays a role in the content of obsessive thoughts or compulsive behaviors (Matsunaga & Seedat, 2011).

An individual with OCD might believe that she has to touch the doorway with her left hand whenever she enters a room and count her steps as she walks. If she does not complete this ritual, she may be overcome with a sense of fear that something terrible will happen (Victor & Bernstein, 2009).

What is the etiology of obsessive-compulsive disorder? In terms of biological factors, there seems to be a genetic component (Alonso & others, 2012; Angoa-Perez & others, 2012). Also, brain-imaging studies have suggested neurological links for OCD (Hou & others, 2012; Stern & others, 2012). One neuroscientific analysis is that the frontal cortex or basal ganglia are so active in OCD that numerous impulses reach the thalamus, generating obsessive thoughts or compulsive actions (Rotge & others, 2009).

In one study, fMRI was used to examine the brain activity of individuals with OCD before and after treatment (Nakao & others, 2005). Following effective treatment, a number of areas in the frontal cortex showed decreased activation. Interestingly, the amygdala, which is associated with the experience of anxiety, may be smaller in individuals with OCD compared to those who do not have the disorder (Atmaca & others, 2008). Low levels of the neurotransmitters serotonin and dopamine likely are involved in the brain pathways linked with OCD (Goljevscek & Carvalho, 2011; Soomro, 2012).

In terms of psychological factors, OCD sometimes occurs during a period of life stress such as that surrounding the birth of a child or a change in occupational or marital status (Uguz & others, 2007). According to the cognitive perspective, what differentiates individuals with OCD from those who do not have it is the ability to turn off negative, intrusive thoughts by ignoring or effectively dismissing them (Leahy, Holland, & McGinn, 2012; C. Williams, 2012).

**obsessive-compulsive disorder (OCD)**
Anxiety disorder in which the individual has anxiety-provoking thoughts that will not go away and/or urges to perform repetitive, ritualistic behaviors to prevent or produce some future situation.

## Post-Traumatic Stress Disorder

If you have ever been in even a minor car accident, you may have had a nightmare or two about it. You might have even found yourself reliving the experience for some time. This normal recovery process takes on a particularly devastating character in post-traumatic stress disorder. **Post-traumatic stress disorder (PTSD)** is an anxiety disorder that develops through exposure to a traumatic event that overwhelms the person's abilities to cope (Beidel, Bulik, & Stanley, 2012). The symptoms of PTSD vary but include:

**post-traumatic stress disorder (PTSD)**
Anxiety disorder that develops through exposure to a traumatic event, a severely oppressive situation, cruel abuse, or a natural or an unnatural disaster.

- Flashbacks in which the individual relives the event. A flashback can make the person lose touch with reality and reenact the event for seconds, hours, or, very rarely, days. A person having a flashback—which can come in the form of images, sounds, smells, and/or feelings—usually believes that the traumatic event is happening all over again (Brewin, 2012).

- Avoiding emotional experiences and avoiding talking about emotions with others.

- Reduced ability to feel emotions, often reported as feeling numb, resulting in an inability to experience happiness, sexual desire, or enjoyable interpersonal relationships.

## The Psychological Wounds of War

**P**TSD has been a concern for soldiers who have served in Iraq and Afghanistan (Klemanski & others, 2012; Yoder & others, 2012). In an effort to prevent PTSD, the U.S. military gives troops stress-management training before deployment (Ritchie & others, 2006). Branches of the armed forces station mental health professionals in combat zones around the world to help prevent PTSD and to lessen the effects of the disorder (Rabasca, 2000). These measures appear to be paying off: Researchers have found that PTSD sufferers from the Iraq and Afghanistan wars are generally less likely to be unemployed or incarcerated and more likely to maintain strong social bonds following their term of service than veterans of earlier wars (Fontana & Rosenheck, 2008).

Historically, the stigma associated with psychological disorders has been especially strong within the military ranks, where struggling with a psychological problem is commonly viewed as a sign of weakness or incompetence (Warner & others, 2011). Yet individuals engaged in combat are at considerable risk of developing PTSD, and the disorder can profoundly affect their lives. A survey of almost 3,000 soldiers who had just returned from the Iraq War revealed that 17 percent met the criteria for PTSD (Hoge & others, 2007). This figure is likely an underestimate given the stigma linked to psychological disorders in the military.

In 2008, military psychologist John Fortunato suggested that veterans with PTSD ought to be eligible for the Purple Heart, the prestigious military decoration awarded to those who have been physically wounded or killed in combat (Schogol, 2009). Awarding PTSD sufferers the Purple Heart, Fortunato argued, would not only acknowledge their sacrifice but also reduce the stigma attached to psychological disorders. That year, the military did consider whether PTSD sufferers in its ranks ought to be awarded the Purple Heart. However, the Pentagon decided against awarding the Purple Heart to military personnel with PTSD on the grounds that the disorder is not limited to victims of physical trauma from enemy fire but also can affect eyewitnesses (Schogol, 2009). Still, the fact that the top brass considered the possibility suggests that the military is becoming more aware of the serious problems facing those who are traumatized while serving their country in combat.

- Excessive arousal, resulting in an exaggerated startle response or an inability to sleep.
- Difficulties with memory and concentration.
- Feelings of apprehension, including nervous tremors.
- Impulsive outbursts of behavior, such as aggressiveness, or sudden changes in lifestyle.

PTSD symptoms can follow a trauma immediately or after months or even years (Solomon & others, 2012). Most individuals who are exposed to a traumatic event experience some of the symptoms in the days and weeks following exposure (National Center for PTSD, 2012). However, not every individual exposed to the same event develops PTSD (Brewin & others, 2012; Nemeroff & others, 2006).

*Prior to deployment, U.S. troops receive stress-management training aimed at helping to prevent PTSD and other disorders that might be triggered by the high-stress conditions of war.*

Researchers have examined PTSD associated with various experiences (Harder & others, 2012). These include combat and war-related traumas (Khamis, 2012), sexual abuse and assault (S. Y. Kim & others, 2012), natural disasters such as hurricanes and earthquakes (Sezgin & Punamaki, 2012), and unnatural disasters such as plane crashes and terrorist attacks (Luft & others, 2012).

Clearly, one cause of PTSD is the traumatic event itself (Risbrough & Stein, 2012). However, because not everyone who experiences the same traumatic life event develops PTSD, other factors, aside from the event, must influence a person's vulnerability to the disorder (Gabert-Quillen & others, 2012). These include a history of previous traumatic events and conditions, such as abuse and psychological disorders (Canton-Cortes, Canton, & Cortes, 2012), cultural background as in the case of traumatized refugees (Hinton & others, 2012), and genetic predisposition (Mehta & Binder, 2012; Skelton & others, 2012).

# 3 Mood Disorders

**Mood disorders** are psychological disorders in which there is a primary disturbance of mood (*mood* refers to a prolonged emotion that colors the individual's entire emotional state). This mood disturbance can include cognitive, behavioral, and somatic (physical) symptoms, as well as interpersonal difficulties. In this section we examine the two main types of mood disorders—depressive disorders and bipolar disorder—and consider a tragic correlate of these disorders: suicide.

**mood disorders**
Psychological disorders—the main types of which are depressive disorders and bipolar disorder—in which there is a primary disturbance of mood: prolonged emotion that colors the individual's entire emotional state.

## Depressive Disorders

**depressive disorders**
Mood disorders in which the individual suffers from depression—an unrelenting lack of pleasure in life.

Everyone feels blue sometimes. A romantic breakup, the death of a loved one, or a personal failure can cast a dark cloud over life. Sometimes, however, a person might feel unhappy and not know why. **Depressive disorders** are mood disorders in which the individual suffers from *depression,* an unrelenting lack of pleasure in life. The severity of depressive disorders varies. Some individuals experience what is classified as *major depressive disorder,* whereas others are given the diagnosis of *dysthymic disorder,* a more chronic depression with fewer symptoms than major depression (Wasserman, 2012)

A variety of cultures have recognized depression, and studies have shown that across cultures depression is characterized as involving an absence of joy, low energy, and high levels of sadness (Dritschel & others, 2011; Kahn, 2012). Moreover, culture may influence the ways individuals describe their experience. For instance, people from Eastern cultures may be less likely to talk about their emotional states, and more likely to describe depressive symptoms in terms of bodily feelings and symptoms, than those from Western cultures (Draguns & Tanaka-Matsumi, 2003). Depressive disorders are common, and many successful individuals have been diagnosed with depression. They include musicians Sheryl Crow and Eric Clapton, actors Drew Barrymore, Halle Berry, and Jim Carrey, artist Pablo Picasso, astronaut Buzz Aldrin (the second moon walker), famed American architect Frank Lloyd Wright, and J. K. Rowling, the author of the *Harry Potter* series.

*This painting by Vincent Van Gogh,* Portrait of Dr. Gachet, *reflects the extreme melancholy that characterizes the depressive disorders.*

**major depressive disorder (MDD)** Psychological disorder involving a major depressive episode and depressed characteristics, such as lethargy and hopelessness, for at least two weeks.

**Major depressive disorder (MDD)** involves a significant depressive episode and depressed characteristics, such as lethargy and hopelessness, for at least two weeks. MDD impairs daily functioning, and the National Institute of Mental Health (NIMH) has called it the leading cause of disability in the United States (NIMH, 2008). Ten symptoms (at least five of which must be present during a two-week period) define a major depressive episode:

- Depressed mood most of the day
- Reduced interest or pleasure in all or most activities
- Significant weight loss or gain or significant decrease or interest in appetite
- Trouble sleeping or sleeping too much
- Psychomotor agitation or retardation
- Fatigue or loss of energy
- Feeling worthless or guilty in an excessive or inappropriate manner
- Problems in thinking, concentrating, or making decisions
- Recurrent thoughts of death and suicide
- No history of manic episodes (periods of euphoric mood)

**Dysthymic disorder (DD)** is a mood disorder that is generally more chronic and has fewer symptoms than MDD. The individual is in a depressed mood for most days for at least two years as an adult or at least one year as a child or adolescent (NIMH, 2012). To be classified as having dysthymic disorder, the individual must not have experienced a major depressive episode, and the two-year period of depression must not have been broken by a normal mood lasting more than two months. Two or more of these six symptoms must be present:

**dysthymic disorder (DD)** Mood disorder that is generally more chronic and has fewer symptoms than major depressive disorder.

- Poor appetite or overeating
- Sleep problems
- Low energy or fatigue
- Low self-esteem
- Poor concentration or difficulty making decisions
- Feelings of hopelessness

What are the causes of depressive disorders? A variety of biological, psychological, and sociocultural factors have been implicated in their development.

**BIOLOGICAL FACTORS**   Genetic influences play a role in depression (Goenjian & others, 2012; Sabunciyan & others, 2012). In addition, specific brain structures are involved in depressive disorders. For example, depressed individuals show lower levels of brain activity in a section of the prefrontal cortex that is involved in generating actions (Duman & others, 2012) as well as in regions of the brain associated with the perception of rewards in the environment (Howland, 2012). A depressed person's brain may not recognize opportunities for pleasurable experiences.

Depression also likely involves problems in neurotransmitter regulation. Recall that neurotransmitters are chemicals that carry impulses from neuron to neuron. For smooth brain function, neurotransmitters must ebb and flow, often in harmony with one another. Individuals with major depressive disorder appear to have too few receptors for the neurotransmitters serotonin and norepinephrine (Houston & others, 2012; H. F. Li & others, 2012). Some research suggests that problems in regulating a neurotransmitter called *substance P* might be involved in depression (Munoz & Covenas, 2012). Substance P is thought to play an important role in the psychological experience of pain (Sacerdote & Levrini, 2012).

**PSYCHOLOGICAL FACTORS**   Psychological explanations of depression have drawn on behavioral learning theories and cognitive theories. One behavioral view of depression focuses on *learned helplessness,* which, as we saw in Chapter 5, involves an individual's feelings of powerlessness after exposure to aversive circumstances over which the person has no control. Martin Seligman (1975) proposed that learned helplessness is a reason that some people become depressed. When individuals cannot control their stress, they eventually feel helpless and stop trying to change their situations. This helplessness spirals into hopelessness (Becker-Weidman & others, 2009).

Cognitive explanations of depression focus on the thoughts and beliefs that contribute to this sense of hopelessness (Britton & others, 2012; Jarrett & others, 2012). Psychiatrist Aaron Beck (1967) proposed that negative thoughts reflect self-defeating beliefs that shape depressed individuals' experiences. These habitual negative thoughts magnify and expand depressed persons' negative experiences (Lam, 2012). For example, a depressed individual might overgeneralize about a minor occurrence—say, turning in a work assignment late—and think that he or she is worthless. A depressed person might view a minor setback such as getting a *D* on a paper as the end of the world. The accumulation of such cognitive distortions can lead to depression (T. W. Lee & others, 2011).

The way people think can also influence the course of depression. Depressed individuals may ruminate on negative experiences and negative feelings, playing them over and over again in their minds (Nolen-Hoeksema, 2011). This tendency to ruminate is associated with the development of depression as well as other psychological problems such as binge eating and substance abuse (Cowdrey & Park, 2012; Kuhn & others, 2012).

Another cognitive view of depression focuses on people's attributions—their attempts to explain what caused something to happen (Seidel & others, 2012). Depression is thought to be related to a *pessimistic* attributional style. In this style, individuals regularly explain negative events as having internal causes ("It is my fault I failed the exam"), stable causes ("I'm going to fail again and again"), and global causes ("Failing this exam shows that I won't do well in any of my courses"). Pessimistic attributional style means blaming oneself for negative events and expecting the negative events to recur (Abramson, Seligman, & Teasdale, 1978). This pessimistic style can be contrasted with an *optimistic* attributional style, which is essentially its opposite. Optimists make external attributions for bad things that happen ("I did badly on the test because it's hard to know what a professor wants on the first exam"). They also recognize that these causes can change ("I'll do better on the next one") and that they are specific ("It was only one test"). Optimistic attributional style has been related to lowered depression and decreased suicide risk in a variety of samples (Rasmussen & Wingate, 2012; Tindle & others, 2012).

Having a spouse, roommate, or friend who suffers from depression can increase the risk that an individual will also become depressed (Coyne, 1976; Joiner, Alfano, & Metalsky, 1992; Ruscher & Gotlib, 1988). Such effects are sometimes called *contagion* because they suggest that depression can spread from one person to another (Kiuru & others, 2012). Of course, the term *contagion* here is metaphorical. In fact, research suggests that whether depression and anxiety are contagious depends on the quality of interactions between people. To read more about this topic and its potential role in children's psychological health, see the Intersection.

## SOCIOCULTURAL FACTORS

Individuals with a low socioeconomic status (SES), especially people living in poverty, are more likely to develop depression than their higher-SES counterparts (Boothroyd & others, 2006). A longitudinal study of adults revealed that depression increased as one's standard of living and employment circumstances worsened (Lorant & others, 2007). Studies have found very high rates of depression in Native American groups, among whom poverty, hopelessness, and alcoholism are widespread (Teesson & Vogl, 2006).

Women are nearly twice as likely as men to develop depression (Yuan & others, 2009). As Figure 12.3 shows, this gender difference occurs in many countries (Inaba & others, 2005). Incidence of depression is high, too, among single women who are the heads of households and among young married women who work at unsatisfying, dead-end jobs (Whiffen & Demidenko, 2006). Minority women also are a high-risk group for depression (Diefenbach & others, 2009).

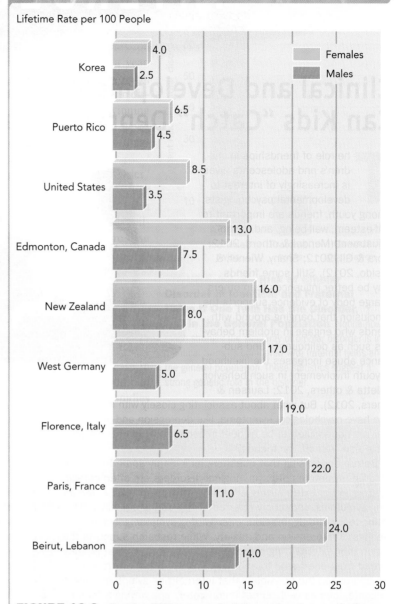

Lifetime Rate per 100 People

Females
Males

Korea 4.0 / 2.5
Puerto Rico 6.5 / 4.5
United States 8.5 / 3.5
Edmonton, Canada 13.0 / 7.5
New Zealand 16.0 / 8.0
West Germany 17.0 / 5.0
Florence, Italy 19.0 / 6.5
Paris, France 22.0 / 11.0
Beirut, Lebanon 24.0 / 14.0

0   5   10   15   20   25   30

**FIGURE 12.3   Gender Differences in Depression Across Cultures**
This graph shows the rates of depression for men and women in nine cultures (Weissman & Olfson, 1995). > *Which cultures have the highest and lowest rates of depression? What might account for these differences?* > *Which cultures have the largest gender difference in depression? What might account for these differences?* > *In order to be diagnosed with depression, a person has to seek treatment for the disorder. How might gender and culture influence a person's willingness to get treatment?*

**bipolar disorder**
Mood disorder characterized by extreme mood swings that include one or more episodes of mania, an overexcited, unrealistically optimistic state.

## Bipolar Disorder

Just as we all have down times, there are times when things seem to be going phenomenally well. For individuals with bipolar disorder, the ups and downs of life take on an extreme and often harmful tone. **Bipolar disorder** is a mood disorder characterized by extreme mood swings that include one or more episodes of *mania*, an overexcited, unrealistically optimistic state. A manic episode is like the flipside of a depressive episode (Goldney, 2012). The person who experiences

*Another gender difference to consider: Why might men show lower levels of depression than women?*

**What to Do**

1. Ask direct, straightforward questions in a calm manner. For example, "Are you thinking about hurting yourself?"

2. Be a good listener and be supportive. Emphasize that unbearable pain can be survived.

3. Take the suicide threat very seriously. Ask questions about the person's feelings, relationships, and thoughts about the type of method to be used. If a gun, pills, rope, or other means is mentioned and a specific plan has been developed, the situation is dangerous. Stay with the person until help arrives.

4. Encourage the person to get professional help and assist him or her in getting help. If the person is willing, take the person to a mental health facility or hospital.

**What Not to Do**

1. Don't ignore the warning signs.

2. Don't refuse to talk about suicide if the person wants to talk about it.

3. Don't react with horror, disapproval, or repulsion.

4. Don't offer false reassurances ("Everything will be all right") or make judgments ("You should be thankful for . . .").

5. Don't abandon the person after the crisis seems to have passed or after professional counseling has begun.

**FIGURE 12.6   When Someone Is Threatening Suicide** Do not ignore the warning signs if you think someone you know is considering suicide. Talk to a counselor if you are reluctant to say anything to the person yourself.

According to the Centers for Disease Control and Prevention (CDC), in 2010, 37,793 people in the United States committed suicide, and suicide was the 10th-highest cause of death in the country (CDC, 2012). There are twice as many suicides as homicides in the United States, and the suicide rate increased 13 percent from 1999 to 2010 (Schmitz & others, 2012). Research indicates that for every completed suicide, 8 to 25 attempted suicides occur (NIMH, 2008). Suicide is the third-leading cause (after automobile accidents and homicides) of death today among U.S. adolescents 13 through 19 years of age (Murphy, Xu, & Kochanek, 2012). Even more shocking, in the United States suicide is the third-leading cause of death among children 10 to 14 years of age (CDC, 2007). Given these grim statistics, psychologists work with individuals to reduce the frequency and intensity of suicidal impulses. Figure 12.6 provides good advice on what to do and what not to do if you encounter someone who is threatening suicide.

What might prompt an individual to end his or her own life? Biological, psychological, and sociocultural circumstances can be contributing factors.

**BIOLOGICAL FACTORS**   Genetic factors appear to play a role in suicide, which tends to run in families (Althoff & others, 2012). The Hemingways are one famous family that has been plagued by suicide. Five Hemingways, spread across generations, committed suicide, including the writer Ernest Hemingway and his granddaughter Margaux, a model and actor. Similarly, in 2009, Nicholas Hughes—a successful marine biologist and the son of Sylvia Plath, a poet who had killed herself—tragically hanged himself.

Studies have linked suicide with low levels of the neurotransmitter serotonin (Lyddon & others, 2012). Individuals who attempt suicide and who have low serotonin levels are 10 times more likely to attempt suicide again than are attempters who have high serotonin levels (Courtet & others, 2004). Poor physical health, especially when it is chronic, is another risk factor for suicide (Webb & others, 2012).

**PSYCHOLOGICAL FACTORS**   Psychological factors that can contribute to suicide include mental disorders and traumas such as sexual abuse (Wanner & others, 2012). Struggling with the stress of a psychological disorder can leave a person feeling hopeless, and the disorder itself may tax the person's ability to cope with life's difficulties. Indeed, approximately 90 percent of individuals who commit suicide are estimated to have a diagnosable mental disorder (NIMH, 2008).

*Note that people whose parents committed suicide may be more likely to consider suicide as an option. So, environment matters.*

An immediate and highly stressful circumstance—such as the loss of a loved one or a job, flunking out of school, or an unwanted pregnancy—can lead people to threaten and/or to commit suicide (Videtic & others, 2009). In addition, substance abuse is linked with suicide more today than in the past (Conner & others, 2012).

In research focusing on suicide notes, Thomas Joiner and his colleagues have found that having a sense of belongingness or of being needed separates individuals who attempt suicide from those who complete it (Joiner, 2005; Joiner, Hollar, & Van Orden, 2006; Joiner & Ribeiro, 2011). Essentially, people who feel that someone will miss them or still need them are less likely than others to complete a suicide (A. R. Smith & others, 2012).

**SOCIOCULTURAL FACTORS**   Chronic economic hardship can be a factor in suicide (Ferretti & Coluccia, 2009; Rojas & Stenberg, 2010). Cultural and ethnic contexts also are related to suicide attempts. In the United States, adolescents' suicide attempts vary across ethnic groups. As Figure 12.7 illustrates, more than 20 percent of American Indian/Alaska Native (AI/AN) female adolescents reported that they had attempted suicide in the previous year, and suicide accounts for almost 20 percent of AI/AN deaths in 15- to 19-year-olds (Goldston & others, 2008). As the figure also shows, African American and non-Latino White males reported the lowest incidence of suicide attempts. A major risk factor in the high rate of suicide attempts by AI/AN adolescents is their elevated rate of alcohol abuse.

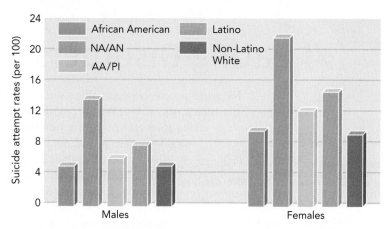

**FIGURE 12.7** **Suicide Attempts by U.S. Adolescents from Different Ethnic Groups** Note that the data shown are for one-year rates of self-reported suicide attempts. NA/AN = Native Americans/Alaska Native; AA/PI = Asian American/Pacific Islander.

Suicide rates vary worldwide; the lowest rates occur in countries with cultural and religious norms against ending one's own life. Among the nations with the highest suicide rates are several eastern European nations—including Belarus, Bulgaria, and Russia—along with Japan and South Korea. According to the World Health Organization (WHO), among the nations with the lowest rates are Haiti, Antigua and Barbuda, Egypt, and Iran (WHO, 2009). Of the 104 nations ranked by the WHO, the United States ranks 40th.

Research has also linked suicide to the culture of honor. Recall that in honor cultures, individuals are more likely to interpret insults as fighting words and to defend their personal honor with aggression. One set of studies examined suicide and depression in the United States, comparing geographic regions that are considered to have a culture of honor (that is, southern states) with other areas. Even accounting for a host of other factors, suicide rates were found to be higher in states with a culture of honor (Osterman & Brown, 2011). The researchers also examined how regions compared in terms of the use of prescription antidepressants and discovered that states with a culture of honor also had lower levels of use of these drugs. It may be that in a culture of honor, seeking treatment for depression is seen as a weakness or a mark of shame.

There are gender differences in suicide as well (Sarma & Kola, 2010). Women are three times more likely than men to attempt suicide. Men, however, are four times more likely than women to complete suicide (Kochanek & others, 2004). Men are also more likely than women to use a firearm in a suicide attempt (Maris, 1998). The highest suicide rate is among non-Latino White men ages 85 and older (NIMH, 2008).

*Men are less likely than women to report being depressed but are more likely to commit suicide. Clearly, depression in men might be underestimated.*

1. To be diagnosed with bipolar disorder, an individual must experience
   A. a manic episode.
   B. a depressive episode.
   C. a manic episode and a depressive episode.
   D. a dysthymic episode.

2. All of the following are a symptom of major depressive disorder except
   A. fatigue.
   B. weight change.
   C. thoughts of death.
   D. substance use.

3. A true statement about suicide and gender is that
   A. women are more likely to attempt suicide than men.
   B. men are more likely to attempt suicide than women.
   C. men and women are equally likely to attempt suicide.
   D. men and women are equally likely to complete suicide.

**APPLY IT!** 4. During his first two college years, Barry has felt "down" most of the time. He has had trouble concentrating and difficulty making decisions. Sometimes he is so overwhelmed with deciding on his major and struggling to focus that he feels hopeless. Otherwise, Barry is doing fairly well; he has no problems with loss of appetite or sleeping, and in general his energy level is fine. Which of the following is most likely to be true of Barry?
   A. Barry is suffering from major depressive disorder.
   B. Barry is entering the depressive phase of bipolar disorder.
   C. Barry has dysthymic disorder.
   D. Barry is experiencing the everyday blues that everyone gets from time to time.

# 4 Eating Disorders

For some people, concerns about weight and body image become a serious, debilitating disorder (Lock, 2012a; Wilson & Zandberg, 2012). For such individuals, the very act of eating is an arena where a variety of complex biological, psychological, and cultural issues are played out, often with tragic consequences.

A number of famous people have coped with eating disorders, including Princess Diana, Ashley Judd, Paula Abdul, Mary-Kate Olsen, and Kelly Clarkson. Eating disorders are characterized by extreme disturbances in eating behavior—from eating very, very little to eating a great deal. In this section we examine three eating disorders—anorexia nervosa, bulimia nervosa, and binge eating disorder.

*Disorders of eating can vary across cultures. In Fiji, a disorder known as* **macake** *involves poor appetite and refusing to eat. Very high levels of social concern meet this refusal, and individuals with macake are strongly motivated to start eating and enjoying food again.*

## Anorexia Nervosa

**anorexia nervosa**
Eating disorder that involves the relentless pursuit of thinness through starvation.

**Anorexia nervosa** is an eating disorder that involves the relentless pursuit of thinness through starvation. Anorexia nervosa is much more common in girls and women than boys and men and affects between 0.5 and 3.7 percent of young women (NIMH, 2011). The American Psychiatric Association (2005) lists these main characteristics of anorexia nervosa:

- Weight less than 85 percent of what is considered normal for age and height, and refusal to maintain weight at a healthy level.
- An intense fear of gaining weight that does not decrease with weight loss.
- A distorted body image (Stewart & others, 2012). Even when individuals with anorexia nervosa are extremely thin, they never think they are thin enough. They weigh themselves frequently, take their body measurements often, and gaze critically at themselves in mirrors.
- *Amenorrhea* (lack of menstruation) in girls who have reached puberty.

Over time, anorexia nervosa can lead to physical changes, such as the growth of fine hair all over the body, thinning of bones and hair, severe constipation, and low blood pressure (NIMH, 2011). Dangerous and even life-threatening complications include damage to the heart and thyroid. Anorexia nervosa is said to have the highest mortality rate (about 5.6 percent of individuals with anorexia nervosa die within 10 years of diagnosis) of any psychological disorder (Hoek, 2006; NIMH, 2011).

Anorexia nervosa typically begins in the teenage years, often following an episode of dieting and some type of life stress (Fitzpatrick, 2012). Most individuals with anorexia nervosa are non-Latino White female adolescents or young adults from well-educated middle- and upper-income families (Darcy, 2012; Dodge, 2012). They are often high-achieving perfectionists (Forbush, Heatherton, & Keel, 2007). Obsessive thinking about weight and compulsive exercise are also related to anorexia nervosa (Hildebrandt & others, 2012).

*Individuals with anorexia nervosa lack personal distress over their symptoms. Recall that personal distress over one's behavior is just one aspect of the definition of abnormal.*

*Uruguayan model Eliana Ramos posed for the camera in her native country. Tragically, the super-thin Ramos died at age 18 in February 2007, two years after this picture was taken, reportedly from health problems associated with anorexia nervosa.*

# Bulimia Nervosa

**Bulimia nervosa** is an eating disorder in which an individual (typically female) consistently follows a binge-and-purge eating pattern. The individual goes on an eating binge and then purges by self-induced vomiting or the use of laxatives. Most people with bulimia nervosa are preoccupied with food, have a strong fear of becoming overweight, and are depressed or anxious (Birgegård, Norring, & Clinton, 2012). Because bulimia nervosa occurs within a normal weight range, the disorder is often difficult to detect. A person with bulimia nervosa usually keeps the disorder a secret and experiences a great deal of self-disgust and shame.

Bulimia nervosa can lead to complications such as a chronic sore throat, kidney problems, dehydration, and gastrointestinal disorders (NIMH, 2011). The disorder is also related to dental problems, as persistent exposure to the stomach acids in vomit can wear away tooth enamel.

Bulimia nervosa typically begins in late adolescence or early adulthood (Levine, 2002). The disorder affects between 1 and 4 percent of young women (NIMH, 2011). Like those with anorexia nervosa, many young women who develop bulimia nervosa are highly perfectionistic (Lampard & others, 2012). At the same time, they tend to have low levels of self-efficacy (Bardone-Cone & others, 2006). In other words, these are young women with very high standards but very low confidence that they can achieve their goals. Impulsivity, negative emotion, and obsessive-compulsive disorder are also related to bulimia (Roncero, Perpina, & Garcia-Soriano, 2011). Bulimia nervosa is associated, too, with a high incidence of sexual and physical abuse in childhood (Lo Sauro & others, 2008).

**bulimia nervosa**
Eating disorder in which an individual (typically a girl or woman) consistently follows a binge-and-purge eating pattern.

Dentists and dental hygienists are sometimes the first to recognize the signs of bulimia nervosa.

Although much more common in women, bulimia can also affect men. Elton John has described his struggles with this eating disorder.

## Anorexia Nervosa and Bulimia Nervosa: Causes and Treatments

What is the etiology (cause) of anorexia nervosa and bulimia nervosa? For many years researchers thought that sociocultural factors, such as media images of very thin women and family pressures, were the central determinants of these disorders (Le Grange & others, 2010). Media images that glorify extreme thinness can indeed influence women's body image, and emphasis on the thin ideal is related to anorexia nervosa and bulimia nervosa (Carr & Peebles, 2012). However, as powerful as these media messages might be, countless females are exposed to media images of unrealistically thin women, but relatively few develop eating disorders. Many young women embark on diets, but comparatively few of them develop eating disorders.

Eating disorders occur in cultures that do not emphasize the ideal of thinness, although the disorders may differ from Western descriptions. For instance, in Eastern cultures, individuals can show the symptoms of anorexia nervosa, but they lack the fear of getting fat that is common in North Americans with the disorder (Pike, Yamamiya, & Konishi, 2011).

Since the 1980s, researchers have increasingly probed the potential biological underpinnings of these disorders, examining in particular the interplay of social and biological factors. Genes play a substantial role in both anorexia nervosa and bulimia nervosa (Lock, 2012b). In fact, genes influence many psychological characteristics (for example, perfectionism, impulsivity, obsessive-compulsive tendencies, and thinness drive) and behaviors (restrained eating, binge eating, self-induced vomiting) that are associated with anorexia nervosa and bulimia nervosa (Mikolajczyk, Grzywacz, & Samochowiec, 2010; Schur, Heckbert, & Goldberg, 2010). These genes are also factors in the regulation of serotonin, and problems in regulating serotonin are related to both anorexia nervosa and bulimia nervosa (Capasso, Putrella, & Milano, 2009).

Even as biological factors play a role in the emergence of eating disorders, eating disorders themselves affect the body, including the brain. Most psychologists believe that while social factors and experiences may play a role in triggering dieting, the physical effects of dieting, bingeing, and purging may change the neural networks that then sustain the disordered pattern, in a kind of vicious cycle (Lock, 2012b).

Although anorexia and bulimia nervosa are serious disorders, recovery is possible (Fitzpatrick, 2012; Treasure, Claudino, & Zucker, 2010). Anorexia nervosa may require hospitalization. The first target of intervention is promoting weight gain, in extreme cases through the use of a feeding tube. A common obstacle in the treatment of anorexia nervosa is that individuals with the disorder deny that anything is wrong. They maintain their belief that thinness and restrictive dieting are correct and not a sign of mental illness (Wilson, Grilo, & Vitousek, 2007). Still, drug therapies and psychotherapy have been shown to be effective in treating anorexia nervosa, as well as bulimia nervosa (Hagman & Frank, 2012; Wilson & Zandberg, 2012).

## Binge Eating Disorder

**binge eating disorder (BED)** Eating disorder characterized by recurrent episodes of eating large amounts of food during which the person feels a lack of control over eating.

**Binge eating disorder (BED)** is characterized by recurrent episodes of consuming large amounts of food during which the person feels a lack of control over eating (Birgegård, Norring, & Clinton, 2012). Unlike an individual with bulimia nervosa, someone with BED does not try to purge. Most individuals with BED are overweight or obese (Carrard, der Linden, & Golay, 2012).

Individuals with BED often eat quickly, eat a great deal when they are not hungry, and eat until they are uncomfortably full. They frequently eat alone because of embarrassment or guilt, and they feel ashamed and disgusted with themselves after overeating. BED is the most common of all eating disorders—affecting men, women, and ethnic groups within the United States more similarly than anorexia nervosa or bulimia nervosa (Azarbad & others, 2010). An estimated 2 to 5 percent of Americans will suffer from BED in their lifetime (NIMH, 2011).

BED is thought to characterize approximately 8 percent of individuals who are obese. Unlike obese individuals who do not suffer from BED, binge eaters are more likely to place great value on their physical appearance, weight, and body shape (Grilo, Masheb, & White, 2010). The complications of BED are those of obesity more generally, including diabetes, hypertension, and cardiovascular disease.

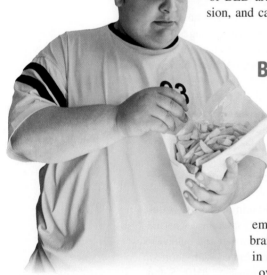

*Unlike individuals with anorexia nervosa or bulimia nervosa, most people with binge eating disorder are overweight or obese.*

### Binge Eating Disorder: Causes and Treatments

Researchers are examining the role of biological and psychological factors in BED. Genes play a role (Akkermann & others, 2012), as does dopamine, the neurotransmitter related to reward pathways in the brain (C. Davis & others, 2010). The fact that binge eating often occurs after stressful events suggests that binge eaters use food to regulate their emotions (Wilson, Grilo, & Vitousek, 2007). The areas of the brain and endocrine system that respond to stress are overactive in individuals with BED (Lo Sauro & others, 2008), and this overactivity leads to high levels of circulating cortisol, the hormone most associated with stress. Individuals with BED may be more likely to perceive events as stressful and then seek to manage that stress by binge eating.

Little research has examined the sociocultural factors in BED. One study examined whether exposure to U.S. culture might increase the risk of developing BED (Swanson & others, 2012). The results showed that Mexicans who immigrated to the United States and Mexican Americans were more likely to develop BED than were Mexicans who lived in Mexico, controlling for a variety of factors (Swanson & others, 2012).

Just as treatment for anorexia nervosa first focuses on weight gain, some believe that treatment for BED should first target weight loss (DeAngelis, 2002). Others argue that individuals with BED must be treated for disordered eating per se, and they insist that if the underlying psychological issues are not addressed, weight loss will not be successful or permanent (de Zwaan & others, 2005; Hay & others, 2009).

1. The main characteristics of anorexia nervosa include all of the following except
   A. absence of menstrual periods after puberty.
   B. distorted image of one's body.
   C. strong fears of weight gain even as weight loss occurs.
   D. intense and persistent tremors.

2. A person with bulimia nervosa typically
   A. thinks a lot about food.
   B. is considerably underweight.
   C. is a male.
   D. is not overly concerned about gaining weight.

3. The most common of all eating disorders is
   A. bulimia nervosa.
   B. anorexia nervosa.
   C. binge eating disorder.
   D. gastrointestinal disease.

APPLY IT! 4. Nancy is a first-year straight-*A* premed major. Nancy's roommate Luci notices that Nancy has lost a great deal of weight and is extremely thin. Luci observes that Nancy works out a lot, rarely finishes meals, and wears bulky sweaters all the time. Luci also notices that Nancy's arms have fine hairs growing on them, and Nancy has mentioned never getting her period anymore. When Luci asks Nancy about her weight loss, Nancy replies that she is very concerned that she not gain the "freshman 15" and is feeling good about her ability to keep up with her work and keep off those extra pounds. Which of the following is the most likely explanation for what is going on with Nancy?
   A. Nancy likely has bulimia nervosa.
   B. Despite her lack of personal distress about her symptoms, Nancy likely has anorexia nervosa.
   C. Nancy has binge eating disorder.
   D. Given Nancy's overall success, it seems unlikely that she is suffering from a psychological disorder.

# 5 Dissociative Disorders

Have you ever been on a long car ride and completely lost track of time, so that you could not even remember a stretch of miles along the road? Have you been so caught up in a daydream that you were unaware of the passage of time? These are examples of normal dissociation. *Dissociation* refers to psychological states in which the person feels disconnected from immediate experience.

**dissociative disorders**
Psychological disorders that involve a sudden loss of memory or change in identity due to the dissociation (separation) of the individual's conscious awareness from previous memories and thoughts.

At the extreme of dissociation are individuals who persistently feel a sense of disconnection. **Dissociative disorders** are psychological disorders that involve a sudden loss of memory or change in identity. Under extreme stress or shock, the individual's conscious awareness becomes dissociated (separated or split) from previous memories and thoughts (Espirito-Santo & Pio-Abreu, 2009). Individuals who develop dissociative disorders may have problems putting together different aspects of consciousness, so that experiences at different levels of awareness might be felt as if they are happening to someone else (Dell & O'Neil, 2007).

Psychologists believe that dissociation is a way of dealing with extreme stress (Brand & others, 2012). Through dissociation the individual mentally protects his or her conscious self from the traumatic event. Dissociative disorders often occur in individuals who also show signs of PTSD (Lanius & others, 2012). Both psychological disorders are thought to be rooted, in part, in extremely traumatic life events (Foote & others, 2006). The notion that dissociative disorders are related to problems in pulling together emotional memories is supported by findings showing lower volume in the hippocampus and amygdala in individuals with dissociative disorders (Vermetten & others, 2006). The hippocampus is especially involved in consolidating memory and organizing life experience into a coherent whole (Spiegel, 2006).

 *In dissociative disorders, consciousness (see Chapter 4) is split off from experience—the "stream of consciousness" is disrupted. Hypnosis is often used to treat dissociative disorders.*

Dissociative disorders are perhaps the most controversial of all diagnostic categories, with some psychologists believing that they are often mistakenly diagnosed (Freeland & others, 1993) and others arguing that they are underdiagnosed (Sar, Akyuz, & Dogan, 2007; Spiegel, 2006). Three kinds of dissociative disorders are dissociative amnesia, dissociative fugue, and dissociative identity disorder.

*The study on dissociative disorders in Uganda from earlier in this chapter found agreement among respondents that dissociative states are brought on by trauma.*

## Dissociative Amnesia and Dissociative Fugue

Recall from Chapter 6 that amnesia is the inability to recall important events (Markowitsch & Staniloiu, 2012). Amnesia can result from a blow to the head that produces trauma in the brain. **Dissociative amnesia** is a type of amnesia characterized by extreme memory loss that stems from extensive psychological stress. People experiencing dissociative amnesia remember everyday tasks like how to hail a cab and use a phone. They forget only aspects of their own identity and autobiographical experiences.

**dissociative amnesia**
Dissociative disorder characterized by extreme memory loss that is caused by extensive psychological stress.

One case of dissociative amnesia involved a 28-year-old married woman who had given birth to her sixth child four months before (Tharoor & others, 2007). After she delivered the child, her family noticed that she did not acknowledge her newborn as her own baby and that she had neither a recollection of having given birth nor a sense of her own identity. She took care of the baby as advised by her family members but maintained a belief that although she had been pregnant, she had not given birth. Under the influence of sodium pentothal (a narcotic sometimes called "truth serum" because it renders people talkative and likely to share information), the young mother eventually described how she had not wanted to continue her sixth pregnancy, but her spouse, who lived in another country, had refused to consent to an abortion. She described herself as exhausted by the pregnancy. Eventually, through hypnosis and memory exercises, the woman recovered autobiographical memory for her identity as well as for the experience of having given birth.

*Matt Damon's character, Jason Bourne, in the Bourne films is named after Ansel Bourne, who in 1887 became the first known real-life case of dissociative fugue.*

**Dissociative fugue** (*fugue* means "flight") is a dissociative disorder in which the individual not only develops amnesia but also unexpectedly travels away from home and sometimes assumes a new identity. What makes dissociative fugue different from dissociative amnesia is this tendency to run away.

**dissociative fugue**
Dissociative disorder in which the individual not only develops amnesia but also unexpectedly travels away from home and assumes a new identity.

A recent case of dissociative fugue involved the disappearance of a middle-school teacher in New York City. Twenty-three-year-old Hannah Upp disappeared while out for a run on August 28, 2008 (Marx & Didziulis, 2009). She had no wallet, no identification, no cell phone, and no money. Her family, friends, and roommates posted flyers around the city and messages on the Internet. As days went by, they became increasingly concerned that something terrible had happened. Finally, Hannah was found floating face down in the New York harbor on September 16, sunburned and dehydrated but alive. She remembered nothing of her experiences. To her, it felt like she had gone out for a run and 10 minutes later was being pulled from the harbor. To this day, she does not know what event might have led to her dissociative fugue, nor does she remember how she survived during her two-week disappearance.

*At one point during her fugue, Hannah was approached by someone who asked if she was the Hannah everyone was looking for, and she answered no.*

## Dissociative Identity Disorder

**dissociative identity disorder (DID)**
Formerly called multiple personality disorder, a dissociative disorder in which the individual has two or more distinct personalities or selves, each with its own memories, behaviors, and relationships.

**Dissociative identity disorder (DID),** formerly called *multiple personality disorder,* is the most dramatic, least common, and most controversial dissociative disorder. Individuals with this disorder have two or more distinct personalities or identities (Belli & others, 2012). Each identity has its own memories, behaviors, and relationships. One identity dominates at one time, another takes over at another time. Individuals sometimes report that a wall of amnesia separates their different identities (Dale & others, 2009); however, research suggests that memory does transfer across these identities, even if the person believes it does not (Kong, Allen, & Glisky, 2008). The shift between identities usually occurs under distress (Sar & others, 2007) but sometimes can also be controlled by the person (Kong, Allen, & Glisky, 2008).

A famous real-life example of dissociative identity disorder is the "three faces of Eve" case, based on the life of a woman named Chris Sizemore (Thigpen & Cleckley, 1957) (Figure 12.8). Eve White was the original dominant personality. She had no knowledge of her second personality, Eve Black, although Eve Black had been alternating with Eve White for a number of years. Eve White was bland, quiet, and serious. By contrast, Eve Black was carefree, mischievous, and uninhibited. Eve Black would emerge at the most inappropriate times, leaving Eve White with hangovers, bills, and a reputa-

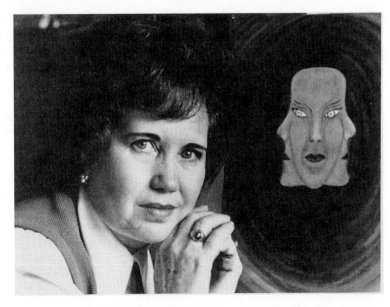

**FIGURE 12.8** **The Three Faces of Eve** Chris Sizemore, the subject of the 1950s book and film *The Three Faces of Eve,* is shown here with a work she painted, titled *Three Faces in One.*

tion in local bars that she could not explain. During treatment, a third personality emerged: Jane. More mature than the other two, Jane seems to have developed as a result of therapy. More recently, former Heisman Trophy winner and legendary NFL running back Herschel Walker (2008) revealed his experience with dissociative disorder in his book *Breaking Free: My Life with Dissociative Identity Disorder.*

Research on dissociative identity disorder links a high rate of extraordinarily severe sexual or physical abuse during early childhood to the condition (Ross & Ness, 2010). Some psychologists believe that a child can cope with intense trauma by dissociating from the experience and developing other alternate selves as protectors. Sexual abuse has occurred in as many as 70 percent or more of dissociative identity disorder cases (Foote & others, 2006); however, the majority of individuals who have been sexually abused do not develop dissociative identity disorder. The vast majority of individuals with dissociative identity disorder are women. A genetic predisposition might also exist, as the disorder tends to run in families (Dell & Eisenhower, 1990).

Until the 1980s, only about 300 cases of dissociative identity disorder had ever been reported (Suinn, 1984). In the past 30 years, hundreds more cases have been diagnosed. Social cognitive approaches point out that diagnoses have tended to increase whenever the popular media present a case, as in the miniseries *Sybil* and the Showtime drama *United States of Tara.* From this perspective, individuals develop multiple identities through social contagion. After exposure to these examples, people may be more likely to view multiple identities as a real condition. Some experts believe, in fact, that dissociative identity disorder is a *social construction*—that it represents a category some people adopt to make sense of their experiences (Spanos, 1996). Rather than being a single person with many conflicting feelings, wishes, and potentially awful experiences, the individual compartmentalizes different aspects of the self into independent identities. In some cases, therapists have been accused of creating alternate personalities. Encountering an individual who appears to have a fragmented sense of self, the therapist may begin to treat each fragment as its own "personality" (Spiegel, 2006).

*Therapists and patients are making attributions to understand abnormal behavior.*

Cross-cultural comparisons can shed light on whether dissociative identity disorder is primarily a response to traumatic events or the result of a social cognitive factor like social contagion. If dissociation is a response to trauma, individuals with similar levels of traumatic experience should show similar degrees of dissociation, regardless of their exposure to cultural messages about dissociation. In China, the popular media *do not* commonly portray individuals with dissociative disorder, and professional knowledge of the disorder is rare. One study comparing individuals from China and Canada (where dissociative identity disorder is a widely publicized condition) found reports of traumatic experience to be similar across groups and to relate to dissociative experiences similarly as well (Ross & others, 2008), casting some doubt on the notion that dissociative experiences are entirely a product of social contagion.

self-quiz

1. Dissociative identity disorder is associated with unusually high rates of
   A. anxiety.
   B. abuse during early childhood.
   C. depression.
   D. divorce.

2. Someone who suffers memory loss after a psychological trauma is said to have
   A. dissociative identity disorder.
   B. dissociative fugue.
   C. dissociative amnesia.
   D. schizophrenia.

3. In cases of dissociative fugue, the individual not only experiences amnesia but also
   A. has frequent thoughts of suicide.
   B. takes on multiple different identities.
   C. refuses to leave his or her home.
   D. travels away from home.

**APPLY IT!** 4. Eddie often loses track of time. He is sometimes late for appointments because he is so engrossed in whatever he is doing. While working on a term paper in the library, he gets so caught up in what he is reading that he is shocked when he looks up and sees that the sun has set and it is night. Which of the following best describes Eddie?
   A. Eddie is showing signs of dissociative identity disorder.
   B. Eddie is showing signs of dissociative fugue.
   C. Eddie is showing normal dissociative states.
   D. Eddie is at risk for dissociative amnesia.

# 6 Schizophrenia

Have you had the experience of watching a movie and suddenly noticing that the film bears an uncanny resemblance to your life? Have you ever listened to a radio talk show and realized that the host was saying exactly what you were just thinking? Do these moments mean something special about you, or are they coincidences? For people with schizophrenia, such experiences may take on special and personal meaning.

**Schizophrenia** is a severe psychological disorder that is characterized by highly disordered thought processes. These disordered thoughts are referred to as *psychotic* because they are far removed from reality. The world of the person with schizophrenia is deeply frightening and chaotic.

Schizophrenia is usually diagnosed in early adulthood, around age 18 for men and 25 for women. Individuals with schizophrenia may see things that are not there, hear voices inside their heads, and live in a strange world of twisted logic. They may say odd things, show inappropriate emotion, and move their bodies in peculiar ways. Often, they are socially withdrawn and isolated.

*Seeking treatment for schizophrenia takes courage. It requires that individuals accept that their perception of the world—their very sense of reality—is mistaken.*

It is difficult to imagine the ordeal of people living with schizophrenia, who comprise about half of the patients in psychiatric hospitals. The suicide risk for individuals with schizophrenia is eight times that for the general population (Pompili & others, 2007). For many with the disorder, controlling it means using powerful medications to combat symptoms. The most common cause of relapse is that individuals stop taking their medication. They might do so because they feel better and believe they no longer need the drugs, they do not realize that their thoughts are disordered, or the side effects of the medications are too unpleasant.

**schizophrenia** Severe psychological disorder characterized by highly disordered thought processes; individuals suffering from schizophrenia may be referred to as psychotic because they are so far removed from reality.

## Symptoms of Schizophrenia

Psychologists generally classify the symptoms of schizophrenia as positive symptoms, negative symptoms, and cognitive deficits (NIMH, 2008).

**POSITIVE SYMPTOMS** The positive symptoms of schizophrenia are marked by a distortion or an excess of normal function. They are "positive" because they reflect something added above and beyond normal behavior. Positive symptoms of schizophrenia include hallucinations, delusions, thought disorders, and disorders of movement.

**Hallucinations** are sensory experiences that occur in the absence of real stimuli. Hallucinations are usually auditory—the person might complain of hearing voices—or visual, and much less commonly they can be experienced as smells or tastes (Bhatia & others, 2009). Culture affects the form hallucinations take, as well as their content and sensory modality—that is, whether the hallucinations are visual, auditory, or manifest as smells or tastes (Bauer & others, 2011). Visual hallucinations involve seeing things that are not there, as in the case of Moe Armstrong. At the age of 21, while serving in Vietnam as a Marine medical corpsman, Armstrong experienced a psychotic break. Dead Vietcong soldiers appeared to talk to him and beg him for help and did not seem to realize that they were dead. Armstrong, now a successful businessman and a sought-after public speaker who holds two master's degrees, relies on medication to keep such experiences at bay (Bonfatti, 2005).

**Delusions** are false, unusual, and sometimes magical beliefs that are not part of an individual's culture. A delusional person might think that he is Jesus Christ or Muhammad; another might imagine that her thoughts are being broadcast over the radio. It is crucial to distinguish delusions from cultural ideas such as the religious belief that a person can have divine visions or communicate personally with a deity. Generally, psychology and psychiatry do not treat these ideas as delusional.

For individuals with schizophrenia, delusional beliefs that might seem completely illogical to the outsider are experienced as all too real. At one point in his life, Bill Garrett (from the chapter-opening vignette) was convinced that a blister on his hand was a sign of gangrene. So strong was his belief that he tried to cut off his hand with a knife, before being stopped by his family (M. Park, 2009).

*Thought disorder* refers to the unusual, sometimes bizarre thought processes that are characteristic positive symptoms of schizophrenia. The thoughts of persons with schizophrenia can be disorganized and confused. Often individuals with schizophrenia do not make sense when they talk or write. For example, someone with schizophrenia might say, "Well, Rocky, babe, happening, but where, when, up, top, side, over, you know, out of the way, that's it. Sign off." These incoherent, loose word associations, called *word salad,* have no meaning for the listener. The individual might also make up new words (Kerns & others, 1999). In addition, a person with schizophrenia can show **referential thinking,** which means giving personal meaning to completely random events. For instance, the individual might believe that a traffic light has turned red because he or she is in a hurry.

A final type of positive symptom is *disorders of movement.* A person with schizophrenia may show unusual mannerisms, body movements, and facial expressions. The individual may repeat certain motions over and over or, in extreme cases, may become catatonic. **Catatonia** is a state of immobility and unresponsiveness that lasts for long periods of time (Figure 12.9).

## NEGATIVE SYMPTOMS

Whereas schizophrenia's positive symptoms are characterized by a distortion or an excess of normal functions, schizophrenia's negative symptoms reflect social withdrawal, behavioral deficits, and the loss or decrease of normal functions. One negative symptom is **flat affect,** which means the display of little or no emotion (LePage & others, 2011). Individuals with schizophrenia also may be lacking in the ability to read the emotions of others (Chambon, Baudouin, & Franck, 2006). They may experience a lack of positive emotional experience in daily life and show a deficient ability to plan, initiate, and engage in goal-directed behavior.

**hallucinations**
Sensory experiences that occur in the absence of real stimuli.

**delusions**
False, unusual, and sometimes magical beliefs that are not part of an individual's culture.

**referential thinking**
Ascribing personal meaning to completely random events.

**catatonia**
State of immobility and unresponsiveness lasting for long periods of time.

**flat affect**
The display of little or no emotion—a common negative symptom of schizophrenia.

**FIGURE 12.9** **Disorders of Movement in Schizophrenia** Unusual motor behaviors are positive symptoms of schizophrenia. Individuals may cease to move altogether (a state called catatonia), sometimes holding bizarre postures.

*Because negative symptoms are not as obviously part of a psychiatric illness, people with schizophrenia may be perceived as lazy and unwilling to better their lives.*

**COGNITIVE SYMPTOMS**  Cognitive symptoms of schizophrenia include difficulty sustaining attention, problems holding information in memory, and inability to interpret information and make decisions (Sitnikova, Goff, & Kuperberg, 2009; Torniainen & others, 2012). These symptoms may be subtle and are often detected only through neuropsychological tests. Researchers now recognize that to understand schizophrenia's cognitive symptoms fully, measures of these symptoms must be tailored to particular cultural contexts (Mehta & others, 2011).

## Causes of Schizophrenia

A great deal of research has investigated schizophrenia's causes, including biological, psychological, and sociocultural factors involved in the disorder.

**BIOLOGICAL FACTORS**  Research provides strong support for biological explanations of schizophrenia. Especially compelling is the evidence for a genetic predisposition (Tao & others, 2012). However, structural abnormalities and neurotransmitters also are linked to this severe psychological disorder (Perez-Costas & others, 2012; Sugranyes & others, 2012).

*Heredity*  Research supports the notion that schizophrenia is at least partially due to genetic factors (Vasco, Cardinale, & Polonia, 2012). As genetic similarity to a person with schizophrenia increases, so does a person's risk of developing schizophrenia, as Figure 12.10 shows (Cardno & Gottesman, 2000). Such data strongly suggest that genetic factors play a role in schizophrenia. Researchers are seeking to pinpoint the chromosomal

---

PSYCHOLOGICAL INQUIRY

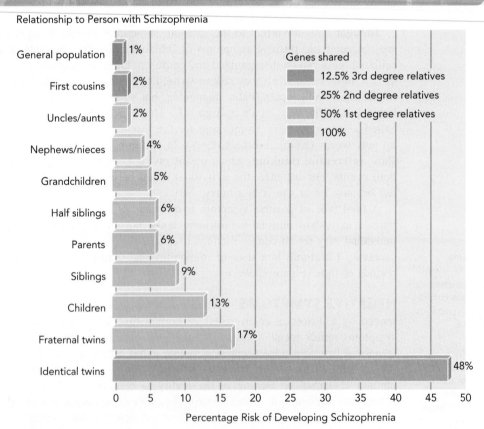

**FIGURE 12.10  Lifetime Risk of Developing Schizophrenia According to Genetic Relatedness**  As genetic relatedness to an individual with schizophrenia increases, so does the risk of developing schizophrenia. > *Which familial relationships have the lowest and highest level of genetic overlap?* > *What is the difference in genetic overlap between identical twins and non-twin siblings?* > *What is the difference in risk of schizophrenia between identical twins and non-twin siblings?*

Relationship to Person with Schizophrenia

General population — 1%
First cousins — 2%
Uncles/aunts — 2%
Nephews/nieces — 4%
Grandchildren — 5%
Half siblings — 6%
Parents — 6%
Siblings — 9%
Children — 13%
Fraternal twins — 17%
Identical twins — 48%

Genes shared
12.5% 3rd degree relatives
25% 2nd degree relatives
50% 1st degree relatives
100%

Percentage Risk of Developing Schizophrenia

location of genes involved in susceptibility to schizophrenia (Crowley & others, 2012; van Beveren & others, 2012).

### Structural Brain Abnormalities

Studies have found structural brain abnormalities in people with schizophrenia. Imaging techniques such as MRI scans clearly show enlarged ventricles in the brain (Rais & others, 2012). Ventricles are fluid-filled spaces, and enlargement of the ventricles indicates the deterioration in other brain tissue. Individuals with schizophrenia also have a small frontal cortex (the area in which thinking, planning, and decision making take place) and show less activity in this area than individuals who do not have schizophrenia (Cotter & others, 2002).

Still, the differences between the brains of healthy individuals and those with schizophrenia are small (NIMH, 2008). Microscopic studies of brain tissue after death reveal small changes in the distribution or characteristics of brain cells in persons with schizophrenia. It appears that many of these changes occurred prenatally because they are not accompanied by glial cells, which are always present when a brain injury occurs after birth. It may be that problems in prenatal development such as infections (A. S. Brown, 2006) predispose a brain to developing schizophrenic symptoms during puberty and young adulthood (Fatemi & Folsom, 2009).

### Problems in Neurotransmitter Regulation

An early biological explanation for schizophrenia linked excess dopamine production to schizophrenia. The link between dopamine and psychotic symptoms was first noticed when the drug L-dopa (which increases dopamine levels) was given to individuals as a treatment for Parkinson disease. In addition to relieving their Parkinson symptoms, L-dopa caused some individuals to experience disturbed thoughts (Janowsky, Addario, & Risch, 1987). Furthermore, drugs that reduce psychotic symptoms often block dopamine (Kapur, 2003). Whether it is differences in the amount, the production, or the uptake of dopamine, there is good evidence that dopamine plays a role in schizophrenia (Brito-Melo & others, 2012; Howes & others, 2012).

As noted in the chapters about states of consciousness (Chapter 4) and learning (Chapter 5), dopamine is a "feel good" neurotransmitter that helps us recognize rewarding stimuli in the environment. As described in the chapter on personality (Chapter 10), dopamine is related to being outgoing and sociable. How can a neurotransmitter that is associated with good things play a crucial role in the most devastating psychological disorder?

*Excess dopamine basically tells the person that everything is important.*

One way to think about this puzzle is to view dopamine as a neurochemical messenger that in effect shouts out, "Hey! This is important!" whenever we encounter opportunities for reward. Imagine what it might be like to be bombarded with such messages about even the smallest details of life (Kapur, 2003). The person's own thoughts might take on such dramatic proportions that they sound like someone else's voice talking inside the person's head. Fleeting ideas such as "It's raining today because I didn't bring my umbrella to work" suddenly seem not silly but true. Shitij Kapur (2003) has suggested that hallucinations, delusions, and referential thinking may be expressions of the individual's attempts to make sense of such extraordinary feelings.

A problem with the dopamine explanation of schizophrenia is that antipsychotic drugs reduce dopamine levels very quickly, but delusional beliefs take much longer to disappear. Even after dopamine levels are balanced, a person might still cling to the bizarre belief that members of a powerful conspiracy are watching his every move. If dopamine causes these symptoms, why do the symptoms persist even after the dopamine is under control? According to Kapur, delusions serve as explanatory schemes that have helped the person make sense of the random and chaotic experiences caused by out-of-control dopamine. Bizarre beliefs might disappear only after experience demonstrates that such schemes no longer carry their explanatory power (Kapur, 2003). That is, with time, experience, and therapy, the person might come to realize that there is, in fact, no conspiracy.

## PSYCHOLOGICAL FACTORS

Psychologists used to explain schizophrenia as rooted in an individual's difficult childhood experiences with parents. Such explanations have mostly fallen by the wayside, but contemporary theorists do recognize that stress may contribute to the development of this disorder. The **diathesis-stress model** argues that a combination of biogenetic disposition and stress causes schizophrenia (Meehl, 1962). (*Diathesis* means "physical vulnerability or predisposition to a particular disorder.") For instance, genetic characteristics might produce schizophrenia only when (and if) the individual experiences extreme stress.

*Recall that Moe Armstrong experienced his first symptoms during the extremely stressful experience of the Vietnam War.*

**diathesis-stress model**
View of schizophrenia emphasizing that a combination of biogenetic disposition and stress causes the disorder.

## SOCIOCULTURAL FACTORS

A fascinating finding on sociocultural factors in schizophrenia is a consistent difference in the course of schizophrenia over time in developing versus developed nations. Specifically, individuals with schizophrenia in developing, nonindustrialized nations are more likely to show indications of recovery over time compared to those in developed, industrialized nations (Bhugra, 2006; Jablensky, 2000; Myers, 2010). Whether measured in symptoms, disturbances in thought, or the ability to engage in productive work, individuals in less developed countries appear to do better than their counterparts in developed nations.

This difference is puzzling. Some experts argue that developing nations must be misdiagnosing more individuals or are better off than the label "developing" implies (Burns, 2009). Other commentators look to differences in cultural beliefs and practices to understand these effects. For instance, it might be that in more developed nations (such as the United States), there is not a very strong belief that individuals diagnosed with schizophrenia *can* recover (Luhrmann, 2007). In addition, cultures vary in terms of their beliefs about and responses to symptoms. In Chandigarh, India, for example, where some of the developing-nation data were collected, visual hallucinations were not viewed as very different from commonplace religious experiences (Luhrmann, 2007). Moreover, in developing nations, families remained involved in individuals' lives after diagnosis, and many families lived in close-knit communities where care of their loved one was not so burdensome (Hopper & Wanderling, 2000). The fact that culture matters to schizophrenia highlights the role of cultural context in psychological disorders. Consider that even if individuals with schizophrenia were found to share some common brain characteristics, these similar brains would have different experiences and different outcomes as a result of culture.

In developed nations, schizophrenia is strongly associated with poverty, but it is not clear if poverty increases the likelihood of experiencing the disorder (Luhrmann, 2007). Marriage, warm and supportive friends (Jablensky & others, 1992; Wiersma & others, 1998), and employment are related to better outcomes for people diagnosed with schizophrenia (Rosen & Garety, 2005). At the very least, this research suggests that some individuals with schizophrenia enjoy marriage, productive work, and friendships (Drake, Levine, & Laska, 2007; Fleischhaker & others, 2005; Marshall & Rathbone, 2006).

**Do It!**

If you have never met anyone with schizophrenia, why not get to know Moe Armstrong online? He has a blog at www.moearmstrong.com/Site/Welcome.html and a speech on YouTube at www.youtube.com/watch?v=p-_j1ZNKzsg.

self-quiz

1. A negative symptom of schizophrenia is
   A. hallucinations.
   B. flat affect.
   C. delusions.
   D. catatonia.

2. Joel believes that he has superhuman powers. He is likely suffering from
   A. hallucinations.
   B. delusions.
   C. negative symptoms.
   D. referential thinking.

3. The biological causes of schizophrenia include

   A. problems with the body's regulation of dopamine.
   B. abnormalities in brain structure such as enlarged ventricles and a small frontal cortex.
   C. both A and B
   D. neither A nor B

**APPLY IT!** 4. During a psychiatric hospital internship, Tara approaches a young man sitting alone in a corner, and they have a short conversation. He asks her if she is with the government, and she tells him that she is not. She asks him a few

questions and walks away. She tells her advisor later that what disturbed her about the conversation was not so much what the young man said, but that she had this feeling that he just was not really there. Tara was noticing the _____ symptoms of schizophrenia.
A. positive
B. negative
C. cognitive
D. genetic

# 7 Personality Disorders

Imagine that your personality—the very thing about you that makes you *you*—is the core of your life difficulties. That is what happens with **personality disorders,** which are chronic, maladaptive cognitive-behavioral patterns that are thoroughly integrated into an individual's personality. Personality disorders are relatively common. In one study of a representative U.S. sample, researchers found that 15 percent had a personality disorder (Grant & others, 2004).

The *DSM-IV* lists 10 different personality disorders. Proposed changes to the classification of personality disorders in the *DSM-V* are radical (Millon, 2012; Skodol, 2012a, 2012b). They call for eliminating four or five of these personality disorders, such as paranoid and histrionic, and deleting the disorders' diagnostic criteria (Frances & Widiger, 2012; Skodol, 2012a, 2012b). Figure 12.11 shows the proposed personality disorder categories for the *DSM-V*.

Here we survey the two personality disorders that have been the object of the greatest study: antisocial personality disorder and borderline personality disorder. Both will likely be kept in the *DSM-V*.

**personality disorders**
Chronic, maladaptive cognitive-behavioral patterns that are thoroughly integrated into an individual's personality.

## Antisocial Personality Disorder

**Antisocial personality disorder (ASPD)** is a psychological disorder characterized by guiltlessness, law-breaking, exploitation of others, irresponsibility, and deceit. Although they may be superficially charming, individuals with ASPD do not play by the rules, and

**antisocial personality disorder (ASPD)**
Psychological disorder characterized by guiltlessness, law-breaking, exploitation of others, irresponsibility, and deceit.

| Personality Disorder | Characteristics |
|---|---|
| Antisocial | Guiltless law-breaking; manipulative, deceitful, callous, hostile, risk-taking, impulsive, irresponsible behavior |
| Avoidant | Socially detached and withdrawn individual who avoids intimacy with others; low levels of positive emotion, high levels of anxiety |
| Borderline | Emotionally unstable and intense, impulsive, risk-taking, hostile, and anxious individual; experiences fear of abandonment, depression, and internal feelings of emptiness |
| Narcissistic | Unrealistic grandiose sense of self-importance, attention-seeking, difficulty taking criticism, lack of empathy for others |
| Obsessive-Compulsive | Rigid perfectionism and adherence to a strict moral code; experiences a great deal of anxiety unless things are "just right" and may be obsessed with rules; excessively stubborn, rigid, and moralistic (Note: This is not the same as the anxiety disorder discussed earlier in this chapter.) |
| Schizotypal | Eccentric beliefs, cognitive and perceptual distortions, unusual beliefs and experiences, similar to delusions; emotionally restricted, socially withdrawn, suspicious |
| Personality Disorder Trait Specified | Extreme trait profile, with personality traits contributing to problems in the self (including sense of identity and self-direction) as well as in social relationships |

**FIGURE 12.11 Personality Disorder Diagnoses Proposed for the *DSM-V*** The newest version of the *DSM* might contain these seven personality disorders (American Psychiatric Association, 2012). Note how these descriptions make use of the personality traits presented in Chapter 10.

Reprinted with permission from the *Diagnostic and Statistical Manual of Mental Disorders*, Fourth Edition, Text Revision. Copyright © 2000 American Psychiatric Association.

they often lead a life of crime and violence. ASPD is far more common in men than in women and is related to criminal behavior, vandalism, substance abuse, and alcoholism (Cale & Lilienfeld, 2002).

The *DSM-IV* criteria for antisocial personality disorder include

- Failure to conform to social norms or obey the law
- Deceitfulness, lying, using aliases, or conning others for personal profit or pleasure
- Impulsivity or failure to plan ahead
- Irritability and aggressiveness; getting into physical fights or perpetrating assaults
- Reckless disregard for the safety of self or others
- Consistent irresponsibility, inconsistent work behavior; not paying bills
- Lack of remorse, indifference to the pain of others, or rationalizing; hurting or mistreating another person

Generally, ASPD is not diagnosed unless a person has shown persistent antisocial behavior before the age of 15.

Although ASPD is associated with criminal behavior, not all individuals with ASPD engage in crime, and not all criminals suffer from ASPD. Some individuals with ASPD can have successful careers. There are antisocial physicians, clergy members, lawyers, and just about any other occupation. Still, such individuals tend to be exploitative of others, and they break the rules, even if they are never caught.

What is the etiology of ASPD? Biological factors include genetic, brain, and autonomic nervous system differences. We consider these in turn.

ASPD is genetically heritable (Nordstrom & others, 2012). Certain genetic characteristics associated with ASPD may interact with testosterone (the hormone most associated with aggressive behavior) to promote antisocial behavior (Sjoberg & others, 2008). Although the experience of childhood abuse may be implicated in ASPD, there is evidence that genetic differences may distinguish abused children who go on to commit violent acts themselves from those who do not (Caspi & others, 2002).

In terms of the brain, research has linked ASPD to low levels of activation in the prefrontal cortex and has related these brain differences to poor decision making and problems in learning (Raine & others, 2000). With regard to the autonomic nervous system, researchers have found that individuals with ASPD are less stressed than others by aversive circumstances, including punishment (Fung & others, 2005), and that they have the ability to keep their cool while engaging in deception (Verschuere & others, 2005). The underaroused autonomic nervous system may be a key difference between adolescents who become antisocial adults and those whose behavior improves during adulthood (Raine, Venables, & Williams, 1990).

*Lack of autonomic nervous system activity suggests why individuals with ASPD might be able to fool a polygraph (lie detector).*

The term *psychopath* is sometimes used to refer to a subgroup of individuals with ASPD (Pham, 2012). Psychopaths are remorseless predators who engage in violence to get what they want. Examples of psychopaths include serial killers John Wayne Gacy, who murdered 33 boys and young men, and Ted Bundy, who confessed to murdering at least 30 young women. Psychopaths tend to show less prefrontal activation than normal individuals and to have structural abnormalities in the amygdala, as well as the hippocampus, the brain structure most closely associated with memory (Weber & others, 2008). Importantly, these brain differences are most pronounced in "unsuccessful psychopaths"—individuals who have been arrested

*John Wayne Gacy (top) and Ted Bundy (bottom) exemplify the subgroup of people with ASPD who are also psychopathic.*

for their behaviors (Yang & others, 2005). In contrast, "successful psychopaths"—individuals who have engaged in antisocial behavior but have not gotten caught—are more similar to healthy controls in terms of brain structure and function. However, in their behavior, successful psychopaths demonstrate a lack of empathy and a willingness to act immorally; they victimize others to enrich their own lives. Psychopaths show deficiencies in learning about fear and have difficulty processing information related to the distress of others, such as sad or fearful faces (Dolan & Fullam, 2006).

A key challenge in treating individuals with ASPD, including psychopaths, is their ability to con even sophisticated mental health professionals. Many never seek therapy, and others end up in prison, where treatment is rarely an option.

*Their functioning frontal lobes might help successful psychopaths avoid getting caught.*

## Borderline Personality Disorder

According to the *DSM-IV,* **borderline personality disorder (BPD)** is a pervasive pattern of instability in interpersonal relationships, self-image, and emotions, and of marked impulsivity beginning by early adulthood and present in various contexts. Individuals with BPD are insecure, impulsive, and emotional (Hooley, Cole, & Gironde, 2012). BPD is related to self-harming behaviors such as *cutting* (injuring oneself with a sharp object but without suicidal intent) and also to suicide (Soloff & others, 1994).

The *DSM-IV* specifies that BPD is indicated by the presence of five or more of the following symptoms:

- Frantic efforts to avoid being abandoned
- Unstable and intense interpersonal relationships characterized by extreme shifts between idealization and devaluation
- Markedly and persistently unstable self-image or sense of self
- Impulsivity in at least two areas that are potentially self-damaging (for example, spending, sex, substance abuse, reckless driving, and binge eating)
- Recurrent suicidal behavior, gestures, or threats or self-mutilating behavior
- Unstable and extreme emotional responses
- Chronic feelings of emptiness
- Inappropriate, intense anger or difficulty controlling anger
- Temporary stress-related paranoia (a pattern of disturbed thought featuring delusions of grandeur or persecution) or severe dissociative symptoms

Individuals with BPD are prone to wild mood swings and very sensitive to how others treat them. They often feel as if they are riding a nonstop emotional roller-coaster (Selby & others, 2009), and their loved ones may have to work hard to avoid upsetting them. Individuals with BPD tend to see the world in black-and-white terms, a thinking style called *splitting*. For example, they typically view other people as either hated enemies with no positive qualities or as beloved, idealized friends who can do no wrong.

Borderline personality disorder is far more common in women than men. Women make up 75 percent of those with the disorder (Korzekwa & others, 2008; Oltmanns & Powers, 2012).

The potential causes of BPD are likely complex and include biological factors as well as childhood experiences. The role of genes in BPD has been demonstrated in a variety of studies and across cultures (Mulder, 2012). The heritability of BPD is about 40 percent (Distel & others, 2008).

Many individuals with borderline personality disorder report experiences of childhood sexual abuse, as well as physical abuse and neglect (Al-Alem & Omar, 2008; De Fruyt & De Clercq, 2012). It is not clear, however, whether abuse is a primary cause of the disorder (Trull & Widiger, 2003). Childhood abuse experiences may combine with genetic factors in promoting BPD.

**borderline personality disorder (BPD)** Psychological disorder characterized by a pervasive pattern of instability in interpersonal relationships, self-image, and emotions, and of marked impulsivity beginning by early adulthood and present in a variety of contexts.

**EXPERIENCE IT!**
Borderline Personality Disorder

*Movie depictions of BPD include* Fatal Attraction, Single White Female, *and* Obsessed. *Where these films get it wrong is that they show BPD as leading to more harm to others than to the self.*

*This would be a diathesis-stress model explanation for BPD.*

Cognitive factors associated with BPD include a tendency to hold a set of irrational beliefs (Leahy & McGinn, 2012). These include thinking that one is powerless and innately unacceptable and that other people are dangerous and hostile (Arntz, 2005). Individuals with BPD also display *hypervigilance:* the tendency to be constantly on the alert, looking for threatening information in the environment (Sieswerda & others, 2007).

Up until 20 years ago, experts thought that BPD was untreatable. More recent evidence, however, suggests that many individuals with BPD show improvement over time—as many as 50 percent within two years of starting treatment (Gunderson, 2008). One key aspect of successful treatment appears to be a reduction in social stress, such as that due to leaving an abusive romantic partner or establishing a sense of trust in a therapist (Gunderson & others, 2003).

To recognize the severe toll of BPD on those suffering from it (and on their families and friends), in 2008 the U.S. House of Representatives declared May to be National Borderline Personality Disorder Awareness Month.

## self-quiz

1. Individuals with ASPD
   A. are incapable of having successful careers.
   B. are typically women.
   C. are typically men.
   D. rarely engage in criminal behavior.

2. People with BPD
   A. pay little attention to how others treat them.
   B. rarely have problems with anger or strong emotion.
   C. tend to have suicidal thoughts or engage in self-harming actions.
   D. tend to have a balanced viewpoint of people and things rather than to see them as all black or all white.

3. All of the following are true of BPD except
   A. BPD can be caused by a combination of nature and nurture—genetic inheritance and childhood experience.
   B. Recent research has shown that people with BPD respond positively to treatment.
   C. A common symptom of BPD is impulsive behavior such as binge eating and reckless driving.
   D. BPD is far more common in men than women.

**APPLY IT!** 4. Your new friend Maureen tells you that she was diagnosed with borderline personality disorder at the age of 23. She feels hopeless when she considers that her mood swings and unstable self-esteem are part of her very personality. Despairing, she asks, "How will I ever change?" Which of the following statements about Maureen's condition is accurate?
   A. Maureen should seek therapy and strive to improve her relationships with others, as BPD is treatable.
   B. Maureen's concerns are realistic, because a personality disorder like BPD is unlikely to change.
   C. Maureen should seek treatment for BPD because there is a high likelihood that she will end up committing a criminal act.
   D. Maureen is right to be concerned, because BPD is most often caused by genetic factors.

# 8 Combatting Stigma

Putting a label on a person with a psychological disorder can make the disorder seem like something that happens only to other people (Baumann, 2007). The truth is that psychological disorders are not just about other people; they are about people, period. Over 26 percent of Americans ages 18 and older suffer from a diagnosable psychological disorder in a given year—an estimated 57.7 million U.S. adults (Kessler & others, 2005; NIMH, 2008). Chances are that you or someone you know will experience a psychological disorder. Figure 12.12 shows how common many psychological disorders are in the United States.

A classic and controversial study illustrates that labels of psychological disorder can be "sticky"—hard to remove once they are applied to a person. David Rosenhan (1973) recruited eight adults (including a stay-at-home mother, a psychology graduate student, a pediatrician, and some psychiatrists), none with a psychological disorder, to see a psychiatrist at various hospitals. These "pseudo-patients" were instructed to act normally except to complain about hearing voices that said things like "empty" and "thud." All eight expressed an interest in leaving the hospital and behaved cooperatively. Nevertheless, all eight were labeled with schizophrenia and kept in the hospital from 3 to 52 days. None of the mental health professionals they encountered ever questioned the diagnosis that was given to these individuals, and all were discharged with the label "schizophrenia in remission." The label "schizophrenia" had stuck to the pseudo-patients and caused the professionals around them to interpret their quite normal behavior as abnormal. Clearly, once a person has been labeled with a psychological disorder, that label colors how others perceive everything else he or she does.

Labels of psychological disorder carry with them a wide array of implications for the individual. Is the person still able to be a good friend? A good parent? A competent worker? A significant concern for individuals with psychological disorders is the negative attitudes that others might have about people struggling with mental illness (Phelan & Basow, 2007). Stigma can be a barrier for individuals coping with a psychological disorder, as well as for their families and loved ones (Corrigan, 2007; Hinshaw, 2007). Negative attitudes about individuals with psychological disorders are common in many cultures, and cultural norms and values influence these attitudes (Abdullah & Brown, 2011). Fear of stigma can prevent individuals from seeking treatment and from talking about their problems with family and friends.

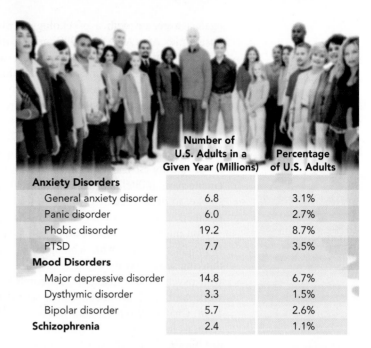

| | Number of U.S. Adults in a Given Year (Millions) | Percentage of U.S. Adults |
|---|---|---|
| **Anxiety Disorders** | | |
| General anxiety disorder | 6.8 | 3.1% |
| Panic disorder | 6.0 | 2.7% |
| Phobic disorder | 19.2 | 8.7% |
| PTSD | 7.7 | 3.5% |
| **Mood Disorders** | | |
| Major depressive disorder | 14.8 | 6.7% |
| Dysthymic disorder | 3.3 | 1.5% |
| Bipolar disorder | 5.7 | 2.6% |
| **Schizophrenia** | 2.4 | 1.1% |

**FIGURE 12.12** **The 12-Month Prevalence of the Most Common Psychological Disorders** If you add up the numbers in this figure, you will see that the totals are higher than the numbers given in the text. The explanation is that people are frequently diagnosed with more than one psychological disorder. An individual who has both a depressive and an anxiety disorder would be counted in both of those categories.

# Consequences of Stigma

The stigma attached to psychological disorders can provoke prejudice and discrimination toward individuals who are struggling with these problems, thus complicating an already difficult situation. Having a disorder and experiencing the stigma associated with it can also negatively affect the physical health of such individuals.

**PREJUDICE AND DISCRIMINATION** Labels of psychological disorders can be damaging because they may lead to negative stereotypes, which play a role in prejudice. For example, the label "schizophrenic" often has negative connotations such as "frightening" and "dangerous."

Vivid cases of extremely harmful behavior by individuals with psychological disorders can perpetuate the stereotype that people with such disorders are violent. For example, Cho Seung-Hui, a 23-year-old college student, murdered 32 students and faculty at Virginia Tech University in April 2007 before killing himself. The widely reported fact that Cho had struggled with psychological disorders throughout his life may have reinforced the notion that individuals with disorders are dangerous. In fact, however, people with psychological disorders (especially those in treatment) are no more likely to commit violent acts than the general population. Cho was no more representative of people with psychological disorders than he was representative of students at Virginia Tech.

Individuals with psychological disorders are often aware of the negative stigma attached to these conditions and may themselves have previously held such negative attitudes. Seeking the assistance they need may involve accepting a stigmatized identity (Thornicroft & others, 2009; Yen & others, 2009). Even mental health professionals can fall prey to prejudicial attitudes toward those who are coping with psychological disorders (Nordt, Rossler, & Lauber, 2006). Improved knowledge about the neurobiological and genetic processes involved in many psychological disorders appears to be a promising direction for interventions to reduce such prejudice. Research shows that information about the role of genes in these disorders reduces prejudicial attitudes (WonPat-Borja & others, 2012).

Among the most feared aspects of stigma is discrimination, or acting prejudicially toward a person who is a member of a stigmatized group. In the workplace, discrimination against a person with a psychological disorder violates the law. The Americans with Disabilities Act (ADA) of 1990 made it illegal to refuse employment or a promotion to someone with a psychological disorder when the person's condition does not prevent performance of the job's essential functions (Cleveland, Barnes-Farrell, & Ratz, 1997). A person's appearance or behavior may be unusual or irritating, but as long as that individual is able to complete the duties required of a position, employment or promotion cannot be denied.

**PHYSICAL HEALTH**   Individuals with psychological disorders are more likely to be physically ill and two times more likely to die than their psychologically healthy counterparts (Gittelman, 2008; Kumar, 2004). They are also more likely to be obese, to smoke, to drink excessively, and to lead sedentary lives (Kim & others, 2007; Lindwall & others, 2007; Mykletun & others, 2007; Osborn, Nazareth, & King, 2006).

You might be thinking that these physical health issues are the least of their worries. If people struggling with schizophrenia want to smoke, why not let them? This type of thinking sells short the capacity of psychological and psychiatric treatments to help those with psychological disorders. Research has shown that health-promotion programs can work well for individuals with a severe psychological disorder (Addington & others, 1998; Chafetz & others, 2008). When we disregard the potential of physical health interventions for people with psychological disorders to make positive life changes, we reveal our biases.

# Overcoming Stigma

How can we combat the stigma of psychological disorders? One obstacle to changing people's attitudes toward individuals with psychological disorders is that mental illness is often "invisible." That is, sometimes a person we know can have a disorder without our being aware. We may be unaware of *many* good lives around us that are being lived under a cloud of psychological disorder, because worries about being stigmatized keep the affected individuals from "coming out." Thus, stigma leads to a catch-22: Positive examples of individuals coping with psychological disorders are often missing from our experience because those who are doing well shun public disclosure of their disorders (Jensen & Wadkins, 2007).

A critical step toward eliminating stigma is to resist thinking of people with disorders as limited by their condition. Instead, it is vital to recognize their strengths—both in confronting their disorder and in carrying on despite their problems—and their achievements. By creating a positive environment for people with disorders, we encourage more of them to become confidently "visible" and empower them to be positive role models.

When Milton Greek arrived at Ohio University in the 1980s as a young undergraduate, he had an ambitious goal: "to discover a psychological code that people should live by, to create world peace" (Carey, 2011a). He became known as a person with very strange ideas. By his senior year, Milt was in a failing marriage and was convinced that he had met God one day on the street and Jesus a few days later. Although he was a lifelong atheist, his delusions took on a distinctive religious character. He believed the Rapture would occur at any moment and that he himself was the anti-Christ. He heard voices no one else did and saw things that were not there. Eventually diagnosed with schizophrenia, Milt began taking medication and started to put his life back together. While in graduate school, he stopped taking his medications when things seemed to be going well, only to have a close friend give him a reality check. "When she used the word 'hallucination' I knew it was true," he said (Carey, 2011a).

Today Milt is a 49-year-old, happily married computer programmer. He takes medications to control his symptoms and seems again to have found a mission in life. This time it is about making a difference in the lives of others by sharing his story as a man with schizophrenia. Along with a small group of other people with serious psychiatric disorders, Milt has "come out" and related his experiences to combat stigma, providing hope for others who are suffering with psychological disorders and helping psychologists who are interested in experiences like his.

After reading this chapter, you know that many admired individuals have dealt with psychological disorders. Their diagnoses do not detract from their accomplishments. To the contrary, their accomplishments are all the more remarkable in the context of the challenges they have faced.

## self-quiz

1. The percentage of Americans 18 years of age and older who suffer from a diagnosable psychological disorder in a given year is closest to
   A. 15 percent.
   B. 26 percent.
   C. 40 percent.
   D. 46 percent.

2. The stigma attached to psychological disorders can have implications for
   A. the physical health of an individual with such a disorder.
   B. the psychological well-being of an individual with such a disorder.
   C. other people's attitudes and behaviors toward the individual with such a disorder.
   D. all of the above

3. Labeling psychological disorders can lead to damaging
   A. stereotyping.
   B. discrimination.
   C. prejudice.
   D. all of the above

APPLY IT! 4. Liliana has applied for a job after graduation doing data entry for a polling firm. During her second interview, Liliana asks the human resources manager whether the job's health benefits include prescription drug coverage, as she is on anti-anxiety medication for generalized anxiety disorder. Which of the following statements is most applicable, legally and otherwise, in light of Liliana's request?
   A. The human resources manager should tell the hiring committee to avoid hiring Liliana because she has a psychological disorder.
   B. It is illegal for the firm to deny Liliana employment simply because she has a psychological disorder.
   C. Liliana should not have asked that question, because she will not be hired.
   D. Liliana must be given the job, or the firm could face a lawsuit.

## SUMMARY

### ① Defining and Explaining Abnormal Behavior

Abnormal behavior is deviant, maladaptive, or personally distressful. Theoretical perspectives on the causes of psychological disorders include biological, psychological, sociocultural, and biopsychosocial approaches.

Biological approaches to disorders describe psychological disorders as diseases with origins in structural, biochemical, and genetic factors. Psychological approaches include the behavioral, social cognitive, and trait perspectives. Sociocultural approaches place emphasis on the larger social context in which a person lives, including marriage, socioeconomic status, ethnicity, gender, and culture. Biopsychosocial approaches view the interactions among biological, psychological, and social factors as significant forces in producing both normal and abnormal behavior.

The classification of disorders provides a shorthand for communication, allows clinicians to make predictions about disorders, and helps them to decide on appropriate treatment. The *Diagnostic and Statistical Manual of Mental Disorders (DSM)* is the classification system clinicians use to diagnose psychological disorders. Some psychologists contend that the *DSM-IV* perpetuates the medical model of psychological disorders, labels everyday problems as psychological disorders, and fails to address strengths.

### ② Anxiety Disorders

Generalized anxiety disorder is anxiety that persists for at least six months with no specific reason for the anxiety. Panic disorder involves attacks marked by the sudden onset of intense terror. Biological, psychological, and sociocultural factors may contribute to the development of panic disorder.

Phobic disorders involve an irrational, overwhelming fear of a particular object, such as snakes, or a situation, such as flying. Obsessive-compulsive disorder is an anxiety disorder in which the individual has anxiety-provoking thoughts that will not go away (obsession) and/or urges to perform repetitive, ritualistic behaviors to prevent or produce some future situation (compulsion). Post-traumatic stress disorder (PTSD) is an anxiety disorder that develops through exposure to traumatic events, sexual abuse and assault, and natural and unnatural disasters. Symptoms include flashbacks, emotional avoidance, emotional numbing, and excessive arousal. A variety of experiential, psychological, and genetic factors have been shown to relate to these disorders.

### ③ Mood Disorders

Two types of mood disorders are depressive disorders and bipolar disorder.

The depressive disorders include major depressive disorder and dysthymic disorder. In major depressive disorder, the individual experiences a serious depressive episode and depressed characteristics such as lethargy and hopelessness. Dysthymic disorder is generally more chronic and has fewer symptoms than major depressive disorder.

Biological explanations of depressive disorders focus on heredity, neurophysiological abnormalities, and neurotransmitter deregulation. Psychological explanations include behavioral and cognitive perspectives. Sociocultural explanations emphasize socioeconomic and ethnic factors, as well as gender.

Bipolar disorder is characterized by extreme mood swings that include one or more episodes of mania (an overexcited, unrealistic, optimistic state). Most individuals with bipolar disorder go through multiple cycles of depression interspersed with mania. Genetic influences are stronger predictors of bipolar disorder than depressive disorder, and biological processes are also a factor in bipolar disorder.

Severe depression and other psychological disorders can cause individuals to want to end their lives. Theorists have proposed biological, psychological, and sociocultural explanations of suicide.

## 4 Eating Disorders

Three eating disorders are anorexia nervosa, bulimia nervosa, and binge eating disorder. Anorexia nervosa is characterized by extreme underweight and starvation. The disorder is related to perfectionism and obsessive-compulsive tendencies. Bulimia nervosa involves a pattern of binge eating followed by purging through self-induced vomiting. In contrast, binge eating disorder involves binge eating without purging.

Anorexia nervosa and bulimia nervosa are much more common in women than men, but there is no gender difference in binge eating disorder. Although sociocultural factors were once thought to be primary in explaining eating disorders, more recent evidence points to the role of biological factors.

## 5 Dissociative Disorders

Dissociative amnesia entails memory loss caused by extensive psychological stress. Dissociative fugue also involves memory loss, but individuals with this disorder unexpectedly travel away from home or work, sometimes assume a new identity, and do not remember the old one. In dissociative identity disorder, formerly called multiple personality disorder, two or more distinct personalities are present in the same individual.

## 6 Schizophrenia

Schizophrenia is a severe psychological disorder characterized by highly disordered thought processes. Positive symptoms of schizophrenia are behaviors and experiences that are present in individuals with schizophrenia but absent in healthy people; they include hallucinations and delusions. Negative symptoms of schizophrenia are behaviors and experiences that are part of healthy human life that are absent for those with this disorder; they include flat affect and an inability to plan or engage in goal-directed behavior.

Biological factors (heredity, structural brain abnormalities, and problems in neurotransmitter regulation, especially dopamine), psychological factors (diathesis-stress model), and sociocultural factors may be involved in schizophrenia. Psychological and sociocultural factors are not viewed as stand-alone causes of schizophrenia, but they are related to the course of the disorder.

## 7 Personality Disorders

Personality disorders are chronic, maladaptive cognitive-behavioral patterns that are thoroughly integrated into an individual's personality. Two common types are antisocial personality disorder (ASPD) and borderline personality disorder (BPD).

Antisocial personality disorder is characterized by guiltlessness, law-breaking, exploitation of others, irresponsibility, and deceit. Individuals with this disorder often lead a life of crime and violence. Psychopaths—remorseless predators who engage in violence to get what they want—are a subgroup of individuals with ASPD.

Borderline personality disorder is a pervasive pattern of instability in interpersonal relationships, self-image, and emotions, and of marked impulsivity beginning by early adulthood and present in a variety of contexts. This disorder is related to self-harming behaviors such as cutting and suicide.

Biological factors for ASPD include genetic, brain, and autonomic nervous system differences. The potential causes of BPD are complex and include biological and cognitive factors as well as childhood experiences.

## 8 Combatting Stigma

Stigma can create a significant barrier for people coping with a psychological disorder, as well as for their loved ones. Fear of being labeled can prevent individuals with a disorder from getting treatment and from talking about their problems with family and friends. In addition, the stigma attached to psychological disorders can lead to prejudice and discrimination toward individuals who are struggling with these problems. Having a disorder and experiencing the stigma associated with it can also negatively affect the physical health of such individuals.

We can help to combat stigma by acknowledging the strengths and the achievements of individuals coping with psychological disorders. By creating a positive environment for people with disorders, we encourage them to be open about their struggles and to thrive, with the result that they can become positive role models for others.

## KEY TERMS

abnormal behavior, p. 441

medical model, p. 443

*DSM-IV,* p. 444

attention deficit hyperactivity disorder (ADHD), p. 446

anxiety disorders, p. 448

generalized anxiety disorder, p. 448

panic disorder, p. 449

phobic disorder (phobia), p. 450

obsessive-compulsive disorder (OCD), p. 452

post-traumatic stress disorder (PTSD), p. 452

mood disorders, p. 454

depressive disorders, p. 454

major depressive disorder (MDD), p. 455

dysthymic disorder (DD), p. 455

bipolar disorder, p. 457

anorexia nervosa, p. 462

bulimia nervosa, p. 463

binge eating disorder (BED), p. 464

dissociative disorders, p. 465

dissociative amnesia, p. 466

dissociative fugue, p. 466

dissociative identity disorder (DID), p. 466

schizophrenia, p. 468

hallucinations, p. 469

delusions, p. 469

referential thinking, p. 469

catatonia, p. 469

flat affect, p. 469

diathesis-stress model, p. 472

personality disorders, p. 473

antisocial personality disorder (ASPD), p. 473

borderline personality disorder (BPD), p. 475

## Multiple Choice

1. The name for a mark of shame that may cause people to avoid, or act negatively toward, an individual is
   A. disfigurement.
   B. mortification.
   C. stigma.
   D. prejudice.

2. Feeling an overwhelming sense of dread and worry without a specific cause is known as
   A. obsessive-compulsive disorder.
   B. generalized anxiety disorder.
   C. phobic disorder.
   D. panic disorder.

3. A characteristic of post-traumatic stress disorder is
   A. panic attacks.
   B. an exaggerated startle response.
   C. persistent nervousness about a variety of things.
   D. extreme fear of an object or place.

4. All of the following are a mood disorder except
   A. generalized anxiety disorder.
   B. dysthymic disorder.
   C. major depressive disorder.
   D. bipolar disorder.

5. The diagnostic criteria for major depressive disorder include the standard that a depressive episode must last at least
   A. one week.
   B. two weeks.
   C. two months.
   D. two years.

6. Insistently focusing on being depressed is characteristic of
   A. catastrophic thinking.
   B. a ruminative coping style.
   C. dysthymic disorder.
   D. learned helplessness.

7. The eating disorder that involves binge eating followed by purging through self-induced vomiting is
   A. binge eating disorder.
   B. bulimia nervosa.
   C. anorexia nervosa.
   D. compulsive eating disorder.

8. A dissociative disorder accompanied by unexpected sudden travel is
   A. dissociate disorder.
   B. dissociative amnesia.
   C. dissociative identity disorder.
   D. dissociative fugue.

9. _____ symptoms of schizophrenia reflect a loss of normal functioning, while _____ symptoms reflect the addition of abnormal functioning.
   A. Cognitive; behavioral
   B. Behavioral; cognitive
   C. Positive; negative
   D. Negative; positive

10. Antisocial personality disorder is characterized by _____, whereas borderline personality disorder is characterized by _____.
    A. avoidance of impulsive behavior; avoidance of physical aggression
    B. avoidance of physical aggression; avoidance of impulsive behavior
    C. a tendency to harm oneself; violence toward others
    D. violence toward others; a tendency to harm oneself

## Apply It!

11. What is the diathesis-stress model? In the text this model was applied to schizophrenia. Apply it to one eating disorder and one anxiety disorder.

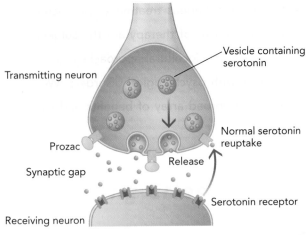

**FIGURE 13.1** **How the Antidepressant Prozac Works**
Secreted by a transmitting neuron, serotonin moves across the synaptic gap and binds to receptors in a receiving neuron. Excess serotonin in the synaptic gap is normally reabsorbed by the transmitting neuron. The antidepressant Prozac blocks this reuptake of serotonin by the transmitting neuron, however, leaving excess serotonin in the synaptic gap. The excess serotonin is transmitted to the receiving neuron and circulated through the brain. The result is a reduction of the serotonin deficit found in depressed individuals.

temporarily for symptomatic relief. Too often, they are overused and can become addictive (Lader, 2012; Marazziti, Carlini, & Dell'osso, 2012).

**ANTIDEPRESSANT DRUGS** **Antidepressant drugs** regulate mood. The three main classes of antidepressant drugs are tricyclics, such as Elavil; monoamine oxidase (MAO) inhibitors, such as Nardil; and selective serotonin reuptake inhibitors, such as Prozac. These antidepressants are all thought to help depressed mood through their effects on neurotransmitters in the brain. In different ways, they all allow the depressed person's brain to increase or maintain its level of important neurotransmitters, especially serotonin and norepinephrine.

*Tricyclics,* so-called because of their three-ringed molecular structure, are believed to work by increasing the level of certain neurotransmitters, especially norepinephrine and serotonin (Taurines & others, 2011). You might recall the role of low serotonin levels in negative mood (Chapter 10) and aggression (Chapter 11). Tricyclics reduce the symptoms of depression in approximately 60 to 70 percent of cases. Tricyclics usually take two to four weeks to improve mood. Adverse side effects may include restlessness, faintness, trembling, sleepiness, and memory difficulties. A recent meta-analysis of 30 years of studies concluded that the older antidepressant drugs, such as the tricyclics, reduced depression more effectively than the newer antidepressant drugs (Undurraga & Baldessarini, 2012).

Related to the tricyclics are *tetracyclic antidepressants,* named for their four-ringed structure. Tetracyclics are also called *noradrenergic and specific serotonergic antidepressants,* or NaSSAs. These drugs have effects on both norepinephrine and serotonin, enhancing brain levels of these neurotransmitters. One recent analysis found that the tetracylic Remeron (mertazapine) was more effective in reducing depression than any other antidepressant drug (Cipriani & others, 2010).

*MAO inhibitors* are thought to work by blocking the enzyme monoamine oxidase, which breaks down the neurotransmitters serotonin and norepinephrine in the brain (Meyer, 2012). Scientists believe that the blocking action of MAO inhibitors allows these neurotransmitters to stick around and help regulate mood. MAO inhibitors are not as widely used as tricyclics because potentially they are more harmful. However, some individuals who do not improve with tricyclics do respond to MAO inhibitors. MAO inhibitors may be especially risky because of their potential interactions with certain foods and drugs (Nishida & others, 2009). Cheese and other fermented foods—including alcoholic beverages, such as red wine—can interact with the inhibitors to raise blood pressure and, over time, cause a stroke.

In recent years psychiatrists have increasingly prescribed a type of antidepressant drug called *selective serotonin reuptake inhibitors (SSRIs).* SSRIs target serotonin and work mainly by interfering with the reabsorption of serotonin in the brain (Fooladi, Bell, & Davis, 2012). Figure 13.1 shows this process.

Three widely prescribed SSRIs are Prozac (fluoxetine), Paxil (paroxetine), and Zoloft (sertraline). The increased prescription of these drugs reflects their effectiveness in reducing the symptoms of depression with fewer side effects than other antidepressants (Fields, 2013). Nonetheless, they can have side effects, including insomnia, anxiety, headache, and impaired sexual functioning (Keeton, Kolos, & Walkup, 2009) and produce severe withdrawal symptoms if the individual abruptly stops taking them (Kurose & others, 2012).

**antidepressant drugs**
Drugs that regulate mood.

*As their name suggests, these drugs selectively inhibit the reuptake of serotonin.*

*Effexor is also commonly prescribed for depression. It inhibits the reuptake of serotonin and norepinephrine and is thus called a* serotonin-norepinephrine reuptake inhibitor, *or SNRI.*

A recent large-scale U.S. study revealed that the number of individuals taking antidepressants rose nearly 400 percent among all ages between 1988 and 2008, with 11 percent of individuals 12 years and older taking an antidepressant in 2008 (Pratt, Brody, & Gu, 2011). In this study, more than 60 percent of individuals in the United States reported that they have been taking antidepressants for two years or longer, and 14 percent for 10 years or longer.

Beyond their usefulness in treating mood disorders, antidepressant drugs are often effective for a number of anxiety disorders, as well as some eating and sleep disorders (Bernardy & others, 2012; Wu & others, 2012). Increasingly, antidepressants are prescribed for other common problems, such as chronic pain. Such prescriptions are called "off label" because they involve using a drug for reasons other than those recommended. In fact, in 2005, less than half of the individuals in the United States who had taken prescribed antidepressants were doing so for depression (Olfson & Marcus, 2009).

**Lithium** is widely used to treat bipolar disorder. Lithium is the lightest of the solid elements in the periodic table of elements. If you have ever used a lithium battery (or are a fan of Nirvana or Evanescence), you know that lithium has uses beyond treating psychological disorders. The amount of lithium that circulates in the bloodstream must be carefully monitored because the effective dosage is precariously close to toxic levels. Kidney and thyroid gland complications as well as weight gain can arise as a consequence of lithium therapy (Bauer & others, 2007). Lithium is thought to stabilize moods by influencing norepinephrine and serotonin, but the exact mechanism of its effect is unknown (Ago & others, 2012). The effectiveness of lithium depends on the person's staying on the medication. Some consumers may be troubled by the association between lithium and weight gain, and others may go off the drug when they are feeling well.

The use of antidepressant drugs to treat depression in children is controversial. To read more about this issue, see Challenge Your Thinking.

### ANTIPSYCHOTIC DRUGS
**Antipsychotic drugs** are powerful drugs that diminish agitated behavior, reduce tension, decrease hallucinations, improve social behavior, and produce better sleep patterns in individuals who have a severe psychological disorder, especially schizophrenia (Guo & others, 2012). Before antipsychotic drugs were developed in the 1950s, few, if any, interventions brought relief from the torment of psychotic symptoms.

*Neuroleptics* are the most extensively used class of antipsychotic drugs (Garver, 2006). When taken in sufficient doses, neuroleptics reduce schizophrenic symptoms (Nasrallah & others, 2009). The most widely accepted explanation for the effectiveness of neuroleptics is their ability to block dopamine's action in the brain (Zhai, Miller, & Sammis, 2012).

Neuroleptics do not cure schizophrenia; they treat its symptoms, not its causes. If an individual with schizophrenia stops taking the drug, the symptoms return. Neuroleptic drugs have substantially reduced the length of hospital stays for individuals with schizophrenia. However, when these individuals are able to return to the community (because the drug therapy reduces their symptoms), many have difficulty coping with the demands of society. In the absence of symptoms, many struggle to justify to themselves that they should continue to take the very medications that have reduced their symptoms, particularly because neuroleptic drugs can have severe side effects, including stroke. Drugs that treat disturbed thought by reducing dopamine can also induce a lack of pleasure (Kapur, 2003).

Another potential side effect of neuroleptic drugs is *tardive dyskinesia,* a neurological disorder characterized by involuntary random movements of the facial muscles,

**lithium**
The lightest of the solid elements in the periodic table of elements, widely used to treat bipolar disorder.

*The diagnosis of bipolar disorder may be made because the person is responsive to lithium.*

**antipsychotic drugs**
Powerful drugs that diminish agitated behavior, reduce tension, decrease hallucinations, improve social behavior, and produce better sleep patterns in individuals with a severe psychological disorder, especially schizophrenia.

*Recall from Chapter 12 that people with schizophrenia have difficulty regulating the neurotransmitter dopamine, which is associated with the experience of reward.*

AND THEN THEY GAVE ME THIS NEW DRUG AND I THOUGHT WHAT THE HECK, WHY NOT, I'VE TAKEN EVERYTHING ELSE ...

*LAB RAT REHAB*
Used by permission of CartoonStock, www.CartoonStock.com.

# Challenge

## YOUR THINKING

## Do Antidepressants Increase Suicide Risk in Youth?

In 2000, Caitlin McIntosh, a 12-year-old straight-A student, artist, and musician, hanged herself with her shoelaces. Caitlin had been struggling with depression and had begun taking antidepressants shortly before her suicide. Tragic cases such as Caitlin's have stirred deep concerns among parents and mental health professionals. Could the very drugs prescribed to alleviate depression be causing children to become suicidal?

In response to the public unease, the FDA in 2004 reviewed clinical trials of antidepressant use with children (Hammad, 2004). No child in the studies attempted or committed suicide, and there were no differences between the antidepressant and placebo groups on ratings of suicidal thoughts and behaviors. However, children who received antidepressants were two times more likely than those in the placebo groups to spontaneously mention thoughts of suicide, as noted by parents or doctors (the rate of such events was 4 percent in the antidepressant group versus 2 percent for the placebo group). Based on this difference, the FDA required prescription antidepressants to carry the severest "black box" warning, describing the potential of antidepressants to be associated with suicidal thoughts and behaviors in children and adolescents (FDA, 2004). The warning, which was widely publicized, had a chilling effect: Between March 2004 and June 2005, the number of prescriptions fell 20 percent compared to the same time frame the year before (Rosack, 2007).

Since the advent of the black box warning, a number of studies have shown no link between antidepressants and suicidal thoughts or behavior among youth (Gibbons & others, 2012a,

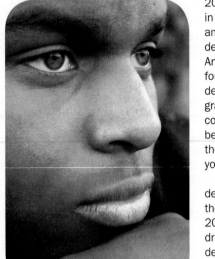

2012b; Sharmila, 2012). Some observers have noted that in the months after the warning took effect, suicide rates among youth increased after having steadily declined for a decade (Bridge & others, 2008; Gibbons & others, 2007). An analysis of data from annual national surveys of youth found that among those who were depressed, reports of delinquent behaviors and illicit drug use increased while grade point average declined in the years after the warning, compared to their levels in the years before (Busch, Golberstein, & Meara, 2011). Such findings could suggest that the black box warning had unexpected consequences on youth struggling with depression.

Perhaps most troubling, there is no strong evidence that depressed adolescents were more likely to receive psychotherapy after the warning took effect (Busch & others, 2010). Such findings are especially disappointing because drug therapy may not be the first-choice treatment for depressed children. Many children and adolescents with depression respond well to psychotherapy alone (Morris, 2012).

This controversy highlights issues we have explored throughout this book. How do we weigh dramatic case study evidence against less vivid scientific data that do not bear out those cases? Are special considerations required when professionals suggest drug therapy in children? How can we best balance the potential benefits and risks of drug treatment? Throughout this debate, the tragedy of suicide looms, and professionals have been moved to change their thinking and practices with regard to treating depression in youth.

### What Do You Think?

- Have antidepressants helped anyone you know? If so, were you aware of negative side effects? Positive side effects? What was the nature of these effects?

- What other events might explain the changes in academic and other outcomes from depressed youth after the black box warning took effect?

---

*Off-label uses of Risperdal include treating aggressive and self-injurious behavior in children, people with autism, and elderly people with dementia.*

tongue, and mouth, as well as extensive twitching of the neck, arms, and legs. Up to 20 percent of individuals with schizophrenia who take neuroleptics develop this disorder. As you may recall from Chapter 12, movement disorders are a positive symptom of schizophrenia, and tardive dyskinesia can also occur in individuals suffering from psychiatric disorders who have not taken neuroleptic drugs (Chouinard, 2006).

Newer antipsychotic drugs called *atypical antipsychotic medications*, introduced in the 1990s, appear to influence dopamine as well as serotonin (Germann, Kurylo, & Han, 2012). The two most widely used medications in this group, Clozaril (clozapine) and Risperdal (risperidone), show promise for reducing

| Psychological Disorder | Drug | Effectiveness | Side Effects |
|---|---|---|---|
| **Everyday Anxiety and Anxiety Disorders** | | | |
| **Everyday Anxiety** | Antianxiety drugs; antidepressant drugs | Substantial improvement short term | Antianxiety drugs: less powerful the longer people take them; may be addictive<br>Antidepressant drugs: see below under depressive disorders |
| **Generalized Anxiety Disorder** | Antianxiety drugs | Not very effective | Less powerful the longer people take them; may be addictive |
| **Panic Disorder** | Antianxiety drugs | About half show improvement | Less powerful the longer people take them; may be addictive |
| **Agoraphobia** | Tricyclic drugs and MAO inhibitors | Majority show improvement | Tricyclics: restlessness, fainting, and trembling<br>MAO inhibitors: toxicity |
| **Specific Phobias** | Antianxiety drugs | Not very effective | Less powerful the longer people take them; may be addictive |
| **Mood Disorders** | | | |
| **Depressive Disorders** | Tricyclic drugs, MAO inhibitors, and SSRI drugs | Majority show moderate improvement | Tricyclics: cardiac problems, mania, confusion, memory loss, fatigue<br>MAO inhibitors: toxicity<br>SSRI drugs: nausea, nervousness, insomnia, and, in a few cases, suicidal thoughts |
| **Bipolar Disorder** | Lithium | Large majority show substantial improvement | Toxicity |
| **Schizophrenic Disorders** | | | |
| **Schizophrenia** | Neuroleptics; atypical antipsychotic medications | Majority show partial improvement | Neuroleptics: irregular heartbeat, low blood pressure, uncontrolled fidgeting, tardive dyskinesia, and immobility of face<br>Atypical antipsychotic medications: less extensive side effects than with neuroleptics, but can have a toxic effect on white blood cells |

**FIGURE 13.2** **Drug Therapy for Psychological Disorders** This figure summarizes the types of drugs used to treat various psychological disorders.

schizophrenia's symptoms without the side effects of neuroleptics (Covell & others, 2012; Nielsen & others, 2012).

Strategies to increase the effectiveness of antipsychotic drugs involve administering small dosages over time rather than a large initial dose, and combining drug therapy with psychotherapy. Along with drug treatment, individuals with schizophrenia may need training in vocational, family, and social skills (Tungpunkom, Maayan, & Soares-Weiser, 2012).

Figure 13.2 lists the drugs used to treat various psychological disorders, their effectiveness, and their side effects. Note that for some anxiety disorders, such as agoraphobia, MAO inhibitors (antidepressant drugs) might be used instead of antianxiety drugs.

# Electroconvulsive Therapy

The goal of **electroconvulsive therapy (ECT)**, commonly called *shock therapy*, is to set off a seizure in the brain, much like what happens spontaneously in some forms of epilepsy. The notion of causing a seizure to help cure a psychological disorder has been around since ancient times. Hippocrates, the ancient Greek father of medicine, first noticed that malaria-induced convulsions would sometimes cure individuals who were thought to be insane (Endler, 1988). Following Hippocrates, many other medical doctors

**electroconvulsive therapy (ECT)**
Also called shock therapy, a treatment, sometimes used for depression, that sets off a seizure in the brain.

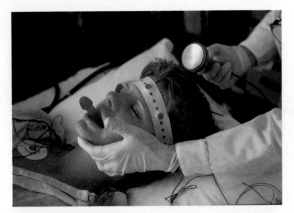

Electroconvulsive therapy (ECT), commonly called shock therapy, causes a seizure in the brain. ECT is given to as many as 100,000 people a year, mainly to treat major depressive disorder.

noted that head traumas, seizures, and convulsions brought on by fever would sometimes lead to the apparent cure of psychological problems.

In the early twentieth century, doctors induced seizures by insulin overdose and other means and used this procedure primarily to treat schizophrenia. In 1937, Ugo Cerletti, an Italian neurologist specializing in epilepsy, developed the procedure by which seizures could be induced using electrical shock. With colleagues, he developed a fast, efficient means of causing seizures in humans, and ECT gained wide use in psychiatric hospitals (Endler, 1988). Unfortunately, in earlier years, ECT was used indiscriminately, sometimes even to punish patients, as in the book and film *One Flew Over the Cuckoo's Nest*.

Today, doctors use ECT primarily to treat severe depression. As many as 100,000 individuals a year undergo ECT, primarily as treatment for major depressive disorder (Mayo Foundation, 2006). Fortunately, the contemporary use of ECT bears little resemblance to its earlier uses. A small electric current lasting for one second or less passes through two electrodes placed on the individual's head. The current stimulates a seizure that lasts for approximately a minute. ECT is given mainly to individuals who have not responded to drug therapy or psychotherapy, and its administration involves little discomfort (Gallegos & others, 2012). The patient receives anesthesia and muscle relaxants before the current is applied; this medication allows the individual to sleep through the procedure, minimizes convulsions, and reduces the risk of physical injury. Increasingly, ECT is applied only to the brain's right side. The individual awakens shortly afterward with no conscious memory of the treatment. A recent study used fMRI to compare brain scans before and after ECT and found that the procedure reduced or weakened connections in the prefrontal cortex (Perrin & others, 2012).

One analysis of studies of the use of ECT found that ECT was as effective as cognitive therapy or drug therapy, with about four of five individuals showing marked improvement in all three therapies (Seligman, 1995). What sets ECT apart from other treatments is the rapid relief it can produce in a person's mood (Merkl, Heuser, & Bajbouj, 2009; Popeo, 2009). ECT may be especially effective as a treatment for acute depression in individuals who are at great risk of suicide (Kellner & others, 2006).

ECT is controversial. Its potential side effects remain a source of debate and contradictory findings (Crowley & others, 2008). These possible effects include memory loss and other cognitive impairments and are generally more severe than drug side effects (Caverzasi & others, 2008). Some individuals treated with ECT report prolonged and profound memory loss (Choi & others, 2011). Side effects are typically lessened if only one side of the brain is stimulated. Despite the potential problems of ECT, some psychiatrists argue that for certain individuals this invasive treatment can have life-enhancing—and even life-saving—benefits (Huuhka & others, 2012; Martinez-Amoros & others, 2012).

More recently, practitioners are treating some forms of depression, as well as other disorders, by applying electrical stimulation in very precise locations in the brain (Luigjes & others, 2012). In *deep brain stimulation*, doctors surgically implant electrodes in the brain that emit signals to alter the brain's electrical circuitry. Deep brain stimulation is being used to treat individuals with treatment-resistant depression and obsessive-compulsive disorder (Chabardès & others, 2012). For instance, deep brain stimulation of the nucleus accumbens (part of the brain's reward pathways) has been effective in treating severe depression (Bewernick & others, 2012).

**psychosurgery**
A biological therapy, with irreversible effects, that involves removal or destruction of brain tissue to improve the individual's adjustment.

## Psychosurgery

**Psychosurgery** is a biological intervention that involves the removal or destruction of brain tissue. Its effects are irreversible.

In the 1930s, Portuguese physician Antonio Egas Moniz developed a new surgical procedure on the brain. In this operation, a surgical instrument was inserted into the brain and rotated, severing fibers that connect the frontal lobe, which is important in higher thought processes, and the thalamus, which plays a key role in emotion. Moniz theorized that by breaking the connections between these structures, the surgeon could alleviate the symptoms of severe mental disorders. In 1949, Moniz received the Nobel Prize for developing this procedure. However, although some patients may have benefited from this surgery, many were left in a vegetable-like state because of the massive assaults on their brain. Moniz himself felt that the procedure should be used with extreme caution and only as a last resort.

*In 1939 a former patient shot Moniz, leaving him a paraplegic; Moniz subsequently retired.*

After hearing about Moniz's work, American physician and neurologist Walter Freeman became the champion of *prefrontal lobotomies* (a term Freeman coined to describe Moniz's procedure). With his colleague James Watts, he performed the first lobotomy in the United States in 1936 (El-Hai, 2005). Freeman developed his own technique, which he performed using a device similar to an ice pick, in surgeries that lasted mere minutes. Throughout the 1950s and 1960s, Freeman, a charismatic showman, traveled the country in a van he called the "lobotomobile," demonstrating the surgery (El-Hai, 2005). Prefrontal lobotomies were conducted on tens of thousands of patients from the 1930s through the 1960s. These numbers speak not only to Freeman's persuasive charm but also to the desperation many physicians felt in treating institutionalized patients with severe psychological disorders (Lerner, 2005).

Subsequent research challenged the effectiveness of lobotomies in enhancing the lives of individuals who had undergone the procedure, pointing instead to the considerable damage that resulted (Landis & Erlick, 1950; Mettler, 1952). Many individuals who received lobotomies suffered permanent and profound brain damage (Whitaker, 2002). Ethical concerns were raised because in many instances, giving consent for the lobotomy was a requirement for release from a mental hospital. Like ECT, lobotomies were used as a form of punishment and control.

By the 1950s drug therapies had emerged as alternatives to lobotomy (Juckel & others, 2009). By the late 1970s new regulations classified the procedure as experimental and established safeguards for patients. In current practice, psychosurgery is more precise (Heller & others, 2006; Kopell, Machado, & Rezai, 2006) and involves making just a small lesion in the amygdala or another part of the limbic system (Fountas & Smith, 2007).

*It makes more sense to target the amygdalae rather than the frontal lobes, considering the functions associated with these brain structures.*

Today, psychosurgery is performed rarely, only as a last resort, and with the utmost caution (Ruck, 2003). Psychiatrists and psychologists recognize that science should tamper with the brain only in extreme cases (Pressman, 1998).

self quiz

1. _____ are used to treat schizophrenia, whereas _____ are used to treat anxiety.
   A. Benzodiazepines; neuroleptics
   B. Neuroleptics; benzodiazepines
   C. MAO inhibitors; tricyclics
   D. Tricyclics; MAO inhibitors

2. Atypical antipsychotic medications work by
   A. increasing the release of presynaptic neurotransmitters.
   B. acting as an antagonist to dopamine.
   C. stopping the reuptake of serotonin.
   D. inhibiting enzymes that break down norepinephrine.

3. A true statement about electroconvulsive therapy is that
   A. it is less effective than medication.
   B. it takes several weeks to see results.
   C. its side effects are more severe than those for medication.
   D. it is painful.

**APPLY IT!** 4. Serena experienced times when her mood was very negative for prolonged periods. She was deeply troubled by her feelings and lacked a sense of pleasure in life. At other times, she felt on top of the world. Antidepressant medications brought her no relief. Finally, her psychiatrist prescribed a different drug, which is helping Serena. Not only have her dark moods leveled out, but she is experiencing more stable positive moods. Which of the following is likely true of Serena's experience?
   A. Serena has a depressive disorder, and the drug is an MAO inhibitor.
   B. Serena has an anxiety disorder, and the drug is a benzodiazipene.
   C. Serena has bipolar disorder, and the drug is lithium.
   D. Serena has an eating disorder, and the drug is an SSRI.

# 2 Psychotherapy

**psychotherapy**
A nonmedical process that helps individuals with psychological disorders recognize and overcome their problems.

Although their ability to prescribe drugs is limited, psychologists and other mental health professionals may provide **psychotherapy,** a nonmedical process that helps individuals with psychological disorders recognize and overcome their problems. Psychotherapy may be given alone or in conjunction with biological therapy administered by psychiatrists and other medical doctors (Davidson, 2009). In many instances, a combination of psychotherapy and medication is a desirable course of treatment (Nolen-Hoeksema, 2011). Unfortunately, even as prescriptions for medications have increased dramatically over the years, the number of people receiving psychotherapy has dropped. According to a recent study, among individuals receiving antidepressant medication, the number in therapy fell from 32 percent in 1996 to less than 20 percent in 2005 (Olfson & Marcus, 2009).

Psychotherapists employ a number of strategies to alleviate symptoms of psychological disorders: talking, interpreting, listening, rewarding, and modeling, for example (Prochaska & Norcross, 2010). Although most psychotherapy is conducted face-to-face, many contemporary therapists communicate with clients through e-mail or text messaging (Berger, Hohl, & Caspar, 2009; Wangberg, Gammon, & Spitznogle, 2007).

Psychotherapy is practiced by a variety of mental health professionals (Figure 13.3). Society retains control over psychotherapy practitioners through state laws that address

| Professional Type | Degree | Education Beyond Bachelor's Degree | Nature of Training |
|---|---|---|---|
| Clinical Psychologist | PhD or PsyD | 5–7 years | Requires both clinical and research training. Includes a 1-year internship in a psychiatric hospital or mental health facility. Some universities have developed PsyD programs, which have a stronger clinical than research emphasis. The PsyD training program takes as long as the clinical psychology PhD program and also requires the equivalent of a 1-year internship. |
| Psychiatrist | MD | 7–9 years | Four years of medical school, plus an internship and residency in psychiatry, is required. A psychiatry residency involves supervision in therapies, including psychotherapy and biomedical therapy. |
| Counseling Psychologist | MA, PhD, PsyD, or EdD | 3–7 years | Similar to clinical psychologist but with emphasis on counseling and therapy. Some counseling psychologists specialize in vocational counseling. Some counselors complete master's degree training, others PhD or EdD training, in graduate schools of psychology or education. |
| School Psychologist | MA, PhD, PsyD, or EdD | 3–7 years | Training in graduate programs of education or psychology. Emphasis on psychological assessment and counseling practices involving students' school-related problems. Training is at the master's or doctoral level. |
| Social Worker | MS W/DSW or PhD | 2–5 years | Graduate work in a school of social work that includes specialized clinical training in mental health facilities. |
| Psychiatric Nurse | RN, MA, or PhD | 0–5 years | Graduate work in a school of nursing with special emphasis on care of mentally disturbed individuals in hospital settings and mental health facilities. |
| Occupational Therapist | BS, MA, or PhD | 0–5 years | Emphasis on occupational training with focus on physically or psychologically handicapped individuals. Stresses getting individuals back into the mainstream of work. |
| Pastoral Counselor | None to PhD or DD (Doctor of Divinity) | 0–5 years | Requires ministerial background and training in psychology. An internship in a mental health facility as a chaplain is recommended. |
| Counselor | MA or MEd | 2 years | Graduate work in a department of psychology or department of education with specialized training in counseling techniques. |

**FIGURE 13.3** **Main Types of Mental Health Professionals** A wide range of professionals with varying levels of training have taken on the challenge of helping people with psychological disorders.

licensing and certification. These laws differ from state to state, but invariably they specify the training the mental health professional must have, and they provide for assessment of an applicant's skill through formal examination. Regardless of their particular occupation, psychotherapists use a range of techniques to help alleviate suffering. This section focuses on four main approaches to psychotherapy: psychodynamic, humanistic, behavioral, and cognitive.

## Psychodynamic Therapies

The **psychodynamic therapies** stress the importance of the unconscious mind, extensive interpretation by the therapist, and the role of early childhood experiences in the development of an individual's problems. The goal of psychodynamic therapies is to help individuals gain insight into the unconscious conflicts that are the source of their problems. Many psychodynamic approaches grew out of Freud's psychoanalytic theory of personality. Today some therapists with a psychodynamic perspective practice Freudian techniques, but others do not (Brusset, 2012; Wolson, 2012).

**psychodynamic therapies** Treatments that stress the importance of the unconscious mind, extensive interpretation by the therapist, and the role of early childhood experiences in the development of an individual's problems.

**PSYCHOANALYSIS**   **Psychoanalysis** is Freud's therapeutic technique for analyzing an individual's unconscious thoughts. Freud believed that a person's current problems could be traced to childhood experiences, many of which involved unconscious sexual conflicts. Only through extensive questioning, probing, and analyzing was Freud able to put together the pieces of the client's personality and help the individual become aware of how these early experiences were affecting present behavior. The psychoanalyst's goal is to bring unconscious conflicts into conscious awareness, thus giving the client insight into his or her core problems and freeing the individual from unconscious influences. To reach the shadowy world of the unconscious, psychoanalytic therapists use the therapeutic techniques of free association, interpretation, dream analysis, analysis of transference, and analysis of resistance.

**psychoanalysis** Freud's therapeutic technique for analyzing an individual's unconscious thoughts.

**Free association** involves encouraging individuals to say aloud whatever comes to mind, no matter how trivial or embarrassing. When Freud detected a person resisting the spontaneous flow of thoughts, he probed further. He believed that the crux of the person's problem probably lurked below this point of resistance. Encouraging people to talk freely, Freud reasoned, would allow their deepest thoughts and feelings to emerge. *Catharsis* is the release of emotional tension a person experiences when reliving an emotionally charged and conflicting experience.

**free association** A psychoanalytic technique that involves encouraging individuals to say aloud whatever comes to mind, no matter how trivial or embarrassing.

*To encourage his patients to relax, Freud had them recline on this couch while he sat in the chair on the left, out of their view.*

**interpretation**
A psychoanalyst's search for symbolic, hidden meanings in what the client says and does during therapy.

**dream analysis**
A psychoanalytic technique for interpreting a person's dreams.

**Interpretation** plays an important role in psychoanalysis. Interpretation means that the analyst does not take the patient's statements and behavior at face value; rather, to understand the source of the person's conflicts, the therapist searches for symbolic, hidden meanings in the individual's words and deeds. From time to time, the therapist suggests possible meanings of the person's statements and behavior.

**Dream analysis** is a psychoanalytic technique for interpreting a person's dreams. Psychoanalysts believe that dreams contain information about unconscious thoughts, wishes, and conflicts (Freud, 1899/1911). From this perspective, dreams provide our unconscious with an outlet to express our unconscious wishes, a mental theater in which our deepest and most secret desires can be played out (Meghnagi, 2011). According to Freud, every dream, even our worst nightmare, contains a hidden, disguised wish. Nightmares might express a wish for punishment, or the sheer horror we feel during the nightmare might itself be the disguise.

Freud distinguished between the dream's manifest content and latent content. *Manifest content* refers to the conscious, remembered aspects of a dream. If you wake up remembering a dream about being back in sixth grade with your teacher scolding you for not turning in your homework, that is the dream's manifest content. *Latent content* refers to the unconscious, hidden aspects that are symbolized by the manifest content. To understand your dream, a psychoanalyst might ask you to free-associate to each of the elements of the manifest content. What comes to your mind when you think of being in sixth grade or of your teacher? According to Freud, the latent meaning of a dream is locked inside the dreamer's unconscious mind. The psychoanalyst's goal is to unlock that secret meaning by having the individual free-associate about the manifest dream elements. The analyst interprets the dream by examining the manifest content for disguised unconscious wishes and needs, especially those that are sexual and aggressive. Dream symbols can mean different things to different dreamers. Freud (1899/1911) recognized that the true meaning of any dream symbol depends on the individual.

*[handwritten note:]* The dreamer "knows" what the dream means, but this meaning is locked in his or her unconscious mind.

Freud believed that transference was an inevitable—and essential—aspect of the analyst–patient relationship. **Transference** is the psychoanalytic term for the client's relating to the analyst in ways that reproduce or relive important relationships in the client's life. A client might interact with an analyst as if the analyst were a parent or lover, for example. Transference can be used therapeutically as a model of how individuals relate to important people in their lives (Faimberg, 2012).

**transference**
A client's relating to the psychoanalyst in ways that reproduce or relive important relationships in the client's life.

**Resistance** is the psychoanalytic term for the client's unconscious defense strategies that prevent the analyst from understanding the person's problems. Resistance occurs because it is painful for the client to bring conflicts into conscious awareness. By resisting analysis, the individual does not have to face the threatening truths that underlie his or her problems (Scharff, 2012). Showing up late or missing sessions, arguing with the psychoanalyst, and faking free associations are examples of resistance. A major goal of the analyst is to break through this resistance.

*[handwritten note:]* Freud would say that the appearance of resistance means that the analyst is getting very close to the truth.

**resistance**
Unconscious defense strategies on the part of a client that prevent the psychoanalyst from understanding the client's problems.

**CONTEMPORARY PSYCHODYNAMIC THERAPIES** Psychodynamic therapy has changed extensively since its beginnings almost a century ago. Nonetheless, many contemporary psychodynamic therapists still probe unconscious thoughts about early childhood experiences to get clues to their clients' current problems, and they try to help individuals gain insight into their emotionally laden, repressed conflicts (Leuzinger-Bohleber & Teising, 2012; Werbart, Forsstrom, & Jeanneau, 2012). However, contemporary psychoanalysts accord more power to the conscious mind and to a person's current relationships, and they generally place less emphasis on sex (Wallerstein, 2012). In addition, clients today rarely lie on a couch as they did in Freud's time (see the photo on the previous page) or see their therapist several times a week, as was the norm in early psychodynamic therapy. Instead, they sit in a comfortable chair facing the therapist, and weekly appointments are typical.

Some contemporary psychodynamic therapists (Caston, 2011; Stern, 2012) focus on the self in social contexts, as Heinz Kohut (1977) recommended. In Kohut's view, early social relationships with attachment figures such as parents are critical. As we develop, we internalize those relationships, and they serve as the basis for our sense of self. Kohut (1977) believed that the therapist's job is to replace unhealthy childhood relationships with the healthy relationship the therapist provides. From Kohut's perspective, the therapist needs to interact with the client in empathic and understanding ways. Empathy and understanding are also cornerstones for humanistic therapies, as we next consider.

# Humanistic Therapies

The underlying philosophy of humanistic therapies is captured by the metaphor of how an acorn, if provided with appropriate conditions, will grow in positive ways, pushing naturally toward its actualization as an oak (Schneider, 2002). **Humanistic therapies** encourage individuals to understand themselves and to grow personally. Humanistic therapies are unique in their emphasis on the person's self-healing capacities. In contrast to psychodynamic therapies, humanistic therapies emphasize conscious rather than unconscious thoughts, the present rather than the past, and growth and self-fulfillment rather than illness.

**humanistic therapies**
Treatments, unique in their emphasis on people's self-healing capacities, that encourage clients to understand themselves and to grow personally.

**Client-centered therapy** (also called *Rogerian therapy* or *nondirective therapy*) is a form of humanistic therapy developed by Carl Rogers (1961, 1980), in which the therapist provides a warm, supportive atmosphere to improve the client's self-concept and to encourage the client to gain insight into problems. Compared with psychodynamic therapies, which emphasize analysis and interpretation by the therapist, client-centered therapy places far more emphasis on the client's self-reflection (Hill, 2000). In client-centered therapy, the goal is not to unlock the deep secrets of the unconscious but rather to help the client identify and understand his or her own genuine feelings (Hazler, 2007). One way to achieve this goal is through active listening and **reflective speech,** a technique in which the therapist mirrors the client's own feelings back to the client. For example, as a woman is describing her grief over the traumatic loss of her husband in a drunk-driving accident, the therapist, noting her voice and facial expression, might suggest, "You sound angry" to help her identify her feelings.

**reflective speech**
A technique in which the therapist mirrors the client's own feelings back to the client.

**client-centered therapy**
Also called Rogerian therapy or nondirective therapy, a form of humanistic therapy, developed by Rogers, in which the therapist provides a warm, supportive atmosphere to improve the client's self-concept and to encourage the client to gain insight into problems.

In Rogers's therapy, the therapist must enter into an authentic relationship with the client, not as a physician diagnosing a disease but as one human being connecting to another. Indeed, in talking about those he was trying to help, Rogers referred to the "client" and eventually to the "person" rather than to the "patient."

Rogers believed that each of us is born with the potential to be fully functioning but that we live in a world in which we are valued only if we live up to conditions of worth. That is, others value us only if we meet certain standards, and we come to apply those standards to ourselves. Each of us needs to feel the positive regard of others, but this positive regard is often conditional—it comes with strings attached. Rogers asserted that each of us requires three essential elements to grow to our full potential: unconditional positive regard, empathy, and genuineness. Let's review these three conditions, which are strongly reflected in Rogerian therapy.

To free a person from conditions of worth, the therapist engages in *unconditional positive regard,* which involves creating a warm, caring environment and never disapproving of the client as a person. Rogers argued that unconditional positive regard provides a context for personal growth and self-acceptance, just as soil, water, and sunshine provide a context for the acorn to become an oak. The Rogerian therapist's role is *nondirective*—that is, he or she does not lead the client to any particular revelation. The therapist is there to listen empathically to the client's problems and to encourage positive self-regard, independent self-appraisal, and decision making.

In addition to unconditional positive regard, Rogers emphasized the importance of empathy and genuineness. Through *empathy* the therapist strives to put himself or herself in the client's shoes—to feel the client's

**To experience Rogerian therapy firsthand, watch a video of Carl Rogers describing his approach and participating in a session with a client at www.viddler.com/v/2b20cab0.**

emotions. *Genuineness* requires the therapist to let the client openly know the therapist's own feelings. Genuineness is meant to coexist with unconditional positive regard. The therapist must provide the client with positive regard no matter what, but at the same time that regard must be a genuine expression of the therapist's true feelings.

The therapist may distinguish between the person's behavior and the person himself or herself. Although the client is always acknowledged as a valuable human being, his or her behavior can be evaluated negatively: "You are a good person but your actions are not." Rogers's positive view of humanity extended to his view of therapists. He believed that by being genuine with the client, the therapist could help the client improve.

1  A month before an examination
2  Two weeks before an examination
3  A week before an examination
4  Five days before an examination
5  Four days before an examination
6  Three days before an examination
7  Two days before an examination
8  One day before an examination
9  The night before an examination
10 On the way to the university on the day of an examination
11 Before the unopened doors of the examination room
12 Awaiting distribution of examination papers
13 The examination paper lies facedown before her
14 In the process of answering an examination paper

**FIGURE 13.4    A Desensitization Hierarchy Involving Test Anxiety** In this hierarchy, the individual begins with her least feared circumstance (a month before the exam) and moves through each of the circumstances until reaching her most feared circumstance (answering the exam questions on test day). At each step, the person replaces fear with deep relaxation and successful visualization.

# Behavior Therapies

Psychodynamic and humanistic methods are sometimes called *insight therapies* because they encourage self-awareness as the path to psychological health. Behavior therapies take a different approach. Insight and self-awareness are not the keys to helping individuals develop more adaptive behavior patterns, behavior therapists say. Rather, behavior therapists offer action-oriented strategies to help people change their behavior (Trull & Prinstein, 2013). Specifically, **behavior therapies,** based on behavioral and social cognitive theories, use principles of learning to reduce or eliminate maladaptive behavior. Behavior therapists say that individuals can become aware of why they are depressed and yet still be depressed. They strive to eliminate the depressed *symptoms* or *behaviors* rather than trying to get individuals to gain insight into, or awareness of, why they are depressed (Miltenberger, 2012).

Although initially based almost exclusively on the learning principles of classical and operant conditioning, behavior therapies have become more diverse (Bankoff & others, 2012; Harned & others, 2012). As social cognitive theory grew in popularity, behavior therapists increasingly included observational learning, cognitive factors, and self-instruction in their treatments (Freedy & others, 2012). In self-instruction, therapists try to get people to change what they say to themselves.

**CLASSICAL CONDITIONING TECHNIQUES** Various techniques of classical conditioning have been used in treating phobias. Among them is **systematic desensitization,** a behavior therapy that treats anxiety by teaching the client to associate deep relaxation with increasingly intense anxiety-producing situations.

Figure 13.4 shows a desensitization hierarchy. *Desensitization* involves exposing someone to a feared situation in a real or an imagined way (Donahue, Odlaug, & Grant, 2011). Desensitization is based on the classical conditioning process of extinction. During extinction, the conditioned stimulus is presented without the unconditioned stimulus, leading to a decreased conditioned response.

In Chapter 5 we saw that aversive conditioning entails repeated pairings of an undesirable behavior with aversive stimuli to decrease the behavior's positive associations. Through aversive conditioning people can learn to avoid such behaviors as smoking, overeating, and drinking alcohol. Electric shocks, nausea-inducing substances, and verbal insults are some of the noxious stimuli used

**behavior therapies** Treatments, based on the behavioral and social cognitive theories, that use principles of learning to reduce or eliminate maladaptive behavior.

**systematic desensitization** A behavior therapy that treats anxiety by teaching the client to associate deep relaxation with increasingly intense anxiety-producing situations.

in aversive conditioning (Sommer & others, 2006). Figure 13.5 illustrates how classical conditioning is the backbone of aversive conditioning.

**OPERANT CONDITIONING TECHNIQUES** The idea behind using operant conditioning as a therapeutic approach is that just as maladaptive behavior patterns are learned, they can be unlearned. Therapy involves conducting a careful analysis of the person's environment to determine which factors need modification. Especially important is changing the consequences of the person's behavior to ensure that healthy, adaptive replacement behaviors are followed by positive reinforcement.

Applied behavior analysis, described in Chapter 5, involves establishing positive reinforcement connections between behaviors and rewards so that individuals engage in appropriate behavior and extinguish inappropriate behavior. Consider, for example, a man with obsessive-compulsive disorder (OCD) who engages in a compulsive ritual such as checking that he has locked the door of his house 10 times every time he leaves his home. If he does not complete his ritual, he is overcome with anxiety that something dreadful will happen. Note that whenever he completes the ritual, nothing dreadful does happen and his anxiety is relieved. His compulsion is a behavior that is reinforced by the relief of anxiety and the fact that nothing dreadful happens. Such a ritual, then, could be viewed as avoidance learning. An operant conditioning–based therapy would involve stopping the behavior to extinguish this avoidance. Specifically, allowing the man to experience the lack of catastrophic consequences in the absence of repeatedly checking the lock, as well as training him to relax, might help to eliminate the compulsive rituals. Indeed, behavior therapy is effective in treating OCD (Bonchek, 2009).

It may strike you as unusual that behavioral approaches do not emphasize gaining insight and self-awareness. However, for the very reason that they do not stress these goals, such treatments may be particularly useful in individuals whose cognitive abilities are limited, such as adults with developmental disabilities or children. Applied behavior analysis can be used, for instance, to treat individuals with autism who engage in self-injurious behaviors such as head banging (LeBlanc & Gillis, 2012).

*Because it does not rely on the cognitive ability of the client, therapy directed at changing behaviors can be remarkably useful.*

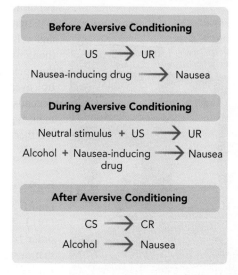

**FIGURE 13.5   Classical Conditioning: The Backbone of Aversive Conditioning** This figure shows how classical conditioning can produce a conditional aversion to alcohol. Recall the abbreviations US (unconditioned stimulus), UR (unconditioned response), CS (conditioned stimulus), and CR (conditioned response). *>What is the conditioned stimulus? >What is the likely effect of alcohol prior to aversion therapy? Is this effect learned or not? >What role, if any, does a person's motivation play in aversive conditioning?*

# Cognitive Therapies

**Cognitive therapies** emphasize that *cognitions,* or thoughts, are the main source of psychological problems, and they attempt to change the individual's feelings and behaviors by changing cognitions. *Cognitive restructuring,* a general concept for changing a pattern of thought that is presumed to be causing maladaptive behavior or emotion, is central to cognitive therapies.

Cognitive therapies differ from psychoanalytic therapies by focusing more on overt symptoms than on deep-seated unconscious thoughts, by providing more structure to the individual's thoughts, and by being less concerned about the origin of the problem.

**cognitive therapies**
Treatments emphasizing that cognitions (thoughts) are the main source of psychological problems and that attempt to change the individual's feelings and behaviors by changing cognitions.

**Aaron Beck (b. 1921)**
*Aaron Beck's method stresses that the goal of therapy should be to help people to recognize and eliminate illogical and self-defeating thinking.*

Compared with humanistic therapies, cognitive therapies provide more of a framework and more analysis, and they are based on specific cognitive techniques.

Cognitive therapists guide individuals in identifying their irrational and self-defeating thoughts. Then they get clients to challenge these thoughts and to consider more positive ways of thinking. Cognitive therapies all involve the basic assumption that human beings have control over their feelings and that how individuals feel about something depends on how they think about it. In this section we examine three main types of cognitive therapy: Albert Ellis's rational-emotive behavior therapy, Aaron Beck's cognitive therapy, and cognitive-behavior therapy.

**RATIONAL-EMOTIVE BEHAVIOR THERAPY** Rational-emotive behavior therapy (REBT) was developed by Albert Ellis (1913–2007), who argued that individuals develop a psychological disorder because of their irrational and self-defeating beliefs. Ellis held that our emotional reactions to life events are a product of our irrational beliefs and expectations along with the central false belief that we cannot control our feelings (1962, 1996, 2000, 2002, 2005). A highly confrontational therapist, Ellis aggressively attacked these irrational beliefs in his practice.

Ellis (2000, 2002) believed that many individuals construct three basic demands for themselves, which he called "musterbating": (1) I absolutely must perform well and win the approval of other people; (2) other people must treat me kindly and fairly; and (3) my life conditions must not be frustrating but rather should be enjoyable. Once people convert their important desires into demands, they often create dysfunctional, exaggerated beliefs such as "Because I'm not performing well, as I absolutely must, I'm an inadequate person."

The goal of REBT is to get the individual to eliminate self-defeating beliefs by rationally examining them (Sava & others, 2009). A client is shown how to dispute his or her dysfunctional beliefs—especially those "musts"—and how to convert them into realistic and logical thoughts. Homework assignments provide opportunities to engage in the new self-talk and to experience the positive results of not viewing life in such a catastrophic way. For Ellis, a successful outcome meant getting the client to live in reality, where life is sometimes tough and bad things happen.

**BECK'S COGNITIVE THERAPY** Aaron Beck (b. 1921) developed a somewhat different form of cognitive therapy to treat psychological problems, especially depression (1976, 1993). A basic assumption Beck makes is that a psychological problem such as depression results when people think illogically about themselves, their world, and the future (2005, 2006). Like Ellis, Beck believes that therapy's goal should be to help people to recognize and discard self-defeating cognitions.

In the initial phases of Beck's therapy, individuals learn to make connections between their patterns of thinking and their emotional responses. From Beck's perspective, emotions are a product of cognitions. By changing cognitions, people can change how they feel. Unfortunately, thoughts that lead to emotions can happen so rapidly that a person is not even aware of them. Thus, the first goal of therapy is to bring these automatic thoughts into awareness so that they can be changed. The therapist helps clients to identify their own automatic thoughts and to keep records of their thought content and emotional reactions.

With the therapist's assistance, clients learn to recognize logical errors in their thinking and to challenge the accuracy of these automatic thoughts. Logical errors in

**rational-emotive behavior therapy (REBT)**
A therapy based on Ellis's assertion that individuals develop a psychological disorder because of irrational and self-defeating beliefs and whose goal is to get clients to eliminate these beliefs by rationally examining them.

*Ellis believed that our thoughts determine all of our emotional responses and that we have the capacity to never be miserable. What do you think?*

**EXPERIENCE IT!**
Virtual Therapy for Agoraphobia

*When was the last time something upset you? What kinds of thoughts did you have about that event or situation?*

## Seeking Therapy?
## There Might Be an App for That

**A**lthough many contemporary therapists communicate with clients through e-mail or text messaging (Berger, Hohl, & Caspar, 2009; Wangberg, Gammon, & Spitznogle, 2007), these are just a taste of how technology is transforming psychological interventions. For example, researchers are developing and studying smartphone applications for therapy (Carey, 2012). Such apps would provide immediate feedback aimed at modifying thoughts and behaviors. Therapy apps could mean access to therapy for millions of people—advice and strategies for managing emotions and changing thoughts at the tap of the screen. An iPad app for art therapy is already available.

Although possibly less portable, *cybertherapy* or *e-therapy* involves getting therapeutic help online (Klein & others, 2010; Murphy, Mitchell, & Hallett, 2011; Postel, de Haan, & de Jong, 2010). E-therapy websites are controversial among mental health professionals, however (Emmelkamp, 2011). For one thing, many of these sites do not include the most basic information about the therapists' qualifications (Norcross & others, 2013). In addition, because cybertherapy occurs at a distance, these sites typically exclude individuals who are having thoughts of suicide. Further, confidentiality, a crucial aspect of the therapeutic relationship, cannot always be guaranteed on a website. On the plus side, though, individuals who are unwilling or unable to seek out face-to-face therapy may be more disposed to get help online (Norcross & others, 2013; Van Voorhees & others, 2009).

E-therapy and therapeutic apps may represent the wave of the future, but for many professionals, human contact is a vital ingredient in psychological healing. Psychiatrist Andrew Garber cautions, "We are built as human beings to figure out our place in the world, to construct a narrative in the context of a relationship that gives meaning to our lives" (Carey, 2012). Technology, in other words, may never replace the power of human conversation.

---

thinking can lead individuals to the following erroneous beliefs (Carson, Butcher, & Mineka, 1996):

- Perceiving the world as harmful while ignoring evidence to the contrary—for example, when a young woman still feels worthless after a friend has just told her how much other people genuinely like her.

- Overgeneralizing on the basis of limited examples, such as a man's seeing himself as worthless because one individual stopped dating him.

- Magnifying the importance of undesirable events, such as seeing being rejected by a love interest as the end of the world.

- Engaging in absolutist thinking like exaggerating the importance of someone's mildly critical comment and perceiving it as proof of total inadequacy.

Figure 13.6 describes some of the most widely used cognitive therapy techniques.

**Do It!**

The Beck Institute maintains a website chronicling the latest developments in cognitive therapy and including a variety of videos of Beck himself. Check out the site at www.beckinstitute.org/.

| Cognitive Therapy Technique | Description | Example |
|---|---|---|
| **Challenge Idiosyncratic Meanings** | Explore personal meaning attached to the client's words and ask the client to consider alternatives. | When a client says he will be "devastated" by his spouse leaving, ask just how he would be devastated and ways he could avoid being devastated. |
| **Question the Evidence** | Systematically examine the evidence for the client's beliefs or assertions. | When a client says she can't live without her spouse, explore how she lived without the spouse before she was married. |
| **Reattribution** | Help the client distribute responsibility for events appropriately. | When a client says that his son's failure in school must be his fault, explore other possibilities, such as the quality of the school. |
| **Examine Options and Alternatives** | Help the client generate alternative actions to maladaptive ones. | If a client considers leaving school, explore whether tutoring or going part-time to school are good alternatives. |
| **Decatastrophize** | Help the client evaluate whether he is overestimating the nature of a situation. | If a client states that failure in a course means he or she must give up the dream of medical school, question whether this is a necessary conclusion. |
| **Fantasize Consequences** | Explore fantasies of a feared situation: if unrealistic, the client may recognize this; if realistic, work on effective coping strategies. | Help a client who fantasizes "falling apart" when asking the boss for a raise to role-play the situation and develop effective skills for making the request. |
| **Examine Advantages and Disadvantages** | Examine advantages and disadvantages of an issue, to instill a broader perspective. | If a client says he "was just born depressed and will always be that way," explore the advantages and disadvantages of holding that perspective versus other perspectives. |
| **Turn Adversity to Advantage** | Explore ways that difficult situations can be transformed into opportunities. | If a client has just been laid off, explore whether this is an opportunity for her to return to school. |
| **Guided Association** | Help the client see connections between different thoughts or ideas. | Draw the connections between a client's anger at his wife for going on a business trip and his fear of being alone. |
| **Scaling** | Ask the client to rate her emotions or thoughts on scales to help gain perspective. | If a client says she was overwhelmed by an emotion, ask her to rate it on a scale from 0 (not at all present) to 100 (I fell down in a faint). |
| **Thought Stopping** | Provide the client with ways of stopping a cascade of negative thoughts. | Teach an anxious client to picture a stop sign or hear a bell when anxious thoughts begin to snowball. |
| **Distraction** | Help the client find benign or positive distractions to take attention away from negative thoughts or emotions temporarily. | Have a client count to 200 by 13s when he feels himself becoming anxious. |
| **Labeling of Distortions** | Provide labels for specific types of distorted thinking to help the client gain more distance and perspective. | Have a client keep a record of the number of times a day she engages in all-or-nothing thinking—seeing things as all bad or all good. |

**FIGURE 13.6  Cognitive Therapy Techniques** Cognitive therapists develop strategies to help change the way people think.

Ellis's and Beck's cognitive therapies share some differences as well as similarities. Ellis's rational-emotive behavior therapy is directive, persuasive, and confrontational; in contrast, Beck's cognitive therapy involves more of an open-ended dialogue between therapist and client. The aim of this dialogue in Beck's approach is to get individuals to reflect on personal issues and discover their own misconceptions. Beck also encourages clients to gather information about themselves and to try out unbiased experiments that reveal the inaccuracies of their beliefs. So whereas Ellis's approach was to bring a sledgehammer down on irrational beliefs, Beck's therapy involves a subtler process of coaxing a client to recognize that these beliefs promote thoughts that influence feelings. One study revealed that Ellis's rational-emotive behavior therapy and

Beck's cognitive therapy were more effective in treating depression than drug therapy (Sava & others, 2009).

**COGNITIVE-BEHAVIOR THERAPY**    **Cognitive-behavior therapy** is a combination of cognitive therapy, with its emphasis on reducing self-defeating thoughts, and behavior therapy, with its emphasis on changing behavior (Reaven & others, 2012; Safir, Wallach, & Bar-Zvi, 2012). An important aspect of cognitive-behavior therapy is *self-efficacy,* Albert Bandura's concept that one can master a situation and produce positive outcomes (1997, 2001, 2008, 2010a, 2010b). Bandura believes that self-efficacy is the key to successful therapy. At each step of the therapy, clients need to bolster their confidence by telling themselves messages such as "I'm going to master my problem," "I can do it," and "I'm improving." As they gain confidence and engage in adaptive behavior, the successes become intrinsically motivating. Before long, individuals persist (with considerable effort) in their attempts to solve personal problems because of the positive outcomes that were set in motion by self-efficacy.

> **cognitive-behavior therapy**
> A therapy that combines cognitive therapy and behavior therapy with the goal of developing the client's self-efficacy.

*Self-instructional methods* are cognitive-behavior techniques aimed at teaching individuals to modify their own behavior (Sharf, 2012). Using self-instructional techniques, cognitive-behavior therapists prompt clients to change what they say to themselves. The therapist gives the client examples of constructive statements, known as reinforcing self-statements, that the client can repeat in order to take positive steps to cope with stress or meet a goal. The therapist also encourages the client to practice the statements through role playing and strengthens these newly acquired skills through reinforcement.

## USE OF COGNITIVE THERAPY TO TREAT PSYCHOLOGICAL DISORDERS

Cognitive therapy has successfully treated some anxiety disorders, mood disorders, schizophrenia, and personality disorders (Britton & others, 2012; Forman & others, 2012; O'Donnell & others, 2012). In many instances, cognitive therapy used with drug therapy is an effective treatment for psychological disorders (Soomro, 2012).

Panic disorder is among the anxiety disorders to which cognitive therapy has been applied (Nations & others, 2011). The central concept in the cognitive model of panic is that individuals catastrophically misinterpret relatively harmless physical or psychological events. In cognitive therapy, the therapist encourages individuals to test the catastrophic misinterpretations by inducing an actual panic attack. The individuals then can test the notion that they will die or go crazy, which they find out is not the case. Cognitive therapy also shows considerable promise in the treatment of post-traumatic stress disorder, especially when therapists encourage clients to relive traumatic experiences so that they can come to grips with the threatening cognitions precipitated by those experiences (Forbes & others, 2012). In addition, cognitive therapy has been successful in treating generalized anxiety disorder, certain phobias, and obsessive-compulsive disorder (Donegan & Dugas, 2012).

One of the earliest applications of cognitive therapy was in the treatment of depression. A number of studies have shown that cognitive therapy can be just as successful as, or in some cases superior to, drug therapy in the treatment of depressive disorders (Sado & others, 2009; Sava & others, 2009). Some studies also have demonstrated that individuals treated with cognitive therapy are less likely to relapse into depression than those treated with drug therapy (Jarrett & others, 2001).

*Plus cognitive therapy lacks the side effects of drug therapies.*

Practitioners have made considerable strides in recent years in applying cognitive therapy to the treatment of schizophrenia. Although not a substitute for drug therapy in the treatment of this disorder, cognitive therapy has been effective in reducing some schizophrenia symptoms, such as belief in delusions and impulsive acting out (Christopher Frueh & others, 2009). Cognitive therapy also has proved effective in treating personality disorders (McMain & Pos, 2007), where the focus has been on changing individuals' core beliefs and reducing their automatic negative thoughts.

So far, we have studied the biological therapies and psychotherapies. The four psychotherapies—psychodynamic, humanistic, behavior, and cognitive—are compared in Figure 13.7.

| | Cause of Problem | Therapy Emphasis | Nature of Therapy and Techniques |
|---|---|---|---|
| Psychodynamic Therapies | Client's problems are symptoms of deep-seated, unresolved unconscious conflicts. | Discover underlying unconscious conflicts and work with client to develop insight. | Psychoanalysis, including free association, dream analysis, resistance, and transference: therapist interprets heavily, operant conditioning. |
| Humanistic Therapies | Client is not functioning at an optimal level of development. | Develop awareness of inherent potential for growth. | Person-centered therapy, including unconditional positive regard, genuineness, accurate empathy, and active listening; self-appreciation emphasized. |
| Behavior Therapies | Client has learned maladaptive behavior patterns. | Learn adaptive behavior patterns through changes in the environment or cognitive processes. | Observation of behavior and its controlling conditions; specific advice given about what should be done; therapies based on classical conditioning, operant conditioning. |
| Cognitive Therapies | Client has developed inappropriate thoughts. | Change feelings and behaviors by changing cognitions. | Conversation with client designed to get him or her to change irrational and self-defeating beliefs. |

**FIGURE 13.7** **Therapy Comparisons** Different therapies address the same problems in very different ways. Many therapists use the tools that seem right for any given client and his or her problems.

# Therapy Integrations

**integrative therapy**
Use of a combination of techniques from different therapies based on the therapist's judgment of which particular methods will provide the greatest benefit for the client.

As many as 50 percent of therapists identify themselves as not adhering to one particular method. Rather, they refer to themselves as "integrative" or "eclectic." **Integrative therapy** is a combination of techniques from different therapies based on the therapist's judgment of which particular methods will provide the greatest benefit for the client (Clarkin, 2012; Prochaska & Norcross, 2010). Integrative therapy is characterized by openness to various ways of applying diverse therapies. For example, a therapist might use a behavioral approach to treat an individual with panic disorder and a cognitive approach to treat a client with major depressive disorder.

Because clients present a wide range of problems, it makes sense for therapists to use the best tools in each case rather than to adopt a "one size fits all" program. Sometimes a given psychological disorder is so difficult to treat that it requires the therapist to bring all of his or her tools to bear (Kozaric-Kovacic, 2008). For example, borderline personality disorder (see Chapter 12) involves emotional instability, impulsivity, and self-harming behaviors. This disorder responds to a therapy called *dialectical behavior therapy,* or *DBT* (Bedics & others, 2012). Like psychodynamic approaches, DBT assumes that early childhood experiences are important to the development of borderline personality disorder. However, DBT employs a variety of techniques, including homework assignments, cognitive interventions, intensive individual therapy, and group sessions involving others with the disorder. Group sessions focus on mindfulness training as well as emotional and interpersonal skills training.

Another integrative method is to combine psychotherapy with drug therapy (Schneier & others, 2012). Combined cognitive therapy and drug therapy has been effective in treating anxiety and depressive disorders (Dunner, 2001), eating disorders (Wilson, Grilo, & Vitousek, 2007), and schizophrenia (Rector & Beck, 2001). This integrative therapy might be conducted by a mental health team that includes a psychiatrist and a clinical psychologist.

*In most U.S. states, psychologists cannot prescribe drugs.*

At their best, integrative therapies are effective, systematic uses of a variety of therapeutic approaches (Prochaska & Norcross, 2010). However, one worry

*"Life's little wonders are too big for me."*

about integrative therapies is that their increased use will result in an unsystematic, haphazard use of therapeutic techniques that some therapists say would be no better than a narrow, dogmatic approach (Lazarus, Beutler, & Norcross, 1992).

Therapy integrations are conceptually compatible with the biopsychosocial model of abnormal behavior described in Chapter 12. That is, many therapists believe that abnormal behavior involves biological, psychological, and social factors. Many single-therapy approaches concentrate on one aspect of the person more than others; for example, drug therapies focus on biological factors, and cognitive therapies probe psychological factors. Therapy integrations take a broader look at individuals' problems, and such breadth is also implied in sociocultural approaches to therapy, our next topic.

*What might the popularity of integrative therapy mean for the training of future psychotherapists?*

self quiz

1. A behavioral therapy technique that is often used for treating phobic disorder is
   A. aversive conditioning.
   B. self-instruction.
   C. systematic desensitization.
   D. counterconditioning.

2. The psychotherapy approach that focuses on the ways in which early childhood relationships have taught people how to behave in current relationships is
   A. client-centered therapy.
   B. psychodynamic therapy.
   C. cognitive therapy.
   D. rational-emotive behavior therapy.

3. The therapy that has unconditional positive regard at its core is
   A. psychodynamic therapy.
   B. cognitive therapy.
   C. dialectical behavior therapy.
   D. client-centered therapy.

**APPLY IT!** 4. Cara has taken a few psychology classes. When she decides to see a therapist for help with her relationship with her mother, she is certain that the therapist will make her lie on a couch and talk about her childhood. When her appointments begin, Cara is surprised that the therapist asks her to just talk about her feelings and offers little feedback. At other times, the therapist talks to Cara about her thoughts and beliefs and gives her homework. On other appointments, the therapist asks Cara about her dreams and childhood. The kind of therapy Cara is getting is
A. cognitive-behavioral.
B. humanistic.
C. psychodynamic.
D. integrative.

## 3 Sociocultural Approaches and Issues in Treatment

In the treatment of psychological disorders, biological therapies change the body, behavior therapies modify behavior, and cognitive therapies alter thinking. This section focuses on sociocultural approaches to the treatment of psychological disorders. These methods view the individual as part of a system of relationships that are influenced by social and cultural factors. We first review common sociocultural approaches and then survey various cultural perspectives on therapy.

**EXPERIENCE IT!**
Using Soccer as Therapy

### Group Therapy

**group therapy**
A sociocultural approach to the treatment of psychological disorders that brings together individuals who share a particular psychological disorder in sessions that are typically led by a mental health professional.

Individuals who share a psychological problem may benefit from observing others cope with a similar problem. In turn, helping others can improve individuals' feelings of competence and efficacy. The sociocultural approach known as **group therapy** brings together individuals who share a psychological disorder in sessions that are typically led by a mental health professional.

Advocates of group therapy point out that individual therapy puts the client outside the normal context of the relationships—family, marital, or peer-group relationships, for example—where many psychological problems develop. Yet such relationships may hold the key to successful therapy, these advocates say. By taking the context of important groups into account, group therapy may be more successful than individual therapy.

Group therapy takes many diverse forms—including psychodynamic, humanistic, behavior, and cognitive therapy—plus approaches that do not reflect the major

*A group of people in therapy together is still a group, so processes described in Chapter 11, such as informational and normative social influence, apply.*

psychotherapeutic perspectives (Corey, 2012; Simon & Sliwka, 2012; Tasca & others, 2011). Six features make group therapy an attractive treatment format (Yalom & Leszcz, 2006):

- *Information:* Individuals receive information about their problems from either the group leader or other group members.
- *Universality:* Many individuals develop the sense that no one else has frightening and unacceptable impulses. In the group, individuals observe that others feel anguish and suffering as well.
- *Altruism:* Group members support one another with advice and sympathy and learn that they have something to offer others.
- *Experience of a positive family group:* A therapy group often resembles a family (in family therapy, the group is a family), with the leaders representing parents and the other members siblings. In this new family, old wounds may be healed and new, more positive family ties may be made.
- *Development of social skills:* Feedback from peers may correct flaws in the individual's interpersonal skills. Self-centered individuals may see that they are self-centered if five other group members inform them about this quality; in one-on-one therapy, the individual might not believe the therapist.
- *Interpersonal learning:* The group can serve as a training ground for practicing new behaviors and relationships. A hostile person may learn that he or she can get along better with others by behaving less aggressively, for example.

# Family and Couples Therapy

Relationships with family members and significant others are certainly an important part of human life. Sometimes these vital relationships can benefit from a helpful outsider. **Family therapy** is group therapy among family members (Wagenaar & Baars, 2012). **Couples therapy** is group therapy involving married or unmarried couples whose major problem lies within their relationship. These approaches stress that although one person may have psychological symptoms, these symptoms are a function of the family or couple relationship (O'Leary, Heyman, & Jongsma, 2012).

**family therapy**
Group therapy
with family
members.

**couples therapy**
Group therapy involving married or unmarried couples whose major problem lies within their relationship.

In family therapy, four of the most widely used techniques are

1. *Validation:* The therapist expresses an understanding and acceptance of each family member's feelings and beliefs and thus validates the person. The therapist finds something positive to say to each family member.
2. *Reframing:* The therapist helps families reframe problems as family problems, not an individual's problems. A delinquent adolescent boy's problems are reframed in terms of how each family member contributed to the situation. The parents' lack of attention to the boy or marital conflict may be involved, for example.
3. *Structural change:* The family therapist tries to restructure the coalitions in a family. In a mother–son coalition, the therapist might suggest that the father take a stronger disciplinarian role to relieve the mother of some burden. Restructuring might be as simple as suggesting that the parents explore satisfying ways of being together, such as going out once a week for a quiet dinner.
4. *Detriangulation:* In some families, one member is the scapegoat for two other members who are in conflict but pretend not to be. For example, parents of a girl with anorexia nervosa might insist that their marriage is fine but find themselves in subtle conflict over how to handle the child. The therapist tries to disentangle, or detriangulate, this situation by shifting attention away from the child to the conflict between the parents.

Couples therapy proceeds similarly to family therapy. Conflict in marriages and in relationships between unmarried individuals frequently involves poor communication. In some instances, communication has broken down entirely. The therapist tries to improve the communication between the partners (Meneses & Greenberg, 2011) and help them understand and solve their problems. Couples therapy addresses diverse problems such as alcohol abuse, jealousy, sexual issues, infidelity, gender roles, two-career families, divorce, remarriage, and the special concerns of stepfamilies (Sandberg & Knestel, 2011).

## Self-Help Support Groups

*Self-help support groups* are voluntary organizations of individuals who get together on a regular basis to discuss topics of common interest. The groups are not conducted by a professional therapist but by a paraprofessional or a member of the common interest group. A *paraprofessional* is an individual who has been taught by a professional to provide some mental health services but who does not have formal mental health training. The paraprofessional may have personally had a disorder; for example, a chemical dependency counselor may also be a person recovering from addiction. The group leader and members provide support to help individuals with their problems.

*"That's precisely what we are talking about, Bob. You cannot simply play dead anytime Vera raises a difficult issue."*

Self-help support groups play a key and valuable role in our nation's mental health (Norcross & others, 2013). A survey in 2002 revealed that for mental health support alone, nearly 7,500 such groups existed in the United States, with more than 1 million members (Goldstrom & others, 2006). In addition to reaching so many people in need of help, these groups are important because they use community resources and are relatively inexpensive. They also serve people who are otherwise less likely to receive help, such as those with a limited education or on a low income.

Self-help support groups provide members with a sympathetic audience for social sharing and emotional release. The social support, role modeling, and sharing of concrete strategies for solving problems that unfold in self-help groups add to their effectiveness. A woman who has been raped might not believe a male therapist who tells her that, with time, she will put the pieces of her shattered life back together. The same message from another rape survivor—someone who has had to work through the same feelings of rage, fear, and violation—might be more believable.

There are myriad self-help groups, including groups for cocaine abusers, dieters, victims of child abuse, and people with various medical conditions (heart disease, cancer, diabetes, and so on). Alcoholics Anonymous (AA) is one of the best-known self-help groups. Mental health professionals often recommend AA for clients struggling with alcoholism (Kaskutas & others, 2009). Some studies show a positive effect for AA, but others do not (Kaskutas, 2009). A recent study found that AA reduced drinking by improving self-efficacy related to not drinking in social contexts, fostering positive changes in social networks, increasing spirituality/religiousness, and reducing negative affect (Kelly & others, 2012).

For individuals who tend to cope by seeking information and affiliation with similar peers, self-help support groups can reduce stress and promote adjustment. However, as with any group therapy, there is a possibility that negative emotions will spread through the group, especially if the members face circumstances that deteriorate over time, as terminal cancer patients do. Group leaders who are sensitive to the spread of negative emotions can minimize such effects.

*Problems such as social contagion and groupthink (see Chapter 11) can arise in support groups.*

In addition to face-to-face groups, a multitude of online support groups has also emerged (Norcross & others, 2013). Online support groups have promise (Ellis & others, 2011), but they can have downsides. In the absence of guidance from a trained professional, members may lack the expertise and knowledge to provide optimal advice. The emergence of pro-anorexia (or "pro-ana") websites, which *promote* anorexia, exemplifies the potentially negative side of the online "support" phenomenon (Bardone-Cone & Cass, 2006).

# Community Mental Health

Community mental health includes services such as medical care, one-on-one counseling, self-help support groups, workshops, and supported residences like halfway houses.

The community mental health movement was born in the 1960s, when society recognized that locking away individuals with psychological disorders and disabilities was inhumane and inappropriate. The deplorable conditions inside some psychiatric facilities spurred the movement as well. The central idea behind the community mental health movement was that individuals with disorders ought to remain within society and with their families and should receive treatment in community mental health centers. This movement also reflected economic concerns, as it was thought that institutionalizing people was more expensive than treating them in the community at large. Thus, with the passage of the Community Mental Health Act of 1963, large numbers of individuals with psychological disorders were transferred from mental institutions to community-based facilities, a process called *deinstitutionalization.* Although at least partially motivated by a desire to help individuals with psychological disorders more effectively, deinstitutionalization has been implicated in rising rates of homelessness. The success of community mental health services depends on the resources and commitment of the communities in which they occur.

Community mental health involves training teachers, ministers, family physicians, nurses, and others who directly interact with community members to offer lay counseling and workshops on topics such as coping with stress, reducing drug use, and assertiveness training (A. Lim & others, 2012). Advocates and providers of community mental health believe that the best way to treat a psychological disorder is through prevention (Feinstein, Richter, & Foster, 2012; Thota & others, 2012).

*How much would you be willing to pay in taxes to support community mental health programs?*

An explicit goal of community mental health is to help people who are disenfranchised from society, such as those living in poverty, to lead happier, more productive lives (Cook & Kilmer, 2012; Simning & others, 2012). A key objective in this effort is empowerment—assisting individuals to develop skills for controlling their own lives. All community mental health programs may rely on financial support from local, state, and federal governments.

## Cultural Perspectives

The psychotherapies discussed earlier in this chapter—psychodynamic, humanistic, behavior, and cognitive—center on the individual. This focus is generally compatible with the needs of people in Western cultures such as the United States, where the emphasis is on the individual rather than the group (family, community, or ethnic group). However, these psychotherapies may not be as effective with people who live in collectivistic cultures that place more importance on the group (Sue & others, 2013). Some psychologists argue that family therapy is likely to be more effective with people in cultures that place a high value on the family, such as Latino and Asian cultures (Guo, 2005). Research shows that adapting or tailoring the therapist relationship to cultural background and to religious/ spiritual orientation improves therapy effectiveness (Norcross, 2011).

If you think about psychotherapy as a conversation among people, you can appreciate the profound and intricate ways culture can influence the psychotherapeutic process. Throughout our exploration of psychology, we have noted the ways in which culture is expressed in language, in our modes of talking to one another, and in the things we talk about. Placing the conversation that is psychotherapy within a cultural framework is enormously complex. Cultures may differ, for instance, in terms of how they view the appropriateness of talking with an elder about personal problems or of talking about one's feelings at all (Asnaani & Hofmann, 2012; Naeem & others, 2009). Cultural issues in therapy include factors such as socioeconomic status, ethnicity, gender, country of

## Clinical and Cultural Psychology: How Can Cognitive-Behavior Therapy Work Across Different Belief Systems?

All therapies seek to help people become psychologically healthier and able to lead more fulfilling lives. What is a psychologically healthy person like? What makes a human life fulfilling? For many people, the answers are provided by culture and especially by religious beliefs. How these cultural and religious values match up with the values inherent in therapeutic approaches is important, especially as Western psychotherapy perspectives spread around the world.

Cognitive-behavior therapy (CBT) involves nudging individuals to question the validity of their beliefs and the reasonableness of their thoughts. From the CBT perspective, changing the ways people think about their life experiences gives them a sense of control over their emotions and reactions. Consider, though, that some of our beliefs are embedded in our cultural worldview, including our cultural and religious beliefs. Clients in therapy might view others' efforts to change such beliefs as judgmental or biased (Asnaani & Hofmann, 2012). As CBT has gained popularity, research has begun to investigate whether and how the values of CBT "fit" in a broad range of cultures.

Cultures and religions differ in terms of how well they match up with the values of CBT. For instance, in one study of college students in India, many felt that the goals of CBT conflicted with their personal, cultural, and religious beliefs (Scorzelli & Reinke-Scorzelli, 1994). Among these students, the notion that individuals might, through therapy, gain greater control over their life was viewed as clashing with cultural and religious values emphasizing that supernatural forces define one's destiny and that a person should live in accord with familial and societal expectations. Similarly, a study in

Pakistan found that students perceived being assertive, talking about one's feelings with an elder, and gaining control over one's feelings and life choices as inconsistent with their religious values (Naeem & others, 2009). In contrast, research in Thailand showed that Buddhists found the goals of CBT to be quite in keeping with their spiritual values. Buddhism views misery as originating in conscious thought, and in this sense, the CBT focus on changing thoughts is well suited to the Buddhist mindset (Reinke-Scorzelli & Scorzelli, 2001).

How might a therapist use CBT with a client whose cultural and religious beliefs clash with the values of CBT? Anu Asnaani and Stefan Hofmann (2012) presented a case study of a woman of Jamaican heritage who was struggling with a psychological disorder. Deeply religious, the woman found that her desire for therapy placed her at odds with her family and friends. In their eyes, her need for therapy signified a weakness of faith. Why did she need therapy? She should put her faith in God and prayer, they insisted. To resolve this conflict, the woman's therapist suggested that she try regarding her therapy as an expression of her spiritual drive toward healing. Through this approach the woman was able to embrace therapy as a means to a spiritual goal. When CBT became part of the healing process embedded in her strong religious faith, she was able to accept that healing could come not only through prayer and the support of a faith community but also through therapy.

\\ **What makes a person psychologically healthy?**

\\ **How does your cultural experience influence your answer?**

---

**cross-cultural competence**
A therapist's assessment of his or her abilities to manage cultural issues in therapy and the client's perception of those abilities.

origin, current culture, and religious beliefs and traditions (Farren, Snee, & McElroy, 2012; Joutsenniemi & others, 2012).

**Cross-cultural competence** refers both to how skilled a therapist feels about being able to manage cultural issues that might arise in therapy and to how the client perceives the therapist's ability (Asnaani & Hofmann, 2012). Dominant features of cross-cultural competence are demonstrating respect for cultural beliefs and practices and balancing the goals of a particular therapeutic approach with the goals and values of a culture. To read more about the issues, see the Intersection.

*When therapists engage with clients in a culturally sensitive way, a key goal is to not immediately assume too much about how culture influences the person. Each person must be treated as an individual.*

**ETHNICITY** Many ethnic minority individuals prefer discussing problems with parents, friends, and relatives rather than mental health professionals (Sue & others, 2013). Might therapy progress best, then, when the therapist and the client are from the same ethnic background? Researchers have found that when there is an ethnic match between the therapist and the client and when ethnic-specific services are provided, clients are less likely to drop out of therapy early and in many cases have better treatment outcomes (Jackson & Greene, 2000). Ethnic-specific services include culturally appropriate greetings and arrangements (for example, serving tea rather than coffee to Chinese American clients), providing flexible hours for treatment, and employing a bicultural/bilingual staff (Nystul, 1999).

 *Would you be comfortable receiving treatment from a therapist who differs from you in ethnic background? In gender? In religious faith?*

Nonetheless, therapy can be effective when the therapist and client are from different ethnic backgrounds if the therapist has excellent clinical skills and is culturally sensitive (Akhtar, 2006). Culturally skilled psychotherapists have good knowledge of their clients' cultural groups, understand sociopolitical influences on clients, and have competence in working with culturally diverse groups (Austad, 2009).

**GENDER** One byproduct of changing gender roles for women and men is reevaluation of the goal of psychotherapy (Gilbert & Kearney, 2006; Nolen-Hoeksema, 2011). Traditionally, the goal has been autonomy or self-determination for the client. However, autonomy and self-determination are often more central to men than to women, whose lives generally are characterized more by relatedness and connection with others. Thus, some psychologists argue that therapy goals should involve increased attention to relatedness and connection with others, especially for women, or should emphasize both autonomy/self-determination and relatedness/connection to others (Notman & Nadelson, 2002).

Feminist therapists believe that traditional psychotherapy continues to carry considerable gender bias and has not adequately addressed the specific concerns of women. Thus, several alternative, nontraditional therapies have arisen that aim to help clients break free from traditional gender roles and stereotypes. In terms of improving clients' lives, the goals of feminist therapists are no different from those of other therapists. However, feminist therapists believe that women must become alert to the possibility of bias and discrimination in their own lives in order to achieve their mental health goals (Herlihy & McCollum, 2007).

## self-quiz

1. A family therapist who attempts to change the alliances among members of a family is using the technique of
   A. reframing.
   B. structural change.
   C. detriangulation.
   D. validation.

2. A paraprofessional is
   A. someone who helps a therapist to conduct therapy.
   B. an unlicensed therapist.
   C. the leader of a therapy group.
   D. someone who has training in helping but lacks formal training as a therapist.

3. Deinstitutionalization is
   A. the release of a convict from the prison system.
   B. the transfer of mental health clients from institutions to community agencies.
   C. the process of having someone admitted to a treatment center against his or her will.
   D. discharging someone with a psychological disorder from treatment.

**APPLY IT!** 4. Frank, an Asian American, is struggling with depression. When he tells a friend that he plans to get therapy, Frank mentions that he hopes the therapist is Asian American. His friend responds that Frank is biased and that he should be open to a therapist from any background. Based on research findings, what is Frank's wisest course of action if he genuinely wants his therapy to succeed?
   A. Frank should insist on an Asian American therapist because he can benefit from counseling only if his therapist shares his ethnicity.
   B. Frank is being close-minded and should take whatever therapist he gets.
   C. Frank should be open to a therapist who understands the cultural issues that might affect Frank's life.
   D. Frank should seek out a therapist who does not share his ethnicity because that way he will be forced to think outside the box.

## 4 The Effectiveness of Psychotherapy

Do individuals who go through therapy get better? Are some approaches more effective than others? How would we know if a therapy worked? During the past several decades, a large volume of research has addressed these questions (Kazdin, 2007).

# Research on the Effectiveness of Psychotherapy

A large body of research points to the conclusion that psychotherapy works (Beck, 2005; Butler & others, 2006; Lambert, 2001; Luborsky & others, 2002). Researchers have carried out hundreds of studies examining the effects of psychotherapy. The strategy used to analyze these diverse studies is meta-analysis, in which the researcher statistically combines the results of many different studies.

Figure 13.8 provides a summary of numerous studies and reviews of research in which clients were randomly assigned to a no-treatment control group, a placebo control group, or a psychotherapy treatment (Lambert, 2001). As can be seen, some individuals who did not get treatment improved. These cases tell us that some psychological symptoms are likely to improve on their own, although it is also possible that these individuals sought help from friends, family, or clergy. Individuals in a placebo control group fared better than untreated individuals, probably because of having contact with a therapist, expectations of being

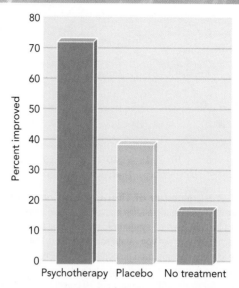

**FIGURE 13.8** **The Effects of Psychotherapy** In a review of studies, more than 70 percent of individuals who saw a therapist improved, whereas less than 40 percent who received a placebo and less than 20 percent who received no treatment improved (Lambert, 2001). *> Why do you think participants in the "no treatment" group improved? > Do these results allow us to make a causal claim about the effectiveness of therapy? Why or why not?*

helped, or the reassurance and support that they got during the study. However, by far the best outcomes occurred for individuals who received psychotherapy.

Individuals contemplating seeing a psychotherapist want to know not only whether psychotherapy works but also which form is most effective. The situation is similar to that of the Dodo bird in *Alice's Adventures in Wonderland*. Dodo was asked to judge the winner of a race. He decided, "Everybody has won and all must have prizes." Many studies of psychotherapy have supported the *Dodo bird hypothesis*—all "win" and all must have "prizes." That is, although research confirms that therapy works, no single therapy has been shown to be significantly better than the others (Hubble & Miller, 2004; Lambert, 2001; Luborsky & others, 2002; Wampold, 2001; Wampold & others, 2011).

Still, research has begun to indicate that certain therapies may work better than others for specific psychological disorders (Gould, Coulson, & Howard, 2012). For example, a recent meta-analysis on anxiety disorders found that for children with an anxiety disorder, psychotherapy was more effective when individual therapy was used and when treatment targeted a specific anxiety disorder, while parental involvement in therapy did not confer any benefits for therapy outcomes (S. Reynolds & others, 2012). The idea that specific therapeutic techniques work best for particular disorders has led to the development of **evidence-based practice.** This relatively new therapeutic approach integrates the best available research with clinical expertise in the context of client characteristics, culture, and preferences (APA Presidential Task Force on Evidence-Based Practice, 2006). From this perspective, decisions about treatment are optimally based on research demonstrating effectiveness (Norcross, 2011).

**evidence-based practice** Integration of the best available research with clinical expertise in the context of client characteristics, culture, and preferences.

How long does it take therapy to work? In one study, clients rated their symptoms, interpersonal relations, and quality of life weekly before each treatment session (Anderson & Lambert, 2001). Figure 13.9 shows that one-third of the individuals had improved outcomes by the 10th session, 50 percent by the 20th session, and 70 percent by the 45th

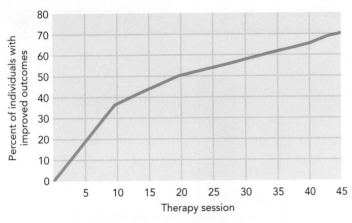

**FIGURE 13.9  Number of Therapy Sessions and Improvement**  In one study, a large number of people undergoing therapy rated their well-being (based on symptoms, interpersonal relations, and quality of life) before each treatment session (Anderson & Lambert, 2001). The percentage of people who showed improved outcomes after each additional session of treatment indicated that about a third of the individuals recovered by the 10th session, 50 percent by the 20th session, and 70 percent by the 45th session.

*The question is whether an individual whose symptoms have been treated can go on to enjoy a productive work life, a rewarding relationship with a romantic partner, and close friendships.*

session. In sum, therapy benefits individuals with psychological problems at least through the first six months of treatment and possibly longer.

## Health and Wellness Benefits of Psychotherapy

Therapy generally targets the relief of psychological symptoms. A therapy is considered effective if it frees a person from the negative effects of psychological disorders. Does therapy have larger implications related to a person's psychological wellness and even physical health?

For example, receiving a cancer diagnosis is stressful for diagnosed individuals. Might psychotherapeutic help aimed at reducing this stress improve patients' ability to cope with the disease? New research indicates that therapy does have such a positive effect. One study revealed that group-based cognitive therapy that focused on sharpening prostate cancer patients' stress management skills was effective in improving their quality of life (Penedo & others, 2006). Another study found that individual cognitive-behavior therapy reduced symptom severity in cancer patients undergoing chemotherapy (Sikorskii & others, 2006).

Psychotherapy might also have benefits for physical health. Depression is associated with coronary heart disease, for example (Linke & others, 2009). Psychotherapy that reduces depression is likely, then, to reduce the risk of heart disease (K. W. Davidson & others, 2006). A research review also revealed evidence of positive effects of psychotherapy on health behavior and physical illness, including habits and ailments such as smoking, chronic pain, chronic fatigue syndrome, and asthma (Eells, 2000).

Psychotherapy might even be a way to prevent psychological and physical problems. In one study (Smit & others, 2006), individuals waiting to see their primary healthcare provider were assigned to receive either physical health treatment as usual or that same treatment plus brief psychotherapy (a simple version of minimal contact cognitive-behavior therapy). The brief psychotherapy included a self-help manual, instructions in mood management, and six short telephone conversations with a prevention worker. The overall rate of depression was significantly lower in the psychotherapy group, and this difference was cost effective. That is, the use of brief psychotherapy as a part of regular physical checkups was psychologically and economically advantageous.

Finally, although typically targeted at relieving distressing symptoms, might psychotherapy enhance psychological well-being? This question is important because the absence of psychological symptoms (the goal of most psychotherapy) is not the same thing as the presence of psychological wellness. Just as an individual who is without serious physical illness is not necessarily at the height of physical health, a person who is relatively free of psychological symptoms still might not show the qualities we associate with psychological thriving. Studies have found that a lack of psychological wellness may predispose individuals to relapse or make them vulnerable to problems (Ryff & Singer, 1998; Ryff, Singer, & Love, 2004; Thunedborg, Black, & Bech, 1995). Research has revealed that individuals who show not only a decrease in symptoms but also an increase in well-being are less prone to relapse (Fava, 2006; Ruini & Fava, 2004).

Recently, therapists have developed a new type of treatment specifically aimed at enhancing well-being. **Well-being therapy (WBT)** is a short-term, problem-focused, directive therapy that encourages clients to accentuate the positive (Fava, 2006; Ruini & Fava, 2009). The first step in WBT is recognizing the positive in one's life when it happens. The initial WBT homework assignment asks clients to monitor their own happiness levels and to keep track of moments of well-being. Clients are encouraged to note even small pleasures—a beautiful spring day, a relaxing chat with a friend, the great taste of morning coffee. Clients then identify thoughts and feelings that are related to the premature ending of these moments. WBT is about learning to notice and savor positive experiences and coming up with ways to promote and celebrate life's good moments. WBT is effective in enhancing well-being, and it may also allow individuals to enjoy sustained recovery from mental disorders (Fava, Ruini, & Belaise, 2007; Ruini & Fava, 2009; Ruini & others, 2006).

**well-being therapy (WBT)** A short-term, problem-focused, directive therapy that encourages clients to accentuate the positive.

## Common Themes in Effective Psychotherapy

In this final section, we look at common threads in successful psychotherapy. Two key ingredients in successful therapy are the therapeutic alliance and client factors.

### THE THERAPEUTIC ALLIANCE

The **therapeutic alliance** is the relationship between the therapist and client. This alliance is an important element of successful psychotherapy (Horvath & others, 2011; Prochaska & Norcross, 2010). A relationship in which the client has confidence and trust in the therapist is essential to effective psychotherapy (Knapp, 2007; McLeod, 2007). The quality of the therapeutic alliance is a significant factor in whether therapy is effective, regardless of the specific type of therapy used (Norcross, 2011).

**therapeutic alliance** The relationship between the therapist and client— an important element of successful psychotherapy.

### CLIENT FACTORS

In all of the meta-analyses of therapeutic outcome studies, one major factor in predicting therapeutic outcome is the client himself or herself. Indeed, the quality of the client's participation is the chief determinant of therapy outcome (McKay, Imel, & Wampold, 2006; Wampold, 2001). Even though the individual may seek therapy from a place of vulnerability, it is that person's strengths, abilities, skills, and motivation that account for therapeutic success (Hubble & Miller, 2004; Wampold & Brown, 2005). In a review of the extensive evidence on therapeutic efficacy, researchers noted, "The data make abundantly clear that therapy does not make clients work, but rather clients make therapy work" (Hubble & Miller, 2004, p. 347). Therapy becomes a catalyst for bringing the person's own strengths to the forefront of his or her life.

Life is complicated and filled with potential pitfalls. We all need help at times, and therapy is one way to improve oneself physically and psychologically—to grow and become the best person we can be. Therapy is as complex as any other human relationship and potentially as rewarding—producing positive changes in one person's life through a meaningful association with another person (Joseph & Linley, 2004).

## SUMMARY

## Biological Therapies

Biological approaches to therapy include drugs, electroconvulsive therapy (ECT), and psychosurgery. Psychotherapeutic drugs that treat psychological disorders fall into three main categories: antianxiety drugs, antidepressant drugs, and antipsychotic drugs.

Benzodiazepines are the most commonly used antianxiety drugs. Antidepressant drugs regulate mood; the three main classes are tricyclics, MAO inhibitors, and SSRI drugs. Lithium is used to treat bipolar disorder. Antipsychotic drugs are administered to treat severe psychological disorders, especially schizophrenia.

Practitioners use electroconvulsive therapy, which triggers a brain seizure, to alleviate severe depression when other interventions have failed. They are also treating some forms of depression through deep brain stimulation, which applies electrical stimulation in precise brain locations. Psychosurgery is an irreversible procedure in which brain tissue is destroyed. Though rarely used today, psychosurgery is more precise now than in the days of prefrontal lobotomies.

## Psychotherapy

Psychotherapy is the process that mental health professionals use to help individuals recognize, define, and overcome their disorders and improve their adjustment. In Freudian psychoanalysis, psychological disorders stem from unresolved unconscious conflicts, believed to originate in early family experiences. A therapist's interpretation of free association, dreams, transference, and resistance provides paths for understanding the client's unconscious conflicts. Although psychodynamic therapy has changed, many contemporary psychodynamic therapists still probe the unconscious mind for early family experiences that might provide clues to clients' current problems.

In humanistic therapies, the analyst encourages clients to understand themselves and to grow personally. Client-centered therapy, developed by Rogers, is a type of humanistic therapy that includes active listening, reflective speech, unconditional positive regard, empathy, and genuineness.

Behavior therapies use learning principles to reduce or eliminate maladaptive behavior. They are based on the behavioral and social cognitive theories of personality. Behavior therapies seek to eliminate symptoms or behaviors rather than to help individuals gain insight into their problems.

The two main behavior therapy techniques based on classical conditioning are systematic desensitization and aversive conditioning. In systematic desensitization, anxiety is treated by getting the individual to associate deep relaxation with increasingly intense anxiety-producing situations. In aversive conditioning, repeated pairings of the undesirable behavior with aversive stimuli decrease the behavior's pleasant associations.

In operant conditioning approaches to behavior therapy, an analysis of the person's environment determines which factors need modification. Applied behavior analysis is the application of operant conditioning to change behavior. Its main goal is to replace maladaptive behaviors with adaptive ones.

Cognitive therapies emphasize that the individual's cognitions (thoughts) are the root of abnormal behavior. Cognitive therapies attempt to change the person's feelings and behaviors by changing cognitions. Three main forms of cognitive therapy are Ellis's rational-emotive behavior therapy (REBT), Beck's cognitive therapy, and cognitive-behavior therapy.

Ellis's approach is based on the idea that individuals develop psychological disorders because of their beliefs, especially irrational beliefs. In Beck's cognitive therapy, the therapist assists the client in learning about logical errors in thinking and guides the client in challenging these thinking errors. Cognitive-behavior therapy combines cognitive and behavior therapy techniques and emphasizes self-efficacy and self-instructional methods.

## Sociocultural Approaches and Issues in Treatment

Group therapies emphasize that relationships can hold the key to successful therapy. Family therapy is group therapy involving family members. Four widely used family therapy techniques are validation, reframing, structural change, and detriangulation. Couples therapy is group therapy with married or unmarried couples whose major problem is within their relationship.

Self-help support groups are voluntary organizations of individuals who get together on a regular basis to discuss topics of common interest. They are conducted without a professional therapist.

The community mental health movement was born out of the belief that the mental healthcare system was not adequately reaching people in poverty and deinstitutionalized individuals. Empowerment is a common goal of community mental health.

Psychotherapies' traditional focus on the individual may be successful in individualistic cultures, but individual-centered psychotherapies may not work as well in collectivistic cultures. Therapy is often more effective when there is an ethnic match between the therapist and the client, although culturally sensitive therapy can be provided by a therapist from a different ethnic background.

The psychotherapeutic emphasis on autonomy may pose a problem for the many women who value connectedness in relationships. Feminist-based therapies emphasize the importance of raising women's awareness of the influence of traditional gender roles and stereotypes in their lives.

As many as 50 percent of practicing therapists refer to themselves as "integrative" or "eclectic." Integrative therapy combines techniques from different therapies based on the therapist's judgment of which methods will provide the greatest benefit.

## 4 The Effectiveness of Psychotherapy

Meta-analysis has found that psychotherapies are successful in treating psychological disorders. Psychotherapy has been shown to help individuals cope with serious physical diseases as well. Evidence-based therapy integrates the best available research with clinical expertise in the context of client characteristics, culture, and preferences. Psychotherapy can aid individuals by alleviating physical symptoms directly or by reducing psychological problems that are related to physical illness.

Brief psychotherapy may be a cost-effective way to prevent serious disorders before they occur. Psychotherapy can also enhance wellness. Individuals who gain in wellness are less likely to fall prey to recurrent problems.

The therapeutic alliance, which involves the professional relationship between the therapist and the client, is key to the success of therapy. Another important factor in determining therapy's success is the client himself or herself.

## KEY TERMS

biological therapies (biomedical therapies), p. 483
antianxiety drugs, p. 483
antidepressant drugs, p. 484
lithium, p. 485
antipsychotic drugs, p. 485
electroconvulsive therapy (ECT), p. 487
psychosurgery, p. 488

psychotherapy, p. 490
psychodynamic therapies, p. 491
psychoanalysis, p. 491
free association, p. 491
interpretation, p. 492
dream analysis, p. 492
transference, p. 492
resistance, p. 492

humanistic therapies, p. 493
client-centered therapy, p. 493
reflective speech, p. 493
behavior therapies, p. 494
systematic desensitization, p. 494
cognitive therapies, p. 495
rational-emotive behavior therapy (REBT), p. 496
cognitive-behavior therapy, p. 499

integrative therapy, p. 500
group therapy, p. 501
family therapy, p. 502
couples therapy, p. 502
cross-cultural competence, p. 505
evidence-based practice, p. 507
well-being therapy (WBT), p. 509
therapeutic alliance, p. 509

## SELF-TEST

### Multiple Choice

1. Prozac is an example of
   A. a benzodiazepine.
   B. a selective serotonin reuptake inhibitor.
   C. a neuroleptic.
   D. a tricyclic.

2. Sharon is seeing a new doctor after various medications have failed to help with her condition. This doctor tells her that many well-designed studies suggest that electroconvulsive therapy is effective in the treatment of
   A. epilepsy.
   B. panic attack disorder.
   C. schizophrenia.
   D. depression.

3. A client who pinches herself each time she has a craving for a cigarette is using the technique of
   A. extinction.
   B. systematic desensitization.
   C. aversive conditioning.
   D. cognitive restructuring.

4. *Catharsis* is a term used to describe
   A. the client's resistance to the therapist's suggestions.
   B. the client's transfer of parental conflicts onto the therapist.
   C. the release of emotions a person experiences when reliving an emotionally charged experience.
   D. the process of redirecting unacceptable motives into a socially acceptable form.

5. Transference is an advantage in the therapeutic situation because
   A. it provides an opportunity to re-create difficult relationships.
   B. it reduces anxiety.
   C. it increases conflict.
   D. it stimulates resistance.

6. According to Freudian dream interpretation, the obvious content of a person's dream hides the true meaning or content of the dream, called the _____ content.
   A. obtuse
   B. subliminal
   C. latent
   D. manifest

7. Cognitive-behavior therapy attempts to produce change by
   A. bringing the unconscious to consciousness.
   B. helping clients unlearn and then relearn specific behaviors.
   C. helping clients develop self-awareness and self-acceptance.
   D. asking clients to give up irrational beliefs.

8. Therapy is most effective during the first
   A. week.
   B. three months.
   C. six months.
   D. year.

9. Helping a family to understand that the problems in their relationships are not exclusively the fault of an individual family member is an example of
   A. reframing.
   B. structural change.
   C. detriangulation.
   D. validation.

10. Self-help support groups
    A. do not play a significant role in promoting the nation's mental health.
    B. rely on community resources.
    C. are relatively expensive to run.
    D. typically serve people who are also receiving help from other sources.

## Apply It!

11. Compare and contrast psychodynamic, humanistic, and cognitive-behavior therapies. For each, give an example of the type of person and problem for which the particular therapy might be best suited.

# 14 Health Psychology

## Does It Take a Village to Lose Weight?

Troubled by the growing problem of obesity, community leaders in the United States are taking steps to help citizens become more active, eat healthier diets, and lose weight (Ockene & others, 2012; Wieland & others, 2012). Some localities have formed community weight-loss clubs through churches and other organizations (Yeary & others, 2012). The town of Lakeland, Florida, sponsored a "Dance Off" and awarded prizes for weight loss (R. Brown, 2012). A child-care center for Native Americans in California started its own vegetable garden, allowing the children to eat fresh vegetables that they themselves had planted and cared for (Sripada, 2012). In the small town of Hernando, Mississippi, a pastor took the drastic step of banning fried chicken from church social events (Hauser, 2012). Communities elsewhere in the world are also banding together to combat obesity. In Ghent, Belgium, city council members declared their community officially vegetarian (at least one day a week) in order to reduce obesity as well as the city's environmental footprint (Mason, 2009).

Embracing a healthy lifestyle is a choice that is made not only by individuals but sometimes by whole communities. Clearly, our physical health is influenced by our contexts, behaviors, motivations, thoughts, and feelings—factors at the very heart of the science of psychology.

The focus of this chapter is health psychology, the field devoted to promoting healthy practices and understanding the psychological processes that underlie health and illness. After first defining the field, we examine the ways psychologists explain the process of making healthy life changes and the resources on which individuals can draw to achieve positive change. Next we survey the psychology of stress and coping and consider psychological perspectives on making wise choices in four vital areas: physical activity, diet, the decision to smoke or not to smoke, and sex. Fittingly, the chapter (and the book) closes with a look at psychology's role in shaping a good life.

# Health Psychology and Behavioral Medicine

**Health psychology** emphasizes psychology's role in establishing and maintaining health and preventing and treating illness. Health psychology reflects the belief that lifestyle choices, behaviors, and psychological characteristics can play important roles in health (Acevedo, 2012; Koenig, King, & Carson, 2012; Marks, 2013; S. E. Taylor, 2012). A related discipline, **behavioral medicine,** is an interdisciplinary field that focuses on developing and integrating behavioral and biomedical knowledge to promote health and reduce illness. The concerns of health psychology and behavioral medicine overlap: Health psychology primarily focuses on behavioral, social, and cognitive factors (Pbert & others, 2012; Rhodes & Mark, 2012; Sheffer & others, 2012), whereas behavioral medicine centers on behavioral, social, and biomedical factors (Hamer, 2012; McBride & others, 2012; Parada & others, 2012).

> **behavioral medicine**
> An interdisciplinary field that focuses on developing and integrating behavioral and biomedical knowledge to promote health and reduce illness; overlaps with and is sometimes indistinguishable from health psychology.

> **health psychology**
> A subfield of psychology that emphasizes psychology's role in establishing and maintaining health and preventing and treating illness.

Related to health psychology and behavioral medicine are the fields of health promotion and public health (Fafard, 2012; Muntaner & others, 2012). *Health promotion* involves helping people change their lifestyle to optimize their health and assisting them in achieving balance in physical, emotional, social, spiritual, and intellectual health and wellness. Health promotion can be a goal of a company's human resources department, as well as state and city health departments, and it is sometimes a specialty for social workers and other members of the helping professions. *Public health* is concerned with studying health and disease in large populations to guide policymakers (Khubchandani & Simmons, 2012). Public health experts identify public health concerns, set priorities, and design interventions for health promotion. An important goal of public health is to ensure that all populations have access to cost-effective healthcare and health promotion services (O'Donnell, 2012; Stav & others, 2012).

A job in health promotion or public health can involve creating attention-grabbing public service advertisements and brochures to alert the public to health-related issues. If you have noticed a "Click It or Ticket" sign on the highway or seen one of thetruth.com's antismoking ads on TV, you have a good feel for what health promotion and public health are all about.

## The Biopsychosocial Model

The interests of health psychologists and behavioral medicine researchers are broad (Accordini & others, 2012; Ferdinand & others, 2012). The biopsychosocial model we examined in Chapter 12 in the context of psychological disorders applies to health psychology as well, because health psychology integrates biological, psychological, and social factors in health (Friedman & Ryff, 2012; Shimizu & others, 2012).

For example, stress is a focal point of study across the broad field of psychology (Manne, 2013). Study of the brain and behavior (Chapter 2 of this book), for instance, acknowledges the impact of stress on the autonomic nervous system. Furthermore, an individual's state of consciousness (Chapter 4), as well as his or her process of thinking about events in particular ways (Chapter 7), can influence the experience of stress. Stressful events also affect our emotions (Chapter 9), which are themselves psychological and physical events. Aspects of our personalities, too, may be associated with stress (Chapter 10) and can influence our health. Finally, social contexts (Chapter 11) can shape both an individual's experience of stress and his or her ability to cope with it.

## Connections Between Mind and Body

From the biopsychosocial perspective, the many diverse aspects of each human being are tightly intertwined. Our bodies and minds are deeply connected, a link introduced in Chapter 1. After suffering a heart attack, one health psychologist ruefully noted that none of his colleagues in the field had thought to ask him whether heart disease was part of his family history, ignoring the obvious question that a medical doctor would ask first. Although the mind is responsible for much of what happens in the body, it is not the only factor. Even as we consider the many ways that psychological processes contribute to health and disease, we must understand that sometimes illness happens for other reasons—affecting even those who have led healthy lives.

While it might be fascinating to think about how the mind may influence bodily health, it is also important to appreciate that the body may influence the mind as well. Health psychology and behavioral medicine are concerned not only with how psychological states influence health, but also with how health and illness may influence the person's psychological experience, including cognitive abilities, stress, and coping (Dedert & others, 2012; Lutwak & Dill, 2012). A person who is feeling psychologically run-down may not realize that the level of fatigue is the beginning stage of an illness. In turn, being physically healthy can be a source of psychological wellness.

**self-quiz**

1. Health psychologists believe that _____ are the key factors in health.
   A. psychological characteristics
   B. lifestyles
   C. behaviors
   D. all of the above

2. According to the text, health psychology overlaps in significant ways with
   A. philosophy.
   B. behavioral medicine.
   C. neuroscience.
   D. behaviorism.

3. The experience of stress can depend on
   A. one's state of consciousness.
   B. one's personality.
   C. one's social situation.
   D. all of the above

**APPLY IT!** 4. Anastasia is committed to getting all A's this semester. In her pursuit of academic excellence, she decides to sleep only three hours a night, to drink a lot of coffee, and to stop wasting time at the gym. She studies nearly 12 hours every night. During finals week, Anastasia is so exhausted that she sleeps through one of her exams and fails another because she cannot concentrate. Which of the following best explains what happened?
   A. Anastasia probably didn't study as hard as she claimed.
   B. Anastasia forgot that the body can affect the functioning of the mind.
   C. Anastasia took too many hard classes this semester.
   D. Anastasia set her goals too high.

# 2 Making Positive Life Changes

One of health psychology's missions is to help individuals identify and implement ways they can effectively change their behaviors for the better (Griffin & others, 2012; S. E. Taylor, 2012). **Health behaviors**—practices that have an impact on physical well-being—include adopting a healthy approach to stress, exercising, eating right, brushing one's teeth, performing breast and testicular exams, not smoking, drinking in moderation

**health behaviors**
Practices that have an impact on physical well-being.

(or not at all), and practicing safe sex. Before exploring what health psychologists have learned about the best ways to make healthy behavioral changes, we first focus on the process of change itself.

# Theoretical Models of Change

In many instances, changing behaviors begins by changing attitudes. Psychologists have sought to understand how changing attitudes can lead to behavioral changes.

A number of theoretical models have addressed the factors that likely play roles in effective health behavior changes. For example, the **theory of reasoned action** suggests that effective change requires individuals to have specific intentions about their behaviors, as well as positive attitudes about a new behavior, and to perceive that their social group looks positively on the new behavior as well (Ajzen, 2012a, 2012b; Ajzen & Albarracin, 2007; Ajzen & Fishbein, 1980, 2005). If, for example, you smoke and want to quit smoking, you will be more successful if you devise an explicit intention of quitting, feel good about it, and believe that your friends support you. Icek Ajzen (pronounced "I-zen") modified the theory of reasoned action to include the fact that not all of our behaviors are under our control. The **theory of planned behavior** includes the basic ideas of the theory of reasoned action but adds the person's perceptions of control over the outcome (Ajzen, 2002, 2012a, 2012b).

The theory of reasoned action and its extension, the theory of planned behavior, have accurately predicted whether individuals successfully enact healthy behaviors (Ajzen & Manstead, 2007), including cancer screening (Ross & others, 2007), HIV prevention (Kalichman, 2007), prevention of smoking and marijuana use in adolescents and binge drinking in college students (Elliott & Ainsworth, 2012; Guo & others, 2007; Lac & others, 2009), exercise (Plotnikoff & others, 2011), healthy eating (Dunn & others, 2011; White & others, 2012), and avoidance of gambling on the part of college students (H. S. Lee, 2012).

**theory of planned behavior**
Theoretical model that includes the basic ideas of the theory of reasoned action but adds the person's perceptions of control over the outcome.

*As we will see later, perceiving that one has control can have important implications for a number of life domains.*

**theory of reasoned action**
Theoretical model stating that effective change requires individuals to have specific intentions about their behaviors, as well as positive attitudes about a new behavior, and to perceive that their social group looks positively on the new behavior as well.

# The Stages of Change Model

The **stages of change model** describes the process by which individuals give up bad habits and adopt healthier lifestyles. The model breaks down behavioral changes into five steps, recognizing that real change does not occur overnight with one monumental decision, even if that night is New Year's Eve (Norcross, Krebs, & Prochaska, 2011; Prochaska, DiClemente, & Norcross, 1992; Prochaska, Norcross, & DiClemente, 1994) (Figure 14.1). Rather, change occurs in progressive stages, each characterized by particular issues and challenges. Those stages are

**stages of change model**
Theoretical model describing a five-step process by which individuals give up bad habits and adopt healthier lifestyles.

*Have you made a healthy life change recently? As we go over these stages, ask yourself whether they apply to your experience.*

- Precontemplation
- Contemplation
- Preparation/Determination
- Action/Willpower
- Maintenance

**PRECONTEMPLATION** The *precontemplation stage* occurs when individuals are not yet genuinely thinking about changing. They may even be unaware that they have a problem behavior. Individuals who drink to excess but are not aware that their drinking is affecting their work may be in the precontemplation phase. At this stage, raising one's consciousness about the problem is crucial.

A woman who smokes may find her consciousness raised by the experience of becoming pregnant. A man who is stopped for drunk driving may be forced to take a good look at his drinking. Similarly, overweight individuals may not recognize their problem

| Stage | Description | Example |
|-------|-------------|---------|
| Precontemplation 1 | Individuals are not yet ready to think about changing and may not be aware that they have a problem that needs to be changed. | Overweight individuals are not aware that they have a weight problem. |
| Contemplation 2 | Individuals acknowledge that they have a problem but may not yet be ready to change. | Overweight individuals know they have a weight problem but aren't yet sure they want to commit to losing weight. |
| Preparation/Determination 3 | Individuals are preparing to take action. | Overweight individuals explore options they can pursue in losing weight. |
| Action/Willpower 4 | Individuals commit to making a behavioral change and enact a plan. | Overweight individuals begin a diet and start an exercise program. |
| Maintenance 5 | Individuals are successful in continuing their behavior change over time. | Overweight individuals are able to stick with their diet and exercise regimens for 6 months. |

**FIGURE 14.1**

**Stages of Change Model Applied to Losing Weight** The stages of change model has been applied to many different health behaviors, including losing weight.

until they see photos of themselves taken at a family reunion or until they learn that an order of a McDonald's Big Mac, large fries, and large chocolate shake amounts to over 2,000 calories, the recommended adult caloric intake for an entire day. If you have seen Morgan Spurlock's documentary film *Super Size Me,* you probably have had your consciousness raised about how harmful fast food can be to health. Spurlock ate every meal at McDonald's for a month. By the end of filming he felt ill, had gained weight (he jumped from 185 to 210 pounds), and could not wait for the experience to end.

It is common for individuals in the precontemplation phase to deny that their behavior is a problem and to defend it, claiming that "I don't drink/smoke/eat that much." Overweight individuals may discover that they do eat "that much" when they start keeping track of calories.

**CONTEMPLATION**   In the *contemplation stage,* individuals acknowledge the problem but may not be ready to commit to change. As the name of the stage suggests, at this point individuals are actively thinking about change. They might reevaluate themselves and the place of this behavior in their life. They understandably may have mixed feelings about giving up a bad habit. For example, how will they deal with missing their friends on a smoke break? Or going out drinking? Or packing a healthy lunch instead of heading to the drive-thru? They may weigh the short-term gains of the harmful behavior against the long-term benefits of changing. As we considered in Chapter 5, future rewards can be difficult to pursue when immediate pleasures beckon. Sure, it would be nice to be thinner, but losing weight is going to take time, and that hot fudge sundae is right there, looking very delicious.

**PREPARATION/DETERMINATION**   In the *preparation/determination stage,* individuals are getting ready to take action. At this point, self-belief and especially beliefs about one's ability to "see it through" are very important. A key consideration is whether individuals truly feel they are ready to change.

During the preparation/determination stage, individuals start thinking concretely about how they might take on their new challenge. For example, they explore options for the best ways to quit smoking or drinking or to start an exercise program. Some smokers might consider trying a nicotine patch or participating in a support group for people

wanting to quit. Individuals who are seeking to lose weight might think about joining a gym or setting the alarm clock for a 6:00 A.M. run.

**ACTION/WILLPOWER** At the *action/ willpower stage,* individuals commit to making a real behavioral change and enact an effective plan. An important challenge at this stage is to find ways to support the new, healthy behavior pattern. One approach is to establish reinforcements or rewards for the new behavior. Individuals who have quit smoking might focus on how much better food tastes after they have given up cigarettes. Successful dieters might treat themselves to a shopping trip to buy new, smaller-size clothes. Acknowledging, enjoying, and celebrating accomplishments can motivate consistent behavior.

Another source of support for new behaviors is the individual's social network (S. E. Taylor, 2012). Friends, family, and members of a support group can help through their encouraging words and behaviors (Antonucci, Birditt, & Ajrouch, 2013; Manne, 2013). Members of a family might all quit smoking at the same time or join the individual in physical activities or healthier eating.

Finally, individuals may focus on alternative behaviors that replace the unhealthy ones. Instead of bar hopping, they might join a group dedicated to activities not associated with drinking alcohol, such as a dance club or community theater group. In other words, effective change also involves avoiding temptations.

*Can you quit smoking if you are spending time with smokers? Can you avoid binge drinking if you regularly go to keg parties?*

**MAINTENANCE** In the *maintenance stage,* individuals successfully avoid temptation and consistently pursue healthy behaviors. They may become skilled at anticipating tempting situations and avoid them or actively prepare for them. If smokers seeking to kick the habit know that they always enjoy a cigarette after a big meal out with friends, they might mentally prepare themselves for that temptation before going out. Successful dieters might post a consciousness-raising photograph on the refrigerator.

At some point, individuals in maintenance may find that actively fighting the urge to indulge in unhealthy behaviors is no longer necessary. *Transcendence* means that they are no longer consciously engaged in maintaining their healthy lifestyle; rather, the lifestyle has become a part of who they are. They are now nonsmokers, healthy eaters, or committed runners.

**relapse**
A return to former unhealthy patterns.

**RELAPSE** One challenge during the maintenance stage is to avoid **relapse,** a return to former unhealthy patterns. Relapse is a common aspect of change, and it can be discouraging. However, the majority of people who eventually do change do not succeed on the first try. Rather, they try and fail and try again, cycling through the five stages several times before achieving a stable, healthy lifestyle. Consequently, individuals who are experts in changing health behavior consider relapse to be normal (Prochaska & Norcross, 2010; Prochaska, Norcross, & DiClemente, 1994).

If you have ever tried to adopt a healthier lifestyle by dieting, starting an exercise program, or quitting smoking, you might know how bad you feel when you experience relapse. One slip, however, does not mean that you are a failure and will never reach your goal. Rather, when a slipup occurs, you have an opportunity to learn, to think about what led to the relapse, and to devise a strategy for preventing it in the future. Successful dieters, for example, do not let one lapse in the doughnut shop ruin the week (Phelan & others, 2003).

*Relapse is a normal part of change. What does this principle suggest about recovery from drug addiction?*

## EVALUATION OF THE STAGES OF CHANGE MODEL

The stages of change model has been applied successfully to a broad range of behaviors. These include cigarette smoking (C. L. Kohler & others, 2008; Schumann & others, 2006), exercise (Lippke & Plotnikoff, 2006), safe-sex practices (Arden & Armitage, 2008; Naar-King & others, 2006), substance use and abuse (DiClemente, 2006; Migneault, Adams, & Read, 2005; Walker & others, 2006), weight loss (MacQueen, Brynes, & Frost, 2002), and return to work (Lam & others, 2010).

Despite its relevance to a variety of behaviors, the stages of change model is controversial (Brug & others, 2004; Joseph, Breslin, & Skinner, 1999). Some critics have questioned whether the stages are mutually exclusive and whether individuals move from one stage to another in the order proposed (Littrell & Girvin, 2002). Critics of the model also point out that it refers more to attitudes that change than to behaviors (West, 2005). On the more positive side, recent evidence suggests that the stages of change model does a good job of capturing the ways that individuals make positive life changes (Lippke & others, 2009; Schuz & others, 2009). A recent meta-analysis of 39 studies that encompassed more than 8,000 psychotherapy clients found that the stages of change model was effective in predicting psychotherapy outcomes (Norcross, Krebs, & Prochaska, 2011).

Experts have argued that the model can be a tool for therapists who are trying to help clients institute healthy behavior patterns. Sometimes, sharing the model with individuals who are trying to change provides them with a useful language for understanding the change process, for reducing uncertainty, and for developing realistic expectations for the difficult journey (Hodgins, 2005; Schuz & others, 2009).

*"Wayne, have you ever given any thought to changing <u>completely</u>?"*

Used by permission of CartoonStock, www.CartoonStock.com.

# 3 Resources for Effective Life Change

Making positive changes to promote health can be very challenging. Fortunately, we all have various psychological, social, and cultural resources at our disposal to help us in the journey to a healthier lifestyle. In this section we consider some of these tools that can help us achieve effective change and, ultimately, a healthier life.

# Motivation

Recall from Chapter 9 that motivation refers to the "why" of behavior. Motivational tools for self-change involve changing for the right reasons. Change is most effective when you are doing it for you—because you want to. An analysis of intervention programs aimed at reducing childhood and adolescent obesity found that those who had joined voluntarily were more likely to lose weight than their counterparts who had been required to join (Stice, Shaw, & Marti, 2006).

Self-determination theory, presented in Chapter 9, distinguishes between intrinsic motivation (doing something because you want to) and extrinsic motivation (doing something for external rewards). Research has shown that creating a context in which people feel more in control, more autonomous, and more competent is associated with enhanced outcomes for a broad array of health behaviors, including controlling diabetes through diet (Bhattacharya, 2012), quitting smoking (Deci & Ryan, 2012), and getting regular physical exercise (Fortier & others, 2012). Individuals are more likely to succeed in their New Year's resolutions if they approach them with a sense of both self-efficacy and autonomy (Koestner & others, 2006).

Planning and goal setting are also crucial to making effective change. Researchers have found that individuals who come up with specific strategies, or **implementation intentions,** for dealing with the challenges of making a life change are more successful than others at navigating change (Armitage, 2006; Prestwich & others, 2012). Setting short-term, achievable goals also allows individuals to experience the emotional payoff of small successes along the way to self-change (R. F. Kushner, 2007). The novice exerciser who catches a glimpse of his new biceps in the mirror gets a mood boost. These feelings of satisfaction can help to motivate continued effort toward achieving health goals (Finch & others, 2005). A recent meta-analysis revealed that implementation intentions were more effective for including healthy food in one's diet but were not as effective in reducing unhealthy eating patterns (Adriaanse & others, 2011).

Enjoying the payoffs of our efforts to change also means that we must monitor our goal progress. As anyone who has watched *The Biggest Loser* will attest, stepping on a scale can be a scary prospect for someone who is trying to lose weight. However, it is important to get feedback on one's progress in the pursuit of any goal. If an individual finds out that she is falling short, she can try to identify areas that need work. On the other hand, discovering that she is doing well can be a potent motivator for future progress.

**implementation intentions**
Specific strategies for dealing with the challenges of making a life change.

*Whether the news is good or bad, information is important for making real progress.*

# Social Relationships

Research has shown, again and again, that social ties are an important, if not the most important, variable in predicting health (Norman & others, 2012). In a landmark study, social isolation had six times the effect on mortality rates that cigarette smoking had (House, Landis, & Umberson, 1988). In another study involving 1,234 cardiac patients, those living alone were nearly twice as likely to have a second heart attack (Case & others, 1992). Loneliness is linked with impaired physical health (cardiovascular disease, for example) (Hawkley & Cacioppo, 2012a, 2012b; Momtaz & others, 2012) and mental health (depression, for example) (Aylaz & others, 2012), and chronic loneliness can lead to an early death (Luo & others, 2012). Being connected to others is crucial to survival. One way that social connections make a difference in our lives is through social support (Antonucci, Birditt, & Ajrouch, 2013).

**Social support** is information and feedback from others indicating that one is loved and cared for, esteemed and valued, and included in a network of communication and mutual obligation. Social support has three types of benefits (S. E. Taylor, 2012):

**social support**
Information and feedback from others indicating that one is loved and cared for, esteemed and valued, and included in a network of communication and mutual obligation.

- *Tangible assistance:* Family and friends can provide goods and services in stressful circumstances, as when gifts of food are given after the death of a loved one.
- *Information:* Individuals who extend support can also recommend specific strategies to help the person under stress cope. Friends may notice that a coworker is overloaded with work and suggest ways of better managing time or delegating tasks.
- *Emotional support:* Individuals under stress often suffer emotionally and may develop depression, anxiety, or loss of self-esteem. Friends and family can reassure the stressed person that he or she is valuable and loved. Knowing that others care allows a person to manage stress with greater assurance.

One way that people gain support during difficult times is through *social sharing*—turning to others who act as a sounding board or a willing ear. Individuals who are striving to make healthy life changes might join a group of others who are also struggling with the same issue. Social sharing can also occur in online support groups.

Sometimes social sharing does not have to be very social to be helpful. James Pennebaker and his colleagues (Pennebaker, 1997a, 1997b, 2004) have demonstrated that writing about traumatic life events for 20 minutes a day over two or three days is associated with improved health, fewer illnesses, greater immune system function, and superior reactions to vaccines. Although writing about trauma is usually linked to increased distress in the short term, over the long run it brings physical and psychological health benefits (Baddeley & Pennebaker, 2011; Frattaroli, 2006; Pennebaker & Chung, 2007, 2011; Smyth, 1998). In most of these studies, the participants were college students writing about their most traumatic life events, and the studies' results suggest that anyone can benefit from writing about negative life events. Subsequent studies have found health benefits for writing about life goals and intensely positive life experiences (Burton & King, 2004, 2008; King, 2002). If you would like to give this simple intervention a try, see Figure 14.2.

Getting support from others is important, but *giving* support can also have benefits. A study of 423 older adult couples who were followed for five years revealed how helping others benefits physical health (S. L. Brown & others, 2003). At the beginning of the study, the couples were asked about the extent to which they had given or received emotional or practical help in the past year. Five years later, those who said they had helped others were half as likely to have died. One possible reason for this finding is that helping others may reduce the output of stress hormones, an effect that improves cardiovascular health and strengthens the immune system (Hackett & others, 2012; Hawkley & Cacioppo, 2012a, 2012b).

Having many different social ties may be especially important during difficult times (Hawkley & Cacioppo, 2012a, 2012b; S. E. Taylor, 2012). People who participate in more diverse social networks—for example, having a close relationship with a partner; interacting with family members, friends, neighbors, and fellow workers; and belonging to social and religious groups—live longer than people with fewer types of social relationships (Vogt & others, 1992). One study investigated the effects of diverse social ties on the susceptibility to getting a common cold (S. Cohen & others, 1998). Individuals reported the extent of their participation in

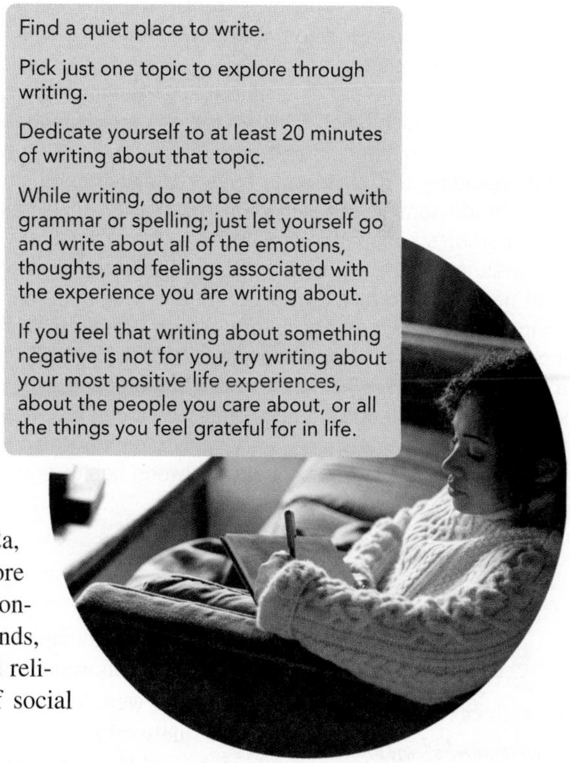

Find a quiet place to write.

Pick just one topic to explore through writing.

Dedicate yourself to at least 20 minutes of writing about that topic.

While writing, do not be concerned with grammar or spelling; just let yourself go and write about all of the emotions, thoughts, and feelings associated with the experience you are writing about.

If you feel that writing about something negative is not for you, try writing about your most positive life experiences, about the people you care about, or all the things you feel grateful for in life.

**FIGURE 14.2  Harnessing the Power of Writing**
Try this simple exercise to explore the health benefits of writing.

# INTERSECTION

## Health and Cross-Cultural Psychology: How Does Culture Influence the Meaning of Social Support?

It is hard to imagine any factor as crucial to human survival as having connections to a social network and friends to provide support in times of need. Yet many studies have been unable to establish a relationship between individuals' perceptions of the levels of compassion and encouragement they have received during stressful times and their physical and psychological functioning (Bolger & Amarel, 2007). How might we understand such research?

Consider that being on the receiving end of social support can mean different things to different people. On the one hand, having someone express support and encouragement during times of stress might give a person a feeling of being genuinely cared for. In this sense, getting help might be *truly helpful*. However, receiving help from another might also make a person feel incompetent: Why am I unable to handle this problem on my own? Culture is one factor that illuminates when and for whom emotional support might come at an emotional cost.

Jiyoung Park and her colleagues (2012) proposed that in Western cultures, which place a high value on personal independence, perceptions of support from others might entail an emotional cost, including concerns about being needy or incompetent. In this cultural context, receiving support may be viewed as threatening a person's sense of independence (Uchida & others, 2008). In contrast, in East Asian cultures that emphasize the interdependent nature of the self, providing and receiving help from others is an important way to enact cultural values. Rather than indicating incompetence or failure, in this context getting help from others is a sign of succeeding at the culturally esteemed goal of being a valued member of one's group. Based on these proposed distinctions between Western and Eastern cultures, Park and her colleagues hypothesized that the link between health and

perceptions of emotional support from others would be especially positive for individuals in East Asian cultures.

To test this prediction, the researchers surveyed over 1,000 adults in Japan and the United States. Participants completed questionnaires measuring stress, emotional support from others, and psychological and physical health. In support of the researchers' predictions, the relationship between perceptions of emotional support and health reports was strong and positive for Japanese but not for U.S. respondents (J. Park & others, 2012). Interestingly, among Japanese participants, support was most likely to be associated with better health reports when individuals were experiencing high levels of stress. These results might indicate that within more interdependent cultures, it is important that support come during times when it is clearly warranted and does not indicate that the person is making unjustifiable demands on the social group (Uchida & others, 2008).

Does this research have a lesson for Westerners? Park and her colleagues suggest that Americans might benefit most from *subtle* forms of support that do not draw attention to their own coping capacities. Specifically, for Westerners, receiving help might be less emotionally costly when it occurs in ways that preserve the supported person's sense of self-efficacy and independence. The researchers liken social support to an insurance policy: Just as insurance provides peace of mind when things are going well, knowing that we have a network of social support may promote health and well-being even when we do not feel the need to use it.

\\ **How and to whom do you typically offer support?**

\\ **When others have supported you in difficult times, how have you felt?**

---

*Ethics guidelines would have dictated the need for the participants' informed consent, meaning that they agreed to be injected with the cold virus.*

12 types of social ties. Then they were given nasal drops containing a cold virus and monitored for the appearance of a cold. Individuals with more diverse social ties were less likely to get a cold than their counterparts with less diverse social networks.

Although such results suggest a powerful role for social connections in health, research findings on the link between social support and health are not always clear-cut. To read more about this issue, see the Intersection.

# Religious Faith

Religious faith is strongly related to maintaining a healthy lifestyle and to good health (Koenig, 2012a, 2012b; Koenig, King, & Carson, 2012). Many religions frown on excess and promote moderation. Indeed, weekly religious attendance relates to a host of healthy behaviors, including not smoking, taking vitamins, walking regularly, wearing seatbelts, exercising strenuously, sleeping soundly, and drinking moderately or not at all (Haber, Koenig, & Jacob, 2011; T. D. Hill & others, 2006). A number of studies have definitively linked religious participation to a longer and healthier life (Campbell, Yoon, & Johnstone, 2009; Koenig, 2012b; Krause, 2006; McCullough & Willoughby, 2009).

Religious participation may also benefit health through its relationship to social support (George, 2009; S. E. Taylor, 2012). Belonging to a faith community may give people access to a warm group of others who are available during times of need. This community is there to provide transportation to the doctor, to check in with the individual during hard times, and simply to stand next to the individual during a worship service, as a fellow member of the community. The social connections promoted by religious activity can forestall anxiety and depression and help to prevent isolation and loneliness (Dein, Cook, & Koenig, 2012; Rosmarin, Krumrei, & Andersson, 2009; Ross & others, 2009a).

Religious faith and spirituality more generally may also be important factors in good health because they provide a sense of life meaning and a buffer against the effects of stressful life events (C. L. Park, 2012). Religious thoughts can play a role in maintaining hope and stimulating motivation for positive life changes. Studies have shown that some individuals with AIDS who lived much longer than expected had used religion as a coping strategy—specific benefits came from participating in religious activities such as praying and attending church services (Ironson & others, 2001)—and that an increase in spirituality after testing positive for HIV is associated with slower disease progression over four years (Ironson, Stuetzle, & Fletcher, 2006). Faith may also help individuals to avoid burnout at work (Murray-Swank & others, 2006) and to negotiate life's difficulties without feeling overwhelmed (Mascaro & Rosen, 2006). Belief in the enduring meaningfulness of one's life can help one keep perspective and see life's hassles in the context of the big picture (C. L. Park, 2012).

*How might these results apply to a person who is not religious?*

# Personality Characteristics

Personality traits are powerful instruments in the self-change toolbox. Here we survey some of the personality characteristics related to health.

**CONSCIENTIOUSNESS**  Recall from Chapter 10 that conscientious individuals are responsible and reliable; they like structure and seeing a task to its completion. Conscientiousness is not the sexiest trait, but it might well be the most important of the big five traits when it comes to health, healthy living, and longevity (Roberts & others, 2009). Various studies show that conscientious people tend to do all the things that they are told are good for their health, such as getting regular exercise, avoiding drinking and smoking, wearing seatbelts, monitoring their blood pressure, and checking smoke detectors (D. B. O'Connor & others, 2009; Rush, Becker, & Curry, 2009; Turiano & others, 2012). Research has also shown that conscientious individuals are not as likely to die as their counterparts who are less conscientious (Fry & Debats, 2009; Iwassa & others, 2008, 2009; Kern & Friedman, 2008; Wilson & others, 2004).

**PERSONAL CONTROL**  Another personality characteristic associated with taking the right steps toward a long, healthy life is a sense of personal control, what we referred to in Chapter 10 as an *internal locus of control* (Baumeister & Alquist, 2009; K. W. Griffin & others, 2012). Feeling in control can reduce stress during difficult times (S. E. Taylor, 2012; Thompson, 2001) and

*A person with a low level of personal control may feel that whatever happens happens—it is meant to be or a matter of (good or bad) luck.*

## How Powerful Is the Power of Positive Thinking?

Research demonstrating the role of psychological variables in health, disease, and mortality is extremely appealing because it gives us a sense we have some control over our physical health. Yet as assuring as such findings might be, these factors are not a psychological recipe for immortality. When scientists find a link between some psychological factor and an important health outcome, the popular media often latch on to the results as if they mean that such factors play a causal role in disease. Such research can sometimes lead to victim blaming: thinking that a person is ill or has died because of a deficit of self-efficacy or optimism.

A compelling case in point is provided by research on "fighting spirit" in combatting breast cancer. In a study published over three decades ago, 69 women were interviewed three months after undergoing surgery for breast cancer (Greer, Morris, & Pettingale, 1979). Based on these interviews, the researchers categorized the women's responses to breast cancer as denial, fighting spirit, quiet resignation, or helplessness. The researchers then followed up on the women five years later to see whether they had experienced a recurrence. The results of the follow-up study showed that women whose responses were characterized by either denial or fighting spirit were less likely to have had a recurrence of cancer. This study led to the conclusion that women with breast cancer should be encouraged to adopt a fighting attitude toward their cancer. The idea that a fighting spirit is important to breast cancer survival continues to hold sway in interventions for women coping with the disease (Coyne & Tennen, 2010).

Crucially, this finding, based on a single study with a relatively small sample, can lead to the development of problem-solving strategies to deal with life's difficulties. An individual with a good sense of personal control might reason, "If I stop smoking now, I will not develop lung cancer."

A sense of personal control has been linked to a lower risk for common chronic diseases such as cancer and cardiovascular disease (Sturmer, Hasselbach, & Amelang, 2006).

*In Chapter 12 we examined the role of learned helplessness in depression. Learned helplessness means believing that one has no control over outcomes in one's life.*

Further, like conscientiousness, a sense of personal control might also help people avoid a risky lifestyle that involves health-compromising behaviors. Consider a study of East German migrants to West Germany who found themselves unemployed (Mittag & Schwarzer, 1993). Individuals in the study often turned to heavy drinking for solace—unless, that is, they had a sense of personal control (as measured by survey items such as "When I'm in trouble, I can rely on my ability to deal with the problem effectively"). Overall, across a wide range of studies, a sense of personal control has been related to emotional well-being, successful coping with a stressful event, healthy behavior change, and good health (Hughes, Berg, & Wiebe, 2012; Little, Snyder, & Wehmeyer, 2006; Sproesser & others, 2011; Stanton, Revenson, & Tennen, 2007; S. E. Taylor, 2012).

**SELF-EFFICACY**    Recall that self-efficacy is an individual's belief that he or she can master a situation and produce positive outcomes. Albert Bandura (1997, 2001, 2010b, 2011a) and others have shown that self-efficacy affects behavior in many situations, ranging from solving personal problems to going on diets. Self-efficacy influences whether individuals try to develop healthy habits, how much effort they expend in coping with stress, how long they persist in the face of obstacles, and how much stress they experience.

Research has shown that self-efficacy is related to success in a wide variety of positive life changes. These include sticking to a New Year's resolution (Norcross, Mrykalo, & Blagys, 2002), achieving weight loss (Byrne, Barry, & Petry, 2012), exercising regularly (Lippke & Plotnikoff, 2006), quitting smoking (Berndt & others, 2012), reducing has not withstood the test of time. Subsequent research, especially studies employing much larger samples, has failed to show any link between adopting a fighting spirit and breast cancer outcomes (Petticrew, Bell, & Hunter, 2002; Phillips & others, 2008; Watson & others, 2005). Although the reality that a fighting spirit does not improve a woman's chances of beating cancer might seem disappointing, many have welcomed this news. As one expert commented, such findings "may help to remove any continuing feelings of guilt or sense of blame for breast cancer relapse from those women who worry because they cannot always maintain a fighting spirit or a positive attitude" (Dobson, 2005, p. 865). The widespread belief that adopting a fighting spirit was key to cancer survival imposed a burden on individuals already dealing with a difficult life experience.

Does this conclusion mean that psychosocial variables have no role to play in disease? Certainly not. One study that found no effect of fighting spirit did show that initial helplessness in response to diagnoses was a predictor of poorer outcomes among women with breast cancer (Watson & others, 2005). Knowing that a person feels helpless early on may prompt professionals to provide much needed information about treatment and the potential for long-term recovery. Indeed, among the factors that (happily) complicate this type of research are that many cancers have effective treatments and that, especially with early detection, relatively few individuals die or experience a recurrence (Coyne & Tennen, 2010). Professionals can also use information about psychological characteristics to build in behavioral supports that might be needed to help a person stick with treatment and optimize her outcomes.

People deal with potentially life-threatening diagnoses in different ways. Dutch swimmer Maarten van der Weijden was diagnosed with leukemia in 2001 at the age of 20 but went on to win Olympic gold in 2008. With respect to his diagnosis, he remarked, "I . . . simply surrendered to the doctors. You always hear those stories that you have to think positively, that you have to fight to survive. This can be a great burden for patients. It has never been proven that you can cure cancer by thinking positively or by fighting" (quoted in Coyne, Tennen, & Ranchor, 2010, p. 40).

**What Do You Think?**

■ In the 1979 study, fighting spirit and denial both were associated with better outcomes. Why do you think people latched on to fighting spirit rather than denial as a key intervention?

■ If someone you love were diagnosed with cancer, how would the research reported here influence the support you would provide to that person?

substance abuse (Goldsmith & others, 2012), practicing safe sex (Buhi & others, 2011), and leading a healthy lifestyle (Axelsson & others, 2012). Recent evidence suggests that self-efficacy is strongly linked to cardiovascular functioning following heart failure and that individuals high in self-efficacy not only are less likely to suffer a second hospitalization due to heart failure but also are likely to live longer (Maeda & others, 2012; Sarkar, Ali, & Whooley, 2009). If there is a problem to be fixed, self-efficacy—having a can-do attitude—is related to finding a solution.

Throughout this book, we have examined the placebo effect as a positive response to a treatment that has no medicinal power. The placebo effect results from the individual's belief in the effectiveness of the treatment. Can you really lose those 10 pounds? Maybe or maybe not, but believing that you can allows you to harness the placebo effect. Self-efficacy is the power of belief in yourself.

*How might culture influence the roles of self-efficacy and personal control in health?*

*HOW OPTIMISM WORKS*

Used by permission of CartoonStock, www.CartoonStock.com.

**OPTIMISM** One factor that is often linked to positive functioning and adjustment is optimism. Researchers have found that optimism is associated with taking proactive steps to protect one's health, while pessimism is linked to engaging in health-compromising behaviors (Carver, Scheier, & Segerstrom, 2010; Ramirez-Maestre, Esteve, & Lopez, 2012). Martin Seligman (1990) views optimism as a matter of how a person explains the causes of bad events. Optimists identify the causes of bad events as external, unstable, and specific, whereas pessimists identify them as internal, stable, and global. Studies have associated explaining life events optimistically with positive outcomes, including a better quality of life (Jowsey & others, 2012; Reivich & Gillham, 2002).

Other researchers define optimism as the expectancy that good things are more likely and that bad things are less likely to occur in the future (Carver & Scheier, 2009). This view focuses on how people pursue their goals and values. Even when faced with misfortune, optimists keep working to reach their goals, whereas pessimists give up.

Numerous studies reveal that optimists generally function more effectively and are physically and mentally healthier than pessimists (Boehm & Kubzansky, 2012; Tindle & others, 2012). Optimism has been linked to more effective immune system functioning and better health (O'Donovon & others, 2009; Segerstrom & Sephton, 2010). Optimism can also be a powerful tool against hopelessness and is associated with decreased thoughts of suicide in adolescents and emerging adults (Ayub, 2009; Hirsch, Conner, & Duberstein, 2007; Nauta & others, 2012). And a recent study of centenarians (people who live to be 100 or more years of age) revealed that those who were in better health had a higher level of optimism than their pessimistic counterparts (Tigani & others, 2012).

As you think about the traits we have examined—conscientiousness, personal control, self-efficacy, and optimism—and their relationship to good health, an important practical tip to keep in mind is that you can *cultivate* these qualities. Studies show that even conscientiousness, the most stable of these characteristics, can increase, especially in young adulthood.

Interestingly, research results pointing to the links between various personality characteristics and better health outcomes can sometimes create a burden on individuals who are struggling with illness. To read about this issue, see Challenge Your Thinking on p. 524.

## self-quiz

1. All of the following are powerful tools for self-change *except*
   A. ethnic heritage.
   B. religious faith.
   C. personality traits.
   D. motivation.

2. The benefits of social support include all of the following *except*
   A. information.
   B. tangible assistance.
   C. emotional support.
   D. victim blaming.

3. According to Seligman, optimists explain the causes of bad events as
   A. external.
   B. internal.
   C. global.
   D. stable.

**APPLY IT!** 4. Daniel was recently diagnosed with diabetes. His doctor gave him a new diet to control his condition. Which of the following situations offers the *best* chances that Daniel will stick with the diet?
   A. Daniel loves junk food and does not want to follow the diet, but his mother and aunt, both diabetics, are pressuring him to follow the doctor's recommendations.
   B. Daniel has always had trouble following through on doing what is good for him, though he says he wants more structure in his life.
   C. Clark, Daniel's roommate, has a diabetic brother, and Clark tells Daniel about how his brother has coped and what diet he follows; Clark offers to introduce them.
   D. Daniel has a pessimistic personality and expects things to work out badly.

# 4 Toward a Healthier Mind (and Body): Controlling Stress

If you could change one thing about your behavior, what would you choose? Would the change perhaps have to do with feeling stressed out much of the time? Maybe you wish you could stop facing every daily challenge with tension. Let's look at the problems that can arise when you feel chronically stressed and the ways you can better manage your stress.

## Stress and Its Stages

*Getting married, having a baby, graduating from college—although positive life events, these achievements can be stressful because they are also major life changes.*

As described in Chapter 2, stress is the response to environmental stressors, the circumstances and events that threaten individuals and tax their coping abilities. Hans Selye (1974, 1983), the founder of stress research, focused on the body's response to stressors, especially the wear and tear due to the demands placed on the body. After observing patients with different problems—the death of someone close, loss of income, arrest for embezzlement—Selye concluded that any number of environmental events or

**general adaptation syndrome (GAS)** Selye's term for the common effects of stressful demands on the body, consisting of three stages: alarm, resistance, and exhaustion.

stimuli would produce the same stress symptoms: loss of appetite, muscular weakness, and decreased interest in the world.

**General adaptation syndrome (GAS)** is Selye's term for the common effects on the body when demands are placed on it (Figure 14.3). The GAS consists of three stages: alarm, resistance, and exhaustion. Selye's model is especially useful in helping us understand the link between stress and health.

The body's first reaction to a stressor, in the *alarm stage,* is a temporary state of shock during which resistance to illness and stress falls below normal limits. In trying to cope with the initial effects of stress, the body releases hormones that, in a short time, adversely affect the functioning of the immune system, the body's network of natural defenses. During this time the individual is prone to infections from illness and injury.

In the *resistance stage* of Selye's general adaptation syndrome, glands throughout the body manufacture different hormones that protect the individual. Endocrine and sympathetic nervous system activity are not as high as in the alarm stage, although they still are elevated. During the resistance stage, the body's immune system can fight off infection with remarkable efficiency. Similarly, hormones that reduce the inflammation normally associated with injury circulate at high levels.

If the body's all-out effort to combat stress fails and the stress persists, the individual moves into the *exhaustion stage.* At this point, wear and tear takes its toll—the person might collapse in exhaustion, and vulnerability to disease increases. Serious, possibly irreversible damage to the body—such as a heart attack or even death—may occur.

The body system that plays the greatest role in Selye's GAS model is the **hypothalamic-pituitary-adrenal axis (HPA axis).** The HPA axis is a complex set of interactions among the hypothalamus (part of the brain's limbic system), the pituitary gland (the master gland of the endocrine system), and the adrenal glands (endocrine system glands located on top of each kidney). The HPA axis regulates various body processes, including digestion, immune system responses, emotion, and energy expenditure. The axis also controls reactions to stressful events, and these responses will be our focus here.

When the brain detects a threat in the environment, it signals the hypothalamus to release corticotropin-releasing hormone (CRH). In turn, CRH stimulates the pituitary gland to produce another hormone that causes the adrenal glands to release cortisol. Cortisol is itself the "stress hormone" that directs cells to make sugar, fat, and protein available so the body can take quick action. Cortisol also suppresses the immune system.

In Chapter 2 we distinguished between acute stress and chronic stress. Acute stress can sometimes be adaptive, and in acute stress cortisol plays an important role in helping us to take the necessary action to avoid dire consequences. Typically, once the body has dealt with a given stressor, our cortisol level returns to normal. However, under chronic stress, the HPA axis can remain activated over the long haul.

The activity of the HPA axis varies from one person to the next. These differences may be explained by genes as well as by particular stressful experiences (Boersma & others, 2012). Research with rats and humans has shown that prenatal stress can influence the development of the HPA axis (Green & others, 2011; O'Connor & others, 2012; Peters & others, 2012). When the HPA is chronically active, various systems in the body suffer.

## Stress and the Immune System

Chronic stress can have serious implications for the body, in particular the immune system. Interest in links between the immune system and stress spawned a new field of scientific inquiry, **psychoneuroimmunology,** which explores connections among psychological

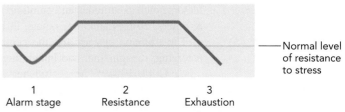

1 Alarm stage  2 Resistance  3 Exhaustion

—— Normal level of resistance to stress

**FIGURE 14.3  Selye's General Adaptation Syndrome** The general adaptation syndrome (GAS) describes an individual's response to stress in terms of three stages: (1) alarm, in which the body mobilizes its resources; (2) resistance, in which the body strives mightily to endure the stressor; and (3) exhaustion, in which resistance becomes depleted.

**hypothalamic-pituitary-adrenal axis (HPA axis)** The complex set of interactions among the hypothalamus, the pituitary gland, and the adrenal glands that regulates various body processes and controls reactions to stressful events.

*EXPERIENCE IT!* Chronic Stress and the Brain

**psychoneuroimmunology** A new field of scientific inquiry that explores connections among psychological factors (such as attitudes and emotions), the nervous system, and the immune system.

factors (such as attitudes and emotions), the nervous system, and the immune system (Cho & others, 2012; Lamkin & others, 2012; Stowell, Robles, & Kane, 2013).

The immune system and the central nervous system are similar in their modes of receiving, recognizing, and integrating signals from the external environment (Sternberg & Gold, 1996). The central nervous system and the immune system both possess "sensory" elements that receive information from the environment and other parts of the body, and "motor" elements that carry out an appropriate response. Both systems also rely on chemical mediators for communication. A key hormone shared by the central nervous system and the immune system is corticotropin-releasing hormone (CRH), which is produced in the hypothalamus, as we saw above, and unites the stress and immune responses.

*Recall from Chapter 5 that the immune system can learn through classical conditioning.*

Stress can profoundly influence the immune system (Broadbent & Koschwanez, 2012; Haroon, Raison, & Miller, 2012). Acute stressors (sudden, stressful, one-time life events) can produce immunological changes. For example, in relatively healthy HIV-infected individuals, as well as in individuals with cancer, acute stressors are associated with poorer immune system functioning (McIntosh & Rosselli, 2012; Pant & Ramaswamy, 2009). In addition to acute stressors, chronic stressors (long-lasting agents of stress) are associated with an increasing downturn in immune system responsiveness (Pervanidou & Chrousos, 2012). This effect has been documented in a number of circumstances that include worries about living next to a damaged nuclear reactor, failures in close relationships (divorce, separation, and marital distress), negative relationships with family and friends, and burdensome caregiving for a family member with a progressive illness (Friedman & others, 2012; Gouin & others, 2012).

Researchers hope to determine the precise links among psychological factors, the brain, and the immune system (DeWitt & others, 2012; Facciabene, Motz, & Coukos, 2012). Preliminary hypotheses about the interaction that causes vulnerability to disease include:

- Stressful experiences lower the efficiency of immune systems, making individuals more susceptible to disease.

- Stress directly promotes disease-producing processes.

- Stressful experiences may cause the activation of dormant viruses that diminish the individual's ability to cope with disease.

These hypotheses may lead to clues for more successful treatments for some of the most challenging diseases to conquer, AIDS and cancer among them (Hill, Rosenbloom, & Nowak, 2012; Vigano & others, 2012).

Sheldon Cohen and his colleagues have carried out a number of studies on the effects of stress, emotion, and social support on immunity and susceptibility to infectious disease (Cohen & Janicki-Deverts, 2009; Cohen & Lemay, 2007; S. Cohen & others, 2009, 2012; Sneed & others, 2012). In one such study, Cohen and his colleagues (1998) focused on 276 adults who were exposed to viruses and then quarantined for five days. Figure 14.4 shows the dramatic results. The longer the participants had experienced major stress in their lives before the study, the more likely they were to catch a cold. Cohen concluded that stress-triggered changes in the immune system and hormones might create greater vulnerability to infection. These findings suggest that when we are under stress, we need to take better care of ourselves than usual (S. Cohen & others, 2009, 2012).

*Meditation, described in Chapter 4, is a great way to cope with stress and has positive benefits for the immune system.*

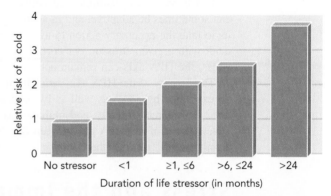

**FIGURE 14.4** **Stress and the Risk of Developing a Cold** In a study by Cohen and others (1998), the longer individuals had a life stressor, the more likely they were to develop a cold. The four-point scale is based on the odds (0 = lower; 4 = higher) of getting a cold.

# Stress and Cardiovascular Disease

There is also reason to believe that stress increases an individual's risk for cardiovascular disease (Emery, Anderson, & Goodwin, 2013; Hollander & others, 2012). Chronic emotional stress is associated with high blood pressure, heart disease, and early death (Schulz, 2007). Apparently, the adrenaline surge caused by severe emotional stress causes the blood to clot more rapidly—and blood clotting is a major factor in heart attacks (Strike & others, 2006). Emotional stress can contribute to cardiovascular disease in other ways. Individuals who have had major life changes (such as the death of a spouse and the loss of a job) have a higher incidence of cardiovascular disease and early death (Mostofsky & others, 2012; S. E. Taylor, 2012). People in a chronically stressed condition, such as that stemming from work stress or prolonged loneliness, are also more likely to take up smoking, start overeating, and avoid exercising, behaviors linked with cardiovascular disease (Steptoe & Kivimaki, 2012; Zimmerman, 2012).

Just as personality characteristics such as a sense of control or self-efficacy can help buffer an individual against stress, other personality characteristics have been shown to worsen stress, with special significance for cardiovascular illness. In particular, people who are impatient or quick to anger or who display frequent hostility have an increased risk for cardiovascular disease (Ohira & others, 2012).

In the late 1950s, a secretary for two California cardiologists, Meyer Friedman and Ray Rosenman, observed that the chairs in their waiting rooms were tattered and worn, but only on the front edges. The cardiologists had also noticed the impatience of their cardiac patients, who often arrived exactly on time and were in a great hurry to leave. Intrigued by this consistency, they conducted a study of 3,000 healthy men between the ages of 35 and 59 over eight years to find out whether people with certain behavioral characteristics might be prone to heart problems (Friedman & Rosenman, 1974). During the eight years, one group of men had twice as many heart attacks or other forms of heart disease as the other men. Further, autopsies of the men who died revealed that this same group had coronary arteries that were more obstructed than those of the other men.

Friedman and Rosenman described the common personality characteristics of the men who developed coronary disease as the **Type A behavior pattern.** They theorized that a cluster of characteristics—being excessively competitive, hard-driven, impatient, and hostile—is related to the incidence of heart disease. Rosenman and Friedman labeled the behavior of the healthier group, who were typically relaxed and easygoing, the **Type B behavior pattern.**

**Type A behavior pattern**
A cluster of characteristics—including being excessively competitive, hard-driven, impatient, and hostile—that are related to a higher incidence of heart disease.

**Type B behavior pattern**
A cluster of characteristics—including being relaxed and easygoing—that are related to a lower incidence of heart disease.

Further research on the link between Type A behavior and coronary disease indicates that the association is not as strong as Friedman and Rosenman believed (Suls & Swain, 1998; R. B. Williams, 2001, 2002). However, researchers have found that certain components of Type A behavior are more precisely linked with coronary risk (Spielberger, 2004). The Type A behavior component most consistently associated with coronary problems is hostility (Ohira & others, 2012). People who are hostile outwardly or who turn anger inward are more likely to develop heart disease than their less angry counterparts (Eng & others, 2003; K. A. Matthews & others, 2004). Such people have been called "hot reactors" because of their intense physiological reactions to stress: Their hearts race, their breathing quickens, and their muscles tense up. One study found that hostility was a better predictor of coronary heart disease in older men than smoking, drinking, high caloric intake, or high levels of LDL cholesterol (Niaura & others, 2002).

There has been increased interest in the **Type D behavior pattern,** which describes individuals who are generally distressed, frequently experience negative emotions, and are socially inhibited (Beutel & others, 2012; Cosci, 2012; Molloy & others, 2012). Even after adjustment for depression, Type D individuals face a threefold increased risk of adverse cardiovascular outcomes (Denollet & Conraads, 2011). A recent meta-analysis also found that Type D persons with cardiovascular disease are at a higher risk for major adverse cardiac events and have a lower health-related quality of life (O'Dell & others, 2011).

**Type D behavior pattern**
A cluster of characteristics—including being generally distressed, having negative emotions, and being socially inhibited—that are related to adverse cardiovascular outcomes.

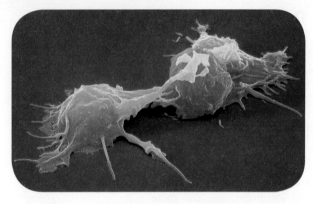

**FIGURE 14.5** **NK Cells and Cancer** Two natural killer (NK) cells (*yellow*) are shown attacking a leukemia cell (*red*). Notice the blisters that the leukemia cell has developed to defend itself. Nonetheless, the NK cells are surrounding the leukemia cell and are about to destroy it.

# Stress and Cancer

Given the association of stress with poor health behaviors such as smoking, it is not surprising that stress has also been related to cancer risk (Nezu & others, 2013). Stress sets in motion biological changes involving the autonomic, endocrine, and immune systems. If the immune system is not compromised, it appears to help provide resistance to cancer and slow its progression. Researchers have found, however, that the physiological effects of stress inhibit a number of cellular immune responses (Hayakawa, 2012). Cancer patients show diminished natural killer cell (NK-cell) activity in the blood (Rosental & others, 2012) (Figure 14.5). Low NK-cell activity is linked with the development of further malignancies, and the length of survival for the cancer patient is related to NK-cell activity (Buchser & others, 2012).

Thus, stress is clearly a factor not only in immune system functioning and cardiovascular health but also in the risk for cancer. In light of these links, understanding the psychological processes by which individuals can effectively handle stressful circumstances is a crucial topic in health psychology (Stowell, Robles, & Kane, 2013).

# Cognitive Appraisal and Coping with Stress

What stresses you out? Stressors can be anything from losing irreplaceable notes from a class, to being yelled at by a friend, to failing a test, to being in a car wreck.

*Let's face it. Just reading about the negative effects of stress can be stressful.*

Although everyone's body may respond similarly to stressors, not everyone perceives the same events as stressful. Whether an experience "stresses you out" depends on how you think about that experience (Rogers & Maytan, 2012). For example, you may perceive an upcoming job interview as a threatening obligation, whereas your roommate may perceive it as a challenging opportunity—a chance to shine. You might view a *D* on a paper as a crushing blow; your roommate may view the same grade as an incentive to work harder. To some degree, then, what is stressful depends on how one thinks about events (Schroder & others, 2012; Visser & others, 2012).

**cognitive appraisal**
Individuals' interpretation of the events in their life as harmful, threatening, or challenging and their determination of whether they have the resources to cope effectively with the events.

**coping**
A kind of problem solving that involves managing taxing circumstances, expending effort to solve life's problems, and seeking to master or reduce stress.

**STEPS IN COGNITIVE APPRAISAL** **Cognitive appraisal** refers to an individual's interpretation of an event as either harmful, threatening, or challenging, and the person's determination of whether he or she has the resources to cope effectively with the event. **Coping** is essentially a kind of problem solving. It involves managing taxing circumstances, expending effort to solve life's problems, and seeking to master or reduce stress.

Richard Lazarus articulated the importance of cognitive appraisal to stress and coping (1993, 2000). In Lazarus's view, people appraise events in two steps: primary appraisal and secondary appraisal. In *primary appraisal,* individuals interpret whether an event involves *harm or loss* that has already occurred, a *threat* of some future danger, or a *challenge* to be overcome. Lazarus believed that perceiving a stressor as a challenge to be overcome rather than as a threat is a good strategy for reducing stress. To understand Lazarus's concept of primary appraisal, consider two students, each with a failing grade in a psychology class at midterm. Sam is almost frozen by the stress of the low grade and looks at the rest of the term as a threatening prospect. In contrast, Pam does not become overwhelmed by the harm already done and the threat of future failures. She sees the low grade as a challenge that she can address and overcome.

In *secondary appraisal,* individuals evaluate their resources and determine how effectively they can be marshaled to cope with the event. This appraisal is secondary because it both comes after primary appraisal and depends on the degree to which the event is appraised as harmful, threatening, or challenging. Sam might have some helpful resources for coping with his low midterm grade, but he views the stressful circumstance as so harmful and threatening that he does not take stock of and use his resources. Pam, in contrast, evaluates the resources she can call on to improve her grade. These include asking the instructor for suggestions about how to improve her studying for the tests, managing time to include more study hours, and consulting with high-achieving classmates.

**TYPES OF COPING**    Research has identified two types of coping. **Problem-focused coping** is the cognitive strategy of squarely facing one's troubles and trying to solve them. For example, if you are having trouble with a class, you might go to the campus study skills center and sign up for a program to learn how to study more effectively. Having done so, you have faced your problem and attempted to do something about it. Problem-focused coping might involve coming up with goals and implementation intentions, the problem-solving steps we examined earlier in this chapter.

**problem-focused coping**
The cognitive strategy of squarely facing one's troubles and trying to solve them.

**Emotion-focused coping** entails responding to the stress that one is feeling—trying to manage the emotional reaction—rather than confronting the root problem. If you use emotion-focused coping, you might avoid going to a class that is a problem for you. Instead, you might say the class does not matter, deny that you are having difficulty with it, joke about it with your friends, or pray that you will do better.

**emotion-focused coping**
The coping strategy that involves responding to the stress that one is feeling—trying to manage one's emotional reaction—rather than focusing on the root problem itself.

In some circumstances, emotion-focused coping can be beneficial in dealing with life's problems. Denial is one of the main protective psychological mechanisms for navigating the flood of feelings that occurs when the reality of death or dying becomes too great. For example, one study found that following the death of a loved one, bereaved individuals who directed their attention away from their negative feelings had fewer health problems and were rated as better adjusted by their friends, compared to bereaved individuals who did not use this coping strategy (Coifman & others, 2007). Denial can be used to avoid the destructive impact of shock by postponing the time when one has to deal with stress. In other circumstances, however, emotion-focused coping can be a problem. Denying that the person you dated does not love you anymore when he or she has become engaged to someone else keeps you from getting on with life.

*Emotion-focused coping can be adaptive in situations in which there is no solution to a problem, such as grieving over a loved one's death, when in fact it makes sense to focus on feeling better and accepting the present circumstances.*

Many individuals successfully use both problem-focused and emotion-focused coping when adjusting to a stressful circumstance. For example, in one study, individuals said they employed both problem-focused and emotion-focused coping strategies in 98 percent of the stressful situations they encounter (Folkman & Lazarus, 1980). Over the long term, though, problem-focused coping rather than emotion-focused coping usually works best (Nagase & others, 2009).

## Strategies for Successful Coping

A stressful circumstance becomes considerably less stressful when a person successfully copes with it. Effective coping is associated with a sense of personal control, a healthy immune system, personal resources, and positive emotions.

Multiple coping strategies often work better than a single strategy, as is true with any problem-solving challenge (Folkman & Moskowitz, 2004). People who have experienced a stressful life event or a cluster of difficulties might actively embrace problem solving and consistently take advantage of opportunities for positive experiences, even in the context of the bad times they are going through. Positive emotion can give them a sense of the big picture, help them devise possible solutions, and allow them to make creative connections.

Optimism can play a strong role in effective coping (Z. E. Taylor & others, 2012). Lisa Aspinwall has found, for example, that optimistic people are more likely to attend to and remember potentially threatening health-related information than are pessimists (Aspinwall, 1998; 2011; Aspinwall, Leaf, & Leachman, 2009; Aspinwall & Pengchit, 2012). Aspinwall views optimism as a resource that allows individuals to engage constructively with potentially frightening information. Optimists are more likely than others to seek out genetic testing in order to learn about their risk for disease (Aspinwall & others, 2012). Optimists engage with life from a place of strength, so when an optimist finds out, for instance, that a favorite pastime, tanning, is related to an elevated risk of skin cancer, the information is important but not overwhelming. In contrast, pessimists are already living in a bleak world and prefer not to hear more bad news.

*Optimists are not just denying that anything bad can happen. They are actively engaged with reality, even when it contains threatening news.*

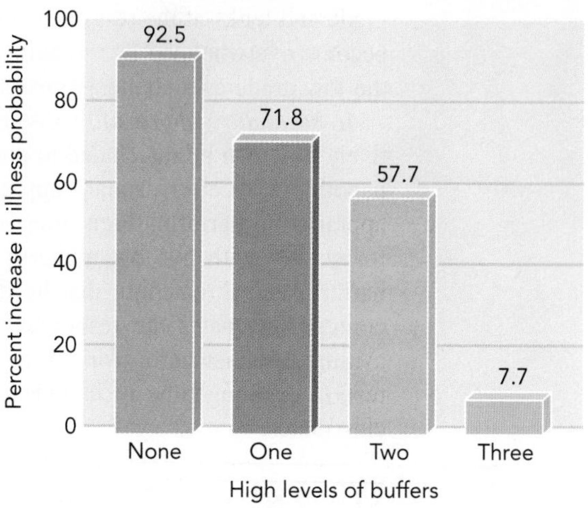

**FIGURE 14.6  Illness in High-Stress Business Executives** In one study of high-stress business executives, a low level of all three buffers (hardiness, exercise, and social support) involved a high probability of at least one serious illness in that year. High levels of one, two, and all three buffers decreased the likelihood of at least one serious illness occurring in the year of the study.

Another personality trait that appears to promote thriving during difficult times is hardiness. **Hardiness** is characterized by a sense of commitment rather than alienation, and of control rather than powerlessness, as well as a perception of problems as challenges rather than threats (Maddi & others, 2006). Hardiness is the trait displayed by the basketball player whose team is down by two points with seconds remaining on the clock when he shouts, "Coach! Give me the ball!" Many of us would shrink from such a high-pressure moment.

The links among hardiness, stress, and illness were the focus of the Chicago Stress Project, which studied male business executives 32 to 65 years of age over a five-year period (Kobasa, Maddi, & Kahn, 1982; Maddi, 1998). During the five years, most of the executives experienced stressful events such as divorce, job transfers, a close friend's death, inferior work-performance evaluations, and reporting to an unpleasant boss. Figure 14.6 shows how hardiness buffered these individuals from stress-related illness (Kobasa & others, 1986).

Other researchers also have found support for the role of hardiness in illness and health (Hystad, Eid, & Brevik, 2011; M. K. Taylor & others, 2012). The results of hardiness research suggest the power of multiple factors, rather than any single factor, in cushioning individuals against stress and maintaining their health (Maddi, 1998, 2008).

**hardiness**
A personality trait characterized by a sense of commitment rather than alienation and of control rather than powerlessness; a perception of problems as challenges rather than threats.

## Stress Management Programs

"Avoid stress" may be good advice, but life is full of potentially stressful experiences. Sometimes just checking e-mail or answering a phone can be an invitation for stress.

Because many people have difficulty regulating stress, psychologists have developed techniques that individuals can learn (Artemiadis & others, 2012; Pollard, 2012). **Stress management programs** teach individuals how to appraise stressful events, develop coping skills, and put these skills to practical use. Some stress management programs teach a range of techniques to handle stress; others focus on a specific technique, such as relaxation or assertiveness training.

**stress management program**
A regimen that teaches individuals how to appraise stressful events, how to develop skills for coping with stress, and how to put these skills into use in everyday life.

Stress management programs are often taught through workshops, which are becoming more common in the workplace (Jensen & others, 2012; S. E. Taylor, 2012). Aware of the high cost in lost productivity due to stress-related disorders, many organizations have become increasingly motivated to help their workers identify and cope with stressful circumstances. Colleges and universities similarly run stress management programs for students.

Do stress management programs work? In one study, researchers randomly assigned men and women with hypertension (blood pressure greater than 140/90) to one of three groups (Linden, Lenz, & Con, 2001). One group received 10 hours of individual stress management training; a second group was placed in a wait-list control group and eventually received stress management training; and a third group (a control group) received no such training. The two groups that received the stress management training showed significantly reduced blood pressure. The control group experienced no reduction in blood pressure. Also, the reduced blood pressure in the first two groups was linked to a reported decrease in psychological stress and improved ability to cope with anger (Linden, Lenz, & Con, 2001).

Coping effectively with stress is essential for physical and mental health (Cox & others, 2012; Xanthopoulos & Daniel, 2013). Still, there is a lot more we can do to promote our health. Healthful living—establishing healthy habits and evaluating and changing behaviors that interfere with good health—helps us avoid the damaging effects of stress (Emery, Anderson, & Goodwin, 2013). Just as the biopsychosocial perspective predicts, healthy changes in one area of life can have benefits that flow to other areas.

*"Dean, for you, the stress management seminar is not, I repeat, not optional."*

Used by permission of CartoonStock, www.CartoonStock.com.

**self-quiz**

1. Selye's term for the pattern of common effects on the body when demands are placed on it is
   A. exhaustion syndrome.
   B. the Type A behavior pattern.
   C. the Type B behavior pattern.
   D. general adaptation syndrome.

2. A personality trait that is characterized by a sense of commitment and control, as well as by a perception of problems as challenges rather than threats, is
   A. self-efficacy.
   B. self-determination.
   C. hardiness.
   D. self-confidence.

3. Dealing with difficult circumstances, expending effort to solve life's problems, and seeking to control or reduce stress are key aspects of
   A. coping.
   B. cognitive appraisal.
   C. primary appraisal.
   D. secondary appraisal.

**APPLY IT!** 4. In addition to taking a full load of classes, Bonnie works at two part-time jobs and helps her sister care for two toddlers. Bonnie is achievement oriented and strives to get A's in all of her courses. Because of her many commitments, she is often in a hurry and regularly does more than one thing at a time, but she tells people that she enjoys her busy routine. Which answer best assesses whether Bonnie is Type A and at risk for cardiovascular disease?

A. Bonnie's hurriedness and achievement orientation indicate that she is Type A and probably at risk for cardiovascular disease.
B. Although Bonnie may experience stress, the lack of hostility mentioned in this description suggests that she is not Type A or at risk for cardiovascular disease.
C. Bonnie is a "hot reactor" and thus at risk for cardiovascular disease.
D. Bonnie is Type A, but her enjoyment of life means that she is not at risk for cardiovascular disease.

# 5  Toward a Healthier Body (and Mind): Behaving as If Your Life Depends upon It

There is no escaping it: Getting stress under control is crucial for a healthy mind and body. It is also important to make wise behavioral choices in four additional life domains where healthy habits can benefit both body and mind. In this section we examine the advantages of becoming physically active, eating right, quitting smoking, and practicing safe sex.

# Becoming Physically Active

Imagine that there was a time when, to change a TV channel, people had to get up and walk a few feet to turn a knob. Consider the time when people physically had to go to the library and hunt through card catalogs and shelves to find information rather than going online and googling. As our daily tasks have gotten increasingly easy, we have become less active, and inactivity is a serious health problem (Acevedo, 2012).

Any activity that expends physical energy can be part of a healthy lifestyle. It can be as simple as taking the stairs instead of an elevator, walking or biking to class instead of driving, or getting up and dancing instead of sitting at the bar. One study of older adults revealed that the more they expended energy in daily activities, the longer they were likely to live (Manini & others, 2006).

In addition to its link to longevity, physical activity corresponds with other positive outcomes, including a lower probability of developing cardiovascular disease and cancer (Eheman & others, 2012; Emery, Anderson, & Goodwin, 2013), weight loss in overweight individuals (Stehr & von Lengerke, 2012), improved cognitive functioning (Etnier & Labban, 2012), positive coping with stress (Hamer, 2012), and increased self-esteem and body image (Ginis, Bassett, & Conlin, 2012). Physical exercise also reduces levels of anxiety (Petruzzello, 2012) and depression (Herring & others, 2012). Even a real pig benefits from exercise; Figure 14.7 shows the positive effects of physical activity in hogs. Being physically active is like investing energy in a wellness bank account: Activity enhances physical well-being and gives us the ability to face life's potential stressors energetically.

**FIGURE 14.7   The Jogging Hog Experiment** Jogging hogs reveal the dramatic effects of exercise on health. In one investigation, a group of hogs was trained to run approximately 100 miles per week (Bloor & White, 1983). Then the researchers narrowed the arteries that supplied blood to the hogs' hearts. The hearts of the jogging hogs developed extensive alternate pathways for blood supply, and 42 percent of the threatened heart tissue was salvaged, compared with only 17 percent in a control group of non-jogging hogs.

Exercise is one special type of physical activity. **Exercise** formally refers to structured activities whose goal is to improve health. Although exercise designed to strengthen muscles and bones or to improve flexibility is important to fitness, many health experts stress the benefits of **aerobic exercise,** which is sustained activity—jogging, swimming, or cycling, for example—that stimulates heart and lung functioning.

In one study, exercise meant the difference between life and death for middle-aged and older adults (Blair & others, 1989). More than 10,000 men and women were divided into categories of low fitness, medium fitness, and high fitness (Blair & others, 1989). Then they were studied over eight years. As shown in Figure 14.8, sedentary participants (low fitness) were more than twice as likely to die during the study's eight-year time span than those who were moderately fit, and more than three times as likely to die as those who were highly fit. The positive effects of physical fitness occurred for both men and women. Further, another study revealed that adults aged 60 and over who were in the lowest fifth in terms of physical fitness as determined by a treadmill test were four times more likely to die over a 12-year period than their counterparts who were in the top fifth of physical fitness (Sui & others, 2007). This study also showed that older adults who were overweight but physically fit had a lower mortality risk over the 12 years than their normal-weight counterparts who were low in fitness (Sui & others, 2007). In addition, a longitudinal study found that men who exercised regularly at 72 years of age had a 30 percent higher probability of being alive at 90 years of age than their sedentary counterparts (Yates & others, 2008).

Health experts recommend that adults engage in at least 30 minutes of moderate physical activity on most, preferably all, days of the week and that

**exercise**
Structured activities whose goal is to improve health.

**aerobic exercise**
Sustained activity—jogging, swimming, or cycling, for example—that stimulates heart and lung functioning.

Fitness here refers to the body's ability to supply fuel during sustained physical activity.

Make time in your day to exercise. It might mean waking up earlier or forgoing watching TV. The benefits are well worth it.

children exercise for 60 minutes daily. Most specialists advise that exercisers raise their heart rate to at least 60 percent of their maximum rate. Only about one-fifth of adults are active at these recommended levels. Figure 14.9 lists physical activities that qualify as moderate and, for comparison, vigorous. Research suggests that both moderate and intense activities may produce important physical and psychological gains and improve quality of life (Focht, 2012).

One often-welcome payoff for increasing physical activity is weight loss. Frequently, researchers have found that the most effective component of weight-loss programs is regular exercise (Stehr & von Lengerke, 2012). Another way to combat weight problems is through changes in diet.

## Eating Right

Americans' biggest health risk is being overweight or obese. The Centers for Disease Control and Prevention (CDC) uses the labels "overweight" and "obese" for ranges of weight that are greater than what experts consider healthy for an individual's height (CDC, 2012c). In recent years, the percentage of overweight or obese individuals has been increasing at a stunning rate. In 1960, less than 50 percent of U.S. adults were overweight

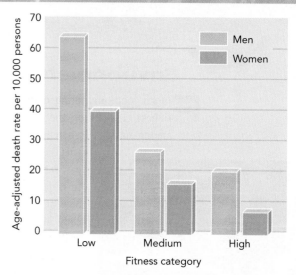

**PSYCHOLOGICAL INQUIRY**

**FIGURE 14.8  Physical Fitness and Mortality** This graph presents the results of an eight-year longitudinal study of more than 10,000 men and women (Blair & others, 1989). The horizontal, or X, axis shows the participants divided by their levels of fitness as well as their sex. The vertical, or Y, axis shows the death rates. **> Which groups had the highest and lowest death rates? > Comparing the results for men and women, what role does biological sex play in mortality? > This is a correlational study, so causation cannot be assumed. What third variables (see Chapter 1) might explain the results?**

| Moderate | Vigorous |
|---|---|
| Walking briskly (3–4 mph) | Walking briskly uphill or with a load |
| Swimming, moderate effort | Swimming, fast treading crawl |
| Cycling for pleasure or transportation (≤10 mph) | Cycling, fast or racing (>10 mph) |
| Racket sports, table tennis | Racket sports, singles tennis, racketball |
| Conditioning exercise, general calisthenics | Conditioning exercise, stair ergometer, ski machine |
| Golf, pulling cart or carrying clubs | Golf, practice at driving range |
| Canoeing, leisurely (2.0–3.9 mph) | Canoeing, rapidly (≥4 mph) |
| Home care, general cleaning | Moving furniture |
| Mowing lawn, power mower | Mowing lawn, hand mower |
| Home repair, painting | Fix-up projects |

**FIGURE 14.9  Moderate and Vigorous Physical Activities** At minimum, adults should strive for 30 minutes of moderate activity each day. That activity can become even more beneficial if we "pump it up" to vigorous.

# PSYCHOLOGY IN OUR WORLD

## Environments That Support Active Lifestyles

French food—featuring delicious cheeses, heavy sauces, and buttery pastries—is one of the richest cuisines on the planet. Yet the obesity rate in France is 11.5 percent, which ranks 28th among nations in a report by the Organisation for Economic Co-operation and Development

(OECD, 2012). In comparison, the United States ranks first, with nearly 34 percent of the population qualifying as obese. Part of the gap may be due to differences in food portions (Rozin & others, 2003), but another factor is how people get to their food. In the United States grocery shopping typically involves a trip in a car, whereas in France individuals are more likely to walk or ride a bicycle (Ferrières, 2004).

A major obstacle to promoting exercise in the United States is that many U.S. cities are not designed in ways that promote walking or cycling. Advocates for change say that by making life too easy and too accommodating to cars and drivers, urban designers have created an *obesogenic* (obesity-promoting) environment—a context where it is challenging for people to engage in healthy activities (Henderson, 2008; Lydon & others, 2011). Countries such as the Netherlands and Denmark have adopted urban planning strategies that promote walking and biking and discourage car use. In the Netherlands, 60 percent of all journeys taken by people over age 60 are by bicycle (Henderson, 2008).

Environmental contexts that invite physical activity increase activity levels. For example, one quasi-experimental study examined the effects of changes to the physical environment on activity. The study focused on an urban neighborhood in which a greenway (a biking and walking trail) was retrofitted to connect with pedestrian sidewalks. Researchers counted the number of people outside engaging in physical activity in that neighborhood for a two-hour period at various times over two years. Compared to two other similar neighborhoods, the neighborhood with the trail featured more people walking and biking (Fitzhugh, Bassett, & Evans, 2010). Environmental characteristics that welcome physical activity are also associated with health and wellness. In one study, elderly people who lived near parks, tree-lined streets, and areas for taking walks showed higher longevity over a five-year study period (Takano, Nakamura, & Watanabe, 2002).

Other aspects of city design can influence obesity rates, including access to nutritious foods (Lydon & others, 2011) and the perceived safety of neighborhoods (Eisenstein & others, 2011). By shedding light on how environmental factors influence healthy lifestyles, research on human behavior can meaningfully impact public policy.

or obese, and this figure changed little from 1960 to 1980. However, as Figure 14.10 illustrates, from 2009 to 2010, 69 percent of U.S. adults were overweight or obese, with 35 percent of those in the obese category (Flegal & others, 2012). In the relevant study, females were less likely to be overweight or obese than were males (64 percent versus 74 percent). And when non-Latino White, African American, and Latino adult females and males were compared, African American females and Latino males were the most overweight or obese (82 percent), while non-Latino White females (59.5 percent) were the least overweight or obese.

Exercising regularly is one great way to lose weight. Making healthy dietary choices is another (Corsica & Perri, 2013; Nicklas & others, 2012). Eating right means selecting

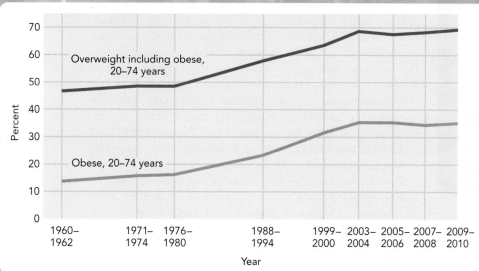

**FIGURE 14.10** **Changes in the Percentage of U.S. Adults 20 to 74 Years of Age Classified as Overweight or Obese, 1960–2010** Being overweight or obese poses the greatest overall health risk for Americans today. In this graph, the vertical, or Y, axis shows the percentage of people considered overweight or obese, and the horizontal, or X, axis shows the years for these values. >*Thinking of these lines as data points, is time positively or negatively correlated with overweight/obesity? Why?* >*Find the year of your birth on the X axis. How has the body weight of Americans changed during your lifetime?* >*What years show the steepest rise in weight gain? What factors might explain this increase?*

sensible, nutritious foods that maximize health and wellness. Despite our seemingly boundless food options, many of us are unhealthy eaters. We take in too much sugar and not enough foods high in vitamins, minerals, and fiber, such as fruits, vegetables, and grains. We eat too much fast food and too few well-balanced meals—choices that increase our fat and cholesterol intake, both of which are implicated in long-term health problems (Barnes & Kimbro, 2012).

Healthy eating means incorporating tasty, healthy foods into meals and snacks. Healthy eating is not just about weight loss but also about committing to lifelong healthy food habits. Several health goals can be accomplished through a sound nutritional plan. Not only does a well-balanced diet provide more energy, but it also can lower blood pressure and lessen the risk for cancer (Eguchi & others, 2012; Eheman & others, 2012). Two recent studies totaling more than 110,000 U.S. adults found that a high level of red meat consumption was linked to an increased risk of earlier death due to cardiovascular disease and cancer (Pan & others, 2012).

Losing weight and opting for healthier foods can be difficult, especially when one is just starting out. Many weight-loss fads promise weight loss with no effort, no hunger, and no real change in one's food consumption. These promises are unrealistic. Making genuine, enduring changes in eating behavior is hard work—but this does not mean that pessimism is required. Rather, positive expectations and self-efficacy are important because the task at hand is challenging.

The National Weight Control Registry is an ongoing study of people who have lost at least 40 pounds and kept it off for at least two years. Research on these successful dieters gives us important tips on how people who keep the weight off achieve this goal (L. G. Ogden & others, 2012; Raynor & others, 2005). Successful dieters show consistency in what they eat, sticking to the same regimen even on weekends and during holidays (Gorin & others, 2004). A study of approximately 2,000 U.S. adults found that exercising 30 minutes a day, planning meals, and weighing themselves daily were the main strategies of successful dieters (Kruger, Blanck, & Gillespie, 2006).

*One key practice is eating breakfast, especially whole-grain cereals.*

The truth is that keeping weight off is an ongoing process. Moreover, the longer a dieter keeps the weight off, the less likely he or she is to gain it back (McGuire & others, 1999). Further, recent research suggests that making small changes in the availability of junk food can have an impact on eating and weight (Rozin & others, 2011).

*So, just don't buy the junk food! If it is not around, you won't eat it.*

# Quitting Smoking

Another health-related goal is giving up smoking. Evidence from a number of studies underscores the dangers of smoking and being around smokers (American Cancer Society, 2012). For example, smoking is linked to 30 percent of cancer deaths, 21 percent of heart disease deaths, and 82 percent of chronic pulmonary disease deaths. Secondhand smoke is implicated in as many as 9,000 lung cancer deaths a year. Children of smokers are at special risk for respiratory and middle-ear diseases (Accordini & others, 2012; Bisgaard, Jensen, & Bonnelykke, 2012).

Fewer people smoke today than in the past, and almost half of the living adults who ever smoked have quit. In 2010, 19.3 percent of all adults in the United States smoked, with men being more likely to smoke (21.5 percent) than women (17.3 percent) (CDC, 2012a). Although these numbers represent a substantial decline from 40 years ago, when 50 percent of men smoked, many individuals still smoke.

Quitting smoking has enormous health benefits. Figure 14.11 shows that when individuals kick the habit, their risk of fatal lung cancer declines over time. There is little doubt that most smokers would like to quit, but their nicotine addiction makes quitting a challenge. Nicotine, the active drug in cigarettes, is a stimulant that increases the smoker's energy and alertness, a pleasurable and reinforcing experience. In addition, nicotine stimulates neurotransmitters that have a calming or pain-reducing effect (Johnstone & others, 2006).

Research confirms that giving up smoking can be difficult, especially in the early days of quitting (McCarthy & others, 2006). There are various ways to quit (Cahill, Stead, & Lancaster, 2012; Sachs & others, 2012; Tahiri & others, 2012), including:

*If you smoke, quit. Many smokers believe that they have to wait for the "perfect time" to quit—a moment when life is not stressful. The truth is that any moment is a good moment to quit smoking. Every cigarette you avoid smoking is a step in the right direction.*

- *Going cold turkey:* Some individuals succeed by stopping smoking without making any major lifestyle changes. They decide they are going to quit, and they do. Lighter smokers usually have more success with this approach than heavier smokers.

- *Using a substitute source of nicotine:* Nicotine gum, the nicotine patch, the nicotine inhaler, and nicotine spray work on the principle of supplying small amounts of nicotine to diminish the intensity of withdrawal (Larzelere & Williams, 2012). *Nicotine gum,* available without a prescription, delivers nicotine orally when an individual gets the urge to smoke. The *nicotine patch* is a nonprescription adhesive pad that releases a steady dose of nicotine to the individual. The dose is gradually reduced over an 8- to 12-week period. *Nicotine spray* delivers a half-milligram squirt of nicotine to each nostril. The usual dosage is one to two administrations per hour and then as needed to reduce cravings. The spray is typically used for three to six months. Success rates for nicotine substitutes are encouraging. All of these nicotine replacement therapies enhance the chances of quitting and remaining smoke-free.

- *Seeking therapeutic help:* Some smokers get professional help to kick the habit. Therapies for helping smokers quit include prescribing medication such as antidepressants and teaching behaviorally based therapeutic techniques. Bupropion SR, an antidepressant sold as Zyban, helps smokers control their cravings while they ease off nicotine.

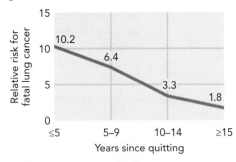

**FIGURE 14.11** **Fatal Lung Cancer and Years Since Quitting Smoking** One study compared more than 43,000 former male smokers with almost 60,000 males who had never smoked (Enstrom, 1999). For comparison purposes, a zero level was assigned as the risk for fatal lung cancer for men who had never smoked. Over time, the relative risk for former smokers declined, but even after 15 years it was still above that of nonsmokers.

Zyban works at the neurotransmitter level in the brain by inhibiting the uptake of dopamine, serotonin, and norepinephrine. Smokers using Zyban to quit have had a 21 percent average success rate after 12 months of taking the antidepressant (Paluck & others, 2006), which is similar to results for individuals using nicotine replacement. More recently, varenicline (trade name Chantix) was approved to help smokers quit. This drug partially blocks nicotine receptors, reducing cravings and also decreasing the pleasurable sensations of smoking. Varenicline, especially when combined with counseling/psychotherapy, is more effective for smoking cessation than bupropion SR (Garrison & Dugan, 2009).

No one method for quitting smoking is foolproof (Fant & others, 2009). Often a combination of approaches is the best strategy. Furthermore, quitting for good typically requires more than one try, as the stages of change model suggests.

# Practicing Safe Sex

One certainty in the human experience is that satisfying sexual experiences are part of a happy life. Sexual behavior also has important implications for physical health. In Chapter 9, we examined research findings on unplanned pregnancy and on educational approaches that can help prevent teen pregnancy. Here we look at another aspect of sexuality: protecting oneself from sexually transmitted infections (STIs). Naturally, by not having sex, individuals can avoid both unplanned pregnancy and STIs. However, even for those whose goal is abstinence, knowledge about preventing unwanted pregnancy and STIs is important, because as the stages of change model suggests, we sometimes fall short of our goals.

## PROTECTING AGAINST SEXUALLY TRANSMITTED INFECTIONS

A **sexually transmitted infection (STI)** is an infection that is contracted primarily through sexual activity—vaginal intercourse as well as oral and anal sex. STIs affect about one of every six adults (CDC, 2012d). Some STIs are bacterial in origin, as in the case of gonorrhea and syphilis, and others are caused by viruses, as in the case of genital herpes and AIDS. STIs are an important health concern because they can have implications for a person's future fertility, risk of cancer, and life expectancy.

No single STI has had a greater impact on sexual behavior in the past decades than AIDS (Campbell, 2009). **Acquired immune deficiency syndrome (AIDS)** is caused by the sexually transmitted human immunodeficiency virus (HIV), which destroys the body's immune system. Without treatment, most people who contract AIDS are vulnerable to germs that a normal immune system can destroy. Through 2009, 619,400 AIDS deaths had occurred in the United States since the epidemic began, including more than 17,000 in 2009 (CDC, 2012b). In 2010, more than 47,000 new HIV infections were reported in the United States.

Recent improvements in drug therapies have given rise to the view that AIDS is a chronic rather than a terminal condition. However, responses to treatment vary among individuals, and keeping up with the cocktail of drugs necessary to fight HIV continuously is challenging. The treatment known as *highly active antiretroviral therapy* (HAART) can involve taking between 6 and 22 pills each day, although the FDA has approved the first one-pill-per-day treatment for AIDS (Onen & others, 2009).

Because of increased education and improved drug therapies, deaths due to AIDS have begun to decline in the United States (CDC, 2012b). There are no solid estimates for the life expectancy of someone who is HIV-positive because the existing treatments have been around for only about a decade. Even in this era of treatment advances, however, AIDS remains incurable. Importantly, it has been estimated that as many as one-half of HIV-positive individuals are not in treatment and that one-fifth do not know that they have contracted the virus (CDC, 2012b). Globally, HIV/AIDS rates have remained alarmingly high. Recent estimates in 2010 indicate that approximately 34 million people

**sexually transmitted infection (STI)**
An infection that is contracted primarily through sexual activity—vaginal intercourse as well as oral and anal sex.

**acquired immune deficiency syndrome (AIDS)**
A sexually transmitted infection, caused by the human immunodeficiency virus (HIV), that destroys the body's immune system.

worldwide are living with HIV. These data reveal increases of 8 million from 1990 and of 27 million from 2000 (UNAIDS, 2012).

All sexually active people are at risk of contracting HIV and other STIs. The only 100 percent safe behavior is abstinence from sex, which many individuals do not view as an option. Sensual activities such as cuddling, massage, and mutual masturbation (without the exchange of bodily fluids) present no risk of developing an STI. Sexual activities that involve penetration, including vaginal or anal intercourse as well as oral sex, are riskier behaviors that can be made less risky with the use of proper protection.

*Anyone who thinks that condom use is inconvenient might well consider which is more convenient—using a condom or contracting gonorrhea or HIV.*

In your own sexual experience, it may be difficult to gauge the accuracy of a partner's estimates of risk and his or her HIV status. The wisest course is always to protect yourself from infection by using a latex condom. When correctly used, latex condoms help to block the transmission of many STIs. Condoms are most effective in preventing gonorrhea, syphilis, chlamydia, and AIDS. Research suggests that consistent condom use also significantly reduces the risk that males will transmit to their female partners the human papilloma virus (HPV), some types of which can cause cervical cancer (Miksis, 2008). Although condoms are less effective against the spread of herpes than against other STIs, consistent condom use reduces the risk of herpes infection for both men and women (Stanaway & others, 2012).

Research has shown that safe-sex programs are especially effective if they include the eroticization of condom use—that is, making condoms part of the sensual experience of foreplay (Scott-Sheldon & Johnson, 2006). Analyses of HIV prevention programs (including over 350 intervention groups and 100 control groups) by Dolores Albarracin and her colleagues have produced important recommendations for the best ways to influence behavior (Albarracin, Durantini, & Earl, 2006; Albarracin & others, 2005, 2008; Durantini & Albarracin, 2009, 2012). The studies have found that fear tactics are relatively less effective and that programs emphasizing active skill building (for example, role playing the use of condoms), self-efficacy, and positive attitudes about condom use are successful with most groups.

1. Regular physical activity and, in particular, exercise are associated with all of the following *except*
   A. weight loss.
   B. increased self-esteem.
   C. less incidence of depression.
   D. premature death in middle-age and older adults.

2. The biggest health risk facing most Americans today is
   A. heart disease.
   B. cancer.
   C. overweight and obesity.
   D. stress.

3. Typically, the *best* approach to quitting smoking is to
   A. go cold turkey.
   B. use a nicotine patch.
   C. use a combination of methods.
   D. get help from a therapist.

**APPLY IT!** 4. J. C. and Veronica promote student health causes on their college campus. This year, they are targeting wise sexual choices. Which of the following is the most promising strategy for their campaign?

A. They should focus on fear of disease as a motivator for condom use.
B. They should focus on promoting non-risky sexual activities, eroticizing condom use, and teaching students skills for effective condom use, reminding students that even if they do not intend to have sex, it is best to be safe.
C. They should focus only on students who are already engaging in sexual behavior.
D. They should encourage students, before having sex, simply to ask their partners how many sexual partners they have had.

# 6 Psychology and Your Good Life

In this discussion of health psychology, we have examined how the mental and physical aspects of your existence intertwine and influence each other. The field of health psychology illustrates how all of the various areas of psychology converge to reveal that interplay.

As a human being, you are both a physical entity and a system of mental processes that are themselves reflected in that most complex of physical organs, the brain. At every

*An experience as deceptively simple as taking in and perceiving a sunset becomes stunningly complex in the context of a human life.*

moment, both body and mind are present and affecting each other. Caring for your brain and mind—the resources that make it possible for you to read this book, study for tests, listen to lectures, fall in love, share with friends, help others, and make a difference in the world—is worthy of being a life mission.

Many pages ago, we defined psychology as the scientific study of behavior and mental processes, broadly meaning the things we do, think, and feel. Reflect for a moment on the psychological dimensions of vision. When we studied the human visual system, we examined the processes by which those amazing sense organs, our eyes, detect color, light, dark, shape, and depth. We probed the ways that the brain takes that information and turns it into perception—how a pattern of colors, shapes, and light come to be perceived as a flower, a fall day, a sunset. Visual systems, we discovered, are generally the same from one person to the next. Thus, you can memorize the different parts of the human eye and know that your understanding is true for just about all the human eyes you will encounter in life.

However, even something as deceptively simple as perceiving a sunset through the sense of vision becomes amazingly complex when we put it in the context of a human life. Is that sunset the first you see while on your honeymoon, or right after a painful romantic breakup, or as a new parent? Placing even the most ordinary moment in the context of a human life renders it extraordinary and fascinating.

This fascination is a primary motivation for the science of psychology itself. Humans have always pondered the mysteries of behavior, thought, and emotion. Why do we do the things we do? How do we think and feel? In this book, we have explored the broad range of topics that have interested psychologists throughout the history of this young science.

Coming to the close of this introduction to psychology allows you to take stock of what psychology has come to mean to you now, as well as to consider what it might mean to you in the future. Whether or not you continue coursework in psychology, this book has highlighted opportunities for your future exploration about yourself and your world. In each of the real-life examples of human experience described in these pages—moments of heroism, weakness, joy, pain, and more—psychology has had a lesson to share with respect to the person that is you. Making the most of what you have learned about psychology means making the most of yourself and your life.

## Do It!

Turn to the Table of Contents of this book. Which chapter or topic did you find most interesting? Go to your school's library and locate the journals that are devoted to that subject (you can ask a librarian for help). Browse a recent issue. What specific topics are scientists studying? If a particular study described in this book sounded interesting, you can probably obtain it online. Do a Google "Scholar" search on the authors and take a look at the original article. What did the authors conclude? What did you learn?

## SUMMARY

### 1 Health Psychology and Behavioral Medicine

Health psychology emphasizes biological, psychological, and social factors in human health. Closely aligned with health psychology is behavioral medicine, which combines medical and behavioral knowledge to reduce illness and promote health. These approaches demonstrate the biopsychosocial model by examining the interaction of biological, psychological, and social variables as they relate to health and illness. Stress is an example of a biological, psychological, and social construct.

Health psychology and behavioral medicine bring the relationship of the mind and body to the forefront. These approaches examine the reciprocal mind–body relationship: how the body is influenced by psychological states and how mental life is influenced by physical health.

### 2 Making Positive Life Changes

The theory of reasoned action suggests that we can make changes by devising specific intentions for behavioral change. We are more likely to follow through on our intentions if we feel good about the change and if we believe that others around us also support the change. The theory of planned behavior incorporates these factors as well as our perceptions of control over the behavior.

The stages of change model posits that personal change occurs in a series of five steps: precontemplation, contemplation, preparation/determination, action/willpower, and maintenance. Each stage has its own challenges. Relapse is a natural part of the journey toward change.

## ③ Resources for Effective Life Change

Motivation is an important part of sustaining behavioral change. Change is more effective when people do it for intrinsic reasons (because they want to) rather than extrinsic reasons (to gain rewards). Implementation intentions are the specific ways individuals plan to institute changes.

Social relationships are strongly associated with health and survival. Social support refers to the aid provided by others to a person in need. Support can take the form of tangible assistance, information, or emotional support. Social support is strongly related to functioning and coping with stress.

Religious faith is associated with enhanced health. One reason for this connection is that religions often frown on excess and promote healthy behavior. In addition, religious participation allows individuals to benefit from a social group, and religion provides a meaning system on which to rely in times of difficulty.

Personality characteristics related to positive health behaviors include conscientiousness, personal control, self-efficacy, and optimism. Conscientious individuals are likely to engage in healthy behaviors and live longer. Personal control is associated with better coping with stress. Self-efficacy is the person's belief in his or her own ability to master a situation and produce positive outcomes. Optimism refers to a particular explanatory style as well as to the inclination to have positive expectations for the future. Studies have shown that both of these types of optimism relate to positive health outcomes.

## ④ Toward a Healthier Mind (and Body): Controlling Stress

Stress is the response of individuals when life circumstances threaten them and tax their ability to cope. Selye characterized the stress response with his concept of a general adaptation syndrome (GAS), which has three stages: alarm, resistance, and exhaustion.

Chronic stress takes a toll on the body's natural disease-fighting abilities. Stress is also related to cardiovascular disease and cancer.

To kick the stress habit means remembering that stress is a product of how we think about events in our lives. Taking control of our appraisals allows us to see potentially threatening events as challenges. Hardiness is associated with thriving during stressful times.

The Type A behavior pattern, particularly the hostility component, is associated with stressing out angrily when things are going badly. This hostility leads to poor health outcomes. There is growing interest in the Type D behavior pattern, seen in individuals who experience generalized and frequent distress, negative emotions, and social inhibition; research has associated this pattern with an elevated risk of cardiovascular problems. When a person is unable to manage stress alone, stress management programs provide options for relief.

## ⑤ Toward a Healthier Body (and Mind): Behaving as If Your Life Depends upon It

Exercise has many positive psychological and physical benefits. Tips for increasing one's activity level include starting small by making changes in one's routine to incorporate physical activity and keeping track of progress.

Overweight and obesity pose the greatest health risks to Americans today. They can be largely avoided by eating right, which means selecting nutritious foods and maintaining healthy eating habits for a lifetime, not just while on a diet. A combination of healthy eating and exercise is the best way to achieve weight loss.

Despite widespread knowledge that smoking causes cancer, some people still smoke. Methods of quitting include going cold turkey, using a substitute source of nicotine, and seeking therapy. Quitting for good is difficult and usually takes more than one try. Usually a combination of methods is the best strategy for quitting.

Practicing safe sex is another aspect of health behavior of interest to health psychologists. Condoms help prevent both unwanted pregnancy and the transmission of sexually transmitted infections (STIs). Interventions to promote condom use are most successful when they include making condom use sexy, promoting contraceptive skills and self-efficacy, and encouraging positive attitudes about condoms.

## ⑥ Psychology and Your Good Life

Psychology is all about you. This book has aimed to show the relevance of psychology to your health and wellness and to help you appreciate the many, and deep, connections between this comparatively new science and your life.

## KEY TERMS

health psychology, p. 514
behavioral medicine, p. 514
health behaviors, p. 515
theory of reasoned action, p. 516
theory of planned behavior, p. 516
stages of change model, p. 516
relapse, p. 518

implementation intentions, p. 520
social support, p. 521
general adaptation syndrome (GAS), p. 527
hypothalamic-pituitary-adrenal axis (HPA axis), p. 527
psychoneuroimmunology, p. 527
Type A behavior pattern, p. 529

Type B behavior pattern, p. 529
Type D behavior pattern, p. 529
cognitive appraisal, p. 530
coping, p. 530
problem-focused coping, p. 531
emotion-focused coping, p. 531
hardiness, p. 532

stress management program, p. 532
exercise, p. 534
aerobic exercise, p. 534
sexually transmitted infection (STI), p. 539
acquired immune deficiency syndrome (AIDS), p. 539

## Multiple Choice

1. If you are involved in the process of trying to change a maladaptive behavior, the stage in which you would most likely expend the most energy and effort is the
   A. preparation stage.
   B. contemplation stage.
   C. action stage.
   D. maintenance stage.

2. Individuals who have high self-efficacy are *least* likely to
   A. carry on when faced with challenges.
   B. expend effort in coping with stress.
   C. experience less stress in challenging situations.
   D. perceive that they have no control over the situation.

3. A distinct physiological pattern emerges when people are exposed to strong and prolonged stress. Selye labeled this response pattern the
   A. transactional stress response (TSR).
   B. two-factor theory of stress.
   C. general adaptation syndrome (GAS).
   D. chronic stress response (CSR).

4. When a rat is first introduced to an overcrowded cage, it will likely enter the _____ stage of the general adaptation syndrome.
   A. alarm
   B. resistance
   C. exhaustion
   D. none of the above

5. Numerous research studies support the idea that perhaps the most important variable in predicting health is
   A. life goals.
   B. social ties.
   C. consistent safe-sex practices.
   D. independence.

6. Religious faith is related to health because it promotes or is associated with all of the following *except*
   A. increased social support.
   B. sturdy moral fiber.
   C. a sense of meaning in life.
   D. moderation.

7. The aspect of Type A behavior that research most consistently associates with coronary problems is
   A. neuroticism.
   B. pessimism.
   C. conscientiousness.
   D. hostility.

8. According to the text, smoking contributes to all of the following *except*
   A. increased risk of middle-ear disease in children.
   B. death from cancer.
   C. death from heart disease.
   D. death from accidents.

9. A person who tries to quit smoking cold turkey is
   A. pairing unpleasant consequences (like smoking until he or she feels nauseated) with the undesirable behavior (smoking).
   B. taking antipsychotic drugs.
   C. trying to stop without making any major lifestyle changes.
   D. using nicotine substitutes.

10. The most probable reason that the United States has one of the highest rates of adolescent pregnancy in the developed world is that
    A. the contraceptive methods used by U.S. adolescents have higher failure rates than those used by adolescents in other developed countries.
    B. U.S. adolescents learn more about sex through school programs than do adolescents in other developed countries.
    C. U.S. adolescents are more sexually active than are adolescents in other developed countries.
    D. compared to other nations, the United States has less comprehensive sex education and less use and availability of condoms.

## Apply It!

11. Cory is interested in becoming more physically active. Using the stages of change model, outline a plan for Cory to achieve his goal.

# answers
## to self-quizzes and self-tests

### Chapter 1

Page 8:     1. A; 2. C; 3. B; 4. B
Page 13:    1. C; 2. D; 3. D; 4. C
Page 17:    1. D; 2. D; 3. B; 4. B
Page 29:    1. B; 2. B; 3. B; 4. A
Page 32:    1. C; 2. B; 3. A; 4. A
Page 37:    1. C; 2. D; 3. B; 4. B
Page 41:    1. A; 2. A; 3. B; 4. A; 5. B; 6. D;
            7. D; 8. D; 9. B; 10. A

### Chapter 2

Page 47:    1. B; 2. D; 3. C; 4. A
Page 56:    1. D; 2. D; 3. A; 4. B
Page 71:    1. B; 2. C; 3. B; 4. C
Page 73:    1. A; 2. C; 3. D; 4. C
Page 76:    1. B; 2. C; 3. A; 4. B
Page 81:    1. C; 2. C; 3. C; 4. A
Page 83:    1. B; 2. B; 3. B; 4. B; 5. B; 6. A;
            7. D; 8. D; 9. C; 10. B

### Chapter 3

Page 95:     1. C; 2. B; 3. A; 4. D
Page 108:    1. D; 2. A; 3. A; 4. B
Page 114:    1. A; 2. C; 3. B; 4. B
Page 122:    1. B; 2. B; 3. B; 4. B
Page 124:    1. B; 2. C; 3. C; 4. D; 5. C; 6. A;
             7. B; 8. B; 9. C; 10. B

### Chapter 4

Page 133:    1. B; 2. A; 3. C; 4. B
Page 145:    1. D; 2. B; 3. B; 4. B
Page 157:    1. D; 2. D; 3. A; 4. C
Page 160:    1. A; 2. D; 3. D; 4. C
Page 163:    1. B; 2. D; 3. A; 4. C
Pages 164–165:   1. A; 2. B; 3. C; 4. B; 5. B;
                 6. D; 7. D; 8. D; 9. C; 10. D

### Chapter 5

Page 169:    1. A; 2. C; 3. C; 4. C
Page 177:    1. B; 2. A; 3. D; 4. B
Page 188:    1. D; 2. B; 3. D; 4. A
Page 190:    1. B; 2. C; 3. B; 4. A
Page 194:    1. C; 2. B; 3. A; 4. A
Page 198:    1. D; 2. C; 3. B; 4. B
Page 200:    1. B; 2. C; 3. A; 4. C; 5. A; 6. C;
             7. A; 8. B; 9. D; 10. B

### Chapter 6

Page 203:    1. D; 2. B; 3. A; 4. A
Page 206:    1. C; 2. D; 3. C; 4. B
Page 220:    1. D; 2. A; 3. B; 4. B
Page 230:    1. C; 2. A; 3. D; 4. B
Page 234:    1. B; 2. D; 3. B; 4. B
Page 239:    1. D; 2. A; 3. B; 4. A
Pages 240–241:   1. A; 2. A; 3. B; 4. D; 5. A;
                 6. C; 7. C; 8. A; 9. B; 10. A

### Chapter 7

Page 245:    1. D; 2. C; 3. D; 4. C
Page 255:    1. C; 2. A; 3. B; 4. D
Page 266:    1. D; 2. B; 3. C; 4. A
Page 275:    1. D; 2. B; 3. B; 4. B
Page 277:    1. A; 2. A; 3. C; 4. A; 5. D; 6. B;
             7. C; 8. B; 9. B; 10. A

### Chapter 8

Page 283:    1. A; 2. C; 3. C; 4. D
Page 293:    1. B; 2. A; 3. B; 4. C
Page 302:    1. A; 2. B; 3. C; 4. B
Page 312:    1. B; 2. D; 3. C; 4. C
Page 315:    1. B; 2. D; 3. B; 4. A
Page 318:    1. C; 2. D; 3. B; 4. C
Page 320:    1. B; 2. B; 3. C; 4. C
Page 323:    1. A; 2. C; 3. D; 4. A; 5. C;
             6. D; 7. C; 8. A; 9. D; 10. A

### Chapter 9

Page 327:    1. D; 2. B; 3. D; 4. B
Page 339:    1. C; 2. A; 3. D; 4. D
Page 345:    1. C; 2. C; 3. C; 4. C
Page 356:    1. B; 2. B; 3. A; 4. D
Page 358:    1. A; 2. C; 3. A; 4. A
Page 360:    1. D; 2. C; 3. D; 4. C; 5. D; 6. C;
             7. B; 8. A; 9. B; 10. D

### Chapter 10

Page 370:    1. D; 2. C; 3. D; 4. C
Page 373:    1. B; 2. C; 3. B; 4. D
Page 380:    1. B; 2. D; 3. D; 4. B
Page 382:    1. B; 2. D; 3. C; 4. A

### Chapter 11 (continued)

Page 387:    1. B; 2. C; 3. A; 4. B
Page 391:    1. B; 2. C; 3. D; 4. C
Page 397:    1. B; 2. A; 3. D; 4. B
Page 399:    1. A; 2. B; 3. C; 4. D; 5. B; 6. B;
             7. D; 8. B; 9. A; 10. D

### Chapter 11

Page 409:    1. D; 2. A; 3. C; 4. B
Page 418:    1. D; 2. C; 3. A; 4. C
Page 428:    1. B; 2. B; 3. C; 4. C
Page 433:    1. C; 2. C; 3. D; 4. B
Page 437:    1. C; 2. C; 3. D; 4. B
Page 439:    1. C; 2. B; 3. B; 4. A; 5. D; 6. B;
             7. D; 8. C; 9. C; 10. C

### Chapter 12

Page 448:    1. A; 2. C; 3. B; 4. A
Page 454:    1. D; 2. C; 3. B; 4. C
Page 461:    1. A; 2. D; 3. A; 4. C
Page 465:    1. D; 2. A; 3. C; 4. B
Page 468:    1. B; 2. C; 3. D; 4. C
Page 472:    1. B; 2. B; 3. C; 4. B
Page 476:    1. C; 2. C; 3. D; 4. A
Page 479:    1. B; 2. D; 3. D; 4. B
Page 481:    1. C; 2. D; 3. B; 4. A; 5. B; 6. B;
             7. B; 8. D; 9. D; 10. D

### Chapter 13

Page 489:    1. B; 2. B; 3. C; 4. C
Page 501:    1. C; 2. B; 3. D; 4. D
Page 506:    1. B; 2. D; 3. B; 4. C
Page 510:    1. D; 2. B; 3. C; 4. B
Pages 511–512:   1. B; 2. D; 3. C; 4. C; 5. A;
                 6. C; 7. B; 8. C; 9. A; 10. B

### Chapter 14

Page 515:    1. D; 2. B; 3. D; 4. B
Page 519:    1. D; 2. B; 3. B; 4. A
Page 526:    1. A; 2. D; 3. A; 4. C
Page 533:    1. D; 2. C; 3. A; 4. B
Page 540:    1. D; 2. C; 3. C; 4. B
Page 543:    1. C; 2. D; 3. C; 4. A; 5. B; 6. B;
             7. D; 8. D; 9. C; 10. D

# glossary

## A

**abnormal behavior** Behavior that is deviant, maladaptive, or personally distressful over a relatively long period of time.

**absolute threshold** The minimum amount of stimulus energy that a person can detect.

**accommodation** An individual's adjustment of his or her schemas to new information.

**acquired immune deficiency syndrome (AIDS)** A sexually transmitted infection, caused by the human immunodeficiency virus (HIV), that destroys the body's immune system.

**acquisition** The initial learning of the connection between the unconditioned stimulus and the conditioned stimulus when these two stimuli are paired.

**action potential** The brief wave of positive electrical charge that sweeps down the axon.

**activation-synthesis theory** Theory that dreaming occurs when the cerebral cortex synthesizes neural signals generated from activity in the lower part of the brain and that dreams result from the brain's attempts to find logic in random brain activity that occurs during sleep.

**addiction** Either a physical or a psychological dependence, or both, on a drug.

**adrenal glands** Glands at the top of each kidney that are responsible for regulating moods, energy level, and the ability to cope with stress.

**aerobic exercise** Sustained activity—jogging, swimming, or cycling, for example—that stimulates heart and lung functioning.

**affectionate love** Love that occurs when an individual has a deep, caring affection for another person and desires to have that person near; also called companionate love.

**afferent nerves** Also called sensory nerves; nerves that carry information about the external environment to the brain and spinal cord via sensory receptors.

**aggression** Social behavior whose objective is to harm someone, either physically or verbally.

**agonist** A drug that mimics or increases a neurotransmitter's effects.

**alcoholism** Disorder that involves long-term, repeated, uncontrolled, compulsive, and excessive use of alcoholic beverages and that impairs the drinker's health and social relationships.

**algorithms** Strategies—including formulas, instructions, and the testing of all possible solutions—that guarantee a solution to a problem.

**all-or-nothing principle** The principle that once the electrical impulse reaches a certain level of intensity (its threshold), it fires and moves all the way down the axon without losing any intensity.

**altruism** Unselfish interest in helping another person.

**amnesia** The loss of memory.

**amygdala** An almond-shaped structure within the base of the temporal lobe that is involved in the discrimination of objects that are necessary for the organism's survival, such as appropriate food, mates, and social rivals.

**androgens** The class of sex hormones that predominate in males, produced by the testes in males and by the adrenal glands in both males and females.

**anorexia nervosa** Eating disorder that involves the relentless pursuit of thinness through starvation.

**antagonist** A drug that blocks a neurotransmitter's effects.

**anterograde amnesia** A memory disorder that affects the retention of new information and events.

**antianxiety drugs** Commonly known as tranquilizers, drugs that reduce anxiety by making individuals calmer and less excitable.

**antidepressant drugs** Drugs that regulate mood.

**antipsychotic drugs** Powerful drugs that diminish agitated behavior, reduce tension, decrease hallucinations, improve social behavior, and produce better sleep patterns in individuals with a severe psychological disorder, especially schizophrenia.

**antisocial personality disorder (ASPD)** Psychological disorder characterized by guiltlessness, law-breaking, exploitation of others, irresponsibility, and deceit.

**anxiety disorders** Disabling (uncontrollable and disruptive) psychological disorders that feature motor tension, hyperactivity, and apprehensive expectations and thoughts.

**anxious attachment style** An attachment style that describes adults who demand closeness, are less trusting, and are more emotional, jealous, and possessive.

**apparent movement** The perception that a stationary object is moving.

**applied behavior analysis (behavior modification)** The use of operant conditioning principles to change human behavior.

**archetypes** Jung's term for emotionally laden ideas and images in the collective unconscious that have rich and symbolic meaning for all people.

**artificial intelligence (AI)** A scientific field that focuses on creating machines capable of performing activities that require intelligence when they are done by people.

**assimilation** An individual's incorporation of new information into existing knowledge.

**association cortex** Sometimes called association areas, the region of the cerebral cortex that is the site of the highest intellectual functions, such as thinking and problem solving.

**associative learning** Learning that occurs when an organism makes a connection, or an association, between two events.

**Atkinson-Shiffrin theory** Theory stating that memory storage involves three separate systems: sensory memory, short-term memory, and long-term memory.

**attention deficit hyperactivity disorder (ADHD)** One of the most common psychological disorders of childhood, in which individuals show one or more of the following: inattention, hyperactivity, and impulsivity.

**attitudes** An individual's opinions and beliefs about people, objects, and ideas—how the person feels about the world.

**attribution theory** The view that people are motivated to discover the underlying causes of behavior as part of their effort to make sense of the behavior.

**auditory nerve** The nerve structure that receives information about sound from the hair cells of the inner ear and carries these neural impulses to the brain's auditory areas.

**authoritarian parenting** A restrictive, punitive style in which the parent exhorts the child to follow the parent's directions and to value hard work and effort.

**authoritative parenting** A parenting style that encourages the child to be independent but that still places limits and controls on behavior.

**autobiographical memory** A special form of episodic memory, consisting of a person's recollections of his or her life experiences.

**automatic processes** States of consciousness that require little attention and do not interfere with other ongoing activities.

**autonomic nervous system** The body system that takes messages to and from the body's internal organs, monitoring such processes as breathing, heart rate, and digestion.

**availability heuristic** A prediction about the probability of an event based on the ease of recalling or imagining similar events.

**aversive conditioning** A form of treatment that consists of repeated pairings of a stimulus with a very unpleasant stimulus.

**avoidance learning** An organism's learning that it can altogether avoid a negative stimulus by making a particular response.

**avoidant attachment style** An attachment style that describes adults who are hesitant about getting involved in romantic relationships and, once in a relationship, tend to distance themselves from their partner.

**axon** The part of the neuron that carries information away from the cell body toward other cells.

## B

**barbiturates** Depressant drugs, such as Nembutal and Seconal, that decrease central nervous system activity.

**basal ganglia** Large neuron clusters located above the thalamus and under the cerebral cortex that work with the cerebellum and the cerebral cortex to control and coordinate voluntary movements.

**base rate fallacy** The tendency to ignore information about general principles in favor of very specific but vivid information.

**behavior** Everything we do that can be directly observed.

**behavioral approach** An approach to psychology emphasizing the scientific study of observable behavioral responses and their environmental determinants.

**behavioral genetics** The study of the inherited underpinnings of behavioral characteristics.

**behavioral medicine** An interdisciplinary field that focuses on developing and integrating behavioral and biomedical knowledge to promote health and reduce illness; overlaps with and is sometimes indistinguishable from health psychology.

**behaviorism** A theory of learning that focuses solely on observable behaviors, discounting the importance of such mental activity as thinking, wishing, and hoping.

**behavior therapies** Treatments, based on the behavioral and social cognitive theories of learning and personality, that use principles of learning to reduce or eliminate maladaptive behavior.

**big five factors of personality** The five broad traits that are thought to describe the main dimensions of personality: openness to experience, conscientiousness, extraversion, agreeableness, and neuroticism (emotional instability).

**binding** In the sense of vision, the bringing together and integration of what is processed by different neural pathways or cells.

**binge eating disorder (BED)** Eating disorder characterized by recurrent episodes of consuming large amounts of food during which the person feels a lack of control over eating.

**binocular cues** Depth cues that depend on the combination of the images in the left and right eyes and on the way the two eyes work together.

**biological approach** An approach to psychology focusing on the body, especially the brain and nervous system.

**biological rhythms** Periodic physiological fluctuations in the body, such as the rise and fall of hormones and accelerated/decelerated cycles of brain activity, that can influence behavior.

**biological therapies** Also called biomedical therapies, treatments that reduce or eliminate the symptoms of psychological disorders by altering aspects of body functioning.

**bipolar disorder** Mood disorder characterized by extreme mood swings that include one or more episodes of mania, an overexcited, unrealistically optimistic state.

**borderline personality disorder (BPD)** Psychological disorder characterized by a pervasive pattern of instability in interpersonal relationships, self-image, and emotions, and of marked impulsivity beginning by early adulthood and present in a variety of contexts.

**bottom-up processing** The operation in sensation and perception in which sensory receptors register information about the external environment and send it up to the brain for interpretation.

**brain stem** The stemlike brain area that includes much of the hindbrain (excluding the cerebellum) and the midbrain; connects with the spinal cord at its lower end and then extends upward to encase the reticular formation in the midbrain.

**broaden-and-build model** Fredrickson's model of positive emotion, stating that the function of positive emotions lies in their effects on an individual's attention and ability to build resources.

**bulimia nervosa** Eating disorder in which an individual (typically female) consistently follows a binge-and-purge eating pattern.

**bystander effect** The tendency for an individual who observes an emergency to help less when other people are present than when the observer is alone.

## C

**Cannon-Bard theory** The proposition that emotion and physiological reactions occur simultaneously.

**case study or case history** An in-depth look at a single individual.

**catatonia** State of immobility and unresponsiveness, lasting for long periods of time.

**cell body** The part of the neuron that contains the nucleus, which directs the manufacture of substances that the neuron needs for growth and maintenance.

**central nervous system (CNS)** The brain and spinal cord.

**cerebral cortex** Part of the forebrain, the outer layer of the brain, responsible for the most complex mental functions, such as thinking and planning.

**chromosomes** In the human cell, threadlike structures that come in 23 pairs, one member of each pair originating from each parent, and that contain DNA.

**circadian rhythms** Daily behavioral or physiological cycles that involve the sleep/wake cycle, body temperature, blood pressure, and blood sugar level.

**classical conditioning** Learning process in which a neutral stimulus becomes associated with an innately meaningful stimulus and acquires the capacity to elicit a similar response.

**client-centered therapy** Also called Rogerian therapy or nondirective therapy, a form of humanistic therapy, developed by Rogers, in which the therapist provides a warm, supportive atmosphere to improve the client's self-concept and to encourage the client to gain insight into problems.

**cognition** The way in which information is processed and manipulated in remembering, thinking, and knowing.

**cognitive affective processing systems (CAPS)** Mischel's theoretical model for describing that individuals' thoughts and emotions about themselves and the world affect their behavior and become linked in ways that matter to that behavior.

**cognitive appraisal** Individuals' interpretation of the events in their life as harmful, threatening, or challenging and their determination of whether they have the resources to cope effectively with the events.

**cognitive approach** An approach to psychology emphasizing the mental processes involved in knowing: how we direct our attention, perceive, remember, think, and solve problems.

**cognitive-behavior therapy** A therapy that combines cognitive therapy and behavior therapy with the goal of developing self-efficacy.

**cognitive dissonance** An individual's psychological discomfort (dissonance) caused by two inconsistent thoughts.

**cognitive theory of dreaming** Theory proposing that we can understand dreaming by applying the same cognitive concepts we use in studying the waking mind.

**cognitive therapies** Treatments that point to cognitions (thoughts) as the main source of psychological problems and that attempt to change the individual's feelings and behaviors by changing cognitions.

**collective unconscious** Jung's term for the impersonal, deepest layer of the unconscious mind, shared by all human beings because of their common ancestral past.

**concept** A mental category that is used to group objects, events, and characteristics.

**concrete operational stage** Piaget's third stage of cognitive development, lasting from about 7 to 11 years of age, during which the individual uses operations and replaces intuitive reasoning with logical reasoning in concrete situations.

**conditioned response (CR)** The learned response to the conditioned stimulus that occurs after a conditioned stimulus–unconditioned stimulus pairing.

**conditioned stimulus (CS)** A previously neutral stimulus that eventually elicits a conditioned response after being paired with the unconditioned stimulus.

**conditions of worth** The standards that the individual must live up to in order to receive positive regard from others.

**cones** The receptor cells in the retina that allow for color perception.

**confederate** A person who is given a role to play in a study so that the social context can be manipulated.

**confirmation bias** The tendency to search for and use information that supports one's ideas rather than refutes them.

**conformity** A change in a person's behavior to coincide more closely with a group standard.

**connectionism** Also called parallel distributed processing (PDP), the theory that memory is stored throughout the brain in connections among neurons, several of which may work together to process a single memory.

**consciousness** An individual's awareness of external events and internal sensations under a condition of arousal, including awareness of the self and thoughts about one's experiences.

**control group** The participants in an experiment who are as much like the experimental group as possible and who are treated in every way like the experimental group except for a manipulated factor, the independent variable.

**controlled processes** The most alert states of human consciousness, during which individuals actively focus their efforts toward a goal.

**convergence** A binocular cue to depth and distance in which the muscle movements in an individual's two eyes provide information about how deep and/or far away something is.

**convergent thinking** Thinking that produces the single best solution to a problem.

**coping** Managing taxing circumstances, expending effort to solve life's problems, and seeking to master or reduce stress.

**corpus callosum** The large bundle of axons that connects the brain's two hemispheres, responsible for relaying information between the two sides.

**correlational research** Research that examines the relationships between variables, whose purpose is to examine whether and how two variables change together.

**counterconditioning** A classical conditioning procedure for changing the relationship between a conditioned stimulus and its conditioned response.

**couples therapy** Group therapy with married or unmarried couples whose major problem lies within their relationship.

**creativity** The ability to think about something in novel and unusual ways and to devise unconventional solutions to problems.

**critical thinking** The process of thinking deeply and actively, asking questions, and evaluating the evidence.

**cross-cultural competence** A therapist's assessment of his or her abilities to manage cultural issues in therapy and the client's perception of those abilities.

**cross-sectional design** A research design in which a group of people are assessed on a psychological variable at one point in time.

**culture-fair tests** Intelligence tests that are intended to be culturally unbiased.

## D

**decay theory** Theory stating that when an individual learns something new, a neurochemical memory trace forms, but over time this trace disintegrates; suggests that the passage of time always increases forgetting.

**decision making** The mental activity of evaluating alternatives and choosing among them.

**deductive reasoning** Reasoning from a general case that is known to be true to a specific instance.

**defense mechanisms** Tactics the ego uses to reduce anxiety by unconsciously distorting reality.

**deindividuation** The reduction in personal identity and erosion of the sense of personal responsibility when one is part of a group.

**delusions** False, unusual, and sometimes magical beliefs that are not part of an individual's culture.

**demand characteristics** Any aspects of a study that communicate to the participants how the experimenter wants them to behave.

**dendrites** Treelike fibers projecting from a neuron, which receive information and orient it toward the neuron's cell body.

**deoxyribonucleic acid (DNA)** A complex molecule in the cell's chromosomes that carries genetic information.

**dependent variable** The outcome; the factor that can change in an experiment in response to changes in the independent variable.

**depressants** Psychoactive drugs that slow down mental and physical activity.

**depressive disorders** Mood disorders in which the individual suffers from depression—an unrelenting lack of pleasure in life.

**depth perception** The ability to perceive objects three-dimensionally.

**development** The pattern of continuity and change in human capabilities that occurs throughout life, involving both growth and decline.

**diathesis-stress model** View of schizophrenia emphasizing that a combination of biogenetic disposition and stress causes the disorder.

**difference threshold** The degree of difference that must exist between two stimuli before the difference is detected.

**discrimination** An unjustified negative or harmful action toward a member of a group simply because the person belongs to that group.

**discrimination (classical conditioning)** The process of learning to respond to certain stimuli and not others.

**discrimination (operant conditioning)** Responding appropriately to stimuli that signal that a behavior will or will not be reinforced.

**display rules** Sociocultural standards that determine when, where, and how emotions should be expressed.

**dissociative amnesia** Dissociative disorder characterized by extreme memory loss that is caused by extensive psychological stress.

**dissociative disorders** Psychological disorders that involve a sudden loss of memory or change in identity due to the dissociation (separation) of the individual's conscious awareness from previous memories and thoughts.

**dissociative fugue** Dissociative disorder in which the individual not only develops amnesia but also unexpectedly travels away from home and assumes a new identity.

**dissociative identity disorder (DID)** Formerly called multiple personality disorder, a dissociative disorder in which the individual has two or more distinct personalities or selves, each with its own memories, behaviors, and relationships.

**divergent thinking** Thinking that produces many solutions to the same problem.

**divided attention** Concentrating on more than one activity at the same time.

**divided consciousness view of hypnosis** Hilgard's view that hypnosis involves a splitting of consciousness into two separate components, one of which follows the hypnotist's commands and the other of which acts as a "hidden observer."

**double-blind experiment** An experimental design in which neither the experimenter nor the participants are aware of which participants are in the experimental group and which are in the control group until the results are calculated.

**dream analysis** A psychoanalytic technique for interpreting a person's dreams.

**drive** An aroused state that occurs because of a physiological need.

**DSM-IV** The *Diagnostic and Statistical Manual of Mental Disorders,* Fourth Edition; the major classification of psychological disorders in the United States.

**dysthymic disorder (DD)** Mood disorder that is generally more chronic and has fewer symptoms than major depressive disorder.

## E

**efferent nerves** Also called motor nerves; nerves that carry information out of the brain and spinal cord to other areas of the body.

**ego** The Freudian structure of personality that deals with the demands of reality.

**egoism** Giving to another person to ensure reciprocity; to gain self-esteem; to present oneself as powerful, competent, or caring; or to avoid social and self-censure for failing to live up to society's expectations.

**elaboration** The formation of a number of different connections around a stimulus at a given level of memory encoding.

**elaboration likelihood model** Theory identifying two ways to persuade: a central route and a peripheral route.

**electroconvulsive therapy (ECT)** Also called shock therapy, a treatment, commonly used for depression, that sets off a seizure in the brain.

**emerging adulthood** The transitional period from adolescence to adulthood, spanning approximately 18 to 25 years of age.

**emotion** Feeling, or affect, that can involve physiological arousal (such as a fast heartbeat), conscious experience (thinking about being in love with someone), and behavioral expression (a smile or grimace).

**emotion-focused coping** The coping strategy that involves responding to the stress that one is feeling—trying to manage one's emotional reaction—rather than focusing on the root problem itself.

**empathy** A feeling of oneness with the emotional state of another person.

**empirically keyed test** A type of self-report test that presents many questionnaire items to two groups that are known to be different in some central way.

**empirical method** Gaining knowledge through the observation of events, the collection of data, and logical reasoning.

**encoding** The first step in memory; the process by which information gets into memory storage.

**endocrine system** The body system consisting of a set of glands that regulate the activities of certain organs by releasing their chemical products into the bloodstream.

**episodic memory** The retention of information about the where, when, and what of life's happenings—that is, how individuals remember life's episodes.

**estrogens** The class of sex hormones that predominate in females, produced mainly by the ovaries.

**ethnocentrism** The tendency to favor one's own ethnic group over other groups.

**evidence-based practice** Integration of the best available research with clinical expertise in the context of client characteristics, culture, and preferences.

**evolutionary approach** An approach to psychology centered on evolutionary ideas such as adaptation, reproduction, and natural selection as the basis for explaining specific human behaviors.

**exercise** Structured activities whose goal is to improve health.

**experiment** A carefully regulated procedure in which the researcher manipulates one or more variables that are believed to influence some other variable.

**experimental group** The participants in an experiment who receive the drug or other treatment under study—that is, those who are exposed to the change that the independent variable represents.

**experimenter bias** The influence of the experimenter's expectations on the outcome of research.

**explicit memory (declarative memory)** The conscious recollection of information, such as specific facts or events and, at least in humans, information that can be verbally communicated.

**external validity** The degree to which an experimental design actually reflects the real-world issues it is supposed to address.

**extinction (classical conditioning)** The weakening of the conditioned response when the unconditioned stimulus is absent.

**extinction (operant conditioning)** Decreases in the frequency of a behavior when the behavior is no longer reinforced.

**extrinsic motivation** Motivation that involves external incentives such as rewards and punishments.

## F

**face validity** The extent to which a test item appears to fit the particular trait it is measuring.

**facial feedback hypothesis** The idea that facial expressions can influence emotions as well as reflect them.

**false consensus effect** Observers' overestimation of the degree to which everybody else thinks or acts the way they do.

**family therapy** Group therapy with family members.

**feature detectors** Neurons in the brain's visual system that respond to particular features of a stimulus.

**figure-ground relationship** The principle by which we organize the perceptual field into stimuli that stand out (figure) and those that are left over (ground).

**fixation** Using a prior strategy and failing to look at a problem from a fresh new perspective.

**flashbulb memory** The memory of emotionally significant events that people often recall with more accuracy and vivid imagery than everyday events.

**flat affect** The display of little or no emotion—a common negative symptom of schizophrenia.

**forebrain** The brain's largest division and its most forward part.

**formal operational stage** Piaget's fourth stage of cognitive development, which begins at 11 to 15 years of age and continues through the adult years; it features thinking about things that are not concrete, making predictions, and using logic to come up with hypotheses about the future.

**free association** A psychoanalytic technique that involves encouraging individuals to say aloud whatever comes to mind, no matter how trivial or embarrassing.

**frequency theory** Theory on how the inner ear registers the frequency of sound, stating that the perception of a sound's frequency depends on how often the auditory nerve fires.

**frontal lobes** The portion of the cerebral cortex behind the forehead, involved in personality, intelligence, and the control of voluntary muscles.

**functional fixedness** Failing to solve a problem as a result of fixation on a thing's usual functions.

**functionalism** James's approach to mental processes, emphasizing the functions and purposes of the mind and behavior in the individual's adaptation to the environment.

**fundamental attribution error** Observers' overestimation of the importance of internal traits and underestimation of the importance of external situations when they seek explanations of an actor's behavior.

## G

**gender** The social and psychological aspects of being female or male.

**gender roles** Roles that reflect the individual's expectations for how females and males should think, act, and feel.

**gender similarities hypothesis** Hyde's proposition that men and women (and boys and girls) are much more similar than they are different.

**general adaptation syndrome (GAS)** Selye's term for the common effects of stressful demands on the body, consisting of three stages: alarm, resistance, and exhaustion.

**generalization (classical conditioning)** The tendency of a new stimulus that is similar to the original conditioned stimulus to elicit a response that is similar to the conditioned response.

**generalization (operant conditioning)** Performing a reinforced behavior in a different situation.

**generalized anxiety disorder** Psychological disorder marked by persistent anxiety for at least 6 months, and in which the individual is unable to specify the reasons for the anxiety.

**genes** The units of hereditary information, consisting of short segments of chromosomes composed of DNA.

**genotype** An individual's genetic heritage; his or her actual genetic material.

**gestalt psychology** A school of thought interested in how people naturally organize their perceptions according to certain patterns.

**gifted** Possessing high intelligence (an IQ of 130 or higher) and/or superior talent in a particular area.

**glands** Organs or tissues in the body that create chemicals that control many bodily functions.

**glial cells** The second of two types of cells in the nervous system; glial cells (also called glia) provide support, nutritional benefits, and other functions and keep neurons running smoothly.

**group polarization effect** The solidification and further strengthening of an individual's position as a consequence of a group discussion.

**group therapy** A sociocultural approach to the treatment of psychological disorders that brings together individuals who share a particular psychological disorder in sessions that are typically led by a mental health professional.

**groupthink** The impaired group decision making that occurs when making the right decision is less important than maintaining group harmony.

## H

**habituation** Decreased responsiveness to a stimulus after repeated presentations.

**hallucinations** Sensory experiences that occur in the absence of real stimuli.

**hallucinogens** Psychoactive drugs that modify a person's perceptual experiences and produce visual images that are not real.

**hardiness** A personality trait characterized by a sense of commitment rather than alienation and of control rather than powerlessness; a perception of problems as challenges rather than threats.

**health behaviors** Practices that have an impact on physical well-being.

**health psychology** A subfield of psychology that emphasizes psychology's role in establishing and maintaining health and preventing and treating illness.

**heritability** The proportion of observable differences in a group that can be explained by differences in the genes of the group's members.

**heuristics** Shortcut strategies or guidelines that suggest a solution to a problem but do not guarantee an answer.

**hierarchy of needs** Maslow's theory that human needs must be satisfied in the following sequence: physiological needs, safety, love and belongingness, esteem, and self-actualization.

**hindbrain** Located at the skull's rear, the lowest portion of the brain, consisting of the medulla, cerebellum, and pons.

**hindsight bias** The tendency to report falsely, after the fact, that one has accurately predicted an outcome.

**hippocampus** The structure in the limbic system that has a special role in the storage of memories.

**homeostasis** The body's tendency to maintain an equilibrium, or steady state.

**hormones** Chemical messengers that are produced by the endocrine glands and carried by the bloodstream to all parts of the body.

**humanistic approach** An approach to psychology emphasizing a person's positive qualities, the capacity for positive growth, and the freedom to choose any destiny.

**humanistic perspectives** Theoretical views stressing a person's capacity for personal growth and positive human qualities.

**humanistic therapies** Treatments, unique in their emphasis on people's self-healing capacities, that encourage clients to understand themselves and to grow personally.

**human sexual response pattern** According to Masters and Johnson, the characteristic sequence of physiological changes that humans experience during sexual activity, consisting of four phases: excitement, plateau, orgasm, and resolution.

**hypnosis** An altered state of consciousness or a psychological state of altered attention and expectation in which the individual is unusually receptive to suggestions.

**hypothalamic-pituitary-adrenal axis (HPA axis)** The complex set of interactions among the hypothalamus, the pituitary gland, and the adrenal glands that regulate various body processes and control reactions to stressful events.

**hypothalamus** A small forebrain structure, located just below the thalamus, that monitors three pleasurable activities—eating, drinking, and sex—as well as emotion, stress, and reward.

**hypothesis** A testable prediction that derives logically from a theory.

## I

**id** The part of the person that Freud called the "it," consisting of unconscious drives; the individual's reservoir of sexual energy.

**implementation intentions** Specific strategies for dealing with the challenges of making a life change.

**implicit memory (nondeclarative memory)** Memory in which behavior is affected by prior experience without a conscious recollection of that experience.

**independent variable** A manipulated experimental factor; the variable that the experimenter changes to see what its effects are.

**individual psychology** Adler's view that people are motivated by purposes and goals and that perfection, not pleasure, is thus the key motivator in human life.

**inductive reasoning** Reasoning from specific observations to make generalizations.

**infant attachment** The close emotional bond between an infant and its caregiver.

**infinite generativity** The ability of language to produce an endless number of meaningful sentences.

**informational social influence** The influence other people have on us because we want to be right.

**inner ear** The part of the ear that includes the oval window, cochlea, and basilar membrane and whose function is to convert sound waves into neural impulses and send them to the brain.

**insight learning** A form of problem solving in which the organism develops a sudden insight into or understanding of a problem's solution.

**instinct** An innate (unlearned) biological pattern of behavior that is assumed to be universal throughout a species.

**instinctive drift** The tendency of animals to revert to instinctive behavior that interferes with learning.

**integrative therapy** A combination of techniques from different therapies based on the therapist's judgment of which particular methods will provide the greatest benefit for the client.

**intellectual disability** A condition of limited mental ability in which an individual has a low IQ, usually below 70 on a traditional intelligence test, and has difficulty adapting to everyday life.

**intelligence** All-purpose ability to do well on cognitive tasks, to solve problems, and to learn from experience.

**intelligence quotient (IQ)** An individual's mental age divided by chronological age multiplied by 100.

**interference theory** The theory that people forget not because memories are lost from storage but because other information gets in the way of what they want to remember.

**internal validity** The degree to which changes in the dependent variable are due to the manipulation of the independent variable.

**interpretation** A psychoanalyst's search for symbolic, hidden meanings in what the client says and does during therapy.

**intrinsic motivation** Motivation based on internal factors such as organismic needs (competence, relatedness, and autonomy), as well as curiosity, challenge, and fun.

**investment model** A model of long-term relationships that examines the ways that commitment, investment, and the availability of attractive alternative partners predict satisfaction and stability in relationships.

## J

**James-Lange theory** The theory that emotion results from physiological states triggered by stimuli in the environment.

## K

**kinesthetic senses** Senses that provide information about movement, posture, and orientation.

## L

**language** A form of communication—whether spoken, written, or signed—that is based on a system of symbols.

**latent content** According to Freud, a dream's hidden content; its unconscious and true meaning.

**latent learning (implicit learning)** Unreinforced learning that is not immediately reflected in behavior.

**law of effect** Thorndike's law stating that behaviors followed by positive outcomes are strengthened and that behaviors followed by negative outcomes are weakened.

**learned helplessness** Through experience with unavoidable aversive stimuli, an organism learns that it has no control over negative outcomes.

**learning** A systematic, relatively permanent change in behavior that occurs through experience.

**levels of processing** A continuum of memory processing from shallow to intermediate to deep, with deeper processing producing better memory.

**limbic system** A loosely connected network of structures under the cerebral cortex, important in both memory and emotion. Its two principal structures are the amygdala and the hippocampus.

**lithium** The lightest of the solid elements in the periodic table of elements, widely used to treat bipolar disorder.

**longitudinal design** A special kind of systematic observation, used by correlational researchers, that involves obtaining measures of the variables of interest in multiple waves over time.

**long-term memory** A relatively permanent type of memory that stores huge amounts of information for a long time.

## M

**major depressive disorder (MDD)** Psychological disorder involving a major depressive episode and depressed characteristics, such as lethargy and hopelessness, for at least two weeks.

**manifest content** According to Freud, the surface content of a dream, containing dream symbols that disguise the dream's true meaning.

**medical model** The view that psychological disorders are medical diseases with a biological origin.

**meditation** The attainment of a peaceful state of mind in which thoughts are not occupied by worry; the meditator is mindfully present to his or her thoughts and feelings but is not consumed by them.

**memory** The retention of information or experience over time as the result of three key processes: encoding, storage, and retrieval.

**mental age (MA)** An individual's level of mental development relative to that of others.

**mental processes** The thoughts, feelings, and motives that people experience privately but that cannot be observed directly.

**mere exposure effect** The phenomenon that the more individuals encounter someone or something, the more probable it is that they will start liking the person or thing even if they do not realize they have seen it before.

**midbrain** Located between the hindbrain and forebrain, an area in which many nerve-fiber systems ascend and descend to connect the higher and lower portions of the brain; in particular, the midbrain relays information between the brain and the eyes and ears.

**middle ear** The part of the ear that channels sound through the eardrum, hammer, anvil, and stirrup to the inner ear.

**mindfulness** The state of being alert and mentally present for one's everyday activities.

**Minnesota Multiphasic Personality Inventory (MMPI)** The most widely used and researched empirically keyed self-report personality test.

**monocular cues** Powerful depth cues available from the image in one eye, either the right or the left.

**mood disorders** Psychological disorders—the main types of which are depressive disorders and bipolar disorder—in which there is a primary disturbance of mood: prolonged emotion that colors the individual's entire emotional state.

**morphology** A language's rules for word formation.

**motivated forgetting** Forgetting that occurs when something is so painful or anxiety-laden that remembering it is intolerable.

**motivation** The force that moves people to behave, think, and feel the way they do.

**motor cortex** A region in the cerebral cortex, located just behind the frontal lobes, that processes information about voluntary movement.

**myelin sheath** A layer of fat cells that encases and insulates most axons.

## N

**naturalistic observation** The observation of behavior in a real-world setting.

**natural selection** Darwin's principle of an evolutionary process in which organisms that are best adapted to their environment will survive and produce offspring.

**nature** An individual's biological inheritance, especially his or her genes.

**need** A deprivation that energizes the drive to eliminate or reduce the deprivation.

**negative punishment** The removal of a stimulus following a given behavior in order to decrease the frequency of that behavior.

**negative reinforcement** The removal of a stimulus following a given behavior in order to increase the frequency of that behavior.

**neglectful parenting** A parenting style characterized by a lack of parental involvement in the child's life.

**neocortex** The outermost part of the cerebral cortex, making up 80 percent of the human brain's cortex.

**nervous system** The body's electrochemical communication circuitry.

**neural networks** Networks of nerve cells that integrate sensory input and motor output.

**neurons** One of two types of cells in the nervous system; neurons are the nerve cells that handle the information-processing function.

**neuroscience** The scientific study of the structure, function, development, genetics, and biochemistry of the nervous system, emphasizing that the brain and nervous system are central to understanding behavior, thought, and emotion.

**neurotransmitters** Chemical substances that are stored in very tiny sacs within the neuron's terminal buttons and involved in transmitting information across a synaptic gap to the next neuron.

**noise** Irrelevant and competing stimuli—not only sounds but also any distracting stimuli for the senses.

**normal distribution** A symmetrical, bell-shaped curve, with a majority of test scores (or other data) falling in the middle of the possible range and few scores (or other data points) appearing toward the extremes.

**normative social influence** The influence others have on us because we want them to like us.

**nurture** An individual's environmental and social experiences.

## O

**obedience** Behavior that complies with the explicit demands of the individual in authority.

**object permanence** Piaget's term for the crucial accomplishment of understanding that objects and events continue to exist even when they cannot directly be seen, heard, or touched.

**observational learning** Learning that occurs through observing and imitating another's behavior.

**obsessive-compulsive disorder (OCD)** Anxiety disorder in which the individual has anxiety-provoking thoughts that will not go away and/or urges to perform repetitive, ritualistic behaviors to prevent or produce some future situation.

**occipital lobes** Structures located at the back of the head that respond to visual stimuli.

**Oedipus complex** According to Freud, a boy's intense desire to replace his father and enjoy the affections of his mother.

**olfactory epithelium** The lining of the roof of the nasal cavity, containing a sheet of receptor cells for smell.

**open-mindedness** The state of being receptive to other ways of looking at things.

**operant conditioning (instrumental conditioning)** A form of associative learning in which the consequences of a behavior change the probability of the behavior's occurrence.

**operational definition** A definition that provides an objective description of how a variable is going to be measured and observed in a particular study.

**opiates** Opium and its derivatives; narcotic drugs that depress activity in the central nervous system and eliminate pain.

**opponent-process theory** Theory stating that cells in the visual system respond to complementary pairs of red-green and blue-yellow colors; a given cell might be excited by red and inhibited by green, whereas another cell might be excited by yellow and inhibited by blue.

**optic nerve** The structure at the back of the eye, made up of axons of the ganglion cells, that carries visual information to the brain for further processing.

**outer ear** The outermost part of the ear, consisting of the pinna and the external auditory canal.

**ovaries** Sex-related endocrine glands that produce hormones involved in women's sexual development and reproduction.

**overt aggression** Physical or verbal behavior that directly harms another person.

## P

**pain** The sensation that warns an individual of damage to the body.

**pancreas** A dual-purpose gland under the stomach that performs both digestive and endocrine functions.

**panic disorder** Anxiety disorder in which the individual experiences recurrent, sudden onsets of intense apprehension or terror, often without warning and with no specific cause.

**papillae** Rounded bumps above the tongue's surface that contain the taste buds, the receptors for taste.

**parallel processing** The simultaneous distribution of information across different neural pathways.

**parasympathetic nervous system** The part of the autonomic nervous system that calms the body.

**parietal lobes** Structures at the top and toward the rear of the head that are involved in registering spatial location, attention, and motor control.

**perception** The process of organizing and interpreting sensory information so that it makes sense.

**perceptual constancy** The recognition that objects are constant and unchanging even though sensory input about them is changing.

**perceptual set** A predisposition or readiness to perceive something in a particular way.

**peripheral nervous system (PNS)** The network of nerves that connects the brain and spinal cord to other parts of the body.

**permissive parenting** A parenting style characterized by the placement of few limits on the child's behavior.

**personality** A pattern of enduring, distinctive thoughts, emotions, and behaviors that characterize the way an individual adapts to the world.

**personality disorders** Chronic, maladaptive cognitive-behavioral patterns that are thoroughly integrated into an individual's personality.

**personological and life story perspectives** Theoretical views stressing that the way to understand the person is to focus on his or her life history and life story.

**phenotype** An individual's observable characteristics.

**phobic disorder (phobia)** Anxiety disorder characterized by an irrational, overwhelming, persistent fear of a particular object or situation.

**phonology** A language's sound system.

**physical dependence** The physiological need for a drug that causes unpleasant withdrawal symptoms such as physical pain and a craving for the drug when it is discontinued.

**pituitary gland** A pea-sized gland just beneath the hypothalamus that controls growth and regulates other glands.

**placebo** In a drug study, a harmless substance that has no physiological effect, given to participants in a control group so that they are treated identically to the experimental group except for the active agent.

**placebo effect** The situation where participants' expectations, rather than the experimental treatment, produce an experimental outcome.

**place theory** Theory on how the inner ear registers the frequency of sound, stating that each frequency produces vibrations at a particular spot on the basilar membrane.

**plasticity** The brain's special capacity for change.

**polygraph** A machine, commonly called a lie detector, that monitors changes in the body, and is used to try to determine whether someone is lying.

**population** The entire group about which the researcher wants to draw conclusions.

**positive affect** Pleasant emotions such as joy, happiness, and interest.

**positive illusions** Favorable views of the self that are not necessarily rooted in reality.

**positive punishment** The presentation of a stimulus following a given behavior in order to decrease the frequency of that behavior.

**positive reinforcement** The presentation of a stimulus following a given behavior in order to increase the frequency of that behavior.

**post-traumatic stress disorder (PTSD)** Anxiety disorder that develops through exposure to a traumatic event, a severely oppressive situation, cruel abuse, or a natural or unnatural disaster.

**pragmatics** The useful character of language and the ability of language to communicate even more meaning than is verbalized.

**preferential looking** A research technique that involves giving an infant a choice of what object to look at.

**prefrontal cortex** An important part of the frontal lobes that is involved in higher cognitive functions such as planning, reasoning, and self-control.

**prejudice** An unjustified negative attitude toward an individual based on the individual's membership in a group.

**preoperational stage** Piaget's second stage of cognitive development, lasting from about 2 to 7 years of age, during which thought is more symbolic than sensorimotor thought.

**preparedness** The species-specific biological predisposition to learn in certain ways but not others.

**primary reinforcer** A reinforcer that is innately satisfying; one that does not take any learning on the organism's part to make it pleasurable.

**priming** The activation of information that people already have in storage to help them remember new information better and faster.

**proactive interference** Situation in which material that was learned earlier disrupts the recall of material that was learned later.

**problem-focused coping** The coping strategy of squarely facing one's troubles and trying to solve them.

**problem solving** The mental process of finding an appropriate way to attain a goal when the goal is not readily available.

**procedural memory** Memory for skills.

**projective test** A personality assessment test that presents individuals with an ambiguous stimulus and asks them to describe it or tell a story about it—to project their own meaning onto the stimulus.

**prosocial behavior** Behavior that is intended to benefit other people.

**prospective memory** Remembering information about doing something in the future; includes memory for intentions.

**prototype model** A model emphasizing that when people evaluate whether a given item reflects a certain concept, they compare the item with the most typical item(s) in that category and look for a "family resemblance" with that item's properties.

**psychoactive drugs** Drugs that act on the nervous system to alter consciousness, modify perception, and change moods.

**psychoanalysis** Freud's therapeutic technique for analyzing an individual's unconscious thoughts.

**psychodynamic approach** An approach to psychology emphasizing unconscious thought, the conflict between biological drives (such as the drive for sex) and society's demands, and early childhood family experiences.

**psychodynamic perspectives** Theoretical views emphasizing that personality is primarily unconscious (beyond awareness).

**psychodynamic therapies** Treatments that stress the importance of the unconscious mind, extensive interpretation by the therapist, and the role of early childhood experiences in the development of an individual's problems.

**psychological dependence** The strong desire to repeat the use of a drug for emotional reasons, such as a feeling of well-being and reduction of stress.

**psychology** The scientific study of behavior and mental processes.

**psychoneuroimmunology** A new field of scientific inquiry that explores connections among psychological factors (such as attitudes and emotions), the nervous system, and the immune system.

**psychosurgery** A biological therapy, with irreversible effects, that involves removal or destruction of brain tissue to improve the individual's adjustment.

**psychotherapy** A nonmedical process that helps individuals with psychological disorders recognize and overcome their problems.

**puberty** A period of rapid skeletal and sexual maturation that occurs mainly in early adolescence.

**punishment** A consequence that decreases the likelihood that a behavior will occur.

# R

**random assignment** Researchers' assignment of participants to groups by chance, to reduce the likelihood that an experiment's results will be due to preexisting differences between groups.

**random sample** A sample that gives every member of the population an equal chance of being selected.

**rational-emotive behavior therapy (REBT)** A therapy based on Ellis's assertion that individuals develop a psychological disorder because of irrational and self-defeating beliefs and whose goal is to get clients to eliminate these beliefs by rationally examining them.

**reasoning** The mental activity of transforming information to reach conclusions.

**referential thinking** Ascribing personal meaning to completely random events.

**reflective speech** A technique in which the therapist mirrors the client's own feelings back to the client.

**reinforcement** The process by which a stimulus or an event (a reinforcer) following a particular behavior increases the probability that the behavior will happen again.

**relapse** A return to former unhealthy patterns.

**relational aggression** Behavior that is meant to harm the social standing of another person.

**reliability** The extent to which a test yields a consistent, reproducible measure of performance.

**REM sleep** An active stage of sleep during which dreaming occurs.

**representativeness heuristic** The tendency to make judgments about group membership based on physical appearances or the match between a person and one's stereotype of a group rather than on available base rate information.

**research participant bias** In an experiment, the influence of participants' expectations, and of their thoughts on how they should behave, on their behavior.

**resilience** A person's ability to recover from or adapt to difficult times.

**resistance** A client's unconscious defense strategies that interfere with the psychoanalyst's understanding of the individual's problems.

**resting potential** The stable, negative charge of an inactive neuron.

**reticular formation** A system in the midbrain comprising a diffuse collection of neurons involved in stereotyped patterns of behavior such as walking, sleeping, and turning to attend to a sudden noise.

**retina** The multilayered light-sensitive surface in the eye that records electromagnetic energy and converts it to neural impulses for processing in the brain.

**retrieval** The memory process that occurs when information that was retained in memory comes out of storage.

**retroactive interference** Situation in which material that was learned later disrupts the retrieval of information that was learned earlier.

**retrograde amnesia** Memory loss for a segment of the past but not for new events.

**retrospective memory** Remembering information from the past.

**risky shift** The tendency for a group decision to be riskier than the average decision made by the individual group members.

**rods** The receptor cells in the retina that are sensitive to light but not very useful for color vision.

**romantic love** Love with strong components of sexuality and infatuation, often predominant in the early part of a love relationship; also called passionate love.

**Rorschach inkblot test** A famous projective test that uses an individual's perception of inkblots to determine his or her personality.

# S

**sample** The subset of the population chosen by the investigator for study.

**schedules of reinforcement** Specific patterns that determine when a behavior will be reinforced.

**schema** A preexisting mental concept or framework that helps people to organize and interpret information. Schemas from prior encounters with the environment influence the way individuals encode, make inferences about, and retrieve information.

**schizophrenia** Severe psychological disorder characterized by highly disordered thought processes; individuals suffering from schizophrenia may be referred to as psychotic because they are so far removed from reality.

**science** The use of systematic methods to observe the natural world, including human behavior, and to draw conclusions.

**script** A schema for an event, often containing information about physical features, people, and typical occurrences.

**secondary reinforcer** A reinforcer that acquires its positive value through an organism's experience; a secondary reinforcer is a learned or conditioned reinforcer.

**secure attachment** The ways that infants use their caregiver, usually their mother, as a secure base from which to explore the environment.

**secure attachment style** An attachment style that describes adults who have positive views of relationships, find it easy to get close to others, and are not overly concerned or stressed out about their romantic relationships.

**selective attention** The act of focusing on a specific aspect of experience while ignoring others.

**self-actualization** The motivation to develop one's full potential as a human being—the highest and most elusive of Maslow's proposed needs.

**self-determination theory** Deci and Ryan's theory asserting that all humans have three basic, innate organismic needs: competence, relatedness, and autonomy.

**self-efficacy** The belief that one can master a situation and produce positive change.

**self-perception theory** Bem's theory on how behaviors influence attitudes, stating that individuals make inferences about their attitudes by perceiving their behavior.

**self-regulation** The process by which an organism effortfully controls its behavior in order to pursue important objectives.

**self-report test** Also called an objective test or an inventory, a method of measuring personality characteristics that directly asks people whether specific items describe their personality traits.

**self-serving bias** The tendency to take credit for one's own successes and to deny responsibility for one's own failures.

**semantic memory** A person's knowledge about the world.

**semantics** The meaning of words and sentences in a particular language.

**semicircular canals** Three fluid-filled circular tubes in the inner ear containing the sensory receptors that detect head motion caused when an individual tilts or moves the head and/or the body.

**sensation** The process of receiving stimulus energies from the external environment and transforming those energies into neural energy.

**sensorimotor stage** Piaget's first stage of cognitive development, lasting from birth to about 2 years of age, during which infants construct an understanding of the world by coordinating sensory experiences with motor (physical) actions.

**sensory adaptation** A change in the responsiveness of the sensory system based on the average level of surrounding stimulation.

**sensory memory** Memory system that involves holding information from the world in its original sensory form for only an instant, not much longer than the brief time it is exposed to the visual, auditory, and other senses.

**sensory receptors** Specialized cells that detect stimulus information and transmit it to sensory (afferent) nerves and the brain.

**serial position effect** The tendency to recall the items at the beginning and end of a list more readily than those in the middle.

**set point** The weight maintained when the individual makes no effort to gain or lose weight.

**sexual harassment** Unwelcome behavior of a sexual nature that offends, humiliates, or intimidates another person.

**sexually transmitted infection (STI)** An infection that is contracted primarily through sexual activity—vaginal intercourse as well as oral and anal sex.

**sexual orientation** The direction of an individual's erotic interests, today viewed as a continuum from exclusive male–female relations to exclusive same-sex relations.

**shaping** Rewarding successive approximations of a desired behavior.

**short-term memory** Limited-capacity memory system in which information is usually retained for only as long as 30 seconds unless strategies are used to retain it longer.

**signal detection theory** An approach to perception that focuses on decision making about stimuli in the presence of uncertainty.

**sleep** A natural state of rest for the body and mind that involves the reversible loss of consciousness.

**social cognitive behavior view of hypnosis** The perspective that hypnosis is a normal state in which the hypnotized person behaves the way he or she believes that a hypnotized person should behave.

**social cognitive perspectives** Theoretical views emphasizing conscious awareness, beliefs, expectations, and goals.

**social comparison** The process by which individuals evaluate their thoughts, feelings, behaviors, and abilities in relation to others.

**social contagion** Imitative behavior involving the spread of behavior, emotions, and ideas.

**social exchange theory** The view of social relationships as involving an exchange of goods, the objective of which is to minimize costs and maximize benefits.

**social facilitation** Improvement in an individual's performance because of the presence of others.

**social identity** The way individuals define themselves in terms of their group membership.

**social identity theory** The view that social identity is a crucial part of self-image and a valuable source of positive feelings about oneself.

**social loafing** Each person's tendency to exert less effort in a group because of reduced accountability for individual effort.

**social psychology** The study of how people think about, influence, and relate to other people.

**social support** Information and feedback from others indicating that one is loved and cared for, esteemed and valued, and included in a network of communication and mutual obligation.

**sociocultural approach** An approach to psychology that examines the ways in which social and cultural environments influence behavior.

**somatic nervous system** The body system consisting of the sensory nerves, whose function is to convey information from the skin and muscles to the central nervous system about conditions such as pain and temperature, and the motor nerves, whose function is to tell muscles what to do.

**somatosensory cortex** A region in the cerebral cortex that processes information about body sensations, located at the front of the parietal lobes.

**spontaneous recovery** The process in classical conditioning by which a conditioned response can recur after a time delay, without further conditioning.

**stages of change model** Theoretical model describing a five-step process by which individuals give up bad habits and adopt healthier lifestyles.

**standardization** The development of uniform procedures for administering and scoring a test, and the creation of norms (performance standards) for the test.

**stem cells** Unique primitive cells that have the capacity to develop into most types of human cells.

**stereotype** A generalization about a group's characteristics that does not consider any variations from one individual to another.

**stereotype threat** An individual's fast-acting, self-fulfilling fear of being judged based on a negative stereotype about his or her group.

**stimulants** Psychoactive drugs, including caffeine, nicotine, amphetamines, and cocaine, that that increase the central nervous system's activity.

**storage** The retention of information over time and how this information is represented in memory.

**stream of consciousness** Term used by William James to describe the mind as a continuous flow of changing sensations, images, thoughts, and feelings.

**stress** The responses of individuals to environmental stressors.

**stress management program** A regimen that teaches individuals how to appraise stressful events, how to develop skills for coping with stress, and how to put these skills into use in everyday life.

**stressors** Circumstances and events that threaten individuals and tax their coping abilities and that cause physiological changes to ready the body to handle the assault of stress.

**structuralism** Wundt's approach to discovering the basic elements, or structures, of mental processes.

**subgoaling** Setting intermediate goals or intermediate problems in order to be in a better position for reaching the final goal or solution.

**subjective well-being** A person's assessment of his or her own level of positive affect relative to negative affect, and an evaluation of his or her life in general.

**subliminal perception** The detection of information below the level of conscious awareness.

**superego** The Freudian structure of personality that serves as the harsh internal judge of our behavior; what we often call conscience.

**suprachiasmatic nucleus (SCN)** A small brain structure that uses input from the retina to synchronize its own rhythm with the daily cycle of light and dark; the body's way of monitoring the change from day to night.

**sustained attention** The ability to maintain attention to a selected stimulus for a prolonged period of time.

**sympathetic nervous system** The part of the autonomic nervous system that arouses the body to mobilize it for action and thus is involved in the experience of stress.

**synapses** Tiny spaces between neurons; the gaps between neurons are referred to as synaptic gaps.

**syntax** A language's rules for combining words to form acceptable phrases and sentences.

**systematic desensitization** A behavior therapy that treats anxiety by teaching the client to associate deep relaxation with increasingly intense anxiety-producing situations.

**T**

**temperament** An individual's behavioral style and characteristic way of responding.

**temporal lobes** Structures in the cerebral cortex that are located just above the ears and are involved in hearing, language processing, and memory.

**testes** Sex-related endocrine glands in the scrotum that produce hormones involved in men's sexual development and reproduction.

**thalamus** The forebrain structure that sits at the top of the brain stem in the brain's central core and serves as an important relay station.

**Thematic Apperception Test (TAT)** A projective test that is designed to elicit stories that reveal something about an individual's personality.

**theory** A broad idea or set of closely related ideas that attempts to explain observations and to make predictions about future observations.

**theory of mind** Individuals' understanding that they and others think, feel, perceive, and have private experiences.

**theory of planned behavior** Theoretical model that includes the basic ideas of the theory of reasoned action but adds the person's perceptions of control over the outcome.

**theory of reasoned action** Theoretical model stating that effective change requires individuals to have specific intentions about their behaviors, as well as positive attitudes about a new behavior, and to perceive that their social group looks positively on the new behavior as well.

**therapeutic alliance** The relationship between the therapist and client—an important element of successful psychotherapy.

**thermoreceptors** Sensory nerve endings under the skin that respond to changes in temperature at or near the skin and provide input to keep the body's temperature at 98.6 degrees Fahrenheit.

**thinking** The process of manipulating information mentally by forming concepts, solving problems, making decisions, and reflecting critically or creatively.

**third variable problem** The circumstance where a variable that has not been measured accounts for the relationship between two other variables. Third variables are also known as confounds.

**tip-of-the-tongue (TOT) phenomenon** A type of effortful retrieval associated with a person's feeling that he or she knows something (say, a word or a name) but cannot quite pull it out of memory.

**tolerance** The need to take increasing amounts of a drug to get the same effect.

**top-down processing** The operation in sensation and perception, launched by cognitive processing at the brain's higher levels, that allows the organism to sense what is happening and to apply that framework to information from the world.

**trait theories** Theoretical views stressing that personality consists of broad, enduring dispositions (traits) that tend to lead to characteristic responses.

**tranquilizers** Depressant drugs, such as Valium and Xanax, that reduce anxiety and induce relaxation.

**transference** A client's relating to the psychoanalyst in ways that reproduce or relive important relationships in the individual's life.

**triarchic theory of intelligence** Sternberg's theory that intelligence comes in three forms: analytical, creative, and practical.

**trichromatic theory** Theory stating that color perception is produced by three types of cone receptors in the retina that are particularly sensitive to different, but overlapping, ranges of wavelengths.

**two-factor theory of emotion** Schachter and Singer's theory that emotion is determined by two factors: physiological arousal and cognitive labeling.

**Type A behavior pattern** A cluster of characteristics—including being excessively competitive, hard-driven, impatient, and hostile—that are related to a higher incidence of heart disease.

**Type B behavior pattern** A cluster of characteristics—including being relaxed and easygoing—that are related to a lower incidence of heart disease.

**Type D behavior pattern** A cluster of characteristics—including being generally distressed, having negative emotions, and being socially inhibited—that are related to adverse cardiovascular outcomes.

**U**

**unconditional positive regard** Rogers's construct referring to the individual's need to be accepted, valued, and treated positively regardless of his or her behavior.

**unconditioned response (UR)** An unlearned reaction that is automatically elicited by the unconditioned stimulus.

**unconditioned stimulus (US)** A stimulus that produces a response without prior learning.

**unconscious thought** According to Freud, a reservoir of unacceptable wishes, feelings, and thoughts that are beyond conscious awareness.

**V**

**validity** The soundness of the conclusions that a researcher draws from an experiment. In the realm of testing, the extent to which a test measures what it is intended to measure.

**variable** Anything that can change.

**visual cortex** Located in the occipital lobe, the part of the cerebral cortex involved in vision.

**vestibular sense** Sense that provides information about balance and movement.

**volley principle** Principle addressing limitations of the frequency theory of hearing, stating that a cluster of nerve cells can fire neural impulses in rapid succession, producing a volley of impulses.

**W**

**Weber's law** The principle that two stimuli must differ by a constant minimum percentage (rather than a constant amount) to be perceived as different.

**well-being therapy (WBT)** A short-term (eight sessions), problem-focused, directive therapy that encourages clients to accentuate the positive.

**wisdom** Expert knowledge about the practical aspects of life.

**working memory** A combination of components, including short-term memory and attention, that allow individuals to hold information temporarily as they perform cognitive tasks; a kind of mental workbench on which the brain manipulates and assembles information to guide understanding, decision making, and problem solving.

**Y**

**Yerkes-Dodson law** The psychological principle stating that performance is best under conditions of moderate arousal rather than either low or high arousal.

Berkowitz, L., & LePage, A. (1996). Weapons as aggression-eliciting stimuli. In S. Fein & S. Spencer (Eds.), *Readings in social psychology: The art and science of research* (pp. 67–73). Boston: Houghton Mifflin.

Bernardy, N. C., Lund, B. C., Alexander, B., & Friedman, M. J. (2012). Prescribing trends in veterans with posttraumatic stress disorder. *Journal of Clinical Psychiatry, 73,* 297–319.

Berndt, N. C., Hayes, A. F., Verboon, P., Lechner, L., Bolman, C., & De Vries, H. (2012). Self-efficacy mediates the impact of craving on smoking abstinence in low to moderately anxious patients: Results of a moderated mediation approach. *Psychology of Addictive Behaviors.* (in press)

Berntsen, D., & Rubin, D. C. (2002). Emotionally charged autobiographical memories across the life span: The recall of happy, sad, traumatic, and involuntary memories. *Psychology and Aging, 17,* 636–652.

Berridge, K. C., & Kringelbach, M. L. (2008). Affective neuroscience of pleasure: Reward in humans and animals. *Psychopharmacology, 199,* 457–480.

Berscheid, E. (1988). Some comments on love's anatomy. Or, whatever happened to an old-fashioned lust? In R. J. Sternberg & M. L. Barnes (Eds.), *Anatomy of love.* New Haven, CT: Yale University Press.

Berscheid, E. (2000). Attraction. In A. Kazdin (Ed.), *Encyclopedia of psychology.* Washington, DC, & New York: American Psychological Association and Oxford University Press.

Berscheid, E. (2010). Love in the fourth dimension. *Annual Review of Psychology* (vol. 61). Palo Alto, CA: Annual Reviews.

Berscheid, E., & Regan, P. C. (2005). *The psychology of interpersonal relationships.* New York: Prentice-Hall.

Berthet, A., & others. (2012). L-dopa impairs proteasome activity in Parkinsonism through D1 dopamine receptor. *Journal of Neuroscience.* (in press)

Bertrand, M., & Mullainathan, S. (2004). Are Emily and Greg more employable than Lakisha and Jamal? A field experiment on labor market discrimination. *American Economic Review, 94,* 991–1013.

Besedovsky, L., Lange, T., & Born, J. (2012). Sleep and immune function. *European Journal of Physiology, 463,* 121–137.

Beutel, M. E., & others. (2012). Type D personality as a cardiovascular risk marker in the general population: Results from the Gutenberg study. *Psychotherapy and Psychosomatics, 81,* 108–117.

Bewernick, B. H., Kayser, S., Sturm, V., & Schlaepfer, T. E. (2012). Long-term effects of nucleus accumbens deep brain stimulation in treatment-resistant depression: Evidence for sustained efficacy. *Neuropsychopharmacology.* doi: 10.1038/npp.2012.44

Beydoun, M. A., & Wang, Y. (2009). Gender-ethnic disparity in BMI and waist circumference distribution shifts in U.S. adults. *Obesity, 17,* 169–176.

Bhatia, T., Garg, K., Pogue-Geile, M., Nimaonkar, V. L., & Deshpande, S. N. (2009). Executive functions and cognitive deficits in schizophrenia: Comparisons between probands, parents, and controls in India. *Journal of Postgraduate Medicine, 55,* 3–7.

Bhattacharya, G. (2012). Psychosocial impacts of type 2 diabetes self-management in a rural African-American population. *Journal of Immigrant and Minority Health.* doi: 10.1007/s10903-012-9585-7

Bhugra, D. (2006). Severe mental illness across cultures. *Acta Psychiatrica Scandinavica, 113,* 17–23.

Bielak, A. A. M., Anstey, K. J., Christensen, H., & Windsor, T. D. (2012). Activity engagement is related to level, but not change in cognitive ability across adulthood. *Psychology and Aging, 27,* 219–228.

Biernat, M., & Deaux, K. (2012). History of social psychology research on gender. In A. W. Kruglanski & W. Stroebe (Eds.), *Handbook of the history of social psychology.* New York: Psychology Press.

Billig, M. (2012). The notion of "prejudice": Some rhetorical and ideological aspects. In J. Dixon & M. Levine (Eds.), *Beyond prejudice: Extending the social psychology of conflict, inequality, and social change* (pp. 139–157). Cambridge, England: Cambridge University Press.

Birditt, K. S., & Fingerman, K. L. (2003). Age and gender differences in adults' descriptions of emotional reactions to interpersonal problems. *Journals of Gerontology: Series B: Psychological Sciences and Social Sciences, 58B,* 237–245.

Birgegård, A., Norring, C., & Clinton, D. (2012). DSM-IV versus DSM-5: Implementation of proposed DSM-5 criteria in a large natural database. *International Journal of Eating Disorders, 45,* 353–361.

Bisgaard, H., Jensen, S. M., & Bonnelykke, K. (2012). Interaction between asthma and lung function growth in early life. *American Journal of Respiratory and Critical Care Medicine.* (in press)

Biswas-Diener, R., Vitterso, J., & Diener, E. (2005). Most people are pretty happy, but there is cultural variation: The Inughuit, the Amish, and the Maasai. *Journal of Happiness Studies, 6,* 205–226.

Bjork, R. A., Dunlosky, J., & Kornell, N. (2013). Self-regulated learning: Beliefs, techniques, and illusions. *Annual Review of Psychology* (vol. 64). Palo Alto, CA: Annual Reviews.

Bjorklund, D. F. (2012). *Children's thinking* (5th ed.). Boston: Cengage.

BKA. (2006). German federal crime statistics (German). www.bka.de/pks/pks2004/index2.html

Blader, J. C. (2006). Pharmacotherapy and postdischarge outcomes of child inpatients admitted for aggressive behavior. *Journal of Clinical Psychopharmacology, 26,* 419–425.

Blagrove, M., & Akehurst, L. (2000). Personality and dream recall frequency: Further negative findings. *Dreaming, 10,* 139–148.

Blagrove, M., & others. (2011). Assessing the dream-lag effect for REM and NREM stage 2 dreams. *PLoS One, 6* (10), e26708.

Blakemore, J. E. O., Berenbaum, S. E., & Liben, L. S. (2009). *Gender development.* New York: Psychology Press.

Blanco, C., & others. (2012). Differences among major depressive disorder with and without co-occurring substance use disorders and substance-induced depressive disorder: Results from the National Epidemiologic Survey on Alcohol and Related Conditions. *Journal of Clinical Psychiatry.* (in press)

Blanco, M., & others. (2009). *Investigating critical incidents, driver restart period, sleep quantity, and crash countermeasures in commercial operations using naturalistic data collection: A final report* (Contract No. DTFH61-01-00049, Task Order #23). Washington, DC: Federal Motor Carrier Safety Administration.

Blanton, H., Jaccard, J., Klick, J., Mellers, B., Mitchell, G., & Tetlock, P. E. (2009). Strong claims and weak evidence: Reassessing the predictive validity of the IAT. *Journal of Applied Psychology, 94,* 567–582.

Blass, R. B. (2012). The ego according to Klein: Return to Freud and beyond. *International Journal of Psychoanalysis, 93,* 151–166.

Blass, T. (2007). Unsupported allegations about a link between Milgram and the CIA: Tortured reasoning in *A Question of Torture. Journal of the History of the Behavioral Sciences, 43,* 199–203.

Blickle, G., Wendel, S., & Ferris, G. R. (2010). Political skill as moderator of personality—Job performance relationships in socioanalytic theory: Test of the getting ahead motive in automobile sales. *Journal of Vocational Behavior, 76,* 326–335.

Block, J. (1982). Assimilation, accommodation, and the dynamics of personality development. *Child Development, 53,* 281–295.

Block, J. (2010). The five-factor framing of personality and beyond: Some ruminations. *Psychological Inquiry, 21,* 2–25.

Block, J., & Kremen, A. M. (1996). IQ and ego-resiliency: Conceptual and empirical connections and separateness. *Journal of Personality and Social Psychology, 70,* 349–361.

Block, S. D., Shestowsky, D., Segovi+47a, D. A., Goodman, G. S., Schaaf, J. M., & Alexander, K. W. (2012). "That never happened": Adults' discernment of children's true and false memory reports. *Law and Human Behavior.* (in press)

Bloom, B. (1985). *Developing talent in young people.* New York: Ballantine.

Bloom B., & Cohen, R. A. (2007). Summary health statistics for U.S. children: National Health Interview Survey, 2006. National Center for Health Statistics. *Vital Health Statistics, 10* (234).

Bloom, F., Nelson, C. A., & Lazerson, A. (2001). *Brain, mind, and behavior* (3rd ed.). New York: Worth.

Bloom, M. (2005). *Dying to kill: The allure of suicide terrorism.* New York: Columbia University Press.

Bloom, P. (2004). Myths of word learning. In D. G. Hall & S. R. Waxman (Eds.), *Weaving a lexicon* (pp. 205–224). Cambridge, MA: MIT Press.

Bloor, C., & White, F. (1983). Unpublished manuscript. La Jolla: University of California, San Diego.

Blumenfeld, P. C., Kempler, T. M., & Krajcik, J. S. (2006). Motivation and cognitive engagement in learning environments. In R. K. Sawyer (Ed.), *The Cambridge handbook of learning sciences.* New York: Cambridge University Press.

Boals, A., & Rubin, D. C. (2011). The integration of emotions in traumatic memories: Cognitive-emotional distinctiveness and posttraumatic stress disorder. *Applied Cognitive Psychology, 25,* 811–816.

Boeddeker, N., & Hemmi, J. M. (2010). Visual gaze control during peering flight manoeuvres in honeybees. *Proceedings. Biological Sciences, 277,* 1209–1217.

Boehm, J. K., & Kubzansky, L. D. (2012). The heart's content: The association between positive psychological well-being and cardiovascular health. *Psychological Bulletin.* doi: 10.1037/a0027448

Boeninger, D. K., Shiraishi, R. W., Aldwin, C. M., & Spiro, A. (2009). Why do older men report lower stress ratings? Findings from the Normative Aging Study. *International Journal of Aging and Human Development, 2,* 149–170.

Boersma, G. J., & others. (2012). Models and mechanisms of metabolic regulation: Genes, stress, and the HPA and HPG axes. *Hormone and Metabolic Research.* doi: 10.1055/s-0032-1311576

Bogaert, A. F. (2000). Birth order and sexual orientation in a national probability sample. *Journal of Sex Research, 37,* 361–368.

Bohbot, V. D., Anderson, N., Trowbridge, A., Sham, R., Konishi, K., Kurdi, V., & Behrer, L. (2011, November 16). *A spatial memory intervention program aimed at stimulating the hippocampus while controlling for caudate nucleus-dependent response strategies led to significant improvements on independent virtual navigation tasks in healthy elderly.* Society for Neuroscience Convention. Washington, DC.

Bolger, N., & Amarel, D. (2007). Effects of social support visibility on adjustment to stress: Experimental evidence. *Journal of Personality and Social Psychology, 92,* 458–475.

Bolhuis, J. J., Brown, G. R., Richardson, R. C., & Laland, K. N. (2011). Darwin in mind: New opportunities in evolutionary psychology. *PLoS Biology, 9* (7), e1001109.

Bonanno, G. A. (2004). Loss, trauma, and human resilience: Have we underestimated the human capacity to thrive after extremely aversive events? *American Psychologist, 59,* 20–28.

Bonanno, G. A. (2005). Resilience in the face of potential trauma. *Current Directions in Psychological Science, 14,* 135–138.

Bonanno, G. A., Westphal, M., Mancini, A. D. (2011). Resilience to loss and potential trauma. *Annual Review of Clinical Psychology, 7,* 511–535.

Bonchek, A. (2009). What's broken with cognitive behavior therapy treatment of obsessive-compulsive disorder and how to fix it. *American Journal of Psychotherapy, 63,* 69–86.

Bond, R., & Smith, P. B. (1996). Culture and conformity: A meta-analysis of studies using Asch's (1952, 1956) line judgment task. *Psychological Bulletin, 119,* 111–137.

Bonds-Raache, J., & Raache, J. (2012). *Research methods.* Upper Saddle River, NJ: Pearson.

Bonfatti, J. F. (2005). Hope holds the key: Finding inspiration. *Schizophrenia Digest* (Summer), 31–34.

Bonney, C. R., & Sternberg, R. J. (2011). Teaching and learning to think critically. In R. E. Mayer & P. A. Alexander (Eds.), *Handbook of research on learning and instruction.* New York: Routledge.

Boothroyd, R. A., Best, K. A., Giard, J. A., Stiles, P. G., Suleski, J., Ort, R., & White, R. (2006). Poor and depressed, The tip of the iceberg: The unmet needs of enrollees in an indigent health care plan. *Adminstration and Policy in Mental Health and Mental Health Services Research, 33,* 172–181.

**Borden, W., & Clark, J. J.** (2012). Contemporary psychodynamic theory, research, and practice: Implications for evidence-based intervention. In T. L. Rzepnicki, S. G. McCracken, & H. E. Briggs (Eds.), *From task-centered social work to evidence-based and integrative practice: Reflections on history and implementation* (pp. 65–87). Chicago: Lyceum Books.

**Bornstein, R. F.** (2012). Rorschach score validation as a model for 21st century personality assessment. *Journal of Personality Assessment, 94,* 26–38.

**Borst, A., Haag, J., & Reiff, D. F.** (2010). Fly motion vision. *Annual Review of Neuroscience* (vol. 33). Palo Alto, CA: Annual Reviews.

**Boschen, M. J.** (2012). Pregabalin: Dose-response relationship in generalized anxiety disorder. *Pharmacopsychiatry, 45,* 51–56.

**Bosson, J. K., & Swann, W. B.** (2009). Self-esteem. In M. R. Leary & R. H. Hoyle (Eds.), *Handbook of individual differences in social behavior* (pp. 527–546). New York: Guilford.

**Bouchard, S. M., Brown, T. G., & Nadeau, L.** (2012). Decision-making capacities and affective reward anticipation in DWI recidivists compared to non-offenders: A preliminary study. *Accident: Analysis and Prevention, 45,* 580–587.

**Bouchard, T. J., Jr., & Loehlin, J. C.** (2001). Genes, evolution, and personality. *Behavior Genetics, 31,* 243–273.

**Bouchard, T. J., Lykken, D. T., Tellegen, A., & McGue, M.** (1996). Genes, drives, environment, and experience. In D. Lubinski & C. Benbow (Eds.), *Psychometrics and social issues concerning intellectual talent.* Baltimore: Johns Hopkins University Press.

**Bourque, F., van der Ven, E., Fusar-Poli, P., & Malla, A.** (2012). Immigration, social environment, and onset of psychotic disorders. *Current Pharmaceutical Design, 18,* 518–526.

**Bow, J. N., Flens, J. R., & Gould, J. W.** (2010). MMPI-2 and MCMI-III in forensic evaluations: A survey of psychologists. *Journal of Forensic Psychology Practice, 10,* 37–52.

**Bowlby, J.** (1969). *Attachment and loss* (vol. 1). London: Hogarth Press.

**Bowlby, J.** (1989). *Secure and insecure attachment.* New York: Basic Books.

**Bowman, N. A.** (2010). College diversity experiences and cognitive development: A meta-analysis. *Review of Educational Research, 80,* 4–33.

**Boyd, J. H.** (2008). Have we found the holy grail? Theory of mind as a unifying concept. *Journal of Religion and Health, 47,* 366–385.

**Boywitt, C. D., & Meiser, T.** (2012). The role of attention for context-context binding of intrinsic and extrinsic features. *Journal of Experimental Psychology: Learning, Memory, and Cognition.* doi: 10.1037/a0026988.

**Brabec, J., & others.** (2011). Volume of the amygdala is reduced in patients with narcolepsy—a structural MRI study. *Neuroendocrinology Letters, 32,* 652–656.

**Brackett, M. A., Rivers, S. E., & Salovey, P.** (2011). Emotional intelligence: Implications for personal, social, academic, and workplace success. *Social and Personality Psychology Compass, 5,* 88–103.

**Brakel, T. M., Dijkstra, A., & Buunk, A. P.** (2012). Effects of the source of social comparison information on former cancer patients' quality of life. *British Journal of Health Psychology.* doi: 10.1111/j.2044-8287.2012.02064.x

**Brand, B. L., Lanius, R., Vermetten, E., Loewenstein, R. J., & Spiegel, D.** (2012). Where are we going? An update on assessment, treatment, and neurobiological research in dissociative disorders as we move toward DSM-5. *Journal of Trauma and Dissociation, 13* (1), 9–31.

**Brannon, L.** (1999). *Gender: Psychological perspectives* (2nd ed.). Boston: Allyn & Bacon.

**Bransford, J., & others.** (2006). Learning theories and education: Toward a decade of synergy. In P. A. Alexander & P.H. Winne (Eds.), *Handbook of educational psychology* (2nd ed.). Mahwah, NJ: Erlbaum.

**Brass, M., Schmitt, R. M., Spengler, S., & Gergely, G.** (2007). Investigation action understanding: Inferential processes vs. action simulation. *Current Biology, 17,* 2117–2121.

**Braucher, J., Cohen, D., & Lawless, R. M.** (2012). Race, attorney Influence, and bankruptcy chapter choice. *Journal of Empirical Legal Studies,* forthcoming, Arizona Legal Studies Discussion Paper No. 12-02. Available at SSRN: http://papers.ssrn.com/sol3/papers.cfm?abstract_id=1989039 (accessed May 22, 2012)

**Braun, M. H., Lukowiak, K., Karnik, V., & Lukowiak, K.** (2012). Differences in neuronal activity explain differences in memory forming abilities of different populations of *Lymnaea stagnalis. Neurobiology of Learning and Memory, 97,* 173–182.

**Braunstein, G. D.** (2007). Management of female sexual dysfunction in postmenopausal women by testosterone administration: Safety issues and controversies. *Journal of Sexual Medicine, 4,* 859–866.

**Breland, K., & Breland, M.** (1961). The misbehavior of organisms. *American Psychologist,16,* 681–684.

**Brendgen, M., Boivin, M., Vitaro, F., Bukowski, W. M., Dionne, G., Tremblay, R. E., & Perusse, D.** (2008). Linkages between children's and their friends' social and physical aggression: Evidence for a gene–environment interaction? *Child Development, 79,* 13–29.

**Brewer, J. B., Zuo, Z., Desmond, J. E., Glover, G. H., & Gabrieli, J. D. E.** (1998). Making memories: Brain activity that predicts how well visual experience will be remembered. *Science, 281,* 1185–1187.

**Brewer, N., Barnes, J., & Sauer, J.** (2011). The effects of peripheral message cues on clinicians' judgments about clients' psychological status. *British Journal of Clinical Psychology. 50,* 67–83.

**Brewer, N., & Wells, G. L.** (2011). Eyewitness identification. *Current Directions in Psychological Science, 20,* 24–27.

**Brewin, C. R.** (2012). A theoretical framework for understanding recovered memory experiences. *Nebraska Symposium on Motivation, 58,* 148–173.

**Brewin, C. R., Andrews, B., Hejdenberg, J., & Stewart, L.** (2012). Objective predictors of delayed-onset post-traumatic stress disorder occurring after military discharge. *Psychological Medicine.* (in press)

**Brickman, P., & Campbell, D. T.** (1971). Hedonic relativism and planning the good society. In M. H. Appley (Ed.), *Adaptation-level theory* (pp. 287–302). New York: Academic.

**Bridge, J. A., & others.** (2008). Suicide trends among youth aged 10 to 19 years in the United States, 1996–2005. *Journal of the American Medical Association, 300,* 1025–1026.

**Brigham, J. C.** (1986). Race and eyewitness identifications. In S. Worschel & W. G. Austin (Eds.), *Psychology of intergroup relations.* Chicago: Nelson-Hall.

**Brigham, J. C., Bennett, L. B., Meissner, C. A., & Mitchell, T. L.** (2007). The influence of race on eyewitness memory. In R. C. L. Lindsay, D. F. Ross, J. D. Read, & M. P. Toglia (Eds.), *The handbook of eyewitness memory* (vol. 2). Mahwah, NJ: Erlbaum.

**Brink, S.** (2001, May 7). Your brain on alcohol. *U.S. News & World Report, 130* (18), 50–57.

**Brinol, P., & Petty, R. E.** (2012). History of attitudes and persuasion research. In A. W. Kruglanski & W. Stroebe (Eds.), *Handbook of the history of social psychology.* New York: Psychology Press.

**Brito-Melo, G. E., & others.** (2012). Increase in dopaminergic, but not serotoninergic, receptors in T-cells as a marker for schizophrenia severity. *Journal of Psychiatric Research.* (in press)

**Britton, W. B., Shahar, B., Szepsenwol, O., & Jacobs, W. J.** (2012). Mindfulness-based cognitive therapy improves emotional reactivity to social stress: Results from a randomized controlled trial. *Behavior Therapy, 43,* 365–380.

**Broadbent, E., & Koschwanez, H. E.** (2012). The psychology of wound healing. *Current Opinion in Psychiatry, 25,* 135–140.

**Broberg, D. J., & Bernstein, I. L.** (1987). Candy as a scapegoat in the prevention of food aversions in children receiving chemotherapy. *Cancer, 60,* 2344–2347.

**Brodbeck, F. C., Guillaume, Y. R. F., & Lee, N.** (2011). Ethnic diversity as a multilevel construct: The combined effects of dissimilarity, group diversity, and societal status on learning performance in work groups. *Journal of Cross-Cultural Psychology, 42,* 1198–1218.

**Brody, L. R.** (1999). Gender emotion and the family. Cambridge, MA: Harvard University Press.

**Brody, N.** (2007). Does education influence intelligence? In P. C. Kyllonen, R. D. Roberts, & L. Stankov (Eds.), *Extending intelligence.* Mahwah, NJ: Erlbaum.

**Brody, S., & Costa, R. M.** (2009). Satisfaction (sexual, life, relationship, and mental health) is associated directly with penile-vaginal intercourse, but inversely with other sexual behavior frequencies. *Journal of Sexual Medicine, 6,* 1947–1954.

**Brooker, R. J.** (2012). *Genetics* (4th ed.). New York: McGraw-Hill.

**Brooks, J. G., & Brooks, M. G.** (2001). *In search of understanding: The case for the constructivist classroom.* Upper Saddle River, NJ: Prentice-Hall.

**Brosschot, J. F., Verkuil, B., & Thayer, J. F.** (2010). Conscious and unconscious perseverative cognition: Is a large part of the prolonged physiological activity due to unconscious stress? *Journal of Psychosomatic Research, 69,* 407–416.

**Brown, A. R., & others.** (2011). Aversive, appetitive, and flavor avoidance responses in the presence of contextual cues. *Learning and Behavior, 39,* 95–103.

**Brown, A. S.** (2006). Prenatal infection as a risk factor for schizophrenia. *Schizophrenia Bulletin, 32,* 200–202.

**Brown, D.** (2007). Evidence-based hypnotherapy for asthma: A critical review. *International Journal of Clinical and Experimental Hypnosis, 55,* 220–249.

**Brown, P., & Tierney, C.** (2011). Media role in violence and the dynamics of bullying. *Pediatric Reviews, 32,* 453–454.

**Brown, P. L., & Jenkins, H. M.** (2009). On the law of effect. In D. Shanks (Ed.), *Psychology of learning.* Thousand Oaks, CA: Sage.

**Brown, R.** (1973). *A first language: The early stages.* Cambridge, MA: Harvard University Press.

**Brown, R.** (2012, February 6). Let's Move Dance-Off will give prizes for weight loss. *The Ledger.* www.theledger.com/article/20120206/NEWS/120209512 (accessed May 30, 2012)

**Brown, S. L., Nesse, R. N., Vinokur, A. D., & Smith, D. M.** (2003). Providing social support may be more beneficial than receiving it: Results from a prospective study of mortality. *Psychological Science, 14,* 320–327.

**Bruce, D.** (1989). Functional explanations of memory. In L. W. Poon, D. C. Rubin, & B. A. Wilson (Eds.), *Everyday cognition in adulthood and late life* (pp. 44–58). Cambridge, England: Cambridge University Press.

**Brüchmiller, K., Margraf, J., & Schneider, S.** (2012). Is ADHD diagnosed in accord with diagnostic criteria? Overdiagnosis and influence of client gender on diagnosis. *Journal of Consulting and Clinical Psychology, 80,* 128–138.

**Bruck, M., & Ceci, S. J.** (2012). Forensic developmental psychology in the courtroom. In D. Faust & M. Ziskin (Eds.), *Coping with psychiatric and psychological testimony.* New York: Cambridge University Press.

**Brug, J., Conner, M., Harré, N., Kremers, S., McKellar, S., & Whitelaw, S.** (2004). The transtheoretical model and stages of change: A critique. Observations by five commentators on the paper by Adams, J. and White, M. (2004) Why don't stage-based activity promotion interventions work? *Health Education Research, 20,* 244–258.

**Brumberg, J. S., & Guenther, F. H.** (2010). Development of speech prostheses: Current status and recent advances. *Expert Review of Medical Devices, 7,* 667–679.

**Brummett, B. H., Boyle, S. H., Kuhn, C. M., Siegler, I. C., & Williams, R. B.** (2008). Associations among central nervous system serotonergic function and neuroticism are moderated by gender. *Biological Psychology, 78,* 200–203.

**Bruning, R. H., Schraw, G. J., Norby, M. M., & Ronning, R. R.** (2004). *Cognitive psychology and instruction* (4th ed.). Upper Saddle River, NJ: Prentice-Hall.

Brunstein, J. (1993). Personal goals and subjective well-being: A longitudinal study. *Journal of Personality and Social Psychology, 65,* 1061–1070.

Brunstein, J., & Maier, G. W. (2005). Implicit and self-attributed motives to achieve: Two separate but inter-acting needs. *Journal of Personality and Social Psychology, 89,* 205–222.

Brusset, B. (2012). The therapeutic action of psychoanalysis. *International Journal of Psychoanalysis, 93,* 427–442.

Bryan, S. M. (2012, January 28). Wolves' senses tapped to keep them clear of cattle. *Associated Press.* http://bangordailynews.com/2012/01/28/outdoors/wolves-senses-tapped-to-keep-them-clear-of-cattle/ (accessed April 12, 2012)

Bucherelli, C., Baldi, E., Mariottini, C., Passani, M. B., & Blandina, P. (2006). Aversive memory reactivation engages in the amygdala only some neurotransmitters involved in consolidation. *Learning and Memory, 13,* 426–430.

Buchser, W. J., Laskow, T. C., Pavlik, P. J., Lin, H. M., & Lotze, M. T. (2012). Cell-mediated autophagy promotes cancer cell survival. *Cancer Research, 72* (12), 1–10.

Bueno, J. L., & Bueno, J. L. S. (2011). Serial conditional discrimination and temporal bisection in rats selectively lesioned in the dentate gyrus. *Behavioral Processes, 86,* 345–358.

Buhi, E. R., Goodson, P., Neilands, T. B., & Blunt, H. (2011). Adolescent sexual abstinence: A test of an integrative theoretical framework. *Health Education and Behavior, 38,* 63–79.

Burgdorf, J., & Panksepp, J. (2006). The neurobiology of positive emotions. *Neuroscience and Biobehavioral Reviews, 30,* 173–187.

Burger, J. (2009). Replicating Milgram: Would people still obey today? *American Psychologist, 64,* 1–11.

Burgess, D. J., Joseph, A., van Ryn, M., & Carnes, M. (2012). Does stereotype threat affect women in academic medicine? *Academic Medicine, 87* (4), 506–512.

Burk, W. J., Denissen, J., Van Doorn, M. D., Branje, S. J. T., & Laursen, B. (2009). The vicissitudes of conflict measurement: Stability and reliability in the frequency of disagreements. *European Psychologist, 14,* 153–159.

Burke, B. L., Martens, A., & Faucher, E. H. (2010). Two decades of terror management theory: A meta-analysis of mortality salience research. *Personality and Social Psychology Review, 14,* 155–195.

Burks, D. J., & Kobus, A. M. (2012). The legacy of altruism in health care: The promotion of empathy, prosociality, and humanism. *Medical Education, 46,* 317–325.

Burns, J. (2009). Dispelling a myth: Developing world poverty, inequality, violence, and social fragmentation are not good for outcome in schizophrenia. *African Journal of Psychiatry, 12,* 200–205.

Burston, D. (2012). Psychoanalysis and psychiatry in the twenty-first century: Historical reflections. *Psychoanalytic Review, 99,* 63–80.

Burton, C. M., & King, L. A. (2004). The health benefits of writing about peak experiences. *Journal of Research in Personality, 38,* 150–163.

Burton, C. M., & King, L. A. (2008). The effects of (very) brief writing on health: The 2-minute miracle. *British Journal of Health Psychology, 13,* 9–14.

Buscemi, L., & Turchi, C. (2011). An overview of genetic susceptibility to alcoholism. *Medicine, Science, and the Law, 51, Suppl. 1,* S2–S6.

Busch, H., & Hofer, J. (2012). Self-regulation and milestones of adult development: Intimacy and generativity. *Developmental Psychology, 48,* 282–293.

Busch, S. H., Frank, R. G., Martin, A., & Barry, C. L. (2010). Antidepressants and suicide risk: How did specific information on FDA safety warnings affect treatment patterns? *Psychiatric Services, 61,* 11–16.

Busch, S. H., Golberstein, E., & Meara, E. (2011). *The FDA and ABCs: The unintended consequences of antidepressant warnings on human capital.* Working Paper 17426. Cambridge, MA: National Bureau of Economic Research. ww.nber.org/papers/w17426 (accessed May 29, 2012)

Bushman, B. J., & Anderson, C. A. (2007). Measuring the strength of the effect of violent media on aggression. *American Psychologist, 62,* 253–254.

Bushman, B. J., Wang, M. C., & Anderson, C. A. (2005). Is the curve relating temperature to aggression linear or curvilinear? Assaults and temperature in Minneapolis reexamined. *Journal of Personality and Social Psychology, 89,* 62–66.

Bushman, L., & Huesman, L. R. (2012). Effects of media violence on aggression. In D. G. Singer & J. L. Singer (Eds.), *Handbook of children and the media* (2nd ed.). Thousand Oaks, CA: Sage.

Buss, D. M. (2009). How can evolutionary psychology successfully explain personality and individual differences? *Perspectives on Psychological Science, 4,* 359–366.

Buss, D. M. (2012). *Evolutionary psychology* (4th ed.). Boston: Allyn & Bacon.

Bussey, K., & Bandura, A. (2004). Social cognitive theory of gender development and functioning. In A. H. Eagly, A. Beall, & R. Sternberg (Eds.), *The psychology of gender* (2nd ed., pp. 92–119). New York: Guilford.

Bussy, G., Charrin, E., Brun, A., Curi, A., & des Portes, V. (2011). Implicit procedural learning in fragile X and Down syndrome. *Journal of Intellectual Disabilities Research, 55,* 521–528.

Butcher, J. N. (2010). Personality assessment from the nineteenth century to the early twenty-first century: Past achievements and contemporary challenges. *Annual Review of Psychology* (vol. 61). Palo Alto, CA: Annual Reviews.

Butcher, J. N., Beutler, L. E., Harwood, T. M., & Blau, K. (2011). The MMPI-2. In T. M. Harwood, L. E. Beutler, & G. Groth-Marnat (Eds.), *Integrative assessment of adult personality* (3rd ed.). New York: Guilford.

Butler, A. C., Chapman, J. E., Forman, E. M., & Beck, A. T. (2006). The empirical status of cognitive-behavioral therapy: A review of meta-analyses. *Clinical Psychology Review, 26,* 17–31.

Butovskaya, M. L., & others. (2012). Aggression, digit ratio, and variation in the androgen receptor, serotonin transporter, and dopamine D4 receptor genes in Africa foragers: The Hadza. *Behavior Genetics.* (in press)

Buttenschøn, H. N., & others. (2011). The norepinephrine transporter gene is a candidate gene for panic disorder. *Journal of Neural Transmission, 118,* 969–976.

Buunk, B. P., & Van Yperen, N. W. (1991). Referential comparisons, relational comparisons, and exchange orientation: Their relation to marital satisfaction. *Personality and Social Psychology Bulletin, 17,* 709–717.

Byard, R. W., & Krous, H. F. (2004). Research and sudden infant death syndrome: Definitions, diagnostic difficulties and discrepancies. *Journal of Paediatrics and Child Health, 40,* 419–421.

Byrne, R. W., Hobaiter, C., & Klailova, M. (2011). Local traditions in gorilla manual skill: Evidence for observational learning of behavioral organization. *Animal Cognition, 14,* 683–693.

Byrne, S., Barry, D., & Petry, N. M. (2012). Predictors of weight loss success. Exercise vs. dietary self-efficacy and treatment attendance. *Appetite, 58,* 695–698.

## C

Cabeza, R. (2002). Hemispheric asymmetry reduction in older adults: The HAROLD model. *Psychology and Aging, 17,* 85–100.

Cahill, K., Stead, L. F., & Lancaster, T. (2012). Nicotine receptor partial agonists for smoking cessation. *Cochrane Database of Systematic Reviews, 4,* CD006103.

Cai, H., Sedikides, C., Gaertner, L., Wang, C., Carvallo, M., Xu, Y., O'Mara, E. M., & Jackson, L. E. (2011). Tactical self-enhancement in China: Is modesty at the service of self-enhancement in East Asian culture? *Social Psychological and Personality Science, 2,* 59–64.

Caillouet, B. A., Boccaccini, M. T., Varela, J. G., Davis, R. D., & Rostow, C. D. (2010). Predictive validity of the MMPI-2 PSY-5 scales and facets for law enforcement officer employment outcomes. *Criminal Justice and Behavior, 37,* 217–238.

Cale, E. M., & Lilienfeld, S. O. (2002). Sex differences in psychopathy and antisocial personality disorder: A review and integration. *Clinical Psychology Review, 22,* 1179–1207.

Calmes, J. (2012, May 23). When a boy found a familiar feel in a pat of the head of state. *New York Times.* www.nytimes.com/2012/05/24/us/politics/indelible-image-of-a-boys-pat-on-obamas-head-hangs-in-white-house.html?_r=1 (accessed May 29, 2012)

Calvo-Merino, B., Grezes, J., Glaser, D. E., Passingham, R. E., & Haggard, P. (2006). Seeing or doing? Influence of visual and motor familiarity inaction observation. *Current Biology, 16,* 1905–1910.

Campbell, C. A. (2009). AIDS. In D. Carr (Ed.), *Encyclopedia of the life course and human development.* Boston: Gale Cengage.

Campbell, J. D., Yoon, D. P., & Johnstone, B. (2009). Determining relationships between physical health and spiritual experience, religious practice, and congregational support in a heterogeneous sample. *Journal of Religion and Health, 21* (2), 127–136.

Campbell, L., Campbell, B., & Dickinson, D. (2004). *Teaching and learning through multiple intelligences.* Boston: Allyn & Bacon.

Canadian Statistics. (2005). Crime in Canada. www.statcan.ca/Daily/English/050721/d050721a.htmltitle=Crime in Canada.

Canli, T. (2008a). Toward a neurogenetic theory of neuroticism. In D. W. Pfaff & B. L. Kieffer (Eds.), *Molecular and biophysical mechanisms of arousal, alertness, and attention* (pp. 153–174). Malden, MA: Blackwell.

Canli, T. (2008b). Toward a "molecular psychology" of personality. In O. P. John, R. W. Robins, & L. A. Pervin (Eds.), *Handbook of personality theory and research* (3rd ed., pp. 311–327). New York: Guilford.

Canli, T., Sivers, H., Whitfield, S. L., Gotlib, I. H., & Gabrieli, J. D. E. (2002). Amygdala response to happy faces as a function of extraversion. *Science, 296,* 2191.

Cannon, M. J., Dominique, Y., O'Leary, L. A., Sniezek, J. E., & Floyd, R. L. (2012). Characteristics and behaviors of mothers who have a child with fetal alcohol syndrome. *Neurotoxicology and Teratology, 34,* 90–95.

Cannon, W. B. (1927). The James-Lange theory of emotions: A critical examination and an alternative theory. *American Journal of Psychology, 39,* 106–124.

Canton-Cortes, D., Canton, J., & Cortes, M. R. (2012). The interactive effect of blame attribution with characteristics of child sexual abuse on posttraumatic stress disorder. *Journal of Nervous and Mental Disease, 200,* 329–335.

Cantor, N., & Sanderson, C. A. (1999). Life task participation and well-being: The importance of taking part in daily life. In D. Kahneman, E. Diener, & N. Schwarz (Eds.), *Well-being: The foundations of hedonic psychology* (pp. 230–243). New York: Russell Sage Foundation.

Cantu, R. (2003). Brain injury-related fatalities in American football, 1945–1999. *Neurosurgery, 52,* 846–853.

Capasso, A., Putrella, C., & Milano, W. (2009). Recent clinical aspects of eating disorders. *Reviews on Recent Clinical Trials, 4,* 63–69.

Caporeal, L. R. (2007). Evolution. In A. W. Kruglanski & E. T. Higgins (Eds.), *Social psychology* (2nd ed.). New York: Guilford.

Capps, D. (2004). A psychobiography of Jesus. In J. H. Ellens & W. G. Rollins (Eds.), *Psychology and the Bible: A new way to read the scriptures, Vol. 4, From Jesus to Christ* (pp. 59–70). Westport, CT: Praeger.

Caprara, G. V., Alessandri, G., Di Giunta, L., Panerai, L., & Eisenberg, N. (2010). The contribution of agreeableness and self-efficacy beliefs to prosociality. *European Journal of Personality, 24,* 36–55.

Caprara, G. V., Alessandri, G., & Eisenberg, N. (2012). Prosociality: The contribution of traits, values, and self-efficacy beliefs. *Journal of Personality and Social Psychology, 102,* 1289–1303.

Caputi, M., Lecce, S., Pagnin, A., & Banerjee, R. (2012). Longitudinal effects of theory of mind on later peer relations: The role of prosocial behavior. *Developmental Psychology, 48,* 257–270.

Cardinali, D. P., Srinivasan, V., Brzezinski, A., & Brown, G. M. (2011). Melatonin and its analogs in insomnia and depression. *Journal of Pineal Research.* doi: 10.1111/j.1600-079X.2011.00962.x

**Cardno, A. G., & Gottesman, I. I.** (2000). Twin studies of schizophrenia: From bow-and-arrow concordances to Star Wars Mx and functional genomics. *American Journal of Medical Genetics, 97,* 12–17.

**Cardno, A. G., & others.** (2012). A twin study of schizoaffective—mania, schizoaffective—depression, and other psychotic symptoms. *American Journal of Medical Genetics B: Neuropsychiatric Genetics, 159B,* 172–182.

**Carey, B.** (2009, August 9). After injury, fighting to regain a sense of self. *New York Times.* www.nytimes.com/2009/08/09/health/research/09brain.html

**Carey, B.** (2011, January 6). Journal's paper on ESP expected to prompt outrage. *New York Times,* A1.

**Carey, B.** (2011a, November 25). Finding purpose after living with delusion. *New York Times,* A1.

**Carey, B.** (2012, February 14). The therapist may see you anytime, anywhere. *New York Times,* D1.

**Caricati, L.** (2011). Upward and downward social comparison in the intermediate-status group: The role of social stratification stability. *British Journal of Social Psychology.* doi: 10.1111/j.2044-8309.2011.02054.x

**Carlo, G., Knight, G. P., McGinley, M., & Hayes, R.** (2011). The roles of parental inductions, moral emotions, and moral cognitions in prosocial tendencies among Mexican American and European American early adolescents. *Journal of Early Adolescence, 31,* 757–781.

**Carlson, S. M.** (2011). Introduction to special issue: Executive function. *Journal of Experimental Child Psychology, 108,* 411–413.

**Carmona, J. E., Holland, A. K., & Harrison, D. W.** (2009). Extending the functional cerebral theory of emotion to the vestibular modality: A systematic and integrative approach. *Psychological Bulletin, 135,* 286–302.

**Carnahan, T., & McFarland, S.** (2007). Revisiting the Stanford prison experiment: Could participant self-selection have led to the cruelty? *Personality and Social Psychology Bulletin, 33,* 603–614.

**Carnell, S., Gibson, C., Benson, L., Ochner, C. N., & Geliebter, A.** (2012). Neuroimaging and obesity: Current knowledge and future directions. *Obesity Reviews, 13,* 43–56.

**Carney, D. R., Colvin, C. R., & Hall, J. A.** (2007). A thin slice perspective on the accuracy of first impressions. *Journal of Research in Personality, 41,* 1054–1072.

**Carpenter, S. K., & DeLosh, E. L.** (2006). Impoverished cue support enhances subsequent retention: Support for the elaborative retrieval explanation of the testing effect. *Memory and Cognition, 34,* 268–276.

**Carprara, G. V., Gagnani, C., Alessandri, G., Steca, P., Gigantesco, A., Sforza, L. l., & Stazi, M. A.** (2009). Human optimal functioning: The genetics of positive orientation towards self, life, and the future. *Behavior Genetics, 39,* 277–284.

**Carr, R., & Peebles, R.** (2012). Developmental considerations of media exposure risk for eating disorders. In J. Lock (Ed.), *Oxford handbook of child and adolescent eating disorders: Developmental perspectives.* New York: Oxford University Press.

**Carrard, I., der Linden, M. V., & Golay, A.** (2012). Comparison of obese and nonobese individuals with binge eating disorder: Delicate boundary between binge eating disorder and non-purging bulimia nervosa. *European Eating Disorders Review.* doi: 10.1002/erv.2174

**Carrieri, V.** (2012). Social comparison and subjective well-being: Does the health of others matter? *Bulletin of Economic Research, 64,* 31–55.

**Carroll, J. L.** (2013). *Sexuality now* (4th ed.). Boston: Cengage.

**Carskadon, M. A.** (2006, March). *Too little, too late: Sleep bioregulatory processes across adolescence.* Paper presented at the meeting of the Society for Research on Adolescence, San Francisco.

**Carskadon, M. A.** (2011a). Sleep in adolescents: The perfect storm. *Pediatric Clinics of North America, 58,* 637–647.

**Carskadon, M. A.** (2011b). Sleep's effects on cognition and learning in adolescence. *Progress in Brain Research, 190,* 137–143.

**Carson, R. C., Butcher, J. N., & Mineka, S.** (1996). *Abnormal psychology and life* (10th ed.). New York: HarperCollins.

**Carstensen, L. L.** (2006). The influence of a sense of time on human development. *Science, 312,* 1913–1915.

**Carstensen, L. L., Turan, B., Scheibe, S., Ram, N., Ersner-Hershfield, H., Samanez-Larkin, G. R., Brooks, K. P., & Nesselroade, J. R.** (2011). Emotional experience improves with age: Evidence based on over 10 years of experience sampling. *Psychology and Aging, 26,* 21–33.

**Carter, C. S., Pournajafi-Nazarloo, H., Kramer, K. M., Ziegler, T. E., White-Traut, R., Bello, D., & Schwertz, D.** (2007). Oxytocin: Behavioral associations and potential as a salivary biomarker. *Annals of the New York Academy of Sciences, 1098,* 312–322.

**Carter, R.** (1998). *Mapping the mind.* Berkeley: University of California Press.

**Cartmill, E. A., Demir, O. E., & Goldin-Meadow, S.** (2011). Studying gesture. In E. Hoff (Ed.), *Research methods in child language.* New York: Wiley.

**Carver, C. S., & Connor-Smith, J.** (2010). Personality and coping. *Annual Review of Psychology* (vol. 61). Palo Alto, CA: Annual Reviews.

**Carver, C. S., & Scheier, M. F.** (2000). Origins and functions of positive and negative affect: A control process view. In E. T. Higgins & A. W. Kruglanski (Eds.), *Motivational science: Social and personality perspectives* (pp. 256–272). New York: Psychology Press.

**Carver, C. S., & Scheier, M. F.** (2009). Optimism. In M. R. Levy & R. H. Hoyle (Eds.), *Handbook of individual differences in social behavior* (pp. 330–342). New York: Guilford.

**Carver, C. S., Scheier, M. F., & Segerstrom, S. C.** (2010). Optimism. *Clinical Psychology Review, 30,* 879–889.

**Casalin, S., Luyten, P., Vliegen, N., & Meurs, P.** (2012). The structure and stability of temperament from infancy to toddlerhood: A one-year prospective study. *Infant Behavior & Development, 35,* 94–108.

**Case, R. B., Moss, A. J., Case, N., McDermott, M., & Eberly, S.** (1992). Living alone after myocardial infarction. Impact on prognosis. *Journal of the American Medical Association, 267,* 515–519.

**Caserta, M., Lund, D., Utz, R., & de Vries, B.** (2009). Stress-related growth among the recently bereaved. *Aging & Mental Health, 13,* 463–476.

**Casey, B. J., Jones, R. M., & Somerville, L. H.** (2011). Braking and accelerating of the adolescent brain. *Journal of Research on Adolescence, 21,* 21–33.

**Casey, B. J., & others.** (2011). Behavioral and neural correlates of delay of gratification 40 years later. *Proceedings of the National Academy of Sciences USA, 108,* 14998–15003.

**Caspi, A., Hariri, A. R., Holmes, A., Uher, R., & Moffitt, T. E.** (2011). Genetic sensitivity to the environment: The case of the serotonin transporter gene and its implications for studying complex diseases and traits. In K. A. Dodge & M. Rutter (Eds.), *Gene-environment interaction and developmental psychopathology.* New York: Guilford.

**Caspi, A., McClay, J., Moffitt, T. E., Mill, J., Martin, J., Craig, I. W., Taylor, A., & Poulton, R.** (2002). Role of genotype in the cycle of violence in maltreated children. *Science, 297,* 851–854.

**Caston, J.** (2011). Agency as a psychoanalytic idea. *Journal of the American Psychoanalytic Association, 59,* 907–938.

**Cathers-Schiffman, T. A., & Thompson, M. S.** (2007). Assessment of English- and Spanish-speaking students with the WISC-III and Leiter-R. *Journal of Psychoeducational Assessment, 25,* 41–52.

**Caverzasi, E., & others.** (2008). Complications in major depressive disorder therapy: A review of magnetic resonance spectroscopy studies. *Functional Neurology, 23,* 129–132.

**Cavina-Pratesi, C., Kentridge, R. W., Heywood, C. A., & Milner, A. D.** (2010). Separate channels for processing form, texture, and color: Evidence from fMRI adaptation and visual object agnosia. *Cerebral Cortex, 20* (10), 2319–2332.

**Centers for Disease Control and Prevention (CDC).** (2007, September 7). Suicide trends among youths and young adults aged 10–24 Years—United States, 1990–2004. *Morbidity and Mortality Weekly Report, 56,* 905–908.

**Centers for Disease Control and Prevention (CDC).** (2009). *Obesity: Halting the epidemic by making health easier.* Atlanta: Author.

**Centers for Disease Control and Prevention (CDC).** (2011). *Concussion in sports.* www.cdc.gov/concussion/sports/index.html

**Centers for Disease Control and Prevention (CDC).** (2011a). Vital signs: Current cigarette smoking among adults aged ≥ 18 years—United States, 2005–2010. *Morbidity and Mortality Weekly Reports, 60* (35). Atlanta: Author.

**Centers for Disease Control and Prevention (CDC).** (2012). Table B. Deaths and death rates for 2010. . . *National Vital Statistics Reports, 60* (4), 31.

**Centers for Disease Control and Prevention (CDC).** (2012a). *Adult cigarette smoking in the United States: Current estimate.* www.cdc.gov/tobacco/data_statistics/fact_sheets/adult_data/cig_smoking/index.htm (accessed June 1, 2012)

**Centers for Disease Control and Prevention (CDC).** (2012b). *HIV in the United States: At a glance.* www.cdc.gov/hiv/resources/factsheets/us.htm (accessed May 5, 2012)

**Centers for Disease Control and Prevention (CDC).** (2012c). *Overweight and obesity.* Atlanta: Author.

**Centers for Disease Control and Prevention (CDC).** (2012d). *Sexually transmitted diseases (STDs).* www.cdc.gov/std/default.htm (accessed May 5, 2012)

**Chabardès, S., & others.** (2012). Deep brain stimulation for obsessive compulsive disorder: Subthalamic nucleus target. *World Neurosurgery.* doi: 10.1016/j.wneu.2012.03.010

**Chabris, C., & Simons, D.** (2010). *The invisible gorilla, and other ways our intuitions deceive us.* New York: Crown.

**Chae, Y., Goodman, G. S., Bederian-Gardner, D., & Lindsay, A.** (2011). Methodological issues and practical strategies in research on child maltreatment victims' abilities and experiences as witnesses. *Child Abuse & Neglect, 35,* 240–248.

**Chafetz, L., White, M., Collins-Bride, G., Cooper, B. A., & Nickens, J.** (2008). Clinical trial of wellness training: Health promotion for severely mentally ill adults. *Journal of Nervous and Mental Disease, 196,* 475–483.

**Chambon, V., Baudouin, J., & Franck, N.** (2006). The role of configural information in facial emotion recognition in schizophrenia. *Neuropsychologia, 44,* 2437–2444.

**Chance, P.** (2009). *Learning and behavior* (6th ed.). Belmont, CA: Cengage.

**Chandra, A., Mosher, W. D., Copen, C., & Sionean, C.** (2011). Sexual behavior, sexual attraction, and sexual identity in the United States: Data from the 2006–2008 National Survey of Family Growth. *National Health Statistics Reports, 36,* 1–36.

**Chang, A. C.** (2012). Primary prevention of sudden cardiac death of the young athlete: The controversy about the screening electrocardiogram and its innovative artificial intelligence solution. *Pediatric Cardiology, 33* (3), 428–433.

**Chang, Z., Lichtenstein, P., & Larsson, H.** (2012). The effects of childhood ADHD symptoms on early-onset substance use: A Swedish twin study. *Journal of Abnormal Child Psychology, 40,* 425–435.

**Chao, R.** (2001). Extending research on the consequences of parenting style for Chinese Americans and European Americans. *Child Development, 72,* 1832–1843.

**Chao, R. K.** (2007, March). *Research with Asian Americans: Looking back and moving forward.* Paper presented at the meeting of the Society for Research in Child Development, Boston.

**Chao, R. K., & Otsuki-Clutter, M.** (2011). Racial and ethnic differences: Sociocultural and contextual explanations. *Journal of Research on Adolescence, 21,* 47–60.

**Charles, S. T., & Carstensen, L. L.** (2010). Social and emotional aging. *Annual Review of Psychology* (vol. 61). Palo Alto, CA: Annual Reviews.

**Chaves, J. F.** (2000). Hypnosis. In A. Kazdin (Ed.), *Encyclopedia of psychology.* Washington, DC, & New York: American Psychological Association and Oxford University Press.

**Cheah, C. S. L., & Leung, C. Y. Y.** (2011). The social development of immigrant children: A focus on Asian and Hispanic children in the U.S. In P. K.

Smith & C. H. Hart (Eds.), *Wiley-Blackwell handbook of childhood social development* (2nd ed.). New York: Wiley.

**Chen, L., & others.** (2011). Fine-scale functional connectivity in somatosensory cortex revealed by high-resolution fMRI. *Magnetic Resonance Imaging, 29,* 1330–1337.

**Chen, P., & Jacobson, K. C.** (2012). Developmental trajectories of substance use from early adolescence to young adulthood: Gender and racial/ethnic differences. *Journal of Adolescent Health, 50,* 154–163.

**Cheng, C. M., & Huang, C. L.** (2011). Processes of conscious and unconscious memory: Evidence from current research on dissociation of memories within a test. *American Journal of Psychology, 124,* 421–440.

**Chess, S., & Thomas, A.** (1977). Temperamental individuality from childhood to adolescence. *Journal of Child Psychiatry, 16,* 218–226.

**Chica, A. B., & Bartolomeo, P.** (2012). Attentional routes to conscious perception. *Frontiers in Psychology, 3,* 1.

**Chichilnisky, E. J.** (2007). Information processing in the retina. *Annual Review of Neuroscience* (vol. 30). Palo Alto, CA: Annual Reviews.

**Chivers, M. L., Seto, M. C., & Blanchard, R.** (2007). Gender and sexual orientation differences in sexual response to sexual activities versus gender of actors in sexual films. *Journal of Personality and Social Psychology, 93,* 1108–1121.

**Cho, H. J., Bower, J. E., Kiefe, C. I., Seeman, T. E., & Irwin, M. R.** (2012). Early life stress and inflammatory mechanisms of fatigue in the Coronary Artery Development in Young Adults (CARDIA) Study. *Brain, Behavior, and Immunity.* (in press)

**Choi, J., Lisanby, S. H., Medalia, A., & Prudic, J.** (2011). A conceptual introduction to cognitive remediation for memory deficits associated with right unilateral electroconvulsive therapy. *Journal of ECT, 27,* 286–291.

**Choi, J. K., & Bowles, S.** (2007). The co-evolution of parochial altruism and war. *Science, 318,* 636–640.

**Chomsky, N.** (1975). *Reflections on language.* New York: Pantheon.

**Chorost, M.** (2011). *The worldwide mind: The coming integration of humans and machines.* New York: Free Press.

**Chou, H. T., & Edge, N.** (2012). "They are happier and having better lives than I am": The impact of using Facebook on perceptions of others' lives. *Cyberpsychology, Behavior, and Social Networking, 15,* 117–122.

**Chouinard, G.** (2006). Interrelations between psychiatric symptoms and drug-induced movement disorder. *Journal of Psychiatry and Neuroscience, 31,* 177–180.

**Christensen, L. B., Johnson, R. B., & Turner, L.** (2011). *Research design, methods, and analysis* (11th ed.). Upper Saddle River, NJ: Prentice-Hall.

**Christopher Frueh, B., Grubaugh, A. L., Cusack, K. J., Kimble, M. O., Elhai, J. D., & Knapp, R. G.** (2009). Exposure-based cognitive-behavioral treatment of PTSD in adults with schizophrenia or schizoaffective disorder: A pilot study. *Journal of Anxiety Disorders, 23,* 665–675.

**Chronicle of Higher Education.** (2011, August 21). Forecast for growth on campuses: More women, minorities. *Almanac of higher education 2011.* http://chronicle.com/article/Forecast-for-Growth-on/128272/

**Chu, Y., & MacGregor, J. N.** (2011). Human performance in insight problem solving: A review. *Journal of Problem Solving, 3,* 119–150.

**Chun, D.** (2010, August 17). For researchers, girl's pain-free life a study in genetic mutation. *Gainesville Sun.* www.gainesville.com/article/20100817/articles/100819454

**Chun, M. M., Turk-Browne, N., & Golomb, J.** (2011). Toward a taxonomy of attention. *Annual Review of Psychology* (vol. 62). Palo Alto, CA: Annual Reviews.

**Chung, T., & others.** (2012). Drinking frequency as a brief screen for adolescent alcohol problems. *Pediatrics, 129* (2), 205–212.

**Church, R. M., & Kirkpatrick, K.** (2001). Theories of conditioning and timing. In R. R. Mowrer & S. B. Klein (Eds.), *Handbook of contemporary learning theories.* Mahwah, NJ: Erlbaum.

**Cialdini, R. B.** (1991). Altruism or egoism? That is (still) the question. *Psychological Inquiry, 2,* 124–126.

**Cialdini, R. B.** (1993). *Influence: Science and practice.* New York: HarperCollins.

**Cialdini, R. B., Vincent, J. E., Lewis, S. K., Catalan, J., Wheeler, D., & Darby, B. L.** (1975). Reciprocal concessions procedure for inducing compliance: The door-in-the-face technique. *Journal of Personality and Social Psychology, 31,* 206–215.

**Cicchetti, D., & Rogosch, F. A.** (2012). Gene × environment interaction and resilience: Effects of child maltreatment and serotonin, corticotropin releasing hormone, dopamine, and oxytocin genes. *Development and Psychopathology, 24,* 411–427.

**Cipriani, A., La Ferla, T., Furukawa, T. A., Signoretti, A., Nakagawa, A., Churchill, R., McGuire, H., & Barbui, C.** (2010). Sertraline versus other antidepressive agents for depression. *Cochrane Database of Systematic Reviews,* 4: CD006117. doi: 10.1002/14651858.CD006117.pub4

**Clark, B.** (2008). *Growing up gifted* (7th ed.). Upper Saddle River, NJ: Prentice-Hall.

**Clark, D. A., & Beck, A. T.** (2011). *Cognitive therapy of anxiety disorders.* New York: Guilford.

**Clark, M. S., & Chrisman, K.** (1994). Resource allocation in intimate relationships: Trying to make sense of a confusing literature. In M. J. Lerner & G. Mikula (Eds.), *Entitlement and the affectional bond: Justice in close relationships* (pp. 65–88). New York: Plenum.

**Clark, R. D., & Hatfield, E.** (1989). Gender differences in receptivity to sexual offers. *Journal of Psychology and Human Sexuality, 2,* 39–55.

**Clarkin, J. F.** (2012). An integrated approach to psychotherapy techniques for patients with personality disorder. *Journal of Personality Disorders, 26,* 43–62.

**Clearfield, M. W.** (2011). Learning to walk changes infants' social interactions. *Infant Behavior & Development, 34,* 15–25.

**Cleeremans, A., & Sarrazin, J. C.** (2007). Time, action, and consciousness. *Human Movement Science, 26,* 180–202.

**Cleveland, J. N., Barnes-Farrell, J. L., & Ratz, J. M.** (1997). Accommodation in the workplace. *Human Resource Management Review, 7,* 77–107.

**Clore, G. L., & Palmer, J.** (2009). Affective guidance of intelligent agents: How emotion controls cognition. *Cognitive Systems Research, 10,* 21–30.

**Close, C. E., Roberts, P. L., & Berger, R. E.** (1990). Cigarettes, alcohol, and marijuana are related to pyospermia in infertile men. *Journal of Urology, 144,* 900–903.

**Cloud, J.** (2008, August 27). Failing our geniuses. *Time,* 40–47.

**CNN Poll.** (2006, December 12). Most Americans see lingering racism—in others. www.cnn.com/2006/US/12/12/racism.poll/index.html (accessed May 22, 2012)

**Cobb, S., & Battin, B.** (2004). Second-impact syndrome. *Journal of School Nursing, 20,* 262–267.

**Cohen, D.** (2001). Cultural variation: Considerations and implications. *Psychological Bulletin, 127,* 451–471.

**Cohen, D., Nisbett, R. E., Bowdle, B. F., & Schwarz, N.** (1996). Insult, aggression, and the southern culture of honor: An "experimental ethnography." *Journal of Personality and Social Psychology, 70,* 945–960.

**Cohen, F., & Solomon, S.** (2011). The politics of mortal terror. *Current Directions in Psychological Science, 20,* 316–320.

**Cohen, S.** (2011, August 20). Joplin tornado volunteers seek out owners of 27,000 photos found in rubble. www.huffingtonpost.com/2011/08/20/reuniting-tornado-victims_n_932115.html (accessed May 13, 2012)

**Cohen, S., Doyle, W. J., Alper, C. M., Janicki-Deverts, D., & Turner, R. B.** (2009). Sleep habits and susceptibility to the common cold. *Archives of Internal Medicine, 169,* 62–67.

**Cohen, S., Frank, E., Doyle, W., Skoner, D. P., Rabin, B. S., & Gwaltney, J. M.** (1998). Types of stressors that increase susceptibility to the common cold in healthy adults. *Health Psychology, 17,* 214–223.

**Cohen, S., & Janicki-Deverts, D.** (2009). Can we improve our physical health by altering our social

networks? *Perspectives on Psychological Science, 4* (4), 375–378.

**Cohen, S., & Lemay, E.** (2007). Why would social networks be linked to affect and health practices? *Health Psychology, 27,* 410–417.

**Cohen, S., & others.** (2012). Chronic stress, glucocorticoid receptor resistance, inflammation, and disease risk. *Proceedings of the National Academy of Sciences USA, 109* (16), 5995–5999.

**Coifman, K. G., Bonanno, G. A., Ray, R. D., & Gross, J. J.** (2007). Does repressing coping promote resilience? Affective-autonomic response discrepancy during bereavement. *Journal of Personality and Social Psychology, 92,* 745–758.

**Colapinto, J.** (2000). *As nature made him.* New York: HarperAcademic.

**Collin, G. B., & others.** (2012). Meckelin is necessary for photoreceptor intraciliary transport and outer segment morphogenesis. *Investigative Ophthalmology and Visual Science.* (in press)

**Collins, W. A., Maccoby, E. E., Steinberg, L., Hetherington, E. M., & Bornstein, M. H.** (2000). Contemporary research on parenting: The case for nature and nurture. *American Psychologist, 55,* 218–232.

**Colrain, I. M., & Baker, F. C.** (2011). Sleep EEG, the clearest window through which to view adolescent brain development. *Sleep, 34,* 1287–1288.

**Colrain, I. M., & Baker, F. C.** (2012). Editorial focus: The maturational trajectories of NREM and REM sleep durations differ across adolescence on both school-night and weekend sleep. *American Journal of Physiology: Regulatory, Integrative, and Comparative Physiology, 302* (5), R531–R532.

***Commonwealth of Massachusetts v. Porter 31285-330.*** (1993, Massachusetts).

**Compton, J., & Pfau, M.** (2008). Inoculating against pro-plagiarism justifications: Rational and affective strategies. *Journal of Applied Communication Research, 36,* 98–119.

**Compton, J. A., & Pfau, M.** (2004). Use of inoculation to foster resistance to credit card marketing targeting college students. *Journal of Applied Communication Research, 32,* 343–364.

**Compton, W. C., & Hoffman, E.** (2013). *Positive psychology* (2nd ed.). Boston: Cengage.

**Comstock, G.** (2012). The use of television and other film-related media. In D. G. Singer & J. L. Singer (Eds.), *Handbook of children and the media* (2nd ed.). Thousand Oaks, CA: Sage.

**Conley, T. D.** (2011). Perceived proposer personality characteristics and gender differences in acceptance of casual sex offers. *Journal of Personality and Social Psychology, 100,* 309–329.

**Conley, T. D., Moors, A. C., Matsick, J. L., Ziegler, A., & Valentine, B. A.** (2011). Women, men and the bedroom: Methodological and conceptual insights that narrow, reframe, and eliminate gender differences in sexuality. *Current Directions in Psychological Science, 20,* 296–300.

**Connellan, J., Baron-Cohen, S., Wheelwright, S., Batki, A., & Ahluwalia, J.** (2000). Sex differences in human neonatal social perception. *Infant Behavior & Development, 23,* 113–118.

**Conner, K. R., Wood, J., Pisani, A. R., & Kemp, J.** (2012). Evaluation of a suicide prevention training curriculum for substance abuse treatment providers based on treatment improvement protocol number 50. *Journal of Substance Abuse and Treatment.* (in press)

**Constantine, N. A.** (2008). Converging evidence leaves policy behind: Sex education in the United States. *Journal of Adolescent Health, 42,* 324–326.

**Constantinidou, F., & Baker, S.** (2002). Stimulus modality and verbal learning performance in normal aging. *Brain and Language, 82,* 296–311.

**Conway, M., & Rubin, D.** (1993). The structure of autobiographical memory. In A. F. Collins, S. E. Gathercole, M. A. Conway, & P. E. Morris (Eds.), *Theories of memory.* Hillsdale, NJ: Erlbaum.

**Cook, J. R., & Kilmer, R. P.** (2012). Systems of care: New partnerships for community psychology. *American Journal of Community Psychology, 49* (3-4), 393–403.

**Cooper, R. M., & Zubek, J. P.** (1958). Effects of enriched and restricted early environments on the learning ability of bright and dull rats. *Canadian Journal of Psychology, 12,* 159–164.

Cooper, Z. D., Jones, J. D., & Comer, S. D. (2012). Glial modulators: A novel pharmaceutical approach to altering behavioral effects of abused substances. *Expert Opinion on Investigational Drugs, 21,* 169–178.

Copeland, D. E., Radvansky, G. A., & Goodwin, K. A. (2009). A novel study: Forgetting curves and the reminiscence bump. *Memory, 17,* 323–336.

Copen, C. E., Daniels, K., Vespa, J., & Mosher, W. D. (2012). First marriages in the United States: Data from the 2006–2010 National Survey of Family Growth. *National health statistics reports* (no. 49). Hyattsville, MD: National Center for Health Statistics.

Corey, G. (2012). *Theory and practice of group counseling* (8th ed.). Boston: Cengage.

Corr, P. J. (2008). Reinforcement sensitivity theory (RST): Introduction. In P. J. Corr (Ed.), *The reinforcement sensitivity theory of personality* (pp. 1–43). New York: Cambridge University Press.

Correa, T., Hinsley, A. W., & de Zuniga, H. G. (2010). Who interacts on the web?: The intersection of users' personality and social media use. *Computers in Human Behavior, 26,* 247–253.

Corrigan, P. W. (2007). How clinical diagnosis might exacerbate the stigma of mental illness. *Social Work, 52,* 31–39.

Corsica, J. A., & Perri, M. G. (2013). Understanding and managing obesity. In I. B. Weiner & others (Eds.), *Handbook of psychology* (2nd ed., vol. 9). New York; Wiley.

Cosci, F. (2012). Assessment of personality in psychosomatic medicine: Current concepts. *Advances in Psychosomatic Medicine, 32,* 133–159.

Cosmides, L. (2011). Evolutionary psychology. *Annual Review of Psychology* (vol. 62). Palo Alto, CA: Annual Reviews.

Costa, A., Carlesimo, G. A., & Caltagirone, C. (2012). Prospective memory functioning: A new area of investigation in the clinical neuropsychology and rehabilitation of Parkinson's disease and mild cognitive impairment. *Neurological Sciences.* doi: 10.1007/s10072-012-0935-y

Costa, P. T., & McCrae, R. R. (1992). *Revised NEO personality inventory.* Odessa, FL: Psychological Assessment Resources.

Costa, P. T., & McCrae, R. R. (2006). Age changes in personality and their origins: Comment on Roberts, Walter, and Viechtbauer (2006). *Psychological Bulletin, 132,* 26–28.

Costa, P. T., Terraciano, A., McCrae, R. R., Scally, M., & Abecasis, G. (2010). An alternative to the search for single polymorphisms: Toward molecular personality scales for the five-factor model. *Journal of Personality and Social Psychology, 99* (6), 1014–1024.

Cotter, D., Mackay, D., Chana, G., Beasley, C., Landau, S., & Everall, I. P. (2002). Reduced neuronal size and glial density in area 9 of the dorsolateral prefrontal cortex in subjects with major depressive disorder. *Cerebral Cortex, 12,* 386–394.

Cotugno, G., & others. (2011). Adherence to diet and quality of life in patients with phenylketonuria. *Acta Pediatrica, 100* (8), 1144–1149.

Couillard-Despres, S., Iglseder, B., & Aigner, L. (2011). Neurogenesis, cellular plasticity, and cognition: The impact of stem cells in the adult and aging brain. *Gerontology, 57,* 559–564.

Courtet, P., & others. (2004). Serotonin transporter gene may be involved in short-term risk of subsequent suicide attempts. *Biological Psychiatry, 55,* 46–51.

Covell, N. H., & others. (2012). Effectiveness of switching from long-acting injectable fluphenazine or haloperidol decanoate to long-acting injectable risperidone microspheres: An open-label randomized controlled trial. *Journal of Clinical Psychology, 73* (5), 669–675.

Cowan, M. K. (2013). *Microbiology fundamentals.* New York: McGraw-Hill.

Cowan, N. (2008). What are the differences between long-term, short-term, and working memory? In W. S. Sossin, L. C. Lacaille, V. F. Castellucci, & S. Belleville (Eds.), *Progress in Brain Research, 169,* 323–338.

Cowan, N. (2010). The magical mystery four: How is working memory capacity limited, and why? *Current Directions in Psychological Science, 19,* 51–57.

Cowan, N., Li, D., Moffitt, A., Becker, T. M., Martin, E. A., Saults, J. S., & Christ, S. E. (2011a). A neural region of abstract working memory. *Journal of Cognitive Neuroscience, 23,* 2852–2863.

Cowan, N., Morey, C. C., AuBuchon, A. M., Zwilling, C. E., Gilchrist, A. L., & Saults, J. S. (2011b). New insights into an old problem: Distinguishing storage from processing in the development of working memory. In P. Barrouillet & V. Gaillard (Eds.), *Cognitive development and working memory: A dialogue between neo-Piagetian theories and cognitive approaches* (pp. 137–150). Hove, England: Psychology Press.

Cowan, N., Rouder, J. N., Blume, C. L., & Saults, J. S. (2012). Models of verbal working memory capacity: What does it take to make them work? *Psychological Review.* (in press)

Cowan, R. L., Roberts, D. M., & Joers, J. M. (2008). Neuroimaging in human MDMA (Ecstasy) users. *Annals of the New York Academy of Sciences, 1139,* 291–298.

Cowdrey, F. A., & Park, R. J. (2012). The role of experiential avoidance, rumination, and mindfulness in eating disorders. *Eating Behaviors, 13,* 100–105.

Cox, K. S., Wilt, J., Olson, B., & McAdams, D. P. (2010). Generativity, the Big Five, and psychosocial adaptation in midlife adults. *Journal of Personality, 78,* 1185–1208.

Cox, R. E., & Bryant, R. A. (2008) Advances in hypnosis research: Methods, designs, and contributions of intrinsic and instrumental hypnosis. In M. R. Nash & A. J. Barnier (Eds.), *The Oxford handbook of hypnosis: Research theory and practice* (pp. 311–336). New York: Oxford University Press.

Cox, T. L., & others. (2012). Stress management–augmented behavioral weight loss intervention for African American women: A pilot, randomized controlled trial. *Health Education and Behavior.* (in press)

Coyne, J. C. (1976). Toward an interactional description of depression. *Psychiatry, 39,* 28–40.

Coyne, J. C., & Tennen, H. (2010). Positive psychology in cancer care: Bad science, exaggerated claims, and unproven medicine. *Annals of Behavioral Medicine, 39,* 16–26.

Coyne, J., Tennen, H., & Ranchor, A. V. (2010). Positive psychology and cancer care: A story line resistant to evidence. *Annals of Behavioral Medicine, 39,* 35–42.

Coyne, S. M., Robinson, S. L., & Nelson, D. A. (2010). Does reality backbite? Physical, verbal, and relational aggression in reality television programs. *Journal of Broadcasting & Electronic Media, 54,* 282–298.

Craik, F. I. M., & Lockhart, R. S. (1972). Levels of processing: A framework for memory research. *Journal of Verbal Learning and Verbal Behavior, 11,* 671–684.

Craik, F. I. M., & Tulving, E. (1975). Depth of processing and retention of words in episodic memory. *Journal of Experimental Psychology: General, 104,* 268–294.

Cramer, P. (2008a). Longitudinal study of defense mechanisms: Late childhood to late adolescence. *Journal of Personality, 75,* 1–23.

Cramer, P. (2008b). Seven pillars of defense mechanism theory. *Social and Personality Psychology Compass, 2,* 1963–1981.

Cramer, P. (2009). The development of defense mechanisms from pre-adolescence to early adulthood: Do IQ and social class matter? A longitudinal study. *Journal of Research in Personality, 43,* 464–471.

Cramer, P., & Jones, C. J. (2007). Defense mechanisms predict differential lifespan change in self-control and self-acceptance. *Journal of Research in Personality, 41,* 841–855.

Crandall, C. S. (2004). Social contagion of binge eating. In R. M. Kowalski & M. R. Leary (Eds.), *The interface of social and clinical psychology: Key readings* (pp. 99–115). New York: Psychology Press.

Crede, M., Harms, P., Niehorster, S., & Gaye-Valentine, A. (2012). An evaluation of the consequences of using short measures of the big five personality traits. *Journal of Personality and Social Psychology, 102* (4), 874–888.

Crenshaw, M. (2007). Explaining suicide terrorism: A review essay. *Security Studies, 16,* 133–162.

Crisafulli, C., & others. (2012). Case-control association study of 14 variants of CREB1, CREBBP, and CREM on diagnosis and treatment outcome in major depressive disorder and bipolar disorder. *Psychiatry Research.* doi: 10.1016/j.psychres.2011.08.022

Crocker, J., Major, B., & Steele, C. (1998). Social stigma. In D. T. Gilbert, S. T. Fiske, & G. Lindzey (Eds.), *Handbook of social psychology* (4th ed., vol. 2). New York: McGraw-Hill.

Croft, W. (2012). *Verbs: Aspect and causal structure.* New York: Oxford University Press.

Cronbach, L. J. (1957). The two disciplines of scientific psychology. *American Psychologist, 12,* 671–684.

Crowley, J. J. (2012). Deep resequencing and association analysis of schizophrenia candidate genes. *Molecular Psychiatry.* (in press)

Crowley, K., Pickle, J., Dale, R., & Fattal, O. (2008). A critical examination of bifrontal electroconvulsive therapy: Clinical efficacy, cognitive side effects, and directions for future research. *Journal of ECT, 24,* 268–271.

Crowley, S. J., & Carskadon, M. A. (2010). Modifications to weekend recovery sleep delay circadian phase in older adolescents. *Chronobiology International, 27,* 1469–1492.

Csikszentmihalyi, M. (1990). *Flow: The psychology of optimal experience.* New York: HarperPerennial.

Cullen, K. (2010, January 14). The untouchable mean girls. *Boston Globe.* www.boston.com/news/local/massachusetts/articles/2010/01/24/the_untouchable_mean_girls/ (accessed May 21, 2012)

Cumming, E., & Henry, W. E. (1961). *Growing older: The process of disengagement.* New York: Basic.

Cunningham, R. L., & McGinnis, M. Y. (2007). Factors influencing aggression toward females by male rats exposed to anabolic androgenic steroids during puberty. *Hormones and Behavior, 51,* 135–141.

Curtis, M. A., Kam, M., & Faull, R. L. (2011). Neurogenesis in humans. *European Journal of Neuroscience, 33,* 1170–1174.

Curtiss, S. (1977). *Genie.* New York: Academic.

## D

Dale, K. Y., Berg, R., Elden, A., Odegard, A., & Holte, A. (2009). Testing the diagnosis of dissociative identity disorder through measures of dissociation, absorption, hypnotizability, and PTSD: A Norwegian pilot study. *Journal of Trauma and Dissociation, 10,* 102–112.

Damon, W. (2008). *The path to purpose: Helping our children find their calling in life.* New York: Free Press.

Damsa, C., Kosel, M., & Moussally, J. (2009). Current status of brain imaging in anxiety disorders. *Current Opinion in Psychiatry, 22,* 96–110.

Danner, D. D., Snowdon, D. A., & Friesen, W. V. (2001). Positive emotions in early life and longevity: Findings from the Nun Study. *Journal of Personality and Social Psychology, 80,* 804–813.

Darcq, E., & others. (2011). RSK2 signaling in brain habenula contributes to place aversive learning. *Learning and Memory, 18,* 574–578.

Darcy, E. (2012). Gender issues in child and adolescent eating disorders. In J. Lock (Ed.), *Oxford handbook of child and adolescent eating disorders: Developmental perspectives.* New York: Oxford University Press.

Darley, J. M., & Latané, B. (1968). Bystander intervention in emergencies: Diffusion of responsibility. *Journal of Personality and Social Psychology, 8,* 377–383.

Darling, S., Allen, R. J., Havelka, J., Campbell, A., & Rattray, E. (2012). Visuospatial bootstrapping: Long-term memory representations are necessary for implicit binding of verbal and visuospatial working memory. *Psychonomic Bulletin & Review, 19* (2), 258–263.

Darwin, C. (1965). *The expression of the emotions in man and animals.* Chicago: University of Chicago Press. (original work published 1872)

Darwin, C. (1979). *The origin of species.* New York: Avenal Books. (original work published 1859)

da Silva Cais, C. F., Stefanello, S., Fabrício Mauro, M. L., Vaz Scavacini de Freitas, G., & Botega, N. J. (2009). Factors associated with repeated suicide attempts: Preliminary results of the WHO Multisite Intervention Study on Suicidal Behavior (SUPRE-MISS) from Campinas, Brazil. *Crisis: The Journal of Crisis Intervention and Suicide Prevention, 30,* 73–78.

**DatingSitesReviews.com.** (2012). *Current online dating and dating services facts & statistics.* www.datingsitesreviews.com/staticpages/index.php?page=online-dating-industry-facts-statistics (accessed May 22, 2012)

**D'Ausilio, A., Altenmuller, E., Olivetti, B. M., & Lotze, M.** (2006). Cross-modal plasticity of motor cortex while listening to a rehearsed musical piece. *European Journal of Neuroscience, 24,* 955–958.

**Davidson, J. R.** (2009). First-line pharmacotherapy approaches for generalized anxiety disorder. *Journal of Clinical Psychiatry, 70, Suppl. 2,* S25–S31.

**Davidson, K. W., & others.** (2006). Assessment and treatment of depression in patients with cardiovascular disease: National Heart, Lung, and Blood Institute Working Group Report. *Psychosomatic Medicine, 68,* 645–650.

**Davidson, R. J.** (2000). Affective style, psychopathology, and resilience: Brain mechanisms and plasticity. *American Psychologist, 55,* 196–214.

**Davidson, R. J.** (2005). Neural substrates of affective style and value. In Y. Christen (Series Ed.) & J.-P. Changeux, A. R. Damasio, W. Singer, & Y. Christen (Vol. Eds.), *Research and perspectives in neurosciences: Neurobiology of human values* (pp. 67–90). Germany: Springer-Verlag.

**Davidson, R. J., & Begley, S.** (2012). *The emotional life of your brain.* New York; Hudson Street.

**Davidson, R. J., Kabat-Zinn, J., Schumacher, J., Rosenkranz, M. M., Daniel, S., Saki, F., Urbanowski, F., Harrington, A., Bonus, K., & Sheridan, J. F.** (2003). Alterations in brain and immune function produced by mindfulness meditation. *Psychosomatic Medicine, 65* (4), 564–570.

**Davidson, R. J., Scherer, K. R., & Goldsmith, H. H. (Eds.).** (2002). *Handbook of affective sciences.* New York: Oxford University Press.

**Davidson, R. J., Shackman, A., & Pizzagalli, D.** (2002). The functional neuroanatomy of emotion and affective style. In R. J. Davidson, K. R. Scherer, & H. H. Goldsmith (Eds.), *Handbook of affective sciences.* New York: Oxford University Press.

**Davis, C., Patte, K., Curtis, C., & Reid, C.** (2010). Immediate pleasures and future consequences: A neuropsychological study of binge eating and obesity. *Appetite, 54,* 208–213.

**Davis, C. M., & Riley, A. L.** (2010). Conditioned taste aversion learning: Implications for animal models of drug abuse. *Annals of the New York Academy of Sciences, 1187,* 247–275.

**Davis, J. I., Senghas, A., & Ochsner, K. N.** (2009). How does facial feedback modulate emotional experience? *Journal of Research in Personality, 43* (5), 822–829.

**DeAngelis, T.** (2002). Binge-eating disorder: What's the best treatment? *Monitor on Psychology, 33.* www.apa.org/monitor/mar02/binge.html (accessed May 24, 2012)

**Deary, I. J.** (2012). Intelligence. *Annual Review of Intelligence* (vol. 63). Palo Alto, CA: Annual Reviews.

**De Biasi, M., & Dani, J. A.** (2011). Reward, addiction, and withdrawal to nicotine. *Annual Review of Neuroscience,* (vol. 34). Palo Alto, CA: Annual Reviews.

**Debiec, J., & LeDoux, J. E.** (2006). Noradrenergic signaling in the amygdale contributes to the reconsolidation of fear memory: Treatment implications for PTSD. *Annals of the New York Academy of Science, 1071,* 521–524.

**Deci, E., & Ryan, R.** (1994). Promoting self-determined education. *Scandinavian Journal of Educational Research, 38,* 3–14.

**Deci, E. L., & Ryan, R. M.** (2000). The "what" and "why" of goal pursuits: Human needs and the self-determination of behavior. *Psychological Inquiry, 4,* 227–268.

**Deci, E. L., & Ryan, R. M. (Eds.).** (2002). *Handbook of self-determination research.* Rochester, NY: University of Rochester Press.

**Deci, E. L., & Ryan, R. M.** (2012). Self-determination theory in health care and its relations to motivational interviewing: A few comments. *International Journal of Behavioral Nutrition and Physical Activity, 9,* 24.

**De Cort, K., Griez, E., Büchler, M., & Schruers, K.** (2012). The role of "interoceptive" fear conditioning in the development of panic disorder. *Behavior Therapy, 43,* 203–215.

**Dedert, E., & others.** (2012). Stress, coping, and circadian disruption among women awaiting breast cancer surgery. *Annals of Behavior Medicine.* (in press)

**De Dreu, K. W., Greer, L. L., Hendgraaf, M. J. J., Shalvi, S., Van Kleef, G. A., Baas, M., Ten Velden, F. S., Van Dijk, E., & Feith, S. W. W.** (2010). The neuropeptide oxytocin regulates parochial altruism intergroup conflict among humans. *Science, 328,* 1408–1411.

**De Fruyt, F., & De Clercq, B.** (2012). Childhood antecedents of personality disorders. In T. Widiger (Ed.), *Oxford handbook of personality disorders.* New York: Oxford University Press.

**Degnin, F. D.** (2009). Difficult patients, overmedication, and groupthink. *Journal of Clinical Ethics, 20,* 64–74.

**de Graaf, T. A., Hsieh, P.-J., & Sack, A. T.** (2012). The "correlates" in neural correlates of consciousness. *Neuroscience and Biobehavioral Reviews, 36,* 191–197.

**Dehaene, S., & Changeux, J. P.** (2011). Experimental and theoretical approaches to conscious processing. *Neuron, 70,* 200–207.

**Dehaene, S., Changeux, J., Naccache, L., Sackur, J., & Sergent, C.** (2006). Conscious, preconscious, and subliminal processing: A testable taxonomy. *Trends in Cognitive Sciences, 10,* 204–211.

**Dein, S., Cook, C. C. H., & Koenig, H. G.** (2012). Religion, spirituality, and mental health: Current controversies and future directions. *Journal of Nervous and Mental Disease.* (in press)

**De Koninck, J.** (2012). Sleep, dreams, and dreaming. In C. M. Morin & C. A. Espie (Eds.), *Oxford handbook of sleep and sleep disorders.* New York: Oxford University Press.

**de Lange, F. P., van Gaal, S., Lamme, V. A., & Dehaene, S.** (2011). How awareness changes the relative weights of evidence during human decision-making. *PLoS One, 9* (11), e1001203.

**Del Corso, J. J., & Rehfuss, M. C., & Galvin, K.** (2011). Striving to adapt: Addressing Adler's work task in the 21st century. *Journal of Individual Psychology, 67,* 88–106.

**Del Cul, A., Dehaene, S., Reyes, P., Bravo, E., & Slachevsky, A.** (2009). Causal role of prefrontal cortex in the threshold for access to consciousness. *Brain, 132,* 2531–2540.

**Dell, P. F., & Eisenhower, J. W.** (1990). Adolescent multiple personality disorder: A preliminary study of eleven cases. *Journal of the American Academy of Child & Adolescent Psychiatry, 29,* 359–366.

**Dell, P. F., & O'Neil, J. A. (Eds.).** (2007). *Dissociation and the dissociative disorders: DSM-V and beyond.* New York: Routledge.

**Dell'osso, B., & Lader, M.** (2012). Do benzodiazepines still deserve a major role in the treatment of psychiatric disorders? A critical reappraisal. *European Psychiatry.* doi : 10.1016/j.eurpsy.2011.11.003

**Delprado, J., & others.** (2012). Clinical measures of prospective memory in amnestic mild cognitive impairment. *Journal of the International Neuropsychological Society, 18* (2) 295–304.

**DeMarree, K. G., & Petty, R. E.** (2007). The elaboration likelihood model of persuasion. In R. F. Baumeister & K. D. Vohs (Eds.), *Encyclopedia of social psychology.* Thousand Oaks, CA: Sage.

**Dennis, A.** (2005). Osama bin Laden: The sum of all fears. In W. T. Schultz (Ed.), *Handbook of psychobiography* (pp. 311–322). Oxford, England: Oxford University Press.

**Denollet, J., & Conraads, V. M.** (2011). Type D personality and vulnerability to adverse outcomes of heart disease. *Cleveland Clinic Journal of Medicine, 78, Suppl. 1,* S13–S19.

**Depue, R. A., & Collins, P. F.** (1999). Neurobiology of the structure of personality: Dopamine, facilitation of incentive motivation, and extraversion. *Behavioural and Brain Sciences, 22,* 491–569.

**De Raad, B., Barelds, D. P. H., Levert, E., Ostendorf, F., Mlacic, B., Di Blas, L., Hrebickova, M., Perugini, M., Church, A. T., & Katigbak, M. S.** (2010). Only three factors of personality description are fully replicable across languages: A comparison of 14 trait taxonomies. *Journal of Personality and Social Psychology, 98,* 160–173.

**Derks, D., Bos, A. E. R., & von Grumbkow, J.** (2008). Emoticons in computer-mediated communication: Social motives and social context. *CyberPsychology & Behavior, 11,* 99–101.

**Derryberry, D., & Reed, M.** (2002). Information processing approaches to individual differences in emotional reactivity. In R. J. Davidson, K. R. Scherer, & H. H. Goldsmith (Eds.), *Handbook of affective sciences.* New York: Oxford University Press.

**De Vos, J.** (2010). From Milgram to Zimbardo: The double birth of postwar psychology/psychologization. *History of the Human Sciences, 23,* 156–175.

**de Waal, F. B. M., Leimgruber, K., & Greenberg, A. R.** (2008). Giving is self-rewarding for monkeys. *PNAS Proceedings of the National Academy of Sciences USA, 105,* 13685–13689.

**DeWall, C. N., Twenge, J. M., Gitter, S. A., & Baumeister, R. F.** (2009). It's the thought that counts: The role of hostile cognition in shaping aggressive responses to social exclusion. *Journal of Personality and Social Psychology, 96,* 45–59.

**de Wit, S., Niry, D., Wariyar, R., Aitken, M. R., & Dickinson, A.** (2007). Stimulus–outcome interactions during instrumental discrimination learning by rats and humans. *Journal of Experimental Psychology: Animal Behavioral Processes, 33,* 1–11.

**DeWitt, J. C., Peden-Adams, M. M., Keil, D. E., & Dietert, R. R.** (2012). Current status of developmental immunotoxicity: Early life-patterns and testing. *Toxicologic Pathology, 40,* 230–236.

**DeYoung, C. G.** (2010). Personality neuroscience and the biology of traits. *Social and Personality Psychology Compass, 4,* 1165–1180.

**DeYoung, C. G., Hirsh, J. B., Shane, M. S., Papademetris, X., Rajeevan, N., & Gray, J. R.** (2010). Testing predictions from personality neuroscience: Brain structure and the big five. *Psychological Science, 21,* 820–828.

**de Zwaan, M., Mitchell, J. E., Crosby, R. D., Mussell, M. P., Raymond, N. C., Specker, S. M., & Seim, H. C.** (2005). Short-term cognitive behavioral treatment does not improve outcome of a comprehensive very-low-calorie diet program in obese women with binge eating disorder. *Behavior Therapy, 36,* 89–99.

**Dhillon, S.** (2012). Aripiprazole: A review of its use in the management of mania in adults with bipolar 1 disorder. *Drugs, 72,* 133–162.

**Diamond, A.** (2013). Executive functioning. *Annual Review of Psychology* (vol. 64). Palo Alto, CA: Annual Reviews.

**Diamond, L. M.** (2008). *Sexual fluidity: Understanding women's love and desire.* Cambridge, MA: Harvard University Press.

**Diamond, L. M.** (2013). Concepts of female sexual orientation. In C. Patterson & A. R. D'Augelli (Eds.), *The psychology sexual orientation.* New York: Cambridge University Press.

**Diamond, M., & Sigmundson, H. K.** (1997). Sex reassignment at birth. *Archives of Pediatric and Adolescent Medicine, 151,* 298–304.

**Diaper, A., & others.** (2012). Evaluation of the effects of venlafaxine and pregabalin on the carbon dioxide inhalation models of generalized anxiety disorder. *Journal of Psychopharmacology.* doi:10.1177/0269881112443742

**Dick, D. M.** (2011). Gene-environment interaction in psychological traits and disorders. *Annual Review of Clinical Psychology* (vol. 7). Palo Alto, CA: Annual Reviews.

**Dick, D. M., & others.** (2011). CHRM2, parenting monitoring, and adolescent externalizing behavior: Evidence for gene–environment interaction. *Psychological Science, 22,* 481–489.

**Dickson, R. A., Pillemer, D. B., & Bruehl, E. C.** (2011). The reminiscence bump for salient personal memories: Is a cultural life script required? *Memory and Cognition, 39,* 977–991.

**DiClemente, C. C.** (2006). Natural change and the troublesome use of substances: A life-course perspective. In W. R. Miller & K. M. Carroll (Eds.), *Rethinking substance abuse: What the science shows, and what we should do about it* (pp. 81–96). New York: Guilford.

**DiCorcia, J. A., & Tronick, E.** (2011). Quotidian resilience: Exploring mechanisms that drive resilience from a perspective of everyday stress and coping. *Neuroscience and Biobehavioral Reviews, 35,* 1593–1602.

**Diefenbach, G. J., Disch, W. B., Robinson, J. T., Baez, E., & Coman, E.** (2009). Anxious depression among Puerto Rican and African American older adults. *Aging and Mental Health, 13,* 118–126.

**Diekelmann, S., Wilhelm, I., & Born, J.** (2009). The whats and whens of sleep-dependent memory consolidation. *Sleep Medicine Reviews, 13,* 309–321.

**Dien, J.** (2009). A tale of two recognition systems: Implications of the fusiform face area and the visual work farm area for lateralized object recognition models. *Neuropsychologia, 47,* 1–16.

**Diener, E.** (1999). Introduction to the special section on the structure of emotion. *Journal of Personality and Social Psychology, 76,* 803–804.

**Diener, E.** (2000). Subjective well-being: The science of happiness and a proposal for a national index. *American Psychologist, 55,* 34–43.

**Diener, E., & Chan, M. Y.** (2011). Happy people live longer: Subjective well-being contributes to health and well-being. *Applied Psychology: Health and Well-Being, 3,* 1–43.

**Diener, E., & Diener, C.** (1996). Most people are happy. *Psychological Science, 7,* 181–185.

**Diener, E., Emmons, R. A., Larsen, R. J., & Griffin, S.** (1985). The Satisfaction with Life Scale. *Journal of Personality Assessment, 49,* 71–75.

**Diener, E., Kesebir, P., & Tov, W.** (2009). Happiness. In M. R. Leary & R. H. Hoyle (Eds.), *Handbook of individual differences in social behavior* (pp. 147–160). New York: Guilford.

**Diener, E., Ng, W., Harter, J., & Arora, R.** (2010). Wealth and happiness across the world: Material prosperity predicts life evaluation, whereas psychosocial prosperity predicts positive feeling. *Journal of Personality and Social Psychology, 99,* 52–61.

**Diener, E., & Seligman, M. E. P.** (2002). Very happy people. *Psychological Science, 13,* 81–84.

**Digman, J. M.** (1990). Personality structure: Emergence of the five-factor model. *Annual Review of Psychology, 41,* 417–440.

**Dijksterhuis, A., Bos, M. W., Van der Leij, A., & Van Baaren, R. B.** (2009). Predicting soccer matches after unconscious and conscious thought as a function of expertise. *Psychological Science, 20,* 1381–1387.

**Dijksterhuis, A., & Nordgren, L. F.** (2006). A theory of unconscious thought. *Perspectives on Psychological Science, 1,* 95–109.

**Dijksterhuis, A., & Van Knippenberg, A.** (1998). The relation between perception and behavior or how to win a game of Trivial Pursuit. *Journal of Personality and Social Psychology, 74,* 865–877.

**Dion, K. K., & Dion, K. L.** (2001). Gender and relationships. In R. K. Unger (Ed.), *Handbook of the psychology of women and gender* (pp. 256–271). Hoboken, NJ: Wiley.

**Distel, M. A., Trull, T. J., Derom, C. A., Thiery, E. W., Grimmer, M. A., Martin, N. G., Willemsen, G., & Dittmar, H., Halliwell, E., & Ive, S.** (2006). Does Barbie make girls want to be thin? The effect of experimental exposure to images of dolls on the body image of 5–8-year-old girls. *Developmental Psychology, 42,* 283–292.

**Dixon, R. M. W.** (2012). *Basic linguistic theory* (vol. 3). New York: Oxford University Press.

**Dobson, R.** (2005). "Fighting spirit" after cancer diagnosis does not improve outcome. *British Medical Journal, 330,* 865.

**Dodge, E.** (2012). Family evolution and process during the child and adolescent years in eating disorders. In J. Lock (Ed.), *Oxford handbook of child and adolescent eating disorders: Developmental perspectives.* New York: Oxford University Press.

**Dolan, M., & Fullam, R.** (2006). Face affect recognition deficits in personality disordered offenders: Associate with psychopathy. *Psychological Medicine, 36,* 1563–1569.

**Dollard, J., Doob, L. W., Miller, N. E., Mowrer, O. H., & Sears, R. R.** (1939). *Frustration and aggression.* New Haven, CT: Yale University Press.

**Domhoff, G. W.** (2007). Realistic simulation and bizarreness in dream content: Past findings and suggestions for future research. In D. Barrett & P. McNamara (Eds.), *The new science of dreaming: Content, recall, and personality correlates* (vol. 2, pp. 1–27). Westport, CT: Praeger.

**Domhoff, G. W.** (2011). The neural substrate for dreaming: Is it a subsystem of the default network? *Consciousness and Cognition, 20,* 1163–1174.

**Domjan, M.** (2005). Pavlovian conditioning: A functional perspective. *Annual Review of Psychology* (vol. 56). Palo Alto, CA: Annual Reviews.

**Domjan, M.** (2010). *The principles of learning and behavior* (6th ed.). Boston: Cengage.

**Donahue, C. B., Odlaug, B. L., & Grant, J. E.** (2011). Compulsive buying treated with motivational interviewing and imaginal desensitization. *Annals of Clinical Psychology, 23,* 226–227.

**Donegan, E., & Dugas, M. J.** (2012). Generalized anxiety disorder: A comparison of symptom change in adults receiving cognitive-behavioral therapy of applied relaxation. *Journal of Consulting and Clinical Psychology, 80* (3), 490–496.

**Donnellan, M. B., Larsen-Rife, D., & Conger, R. D.** (2005). Personality, family history, and competence in early adult romantic relationships. *Journal of Personality and Social Psychology, 88,* 562–576.

**Donnellan, M. B., Lucas, R. E., & Fleeson, W.** (2009). Introduction to personality and assessment at age 40: Reflections on the legacy of the person-situation debate and the future of person-situation integration. *Journal of Research in Personality, 43,* 117–119.

**Doolan, A. W., Day, D. D., Maerlender, A. C., Goforth, M., & Gunnar, B. P.** (2012). A review of return to play issues and sports-related concussion. *Annals of Biomedical Engineering, 40,* 106–113.

**Dorn, L. H., & Biro, F. M.** (2011). Puberty and its measurement: A decade in review. *Journal of Research on Adolescence, 21,* 180–195.

**Dossey, L.** (2011). Why are scientists afraid of Daryl Bem? *Explore: The Journal of Science and Healing, 7,* 127–137.

**Dourley, J.** (2011). Jung's equation of the ground of being with the ground of psyche. *Journal of Analytical Psychology, 56,* 514–531.

**Dovidio, J. F., Kawakami, K., & Gaertner, S. L.** (2002). Implicit and explicit prejudice and interracial interaction. *Journal of Personality and Social Psychology, 82,* 62–68.

**Dovidio, J. F., Newheiser, A.-K., & Leyens, J.-P.** (2012). History of intergroup relations research. In A. W. Kruglanski & W. Stroebe (Eds.), *Handbook of the history of social psychology.* New York: Psychology Press.

**Dovidio, J. F., Saguy, T., Gaertner, S. L., & Thomas, E. L.** (2012). From attitudes to (in)action: The darker side of "we." In J. Dixon, M. Keynes, & M. Levine (Eds.), *Beyond prejudice.* New York; Cambridge University Press.

**Draguns, J. G., & Tanaka-Matsumi, J.** (2003). Assessment of psychopathology across and within cultures: Issues and findings. *Behavior Research and Therapy, 41,* 755–776.

**Drake, C., Levine, R., & Laska, E. A.** (2007). Identifying prognostic factors that predict recovery in the presence of loss to follow-up. In K. Hopper, G. Harrison, A. Janca, & N. Sartorius (Eds.), *Recovery from schizophrenia: An international perspective: A report from the WHO Collaborative Project, the international study of schizophrenia* (pp. 69–72). New York: Oxford University Press.

**Dritschel, B., Kao, C., Astell, A., Neufeind, J., & Lai, T.** (2011). How are depression and autobiographical memory retrieval related to culture? *Journal of Abnormal Psychology, 120,* 969–974.

**Duenas, J., & others.** (2011, August). Neuroscience robotics to investigate multisensory integration and bodily awareness. *Conference Proceedings: Annual International Conference of the IEEE Engineering in Medicine and Biology Society,* 8348–8352.

**Duman, R. S., Li, N., Liu, R. J., Duric, V., & Aghajanian, G.** (2012). Signaling pathways underlying the rapid antidepressant actions of ketamine. *Neuropharmacology, 62,* 35–41.

**Dunbar, R. I. M., & Shultz, S.** (2007). Evolution in the social brain. *Science, 317,* 1344–1347.

**Duncan, A. E., Scherrer, J., Fu, Q., Bucholz, K. K., Heath, A. C., True, W. R., Haber, J. R., Howell, D., & Jacob, T.** (2006). Exposure to paternal alcoholism does not predict development of alcohol-use disorders in offspring: Evidence from an offspring-of-twins study. *Journal of Studies on Alcohol, 67,* 649–656.

**Dunkel Schetter, C.** (2011). Psychological science in the study of pregnancy and birth. *Annual Review of Psychology* (vol. 62). Palo Alto, CA: Annual Reviews.

**Dunn, E. W., Aknin, L. B., & Norton, M. I.** (2008). Spending money on others promotes happiness. *Science, 319,* 1687–1688.

**Dunn, K. I., Mohr, P., Wilson, C. J., & Wittert, G. A.** (2011). Determinants of fast-food consumption: An application of the theory of planned behavior. *Appetite, 57,* 349–357.

**Dunner, D. L.** (2001). Acute and maintenance treatment of chronic depression. *Journal of Clinical Psychiatry, 62, Suppl. 6,* 10–16.

**Dupoux, E., de Gardelle, V., & Kouider, S.** (2008). Subliminal speech perception and auditory streaming. *Cognition, 109,* 267–273.

**Dupre, K. E., & Barling, J.** (2006). Predicting and preventing supervisory workplace aggression. *Journal of Occupational Health Psychology, 11,* 13–26.

**Durantini, M. R., & Albarracin, D.** (2009). Material and social incentives to participation in behavioral interventions: A meta-analysis of gender disparities in enrollment and retention in experimental HIV prevention interventions. *Health Psychology, 28* (5), 631–640.

**Durantini, M. R., & Albarracin, D.** (2012). Men and women have specific needs that facilitate enrollment in HIV-prevention counseling. *AIDS Care.* (in press)

**Duvarci, S., Nader, K., & LeDoux, J. E.** (2008). De novo mRNA synthesis is required for both consolidation and reconsolidation of fear memories in the amygdala. *Learning and Memory, 15,* 747–755.

**Dweck, C. S.** (2006). *Mindset.* New York: Random House.

**Dweck, C. S.** (2012). Social development. In P. Zelazo (Ed.), *Oxford handbook of developmental psychology.* New York: Oxford University Press.

## E

**Eagly, A. H.** (2009). The his and hers of prosocial behavior: An examination of the social psychology of gender. *American Psychologist, 64* (8), 644–658.

**Eagly, A. H.** (2012). Science, feminism, and the investigation of gender. In R. W. Proctor & E. J. Capaldi (Eds.), *Psychology of science: Implicit and explicit reasoning.* New York: Oxford University Press.

**Eagly, A. H., & Crowley, M.** (1986). Gender and helping behavior: A meta-analytic review of the social psychological literature. *Psychological Bulletin, 100,* 283–308.

**Eagly, A. H., & Wood, W.** (2010). Gender roles in a biosocial world. In P. van Lange, A. Kruglanski, & E. T. Higgins (Eds.), *Handbook of theories in social psychology.* Thousand Oaks, CA: Sage.

**Eagly, A. H., & Wood, W.** (2011). Feminism and the evolution of sex differences and similarities. *Sex Roles, 64,* 9–10.

**Eagly, A. H., & Wood, W.** (2012). Social role theory. In P. A. M. Van Langue, A. W. Kruglanski, & E. T. Higgins (Eds.), *Handbook of theories of social psychology* (pp. 458–476). Thousand Oaks, CA: Sage.

**Eastwick, P. W., & Finkel, E.** (2008). Sex differences in mate preferences revisited: Do people know what they initially desire in a romantic partner? *Journal of Personality and Social Psychology, 94,* 245–264.

**Eaton, D. K., & others.** (2008). Youth risk behavior surveillance—United States, 2007. *Morbidity and Mortality Weekly Reports, 57,* 1–131.

**Eckert, A., Schmitt, K., & Gotz, J.** (2011). Mitochondrial dysfunction—the beginning of the end in Alzheimer's disease? Separate and synergistic models of tau and amyloid-*B* toxicity. *Alzheimer's Research and Therapy, 3* (2),15.

**Edinger, J. D., & Morin, C. M.** (2012). Sleep disorders classification and diagnosis. In C. M. Morin & C. A. Espie (Eds.), *Oxford handbook of sleep and sleep disorders.* New York: Oxford University Press.

**Eells, T. D.** (2000). Can therapy affect physical health? *Journal of Psychotherapy Practice and Research, 9,* 100–104.

**Eggum, N. D., Eisenberg, N., Kao, K., Spinrad, T. L., Bolnick, R., Hofer, C., Kupfer, A. S., & Fabricius, W. V.** (2011). Emotion understanding, theory of mind, and prosocial orientation: Relations over time in early childhood. *Journal of Positive Psychology, 6*, 4–16.

**Eguchi, E., & others.** (2012). Healthy lifestyle behaviors and cardiovascular mortality among Japanese men and women: The Japan collaborative cohort study. *European Heart Journal, 33*, 467–477.

**Eheman, C., & others.** (2012). Annual report to the nation on the status of cancer, 1975–2008, featuring cancers associated with excess weight and lack of sufficient physical activity. *Cancer, 118*, 2338–2366.

**Eich, E.** (2007). Mood, memory, and the concept of context. In H. L. Roediger, Y. Dubai, & S. Fitzpatrick (Eds.), *Science of memory: Concepts.* New York: Oxford University Press.

**Eidelman, P., Gershon, A., McGlinchey, E., & Harvey, A. G.** (2012). Sleep and psychopathology. In C. M. Morin & C. A. Espie (Eds.), *Oxford handbook of sleep and sleep disorders.* New York: Oxford University Press.

**Eimes, D. G., Kantowitz, B. H., & Roediger, H. L.** (2012). *Research methods in psychology* (9th ed.). Boston: Cengage.

**Ein-Gar, D., Shiv, B., & Tormala, Z. L.** (2012). When blemishing leads to blossoming: The positive effect of negative information. *Journal of Consumer Research, 38*, 846–859.

**Eisenberg, N., Cumberland, A., Guthrie, I. K., Murphy, B. C., & Shepard, S. A.** (2005). Age changes in prosocial responding and moral reasoning in adolescence and early adulthood. *Journal of Research on Adolescence, 15*, 235–260.

**Eisenberg, N., Guthrie, I. K., Cumberland, A., Murphy, B. C., Shepard, S. A., Zhou, Q., & Carlo, G.** (2002). Prosocial development in early adulthood: A longitudinal study. *Journal of Personality and Social Psychology, 82*, 993–1006.

**Eisenstein, A. R., Prohaska, T. R., Kruger, J., Satariano, W. A., Hooker, S., Buchner, D., Kealey, M., & Hunter, R. H.** (2011). Environmental correlates of overweight and obesity in community residing older adults. *Journal of Aging and Health, 23*, 994–1009.

**Eiser, J. R.** (2012). History of social judgment research. In A. W. Kruglanski & W. Stroebe (Eds.), *Handbook of the history of social psychology.* New York: Psychology Press.

**Eivers, A. R., Brendgen, M., Vitaro, F., & Borge, A. I. H.** (2012). Concurrent and longitudinal links between children's and their friends' antisocial and prosocial behavior in preschool. *Early Childhood Research Quarterly, 27*, 137–146.

**Ekman, P.** (1980). *The face of man.* New York: Garland.

**Ekman, P.** (1996). Lying and deception. In N. L. Stein, C. Brainerd, P. A. Ornstein, & B. Tversky (Eds.), *Memory for everyday emotional events.* Mahwah, NJ: Erlbaum.

**Ekman, P.** (2003). Emotions inside out: 130 years after Darwin's "The expression of emotions in man and animal." *Annals of the New York Academy of Science, 1000*, 1–6.

**Ekman, P., Davidson, R. J., & Friesen, W. V.** (1990). The Duchenne smile: Emotional expression and brain physiology: II. *Journal of Personality and Social Psychology, 58*, 342–353.

**Ekman, P., & Friesen, W. V.** (1969). The repertoire of nonverbal behavior: Categories, origins, usage, and coding. *Semiotica, 1*, 49–98.

**Ekman, P., & Friesen, W. V.** (1971). Constants across cultures in the face and emotion. *Journal of Personality and Social Psychology, 17*, 124–129.

**Ekman, P., Levenson, R. W., & Friesen, W. V.** (1983). Autonomic nervous system activity distinguishes among emotions. *Science, 223*, 1208–1210.

**Ekman, P., & O'Sullivan, M.** (1991). Facial expressions: Methods, means, and moues. In R. S. Feldman & B. Rime (Eds.), *Fundamentals of nonverbal behavior.* Cambridge, England: Cambridge University Press.

**Elbert, T.** (2012). Pain from brain: Can we remodel neural circuitry that generates phantom limb pain and other forms of neuropathic pain? *Neuroscience Letters, 507*, 95–96.

**Eley, T. C., & others.** (2004). Gene-environment interaction analysis of serotonin system markers with adolescent depression. *Molecular Psychiatry, 9*, 908–915.

**El-Hai, J.** (2005). *The lobotomist: A maverick medical genius and his tragic quest to rid the world of mental illness.* Hoboken, NJ: Wiley.

**Ellender, T. J., & others.** (2011). Differential modulation of excitatory and inhibitory striatal synaptic transmission by histamine. *Journal of Neuroscience, 31*, 15340–15351.

**Elliott, M. A., & Ainsworth, K.** (2012). Predicting university undergraduates' binge-drinking behavior: A comparative test of the one- and two-component theories of planned behavior. *Addictive Behaviors, 37*, 92–101.

**Elliott, T., Kuang, X., Shadbolt, N. R., & Zauner, K. P.** (2009). Adaptation in multisensory neurons: Impact of cross-modal enhancement. *Network, 20*, 1–31.

**Ellis, A.** (1962). *Reason and emotion in psychotherapy.* New York: Lyle Stuart.

**Ellis, A.** (1996). A rational-emotive behavior therapist's perspective on Ruth. In G. Corey (Ed.), *Case approach to counseling and psychotherapy.* Pacific Grove, CA: Brooks/Cole.

**Ellis, A.** (2000). Rational emotive behavior therapy. In A. Kazdin (Ed.), *Encyclopedia of psychology.* Washington, DC, & New York: American Psychological Association and Oxford University Press.

**Ellis, A.** (2002). Rational emotive behavior therapy. In M. Hersen & W. H. Sledge (Eds.), *Encyclopedia of psychotherapy.* San Diego: Academic.

**Ellis, A.** (2005). Why I (really) became a therapist. *Journal of Clinical Psychology, 61*, 945–948.

**Ellis, L. A., Campbell, A. J., Sethi, S., & O'Dea, B. M.** (2011). Comparative randomized trial of an online cognitive-behavioral therapy program and an online support group for depression and anxiety. *Journal of CyberTherapy and Rehabilitation, 4*, 461–467.

**Elms, A. C.** (2005). Freud as Leonardo: Why the first psychobiography went wrong. In W. T. Schultz (Ed.), *The handbook of psychobiography* (pp. 210–222). New York: Oxford University Press.

**Elms, A. C., & Heller, B.** (2005). Twelve ways to say "lonesome": Assessing error and control in the music of Elvis Presley. In W. T. Schultz (Ed.), *Handbook of psychobiography* (pp. 142–157). Oxford, England: Oxford University Press.

**Ely, R. J., Thomas, D. A., & Padavic, I.** (2007). *Team learning and the link between racial diversity and performance.* Unpublished manuscript, Harvard Business School, Boston.

**Emery, C., Anderson, D. R., & Goodwin, C. L.** (2013). Coronary heart disease and hypertension. In I. B. Weiner & others (Eds.), *Handbook of psychology* (2nd ed., vol. 9). New York: Wiley.

**Emes, R. D., & Grant, S. G. N.** (2012). Evolution of synaptic complexity and diversity. *Annual Review of Neuroscience* (vol. 35). Palo Alto, CA: Annual Reviews.

**Emmelkamp, P. M.** (2011). Effectiveness of cybertherapy in mental health: A critical appraisal. In B. K. Wiederhold, S. Bouchard, & G. Riva (Eds.), *Annual Review of Cybertherapy and Telemedicine: Advanced Technologies in Behavioral, Social, and Neurosciences, 9*, 6–9.

**Emmons, R. A., & Diener, E.** (1986). Situation selection as a moderator of response consistency and stability. *Journal of Personality and Social Psychology, 51*, 1013–1019.

**Emmons, R. A., & King, L. A.** (1988). Conflict among personal strivings: Immediate and long-term implications for psychological and physical well-being. *Journal of Personality and Social Psychology, 48*, 1040–1048.

**Emmons, R. A., & McCullough, M. E.** (2003). Counting blessings versus burdens: An experimental investigation of gratitude and subjective well-being in daily life. *Journal of Personality and Social Psychology, 84*, 377–389.

**Emmons, R. A., & McCullough, M. E. (Eds.).** (2004). *The psychology of gratitude.* New York: Oxford University Press.

**Endler, N. S.** (1988). The origins of electroconvulsive therapy (ECT). *Convulsive Therapy, 4*, 5–23.

**Engel, A. K., & Singer, W.** (2001). Temporal binding and the neural correlates of sensory awareness. *Trends in Cognitive Science, 5*, 16–25.

**Enger, E., Ross, F. C., & Bailey, D.** (2012). *Concepts in biology* (14th ed.). New York: McGraw-Hill.

**Englander, E. K.** (2006). *Understanding violence* (3rd ed.). Mahwah, NJ: Erlbaum.

**Ensembl Human.** (2008). *Explore the Homo sapiens genome.* www.ensembl.org/Homo_sapiens/index.html

**Enstrom, J. E.** (1999). Smoking cessation and mortality trends among two United States populations. *Journal of Clinical Epidemiology, 52*, 813–825.

**Erickson, K. I., Miller, D. L., & Roecklein, K. A.** (2012). The aging hippocampus: Interactions between exercise, depression, and BDNF. *Neuroscientist, 18*, 82–97.

**Erickson, K. I., & others** (2011). Exercise training increases the size of the hippocampus and improves memory. *Proceedings of the National Academy of Sciences USA, 108*, 3017–3022.

**Eriksen, J., Jorgensen, T. N., & Gether, U.** (2010). Regulation of the dopamine transporter function by protein-protein interactions: New discoveries and methodological challenges. *Journal of Neurochemistry, 113*, 27–41.

**Erikson, E. H.** (1968). *Identity: Youth and crisis.* New York: Norton.

**Erikson, E. H.** (1969). *Gandhi's truth.* New York: Norton.

**Esler, M., Eikelis, N., Schlaich, M., Lambert, G., Alvarenga, M., Kaye, D., El-Osta, A., Guo, L., Barton, D., Pier, C., Brenchley, C., Dawood, T., Jennings, G., & Lambert, E.** (2009). Human sympathetic nerve biology: Parallel influences of stress and epigenetics in essential hypertension and panic disorder. In R. Kvetňanský, G. Aguilera, D. Goldstein, D. Jezova, O. Krizanova, E. L. Sabban, & K. Pacak (Eds.), *Stress, neurotransmitters, and hormones: Neuroendocrine and genetic mechanisms* (pp. 338–348). New York: New York Academy of Sciences.

**Espana, R. A., & Scammell, T. E.** (2011). Sleep neurobiology from a clinical perspective. *Sleep, 34*, 845–858.

**Espirito-Santo, H., & Pio-Abreu, J. L.** (2009). Psychiatric symptoms and dissociation in conversion, somatization, and dissociative disorders. *Australian and New Zealand Journal of Psychiatry, 43*, 270–276.

**Esposito, E. A., Grigorenko, E. L., & Sternberg, R. J.** (2012). The nature-nurture issue: An illustration using behavior-genetic research on cognitive development. In A. Slater & J. Gavin-Bremmer (Eds.), *An introduction to developmental psychology* (2nd ed.). New York: Wiley-Blackwell.

**Etnier, J. L., & Labban, J. D.** (2012). Physical activity and cognitive function: Theoretical bases, mechanisms, and moderators. In E. O. Acevedo (Ed.), *Oxford handbook of exercise psychology.* New York: Oxford University Press.

**Evans, B. G., & Iverson, P.** (2007). Plasticity in vowel perception and production: A study of accent change in young adults. *Journal of the Acoustical Society of America, 121* (6), 3814–3826.

**Evans, D. E., & Rothbart, M. K.** (2009). A two-factor model of temperament. *Personality and Individual Differences, 47*, 565–570.

**Evans, J.** (2012). Dual-process theories of reasoning: Facts and fallacies. In K. J. Holyoak & R. G. Morrison (Eds.), *Oxford handbook of thinking and reasoning.* New York: Oxford University Press.

**Evans, J. S. B. T.** (2002). Logic and human reasoning: An assessment of the deduction paradigm. *Psychological Bulletin, 128*, 978–996.

**Evans, J. S. B. T.** (2010). *Thinking twice: Two minds in one brain.* Oxford University Press.

**Eysenck, H. J.** (1967). *The biological basis of personality.* Springfield, IL: Thomas.

## F

**Facciabene, A., Motz, G. T., & Coukos, G.** (2012). T-regulatory cells: Key players in tumor immune escape and angiogenesis. *Cancer Research, 72*, 2162–2171.

**Fafard, P.** (2012). Public health understandings of policy and power: Lessons from INSITE. *Journal of Urban Health.* doi: 10.1007/s11524-012-9698-2

**Fagen, J. L., & Anderson, P. B.** (2011). Constructing masculinity in response to women's sexual advances. *Archives of Sexual Behavior, 41* (1), 261–270.

**Fagerlund, M., Estrada, C. P., Jaff, N., Svensson, M., & Brundin, L.** (2012). Neural stem/progenitor cells transplanted to the hypoglossal nucleus integrates with the host CNS in adult rats and promotes motor neuron survival. *Cell Transplantation.* (in press)

**Fahlman, S. E.** (2003). *Smiley lore.* www.cs.cmu.edu/~sef/sefSmiley.htm (accessed May 7, 2012)

**Faimberg, H.** (2012). Listening to the psychic consequences of Nazism in psychoanalytic patients. *Psychoanalytic Quarterly, 81,* 157–169.

**Fairchild Bridal Group.** (2005). *The American wedding.* New York: Author. www.sellthebride.com/documents/americanweddingsurvey.pdf

**Fairweather, E., & Cramond, B.** (2011). Infusing creative and critical thinking into the classroom. In R. A. Beghetto & J. C. Kaufman (Eds.), *Nurturing creativity in the classroom.* New York: Cambridge University Press.

**Falk, C. F., Heine, S. J., Yuki, M., & Takemura, K.** (2009). Why do Westerners self-enhance more than East Asians? *European Journal of Personality, 23,* 183–203.

**Family and Youth Services Bureau.** (2004). *Fact sheet: Section 510 state abstinence education program.* Bethesda, MD: U.S. Department of Health and Human Services.

**Fant, R. V., Buchhalter, A. R., Buchman, A. C., & Heningfield, J. E.** (2009). Pharmacotherapy for tobacco dependence. *Handbook of Experimental Pharmacology, 192,* 487–510.

**Farrant, B. M., Devine, T. A. J., Maybery, M. T., & Fletcher, J.** (2012). Empathy, perspective taking and prosocial behaviour: The importance of parenting practices. *Infant and Child Development, 21,* 175–188.

**Farren, C. K., Snee, L., & McElroy, S.** (2011). Gender differences in outcome at 2-year follow-up of treated bipolar and depressed alcoholics. *Journal of Studies on Alcohol and Drugs, 72,* 872–880.

**Farris, M.** (2009, November 2). *Man donates kidney to complete stranger.* www.wwltv.com/home/wwl110209cbstranger-68784452.html (accessed May 19, 2012)

**Fatemi, S. H., & Folsom, T. D.** (2009). The neurodevelopmental hypothesis of schizophrenia, revisited. *Schizophrenia Bulletin, 35,* 528–548.

**Faugeras, F., & others.** (2012). Event related potentials elicited by violations of auditory regularities in patients with impaired consciousness. *Neuropsychologia, 50,* 403–418.

**Fava, G. A., Ruini, C., & Belaise, C.** (2007). The concept of recovery in depression. *Psychological Medicine, 37,* 307–317.

**Faymonville, M. E., Boly, M., & Laureys, S.** (2006). Functional neuroanatomy of the hypnotic state. *Journal of Physiology, Paris, 99,* 463–469.

**Fazio, R. H., Chen, J., McDonel, E. C., & Sherman, S. J.** (1982). Attitude accessibility, attitude-behavior consistency, and the strength of the object-evaluation association. *Journal of Experimental Social Psychology, 18,* 339–357.

**Fazio, R. H., & Olsen, A.** (2007). Attitudes. In M. A. Hogg & J. Cooper (Eds.), *The Sage handbook of social psychology* (concise 2nd ed.). Thousand Oaks, CA: Sage.

**Federal Bureau of Investigation (FBI).** (2012). *Expanded homicide data.* www.fbi.gov/about-us/cjis/ucr/crime-in-the-u.s/2010/crime-in-the-u.s.-2010/offenses-known-to-law-enforcement/expanded/expandhomicidemain (accessed May 21, 2012)

**Federal Emergency Management Agency (FEMA).** (2003, July 10). *Disaster search canine readiness evaluation process.* Washington, DC: Author.

**Fei-Fei, L., Iyer, A., Koch, C., & Perona, P.** (2007). What do we perceive in a glance at a real-world scene? *Journal of Vision, 7,* 10.

**Fein, S., Goethals, G. R., Kassin, S. M., & Cross, J.** (1993, August). *Social influence and presidential debates.* Paper presented at the meeting of the American Psychological Association, Toronto.

**Feinstein, E. C., Richter, L., & Foster, S. E.** (2012). Addressing the critical health problem of adolescent substance use through health care, research, and public policy. *Journal of Adolescent Health, 50,* 431–436.

**Ferdinand, K. C., & others.** (2012). Community-based approaches to prevention and management of hypertension and cardiovascular disease. *Journal of Clinical Hypertension, 14,* 336–343.

**Ferguson, C. J., & Garza, A.** (2011). Call of (civic) duty: Action games and civic behavior in a large sample of youth. *Computers in Human Behavior, 27,* 770–775.

**Ferguson, C. J., & Kilburn, J.** (2010). Much ado about nothing: The misestimation and overinterpretation of violent video game effects in Eastern and Western nations: Comment on Anderson et al. (2010). *Psychological Bulletin, 136,* 174–178.

**Ferguson, C. J., Rueda, S. M., Cruz, A. M., Ferguson, D. E., Fritz, S., & Smith, S. M.** (2008). Violent video games and aggression: Causal relationship or byproduct of family violence and intrinsic violence motivation? *Criminal Justice and Behavior, 35,* 311–332.

**Ferguson, E., & Bibby, P. A.** (2012). Openness to experience and all-cause mortality: A meta-analysis and r(equivalent) from risk ratio and odds ratios. *British Journal of Health Psychology, 17,* 85–102.

**Feri, F., Meléndez-Jiménez, M. A., Ponti, G., & Vega-Redondo, F.** (2011). Error cascades in observational learning: An experiment on the Chinos game. *Games and Economic Behavior, 73,* 136–146.

**Ferretti, F., & Coluccia, A.** (2009). Socio-economic factors and suicide rates in European Union countries. *Legal Medicine, 11, Suppl. 1,* S92–S94.

**Ferrie, J. E., & others.** (2011). Change in sleep duration and cognitive function: Findings from the Whitehall II Study. *Sleep, 34,* 565–573.

**Ferrières, J.** (2004). The French paradox; Lessons for other countries. *Heart, 90* (1), 107–111.

**Festinger, L.** (1954). A theory of social comparison processes. *Human Relations, 7,* 117–140.

**Festinger, L.** (1957). *A theory of cognitive dissonance.* Evanston, IL: Row Peterson.

**Festinger, L., & Carlsmith, J. M.** (1959). Cognitive consequences of forced compliance. *Journal of Abnormal and Social Psychology, 58,* 203–211.

**Field, T. M., Diego, M., & Hernandez-Reif, M.** (2011). Potential underlying mechanisms for greater weight gain in massaged preterm infants. *Infant Behavior & Development, 34,* 383–389.

**Fields, R.** (2013). *Drugs in perspective* (8th ed.). New York: McGraw-Hill.

**Fiese, B. H., Foley, K. P., & Spagnola, M.** (2006). Routine and ritual elements in family mealtimes: Contexts for child well-being and family identity. *New Directions in Child and Adolescent Development, 111,* 67–89.

**Fietta, P., & Fietta, P.** (2011). The neurobiology of human memory. *Theoretical Biology Forum, 104,* 69–87.

**Fifer, W. P., & Myers, M. M.** (2002) Sudden fetal and infant deaths: Shared observations and distinctive features. *Seminar in Perinatology, 26,* 89–96.

**Finch, E. A., Linde, J. A., Jeffery, R. W., Rothman, A. J., King, C. M., & Levy, R. L.** (2005). The effects of outcome expectations and satisfaction on weight loss and maintenance: Correlational and experimental analyses—a randomized trial. *Health Psychology, 24* (6), 608–616.

**Fingerhut, A. W., & Peplau, L. A.** (2013). Same-sex romantic relationships. In C. J. Patterson & A. R. D'Augelli (Eds.), *The psychology of sexual orientation.* New York: Cambridge University Press.

**Fischer, R.** (2006). Congruence and functions of personal and cultural values: Do my values reflect my culture's values? *Personality and Social Psychology Bulletin, 32,* 1419–1431.

**Fisher, T. D., Moore, Z. T., & Pittenger, M. J.** (2012). Sex on the brain? An examination of frequency of sexual cognitions as a function of gender, erotophilia, and social desirability. *Journal of Sex Research, 49,* 69–77.

**Fitzhugh, E. C., Bassett, D. R., & Evans, M. F.** (2010). Urban trails and physical activity: A natural experiment. *American Journal of Preventive Medicine, 39,* 259–262.

**Fitzpatrick, K. K.** (2012). Developmental considerations when treating anorexia nervosa in adolescents and young adults. In J. Lock (Ed.), *Oxford handbook of child and adolescent eating disorders: Developmental perspectives.* New York: Oxford University Press.

**Fivush, R.** (2011). The development of autobiographical memory. *Annual Review of Psychology* (vol. 62). Palo Alto, CA: Annual Reviews.

**Flegal, K. M., Carroll, M. D., Kit, B. K., & Ogden, C. L.** (2012). Prevalence of obesity and trends in the distribution of body mass index among U.S. adults, 1999–2010. *Journal of the American Medical Association, 307,* 491–497.

**Fleischhaker, S., Schulz, E., Tepper, K., Martin, M., Hennighausen, K., & Remschmidt, H.** (2005). Long-term course of adolescent schizophrenia. *Schizophrenia Bulletin, 31,* 769–780.

**Fleischmann, F., Phalet, K., & Klein, O.** (2011). Religious affiliation and politicization in the face of discrimination: Support for political Islam and political action among the Turkish and Moroccan second generation in Europe. *British Journal of Social Psychology, 50,* 628–648.

**Fleming, L., & Davidson, J. R.** (2012). Sleep and medical disorders. In C. M. Morin & C. A. Espie (Eds.), *Oxford handbook of sleep and sleep disorders.* New York: Oxford University Press.

**Fleuret, F., & others.** (2011). Comparing machines and humans on a visual categorization test. *Proceedings of the National Academy of Sciences USA, 108,* 17621–17625.

**Flint, M. S., Baum, A., Chambers, W. H., & Jenkins, F. J.** (2007). Induction of DNA damage, alteration of DNA repair, and transcriptional activation by stress hormones. *Psychoneuroendocrinology, 32,* 470–479.

**Flom, R., & Bahrick, L. E.** (2010). The effects of intersensory redundancy on attention and memory: Infants' long-term memory for orientation in audiovisual events. *Developmental Psychology, 46,* 428–436.

**Flor, H., & Diers, M.** (2009). Sensorimotor training and cortical reorganization. *NeuroRehabilitation, 25,* 19–27.

**Flynn, J. R.** (1999). Searching for justice: The discovery of IQ gains over time. *American Psychologist, 54,* 5–20.

**Flynn, J. R.** (2011). Secular changes in intelligence. In R. J. Sternberg & S. B. Kaufman (Eds.), *Handbook of intelligence* (pp. 647–665). New York: Cambridge University Press.

**Foa, E. B.** (2011). Prolonged exposure therapy: Past, present, and future. *Depression and Anxiety, 28,* 1043–1047.

**Focht, B. C.** (2012). Exercise and health-related quality of life. In E. O. Acevedo (Ed.), *Oxford handbook of exercise psychology.* New York: Oxford University Press.

**Fodor, I., & Epstein, J.** (2002). Agoraphobia, panic disorder, and gender. In J. Worell (Ed.), *Encyclopedia of women and gender.* San Diego: Academic.

**Foell, J., Bekrater-Bodmann, R., Flor, H., & Cole, J.** (2011). Phantom limb after lower limb trauma: Origins and treatments. *International Journal of Lower Extremity Wounds, 10,* 224–235.

**Foer, J.** (2008). The unspeakable odyssey of the motionless boy. *Esquire.* http://www.esquire.com/features/unspeakable-odyssey-motionless-boy-1008

**Fok, H., Hui, C., Bond, M. H., Matsumoto, D., & Yoo, S. H.** (2008). Integrating personality, context, relationship, and emotion type into a model of display rules. *Journal of Research in Personality, 42,* 133–150.

**Foley, J. A., Kaschel, R., Logie, R. H., & Della Sala, S.** (2011). Dual-task performance in Alzheimer's disease, mild cognitive impairment, and normal aging. *Archives of Clinical Neuropsychology, 26,* 340–348.

**Folkman, S., & Lazarus, R. S.** (1980). An analysis of coping in a middle-aged community sample. *Journal of Health and Social Behavior, 21,* 219–239.

**Folkman, S., & Moskowitz, J. T.** (2004). Coping: Pitfalls and promises. *Annual Review of Psychology* (vol. 54). Palo Alto, CA: Annual Reviews.

**Fondell, E., & others.** (2011). Short natural sleep is associated with higher T cell and lower NK cell activities. *Brain, Behavior, and Immunity, 25,* 1367–1375.

**Fontana, A., & Rosenheck, R.** (2008). Treatment-seeking veterans of Iraq and Afghanistan: Comparison with veterans of previous wars. *Journal of Nervous and Mental Disease, 196,* 513–521.

**Fontana, A. P., & others.** (2011). Role of the parietal cortex in predicting incoming actions. *NeuroImage, 59,* 556–564.

Fontana, M. A., & Wohlgemuth, S. D. (2010). The surgical treatment of metabolic disease and morbid obesity. *Gastroenterology Clinics of North America, 39*, 125–133.

Fooladi, E., Bell, R. J., & Davis, S. R. (2012). Management strategies in SSRI-associated dysfunction in women at midlife. *Climacteric.* (in press)

Foote, B., Smolin, Y., Kaplan, M., Legatt, M. E., & Lipschitz, D. (2006). Prevalence of dissociative disorders in psychiatric outpatients. *American Journal of Psychiatry, 163*, 566–568.

Forbes, D., & others. (2012). A multisite randomized controlled effectiveness trial of cognitive processing therapy for military-related posttraumatic stress disorder. *Journal of Anxiety Disorders, 26*, 442–452.

Forbush, K., Heatherton, T. F., & Keel, P. K. (2007). Relationships between perfectionism and specific disordered eating behaviors. *International Journal of Eating Disorders, 40*, 37–41.

Forgas, J. P., Fiedler, K., & Sedikides, C. (Eds.). (2012). *Social thinking and interpersonal behavior.* New York: Psychology Press.

Forman, E. M., & others. (2012). Using session-by-session measurement to compare mechanisms of action for acceptance and commitment therapy and cognitive therapy. *Behavior Therapy, 43*, 341–354.

Forman-Hoffman, V. L., & Cunningham, C. L. (2008). Geographical clustering of eating disordered behaviors in U.S. high school students. *International Journal of Eating Disorders, 41*, 209–214.

Forsythe, C., Bernard, M. L., & Goldsmith, T. E. (Eds.). (2006). *Cognitive systems.* Mahwah, NJ: Erlbaum.

Fortier, M. S., Duda, J. L., Guerin, E., & Texeira, P. J. (2012). Promoting physical activity: Development and testing of self-determination theory-based interventions. *International Journal of Behavioral Nutrition and Physical Activity.* doi:10.1186/1479-5868-9-20

Fotuhi, O., & others. (2012). Patterns of cognitive dissonance-reducing beliefs among smokers: A longitudinal analysis from the International Tobacco Control (ITC) four country survey. *Tobacco Control.* doi:10.1136/tobaccocontrol-2011-050139

Fountas, K. N., & Smith, J. R. (2007). Historical evolution of stereotactic amygdalotomy for the management of severe aggression. *Journal of Neurosurgery, 106*, 710–713.

Fountoulakis, K. N. (2012). The possible involvement of NMDA glutamate receptor in the etiopathogenesis of bipolar disorder. *Current Pharmaceutical Design, 18*, 1605–1608.

Fox, R., & Millam, J. R. (2010). The use of ratings and direct behavioural observation to measure temperament traits in cockatiels (*nymphicus hollandicus*). *Ethology, 116*, 59–75.

Frances, A. J., & Widiger, T. (2012). Psychiatric diagnosis: Lessons from the *DSM-IV* past and cautions for the *DSM-5* future. *Annual Review of Clinical Psychology* (vol. 8). Palo Alto, CA: Annual Reviews.

Frank, M. G. (2006). The mystery of sleep function: Current perspectives and future directions. *Reviews in the Neurosciences. 17*, 375–392.

Frank, M. G., & Benington J. H. (2006). The role of sleep in memory consolidation and brain plasticity: Dream or reality? *Neuroscientist, 12*, 477–488.

Frankl, V. E. (1984). *Man's search for meaning* (3rd ed.). New York: First Washington Square Press. (original work published 1946)

Frattaroli, J. (2006). Experimental disclosure and its moderators: A meta-analysis. *Psychological Bulletin, 132*, 823–865.

Frazier, P., Keenan, A., Anders, S., Perera, S., Shallcross, S., & Hintz, S. (2011). Perceived past, present, and future control and adjustment to stressful life events. *Journal of Personality and Social Psychology, 100*, 749–765.

Frazier, T. W. (2012). Friends not foes: Combined risperidone and behavior therapy for irritability in autism. *Journal of the American Academy of Child and Adolescent Psychiatry, 51*, 129–131.

Fredrick, S., & Loewenstein, G. (1999). Hedonic adaptation. In D. Kahneman, E. Diener, & N. Schwarz (Eds.), *Well-being: The foundations of hedonic psychology* (pp. 302–329). New York: Russell Sage Foundation.

Fredrickson, B. L. (1998). What good are positive emotions? *Review of General Psychology, 2*, 300–319.

Fredrickson, B. L. (2001). The role of positive emotions in positive psychology. *American Psychologist, 56*, 218–226.

Fredrickson, B. L. (2006). Unpacking positive emotions: Investigating the seeds of human flourishing. *Journal of Positive Psychology, 1*, 57–60.

Fredrickson, B. L. (2009). *Positivity.* New York: Crown.

Fredrickson, B. L., Tugade, M. M., Waugh, C. E., & Larkin, G. R. (2003). What good are positive emotions in crisis? A prospective study of resilience and emotions following the terrorist attacks on the United States on September 11th, 2001. *Journal of Personality and Social Psychology, 84*, 365–376.

Freed, C. R., Zhou, W., & Breeze, R. E. (2011). Dopamine cell transplantation for Parkinson disease: The importance of controlled clinical trials. *Neurotherapeutics, 8*, 549–561.

Freedman, J. L., & Fraser, S. C. (1966). Compliance without pressure: The foot-in-the-door technique. *Journal of Personality and Social Psychology, 4*, 195–202.

Freedy, J. R., Carek, P. J., Diaz, V. A., & Thiedke, C. C. (2012). Integrating cognitive therapy into management of depression. *American Family Physician, 85*, 686–687.

Freeland, A., Manchanda, R., Chiu, S., Sharma, V., & Merskey, H. (1993). Four cases of supposed multiple personality disorder: Evidence of unjustified diagnoses. *Canadian Journal of Psychiatry, 38*, 245–247.

Freeman, D., & Freeman, J. (2012). *Anxiety.* New York: Oxford University Press.

French, C. C. (2010). Missing the point? In S. Krippner & H. L. Friedman (Eds.), *Debating psychic experience: Human potential or human illusion?* (pp. 149–151). Santa Barbara, CA: Praeger/ABC-CLIO.

Frenda, S. J., Nichols, R. M., & Loftus, E. F. (2011). Current issues and advances in misinformation research. *Current Directions in Psychological Science, 20*, 20–23.

Frensch, K. M., Pratt, M. W., & Norris, J. E. (2007). Foundations of generativity: Personal and family correlates of emerging adults' generative life-story themes. *Journal of Research in Personality, 41*, 45–62.

Freud, S. (1911). *The interpretation of dreams* (3rd ed.). A. A. Brill (Trans.). New York: Macmillan. (original work published 1899)

Freud, S. (1917). *A general introduction to psychoanalysis.* New York: Washington Square Press.

Freud, S. (1996). Number 23091. In R. Andrews, M. Seidel, & M. Biggs, (Eds.), *Columbia world of quotations.* New York: Columbia University Press. (original work published 1918)

Fried, S. (2008, October 9). Commentary in "Think fat just hangs around, does nothing." *USA Today*, 6D.

Friedenberg, J., & Silverman, G. (2012). *Cognitive science: An introduction to the study of mind* (2nd ed.). Thousand Oaks, CA: Sage.

Friedman, E. M., Karlamangia, A. S., Almeida, D. M., & Seeman, T. E. (2012). Social strain and cortisol regulation in midlife in the U.S. *Social Science and Medicine, 74*, 607–615.

Friedman, E. M., & Ryff, C. O. (2012). Living well with medical comorbidities: A biopsychosocial perspective. *Journals of Gerontology B: Psychological Sciences and Social Sciences.* (in press)

Friedman, M., & Rosenman, R. (1974). *Type A behavior and your heart.* New York: Knopf.

Friedman, R., Myers, P., & Benson, H. (1998). Meditation and the relaxation response. In H. S. Friedman (Ed.), *Encyclopedia of mental health* (vol. 2). San Diego: Academic.

Frijda, N. H. (2007). *The laws of emotion.* Mahwah, NJ: Erlbaum.

Fromm, E. (1947). *Man for himself.* New York: Holt, Rinehart & Winston.

Fromm, E. (1973). *The anatomy of human destructiveness.* New York: Fawcett.

Fryberg, S. A., & Markus, H. R. (2003). On being American Indian: Current and possible selves. *Self and Identity, 2*, 325–344.

Fujiwara, E., Levine, B., & Anderson, A. K. (2008). Intact implicit and reduced explicit memory for negative self-related information in repressive coping. *Cognitive, Affective, and Behavioral Neuroscience, 8*, 254–263.

Fulmer, C. A., & others. (2010). On "feeling right" in cultural contexts: How person-culture match affects self-esteem and subjective well-being. *Psychological Science, 21*, 1563–1569.

Fultz, J., Batson, C. D., Fortenbach, V. A., McCarthy, P. M., & Varney, L. L. (1986). Social evaluation and the empathy-altruism hypothesis. *Journal of Personality and Social Psychology, 50*, 761–769.

Funder, D. C. (2009). Persons, behaviors, and situations: An agenda for personality psychology in the postwar era. *Journal of Research in Personality, 43*, 120–126.

Fung, M. T., Raine, A., Loeber, R., Lynam, D. R., Steinhauer, S. R., Venables, P. H., & Stouthamer-Loeber, M. (2005). Reduced electrodermal activity in psychopathy-prone adolescents. *Journal of Abnormal Psychology, 114*, 187–196.

Furlong, M., & McGilloway, S. (2012). The Incredible Years Parenting Program in Ireland: A qualitative analysis of the experience of disadvantaged parents. *Clinical Child Psychology and Psychiatry.* (in press)

## G

Gabert-Quillen, C. A., & others. (2012). The impact of social support on the relationship between trauma history and PTSD symptoms in motor vehicle accident victims. *International Journal of Stress Management, 19*, 69–79.

Gaig, C., & Iranzo, A. (2012). Sleep-disordered breathing in neurogenerative diseases. *Current Neurology and Neuroscience Reports, 12* (2), 205–217.

Gaines, S. O. (2012). Stereotyping, prejudice, and discrimination revisited: From Willliam James to W. E. B. Du Bois. In J. Dixon, M. Keynes, & M. Levine (Eds.), *Beyond prejudice.* New York: Cambridge University Press.

Gainotti, G. (2012). Unconscious processing of emotions and the right hemisphere. *Neuropsychologia, 50*, 205–218.

Galambos, N. L., Howard, A. L., & Maggs, J. L. (2011). Rise and fall of sleep quality with student experiences across the first year of the university. *Journal of Research on Adolescence, 21*, 342–349.

Gale, C. R., Deary, I. J., Boyle, S. H., Barefoot, J., Mortensen, L. H., & Batty, G. D. (2008). Cognitive ability in early adulthood and risk of 5 specific psychiatric disorders in middle age: The Vietnam Experience Study. *Archives of General Psychiatry, 65*, 1410–1418.

Gallagher, K. E., & Parrott, D. J. (2010). Influence of heavy episodic drinking on the relation between men's locus of control and aggression toward intimate partners. *Journal of Studies on Alcohol and Drugs, 71*, 299–306.

Gallegos, J., & others. (2012). Decreasing adverse outcomes of unmodified electroconvulsive therapy: Suggestions and possibilities. *Journal of ECT.* (in press)

Gallese, V., Gernsbacher, M. A., Heyes, C., Hickok, G., & Iacoboni, M. (2011). Mirror neuron forum. *Perspectives on Psychological Science, 6*, 369–407.

Gallina, P., & others. (2011). Progress in restorative neurosurgery: Human fetal striatal transplantation in Huntington's disease. Reviews. *Journal of Neurosurgical Science, 55*, 371–381.

Gao, D., & Vasconcelos, N. (2009). Decision-theoretic saliency: Computational principles, biological plausibility, and implications for neurophysiology. *Neural Computation, 21*, 239–271.

Gao, Y. J., & Ji, R. R. (2010). Chemokines, neuronal-glial interactions, and central processing of neuropathic pain. *Pharmacology & Therapeutics, 126* (1), 56–68.

Garb, H. N., Wood, J. M., Nezworski, M. T., Grove, W. M., & Stejskal, W. J. (2001). Toward a resolution of the Rorschach controversy. *Psychological Assessment, 13*, 433–448.

Garcia, J. (1989). Food for Tolman: Cognition and cathexis in concert. In T. Archer & L. Nilsson (Eds.), *Aversion, avoidance, and anxiety.* Mahwah, NJ: Erlbaum.

Garcia, J., Ervin, F. E., & Koelling, R. A. (1966). Learning with prolonged delay of reinforcement. *Psychonomic Science, 5*, 121–122.

Garcia, J., & Koelling, R. A. (1966). Relation of cue to consequence in avoidance learning. *Psychonomic Science, 4,* 123–124.

Garcia, J., & Koelling, R. A. (2009). Specific hungers and poison avoidance as adaptive specializations of learning. In D. Shanks (Ed.), *Psychology of learning.* Thousand Oaks, CA: Sage.

Gardner, H. (1983). *Frames of mind.* New York: Basic Books.

Gardner, H. (1993). *Multiple intelligences.* New York: Basic Books.

Gardner, H. (2002). The pursuit of excellence through education. In M. Ferrari (Ed.), *Learning from extraordinary minds.* Mahwah, NJ: Erlbaum.

Garfield, C. F., Dorsey, E. R., Zhu, S., Huskamp, H. A., Conti, R., Dusetzina, S. B., Higashi, A., Perrin, J. M., Kornfield, R., & Alexander, G. C. (2012). Trends in attention deficit hyperactivity disorder ambulatory diagnosis and medical treatment in the United States, 2000–2010. *Academic Pediatrics, 12,* 110–116.

Garrett, B. L. (2011). *Convicting the innocent: Where criminal prosecutions go wrong.* Cambridge, MA: Harvard University Press.

Garrison, G. D., & Dugan, S. E. (2009). Varenicline: A first-line treatment for smoking cessation. *Clinical Therapeutics, 31,* 463–491.

Gartland, N., O'Connor, D. B., & Lawton, R. (2012). The effects of conscientiousness on the appraisals of daily stressors. *Stress and Health, 28,* 80–86.

Garver, D. L. (2006). Evolution of antipsychotic intervention in the schizophrenic psychosis. *Current Drug Targets, 7,* 1205–1215.

Gathercole, S. E., & Alloway, T. P. (2008). *Working memory and learning: A practical guide.* Thousand Oaks, CA: Sage.

Gavlak, D. (2009, April 12). Jordan honor killing: Man confesses to brutally stabbing to death pregnant sister. www.huffingtonpost.com/2009/04/12/jordan-honor-killing-man-_n_185977.html (accessed May 19 2012)

Gazzaley, A., & Nobre, A. C. (2012). Top-down modulation bridging selective attention and working memory. *Trends in Cognitive Science, 16* (2), 129–135.

Geary, D. C. (2004). *Origin of mind: Evolution of brain, cognition, and intelligence.* Washington, DC: American Psychological Association.

Geary, D. C. (2006). Evolutionary developmental psychology: Current status and future directions. *Developmental Review, 26,* 113–119.

Gehrman, P., Findley, J., & Perlis, M. (2012). Insomnia I: Etiology and conceptualization. In C. M. Morin & C. A. Espie (Eds.), *Oxford handbook of sleep and sleep disorders.* New York: Oxford University Press.

Gelder, B. D., Meeren, H. K., Righart, R., Stock, J. V., van de Riet, W. A., & Tamietto, M. (2006). Beyond the face: Exploring rapid influences of context on face processing. *Progress in Brain Research, 155PB,* 37–48.

Gelfand, M., & others. (2012). The cultural contagion of conflict. *Philosophical Transactions of the Royal Society of London, 367,* 692–703.

Geller, E. S. (2002).The challenge of increasing proenvironmental behavior. In R. B. Bechtel & A. Churchman (Eds.), *Handbook of environmental psychology* (pp. 525–540). Hoboken, NJ: Wiley.

Geller, E. S. (2006). Occupational injury prevention and applied behavior analysis. In A. C. Gielen, D. A. Sleet, & R. J. DiClemente (Eds.), *Injury and violence prevention: Behavioral science theories, methods, and applications* (pp. 297–322). San Francisco: Jossey-Bass.

George, L. G., Helson, R., & John, O. P. (2011). The "CEO" of women's work lives: How big five conscientiousness, extraversion, and openness predict 50 years of work experiences in a changing sociocultural context. *Journal of Personality and Social Psychology, 101,* 812–830.

George, L. K. (2009). Religiousness and spirituality, later life. In D. Carr (Ed.), *Encyclopedia of the life course and human adjustment.* Boston: Gale Cengage.

Geraerts, E., Lindsay, D. S., Merckelbach, H., Jelicic, M., Raymaekers, L., Arnold, M. M., & Schooler, J. W. (2009). Cognitive mechanisms underlying recovered-memory experiences of childhood sexual abuse. *Psychological Science, 20,* 92–98.

Germain, A. (2012). Parasomnias I: Nightmares. In C. M. Morin & C. A. Espie (Eds.), *Oxford handbook of sleep and sleep disorders.* New York: Oxford University Press.

Germann, D., Kurylo, N., & Han, F. (2012). Risperidone. *Profiles of Drug Substances and Excipients, 37,* 313–361.

Gernsbacher, M. A., Stevenson, J. L., & Schweigart, E. K. (2012). Mirror neurons in humans? A critical review. *Social Neuroscience.* (in press)

Gershman, S. J., Blei, D. M., & Niv, Y. (2010). Context, learning, and extinction. *Psychological Review, 117,* 197–209.

Giang, D. W., & others. (1996). Conditioning of cyclophosphamide-induced leukopenia in humans. *Journal of Neuropsychiatry and Clinical Neuroscience, 8,* 194–201.

Gibbons, R. D., Brown, C. H., Hur, K., Davis, J. M., & Mann, J. J. (2012a). Suicidal thoughts and behavior with antidepressant treatment. *Archives of General Psychiatry.* (in press)

Gibbons, R. D., Brown, C. H., Hur, K., Marcus, S. M., Bhaumik, D. K., Erkens, J. A., Herings, R. M. C., & Mann, J. J. (2007). Early evidence on the effects of regulators' suicidality warnings on SSRI prescriptions and suicide in children and adolescents. *American Journal of Psychiatry, 164,* 1356–1363.

Gibbons, R. D., Hur, K., Brown, C. H., Davis, J. M., & Mann, J. J. (2012b). Benefits from antidepressants: Synthesis of 6-week patient-level outcomes from double-blind placebo-controlled randomized trials of fluoxetine and venlafaxine. *Archives of General Psychiatry.* (in press)

Gigerenzer, G., & Gaissmaier, W. (2011). Heuristic decision making. *Annual Review of Psychology* (vol. 62). Palo Alto, CA: Annual Reviews.

Gilbert, A. L., Regier, T., Kay, P., & Ivry, R. B. (2006). Whorf hypothesis is supported in the right visual field but not the left. *Proceedings of the National Academy of Sciences USA, 103* (2), 489–494.

Gilbert, D. T., & Malone, P. S. (1995). The correspondence bias. *Psychological Bulletin, 117,* 21–38.

Gilbert, L. A., & Kearney, L. K. (2006). The psychotherapeutic relationship as a positive and powerful resource for girls and women. In J. Worell & C. D. Goodheart (Eds.), *Handbook of girls' and women's psychological health: Gender and well-being across the lifespan.* New York: Oxford University Press.

Giletta, M., & others. (2012). Friendship context matters: Examining the domain specificity of alcohol and depression socialization among adolescents. *Journal of Abnormal Child Psychology.* doi: 10.1007/s10802-012-9625-8

Gillath, O., Sesko, A. K., Shaver, P. R., & Chun, D. S. (2010). Attachment, authenticity, and honesty: Dispositional and experimentally induced security can reduce self- and other-deception. *Journal of Personality and Social Psychology, 98,* 841–855.

Gilligan, C. (1982). *In a different voice.* Cambridge, MA: Harvard University Press.

Gil-Mohapel, J., Simpson, J. M., Ghilan, M., & Christie, B. R. (2011). Neurogenesis in Huntington's disease: Can studying adult neurogenesis lead to the development of new therapeutic strategies? *Brain Research, 1406,* 84–105.

Gil-Mohapel, J., Simpson, J. M., Titerness, A. K., & Christie, B. R. (2010). Characterization of the neurogenesis quiet zone in the rodent brain: Effects of age and exercise. *European Journal of Neuroscience, 31,* 797–807.

Ginis, K. A. M., Bassett, R. L., & Conlin, C. (2012). Body image and exercise. In E. O. Acevedo (Ed.), *Oxford handbook of exercise psychology.* New York: Oxford University Press.

Gittelman, M. (2008). Editor's introduction: Why are the mentally ill dying? *International Journal of Mental Health, 37,* 3–12.

Glasford, D. E., & Calcagno, J. (2012). The conflict of harmony: Intergroup contact, commonality and political solidarity between minority groups. *Journal of Experimental Social Psychology, 48,* 323–328.

Glaw, X. M., Garrick, T. M., Terwee, P. J., Patching, J. R., Blake, H., & Harper, C. (2009). Brain donation: Who and why? *Cell and Tissue Banking, 10,* 241–246.

Gleitman, L., & Papafragou, A. (2012). Language and thought. In K. J. Holyoak & R. G. Morrison (Eds.), *Oxford handbook of thinking and reasoning.* New York: Oxford University Press.

Glenberg, A. M. (2011a). Introduction to the mirror neuron forum. *Perspectives on Psychological Science, 6,* 363–368.

Glenberg, A. M. (2011b). Positions in the mirror are closer than they appear. *Perspectives on Psychological Science, 6,* 408–410.

Glenn, D. (2010, February 5). Divided attention. *Chronicle of Higher Education, 56,* B5–B8.

Glick, P., & Fiske, S. T. (2012). An ambivalent alliance: Hostile and benevolent sexism in contemporary justifications for gender inequality. In J. Dixon, M. Keynes, & M. Levine (Eds.), *Beyond prejudice.* New York: Cambridge University Press.

Gobet, F., & Clarkson, G. (2004). Chunks in expert memory: Evidence for the magical number four . . . or is it two? *Memory, 12,* 732–747.

Godden, D. R., & Baddeley, A. D. (1975). Context-dependent memory in two natural environments: On land and under water. *British Journal of Psychology, 66,* 325–331.

Goldin-Meadow, S., & Cook, S. W. (2012). Gesture in thought. In K. J. Holyoak & R. G. Morrison (Eds.), *Oxford handbook of thinking and reasoning.* New York: Oxford University Press.

Goldsmith, A. A., Thompson, R. D., Black, J. J., Tran, G. Q., & Smith, J. P. (2012). Drinking refusal self-efficacy and tension-reduction alcohol expectancies moderating the relationship between generalized anxiety and drinking behaviors in young adult drinkers. *Psychology of Addictive Behaviors, 26,* 59–67.

Goodman, G. S. (1991). Stress and children's testimony: Commentary on Peters. In J. Doris (Ed.), *The suggestibility of children's recollections* (pp. 77–82). Washington, DC: American Psychological Association.

Goodman, G. S., Quas, J. A., Batterman-Faunce, J. M., Riddlesberger, M., & Kuhn, J. (1997). Children's reactions to and memory for a stressful experience: Influences of age, knowledge, anatomical dolls, and parental attachment. *Applied Developmental Sciences, 1,* 54–75.

Goebel, M. U., Trebst, A. E., Steiner, J., Xie, Y. F., Exton, M. S., and others. (2002). Behavioral conditioning of immunosuppression is possible in humans. *Federation of American Societies for Experimental Biology Journal, 16,* 1869–1873.

Goel, A. K., & Davies, J. (2011). Artificial intelligence. In R. J. Sternberg & S. B. Kaufman (Eds.), *Handbook of intelligence.* New York: Cambridge University Press.

Goenjian, A. K., & others. (2012). Association of TPH1, TPH2, and 5HTTLPR with PTSD and depressive symptoms. *Journal of Affective Disorders.* doi.org/10.1016/j.jad.2012.02.015

Goethals, G. R., & Demorest, A. P. (1995). The risky shift is a sure bet. In M. E. Ware & D. E. Johnson (Eds.), *Demonstrations and activities in teaching of psychology* (vol. 3). Mahwah, NJ: Erlbaum.

Goldberg, R. (2010). *Drugs across the spectrum* (6th ed.). Boston: Cengage.

Goldfield, B. A., & Snow, C. E. (2009). Individual differences: Implications for the study of language acquisition. In J. Berko Gleason & N. Ratner (Eds.), *The development of language* (7th ed.). Boston: Allyn & Bacon.

Goldman, M. S. (2009). Memory without feedback in a neural network. *Neuron, 61,* 621–634.

Goldney, R. D. (2012). From mania to melancholia to the bipolar disorders spectrum: A brief history of the controversy. *Australian and New Zealand Journal of Psychiatry, 46,* 306–312.

Goldschmidt, L., Richardson, G. A., Willford, J., & Day, N. L. (2008). Prenatal marijuana exposure and intelligence test performance at age 6. *Journal of the American Academy of Child and Adolescent Psychiatry, 47,* 254–263.

Goldstein, E. B. (2010). *Sensation and perception* (8th ed.). Boston: Cengage.

Goldstein, M. H., King, A. P., & West, M. J. (2003). Social interaction shapes babbling: Testing parallels between birdsong and speech. *Proceedings of the*

*National Academy of Sciences USA, 100* (13), 8030–8035.

Goldston, D. B., Molock, S. D., Whibbeck, L. B., Murakami, J. L., Zayas, L. H., & Hall, G. C. (2008). Cultural considerations in adolescent suicide prevention and psychosocial treatment. *American Psychologist, 63,* 14–31.

Goldstrom, I. D., Campbell, J., Rogers, J. A., Lambert, D. B., Blacklow, B., Henderson, M. J., & Manderscheid, R. W. (2006). National estimates for mental health mutual support groups, self-help organizations, and consumer-operated services. *Administration and Policy in Mental Health, 33,* 92–103.

Goleman, D., Kaufman, P., & Ray, M. (1993). *The creative mind.* New York: Plume.

Goljevscek, S., & Carvalho, L. A. (2011). Current management of obsessive and phobic states. *Neuropsychiatric Diseases and Treatment, 7,* 599–610.

Gonda, X., & others. (2009). Association of the s allele of the 5-HTTLPR with neuroticism-related traits and temperaments in a psychiatrically healthy population. *European Archives of Psychiatry and Clinical Neuroscience, 259,* 106–113.

Gonzalez-Maeso, J., & Sealfon, S. C. (2009). Psychedelics and schizophrenia. *Trends in Neuroscience, 32,* 225–232.

Gonzalez-Vallejo, C., Lassiter, G. D., Bellezza, F. S., & Lindberg, M. J. (2008). "Save angels perhaps": A critical examination of unconscious thought theory and the deliberation-without-attention effect. *Review of General Psychology, 12,* 282–296.

Goode, E., & Schwartz, J. (2011, August 28). Police lineups start to face fact: Eyes can lie. *New York Times,* A1.

Gooding, P. A., Hurst, A., Johnson, J., & Tarrier, N. (2012). Psychological resilience in young and older adults. *International Journal of Geriatric Psychiatry, 27,* 262–270.

Goodman, G. S. (2005). Wailing babies in her wake. *American Psychologist, 60,* 872–881.

Goodman, G. S. (2006). Children's eyewitness memory: A modern history and contemporary commentary. *Journal of Social Issues, 62,* 811–832.

Goosens, K. A. (2011). Hippocampal regulation of aversive memories. *21,* 460–466.

Gorin, A., Phelan, S., Wing, R. R., & Hill, J. O. (2004). Promoting long-term weight control: Does dieting consistency matter? *International Journal of Obesity Related Metabolic Disorder, 28,* 278–281.

Gosling, S. D. (2008a). *Snoop: What your stuff says about you.* New York: Basic.

Gosling, S. D. (2008b). Personality in nonhuman animals. *Social and Personality Psychology Compass, 2,* 985–1001.

Gosling, S. D., & John, O. P. (1999). Personality dimensions in nonhuman animals: A cross-species review. *Current Directions in Psychological Science, 8,* 69–75.

Gosling, S. D., Kwan, V. S. Y., & John, O. (2003). A dog's got personality: A cross-species comparison of personality judgments in dogs and humans. *Journal of Personality and Social Psychology, 85,* 1161–1169.

Gottlieb, G. (2007). Probabilistic epigenesis. *Developmental Science, 10,* 1–11.

Gottman, J. (2006, April, 29). Secrets of long term love. *New Scientist, 2549,* 40.

Gottman, J. M., Swanson, C., & Swanson, K. (2002). A general systems theory of marriage: Nonlinear difference equation modeling of marital interaction. *Personality and Social Psychology Review, 6,* 326–340.

Gottsegen, D. (2011). Hypnosis for functional abdominal pain. *American Journal of Clinical Hypnosis, 54,* 56–69.

Gouin, J. P., & others. (2012). Chronic stress, daily stressors, and circulating inflammatory markers. *Health Psychology, 31,* 264–268.

Gould, R. L., Coulson, M. C., & Howard, R. J. (2012). Efficacy of cognitive behavioral therapy for anxiety disorders in older people: A meta-analysis and meta-regression of randomized controlled trials. *Journal of the American Geriatric Society, 60,* 218–229.

Graber, J. A., Brooks-Gunn, J., & Warren, M. P. (2006). Pubertal effects on adjustment in girls: Moving from demonstrating effects to identifying pathways. *Journal of Youth and Adolescence, 35,* 391–401.

Graham, J., Nosek, B. A., Haidt, J., Iyer, R., Koleva, S., & Ditto, P. H. (2011). Mapping the moral domain. *Journal of Personality and Social Psychology, 101,* 366–385.

Graham, J. R. (2012). *MMPI-2: Assessing personality and psychopathology.* New York: Oxford University Press.

Grant, B. F., Stinson, F. S., Dawson, D. A., Chou, P., Dufour, M. C., Compton, W., Pickering, R. P., & Kaplan, K. (2004). Prevalence and co-occurrence of substance use disorders and independent mood and anxiety disorders: Results from the national epidemiologic survey on alcohol and related conditions. *Archives of General Psychiatry, 61,* 807–816.

Gravetter, F. J., & Forzano, L. B. (2012). *Research methods for the behavioral sciences* (4th ed.). Boston: Cengage.

Gray, J. A. (1987). *The psychology of fear and stress.* Cambridge, England: Cambridge University Press.

Gray, J. A., & McNaughton, N. (2000). *The neuropsychology of anxiety: An enquiry into the functions of the septo-hippocampal system.* Oxford, England: Oxford University Press.

Graziano, M. S. A., & Kastner, S. (2011). Human consciousness and its relationship to social neuroscience: A novel hypothesis. *Cognitive Neuroscience, 2,* 98–113.

Graziano, W. G., & Tobin, R. M. (2009). Agreeableness. In M. R. Leary & R. H. Hoyle (Eds.), *Handbook of individual differences in social behavior* (pp. 46–61). New York: Guilford.

Green, J. P., Page, R. A., Handley, G. W., & Rasekhy, R. (2005). The "hidden observer" and ideomotor responding: A real–simulator comparison. *Contemporary Hypnosis, 22,* 123–137.

Green, M. K., & others. (2011). Prenatal stress induces long term stress vulnerability, compromising stress response systems in the brain and impairing extinction of conditioned fear after adult stress. *Neuroscience, 192,* 438–451.

Greenberg, J. (2008). Understanding the vital human quest for self-esteem. *Perspectives on Psychological Science, 3,* 48–55.

Greenberg, J., & Kosloff, S. (2008). Terror management theory: Implications for understanding prejudice, stereotyping, intergroup conflict, and political attitudes. *Social and Personality Psychology Compass, 2,* 1881–1894.

Greene, R. L. (2011). MMPI-2/MMPI-2-RF (3rd ed.). Upper Saddle River, NJ: Pearson.

Greenwald, A. G., Poehlman, T. A., Uhlmann, E., & Banaji, M. R. (2009). Understanding and using the Implicit Association Test: III. Meta-analysis of predictive validity. *Journal of Personality and Social Psychology, 97,* 17–41.

Greer, S., Morris, T., & Pettingale, K. W. (1979). Psychological response to breast cancer: Effect on outcome. *Lancet, 314,* 785–787.

Greeson, J. M., Lewis, J. G., Achanzar, K., Zimmerman, E., Young K. H., & Suarez, E. C. (2009). Stress-induced changes in the expression of monocytic beta-2-integrins: The impact of arousal of negative affect and adrenergic responses to the Anger Recall interview. *Brain, Behavior, and Immunity, 23,* 251–256.

Gregan, M. J., Nelson, P. B., & Oxenham, A. (2011). Behavioral estimates of basilar-membrane compression: Additivity of forward masking in noise-masked normal-hearing listeners. *Journal of the Acoustical Society of America, 130,* 2835–2844.

Gregerson, M., Kaufman, J. C., & Snyder, H. (Eds.). (2012). *Teaching creatively and teaching creativity.* New York: Springer.

Gregg, A. P., & Sedikides, C. (2010). Narcissistic fragility: Rethinking its link to explicit and implicit self-esteem. *Self and Identity, 9,* 142–146.

Gregory, A. M., Ball, H. A., & Button, T. M. M. (2011). Behavioral genetics. In P. K. Smith & C. H. Hart (Eds.), *Wiley-Blackwell handbook of childhood social development* (2nd ed.). New York: Wiley.

Greitemeyer, T. (2009). Effects of songs with prosocial lyrics on prosocial thoughts, affect, and behavior. *Journal of Experimental Social Psychology, 45,* 186–190.

Greitemeyer, T., & Osswald, S. (2010). Effects of prosocial video games on prosocial behavior. *Journal of Personality and Social Psychology, 98,* 211–221.

Greitemeyer, T., & Osswald, S. (2011). Playing prosocial video games increases the accessibility of prosocial thoughts. *Journal of Social Psychology, 151,* 121–128.

Griffin, D. (2012). Judgment heuristics. In K. J. Holyoak & R. G. Morrison (Eds.), *Oxford handbook of thinking and reasoning.* New York: Oxford University Press.

Griffin, K. W., & others. (2012). Long-term effects of self-control on alcohol use and sexual behavior among urban minority young women. *International Journal of Environmental Research and Public Health, 9,* 1–23.

Griffith, R. L., & Converse, P. D. (2011). The rules of evidence and the prevalence of applicant faking. In M. Ziegler, C. MacCann, & R. Roberts (Eds.), *New perspectives on faking in personality assessment.* New York: Oxford University Press.

Grigorenko, E. L., Jarvin, L., Tan, M., & Sternberg, R. J. (2009). Something new in the garden: Assessing creativity in academic domains. *Psychology Science Quarterly, 50* (2), 295–307.

Grigoryan, G., Korkotian, E., & Segal, M. (2012). Selective facilitation of LPTP in the ventral hippocampus by calcium stores. *Hippocampus.* doi: 10.1002/hipo.22000.

Griguoli, M., & Cherubini, A. (2012). Regulation of hippocampal inhibitory circuits by nicotinic acetylcholine receptors. *Journal of Physiology, 590,* 655–666.

Grilo, C. M., Masheb, R. M., & White, M. A. (2010). Significance of overvaluation of shape/weight in binge-eating disorder: Comparative study with overweight and bulimia nervosa. *Obesity, 18,* 499–504.

Grubin, D. (2010). The polygraph and forensic psychiatry. *Journal of the American Academy of Psychology and Law, 38,* 446–451.

Grubin, D., & Madsen, L. (2006). Accuracy and utility of post-conviction polygraph testing of sex offenders. *British Journal of Psychiatry, 188,* 479–483.

Grundy, S. M. (2012). Pre-diabetes, metabolic syndrome, and cardiovascular disease. *Journal of the American College of Cardiology, 59,* 635–643.

Grusec, J. E. (2011). Socialization processes in the family: Social and emotional development. *Annual Review of Psychology* (vol. 62). Palo Alto, CA: Annual Reviews.

Guérard, K., Tremblay, S., & Saint-Aubin, J. (2009). The processing of spatial information in short-term memory: Insights from eye-tracking the path length effect. *Acta Psychologica, 132,* 136–144.

Guillaume, Y. R. F., Brodbeck, F. C., & Riketta, M. (2012). Surface- and deep-level dissimilarity effects on social integration and individual related outcomes in work groups: A meta-analytic integration. *Journal of Occupational and Organizational Psychology, 85,* 80–115.

Gunderson, J. (2008). Borderline personality disorder: An overview. *Social Work in Mental Health, 6,* 5–12.

Gunderson, J. G., Bender, D., Sanislow, C., Yen, S., Rettew, J. B., Dolan-Sewell, R., Dyck, I., Morey, L. C., McGlashan, T. H., Shea, M. T., & Skodol, A. E. (2003). Plausibility and possible determinants of sudden "remissions" in borderline patients. *Psychiatry: Interpersonal and Biological Processes, 66,* 111–119.

Gunty, A. L., Frazier, P. A., Tennen, H., Tomich, P., Tashiro, T., & Park, C. (2011). Moderators of the relation between perceived and actual posttraumatic growth. *Psychological Trauma: Theory, Research, Practice, and Policy, 3,* 61–66.

Guo, Q., Johnson, C. A., Unger, J. B., Lee, L., Xie, B., Chou, C. P., Palmer, P. H., Sun, P., Gallaher, P., & Pentz, M. (2007). Utility of theory of reasoned action and theory of planned behavior for predicting Chinese adolescent smoking. *Addictive Behaviors, 32,* 1066–1081.

Guo, X., & others. (2012). Effects of antipsychotic medications on quality of life and psychosocial functioning in patients with early-stage schizophrenia: 1-year follow-up naturalistic study. *Comprehensive Psychiatry.* (in press)

Guo, Y. (2005). Filial therapy for children's behavioral and emotional problems in mainland China. *Journal of Child and Adolescent Psychiatric Nursing, 18,* 171–180.

**Gurin, P., Dey, E. L., Hurtado, S., & Gurin, G.** (2002). Diversity and higher education: Theory and impact on educational outcomes. *Harvard Educational Review, 72,* 330–366.

**Guttmacher Institute.** (2010, January). *Facts on American teens' sexual and reproductive health.* Washington, DC: Author.

# H

**Haas, B. W., Omura, K., Constable, R. T., & Canli, T.** (2007). Emotional conflict and neuroticism: Personality-dependent activation in the amygdala and subgenual anterior cingulate. *Behavioral Neuroscience, 121,* 249–256.

**Haase, S. J., & Fisk, G. D.** (2011). A comparison of signal detection theory to objective threshold/strategic model of unconscious perception. *Perceptual and Motor Skills, 113,* 242–256.

**Habeck, C., Rakitin, B. C., Moeller, J., Scarmeas, N., Zarahn, E., Brown, T., & Stern, Y.** (2004). An event-related fMRI study of the neurobehavioral impact of sleep deprivation on performance of a delayed-match-to-sample task. *Brain Research, 18,* 306–321.

**Haber, J. R., Koenig, L. B., & Jacob, T.** (2011). Alcoholism, personality, religion/spirituality: An integrative review. *Current Drug Abuse Reviews, 4,* 250–260.

**Hackett, R. A., Hamer, M., Endrighi, R., Brydon, L., & Steptoe, A.** (2012). Loneliness and stress-related inflammatory and neuroendocrine responses in older men and women. *Psychoneuroimmunology.* (in press)

**Hagman, J. O., & Frank, G. K. W.** (2012). Developmental concerns in psychopharmacological treatment of children and adolescents with eating disorders. In J. Lock (Ed.), *Oxford handbook of child and adolescent eating disorders: Developmental perspectives.* New York: Oxford University Press.

**Hahn, D. B., Payne, W. A., & Lucas, E. B.** (2013). *Focus on health* (11th ed.). New York: McGraw-Hill.

**Hahn, U., & Oaksford, M.** (2012). Rational argument. In K. J. Holyoak & R. G. Morrison (Eds.), *Oxford handbook of thinking and reasoning.* New York: Oxford University Press.

**Haidle, M. N.** (2010). Working memory capacity and the evolution of modern cognitive capacities—implications from animal and early human tool use. *Current Anthropology 51/S1 Working memory: Beyond language and symbolism, Wenner-Gren Symposium, Suppl. 1,* S149–S166.

**Halberstadt, J.** (2010). Dumb but lucky: Fortuitous affect cues and their disruption by analytic thought. *Social and Personality Psychology Compass, 4,* 64–76.

**Hald, G. M., Malamuth, N. M., & Yuen, C.** (2010). Pornography and attitudes supporting violence against women: Revisiting the relationship in nonexperimental studies. *Aggressive Behavior, 36,* 14–20.

**Hales, D.** (2011). *An invitation to health* (14th ed.). Boston: Cengage.

**Halford, J. C., & others.** (2011). Serotonergic anti-obesity agents: Past experience and future prospects. *Drugs, 71,* 2247–2255.

**Halgunseth, L. C., Ispa, J. M., & Rudy, D.** (2006). Parental control in Latino families: An integrated review of the literature. *Child Development, 77,* 1282–1297.

**Hall, C., Hogue, T., & Guo, K.** (2011). Differential gaze behavior towards sexually preferred and non-preferred human figures. *Journal of Sexual Research, 48,* 461–469.

**Hall, J. A., & Matsumoto, D.** (2004). Gender differences in judgments of multiple emotions from facial expressions. *Emotion, l4,* 201–206.

**Hall, J. A., Park, N., Song, H., & Cody, M. J.** (2010). Strategic misrepresentation in online dating: The effects of gender, self-monitoring, and personality traits. *Journal of Social and Personal Relationships, 27,* 117–135.

**Hallahan, D. P., Kauffman, J. M., & Pullen, P. C.** (2012). *Exceptional learners* (12th ed). Boston: Allyn & Bacon.

**Halpern, D. F., Benbow, C. P. Geary, D. C., Gur, R. C., Hyde, J. S., & Gernsbache, M. A.** (2007). The science of sex differences in science and mathematics. *Psychological Science in the Public Interest, 8,* 1–51.

**Hamer, M.** (2012). Psychoneuroimmunology and physical activity. In E. O. Acevedo (Ed.), *Oxford handbook of exercise psychology.* New York: Oxford University Press.

**Hammad, T. A.** (2004, September 13). *Results of the analysis of suicidality in pediatric trials of newer antidepressants.* Presentation at the U.S. Food and Drug Administration, Psychopharmacologic Drugs Advisory Committee and the Pediatric Advisory Committee. www.fda.gov/ohrms/dockets/ac/04/slides/2004-4065S1_08_FDA-Hammad.htm (accessed May 29, 2012)

**Hammond, D. C.** (2010). Hypnosis in the treatment of anxiety- and stress-related disorders. *Expert Review of Neurotherapeutics, 10,* 263–273.

**Hampton, J.** (2008). Abstinence-only programs under fire. *Journal of the American Medical Association, 17,* 2013–2015.

**Han, R., Shi, J.,Yong, W., & Wang, W.** (2012). Intelligence and prosocial behavior: Do smart children really act nice? *Current Psychology, 31,* 88–101.

**Han, S., O'Connor, A. R., Eslick, A. N., & Dobbins, I. G.** (2012). The role of the left ventrolateral prefrontal cortex during episodic decisions: Semantic elaboration or resolution of an episodic interference. *Journal of Cognitive Neuroscience, 24,* 223–234.

**Han, S., & others.** (2012). $Na_V1.1$ channels are critical for intercellular communication in the suprachiasmatic nucleus and for normal circadian rhythms. *Proceedings of the National Academy of Sciences USA.* doi: 10.1073/pnas.1115729109

**Haney, C., Banks, C., & Zimbardo, P.** (1973). Interpersonal dynamics in a simulated prison. *International Journal of Criminology and Penology, 1,* 69–97.

**Hanley, J. R.** (2011). Why are the names of people associated with so many phonological retrieval failures. *Psychonomic Bulletin and Review, 18,* 612–617.

**Hannum, R. D., Rosellini, R. A., & Seligman, M. E. P.** (1976). Learned helplessness in the rat: Retention and immunization. *Developmental Psychology, 12,* 449–454.

**Hanowski, R. J., Olson, R. L., Hickman, J. S., & Bocanegra, J.** (2009, September). *Driver distraction in commercial vehicle operations.* Paper presented at the First International Conference on Driver Distraction and Inattention, Gothenburg, Sweden.

**Hanscombe, K. B., & others.** (2011). Socioeconomic status (SES) and children's intelligence (IQ): In a UK-representative sample SES moderates the environmental, not genetic, effect on IQ. *PLoS One, 7* (2), E30320.

**Hansen, K. B., Vilsboll, T., Bagger, J. L., Holst, J. J., & Knop, F. K.** (2012). Impaired incretin-inducted amplification of insulin secretion after glucose homeostatic dysregulation in healthy subjects. *Journal of Clinical Endocrinology and Metabolism, 97* (4), 1363–1370.

**Hansen, K. E., & Pronin, E.** (2012). Illusions of self-knowledge. In S. Vazire & T. D. Wilson (Eds.), *Handbook of self knowledge.* New York: Guilford.

**Harder, V. S., & others.** (2012). Multiple traumas, post-election violence, and posttraumatic stress among impoverished Kenyan youth. *Journal of Traumatic Stress, 25,* 64–70.

**Hardy, S. A., & Carlo, G.** (2011). Moral identity: What is it, how does it develop, and is it linked to moral action? *Child Development Perspectives, 5,* 212–218.

**Harker, L. A., & Keltner, D.** (2001). Expressions of positive emotion in women's college yearbook pictures and their relationship to personality and life outcomes across adulthood. *Journal of Personality and Social Psychology, 80,* 112–124.

**Harlow, H. F.** (1958). The nature of love. *American Psychologist, 13,* 673–685.

**Harman, D.** (1956). Aging: A theory based on free radical and radiation chemistry. *Journal of Gerontology, 11,* 298–300.

**Harned, E. S., Korslund, K. E., Foa, E. B., & Linehan, M. M.** (2012). Treating PTSD in suicidal and self-injuring women with borderline personality disorder: Development and preliminary evaluation of dialectical behavior therapy prolonged exposure protocol. *Behavior Research and Therapy, 50,* 381–386.

**Haroon, E., Raison, C. L., & Miller, A. H.** (2012). Psychoneuroimmunology meets neuropsychopharmacology: Translational implications of the impact of inflammation on behavior. *Neuropsychopharmacology, 37,* 137–162.

**Harpaz, Y., Levkovitz, Y., & Lavidor, M.** (2009). Lexical ambiguity resolution in Wernicke's area and its right homologue. *Cortex, 45* (9), 1097–1103.

**Harris, A. E.** (2011). The relational tradition: Landscape and canon. *Journal of the American Psychoanalytic Association, 59,* 701–736.

**Harris, D. M., & Kay, J.** (1995). I recognize your face but I can't remember your name: Is it because names are unique? *British Journal of Psychology, 86,* 345–358.

**Harris, J. A.** (2006). Elemental representations of stimuli in associative learning. *Psychological Review, 113,* 584–605.

**Harris, J. A., Andrew, B. J., & Livesey, E. J.** (2012). The content of compound conditioning. *Journal of Experimental Psychology: Animal Behavior and Processes, 38* (2), 157–166.

**Harris, J. J., & Attwell, D.** (2012). The energetics of CNS white matter. *Journal of Neuroscience, 32,* 356–371.

**Harris, J. R.** (1998). *The nurture assumption: Why children turn out the way they do.* New York: Free Press.

**Harris, J. R.** (2009). *The nurture assumption* (rev. and updated edition). New York: Free Press.

**Harris Interactive.** (2011). *Consumers begin to "go social" for gift recommendations.* www.harrisinteractive.com/NewsRoom/HarrisPolls/tabid/447/mid/1508/articleId/925/ctl/ReadCustom%20Default/Default.aspx (accessed May 6, 2012)

**Harrison, M. A., & Shortall, J. C.** (2011). Women and men in love: Who really feels it and says it first? *Journal of Social Psychology, 151,* 727–736.

**Harrison, Y.** (2012). The functions of sleep. In C. M. Morin & C. A. Espie (Eds.), *Oxford handbook of sleep and sleep disorders.* New York: Oxford University Press.

**Harro, J., Merenakk, L., Nordquist, N., Konstabel, K., Comasco, E., & Oreland, L.** (2009). Personality and the serotonin transporter gene: Associations in a longitudinal population-based study. *Biological Psychology, 81,* 9–13.

**Hart, C. L., Ksir, C. J., & Ray, O. S.** (2011). *Drugs, society, and human behavior* (14th ed.). New York: McGraw-Hill.

**Hartenbaum, N., & others.** (2006). Sleep apnea and commercial motor vehicle operators. *Chest, 130,* 902–905.

**Hartmann, E.** (1993). Nightmares. In M. A. Carskadon (Ed.), *Encyclopedia of sleep and dreams.* New York: Macmillan.

**Haselton, M. G.** (2006, April 29). How to pick a perfect mate. *New Scientist, 2549,* 36.

**Haslam, S. A., & Reicher, S.** (2003). Beyond Stanford: Questioning a role-based explanation of tyranny. *SPSP Dialogue, 18,* 22–25.

**Haslam, S. A., Reicher, S. D., & Reynolds, K. J.** (2012). Identity, influence, and change: Rediscovering John Turner's vision for social psychology. *British Journal of Social Psychology.* doi: 10.1111/j.2044-8309.2011.02091.x

**Hauk, O., & Pulvermuller, F.** (2011). The lateralization of motor cortex activation in action-words. *Frontiers of Human Neuroscience, 5,* 149.

**Haun, D. B. M., Rapold, C. J., Janzen, G., & Levinson, S. C.** (2011). Plasticity of human spatial cognition: Spatial language and cognition covary across cultures. *Cognition, 119,* 70–80.

**Hauser, A.** (2012, January 18). One Mississippi town's inspiring fight against obesity. *Everyday Health.* www.everydayhealth.com/weight/one-mississippi-towns-inspiring-fight-against-obesity.aspx (accessed May 30, 2012)

**Hawkins-Gilligan, J., Dygdon, J. A., & Conger, A. J.** (2011). Examining the nature of fear of flying. *Aviation, Space, and Environmental Medicine, 82,* 964–971.

**Hawkley, L. C., & Cacioppo, J. T.** (2012a). Loneliness and health. In M. Gellman & J. R. Turner (Eds.), *Encyclopedia of behavioral medicine.* New York: Springer.

**Hawkley, L. C., & Cacioppo, J. T.** (2012b). Social connection and relationships in successful aging. In J. M. Rippe (Ed.), *Encyclopedia of lifestyle medicine and health.* Thousand Oaks, CA: Sage.

**Hay, P. P., Bacaltchuk, J., Stefano, S., & Kashyap, P.** (2009). Psychological treatments for bulimia nervosa and binging. *Cochrane Database of Systematic Reviews, 4,* CD000562.

Hayakawa, Y. (2012). Targeting NKG2D in tumor surveillance. *Expert Opinion on Therapeutic Targets, 16* (6), 587–599.

Hayatbakhsh, M. R., & others. (2012). Birth outcomes associated with cannabis use before and during pregnancy. *Pediatric Research, 71,* 215–219.

Hayes, J. E., & Keast, R. S. J. (2011). Two decades of supertasting: Where do we stand? *Physiology and Behavior.* doi: 10.1016/j.physbeh.2011.08.003

Hayflick, L. (1977). The cellular basis for biological aging. In C. E. Finch & L. Hayflick (Eds.), *Handbook of the biology of aging.* New York: Van Nostrand.

Hazler, R. J. (2007). Person-centered therapy. In D. Capuzzi & D. Gross (Eds.), *Counseling and psychotherapy* (4th ed.). Upper Saddle River, NJ: Prentice-Hall.

Hearold, S. (1986). A synthesis of 1043 effects of television on social behavior. In G. Comstock (Ed.), *Public communication of behavior* (pp. 65–133). San Diego: Academic.

Hebb, D. O. (1949). *The organization of behavior: A neuropsychological theory.* New York: Wiley.

Hebb, D. O. (1980). *Essay on mind.* Mahwah, NJ: Erlbaum.

Heffner, K. L. (2011). Neuroendocrine effects of stress on immunity in the elderly: Implications for inflammatory disease. *Immunology and Allergy Clinics of North America, 31,* 95–108.

Heidegger, M. (1962). *Being and time.* New York, NY: Harper & Row. (original work published 1927)

Heider, F. (1958). *The psychology of interpersonal relations.* Hoboken, NJ: Wiley.

Heiman, G. W. (2011). *Basic statistics for the behavioral sciences* (6th ed.). Boston: Cengage.

Heine, S. J. (2005). Constructing good selves in Japan and North America. In R. M. Sorrentino, D. Cohen, J. M. Olson, & M. P. Zanna (Eds.), *Cultural and social behavior: The Ontario symposium* (vol. 10, pp. 95–116). Mahwah, NJ: Erlbaum.

Heine, S. J., & Hamamura, T. (2007). In search of East Asian self-enhancement. *Personality and Social Psychology Review, 11,* 1–24.

Heine, S. J., & Raineri, A. (2009). Self-improving motivations and collectivism: The case of Chileans. *Journal of Cross-Cultural Psychology, 40,* 158–163.

Heller, A. C., Amar, A. P., Liu, C. Y., & Apuzzo, M. L. (2006). Surgery of the mind and mood: A mosaic of issues in time and evolution. *Neurosurgery, 59,* 720–733.

Helsen, K., Goubert, L., Peters, M. L., & Vlaeyen, J. W. S. (2011). Observational learning and pain-related fear: An experimental study with colored cold pressor tasks. *Journal of Pain, 12,* 1230–1239.

Helzer, E. G., & Dunning, D. (2012). On motivated reasoning and self-belief. In S. Vazire & T. D. Wilson (Eds.), *Handbook of self knowledge.* New York: Guilford.

Henderson, M. (2008, February 18). Welcome to the town that will make you lose weight. *Times Online.* www.transitionpenwith.org.uk/news/04-08-08/welcome-town-will-make-you-lose-weight (accessed June 1, 2012)

Henderson, V. W. (2011). Gonadal hormones and cognitive aging: A midlife perspective. *Women's Health, 7* (1), 81–93.

Hennessey, B. A. (2011). Intrinsic motivation and creativity: Have we come full circle? In R. A. Beghetto & J. C. Kaufman (Eds.), *Nurturing creativity in the classroom.* New York: Cambridge University Press.

Henrich, J., Ensminger, J., McElreath, R., Barr, A., Barrett, C., Bolyanatz, A., Cardenas, J. C., Gurven, M., Gwako, E., Henrich, N., Lesorogoi, C., Marlowe, F., Tracer, D., & Ziker, J. (2010). Markets, religion, community size, and the evolution of fairness and punishment. *Science, 327,* 1480–1484.

Henry, J. D., MacLeod, M. S., Phillips, L. H., & Crawford, J. R. (2004). A meta-analytic review of prospective memory and aging. *Psychology and Aging, 19,* 27–39.

Hepper, E. G., & Sedikides, C. (2010). Self-enhancing feedback. In R. Sutton, M. Hornsey, & K. Douglas (Eds.), *Feedback: The handbook of praise, criticism, and advice.* Bern, Switzerland: Peter Lang.

Hepting, U., & Solle, R. (1973). Sex-specific differences in color coding. *Archiv fur Psychologie, 125* (2-3), 184–202.

Herberstein, M. E., & Kemp, D. J. (2012). A clearer view from fuzzy images. *Science, 335,* 409–410.

Herbert, J. (1988). The physiology of aggression. In J. Groebel & R. Hinde (Eds.), *Aggression and war: The biological and social bases.* New York: Cambridge University Press.

Herlihy, B., & McCollum, V. (2007). Feminist theory. In D. Capuzzi & D. Gross (Eds.), *Counseling and psychotherapy* (4th ed.). Upper Saddle River, NJ: Prentice-Hall.

Herman, D., Macknight, J. M., Stromwall, A. E., & Mistry, D. J. (2011). The international athlete—advances in management of jet lag disorder and anti-doping policy. *Clinical Sports Medicine, 30,* 641–659.

Hermundstad, A. M., Brown, K. S., Bassett, D. S., & Carlson, J. M. (2011). Learning, memory, and the role of neural network architecture. *PLoS Computational Biology, 7,* e1002063.

Herring, M. P., Puetz, T. W., O'Connor, P. J., & Dishman, P. K. (2012). Effect of exercise training on depressive symptoms among patients with a chronic illness: A systematic review and meta-analysis of randomized controlled conditions. *Archives of Internal Medicine, 172,* 101–111.

Hertwig, R., & Ortmann, A. (2008). Deception in experiments: Revisiting the arguments in its defense. *Ethics and Behavior, 18,* 59–92.

Herzog, H. (2006). Forty-two thousand and one dalmatians: Fads, social contagion, and dog breed popularity. *Society & Animals, 14,* 383–397.

Heward, W. L. (2013). *Exceptional children* (10th ed.). Upper Saddle River, NJ: Merrill.

Hewlin, P. F. (2009). Wearing the cloak: Antecedents and consequences of creating facades of conformity. *Journal of Applied Psychology, 94,* 727–741.

Heyes, C. (2010). Mesmerizing mirror neurons. *NeuroImage, 51,* 789–791.

Hibbard, S., Porcerelli, J., Kamoo, R., Schwartz, M., & Abell, S. (2010). Defense and object relational maturity on thematic apperception test scales indicate levels of personality organization. *Journal of Personality Assessment, 92,* 241–253.

Hickok, G. (2009). Eight problems for the mirror neuron theory of action understanding in monkeys and humans. *Journal of Cognitive Neuroscience, 17,* 282–293.

Hickok, G., & Hauser, M. (2010). (Mis)understanding mirror neurons. *Current Biology, 20,* 593–594.

Hicks, J. A., Cicero, D. C., Trent, J., Burton, C. M., & King, L. A. (2010). Positive affect, intuition, and the feeling of meaning. *Journal of Personality and Social Psychology, 98* (6), 967–979.

Hicks, J. A., Trent, J., Davis, W., & King, L. A. (2012). Positive affect, meaning in life, and future time perspective: An application of Socioemotional Selectivity Theory. *Psychology and Aging, 27,* 181–189.

Hidaka, B. H. (2012). Depression as a disease of modernity: Explanations for increasing prevalence. *Journal of Affective Disorders.* (in press)

Hildebrandt, T., Bacow, T., Markella, M., & Loeb, K. L. (2012). Anxiety in anorexia nervosa and its management using family-based treatment. *European Eating Disorders Review, 20,* e1–e16.

Hilgard, E. R. (1977). *Divided consciousness: Multiple controls in human thought and action.* New York: Wiley.

Hilgard, E. R. (1992). Dissociation and theories of hypnosis. In E. Fromm & M. R. Nash (Eds.), *Contemporary hypnosis research.* New York: Guilford.

Hill, A. L., Rosenbloom, D. I., & Nowak, M. A. (2012). Evolutionary dynamics of HIV at multiple spatial and temporal scales. *Journal of Molecular Biology, 90,* 543–561.

Hill, C. E. (2000). Client-centered therapy. In A. Kazdin (Ed.), *Encyclopedia of psychology.* Washington, DC, & New York: American Psychological Association and Oxford University Press.

Hill, P. L., Jackson, J. J., Roberts, B. W., Lapsley, D. K., & Brandenberger, J. W. (2011). Change you can believe in: Changes in goal setting during emerging and young adulthood predict later adult well-being. *Social Psychological and Personality Science, 2,* 123–131.

Hill, T. D., Burdette, A. M., Ellison, C. G., & Musick, M. A. (2006). Religious attendance and the health behaviors of Texas adults. *Preventive Medicine: An International Journal Devoted to Practice and Theory, 42,* 309–312.

Hingson, R. W., Heeren, T., & Winter, M. R. (2006). Age at drinking onset and alcohol dependence: Age of onset, duration, and severity. *Archives of Pediatric and Adolescent Medicine, 160,* 739–746.

Hinshaw, S. P. (2007). *The mark of shame: Stigma of mental illness and an agenda for change.* New York: Oxford University Press.

Hinton, D., Kredlow, B. A., Bui, E., Pollack, M., & Hofmann, S. (2012). Treatment change of somatic symptoms and cultural syndromes among Cambodian refugees with PTSD. *Depression and Anxiety, 29,* 148–155.

Hirata, A., & Castro-Alamancos, M. A. (2010). Neocortex network activation and deactivation states controlled by the thalamus. *Journal of Neurophysiology, 103* (3), 1147–1157.

Hirsch, J. K., Conner, K. R., & Duberstein, P. R. (2007). Optimism and suicide ideation among young college students. *Archives of Suicide Research, 11,* 177–185.

Ho, M. L., & Brass, S. D. (2011). Obstructive sleep apnea. *Neurology International, 3,* e15.

Ho, Y. J., Ho, S. C., Pawlak, C. R., & Yeh, K. Y. (2011). Effects of D-cycloserine on MPTP-induced behavioral and neurological changes: Potential for treatment of Parkinson's disease dementia. *Behavioral Brain Research, 219,* 280–290.

Hobara, M. (2005). Beliefs about appropriate pain behavior: Cross-cultural and sex differences between Japanese and Euro-Americans. *European Journal of Pain, 9,* 389–393.

Hobson, A., & Voss, U. (2011). A mind to go out of: Reflections on primary and secondary consciousness. *Consciousness and Cognition, 20,* 993–997.

Hobson, J. A. (1999). Dreams. In R. Conlan (Ed.), *States of mind.* New York: Wiley.

Hobson, J. A. (2000). Dreams: Physiology. In A. Kazdin (Ed.), *Encyclopedia of psychology.* Washington, DC, & New York: American Psychological Association and Oxford University Press.

Hobson, J. A. (2002). *Dreaming.* New York: Oxford University Press.

Hobson, J. A. (2004). Freud returns? Like a bad dream. *Scientific American, 290,* 89.

Hobson, J. A., Pace-Schott, E. F., & Stickgold, R. (2000). Dreaming and the brain. *Behavior and Brain Sciences, 23,* 793–842.

Hock, R. R. (2012). *Human sexuality* (3rd ed.). Upper Saddle River, NJ: Pearson.

Hockett, C. F. (1960). The origin of speech. *Scientific American, 203,* 88–96.

Hodapp, R. M., Griffin, M. M., Burke, M. M., & Fisher, M. H. (2011). Intellectual disabilities. In R. J. Sternberg & S. B. Kaufman (Eds.), *Handbook of intelligence.* New York: Cambridge University Press.

Hodgins, D. C. (2005). Weighing the pros and cons of changing change models: A comment on West (2005). *Addiction, 100,* 1042–1043.

Hodson, G., & Busseri, M. A. (2012). Bright minds and dark attitudes: Lower cognitive ability predicts greater prejudice through right-wing ideology and lower intergroup contact. *Psychological Science, 23* (2), 187–195.

Hoefnagels, M. (2012). *Biology* (2nd ed.). New York: McGraw-Hill.

Hoek, H. W. (2006). Incidence, prevalence and mortality of anorexia nervosa and other eating disorders. *Current Opinion in Psychiatry, 19,* 389–394.

Hoffman, J. (2012, February 23). Trying to find a cry of desperation amid Facebook drama. *New York Times,* A1.

Hogan, E. H., Hornick, B. A., & Bouchoux, A. (2002). Focus on communications: Communicating the message: Clarifying the controversies about caffeine. *Nutrition Today, 37,* 28–35.

Hogan, R. (2006). *Personality and the fate of organizations.* Mahwah, NJ: Erlbaum.

Hogan, R. (2009). Much ado about nothing. *Journal of Research in Personality, 43,* 249.

Hoge, C. W., Terhakoian, A., Castro, C. A., Messer, S. C., & Engel, C. C. (2007). Association of posttraumatic stress disorder with somatic symptoms, health care visits, and absenteeism among Iraq War veterans. *American Journal of Psychiatry, 164,* 150–153.

Hogg, M. A. (2012). Social identity and the psychology of groups. In M. R. Leary & J. P. Tangney (Eds.), *Handbook of self and identity.* New York: Guilford.

**Holden, R. R., & Book, A. S.** (2011). Faking does distort self-report personality assessment. In M. Ziegler, C. MacCann, & R. Roberts (Eds.), *New perspectives on faking in personality assessment.* New York: Oxford University Press.

**Holland, A. C., Addis, D. R., & Kensinger, E. A.** (2011). The neural correlates of specific versus general autobiographical memory construction and elaboration. *Neuropsychologia, 49,* 3164–3177.

**Holland, A. S., & Roisman, G. I.** (2010). Adult attachment security and young adults' dating relationships over time: Self-reported, observational, and physiological evidence. *Developmental Psychology, 46,* 552–557.

**Holland, P. C.** (1996). The effects of intertrial and feature-target intervals on operant serial feature-positive discrimination learning. *Animal Learning & Behavior, 24,* 411–428.

**Hollander, A. C., & others.** (2012). Longitudinal study of mortality among refugees in Sweden. *International Journal of Epidemiology.* doi: 10.1093/ije/dys072

**Hollich, G.** (2006). Combining techniques to reveal emergent effects in infants' segmentation, word learning, and grammar. *Language and Speech, 49,* 3–19.

**Holmes, J.** (2011). Superego: An attachment perspective. *International Journal of Psychoanalysis, 92,* 1221–1240.

**Holmes, J. G., Miller, D. T., & Lerner, M. J.** (2002). Committing altruism under the cloak of self-interest: The exchange fiction. *Journal of Experimental Social Psychology, 38* (2), 144–151.

**Holmes, L. B., & Westgate, M. N.** (2011). Inclusion and exclusion criteria for malformations in newborn infants exposed to potential teratogens. *Birth Defects Research. Part A. Clinical and Molecular Teratology, 91* (9), 807–812.

**Holmes, S.** (1993). Food avoidance in patients undergoing cancer chemotherapy. *Support Care Cancer, 1* (6), 326–330.

**Holsboer, F., & Ising, M.** (2010). Stress hormones and stress regulation: Biological role and behavioral effects. *Annual Review of Psychology* (vol. 61). Palo Alto, CA: Annual Reviews.

**Holzschneider, K., & Mulert, C.** (2011). Neuroimaging in anxiety disorders. *Dialogues in Clinical Neuroscience, 13,* 453–461.

**Holyoak, K. J., & Morrison, R. G. (Eds.).** (2012). *Oxford handbook of thinking and reasoning.* New York: Oxford University Press.

**Hong, S. W., & Shevell, S. K.** (2009). Color-binding errors during rivalrous suppression of form. *Psychological Science, 20,* 1084–1091.

**Honts, C.** (1998, June). Commentary. *APA Monitor,* 30.

**Hooley, J. M., Cole, S. H., & Gironde, S.** (2012). Borderline personality disorder. In T. Widiger (Ed.), *Oxford handbook of personality disorders.* New York: Oxford University Press.

**Hooper, J., & Teresi, D.** (1993). *The 3-pound universe.* New York: Tarcher/Putnam.

**Hopf, F. W., & others.** (2010). Reduced nucleus accumbens SK channel activity enhances alcohol seeking abstinence. *Neuron, 65,* 682–694.

**Hopper, K., & Wanderling, J.** (2000). Revisiting the developed versus developing country distinction in course and outcome in schizophrenia: Results from ISoS, the WHO collaborative followup project. *Schizophrenia Bulletin, 26,* 835–846.

**Horn, J. L., & Cattell, R. B.** (1967). Age differences in fluid and crystallized intelligence. *Acta Psychologica, 26,* 107–129.

**Horner, V., Carter, J. D., Suchak, M., & de Waal, F. B.** (2011). Spontaneous prosocial choice by chimpanzees. *Proceedings of the National Academy of Sciences USA, 108,* 13847–13851.

**Horney, K.** (1945). *Our inner conflicts.* New York: Norton.

**Horney, K.** (1967). *Feminine psychology (collected essays, 1922–1937).* New York: Norton.

**Hornickel, J., Skoe, E., & Kraus, N.** (2009). Subcortical laterality of speech encoding. *Audiology and Neuro-Otology, 14,* 198–207.

**Horvath, A. O., Del Re, A. C., Flückiger, C., & Symonds, D.** (2011). Alliance in individual psychotherapy. *Psychotherapy, 48* (1), 9–16.

**Hosp, J. A., Pekanovic, A., Rioult-Pedotti, M. S., & Luft, A. R.** (2011). Dopaminergic projections from midbrain to primary motor cortex mediate motor skill learning. *Journal of Neuroscience, 31,* 2481–2487.

**Hoss, R. A., & Langlois, J. H.** (2003). Infants prefer attractive faces. In O. Pascalis & A. Slater (Eds.), *The development of face processing in infancy and early childhood: Current perspectives* (pp. 27–38). Hauppauge, NY: Nova Science Publishers.

**Hotard, S. R., McFatter, R. M., McWhirter, R. M., & Stegall, M. E.** (1989). Interactive effects of extraversion, neuroticism, and social relationships on subjective well-being. *Journal of Personality and Social Psychology, 57,* 321–331.

**Hou, J., & others.** (2012). Localization of cerebral functional deficits in patients with obsessive-compulsive disorder: A resting-state fMRI study. *Journal of Affective Disorders, 138,* 313–321.

**House, J. S., Landis, K. R., & Umberson, D.** (1988). Social relationships and health. *Science, 241,* 540–545.

**Houser-Marko, L., & Sheldon, K. M.** (2008). Eyes on the prize or nose to the grindstone? The effects of level of goal evaluation on mood and motivation. *Personality and Social Psychology Bulletin, 34,* 1556–1569.

**Houston, J. P., & others.** (2012). Association of common variations in the norepinephrine transporter gene with response to olanzapine-fluoxetine combination versus continued fluoxetine treatment in patients with treatment-resistant depression: A candidate gene analysis. *Journal of Clinical Psychiatry.* (in press)

**Hovland, C. I., Janis, I. L., & Kelley, H. H.** (1953). *Communication and persuasion.* New Haven, CT: Yale University Press.

**Howell, D. C.** (2013). *Statistical methods for psychology* (8th ed.). Boston: Cengage. (in press)

**Howes, M. B.** (2006). *Human memory.* Thousand Oaks, CA: Sage.

**Howes, O. D., & others.** (2012). The nature of dopamine dysfunction in schizophrenia and what this means for treatment: Meta-analysis of imaging studies. *Archives of General Psychiatry.* (in press)

**Howland, R. H.** (2012). The use of dopaminergic and stimulant drugs for the treatment of depression. *Journal of Psychosocial Nursing and Mental Health Services, 50,* 11–14.

**Hoyer, D., Hannon, J. P., & Martin, G. R.** (2002). Molecular, pharmacological, and functional diversity of 5-HT receptors. *Pharmacology, Biochemistry, and Behavior, 71,* 533–554.

**Hsieh, L. T., Hung, D. L., Tzeng, O. J., Lee, J. R., & Cheng, S. K.** (2009). An event-related potential investigation of the processing of remember/forget cues and item encoding in item-method directed forgetting. *Brain Research, 1250,* 190–201.

**Hsu, L., & others.** (2012). Social anxiety among East Asians in North America: East Asian socialization or the challenge of acculturation? *Cultural Diversity and Ethnic Minority Psychology, 18,* 181–191.

**Hu, S., & Kuh, G. D.** (2003). Diversity learning experiences and college student learning and development. *Journal of College Student Development, 44,* 320–334.

**Huang, C. C., & Chang, Y. C.** (2009). The long-term effects of febrile seizures on the hippocampal neuronal plasticity—clinical and experimental evidence. *Brain Development, 31,* 383–387.

**Huart, C., Collet, S., & Rombaux, P.** (2009). Chemosensory pathways: From periphery to cortex. *B-ENT, 5, Suppl. 13,* S3–S9.

**Hubble, M. A., & Miller, S. D.** (2004). The client: Psychotherapy's missing link for promoting a positive psychology. In A. Linley & S. Joseph (Eds.), *Positive psychology in practice* (pp. 335–353). Hoboken, NJ: Wiley.

**Hubel, D. H., & Wiesel, T. N.** (1963). Receptive fields of cells in striate cortex of very young, visually inexperienced kittens. *Journal of Neurophysiology, 26,* 994–1002.

**Hudak, M. L., & others.** (2012). Neonatal drug withdrawal. *Pediatrics, 129,* e540–e560.

**Huff, C. R.** (2002). What can we learn from other nations about the problem of wrongful conviction? *Judicature, 86,* 91–97.

**Hughes, A. E., Berg, C. A., & Wiebe, D. J.** (2012). Emotional processing and self-control in adolescents with type 1 diabetes. *Journal of Pediatric Psychology.* (in press)

**Hull, E. M., & Dominguez, J. M.** (2006). Getting his act together: Roles of glutamate, nitric oxide, and dopamine in the medial preoptic area. *Brain Research, 1126,* 66–75 .

**Human, L. J., & Biesanz, J. C.** (2011). Through the looking glass clearly: Accuracy and assumed similarity in well-adjusted individuals' first impressions. *Journal of Personality and Social Psychology, 100,* 349–364.

**Human, L. J., Biesanz, J. C., Parisotto, K. L., & Dunn, E. W.** (2012). Your best self helps reveal your true self: Positive self-presentation leads to more accurate personality impressions. *Social Psychological and Personality Science, 3,* 23–30.

**Humphrey, N.** (2000). How to solve the mind–body problem. *Journal of Consciousness Studies, 7,* 5–20.

**Humphrey, N.** (2006). *Seeing red: A study in consciousness.* Cambridge, MA; Harvard University Press.

**Hunsley, J., & Bailey, J. M.** (2001). Whither the Rorschach? An analysis of the evidence. *Psychological Assessment, 13,* 472–485.

**Hunt, H. T.** (2012). A collective unconscious reconsidered: Jung's archetypal imagination in the light of contemporary psychology and social science. *Journal of Analytical Psychology, 57,* 76–98.

**Hunt, R. R., & Ellis, H. C.** (2004). *Fundamentals of cognitive psychology* (7th ed.). New York: McGraw-Hill.

**Huttenlocher, P. R.** (1999). Dendritic synaptic development in human cerebral cortex: Time course and critical periods. *Developmental Neuropsychology, 16,* 347–349.

**Huuhka, K., & others.** (2012). One-year follow-up after discontinuing maintenance electroconvulsive therapy. *Journal of ECT.* (in press)

**Hwang, J. Y., & others.** (2012). Multidimensional comparison of personality characteristics of the big five model, impulsiveness, and affect in pathological gambling and obsessive-compulsive disorder. *Journal of Gambling Studies.* (in press)

**Hyde, J. S.** (2005). The gender similarities hypothesis. *American Psychologist, 60,* 581–592.

**Hyde, J. S.** (2006). Gender similarities in mathematics and science. *Science, 314,* 599–600.

**Hyde, J. S.** (2007). New directions in the study of gender similarities and differences. *Current Directions in Psychological Science, 16,* 259–263.

**Hyde, J. S., & DeLamater, J. D.** (2011). *Understanding human sexuality* (11th ed.). New York: McGraw-Hill.

**Hyde, L. W., Shaw, D. S., & Moilanen, K. L.** (2010). Developmental precursors of moral disengagement and the role of moral disengagement in the development of antisocial behavior. *Journal of Abnormal Child Psychology, 38,* 197–209.

**Hyland, M. E.** (2011). Motivation and placebos: Do different mechanisms occur in different contexts. *Philosophical Transactioins of the Royal Society of London. Series B, Biological Sciences, 366,* 1828–1837.

**Hyman, R.** (2010). Meta-analysis that conceals more than it reveals: Comment on Storm et al. (2010). *Psychological Bulletin, 136,* 486–490.

**Hyman, S.** (2001, October 23). *Basic and clinical neuroscience in the post-genomic era.* Paper presented at the centennial symposium on the Celebration of Excellence in Neuroscience, Rockefeller University, New York City.

**Hyman, S. E.** (2010). The diagnosis of mental disorders: The problem of reification. *Annual Review of Clinical Psychology* (vol. 6). Palo Alto, CA: Annual Reviews.

**Hystad, S. W., Eid, J., & Brevik, J. L.** (2011). Effects of psychological hardiness, job demands, and job control on sickness absence: A prospective study. *Journal of Occupational Health Psychology, 16* (3), 265–278.

## I

**Iacoboni, M.** (2009). Imitation, empathy, and mirror neurons. *Annual Review of Psychology* (vol. 60). Palo Alto, CA: Annual Reviews.

**Iacono, W. G., & Lykken, D. T.** (1997). The validity of the lie detector: Two surveys of scientific opinion. *Journal of Applied Psychology, 82,* 426–433.

**Iannilli, E., & others.** (2012). Taste laterality studied by means of umani and salt stimuli: An fMRI study. *NeuroImage, 60* (1), 426–435.

**Ibrahim, R., & Eviatar, Z.** (2012). The contribution of the two hemispheres to lexical decision in different languages. *Behavior and Brain Functioning, 8,* 3.

**Iemmola, F., & Ciani, A. C.** (2009). New evidence of genetic factors influencing sexual orientation in men:

Female fecundity increase in the maternal line. *Archives of Sexual Behavior, 38*, 393–399.

Iglesias, P. A. (2012). A systems biology view of adaptation in sensory mechanisms. *Advances in Experimental Medicine and Biology, 736*, 499–516.

Ikeda, B. E., Collins, C. E., Alvaro, F., Marshall, G., & Garg, M. L. (2006). Well-being and nutrition-related side effects in children undergoing chemotherapy. *Nutrition and Dietetics, 63*, 227–239.

Ikeda, K., Sekiguchi, T., & Hayashi, A. (2010). Concentrated pitch discrimination modulates auditory brainstem responses during contralateral noise exposure. *NeuroReport, 21*, 359–366.

Imada, T. (2012). Cultural narratives of individualism and collectivism: A content analysis of textbook stories in the United States and Japan. *Journal of Cross-Cultural Psychology, 43*, 576–591.

Imada, T., & Ellsworth, P. C. (2011). Proud Americans and lucky Japanese: Cultural differences in appraisal and corresponding emotion. *Emotion, 11*, 329–345.

Imeri, L., & Opp, M. R. (2009). How (and why) the immune system makes us sleep. *Nature Reviews: Neuroscience, 10*, 199–210.

Inaba, A., Thoits, P. A., Ueno, K., Gove, W. R., Evenson, R. J., & Sloan, M. (2005). Depression in the United States and Japan: Gender, marital status, and SES patterns. *Social Science & Medicine, 61*, 2280–2292.

Insko, C. A., & Wilson, M. (1977). Interpersonal attraction as a function of social interaction. *Journal of Personality and Social Psychology, 35*, 903–911.

Ironson, G., Solomon, G., Balbin, E., O'Cleirigh, C., George, A., Schneiderman, N., & Woods, T. (2001, March). *Religious behavior, religious coping, and compassionate view of others is associated with long-term survival with AIDS.* Paper presented at the meeting of the American Psychosomatic Society, Monterey, CA.

Ironson, G., Stuetzle, R., & Fletcher, M. A. (2006). An increase in religiousness/spirituality occurs after HIV diagnosis and predicts slower disease progression over 4 years in people with HIV. *Journal of General Internal Medicine, 21*, S62–S68.

Irwin, M. R., Wang, M., Campomayor, C. O., Coliado-Hidalgo, A., & Cole, S. (2006). Sleep deprivation and activation of morning levels of cellular and genomic markers of inflammation. *Archives of Internal Medicine, 166*, 1756–1762.

Ishikawa, Y., & others. (2012). The primary brain vesicles revisited: Are the three primary vesicles (forebrain/midbrain/hindbrain) universal in vertebrates? *Brain, Behavior, and Evolution.* (in press)

Iturbide, M. I., Raffaelli, M., & Carlo, G. (2009). Protective effects of ethnic identity on Mexican American college students' psychological well-being. *Hispanic Journal of Behavioral Sciences, 31*, 536–552.

Iwassa, H., Masul, Y., Gondo, Y., Inagaki, H., Kawaal, C., & Suzuki, T. (2008). Personality and all-cause mortality among older adults dwelling in a Japanese community: A five-year population-based prospective study. *American Journal of Geriatric Psychiatry, 16*, 399–405.

Iwassa, H., & others. (2009). Personality and participation in mass health checkups among Japanese community-dwelling elderly. *Journal of Psychosomatic Research, 66*, 155–159.

Izard, C. E. (2009). Emotion theory and research: Highlights, unanswered questions, and emerging issues. *Annual Review of Psychology* (vol. 60). Palo Alto, CA: Annual Reviews.

J

Jablensky, E. (2000). Epidemiology of schizophrenia: The global burden of disease and disability. *European Archives of Psychiatry and Clinical Neuroscience, 250*, 274–285.

Jablensky, E., Sartorius, N., Ernberg, G., & others. (1992). Schizophrenia: Manifestations, incidence and course in different cultures: A World Health Organization 10-country study. *Psychological Medicine, Monograph Suppl. 20*, 1–97.

Jacinto, G. A., & Edwards, B. L. (2011). Therapeutic stages of forgiveness and self-forgiveness. *Journal of Human Behavior in the Social Environment, 21*, 423–437.

Jackendoff, R. (2012). *A user's guide to thought and meaning.* New York: Oxford University Press.

Jackson, G. (2010). Come fly with me: Jet lag and melatonin. *International Journal of Clinical Practice, 64*, 135.

Jackson, L. C., & Greene, B. (2000). *Psychotherapy with African-American women.* New York: Guilford.

Jackson, M. L., & others. (2011). The effect of sleep deprivation on BOLD activity elicited by a divided attention task. *Brain Imaging and Behavior, 5*, 97–108.

Jackson, N. W. (2012). Equal discussion of significant findings? Possible confirmation bias in study of alcohol advertising. *Alcohol and Alcoholism, 47*, 79.

Jackson, S. L. (2012). *Research methods: A critical thinking approach* (4th ed.). Boston: Cengage.

Jacobs, T. L., Epel, E. S., Lin, J., Blackburn, E. H., Wolkowitz, O. M., Bridwell, D. A., Zanesco, A. P., Aichele, S. R., Sahdra, B. K., MacLean, K. A., King, B. G., Shaver, P. R., Rosenberg, E. L., Ferrer, E., Wallace, B. A., & Saron, C. D. (2011). Intensive meditation training, immune cell telomerase activity, and psychological mediators. *Psychoneuroendocrinology, 36*, 664–681.

Jacobsen, P. B., Bovbjerg, D. H., Schwartz, M. D., Andrykowski, M. A., Futterman, A. D., Gilewski, T., Norton, L., & Redd, W. H. (1993). Formation of food aversions in cancer patients receiving repeated infusions of chemotherapy. *Behavior Reseach Therapy, 31* (8), 739–748.

Jaeger, S. R., Bava, C. M., Worch, T., Dawson, J., & Marshall, D. W. (2011). The food choice kaleidoscope: A framework for structured description of product, place, and person as sources of variation in food choices. *Appetite, 56*, 412–423.

Jaeggi, S. M., Buschkuehl, M., Jonides, J., & Perrig, W. J. (2008). Improving fluid intelligence with training on working memory. *Proceedings of the National Academy of Sciences USA, 105* (19), 6829–6833.

Jakupcak, M., Salters, K., Gratz, K. L., & Roemer, L. (2003). Masculinity and emotionality: An investigation of men's primary and secondary emotional responding. *Sex Roles, 49*, 111–120.

James, W. (1950). *Principles of psychology.* New York: Dover. (original work published 1890)

Jameson, D., & Hurvich, L. M. (1989). Essay concerning color constancy. *Annual Review of Psychology* (vol. 40). Palo Alto, CA: Annual Reviews.

Jan, J. E., & others. (2012). Neurophysiology of circadian rhythm sleep disorders of children with neurodevelopmental disabilities. *European Journal of Pediatric Neurology.* (in press)

Janak, P. H., Bowers, M. S., & Corbit, L. H. (2012). Compound stimulus presentation and the norepinephrine reuptake inhibitor Atomoxetine enhance long-term extinction of cocaine-seeking behavior. *Neuropsychopharmacology, 37*, 975–985.

Jang, K. L., Livesley, W. J., & Vernon, P. A. (1996). Heritability of the big five personality dimensions and their facets: A twin study. *Journal of Personality, 64*, 577–591.

Janis, I. (1972). *Victims of groupthink: A psychological study of foreign-policy decisions and fiascos.* Boston: Houghton Mifflin.

Janis, I. L., & Hovland, C. I. (1959). An overview of persuasability research. In C. I. Hovland & I. L. Janis (Eds.), *Personality and persuasability* (pp. 1–26). New Haven, CT: Yale University Press.

Janowsky, D. S., Addario, D., & Risch, S. C. (1987). *Psychopharmacology case studies* (2nd ed.). New York: Guilford.

Jarrett, C. (2011). Ouch! The different ways people experience pain. *The Psychologist, 24*, Part 6.

Jarrett, R. B., Kraft, D., Doyle, J., Foster, B. M., Eaves, G. G., & Silver, P. C. (2001). Preventing recurrent depression using cognitive therapy with and without a continuation phase: A randomized clinical trial. *Archives of General Psychiatry, 58*, 381–388.

Jarrett, R. B., & others. (2012). Cognitive reactivity, dysfunctional attitudes, and depressive relapse and recurrence in cognitive therapy responders. *Behavior Research and Therapy, 50*, 280–286.

Jaspal, R., & Cinnirella, M. (2012). Identity processes, threat, and interpersonal relations: Accounts from British Muslim gay men. *Journal of Homosexuality, 59*, 215–240.

Jensen, L. W., & Wadkins, T. A. (2007). Mental health success stories: Finding paths to recovery. *Issues in Mental Health Nursing, 28*, 325–340.

Jensen, M. P. (2009). The neurophysiology of pain perception and hypnotic analgesia: Implications for clinical practice. *American Journal of Clinical Hypnosis, 51*, 123–148.

Jensen, S. E., & others. (2012). Cognitive-behavioral stress management and psychological well-being in HIV+ racial/ethnic minority women with human papillomavirus. *Health Psychology.* (in press)

Jensen-Campbell, L. A., & Malcolm, K. T. (2007). The importance of conscientiousness in adolescent interpersonal relationships. *Personality and Social Psychology Bulletin, 33*, 368–383.

Jeong, J., Kim, D. J., Kim, S. Y., Chae, J. H., Go, H. J., & Kim, K. S. (2001). Effect of total sleep deprivation on the dimensional complexity of the waking EEG. *Sleep, 15*, 197–202.

Jeon-Slaughter, H. (2012, March). Economic factors in patients' nonadherence to antidepressant treatment. *Social Psychiatry and Psychiatric Epidemiology*, 1–14. doi: 10.1007/s00127-012-0497-6

Jernelov, S., & others. (2012). Efficacy of a behavioral self-help treatment with or without therapist guidance for co-morbid and primary insomnia—a randomized controlled trial. *BMC Psychiatry.* doi: 10.1186/1471-244X-12-5

Jia, F., Goldstein, P. A., & Harrison, N. L. (2009). The modulation of synaptic GABA (A) receptors in the thalamus by eszopiclone and zolpidem. *Journal of Pharmacology and Experimental Therapeutics, 328*, 1000–1006.

Joel, S., MacDonald, G., Shimotomai, A. (2011). Conflicting pressures on romantic relationship commitment for anxiously attached individuals. *Journal of Personality, 79*, 51–73.

Johansen, J. P., Wolff, S. B., Luthi, A., & LeDoux, J. E. (2012). Controlling the elements: An optogenetic approach to understanding the neural circuits of fear. *Biological Psychiatry.* (in press)

John, D. A., & others. (2012). Does an immigrant health paradox exist among Asian Americans? Associations of nativity and occupational class with self-treated health and mental disorders. *Social Science and Medicine.* (in press)

Johnson, C. S. (2011). Addressing the moral agency of culturally specific care perspectives. *Journal of Moral Education, 40*, 471–489.

Johnson, G. B. (2012). *The living world* (7th ed.). New York: McGraw-Hill.

Johnson, J. S., & Newport, E. L. (1991). Critical period effects on universal properties of language: The status of subjacency in the acquisition of a second language. *Cognition, 39*, 215–258.

Johnson, J. T., Robinson, M., & Mitchell, E. B. (2004). Inferences about the authentic self: When do actions say more than mental states? *Journal of Personality and Social Psychology, 87*, 615–630.

Johnson, L. R., McGuire, J., Lazarus, R., & Palmer, A. A. (2012). Pavlovian fear memory circuits and phenotype models of PTSD. *Neuropharmacology, 62*, 638–646.

Johnson, S. K., & Halpern, A. R. (2012). Semantic priming of familiar songs. *Memory and Cognition, 40* (4), 579–593.

Johnston, L. D., O'Malley, P. M., Bachman, J. G., & Schulenberg, J. E. (2008). *Monitoring the Future national survey results on drug use, 1975–2007.* Bethesda, MD: National Institute on Drug Abuse.

Johnston, L. D., O'Malley, P. M., Bachman, J. G., & Schulenberg, J. E. (2009). *Monitoring the Future: National results on adolescent drug use: Overview of key findings, 2008.* Bethesda, MD: National Institute on Drug Abuse.

Johnston, L. D., O'Malley, P. M., Bachman, J. G., & Schulenberg, J. E. (2012). *Monitoring the Future national results on adolescent drug use: Overview of key findings, 2011.* Ann Arbor: Institute for Social Research, University of Michigan.

Johnstone, E., Benowitz, N., Cargill, A., Jacob, R., Hinks, L., Day, I., Murphy, M., & Walton, R. (2006). Determinants of the rate of nicotine metabolism and the effects on smoking behavior. *Clinical Pharmacology and Therapeutics, 80*, 319–330.

Joiner, T. E. (2005). *Why people die by suicide*. Cambridge, MA: Harvard University Press.

Joiner, T. E., Alfano, M. S., & Metalsky, G. I. (1992). When depression breeds contempt: Reassurance seeking, self-esteem, and rejection of depressed college students by their roommates. *Journal of Abnormal Psychology, 101*, 165–173.

Joiner, T. E., Hollar, D., & Van Orden, K. (2006). On Buckeyes, Gators, Super Bowl Sunday, and the miracle on ice: "Pulling together" is associated with lower suicide rates. *Journal of Social & Clinical Psychology, 25*, 179–195.

Joiner, T. E., & Ribeiro, J. D. (2012). Assessment and management of suicidal behavior in children and adolescents. *Pediatric Annals, 40*, 319–324.

Jones, E. E. (1998). Major developments in five decades of social psychology. In D. T. Gilbert, S. T. Fiske, & G. Lindzey (Eds.), *Handbook of social psychology* (4th ed., vol. 1). New York: McGraw-Hill.

Jones, E. E., & Harris, V. A. (1967). The attribution of attitudes. *Journal of Experimental Social Psychology, 3*, 1–24.

Joscelyne, A., & Kehoe, E. J. (2007). Time and stimulus specificity in extinction of the conditioned nictitating membrane response in the rabbit (*Oryctolagus cuniculus*). *Behavioral Neuroscience, 121*, 50–62.

Joseph, J. (2006). *The missing gene*. New York: Algora.

Joseph, J., Breslin, C., & Skinner, H. (1999). Critical perspectives on the transtheoretical model and stages of change. In J. A. Tucker, D. M. Donovan, & G. A. Marlatt (Eds.), *Changing addictive behavior: Bridging clinical and public health strategies* (pp. 160–190). New York: Guilford.

Joseph, S., & Linley, P. A. (2004). Positive therapy: A positive psychological approach to therapeutic practice. In P. A. Linley & S. Joseph (Eds.), *Positive psychology in practice* (pp. 354–368). Hoboken, NJ: Wiley.

Jost, J. T., Glaser, J., Kruglanski, A. W., & Sulloway, F. J. (2003). Political conservatism as motivated social cognition. *Psychological Bulletin, 129*, 339–375.

Joubert, O. R., Fize, D., Rousselet, G. A., & Fabre-Thorpe, M. (2008). Early interference of context congruence on object processing in rapid visual categorization of natural scences. *Journal of Vision, 8*, 1–18.

Joutsenniemi, K., & others. (2012). Prediction of the outcome of short- and long-term psychotherapy based on socio-demographic factors. *Journal of Affective Disorders*. doi: 10.1016/j.jad.2012.03.027

Juckel, G., Uhl, I., Padberg, F., Brune, M., & Winter, C. (2009). Psychosugery and deep brain stimulation as ultima ratio treatment for refractory depression. *European Archives of Psychiatry and Clinical Neuroscience, 259*, 1–7.

Judd, F. K., Hickey, M., & Bryant, C. (2011). Depression and midlife: Are we overpathologising the menopause? *Journal of Affective Disorders, 136* (3),199–211.

Jung, C. (1917). *Analytic psychology*. New York: Moffat, Yard.

## K

Kabat-Zinn, J. (2006). Coming to our senses: Healing ourselves and the world through mindfulness. New York, NY: Hyperion.

Kabat-Zinn, J. (2009, March 18). This analog life; Reconnecting with what is important in an always uncertain world. Presentation at the 7th Annual Conference at the Center for Mindful Meditation, Worcester, MA.

Kabat-Zinn, J., & Davidson, R. (Eds.). (2012). *The mind's own physician*. Berkeley, CA: New Harbinger.

Kabat-Zinn, J., Wheeler, E., Light, T., Skillings, A., Scharf, M. J., Cropley, T. G., Hosmer, D., & Bernhard, J. D. (1998). Influence of a mindfulness meditation-based stress reduction intervention on rates of skin clearing in patients with moderate to severe psoriasis undergoing phototherapy (UVB) and photochemotherapy (PUVA). *Psychosomatic Medicine, 60*, 625–632.

Kagan, J. (2008). The biological contributions to temperaments and emotions. *European Journal of Developmental Science, 2*, 38–51.

Kahana, M. J. (2012). *Foundations of human* memory. New York: Oxford University Press.

Kahn, A., & others. (1992) Sleep and cardiorespiratory characteristics of infant victim of sudden death: A prospective case-control study. *Sleep, 15*, 287–292.

Kahn, J. P. (2012). *Angst*. New York: Oxford University Press.

Kahneman, D., & Klein, G. (2009). Conditions for intuitive experience: A failure to disagree. *American Psychologist, 64*, 515–526.

Kahneman, D., Lovallo, D., & Sibony, O. (2011). Before you make that big decision . . . *Harvard Business Review, 89*, 50–60.

Kalat, J. W., & Shiota, M. N. (2012). *Emotion* (2nd ed.). Boston: Cengage.

Kalichman, S. C. (2007). The theory of reasoned action and advances in HIV/AIDS prevention. In I. Ajzen, D. Albarracin, & R. Hornik (Eds.), *Prediction and change of health behavior*. Mahwah, NJ: Erlbaum.

Kalivas, P. W. (2007). Neurobiology of cocaine addiction: Implications for new pharmacotherapy. *American Journal of Addiction, 16*, 71–78.

Kalmbach, A., Hedrick, T., & Waters, J. (2012). Selective optogenetic stimulation of cholinergic axons in the neocortex. *Journal of Neurophysiology*. (in press)

Kamin, L. J. (1968). Attention-like processes in classical conditioning. In M. R. Jones (Ed.), *Miami symposium on the prediction of behavior: Aversive stimuli*. Coral Gables, FL: University of Miami Press.

Kammrath, L. K., & Scholer, A. A. (2012). The cognitive-affective processing system. In I. B. Weiner, H. A. Tennen, & J. Suls (Eds.), *Handbook of psychology: Personality and social psychology* (2nd ed., vol. 5). New York: Wiley.

Kandel, E. R., & Schwartz, J. H. (1982). Molecular biology of learning: Modulation of transmitter release. *Science, 218*, 433–443.

Kaneshanathan, A., Prime, K., Hay, P. E., & Oakeshott, P. (2012). Sex and relationship education: Did you get it? *Sexually Transmitted Infections*. doi:10.1136/sextrans-2012-050499

Kang, Y., Williams, L. E., Clark, M. S., Gray, J. R., & Bargh, J. A. (2010). Physical temperature effects on trust behavior: The role of insula. *Social Cognitive and Affective Neuroscience, 6*, 507–515.

Kanwisher, N. (2006). Neuroscience: What's in a face? *Science, 311*, 617–618.

Kapur, S. (2003). Psychosis as a state of aberrant salience: A framework linking biology, phenomenology, and pharmacology. *American Journal of Psychiatry, 160*, 13–23.

Karau, S. J., & Williams, K. D. (1993). Social loafing: A meta-analytic review and theoretical integration. *Journal of Personality and Social Psychology, 65*, 681–706.

Karg, K., & Sen, S. (2012). Gene x environment interaction models in psychiatric genetics. *Current Topics in Behavioral Neuroscience*. (in press)

Karsten, J., & others. (2012). The state effect of depressive and anxiety disorders and the big five personality traits. *Journal of Psychiatric Research, 46* (5), 644–650.

Kaschel, R., Logie, R. H., Kazen, M., & Della Sala, S. (2009). Alzheimer's disease, but not aging or depression, affects dual-tasking. *Journal of Neurology, 256*, 1860–1868.

Kashima, E. S. (2010). Culture and terror management: What is "culture" in cultural psychology and terror management theory? *Social and Personality Psychology Compass, 4*, 164–173.

Kaskutas, L. A. (2009). Alcoholics Anonymous effectiveness: Faith meets science. *Journal of Addictive Diseases, 28*, 145–157.

Kaskutas, L. A., Subbaraman, M. S., Witbordt, J., & Zemore, S. E. (2009). Effectiveness of making Alcoholics Anonymous easier: A group format 12-step facilitation approach. *Journal of Substance Abuse Treatment, 28*, 145–157.

Kasser, T. (2011). Cultural values and the well-being of future generations: A cross-national study. *Journal of Cross-Cultural Psychology, 42*, 206–215.

Kasser, T., & Ryan, R. M. (1993). A dark side of the American dream: Correlates of financial success as a central life aspiration. *Journal of Personality and Social Psychology, 65*, 410–422.

Kasser, T., & Ryan, R. M. (1996). Further examining the American dream: Differential correlates of intrinsic and extrinsic goals. *Personality and Social Psychology Bulletin, 22*, 280–287.

Kasser, T., Ryan, R. M., Couchman, C. E., & Sheldon, K. M. (2004). Materialistic values: Their causes and consequences. In T. Kasser & A. D. Kanner (Eds.), *Psychology and consumer culture: The struggle for a good life in a materialistic world* (pp. 11–28). Washington, DC: American Psychological Association.

Kasser, T., & Sharma, Y. S. (1999). Reproductive freedom, educational equality, and females' preference for resource-acquisition characteristics in mates. *Psychological Science, 10*, 374–377.

Kato, I., & others. (2003). Incomplete arousal processes in infants who were victims of sudden death. *American Journal of Respiratory Critical Care Medicine 168*, 1298–1303.

Katz, J. N. (1995). *The invention of heterosexuality*. New York: Dutton.

Kaufman, J. C., & Sternberg, R. J. (2010). *The Cambridge handbook of creativity*. New York: Cambridge University Press.

Kazdin, A. E. (2007). Mediators and mechanisms of change in psychotherapy change. *Annual Review of Clinical Psychology* (vol. 3). Palo Alto, CA: Annual Reviews.

Keen, R. (2011). The development of problem solving in young children: A critical cognitive skill. *Annual Review of Psychology* (vol. 62). Palo Alto, CA: Annual Reviews.

Keeton, C. P., Kolos, A. C., & Walkup, J. T. (2009). Pediatric generalized anxiety disorder: Epidemiology, diagnosis, and management. *Pediatric Drugs, 11*, 171–183.

Keillor, J. M., Barrett, A. M., Crucian, G. P., Kortenkamp, S., & Heilman, K. M. (2002). Emotional experience and perception in the absence of facial feedback. *Journal of the International Neuropsychological Society, 8*, 130–135.

Kellerman, A. L., & others. (1993). Gun ownership as a risk factor for homicide in the home. *New England Journal of Medicine, 329*, 1084–1091.

Kelley, H. H. (1973). The processes of causal attribution. *American Psychologist, 28*, 107–128.

Kellner, C. H., Knapp, R. G., Petrides, G., Rummans, T. A., Husain, M. M., Rasmussen, K., Mueller, M., Bernstein, H. J., O'Connor, K., Smith, G., Biggs, M., Bailine, S. H., Malur, C., Yim, E., McClintock, S., Sampson, S., & Fink, M. (2006). Continuation electroconvulsive therapy vs pharmacotherapy for relapse prevention in major depression: A multisite study from the Consortium for Research in Electroconvulsive Therapy (CORE). *Archives of General Psychiatry, 63*, 1337–1344.

Kelly, G. F. (2006). *Sexuality today* (8th ed.). New York: McGraw-Hill.

Kelly, J. F., Hoeppner, B., Sout, R. L., & Pagano, M. (2012). Determining the relative importance of the mechanisms of behavior change within Alcoholics Anonymous: A multiplier mediator analysis. *Addiction, 107*, 289–299.

Kelly, J. R., & Agnew, C. R. (2012). Behavior and behavioral assessment. In K. Deaux & M. Snyder (Eds.), *Oxford handbook of personality and social psychology*. New York: Oxford University Press.

Kendler, K. S., Gardner, C., & Dick, D. M. (2011). Predicting alcohol consumption in adolescence from alcohol-specific and general externalizing genetic risk factors, key environmental factors, and their interaction. *Psychological Medicine, 41*, 1507–1516.

Kenrick, D. T., & Cohen, A. B. (2012). History of evolutionary social psychology. In A. W. Kruglanski & W. Stroebe (Eds.), *Handbook of the history of social psychology*. New York: Psychology Press.

Keogh, R., & Pearson, J. (2011). Mental imagery and visual working memory. *PLoS One, 6* (12), E29221.

Kerger, S., Martin, R., & Brunner, M. (2011). How can we enhance girls' interests in scientific topics? *British Journal of Educational Psychology, 81*, 606–628.

Kerkhof, I., Vansteenwegen, D., Baeyens, F., & Hermans, D. (2011). Counterconditioning: An effective technique for changing conditioned preferences. *Experimental Psychology, 58*, 31–38.

Kern, M. L., & Friedman, H. S. (2008). Do conscientious individuals live longer? A quantitative review. *Health Psychology, 27*, 505–512.

Kerns, J. G., Berenbaum, H., Barch, D. M., Banich, M. T., & Stolar, N. (1999). Word production in schizophrenia and its relationship to positive symptoms. *Psychiatry Research, 87,* 29–37.

Kessler, R. C., Chiu, W. T., Demler, O., & Walters, E. E. (2005). Prevalence, severity, and comorbidity of twelve-month DSM-IV disorders in the National Comorbidity Survey Replication (NCS-R). *Archives of General Psychiatry, 62,* 617–627.

Khamis, V. (2012). Impact of war, religiosity, and ideology on PTSD and psychiatric disorders in adolescents from Gaza Strip and South Lebanon. *Social Science and Medicine.* (in press)

Khare, K., & others. (2012). Accelerated MR imaging using compressive sensing with no free parameters. *Magnetic Resonance Imaging.* doi: 10.1002/mrm.24143

Khodarahimi, S., & Ogletree, S. L. (2011). Birth order, family size, and positive pathological constructs: What roles do they play for Iranian adolescents and young adults? *Journal of Individual Psychology, 67,* 41–56.

Khubchandani, J., & Simmons, R. (2012). Going global: Building a foundation for global health promotion research to practice. *Health Promotion Practices, 13,* 293–297.

Khurana, V. G., & Kaye, A. H. (2012). An overview of concussion in sport. *Journal of Clinical Neuroscience, 19,* 1–11.

Kihlstrom, J. (2005). Is hypnosis an altered state of consciousness or what?: Comment. *Contemporary Hypnosis, 22,* 34–38.

Killeen, P. R., Posadas-Sanchez, D., Johansen, E. B., & Thrailkill, E. A. (2009). Progressive ratio schedules of reinforcement. *Journal of Experimental Psychology: Animal Behavioral Processes, 35,* 35–50.

Killgore, W. D. S., Killgore, D. B., Day, L. M., Li, C., Kamimori, G. H., & Balkin, T. J. (2007). The effects of 53 hours of sleep deprivation on moral judgment. *SLEEP, 30,* 345–352.

Kilner, J. M., & Frith, C. D. (2008). Action observation: Inferring intentions without mirror neurons. *Current Biology, 18,* R32–R33.

Kim, H. (2011). Differential neural activity in the recognition of old and new events: An activation likelihood estimation meta-analysis. *Human Brain Mapping.* doi: 10.1002/hbm.21474.

Kim, J. Y., Oh, D. J., Yoon, T. Y., Choi, J. M., & Choe, B. K. (2007). The impacts of obesity on psychological well-being: A cross-sectional study about depressive mood and quality of life. *Journal of Preventive Medicine and Public Health, 40,* 191–195.

Kim, S. Y., & others. (2012). Resting cerebral glucose metabolism and perfusion patterns in women with posttraumatic stress disorder related to sexual assault. *Psychiatry Research.* (in press)

Kim, W., Woo, J. S., & Kim, W. (2012). Disrupted circadian rhythm in night shift workers: What can we do? *International Journal of Cardiology, 154* (1), 94–95.

Kimmel, A. J. (2012). Deception in research. In S. J. Knapp, M. C. Gottlieb, M. M. Handelsman, & L. D. VandeCreek (Eds.), *APA handbook of ethics in psychology: Practice, teaching, and research* (vol. 2, pp. 401–421). Washington, DC: American Psychological Association.

King, B. M. (2012). *Human sexuality today* (7th ed.). Upper Saddle River, NJ: Pearson.

King, L. A. (2002). Gain without pain: Expressive writing and self regulation. In S. J. Lepore & J. Smyth (Eds.), *The writing cure.* Washington, DC: American Psychological Association.

King, L. A. (2003). Measures and meanings: The use of qualitative data in social and personality psychology. In C. Sansone, C. Morf, & A. Panter (Eds.), *Handbook of methods in social psychology* (pp. 173–194). New York: Sage.

King, L. A. (2008). Personal goals and life dreams: Positive psychology and motivation in daily life. In W. Gardner & J. Shah (Eds.), *Handbook of motivation science* (pp. 518–532). New York: Guilford.

King, L. A., & Broyles, S. (1997). Wishes, gender, personality, and well-being. *Journal of Personality, 65,* 50–75.

King, L. A., & Hicks, J. A. (2006). Narrating the self in the past and the future: Implications for maturity. *Research in Human Development, 3,* 121–138.

King, L. A., & Hicks, J. A. (2007). Whatever happened to "what might have been"? Regret, happiness, and maturity. *American Psychologist, 62,* 625–636.

King, L. A., & Hicks, J. A. (2012). Positive affect and meaning in life: The intersection of hedonism and eudaimonia. In P. T. Wong, (Ed.), *The human quest for meaning* (2nd ed., pp. 125–142). New York: Routledge.

King, L. A., Hicks, J. A., & Abdelkhalik, J. (2009). Death, life, scarcity, and value: An alternative approach to the meaning of death. *Psychological Science, 20,* 1459–1462.

King, L. A., Hicks, J. A., Krull, J., & Del Gaiso, A. K. (2006). Positive affect and the experience of meaning in life. *Journal of Personality and Social Psychology, 90,* 179–196.

King, L. A., Scollon, C. K., Ramsey, C. M., & Williams, T. (2000). Stories of life transition: Happy endings, subjective well-being, and ego development in parents of children with Down syndrome. *Journal of Research in Personality, 34,* 509–536.

King, L. A., & Smith, S. N. (2005). Happy, mature, and gay: Intimacy, power, and difficult times in coming out stories. *Journal of Research in Personality, 39,* 278–298.

King, L. A., & Trent, J. (2012). Personality strengths. In H. Tennen & J. M. Suls (Eds.), *Handbook of psychology: Personality and social psychology* (vol. 5). New York: Wiley.

King, P. E., Ramos, J. S., & Clardy, C. E. (2012). Searching for the sacred: Religious and spiritual development among adolescents. In K. I. Pargament, J. Exline, & J. Jones (Eds.), *APA handbook of psychology, religion, and spiritualitiy.* Washington, DC: American Psychological Association.

Kinney, H. (2009). Neuropathology provides new insight in the pathogenesis of the sudden infant death syndrome. *Acta Neuropathologica, 117,* 247–255.

Kinsey, A. C., Martin, C. E., & Pomeroy, W. B. (1953). *Sexual behavior in the human female.* Philadelphia: Saunders.

Kinsey, A. C., Pomeroy, W. B., & Martin, C. E. (1948). *Sexual behavior in the human male.* Philadelphia: Saunders.

Kirby, D. B. (2008). The impact of abstinence and comprehensive sex and STD/HIV education programs on adolescent sexual behavior. *Sexuality Research & Social Policy, 5,* 18–27.

Kirsch, I. (2011). The altered state issue: Dead or alive? *International Journal of Clinical and Experimental Hyponosis, 59,* 350–362.

Kissileff, H. R., & others. (2012). Leptin reverses declines in satiation in weight-reduced obese humans. *American Journal of Clinical Nutrition, 95,* 309–317.

Kitayama, S., & Bowman, N. A. (2010). Cultural consequences of voluntary settlement in the frontier: Evidence and implications. In M. Schaller, A. Norenzayan, S. J. Heine, T. Yamagishi, & T. Kameda (Eds.), *Evolution, culture, and the human mind* (pp. 205–227). New York: Psychology Press.

Kitayama, S., & Cohen, D. (Eds.). (2007). *Handbook of cultural psychology.* New York: Guilford.

Kiuru, N., Burk, W. J., Laursen, B., Nurmi, J. E., & Salmela-Aro, K. (2012). Is depression contagious? A test of alternative peer socialization mechanisms of depressive symptoms in adolescent peer networks. *Journal of Adolescent Health, 50,* 250–255.

Klein, B., & others. (2010). A therapist-assisted cognitive behavior therapy internet intervention for posttraumatic stress disorder: Pre-, post-, and 3-month follow-up results from an open trial. *Journal of Anxiety Disorders, 24,* 635–644.

Klein, S. B. (2009). *Learning.* Thousand Oaks, CA: Sage.

Klemanski, D. H., & others. (2012). Emotion-related regulatory difficulties contribute to negative psychological outcomes in active-duty Iraq War soldiers with and without posttraumatic stress disorder. *Depression and Anxiety.* doi: 10.1002/da.21914

Klemfuss, J. Z., & Ceci, S. J. (2012a). An empirical approach to children's testimonial competence. *Developmental Review.* (in press)

Klemfuss, J. Z., & Ceci, S. J. (2012b). The law and science of children's testimonial competence. In R. Holliday & T. Marche (Eds.), *Child forensic psychology.* New York: Macmillan.

Klimstra, T. A., Hale, W. W., Raaijmakers, Q. A., Branje, S. J., & Meeus, W. H. (2009). Maturation of personality in adolescence. *Journal of Personality and Social Psychology, 96,* 898–912.

Klimstra, T. A., Luyckx, K., Hale, W. A., Frijns, T., van Lier, P. A. C., & Meeus, W. H. J. (2010). Short-term fluctuations in identity: Introducing a micro-level approach to identity formation. *Journal of Personality and Social Psychology, 99,* 191–202.

Klinesmith, J., Kasser, T., & McAndrew, F. T. (2006). Guns, testosterone, and aggression: An experimental test of a mediational hypothesis. *Psychological Science, 17,* 568–571.

Klosterhalfen, S., Rüttgers, A., Krumrey, E., Otto, B., Stockhorst, U., Riepl, R. L., Probst, T., & Enck, P. (2000). Pavlovian conditioning of taste aversion using a motion sickness paradigm. *Psychosomatic Medicine, 62,* 671–677.

Klucharev, V., Hytonen, K., Rijpkema, M., Smidts, A., & Fernandez, G. (2009). Reinforcement learning signal predicts social conformity. *Neuron, 61,* 140–151.

Kluge, C., & others. (2011). Plasticity of human auditory-evoked fields induced by shock conditioning and contingency reversal. *Proceedings of the National Academy of Sciences USA, 108,* 12545–12550.

Knapp, H. (2007). *Therapeutic communication.* Thousand Oaks, CA: Sage.

Knapp, S., & VandeCreek, L. (2000). Recovered memories of childhood abuse: Is there an underlying consensus. *Professional Psychology: Research and Practice, 31,* 365–371.

Knight, D. C., Lewis, E. P., & Wood, K. H. (2011). Conditioned diminution of the unconditioned skin conductance response. *Behavioral Neuroscience, 125,* 626–631.

Knott, V., McIntosh, J., Millar, A., Fisher, D., Villeneuve, C., Ilivitsky, V., & Horn, E. (2006). Nicotine and smoker status moderate brain and electric and mood activation induced by ketamine, an N-methyl-d-aspartate (NMDA) receptor antagonist. *Pharmacology, Biochemistry, and Behavior, 85,* 228–242.

Knowles, E. S., Nolan, J., & Riner, D. D. (2007). Resistance to persuasion. In R. Baumeister & K. Vohs (Eds.), *Encyclopedia of social psychology.* Newbury Park, CA: Sage.

Knox, W. B., Otto, A. R., Stone, P., & Love, B. C. (2011). The nature of belief-directed exploratory choice in human decision-making. *Frontiers in Psychology, 2,* 398.

Kobasa, S., Maddi, S., & Kahn, S. (1982). Hardiness and health: A prospective study. *Journal of Personality and Social Psychology, 42,* 168–177.

Kobasa, S. C., Maddi, S. R., Puccetti, M. C., & Zola, M. (1986). Relative effectiveness of hardiness, exercise, and social support as resources against illness. *Journal of Psychosomatic Research, 29,* 525–533.

Koch, C. (2011). Neuroscience of consciousness. *Annual Review of Psychology* (vol. 62). Palo Alto, CA: Annual Reviews.

Kochanek, K. D., Murphy, S. L. Anderson, R. N., & Scott, C. (2004, October 12). Deaths: Final data for 2002. *National Vital Statistics Reports, 53* (5). Washington, DC: U.S. Department of Health and Human Services.

Kochanska, G., Aksan, N., Prisco, T. R., & Adams, E. E. (2008). Mother-child and father-child mutually responsive orientation in the first two years and children's outcomes at preschool age: Mechanisms of influence. *Child Development, 79,* 30–44.

Koelkebeck, K., Hirao, K., Kawada, R., Miyata, J., Saze, T., Ubukata, S., Itakura, S., Kanakogi, Y., Ohrmann, P., Bauer, J., Pedersen, A., Sawamoto, N., Fukuyama, H., Takahashi, H., & Murai, T. (2011). Transcultural differences in brain activation patterns during theory of mind (ToM) task performance in Japanese and Caucasian participants. *Social Neuroscience, 6,* 615–626.

Koelsch, S., Enge, J., & Jentschke, S. (2012). Cardiac signatures of personality. *PLoS One, 7* (2), e31441.

Koenig, A. M., Eagly, A. H., Mitchell, A. A., & Ristikari, T. (2011). Are leader stereotypes masculine? A meta-analysis of three research paradigms. *Psychological Bulletin, 137,* 616–642.

Koenig, H., King, D., & Carson, V. B. (Eds.). (2012). *Handbook of religion and health* (2nd ed.). New York: Oxford University Press.

Koenig, H. G. (2012a). Religious versus conventional psychotherapy for major depression in patients with chronic medical illness: Rationale, methods, and preliminary results. *Depression Research and Treatment.* (in press)

Koenig, H. G. (2012b). Why do research on spirituality and health, and what do the results mean? *Journal of Religion and Health.* (in press)

Koenis, M. M., & others. (2011). Does sleep restore the topology of functional brain networks. *Human Brain Mapping.* doi: 10.1002/hbm.21455

Koepp, M. J., Hammers, A., Lawrence, A. D., Asselin, M. C., Grasby, P. M., & Bench, C. J. (2009). Evidence for endogenous opioid release in the amygdale during positive emotion. *NeuroImage, 44,* 252–256.

Koerner, A. (2012). Social cognition and family communication. In D. R. Roskos-Ewoldsen & J. L. Monahan (Eds.), *Communication and social cognition.* New York: Psychology Press.

Koestner, R., Horberg, E. J., Gaudreau, P., Powers, T., Di Dio, P., Bryan, C., Jochum, R., & Salter, N. (2006). Bolstering implementation plans for the long haul: The benefits of simultaneously boosting self-concordance or self-efficacy. *Personality and Social Psychology Bulletin, 32,* 1547–1558.

Kohlberg, L. (1958). *The development on modes of moral thinking and choice in the years 10 to 16.* Unpublished doctoral dissertation, University of Chicago.

Kohlberg, L. (1986). A current statement on some theoretical issues. In S. Modgil & C. Modgil (Eds.), *Lawrence Kohlberg.* Philadelphia: Falmer.

Kohler, C. L., Schoenberger, Y., Tseng, T., & Ross, L. (2008). Correlates of transitions in stage of change for quitting among adolescent smokers. *Addictive Behaviors, 33,* 1615–1618.

Köhler, W. (1925). *The mentality of apes.* New York: Harcourt Brace Jovanovich.

Kohut, H. (1977). *Restoration of the self.* New York: International Universities Press.

Kok, B. E., Catalino, L. I., & Fredrickson, B. L. (2008). The broadening, building, buffering effects of positive emotion. In S. J. Lopez (Ed.), *Positive psychology: Exploring the best of people* (vol. 3). Westport, CT: Greenwood.

Komiyama, O., Kawara, M., & De Laat, A. (2007). Ethnic differences regarding tactile and pain thresholds in the trigeminal region. *Journal of Pain, 8,* 363–369.

Komsi, N., Räikkönen, K., Pesonen, A., Heinonen, K., Keskivaara, P., Järvenpää, A., & Strandberg, T. E. (2006). Continuity of temperament from infancy to middle childhood. *Infant Behavior & Development, 29,* 494–508.

Kong, L. L., Allen, J. J. B., & Glisky, E. L. (2008). Interidentity memory transfer in dissociative identity disorder. *Journal of Abnormal Psychology, 117,* 686–692.

Koob, G. F. (2006). The neurobiology of addiction: A neuroadaptational view. *Addiction, 101, Suppl. 1,* S23–S30.

Kooij, S. J., & others. (2010). European consensus statement on diagnosis and treatment of adult ADHD: The European Network Adult ADHD. *BMC Psychiatry, 10,* 67–72.

Kopell, B. H., Machado, A. G., & Rezai, A. R. (2006). Not your father's lobotomy: Psychiatric surgery revisited. *Clinical Neurosurgery, 52,* 315–330.

Kort-Butler, L. A., & Hagewen, K. J. (2011). School-based extracurricular activity involvement and adolescent self-esteem: A growth-curve analysis. *Journal of Youth and Adolescence, 40,* 568–581.

Korzekwa, M. I., Dell, P. F., Links, P. S., Thabane, L., & Webb, S. P. (2008). Estimating the prevalence of borderline personality disorder in psychiatric outpatients using a two-phase procedure. *Comprehensive Psychiatry, 49* (4), 380–386.

Kosslyn, S. M., Thompson, W. L., Kim, I. J., Rauch, S. L., & Alpert, N. M. (1996). Individual differences in cerebral blood flow in Area 17 predict the time to evaluate visualized letters. *Journal of Cognitive Neuroscience, 8,* 78–82.

Kotsis, V., Stabouli, S., Papakatsika, S., Rizos, Z., & Parati, G. (2010). Mechanisms of obesity-induced hypertension. *Hypertension Research, 33,* 386–393.

Kotter-Grühn, D., & Smith, J. (2011). When time is running out: Changes in positive future perception and their relationships to changes in well-being in old age. *Psychology and Aging, 26,* 381–387.

Kovacs, A. M. (2009). Early bilingualism enhances mechanisms of false-belief reasoning. *Developmental Science, 12,* 48–54.

Kozaric-Kovacic, D. (2008). Integrative psychotherapy. *Psychiatria Danubina, 20,* 352–363.

Koziorynska, E. L., & Rodriquez, A. J. (2011). Narcolepsy: Clinical approach to etiology, diagnosis, and treatment. *Reviews in Neurological Diseases, 8,* e97–e106.

Kraft, E. (2012). Cognitive function, physical activity, and aging: Possible biological links and implications for multimodal interventions. *Aging, Neuropsychology, and Cognition, 19,* 248–263.

Kraft, J. M., Kulkarni, A., Hsia, J., Jamieson, D. J., & Warner, L. (2012). Sex education and adolescent sexual behavior: Do community characteristics matter? *Contraception.* (in press)

Kregel, K. C., & Zhang, H. J. (2006). An integrated view of oxidative stress in aging: Basic mechanisms, functional effects, and pathological considerations. *Journal of Physiology, 292,* R18–R36.

Kring, A. M., Davison, G. C., Neale, J. M., & Johnson, S. L. (2007). *Abnormal psychology* (10th ed.). New York: Wiley.

Kringelbach, M. L. (2005). The human orbitofrontal cortex: Linking reward to hedonic experience. *Nature Reviews Neuroscience, 6,* 691–702.

Krishnamurthy, R., Archer, R. P., & Groth-Marnat, G. (2011). The Rorschach and performance-based assessment. In T. M. Harwood, L. E. Beutler, & G. Groth-Marnat (Eds.), *Integrative assessment of adult personality* (3rd ed.). New York: Guilford.

Kristen, S., Thoermer, C., Hofer, T., Aschersleben, G., & Sodian, B. (2006). Skalierung von "theory of mind"–Aufgaben [Validation of the "theory of mind" scale]. *Zeitschrift für Entwicklungspsychologie und Padagogische Psychologie, 38,* 186–195.

Kroger, J., Martinussen, M., & Marcia, J. E. (2010). Identity status change during adolescence and young adulthood: A meta-analysis. *Journal of Adolescence, 33,* 683–698.

Kross, E., Mischel, W., & Shoda, Y. (2010). Enabling self-control: A cognitive affective processing system (CAPS) approach to problematic behavior. In J. Maddux & J. Tangney (Eds.), *Social psychological foundations of clinical psychology.* New York: Guilford.

Krueger, R. F., Markon, K. E., & Bouchard, T. J. (2003). The extended genotype: The heritability of personality accounts for the heritability of recalled family environments in twins reared apart. *Journal of Personality, 71,* 809–833.

Kruger, J., Blanck, H. M., & Gillespie, C. (2006). Dietary and physical activity behaviors among adults successful at weight loss maintenance. *International Journal of Behavioral Nutrition and Physical Activity, 3,* 17.

Kruglanski, A. W., Chen, X., Dechesne, M., Fishman, S., & Orehek, E. (2009). Fully committed: Suicide bombers' motivation and the quest for personal significance. *Political Psychology, 30,* 331–357.

Kruglanski, A. W., Gelfand, M., & Gunaratna, R. (2012). Terrorism as means to an end: How political violence bestows significance. In M. Mikulincer & P. Shaver (Eds.), *Meaning, mortality, and choice: The social psychology of existential concerns.* Washington, DC: American Psychological Association.

Kruglanski, A. W., & Orehek, E. (2011). The role of the quest for personal significance in motivating terrorism. In J. P. Forgas, A. W. Kruglanski, & K. D. Williams (Eds.), *The psychology of social conflict and aggression* (pp. 153–164). New York: Psychology Press.

Kruglanski, A. W., Sharvit, K., & Fishman, S. (2011). Workings of the terrorist mind: Its individual, group, and organizational psychologies. In D. Bar-Tal (Ed.), *Intergroup conflicts and their resolution: A social psychological perspective* (pp. 195–216). New York: Psychology Press.

Kruschke, J. K. (2011). Bayesian assessment of null values via parameter estimation and model comparison. *Perspectives on Psychological Science, 6,* 299–312.

Kübler-Ross, E. (1969). *On death and dying.* New York: Simon & Schuster.

Kuhl, P. K. (1993). Infant speech perception: A window on psycholinguistic development. *International Journal of Psycholinguistics, 9,* 33–56.

Kuhl, P. K. (2000). A new view of language acquisition. *Proceedings of the National Academy of Sciences USA, 97,* 11850–11857.

Kuhl, P. K. (2007). Is speech learning "gated" by the social brain? *Developmental Science, 10,* 110–120.

Kuhl, P. K. (2009). Linking infant speech perception to language acquisition: Phonetic learning predicts language growth. In J. Colombo, P. McCardle, & L. Freund (Eds.), *Infant pathways to language.* New York: Psychology Press.

Kuhl, P. K. (2011a). Early language learning and literacy: Neuroscience implications for education. *Mind, Brain, and Education, 5,* 128–142.

Kuhl, P. K. (2011b). Social mechanisms in early language acquisition: Understanding integrated brain systems supporting language. In J. Decety & J. Cacioppo (Eds.), *The Oxford handbook of social neuroscience.* New York: Oxford University Press.

Kuhn, D. (2008). Formal operations from a twenty-first century perspective. *Human Development, 51,* 48–55.

Kuhn, S., & Gallinat, J. (2011). A quantitative meta-analysis on cue-induced male sexual arousal. *Journal of Sexual Medicine, 8,* 2269–2275.

Kuhn, S., Vanderhasselt, M. A., De Raedt, R., & Gallinat, J. (2012). Why ruminators won't stop: The structural and resting state correlates of rumination and its relation to depression. *Journal of Affective Disorders.* doi: 10.1016/j.jad.2012.03.024

Kulkofsky, S., & others (2011). Cultural variation In the correlates of flashbulb memories: An investigation in five countries. *Memory, 19,* 233–240.

Kumar, C. T. S. (2004). Physical illness and schizophrenia. *British Journal of Psychiatry, 184,* 541.

Kuper, K., Groh-Bordin, C., Zimmer, H. D., & Ecker, U. K. (2012). Electrophysiological correlates of exemplar-specific processes in implicit and explicit memory. *Cognitive, Affective, and Behavioral Neuroscience, 12,* 52–64.

Kurose, K., & others. (2012). Genome-wide association study of SSRI/SNRI-induced sexual dysfunction in a Japanese cohort with major depression. *Psychiatry Research.* (in press)

Kurson, R. (2007). *Crashing through: A true story of risk, adventure, and the man who dared to see.* New York: Random House.

Kushner, R. F. (2007). Obesity management. *Gastroenterology Clinics of North America, 36,* 191–210.

Kusurkar, R. A., & others. (2012). How motivation affects academic performance: A structural equation modeling analysis. *Advances in Health Science Education: Theory and Practice.* (in press)

Kuyper, P. (1972). The cocktail party effect. *Audiology, 11,* 277–282.

Kwok, D. W., & Boakes, R. A. (2012). Blocking of acquisition of a taste aversion by a context experienced prior to the taste. *Behavioral Processes, 89,* 27–29.

## L

Lachman, M. E., Rocke, C., Rosnick, C., & Ryff, C. D. (2008). Realism and illusion in Americans' temporal views of their life satisfaction: Age differences in reconstructing the past and anticipating the future. *Psychological Science, 19,* 89–897.

Lack, L. C., & Wright, H. R. (2012). Circadian rhythm disorders I: Phase-advanced and phase-delayed syndromes. In C. M. Morin & C. A. Espie (Eds.), *Oxford handbook of sleep and sleep disorders.* New York: Oxford University Press.

Lader, M. (2012). Dependence and withdrawal: Comparison of the benzodiazepines and selective serotonin re-uptake inhibitors. *Addiction, 107,* 909–910.

Lahey, B. B., & others. (2011). Interactions between early parenting and a polymorphism of the child's dopamine transporter genes in predicting future child conduct disorder symptoms. *Journal of Abnormal Psychology, 120,* 33–45.

Laible, D. J., & Thompson, R. A. (2000). Mother–child discourse, attachment security, shared positive affect, and early conscience development. *Child Development, 71,* 1424–1440.

Laible, D. J., & Thompson, R. A. (2002). Mother–child conflict in the toddler years: Lessons in emotion, morality, and relationships. *Child Development, 73,* 1187–1203.

Lam, C. S., Wiley, A. H., Siu, A., & Emmett, J. (2010). Assessing readiness to work from a stages of change perspective: Implications for return to work. *Work, 37,* 321–329.

Lam, R. (2012). *Depression* (2nd ed.). New York: Oxford University Press.

Lambert, M. J. (2001). The effectiveness of psychotherapy: What a century of research tells us about the effects of treatment. *Psychotherapeutically speaking—Updates from the Division of Psychotherapy* (29). Washington, DC: American Psychological Association.

Laming, D. (2010). Serial position curves in free recall. *Psychological Review, 117,* 93–133.

Lamkin, D. M., & others. (2012). Chronic stress enhances progression of acute lymphoblastic leukemia via *b*-adrenergic signaling. *Brain, Behavior, and Immunity, 26,* 635–641.

Lamoureux, P. L., O'Toole, M. R., Heidemann, S. R., & Miller, K. E. (2010). Slowing of axonal regeneration is correlated with increased axonal viscosity during aging. *BMC Neuroscience, 11,* ArtID 140.

Lampard, A. M., Byrne, S. M., McLean, N., & Fursland, A. (2012). The Eating Disorder Inventory-2 perfectionism scale: Factor structure and associations with dietary restraint and weight and shape concern in eating disorders. *Eating Behaviors, 13,* 49–53.

Landgren, S., & others. (2011). Reward-related gender and personality traits in alcohol-dependent individuals: A pilot case control study. *Neuropsychobiology, 64,* 38–46.

Landis, C., & Erlick, D. (1950). An analysis of the Porteus Maze Test as affected by psychosurgery. *American Journal of Psychology, 63,* 557–566.

Landler, M. (2012, January 30). From Biden, a vivid account of Bin Laden raid. *New York Times.* http://thecaucus.blogs.nytimes.com/2012/01/30/from-biden-a-vivid-account-of-bin-laden-decision/ (accessed June 14, 2012)

Lane, S. M., & Schooler, J. W. (2004). Skimming the surface: Verbal overshadowing of analogical retrieval. *Psychological Science, 15,* 715–719.

Lange, C. G. (1922). *The emotions.* Baltimore: Williams & Wilkins.

Langer, E., Blank, A., & Chanowitz, B. (1978). The mindlessness of ostensibly thoughtful action: The role of "placebic" information in interpersonal interaction. *Journal of Personality and Social Psychology, 36* (6), 635–642.

Langer, E. J. (1997). *The power of mindful learning.* Reading, MA: Addison-Wesley.

Langer, E. J. (2000). Mindful learning. *Current Directions in Psychological Science, 9,* 220–223.

Langer, E. J. (2005). *On becoming an artist.* New York: Ballantine.

Langer, J. J. (1991). *Holocaust testimonies: The ruins of memory.* New Haven, CT: Yale University Press.

Langlois, J. H., Kalakanis, L., Rubenstein, A. J., Larson, A., Hallam, M., & Smoot, M. (2000). Maxims or myths of beauty? A meta-analytic and theoretical review. *Psychological Bulletin, 126,* 390–423.

Langlois, J. H., Roggman, L. A., & Musselman, L. (1994). What is average and what is not average about attractive faces? *Psychological Science, 5,* 214–220.

Langstrom, N., Rahman, Q., Carlstrom, E., & Lichtenstein, P. (2010). Genetic and environmental effects on same-sex sexual behaviour: A population study of twins in Sweden. *Archives of Sexual Behavior, 39,* 75–80.

Lanius, R. A., Brand, B., Vermetten, E., Frewen, P. A., & Spiegel, D. (2012). The dissociative subtype of posttraumatic stress disorder: Rationale, clinical and neurobiological evidence, and implications. *Depression and Anxiety, 16,* 1–8.

Lapid, H., & others. (2011). Neural activity at the human olfactory epithelium reflects olfactory perception. *Nature Neuroscience, 14,* 1455–1461.

Larzelere, M. M., & Williams, D. E. (2012). Promoting smoking cessation. *American Family Physician, 85,* 591–598.

Lashley, K. (1950). In search of the engram. In *Symposium of the Society for Experimental Biology* (vol. 4). New York: Cambridge University Press.

Latané, B. (1981). The psychology of social impact. *American Psychologist, 36,* 343–356.

Laureys, S., & Schiff, N. D. (2012). Coma and consciousness: Paradigms (re)framed by neuroimaging. *NeuroImage.* doi: 10.1016/j.neuroimage. 2011.12.041

Laursen, B., Hafen, C. A., Kerr, M., & Stattin, H. (2012). Friend influence over adolescent problem behaviors as a function of relative peer acceptance: To be liked is to be emulated. *Journal of Abnormal Psychology, 121,* 88–94.

Law, R., & others. (2011). The relationship between retrieval-induced forgetting, anxiety, and personality. *Anxiety, Stress, and Coping.* (in press)

Lazard, D. S., Collette, J. L., & Perrot, X. (2012). Speech processing: From peripheral to hemispheric asymmetry of the auditory system. *Laryngoscope, 122,* 167–173.

Lazarus, A. A., Beutler, L. E., & Norcross, J. C. (1992). The future of technical eclecticism. *Psychotherapy, 29,* 11–20.

Lazarus, R. S. (1991). On the primacy of cognition. *American Psychologist, 39,* 124–129.

Lazarus, R. S. (1993). Coping theory and research: Past, present, and future. *Psychosomatic Medicine, 55,* 234–247.

Lazarus, R. S. (2000). Toward better research on stress and coping. *American Psychologist, 55,* 665–673.

Lazarus, R. S. (2003). Does the positive psychology movement have legs? *Psychological Inquiry, 14,* 93–109.

Leahy, R. L., Holland, S. J. F., & McGinn, L. K. (2012). *Treatment plans and interventions for depression and anxiety disorders* (2nd ed.). New York: Guilford.

Leahy, R. L., & McGinn, L. K. (2012). Cognitive therapy for personality disorders. In T. Widiger (Ed.), *Oxford handbook of personality disorders.* New York: Oxford University Press.

Leary, M. R. (2012). *Introduction to behavioral methods* (6th ed.). Upper Saddle River, NJ: Pearson.

Leary, M. R., & Guadagno, J. (2011). The sociometer, self-esteem, and the regulation of interpersonal behavior. In K. D. Vohs & R. F. Baumeister (Eds.), *Handbook of self-regulation: Research, theory, and applications* (2nd ed., pp. 339–354). New York: Guilford.

Leary, M. R., & Hoyle, R. H. (Eds.). (2009a). *Handbook of individual differences in social behavior.* New York: Guilford.

Leary, M. R., & Hoyle, R. H. (Eds.). (2009b). Situations, dispositions, and the study of social behavior. In M. R. Leary & R. H. Hoyle (Eds.), *Handbook of individual differences in social behavior* (pp. 3–11). New York: Guilford.

LeBel, E. P., & Peters, K. R. (2011). Fearing the future of empirical psychology: Bem's (2011) evidence for psi as a case study of deficiencies in modal research practice. *Review of General Psychology, 15,* 371–379.

LeBlanc, L. A., & Gillis, J. M. (2012). Behavioral interventions for children with autism spectrum disorders. *Pediatric Clinics of North America, 59,* 147–164.

LeBoeuf, R. A., & Shafir, E. (2012). Decision making. In K. J. Holyoak & R. G. Morrison (Eds.), *Oxford handbook of thinking and reasoning.* New York: Oxford University Press.

Lecce, S., Caputi, M., & Hughes, C. (2011). Does sensitivity to criticism mediate the relationship between theory of mind and academic achievement? *Journal of Experimental Child Psychology, 110,* 313–331.

LeDoux, J. E. (1996). *The emotional brain: The mysterious underpinnings of emotional life.* New York: Simon & Schuster.

LeDoux, J. E. (2000). Emotion circuits in the brain. *Annual Review of Neuroscience, 23,* 155–184.

LeDoux, J. E. (2001). *Emotion, memory, and the brain.* www.cns.nyu.edu/ledoux/overview.htm (accessed May 7, 2012)

LeDoux, J. E. (2002). *The synaptic self.* New York: Viking.

LeDoux, J. E. (2008). Amygdala. *Scholarpedia, 3,* 2698.

LeDoux, J. E. (2012). Evolution of human emotion: A view through fear. *Progress in Brain Research, 195,* 431–442.

Lee, A. K., & Bishop, J. R. (2011). Pharmacogenetics of leptin in antipsychotic-associated weight gain and obesity-related complications. *Pharmacogenetics, 12,* 999–1016.

Lee, H. A., & Lee, S. H. (2012). Hierarchy of direction-tuned motion adaptation in human visual cortex. *Journal of Neurophysiology.* (in press)

Lee, H. S. (2012). Predicting and understanding undergraduate students' intention to gamble in a casino using an extended model of the theory of reasoned action and the theory of planned behavior. *Journal of Gambling Studies.* (in press)

Lee, K. A., & Rosen, E. A. (2012). Sleep and human development. In C. M. Morin & C. A. Espie (Eds.), *Oxford handbook of sleep and sleep disorders.* New York: Oxford University Press.

Lee, T. W., Yu, Y. W., Chen, M. C., & Chen, T. J. (2011). Cortical mechanisms of the symptomatology in major depressive disorder: An EEG study. *Journal of Affective Disorders, 131,* 243–250.

Leedy, P. D., & Ormrod, J. E. (2010). *Practical research* (9th ed.). Upper Saddle River, NJ: Prentice-Hall.

Le Grange, D., Lock, J., Loeb, K., & Nicholls, D. (2010). Academy for Eating Disorders position paper: The role of the family in eating disorders. *International Journal of Eating Disorders, 43,* 1–5.

Leigh, E. G. (2010). The group selection controversy. *Journal of Evolutionary Biology, 23,* 6–19.

Lenglet, C., & others. (2012). Comprehensive in vivo mapping of the human basal ganglia and thalamic connectome in individuals using 7T MRI. *PLoS One.* (in press)

Lenneberg, E. H., Rebelsky, F. G., & Nichols, I. A. (1965). The vocalization of infants born to deaf and hearing parents. *Human Development, 8,* 23–37.

Leo, J. L. (2005). Editorial: Methylphenidate-induced neuropathology in the developing rat brain: Implications for humans. *Ethical Human Psychology and Psychiatry, 7,* 107–116.

Lepage, J. F., & Theoret, H. (2010). Brain connectivity: Finding a cause. *Current Biology, 20,* R66–R67.

Lepage, M., Sergerie, K., Benoit, A., Czechowska, Y., Dickie, E., & Armony, J. L. (2011). Emotional face processing and flat affect in schizophrenia: Functional and structural neural correlates. *Psychological Medicine, 41,* 1833–1844.

Lerner, B. H. (2005). Last-ditch medical therapy—revisiting lobotomy. *New England Journal of Medicine, 353,* 119–121.

Letvin, N. L. (2007). Progress and obstacles in the development of an AIDS vaccine. *Nature Reviews: Immunology, 6,* 930–939.

Leung, A. K., Maddux, W. W., Galinsky, A. D., & Chiu, C. (2008). Multicultural experience enhances creativity. *American Psychologist, 63,* 169–181.

Leuzinger-Bohleber, M., & Teising, M. (2012). "Without being in psychoanalysis I would never have dared to become pregnant": Psychoanalytical observations in a multidisciplinary study concerning a woman undergoing prenatal diagnostics. *International Journal of Psychoanalysis, 93,* 293–315.

Leventhal, H., & Tomarken, A. J. (1986). Emotion: Today's problems. *Annual Review of Psychology* (vol. 37). Palo Alto, CA: Annual Reviews.

Levin, C. (2010). The mind as a complex internal object: Inner estrangement. *Psychoanalytic Quarterly, 79,* 95–27.

Levine, B., Svoboda, E., Turner, G. R., Mandic, M., & Mackey, A. (2009). Behavioral and functional neuroanatomical correlates of anterograde autobiographical memory in isolated retrograde amnesic patient M.L. *Neuropsychologia, 47* (11), 2188–2196.

Levine, J. M. (2000). Groups: Group processes. In A. E. Kazdin (Ed.), *Encyclopedia of psychology* (vol. 4, pp. 26–31). Washington, DC: American Psychological Association.

Levine, F. M. & De Simone, L. L. (1991). The effects of experimenter gender on pain report in male and female subjects. *Pain, 44,* 69–72.

Levine, J. M., & Moreland, R. L. (2012). History of intergroup relations research. In A. W. Kruglanski & W. Stroebe (Eds.), *Handbook of the history of social psychology.* New York: Psychology Press.

Levine, M., Cassidy, C., & Jentzsch, I. (2010). The implicit identity effect: Identity primes, group size, and helping. *British Journal of Social Psychology, 49,* 785–802.

Levine, R. L. (2002). Endocrine aspects of eating disorders in adolescents. *Adolescent Medicine, 13,* 129–144.

Levine, S. C., Ratliff, K. R., Huttenlocher, J., & Cannon, J. (2012). Early puzzle play: A predictor of preschoolers' spatial transformation skill. *Developmental Psychology, 48,* 530–542.

Levinthal, C. F. (2010). *Drugs, behavior, and modern society* (6th ed.). Upper Saddle River, NJ: Prentice-Hall.

Levy, B. R., Slade, M. D., & Kasl, S. V. (2002). Increased longevity by positive self-perceptions of aging. *Journal of Personality and Social Psychology, 83,* 261–270.

Lew, M. W., & others. (2011). Use of preoperative hypnosis to reduce postoperative pain and anesthesia-related side effects. *International Journal of Clinical and Experimental Hypnosis, 59,* 406–423.

Lewald, J., & Getzmann, S. (2011). When and where of auditory spatial processing in cortex: A novel approach using electromyography. *PLoS One, 6* (9), e25146.

Lewis, A., Williams, P., Lawrence, O., Wong, R. O., & Brockerhoff, S. E. (2010). Wild-type cone photoreceptors persist despite neighboring mutant cone degeneration. *Journal of Neuroscience, 30,* 382–389.

Lewis, P. A., Cairney, S., Manning, L., & Critchley, H. D. (2011). The impact of overnight consolidation upon memory for emotional and neutral encoding contexts. *Neuropsychologia, 49,* 2619–2629.

Lewkowicz, D. J. (2010). Infant perception of audiovisual speech synchrony. *Developmental Psychology, 46,* 66–77.

Lewkowicz, D. J., & Hansen-Tift, A. M. (2012). Infants deploy selective attention to the mouth of a talking face when learning speech. *PNAS Proceedings of the National Academy of Sciences USA, 109,* 1431–1436.

Li, H. F., & others. (2012). The relationship between single nucleotide polymorphism in 5-HT2A signal transduction-related genes and the response efficacy to selective serotonin reuptake inhibitor treatments in Chinese patients with major depressive disorder. *Genetic Testing and Molecular Biomarkers.* (in press)

Li, Y., & Epley, N. (2009). When the best appears to be saved for last: Serial position effects on choice. *Journal of Behavioral Decision Making, 22,* 378–389.

Li, Y. J., Johnson, K., Cohen, A. B., Williams, M. J., Knowles, E. D., & Chen, Z. (2012). Fundamental(ist) attribution error: Protestants are dispositionally focused. *Journal of Personality and Social Psychology, 102,* 281–290.

Liang, B., Williams, L. M., & Siegel, J. A. (2006). Relational outcomes of childhood sexual trauma in female survivors: A longitudinal study. *Journal of Interpersonal Violence, 21,* 42–57.

Libedinsky, C., & others. (2011). Sleep deprivation alters valuation signals in the ventromedial prefrontal cortex. *Frontiers in Behavioral Science.* doi: 10.3389/fnbeh.2011.00070

Lichstein, K. L., Vander Wal, G. S., & Dillon, H. R. (2012). Insomnia III: Therapeutic approaches. In C. M. Morin & C. A. Espie (Eds.), *Oxford handbook of sleep and sleep disorders.* New York: Oxford University Press.

Lieberman, M. A. (2012). *Human learning and memory.* New York: Cambridge University Press.

Light, S. N., Goldsmith, H. H., Coan, J. A., Frye, C., & Davidson, R. J. (2009). Dynamic variation in pleasure in children predicts non-linear change in lateral frontal activity. *Developmental Psychology, 45,* 525–533.

Light, S. N., & others. (2011). Reduced right ventrolateral prefrontal cortex activity while inhibiting positive affect is associated with improvement in hedonic capacity after 8 weeks of antidepressant treatment in major depressive disorder. *Biological Psychiatry, 70,* 962–968.

Lilienfeld, S. O., Wood, J. M., & Garb, H. N. (2000, November). The scientific status of projective techniques. *Psychological Science in the Public Interest, 1* (2).

Lim, A., & others. (2012). Effects of workshop trainings on evidence-based practice knowledge and attitudes among youth community mental health providers. *Behavior Research and Therapy, 50,* 397–406.

Lim, S. C., Kyung, K. U., & Kwon, D. S. (2012). Effect of frequency difference on sensitivity of beats perception. *Experimental Brain Research, 216,* 11–19.

Lin, L. (2009). Breadth-biased versus focused cognitive control in media multitasking behaviors. *Proceedings of the National Academy of Sciences USA, 106,* 15521–15522.

Linden, W., Lenz, J. W., & Con, A. H. (2001). Individualized stress management for primary hypertension: A randomized trial. *Archives of Internal Medicine, 161,* 1071–1080.

Lindwall, M., Rennemark, M., Halling, A., Berglund, J., & Hassmen, P. (2007). Depression and exercise in elderly men and women: Findings from the Swedish national study on aging and care. *Journal of Aging and Physical Activity, 15,* 41–55.

Lingjaerde, O., Foreland, A. R., & Engvik, H. (2001). Personality structure in patients with winter depression, assessed in a depression-free state according to the five-factor model of personality. *Journal of Affective Disorders, 62,* 165–174.

Linke, S. E., & others. (2009). Depressive symptom dimensions and cardiovascular prognosis among women with suspected myocardial ischemia: A report from the National Heart, Lung, and Blood Institute-sponsored women's Ischemia Syndrome Foundation. *Archives of General Psychiatry, 66,* 499–507.

Linnman, C., & others. (2012). Resting amygdala and medial prefrontal metabolism predicts functional activation of the fear extinction circuit. *American Journal of Psychiatry, 169* (4), 415–423.

Lippke, S., Ziegelmann, J. P., Schwarzer, R., & Velicer, W. F. (2009). Validity of stage assessment in the adoption and maintenance of physical activity and fruit and vegetable consumption. *Health Psychology, 28,* 183–193.

Liszkowski, U., Schäfer, M., Carpenter, M., & Tomasello, M. (2009). Prelinguistic infants, but not chimpanzees, communicate about absent entities. *Psychological Science, 20,* 654–660.

Lissek, S., Rabin, S., Heller, R. E., Lukenbaugh, D., Geraci, M., Pine, D. S., & Grillon, C. (2010). Overgeneralization of conditioned fear as a pathogenic marker of panic disorder. *American Journal of Psychiatry, 167,* 47–55.

Little, K. Y., Zhang, L., & Cook, E. (2006). Fluoxetine-induced alterations in human platelet serotonin transporter expression: Serotonin transporter polymorphism effects. *Psychiatry and Neuroscience, 31,* 333–339.

Little, T. D., Snyder, C. R., & Wehmeyer, M. (2006). The agentic self: On the nature and origins of personal agency across the life span. In D. K. Mroczek & T. D. Little (Eds.), *Handbook of personality development.* Mahwah, NJ: Erlbaum.

Littlefield, A. K., & Sher, K. J. (2010). Alcohol use disorders in young adulthood. In J. E. Grant (Ed.), *Young adult mental health* (pp. 292–310). New York: Oxford University Press.

Littlefield, A. K., & Sher, K. J. (2012). Smoking desistance and personality change in emerging and young adulthood. *Nicotine & Tobacco Research, 14,* 338–342.

Littrell, J. H., & Girvin, H. (2002). Stages of change: A critique. *Behavior Modification, 26,* 223–273.

Liu, C. M., & others. (2012). SOAP3: Ultra-fast GPU-based parallel alignment tool for short reads. *Bioinformatics.* doi:10.1093/bioinformatics/bts061

Liu, F., & Er, M. J. (2012). A novel efficient algorithm for self-generating fuzzy neural networkwith applications. *International Journal of Neural Systems, 22* (1), 21–35.

Liu, K. S., & others. (2011). RIM-binding protein, a central part of the active zone, is essential for neurotransmitter release. *Science, 334,* 1565–1569.

Lo, S. (2008). The nonverbal communication functions of emotions in computer-mediated communication. *Cyber Psychology & Behavior, 11,* 595–597.

Lobo, F. A., & Schraag, S. (2011). Limitations of anesthesia depth monitoring. *Current Opinion in Anesthesia, 24,* 657–664.

Lock, J. (Ed.). (2012a). *Oxford handbook of child and adolescent eating disorders: Developmental perspectives.* New York: Oxford University Press.

Lock, J. (2012c). Developmental translational research: Adolescence, brain circuitry, cognitive processes, and eating disorders. In J. Lock (Ed.), *Oxford handbook of child and adolescent eating disorders.* New York: Oxford University Press.

Loftus, E. F. (1975). Spreading activation within semantic categories. *Journal of Experimental Psychology, 104,* 234–240.

Loftus, E. F. (1993). Psychologists in the eyewitness world. *American Psychologist, 48,* 550–552.

Longo, D. A., Lent, R. W., & Brown, S. D. (1992). Social cognitive variables in the prediction of client motivation and attribution. *Journal of Counseling Psychology, 39,* 447–452.

Lopez, K. N., & Knudson, J. D. (2012). Obesity: From agricultural revolution to the contemporary pediatric epidemic. *Congenital Heart Disease, 7* (2), 189–199.

Lorant, V., Croux, C., Weich, S., Deliege, D., Mackenbach, J., & Ansseau, M. (2007). Depression and socioeconomic risk factors: 7-year longitudinal population study. *British Journal of Psychiatry, 190,* 293–298.

Lo Sauro, C., Ravaldi, C., Cabras, P. L., Faravelli, C., & Ricca, V. (2008). Stress, hypothalamic-pituitary-adrenal axis, and eating disorders. *Neuropsychobiology, 57,* 95–115.

LoSavio, S. T., Cohen, L. H., Laurenceau, J., Dasch, K. B., Parrish, B. P., & Park, C. L. (2011). Reports of stress-related growth from daily negative events. *Journal of Social and Clinical Psychology, 30,* 760–785.

Lovheim, H. (2012). A new three-dimensional model for emotions and monoamine neurotransmitters. *Medical Hypotheses, 78,* 341–348.

Lowmaster, S. E., & Morey, L. C. (2012). Predicting law enforcement officer job performance with the Personality Assessment Inventory. *Journal of Personality Assessment, 94* (3), 254–261.

Lu, P. H., & others. (2011). Age-related slowing in cognitive processing speed is associated with myelin integrity in a very healthy elderly sample. *Journal of Clinical and Experimental Neuropsychology, 33,* 1059–1068.

Lubinski, D., Benbow, C. P., Webb, R. M., & Bleske-Rechek, A. (2006). Tracking exceptional human capital over two decades. *Psychological Science, 17,* 194–199.

Lubinski, D., Webb, R. M., Morelock, M. J., & Benbow, C. P. (2001). Top 1 in 10,000: A 10-year follow-up of the profoundly gifted. *Journal of Applied Psychology, 86,* 718–729.

Luborsky, L., Rosenthal, R., Diguer, L., Andrusyna, T. P., Berman, J. S., Levitt, J. T., Seligman, D. A., & Krause, E. D. (2002). The dodo bird verdict is alive and well—mostly. *Clinical Psychology: Science and Practice, 9,* 2–12.

Lucas, R. E., & Baird, B. (2004). Extraversion and emotional reactivity. *Journal of Personality and Social Psychology, 86,* 473–485.

Lüdtke, O., Roberts, B. W., Trautwein, U., & Nagy, G. (2011). A random walk down university avenue: Life paths, life events, and personality trait change at the transition to university life. *Journal of Personality and Social Psychology, 101,* 620–637.

Luft, B. J., & others. (2012). Exposure, probable PTSD, and lower respiratory illness among World Trade Center rescue, recovery, and clean-up workers. *Psychological Medicine, 42,* 1069–1079.

Luhrmann, T. M. (2007). Social defeat and the culture of chronicity: Or, why schizophrenia does so well over there and so badly here. *Culture, Medicine and Psychiatry, 31,* 135–172.

Luigjes, J., & others. (2012). Surgery for psychiatric disorders. *World Neurosurgery.* doi: 10.1016/j.wneu.2012.03.009

Lund, H. G., Reider, B. D., Whiting, A. B., & Prichard, J. R. (2010). Sleep patterns and predictors of disturbed sleep in a large population of college students. *Journal of Adolescent Health, 46,* 124–132.

Luo, Y., & Baillargeon, R. (2005). Can a self-propelled box have a goal? Psychological reasoning in 5-month-old infants. *Psychological Science, 16,* 601–608.

Luo, Y., Hawkley, L. C., Waite, L. J., & Cacioppo, J. T. (2012). Loneliness, health, and mortality in old age: A national longitudinal study. *Social Science and Medicine, 74,* 907–914.

Luo, Y., Kaufman, L., & Baillargeon, R. (2009). Young infants' reasoning about physical events involving inert and self-propelled objects. *Cognitive Psychology, 58,* 441–486.

Luria, A. R. (1973). *The working brain.* New York: Penguin.

Lutwak, N., & Dill, C. (2012). Depression and cardio-vascular disease in women. *Journal of Women's Health.* doi:10.1089/jwh.2012.3626

Lyddon, R., & others. (2012). Serotonin 2c receptor RNA editing in major depression and suicide. *World Journal of Biological Psychiatry.* (in press)

Lydon, C. A., Rohmeier, K. D., Yi, S. C., Mattaini, M. A., & Williams, W. L. (2011). How far do you have to go to get a cheeseburger around here? The realities of an environmental design approach to curbing the consumption of fast-food. *Behavior and Social Issues, 20,* 6–23.

Lynn, S. J., & Green, J. P. (2011). The sociocognitive and dissociation theories of hypnosis: Toward a rapproachement. *International Journal of Clinical and Experimental Hypnosis, 59,* 277–293.

Lynn, S. J., Green, J. P., Accaradi, M., & Cleere, C. (2010). Hypnosis and smoking cessation: The state of the science. *American Journal of Clinical Hypnosis, 52,* 177–181.

Lyons, D. M., & others. (2010). Stress coping stimulates hippocampal neurogenesis in adult monkeys. *Proceedings of the National Academy of Sciences USA, 107,* 14823–14827.

Lyubomirsky, S. (2008). The how of happiness: A scientific approach to getting the life you want. New York: Penguin.

Lyubomirsky, S. (2011). *The way to happiness: Action plan for a happy life.* Yehuda, Israel: Kinneret.

Lyubomirsky, S. (2013). *The myth of happiness.* New York: Penguin.

Lyubomirsky, S., Boehm, J. K., Kasri, F., & Zehm, K. (2011a). The cognitive and hedonic costs of dwelling on achievement-related negative experiences: Implications for enduring happiness and unhappiness. *Emotion, 11,* 1152–1167.

Lyubomirsky, S., Dickerhoof, R., Boehm, J. K., & Sheldon, K. M. (2011b). Becoming happier takes both a will and a proper way: An experimental longitudinal intervention to boost well-being. *Emotion, 11,* 391–402.

## M

Machado, G. M., Oliveira, M. M., & Fernandes, L. A. (2009). A physiologically-based model for simulation of color vision deficiency. *IEEE Transactions on Visualization and Computer Graphics, 15,* 1291–1298.

Maccoby, E. E. (2002). Gender and group processes. *Current Directions in Psychological Science, 11,* 54–58.

MacDonald, C., Bore, M., & Munro, D. (2008). Values in action scale and the Big 5: An empirical indication of structure. *Journal of Research in Personality, 42,* 787–799.

MacQueen, C. E., Brynes, A. E., & Frost, G. S. (2002). Treating obesity: A follow-up study. Can the stages of change model be used as a postal screening tool? *Journal of Human Nutrition and Dietetics, 15* (1), 3–7.

Madden, D. J., Gottlob, L. R., Denny, L. L., Turkington, T. G., Provenzale, J. M., Hawk, T. C., & others. (1999). Aging and recognition memory: Changes in regional cerebral blood flow associated with components of reaction time distributions. *Journal of Cognitive Neuroscience, 11,* 511–520.

Maddi, S. (1998). Hardiness. In H. S. Friedman (Ed.), *Encyclopedia of mental health* (vol. 3). San Diego: Academic.

Maddi, S. R. (2008). The courage and strategies of hardiness as helpful in growing despite major, disruptive stresses. *American Psychologist, 63,* 563–564.

Maddi, S. R., Harvey, R. H., Khoshaba, D. M., Lu, J. L., Persico, M., & Brow, M. (2006). The personality construct of hardiness, III: Relationships with repression, innovativeness, authoritarianism, and performance. *Journal of Personality, 74,* 575–597.

Maddock, R. J., Buonocore, M. H. Copeland, L. E., & Richards, A. L. (2009). Elevated brain lactate responses to neural activation in panic disorder: A dynamic 1H-MRS study. *Molecular Psychiatry, 14,* 537–545.

Madhyastha, T. M., Hamaker, E. L. & Gottman, J. M. (2011). Investigating spousal influence using moment-to-moment affect data from marital conflict. *Journal of Family Psychology, 25,* 292–300.

Maeda, U., Shen, B. J., Schwarz, E. R., Farrell, K. A., & Mallon, S. (2012). Self-efficacy mediates the associations of social support and depression with treatment adherence in heart failure patients. *International Journal of Behavioral Medicine.* (in press)

Maes, H. H. M., Neal, M. C., & Eaves, L. J. (1997). Genetic and environmental factors in relative body weight and human adiposity. *Behavior Genetics, 27,* 325–351.

Magon, N., & Kaira, S. (2011). The orgasmic history of oxytocin: Love, lust, and labor. *Indian Journal of Endocrinology and Metabolism, 15, Suppl. 3,* S156–S161.

Maguire, E. A., Gadian, G. D., Johnsrude, I. S., Good, C. D., Ashburner, J., Frackowiak, R. S. J., & Frith, C. D. (2000). Navigation-related structural change in the hippocampi of taxi drivers. *Proceedings of the National Academy of Sciences USA, 97,* 4398–4403.

Mahbub, S., Brubaker, A. L., & Kovacs, E. J. (2011). Aging of the innate immune system: An update. *Current Immunology Reviews, 7,* 104–115.

Mahler, D. A., Murray, J. A., Waterman, L. A., Ward, J., Kraemer, W. J., Zhang, X., & Baird, J. C. (2009). Endogenous opioids modify dyspnea during treadmill exercise in patients with COPD. *European Respiratory Journal, 33,* 771–777.

Mahmoud, F. A., Aktas, A., Walsh, D., & Hullihen, B. (2011). A pilot study of taste changes among hospice inpatients with advanced cancer. *American Journal of Hospice and Palliative Care, 28,* 487–492.

Maier, N. R. F. (1931). Reasoning in humans. *Journal of Comparative Psychology, 12,* 181–194.

Makransky, G., Mortensen, E. L., & Glas, C. A. (2012). Improving personality facet scores with multidimensional computer adaptive testing: An illustration with the Neo Pi-R. *Assessment.* (in press)

Malamuth, N. M., Addison, T., & Koss, M. (2000). Pornography and sexual aggression: Are there reliable effects and can we understand them? *Annual Review of Sex Research, 11,* 26–91.

Malcolm-Smith, S., Solms, M., Turnbull, O., & Tredoux, C. (2008). Threat in dreams: An adaptation? *Consciousness and cognition, 17,* 1281–1291.

Malhotra, R. K., & Desai, A. K. (2010). Healthy brain aging: what has sleep got to do with it? *Clinics in Geriatric Medicine, 26,* 46–56.

Malloy, L. C., Lyon, T. D., & Quas, J. A. (2007). Filial dependency and recantation of child sexual abuse allegations. *Journal of the American Academy of Child & Adolescent Psychiatry, 46,* 162–170.

Malmberg, K. J., Criss, A. H., Gangwani, T. H., & Shiffrin, R. M. (2012). Overcoming the negative consequences of interference from recognition memory testing. *Psychological Science, 23* (2),115–119.

Mambou, E. (2011). South Africans and Mexicans in Florida: Intergroup conflict. *Journal of Black Studies, 42,* 379–388.

Mancini, A. D., & Bonanno, G. A. (2009). Predictors and parameters of resilience to loss: Toward an individual difference model. *Journal of Personality, 77,* 1805–1832.

Mandal, I., & Sairam, N. (2012). Accurate prediction of coronary artery disease using reliable diagnosis system. *Journal of Medical Systems.* (in press)

Mandler, G. (1980). Recognizing: The judgment of previous occurrence. *Psychological Review, 87,* 252–271.

Maner, J. K., Luce, C. L., Neuberg, S. L., Cialdini, R. B., Brown, S., & Sagarin, B. J. (2002). The effects of perspective taking on motivations for helping: Still no evidence for altruism. *Personality and Social Psychology Bulletin, 28,* 1601–1610.

Manini, T. M., & others. (2006). Daily activity energy expenditure and mortality among older adults. *Journal of the American Medical Association, 296,* 216–218.

Manne, S. (2013). Coping and social support. In I. B. Weiner & others (Eds.), *Handbook of psychology* (2nd ed., vol. 9). New York: Wiley.

Manto, M., & others. (2012). Consensus paper: Roles of cerebellum in motor control—the diversity of ideas on cerebellar involvement in movement. *Cerebellum.* (in press)

Mantonakis, A., Rodero, P., Lesschaeve, I., & Hastie, R. (2009). Order in choice: Effects of serial position on preferences. *Psychological Science, 20,* 1309–1312.

Mantzoros, C. S., & others. (2011). Leptin in human physiology and pathophysiology. *American Journal of Physiology, Endocrinology, and Metabolism, 301,* E567–E584.

Manusov, V. (2012). Attributions and communication: Out of our heads and into behavior. In D. R. Roskos-Ewoldsen & J. L. Monahan (Eds.), *Communication and social cognition.* New York: Psychology Press.

Maoz, I. (2012). Contact and social change in an ongoing asymmetrical conflict: Four social-psychological models of reconciliation-aimed planned encounters between Israeli Jews and Palestinians. In J. Dixon, M. Keynes, & M. Levine (Eds.), *Beyond prejudice.* New York: Cambridge University Press.

Mar, R. A., Mason, M. F., & Litvack, A. (2012). How daydreaming relates to life satisfaction, loneliness, and social support: The importance of gender and daydream content. *Consciousness and Cognition, 21* (1), 401–407.

Marazziti, D., Carlini, M., & Dell'osso, L. (2012). Treatment strategies of obsessive-compulsive disorder and panic disorder/agoraphobia. *Current Topics in Medicinal Chemistry, 12,* 238–253.

Marchiori, D., & Warglien, M. (2011, December). Neural network models of learning and categorization in multi-game experiments. *Frontiers in Neuroscience, 5,* 139.

Marcia, J. E. (1980). Ego identity development. In J. Adelson (Ed.), *Handbook of adolescent psychology.* New York: Wiley.

Marcia, J. E. (2002). Identity and psychosocial development in adulthood. *Identity, 2,* 7–28.

Marcus, D. K., Norris, A. L., & Coccaro, E. F. (2012). The latent structure of attention deficit/hyperactivity disorder in an adult sample. *Journal of Psychiatric Research.* (in press)

Marcus, G. F. (2001). *The algebraic mind.* Cambridge, MA: MIT Press.

Marewski, J. N., & Schooler, L. J. (2011). Cognitive niches: An ecological model of strategy selection. *Psychological Review, 118,* 393–437.

Marine, A., Rutosalainen, J., Serra, C., & Verbeek, J. (2006). Preventing occupational stress in healthcare workers. *Cochrane Database System Review, 18* (4), CD002892.

Marinkovic, K., & others. (2011). Right hemisphere has the last laugh: Neural dynamics of joke appreciation. *Cognitive and Affective Behavioral Neuroscience, 11,* 113–130.

Maris, R. W. (1998). Suicide. In H. S. Friedman (Ed.), *Encyclopedia of mental health* (vol. 3). San Diego: Academic.

Markham, C. M., & others. (2012). Sexual risk avoidance and sexual risk reduction interventions for middle school youth: A randomized controlled trial. *Journal of Adolescent Health, 50,* 279–288.

Markovits, H., Forgues, H. L., & Brunet, M. L. (2012). More evidence for a dual-process model of conditional reasoning. *Memory and Cognition.* doi: 10.3758/s13421-012-0186-4

Markowitsch, H. J., & Staniloiu, A. (2012). Amnesic disorders. *Lancet.* (in press)

Marks, A. K. Patton, F., & Coll, C. G. (2011). Being bicultural: A mixed-methods study of adolescents' implicitly and explicitly measured multiethnic identities. *Developmental Psychology, 47,* 270–288.

Marks, D. F. (2013). Health psychology: Overview. In I. B. Weiner & others (Eds.), *Handbook of psychology* (2nd ed., vol. 9). New York: Wiley.

Marlow, A. (1999). *How to stop time: Heroin from A to Z.* New York: Basic Books.

Marshall, D. S. (1971). Sexual behavior in Mangaia. In D. S. Marshall & R. C. Suggs (Eds.), *Human sexual behavior: Variations in the ethnographic spectrum* (pp. 103–162). New York: Basic Books.

Marshall, M., & Rathbone, J. (2006). Early intervention for psychosis. *Cochrane Database of Systematic Reviews, 4,* CD004718.

Marston, O. J., & others. (2011). Neuropeptide Y cells represent a distinct glucose-sensing population in the lateral hypothalamus. *Endocrinology, 152,* 4046–4052.

**Martin, C. L., & Ruble, D. N.** (2010). Patterns of gender development. *Annual Review of Psychology* (vol. 61). Palo Alto, CA: Annual Reviews.

**Martin, G. L., & Pear, J.** (2011). *Behavior modification* (9th ed.). Upper Saddle River, NJ: Pearson.

**Martinez, E.** (2009, December 2). Richmond High gang rape: Six plead not guilty to raping teen while others watched. *CBS News.* www.cbsnews.com/8301-504083_162-5697503-504083.html?tag=mncol;lst;4 (accessed May 19, 2012)

**Martinez-Amoros, E., & others.** (2012). Long-term treatment strategies in major depression: A 2-year prospective naturalistic follow-up after successful electroconvulsive therapy. *Journal of ECT, 28* (2), 92–97.

**Maruyama, Y., Pereira, M., Margolskee, R. F., Chaudhari, N., & Roper, S. D.** (2006). Umami responses in mouse taste cells indicate more than one receptor. *Journal of Neuroscience, 26,* 2227–2234.

**Marx, R. F., & Didziulis, V.** (2009, March 1). A life, interrupted. *New York Times.*

**Marzano. C., & others.** (2011). Recalling and forgetting dreams: Theta and alpha oscillations during sleep predict subsequent dream recall. *Journal of Neuroscience, 31,* 6674–6683.

**Mascaro, N., & Rosen, D. H.** (2006). The role of existential meaning as a buffer against stress. *Journal of Humanistic Psychology, 46,* 168–190.

**Mash, E. J., & Wolfe, D. A.** (2013). *Abnormal child psychology* (5th ed.). Boston: Cengage.

**Maslow, A. H.** (1954). *Motivation and personality.* New York: Harper & Row.

**Maslow, A. H.** (1971). *The farther reaches of human nature.* New York: Viking.

**Mason, C.** (2009, May 12). Belgian city plans "veggie" days. *BBC.* http://news.bbc.co.uk/2/hi/europe/8046970.stm (accessed May 30, 2012)

**Massa, L. J., & Mayer, R. E.** (2006). Testing the ATI hypothesis: Should multimedia instruction accommodate verbalizer-visualizer cognitive style? *Learning and Individual Differences, 16,* 321–336.

**Masten, A. S.** (2006). Developmental psychopathology: Pathways to the future. *International Journal of Behavioral Development, 31,* 46–53.

**Masten, A. S.** (2009). Ordinary magic: Lessons from research on human development. *Education Canada, 49,* 28–32.

**Masters, W. H., & Johnson, V. E.** (1966). *Human sexual response.* Boston: Little, Brown.

**Masuda, T., & Nisbett, R. E.** (2001). Attending holistically vs. analytically: Comparing the context sensitivity of Japanese and Americans. *Journal of Personality and Social Psychology, 81,* 922–934.

**Masuda, T., & Nisbett, R. E.** (2006). Culture and change blindness. *Trends in Cognitive Science, 30,* 381–399.

**Mather, K. A., Jorm, A. F., Parslow, R. A., & Christensen, H.** (2011). Is telomere length a biomarker of aging? A review. *Journals of Gerontology A: Biological Sciences and Medical Sciences, 66A,* 202–213.

**Matos, A. P., Ferreira, J. A., & Haase, R. F.** (2012). Television and aggression: A test of a mediated model with a sample of Portuguese students. *Journal of Social Psychology, 152,* 75–91.

**Matsumoto, D., & Juang, L.** (2013). *Culture and psychology* (5th ed.). Boston: Cengage.

**Matsunaga, H., & Seedat, S.** (2011). Obsessive-compulsive spectrum disorders: Cross-national and ethnic issues. In E. Hollander, J. Zohar, P. J. Sirovatka, & D. A. Regier (Eds.), *Obsessive-compulsive spectrum disorders: Refining the research agenda for DSM-V* (pp. 205–221). Washington, DC: American Psychiatric Association.

**Mattes, K., Spezio, M., Kim, H., Todorov, A., Adolphs, R., & Alvarez, R. M.** (2010). Predicting election outcomes from positive and negative trait assessments of candidate images. *Political Psychology, 31,* 41–58.

**Matthews, J., & Moran, A.** (2011). Physical activity and self-regulation strategy use in adolescents. *American Journal of Health Behavior, 35,* 807–814.

**Matthews, K., & Gallo, L. C.** (2011). Psychological perspectives on the association of socioeconomic status and physical health. *Annual Review of Psychology* (vol. 62). Palo Alto, CA: Annual Reviews.

**Matzel, L. D., & Kolata, S.** (2010). Selective attention, working memory, and animal intelligence. *Neuroscience and Biobehavioral Reviews, 34,* 23–30.

**Maxfield, M., Pyszczynski, T., Greenberg, J., Pepin, R., & Davis, H. P.** (2012). The moderating role of executive functioning in older adults' responses to a reminder of mortality. *Psychology and Aging, 27,* 256–263

**Maxwell, W. L.** (2012). Traumatic brain injury in the neonate, child, and adolescent human: An overview of pathology. *International Journal of Developmental Neuroscience.* (in press)

**May, M.** (2003). *Vision diary.* http://www.guardian.co.uk/g2/ story/0,3604,1029268,00.html (accessed October 11, 2006)

**May, P. A., & Gossage, J. P.** (2011). Maternal risk factors for fetal alcohol spectrum disorders: Not as simple as it might seem. *Alcohol Research & Health, 34,* 15–26.

**Mayer, R.** (2000). Problem solving. In M. A. Runco & S. Pritzker (Eds.), *Encyclopedia of psychology.* San Diego: Academic.

**Mayer, R. E.** (2011). *Applying the science of learning.* Boston: Allyn & Bacon.

**Mayo Foundation.** (2006). *Electroconvulsive therapy (ECT): Treating severe depression and mental illness.* Rochester, MN: Author. www.mayoclinic.com/health/electroconvulsive-therapy/MY00129 (accessed May 29, 2012)

**McAdams, D. P.** (1989). *Intimacy: The need to be close.* New York: Doubleday.

**McAdams, D. P.** (2001). The psychology of life stories. *Review of General Psychology, 5,* 100–122.

**McAdams, D. P.** (2006). *The redemptive self: Stories Americans live by.* New York: Oxford University Press.

**McAdams, D. P.** (2007, April 10). Understanding behavior (letter to the editor). *New York Times.* http://query.nytimes.com/gst/fullpage.html?res=9C0CE7DA153FF933A25757C0A9619C8B63&n=Top%2fReference%2fTimes%20Topics%2fSubjects%2fT%2fTerrorism (accessed May 21, 2012)

**McAdams, D. P.** (2009). *The person* (5th ed.). New York: Wiley.

**McAdams, D. P.** (2011a). Life narratives. In K. L. Fingerman, C. A. Berg, J. Smith, & T. C. Antonucci (Eds.), *Handbook of lifespan development.* New York: Springer.

**McAdams, D. P.** (2011b). Narrative identity. In S. J. Schwartz, K. Luyckx, & V. L. Vignoles (Eds.), *Handbook of identity theory and research.* New York: Springer.

**McAdams, D. P.** (2012). Exploring psychological themes through life narrative accounts. In J. A. Holstein & J. F. Gubrium (Eds.), *Varieties of narrative analysis.* Thousand Oaks, CA: Sage.

**McAdams, D. P., & Bryant, F. B.** (1987). Intimacy motivation and subjective mental health in a nationwide sample. *Journal of Personality, 55,* 395–413.

**McAdams, D. P., & Olson, B. D.** (2010). Personality development: Continuity and change. *Annual Review of Psychology* (vol. 61). Palo Alto, CA: Annual Reviews.

**McBride, C. M., Bryan, A. D., Bray, M. S., Swan, G. E., & Green, E. D.** (2012). Health behavior change: Can genomics improve behavior adherence? *American Journal of Public Health, 102,* 401–405.

**McCarthy, D. E., Piasecki, T. M., Fiore, M. C., & Baker, T. B.** (2006). Life before and after quitting smoking: An electronic diary study. *Journal of Abnormal Psychology, 115,* 454–466.

**McClelland, J. L.** (2011). Memory as a constructive process: The parallel-distributed processing approach. In S. Nalbantian, P. Matthews, & J. L. McClelland (Eds.), *The memory process.* Cambridge, MA: MIT Press.

**McClelland, J. L., & Rumelhart, D. E.** (2009). Why there are complementary learning systems in the hippocampus and neocortex: Insights from the successes and failures of connectionist models of learning and memory. In D. Shanks (Ed.), *Psychology of learning.* Thousand Oaks, CA: Sage.

**McClelland, J. L., & others.** (2010). Letting structure emerge: Connectionist and dynamical systems approaches to cognition. *Trends in Cognitive Science, 14,* 348–356.

**McConnell, A. R., & Brown, C. M.** (2010). Dissonance averted: Self-concept organization moderates the effect of hypocrisy on attitude change. *Journal of Experimental Social Psychology, 46,* 361–366.

**McCrae, R. R., Harwood, T. M., & Kelly, S. L.** (2011). The NEO inventories. In T. M. Harwood, L. E. Beutler, & G. Groth-Marnat (Eds.), *Integrative assessment of adult personality* (3rd ed.). New York: Guilford.

**McCrae, R. R., & Sutin, A. R.** (2007). New frontiers for the five factor model: A preview of the literature. *Social and Personality Psychology Compass, 1,* 423–440.

**McCrae, R. R., & Sutin, A. R.** (2009). Openness to experience. In M. R. Leary & R. H. Hoyle (Eds.), *Handbook of individual differences in social behavior* (pp. 257–273). New York: Guilford.

**McCulloch, K. C., Ferguson, M. J., Kawada, C. C. K., & Bargh, J. A.** (2008). Taking a closer look: On the operation of nonconscious impression formation. *Journal of Experimental Social Psychology, 44,* 614–623.

**McCullough, M. E., Bono, G., & Root, L. M.** (2007). Rumination, emotion, and forgiveness: Three longitudinal studies. *Journal of Personality and Social Psychology, 92,* 490–505.

**McCullough, M. E., Emmons, R. A., & Tsang, J.** (2002). The grateful disposition: A conceptual and empirical topography. *Journal of Personality and Social Psychology, 82,* 112–127.

**McCullough, M. E., Kurzban, R., & Tabak, B. A.** (2011). Evolved mechanisms for revenge and forgiveness. In M. Mikulincer & P. R. Shaver (Eds.), *Human aggression and violence: Causes, manifestations, and consequences* (pp. 221–239). Washington, DC: American Psychological Association.

**McCullough, M. E., Luna, L. R., Berry, J. W., Tabak, B. A., & Bono, G.** (2010). On the form and function of forgiving: Modeling the time–forgiveness relationship and testing the valuable relationships hypothesis. *Emotion, 10,* 358–376.

**McCullough, M. E., & Willoughby, B. L.** (2009). Religion, self-regulation, and self-control: Associations, explanations, and implications. *Psychological Bulletin, 135,* 69–93.

**McDaniel, M. A., & Einstein, G. O.** (2007). *Prospective memory: An overview and synthesis of an emerging field.* Thousand Oaks, CA: Sage.

**McDermott, R.** (2009). Medical decision making: Lessons from psychology. *Urologic Oncology, 26,* 665–668.

**McDonald, M., Asher, B. D., Kerr, N. L., & Navarrete, C. D.** (2011). Fertility and intergroup bias in racial and minimal-group contexts: Evidence for shared architecture. *Psychological Science, 22,* 860–865.

**McFadden, S. H., & Basting, A. D.** (2010). Healthy aging persons and their brains: Promoting resilience through creative engagement. *Clinics in Geriatric Medicine, 26,* 149–161.

**McGhee, K. E., & Travis, J.** (2010). Repeatable behavioural type and stable dominance rank in the bluefin killifish. *Animal Behaviour, 79,* 497–507.

**McGuire, M. T., Wing, R. R., Klem, M. L., Lang, W., & Hill, J. O.** (1999). What predicts weight regain in a group of successful weight losers? *Journal of Consulting and Clinical Psychology, 67,* 177–185.

**McGuire, W. J.** (2003). Doing psychology my way. In R. J. Sternberg (Ed.), *Psychologists defying the crowd: Stories of those who battled the establishment and won* (pp. 119–137). Washington, DC: American Psychological Association.

**McGuire, W. J., & Papageorgis, D.** (1961). The relative efficacy of various types of prior belief-defense in producing immunity against persuasion. *Public Opinion Quarterly, 26,* 24–34.

**McIntosh, R. C., & Rosselli, M.** (2012). Stress and coping in women living with HIV: A meta-analytic review. *AIDS Behavior.* doi: 10.1007/s10461-012-0166-5

**McIntosh, W. D., Harlow, T. F., & Martin, L. L.** (1995). Linkers and non-linkers: Goal beliefs as a moderator of the effects of everyday hassles on rumination, depression, and physical complaints. *Journal of Applied Social Psychology, 25,* 1231–1244.

**McKay, K. M., Imel, Z. E., & Wampold, B. E.** (2006). Psychiatrist effects in the psychopharmacological treatment of depression. *Journal of Affective Disorders, 92,* 287–290.

**McLeod, J.** (2007). *Counseling skill.* New York: McGraw-Hill.

**McMahan, E. A., & Estes, D.** (2011). Hedonic versus eudaimonic conceptions of well-being: Evidence of

National Center for PTSD. (2012). *Gateway to post traumatic stress disorder information.* www.ptsdinfo.org/ (accessed April 20, 2012)

National Institute of Mental Health (NIMH). (2008). *The numbers count: Mental disorders in America.* Bethesda, MD: U.S. Department of Health and Human Services. www.nimh.nih.gov/health/publications/the-numbers-count-mental-disorders-in-america/index.shtml (accessed May 24, 2012)

National Institute of Mental Health (NIMH). (2011). *Eating disorders.* Bethesda, MD: Author.

National Institute of Mental Health (NIMH). (2012). *Depression.* www.nimh.nih.gov/health/publications/depression/complete-index.shtml (accessed May 25, 2012)

National Institute on Drug Abuse (NIDA). (2009). *Research report series—MDMA (Ecstasy) abuse.* Bethesda, MD: Author.

National Sleep Foundation. (2007, March 6). *Stressed-out American women have no time for sleep.* Washington, DC: Author.

National Sleep Foundation. (2011). *Annual Sleep in America poll exploring connections with communications and communications technology use and sleep.* Washington, DC: Author.

Nations, K. R., & others. (2012). Evaluation of the glycine transporter inhibitor org 25935 as augmentation to cognitive-behavioral therapy for panic disorder: A multicenter, randomized, double-blind, placebo trial. *Journal of Clinical Psychology.* (in press)

Naumann, L. P., Vazire, S., Rentfrow, P. J., & Gosling, S. D. (2009). Personality judgments based on physical appearance. *Personality and Social Psychology Bulletin, 35,* 1661–1671.

Nauta, M. H., & others. (2012). Preventing mood and anxiety disorders in youth: A multi-centre RCT in the high risk offspring of depressed and anxious patients. *BMC Psychiatry, 12* (1), 31.

Nay, W. R. (2012). *Taking charge of anger* (2nd ed.). New York: Guilford.

Needham, A., Barrett, T., & Peterman, K. (2002). A pick-me-up for infants' exploratory skills: Early simulated experiences reaching for objects using "sticky mittens" enhances young infants' object exploration skills. *Infant Behavior and Development, 25,* 279–295.

Negriff, S., Susman, E. J., & Trickett, P. K. (2011). The development pathway from pubertal timing to delinquency and sexual activity from early to late adolescence. *Journal of Youth and Adolescence, 40* (10), 1343–1356.

Neikrug, A. B., & Ancoli-Israel, S. (2010). Sleep disorders in the older adult: A mini-review. *Gerontology, 56,* 181–189.

Nelson, C. A. (2011). Brain development and behavior. In A. M. Rudolph, C. Rudolph, L. First, G. Lister, & A. A. Gershon (Eds.), *Rudolph's pediatrics* (22nd ed.). New York: McGraw-Hill.

Nelson, K. (1993). The psychological and social origins of autobiographical memory. *Psychological Science, 4,* 7–14.

Nemeroff, C. B., Bremner, J. D., Foa, E. B., Mayberg, H. S., North, C. S., & Stein, M. B. (2006). Posttraumatic stress disorder: A state-of-the-science review. *Journal of Psychiatric Research, 40* (1), 1–21.

Nestler, S., Blank, H., & Egloff, B. (2010). Hindsight ≠ hindsight: Experimentally induced dissociations between hindsight components. *Journal of Experimental Psychology: Learning, Memory, and Cognition, 36,* 1399–1413.

Nestler, S., Blank, H., & von Collani, G. (2008). Hindsight bias doesn't always come easy: Causal models, cognitive effort, and creeping determinism. *Journal of Experimental Psychology: Learning, Memory, and Cognition, 34,* 1043–1054.

Nett, E. J., & others. (2012). Four-dimensional phase contrast MRI with accelerated dual velocity coding. *Journal of Magnetic Resonance Imaging.* doi: 10.1002/jmri.23588

Nettle, D. (2006). The evolution of personality variations in humans and other animals. *American Psychologist, 61,* 622–631.

Neufeld, J., & others. (2012). The neural correlates of colored music: A functional MRI investigation of auditory-visual synesthesia. *Neuropsychologia, 50,* 85–89.

Neukrug, E. S., & Fawcett, R. C. (2010). *Essentials of testing and assessment* (2nd ed.). Boston: Cengage.

Neumann, I. D., Veenema, A. H., & Beiderbeck, D. I. (2010). Aggression and anxiety: Social context and neurobiological links. *Frontiers in Behavioral Neuroscience, 30,* 4–12.

Nevels, R. M., Dehon, E. E., Alexander, K., & Gontkovsky, S. T. (2010). Psychopharmacology of aggression in children and adolescents with primary neuropsychiatric disorders: A review of current and potentially promising treatment options. *Experimental and Clinical Psychopharmacology, 18,* 184–201.

Neville, H. J. (2006). Different profiles of plasticity within human cognition. In Y. Munakata & M. H. Johnson (Eds.), *Attention and performance.* Oxford, England: Oxford University Press.

Nevsimalova, S. (2009). Narcolepsy in childhood. *Sleep Medicine Reviews, 13,* 169–180.

Nezu, A., Nezu, C. M., Felgoise, S. H., & Greenberg, L. M. (2013). Psychosocial oncology. In I. B. Weiner & others (Eds.), *Handbook of psychology* (2nd ed., vol. 9). New York: Wiley.

Niaura, R., Todaro, J. F., Strood, L., Spiro, A., Ward, K. D., & Weiss, S. (2002). Hostility, the metabolic syndrome, and incident coronary heart disease. *Health Psychology, 21,* 588–593.

Nickerson, R. S., & Adams, M. J. (1979). Long-term memory for a common object. *Cognitive Psychology, 11,* 287–307.

Nicklas, J. M., & others. (2012). Successful weight loss among obese U.S. adults. *American Journal of Preventive Medicine, 42,* 481–485.

Nicoleau, C., Viegas, P., Peschanski, M., & Perrier, A. L. (2011). Human pluripotent stem cell therapy for Huntington's disease. *Neurotherapeutics, 8,* 562–576.

Nicolle, A., Symmonds, M., & Dolan, R. J. (2011). Optimistic biases in observational learning of value. *Cognition, 119,* 394–402.

Nielsen, J., & others. (2012). Geographical and temporal variations in clozapine prescription for schizophrenia. *European Neuropsychopharmacology.* doi: 10.1016/j.euroneuro.2012.03.003

Nielsen, M. B., & Einarsen, S. (2012). Prospective relationships between workplace sexual harassment and psychological distress. *Occupational Medicine.* doi: 10.1093/occmed/kqs010

Nieto, S., & Bode, P. (2012). *Affirming diversity* (6th ed.). Boston: Allyn & Bacon.

Nijstad, B. (2009). *Group performance.* New York: Psychology Press.

Nillni, Y. I., Berenz, E. C., Rohan, K. J., & Zvolensky, M. J. (2012). Sex differences in panic-relevant responding to a 10% carbon dioxide–enriched air biological challenge. *Journal of Anxiety Disorders, 26,* 165–172.

Nilsson, H., Juslin, P., & Olsson, H. (2008). Exemplars in the mist: The cognitive substrate of the representativeness heuristic. *Scandinavian Journal of Psychology, 49,* 201–212.

Ni Mhaolain, A. M., & others. (2012). Subjective well-being amongst community-dwelling elders: What determines satisfaction with life? Findings from the Dublin Healthy Aging Study. *International Psychogeriatrics, 24,* 316–323.

Nisbett, R. E., Aronson, J., Blair, C., Dickens, W., Flynn, J., Halpern, D. F., & Turkheimer, E. (2012). Intelligence: New findings and theoretical developments. *American Psychologist, 67,* 130–159.

Nisbett, R. E., & Ross, L. (1980). *Human inference.* Upper Saddle River, NJ: Prentice-Hall.

Nishida, A., Miyaoka, T., Inagaki, T., & Horiguchi, J. (2009). New approaches to antidepressant drug design: Cytokine-regulated pathways. *Current Pharmaceutical Design, 15,* 1683–1687.

Noftle, E. E., & Robins, R. W. (2007). Personality predictors of academic outcomes: Big five correlates of GPA and SAT scores. *Journal of Personality and Social Psychology, 93,* 116–130.

Nolen-Hoeksema, S. (2011). *Abnormal psychology* (5th ed.). New York: McGraw-Hill.

Norcross, J. C. (Ed.). (2011). *Psychotherapy relationships that work.* New York: Oxford University Press.

Norcross, J. C., Campbell, L. M., Grohol, J. M., Santrock, J. W., Seagea, F., & Sommer, R. (2013). *Self-help that works: Evidence-based resources for the public and professionals* (4th ed.). New York: Oxford University Press.

Norcross, J. C., Krebs, P. M., & Prochaska, J. O. (2011). Stages of change. *Journal of Clinical Psychology, 67,* 143–154.

Norcross, J. C., Mrykalo, M. S., & Blagys, M. D. (2002). Auld lang syne: Success predictors, change processes, and self-reported outcomes of New Year's resolvers and nonresolvers. *Journal of Clinical Psychology, 58,* 397–405.

Nordgren, L. F., & Dijksterhuis, A. P. (2009). The devil is in the deliberation: Thinking too much reduces preference consistency. *Journal of Consumer Research, 36,* 39–46.

Nordstrom, B. R., & others. (2011). Neurocriminology. *Advances in Genetics, 75,* 255–283.

Nordt, C., Rossler, W., & Lauber, C. (2006). Attitudes of mental health professionals toward people with schizophrenia and major depression. *Schizophrenia Bulletin, 32,* 709–714.

Norman, G. J., DeVries, A. C., Hawkley, L. C., Cacioppo, J. T., & Bernston, G. G. (2012). Social influences on physiological processes: A focus on health. In R. Wright & G. Gendolla (Eds.), *Motivation perspectives in cardiovascular response.* Washington, DC: American Psychological Association.

North, M. S., & Fiske, S. T. (2012). History of social cognition. In A. W. Kruglanski & W. Stroebe (Eds.), *Handbook of the history of social psychology.* New York: Psychology Press.

Nosek, B. A., & Banaji, M. R. (2007). Implicit attitude. In P. Wilken, T. Bayne, & A. Cleeremans (Eds.), *Oxford companion to consciousness.* Oxford: Oxford University Press.

Nosko, A., Tieu, T. T., Lawford, H., & Pratt, M. W. (2011). How do I love thee? Let me count the ways: Parenting during adolescence, attachment styles, and romantic narratives in emerging adulthood. *Developmental Psychology, 47,* 645–657.

Notman, M. T., & Nadelson, C. C. (2002). Women's issues. In M. Hersen & W. H. Sledge (Eds.), *Encyclopedia of psychotherapy.* San Diego: Academic.

Nowak, M. A., Page, K. M., & Sigmund, K. (2000). Fairness versus reason in the ultimatum game. *Science, 289,* 1773–1775.

Nowotny, M., & Gummer, A. W. (2011). Vibration responses of the organ of Corti and the tectorial membrane to electrical stimulation. *Journal of the Acoustical Society of America, 130,* 3852.

NPD Group. (2011, January 27). *U.S. toy industry retail sales generated $21.87 billion In 2010.* Port Washington, NY: Author. www.npd.com/press/releases/press_110127.html (accessed May 6, 2012)

Nunez, N., McCrea, S. M., & Culhane, S. E. (2011). Jury decision making research: Are researchers focusing on the mouse and not the elephant in the room? *Behavioral Science and the Law, 29,* 439–451.

Nunez, P. L. (2012). Nested hierarchy, small worlds, brain complexity, and emergence. *Physics of Life Reviews.* doi: 10.1016/j.plrev.2011.12.012

Nyberg, L. (2004, August). *Imaging cognition.* Paper presented at the 28th International Congress of Psychology, Beijing, China.

## O

Oakley, D. A., & Halligan, P. W. (2011). Using hypnosis to gain insights into healthy and pathological cognitive functioning. *Consciousness and Cognition, 20* (2), 328–331.

O'Barr, W. M. (2006). Multiculturalism in the marketplace: Targeting Latinas, African American women, and gay consumers. *Advertising and Society Review, 7* (4).

Ockene, I. S., & others. (2012). Outcomes of a Latino community-based intervention for the prevention of diabetes: The Lawrence Latino Diabetes Prevention Project. *American Journal of Public Health, 102,* 336–342.

O'Connor, D. B., Conner, M., Jones, F., McMillan, B., & Ferguson, E. (2009). Exploring the benefits of conscientiousness: An investigation of the role of daily stressors and health behaviors. *Annals of Behavioral Medicine, 37* (2), 184–196.

**O'Connor, T. G., Bergman, K., Sarkar, P., & Glover, V.** (2012). Prenatal cortisol exposure predicts infant cortisol response to acute stress. *Developmental Psychobiology.* doi: 10.1002/dev.21007

**O'Dell, K. R., Masters, K. S., Spielmans, G. I., & Maisto, S. A.** (2011). Does type-D personality predict outcomes among patients with cardiovascular disease? A meta-analytic review. *Journal of Psychosomatic Research, 71,* 199–206.

**O'Donnell, M. L., & others.** (2012). Stepped early psychological intervention for posttraumatic stress disorder, other anxiety disorders, and depression following serious injury. *Journal of Traumatic Stress, 25,* 125–133.

**O'Donnell, M. P.** (2012). Financial incentives for workplace health promotion: What is equitable, what is sustainable, and what drives healthy behaviors? *American Journal of Health Promotion, 26* (5), iv–vii.

**O'Donovan, A., & others.** (2009). Pessimism correlates with leukocyte telomere shortness and elevated interleukin-6 in post-menopausal women. *Brain, Behavior, and Immunity, 23,* 446–449.

**OECD.** (2010). *Obesity and the economics of prevention—Fit or fat.* Paris: Author.

**OECD.** (2012). *Obesity update 2012.* Paris: Author. www.oecd.org/dataoecd/1/61/49716427.pdf (accessed June 1, 2012)

**OECD Family Database.** (2010). *SF3.1 Marriage and divorce rates.* Paris: Organisation for Economic Cooperation and Development, Directorate of Employment, Labour and Social Affairs.

**Oerlemans, W. G., Bakker, A. B., & Veenhoven, R.** (2011). Finding the key to happy aging: A day reconstruction of happiness. *Journals of Gerontology B: Psychological Sciences and Social Sciences, 66B,* 665–674.

**Ogden, C. L., Carroll, M. D., Kit, B. K., & Flegal, K. M.** (2012, January). Prevalence of obesity in the United States, 2009–2010. *NCHS Data Brief, 82.*

**Ogilvie, R. D., & Wilkinson, R. T.** (1988). Behavioral versus EEG-based monitoring of all-night sleep/wake patterns. *Sleep, 11* (2), 139–155.

**Ohira, T., & others.** (2012). Associations of anger, anxiety, and depressive symptoms with carotid arterial wall thickness: The multi-ethnic study of atherosclerosis. *Psychosomatic Medicine.* doi: 10.1097/PSY.0b013e31824f6267

**Ohman, A., & Mineka, S.** (2001). Fears, phobias, and preparedness: Toward an evolved module of fear and fear learning. *Psychological Review, 108,* 483–522.

**Ohman, A., & Mineka, S.** (2003). The malicious serpent: Snakes as a prototypical stimulus for an evolved module of fear. *Current Directions in Psychological Science, 12,* 5–9.

**Ohman, A., & Soares, J. J. P.** (1998). Emotional conditioning to masked stimuli: Expectancies for aversive outcomes following nonrecognized fear-relevant stimuli. *Journal of Experimental Psychology, 127,* 69–82.

**Oishi, S., Miao, F. F., Koo, M., Kisling, J., & Ratliff, K. A.** (2012). Residential mobility breeds familiarity seeking. *Journal of Personality and Social Psychology, 102,* 149–162.

**Okano, K., & others.** (2012). Retinal cone and rod photoreceptor cells exhibit differential susceptibility to light-induced change. *Journal of Neurochemistry.* (in press)

**Olbrich, D., & Dittmar, M.** (2011). Older poor-sleeping women display a smaller evening increase in melatonin secretion and lower values of melatonin and core body temperature than good sleepers. *Chronobiology International, 28,* 681–689.

**Olds, J. M.** (1958). Self-stimulation experiments and differential reward systems. In H. H. Jasper, L. D. Proctor, R. S. Knighton, W. C. Noshay, & R. T. Costello (Eds.), *Reticular formation of the brain.* Boston: Little, Brown.

**Olds, J. M., & Milner, P. M.** (1954). Positive reinforcement produced by electrical stimulation of the septal area and other areas of the rat brain. *Journal of Comparative and Physiological Psychology, 47,* 419–427.

**O'Leary, K. D., Heyman, R. E., & Jongsma, A. E.** (2012). *The couples psychotherapy treatment planner.* New York: Wiley.

**Olfson, M., & Marcus, S. C.** (2009). National patterns in antidepressant medication treatment. *Archives of General Psychiatry, 66,* 848–856.

**Oliver, P. L., & others.** (2012). Disrupted circadian rhythms in a mouse model of schizophrenia. *Current Biology, 22* (4), 314–319.

**Olma, M. C., & others.** (2011). Excitability changes in the visual cortex quantified with signal detection analysis. *Restorative Neurology and Neuroscience.* doi: 10.3233/RNN-2011-607

**Olness, K., & Ader, R.** (1992). Conditioning as an adjunct in the pharmacotherapy of lupus erythematosus. *Journal of Developmental and Behavioral Pediatrics, 13,* 124–125.

**Olson, J. M., & Stone, J.** (2005). The influence of behavior on attitudes. In D. Albarracin, B. T. Johnson, & M. P. Zanna (Eds.), *The handbook of attitudes* (pp. 223–271). Mahwah, NJ: Erlbaum.

**Oltmanns, T. F., & Emery, R. E.** (2013). *Abnormal psychology* (7th ed.). Upper Saddle River, NJ: Pearson.

**Oltmanns, T. F., & Powers, A. D.** (2012). Gender and personality disorders. In T. Widiger (Ed.), *Oxford handbook of personality disorders.* New York: Oxford University Press.

**"100 best companies to work for."** (2012). CNN Money. http://money.cnn.com/magazines/fortune/best-companies/2012/full_list/ (accessed May 3, 2012)

**Onen, N. F., Overton, E. T., Presti, R., Blair, C., Powderly, W. G., & Mondy, K.** (2009). Sub-optimal CD4 recovery on long-term suppressive highly active antiretroviral therapy is associated with favorable outcome. *HIV Medicine, 10* (7), 439–446.

**Ong, A. D., Fuller-Rowell, T. E., & Bonanno, G. A.** (2010). Prospective predictors of positive emotions following spousal loss. *Psychology and Aging, 25,* 653–660.

**Onifer, S. M., Smith, G. M., & Fouad, K.** (2011). Plasticity after spinal cord injury: Relevance to recovery and approaches to facilitate it. *Neurotherapeutics, 8,* 283–293.

**Onwudiwe, N. C., Stuart, B., Zuckerman, I. H., & Sorkin, J. D.** (2011). Obesity and Medicare expenditure: Accounting for age-related height loss. *Obesity, 19,* 204–211.

**Ophir, E., Nass, C., & Wagner, A. D.** (2009). Cognitive control in media multitaskers. *Proceedings of the National Academy of Sciences USA, 106,* 15583–15587.

**Oral, E., Aydin, N., Gulec, M., & Oral, M.** (2012). Panic disorder and subthreshold panic in the light of comorbidity: A follow-up study. *Comprehensive Psychiatry.* (in press)

**Orom, H., & Cervone, D.** (2009). Personality dynamics, meaning, and idiosyncrasy: Identifying cross-situational coherence by assessing personality architecture. *Journal of Research in Personality, 43,* 228–240.

**Osborn, D. P. J., Nazareth, I., & King, M. B.** (2006). Risk of coronary heart disease in people with severe mental illness: Cross-sectional comparative study in primary care. *British Journal of Psychiatry, 188,* 271–277.

**Osterman, L. L., & Brown, R. P.** (2011). Culture of honor and violence against the self. *Personality and Social Psychology Bulletin, 37,* 1611–1623.

**Ostir, G. V., Markides, K. S., Black, S. A., & Goodwin, J. S.** (2000). Emotional well-being predicts subsequent functional independence and survival. *Journal of the American Geriatrics Society, 48,* 473–478.

**Otake, K., Shimai, S., Tanaka-Matsumi, J., Otsui, K., & Fredrickson, B. L.** (2006). Happy people becoming happier through kindness: A counting kindnesses intervention. *Journal of Happiness Studies, 7,* 361–375.

**Otonari, J., & others.** (2012). Neuroticism and extraversion personality traits, health behaviors, and subjective well-being: The Fukuoka Study (Japan). *Quality of Life Research.* (in press)

**Owens, J. A., Belon, K., & Moss, P.** (2010). Impact of delaying school start time on adolescent sleep, mood, and behavior. *Archives of Pediatric and Adolescent Medicine, 164,* 608–614.

**Oyserman, D., Kemmelmeier, M., Fryberg, St., Brosh, H., & Hart-Johnson, T.** (2003). Racial-ethnic self-schemas. *Social Psychology Quarterly, 66,* 333–347.

**Oztekin, I., & Badre, D.** (2011). Distributed patterns of brain activity that lead to forgetting. *Frontiers in Human Neuroscience, 5,* 1–8.

**P**

**Packer, D. J.** (2008). Identifying systematic disobedience in Milgram's obedience experiments: A meta-analytic review. *Perspectives on Psychological Science, 3,* 301–304.

**Packer, D. J.** (2009). Avoiding groupthink: Whereas weakly identified members stay silent, strongly identified members dissent about collective matters. *Psychological Science, 20,* 546–548.

**Pagano, R. R.** (2013). *Understanding statistics in the behavioral sciences* (10th ed.). Boston: Cengage. (in press)

**Paivio, A.** (1971). *Imagery and verbal processes.* New York: Holt, Rinehart & Winston.

**Paivio, A.** (1986). *Mental representations: A dual coding approach.* New York: Oxford University Press.

**Paivio, A.** (2007). *Mind and its evolution.* Mahwah, NJ: Erlbaum.

**Paivio, A., & Sadoski, M.** (2011). Lexicons, contexts, events, and images: Commentary on Elman (2009) from the perspective of dual coding theory. *Cognitive Science, 35,* 198–209.

**Paluck, E. C., McCormack, J. P., Ensom, M. H. H., Levine, M., Soon, J. A., & Fielding, D. W.** (2006). Outcomes of bupropion therapy for smoking cessation during routine clinical use. *Annals of Pharmacotherapy, 40,* 185–190.

**Pan, A., & others.** (2012). Red meat consumption and mortality: Results from 2 prospective cohort studies. *Archives of Internal Medicine, 172,* 555–563.

**Pan, B. A.** (2011). Assessing vocabulary skills. In E. Hoff (Ed.), *Research methods in child language.* New York: Wiley.

**Pan, B. A., & Uccelli, P.** (2009). Semantic development. In J. Berko Gleason & N. Ratner (Eds.), *The development of language* (7th ed.). Boston: Allyn & Bacon.

**Pant, S., & Ramaswamy, B.** (2009). Association of major stressors with elevated risk of breast cancer incidence or relapse. *Drugs Today, 45,* 115–126.

**Pappas, S.** (2012, January 26). Low IQ & conservative beliefs linked to prejudice. *LiveScience.com.* www.livescience.com/18132-intelligence-social-conservatism-racism.html (accessed May 3, 2012)

**Parada, H., Horton, L. A., Cherrington, A., Ibarra, L., & Ayala, G. X.** (2012). Correlates of medication nonadherence among Latinos with type 2 diabetes. *Diabetes Education.* doi: 10.1177/0145721712445215

**Paralympic Movement.** (2012). Believe in yourself. www.paralympic.org/BelieveInYourself/OurHeroes (accessed June 9, 2012)

**Parati, G., Lombardi. C., & Narkiewicz, K.** (2007). Sleep apnea: Epidemiology, pathophysiology, and relation to cardiovascular risk. *American Journal of Physiology: Regulatory, Integrative and Comparative Physiology, 293,* R1671–R1683.

**Park, C. L.** (2012). Meaning making in cancer survivorship. In P. T. P. Wong (Ed.), *Handbook of meaning* (2nd ed.). Thousand Oaks, CA: Sage.

**Park, D. H., Eve, D. J., Borlongan, C. V., Klasko, S. K., Cruz, L. E., & Sanberg, P. R.** (2009). From the basics to application of cell therapy, a steppingstone to the conquest of neurodegeneration: A meeting report. *Medical Science Monitor, 15,* RA23–31.

**Park, J., Kitayama, S., Karasawa, M., Curhan, K., Markus, H. R., Kawakami, N., Miyamoto, Y., Love, G. D., Coe, C. L., & Ryff, C. D.** (2012). Clarifying the links between social support and health: Culture, stress, and neuroticism matter. *Journal of Health Psychology.* doi: 10.1177/1359105312439731

**Park, M.** (2009, April 4). Teen tries to quiet the voices caused by schizophrenia. *CNN.com* www.cnn.com/2009/HEALTH/04/24/schizophrenia.soloist.brain/index.html (accessed May 22, 2012)

**Park, S., Holloway, S. D., Arendtsz, A., & Bempechat, J.** (2012). What makes students engaged in learning? A time-use study of within- and between-individual predictors of emotional engagement in low-performing schools. *Journal of Youth and Adolescence, 41,* 390–401.

**Parker, P. S.** (2006). *Race, gender, and leadership.* Mahwah, NJ: Erlbaum.

**Parks, M. R.** (2007). *Personal relationships and personal networks.* Mahwah, NJ: Erlbaum.

Parry, A., & Matthews, P. M. (2002). Functional magnetic resonance imaging: A window into the brain. *Interdisciplinary Science Reviews, 27*, 50–60.

Pasi, M., Pogessi, A., & Pantoni, L. (2011). The use of CT in dementia. *International Psychogeriatrics, 23, Suppl. 2*, S6–S12.

Pascalls, O., & Kelly, D. J. (2008). Face processing. In M. M. Haith & J. B. Benson (Eds.), *Encyclopedia of infant and early childhood development*. Oxford, England: Elsevier.

Pashler, H., McDaniel, M., Rohrer, D., & Bjork, R. (2008). Learning styles: Concepts and evidence. *Psychological Science in the Public Interest, 9*, 105–119.

Patalano, A. L., Wengrovitz, S. M., & Sharpes, K. M. (2009). The influence of category coherence on inference about cross-classified entities. *Memory and Cognition, 37*, 21–38.

Patel, S. R., & others. (2012). A prospective study of sleep deprivation and pneumonia risk in women. *Sleep, 35*, 97–101.

Patell, E. A., Cooper, H., & Robinson, J. C. (2008). The effects of choice on intrinsic motivation and related outcomes: A meta-analysis of research findings. *Psychological Bulletin, 134*, 270–300.

Patterson, C. J. (2012). Family lives of lesbian and gay adults. In G. W. Petersen & K. R. Bush (Eds.), *Handbook of marriage and the family*. New York: Springer.

Patterson, C. J. (2012a). Sexual minority youth with sexual minority parents. In A. Ben-Arieh & others (Eds.), *Handbook of child research*. Thousand Oaks, CA: Sage.

Patterson, C. J., & Farr, R. H. (2012). Children of lesbian and gay parents: Reflections on the research–policy interface. In H. R. Schaffer & K. Durkin (Eds.), *Blackwell handbook of developmental psychology in action*. New York: Wiley-Blackwell.

Patterson, C. J., & Wainwright, J. L. (2010). Adolescents with same-sex parents: Findings from the National Longitudinal Study of Adolescent Health. In D. Brodzinsky, A. Pertman, & D. Kunz (Eds.), *Lesbian and gay adoption: A new American reality*. New York: Oxford University Press.

Pattillo, R. (2010). Are students as good at multitasking as they think? *Nurse Educator, 35*, 24.

Paul, M. A., Gray, G. W., Lieberman, H. R., Love, R. J., Miller, J. C., Trouborst, M., & Arendt, J. (2011). Phase advance with separate and combined melatonin and light treatment. *Psychopharmacology, 214*, 515–523.

Paulus, P. B. (1989). An overview and evaluation of group influence. In P. B. Paulus (Ed.), *Psychology of group influence*. Mahwah, NJ: Erlbaum.

Paunonen, S., Jackson, D., Trzebinski, J., & Forserling, F. (1992). Personality structures across cultures: A multimethod evaluation. *Journal of Personality and Social Psychology, 62*, 447–456.

Paus, T., Toro, R., Leonard, G., Lerner, J. V., Lerner, R. M., Perron, M., Pike, G. B., Richer, L., Steinberg, L., Veillete, S., & Pausova, Z. (2008). Morphological properties of the action-observation cortical network in adolescents with low and high resistance to peer influence. *Social Neuroscience, 3*, 303–316.

Pavlov, I. P. (1927). *Conditioned reflexes*. G. V. Anrep (Trans.). New York: Dover.

Pavot, W., & Diener, E. (2008). The Satisfaction with Life Scale and the emerging construct of life satisfaction. *Journal of Positive Psychology, 3*, 137–152.

Pbert, L., & others. (2012). Effect of mindfulness training on asthma quality of life and lung function: A randomized controlled trial. *Thorax*. doi:10.1136/thoraxjnl-2011-200253

Pearce, J. M., & Hall, G. (2009). A model for stimulus generalization in Pavlovian conditioning. In D. Shanks (Ed.), *Psychology of learning*. Thousand Oaks, CA: Sage.

Pearson, N. J., Johnson, L. L., & Nahin, R. L. (2006). Insomnia, trouble sleeping, and complementary and alternative medicine: Analysis of the 2002 National Health Interview Survey data. *Archives of Internal Medicine, 166*, 1775–1782.

Pedroso, I., & others. (2012). Common genetic variants and gene-expression changes associated with bipolar disorder are over-represented in brain signaling pathway genes. *Biological Psychiatry*. doi: 10.1016/j.biopsych.2011.12.031

Peigneux, P., Urbain, C., & Schmitz, R. (2012). Sleep and the brain. In C. M. Morin & C. A. Espie (Eds.), *Oxford handbook of sleep and sleep disorders*. New York: Oxford University Press.

Peleg, G., Katzier, G., Peleg, O., Kamara, M., Brodskey, L., Hel-Or, H., Keren, D., & Nevo, E. (2006). Hereditary family signature of facial expression. *Proceedings of the National Academy of Sciences USA, 103*, 15921–15926.

Pelleymounter, M. A., & others. (1995). Effects of the obese gene product on body weight regulation in ob/ob mice. *Science, 269*, 540–543.

Penedo, F. J., Molton, I., Dahn, J. R., Shen, B. J., Kinsigner, D., Traeger, L., Siegel, S., Schneiderman, N., & Antoni, M. (2006). A randomized clinical trial of group-based cognitive-behavioral stress management in localized prostate cancer: Development of stress management skills improves quality of life and benefit finding. *Annals of Behavioral Medicine, 31*, 261–270.

Penfield, W. (1947). Some observations in the cerebral cortex of man. *Proceedings of the Royal Society, 134*, 349.

Pennebaker, J. W. (1997a). *Opening up: The healing power of expressing emotions* (rev. ed.). New York: Guilford.

Pennebaker, J. W. (1997b). Writing about emotional experiences as a therapeutic experience. *Psychological Science, 8*, 162–166.

Pennebaker, J. W. (2004). *Writing to heal: A guided journal for recovering from trauma and emotional upheaval*. Oakland, CA: New Harbinger.

Pennebaker, J. W., & Chung, C. K. (2007). Expressive writing, emotional upheavals, and health. In H. S. Friedman & R. C. Silver (Eds.), *Foundations of health psychology* (pp. 263–284). New York: Oxford University Press.

Pennebaker, J. W., & Chung, C. K. (2011). Expressive writing and its links to mental and physical health. In H. S. Friedman (Ed.), *Oxford handbook of health psychology*. New York: Oxford University Press.

Peplau, L. A., & Fingerhut, A. W. (2007). The close relationships of lesbians and gay men. *Annual Review of Psychology* (vol. 58). Palo Alto, CA: Annual Reviews.

Perez-Costas, E., Melendez-Ferro, M., & Roberts, R. C. (2010). Basal ganglia pathology in schizophrenia: Dopamine connections and anomalies. *Journal of Neurochemistry, 113*, 287–302.

Perez-Costas, E., & others. (2012). Dopamine pathology in schizophrenia: Analysis of total and phosphorylated tyrosine hydroxylase in the substantia nigra. *Frontiers in Psychology*. (in press)

Perkins, A. M., Inchley-Mort, S. L., Pickering, A. D., Corr, P. J., & Burgess, A. P. (2012). A facial expression for anxiety. *Journal of Personality and Social Psychology, 102* (5), 910–924.

Perkins, D. (1994, September). Creativity by design. *Educational Leadership*, 18–25.

Perrin, J. S., Merz, S., Bennett, D. M., Currie, J., Steele, D. J., Reid, I. C., & Schwarzbauer, C. (2012). Electroconvulsive therapy reduces frontal cortical connectivity in severe depressive disorder. *Proceedings of the National Academy of Sciences USA, 109*, 5464–5468.

Pert, C. B. (1999). *Molecules of emotion*. New York: Simon & Schuster.

Pert, C. B., & Snyder, S. H. (1973). Opiate receptor: Demonstration in a nervous tissue. *Science, 179*, 1011.

Pervanidou, P., & Chrousos, G. P. (2012). Metabolic consequences of stress during childhood and adolescence. *Metabolism, 61*, 611–619.

Peters, J. L., & others. (2012). Prenatal negative life events increase cord blood IgE: Interactions with dust mite allergen and maternal atopy. *Allergy, 67*, 545–551.

Petersen, J. L., & Hyde, J. S. (2010). A meta-analytic review of research on gender differences in sexuality, 1973–2007. *Psychological Bulletin, 136*, 21–38.

Peterson, C. C., Garnett, M., Kelly, A., & Attwood, T. (2009). Everyday social and conversation applications of theory-of-mind understanding by children with autism-spectrum disorders or typical development. *European Child and Adolescent Psychology, 18*, 105–115.

Peterson, M. H., Griffith, R. L., Isaacson, J. A., O'Connell, M. S., & Mangos, P. M. (2011). Applicant faking, social desirability, and the prediction of counterproductive work behaviors. *Human Performance, 24*, 270–290.

Petri, H. L., & Govern, J. M. (2013). *Motivation* (6th ed.). Boston: Cengage.

Petruzzello, S. J. (2012). The ultimate tranquilizer: Exercise and its influence on anxiety. In E. O. Acevedo (Ed.), *Oxford handbook of exercise psychology*. New York: Oxford University Press.

Petticrew, M., Bell, R., & Hunter, D. (2002). Influence of psychological coping on survival and recurrence in people with cancer: Systematic review. *British Medical Journal, 325*, 1066–1069.

Pettigrew, T. F., & Tropp, L. R. (2006). A meta-analytic test of intergroup contact theory. *Journal of Personality and Social Psychology, 90*, 751–783.

Petty, R. E., & Brinol, P. (2008). Persuasion: From single to multiple to metacognitive processes. *Perspectives on Psychological Science, 3*, 137–147.

Petty, R. E., & Cacioppo, J. T. (1986). The elaboration likelihood of persuasion. In L. Berkowitz (Ed.), *Advances in experimental social psychology* (vol. 19). New York: Academic.

Pezdek, K. (2003). Event memory and autobiographical memory for the events of September 11, 2001. *Applied Cognitive Psychology, 17*, 1033–1045.

Pezzo, M. V. (2011). Hindsight bias: A primer for motivational researchers. *Social and Personality Psychology Compass, 5*, 665–678.

Pham, T. H. (2012). Psychology and traumatic stress. *Journal of Personality Disorders, 26*, 213–225.

Phaneuf, L., & McIntyre, L. L. (2007). Effects of individualized video feedback combined with group parent training on inappropriate maternal behavior. *Journal of Applied Behavior Analysis, 40* (4), 737–741.

Phelan, J. E., & Basow, S. A. (2007). College students' attitudes toward mental illness: An examination of the stigma process. *Journal of Applied Social Psychology, 37*, 2877–2902.

Phelan, S., Hill, J. O., Lang, W., Dibello, J. R., & Wing, R. R. (2003). Recovery from relapse among successful weight maintainers. *American Journal of Clinical Nutrition, 78*, 1079–1084.

Phillips, A. C., Batty, G. D., van Zanten, J. C. S., Veldhuijzen, M., Laust, H., Deary, I. J., Calvin, C. M., & Carroll, D. (2011). Cognitive ability in early adulthood is associated with systemic inflammation in middle age: The Vietnam experience study. *Brain, Behavior, and Immunity, 25*, 298–301.

Phillips, D. A., & Lowenstein, A. E. (2011). Early child care, education, and development. *Annual Review of Psychology* (vol. 62). Palo Alto, CA: Annual Reviews.

Phillips, K., Osborne, R. H., Giles, G. G., Dite, G., Apicella, C., Hopper, J. L., & Milne, R. L. (2008). Population-based prospective cohort study of psychosocial factors and survival of young Australian women with breast cancer. *Journal of Clinical Oncology, 26*, Suppl. 9584.

Phillips, K. J., & Mudford, O. C. (2008). Functional analysis skills training for residential caregivers. *Behavioral Interventions, 23* (1), 1–12.

Piaget, J. (1952). *The origins of intelligence in children*. New York: Oxford University Press.

Piber-Dabrowska, K., Sedek, G., & Kofta, M. (2010). The cognitive nature of prejudiced individuals. In T. Maruszewski, M. Fajkowska, & M. W. Eysenck (Eds.), *Personality from biological, cognitive, and social perspectives* (pp. 145–171). Clinton Corners, NY: Eliot Werner.

Pickering, A. D., & Smillie, L. D. (2008). The behavioral activation system: Challenges and opportunities. In P. J. Corr (Ed.), *The reinforcement sensitivity theory of personality* (pp. 120–154). New York: Cambridge University Press.

Pierce, B. H., & Gallo, D. A. (2011). Encoding modality can affect memory accuracy via retrieval orientation. *Journal of Experimental Psychology: Learning, Memory, and Cognition, 37*, 516–521.

Piff, P. K., Kraus, M. W., Côté, S., Cheng, B. H., & Keltner, D. (2010). Having less, giving more: The influence of social class on prosocial behavior. *Journal of Personality and Social Psychology, 99*, 771–784.

Pike, J. J., & Jennings, N. A. (2005). The effects of commercials on children's perceptions of gender appropriate toy use. *Sex Roles, 52*, 83–91.

Pike, K. M., Yamamiya, Y., & Konishi, H. (2011). Eating disorders in Japan: Cultural context, clinical features, and future directions. In R. H. Striegel-Moore, S. A. Wonderlich, B. T. Walsh, & J. E. Mitchell (Eds.), *Developing an evidence-based classification of eating disorders: Scientific findings for DSM-5* (pp. 335–349). Washington, DC: American Psychiatric Association.

Pilecki, B., Arentoft, A., & McKay, D. (2011). An evidence-based causal model of panic disorder. *Journal of Anxiety Disorders, 25,* 381–388.

Pillemer, D. B. (1998). *Momentous events: Vivid memories.* Cambridge, MA: Harvard University Press.

Pinel, J. P. J. (2009). *Biopsychology* (7th ed.). Upper Saddle River, NJ: Prentice-Hall.

Pines, A. M., & Maslach, C. (2002). *Experiencing social psychology* (4th ed.). New York: McGraw-Hill.

Pinker, S. (1994). *The language instinct.* New York: HarperCollins.

Piolino, P., Desgranges, B., Clarys, D., Guillery-Girard, B., Taconnat, L., Isingrini, M., & Eustache, F. (2006). Autobiographical memory, autonoetic consciousness, and self-perspective in aging. *Psychology and Aging, 21,* 510–525.

Pirooznia, M., & others. (2012). Data mining approaches for genome-wide association of mood disorders. *Psychiatric Genetics, 22,* 55–61.

Plotnikoff, R. C., & others. (2011). A test of the theory of planned action to explain physical activity in a large population of adolescents from Alberta, Canada. *Journal of Adolescent Health, 49,* 547–549.

Pogue, D. (2012, January 26). Embracing the mothers of invention. *New York Times,* B1.

Poirier, J., & Cobb, N. K. (2012). Social influences as a driver of engagement in a web-based health intervention. *Journal of Medical Internet Research, 14* (1), e36.

Pollard, H. (2012). For people with persistent tension-type neck pain, a multicomponent pain and stress management intervention gives better improvement in ability to control pain and self-efficacy, but not disability, than physical therapy. *Evidence Based Medicine.* (in press)

Pomerantz, E. M., Saxon, J. L., & Oishi, S. (2000). The psychological trade-offs of goal investment. *Journal of Personality and Social Psychology, 79,* 617–630.

Pompili, M., Amador, X. F., Girardi, P., Harkavy-Friedman, J., & others. (2007). Suicide risk in schizophrenia: Learning from the past to change the future. *Annals of General Psychiatry, 6,* 10.

Popeo, D. M. (2009). Electroconvulsive therapy for depressive episodes: A brief review. *Geriatrics, 64,* 9–12.

Popp, A. (2006, November). *Inequality and segregation as correlates of urban crime rates.* Paper presented at the annual meeting of the American Society of Criminology (ASC), Los Angeles.

Porter, S., & ten Brinke, L. (2008). Reading between the lies: Identifying concealed and falsified emotions in universal facial expressions. *Psychological Science, 19,* 508–514.

Posner, J., Russell J., & Peterson, B. S. (2005). The circumplex model of affect: An integrative approach to affective neuroscience, cognitive development, and psychopathology. *Developmental Psychopathology, 17,* 715–734.

Post, J. M., & Panis, L. K. (2011). Crimes of obedience: "Groupthink" at Abu Ghraib. *International Journal of Group Psychotherapy, 61,* 48–66.

Postel, M. G., de Haan, H. A., & de Jong, C. A. (2010). Evaluation of an e-therapy program for problem drinkers: A pilot study. *Substance Use and Misuse, 45* (12), 2059–2075.

Potter, N. N. (2012). Mad, bad, or virtuous? The moral, cultural, and pathologizing features of deviance. *Theory & Psychology, 22,* 23–45.

Powell, D. M., Spencer, M. B., & Petrie, K. J. (2011). Automated collection of fatigue ratings at the top of descent: A practical commercial airline tool. *Aviation, Space, and Environmental Science, 82,* 1037–1041.

Powell, R. A., & Honey, P. L. (2013). *Introduction to learning and behavior* (4th ed.). Boston: Cengage.

Pratt, L. A., Brody, D. J., & Gu, Q. (2011, October). Antidepressant use in persons aged 12 and over: United States 2005–2008. *NCHS Data Brief, 76,* 1–10.

Prescott, J., & others. (2011). Genome-wide association study of relative telomere length. *PLoS One, 10* (5), e19635.

Pressman, J. (1998). *Last resort, Psychosurgery and the limits of medicine.* New York: Cambridge University Press.

Prestwich, A., & others. (2012). Randomized controlled trial of collaborative implementation intentions targeting working adults' physical activity. *Health Psychology.* (in press)

Price, D. D., Finniss, D. G., & Benedetti, F. (2008). A comprehensive review of the placebo effect. *Annual Review of Psychology* (vol. 59). Palo Alto, CA: Annual Reviews.

Prinstein, M. J. (2007). Moderators of peer contagion: A longitudinal examination of depression socialization between adolescents and their best friends. *Journal of Clinical Child and Adolescent Psychology, 36,* 159–170.

Prislin, R., & Crano, W. D. (2012). History of social influence research. In A. W. Kruglanski & W. Stroebe (Eds.), *Handbook of the history of social psychology.* New York: Psychology Press.

Procaccini, C., Jirillo, E., & Matarese, G. (2012). Leptin as a neuromodulator. *Molecular Aspects of Medicine, 33,* 35–45.

Prochaska, J. O., DiClemente, C. C., & Norcross, J. C. (1992). In search of how people change: Applications to addictive behaviors. *American Psychologist, 47,* 1102–1114.

Prochaska, J. O., & Norcross, J. C. (2010). *Systems of psychotherapy* (7th ed.). Pacific Grove, CA: Brooks/Cole.

Prochaska, J. O., Norcross, J. C., & DiClemente, C. C. (1994). *Changing for good: A revolutionary six-stage program for overcoming bad habits and moving your life positively forward.* New York: Avon.

Pronk, T. M., Karremans, J. C., Overbeek, G., Vermulst, A. A., & Wigboldus, D. H. J. (2010). What it takes to forgive: When and why executive functioning facilitates forgiveness. *Journal of Personality and Social Psychology, 98,* 119–131.

Provenzo, E. F. (2002). *Teaching, learning, and schooling in American culture: A critical perspective.* Boston: Allyn & Bacon.

Provine, R. R., Spencer, R. J., & Mandell, D. L. (2007). Emotional expression online: Emoticons punctuate website text messages. *Journal of Language and Social Psychology, 26,* 299–307.

Pryce, C. R., & others. (2011). Helplessness: A systematic translational review of theory and evidence for its relevance to understanding and treating of depression. *Pharmacology and Therapeutics, 132,* 242–267.

Ptak, R., & Schnider, A. (2011). The attention network of the human brain: Relating structural damage associated with spatial neglect to functional imaging correlates of spatial attention. *Neuropsychologia, 49,* 3063–3070.

Puddicombe, A. (2008). Meditation in the workplace. *Management Issues.* http://www.management-issues.com/2008/1/8/opinion/meditation-in-the-workplace.asp (accessed April 2, 2012)

Pukrop, R., Sass, H., & Steinmeyer, E. M. (2000). Circumplex models for the similarity relationships between higher-order factors of personality and personality disorders: An empirical analysis. *Contemporary Psychiatry, 41,* 438–445.

Pull, C. B. (2012). Current status of knowledge about public speaking anxiety. *Current Opinion in Psychiatry, 25,* 32–38.

Puttonen, S., Viitasalo, K., & Harma, M. (2011). Effect of shiftwork on systemic markers of inflammation. *Chronobiology International, 28,* 528–535.

Pyszczynski, T., Greenberg, J., Solomon, S., Arndt, J., & Schimel, J. (2004). Why do people need self-esteem? A theoretical and empirical review. *Psychological Bulletin, 130,* 435–468.

**Q**

Qian, Z. (2009). Mate selection. In D. Carr (Ed.), *Encyclopedia of the life course and human development.* Boston: Gale Cengage.

**R**

Rabasca, L. (2000, June). More psychologists in the trenches. *Monitor on Psychology, 31,* 50–51.

Rachlin, H., & Green, L. (2009). The neural basis of drug craving: An incentive-sensitization theory of addiction. In D. Shanks (Ed.), *Psychology of learning.* Thousand Oaks, CA: Sage.

Racine, M., & others. (2012a). A systematic literature review of 10 years of research on sex/gender and experimental pain perception—Part 1: Are there really differences between women and men? *Pain.* (in press)

Racine, M., & others. (2012b). A systematic literature review of 10 years of research on sex/gender and pain perception—Part 2: Do biopsychosocial factors alter pain sensitivity differently in women and men? *Pain.* (in press)

Racsmany, M., Conway, M. A., & Demeter, G. (2010). Consolidation of episodic memory during sleep: Long-term effects of retrieval practice. *Psychological Science, 21,* 80–85.

Radel, R., Sarrazin, P., & Pelletier, L. (2009). Evidence of subliminally primed motivational orientations: The effects of unconscious motivational processes on the performance of a new motor task. *Journal of Sport and Exercise Psychology, 31,* 657–674.

Radin, D. I. (2006). *Entangled minds: Extrasensory experiences in a quantum reality.* New York: Simon & Schuster.

Raine, A. (2008). From genes to brain to antisocial behavior. *Current Directions in Psychological Science, 17,* 323–328.

Raine, A., Lencz, T., Bihrle, S., LaCasse, L., & Colletti, P. (2000). Reduced prefrontal gray matter volume and reduced autonomic activity in antisocial personality disorder. *Archives of General Psychiatry, 57,* 119–127.

Raine, A., Venables, P. H., & Williams, M. (1990). Relationships between N1, P300 and CNV recorded at age 15 and criminal behavior at age 24. *Psychophysiology, 27,* 567–575.

Rai, T. S., & Fiske, A. P. (2011). Moral psychology is relationship regulation: Moral motives for unity, hierarchy, equality, and proportionality. *Psychological Review, 118,* 57–75.

Rais, M., & others. (2012). Brain volume reductions in medication-naïve patients with schizophrenia in relation to intelligence quotient. *Psychological Medicine.* (in press)

Rajaratnam, S. M., & others. (2011). Sleep disorders, health, and safety in police officers. *Journal of the American Medical Association, 306,* 2567–2578.

Ramachandran, V. S. (2008). Mirror neurons and imitation as the driving force behind "the great leap forward" in human evolution. EDGE: The third culture. www.edge.org/3rd_culture/ramachandran/ramachandran_p1.html.

Ramachandran V. S., & Oberman, L. S. (2006). Broken mirrors: A theory of autism. *Scientific American, 295,* 62–69.

Ramirez-Esparza, N., Gosling, S. D., Benet-Martinez, V., Potter, J. P., & Pennebaker, J. W. (2006). Do bilinguals have two personalities? A special case of cultural frame switching. *Journal of Research in Personality, 40,* 99–120.

Ramirez-Maestre, C., Esteve, R., & Lopez, A. E. (2012). The role of optimism and pessimism in chronic pain patients' adjustment. *Spanish Journal of Psychology, 15,* 286–294.

Ramponi, C., Barnard, P. J., Kherif, F., & Henson, R. N. (2011). Voluntary explicit versus involuntary conceptual memory are associated with dissociable fMRI responses in hippocampus, amygdala, and parietal cortex for emotional and neutral word pairs. *Journal of Cognitive Neuroscience, 23,* 1935–1951.

Ramsey, J. L., Langlois, J. H., Hoss, R. A., Rubenstein, A. J., & Griffin, A. M. (2004). Origins of a stereotype: Categorization of facial attractiveness by 6-month-old infants. *Developmental Science, 7* (2), 201–211.

Rapaport, D. (1967). On the psychoanalytic theory of thinking. In M. M. Gill (Ed.), *The collected papers of David Rapaport.* New York: Basic Books.

Rapaport, S. (1994, November 28). Interview. *U.S. News and World Report,* 94.

Rasmussen, K. A., & Wingate, L. R. (2011). The role of optimism in the interpersonal-psycholgoical theory of suicidal behavior. *Suicide and Life-Threatening Behavior, 41,* 137–148.

Rathunde, K. (2010). Experiential wisdom and optimal experience: Interviews with three distinguished lifelong learners. *Journal of Adult Development, 17,* 81–93.

**Raven, P. H., & others.** (2011). *Biology* (9th ed.). New York: McGraw-Hill.

**Raw, R. K., Wilkie, R. M., Culmer, P. R., & Mon-Williams, M.** (2012). Reduced motor asymmetry in older adults when manually tracing paths. *Experimental Brain Research, 217,* 35–41.

**Ray, W. J.** (2012). *Methods toward a science of behavior and experience* (10th ed.). Boston: Cengage.

**Raynor, H. A., Jeffrey, R. W., Phelan, S., Hill, J. O., & Wing, R. R.** (2005). Amount of food groups variety consumed in the diet and long term weight loss maintenance. *Obesity Research, 13,* 883–890.

**Raz, A.** (2011). Hypnosis: A twilight zone of the top-down variety: Few have never heard of hypnosis but most know little about the potential of this mind-body regulation technique for advancing science. *Trends in Cognitive Science, 15,* 555–557.

**Raz, A., Schwiezer, H. R., Zhu, H., & Bowles, E. N.** (2010). Hypnotic dreams as a lens into hypnotic dynamics. *International Journal of Clinical and Experimental Hypnosis, 58,* 69–81.

**Raznahan, A., & others.** (2011). How does your cortex grow? *Journal of Neuroscience, 31,* 7174–7177.

**Realini, J. P., Buzi, R. S., Smith, P. B., & Martinez, M.** (2010). Evaluation of "big decisions": An abstinence-plus sexuality curriculum. *Journal of Sex & Marital Therapy, 36,* 313–326.

**Realo, A., & Dobewall, H.** (2011). Does life satisfaction change with age? A comparison of Estonia, Finland, Latvia, and Sweden. *Journal of Research in Personality, 45,* 297–308.

**Reaven, J., & others.** (2012). Group cognitive behavior therapy for children with high-functioning autism spectrum disorders and anxiety: A randomized trial. *Journal of Child Psychology and Psychiatry, 53,* 410–419.

**Recanzone, G. H., & Sutter, M. L.** (2008). The biological basis of audition. *Annual Review of Psychology* (vol. 59). Palo Alto, CA: Annual Reviews.

**Rector, N. A., & Beck, A. T.** (2001). Cognitive behavioral therapy for schizophrenia: An empirical review. *Journal of Nervous and Mental Disorders, 189,* 278–287.

**Reed, L. A., & Hicks, P. B.** (2012). Selective auditory attention in adults: Effects of rhythmic structure of the competing language. *Journal of Speech, Language, and Hearing Research.* (in press)

**Reeve, C.** (2000, May 1). Use the body's repair kit. *Time, 155,* 18.

**Reeve, C. L., & Charles, J. E.** (2008). Survey of opinions on the primacy of *g* and social consequences of ability testing: A comparison of expert and non-expert views. *Intelligence, 36,* 681–688.

**Rehfeldt, R. A.** (2011). Toward a technology of derived stimulus relations: An analysis of articles published in the *Journal of Applied Behavior Analysis,* 1992–2009. *Journal of Applied Behavior Analysis, 44,* 109–119.

**Reich, J.** (2009). Avoidant personality disorder and its relationship to social phobia. *Current Psychiatry Reports, 11,* 89–93.

**Reichardt, C. S.** (2009). Quasi-experimental designs. In R. E. Millsap & A. Maydeu-Olivares (Eds.), *The Sage handbook of quantitative methods* (pp. 46–71). Thousand Oaks, CA: Sage.

**Reiman, E. M., Fusselman, M. J., Fox, P. T., & Raichle, M. E.** (1989). Neuroanatomical correlates of anticipatory anxiety. *Science, 243,* 1071–1074.

**Reinhold, J., Mandos, L. A., Rickels, K., & Lohoff, F. W.** (2011). Pharmacological treatment of generalized anxiety disorder. *Expert Opinion on Pharmacotherapy, 12,* 2457–2467.

**Reinke-Scorzelli, M., & Scorzelli, J.** (2001). Cultural sensitivity and cognitive therapy in Thailand. *Journal of Mental Health Counseling, 23,* 85–93.

**Reis, H. T.** (2012). A brief history of relationship research in social psychology. In A. W. Kruglanski & W. Stroebe (Eds.), *Handbook of the history of social psychology.* New York: Psychology Press.

**Reis, H. T., Sheldon, K. M., Gable, S. L., Roscoe, J., & Ryan, R. M.** (2000). Daily well-being: The role of autonomy, competence, and relatedness. *Personality and Social Psychology Bulletin, 26,* 419–435.

**Reis, S. M., & Renzulli, J. S.** (2011). Intellectual giftedness. In R. J. Sternberg & S. B. Kaufman (Eds.), *Handbook of intelligence.* New York: Cambridge University Press.

**Reivich, K., & Gillham, J.** (2003). Learned optimism: The measurement of explanatory style. In S. J. Lopez & C. R. Snyder (Eds.), *Positive psychological assessment: A handbook of models and measures* (pp. 57–74). Washington, DC: American Psychological Association.

**Rendell, P. G., & Craik, F. I. M.** (2000). Virtual week and actual week: Age-related differences in prospective memory. *Applied Cognitive Psychology, 14,* S43–S62.

**Rescorla, R. A.** (1966). Predictability and number of pairings in Pavlovian fear conditioning. *Psychonomic Science, 4,* 383–384.

**Rescorla, R. A.** (1988). Pavlovian conditioning: It's not what you think it is. *American Psychologist, 43,* 151–160.

**Rescorla, R. A.** (2003). Contemporary study of Pavlovian conditioning. *Spanish Journal of Psychology, 6,* 185–195.

**Rescorla, R. A.** (2005). Spontaneous recovery of excitation but not inhibition. *Journal of Experimental Psychology: Animal Behavior Processes, 31,* 277–288.

**Rescorla, R. A.** (2009). A theory of Pavlovian conditioning: Variations in the effectiveness of reinforcement and nonreinforcement. In D. Shanks (Ed.), *Psychology of learning.* Thousand Oaks, CA: Sage.

**Rescorla, R. A., & Wagner, A. R.** (2009). A theory of attention: Variations in the associability of stimuli with reinforcement. In D. Shanks (Ed.), *Psychology of learning.* Thousand Oaks, CA: Sage.

**Reuter-Lorenz, P., & Davidson, R. J.** (1981). Differential contributions of the two cerebral hemispheres to the perception of happy and sad faces. *Neuropsychologia, 19,* 609–613.

**Revelle, W.** (2008). The contribution of reinforcement sensitivity theory to personality theory. In P. J. Corr (Ed.), *The reinforcement sensitivity theory of personality* (pp. 508–527). New York: Cambridge University Press.

**Reynolds, K. J., Haslam, S. A., & Turner, J. C.** (2012). Prejudice, social identity, and social change: Resolving the Allportian problematic. In J. Dixon, M. Keynes, & M. Levine (Eds.), *Beyond prejudice.* New York: Cambridge University Press.

**Reynolds, S., Wilson, C., Austin, J., & Hooper, L.** (2012). Effects of psychotherapy for anxiety in children and adolescents: A meta-analytic review. *Clinical Psychology Review, 32,* 251–262.

**Rhodes, R. E., & Mark, R.** (2012). Social cognitive models. In E. O. Acevedo (Ed.), *Oxford handbook of exercise psychology.* New York: Oxford University Press.

**Richter, M. A., & others.** (2012). Evidence for cortical inhibitory and excitatory dysfunction in obsessive compulsive disorder. *Neuropsychopharmacology.* (in press)

**Riediger, M., & Freund, A. M.** (2006). Focusing and restricting: Two aspects of motivational selectivity in adulthood. *Psychology and Aging, 21,* 173–185.

**Ries, M. L., & others.** (2012). Medial prefrontal functional connectivity—relation to memory self-appraisal accuracy in older adults with and without memory disorders. *Neuropsychologia, 50* (5), 603–611.

**Rips, L. J.** (2011). Causation from perception. *Perspectives on Psychological Science, 6,* 77–97.

**Rips, L. J., Smith, E. E., & Medin, D. L.** (2012). Concepts and categories: Memory, meaning, and metaphysics. In K. J. Holyoak & R. G. Morrison (Eds.), *Oxford handbook of thinking and reasoning.* New York: Oxford University Press.

**Risbrough, V. B., & Stein, M. B.** (2012). Neuropharmacology special issue on posttraumatic stress disorder (PTSD): Current state of the art in clinical and preclinical PTSD. *Neuropharmacology, 62,* 539–541.

**Rissman, J., & Wagner, A. D.** (2012). Distributed representations in memory: Insights from functional brain imaging. *Annual Review of Psychology* (vol. 63). Palo Alto, CA: Annual Reviews.

**Ritchie, E. C., Benedek, D., Malone, R., & Carr-Malone, R.** (2006). Psychiatry and the military: An update. *Psychiatric Clinics of North America, 29,* 695–707.

**Ritskes, R., Ritskes-Hoitinga, M., Stodkilde-Jorgensen, H., Baerentsen, K., & Hartman, T.** (2003). MRI scanning during Zen meditation: The picture of enlightenment? *Constructivism in the Human Sciences, 8* (1), 85–90.

**Ritter, D., & Elsea, M.** (2005). Hot sauce, toy guns, and graffiti: A critical account of current laboratory aggression paradigms. *Aggressive Behavior, 31,* 407–419.

**Rivas-Drake, D.** (2012). Ethnic identity and adjustment: The mediating role of sense of community. *Cultural Diversity and Ethnic Minority Psychology, 18* (2), 210–215.

**Rizzolatti, G., & Fabbri-Destro, M.** (2010). Mirror neurons: From discovery to autism. *Experimental Brain Research, 200,* 233–237.

**Rizzolatti, G., & Sinigaglia, C.** (2010). The functional role of the parieto-frontal mirror circuit: Interpretations and misinterpretations. *Nature Reviews: Neuroscience, 11,* 264–274.

**Robbins, T. W., Gillan, C. M., Smith, D. G., de Wit, S., & Ersche, K. D.** (2012). Neurocognitive endophenotypes of impulsivity and compulsivity: Towards dimensional psychiatry. *Trends in Cognitive Science, 16,* 81–91.

**Roberts, B. W., Jackson, J. J., Fayard, J. V., Edmonds, G., & Meints, J. O.** (2009). Conscientiousness. In M. Leary & R. Hoyle (Eds.), *Handbook of individual differences in social behavior* (pp. 369–381). New York: Guilford.

**Roberts, D. F., Henriksen, L., & Foehr, U. G.** (2009). Adolescence, adolescents, and the media. In R. M. Lerner & L. Steinberg (Eds.), *Handbook of adolescent psychology* (3rd ed.). New York: Wiley.

**Roberts, G., & others.** (2011). Can improving working memory prevent academic difficulties? A school based randomized controlled trial. *BMC Pediatrics.* doi: 10.1186/1471-2431-11-57

**Robertson, E. M.** (2012). New insights in human memory interference and consolidation. *Current Biology, 22,* R66–R71.

**Robinson-Riegler, B., & Robinson-Riegler, G. L.** (2012). *Cognitive psychology: Applying the science of the mind* (3rd ed.). Upper Saddle River, NJ: Pearson.

**Rocha, F. L., Fuzikawa, C., Riera, R., & Hara, C.** (2012). Combination of antidepressants in the treatment of major depressive disorder: A systematic review and meta-analysis. *Journal of Clinical Psychopharmacology, 32* (2), 278–281.

**Rodgers, J. L.** (2007). The shape of things to come: Diagnosing social contagion from adolescent smoking and drinking curves. In T. D. Little, J. A. Bovaird, & N. A. Card (Eds.), *Modeling contextual effects in longitudinal studies* (pp. 343–362). Mahwah, NJ: Erlbaum.

**Rodin, J.** (1984, December). Interview: A sense of control. *Psychology Today,* 38–45.

**Roediger, H. L., & Marsh, E. J.** (2003). Episodic and autobiographical memory. In I. B. Weiner (Ed.), *Handbook of psychology* (vol. 4). New York: Wiley.

**Rogers, C. R.** (1961). *On becoming a person.* Boston: Houghton Mifflin.

**Rogers, C. R.** (1980). *A way of being.* Boston: Houghton Mifflin.

**Rogers, G., & others.** (2009). The harmful health effects of recreational ecstasy: A systematic review of observational evidence. *Health Technology Assessment, 13,* 1–315.

**Rogers, H., & Maytan, M.** (2012). *Mindfulness for the next generation.* New York: Oxford University Press.

**Rohleder, N.** (2012). Acute and chronic stress induced changes in sensitivity of peripheral inflammatory pathways to the signals of multiple stress systems—2011 Curt Richter Award Winner. *Psychoneuroendocrinology.* (in press)

**Rojas, Y., & Stenberg, S. A.** (2010). Early life circumstances and male suicide—a 30-year follow-up of a Stockholm cohort born in 1953. *Social Science Medicine, 70,* 420–427.

**Roncero, M., Perpina, C., & Garcia-Soriano, G.** (2011). Study of obsessive compulsive beliefs: Relationship with eating disorders. *Behavioral and Cognitive Psychotherapy, 39,* 457–470.

**Roos, C. J., Quax, P. H., & Jukema, J. W.** (2012). Cardiovascular metabolic syndrome: Mediators involved in the pathophysiology from obesity to coronary heart disease. *Biomarkers in Medicine, 6,* 35–52.

**Rosack, J.** (2007). Impact of FDA warning questioned in suicide rise. *Psychiatric News, 5,* 1.

**Rose, A. J.** (2002). Co-rumination in the friendships of girls and boys. *Child Development, 73,* 1830–1843.

Rose, A. J., Carlson, W., & Waller, E. M. (2007). Prospective associations of co-rumination with friendship and emotional adjustment: Considering the socioemotional trade-offs of co-rumination. *Developmental Psychology, 43,* 1019–1031.

Rose, A. J., & Smith, R. L. (2009). Sex differences in peer relationships. In K. H. Rubin, W. M. Bukowski, & B. Laursen (Eds.), *Handbook of peer interactions, relationships, and groups.* New York: Guilford.

Rose, N. S., & Craik, F. I. (2012). A processing approach to the working memory/long-term memory distinction: Evidence from the levels-of-processing span task. *Journal of Experimental Psychology: Learning, Memory, and Cognition.* (in press)

Rose, R. J., Koskenvuo, M., Kaprio, J., Sarna, S., & Langinvainio, H. (1988). Shared genes, shared experiences, and similarity of personality: Data from 14,228 adult Finnish co-twins. *Journal of Personality and Social Psychology, 54,* 161–171.

Rosell, D. R., & others. (2010). Increased serotonin 2A receptor availability in the orbitofrontal cortex of physically aggressive personality disordered patients. *Biological Psychiatry, 67* (12), 1154–1162.

Rosen, K., & Garety, P. (2005). Predicting recovery from schizophrenia: A retrospective comparison of characteristics at onset of people with single and multiple episodes. *Schizophrenia Bulletin, 31,* 735–750.

Rosenbaum, R. S., Kohler, S., Schacter, D. L., Moscovitch, M., Westmacott, R., Black, S. E., Gao, F., & Tulving, E. (2005). The case of K.C.: Contributions of a memory-impaired person to memory theory. *Neuropsychologia, 43,* 989–1021.

Rosenhan, D. L. (1973). On being sane in insane places. *Science, 179,* 250–258.

Rosental, B., & others. (2012). The effect of chemotherapy/radiotherapy on cancerous pattern recognition by NK cells. *Current Medicinal Chemistry, 19,* 1780–1791.

Rosenthal, D. G., Learned, N., Liu, Y. H., & Weitzman, M. (2012). Characteristics of fathers with depressed symptoms. *Maternal and Child Health Journal.* (in press)

Rosenthal, E. S. (2012). The utility of EEG, SSEP, and other neurophysiologic tools to guide neurocritical care. *Neurotherapeutics.* (in press)

Rosenthal, R. (1966). *Experimenter effects in behavioral research.* New York: Appleton-Century-Crofts.

Rosenthal, R., & Jacobsen, L. (1968). *Pygmalion in the classroom.* Fort Worth: Harcourt Brace.

Rosmarin, D. H., Krumrei, E. J., & Andersson, G. (2009). Religion as a predictor of psychological distress in two religious communities. *Cognitive Behavior Therapy, 38,* 54–64.

Rosnow, R. L., & Rosenthal, R. (2008). *Beginning behavioral research* (6th ed.). Upper Saddle River, NJ: Prentice-Hall.

Ross, C. A., Keyes, B. B., Yan, H., Wang, Z., Zou, Z., Xu, Y., Chen, J., Zhang, H., & Xiao, Z. (2008). A cross-cultural test of the trauma model of dissociation. *Journal of Trauma & Dissociation, 9,* 35–49.

Ross, C. A., & Ness, L. (2010). Symptom patterns in dissociative identity disorder patients and the general population. *Journal of Trauma and Dissociation, 11,* 458–468.

Ross, J. N., & Coleman, N. M. (2011). Gold digger or video girl: The salience of an emerging hip-hop sexual script. *Culture, Health, and Sexuality, 13,* 157–171.

Ross, K., Handel, P. J., Clark, E. M., & Vander Wal, J. S. (2009a). The relationship between religion and religious coping: Religious coping as a moderator between coping and adjustment. *Journal of Religion and Health. 48* (4), 454–467.

Ross, K. M., Milsom, V. A., Debraganza, N., Gibbons, L. M., Murawski, M. E., & Perri, M. G. (2009b). The contributions of weight loss and increased physical fitness to improvements in health-related quality of life. *Eating Behaviors, 10,* 84–88.

Ross, L., Kohler, C. L., Grimley, D. M., & Anderson-Lewis, C. (2007). The theory of reasoned action and intention to seek cancer information. *American Journal of Health Behavior, 31,* 123–134.

Rossi, E. L. (2009). The psychosocial genomics of therapeutic hypnosis, psychotherapy, and rehabilitation. *American Journal of Clinical Hypnosis, 51,* 281–298.

Rossignol, S., & Frigon, A. (2011). Recovery of locomotion after spinal cord injury: Some facts and mechanisms. *Annual Review of Neuroscience* (vol. 34). Palo Alto, CA: Annual Reviews.

Roten, R. G. (2007). DSM-IV and the taxonomy of roles: How can the taxonomy of roles complement the DSM-IV to create a more holistic diagnostic tool? *The Arts in Psychotherapy, 34,* 53–68.

Rotge, J. Y., & others. (2009). Inverse relationship between thalamic and orbitofrontal volumes in obsessive-compulsive disorder. *Progress in Neuro-Psychopharmacology & Biological Psychiatry, 33,* 682–686.

Rothbaum, F., Kakinuma, M., Nagaoka, R., & Azuma, H. (2007). Attachment and AMAE: Parent–child closeness in the United States and Japan. *Journal of Cross-Cultural Psychology, 38,* 465–486.

Rothbaum, F., Weisz, J., Pott, M., Miyake, K., & Morelli, G. (2000). Attachment and culture: Security in the United States and Japan. *American Psychologist, 55* (10), 1093–1104.

Rouder, J. N., & Morey, R. D. (2009). The nature of psychological thresholds. *Psychological Review, 116,* 655–660.

Rouder, J. N., & Morey, R. D. (2011). A Bayes factor meta-analysis of Bem's ESP claim. *Psychonomic Bulletin & Review, 18,* 682–689.

Rozin, P., Kabnick, K., Pete, E., Fischler, C., & Shields, C. (2003). The ecology of eating: Smaller portion sizes in France than in the United States help explain the French paradox. *Psychological Science, 14,* 450–454.

Rozin, P., Scott, S., Dingley, M., Urbanek, J. K., Jiang, H., & Kaltenbach, M. (2011). Nudge to nobesity I: Minor changes in accessibility decrease food intake. *Judgment and Decision Making, 6,* 323–332.

Rubin, D. C. (2011). The coherence of memories for trauma: Evidence from posttraumatic stress disorder. *Consciousness and Cognition, 20,* 857–865.

Rubin, Z., & Mitchell, C. (1976). Couples research as couples counseling: Some unintended effects of studying close relationships. *American Psychologist, 31,* 17–25.

Ruck, C. (2003). Psychosurgery. *Journal of Neurosurgery, 99,* 1113–1114.

Rudy, D., & Grusec, J. E. (2006). Authoritarian parenting in individualist and collectivist groups: Associations with maternal emotion and cognition and children's self-esteem. *Journal of Family Psychology, 20,* 68–78.

Ruini, C., Belaise, C., Brombin, C., Caffo, E., & Fava, G. A. (2006). Well-being therapy in school settings: A pilot study. *Psychotherapy and Psychosomatics, 75,* 331–336.

Ruini, C., & Fava, G. A. (2004). Clinical applications of well-being therapy. In A. Linley & S. Joseph (Eds.), *Positive psychology in practice* (pp. 371–387). Hoboken, NJ: Wiley.

Ruini, C., & Fava, G. A. (2009). Well-being therapy for generalized anxiety disorder. *Journal of Clinical Psychology, 65,* 510–519.

Runyon, W. M. (2007). *Psychology and historical interpretation.* New York: Oxford University Press.

Rusbult, C. E., Agnew, C. R., & Arriaga, X. B. (2012). The investment model of commitment processes. In P. A. M. Van Lange, A. W. Kruglanski, & E. T. Higgins (Eds.), *Handbook of theories of social psychology* (vol. 2, pp. 218–231). Thousand Oaks, CA: Sage.

Rusbult, C. E., Kumashiro, M., Coolsen, M. K., & Kirchner, J. L. (2004). Interdependence, closeness, and relationships. In D. J. Mashek & A. P. Aaron (Eds.), *Handbook of closeness and intimacy* (pp. 137–161). Mahwah, NJ: Erlbaum.

Ruscher, S. M., & Gotlib, I. H. (1988). Marital interaction patterns of couples with and without a depressed partner. *Behavior Therapy, 19,* 455–470.

Rush, C. C., Becker, S. J., & Curry, J. F. (2009). Personality factors and styles among college students who binge eat and drink. *Psychology of Addictive Behaviors, 23,* 140–145.

Rushton, J. P., & Irwing, P. (2009). A general factor of personality in the Comrey Personality Scales, Minnesota Multiphasic Personality Inventory-2 and the Multicultural Personality Questionnaire. *Personality and Individual Differences, 46,* 437–442.

Rutter, M., & Dodge, K. A. (2011). Gene–environment interaction: State of the science. In K. A. Dodge & M. Rutter (Eds.), *Gene–environment interaction and developmental psychopathology.* New York: Guilford.

Ryan, R. M., & Deci, E. L. (2000). Self-determination theory and the facilitation of intrinsic motivation, social development, and well-being. *American Psychologist, 55,* 68–78.

Ryan, R. M., & Deci, E. L. (2001). On happiness and human potentials: A review of research on hedonic and eudaimonic well-being. *Annual Review of Psychology* (vol. 52). Palo Alto, CA: Annual Reviews.

Ryan, R. M., & Deci, E. L. (2009). Promoting self-determined school engagement, motivation, learning, and well-being. In K. R. Wentzel & A. Wigfield (Eds.), *Handbook of research on schools, schooling, and human development.* New York: Routledge.

Ryan, R. M., & Deci, E. L. (2011). A self-determination theory perspective on social, institutional, cultural, and economic supports for autonomy and their importance for well-being. In V. I. Chirkov, R. M. Ryan, & K. M. Sheldon (Eds.), *Human autonomy in cross-cultural context: Perspectives on the psychology of agency, freedom, and well-being* (pp. 45–64). New York: Springer Science + Business Media.

Ryan, R. M., Huta, V., & Deci, E. L. (2008). Living well: A self-determination theory perspective on eudaimonia. *Journal of Happiness Studies, 9,* 139–170.

Ryckman, R. M. (2013). *Theories of personality* (10th ed.). Boston: Cengage.

Rydell, R. J., & Boucher, K. L. (2010). Capitalizing on multiple social identities to prevent stereotype threat: The moderating role of self-esteem. *Personality and Social Psychology Bulletin, 36,* 239–250.

Ryff, C. D., & Singer, B. (1998). Contours of positive human health. *Psychological Inquiry, 9,* 1–28.

Ryff, C. D., Singer, B. H., & Love, G. D. (2004). Positive health: Connecting well-being with biology. *Philosophical Transactions of the Royal Society of London, 359,* 1383–1394.

Rymer, R. (1993). *Genie.* New York: HarperCollins.

## S

Sabanayagam, C., & Shankar, A. (2010). Sleep duration and cardiovascular disease: Results from the National Health Survey. *Sleep, 33,* 1037–1042.

Sabunciyan, S., & others. (2012). Genome-wide DNA methylation scan in major depressive disorder. *PLoS One, 7* (4), e34451.

Sacco, D. F., & Hugenberg, K. (2009). The look of anger and fear: Facial maturity modulates recognition of fearful and angry expressions. *Emotion, 9,* 39–49.

Sacerdote, P., & Levrini, L. (2012). Peripheral mechanisms of dental pain: The role of substance P. *Mediators of Inflammation.* doi: 10.1155/2012/951920

Sachs, J. (2009). Communication development in infancy. In J. Berko Gleason & N. Ratner (Eds.), *The development of language* (7th ed.). Boston: Allyn & Bacon.

Sachs, R., & others. (2012). Smoking cessation interventions in the pre-admission clinic: Assessing two approaches. *Canadian Journal of Anesthetics.* (in press)

Sack, R. L. (2010). Clinical practice. Jet lag. *New England Journal of Medicine, 362,* 440–447.

Sacks, O. (2006, June 19). Stereo Sue. *New Yorker,* 64–73.

Sado, M., Knapp, M., Yamauchi, K., Fujisawa, D., So, M., Nakagawa, A., Kikuchi, T., & Ono, Y. (2009). Cost-effectiveness of combination therapy versus antidepressant therapy for management of depression in Japan. *Australian and New Zealand Journal of Psychiatry, 43,* 539–547.

Safir, M. P., Wallach, H. S., & Bar-Zvi, M. (2012). Virtual reality cognitive-behavior therapy for public speaking anxiety: One-year follow-up. *Behavior Modification, 36,* 235–246.

Sahly, J., Shaffer, T. W., Erdberg, P., & O'Toole, S. (2011). Rorschach intercoder reliability for protocol-level comprehensive system variables in an international sample. *Journal of Personality Assessment, 93,* 592–596.

Saleem, M., & Anderson, C. A. (2012). The good, the bad, and the ugly of electronic media. In J. Dvoskin, J. L. Skeem, R. W. Novaco, & K. S. Douglas (Eds.), *Applying social science to reduce violent offending.* New York: Oxford University Press.

Salkind, N. J. (2012). *Exploring research* (8th ed.). Upper Saddle River, NJ: Pearson.

housing. *American Journal of Geriatric Psychiatry, 20,* 441–451.

Simon, H. A. (1969). *The sciences of the artificial.* Cambridge, MA: MIT Press.

Simon, W., & Sliwka, P. (2012). Effectiveness of group psychotherapy for adult outpatients traumatized by abuse, neglect, and/or pregnancy loss: A multiple-site, pre-post-follow-up, naturalistic study. *International Journal of Group Psychotherapy, 62,* 283–308.

Simons, D. J., & Chabris, C. F. (1999). Gorillas in our midst: Sustained inattentional blindness for dynamic events. *Perception, 28* (9), 1059–1074.

Simons, D. J., & Chabris, C. F. (2011). What people believe about how memory works: A representative survey of the U.S. population. *PLoS One, 6* (8), e22757.

Simpkins, S. D., Bouffard, S. M., Dearing, E., Kreider, H., Wimer, C., Caronongan, P., & Weiss, H. B. (2009). Adolescent adjustment and patterns of parents' behaviors in early and middle adolescence. *Journal of Research on Adolescence, 19,* 530–557.

Simpson, J. A., & Rholes, W. S. (2010). Attachment and relationships: Milestones and future directions. *Journal of Social and Personal Relationships, 27,* 173–180.

Sin, N. L., & Lyubomirsky, S. (2009). Enhancing well-being and alleviating depressive symptoms with positive psychology interventions: A practice-friendly meta-analysis. *Journal of Clinical Psychology, 65,* 467–487.

Singer, J. A., & Blagov, P. (2004). The integrative function of narrative processing: Autobiographical memory, self-defining memories, and the life story of identity. In D. R. Beike, J. M. Lampinen, & D. A. Behrend (Eds.), *The self and memory* (pp. 117–138). New York: Psychology Press.

Singer, J. A., & Conway, M. A. (2008). Should we forget about forgetting? *Memory Studies, 1,* 279–285.

Singer, J. A., & Conway, M. A. (2011). Reconsidering therapeutic action: Loewald, cognitive neuroscience, and the integration of memory's duality. *International Journal of Psychoanalysis, 92,* 1183–1207.

Singh-Manoux, A., Kivimaki, M., Glymour, M. M., Elbaz, A., Berr, C., Ebmeier, K. P., Ferrie, J. E., & Dugravot, A. (2012). Timing of onset of cognitive decline: Results from Whitehall II prospective cohort study. *British Medical Journal, 344,* 1–8.

Sinn, D. L., Gosling, S. D., & Moltschaniwskyj, N. A. (2008). Development of shy/bold behaviour in squid: Context-specific phenotypes associated with developmental plasticity. *Animal Behaviour, 75,* 433–442.

Sinn, D. L., Moltschaniwskyj, N. A., Wapstra, E., & Dall, S. R. X. (2010). Are behavioral syndromes invariant? Spatiotemporal variation in shy/bold behavior in squid. *Behavioral Ecology and Sociobiology, 64,* 693–702.

Sintov, N. D., & others. (2010). Empirically defined subtypes of alcohol dependence in an Irish family sample. *Drug and Alcohol Dependence, 107,* 230–236.

Sitnikova, T., Goff, D., & Kuperberg, G. R. (2009). Neurocognitive abnormalities during comprehension of real-world goal-directed behaviors in schizophrenia. *Journal of Abnormal Psychology, 118,* 256–277.

Sivacek, J., & Crano, W. D. (1982). Vested interest as a moderator of attitude-behavior consistency. *Journal of Personality and Social Psychology, 43* (2), 210–221.

Sjoberg, R. L., Ducci, F., Barr, C. S., Newman, T. K., Dell'Osso, L., Virkkunen, M., & Goldman, D. (2008). A non-additive interaction of a functional MAO-A VNTR and testosterone predicts antisocial behavior. *Neuropsychopharmacology, 33,* 425–430.

Skelton, K., Ressler, K. J., Norrholm, S. D., Jovanovic, T., & Bradley-Davino, B. (2012). PTSD and gene variants: New pathways and new thinking. *Neuropharmacology, 62,* 628–637.

Skinner, B. F. (1938). *The behavior of organisms: An experimental analysis.* New York: Appleton-Century-Crofts.

Skinner, B. F. (1957). *Verbal behavior.* New York: Appleton-Century-Crofts.

Skodol, A. E. (2012a). Diagnosis and DSM-5: Work in progress. In T. Widiger (Ed.), *Oxford handbook of personality disorders.* New York: Oxford University Press.

Skodol, A. E. (2012b). Personality disorders in DSM-5. *Annual Review of Clinical Psychology* (vol. 8). Palo Alto, CA: Annual Reviews.

Skolin I., Wahlin, Y. B., Broman, D. A., Koivisto Hursti, U., Vikström, L. M., & Hernell, O. (2006). Altered food intake and taste perception in children with cancer after start of chemotherapy: Perspectives of children, parents and nurses. *Supportive Care in Cancer, 14,* 369–378.

Slater, A. M., Riddell, P., Quinn, P. C., Pacalis, O., Lee, K., & Kelly, D. J. (2011). Visual perception. In U. Goswami (Ed.), *Wiley-Blackwell handbook of childhood cognitive development* (2nd ed.). New York: Wiley Blackwell.

Slater, C., & Dymond, S. (2011). Using differential reinforcement to improve equine welfare: Shaping appropriate truck loading and feet handling. *Behavioral Processes, 86,* 329–339.

Sloane, S., Baillargeon, R., & Premack, D. (2012). Do infants have a sense of fairness? *Psychological Science, 23,* 196–204.

Slotnick, S. D., & Schacter, D. L. (2006). The nature of memory related activity in early visual areas. *Neuropsychologia, 44,* 2874–2886.

Smallwood, J., Schooler, J. W., Turk, D. J., Cunningham, S. J., Burns, P., & Macrae, C. N. (2011). Self-reflection and the temporal focus of the wandering mind. *Consciousness and Cognition, 20,* 1120–1126.

Smetana, J. G., Villalobos, M., Rogge, R. D., & Tasopoulos-Chan, M. (2010). Keeping secrets from parents: Daily variations among poor, urban adolescents. *Journal of Adolescence, 33,* 321–331.

Smillie, L. D., Cooper, A., Wilt, J., & Revelle, W. (2012). Do extraverts get more bang for the buck? Refining the affective-reactivity hypothesis of extraversion. *Journal of Personality and Social Psychology.* (in press)

Smit, F., Willemse, G., Koopmanschap, M., Onrust, S., Cuijpers, P., & Beekman, A. (2006). Cost-effectiveness of preventing depression in primary care patients: Randomized trial. *British Journal of Psychiatry, 188,* 330–336.

Smit, Y., & others. (2012). The effectiveness of long-term psychoanalytic psychotherapy—A meta-analysis of randomized controlled trials. *Clinical Psychology Review, 32,* 81–92.

Smith, A. R., & others. (2012). An examination of environmental and genetic contributions to the determinants of suicidal behavior among male twins. *Psychiatry Research.* doi: 10.1016/j.psychres.2012.01.010

Smith, C. P. (Ed.). (1992). *Thematic content analysis for motivation and personality research.* New York: Cambridge University Press.

Smith, H. S. (2010). The role of genomic oxidative-reductive balance as predictor of complex regional pain syndrome development: A novel theory. *Pain Physician, 13,* 79–90.

Smith, J. A., Greer, T., Sheets, T., & Watson, S. (2011). Is there more to yoga than exercise? *Alternative Therapies in Health and Medicine, 17,* 22–29.

Smith, M. C., Bibi, U., & Sheard, D. E. (2003). Evidence for the differential impact of time and emotion on personal and event memories for September 11, 2001. *Applied Cognitive Psychology, 17,* 1047–1055.

Smith, P. K., & Bargh, J. A. (2008). Nonconscious effects of power on basic approach and avoidance tendencies. *Social Cognition, 26,* 1–24.

Smith, R. A., & Davis, S. F. (2010). *Psychologist as detective* (5th ed.). Boston: Cengage.

Smith, R. E., Horn, S. S., & Bayen, U. J. (2012). Prospective memory in young and older adults: The effects of ongoing task load. *Neuropsychology, Development, and Cognition: Aging, Neuropsychology, and Cognition.* (in press)

Smith, R. L., & Rose, A. J. (2011). The "cost of caring" in youths' friendships: Considering associations among social perspective-taking, co-rumination, and empathetic distress. *Developmental Psychology, 47,* 1792–1803.

Smith, R. L., Rose, A. J., & Schwartz-Mette, R. A. (2010). Relational and overt aggression in childhood and adolescence: Clarifying mean-level gender differences and associations with peer acceptance. *Social Development, 19,* 243–269.

Smyth, J. (1998). Written emotional expression: Effect sizes, outcome types, and moderating variables. *Journal of Consulting and Clinical Psychology, 66,* 174–184.

Sneed, R., Cohen, S., Turner, R. B., & Doyle, W. A. (2012). Parenthood and host resistance to the common cold. *Psychosomatic Medicine.* (in press)

Snowden, M., Steinman, L., Mochan, K., Grodstein, F., Prohaska, T. R., Thurman, D. J., Brown, D. R., Laditka, J. N., Soares, J., Zweiback, D. J., Little, D., & Anderson, L. A. (2011). Effect of exercise on cognitive performance in community-dwelling older adults: Review of intervention trials and recommendations for public health practice and research. *Journal of the American Geriatrics Society, 59,* 704–716.

Snowdon, D. A. (2003). Healthy aging and dementia: Findings from the Nun Study. *Annals of Internal Medicine, 139,* 450–454.

Snowdon, D. A. (2007, April). *Aging with grace: Findings from the Nun Study.* Paper presented at the 22nd annual Alzheimer's regional conference, Seattle.

Snyder, C. R., Lopez, S. J., & Pedrotti, J. T. (2010). *Positive psychology.* Thousand Oaks, CA: Sage.

Snyder, J. S., & Cameron, H. A. (2011). Could adult hippocampal neurogenesis be relevant for human behavior? *Behavioural Brain Research.* doi: 10.1016/j.bbr.2011.06.02

Solesio-Jofre, E., & others. (2011). Age effects on retroactive interference during working memory maintenance. *Biological Psychology, 88,* 72–82.

Soloff, P. H., Lis, J. A., Kelly, T., Cornelius, J., & others. (1994). Self-mutilation and suicidal behavior in borderline personality disorder. *Journal of Personality Disorders, 8,* 257–267.

Solomon, S., Greenberg, J., & Pyszczynski, T. (1991). Terror management theory of self-esteem. In C. R Snyder & D. R. Forsyth (Eds.), *Handbook of social and clinical psychology: The health perspective* (pp. 21–40). Elmsford, NY: Pergamon.

Solomon, Z., Horesh, D., Ein-Dor, T., & Ohry, A. (2012). Predictors of PTSD trajectories following captivity: A 35-year longitudinal study. *Psychiatry Research.* (in press)

Sommer, M., Hajak, G., Dohnel, K., Schwerdtner, J., Meinhardt, J., & Muller, J. L. (2006). Integration of emotion and cognition in patients with psychopathy. *Progress in Brain Research, 156C,* 457–466.

Sommer, V., & Vasey, P. L. (Eds.). (2006). *Homosexual behaviour in animals: An evolutionary perspective.* New York: Cambridge University Press.

Song, A. V., & Halpern-Felsher, B. L. (2010). Predictive relationship between adolescent oral and vaginal sex: Results from a prospective, longitudinal study. *Archives of Pediatric and Adolescent Medicine, 165,* 243–249.

Song, S. (2006, March 27). Mind over medicine. *Time, 167,* 13.

Soomro, G. M. (2012). Obsessive-compulsive disorder. *Clinical Evidence.* (in press)

Sotres-Bayon, F., Diaz-Mataix, L., Bush, D. E., & LeDoux, J. E. (2009). Dissociable roles for the ventromedial prefrontal cortex and amygdale in fear extinction: NR2B contribution. *Cerebral Cortex, 19,* 472–482.

South, S. C., & Krueger, R. F. (2008). And interactionist on genetic and environmental contributions to personality. *Social and Personality Psychology Compass, 2,* 929–948.

Spanos, N. P. (1996). *Multiple identities and false memories: A sociocognitive perspective.* Washington, DC: American Psychological Association.

Sparks, J. R., & Areni, C. S. (2008). Style versus substance: Multiple roles of language power in persuasion. *Journal of Applied Social Psychology, 38,* 37–60.

Sparling, P., & Redican, K. (2012). *iHealth: An interactive framework.* New York: McGraw-Hill.

Sparreboom, M., Snik, A. F., & Mylanus, E. A. (2012). Sequential bilateral cochlear implantation in children: Quality of life. *Archives of Otolaryngology—Head and Neck Injury, 138* (2), 134–141.

Sparrow, B., Liu, J., & Wegner, D. M. (2011). Google effects on memory: Cognitive consequences of having information at our fingertips. *Science, 333,* 776–778.

Speakman, J. R., & others. (2011). Set points, settling points, and some alternative models: Theoretical options to understand how genes and environments combine to regulate body adiposity. *Disease Models and Mechanisms, 4,* 733–745.

**Spearman, C.** (1904). "General intelligence" objectively determined and measured. *American Journal of Psychology, 15,* 201–293.

**Specht, J., Egloff, B., & Schmukle, S. C.** (2011). Stability and change of personality across the life course: The impact of age and major life events on mean-level and rank-order stability of the Big Five. *Journal of Personality and Social Psychology, 101,* 862–882.

**Spekhard, A., & Akhmedova, K.** (2005). Talking to terrorists. *Journal of Psychohistory, 33,* 125–156.

**Spence, K. W.** (1938). Gradual versus sudden solution of discrimination problems by chimpanzees. *Journal of Comparative Psychology, 25,* 213–224.

**Spencer, S. J., Steele, C. M., & Quinn, D. M.** (1999). Stereotype threat and women's math performance. *Journal of Experimental Social Psychology, 35,* 4–28.

**Sperling, G.** (1960). The information available in brief presentations. *Psychological Monographs, 74* (11).

**Sperling, R.** (2011). The potential of functional MRI as a biomarker in early Alzheimer's disease. *Neurobiology of Aging, 32, Suppl. 1,* S37–S43.

**Sperry, R. W.** (1968). Hemisphere deconnection and unity in conscious awareness. *American Psychologist, 23,* 723–733.

**Sperry, R. W.** (1974). Lateral specialization in surgically separated hemispheres. In F. O. Schmitt & F. G. Worden (Eds.), *The neurosciences: Third study program.* Cambridge, MA: MIT Press.

**Spiegel, D.** (2006). Editorial: Recognizing traumatic dissociation. *American Journal of Psychiatry, 163,* 566–568.

**Spiegel, D.** (2010). Hypnosis testing. In A. F. Barabasz, K. Olness, R. Boland, & S. Kahn (Eds.), *Medical hypnosis primer: Clinical and research evidence* (pp. 11–18). New York: Routledge/Taylor & Francis.

**Spiegler, M. D., & Guevremont, D. C.** (2010). *Contemporary behavior therapy* (5th ed.). Boston: Cengage.

**Spielberger, C. D.** (2004, August). *Type A behavior, anger-hostility, and heart disease.* Paper presented at the 28th International Congress of Psychology, Beijing, China.

**Sproesser, G., Strohbach, S., Schupp, H., & Renner, B.** (2011). Candy or apple? How self-control resources and motives impact dietary healthiness in women. *Appetite, 56,* 784–787.

**Squire, L.** (1990, June). *Memory and brain systems.* Paper presented at the meeting of the American Psychological Society, Dallas.

**Squire, L.** (2007). Memory systems as a biological concept. In H. L. Roediger, Y. Dudai, & S. Fitzpatrick (Eds.), *Science of memory: Concepts.* New York: Oxford University Press.

**Squire, L. R., & Wixted, J. T.** (2011). The cognitive neuroscience of human memory since H. M. *Annual Review of Neuroscience* (vol. 34). Palo Alto, CA: Annual Reviews.

**Sripada, K.** (2012, April 12). *Childcare update: Success stories from tribal communities.* www.letsmove.gov (accessed May 30, 2012).

**Sriram, N., & Greenwald, A. G.** (2009). The Brief Implicit Association Test. *Experimental Psychology, 56,* 283–204.

**Sroufe, L. A., Coffino, B., & Carlson, E. A.** (2010). Conceptualizing the role of early experience: Lessons from the Minnesota Longitudinal Study. *Developmental Review, 30,* 36–51.

**Stahl, T., Van Laar, C., & Ellemers, N.** (2012). The role of prevention focus under stereotype threat: Initial cognitive mobilization is followed by depletion. *Journal of Personality and Social Psychology.* (in press)

**Stanaway, J. D., & others.** (2012). Case-crossover analysis of condom use and herpes simplex virus type 2 acquisition. *Sexually Transmitted Diseases, 39,* 388–393.

**Standage, M., Gillison, F. B., Ntoumanis, N., & Treasure, D. C.** (2012). Predicting students' physical activity and health-related well-being: A prospective cross-domain investigation of motivation across school physical education and exercise settings. *Journal of Sport and Exercise Psychology, 34,* 37–60.

**Stanford Center for Longevity.** (2012). *Expert consensus on brain health.* http://longevity.stanford.edu/brain-health/expert-consensus-on-brain-health/ (accessed May 6, 2012)

**Stanger-Hall, K. F., & Hall, D. W.** (2011). Abstinence-only education and teen pregnancy rates: Why we need comprehensive sex education in the U.S. *PLoS One, 6* (10), e24658.

**Stangor, C.** (2011). *Research methods for the behavioral sciences* (4th ed.). Boston: Cengage.

**Stankewitz, A., & May, A.** (2011). Increased limbic and brainstem activity during migraine attacks following olfactory stimulation. *Neurology, 77,* 476–482.

**Stanley, J. T., & Isaacowitz, D. M.** (2011). Age-related differences in profiles of mood-change trajectories. *Developmental Psychology, 47,* 318–330.

**Stanovich, K. E.** (2010). *How to think straight about psychology* (9th ed.). Upper Saddle River, NJ: Prentice-Hall.

**Stanovich, K. E.** (2012). On the distinction between rationality and intelligence: Implications for understanding individual differences in reasoning. In K. J. Holyoak & R. G. Morrison (Eds.), *Oxford handbook of thinking and reasoning.* New York: Oxford University Press.

**Stanton, A. L., Revenson, T. A., & Tennen, H.** (2007). Health psychology: Psychological adjustment to chronic disease. *Annual Review of Psychology* (vol. 58). Palo Alto, CA: Annual Reviews.

**Starkstein, S. E.** (2012). Apathy in Parkinson's disease: Diagnostic and etiological dilemmas. *Movement Disorders.* (in press)

**Staub, E., & Vollhardt, J.** (2008). Altruism born of suffering: The roots of caring and helping after victimization and other trauma. *American Journal of Orthopsychiatry, 78,* 267–280.

**Staud, R., Price, D. D., Janicke, D., Andrade, E., Hadjipanayis, A. G., Eaton, W. T., Kaplan, L., & Wallace, M. R.** (2011). Two novel mutations of SCN9A (Nav1.7) are associated with partial congenital insensitivity to pain. *European Journal of Pain, 15,* 223–230.

**Staudinger, U. M., & Gluck, J.** (2011). Psychological wisdom research. *Annual Review of Psychology* (vol. 62). Palo Alto, CA: Annual Reviews.

**Staudt, M.** (2010). Brain plasticity following early life brain injury: Insights from neuroimaging. *Seminars in Perinatology, 34,* 87–92.

**Stay, W. B., Hallenen, T., Lane, J., & Arbesman, M.** (2012). Systematic review of occupational engagement and health outcomes among community-dwelling older adults. *American Journal of Occupational Therapy, 66,* 301–310.

**Steblay, N., Dysart, J., & Wells, G. L.** (2011). Seventy-two tests of the sequential lineup superiority effect: A meta-analysis and policy discussion. *Psychology, Public Policy, and Law, 17,* 99–139.

**Steele, C. M., & Aronson, J.** (1995). Stereotype threat and the intellectual test performance of African-Americans. *Journal of Personality and Social Psychology, 69,* 797–811.

**Steele, C. M., & Aronson, J. A.** (2004). Stereotype threat does not live by Steele and Aronson (1995) alone. *American Psychologist, 59,* 47–48.

**Steger, M. F., & Frazier, P.** (2005). Meaning in life: One link in the chain from religion to well-being. *Journal of Counseling Psychology, 52,* 574–582.

**Stehr, M. D., & von Lengerke, T.** (2012). Preventing weight gain through exercise and physical activity in the elderly: A systematic review. *Maturitas, 72,* 13–22.

**Stein, R.** (2003). *Blinded by the light.* www.theage.com.au/articles/2003/09/01/1062403448264.html?from=storyrhs (accessed July 24, 2012)

**Stenfelt, S.** (2006). Middle ear ossicles motion at hearing thresholds with air conduction and bone conduction stimulation. *Journal of the Acoustical Society of America, 119,* 2848–2858.

**Stephenson, K. M., Schroder, C. M., & Berstchy, G., & Bourgin, P.** (2012). Complex interaction of circadian and non-circadian effects of light on mood: Shedding new light on an old story. *Sleep Medicine Reviews.* (in press)

**Steptoe, A., & Kivimaki, M.** (2012). Stress and cardiovascular disease. *Nature Reviews: Cardiology, 9,* 360–370.

**Stern, B. B.** (2012). Witnessing across time: Accessing the present from the past and the past from the present. *Psychoanalytic Quarterly, 81,* 53–81.

**Stern, E. R., & others.** (2012). Subjective uncertainty and limbic hyperactivation in obsessive-compulsive disorder. *Human Brain Mapping.* (in press)

**Stern, Y., Alexander, G. E., Prohovnik, I., & Mayeux, R.** (1992). Inverse relationship between education and parietotemporal perfusion deficit in Alzheimer's disease. *Annals of Neurology, 32,* 371–375.

**Stern, Y., Scarmeas, N., & Habeck, C.** (2004). Imaging cognitive reserve. *International Journal of Psychology, 39* 18–26.

**Sternberg, E. M., & Gold, P. W.** (1996). The mind–body interaction in disease. *Mysteries of the mind.* New York: Scientific American.

**Sternberg, R. J.** (1986). *Intelligence applied.* Fort Worth: Harcourt Brace.

**Sternberg, R. J. (Ed.).** (2004). Definitions and conceptions of giftedness. Thousand Oaks, CA: Corwin Press.

**Sternberg, R. J.** (2008). The triarchic theory of human intelligence. In N. Salkind (Ed.), *Encyclopedia of educational psychology.* Thousand Oaks, CA: Sage.

**Sternberg, R. J.** (2011). The theory of successful intelligence. In R. J. Sternberg & S. B. Kaufman (Eds.), *Cambridge handbook of intelligence.* New York: Cambridge University Press.

**Sternberg, R. J.** (2012a). Human Intelligence. In V. S. Ramachandran (Ed.), *Encyclopedia of human behavior* (2nd ed.). New York: Elsevier.

**Sternberg, R. J.** (2012b). Intelligence. In I. B. Weiner & others (Eds.), *Handbook of psychology* (2nd ed.). New York: Wiley.

**Sternberg, R. J.** (2012c). Intelligence in its cultural context. In M. Gelfand, C. Y. Chiu, & Y. Y. Hong (Eds.), *Advances in cultures and psychology* (vol. 2). New York: Oxford University Press.

**Sternberg, R. J.** (2012d). Giftedness and ethics. *Gifted Education International.* doi:10.1177/0261429411435050

**Sternberg, R. J., Grigorenko, E. L., & Kidd, K. K.** (2005). Intelligence, race, and genetics. *American Psychologist, 60,* 46–59.

**Sternberg, R. J., & Sternberg, K.** (2012). *Cognitive psychology* (6th ed.). Boston: Cengage.

**Stevens, A. A., Tappon, S. C., Garg, A., & Fair, D. A.** (2012). Functional brain network modularity captures inter- and intra-individual variation in working memory capacity. *PLoS One, 7* (1), e30468.

**Stewart, A. D., & others.** (2012). Body image, shape, and volumetric assessments using 3D whole body laser scanning and 2D digital photography in females with a diagnosed eating disorder: Preliminary novel findings. *British Journal of Psychology, 103,* 183–202.

**Stice, E., Shaw, H., & Marti, C. N.** (2006). A meta-analytic review of obesity prevention programs for children and adolescents: The skinny on interventions that work. *Psychological Bulletin, 132,* 667–691.

**Stickgold, R.** (2001). Watching the sleeping brain watch us: Sensory processing during sleep. *Trends in Neuroscience, 24,* 307–309.

**Stickgold, R., & Walker, M. P.** (2005). Sleep and memory: An ongoing debate. *Sleep, 28,* 1225–1227.

**Stirling, J. D.** (2002). *Introducing neuropsychology.* East Sussex, England: Psychology Press.

**Stoner, J.** (1961). *A comparison of individual and group decisions, including risk.* Unpublished master's thesis, School of Industrial Management, MIT.

**Storm, L., Tressoldi, P. E., & Di Risio, L.** (2010). Meta-analysis of free-response studies, 1992–2008: Assessing the noise reduction model in parapsychology. *Psychological Bulletin, 136,* 471–485.

**Stott, C., Drury, J., & Reicher, S.** (2012). From "prejudice" to collective action. In J. Dixon, M. Keynes, & M. Levine (Eds.), *Beyond prejudice: Extending the social psychology of conflict, inequality, and social change* (pp. 286–303). Cambridge, England: Cambridge University Press.

**Stowell, J. R., Robles, T., & Kane, H. S.** (2013). Psychoneuroimmunology: Mechanisms, individual differences, and interventions. In I. B. Weiner & others (Eds.), *Handbook of psychology* (2nd ed., vol. 9). New York: Wiley.

**Strahan, E., Spencer, S. J., & Zanna, M. P.** (2002). Subliminal priming and persuasion: Striking while the iron is hot. *Journal of Experimental Social Psychology, 38,* 556–568.

**Straube, T., Mothes-Lasch, M., & Miltner, W. H.** (2011). Neural mechanisms of the automatic processing of emotional information from faces and voices. *British Journal of Psychology, 102,* 830–848.

**Streff, F. M., & Geller, E. S.** (1986). Strategies for motivating safety belt use: The application of applied behavior analysis. *Health Education Research, 1* (1), 47–59.

**Strike, P. C., Magid, K., Whitehead, D. L., Brydon, L., Bhattacharyya, M. R., & Steptoe, A.** (2006). Pathophysiological processes underlying emotional triggering of acute cardiac events. *Proceedings of the National Academy of Sciences USA, 103,* 4322–4327.

**Sturmer, T., Hasselbach, P., & Amelang, M.** (2006). Personality, lifestyle, and risk of cardiovascular disease and cancer: Follow-up of population-based cohort. *British Medical Journal, 332,* 1359.

**Subedi, B., & Grossberg, G. T.** (2011). Phantom limb pain: Mechanisms and treatment approaches. *Pain Research and Treatment.* doi: 10.1155/2011/864605

**Sue, D., Sue, D. W., Sue, S., & Sue, D. M.** (2013). *Understanding abnormal behavior* (10th ed.). Boston: Cengage.

**Sueur, C., Deneubourg, J. L., & Petit, O.** (2012). From social network (centralized vs. decentralized) to collective decision-making (unshared vs. shared consensus). *PLoS One, 7* (2), e32566.

**Sugranyes, G., & others.** (2012). Multimodal analyses identify linked functional and white matter abnormalities within the working memory network in schizophrenia. *Schizophrenia Research.* (in press)

**Sui, X., LaMonte, M. J., Laditka, J. N., Hardin, J. W., Chase, N., Hooker, S. P., & Blair, S. N.** (2007). Cardiorespiratory fitness and adiposity as mortality predictors in older adults. *Journal of the American Medical Association, 298,* 2507–2516.

**Suinn, R. M.** (1984). *Fundamentals of abnormal psychology.* Chicago: Nelson-Hall.

**Sullivan, H. S.** (1953). *The interpersonal theory of psychiatry.* New York: Norton.

**Sullivan, R., Wilson, D. A., Feldon, J., Yee, B. K., Meyer, U., Richter-Levin, G., Avi, A., Michael, T., Gruss, M., Bock, J., Helmeke, C., & Braun, K.** (2006). The International Society for Developmental Psychobiology Annual Meeting Symposium: Impact of early life experiences on brain and behavioral development. *Developmental Psychobiology, 48,* 583–602.

**Sullivan, S. J., Mikels, J. A., & Carstensen, L. L.** (2010). You never lose the ages you've been: Affective perspective taking in older adults. *Psychology and Aging, 251,* 229–234.

**Suls, J., & Swain, A.** (1998). Type A–Type B personalities. In H. S. Friedman (Ed.), *Encyclopedia of mental health* (vol. 3). San Diego: Academic.

**Sutin, A. R., Ferrucci, L., Zonderman, A. B., & Terracciano, A.** (2011). Personality and obesity across the adult life span. *Journal of Personality and Social Psychology, 101,* 579–592.

**Swaminathan, S. K., & Freedman, D. J.** (2012). Preferential encoding of visual categories in the parietal cortex compared with the prefrontal cortex. *Nature Neuroscience.* (in press)

**Swanson, S. A., Saito, N., Borges, G., Benjet, C., Aguilar-Gaxiola, S., Medina-Mora, M. E., & Breslan, J.** (2012). Change in binge eating and binge eating disorder associated with migration from Mexico to the US. *Journal of Psychiatric Research, 46,* 31–37.

**Syed, M.** (2010). Developing an integrated self: Academic and ethnic identities among ethnically diverse college students. *Developmental Psychology, 46,* 1590–1604.

**Syed, M., Azmitia, M., & Cooper, C. R.** (2011). Identity and academic success among underrepresented ethnic minorities: An interdisciplinary review and integration. *Journal of Social Issues, 67,* 442–468.

**Szasz, T. S.** (1961). *The myth of mental illness: Foundations of a theory of personal conduct.* New York: Hoeber-Harper.

**T**

**Tacca, M. C.** (2012). Commonalities between perception and cognition. *Frontiers in Psychology.* (in press)

**Taga, K. A., Markey, C. N., & Friedman, H. S.** (2006). A longitudinal investigation of associations between boys' pubertal timing and adult behavioral health and well-being. *Journal of Youth and Adolescence, 35,* 380–390.

**Tagliamonte, S. A., & Denis, D.** (2008). Linguistic ruin? LOL! Instant messaging and teen language. *American Speech, 83,* 3–34.

**Tahiri, M., & others.** (2012). Alternative smoking cessation aids: A meta-analysis of randomized controlled trials. *American Journal of Medicine, 125* (6), 576–584.

**Tajfel, H.** (1978). The achievement of group differentiation. In H. Tajfel (Ed.), *Differentiation between social groups.* London: Academic.

**Takahashi, Y., Roberts, B. W., & Hoshino, T.** (2012). Conscientiousness mediates the relation between perceived socialization and self-rated health. *Psychology and Health,* 1–14.

**Takano, T., Nakamura, K., & Watanabe. M.** (2002). Urban residential environments and senior citizens' longevity in mega-city areas: The importance of walkable green space. *Journal of Epidemiology and Community Health, 56,* 913–916.

**Tamburrini, G., & Mattia, D.** (2011). Disorders of consciousness and communication: Ethical motivations and communication-enabling attributes of consciousness. *Functional Neurology, 26,* (Special Issue: Coma and Consciousness), 51–54.

**Tanaka, J. W., Kaiser, M. D., Butler, S., & Le Grand, R.** (2012). Mixed emotions: Holistic and analytic perception of facial expressions. *Cognition and Emotion.* (in press)

**Tao, R., & others.** (2012). Transcript-specific associations of SLC12A5 (KCC2) in human prefrontal cortex with development, schizophrenic, and affective disorders. *Journal of Neuroscience, 32,* 5216–5522.

**Tarokh, L., & Carskadon, M. A.** (2010). Developmental changes in the human sleep EEG during early adolescence. *Sleep, 33,* 801–809.

**Tarricone, P.** (2011). *The taxonomy of metacognition.* New York: Psychology Press.

**Tarter, R. E., Vanyukov, M., Kirisci, L., Reynolds, M., & Clark, D. B.** (2006). Predictors of marijuana use in adolescents before and after illicit drug use: Examination of the gateway hypothesis. *American Journal of Psychiatry, 163,* 2134–2140.

**Tasca, G. A., Foot, M., Leite, C., Maxwell, H., Balfour, L., & Bissada, H.** (2011) Interpersonal processes in psychodynamic–interpersonal and cognitive behavioral group therapy: A systematic case study of two groups. *Psychotherapy, 48,* 260–273.

**Tasopoulos-Chan, M., Smetana, J. G., & Yau, J. P.** (2009). How much do I tell thee? Strategies for managing information to parents among American adolescents from Chinese, Mexican, and European backgrounds. *Journal of Family Psychology, 23,* 364–374.

**Taurines, R., & others.** (2011). Pharmacotherapy in depressed children and adolescents. *World Journal of Biological Psychiatry, 12, Suppl. 1,* S11–S15.

**Tateno, T., & Robinson, H. P.** (2011). The mechanism of ethanol action on midbrain dopaminergic neuron firing: A dynamic clamp study of the role of I(h) and GABAergic synaptic integration. *Journal of Neurophysiology, 106,* 1901–1922.

**Taupin, P.** (2011). Neurogenic drugs and compounds. *Recent Patents on CNS Drug Discovery, 11,* 35–37.

**Tavris, C., & Wade, C.** (1984). *The longest war: Sex differences in perspective* (2nd ed.). Fort Worth: Harcourt Brace.

**Tay, C., Ang, S., & Van Dyne, L.** (2006). Personality, biographical characteristics, and job interview success: A longitudinal study of the mediating effects of self-efficacy and the moderating effects of internal locus of causality. *Journal of Applied Psychology, 91,* 446–454.

**Tay, L., & Diener, E.** (2011). Needs and subjective well-being around the world. *Journal of Personality and Social Psychology, 101,* 354–365.

**Taylor, J. G.** (2012). Does the corollary discharge of attention exist? *Consciousness and Cognition, 21* (1), 325–339.

**Taylor, M., Bates, G., & Webster, J. D.** (2011). Comparing the properties of two measures of wisdom: Predicting forgiveness and psychological well-being with the Self-Assessed Wisdom Scale (SAWS) and the Three-Dimensional Wisdom Scale (3D-WS). *Experimental Aging Research, 37,* 129–141.

**Taylor, M. K., & others.** (2012). Relationships of hardiness to physical and mental health status in military men: A test of mediated effects. *Journal of Behavioral Medicine.* doi: 10.1007/s10865-011-9387-8

**Taylor, S. E.** (2001). Toward a biology of social support. In C. R. Snyder & S. J. Lopez (Eds.), *Handbook of positive psychology.* New York: Oxford University Press.

**Taylor, S. E.** (2007). Social support. In H. S. Friedman & R. C. Silver (Eds.), *Foundations of health psychology.* New York: Oxford University Press.

**Taylor, S. E.** (2011a). Tend and befriend theory. In A. M. van Lange, A. W., Kruglanski, & E. T. Higgins (Eds.), *Handbook of theories of social psychology.* Thousand Oaks, CA: Sage.

**Taylor, S. E.** (2011b). Affiliation and stress. In S. S. Folkman (Ed.), *Oxford handbook of stress, health, and coping.* New York: Oxford University Press.

**Taylor, S. E.** (2011c). Positive illusions: How ordinary people become extraordinary. In M. A. Gernsbacher, R. W. Pew, L. M. Hough, & J. R. Pomerantz (Eds.), *Psychology and the real world: Essays illustrating fundamental contributions to society* (pp. 224–228). New York: Worth.

**Taylor, S. E.** (2012). *Health psychology* (8th ed.). New York: McGraw-Hill.

**Taylor, S. E., Brown, J. D., Colvin, C. R., Block, J., & Funder, D. C.** (2007). Issue 6: Do positive illusions lead to healthy behavior? In J. A. Nier (Ed.). *Taking sides: Clashing views in social psychology* (2nd ed., pp. 116–137). New York: McGraw-Hill.

**Taylor, S. E., Lerner, J. S., Sherman, D. K., Sage, R. M., & McDowell, N. K.** (2003a). Are self-enhancing cognitions associated with healthy or unhealthy biological profiles? *Journal of Personality and Social Psychology, 85,* 605–615.

**Taylor, S. E., Lerner, J. S., Sherman, D. K., Sage, R. M., & McDowell, N. K.** (2003b). Portrait of the self-enhancer: Well adjusted and well liked or maladjusted and friendless? *Journal of Personality and Social Psychology, 84,* 165–176.

**Taylor, S. E., & Sherman, D. K.** (2008). Self-enhancement and self-affirmation: The consequences of positive self-thoughts for motivation and health. In W. Gardner & J. Shah (Eds.), *Handbook of motivation science.* New York: Guilford.

**Taylor, Z. E., & others.** (2012). Dispositional optimism: A psychological resource for Mexican-origin mothers experiencing economic stress. *Journal of Family Psychology, 26,* 133–139.

**Teesson, M., & Vogl, L.** (2006). Major depressive disorder is common among Native Americans, women, the middle aged, the poor, the widowed, separated, or divorced people. *Evidence-Based Mental Health, 9,* 59.

**Teffer, K., & Semendeferi, K.** (2012). Human prefrontal cortex evolution, development, and pathology. *Progress in Brain Research, 195,* 191–218.

**Teismann, N. A., Lenaghan, P., Stein, J., & Green, A.** (2012). Will the real optic nerve please stand up? *Journal of Ultrasound Medicine, 31,* 130–131.

**ten Bricke, L., Macdonald, S., Porter, S., & O'Connor, B.** (2012). Crocodile tears: Facial, verbal, and body language behaviors associated with genuine and fabricated remorse. *Law and Human Behavior, 36* (1), 51–59.

**Tennie, C., Call, J., & Tomasello, M.** (2010). Evidence for emulation in chimpanzees in social settings using the floating peanut task. *PLoS One, 5* (5), e10544. doi: 10.1371/journal.pone.0010544

**Teodorescu, M., & others.** (2006). Correlates of daytime sleepiness in patients with asthma. *Sleep Medicine, 7,* 607–613.

**Terman, L.** (1925). *Genetic studies of genius: Mental and physical traits of a thousand gifted children* (vol. 1). Stanford, CA: Stanford University Press.

**Terr, L. C.** (1988). What happens to early memories of trauma? *Journal of the American Academy of Child and Adolescent Psychiatry, 27,* 96–104.

**Terry, S.** (2009). *Learning and memory* (4th ed.). Upper Saddle River, NJ: Prentice-Hall.

**Tharoor, H., Dinesh, N., Chauhan, A., Mathew, A., & Sharma, P. S. V. N.** (2007). Dissociative amnesia related to pregnancy. *German Journal of Psychiatry, 10,* 119–121.

**Theeuwes, J., Belopolsky, A., & Olivers, C. N.** (2009). Interactions between working memory, attention, and eye movements. *Acta Psychologica, 132* (2), 106–114.

Thigpen, C. H., & Cleckley, H. M. (1957). *Three faces of Eve*. New York. McGraw-Hill.

Thoeringer, C. K., Ripke, S., Unschuld, P. G., Lucae, S., Ising, M., Bettecken, T., Uhr, M., Keck, M. E., Mueller-Myhsok, B., Holsboer, F., Binder, E. B., & Erhardt, A. (2009). The GABA transporter 1 (SLC6A1): A novel candidate gene for anxiety disorders. *Journal of Neural Transmission, 116*, 649–657.

Thomas, M. S. C., & Johnson, M. H. (2008). New advances in understanding sensitive periods in brain development. *Current Directions in Psychological Science, 17*, 1–5.

Thompson, J., & Manore, M. (2013). *Nutrition for life* (3rd ed.). Upper Saddle River, NJ: Pearson.

Thompson, L., & others. (2005). Dispositional forgiveness of self, others, and situations. *Journal of Personality, 73*, 313–359.

Thomsen, D. K., Pillemer, D. B., & Ivcevic, Z. (2011). Life story chapters, specific memories, and the reminiscence bump. *Memory, 19*, 267–279.

Thomson, D. R., & Milliken, B. (2012). Perceptual distinctiveness produces long-lasting priming of pop-out. *Psychonomic Bulletin and Review, 19* (2), 170–176.

Thorndike, E. L. (1898). *Animal intelligence: An experimental study of the associative processes in animals* (Psychological Review, monograph supplements, no. 8). New York: Macmillan.

Thornicroft, G., Brohan, E., Rose, D., Sartorius, N., Lees, M., & the INDIGO Study Group. (2009). Global pattern of experienced and anticipated discrimination against people with schizophrenia: A cross-sectional survey. *Lancet, 373*, 408–415.

Thota, A. B., & others. (2012). Collaborative care to improve the management of depressive disorders: A community guide systematic review and meta-analysis. *American Journal of Preventive Medicine, 42*, 525–538.

Thunedborg, K., Black, C. H., & Bech, P. (1995). Beyond the Hamilton depression scores in long-term treatment of manic-melancholic patients: Prediction of recurrence of depression by quality of life measurements. *Psychotherapy and Psychosomatics, 64*, 131–140.

Tigani, X., & others. (2012). Self-rated health in centenarians: A nationwide cross-sectional Greek study. *Archives of Gerontology and Geriatrics, 54*, e342–e348.

Timofeev, I. (2011). Neuronal plasticity and thalamocortical sleep and waking oscillations. *Progress in Brain Research, 193*, 121–144.

Tinbergen, N. (1969). *The study of instinct*. New York: Oxford University Press.

Tindle, H., & others. (2012). Optimism, response to treatment of depression, and rehospitalization after coronary artery bypass graft surgery. *Psychosomatic Medicine, 74*, 200–207.

Todorov, A. (2013). Social psychology: Inference and person perception. *Annual Review of Psychology* (vol. 64). Palo Alto, CA: Annual Reviews.

Todorov, A., Mandisodza, A. N., Goren, A., & Hall, C. C. (2005). Inferences of competence from faces predict election outcomes. *Science, 308* (5728), 1623–1626.

Tolman, E. C. (1932). *Purposive behavior in animals and man*. New York: Appleton-Century-Crofts.

Tolman, E. C., & Honzik, C. H. (1930). Degrees of hunger, reward and non-reward, and maze performance in rats. *University of California Publications in Psychology, 4*, 21–256.

tom Dieck, S., & Brandstatter, J. H. (2006). Ribbon synapses in the retina. *Cell Tissue Research, 326*, 339–346.

Tompkins, T. L., & others. (2011). A closer look at co-rumination: Gender, coping, peer functioning, and internalizing/externalizing problems. *Journal of Adolescence, 34*, 801–811.

Tononi, G., & Cirelli, C. (2011). Sleep and synaptic plasticity. *Annual Review of Psychology* (vol. 62). Palo Alto, CA: Annual Reviews.

Topolinski, S., & Strack, F. (2008). Where there's a will—there's no intuition: The unintentional basis of semantic coherence judgments. *Journal of Memory and Language, 58*, 1032–1048.

Topolinski, S., & Strack, F. (2009). Scanning the "fringe of consciousness": What is felt and what is not felt in intuition about semantic coherence. *Consciousness and Cognition, 18* (3), 608–618.

Torniainen, M., & others. (2012). Cognitive impairments in schizophrenia and schizoaffective disorder: Relationship with clinical characteristics. *Journal of Nervous and Mental Disease, 200*, 316–322.

Torres, L., Yznaga, S. D., & Moore, K. M. (2011). Discrimination and Latino psychological distress: The moderating role of ethnic identity exploration and commitment. *American Journal of Orthopsychiatry, 81*, 526–534.

Toyoda, H., & others (2011). Interplay of amygdala and cingulate plasticity in emotional fear. *Neural Plasticity.* doi: 10.1155/2011/813749

Trainor, L. J., Lee, K., & Bosnyak, D. J. (2011). Cortical plasticity in 4-month-old infants: Specific effects of experience with musical timbres. *Brain Topography, 24*, 192–203.

Treasure, J., Claudino, A. M., & Zucker, N. (2010). Eating disorders. *Lancet, 375*, 583–593.

Tremblay, T., Monetta, L., & Joanette, Y. (2009). Complexity and hemispheric abilities: Evidence for a differential impact on semantics and phonology. *Brain and Language, 108*, 67–72.

Triandis, H. C. (2000). Cross-cultural psychology: History of the field. In A. Kazdin (Ed.), *Encyclopedia of psychology*. Washington, DC, & New York: American Psychological Association and Oxford University Press.

Triandis, H. C. (2007). Culture and psychology: A history of the study of their relationship. In S. Kitayama & D. Cohen (Eds.), *Handbook of cultural psychology* (pp. 59–76). New York: Guilford.

Tronson, N. C., & others. (2012). Fear conditioning and extinction: Emotional states encoded by distinct signaling pathways. *Trends in Neuroscience, 35* (3), 145–155.

Tropp, L. R., & Wright, S. C. (2003). Evaluations and perceptions of self, ingroup, and outgroup: Comparisons between Mexican-American and European-American children. *Self and Identity, 2*, 203–221.

Trull, T., & Prinstein, M. (2013). *Clinical psychology* (8th ed.). Boston: Cengage.

Trull, T. J., & Widiger, T. A. (2003). Personality disorders. In I. B. Weiner (Ed.), *Handbook of psychology* (vol. 8). New York: Wiley.

Trull, T. J., & others. (2012). The structure of *Diagnostic and Statistical Manual of Mental Disorders* (4th ed., text revision) personality disorder symptoms in a large national sample. *Personality Disorders.* (in press)

Tryon, R. C. (1940). Genetic differences in maze-learning ability in rats. In *39th Yearbook, National Society for the Study of Education*. Chicago: University of Chicago Press.

Trzesniewski, K. H., & Donnellan, M. B. (2010). Rethinking "generation me": A study of cohort effects from 1976–2006. *Perspectives on Psychological Science, 5*, 58–75.

Tsenkova, V. K., Dienberg Love, G., Singer, B. H., & Ryff, C. D. (2008). Coping and positive affect predict longitudinal change in glycosylated hemoglobin. *Health Psychology, 27, Suppl. 2*, S163–S171.

Tucker-Drob, E. M. (2011). Individual differences methods for randomized experiments. *Psychological Methods, 16*, 298–318.

Tuckman, A. M., Stern, Y., Basner, R. C., & Rakitin, B. C. (2011). The prefrontal model revisited: Double dissociations between young sleep deprived and elderly subjects on cognitive components of performance. *Sleep, 34*, 1039–1050.

Tugade, M. M., Fredrickson, B. L., & Feldman Barrett, L. (2004). Psychological resilience and positive emotional granularity: Examining the benefits of positive emotions on coping and health. *Journal of Personality, 72*, 1161–1190.

Tulving, E. (1972). Episodic and semantic memory. In E. Tulving & W. Donaldson (Eds.), *Origins of memory*. San Diego: Academic.

Tulving, E. (1983). *Elements of episodic memory*. New York: Oxford University Press.

Tulving, E. (1989). Remembering and knowing the past. *American Scientist, 77*, 361–367.

Tulving, E. (2000). Concepts of memory. In E. Tulving & F. I. M. Craik (Eds.), *The Oxford handbook of memory*. New York: Oxford University Press.

Tungpunkom, P., Maayan, N., & Soares-Weiser, K. (2012). Life skills programs for chronic mental illness. *Cochrane Database of Systematic Reviews, 1*, CD000381.

Turiano, N. A., Spiro, A., & Mroczek, D. K. (2012). Openness to experience and mortality in men: Analysis of trait and facets. *Journal of Aging and Health, 24* (4), 654–672.

Turiano, N. A., & others. (2012). Personality trait level and change as predictors of health outcomes: Findings from a national study of Americans (MIDUS). *Journals of Gerontology B: Psychological Sciences and Social Sciences, 67B*, 4–12.

Turkheimer, E. (2011). Genetics and human agency: Comment on Dar-Nimrod and Heine. *Psychological Bulletin, 137*, 825–828.

Turkheimer, E., Haley, A., Waldron, M., D'Onofrio, B., & Gottesman, I. I. (2003). Socioeconomic status modifies heritability of IQ in young children. *Psychological Science, 14*, 623–628.

Turnbull, A., Rutherford-Turnbull, H., Wehmeyer, M., & Shogren, K. A. (2013). *Exceptional lives* (7th ed.). Upper Saddle River, NJ: Merrill.

Turrigiano, G. (2010). Synaptic homeostasis. *Annual Review of Neuroscience* (vol. 33). Palo Alto, CA: Annual Reviews.

Twenge, J. M. (2006). *Generation Me: Why today's young Americans are more confident, assertive, entitled—and more miserable than ever before*. New York: Free Press.

Twenge, J. M., & Campbell, S. M. (2010). Generation Me and the changing world of work. In A. P. Linley, S. Harrington, & N. Garcea (Eds.), *Oxford handbook of positive psychology and work* (pp. 25–35). New York: Oxford University Press.

Tyas, S. L., Salazar, J. C., Snowdon, D. A., Desrosier, M. F., Riley, K. P., Mendiondo, M. S., & Kryscio, R. J. (2007). Transitions to mild cognitive impairments, dementia, and death: Findings from the Nun Study. *American Journal of Epidemiology, 165*, 1231–1238.

Tynes, B. M., Umaña-Taylor, A. J., Rose, C. A., Lin, J., & Anderson, C. J. (2012). Online racial discrimination and the protective function of ethnic identity and self-esteem for African America adolescents. *Developmental Psychology, 48*, 343–355.

## U

Uchida, Y., Kitayama, S., Mesquita, B., Reyes, J. A. S., & Morling, B. (2008). Is perceived emotional support beneficial? Well-being and health in independent and interdependent cultures. *Personality and Social Psychology Bulletin, 34*, 741–754.

Uguz, F., Akman, C., Kaya, N., & Cilli, A. S. (2007). Postpartum-onset obsessive-compulsive disorder: Incidence, clinical features, and related factors. *Journal of Clinical Psychiatry, 68*, 132–138.

Ullman, A. D. (1952). Review of "Antabuse" in the treatment of alcoholism. *Psychological Bulletin, 49*, 557–558.

Umaña-Taylor, A. J., Gonzales-Backen, M. A. & Guimond, A. B. (2009). Latino adolescents' ethnic identity: Is there a developmental progression and does growth in ethnic identity predict growth in self-esteem? *Child Development, 80*, 391–405.

Umaña-Taylor, A. J., Updegraff, K. A., & Gonzales-Bracken, M. A. (2011). Mexican-origin adolescent mothers' stressors and psychological functioning: Examining ethnic identity affirmation and familism as moderators. *Journal of Youth and Adolescence, 40*, 140–157.

Umanath, S., Sarezky, D., & Finger, S. (2011). Sleepwalking through history: Medicine, arts, and courts of law. *Journal of the History of the Neurosciences, 20*, 253–276.

UNAIDS. (2012). *Worldwide HIV and AIDS statistics*. avert.org/worldstats.htm (accessed May 5, 2012)

Underhill, K., Montgomery, P., & Operario, D. (2007). Sexual abstinence programs to prevent HIV infection in high-income countries. *British Medical Journal, 335*, 248.

Undurraga, J., & Baldessarini, R. J. (2012). Randomized, placebo-controlled trials of antidepressants for acute major depression: Thirty-year meta-analytic review. *Neuropsychopharmacology, 37*, 851–864.

United Nations. (2011, July 19). Happiness should have greater role in development policy—UN Member States. *UN News Centre.* www.un.org/apps/news/story.asp?NewsID=39084. (accessed February 22, 2012)

United Nations Office on Drugs and Crime (UNODC). (2011). *World drug report 2011.* Vienna: Author.

United Nations World Youth Report. (2005). *World youth report 2005: Young people today and in 2015.* Geneva, Switzerland: United Nations.

Unkelbach, C. (2007). Reversing the truth effect: Learning the interpretation of processing fluency in judgments of truth. *Journal of Experimental Psychology: Learning, Memory, and Cognition, 33,* 219–230.

Unsworth, N., Brewer, G. A., & Spillers, G. J. (2011). Variation in working memory capacity and episodic memory: Examining the importance of encoding specificity. *Psychonomic Bulletin and Review, 18,* 1113–1118.

Unsworth, N., Spillers, G. J., & Brewer, G. A. (2012). The role of working memory in autobiographical retrieval: Individual differences in strategic search. *Memory, 20* (2), 167–176.

Urbina, S. (2011). Tests of intelligence. In R. J. Sternberg & S. B. Kaufman (Eds.), *Handbook of intelligence.* New York: Cambridge University Press.

Urcelay, G. P., Wheeler, D. S., & Miller, R. R. (2009). Spacing extinction trials alleviates renewal and spontaneous recovery. *Learning and Behavior, 37,* 60–73.

Urry, H. L., Nitschke, J. B., Dolski, I., Jackson, D. C., Dalton, K. M., Mueller, C. J., Rosenkranz, M. A., Ryff, C. D., Singer, B. H., & Davidson, R. J. (2004). Making a life worth living: Neural correlates of well-being. *Psychological Science, 15,* 367–372.

U.S. Bureau of Justice Statistics. (2006). *All crimes in the US in 2004.* Washington, DC: Author.

U.S. Department of Education, National Center for Education Statistics. (2011). *Digest of education statistics, 2010* (NCES 2011-015). Washington, DC: Author.

U.S. Food and Drug Administration. (2004, October 15). *FDA launches a multi-pronged strategy to strengthen safeguards for children treated with antidepressant medications.* News release. Washington, DC: Author.

U.S. Food and Drug Administration. (2009). *Office of Device Evaluation annual report, fiscal year 2008.* Washington, DC: Center for Devices and Radiological Health.

## V

Vail, K. E., Juhl, J., Arndt, J., Routledge, C., Vess, M., & Rutjens, B. (2012). When death is good for life: Considering the positive trajectories of terror management. *Personality and Social Psychology Review.* doi: 10.1177/1088868312440046

Vaillant, G. (2003). A 60-year follow-up of alcoholic men. *Addiction, 98,* 1043–1051.

Vaillières, A., & Bastille-Denis, E. (2012). Circadian rhythm disorders II: Shift-work and jet-lag. In C. M. Morin & C. A. Espie (Eds.), *Oxford handbook of sleep and sleep disorders.* New York: Oxford University Press.

van Beveren, N. J., & others. (2012). Functional gene-expression analysis shows involvement of schizophrenia-relevant pathways in patients with 22q deletion syndrome. *PLoS One, 7* (3), e33352.

van Bokhoven, I., van Goozen, S. H. M., van Engeland, H., Schaal, B., Arseneault, L., Seguin, J. R., Assaad, J., Nagin, D. S., Vitaro, F., & Tremblay, R. E. (2006). Salivary testosterone and aggression, delinquency, and social dominance in a population-based longitudinal study of adolescent males. *Hormones and Behavior, 50,* 118–125.

Vandello, J. A., & Cohen, D. (2004). When believing is seeing: Sustaining norms of violence in cultures of honor. In M. Schaller & C. S. Crandall (Eds.), *The psychological foundations of culture* (pp. 281–304). Mahwah, NJ: Erlbaum.

van der Linden, D., te Nijenhuis, J., & Bakker, A. B. (2010). The general factor of personality: A meta-analysis of Big Five intercorrelations and a criterion-related validity study. *Journal of Research in Personality, 44,* 315–327.

Van de Vliert, E. (2009). *Climate, affluence, and culture.* Cambridge, England: Cambridge University Press.

Van Doorn, G. S., & Taborsky, M. (2012). The evolution of generalized reciprocity on social interaction networks. *Evolution, 66,* 651–664.

van Duijl, M., Cardeña, E., & De Jong, J. (2005). The validity of DSM-IV dissociative disorders categories in South-West Uganda. *Transcultural Psychiatry, 42,* 219–241.

van Gaal, S., & Lamme, V. A. F. (2011). Unconscious high-level information processing: Implications for neurobiological theories of consciousness. *Neuroscientist.* doi: 10.1177/1073858411140407

van Hof, P., van der Kamp, J., & Savelsbergh, G. J. P. (2008). The relation between infants' perception of catchableness and the control of catching. *Developmental Psychology, 44,* 182–194.

van IJzendoorn, M. H., & Bakermans-Kranenburg, M. J. (2010). Invariance of adult attachment across gender, age, culture, and socioeconomic status? *Journal of Social and Personal Relationships, 27,* 200–208.

Van Lange, P. A. M., Rusbult, C. E., Drigotas, S. M., & Arriaga, X. B. (1997). Willingness to sacrifice in close relationships. *Journal of Personality and Social Psychology, 72,* 1373–1395.

Vasco, V. R., Cardinale, G., & Polonia, P. (2012). Deletion of PLCB1 gene in schizophrenia-affected patients. *Journal of Cellular and Molecular Medicine, 16,* 844–851.

Von Polier, G. G., Vloet, T. D., & Herpertz-Dahlmann, B. (2012). ADHD and delinquency—a developmental perspective. *Behavioral Sciences and the Law, 30,* 121–139.

van Pragg, H. (2009). Exercise and the brain: Something to chew on. *Trends in Neuroscience, 32,* 990–998.

van Reedt Dortland, A. K. B., & others. (2012). Personality traits and childhood trauma as correlates of metabolic risk factors: The Netherlands Study of Depression and Anxiety (NESDA). *Progress in Neuropsychopharmacology and Biological Psychiatry, 36,* 85–91.

Van Riper, M. (2007). Families of children with Down syndrome: Responding to "a change in plans" with resilience. *Journal of Pediatric Nursing, 22,* 116–128.

Van Voorhees, B. W., & others. (2009). Randomized clinical trial of an Internet-based depression prevention program for adolescents (Project CATCH-IT) in primary care: 12-week outcomes. *Journal of Developmental and Behavioral Pediatrics, 30,* 23–37.

Vaughn, S., Bos, C. S., & Schumm, J. S. (2003). *Teaching exceptional, diverse, and at-risk students in the general education classroom* (3rd ed.). Boston: Allyn & Bacon.

Vazire, S. (2010). Who knows what about a person? The self-other knowledge asymmetry (SOKA) model. *Journal of Personality and Social Psychology, 98,* 281–300.

Vazquez, J., Hall, S. C., Witkowska, H. E., & Greco, M. A. (2008). Rapid alterations in cortical protein profiles underlie spontaneous sleep and wake bouts. *Journal of Cellular Biochemistry, 105,* 1472–1484.

Vega, V., & Malamuth, N. M. (2007). Predicting sexual aggression: The role of pornography in the context of general and specific risk factors. *Aggressive Behavior, 33,* 104–117.

Ventura, S. J., & Hamilton, B. E. (2011, February). U.S. teenage birth rate resumes decline. *NCHS Data Brief, 58,* 1–3.

Vermetten, E., Schmahl, C., Lindner, S., Loewenstein, R. J., & Bremner, J. D. (2006). Hippocampal and amygdalar volumes in dissociative identity disorder. *American Journal of Psychiatry, 163,* 630–636.

Verschuere, B., Crombez, G., De Clercq, A., & Koster, E. H. W. (2005). Psychopathic traits and autonomic responding to concealed information in a prison sample. *Psychophysiology, 42,* 239–245.

Vetere, G., & others. (2011). Extinction partially reverts structural changes associated with fear memory. *Learning and Memory, 18,* 554–557.

Vetter, I., Kapitzke, D., Hermanussen, S., Moneith, G. R., & Cabot, P. J. (2006). The effects of pH on beta-endorphin and morphine inhibition of calcium transients in dorsal root ganglion neurons. *Journal of Pain, 7,* 488–499.

Vezzali, L., Capozza, D., Stathi, S., & Giovannini, D. (2012). Increasing outgroup trust, reducing infrahumanization, and enhancing future contact intentions via imagined intergroup contact. *Journal of Experimental Social Psychology, 48,* 437–440.

Victor, A. M., & Bernstein, G. A. (2009). Anxiety disorders and posttraumatic stress disorder update. *Psychiatric Clinics of North America, 32,* 57–69.

Videtic, A., Zupanic, T., Pregelj, P., Balazic, J., Tomori, M., & Komel, R. (2009). Suicide, stress, and serotonin receptor 1A promotor polymorphism -1019,G in Slovenian suicide victims. *European Archives of Psychiatry and Clinical Neuroscience, 259,* 234–238.

Vigano, S., Perreau, M., Panaleo, G., & Harari, A. (2012). Positive and negative regulation of cellular immune responses in physiologic conditions and diseases. *Clinical and Developmental Immunology.* doi: 10.1155/2012/485781

Vinberg, M., Mellerup, E., Andersen, P. K., Bennike, B., & Kessing, L. V. (2010). Variations in 5-HTTLPR: Relation to familiar risk of affective disorder, life events, neuroticism, and cortisol. *Progress in Neuro-Psychopharmacology & Biological Psychiatry, 34,* 86–91.

Visser, P. L., Loess, P., Jeglic, E. L., & Hirsch, J. K. (2012). Hope as a moderator of negative life events and depressive symptoms in a diverse sample. *Stress and Health.* doi: 10.1002/smi.2433

Viswanath, B., Maroky, A. S. M., Math, S. B., John, J. P., Benegal, V., Hamza, A., & Chaturvedi, S. K. (2012). Psychological impact of the tsunami on elderly survivors. *American Journal of Geriatric Psychiatry, 20,* 402–407.

Vogelei, R. (2011, March 30). Over 10 billion Social Networking and Online World (SNOW) registered accounts created as of 2010, nearly 4.5 billion which are active. Scottsdale, AZ: Instat.com. www.instat.com/press.asp?ID=3085&sku=IN1004659CM (accessed May 9, 2012)

Vogt, T. M., Mullooly, J. P., Ernst, D., Pople, C. R., & Hollis, J. F. (1992). Social networks as predictors of ischemic heart disease, cancer, stroke, and hypertension. *Journal of Clinical Epidemiology, 45,* 659–666.

von Békésy, G. (1960). Vibratory patterns of the basilar membrane. In E. G. Wever (Ed.), *Experiments in hearing.* New York: McGraw-Hill.

Vong, L., & others. (2011). Leptin action on GABAergic neurons prevents obesity and reduces inhibitory tone to POMC neurons. *Neuron, 71,* 142–154.

Von Neumann, J. (1958). *The computer and the brain.* New Haven, CT: Yale University Press.

Vrachnis, N., & others. (2012). The oxytocin-oxytocin receptor system and its antagonists as tocolytic agents. *International Journal of Endocrinology.* (in press)

Vriends, N., Michael T., Schindler, B., & Margraf, J. (2012). Associative learning in flying phobia. *Journal of Behavior Therapy and Experimental Psychiatry, 43,* 838–843.

Vukovic, J., & others. (2009). Lack of fibulin-3 alters regenerative tissue responses in the primary olfactory pathway. *Matrix Biology, 28,* 406–415.

Vygotsky, L. S. (1962). *Thought and language.* Cambridge, MA: MIT Press.

## W

Waage, S., & others. (2012). Subjective and objective sleepiness among oil rig workers during three different shift schedules. *Sleep Medicine, 13,* 64–72.

Wacker, J., Mueller, E. M., Hennig, J., & Stemmler, G. (2012). How to consistently link extraversion and intelligence to the catechol-O-methyltransferase (COMT) gene: On defining and measuring psychological phenotypes in neurogenetic research. *Journal of Personality and Social Psychology, 102,* 427–444.

Waenke, M., Samochowiecz, J., & Landwehr, J. (2012). Facial politics: Political judgment based on looks. In J. P. Forgas, K. Fiedler, & C. Sedikides (Eds.), *Social thinking and interpersonal behavior.* New York: Psychology Press.

Wagenaar, K., & Baars, J. (2012). Family and family therapy in the Netherlands. *International Review of Psychiatry, 24,* 144–148.

Wagenmakers, E. J., Wetzels, R., Borsboom, D., & van der Maas, H. L. J. (2011). Why psychologists must change the way they analyze their data: The case of psi: Comment on Bem (2011). *Journal of Personality and Social Psychology, 100*, 426–432.

Wagner, A. D., Schacter, D. L., Rotte, M., Koutstaal, B., Maril, A., Dale, A. M., Rosen, B. R., & Buckner, R. L. (1998). Building memories: Remembering and forgetting of verbal experiences as predicted by brain activity. *Science, 281*, 1185–1187.

Wai, J., Lubinski, D., & Benbow, C. P. (2005) Creativity and occupational accomplishments among intellectually precocious youths: An age 13 to age 33 longitudinal study. *Journal of Educational Psychology, 97*, 484–492.

Walker, D. D., Roffman, R. A., Stephens, R. S., Wakana, K., & Berghuis, J. (2006). Motivational enhancement therapy for adolescent marijuana users: A preliminary randomized controlled trial. *Journal of Consulting and Clinical Psychology, 74*, 628–632.

Walker, H. (2008). *Breaking free: My life with dissociative identity disorder.* New York: Simon & Schuster.

Walker, M. P. (2012). The role of sleep and neurocognitive function. In C. M. Morin & C. A. Espie (Eds.), *Oxford handbook of sleep and sleep disorders.* New York: Oxford University Press.

Waller, E. A., Bendel, R. E., & Kaplan, J. (2008). Sleep disorders and the eye. *Mayo Clinic Proceedings, 83*, 1251–1261.

Wallerstein, R. S. (2012). Will psychoanalysis fulfill its promise? *International Journal of Psychoanalysis, 93*, 377–399.

Wallien, M. S. C., Veenstra, R., Kreukels, B. P. C., & Cohen-Kettenis, P. T. (2010). Peer group status of gender dysphoric children: A sociometric study. *Archives of Sexual Behavior, 39*, 553–560.

Walton, K. E., & Roberts, B. W. (2004). On the relationship between substance use and personality traits: Abstainers are not maladjusted. *Journal of Research in Personality, 38*, 515–535.

Wampold, B. E. (2001). *The great psychotherapy debate: Models, methods, and findings.* Mahwah, NJ: Erlbaum.

Wampold, B. E., & Brown, G. S. (2005). Estimating variability in outcomes attributable to therapists: A naturalistic study of outcomes of managed care. *Journal of Consulting and Clinical Psychology, 73*, 914–923.

Wampold, B. E., & others. (2011). Evidence-based treatments for depression and anxiety versus treatment-as-usual: A meta-analysis of direct comparisons. *Clinical Psychology Review, 31*, 1304–1312.

Wan, C., Dach-Gruschow, K., No, S., & Hong, Y. (2011). Self-definitional functions of culture. In A. K. Lueng & C. Y. Chiu (Eds.), *Cultural processes: A social psychological perspective* (pp. 111–135). New York: Cambridge University Press.

Wang, Q. (2006). Earliest recollections of self and others in European American and Taiwanese young adults. *Psychological Science, 17*, 708–714.

Wang, Q. (2009). Once upon a time: Explaining cultural differences in episodic specificity. *Social and Personality Psychology Compass, 3/4*, 413–432.

Wang, Q., Hou, Y., Tang, H., & Wiprovnick, A. (2011). Travelling backwards and forwards in time: Culture and gender in the episodic specificity of past and future events. *Memory, 19*, 103–109.

Wangberg, S. C., Gammon, D., & Spitznogle, K. (2007). In the eyes of the beholder: Exploring psychologists' attitudes towards the use of e-therapy in Norway. *CyberPsychology and Behavior, 10*, 418–423.

Wanner, B., Vitaro, F., Tremblay, R. E., & Turecki, G. (2012). Childhood trajectories of anxiousness and disruptiveness explain the association between early-life adversity and attempted suicide. *Psychological Medicine.* doi: org/10.1017/S0033291712000438

Ward, J., Hall, K., & Haslam, C. (2006). Patterns of memory dysfunction in current and 2-year abstinent MDMA users. *Journal of Clinical and Experimental Neuropsychology, 28*, 306–324.

Warner, C. H., & others. (2011). Importance of anonymity to encourage honest reporting in mental health screening after combat deployment. *Archives of General Psychiatry, 68*, 1065–1071.

Warren, G., Schertler, E., & Bull, P. (2009). Detecting deception from emotional and unemotional cues. *Journal of Nonverbal Behavior, 33*, 59–69.

Wasserman, D. (2012). *Depression* (2nd ed.). New York: Oxford University Press.

Watson, A., El-Deredy, W., Bentley, D. E., Vogt, B. A., & Jones, A. K. (2006). Categories of placebo response in the absence of site-specific stimulation of analgesia. *Pain, 126*, 115–122.

Watson, D. (2001). Positive affectivity: The disposition to experience pleasurable emotional states. In C. R. Snyder & S. J. Lopez (Eds.), *Handbook of positive psychology.* New York: Oxford University Press.

Watson, D., & Clark, L. A. (1997). Extraversion and its positive emotional core. In R. Hogan, J. A. Johnson, & S. R., Briggs (Eds.), *Handbook of personality psychology* (pp. 767–793). San Diego: Academic.

Watson, J. B., & Rayner, R. (1920). Conditioned emotional reactions. *Journal of Experimental Psychology, 3*, 1–14.

Watson, M., Homewood, J., Haviland, J., & Bliss, J. M. (2005). Influence of psychological response on breast cancer survival: A 10-year follow-up of a population-based cohort. *European Journal of Cancer, 41*, 1710–1714.

Way, B. M., & Gurbaxani, B. M. (2008). A genetics primer for social health research. *Social and Personality Psychology Compass, 2*, 785–816.

Weaver, K., Garcia, S. M., Schwarz, N., & Miller, D. T. (2007). Inferring the popularity of an opinion from its familiarity: A repetitive voice can sound like a chorus. *Journal of Personality and Social Psychology, 92*, 821–833.

Webb, R. T., & others. (2012). Suicide risk in primary care patients with major physical diseases: A case-control study. *Archives of General Psychiatry, 69*, 256–264.

Webb, W. B. (2000). Sleep. In A. Kazdin (Ed.), *Encyclopedia of psychology.* Washington, DC, & New York: American Psychological Association and Oxford University Press.

Weber, S., Habel, U., Amunts, K., & Schneider, F. (2008). Structural brain abnormalities in psychopaths—A review. *Behavioral Sciences and the Law, 26*, 7–28.

Webster, J. M., Smith, R. H., Rhodes, A., & Whatley, M. A. (1999). The effect of a favor on public and private compliance: How internalized is the norm of reciprocity? *Basic and Applied Social Psychology, 21*, 251–260.

Wechsler, H., Lee, J. E., Kuo, M., & Lee, H. (2000). College binge drinking in the 1990s—A continuing health problem: Results of the Harvard University School of Public Health 1999 College Alcohol Study. *Journal of American College Health, 48*, 199–210.

Wechsler, H., Lee, J. E., Kuo, M., Seibring, M., Nelson, T. F., & Lee, H. (2002). Trends in college binge drinking during a period of increased prevention efforts: Findings from 4 Harvard School of Public Health college alcohol study surveys: 1993–2001. *Journal of American College Health, 50*, 203–217.

Weger, U. W., Hooper, N., Meier, B. P., & Hopthrow, T. (2012). Mindful maths: Reducing the impact of stereotype threat through a mindfulness exercise. *Consciousness and Cognition, 21*, 471–475.

Weiner, B. (2006). Social motivation, justice, and the moral emotions: An attributional approach. Mahwah, NJ: Erlbaum.

Weiner, I. B. (2004). Rorschach assessment: Current status. In M. Hersen (Ed.), *Comprehensive handbook of psychological assessment* (vol. 2). New York: Wiley.

Weinstein, N., Deci, E. L., & Ryan, R. M. (2011). Motivational determinants of integrating positive and negative past identities. *Journal of Personality and Social Psychology, 100*, 527–544.

Weinstein, N., Ryan, W. S., DeHaan, C. R., Przybylski, A. K., Legate, N., & Ryan, R. M. (2012). Parental autonomy support and discrepancies between implicit and explicit sexual identities: Dynamics of self-acceptance and defense. *Journal of Personality and Social Psychology, 102*, 815–832.

Weinstein, T. A. R., Capitanio, J. P., & Gosling, S. D. (2008). Personality in animals. In O. P. John, R. W.

Robins, & L. A. Pervin (Eds.), *Handbook of personality theory and research* (3rd ed., pp. 328–350). New York: Guilford.

Weir, W. (1984, October 15). Another look at subliminal "facts." *Advertising Age, 46*.

Weiss, A., Bates, T. C., & Luciano, M. (2008). Happiness is a personal(ity) thing: The genetics of personality and well-being in a representative sample. *Psychological Science, 19*, 205–210.

Weiss, A., King, J. E., & Perkins, L. (2006). Personality and subjective well-being in orangutans (*Pongo pygmaeus* and *Pongo abelii*). *Journal of Personality and Social Psychology, 90*, 501–511.

Weissman, M., & Olfson, M. (1995). Depression in women: Implications for health care research. *Science, 269*, 799–801.

Weissman, M. M., & others. (1995). Current rates and symptom profiles of panic disorder in six cross-national studies. *Clinical Neuropharmacology, 18, Suppl. 2*, S1–S6.

Welcome, S. E, Paivio, A., McRae, K., & Joanisse, M. F. (2011). An electrophysiological study of task demands on concreteness effects: Evidence for dual coding theory. *Experimental Brain Research, 312*, 347–358.

Welgampola, M. S., Bradshaw, A., & Halmagyi, G. M. (2011). Practical neurology—4: Dizziness on head movement. *Medical Journal of Australia, 195*, 518–522.

Wellman, H. M. (2011). Developing a theory of mind. In U. Goswami (Ed.), *Wiley-Blackwell handbook of childhood cognitive development* (2nd ed.). New York: Wiley.

Wellman, H. M., Fang, F., Liu, D., Zhu, L., & Liu, L. (2006). Scaling theory-of-mind understandings in Chinese children. *Psychological Science, 17*, 1075–1081.

Wellman, H. M., Fang, F., & Peterson, C. C. (2011). Sequential progressions in a theory-of-mind scale: Longitudinal perspectives. *Child Development, 82*, 780–792.

Wellman, H. M., & Liu, D. (2004). Scaling theory-of-mind tasks. *Child Development, 75*, 523–541.

Wellman, H. M., & Woolley, J. D. (1990). From simple desires to ordinary beliefs: The early development of everyday psychology. *Cognition, 35*, 245–275.

Wells, G. L. (1993). What do we know about eyewitness identification? *American Psychologist, 48*, 553–571.

Wells, G. L., Steblay, N. K., & Dysart, J. E. (2011) *A test if the simultaneous vs. sequential lineup methods: An initial report of the AJS National Eyewitness Identification Field Studies.* Des Moines, IA: American Judicature Society.

Werbart, A., Forsstrom, D., & Jeanneau, M. (2012). Long-term outcomes of psychodynamic residential treatment for severely disturbed young adults: A naturalistic study at a Swedish therapeutic community. *Nordic Journal of Psychiatry.* (in press)

West, R. (2005). Time for a change: Putting the transtheoretical (stages of change) model to rest. *Addiction, 100*, 1036–1039.

Wetherell, M. (2012). The prejudice problematic. In J. Dixon, M. Keynes, & M. Levine (Eds.), *Beyond prejudice.* New York: Cambridge University Press.

Wetzels, R., Matzke, D., Lee, M. D., Rouder, J. N., Iverson, G. J., & Wagenmakers, E. J. (2011). Statistical evidence in experimental psychology: An empirical comparison using 855 t-tests. *Perspectives on Psychological Science, 6*, 291–298.

Wheeler, D. S., & Miller, R. R. (2008). Determinants of cue interactions. *Behavioral Processes, 78*, 191–203.

Whiffen, V. E., & Demidenko, N. (2006). Mood disturbances across the lifespan. In J. Worell & C. D. Goodheart (Eds.), *Handbook of girls' and women's health: Gender and well-being across the lifespan.* New York: Oxford University Press.

Whitaker, J. L., & Bushman, B. J. (2012). "Remain calm. Be kind." Effects of relaxing video games on aggressive and prosocial behavior. *Social Psychological and Personality Science, 3*, 88–92.

Whitaker, R. (2002). *Mad in America: Bad science, bad medicine, and the mistreatment of the mentally ill.* Cambridge, MA: Perseus.

White, K. M., & others. (2012). An extended theory of planned behavior intervention to promote physical

# Credits

## Text and Line Art Credits

### Chapter 2
**Figure 2.3:** From R. Lewis, *Life*, 3rd Ed. Copyright © 1998 The McGraw-Hill Companies, Inc. Reproduced with permission by The McGraw-Hill Companies. **Figure 2.4:** From R. Lewis, *Life*, 3rd Ed. Copyright © 1998 The McGraw-Hill Companies, Inc. Reproduced with permission by The McGraw-Hill Companies. **Figure 2.6:** From *Mapping the Mind* by Rita Carter, 1998. Reprinted by permission of Weidenfeld & Nicholson Ltd, a division of The Orion Publishing Group (London). **Figure 2.11:** From *Brain, Mind, and Behavior* 3e by Floyd Bloom, Charles A. Nelson, and Arlyne Lazerson. © 1985, 1988, 2001 by Educational Broadcasting Corporation. Used with the permission of Worth Publishers. **Figure 2.16:** From *Brain, Mind, and Behavior* 3e by Floyd Bloom, Charles A. Nelson, and Arlyne Lazerson. © 1985, 1988, 2001 by Educational Broadcasting Corporation. Used with the permission of Worth Publishers.

### Chapter 3
**Figure 3.15:** From *Ishihara's Tests for Color Deficiency*. Published by Kanehara Trading, Inc. Tokyo, Japan. Used with permission. **Figure 3.16:** From Atkins/Hilgard/Smith/Hoeksema/Fredrickson. *Atkinson and Hilgard's Introduction to Psychology*, 14e. © 2003 Wadsworth, a part of Cengage Learning, Inc. Reproduced by permission. www.cengage.com/permissions. **Figure 3.23:** From James J. Gibson. *The Perception of the Visual World*. © 1950 Wadsworth, a part of Cengage Learning, Inc. Reproduced by permission. www.cengage.com/permissions. **Figure 3.25:** From *Brain, Mind, and Behavior* 3e by Floyd Bloom, Charles A. Nelson, and Arlyne Lazerson. © 1985, 1988, 2001 by Educational Broadcasting Corporation. Used with the permission of Worth Publishers.

### Chapter 4
**Figure 4.6:** From *Brain, Mind, and Behavior* 3e by Floyd Bloom, Charles A. Nelson, and Arlyne Lazerson. © 1985, 1988, 2001 by Educational Broadcasting Corporation. Used with the permission of Worth Publishers. **Figure 4.9:** From John Santrock, *Adolescence*, 8th Ed. Copyright © 2001 The McGraw-Hill Companies, Inc. Reproduced with permission by The McGraw-Hill Companies. **Figure 4.13:** From *Journal of the American Medical Association*, 272, 1672–1677, 1994 data presented by H. Wechsler, Davenport, et al. Used with permission by American Medical Association.

### Chapter 6
**Figure 6.10:** From John Santrock, *Life-Span Development*, 11th Ed. Copyright © 2008 The McGraw-Hill Companies, Inc. Reproduced with permission by The McGraw-Hill Companies. **Figure 6.13:** From *Human Memory: Theory and Data* by B. Murdock, Jr. © 1974. Lawrence Erlbaum. **Figure 6.17:** David Barker, © Exploratorium, www.exploratorium.edu. Used with permission.

### Chapter 7
**Figure 7.9:** From John Santrock, *Children*, 7th Ed. Copyright © 2003 The McGraw-Hill Companies, Inc. Reproduced with permission by The McGraw-Hill Companies. **Figure 7.11:** From "The Increase in IQ Scores from 1932–1997," by Ulric Neisser. Used with permission. **Figure 7.13:** From John Santrock, *Educational Psychology*. Copyright © 2001 The McGraw-Hill Companies, Inc. Reproduced with permission by The McGraw-Hill Companies.

### Chapter 8
**Figure 8.5:** From John Santrock, *Topical Life-Span Development, 2002*. Copyright © The McGraw-Hill Companies, Inc. Reproduced with permission by The McGraw-Hill Companies. **Figure 8.7:** From John Santrock, *Life-Span Development*, 9th Ed. Copyright © The McGraw-Hill Companies, Inc. Reproduced with permission by The McGraw-Hill Companies. **Figure 8.8 (graphic):** From Grant Jarding. *USA Today*. January 5, 1999. Reprinted with permission. **Figure 8.12:** From John Santrock, *Child Development*, 10th Ed. Copyright © The McGraw-Hill Companies, Inc. Reproduced with permission by The McGraw-Hill Companies. **Figure 8.16:** From John Santrock, *Life-Span Development*, 8th Ed. Copyright © 2002 The McGraw-Hill Companies, Inc. Reproduced with permission by The McGraw-Hill Companies.

### Chapter 9
**Figure 9.5:** From *Sex in America* by John Gagnon. Copyright © 1994 by CSG Enterprises, Inc., Edward O. Laumann, Robert T. Michael, and Gina Kolata. By permission of Little Brown & Company and Brockman, Inc.

### Chapter 10
**Figure 10.1:** From Wrightsman/Sigelman/Sanford. *Psychology: A Scientific Study of Human Behavior*, 5e. © 1979 Wadsworth, a part of Cengage Learning, Inc. Reproduced with permission. www.cengage.com/permissions.

### Chapter 11
**Figure 11.6:** This figure by K. Deaux was published in *Encyclopedia of Women and Gender: Sex Similarities and Differences and the Impact of Society of Gender*, Two-Volume Set, edited by Judith Worell, "Types of Identity." Copyright Elsevier 1969. **Figure 11.7:** Muzafer Sherif et al. Fig labeled "Attitudes Toward the Out-Group Following Competitive and Cooperative Activities." © 1988 by Muzafer Sherif and reprinted by permission of Wesleyan University Press.

### Chapter 12
**Figure 12.3:** From Weissman and Olfson, *Science 269*:779, Figure 1 (1995). Copyright © 1995 American Association for the Advancement of Science. Used with permission. **Figure 12.4:** Reprinted with permission from the *Annual Review of Neuroscience*, Volume 20, © 1997 by Annual Reviews, www.annualreviews.org. **Figure 12.10:** © Irving Gottesman 2004. Used by permission. **Figure 12.12:** Reprinted with permission from the *Diagnostic and Statistical Manual of Mental Disorders*, Fourth Edition, Text Revision. Copyright © 2000 American Psychiatric Association.

### Chapter 13
**Figure 13.6:** Adapted from A. Freeman and M. A. Reinecke, "Cognitive Therapy," in A. S. Gurman, ed., *Essential Psychotherapies*. Adapted with permission of The Guilford Press. **Figure 13.8:** Reprinted with permission of Michael J. Lambert, Brigham Young University. **Figure 13.9:** From "A Survival Analysis of Clinically Significant Change in Outpatient Psychotherapy" by Anderson & Lambert, from *Journal of Clinical Psychology, 57*, 875–888. Copyright © 2001. Reproduced with permission of John Wiley & Sons, Inc.

### Chapter 14
**Figure 14.4:** From H. Selye et al., *The Stress of Life*. Copyright © 1976 The McGraw-Hill Companies, Inc. Reproduced with permission by The McGraw-Hill Companies. **Figure 14.5:** From S. Cohen, E. Frank, W. J. Doyle, D. P. Skoner, B. S. Rabin, and J. M. Gwaltney (1998). "Types of Stressors That Increase Susceptibility to the Common Cold in Adults." *Health Psychology, 17*, 214–233. Copyright © 1998 by the American Psychological Association. Used with permission. **Figure 14.7:** This article was published in *Journal of Psychosomatic Research, Vol. 29*, S. C. Kobasa, S. R. Maddi, M. C. Puccette, and M. A. Zola, pp. 525–533. Copyright Elsevier 1986. Used with permission. **Figure 14.9:** From John Santrock, *Life-Span Development*, 11th Ed. Copyright © 2008 The McGraw-Hill Companies, Inc. Reproduced with permission by The McGraw-Hill Companies.

## Photo Credits

### Chapter 1
**Opener:** © Huntstock/Getty Images; **p. 2 (both):** © Betsie Van Der Meer/Taxi/Getty Images; **p. 5:** © William Thomas Cain/Stringer/Getty Images; **p. 6, p. 7:** © Bettmann/Corbis; **p. 9:** Courtesy of Richard Davidson, University of Wisconsin, Madison. Photo by Jeff Miller; **p. 10 (top):** © Time & Life Pictures/Getty Images; **p. 10 (bottom):** © Rick Diamond/Getty Images for Macy's; **p. 13 (top):** © Creatas/Punchstock; **p. 13 (bottom):** © George Doyle & Ciaran Griffin/Stockbyte/Getty Images; **Fig 1.3 (gift):** © Stockdisc/PunchStock; **Fig 1.3 (woman):** © Masterfile/Royalty Free; **p. 15:** © Peter Ciresa Cires/Index Stock; **p. 18:** © Bettmann/Corbis; **Fig 1.4 (yawning):** © Doug Menuez/Getty Images; **Fig 1.4 (leaning):** © BananaStock/JupiterImages; **Fig 1.4 (reading):** © Veer; **Fig 1.4 (friends):** © Stockbyte/Punchstock; **p. 22:** © Photodisc/PunchStock; **p. 23:** AP Photo/Richard Vogel; **p. 28:** © hana/Datacraft/Getty Images; **p. 29 (left):** © Sapone, Patti/Star Ledger/Corbis; **p. 29 (right):** © Elsa/Staff/Getty Images; **p. 31:** © Eric Audras/Getty Images; **p. 32 (left):** © Michael Nichols/National Geographic/Getty Images; **p. 32 (right):** Courtesy of Barbara Fredrickson, University of North Carolina; **p. 33:** © The McGraw-Hill Companies, Inc./Lars A. Niki, photographer; **p. 36:** American Images Inc./Photodisc/Getty Images; **p. 38:** © PhotoAlto sas/Alamy; **p. 39:** © Andrew Rich/The Agency Collection/Getty Images.

### Chapter 2
**Opener:** © Jordan Siemens/Getty Images; **p. 44:** © Phanie/Photo Researchers, Inc.; **Fig 2.1:** © RubberBall Productions; **p. 48:** © Lawrence Manning/Corbis; **p. 49:** © Mark Hunt/Huntstock/Corbis; **p. 53:** Centers for Disease Control; **p. 54:** © Nora Tejada/Taxi/Getty Images; **Fig 2.8:** © Jonathan Nourok/PhotoEdit; **p. 58:** © David Fraizer/The Image Works; **Fig 2.9:** © Peter Arnold, Inc./Alamy; **Fig 2.10:** © Lennart Nilsson/Albert Bonniers Forlag AB; **Fig 2.13:** © John Whiley, California Institute of Technology, estate of James Olds; **Fig 2.14:** © A. Glauberman/Photo Researchers, Inc; **p. 65:** From: Damasio H., Grabowski T., Frank R., Galaburda A.M., Damasio A.R.: The return of Phineas Gage: Clues about the brain from the skull of a famous patient. *Science, 264*:1102–1105, 1994. Departments of Neurology and Image Analysis Facility, University of Iowa; **p. 69 (left):** © Image Source/Getty Images; **p. 69 (right):** © Comstock Images/Getty Images; **Fig 2.20:** © PhotoAlto/PunchStock; **Fig 2.21:** © Lennart Nilsson/Albert Bonniers Forlag AB; **p. 73:** © Justin K. Aller/Getty Images; **p. 77:** © Foodcollection; **p. 79:** © Enrico Ferorelli; **p. 80:** © Joe Murphy/NBAE via Getty Images.

### Chapter 3
**Opener:** © Philip and Karen Smith/Iconica/Getty Images; **p. 85:** © Ariel Skelley/Riser/Getty Images; **p. 86 (left):** © Ron Austing; Frank Lane Picture Agency/Corbis; **p. 86 (right):** © Image Source/Punchstock; **Fig 3.1 (eye):** © Barbara Penoyar/Getty Images; **Fig 3.1 (ear):** © The McGraw-Hill Companies, Inc./Eric Wise, photographer; **Fig 3.1 (foot):** © The McGraw-Hill Companies, Inc./Jill Braaten, photographer; **Fig 3.1 (smelling):** © ZenShui/Sigrid Olsson/Getty Images; **Fig 3.1 (eating):** © istockphoto.com/Zorani; **p. 88:** © Stockbyte/PunchStock; **p. 89:** © Photodisc; **p. 90:** © Stockdisc; **p. 91:** © SuperStock/AGE Fotostock; **p. 92:** © Burke/Triolo/Brand X Pictures; **p. 94:** © Vstock LLC/Getty Images; **Fig 3.8:** Courtesy of X-Rite, Inc.; **Fig 3.10:** © Omikron/Photo Researchers; **Fig 3.13:** © David A. Tietz/Editorial Image, LLC; **p. 101:** © RubberBall Productions/Getty Images; **Fig 3.20:** © Erich Lessing/Art Resource, NY; **Fig 3.22:** © Steve Allen/Getty Images; **p. 109:** © The Star-Ledger/Saed Hindash/The Image Works; **p. 116:** © John Fedele/Blend Images/Getty Images; **p. 118:** © TWPhoto/Corbis; **p. 119:** © Tom Grill/Photographer's Choice RF/Getty Images; **p. 121 (pitching):** © Lisa Blumenfeld/Getty Images; **Fig 3.31:** © Dominic Rouse/The Image Bank/Getty Images; **Fig 3.31 (inset):** © Lennart Nilsson/Albert Bonniers Forlag AB.

### Chapter 4
**Opener:** © Image Source/AGE Fotostock; **p. 127:** © Comstock/Alamy; **p. 128:** © Image Source/Alamy; **p. 130:** © Jajmo/

# name index

## A

Aalsma, M. C., 299
Abbassi, E., 70
Abbate, C., 234
ABC News, 336
Abdelkhalik, J., 320
Abdullah, T., 477
Abell, S., 395
Abelson, R., 216
Ábrahám, H., 288
Abrams, L., 233
Abramson, L. Y., 456, 463
Accaradi, M., 159
Accordini, S., 514, 538
Acevedo, E. O., 514, 534
Achanzar, K., 349
Acheson, D. T., 449, 450
Ackerman, J. M., 116, 421
Ackerman, P., 411
Adamou, M., 447
Adams, E. E., 317
Adams, H. E., 365
Adams, M. J., 231
Adams, T. B., 519
Addario, D., 471
Addington, D., 478
Addington, J., 478
Addis, D. R., 205
Addison, T., 416
Adelstein, J. S., 388
Ader, R., 174
Adler, A., 367, 368, 369
Adler, N. E., 329
Adolph, K. E., 286
Adolphs, R., 401
Adriaanse, M. A., 520
Aggarwal, N. T., 238
Aggarwal, S., 49
Aghajanian, G., 456
Agnati, L. F., 244
Agnew, C. R., 397, 437
Ago, Y., 485
Agorastos, A., 442, 450, 451
Aguayo, D., 11
Aguilar-Gaxiola, S., 465
Ahluwalia, J., 313
Ahmadi, J., 154
Aichele, S. R., 292
Aigner, L., 75, 293
Aimola Davies, A., 93
Ainsworth, K., 516
Ainsworth, M. D. S., 303
Ainsworth, M. S., 303
Aitken, M. R., 183
Ajrouch, K., 518, 520
Ajzen, I., 406, 516
Akehurst, L., 144
Akhmedova, K., 341
Akhtar, S., 506
Akkermann, K., 464
Akman, C., 452
Aknin, L. B., 14
Aksan, N., 317
Aktas, A., 175
Akturk, U., 520
Akyuz, G., 466, 467
Al-Alem, L., 475
Alanko, K., 336
Albarracin, D., 516, 540
Albert, D., 299
Alberto, P. A., 188
Aldwin, C. M., 321
Alea, 237
Alessandri, G., 317, 375, 390

Alexander, B., 483, 485
Alexander, G. C., 447
Alexander, G. E., 238
Alexander, G. M., 313
Alexander, K., 413
Alexander, K. W., 227
Alexander, M. G., 337
Alfano, M. S., 457
Ali, S., 525
Allen, J. J. B., 221, 467
Allen, K., 338
Allen, R. J., 130
Alloway, T. P., 210
Allport, G. W., 373, 374, 380, 385
Almeida, D. M., 528
Almen, M. S., 330
Alonso, P., 452
Alper, C. M., 528
Alpert, N. M., 57
Alquist, J. L., 523
Alstermark, B., 44
Altemus, M., 450
Altenmuller, E., 48
Altenor, A., 182
Alter, A. L., 405
Althoff, R. R., 460
Alvarenga, M., 449
Alvarez, M. J., 332
Alvarez, R. M., 401
Alvaro, E. M., 516
Alvaro, F., 175
Al-Wer, E., 267
Aly, M., 126
Amano, T., 62, 173, 347
Amar, A. P., 489
Amarel, D., 522
Ambadar, Z., 226
Amelang, M., 524
American Academy of Ophthalmology, 155
American Association of Neurological Surgeons, 74
American Association on Intellectual and Developmental Disabilities, 264
American Cancer Society, 538
American Psychiatric Association, 441, 444, 446, 462, 507
American Psychological Association, 339
Amunts, K., 58, 474
Anastasi, A., 259
Ancoli-Israel, S., 140
Andel, R., 238
Anders, S., 384
Andersen, P. K., 389, 390
Anderson, A. K., 226
Anderson, C. A., 22, 414, 417
Anderson, C. J., 429
Anderson, D. R., 529, 533, 534
Anderson, E. M., 507, 508
Anderson, K. B., 22
Anderson, L. A., 291
Anderson, N., 238
Anderson, N. H., 402
Anderson, P. B., 332
Anderson, R. N, 461
Anderson, V., 73
Anderson-Hanley, C., 301
Anderson-Lewis, C., 516
Andersson, G., 523
Andrade, E., 84
Andre, J. B., 410
Andrew, B. J., 171
Andrews, B., 453

Andrillon, T., 138
Andrusyna, T. P., 507
Andrykowski, M. A., 175
Anestis, M. D., 475
Ang, S., 255, 259, 384
Angel, L., 293
Angermeyer, M. C., 406
Angoa-Perez, M., 452
Ansseau, M., 457
Anstey, K. J., 300
Antoni, M., 508
Antonucci, T. C., 518, 520
Anusic, I., 393
Apicella, C., 525
April, L. B., 171
Apuzzo, M. L., 489
Araton, H., 324
Arbesman, M., 514
Archer, R. P., 395
Arciero, P. J., 301
Arden, M., 519
Areh, I., 228
Arendt, J., 134, 135
Arendtsz, A., 343
Areni, C. S., 408
Arentoft, A., 449, 450
Ariely, D., 35, 357
Armitage, C. J., 519, 520
Armony, J. L., 469
Armor, D. A., 282
Arndt, J., 319
Arnett, J. J., 309
Arntz, A., 476
Aronson, J., 259, 260, 266, 405
Arora, R., 31
Arpan, L., 406
Arps, K., 411
Arriaga, X. B., 437
Arrow, H., 412
Arseneault, L., 413
Artazcoz, L., 136
Artemiadis, A. K., 532
Asch, S. E., 419
Aschersleben, G., 128
Ashburner, J., 44
Ashby, N. J., 131
Asher, B. D., 404
Asherson, P., 447
Asian, H., 520
Asnaani, A., 504, 505
Aspinwall, L. G., 532
Assaad, J., 413
Asselin, M. C., 349
Assido, M., 458
Associated Press, 226
Astell, A., 214, 455
Atkins, D. C., 500
Atkinson, R. C., 207, 221
Atmaca, M., 452
Aton, S. J., 135
Attwell, D., 85
Attwood, T., 129
AuBuchon, A. M., 209
Austad, C. S., 506
Austin, J., 507
Avi, A., 289
Axelsson, M., 525
Ayala, G. X., 514
Aydin, N., 449
Ayduk, O., 386
Aylaz, R., 520
Ayub, M., 504, 505
Ayub, N., 526
Azarbad, L., 464

Azmitia, M., 308
Azuma, H., 304

## B

Baars, B. J., 127
Baars, J., 502
Baas, M., 412
Babiloni, C., 219
Babinski, D. E., 447
Bacaltchuk, J., 465
Bachman, J. G., 146, 149, 153, 155
Bachmann, T., 126
Back, M. D., 361
Bacow, T., 462
Baddeley, A., 209, 210, 211, 223
Baddeley, J. L., 237, 521
Badler, J. B., 106
Badre, D., 232
Baer, J., 254
Baerentsen, K., 161
Baeyens, F., 173
Baez, E., 457
Bagger, J. L., 328
Bahrick, H. P., 212, 213
Bahrick, L. E., 203
Bahrick, P. O., 213
Bailey, D., 71
Bailey, J. M., 338, 339, 394
Bailey, S. J., 436
Bailine, S. H., 488
Baillargeon, R., 298, 299
Baird, B., 130, 378
Baird, J. C., 54
Bajbouj, M., 488
Baker, F. C., 138, 139
Baker, L. A., 413
Baker, S., 197
Baker, T. B., 538
Bakermans-Kranenburg, M. J., 81, 304
Bakker, A. B., 376, 377
Balazic, J., 460
Balbin, E., 523
Balcetis, E., 74
Baldessarini, R. J., 484
Baldi, E., 225
Balfour, L., 502
Balkin, T. J., 136
Ball, H. A., 78
Balliet, D., 5, 376
Balter, M., 210
Banaji, M. R., 431
Bandura, A., 9, 168, 188, 189, 190, 313, 314, 344, 383, 384, 414, 415, 417, 425, 499, 524
Banerjee, R., 129
Banich, M. T., 469
Bankoff, S. M., 494
Banks, C., 423
Banks, J. A., 11
Banthia, R., 141
Banyard, V. L., 225
Barbui, C., 484
Barch, D. M., 469
Bard, P., 347
Bardone-Cone, A. M., 463, 503
Barefoot, J., 300
Barefoot, J. C., 529
Barelds, D. P. H., 377
Bargh, J. A., 116, 132, 215
Barker, A. T., 59
Barker, R. A., 75
Barkley, R., 447

Barling, J., 414
Barloon, T., 449
Barnard, P. J., 219
Barndollar, K., 215
Barnes, A. S., 537
Barnes, J., 408
Barnes, L. L., 238
Barnes-Farrell, J. L., 478
Bar-On, N., 436
Barr, A., 411
Barr, C. S., 474
Barrera, M. E., 287
Barrett, A. M., 350
Barrett, C., 411
Barrett, T., 287
Barrouillet, P., 232, 233
Barry, C. L., 486
Barry, D., 524
Barry, S., 106
Bartels, A., 347
Bartholow, B. D., 414
Bartolomei, F., 127
Bartolomeo, P., 126
Barton, D., 449
Baruh, 1
Bar-Zvi, M., 499
Baser, O., 173
Basner, R. C., 140
Basow, S. A., 477
Bassett, D. R., 536
Bassett, D. S., 245
Bassett, R. L., 534
Bassok, M., 246
Bastille-Denis, E., 134
Bastin, C., 62, 218
Basting, A. D., 281
Bates, G., 301
Bates, T. C., 390
Batki, A., 313
Batson, C. D., 411
Batterman-Faunce, J. M., 226
Battin, B., 74
Battista, J., 74, 74
Batty, G. D., 300
Baudouin, J., 469
Bauer, J. J., 129, 237, 321
Bauer, M. E., 271, 485
Bauer, S. M., 469
Baum, A., 80
Baumann, A. E., 476
Baumeister, R. F., 132, 336, 342,
    414, 523
Baumrind, D., 281, 306
Bava, C. M., 330
Bavelier, D., 9, 44
Baxter, L. R., Jr., 459
Bayen, U. J., 234
Baylor, D., 106
Bayoglu, B., 449
Bazerman, M. H., 226
BBC News, 205
Beaman, A. L., 411
Beasley, C., 471
Beaver, K. M., 280
Bech, P., 509
Beck, A. T., 46, 456, 496, 497, 498,
    500, 507
Becker, D. V., 421
Becker, E., 318
Becker, H., 384
Becker, M., 429
Becker, S. J., 523
Becker, S. W., 412
Becker, T., 482
Becker, T. M., 209
Becker-Weidman, E. G., 456
Bederian-Gardner, D., 226
Bedics, J. D., 500
Bednark, J. G., 247, 251
Beeftink, F., 384
Beekman, A., 508
Beeli, G., 88
Beem, A. L., 389
Begley, S., 161, 349

Behrens, K. Y., 304
Behrer, L., 238
Behrman, B. W., 228
Beidel, D. C., 452
Beiderbeck, D. I., 413
Békésy, G. v., 112
Bekinschtein, T. A., 127
Bekrater-Bodmann, R., 88
Belaise, C., 509
Bell, A. P., 338
Bell, R., 525
Bell, R. J., 484
Bellezza, F. S., 131
Belli, H., 466
Bello, D., 55
Belon, K., 139
Belopolsky, A., 209
Belsky, J., 280
Bem, D., 90, 91, 407
Bempechat, J., 343
Benbow, C. P., 262, 312
Bench, C. J., 349
Bendel, R. E., 134
Bender, D., 476
Bender, T. W., 475
Bendiksen, M., 226
Benedek, D., 453
Benedetti, F., 174, 191
Benegal, V., 450
Benet-Martinez, V., 270
Benham, B., 35
Benington, J. H., 13
Benjamin, A. J., Jr., 414
Benjet, C., 465
Bennett, D. A ., 523
Bennett, D. M., 488
Bennett, L. B., 228
Bennike, B., 389, 390
Benoit, A., 469
Benowitz, N., 538
Benson, E., 298
Benson, H., 161
Benson, J. A., 156
Benson, L., 329
Bentley, D. E., 117
Bereiter, C., 247
Berenbaum, H., 469
Berenbaum, S. E., 354
Berenz, E. C., 450
Berg, C., 375
Berg, C. A., 524
Berg, C. J., 458
Berg, R., 466
Berger, R. E., 155
Berger, T., 490, 497
Berghuis, J., 519
Berglund, J., 478
Bergman, K., 527
Bergman, M. E., 432
Berkman, E. T., 389
Berko Gleason, J., 266, 271, 272
Berkowitz, L., 414
Berman, J. S., 507
Bernard, A., 298
Bernard, M. L., 243
Bernardy, N. C., 483, 485
Berndt, N. C., 524
Bernhard, J. D., 161
Bernstein, G. A., 452
Bernstein, H. J., 488
Bernstein, I. L., 175
Bernston, G. G., 520
Berntsen, D., 223
Berr, C., 301
Berridge, K. C., 349
Berry, J. W., 5
Berscheid, E., 434, 436
Berstchy, G., 133
Berthet, A., 54
Bertin, E., 92
Bertrand, J. W., 384
Bertrand, M., 430
Besedovsky, L., 141
Best, K. A., 457
Bettecken, T., 449

Beutel, M. E., 529
Beutler, L. E., 393, 501
Bewernick, B. H., 488
Beydoun, M. A., 329
Bhatia, T., 469
Bhattacharya, G., 520
Bhattacharyya, M. R., 529
Bhaumik, D. K., 486
Bhugra, D., 472
Bibby, P. A., 375
Bibi, U., 225
Bielak, A. A. M., 300
Bienias, J. L., 523
Biernat, M., 411, 429
Biesanz, J. C., 395
Biggs, M., 488
Bihrle, S., 474, 475
Billig, M., 430
Binder, E. B., 449, 454
Binet, A., 257
Birch, K., 411
Birditt, K., 353, 518, 520
Birgegård, A., 444, 463, 464
Biro, F. M., 63, 289
Bischof, 238
Bisgaard, H., 538
Bishop, J. R., 328
Bissada, H., 502
Biswas-Diener, R., 19, 20
Bjerkeset, O., 478
Bjork, R., 197
Bjork, R. A., 168, 190
Bjorklund, D. F., 11
Black, C. H., 509
Black, J. J., 525
Black, S. A., 22
Black, S. E., 213
Blackburn, E. H., 292
Blacklow, B., 503
Blader, J. C., 413
Blagov, P., 237
Blagrove, M., 138, 144
Blagys, M. D., 524
Blair, C., 259, 260, 266, 539
Blair, S. N., 534
Blake, H., 75
Blakemore, J. E. O., 354
Blanchard, R., 336
Blanck, H. M., 537
Blanco, C., 459
Blanco, M., 94
Blandina, P., 225
Blank, A., 253
Blank, H., 252
Blanton, H., 431
Blass, R. B., 367
Blass, T., 422
Blau, K., 393
Blehar, M. C., 303
Blei, D. M., 172
Bleske-Rechek, A., 262
Blickle, G., 375
Bliss, J. M., 525
Block, G. D., 140
Block, J., 321, 355, 376, 405
Block, S. D., 227
Blocker, A., 84
Bloom, B., 262, 447
Bloom, F., 43, 116, 117
Bloom, M., 341
Bloom, P., 274
Blume, C. L., 209
Blumenfeld, P. C., 343, 344
Blunt, H., 525
Boakes, R. A., 174
Boals, A., 225
Bocanegra, J., 94
Boccaccini, M. T., 393
Bock, J., 289
Bode, P., 30
Boeddeker, N., 106
Boehm, J. K., 357, 526
Boeninger, D. K., 321
Boersma, G. J., 527
Bogaert, A. F., 338

Bohbot, V. D., 238
Boivin, M., 413
Bolea, B., 447
Bolger, N., 522
Bolhuis, J. J., 325
Bolman, C., 524
Bolnick, R., 317
Bolt, S., 257
Boly, M., 158
Bolyanatz, A., 411
Bonam, C., 405
Bonanno, G. A., 320, 531
Bonchek, A., 495
Bond, M. H., 352
Bond, R., 421
Bonds-Raache, J., 26
Bonfatti, J. F., 469
Bonnelykke, K., 538
Bonney, C. R., 3, 253
Bono, G., 5
Bonus, K., 161
Book, A. S., 393
Boomsma, D. I., 389, 475
Boothroyd, R. A., 457
Borden, W., 10
Bore, M., 58
Borge, A. I. H., 316
Borges, G., 465
Borlongan, C. V., 75
Born, J., 135, 141
Bornstein, M. H., 281
Bornstein, R. F., 394
Borsboom, D., 90, 91
Borst, A., 106
Bos, A. E. R., 353
Bos, C. S., 264
Bos, M. W., 250
Boschen, M. J., 449
Bosnyak, D. J., 289
Bosson, J. K., 404
Botega, N. J., 459
Bouazzaoui, B., 293
Bouchard, S. M., 148
Bouchard, T. J., 79, 390
Bouchard, T. J., Jr., 390
Boucher, K. L., 405
Bouchoux, A., 151
Bouffard, S. M., 308
Bourgin, P., 133
Bourque, F., 442
Bovbjerg, D. H., 175
Bow, J. N., 393
Bowdle, B. F., 415
Bower, J. E, 528
Bowers, M. S., 54
Bowlby, J., 303
Bowles, E. N., 158
Bowles, S., 412
Bowman, N. A., 193, 421
Boyd, J. H., 129
Boyle, P. A., 238
Boyle, S. H., 300, 389
Boywitt, C. D., 222
Brabec, J., 142
Brackett, M. A., 265
Bradley-Davino, B., 454
Bradshaw, A., 121
Brakel, T. M., 406
Brammer, G. L., 413
Brand, B., 465
Brand, B. L., 465
Brandenberger, J. W., 309
Brandstatter, J. H., 99
Branje, S. J., 1, 308
Brannon, L., 353
Bransford, J., 253
Brass, M., 48
Brass, S. D., 143
Braucher, J., 430, 431
Braun, K., 289
Braun, M. H., 218
Braunstein, G. D., 331
Bravo, E., 127
Bray, M. S., 514
Breakspear, M., 100

Breeze, R. E., 75
Breland, M., 194
Bremner, J. D., 453, 465
Brenchley, C., 449
Brendgen, M., 316, 413
Breslan, J., 465
Breslin, C., 519
Brevik, J. L., 532
Brewer, G. A., 22, 237
Brewer, J. B., 219
Brewer, N., 229, 408
Brewin, C. R., 452, 453
Brickman, A. M., 301
Brickman, P., 357
Bridge, J. A., 486
Bridwell, D. A., 292
Brigham, J. C., 228, 432
Bright, M., 210
Brink, S., 148
Brinol, P., 406, 407, 408
Brito-Melo, G. E., 471
Britton, W. B., 456, 499
Broadbent, E., 528
Broberg, D. J., 175
Broca, P., 67
Brockerhoff, S. E., 99
Brodbeck, F. C., 193
Brodskey, L., 351
Brody, D. J., 485
Brody, L. R., 353, 354
Brody, N., 266
Brody, S., 336
Brohan, E., 477
Broman, D. A., 175
Brombin, C., 509
Brooker, R. J., 78
Brooks, J. G., 253
Brooks, K. P., 311
Brooks, M. G., 253
Brooks-Gunn, J., 289
Brosh, H., 308
Brosschot, J. F., 131
Brow, M., 532
Brown, A. R., 173
Brown, A. S., 471
Brown, C. H., 486
Brown, C. M., 407
Brown, D., 159
Brown, D. R., 291
Brown, G. M., 141
Brown, G. R., 325
Brown, G. S., 509
Brown, J. D., 405
Brown, K. S., 245
Brown, N. R., 236
Brown, P., 415
Brown, P. L., 178
Brown, R., 271, 513
Brown, R. P., 461
Brown, S., 410
Brown, S. D., 384
Brown, S. L., 521
Brown, T., 136
Brown, T. G., 148
Brown, T. L., 477
Broyles, S., 434
Brubaker, A. L., 292
Bruce, D., 237
Bruce, K., 171
Brüchmiller, K., 447
Bruck, M., 225, 227
Bruehl, E. C., 223
Brug, J., 519
Brumberg, J. S., 125
Brummett, B. H., 389
Brun, A., 219
Brundin, L., 75
Brune, M., 489
Brunet, M. L., 249
Bruning, R. H., 235
Brunner, M., 405
Brunstein, J., 357, 397
Brunstein, J. C., 397
Brusset, B., 491

Bryan, A. D., 514
Bryan, C., 520
Bryant, C., 291
Bryant, F. B., 381
Bryant, R. A., 159
Brydon, L., 521, 529
Brynes, A. E., 519
Brzezinski, A., 141
Bucherelli, C., 225
Buchhalter, A. R., 539
Büchler, M., 450
Buchman, A. C., 539
Buchner, D., 536
Bucholz, K. K., 150
Buchser, W. J., 530
Buckley, T., 411
Bueno, J. L., 180
Bueno, J. L. S., 180
Buhi, E. R., 525
Bui, E., 454
Bukowski, W. M., 413
Bulik, C. M., 452
Bull, P., 347
Buonocore, M. H., 449
Burdette, A. M., 523
Burgdorf, J., 349
Burger, J., 423
Burgess, A. P., 350
Burgess, D. J., 405
Buring, J. E., 534
Burk, W. J., 1, 425, 457
Burke, B. L., 319
Burke, M. M., 264
Burks, D. J., 410, 411
Burney, R., 161
Burns, J., 472
Burns, P., 130
Burrows, L., 215
Burston, D., 367
Burton, C. M., 27, 250, 521
Buscemi, L., 150
Busch, H., 310
Busch, S. H., 486
Buschkuehl, M., 274
Bush, D. E., 348
Bushman, B. J., 22, 414, 417
Bushman, L., 415
Buss, D. M., 8, 10, 120, 325, 376,
   410, 435
Busseri, M. A., 262, 263
Bussey, K., 313, 314
Bussy, G., 219
Butcher, J. N., 393, 497
Butler, A. C., 507
Butler, S., 350
Butovskaya, M. L., 413
Buttenschøn, H. N., 449
Button, T. M. M., 78
Buunk, A. P., 406
Buunk, B. P., 437
Buzi, R. S., 333
Byard, R. W., 143
Byrne, R. W., 189
Byrne, S., 524
Byrne, S. M., 463


C

Cabeza, R., 293
Cabot, P. J., 54
Cabras, P. L., 463, 464
Cacioppo, J. T., 408, 520, 521
Caffo, E., 509
Cahill, K., 538
Cai, H., 11
Caillouet, B. A., 393
Cairney, S., 135
Calcagno, J., 412
Cale, E. M., 474
Call, J., 192
Calmes, J., 189
Caltagirone, C., 233
Calvin, C. M., 300
Calvo-Merino, B., 48

Cameron, H. A., 75
Campbell, A., 130
Campbell, A. J., 503
Campbell, B., 265
Campbell, C. A., 539
Campbell, D. T., 107, 357
Campbell, J., 503
Campbell, J. D., 523
Campbell, L., 265
Campbell, L. M., 482, 497, 503
Campbell, S. M., 4
Campbell, W., 478
Campomayor, C. O., 141
Canli, T., 388
Cannon, J., 289
Cannon, M. J., 285
Cannon, W. B., 328, 347
Canton, J., 454
Canton-Cortes, D., 454
Cantor, N., 238, 386
Cantu, R., 74
Capasso, A., 463
Capitanio, J. P., 377
Caporeal, L. R., 435
Capozza, D., 432
Cappa, S., 219
Caprara, G. V., 317, 375
Caputi, M., 127, 129
Cardeña, E., 443
Cardenas, J. C., 411
Cardinale, G., 470
Cardinali, D. P., 141
Cardno, A. G., 78, 470
Carek, P. J., 494
Carey, B., 42, 90, 212, 478, 497
Cargill, A., 538
Caricati, L., 406
Carlesimo, G. A., 233
Carlini, M., 484
Carlo, G., 308, 316, 317
Carlsmith, J. M., 407
Carlson, E. A., 280, 303, 304
Carlson, J. M., 245
Carlson, S. M., 65
Carlson, W., 458
Carlstrom, E., 338, 339
Carmona, J. E., 70
Carnahan, T., 424
Carnell, S., 329
Carnes, M., 405
Carney, D. R., 394
Caronongan, P., 308
Carpenter, M., 270
Carpenter, S. K., 221
Carprara, G. V., 390
Carr, R., 463
Carrard, I., 464
Carrieri, V., 406
Carrigan, K. A., 174
Carr-Malone, R., 453
Carroll, D., 300
Carroll, J. L., 331
Carroll, M. D., 536
Carskadon, M. A., 139
Carson, R. C., 497
Carson, V. B., 514, 523
Carstensen, L. L., 311
Carter, C. S., 55
Carter, J. D., 410
Carter, R., 61
Cartmill, E. A., 273
Caruso, D. R., 265
Carvalho, L. A., 452
Carvallo, M., 11
Carver, C. S., 344, 375, 525, 526
Casalin, S., 303
Cascant, L., 136
Case, N., 520
Case, R. B., 520
Caserta, M., 321
Casey, B. J., 77, 290, 386
Caspar, F., 490, 497
Caspi, A., 80, 413, 474
Cass, K. M., 503

Cassidy, C., 425
Caston, J., 492
Castro, C. A., 453
Castro-Alamancos, M. A., 115
Catalan, J., 409
Catalino, L. I., 355
Cathers-Schiffman, T. A., 258
Catroppa, C., 73
Cattell, R. B., 300
Cavender, J. H., 221
Caverzasi, E., 488
Cavina-Pratesi, C., 104
Ceci, S. J., 225, 227
Centers for Disease Control and Prevention,
   74, 152, 329, 460, 535, 539
Cerletti, U., 488
Cervone, D., 386
Chabardès, S., 488
Chabris, C., 93
Chabris, C. F., 93, 228
Chae, J. H., 136
Chae, Y., 226
Chafetz, L., 478
Chalk, M., 173
Chambers, W. H., 80
Chambon, V., 469
Chan, M. Y., 15
Chana, G., 471
Chance, P., 187, 194
Chandra, A., 336, 338
Chang, A. C., 245
Chang, Y. C., 73
Chang, Z., 447
Changeux, J., 127
Changeux, J. P., 127
Chanowitz, B., 253
Chao, R. K., 307
Chapman, J. E., 507
Charles, J. E., 266
Charles, S. T., 311
Charrin, E., 219
Chase, N., 534
Chaturvedi, S. K., 450
Chaudhari, N., 118
Chaudhry, H. R., 469
Chauhan, A., 466
Chaves, J. F., 159
Cheah, C. S., 11
Chechneva, O., 47
Chelaru, I. M., 184
Chemero, A., 126
Chen, C. C., 477
Chen, J., 406, 468
Chen, L., 66
Chen, M., 215
Chen, M. C., 456
Chen, P., 149, 150
Chen, T. J., 456
Chen, X., 341
Chen, Z., 403
Cheng, B. H., 342
Cheng, C., 10
Cheng, C. M., 251
Cheng, S. K., 231
Cherian, T., 68
Cherkassky, L., 265
Cherrington, A., 514
Cherubini, A., 53
Chervin, R. D., 139
Chess, S., 302
Chica, A. B., 126
Chiu, C., 192
Chiu, S., 466
Chiu, W. T., 476
Chivers, M. L., 336
Cho, H. J., 528
Choe, B. K., 478
Choi, J., 488
Choi, J. K., 412
Choi, J. M., 478
Chomsky, N., 270, 271
Chorost, M., 125
Chou, C. P., 516
Chou, H. T., 252, 406

Chou, P., 473
Chouinard, G., 486
Chow, T., 331
Chrisman, K., 437
Christ, S. E., 209
Christensen, H., 292, 300
Christensen, L. B., 34
Christie, B. R., 75, 293
Christoff, K., 130
Christopher Frueh, B., 499
Chronicle of Higher Education, 193
Chrousos, G. P., 46, 528
Chu, Y., 192
Chun, D., 84
Chun, D. S., 317
Chun, M. M., 203
Chung, C. K., 521
Chung, H., 514
Chung, T., 149
Church, A. T., 377
Church, R. M., 185
Churchill, R., 484
Cialdini, R. B., 409, 410, 411
Ciani, A. C., 339
Cicchetti, D., 280
Cicero, D. C., 250
Cilli, A. S., 452
Cinnirella, M., 429
Cipriani, A., 484
Cirelli, C., 135
Clardy, C. E., 429
Clark, B., 263
Clark, D. A., 46
Clark, D. B., 155
Clark, E. M., 523
Clark, J. J., 10
Clark, L. A., 377
Clark, M. S., 116, 437
Clark, R. D., 337
Clarkin, J. F., 500
Clarkson, G., 209
Clarys, D., 223
Claudino, A. M., 464
Clearfield, M. W., 286
Cleckley, H. M., 467
Cleere, C., 159
Cleeremans, A., 92
Cleveland, J. N., 478
Clifford, C. W., 347
Clinton, D., 444, 463, 464
Clooney, G., 321, 322
Clore, G. L., 251
Close, C. E., 155
Cloud, J., 263
CNN, 431
Coan, J. A., 349
Cobb, N. K., 425
Cobb, S., 74
Coccaro, E. F., 390, 447
Cody, M. J., 376
Coe, C. L., 343, 522
Coffino, B., 280, 303, 304
Cohen, A. B., 403, 412
Cohen, D., 415, 430, 431
Cohen, F., 341
Cohen, L., 127
Cohen, L. H., 321
Cohen, N., 174
Cohen, R. A., 447
Cohen, S., 201, 521, 528
Cohen-Kettenis, P. T., 313
Coifman, K. G., 531
Colapinto, J., 314
Cole, J., 88
Cole, S., 141
Cole, S. H., 475
Cole, S. W., 565
Coleman, N. M., 332
Coleman, T., 135
Coliado-Hidalgo, A., 141
Coll, C. G., 308
Collet, S., 120
Collette, J. L., 69
Colletti, P., 474, 475

Collin, G. B., 98
Collins, C., 74
Collins, C. E., 175
Collins, P. F., 389
Collins, W. A., 281
Collins-Bride, G., 478
Colrain, I. M., 138, 139
Coluccia, A., 460
Colvin, C. R., 394, 405
Colwell, C. S., 140
Coman, E., 457
Comasco, E., 389
Comer, S. D., 47
Compton, J. A., 409
Compton, W., 473
Compton, W. C., 446
Comstock, G., 415
Comstock, R. D., 74
Comtois, K. A., 500
Con, A. H., 533
Conger, A. J., 173
Conger, R. D., 375
Conley, T. D., 337
Conlin, C., 534
Connellan, J., 313
Conner, K. R., 460, 526
Conner, M., 519, 523
Connor-Smith, J., 375
Conraads, V. M., 529
Conrad, F. G., 236
Constable, R. T., 388
Constantine, N. A., 333
Constantinidou, F., 197
Conti, R., 447
Converse, P. D., 393
Conway, M., 223
Conway, M. A., 135, 237
Cook, C. C. H., 523
Cook, E., 54
Cook, J. R., 504
Cook, S. P., 225
Cook, S. W., 267
Coolidge, F. L., 210, 392
Cooper, A., 378, 389
Cooper, B. A., 478
Cooper, C. R., 308
Cooper, H., 343
Cooper, R. M., 78
Cooper, Z. D., 47
Copeland, D. E., 223
Copeland, L. E., 449
Copen, C., 336, 338
Copen, C. E., 310
Corbit, L. H., 54
Corey, G., 502
Corr, P. J., 350, 389
Correa, T., 375
Corrigan, P. W., 477
Corsica, J., 464
Corsica, J. A., 536
Cortes, I., 136
Cortes, M. R., 454
Cosci, F., 529
Cosmides, L., 10
Costa, A., 233
Costa, L. C., 391
Costa, P. T., 374, 393
Costa, R. M., 336
Côté, S., 342
Cotter, D., 471
Cotugno, G., 280
Couchman, C. E., 16, 343
Couillard-Despres, S., 75, 293
Coukos, G., 528
Coulson, M. C., 507
Coursen, E. L., 158
Courtet, P., 460
Covell, N. H., 487
Covenas, R., 456
Cowan, M. K., 78
Cowan, N., 209, 210
Cowan, R. L., 154
Cowdrey, F. A., 456
Cox, E., 482

Cox, K. S., 310
Cox, R. E., 159
Cox, T. L., 533
Coyne, J., 525
Coyne, J. C., 457, 524, 525
Coyne, S. M., 1
Craig, I. W., 474
Craik, F. I. M., 204, 221, 234
Cramer, P., 365, 369, 397
Cramond, B., 253
Crandall, C. S., 425
Crano, W. D., 406, 407
Crano, W. M., 516
Crawford, J. R., 234
Crede, M., 374
Crenshaw, M., 341
Crimmins, E., 238
Crisafulli, C., 459
Criss, A. H., 232
Critchley, H. D., 135
Crocker, J., 429
Croft, W., 267
Crombez, G., 474
Cropley, T. G., 161
Crosby, R. D., 465
Cross, J., 419
Croux, C., 457
Crowe, M., 238
Crowley, J. J., 471
Crowley, K., 488
Crowley, M., 412
Crowley, S. J., 139
Crucian, G. P., 350
Cruz, A. M., 415, 417
Cruz, L. E., 75
Csikszentmihalyi, M., 5, 355
Cuijpers, P., 508
Culhane, S. E., 426
Cullen, K., 416
Culmer, P. R., 293
Cumberland, A., 316, 317
Cumming, E., 311
Cunningham, C. L., 425
Cunningham, R. L., 413
Cunningham, S. J., 130
Curhan, K., 343, 522
Curi, A., 219
Currie, J., 488
Curry, J. F., 523
Curtis, C., 464
Curtis, M. A., 75, 292
Curtiss, S., 272
Cusack, K. J., 499
Cutler, T., 140
Czechowska, Y., 469

D

Dabringhaus, A., 58
Dach-Gruschow, K., 11
Dackis, C., 154
Dahn, J. R., 508
Dale, K.Y., 466
Dale, R., 488
Dall, S. R. X., 377
Dalton, K. M., 57, 349
Damon, W., 344
Damsa, C., 451
Dani, J. A., 147
Daniel, L. C., 533
Daniel, S., 161
Daniels, K., 310
Danner, D. D., 22
Darby, B. L., 409
Darcq, E., 180
Darcy, E., 462
Darley, J. M., 405, 412
Darling, S., 130
Darwin, C., 7, 351, 449
Dasch, K. B., 321
da Silva Cais, C. F., 459
D'Ausilio, A., 48
Davey, S. L., 228
David, D., 496, 499

Davidson, J. R., 141, 490
Davidson, J. W., 262
Davidson, K. W., 508
Davidson, P. S., 225
Davidson, R., 161
Davidson, R. J., 57, 161, 345, 349, 389
Davies, J., 245, 259
Davis, C., 464
Davis, C. M., 174
Davis, D. E., 5
Davis, H. P., 319
Davis, J. I., 350
Davis, J. M., 486
Davis, R. D., 393
Davis, S. F., 17, 33
Davis, S. R., 484
Davis, W., 311
Davison, G. C., 446
Dawood, T., 449
Dawson, D. A., 473
Dawson, J., 330
Day, D. D., 74
Day, I., 538
Day, L. M., 136
Day, N. L., 155
De Angelis, T., 465
Dearing, E., 308
Deary, I. J., 259, 300
Deaux, K., 411, 429
Debats, D. L., 375, 523
De Biasi, M., 147
Debiec, J., 348
Dechesne, M., 341
Deci, E. L., 16, 342, 343, 344, 355, 520
De Clercq, A., 474
De Clercq, B., 475
De Cort, K., 450
Dedert, E., 515
De Dreu, K. W., 412
De Fruyt, F., 475
de Gardelle, V., 92
de Geus, E. J. C., 389
Degnin, F. D., 427
de Graaf, T. A., 127
DeHaan, C. R., 369
de Haan, H. A., 497
Dehaene, S., 127, 129
Dehon, E. E., 413
Dein, S., 523
de Jong, C. A., 497
De Jong, J., 443
De Koninck, J., 144
De Laat, A., 117
DeLamater, J. D., 333
de Lange, F. P., 129
Del Corso, J. J., 368
Del Cul, A., 127
Del Gaiso, A. K., 375
Deliege, D., 457
Dell, P. F., 465, 467, 475
Della Sala, S., 210
Dell'osso, B., 474, 483, 484
DeLosh, E. L., 221
Delprado, J., 233
Del Re, A. C., 509
DeMarree, K. G., 408
de-Melo-Neto, V. L., 450
Demeter, G., 135
Demidenko, N., 457
Demir, O. E., 273
Demler, O., 476
Demorest, A. P., 426
Deneubourg, J. L., 426
DeNeve, K. M., 22
Deng, W., 47
Denis, D., 353
Denissen, J., 1
Denmark, L., 278
Denollet, J., 529
Depue, R. A., 389
De Raad, B., 377
De Raedt, R., 456
De Ridder, D. T., 520

Derks, D., 353
der Linden, M. V., 464
Derom, C. A., 475
Derryberry, D., 349
Desai, A. K., 140
Desgranges, B., 223
Deshpande, S. N., 469
De Simone, L. L., 117
Desmond, J. E., 219
des Portes, V., 219
Desrosiers, M. F., 22
Devine, T. A. J., 316
Devor, M., 145
De Vos, J., 424
DeVries, A. C., 520
de Vries, B., 321
De Vries, H., 524
de Waal, F. B., 410
de Waal, F. B. M., 410
DeWall, C. N., 414
Dewey, M., 478
De Wit, J. B., 520
de Wit, S., 183, 446
DeWitt, J. C., 528
Dey, E. L., 193
DeYoung, C. G., 58, 388
de Zuniga, H. G., 375
de Zwaan, M., 465
d'Hemecourt, P., 74
Dhillo, W. S., 328
Dhillon, S., 459
Diamond, A., 77
Diamond, L. M., 65, 336, 338
Diamond, M., 314
Diaper, A., 483
Diaz, V. A., 494
Diaz-Mataix, L., 348
Dibello, J. R., 518
Di Blas, L., 377
Dick, D. M., 150, 280, 418
Dickens, W., 259, 260, 266
Dickerhoof, R., 357
Dickert, S., 131
Dickie, E., 469
Dickinson, A., 183
Dickinson, D., 265
Dickson, R. A., 223
DiClemente, C. C., 516, 518, 519
DiCorcia, J. A., 281
Di Dio, P., 520
Didziulis, V., 466
Diefenbach, G. J., 457
Diego, M., 285
Diekelmann, S., 135
Dien, J., 59
Dienberg Love, G., 311
Diener, C., 19
Diener, E., 15, 19, 20, 31, 358, 375,
    377, 385
Diers, M., 88
Dietert, R. R., 528
Di Giunta, L., 375
Digman, J. M., 374
Diguer, L., 507
Dijksterhuis, A. P., 216, 250
Dijkstra, A., 406
Dill, C., 515
Dill, K. E., 417
Dillon, H. R., 141
Dinesh, N., 466
Dingley, M., 537
Dion, K. K., 436
Dion, K. L., 436
Dionne, G., 413
Di Risio, L., 91
Disch, W. B., 457
Dishman, P. K., 534
Distel, M. A., 475
Dite, G., 525
Dittmar, H., 298
Dittmar, M., 140
Ditto, P. H., 316
Dixon, L. B., 523
Dixon, R. M. W., 267

Djousse, L., 534
Dobbins, I. G., 205
Dobewall, H., 311
Dobson, R., 525
Dodge, E., 462
Dodge, K. A., 80
Dogan, O., 466, 467
Dohnel, K., 495
Dolan, M., 475
Dolan, R. J., 189
Dolan-Sewell, R., 476
Dollard, J., 414
Dolski, I., 57, 349
Domhoff, G. W., 130, 144, 145
Dominguez, J. M., 331
Dominique, Y., 285
Domjan, M., 167, 175
Donahue, C. B., 494
Donegan, E., 499
Donnellan, M. B., 4, 375, 385
D'Onofrio, B., 259
Doob, L. W., 414
Doolan, A. W., 74
Dormuth, C. R., 447
Dorn, L. H., 63, 289
Dorr, N., 22
Dorsey, E. R., 447
Dossey, L., 91
Dourley, J., 368
Dovidio, J. F., 428, 429, 431
Doyle, J., 499
Doyle, W., 521, 528
Doyle, W. A., 528
Doyle, W. J., 528
Draguns, J. G., 443, 455
Drake, C., 472
Drasgow, F., 432
Drigotas, S. M., 437
Dritschel, B., 214, 455
Drury, J., 432
Duberstein, P. R., 526
Ducci, F., 474
Duda, J. L., 520
Duenas, J., 126
Dufour, M. C., 473
Dugan, S. E., 539
Dugas, M. J., 499
Dugravot, A., 301
Duman, R. S., 456
Dumoulin, M., 135
Dunbar, R. I. M., 64
Duncan, A. E., 150
Duncan, B. D., 411
Dunkel Schetter, C., 285
Dunlosky, J., 168, 190
Dunn, E. W., 14, 395
Dunn, K. I., 516
Dunner, D. L., 500
Dunning, D., 74, 405
Dupoux, E., 92
Dupré, K. E., 414
Durantini, M. R., 540
Duric, V., 456
Durso, K., 138
Dusetzina, S. B., 447
Duvarci, S., 62, 173, 347, 348
Dweck, C. S., 196, 198, 261
Dyck, I., 476
Dygdon, J. A., 173
Dymond, S., 180
Dysart, J., 229
Dysart, J. E., 229

E

Eagly, A. H., 11, 314, 411, 412, 435
Earl, A., 540
Earl, A. N., 540
Eastwick, P. W., 337
Eaton, D. K., 146
Eaton, W. T., 84
Eaves, G. J., 499
Eaves, L. J., 330
Ebbinghaus, H., 230, 231

Eberly, S., 520
Ebmeier, K. P., 301
Ecker, U. K., 211
Eckert, A., 292
Edge, N., 252, 406
Edinger, J. D., 141
Edmonds, G., 523
Edwards, B. L., 5
Eells, T. D., 508
Egan, K. G., 482
Eggum, N. D., 317
Egloff, B., 252, 281, 361
Eguchi, E., 537
Eheman, C., 534, 537
Eich, E., 223, 225
Eid, J., 532
Eidelman, P., 141
Eikelis, N., 449
Eimes, D. G., 23
Einarsen, S., 432
Ein-Dor, T., 436, 453
Ein-Gar, D., 3
Einstein, A., 194
Einstein, G. O., 219, 234
Eisenberg, N., 316, 317, 375
Eisenhower, J. W., 467
Eisenstein, A. R., 536
Eiser, J. R., 401
Eivers, A. R., 316
Ekman, P., 56, 350, 351, 352
Elbaz, A., 301
Elbert, T., 88
Elden, A., 466
El-Deredy, W., 117
Eley, T. C., 390
el-Guebaly, N., 478
El-Hai, J., 489
Elhai, J. D., 499
Ellemers, N., 405
Ellender, T. J., 53
Elliot, A. J., 343
Elliott, M. A., 516
Elliott, T., 95
Ellis, A., 496, 498
Ellis, H. C., 205
Ellis, L. A., 503
Ellison, C. G., 523
Ellsworth, P., 28
Elms, A. C., 382
El-Osta, A., 449
Elsea, M., 417
Ely, R. J., 193
Emery, C. ., 529, 533, 534
Emery, R. E., 446
Emes, R. D., 44, 51
Emmelkamp, P. M., 497
Emmett, D., 175
Emmons, R. A., 15, 19, 357, 358,
    375, 385
Enck, P., 175
Endler, N. S., 487, 488
Endrighi, R., 521
Eng, P. M., 529
Enge, J., 375
Engel, A. K., 101
Engel, C. C., 453
Enger, E., 71
Englander, E. K., 414
Engvik, H., 376
Ensembl Human, 77
Ensminger, J., 411
Ensom, M. H. H., 539
Enstrom, J. E., 538
Epel, E. S., 292
Epley, N., 221
Epstein, J., 450
Er, M. J., 247
Erci, B., 520
Erdberg, P., 393
Erhardt, A., 449
Erickson, K. I., 238, 291
Eriksen, J., 54
Erikson, E. H., 18, 304, 305, 306, 307,
    309, 310, 311, 367

Erkens, J. A., 486
Erlick, D., 489
Ernst, D., 521
Ersche, K. D., 446
Ersner-Hershfield, H., 311
Ervin, F. E., 195
Escriba-Aguir, V., 136
Esler, M., 449
Eslick, A. N., 205
Espana, R. A., 61
Espirito-Santo, H., 465
Esposito, E. A., 259, 260
Esslen, M., 88
Estes, D., 6
Esteve, R., 525
Estrada, C. P., 75
Etnier, J. L., 534
Eustache, F., 223
Evans, B. G., 274
Evans, D. A., 238, 523
Evans, D. E., 303
Evans, J., 250
Evans, J. S. B. T., 132
Evans, M. F., 536
Eve, D. J., 75
Evenson, R. J., 457
Everall, I. P., 471
Eviatar, Z., 69, 70
Exton, M. S., 174
Eysenck, H. J., 388, 389

F

Fabbri-Destro, M., 48
Fabre-Thorpe, M., 101
Fabrício Mauro, M. L., 459
Fabricius, W. V., 317
Facciabene, A., 528
Fafard, P., 514
Fagen, J. L., 332
Fagerlund, M., 75
Fahlman, S. E., 353
Faimberg, H., 492
Fair, D. A., 218
Fairchild Bridal Group, 1
Fairweather, E., 253
Falk, C. F., 28
Family and Youth Services
    Bureau, 333
Fang, F., 128
Fant, R. V., 539
Faravelli, C., 463, 464
Farr, R. H., 37, 338, 339
Farrant, B. M., 316
Farrell, K. A., 525
Farren, C. K., 505
Fatemi, S. H., 471
Fattal, O., 488
Faucher, E. H., 319
Faugeras, F., 127
Faull, R. L., 75, 292
Fava, G. A., 509
Fawcet, J. P., 413
Fawcett, R. C., 256
Fay, S., 293
Fayard, J. V., 523
Faymonville, M. E., 158
Fazio, R. H., 406
Federal Bureau of Investigation, 416
Federal Emergency Management
    Agency, 166
Fei-Fei, L., 95
Fein, S., 419
Feinberg, E. H., 44, 55
Feinstein, E. C., 504
Feith, S. W. W., 412
Feldman, S., 386
Feldman Barrett, L., 355
Feldon, J., 289
Felgoise, S. H., 530
Ferdinand, K. C., 514
Ferguson, C. J., 415, 417
Ferguson, D. E., 415, 417
Ferguson, E., 375, 523

Ferguson, M. J., 215
Feri, F., 189
Fernandes, L. A., 102
Fernandez, G., 419
Ferreira, J. A., 415
Ferrer, E., 292
Ferretti, F., 460
Ferrie, J. E., 140, 301
Ferrières, J., 536
Ferris, G. R., 375
Ferrucci, L., 379
Festinger, L., 405, 406, 407
Fiedler, K., 401
Field, T. M., 285
Fielding, D. W., 539
Fields, R., 130, 147, 483, 484
Fiese, B. H., 330
Fietta, P., 55, 215
Fifer, W. P., 143
Finch, E. A., 520
Findley, J., 141
Finger, S., 141
Fingerhut, A. W., 338
Fingerman, K. L., 353
Fink, M., 488
Finkel, E., 337
Finnerty, K. L., 1
Finniss, D. G., 191
Fiore, M. C., 538
Fischer, R., 352
Fischler, C., 536
Fishbein, M., 516
Fisher, D., 152
Fisher, M. H., 264
Fisher, T. D., 337
Fishman, S., 341
Fisk, G. D., 92
Fiske, A. P., 316
Fiske, S. T., 402, 432
Fitches, A., 449
Fitzhugh, E. C., 536
Fitzmaurice, G., 529
Fitzpatrick, K. K., 462, 464
Fivush, R., 223
Fize, D., 101
Flanagan, M., 22
Flannery, D. J., 299
Fleeson, W., 385
Flegal, K. M., 536
Fleischhaker, S., 472
Fleischmann, F., 429
Fleming, L., 141
Flens, J. R., 393
Fletcher, J., 316
Fletcher, K., 161
Fletcher, M. A., 523
Fleuret, F., 245
Flint, J., 389
Flint, M. S., 80
Flom, R., 203
Flor, H., 88
Flores, L. Y., 11
Floyd, R. L., 285
Flückiger, C., 509
Flynn, J., 259, 260, 266
Flynn, J. R., 260
Foa, E. B., 453, 494
Focht, B. C., 535
Fodor, I., 450
Foehr, U. G., 417
Foell, J., 88
Foer, J., 125
Fok, H., 352
Foley, J. A., 210
Foley, K. P., 330
Folkman, S., 531
Folsom, T. D., 471
Fondell, E., 135
Fontana, A., 453
Fontana, A. P., 47
Fontana, M. A., 141
Fooladi, E., 484
Foot, M., 502
Foote, B., 465, 467

Forbes, D., 499
Forbes, H. E., 494
Forbush, K., 462
Foreland, A. R., 376
Forgas, J. P., 401
Forgues, H. L., 249
Forman, E. M., 499, 507
Forman-Hoffman, V. L., 425
Forserling, F., 376
Forsstrom, D., 492
Forsyth, J. P., 449, 450
Forsythe, C., 243
Fortenbach, V. A., 411
Fortier, M. S., 520
Forzano, L. B., 3
Foster, B. M., 499
Foster, S. E., 504
Fotuhi, O., 406
Fouad, K., 73
Fountas, K. N., 489
Fountoulakis, K. N., 459
Fox, P. T., 449
Fox, R., 377
Frackowiak, R. S. J., 44
Frances, A. J., 446, 473
Franck, N., 469
Frank, E., 521, 528
Frank, G. K. W., 464
Frank, M. G., 135
Frank, R. G., 486
Frankl, V. E., 23
Fraser, S. C., 409
Frattaroli, J., 521
Frazier, P., 23, 384
Frazier, P. A., 321
Frazier, T. W., 188
Fredrick, S., 357
Fredrickson, B. L., 355
Freed, C. R., 75
Freedman, D. J., 85
Freedman, J. L., 409
Freedy, J. R., 494
Freeland, A., 466
Freeman, D., 448
Freeman, J., 448
Freeston, I. L., 59
Freire, R. C., 450
French, C. C., 90
Frenda, S. J., 228
Frensch, K. M., 282
Freud, A., 364
Freud, S., 5, 10, 131, 143, 362, 363, 364,
    491, 492
Freund, A. M., 291
Frewen, P. A., 465
Frey, M., 519
Fried, S., 330
Friedenberg, J., 10
Friedman, C. K., 417
Friedman, D., 232
Friedman, E. M., 514, 528
Friedman, H. S., 289, 523
Friedman, L., 141
Friedman, M., 529
Friedman, M. J., 483, 485
Friedman, R., 161
Friesen, W. V., 22, 57, 350,
    351, 352
Frigon, A., 73
Frijda, N. H., 349
Frijns, T., 308
Frith, C. D., 44, 48
Fritz, S., 415, 417
Fromm, E., 367, 424
Frost, G., 328
Frost, G. S., 519
Fry, P. S., 375, 523
Fryberg, S. A., 28, 308
Frye, C., 349
Fu, Q., 150
Fujisawa, D., 499
Fujiwara, E., 226
Fukuyama, H., 129
Fullam, R., 475

Fuller-Rowell, T. E., 320
Fulmer, C. A., 376
Fultz, J., 411
Funder, D. C., 385, 405
Fung, M. T., 474
Furlong, M., 418
Fursland, A., 463
Furukawa, T. A., 484
Fusar-Poli, P., 442
Fusselman, M. J., 449
Futterman, A. D., 175
Fuzikawa, C., 390

**G**

Gabert-Quillen, C. A., 454
Gable, S. L., 342, 389
Gabrieli, J. D. E., 219, 388
Gaddis, S., 361
Gadian, G. D., 44
Gaertner, L., 11, 404
Gaertner, S. L., 429, 431
Gage, F. H., 75
Gage, P. T., 65
Gagnani, C., 390
Gagnon, J. H., 335
Gaig, C., 141
Gaines, S. O., 402
Gainotti, G., 69, 131
Gaissmaier, W., 404
Galambos, N. L., 140
Gale, C. R., 300
Galinsky, A. D., 192
Galizio, M., 171
Gallagher, K. E., 149
Gallaher, P., 516
Gallegos, J., 488
Gallese, V., 48
Gallina, P., 75
Gallinat, J., 330, 456
Gallo, D. A., 220
Gallo, L. C., 11
Galvin, K., 368
Gammon, D., 490, 497
Gandhi, M., 18
Gangadhar, B. N., 470
Gangemi, A., 349
Gangwani, T. H., 232
Gannon, K. E., 482
Gao, D., 92
Gao, F., 213
Gao, Y. J., 117
Garaets, 226
Garb, H. N., 394, 395
Garber, A., 497
Garcia, J., 174, 195
Garcia, S. M., 404
Garcia-Marques, L., 332
Garcia-Soriano, G., 463
Gardner, C., 150
Gardner, H., 265
Garefino, A. C., 447
Garety, P., 472
Garfield, C. F., 447
Garg, A., 218
Garg, K., 469
Garg, M. L., 175
Garland, J., 447
Garnett, M., 129
Garrett, B. L., 223, 229
Garrett, W., 440
Garrick, T. M., 75
Garrido, A., 401
Garrison, G. D., 539
Gartland, N., 376
Gartner, A. L., 5
Garver, D. L., 485
Garza, A., 417
Gastfriend, D. R., 173
Gathercole, S. E., 210
Gatz, M., 238, 375
Gaudreau, P., 520
Gavlak, D., 415
Gaye-Valentine, A., 374

Gaziano, J. M., 534
Gazzaley, A., 130
Geary, D. C., 132, 312, 435
Gehrman, P., 141
Gelder, B. D., 351
Gelfand, M., 341, 428
Geliebter, A., 329
Geller, E. S., 188
Gentile, D. A., 417
George, A., 523
George, L. G., 378
George, L. K., 523
Geraci, M., 450
Gerberding, J. L., 379
Gerdes, A. B., 93
Gergely, G., 48
Germain, A., 142
German, T. P., 127
Germann, D., 486
Gerner, R. H., 459
Gernsbache, M. A., 312
Gernsbacher, M. A., 48
Gershman, S. J., 172
Gershon, A., 141
Gertner, Y., 298
Gether, U., 54
Getzmann, S., 113
Geyer, M. A., 376
Ghilan, M., 75, 293
Giang, D. W., 174
Giard, J. A., 457
Gibbons, R. D., 486
Gibson, C., 329
Giel, R., 472
Gigantesco, A., 390
Gigerenzer, G., 404
Gil, J., 458
Gilbert, A. L., 268
Gilbert, D. T., 403
Gilbert, L. A., 506
Gilchrist, A. L., 209
Giles, G. G., 525
Giletta, M., 458
Gilewski, T., 175
Gillan, C. M., 446
Gillath, O., 317
Gillespie, C., 537
Gillette, J. C., 540
Gillham, J., 525
Gilligan, C., 316
Gillis, J. M., 495
Gillison, F. B., 373
Gil-Mohapel, J., 75, 293
Ginis, K. A. M., 534
Gino, F., 226
Giovannini, D., 432
Girden, 32
Gironde, S., 475
Girvin, H., 519
Gittelman, M., 478
Gitter, S. A., 414
Given, B., 508
Given, C., 508
Glas, C. A., 391
Glaser, D. E., 48
Glaser, J., 262
Glasford, D. E., 412
Glasman, L. R., 540
Glaw, X. M., 75
Gleitman, L., 267
Glenberg, A. M., 48
Glenn, A. L., 413
Glenn, D., 204
Glick, P., 432
Glisky, E. L., 225, 467
Glockner, A., 131
Glover, G. H., 219
Glover, V., 527
Glowacki, L., 413
Gluck, J., 301
Glymour, M. M., 301
Gnagy, E. M., 447
Go, H. J., 136
Gobbi, M., 504, 505

Gobet, F., 209
Godden, D. R., 223
Godin, J. J., 377
Goebel, M. U., 174
Goel, A. K., 245
Goenjian, A. K., 456
Goethals, G. R., 419, 426
Goff, D., 470
Goforth, M., 74
Golay, A., 464
Golberstein, E., 486
Gold, P. W., 528
Goldberg, J., 329
Goldberg, J. H., 463
Goldberg, L. R., 374, 376
Goldberg, R., 147
Goldfield, B. A., 272
Goldin-Meadow, S., 267, 273
Goldman, M. S., 55
Goldman, D., 474
Goldney, R. D., 457
Goldschmidt, L., 155
Goldsmith, A. A., 525
Goldsmith, H. H., 345, 349
Goldsmith, T. E., 243
Goldstein, E. B., 86
Goldstein, M. H., 272
Goldstein, P. A., 62
Goldston, D. B., 461
Goldstrom, I. D., 503
Goleman, D., 254
Goljevscek, S., 452
Gollwitzer, P. M., 215
Golomb, J., 203
Gömöri, É., 288
Gonda, X., 389
Gondo, Y., 523
Gontkovsky, S. T., 413
Gonzales-Bracken, M. A., 308
Gonzalez-Maeso, J., 155
Gonzalez-Vallejo, C., 131
Good, C. D., 44
Goodale, M. A., 131
Goode, E., 229
Gooding, P. A., 281
Goodman, G. S., 226, 227
Goodson, P., 525
Goodwin, C. L., 529, 533, 534
Goodwin, J. S., 22
Goodwin, K. A., 223
Goosens, K. A., 225
Goren, A., 401
Gorin, A., 537
Gosling, S. D., 270, 361, 375,
    376, 377
Gossage, J. P., 285
Gotlib, I. H., 388, 457
Gottesman, I. I., 259, 470
Gottlieb, G., 80, 280
Gottman, J. M., 310
Gottsegen, D., 159
Gotz, J., 292
Goubert, L., 189
Gouin, J. P., 528
Gould, J. W., 393
Gould, R. L., 507
Gove, W. R., 457
Govern, J. M., 190
Graber, J. A., 289
Graham, J., 316
Graham, J. R., 393
Grant, B. F., 473
Grant, J. E., 494
Grant, S. G. N., 44, 51
Grasby, P. M., 349
Gratz, K. L., 354
Gravetter, F. J., 3
Gray, G. W., 134, 135
Gray, J. A., 389
Gray, J. R., 58, 116
Graziano, M. S. A., 126
Graziano, W. G., 58
Greco, M. A., 135
Green, A., 100

Green, C. S., 9, 44
Green, E. D., 514
Green, J. P., 157, 159
Green, L., 175
Green, M. K., 527
Greenberg, A. R., 410
Greenberg, J., 319
Greenberg, L. M., 530
Greenberg, L. S., 503
Greene, B., 506
Greene, R. L., 393
Greenwald, A. G., 431
Greenwood, T. A., 376
Greer, L. L., 412
Greer, S., 524
Greer, T., 46
Greeson, J. M., 349
Gregan, M. J., 111
Gregerson, M., 254
Gregg, A. P., 404
Gregory, A. M., 78
Greitemeyer, T., 412, 417
Grezes, J., 48
Griez, E., 450
Griffin, A. M., 401
Griffin, D., 251
Griffin, K. W., 515, 523
Griffin, M. M., 264
Griffin, S., 15, 19
Griffith, R. L., 18, 393
Grigorenko, E. L., 259,
    260, 262
Grigoryan, G., 218
Grigulio, M., 53
Grillon, C., 450
Grilo, C. M., 464, 500
Grimley, D. M., 516
Grimmer, M. A., 475
Grodstein, F., 291
Groh-Bordin, C., 211
Grohol, J. M., 482, 497, 503
Gross, J. J., 531
Grossberg, G. T., 88
Groth-Marnat, G., 395
Grove, W. M., 394
Grubaugh, A. L., 499
Grubin, D., 347
Grundy, S. M., 329
Grusec, J. E., 261, 307
Gruss, M., 289
Gruzelier, J. H., 158
Grzywacz, A., 463
Gscheider, S., 469
Gu, Q., 485
Guadagno, J., 14
Guenther, F. H., 125
Guérard, K., 209
Guerin, E., 520
Guevremont, D. C., 188
Guillaume, Y. R. F., 193
Guillery-Girard, B., 223
Guimond, A. B., 308
Gulec, M., 449
Gummer, A. W., 112
Gump, B. B., 529
Gunaratna, R., 341
Gunderson, J., 476
Gunderson, J. G., 476
Gunnar, B. P., 74
Gunty, A. L., 321
Guo, K., 332
Guo, L., 449
Guo, Q., 516
Guo, S., 376
Guo, X., 485
Guo, Y., 504
Gur, R. C., 312
Gurbaxani, B. M., 390
Gurin, G., 193
Gurin, P., 193
Gurven, M., 411
Guthrie, I. K., 316, 317
Guttmacher Institute, 333
Guttman, N., 182, 183

Gwako, E., 411
Gwaltney, J. M., 521, 528

## H

Haag, J., 106
Haas, B. W., 388
Haase, R. F., 415
Haase, S. J., 92
Haasen, C., 442, 450, 451
Habeck, C., 136, 238
Habel, U., 474
Habenstein, R. W., 261
Haber, J. R., 150, 375, 523
Hackett, R. A., 521
Hadjipanayis, A. G., 84
Hafen, C. A., 309, 458
Hagewen, K. J., 308
Haggard, P., 48
Haidle, M. N., 210
Haidt, J., 316
Hajak, G., 495
Halberstadt, J., 250
Hald, G. M., 416
Hale, W. A., 308
Hale, W. W., 308
Hales, D., 147
Haley, A., 259
Halford, J., 1
Halford, J. C., 329
Halgunseth, L. C., 307
Hall, B., 464
Hall, B. J., 58
Hall, C., 332
Hall, C. C., 401
Hall, D. W., 333
Hall, G., 215
Hall, G. C., 461
Hall, J. A., 261, 353, 376, 394
Hall, K., 154
Hall, S. C., 135
Hallahan, D. P., 263
Hallam, M., 401, 402
Hallenen, T., 514
Hallett, R., 497
Halligan, P. W., 159
Halling, A., 478
Halliwell, E., 298
Halmagyi, G. M., 121
Halpern, A. R., 215
Halpern, D. F., 259, 260, 266, 312
Halpern-Felsher, B. L., 335
Haltigan, J. D., 304
Hamaker, E. L., 310
Hamamura, T., 28
Hamer, M., 514, 521, 534
Hamilton, B. E., 333
Hammad, T. A., 486
Hammers, A., 349
Hammersmith, S. K., 338
Hammond, D. C., 159
Hampton, D., 339
Hampton, J., 333
Hamza, A., 450
Han, F., 486
Han, R., 133, 205, 317
Han, S., 205
Handel, P. J., 523
Handley, G. W., 159
Handy, T. C., 130
Haney, C., 423, 424
Haney, T. L., 529
Hanley, J. R., 233
Hannon, J. P., 54
Hannum, R. D., 182
Hanowski, R. J., 94
Hanscombe, K. B., 259
Hansen, C., 23
Hansen, K. B., 328
Hansen, K. E., 404
Hansen, T., 236

Hansen-Tift, A. M., 287
Hanus, D., 192
Hapke, U., 519
Hara, C., 390
Haraguchi, A., 205
Harari, A., 528
Harder, V. S., 454
Hardin, J. W., 534
Hardy, S. A., 316
Hariri, A. R., 80
Haritou, F., 73
Harker, L. A., 15
Harlaar, N., 336
Harlow, H. F., 303
Harlow, T. F., 357
Harma, M., 134
Harman, D., 292
Harmon-Jones, C., 389
Harmon-Jones, E., 221, 389
Harms, P., 374, 376
Harned, E. S., 494
Haroon, E., 528
Harpaz, Y., 271
Harper, C., 75
Harré, N., 519
Harrington, A., 161
Harris, A. E., 367
Harris, D. M., 204
Harris, J. A., 171
Harris, J. J., 85
Harris, J. R., 281
Harris, K. F., 529
Harris, V. A., 403
Harris Interactive, 298
Harrison, D. W., 70
Harrison, M. A., 436
Harrison, N. L., 62
Harrison, Y., 135
Harro, J., 389
Hart, C. L., 55, 130, 390
Hartenbaum, N., 143
Harter, J., 31
Harter, S., 401, 404
Hart-Johnson, T., 308
Hartman, T., 161
Hartmann, E., 142
Hartwigsen, G., 59
Harvey, A. G., 141
Harvey, O. J., 433
Harvey, R. H., 532
Harvey, T., 65
Harwood, T. M., 393
Haselton, M. G., 120
Haslam, C., 154
Haslam, S. A., 424, 428, 429
Hasselbach, P., 524
Hassmen, P., 478
Hastie, R., 221
Hatfield, E., 337
Hattiangady, B., 75
Hauk, O., 68
Haun, D. B. M., 269
Hauser, A., 513
Hauser, M., 48
Havelka, J., 130, 236
Haviland, J., 525
Hawkins-Gilligan, J., 173
Hawkley, L. C., 520, 521
Hay, P. E., 333
Hay, P. P., 465
Hayakawa, Y., 530
Hayashi, A., 91
Hayatbakhsh, M. R., 155
Hayes, A. F., 524
Hayes, J. E., 119
Hayes, R., 316
Hayflick, L., 291
Hazan, C., 435
Hazler, R. J., 493
He, L., 376
He, Q., 291
He, Z., 298
Hearold, S., 412
Heath, A. C., 150

Heath, C., 418
Heatherton, T. F., 462, 463
Hebb, D. O., 218
Hebert, L. E., 238
Heckbert, S. R., 463
Hedrick, T., 53
Heeren, T., 150
Heffner, K. L., 292
Heidegger, M., 132
Heidemann, S. R., 291
Heider, F., 403
Heilman, K. M., 350
Heiman, G. W., 21
Heiman, J. R., 217
Heine, S. J., 28
Heinen, S. J., 106
Heinonen, K., 303
Hejdenberg, J., 453
Heller, A. C., 489
Heller, R. E., 450
Heller, W., 388
Helmeke, C., 289
Hel-Or, H., 351
Helsen, K, 189
Helson, R., 378
Helzer, E. G., 405
Hemmi, J. M., 106
Henderson, M., 536
Henderson, M. J., 503
Henderson, V. W., 291
Hendgraaf, M. J. J., 412
Heningfield, J. E., 539
Hennessey, B. A., 254
Hennig, J., 389, 391
Hennighausen, K., 472
Henrich, J., 411
Henrich, N., 411
Henriksen, L., 417
Henry, J. D., 234
Henry, P. J., 431
Henry, W. E., 311
Henson, R. N., 219
Hepper, E. G., 404
Hepting, U., 268
Herberstein, M. E., 98
Herbert, J., 413
Hering, E., 102
Herings, R. M. C., 486
Herlihy, B., 506
Herman, D., 135
Herman, K., 11
Hermans, D., 173
Hermanussen, S., 54
Hermundstad, A. M., 245
Hernandez-Reif, M., 285
Hernell, O., 175
Herpertz-Dahlmann, B., 447
Herring, M. P., 534
Herskovits, M. J., 107
Hertwig, R., 35
Hertzman, C., 316
Herzog, H., 425
Hetherington, E. M., 281
Heuser, I., 488
Heward, W. L., 264
Hewlin, P. F., 419
Heyes, C., 48
Heyman, R. E., 502
Heywood, C. A., 104
Hibbard, S., 395
Hickey, M., 291
Hickman, J. S., 94
Hickok, G., 48
Hicks, J. A., 24, 237, 250, 311, 320,
   321, 375
Hicks, P. B., 93
Hickson, M., 328
Hidaka, B. H., 141
Higa, J. J., 184
Higashi, A., 447
Hildebrandt, T., 462
Hilgard, E. R., 158, 159
Hill, A. L., 528
Hill, C. E., 493

Hill, J. O., 518, 537
Hill, P. L., 309
Hill, T. D., 523
Hilpert, J., 10
Hingson, R. W., 150
Hinkin, C. H., 331
Hinks, L., 538
Hinshaw, S. P., 477
Hinsley, A. W., 375
Hinton, D., 454
Hintz, S., 384
Hippocrates, 387
Hirao, K., 129
Hirata, A., 115
Hirsch, J. K., 526, 530
Hirsh, J. B., 58
Hitler, A., 380, 381
Ho, M., 540
Ho, M. L., 143
Ho, S. C., 56
Ho, Y. J., 56
Hobaiter, C., 189
Hobara, M., 117
Hobson, A., 131, 145
Hobson, J. A., 138, 145
Hock, R. R., 338
Hockett, C. F., 270
Hodapp, R. M., 264
Hodgins, D. C., 519
Hodgkins, D. C., 478
Hodson, G., 262, 263
Hoefnagels, M., 87
Hoek, H. W., 462
Hoeppner, B., 503
Hofer, C., 317
Hofer, J., 310
Hofer, T., 128
Hoffman, E., 446
Hoffman, J., 482
Hofman, S. G., 504, 505
Hofmann, S., 454
Hogan, E. H., 151
Hogan, R., 374, 385
Hoge, C. W., 453
Hogg, M. A., 429
Hogue, T., 332
Hohl, E., 490, 497
Holden, R. R., 393
Holland, A. C., 205
Holland, A. K., 70
Holland, A. S., 436
Holland, P. C., 185
Holland, S. J. F., 452
Hollander, A. C., 529
Hollar, D., 460
Hollich, G., 287
Hollis, J. F., 521
Holloway, S. D., 343
Holman, E. A., 281
Holmes, A., 80
Holmes, J., 367
Holmes, J. G., 410
Holmes, L. B., 285
Holmes, S., 175
Holsboer, F., 46, 449
Holst, J. J., 328
Holte, A., 466
Holyoak, K. J., 245
Holzschneider, K., 449
Homewood, J., 525
Honey, P. L., 173, 179
Hong, S. W., 101
Hong, Y., 11
Honts, C., 347
Honzik, C. H., 191
Hood, M., 464
Hood, W. R., 433
Hook, J. N., 5
Hooker, S., 536
Hooker, S. P., 534
Hooley, J. M., 475
Hooper, J., 145
Hooper, L., 507
Hooper, N., 405

Hopf, F. W., 148
Hopper, J. L., 525
Hopper, K., 472
Hopthrow, T., 405
Horberg, E. J., 520
Horesh, D., 453
Horiguchi, J., 484
Horn, E., 152
Horn, J. L., 300
Horn, S. S., 234
Horner, V., 410
Horney, K., 367, 368
Hornick, B. A., 151
Hornickel, J., 271
Horton, L. A., 514
Horvath, A. O., 509
Hoshino, T., 376
Hosmer, D. H., 161
Hosp, J. A., 56
Hoss, R. A., 401
Hotard, S. R., 377
Hottenga, J., 389
Hou, J., 452
Hou, Y., 214
Houlihan, D., 411
House, J. S., 520
Houser-Marko, L., 342, 345
Houston, J. P., 456
Hovland, C. I., 408
Howard, A. L., 140
Howard, R. J., 507
Howe, M. J. A., 262
Howell, D., 150
Howell, D. C., 16
Howes, M. B., 204
Howes, O. D., 471
Howland, R. H., 456
Hox, J. J., 520
Hoyer, D., 54
Hoyle, R. H., 378
Hrebickova, M., 377
Hsia, J., 333
Hsieh, L. T., 231
Hsieh, P.-J., 127
Hsu, L., 451
Hu, S., 193
Huang, C. C., 73
Huang, C. L., 251
Huart, C., 120
Hubble, M. A., 507, 509
Hubel, D. H., 100, 101
Huber, C. G., 442, 450, 451
Hudak, M. L., 483
Huesmann, L. R., 415, 417
Huff, C. R., 230
Hugenberg, K., 350
Hughes, A. E., 524
Hughes, C., 127
Hui, C., 352
Hull, E. M., 331
Hullihen, B., 175
Human, L. J., 395
Humphrey, N., 132
Hung, D. L., 231
Hunsley, J., 394
Hunt, H. T., 368
Hunt, R. R., 205
Hunter, D., 525
Hunter, R. H., 536
Hur, K., 486
Hurst, A., 281
Hurtado, S., 193
Hurvich, L. M., 103
Husain, M. M., 488
Huskamp, H. A., 447
Huta, V., 16
Huttenlocher, J., 289
Huttenlocher, P. R., 288
Huuhka, K., 488
Hwang, J. Y., 376
Hyde, J. S., 312, 314, 333, 336
Hyde, L. W., 317
Hyland, M. E., 174
Hyman, R., 90, 91

Hyman, S., 43
Hystad, S. W., 532
Hytonen, K., 419

I

Iacoboni, M., 48
Iacono, W. G., 347
Iannilli, E., 118
Ibarra, L., 514
Ibrahim, R., 69, 70
Idemudia, S. E., 469
Iemmola, F., 339
Iglesias, P. A., 95
Iglseder, B., 75, 293
Ihori, N., 417
Ijames, S. G., 174
Ikeda, B. E., 175
Ikeda, K., 91
Ilivitsky, V., 152
Imada, R., 28
Imada, T., 403
Imel, Z. E., 509
Imeri, L., 141
Inaba, A., 457
Inagaki, H., 523
Inagaki, T., 484
Inchley-Mort, S. L., 350
INDIGO Study Group, 477
Insko, C. A., 434
Iranzo, A., 141
Ironson, G., 523
Irwin, M. R., 141, 528
Irwing, P., 376
Isa, T., 44
Isaacowitz, D. M., 281, 311
Isaacson, J. A., 18
Ishak, S., 286
Ishikawa, Y., 61
Ising, M., 46, 449
Isingrini, M., 223, 293
Ispa, J. M., 307
Itakura, S., 129
Iturbide, M. I., 308
Ivcevic, Z., 223
Ive, S., 298
Iverson, G. J., 91
Iverson, P., 274
Ivry, R. B., 268
Iwassa, H., 523
Iyer, A., 95
Iyer, R., 316
Izard, C. E., 354
Izumi, Y., 218

J

Jablensky, E., 472
Jaccard, J., 431
Jacinto, G. A., 5
Jackendoff, R., 270
Jackson, D., 376
Jackson, D. C., 57, 349
Jackson, G., 135
Jackson, J. J., 309, 523
Jackson, L. C., 506
Jackson, L. E., 11
Jackson, M. L., 136
Jackson, N. W., 252
Jackson, S. L., 3
Jacob, R., 538
Jacob, T., 150, 375, 523
Jacobs, R. H., 456
Jacobs, T. L., 292
Jacobs, W. J., 456, 499
Jacobsen, L., 402
Jacobsen, P. B., 175
Jacobson, K. C., 149, 150, 413
Jaeger, S. R., 330
Jaeggi, S. M., 274
Jaff, N., 75
Jakupcak, M., 354
Jalinous, R., 59
James, W., 7, 126, 347
Jameson, D., 103

Jamieson, D. J., 333
Jan, J. E., 133
Janak, P. H., 54
Jancke, L., 58, 88
Jang, K. L., 390
Janicke, D., 84
Janicki-Deverts, D., 528
Janis, I., 427
Janis, I. L., 408
Janowsky, D. S., 471
Janson, C., 514, 538
Janzen, G., 269
Jarrett, C., 117
Jarrett, R. B., 456, 499
Järvenpää, A., 303
Jarvin, L., 262
Jarvis, D., 514, 538
Jaspal, R., 429
Jeanneau, M., 492
Jeckel, C. M., 271
Jeffery, R. W., 520, 537
Jeglic, E. L., 530
Jelenchick, L. A., 482
Jenkins, F. J., 80
Jenkins, H. M., 178
Jennings, D. J., 5
Jennings, G., 449
Jennings, N. A., 298
Jensen, L. W., 478
Jensen, M. P., 159
Jensen, S. E., 533
Jensen, S. M., 538
Jensen-Campbell, L. A., 376
Jentschke, S., 375
Jentzsch, I., 425
Jeon, S., 508
Jeong, J., 136
Jeon-Slaughter, H., 443
Jernelov, S., 141
Jewgenow, I., 288
Ji, R. R., 117
Jia, F., 62
Jiang, H., 537
Jiang, P., 47
Jirillo, E., 328
Joanette, Y., 70, 271
Joanisse, M. F., 206
Jochum, R., 520
Joel, S., 436
Joers, J. M., 154
Johansen, E. B., 183
Johansen, J. P., 348
Johansson, B., 238
John, D. A., 442
John, J. P., 450
John, O., 377
John, O. P., 378
John, U., 519
Johnson, B. T., 540
Johnson, C. A., 516
Johnson, C. S., 316
Johnson, G. B., 53, 72
Johnson, J., 281
Johnson, J. S., 274
Johnson, J. T., 404
Johnson, K., 403
Johnson, L. L., 141
Johnson, L. R., 215
Johnson, M. H., 274
Johnson, R. B., 34
Johnson, S. K., 215
Johnson, S. L., 446
Johnson, V. E., 331
Johnson, W. O., 91
Johnson-Laird, P. N., 349
Johnsrude, I. S., 44
Johnston, L. D., 146, 149,
   153, 155
Johnstone, B., 523
Johnstone, E., 538
Joiner, T. E., 457, 460, 475
Joiner, T. E., Jr., 460, 463
Joireman, J., 5
Jones, A. K., 117

Jones, C. J., 397
Jones, E. E., 403
Jones, F., 523
Jones, J., 338
Jones, J. D., 47
Jones, K. L., 285
Jones, R. M., 290, 386
Jones, T., 342
Jongsma, A. E., 502
Jonides, J., 274
Jorgensen, T. N., 54
Jorm, A. F., 292
Joscelyne, A., 172
Joseph, A., 405
Joseph, J., 79, 519
Joseph, S., 509
Jost, J. T., 262
Joubert, O. R., 101
Joutsenniemi, K., 505
Jovanovic, T., 454
Jowsey, 525
Joy, J. E., 156
Juang, L., 11, 28, 196, 443
Juckel, G., 489
Judd, F. K., 291
Juhl, J., 319
Jukema, J. W., 329
Jung, C., 367, 368
Juslin, P., 252

**K**

Kabacoff, 32
Kabat-Zinn, J., 161
Kabnick, K., 536
Kagan, J., 303
Kahana, M. J., 202, 216
Kahlaoui, K., 70
Kahn, A., 143
Kahn, J. P., 455
Kahn, S., 532
Kahneman, D., 250, 251, 357
Kaira, S., 55, 331
Kaiser, M. D., 350
Kakinuma, M., 304
Kalakanis, L., 401, 402
Kalat, J. W., 345
Kalichman, S. C., 516
Kalivas, P. W., 63
Kalish, H. I., 182, 183
Kalmbach, A., 53
Kaltenbach, M., 537
Kam, M., 75, 292
Kamara, M., 351
Kamimori, G. H., 136
Kamin, L. J., 191
Kammrath, L. K., 378
Kamoo, R., 395
Kampman, K. M., 154
Kan, E., 285
Kanakogi, Y., 129
Kandel, E. R., 218
Kane, H. S., 528, 530
Kaneshanathan, A., 333
Kang, S. J., 384
Kang, Y., 116
Kanmaz, E., 452
Kantowitz, B. H., 23
Kanwisher, N., 69
Kao, C., 214, 455
Kao, K., 317
Kapitzke, D., 54
Kaplan, J., 134
Kaplan, K., 473
Kaplan, L., 84
Kaplan, M., 465, 467
Kaprio, J., 79
Kapur, S., 471, 485
Kara, B., 452
Karagogeos, D., 47
Karakula, H., 469
Karasawa, M., 343, 522
Karasik, L. B., 286
Karau, S. J., 426

Karch, K. M., 447
Karg, K., 54, 81
Karlamangia, A. S., 528
Karnik, V., 218
Karpel, M. G., 494
Karremans, J. C., 5
Karsten, J., 375
Kaschel, R., 210
Kashima, E. S., 319
Kashyap, P., 465
Kaskutas, L. A., 503
Kasl, S. V., 311
Kasri, F., 357
Kasser, T., 16, 342, 343, 413,
   414, 435
Kassin, S. M., 419
Kassuba, T., 59
Kastner, S., 86, 126
Katigbak, M. S., 377
Kato, I., 143
Katz, J. N., 339
Katzier, G., 351
Kauffman, J. M., 263
Kaufman, J. C., 254
Kaufman, L., 298
Kaufman, P., 254
Kawaal, C., 523
Kawachi, I., 529
Kawada, C. C. K., 215
Kawada, R., 129
Kawakami, K., 431
Kawakami, N., 343, 522
Kawamoto, M., 452
Kawara, M., 117
Kay, J., 204
Kay, P., 268
Kaya, N., 452
Kaye, A. H., 74
Kaye, D., 449
Kayser, S., 488
Kazdin, A. E., 506
Kazen, M., 210
Kealey, M., 536
Kearney, L. K., 506
Keast, R. S. J., 119
Keck, M. E., 449
Keel, P. K., 462
Keen, R., 287
Keenan, A., 384
Keeton, C. P., 484
Kehoe, E. J., 172
Keil, D. E., 528
Keillor, J. M., 350
Keller, M. C., 194, 338, 339
Kellerman, A. L., 414
Kelley, H. H., 403, 408
Kellner, C. H., 488
Kelly, A., 129
Kelly, D. J., 287
Kelly, G. F., 332
Kelly, J. F., 503
Kelly, J. R., 397
Kelly, S. L., 393
Kelsoe, J. R., 376
Keltner, D. J., 15, 342
Kemmelmeier, M., 308
Kemp, D. J., 98
Kemp, J., 460
Kempler, T. M., 343, 344
Kendler, K. S., 150
Kenrick, D. T., 412, 421
Kensinger, E. A., 205
Kentridge, R. W., 104
Keogh, R., 205
Keren, D., 351
Kerger, S., 405
Kerkhof, I., 173
Kern, M. L., 523
Kerns, J. G., 469
Kerr, M., 309, 458
Kerr, N. L., 404
Kesebir, P., 377
Keshaven, M. S., 470
Keskivaara, P., 303

Kessing, L. V., 389, 390
Kessler, R. C., 476
Keyes, B. B., 468
Khamis, V., 454
Khare, K., 219
Kherif, F., 219
Khodarahimi, S., 369
Khoshaba, D. M., 532
Khubchandani, J., 514
Khurana, V. G., 74
Kidd, K. K., 260
Kiefe, C. I., 528
Kigar, D. L., 65
Kihlstrom, J., 159
Kikuchi, T., 499
Kilburn, J., 417
Killeen, P. R., 183
Killgore, D. B., 136
Killgore, W. D. S., 136
Kilmer, R. P., 504
Kilner, J. M., 48
Kim, D. J., 136
Kim, H., 219, 401
Kim, I. J., 57
Kim, J. Y., 478
Kim, K. S., 136
Kim, N. S., 252
Kim, S. Y., 136, 454
Kim, W., 134
Kim, Y., 343
Kimble, M. O., 499
Kimbro, R. T., 537
Kimmel, A. J., 35
King, A. P., 272
King, B. G., 292
King, B. M., 336
King, C. M., 520
King, D., 514, 523
King, J. E., 377
King, L. A., 23, 24, 27, 237, 250, 311,
   320, 321, 344, 357, 358, 375, 376,
   381, 382, 434, 521
King, M. B., 478
King, M. L., Jr., 432
King, P. E., 429
Kingdon, D., 504, 505
Kinney, H., 143
Kinsey, A. C., 335
Kinsigner, D., 508
Kirby, D. B., 333
Kirisci, L., 155
Kirkpatrick, K., 185
Kirsch, I., 157
Kisling, J., 420
Kissileff, H. R., 329
Kit, B. K., 536
Kitayama, S., 343, 415, 421, 522
Kittredge, A. K., 298
Kiuru, N., 425, 457
Kivimaki, M., 301, 529
Kjelsberg, E., 416
Klailova, M., 189
Klasko, S. K., 75
Klein, B., 497
Klein, D. F., 450
Klein, G., 250, 251
Klein, O., 429
Klein, S. B., 167
Klem, M. L., 537
Klemanski, D. H., 453
Klemfuss, J. Z., 225, 227
Klick, J., 431
Klimstra, T. A., 308
Klinesmith, J., 413, 414
Klosterhalfen, S., 175
Klucharev, V., 419
Kluge, C., 191
Knapp, H., 509
Knapp, M., 499
Knapp, R. G., 488, 499
Knapp, S., 227
Knestel, A., 503
Knight, D. C., 191
Knight, G. P., 316

Knop, F. K., 328
Knott, V., 152
Knowles, E. D., 403
Knowles, E. S., 425
Knox, W. B., 250
Knudson, J. D., 328
Ko, C. H., 477
Ko, C. M., 141
Kobasa, S., 532
Kobasa, S. C., 532
Kobus, A. M., 410, 411
Koch, C., 9, 95, 127
Kochanek, K. D., 460, 461
Kochanska, G., 317
Koelkebeck, K., 129
Koelling, R. A., 174, 195
Koelsch, S., 375
Koenig, A. M., 314
Koenig, H., 514, 523
Koenig, H. G., 523
Koenig, L. B., 375, 523
Koenis, M. M., 136
Koepp, M. J., 349
Koerner, A., 401
Koestner, R., 520
Kofta, M., 262
Kohlberg, L., 315, 316
Kohler, C. L., 516, 519
Kohler, S., 213
Köhler, W., 191, 192
Kohlmann, W., 532
Kohut, H., 367, 492, 493
Kohyama, J., 293
Koivisto Hursti, U., 175
Kok, B. E., 355
Kola, S., 461
Kolata, G., 335
Kolata, S., 203
Koleva, S., 316
Kolos, A. C., 484
Komel, R., 460
Komiyama, O., 117
Komsi, N., 303
Kong, L. L., 467
Konishi, H., 463
Konishi, K., 238
Konstabel, K., 389
Koo, M., 420
Koob, G. F., 147
Kooij, S. J., 447
Koopmanschap, M., 508
Kopell, B. H., 489
Korkotian, E., 218
Kornell, N., 168, 190
Kornfield, R., 447
Korslund, K. E., 494
Kort-Butler, L. A., 308
Kortenkamp, S., 350
Korzekwa, M. I., 475
Koschwanez, H. E., 528
Kosel, M., 451
Koselka, M., 450
Koskenvuo, M., 79
Kosloff, S., 319
Koss, M., 416
Kosslyn, S. M., 57
Koster, E. H. W., 474
Kotsis, V., 143
Kotter-Grühn, D., 311
Kouider, S., 92
Kourtzi, Z., 105
Kovacs, A. M., 267
Kovacs, E. J., 292
Kozaric-Kovacic, D., 500
Koziorynska, E. L., 139
Kraemer, W. J., 54
Kraft, D., 499
Kraft, E., 291
Kraft, J. M., 333
Krajcik, J. S., 343, 344
Kramer, A. F., 301
Kramer, K. M., 55
Kraus, M. W., 342
Kraus, N., 271

Krause, E. D., 507
Krause, N., 523
Kravják, A., 288
Krebs, P. M., 516, 519
Kredlow, B. A., 454
Kregel, K. C., 292
Kreider, H., 308
Kremen, A. M., 355
Kremers, S., 519
Kreukels, B. P. C., 313
Kring, A. M., 446
Kringelbach, M. L., 127, 349
Krings, T., 159
Krishnamurthy, R., 395
Kristen, S., 128
Kroger, J., 307
Kross, E., 386
Krous, H. F., 143
Krsiak, M., 236
Krueger, R. F., 390
Kruger, J., 536, 537
Kruglanski, A. W., 262, 341
Krull, J., 375
Krumrei, E. J., 523
Krumrey, E., 175
Kruschke, J. K., 91
Kryscio, R. J., 22
Ksir, C. J., 55, 130, 390
Kuang, X., 95
Kübler-Ross, E., 319
Kubzansky, L. D., 526, 529
Kudo, T., 140
Kudoh, A., 452
Kudrowitz, B., 298
Kuh, G. D., 193
Kuhl, P. K., 273
Kuhn, C. M., 389
Kuhn, D., 299
Kuhn, J., 226
Kuhn, S., 330, 456
Kulkarni, A., 333
Kulkofsky, S., 224
Kumar, C. T. S., 478
Kuo, M., 149
Kuper, K., 211
Kuperberg, G. R., 470
Kupfer, A. S., 317
Kurdi, V., 238
Kuriyan, A. B., 447
Kurose, K., 484
Kurson, R., 96
Kurth, T., 534
Kurylo, N., 486
Kurzban, R., 5
Kushner, R. F., 520
Kusurkar, R. A., 373
Kuyper, P., 93
Kwan, V. S. Y., 377
Kwok, D. W., 174
Kwon, D. S., 89
Kyrios, M., 452
Kyung, K. U., 89

L

Labban, J. D., 534
Lac, A., 516
LaCasse, L., 474, 475
Lachman, M. E., 311
Lack, L. C., 134
Ladd, B., 317
Lader, M., 483, 484
Laditka, J. N., 291, 534
La Ferla, T., 484
Lahey, B. B., 81
Lai, T., 214, 455
Laible, D. J., 317
Lakenberg, N., 389
Laland, K. N., 325
Lam, C. S., 519
Lam, R., 456
Lambert, D. B., 503
Lambert, E., 449
Lambert, G., 449

Lambert, M. J., 507, 508
Laming, D., 220
Lamkin, D. M., 528
Lamme, V. A., 129
Lamme, V. A. F., 86
LaMonte, M. J., 534
Lamoureux, P. L., 291
Lampard, A. M., 463
Lancaster, T., 538
Landau, S., 471
Landgren, S., 150
Landis, C., 489
Landis, K. R., 520
Landler, M., 427
Landwehr, J., 401
Lane, J., 514
Lane, S. M., 223
Lang, W., 518, 537
Lange, C. G., 347
Lange, T., 141
Langer, E., 253
Langer, E. J., 253
Langer, J. J., 225
Langerock, N., 232, 233
Langinvainio, H., 79
Langlois, J. H., 401, 402
Langstrom, N., 338, 339
Lanius, R., 465
Lanius, R. A., 465
Lapid, H., 119
Lapsley, D. K., 299, 309
Laris, B. A., 333
Larkin, G. R., 355
Larsen, R. J., 15, 19
Larsen-Rife, D., 375
Larson, A., 401, 402
Larsson, H., 447
Larzelere, M. M., 538
Lashley, K., 217, 218
Laska, E. A., 472
Laskow, T. C., 530
Lassiter, G. D., 131
Latané, B., 412, 426
Lauber, C., 477
Laumann, E. O., 335
Laurenceau, J., 321
Laureys, S., 131, 158
Laursen, B., 1, 309, 425, 457, 458
Laust, H., 300
Lavidor, M., 271
Lavie, N., 93
Law, R., 232
Lawford, H., 435
Lawless, R. M., 430, 431
Lawrence, A. D., 349
Lawrence, O., 99
Lawton, R., 376
Lazard, D. S., 69
Lazarus, A. A., 501
Lazarus, R., 215
Lazarus, R. S., 6, 349, 350, 530, 531
Lazerson, A., 43, 116, 117
Leachman, S. A., 532
Leaf, S. L., 532
Leahy, R. L., 452, 476
Leaper, C., 417
Learned, N., 443
Leary, M. R., 3, 14, 25, 342, 378
LeBel, E. P., 90, 91
LeBlanc, L. A., 495
LeBoeuf, R. A., 250
Lecce, S., 127, 129
Lechner, L., 524
LeDoux, J. E., 61, 348, 350
Lee, A. K., 328
Lee, H., 149
Lee, H. A., 106
Lee, H. S., 516
Lee, J. E., 149
Lee, J. R., 231
Lee, K., 289
Lee, K. A., 139
Lee, L., 516
Lee, M. D., 91

Lee, P. J., 236
Lee, S. H., 106
Lee, T. W., 456
Lee, Y., 477
Lee-Chai, A., 215
Leedy, P. D., 32
Lees, M., 477
Legate, N., 369
Legatt, M. E., 465, 467
Le Grand, R., 350
Le Grange, D., 463
Leigh, E. G., 410
Leimbruber, K., 410
Leite, C., 502
Lemay, E., 528
Lenaghan, P., 100
Lencz, T., 474, 475
Lenglet, C., 63
Lenneberg, E. H., 273
Lent, R. W., 384
Lenz, J. W., 533
Leo, J. L., 45
Leonard, G., 290
LePage, A., 414
Lepage, J. F., 59
Lepage, M., 469
Lepak, A., 42
Lerner, B. H., 489
Lerner, J. S., 405
Lerner, J. V., 290
Lerner, M. J., 410
Lerner, R. M., 290
Leskin, G. A., 450
Leslie, A. M., 127
Lesorogoi, C., 411
Lesschaeve, I., 221
Leszcz, M., 502
Leung, A. K., 192
Leung, C. Y. Y., 11
Leuzinger-Bohleber, M., 492
Levenson, R. W., 350
Leventhal, H., 349
Levert, E., 377
Levin, C., 362
Levine, B., 226, 234
Levine, F. M., 117
Levine, J. M., 418, 426
Levine, M., 539
Levine, M., 425
Levine, R., 472
Levine, R. L., 463
Levine, S. C., 289
Levinson, S. C., 269
Levinthal, C. F., 149
Levitt, J. T., 507
Levkovitz, Y., 271
Levrini, L., 456
Levy, B. R., 311
Levy, J. J., 159
Levy, R. L., 520
Lew, M. W., 159
Lewald, J., 113
Lewis, A., 99
Lewis, E. P., 191
Lewis, J., 79
Lewis, J. G., 349
Lewis, P. A., 135
Lewis, S. J., 140
Lewis, S. K., 409
Lewkowicz, D. J., 287
Leyens, J.-P., 428
Li, C., 136
Li, D., 209
Li, H., 457
Li, H. F., 456
Li, N., 456
Li, N. P., 5
Li, Y., 221
Li, Y. J., 403
Liang, B., 225
Libedinsky, C., 136
Liben, L. S., 354
Libertus, M. E., 92
Lichstein, K. L., 141

Lichtenstein, P., 338, 339, 447
Lieberman, H. R., 134, 135
Lieberman, M. A., 202
Lieberman, M. D., 389
Light, S. N., 349
Light, T., 161
Lilienfeld, S. O., 395, 474
Lim, A., 504
Lim, S. C., 89
Lin, H. M., 530
Lin, J., 292, 404, 429
Lin, L., 203
Lindberg, M. J., 131
Linde, J. A., 520
Linden, W., 533
Lindner, S., 465
Lindsay, A., 226
Lindwall, M., 478
Linehan, M. M., 494, 500
Lingjaerde, O., 376
Link, B. G., 477
Linke, S. E., 508
Links, P. S., 475
Linley, P. A., 509
Linnman, C., 348
Liossi, C., 413
Lippke, S., 519, 524
Lipschitz, D., 465, 467
Lipworth, L., 161
Lisanby, S. H., 488
Lissek, S., 450
Liszkowski, U., 270
Little, D., 291
Little, K. Y., 54
Little, T. D., 524
Littlefield, A. K., 149, 379
Littrell, J. H., 519
Litvack, A., 130
Liu, C. M., 244
Liu, C. Y., 489
Liu, D., 128
Liu, F., 247
Liu, J., 211, 413
Liu, K. S., 52
Liu, L., 128
Liu, R. J., 456
Liu, Y. H., 443
Livesey, E. J., 171
Livesley, W. J., 390
Lo, S., 353
Lo, U. G., 47
Lobo, F. A., 131
Lobo, S. A., 286
Lock, J., 462, 463, 464
Lockhart, R. S., 204
Lockwood, P., 393
Loeb, K., 463
Loeb, K. L., 462
Loeber, R., 474
Loehlin, J. C., 390
Loess, P., 530
Loewenstein, G., 357
Loewenstein, R. J., 465
Loftus, E. F., 228
Logie, R. H., 210
Logothetis, N. K., 347
Lohoff, F. W., 483
Lohr, B. A., 365
Lombardi, C., 143
Longo, D. A., 384
Lopes, F. L., 450
Lopez, A. E., 525
Lopez, K. N., 328
Lopez, S. J., 6, 411
Lorant, V., 457
Lorenz, K. Z., 412
Lo Sauro, C., 463, 464
LoSavio, S. T., 321
Lotze, M., 48
Lotze, M. T., 530
Lovallo, D., 251
Love, B. C., 250
Love, G. D., 343, 509, 522
Love, R. J., 134, 135
Lovheim, H., 347

Lowenstein, A., 260, 280
Lowmaster, S. E., 391
Lu, J., 145
Lu, J. L., 532
Lu, P. H., 49
Lubinski, D., 262
Luborsky, L., 507
Lucae, S., 449
Lucas, E. B., 379
Lucas, R. E., 378, 385
Luce, C. L., 410
Luciano, M., 390
Lucksted, A., 523
Lüdtke, O., 281
Luft, A. R., 56
Luft, B. J., 454
Luhrmann, T. M., 472
Luigjes, J., 488
Lukenbaugh, D., 450
Lukowiak, K., 218
Lumpkin, G. T., 375, 376
Luna, L. R., 5
Lund, B. C., 483, 485
Lund, D., 321
Lund, H. G., 140
Luo, Y., 298, 457, 520
Lupu, V., 496, 499
Luria, A. R., 65
Luthi, A., 348
Lutwak, N., 515
Luyckx, K., 308
Luyten, P., 303
Luz, C., 271
Lyddon, R., 460
Lydon, C. A., 536
Lykken, D. T., 79, 347, 356
Lynam, D. R., 474
Lynn, S. J., 157, 159
Lyon, T. D., 227
Lyons, D. M., 75
Lysle, D. T., 174
Lyubomirsky, S., 356, 357

**M**

Maayan, N., 487
MacCann, C., 393
Maccoby, E. E., 281, 313
MacDonald, C., 58
MacDonald, G., 436
Macdonald, J. S. P., 93
Macdonald, S., 347
MacGregor, J. N., 192
Macgregor, S., 338, 339
Machado, A. G., 489
Machado, G. M., 102
Mackay, D., 471
Mackenbach, J., 457
Mackey, A., 234
Mackey, A., 234
Macknight, J. M., 135
MacLean, K. A., 292
MacLeod, M. S., 234
Maclure, M., 447
MacQueen, C. E., 519
Macrae, C. N., 130
Madden, D. J., 293
Maddi, S. R., 532
Maddock, R. J., 449
Maddux, W. W., 192
Madhyastha, T. M., 310
Madsen, L., 347
Maeda, U., 525
Maerlender, A. C., 74
Maes, H. H. M., 330
Maggs, J. L., 140
Magid, K., 529
Magon, N., 55, 331
Maguire, E. A., 44
Mahbub, S., 292
Mahler, D. A., 54
Mahmoud, F. A., 175
Mahowald, M., 142
Maier, G. W., 397
Maier, N. R. F., 248
Maier, S. F., 182

Maisto, S. A., 529
Major, B., 429
Makransky, G., 391
Malamuth, N. M., 416
Malcarne, V. L., 141
Malcolm, K. T., 376
Malcolm-Smith, S., 145
Malhotra, R. K., 140
Malla, A., 442
Mallach, N., 519
Mallon, S., 525
Malloy, L. C., 227
Malmberg, K. J., 232
Malone, P. S., 403
Malone, R., 453
Malur, C., 488
Mambou, E., 428
Manchanda, R., 466
Mancini, A. D., 320
Mancini, F., 349
Mandal, I., 247
Mandell, D. L., 353
Manderscheid, R. W., 503
Mandic, M., 234
Mandisodza, A. N., 401
Mandler, G., 216
Mandos, L. A., 483
Maner, J. K., 410
Mangos, P. M., 18
Manini, T. M., 534
Mann, J. J., 486
Manne, S., 515, 518
Manning, L., 135
Manore, M., 379
Manstead, A. S. R., 516
Manto, M., 61
Mantonakis, A., 221
Mantzoros, C. S., 328
Manusov, V., 403
Maoz, I., 428
Mar, R. A., 130
March, J. S., 456
Marchiori, D., 44
Marcia, J. E., 307, 308
Marcus, D. K., 447
Marcus, G. F., 217, 243
Marcus, S. C., 485, 490
Marcus, S. M., 486
Marewski, J. N., 247
Margolskee, R. F., 118
Margraf, J., 447, 451
Marine, A., 378
Marinkovic, K., 70
Mariottini, C., 225
Maris, R. W., 461
Mark, R., 514
Markella, M., 462
Markesbery, W. R., 22
Markey, C. N., 289
Markham, C. M., 333
Markides, K. S., 22
Markie, D., 449
Markon, K. E., 390
Markovits, H., 249
Markowitsch, H. J., 466
Marks, A. K., 308
Marks, D. F., 514
Marks, J. S., 379
Markus, H. R., 28, 343, 522
Marlow, A., 177
Marlowe, F., 411
Maroky, A. S. M., 450
Marsh, E. J., 223
Marshall, D. S., 332
Marshall, D. W., 330
Marshall, G., 175
Marshall, M., 472
Marston, O. J., 329
Martens, A., 319
Marti, C. N., 520
Martin, A., 486
Martin, C., 375
Martin, C. E., 335
Martin, C. L., 313

Martin, E. A., 209
Martin, G. L., 9, 185, 186
Martin, G. R., 54
Martin, J., 474
Martin, L. L., 357
Martin, M., 472
Martin, N. G., 338, 339, 475
Martin, R., 405
Martinez, E., 412
Martinez, M., 333
Martinez-Amoros, E., 488
Martinovich, Z., 456
Martinussen, M., 307
Maruyama, Y., 118
Marx, R. F., 466
Marzano, C., 138
Mascaro, N., 523
Mash, E. J., 447
Masheb, R. M., 464
Masicampo, E. J., 132
Maslach, C., 419, 424
Maslow, A. H., 10, 27, 340,
    370, 371
Mason, C., 513
Mason, M. F., 130
Massa, L. J., 197
Massey, C., 282
Masten, A. S., 281, 355
Masters, K. S., 529
Masters, W. H., 331
Masuda, T., 94
Masul, Y., 523
Matarese, G., 328
Math, S. B., 450
Mather, K. A., 292
Mathew, A., 466
Matlin, 11, 30, 435
Matos, A. P., 415
Matschinger, H., 406
Matsick, J. L., 337
Matsumoto, D., 11, 28, 196, 352,
    353, 443
Matsunaga, H., 452
Mattaini, M. A., 536
Mattes, K., 401
Matthews, J., 190
Matthews, K., 11
Matthews, K. A., 529
Matthews, P. M., 58
Mattia, D., 132
Mattson, S. N., 285
Matzel, L. D., 203
Matzke, D., 91
Maurer, D., 287
Maxfield, M., 319
Maxwell, H., 502
Maxwell, W. L., 73
May, A., 120
May, M., 122
May, P. A., 285
May, P. J., 114
Mayberg, H. S., 453
Maybery, M. T., 316
Mayer, J. D., 265
Mayer, R., 246
Mayer, R. E., 168, 197
Mayeux, R., 238
Mayo Foundation, 488
Maytan, M., 530
Mazziotta, J. C., 459
McAdams, D. P., 224, 237, 310, 321,
    380, 381, 424, 469
McAndrew, F. T., 413, 414
McBride, C. M., 514
McCabe, J., 217
McCarthy, D. E., 538
McCarthy, P. M., 411
McCauley, C., 422
McClay, J., 474
McClelland, J. L., 216, 217
McClelland, M. M., 384
McClintock, M., 488
McCollum, V., 506
McConnell, A. R., 407
McCorkle, R., 508

McCormack, J. P., 539
McCoy, C., 74
McCrae, R. R., 373, 374, 375, 393
McCrea, S. M., 426
McCulloch, K. C., 215
McCullough, M. E., 5, 357, 375, 523
McDaniel, M., 197
McDaniel, M. A., 219, 234
McDermott, M., 520
McDermott, R., 252
McDonald, M., 404
McDonel, E. C., 406
McDowell, N. K., 405
McElreath, R., 411
McElroy, S., 505
McFadden, S. H., 281
McFarland, S., 424
McFatter, R. M., 377
McGhee, K. E., 377
McGilloway, S., 418
McGinley, M., 316
McGinn, L. K., 452, 476
McGinnis, M. Y., 413
McGlashan, T. H., 476
McGlinchey, E., 141
McGue, M., 79
McGuire, H., 484
McGuire, J., 215
McGuire, M. T., 537
McGuire, W. J., 409
McIntosh, J., 152
McIntosh, R. C., 528
McIntosh, W. D., 357
McIntyre, L. L., 188
McKay, D., 449, 450
McKay, K. M., 509
McKellar, S., 519
McLaren, D., 138
McLean, N., 463
McLeod, J., 509
McMahan, E. A., 6
McMahon, D. B., 101
McMains, S., 86, 499
McMillan, B., 523
McNamara, M., 142
McNamara, P., 138
McNaughton, N., 389
McNulty, J. K., 5
McRae, K., 206
McWhirter, R. M., 377
McWilliams, L. A., 436
Meara, E., 486
Medalia, A., 488
Medin, D. L., 245
Medina-Mora, M. E., 465
Medley-Rath, S. R., 334
MedlinePlus, 150
Medoff, D. R., 523
Meehan, W. P., 74
Meehl, P., 472
Meeren, H. K., 351
Meeus, W. H., 308
Meeus, W. H. J., 308
Meghnagi, D., 492
Mehta, D., 454
Mehta, U. M., 470
Meier, B. P., 405
Meinhardt, J., 495
Meints, J. O., 523
Meiser, T., 222
Meissner, C. A., 228
Meister, I. G., 159
Mejia-Arauz, R., 196
Melendez-Ferro, M., 54
Meléndez-Jiménez, M. A., 189
Mellers, B., 431
Mellerup, E., 389, 390
Melton, L., 237, 238
Meltzer, L. J., 139
Melzack, R., 117
Mendel, G., 77, 78
Mendel, J. R., 458
Mendel, R., 252
Mendes, D. M., 370

Mendes, N., 192
Mendes, W. B., 426
Mendes de Leon, C. F., 238
Mendes de Leon, D. F., 523
Mendez, M. F., 331
Mendiondo, M. S., 22
Meneses, C. W., 503
Meng, M., 68
Meng, X., 457
Menn, L., 266, 273
Mercier, H., 132, 299
Meredith-Owen, W., 368
Merenakk, L., 389
Merkl, A., 488
Mermi, O., 452
Merskey, H., 466
Mertens, I., 476
Merz, M. E., 301
Merz, S., 488
Meshul, C. K., 150
Mesquita, B., 352, 522
Messenger, J. C., 332
Messer, S. C., 453
Mesulam, M., 64
Metalsky, G. I., 457
Metcalfe, J., 233, 386
Mettler, F. A., 489
Meurs, P., 303
Meyer, C., 519
Meyer, J. H., 54, 484
Meyer, K., 86
Meyer, P. J., 150
Meyer, U., 289
Mezzasalma, M. A., 450
Miacic, B., 376
Miao, F. F., 420
Michael, R. T., 335
Michael, T., 289, 451
Michalik, N. M., 317
Middeldorp, C. M., 389
Migneault, J. P., 519
Mikels, J. A., 311
Mikolajczyk, E., 463
Miksis, S., 540
Mikulincer, M., 435, 436
Milano, W., 463
Milgram, S., 422, 423
Mill, J., 474
Millam, J. R., 377
Millar, A., 152
Miller, A. G., 422
Miller, A. H., 528
Miller, A. J., 5
Miller, D. B., 139
Miller, D. L., 238
Miller, D. T., 404, 410
Miller, G., 90, 91
Miller, G. A., 208
Miller, G. E., 376
Miller, J., 485
Miller, J. C., 134, 135
Miller, J. J., 161
Miller, K. E., 291
Miller, N. E., 36, 414
Miller, R. R., 171, 172
Miller, S. D., 507, 509
Milliken, B., 215
Milling, L. S., 158
Millon, T., 473
Milne, R. L., 525
Milner, A. D., 104, 131
Milner, P. M., 63
Milsom, V. A., 572
Miltenberger, R. G., 9, 167, 187, 494
Miltner, W. H., 131
Mindel, C. H., 261
Mindell, J. A., 139
Mineka, S., 195, 497
Ming, G. L., 75, 293
Miniussi, C., 219
Mirilas, P., 117
Mischel, W., 384, 385, 386
Miserandino, M., 373
Mistry, D. J., 135

Mitchell, A. A., 314
Mitchell, C., 33
Mitchell, D., 497
Mitchell, E. B., 404
Mitchell, G., 431
Mitchell, J. E., 465
Mitchell, T. L., 228
Mittag, W., 524
Miyake, K., 304
Miyamoto, Y., 94, 343, 522
Miyaoka, T., 484
Miyata, J., 129
Mizunami, M., 170
Mlacic, B., 377
Moberly, N. J., 251
Mochan, K., 291
Moeller, J., 136
Moffitt, A., 209
Moffitt, T. E., 80, 413, 474
Mogan, C., 452
Mohr, P., 516
Mohring, W., 92
Moilanen, K. L., 317
Mokdad, A. H., 379
Molet, M., 250
Molina, B. S. G., 447
Molloy, G. J., 529
Molock, S. D., 461
Molton, I., 508
Moltschaniwskyj, N. A., 377
Momtaz, Y. A., 520
Moncrieff, J., 447
Mondy, K., 539
Moneith, G. R., 54
Monetta, L., 271
Money, J., 314
Moniz, A. E., 489
Monk, T. H., 136
Montgomery, E., 281
Montgomery, P., 333
Mon-Williams, M., 293
Moore, B. S., 386
Moore, D. G., 262
Moore, K. M., 429
Moore, Z. T., 337
Moors, A. C., 337
Mora, T., 458
Moran, A., 190
Moreland, R. L., 418
Morelli, G., 304
Morelock, M. J., 262
Moreno, M. A., 482
Morewedge, C. K., 250
Morey, C. C., 209
Morey, L. C., 391, 476
Morey, R. D., 90, 91, 92
Morgan, C., 395
Morgan, C. D., 381
Morgan, H., 368
Morin, C. M., 141
Morin, O., 410
Morley, K. I., 338, 339
Morling, B., 522
Morris, J., 486
Morris, M. W., 403
Morris, T., 524
Morrison, F. J., 384
Morrison, G. S., 260
Morrison, R. G., 245
Morrow, R. L., 447
Morse, S., 73
Morsella, E., 132, 215
Mortensen, C. R., 421
Mortensen, E. L., 391
Mortensen, L. H., 300
Mortimer, J., 238
Mortimer, J. A., 22
Morua, S. D., 447
Moscovici, S., 426
Moscovitch, M., 213
Moses, E., 449, 450
Mosher, W. D., 310, 336, 338
Moskowitz, J. T., 531
Moss, A. J., 520
Moss, C., 328

Moss, P., 139
Mostofsky, E., 529
Mothes-Lasch, M., 131
Mott, M., 194
Motz, G. T., 528
Moussally, J., 451
Mowrer, O. H., 414
Mroczek, D. K., 311
Mrykalo, M. S., 524
Mu, Y., 75
Mudford, O. C., 188
Mueller, C. J., 57, 349
Mueller, D. L., 120
Mueller, E. M., 389, 391
Mueller, M., 488
Mueller-Myhsok, B., 449
Mulder, R. T., 475
Mulert, C., 449
Mullainathan, S., 430
Muller, J. L., 495
Muller, U., 447
Mullooly, J. P., 521
Munafo, M. R., 389
Munakata, Y., 77
Munch, E., 449
Munoz, M., 456
Munro, D., 58
Munroe, M., 160, 161
Muntaner, C., 514
Murai, T., 129
Murakami, J. L., 461
Murphy, B. C., 316, 317
Murphy, K., 514
Murphy, L., 497
Murphy, M., 538
Murphy, M. L., 376
Murphy, N. A., 261
Murphy, S. L., 460, 461
Murray, D. R., 421
Murray, H., 380, 395
Murray, H. A., 381
Murray, J. A., 54
Murray-Swank, A. B., 523
Musick, M. A., 523
Mussell, M. P., 465
Musselman, L., 402
Musso, M. W., 258
Myers, M. M., 143
Myers, N. L., 472
Myers, P., 161
Myers, S. L., 23
Mykletun, A., 478
Mylanus, E. A., 112

## N

Naar-King, S., 519
Nabeyama, M., 452
Nabi, R. L., 1
Naccache, L., 127
Nadeau, L., 148
Nadelson, C. C., 506
Nader, K., 348
Naeem, F., 504, 505
Nagaoka, R., 304
Nagase, Y., 531
Nagin, D. S., 413
Nagy, G., 281
Nahin, R. L., 141
Naidoo, N., 135
Naismith, S. L., 140
Nakagawa, A., 452, 484, 499
Nakamura, K., 536
Nakamura, T. J., 140
Nakamura, W., 140
Nakao, T., 452
Nakatani, E., 452
Nardi, A. E., 450
Narkiewicz, K., 143
Narr, K. L., 285
Nascimento, I., 450
Nash, J. R., 451
Nash, M. R., 158, 159
Nasrallah, H. A., 485
Nass, C., 204

National Center for Health Statistics, 149, 335
National Center for Post-Traumatic Stress Disorder, 453
National Highway Traffic Safety Administration, 149
National Institute of Mental Health, 451, 455, 459, 460, 461, 462, 463, 464, 468, 471, 476
National Institute on Drug Abuse, 154
National Sleep Foundation, 136, 141
Nations, K. R., 499
Naumann, L. P., 375, 376
Nauta, M. H., 459, 526
Navarrete, C. D., 404
Navarro, R. L., 339
Nay, W. R., 46
Nazareth, I., 478
Neal, M. C., 330
Neale, J. M., 446
Needham, A., 287
Negriff, S., 289
Neikrug, A. B., 140
Neilands, T. B., 525
Nelson, C. A., 43, 44, 116, 117
Nelson, D. A., 1
Nelson, K., 237
Nelson, P. B., 111
Nelson, P. T., 22
Nelson, T. F., 149
Nemeroff, C. B., 453
Ness, L., 467
Nesse, R. N., 521
Nesselroade, J. R., 311
Nestler, S., 252
Nett, E. J., 219
Nettle, D., 376
Neuberg, S. L., 410, 421
Neufeind, J., 214, 455
Neufeld, J., 88
Neukrug, E. S., 256
Neumann, I. D., 413
Nevels, R. M., 413
Neville, H. J., 274
Nevo, E., 351
Nevsimalova, S., 142
Newheiser, A.-K., 428
Newman, T. K., 474
Newport, E. L., 274
Nezu, A., 530
Nezu, C. M., 530
Nezworski, M. T., 394
Ng, 1
Ng, E., 514
Ng, W., 31
Niaura, R., 529
Nicholls, D., 463
Nichols, I. A., 273
Nichols, R. M., 228
Nickens, J., 478
Nickerson, R. S., 231
Nicklas, J. M., 536
Nicoleau, C., 75
Nicolle, A., 189
Niehorster, S., 374
Nielsen, J., 487
Nielsen, M. B., 432
Nienhuis, F. J., 472
Nieto, S., 30
Nijstad, B., 426
Nillni, Y. I., 450
Nilsson, H., 252
Nimaonkar, V. L., 469
Ni Mhaolain, A. M., 377
Nimon, J. P., 301
Niry, D., 183
Nisbett, R. E., 94, 251, 259, 260, 266, 415
Nishida, A., 484
Nitschke, J. B., 57, 349
Niv, Y., 172
No, S., 11
Nobre, A. C., 130
Nocera, C. C., 116

Noftle, E. E., 376
Nolan, J., 425
Nolen-Hoeksema, S., 456, 490, 506
Norby, M. M., 235
Norcross, J. C., 482, 490, 497, 500, 501, 503, 504, 507, 509, 516, 518, 519, 524
Nordgren, L. F., 250
Nordquist, N., 389
Nordstrom, B. R., 413, 474
Nordt, C., 477
Noreika, V., 131
Norman, G. J., 520
Norrholm, S. D., 454
Norring, C., 444, 463, 464
Norris, A. L., 447
Norris, J. E., 282
North, C. S., 453
North, M. S., 402
Norton, L., 175
Norton, M. I., 14, 35
Nosek, B., 263
Nosek, B. A., 316, 431
Nosko, A., 435
Notman, M. T., 506
Novick, L. R., 246
Nowak, M. A., 410, 528
Nowotny, M., 112
Noyes, R., Jr., 449
NPD Group, 298
Ntoumanis, N., 373
Nunez, N., 426
Nunez, P. L., 244
Nurmi, J. E., 425, 457
Nusbaum, E. C., 375
Nutt, D. J., 451
Nyberg, L., 58
Nystul, M. S., 506

O

Oakeshott, P., 333
Oakley, D. A., 159
Oaksford, M., 249
Obama, B., 76, 407
O'Barr, W. M., 339
Oberman, L. S., 48
Obler, L. K., 274
O'Callaghan, J. P., 139
Ochner, C. N., 329
Ochsner, K. N., 350
Ockene, I. S., 513
O'Cleirigh, C., 523
O'Connell, M. S., 18
O'Connor, A., 375
O'Connor, A. R., 205
O'Connor, B., 347
O'Connor, D. B., 376, 523
O'Connor, K., 488
O'Connor, M. J., 285
O'Connor, P. J., 534
O'Connor, T. G., 527
Odbert, H., 374
O'Dea, B. M., 503
Odegard, A., 466
O'Dell, K. R., 529
Odlaug, B. L., 494
O'Donnell, M. L., 499
O'Donnell, M. P., 514
O'Donovan, A., 526
OECD, 1, 329
Oerlemans, W. G., 377
Ogden, C. L., 536, 537
Ogilvie, R. D., 131
Ogletree, S. L., 369
Oh, D. J., 478
Ohira, T., 529
Ohman, A., 195
Ohrmann, P., 129
Ohry, A., 453
Oishi, S., 358, 420
Ojeda, L., 11
Okano, K., 99
Okribelashvili, N., 469

Okuma, N., 301
Olajossy-Hilkesberger, L., 469
Olbrich, D., 140
Olds, J. M., 63
O'Leary, K. D., 502
O'Leary, L. A., 285
Olfson, M., 485, 490
Oliveira, M. M., 102
Oliver, P. L., 133
Olivers, C. N., 209
Olivetti, B. M., 48
Olma, M. C., 92
Olness, K., 174
Olsen, A., 406
Olson, B., 310
Olson, B. D., 380
Olson, C. R., 101
Olson, J. M., 407
Olson, R. L., 94
Olsson, H., 252
Oltmanns, T. F., 446, 475
O'Malley, P. M., 146, 149, 153, 155
Omar, H. A., 475
O'Mara, E. M., 11
Omura, K., 388
Oncu, F., 466
Ondersma, S., 519
O'Neil, J. A., 465
Onen, N. F., 539
Ong, A. D., 320
Onifer, S. M., 73
Ono, Y., 499
Onrust, S., 508
Onwudiwe, N. C., 291
Operario, D., 333
Ophir, E., 204
Opp, M. R., 141
Oral, E., 449
Oral, M., 449
Orehek, E., 341
Oreland, L., 389
Organisation for Economic Co-operation and Development, 536
Ormerod, A. J., 432
Ormrod, J. E., 32
Orom, H., 386
Ort, R., 457
Ortmann, A., 35
Osborn, D. P. J., 478
Osborne, R. H., 525
Oslin, D. M., 154
Osswald, S., 417
Ostendorf, F., 377
Osterman, L. L., 461
Ostir, G. V., 22
O'Sullivan, M., 350
Otake, K., 355
Otonari, J., 377
O'Toole, M. R., 291
O'Toole, S., 393
Otsui, K., 355
Otsuki-Clutter, M., 307
Otto, A. R., 250
Otto, B., 175
Overbeek, G., 5
Overland, S., 478
Overton, E. T., 539
Owens, J. A., 139
Oxenham, A., 111
Oxenham, A. J., 112
Oyserman, D., 308
Ozdemir, H. N., 452
Ozler, S., 452
Ozler, Z., 452
Oztekin, I., 232
Ozturk, H., 520

P

Pace-Schott, E. F., 145
Pacheco-Lopez, G., 174
Packer, D. J., 423, 427
Padavic, I., 193

Padberg, F., 489
Pagano, M., 503
Pagano, R. R., 21
Page, K. M., 410
Page, R. A., 159
Pagnin, A., 129
Paivio, A., 206
Palmer, A. A., 215
Palmer, J., 251
Palmer, P. H., 516
Palmieri, P. A., 432
Paluck, E. C., 539
Pan, A., 537
Pan, B. A., 267, 272
Panaleo, G., 528
Panerai, L., 375
Panis, L. K., 427
Panksepp, J., 349
Pant, S., 528
Pantalone, D. W., 494
Pantoni, L., 57
Papademetris, X., 58
Papafragou, A., 267
Papageorgis, D., 409
Papakatsika, S., 143
Pappas, S., 263
Parada, H., 514
Paradise, R., 196
Paralympic Movement, 342
Parati, G., 143
Pare, D., 62, 173, 347
Parisotto, K. L., 395
Park, C., 321
Park, C. L., 321, 523
Park, D. H., 75
Park, J., 343, 522
Park, M., 440, 469
Park, N., 376
Park, R. J., 456
Park, S., 343
Parker, A. C., 304
Parker, P. S., 432
Parks, M. R., 429
Parks, R., 400
Parrish, B. P., 321
Parrott, D. J., 149
Parry, A., 58
Parslow, R. A., 292
Parsons, J. T., 519
Pascalls, O., 287
Pashler, H., 197
Pasi, M., 57
Pasqualetti, P., 219
Passani, M. B., 225
Passingham, R. E., 48
Patalano, A. L., 246
Patching, J. R., 75
Patel, S. R., 141
Patell, E. A., 343
Patte, K., 464
Patterson, C. J., 37, 338, 339
Pattillo, R., 204
Patton, F., 308
Paul, M. A., 134, 135
Pauli, P., 93
Paunonen, S., 376
Paus, T., 290
Pausova, Z., 290
Pavlik, P. J., 530
Pavlov, I. P., 169, 170, 171, 172
Pavot, W., 15
Pawlak, C. R., 56
Payne, W. A., 379
Pbert, L., 514
Pear, J., 9, 185, 186
Pearce, J. M., 215
Pearson, J., 205
Pearson, N. J., 141
Peck, C., 405
Peden-Adams, M. M., 528
Pedersen, A., 129
Pedersen, N. L., 238, 375
Pedroso, I., 459

Pedrotti, J. T., 6, 411
Peebles, R., 463
Peigneux, P., 139
Pekanovic, A., 56
Peleg, G., 351
Peleg, O., 351
Pelham, W. E., Jr., 447
Pelletier, L., 92
Pelleymounter, M. A., 328
Pence, B. D., 301
Penedo, F. J., 508
Penfield, W., 66
Peng, A. C., 384
Peng, K., 403
Pengchit, W., 532
Pennebaker, J. W., 270, 521
Pentz, M., 516
Pepin, R., 319
Peplau, L. A., 338
Pereira, M., 118
Perera, S., 384
Peres, K. G., 391
Perez, N., 159
Perez-Costas, E., 54, 470
Perkins, A. M., 350
Perkins, D., 254
Perkins, L., 377
Perl, T., 291
Perlis, M., 141
Perona, P., 95
Perpina, C., 463
Perreau, M., 528
Perri, M. G., 536
Perrier, A. L., 75
Perrig, W. J., 274
Perrin, J. M., 447
Perrin, J. S., 488
Perron, M., 290
Perrot, X., 69
Persico, M., 532
Pert, C. B., 54
Perugini, M., 377
Perusse, D., 413
Pervanidou, P., 46, 528
Peschanski, M., 75
Pesonen, A., 303
Pete, E., 536
Peterman, K., 287
Peters, J. L., 527
Peters, K. R., 90, 91
Peters, M. L., 189
Petersen, J. L., 336
Peterson, B. S., 354
Peterson, C. C., 128, 129
Peterson, M. H., 18
Petit, O., 426
Petri, H. L., 190
Petrides, G., 488
Petrie, K. J., 134
Petruzzello, S. J., 534
Petry, N. M., 524
Petticrew, M., 525
Pettigrew, T. F., 433
Pettinati, H. M., 154
Pettingale, K. W., 524
Petty, R. E., 406, 407, 408
Pezdek, K., 224
Pezhouh, M. K., 22
Pezzo, M. V., 252
Pfau, M., 409
Pfingst, B. E., 112
Phalet, K., 429
Pham, T. H., 474
Phaneuf, L., 188
Phelan, J. C., 477
Phelan, J. E., 477
Phelan, S., 518, 537
Phelps, M. E., 459
Phillips, A. C., 300
Phillips, D. A., 260, 280
Phillips, K., 525
Phillips, K. J., 188
Phillips, L. H., 234
Phillips, T. J., 150

Piaget, J., 294, 295, 296, 297, 298, 299
Piasecki, T. M., 538
Piber-Dabrowska, K., 262
Pickering, A. D., 350, 389
Pickering, R. P., 473
Pickle, J., 488
Pier, C., 449
Pierce, B. H., 220
Piff, P. K., 342
Pike, G. B., 290
Pike, J. J., 298
Pike, K. M., 463
Pilecki, B., 449, 450
Pillemer, D. B., 223, 237
Pilon, M., 141, 142
Pine, D. S., 450
Pinel, J. P. J., 36
Pines, A. M., 419
Pinker, S., 270
Pinkus, R. T., 393
Pio-Abreu, J. L., 465
Piolino, P., 223
Pirooznia, M., 459
Pisani, A. R., 460
Pittenger, M. J., 337
Pitts, M., 447
Pizzagalli, D., 349
Plotnikoff, R. C., 516, 519, 524
Poehlman, T. A., 431
Pogessi, A., 57
Pogue, D., 242
Pogue-Geile, M., 469
Poirier, J., 425
Polizzi, P., 127
Pollack, M., 454
Pollard, H., 532
Polonia, P., 470
Pomerantz, E. M., 358
Pomeroy, W. B., 335
Pompili, M., 468
Ponitz, C. C., 384
Ponti, G., 189
Popa, D., 62, 173, 347
Pope, C. R., 521
Porcerelli, J., 395
Porter, S., 347
Pos, A. E., 499
Posadas-Sanchez, D., 183
Posner, J., 354
Post, J. M., 427
Postel, M. G., 497
Potenza, M. N., 388
Pott, M., 304
Potter, J. P., 270
Potter, N. N., 442
Pouget, A., 9, 44
Poulton, R., 474
Pournajafi-Nazarloo, H., 55
Powderly, W. G., 539
Powell, D. M., 134
Powell, L. J., 58
Powell, R. A., 173, 179
Powers, A. D., 475
Powers, T., 520
Pratt, L. A., 485
Pratt, M. W., 282, 435
Pregelj, P., 460
Premack, D., 298, 299
Prescott, J., 292
Pressman, J., 489
Presti, R., 539
Preston, T. J., 105
Prestwich, A., 520
Price, D. D., 84, 191
Prichard, J. R., 140
Prime, K., 333
Prince, M., 478
Prinstein, M., 494
Prinstein, M. J., 458
Prisco, T. R., 317
Prislin, R., 407
Probst, T., 175
Procaccini, C., 328

Prochaska, J. O., 490, 500, 509, 516, 518, 519
Prohaska, T. R., 291, 536
Prohovnik, I., 238
Pronin, E., 404
Pronk, T. M., 5
Prot, S., 417
Provenzo, E. F., 258
Provine, R. R., 353
Prudic, J., 488
Pryce, C. R., 182
Przybylski, A. K., 369
Ptak, R., 65
Puccetti, M. C., 532
Puddicombe, A., 162
Puetz, T. W., 534
Pukrop, R., 376
Pull, C. B., 451
Pullen, P. C., 263
Pulvermuller, F., 68
Punamaki, R. L., 454
Putrella, C., 463
Puttonen, S., 134
Pyszczynski, T., 319

Q

Qian, Z., 434
Quas, J. A., 226, 227
Quax, P. H., 329
Quinn, D. M., 405

R

Raabe, A., 249
Raache, J., 26
Raaijmakers, Q. A., 308
Rabasca, L., 453
Rabin, B. S., 521, 528
Rabin, S., 450
Rachlin, H., 175
Racine, M., 117
Racsmany, M., 135
Radel, R., 92
Radin, D. I., 91
Radvansky, G. A., 223
Raffaelli, M., 308
Rahman, Q., 338, 339
Rai, T. S., 316
Raichle, M. E., 449
Räikkönen, K., 303
Raine, A., 413, 474, 475
Raineri, A., 28
Rais, M., 471
Raison, C. L., 528
Rajaratnam, S. M., 141
Rajeevan, N., 58
Rakitin, B. C., 136, 140
Raleigh, M., 413
Ram, N., 311
Ramachandran, V. S., 48
Ramaswamy, B., 528
Ramirez-Esparza, N., 270
Ramirez-Maestre, C., 525
Ramos, J. S., 429
Ramponi, C., 219
Ramsey, C. M., 382
Ramsey, E., 125
Ramsey, J. L., 401
Ranchor, A. V., 525
Rao, N., 75
Rapaport, D., 367
Rapaport, S., 293
Rapold, C. J., 269
Rasekhy, R., 159
Rasmussen, K., 488
Rasmussen, K. A., 456
Rathbone, J., 472
Rathunde, K., 282
Ratliff, K. A., 420
Ratliff, K. R., 289
Ratner, N. B., 272
Rattray, E., 130
Ratz, J. M., 478

Rauch, S. L., 57
Ravaldi, C., 463, 464
Raven, P. H., 61
Raw, R. K., 293
Rawson, R., 173
Ray, M., 254
Ray, O. S., 55, 130, 390
Ray, R. D., 531
Ray, W. J., 13, 25
Raymond, N. C., 465
Rayner, R., 173
Raynor, H. A., 537
Raz, A., 158, 160
Raznahan, A., 289
Read, J. P., 519
Realini, J. P., 333
Realo, A., 311
Reaven, J., 499
Rebelsky, F. G., 273
Recanzone, G. H., 101, 113
Rector, N. A., 500
Redd, W. H., 175
Reddon, J. R., 236
Redican, K., 148
Reed, L. A., 93
Reed, M., 349
Reeve, C., 76
Reeve, C. L., 266
Regan, P. C., 436
Regier, T., 268
Rehfeldt, R. A., 9
Rehfuss, M. C., 368
Reich, J., 451
Reichardt, C. S., 25
Reicher, S., 424, 432
Reicher, S. D., 429
Reichle, E. D., 130
Reid, C., 464
Reid, I. C., 488
Reider, B. D., 140
Reiff, D. F., 106
Reiman, E. M., 449
Reimer, B., 314
Reinecke, M. A., 456
Reinhold, J., 483
Reinke-Scorzelli, M., 505
Reis, H. T., 342, 418
Reis, S. M., 262
Reivich, K., 525
Remschmidt, H., 472
Rendell, P. G., 234
Rennemark, M., 478
Renner, B., 524
Rentfrow, P. J., 375, 376
Renzulli, J. S., 262
Rescorla, R. A., 171, 191
Ressler, K. J., 454
Rettew, J. B., 476
Reuter-Lorenz, P., 349
Revelle, W., 377, 378, 389, 391
Revenson, T. A., 524
Rex, S., 159
Reyes, J. A. S., 522
Reyes, P., 127
Reynolds, C. A., 375
Reynolds, K. J., 428, 429
Reynolds, M., 155
Reynolds, S., 507
Rezai, A. R., 489
Rhodes, N., 406
Rhodes, R. E., 514
Rholes, W. S., 316
Ribeiro, J. D., 460
Ricca, V., 463, 464
Richards, A. L., 449
Richardson, G. A., 155
Richardson, R. C., 325
Richer, L., 290
Richter, L., 504
Richter, M. A., 53
Richter-Levin, G., 289
Rickels, K., 483
Riddlesberger, M., 226
Riediger, M., 291

Riepl, R. L., 175
Riera, R., 390
Ries, M. L., 219
Righart, R., 351
Rijpkema, M., 419
Riketta, M., 193
Riley, A. L., 174
Riley, E. P., 285
Riley, K. P., 22
Rimm, E. B., 529
Riner, D. D., 425
Ringman, J., 331
Riolli, L. T., 384
Rioult-Pedotti, M. S., 56
Ripke, S., 449
Rips, L. J., 245, 403
Risbrough, V. B., 454
Risch, S. C., 471
Rissman, J., 71, 211, 219
Ristikari, T., 314
Ritchie, E. C., 453
Ritskes, R., 161
Ritskes-Hoitinga, M., 161
Ritter, D., 417
Ritter, K., 469
Rivas-Drake, D., 429
Rivers, S. E., 265
Rizos, Z., 143
Rizzolatti, G., 48
Robbins, T. W., 446
Roberts, B. W., 281, 309, 376, 523
Roberts, D. F., 417
Roberts, D. M., 154
Roberts, G., 210
Roberts, P. L., 155
Roberts, R., 393
Roberts, R. C., 54
Robertson, E. M., 220
Robins, R. W., 376
Robinson, H. P., 148
Robinson, J. C., 343
Robinson, J. T., 457
Robinson, M., 404
Robinson, S. L., 1
Robinson-Riegler, B., 203, 245
Robinson-Riegler, G. L., 203, 245
Robles, T., 528, 530
Rocha, F. L., 390
Rocke, C., 311
Rodero, P., 221
Rodgers, J. L., 425
Rodin, J., 328, 330
Rodriguez, C., 405
Rodriguez, E. L., 233
Rodriquez, A. J., 139
Roecklein, K. A., 238
Roediger, H. L., 23, 223
Roemer, L., 354
Roffman, R. A., 519
Rogers, C. R., 10, 371, 372, 493
Rogers, G., 154
Rogers, H., 530
Rogers, J. A., 503
Rogers, N. L., 140
Rogge, R. D., 308
Roggman, L. A., 402
Rogoff, B., 196
Rogosch, F. A., 280
Rohan, K. J., 450
Rohaut, B., 127
Rohleder, N., 46
Rohmeier, K. D., 536
Rohrer, D., 197
Roisman, G. I., 436
Rojas, Y., 460
Rolleri, L. A., 333
Rombaux, P., 120
Roncero, M., 463
Ronning, R. R., 235
Roos, C. J., 329
Root, L. M., 5
Roper, S. D., 118
Rorschach, H., 394
Rosack, J., 486

Roscoe, J., 342
Rose, A. J., 416, 458
Rose, C. A., 429
Rose, D., 477
Rose, N. S., 204
Rose, R. J., 79
Rosell, D. R., 413
Rosellini, R. A., 182
Rosen, D. H., 523
Rosen, E. A., 139
Rosen, K., 472
Rosenbaum, R. S., 213
Rosenberg, E. L., 292
Rosenbloom, D. I., 528
Rosenfeld, J., 73
Rosenhan, D. L., 476
Rosenheck, R., 453
Rosenkranz, M. A., 57, 349
Rosenkranz, M. M., 161
Rosenman, R., 529
Rosental, B., 530
Rosenthal, D. G., 443
Rosenthal, E. S., 56
Rosenthal, R., 25, 26, 402, 507
Roskos-Ewoldsen, D. R., 406
Rosmarin, D. H., 523
Rosnick, C., 311
Rosnow, R. L., 25
Ross, C. A., 467, 468
Ross, D., 189, 414, 415
Ross, F. C., 71
Ross, J. N., 332
Ross, K., 523
Ross, L., 251, 516, 519
Ross, S. A., 189, 414, 415
Rossaint, R., 159
Rosselli, M., 528
Rossi, E. L., 159
Rossi, S., 219
Rossini, P. M., 219
Rossler, W., 477
Rostow, C. D., 393
Roten, R. G., 446
Rotge, J. Y., 452
Rothbart, M. K., 303
Rothbaum, F., 304
Rothman, A. J., 520
Rothstein, H. R., 417
Rothwell, J. C., 59
Rouder, J. N., 90, 91, 92, 209
Rousselet, G. A., 101
Roussotte, F., 285
Routledge, C., 319
Rozin, P., 536, 537
Rubenstein, A. J., 401, 402
Rubin, D., 223
Rubin, D. C., 223, 225
Rubin, Z., 33
Ruble, D. N., 313, 405
Ruck, C., 489
Rudaleviciene, P., 469
Rudy, D., 307
Rueda, S. M., 415, 417
Ruini, C., 509
Rumelhart, D. E., 217
Rummans, T. A., 488
Rumpf, H., 519
Runyon, W. M., 382
Rusbult, C. E., 437
Ruscher, S. M., 457
Rush, C. C., 523
Rushton, J. P., 376
Russell, J., 354
Rutherford-Turnbull, H., 264
Rutjens, B., 319
Rutosalainen, J., 378
Rutte, C. G., 384
Rutter, M., 80
Rüttgers, A., 175
Ryan, R. M., 16, 342, 343, 344, 355, 369, 520
Ryan, W. S., 369
Ryckman, R. M., 372

Rydell, R. J., 405
Ryff, C. D., 57, 311, 343, 349, 509, 522
Ryff, C. O., 514
Rymer, R., 272

S

Sabanayagam, C., 141
Sabunciyan, S., 456
Sacco, D. F., 350
Sacerdote, P., 456
Sachs, J., 274
Sachs, M., 538
Sack, A. T., 127
Sack, R. L., 135
Sackett, A. M., 282
Sacks, O., 106, 122
Sackur, J., 127
Sadler, G. R., 141
Sado, M., 499
Sadoski, M., 206
Safir, M. P., 499
Sagan, C., 90
Sagarin, B. J., 410
Sage, R. M., 405
Saguy, T., 429
Sahdra, B. K., 292
Sahly, J., 393
Saint-Aubin, J., 209
Sairam, N., 247
Saito, N., 465
Sakaeda, A. R., 237
Sakamoto, A., 417
Saki, F., 161
Salazar, J. C., 22
Saleem, M., 417
Salkind, N. J., 17
Salmela-Aro, K., 425, 457
Salminen, N. H., 114
Salovey, P., 265
Salter, N., 520
Salters, K., 354
Salthouse, T. A., 301
Salu, Y., 330
Salvia, J., 257
Samanez-Larkin, G. R., 311
Sammis, G., 485
Samochowiecz, J., 401, 463
Sampson, S., 488
Sanberg, P. R., 75
Sanchez, D., 405
Sandberg, J. G., 503
Sanderson, C. A., 238
Sandler, I., 281
Sandnabba, N. K., 336
Sandomir, R. S., 74
Sanislow, C., 476
SantaCruz, K. S., 22
Santrock, J. W., 482, 497, 503
Santtila, P., 336
Saper, C. B., 145
Sapir, E., 268
Sapolsky, R. M., 46
Sar, V., 466, 467
Sarezky, D., 141
Sarkar, P., 527
Sarkar, U., 525
Sarma, K., 461
Sarna, S., 79
Saroglou, V., 376
Saron, C. D., 292
Sarrazin, J. C., 92
Sarrazin, P., 92
Sartorius, N., 477
Sass, H., 376
Satariano, W. A., 536
Sauer, J., 408
Saul, S., 142
Saults, J. S., 209
Sava, F. A., 496, 499
Savage, J., 414, 415, 417
Savelsbergh, G. J. P., 287

Savin, H. B., 424
Savoy, H. B., 339
Savvaki, M., 47
Sawamoto, N., 129
Sawatzky, R. G., 384
Saxe, L., 347
Saxe, R., 58
Saxon, J. L., 358
Sayette, M. A., 130
Saze, T., 129
Scammell, T. E., 61
Scardamalia, M., 247
Scarmeas, N., 136, 238
Scarr, S., 258, 281
Schaaf, J. M., 227
Schaal, B., 413
Schachter, S., 349
Schacter, D. L., 202, 213, 214, 234
Schäfer, M., 270
Schaie, K. W., 279, 300, 301
Schaller, M., 411, 421
Schanda, H., 469
Schank, R., 216
Scharf, M. J., 161
Scharff, J. S., 492
Schaubroeck, J. M., 384
Schedlowski, M., 174
Scheibe, S., 311
Scheier, M. F., 344, 525, 526
Schenberg, L. C., 450
Scherer, K. R., 345
Scherrer, J., 150
Schertler, E., 347
Schiefele, U., 249
Schiff, N. D., 131
Schimel, J., 319
Schimmack, U., 393
Schindler, B., 451
Schira, M. M., 100
Schkade, D. A., 357
Schlaepfer, T. E., 488
Schlaich, M., 449
Schlaug, G. D., 58
Schleicher, A., 58
Schmahl, C., 465
Schmeichel, B. J., 389
Schmidt, N. B., 450
Schmidtke, J. I., 388
Schmitt, K., 292
Schmitt, R. M., 48
Schmitz, M., 130, 215
Schmitz, R., 139
Schmitz, W. M., 460
Schmukle, S. C., 281, 361
Schneider, F., 474
Schneider, K. J., 493
Schneider, S., 447
Schneiderman, N., 508, 523
Schneier, F. R., 500
Schnider, A., 65
Schoenberger, Y., 519
Schoenfelder, E., 281
Schogol, J., 453
Scholer, A. A., 378
Scholl, B., 205
Schomerus, G., 406
Schonert-Reichl, K. A., 316
Schooler, J. W., 130, 223, 225, 226, 357
Schooler, L. J., 247
Schraag, S., 131
Schraw, G. J., 235
Schredl, M., 144
Schroder, A., 530
Schroder, C. M., 133
Schruers, K., 450
Schulenberg, J. E., 146, 149, 153, 155
Schultheiss, O. C., 397
Schultz, D. P., 6, 368, 370, 372
Schultz, S. E., 6, 368, 370, 372
Schultz, W. T., 382
Schulz, E., 472
Schulz, R., 529
Schulz-Stubner, S., 159

Schumacher, J., 161
Schumann, A., 519
Schumm, J. S., 264
Schunk, D. H., 188, 190, 247, 344, 384
Schupp, H., 524
Schur, E. A., 463
Schuz, B., 519
Schwab, J. R., 321, 469
Schwartz, B. L., 229, 233
Schwartz, J., 229
Schwartz, J. H., 218
Schwartz, J. M., 459
Schwartz, M., 395
Schwartz, M. D., 175
Schwartz, S., 144
Schwartz-Mette, R. A., 416, 458
Schwarz, E. R., 525
Schwarz, N., 404, 415
Schwarzbauer, C., 488
Schwarzer, R., 519, 524
Schweigart, E. K., 48
Schwerdtner, J., 495
Schwertz, D., 55
Schwiezer, H. R., 158
Scollon, C. K., 382
Scorzelli, J., 505
Scott, C., 461
Scott, R. M., 298
Scott, S., 537
Scott, T. R., 174
Scott-Sheldon, L. A. J., 540
Seagea, F., 482, 497, 503
Sealfon, S. C., 155
Sears, D. O., 431
Sears, R. R., 414
Sedek, G., 262
Sedikides, C., 11, 401, 404
Seedat, S., 452
Seeman, T. E., 528
Seery, M. D., 281
Segal, D. L., 392
Segal, M., 218
Segal, M. E., 422
Segall, M. H., 107
Segerstrom, S. C., 355, 525, 526
Segovia, D. A., 227
Seguin, J. R., 413
Seibert, S. E., 375, 376
Seibring, M., 149
Seibt, J., 135
Seidel, E. M., 456
Seim, H. C., 465
Sekiguchi, T., 91
Selby, E. A., 475
Seligman, D. A., 507
Seligman, M. E. P., 5, 182, 195, 358,
    456, 488, 525
Selin, C. E., 459
Selvaraj, V., 47
Selye, H., 526, 527
Semendeferi, K., 65
Semin, G. R., 401
Sen, S., 54, 81
Senghas, A., 350
Sephton, S. E., 526
Seress, L., 288
Sergent, C., 127
Sergerie, K., 469
Serra, C., 378
Sesko, A. K., 317
Sethi, S., 503
Seto, M. C., 336
Setoh, P., 298
Seymour, K., 347
Sezgin, U., 454
Sforza, L. l., 390
Shackman, A., 349
Shadbolt, N. R., 95
Shaffer, T. W., 393
Shafir, E., 250
Shahaeian, A., 128
Shahar, B., 456, 499
Shalev, I., 116
Shallcross, S., 384

Shalvi, S., 412
Sham, R., 238
Shane, M. S., 58
Shankar, A., 141
Shany, M., 458
Sharf, R. S., 499
Sharma, P. S. V. N., 466
Sharma, V., 466
Sharma, Y. S., 435
Sharmila, D., 486
Sharp, E. S., 375
Sharpes, K. M., 246
Sharvit, K., 341
Shaver, P., 435, 436
Shaver, P. R., 292, 317, 436
Shaw, D. S., 317
Shaw, H., 520
Shea, M. T., 476
Sheard, D. E., 225
Sheets, T., 46
Sheffer, C., 514
Sheikh, J. I., 450
Shekar, S. N., 338, 339
Sheldon, K. M., 10, 16, 342, 343, 345,
    356, 357, 358
Shen, B. J., 508, 525
Shepard, R. N., 228
Shepard, S. A., 316, 317
Sher, K. J., 149, 379
Sheridan, J. F., 161
Sherif, C. W., 433
Sherif, M., 433
Sherman, D., 145
Sherman, D. K., 405
Sherman, S. J., 406
Shestowsky, D., 227
Shetty, A. K., 75
Shevell, S. K., 101
Shi, J., 133, 205, 317
Shibuya, A., 417
Shields, C., 536
Shields, S. A., 352
Shiffrin, R. M., 207, 221, 232
Shih, M., 405
Shimai, S., 355
Shimizu, K., 514
Shimotomai, A., 436
Shiota, M. N., 345
Shiraev, E., 4, 196
Shiraishi, R. W., 321
Shiv, B., 3
Shoda, Y., 386
Shogren, K. A., 264
Shores, J. S., 158
Shors, T. J., 75
Shortall, J. C., 436
Shrater, P., 9, 44
Shu, L. L., 226
Shultz, S., 64
Shushruth, S., 100
Sibley, M. H., 447
Sibony, O., 251
Siebner, H. R., 59
Siegel, J. A., 226
Siegel, J. M., 135, 142
Siegel, J. T., 516
Siegel, M., 270
Siegel, S., 176, 508
Siegler, I. C., 389
Sieswerda, S., 476
Sigmund, K., 410
Sigmundson, H. K., 314
Signoretti, A., 484
Sikorskii, A., 508
Silberstein, M., 126
Silva, P. A., 413
Silva, S. G., 456
Silver, P. C., 499
Silver, R. C., 281
Silverman, R., 10
Silvia, P. J., 375
Simmons, R., 514
Simner, J., 88
Simning, A., 504

Simon, H., 243
Simon, W., 502
Simons, D., 93
Simons, D. J., 93, 228
Simpkins, S. D., 308
Simpson, J. A., 316
Simpson, J. M., 75, 293
Sin, N. L., 357
Singal, G., 68
Singer, B., 509
Singer, B. H., 57, 311, 349, 509
Singer, J. A., 237
Singer, J. E., 349
Singer, W., 101
Singh-Manoux, A., 301
Sinha, P., 68
Sinigaglia, C., 48
Sinn, D. L., 377
Sintov, N. D., 150
Sionean, C., 336, 338
Sitnikova, T., 470
Siu, A., 519
Sivacek, J., 406
Sivers, H., 388
Sjoberg, R. L., 474
Skelton, K., 454
Skillings, A., 161
Skinner, B. F., 9, 178, 179, 180, 271
Skinner, H., 519
Skodol, A. E., 444, 446, 473, 476
Skoe, E., 271
Skoner, D. P., 521, 528
Skowronski, J. J., 404
Slachevsky, A., 127
Slade, M. D., 311
Slagboom, P. E., 389
Slater, C., 180
Slaughter, V., 128
Sliwka, P., 502
Sloan, M., 457
Sloane, S., 298, 299
Sloboda, J. A., 262
Slooff, C. J., 472
Slotnick, S. D., 214
Smallwood, J., 130
Smetana, J. G., 308
Smidts, A., 419
Smillie, L. D., 378, 389
Smit, F., 508
Smith, A. R., 370, 460
Smith, C. P., 381, 397
Smith, D. G., 446
Smith, D. M., 521
Smith, E. E., 245
Smith, G., 488
Smith, G. M., 73
Smith, H. S., 117
Smith, J., 311
Smith, J. A., 46
Smith, J. P., 525
Smith, J. R., 489
Smith, M. C., 225
Smith, P. B., 333, 421
Smith, P. K., 215
Smith, R. A., 17, 33
Smith, R. E., 234
Smith, R. L., 416, 458
Smith, S. M., 415, 417
Smith, S. N., 381
Smith, V., 316
Smith, V. L., 22, 293
Smyth, J., 521
Sneddon, M., 293
Snee, L., 505
Sneed, R., 528
Sniehotta, F. F., 519
Sniezek, J. E., 285
Snik, A. F., 112
Snow, C. E., 272
Snowden, M., 291
Snowdon, D. A., 22, 293
Snyder, C. R., 5, 411, 524

Snyder, H., 254
Snyder, J. S., 75
Snyder, S. H., 54
So, M., 499
Soares, J., 291
Soares, J. J. P., 195
Soares-Weiser, K., 487
Sodian, B., 128
Solesio-Jofre, E., 232
Solle, R., 268
Solms, M., 145
Soloff, P. H., 475
Solomon, G., 523
Solomon, S., 319, 341
Solomon, Z., 453
Somerville, L. H., 290, 386
Sommer, M., 495
Sommer, R., 482, 497, 503
Song, A. V., 335
Song, H., 75, 293, 376
Song, S., 157
Sonnen, J. A., 22
Soomro, G. M., 452, 499
Soon, J. A., 539
Sorkin, J. D., 291
Sotres-Bayon, F., 348
Sout, R. L., 503
South, S. C., 390
Sowell, E. R., 285
Spagnola, M., 330
Spain, E. S., 384
Spanos, N. P., 467
Sparkman, T., 154
Sparks, J. R., 408
Sparling, P., 148
Sparreboom, M., 112
Sparrow, B., 211
Speakman, J. R., 330
Spearman, C., 256
Specht, J., 281
Specker, S. M., 465
Spehar, B., 100
Spekhard, A., 341
Spence, K. W., 192
Spencer, M. B., 134
Spencer, R. J., 353
Spencer, S. J., 92, 405
Spencer-Smith, M., 73
Spengler, S., 48
Sperber, D., 132, 299
Sperling, G., 208
Sperling, R., 58
Sperry, R. W., 68
Spezio, M., 401
Spiegel, D., 158, 465, 466
Spiegler, M. D., 188
Spielberger, C. D., 529
Spielmans, G. I., 529
Spillers, G. J., 22, 237
Spinrad, T. L., 317
Spiro, A., 311, 321, 529
Spitznogle, K., 490, 497
Springer, J., 79
Sproesser, G., 524
Spurlock, M., 517
Squire, L. R., 71, 218, 219
Srinivasan, V., 141
Sripada, K., 513
Sriram, N., 431
Sroufe, L. A., 280, 303, 304
Stabouli, S., 143
Staddon, J. E., 184
Stahl, T., 405
Stanaway, J. D., 540
Standage, M., 373
Stanford Center for Longevity, 301
Stanger-Hall, K. F., 333
Stangor, C., 18
Staniloiu, A., 466
Stankewitz, A., 120
Stanley, J., 262
Stanley, J. T., 281, 311
Stanley, M. A., 452
Stanovich, K. E., 3, 37, 39, 250

Stanton, A. L., 524
Starkstein, S.E., 63
Stathi, S., 432
Stattin, H., 309, 458
Staub, E., 411
Staud, R., 84
Staudinger, U. M., 301
Stavans, M., 298
Stay, W. B., 514
Stazi, M. A., 390
Stead, L. F., 538
Steblay, N., 229
Steblay, N. K., 229
Steca, P., 390
Steele, C., 429
Steele, C. M., 405
Steele, D. J., 488
Stefanello, S., 459
Stefano, S., 465
Stegall, M. E., 377
Steger, M. F., 23
Stehr, M. D., 534, 535
Stein, J., 100
Stein, M. B., 453, 454
Stein, R., 122
Steinberg, L., 281, 290, 299
Steinbrook, R., 347
Steiner, J., 174
Steinhauer, S. R., 474
Steinman, L., 291
Steinmetz, H., 58
Steinmetz, N., 135
Steinmeyer, E. M., 376
Stejskal, W. J., 394
Stemmler, G., 389, 391
Stenberg, S. A., 460
Stenfelt, S., 111
Stephens, R. S., 519
Stephenson, K. M., 133
Steptoe, A., 521, 529
Stern, B. B., 492
Stern, E. R., 452
Stern, W., 257
Stern, Y., 136, 140, 238
Sternberg, E. M., 528
Sternberg, K., 245
Sternberg, R. J., 3, 10, 245, 253, 255,
     259, 260, 262, 265, 266
Stevens, A. A., 218
Stevenson, J. L., 48
Stewart, A. D., 218, 462
Stewart, J., 329
Stewart, L., 453
Stewart, R., 478
Stice, E., 520
Stickgold, R., 131, 138, 145
Stiles, P. G., 457
Stillman, T., 336
Stinson, F. S., 473
Stirling, J. D., 68
Stitt, R. S., 1
Stock, J. V., 351
Stockhorst, U., 175
Stodkilde-Jorgensen, H., 161
Stoel-Gammon, C., 266, 273
Stolar, N., 469
Stompe, T., 469
Stone, J., 405, 407
Stone, P., 250
Stoner, J., 426
Stopfer, J. M., 361
Storm, L., 91
Stott, C., 432
Stouthamer-Loeber, M., 474
Stowell, J. R., 528, 530
Strack, F., 250
Strahan, E., 92
Strandberg, T. E., 303
Straube, T., 131
Streff, F. M., 188
Strike, P. C., 529
Strohbach, S., 524
Stromwall, A. E., 135
Strood, L., 529

Stroup, D. F., 379
Stuart, B., 291
Stuetzle, R., 523
Stuifbergen, A., 384
Sturm, V., 488
Sturmer, T., 524
Suarez, E. C., 349
Subbaraman, M. S., 503
Subedi, B., 88
Suchak, M., 410
Sue, D., 442, 504, 506
Sue, D. M., 442, 504, 506
Sue, D. W., 442, 504, 506
Sue, S., 442, 504, 506
Sueur, C., 426
Sugranyes, G., 470
Sui, X., 534
Suinn, R. M., 467
Suleski, J., 457
Sulik, K. K., 285
Sullivan, H. S., 367
Sullivan, R., 289
Sullivan, S. J., 311
Sulloway, F. J., 262
Suls, J., 529
Sumida, R. M., 459
Sun, P., 516
Sun, Y. E., 293
Surian, L., 270
Susman, E. J., 289
Sutin, A. R., 373, 375, 379
Sutter, M. L., 101, 113
Suzuki, M., 291
Suzuki, T., 523
Svanes, C., 514, 538
Svensson, M., 75
Svoboda, E., 234
Swain, A., 529
Swaminathan, S. K., 85
Swan, G. E., 514
Swann, W. B., 404
Swanson, C., 310
Swanson, J., 142
Swanson, K., 310
Swanson, S. A., 465
Swing, E. L., 417
Syed, M., 308
Symmonds, M., 189
Symonds, D., 509
Szasz, T. S., 446
Szentagotal, A., 496, 499
Szepsenwol, O., 456, 499

T

Tabak, B. A., 5
Taber, J. M., 532
Taborsky, M., 410
Tacca, M. C., 101
Taconnat, L., 223
Tada, K., 452
Tadel, F., 127
Taga, K. A., 289
Tagliamonte, S. A., 353
Tahiri, M., 538
Tajfel, H., 429
Takahashi, H., 129
Takahashi, Y., 376
Takano, T., 536
Takemura, K., 28
Tamburrini, G., 132
Tamietto, M., 351
Tamis-LeMonda, C. S., 286
Tan, M., 262, 293
Tan, M. L., 255
Tanaka, J. W., 350
Tanaka-Matsumi, J., 355, 443, 455
Tang, H., 214
Tang, T. C., 477
Tang, W., 376
Tanner, A., 217
Tanner, J. M., 289
Tao, R., 470
Tappon, S. C., 218

Tarokh, L., 139
Tarricone, P., 126
Tarrier, N., 281
Tarter, R. E., 155
Tasca, G. A., 502
Tashiro, T., 321
Tasopoulos-Chan, M., 308
Tasso, A., 159
Tateno, T., 148
Taupin, P., 75
Taurines, R., 484
Tavris, C., 353
Tay, C., 384
Tay, L., 31
Taylor, A., 474
Taylor, J. G., 126
Taylor, M., 301
Taylor, M. K., 532
Taylor, S., 447
Taylor, S. E., 55, 405, 514, 515, 518,
     521, 523, 524, 529, 533
Taylor, Z. E., 532
Teasdale, J., 456
Teesson, M., 457
Teffer, K., 65
Teising, M., 492
Teismann, N. A., 100
Tellegen, A., 79
Templin, T., 519
ten Brinke, L., 347
te Nijenhuis, J., 376
Tennen, H., 321, 524, 525
Tennie, C., 192
Ten Velden, F. S., 412
Teodorescu, M., 141
Tepper, K., 472
Teresi, D., 145
Terhakoian, A., 453
Terman, L., 261
Terr, L. C., 225
Terracciano, A., 379
Terry, S., 204
Terwee, P. J., 75
Tetlock, P. E., 431
Texeira, P. J., 520
Tezcan, E., 452
Thabane, L., 475
Tharoor, H., 466
Thayer, J. F., 131
Theeuwes, J., 209
Theoret, H., 59
Thiedke, C. C., 494
Thiery, E. W., 475
Thiessen, 331
Thigpen, C. H., 467
Thirthalli, J., 470
Thoeringer, C. K., 449
Thoermer, C., 128
Thoits, P. A., 457
Thomas, A., 302
Thomas, D. A., 193
Thomas, E. L., 429
Thomas, M. S. C., 274
Thomas, S., 157
Thome, J., 447
Thompson, J., 379
Thompson, L., 375
Thompson, M., 317
Thompson, M. S., 258
Thompson, R. A., 317
Thompson, R. D., 525
Thompson, S. C., 523
Thompson, W. L., 57
Thomsen, D. K., 223
Thomson, D. R., 215
Thorndike, E. L., 178, 179
Thornicroft, G., 477
Thota, A. B., 504
Thrailkill, E. A., 183
Thron, A., 159
Thunedborg, K., 509
Thurman, D. J., 291
Tierney, C., 415
Tieu, T. T., 435

Tigani, X., 384, 526
Tiitnen, H., 114
Timimi, S., 447
Timofeev, I., 135
Tinbergen, N., 412
Tindle, H., 456, 526
Titchener, E. B., 6
Titerness, A. K., 75
Tobin, R. M., 58
Todaro, J. F., 529
Todorov, A., 401, 402, 403
Tolman, E. C., 190, 191
Tomarken, A. J., 349
Tomasello, M., 192, 270
tom Dieck, S., 99
Tomich, P., 321
Tomori, M., 460
Tompkins, T. L., 458
Tononi, G., 135
Topolinski, S., 250
Tormala, Z. L., 3
Torniainen, M., 470
Toro, R., 290
Torres, L., 429
Tov, W., 377
Toyoda, H., 62
Tracer, D., 411
Traeger, L., 508
Trainor, L. J., 289
Tran, G. Q., 525
Tran, T. V., 261
Trautwein, U., 281
Travis, J., 377
Treasure, D. C., 373
Treasure, J., 464
Trebst, A. E., 174
Tredoux, C., 145
Tremblay, R. E., 413, 460
Tremblay, S., 209
Tremblay, T., 271
Trent, J., 250, 311, 376
Tressoldi, P. E., 91
Triandis, H. C., 28, 343
Trickett, P. K., 289
Tronick, E., 281
Tronson, N. C., 173
Tropp, L. R., 28, 433
Trotschel, R., 215
Trouborst, M., 134, 135
Troutman, A. C., 188
Trowbridge, A., 238
Trudeau, R., 421
True, W. R., 150
Trull, T., 494
Trull, T. J., 446, 475
Tryon, R. C., 78
Trzebinski, J., 376
Trzesniewski, K. H., 4
Tsang, J., 357, 375
Tseng, T., 519
Tsenkova, V. K., 311
Tucker, P., 314
Tucker-Drob, E. M., 30
Tuckman, A. M., 140
Tugade, M. M., 355
Tulving, E., 212, 213, 214, 221
Tungpunkom, P., 487
Turan, B., 311
Turban, D., 342
Turchi, C., 150
Turecki, G., 460
Turiano, N. A., 378, 523
Turk, D. J., 130
Turk-Browne, N., 203
Turkheimer, E., 259, 260, 266, 280, 282
Turnbull, A., 264
Turnbull, O., 145
Turner, G. R., 234
Turner, J. C., 428
Turner, J. M. W., 105
Turner, L., 34
Turner, R. B., 528
Turrigiano, G., 51
Twenge, J. M., 4, 414

Twitchell, G., 331
Tyas, S. L., 22
Tyler, C. W., 100
Tynes, B. M., 429
Tzeng, O. J., 231

## U

Ubukata, S., 129
Uccelli, P., 267, 272
Uchida, Y., 522
Ueno, K., 457
Uguz, F., 452
Uher, R., 80
Uhl, I., 489
Uhlmann, E., 431
Uhr, M., 449
Ullman, A. D., 173
Umaña-Taylor, A. J., 308, 429
Umanath, S., 141
Umberson, D., 520
UNAIDS, 540
Underhill, K., 333
Undurraga, J., 484
Unger, J. B., 516
United Nations, 31
United Nations Office on Drugs and
    Crime, 146, 152
United Nations World Youth
    Report, 152
Unkelbach, C., 251
Unschuld, P. G., 449
Unsworth, N., 22, 237
Updegraff, K. A., 308
Ural, C., 466
Urbain, C., 139
Urbanek, J. K., 537
Urbanowski, F., 161
Urbina, S., 257, 259
Urcelay, G. P., 172
Urry, H. L., 57, 349
U.S. Department of Education, 193
U.S. Food and Drug Administration,
    112, 486
Utts, J., 91
Utz, R., 321

## V

Vaccarino, V., 329
Vail, K. E., 319
Vaillant, G., 150, 151
Vaillières, A., 134
Valença, A. M., 450
Valentine, B. A., 337
Valiente, C., 317
Van Baaren, R. B., 250
van Beveren, N. J., 471
van Bokhoven, I., 413
VandeCreek, L., 227
Vandello, J. A., 415
Vanderhasselt, M. A., 456
van de Riet, W. A, 351
van der Kamp, J., 287
Van der Leij, A., 250
van der Linden, D., 376
van der Maas, H. L. J., 90, 91
van der Ven, E., 442
Vander Wal, G. S., 141
Vander Wal, J. S., 523
Van de Vliert, E., 421
Van Dijk, E., 412
Van Doom, M. D., 1
Van Doorn, G. S., 410
van Duijl, M., 443
van Dyne, L., 255, 259, 384
Van Eerde, W., 384
van Engeland, H., 413
van Gaal, S., 86, 129
van Goozen, S. H. M., 413
van Hof, P., 287
van IJzendoorn, M. H., 81, 304
Van Kleef, G. A., 412

Van Knippenberg, A., 216
Van Laar, C., 405
Van Lange, P. A. M., 437
van Lier, P. A. C., 308
Van Orden, K., 460
van Pragg, H., 75
van Reedt Dortland, A. K. B., 378
Van Riper, M., 264
van Ryn, M., 405
Vansteenwegen, D., 173
Van Voorhees, B. W., 497
Van Yperen, N. W., 437
Vanyukov, M., 155
van Zanten, J. C. S., 300
Vardar, M. K., 466
Varela, J. G., 393
Varjonen, M., 336
Varney, L. L., 411
Varni, J. W., 141
Vasco, V. R., 470
Vasconcelos, F. A., 391
Vasconcelos, N., 92
Vaughn, S., 264
Vazire, S., 361, 375, 376, 394, 395
Vazquez, J., 135
Vaz Scavacini de Freitas, G., 459
Vecchio, F., 219
Veenema, A. H., 413
Veenhoven, R., 377
Veenstra, R., 313
Vega, V., 416
Vega-Redondo, F., 189
Veillete, S., 290
Veldhuijzen, M., 300
Velicer, W. F., 519
Venables, P. H., 474
Ventura, S. J., 333
Veras, A. B., 450
Verbeek, J., 378
Verboon, P., 524
Verkuil, B., 131
Vermetten, E., 465
Vermulst, A. A., 5
Vernon, P. A., 390
Verschuere, B., 474
Vertommen, S., 476
Verweij, K. J. H., 338, 339
Vespa, J., 310
Vess, M., 319
Veszprémi, B., 288
Vetere, G., 173
Vetter, I., 54
Vevea, J. L., 404
Vezzali, L., 432
Vicary, J., 92
Victor, A. M., 452
Videtic, A., 460
Viegas, P., 75
Vigano, S., 528
Viitasalo, K., 134
Vikström, L. M., 175
Villalobos, M., 308
Villegas, R., 136
Villeneuve, C., 152
Vilsboll, T., 328
Vinberg, M., 389, 390
Vincent, J. E., 409
Vincze, A., 288
Vinkers, C. D., 520
Vinokur, A. D., 521
Virkkunen, M., 474
Visser, P. L., 530
Viswanath, B., 450
Vitaro, F., 316, 413, 460
Vitousek, K. M., 464, 500
Vitterso, J., 19, 20
Vlaeyen, J, W. S., 189
Vliegen, N., 303
Vloet, T. D., 447
Vogelei, R., 361
Vogl, L., 457
Vogt, B. A., 117
Vogt, T. M., 521
Vohs, K. D., 463

Vollhardt, J., 411
Volpicelli, J. R., 182
von Collani, G., 252
von der Pahlen, B., 336
Vong, L., 328
von Grumbkow, J., 353
von Helmholtz, H., 102
von Lengerke, T., 534, 535
von Neumann, J., 211, 243
Von Polier, G. G., 447
Voss, U., 131, 145
Vrachnis, N., 55
Vriends, N., 451
Vukovic, J., 119
Vygotsky, L. S., 299

## W

Waage, S., 134
Wacker, J., 389, 391
Wade, C., 353
Wadkins, T. A., 478
Waenke, M., 401
Wagenaar, K., 502
Wagenmakers, E. J., 90, 91
Wagner, A. D., 71, 204, 211, 219
Wagner, A. R., 191
Wahlin, Y. B., 175
Wai, J., 262
Wainright, J. L., 37
Waite, L. J., 520
Wakana, K., 519
Waldron, M., 259
Walker, D. D., 519
Walker, H., 467
Walker, M. P., 135, 138
Walkup, J. T., 484
Wall, S., 303
Wallace, B. A., 292
Wallace, M. R., 84
Wallach, H. S., 499
Waller, E. A., 134
Waller, E. M., 458
Wallerstein, R. S., 492
Wallien, M. S. C., 313
Walsh, D., 175
Walters, E. E., 476
Walton, K. E., 376
Walton, R., 538
Wampold, B. E., 507, 509
Wan, C., 11
Wanderling, J., 472
Wang, C., 11
Wang, M., 141
Wang, M. C., 22
Wang, N. C., 291
Wang, Q., 214
Wang, W., 133, 205, 317
Wang, Y., 329
Wang, Z., 468
Wangberg, S. C., 490, 497
Wanner, B., 460
Wapstra, E., 377
Ward, J., 54, 154
Ward, K. D., 529
Warglien, M., 44
Wariyar, R., 183
Warner, C. H., 453
Warner, L., 333
Warren, G., 347
Warren, M. P., 289
Waschbusch, D. A., 447
Washburn, A. L., 328
Wasserman, D., 455
Waszkiewicz, J. A., 158
Watanabe, H., 170
Watanabe, M., 536
Waterman, L. A., 54
Waters, E., 303
Waters, J., 303
Watkins, E. R., 251
Watson, A., 117
Watson, D., 354, 355, 377
Watson, J. B., 9, 173, 176, 293

Watson, M., 525
Watson, S., 46
Watson, S. J., 156
Watt, C., 90
Watts, J., 489
Waugh, C. E., 355
Way, B. M., 390
Weaver, K., 404
Webb, R. M., 262
Webb, R. T., 460
Webb, S. P., 475
Webb, W. B., 138
Weber, E. H., 92
Weber, S., 474
Webster, J. D., 301
Wechsler, H., 149
Weger, U. W., 405
Wegner, D. M., 211
Wehmeyer, M., 264, 524
Weich, S., 457
Weinberg, M. S., 338
Weiner, B., 403
Weiner, I. B., 394
Weinstein, N., 342, 369
Weinstein, T. A. R., 377
Weir, W., 92
Weiss, A., 377, 390
Weiss, H. B., 308
Weiss, S., 529
Weissman, M. M., 450
Weisz, J., 304
Weitzman, M., 443
Welchman, A. E., 105
Welcome, S. E., 206
Welgampola, M. S., 121
Wellman, H. M., 127, 128
Wells, G. L., 229
Wendel, S., 375
Wengrovitz, S. M., 246
Wentura, D., 130, 215
Werbart, A., 492
West, M. J., 272
West, R., 519
Westen, S. C., 301
Westgate, M. N., 285
Westmacott, R., 213
Westphal, M., 320
Wetherell, M., 432
Wetzels, R., 90, 91
Wheeler, D., 409
Wheeler, D. S., 171, 172
Wheeler, E., 161
Wheelwright, S., 313
Whibeck, L. B., 461
Whiffen, V. E., 457
Whitaker, J. L., 417
Whitaker, R., 489
White, B. J., 433
White, K. M., 516
White, M., 478
White, M. A., 464
White, R., 457
White, R. C., 93
White, R. W., 382
Whitehead, D. L., 529
Whitelaw, S., 519
White-Traut, R., 55
Whitfield, S. L., 388
Whiting, A. B., 140
Whooley, M. A., 525
Whorf, B. L., 268
Wickersham, I. R., 44, 55
Widiger, T., 446, 473
Widiger, T. A., 375, 475
Wiebe, D. J., 524
Wiebe, R. P., 376
Wiedemann, A. U., 519
Wieland, M. L., 513
Wiemer, J., 93
Wiener, J., 458
Wiersma, D., 472
Wiese, H., 58
Wiesel, T. N., 100, 101
Wigboldus, D. H. J., 5

Wijeyekoon, R., 75
Wilcox, T., 313
Wiley, A. H., 519
Wilhelm, I., 135
Wilkie, R. M., 293
Wilkinson, R. T., 131
Willcox, B. J., 291
Willcox, D. C., 291
Willemse, G., 508
Willemsen, G., 475
Willford, J., 155
Williams, C., 452
Williams, D. E., 538
Williams, D. R., 432
Williams, J. D., 158
Williams, K. D., 426
Williams, L. E., 116
Williams, L. M., 225, 226
Williams, M., 474
Williams, M. J., 403
Williams, P., 99
Williams, R. B., 389, 529
Williams, T., 382
Williams, W. L., 536
Willingham, D. T., 197
Willis, J., 402
Willis, S. L., 301
Willis-Owen, S. A., 389
Willoughby, B. L., 523
Wilson, A., 377
Wilson, C., 507
Wilson, C. J., 516
Wilson, D. A., 289
Wilson, G. T., 462, 464, 500
Wilson, J., 449
Wilson, M., 434
Wilson, M. A., 70
Wilson, R., 238
Wilson, R. S., 523
Wilt, J., 310, 377, 378, 389
Wiltermuth, S. S., 34, 35, 418
Wimer, C., 308
Windel, R. C., 458
Windle, M., 458
Windsor, T. D., 300
Windt, J. M., 131
Wing, R. R., 518, 537
Wingate, L. R., 456
Winne, P. H., 344
Winner, E., 261, 263
Winter, C., 489
Winter, D. G., 381
Winter, M. R., 150
Wiprovnick, A., 214
Wiseman, R., 90
Witbordt, J., 503
Witelson, S. F., 65
Witkowska, H. E., 135
Wittert, G. A., 516

Wittlinger, R. P., 213
Wixted, J. T., 71, 219
Wohlgemuth, S. D., 141
Wohlheiter, K., 523
Woike, B. A., 397
Wojtczak, M., 112
Wolchik, S., 281
Wolf, A., 353
Wolfe, D. A., 447
Wolff, S. B., 348
Wolkowitz, O. M., 292
Wolson, P., 491
Wong, D. L., 54
Wong, R. O., 99
WonPat-Borja, A. J., 477
Woo, J. S., 134
Wood, A., 73
Wood, A. H., 11
Wood, D., 376
Wood, J., 460
Wood, J. M., 394, 395
Wood, K. H., 191
Wood, R. L., 413
Wood, W., 314
Woodhead, D., 324
Woods, J. A., 301
Woods, R., 313
Woods, T., 523
Woolfolk, A., 265
Woolley, J. D., 127
Worch, T., 330
World Health Organization, 461
Worthington, E. L., 5
Worthington, R. L., 339
Wrangham, R. W., 413
Wright, H. R., 134
Wright, J. M., 447
Wright, K., 519
Wright, L. W., 365
Wright, M. J., 338, 339
Wright, R. H., 261
Wright, S. C., 28
Wrosch, C., 376
Wu, C. S., 485
Wu, D., 298
Wu, W., 75
Wundt, W., 6, 7
Wynn, T., 210

X

Xanthopoulos, M. S., 533
Xiao, Z., 468
Xie, B., 516
Xie, C., 293
Xie, Y. F., 174
Xu, J., 388, 460
Xu, L., 112
Xu, Y., 11, 468

Y

Yalcin, B., 389
Yalom, I. D., 502
Yamamiya, Y., 463
Yamauchi, K., 499
Yamazaki, S., 140
Yan, H., 468
Yan, J. H., 457
Yancey, C., 414, 415, 417
Yang, L. H., 477
Yang, Y., 285, 413, 475, 523
Yanowitch, R., 390
Yap, K., 452
Yates, B. T., 496, 499
Yates, L. B., 534
Yau, J. P., 308
Yeary, K. H., 513
Yee, B. K., 289
Yeh, K. Y., 56
Yen, C. F., 477
Yen, J. Y., 477
Yen, S., 476
Yeomans, J. S., 61
Yesavage, J. A., 141
Yesilyurt, S., 466
Yi, S. C., 536
Yi, Y., 232
Yildirim, H., 452
Yim, E., 488
Yoder, M., 453
Yonelinas, A. P., 126
Yong, W., 133, 205, 317
Yoo, S. H., 352
Yoon, D. P., 523
Yoon, T. Y., 478
Yopchick, J. E., 252
Yoshioka, K., 452
Yoshiura, T., 452
Yoshizato, C., 452
Young, H., 482
Young, K. H., 349
Young, L. J., 55
Young, S., 447
Young, T., 102
Yrttiaho, S., 114
Ysseldyke, J. E., 257
Yu, F., 457
Yu, Y. W., 456
Yuan, J., 457
Yuen, C., 416
Yuki, M., 28
Yuwiler, A., 413
Yznaga, S. D., 429

Z

Zadra, A., 141, 142, 144
Zaidman-Zait, A., 316
Zajonc, R. B., 349, 350, 426, 434

Zandberg, L. J., 462, 464
Zanesco, A. P., 292
Zanna, M. P., 92
Zarahn, E., 136
Zauner, K. P., 95
Zayas, L. H., 461
Zehm, K., 357
Zeifman, D., 435
Zeitzer, J. M., 141
Zemore, S. E., 503
Zeng, Y., 293
Zhai, H., 485
Zhang, H., 468
Zhang, H. J., 292
Zhang, L., 54
Zhang, L. F., 255, 259
Zhang, X., 54
Zhao, H., 375, 376
Zhao, J., 329
Zhou, N., 112
Zhou, Q., 317
Zhou, W., 75
Zhou, X., 376
Zhu, H., 158
Zhu, L., 128
Zhu, S., 447
Ziegelmann, J. P., 519
Ziegler, A., 337
Ziegler, M., 393
Ziegler, T. E., 55
Zietsch, B. P., 338, 339
Ziker, J., 411
Zilles, K., 58
Zilney, L. A., 147
Zimbardo, P., 423, 424
Zimbardo, P. G., 424
Zimmer, H. D., 211
Zimmerman, B. J., 344
Zimmerman, E., 349
Zimmerman, E. A., 301
Zimmerman, F. H., 529
Zin, W. A., 450
Zola, M., 532
Zollig, J., 234
Zonderman, A. B., 379
Zorumski, C. F., 218
Zou, Z., 468
Zoupi, L., 47
Zubek, J. P., 78
Zucker, N., 464
Zuckerman, I. H., 291
Zuo, Z., 219
Zupanic, T., 460
Zvolensky, M. J., 450
Zweiback, D. J., 291
Zwilling, C. E., 209

# subject index

Note: Page references for key terms are listed in **boldface**. Page references for figures are followed by *f*.

## A

AA (Alcoholics Anonymous), 151, 503
abnormal behavior, **441**–442. *See also* psychological disorders
absentmindedness, 234
absolute threshold, **89**–91, 89*f*, 90*f*
abstinence-only sex education, 333
accommodation, **294**, 321
acetylcholine (ACh), 53, 54, 139
acquaintance, attraction and, 434
acquired immune deficiency syndrome (AIDS), 151, 285, **539**–540
acquisition, in conditioning, **170**–171, 172*f*
action potentials, **51**
    mechanisms of, 51, 51*f*
    sensory receptors and, 85, 87–89, 87*f*, 88*f*
action/willpower stage, 517*f*, 518
activation-synthesis theory, **145**
active deception, 35
acute stress, 46
adaptive characteristics, 7
addiction, 63, **147**
ADHD (attention deficit hyperactivity disorder), **446**, 447
adipose cells, 330
Adler's individual psychology, **368**–369
adolescents
    alcohol use by, 149
    antidepressants and, 486
    brain in, 289–290, 290*f*
    cognitive development in, 295*f*, 297, 299–300
    depression in, 458, 486
    drug use by, 146, 146*f*
    eating disorders in, 462, 463
    egocentrism in, 299
    formal operational thought in, 295*f*, 297
    identity and, 307–309, 307*f*
    oral sex by, 334, 335*f*
    physical development in, 289–290, 289*f*, 290*f*
    pregnancy in, 333, 334*f*
    sleep deprivation in, 139, 140*f*
    suicide by, 460–461, 461*f*, 486
    timing of puberty in, 289, 289*f*
    tobacco use by, 152–153, 153*f*
adrenal glands, **72**, 72*f*, 527
adrenaline (epinephrine), 72, 349
adulthood. *See also* aging
    cognitive development in, 299–302, 301*f*
    marriage in, 310
    physical changes in, 290–293, 292*f*, 293*f*
    sleep in, 140, 140*f*
    socioemotional development in, 309–311
advertising, 92, 176
aerobic exercise, **534**–535, 534*f*, 535*f*
affectionate love, **436**
afferent nerves, **44**
African Americans
    obesity in, 536
    prejudice against, 430–431
    suicide by, 461, 461*f*
afterimages, 102–103, 103*f*
aggression, **412**
    in animals, 412–413
    biological influences in, 412–414

dopamine and, 81
gender and, 416
media violence and, 415–416, 417
neurobiological factors in, 413–414
overt, 416
psychological factors in, 414–415
reducing, 417–418
relational, 416
serotonin and, 390
sociocultural factors in, 415–416
aging
    active development and, 321–322
    biological theories of, 291–292, 292*f*
    brain and, 292–293, 293*f*
    integrity *vs.* despair in, 305*f*, 310–311
    intellectual abilities and, 301
    preserving memory with, 201, 237–238
    prospective memory and, 234
    sleep and, 140, 140*f*
    wisdom and, 301
agonists, **55**
agoraphobia, 449, 487, 487*f*
agreeableness, 58, 375–376, 375*f*
AI (artificial intelligence), **244**–245, 244*f*
AIDS (acquired immune deficiency syndrome), 151, 285, **539**–540
Albert, conditioning demonstration on, 173, 173*f*
alcohol. *See also* psychoactive drugs
    alcoholism, 150–151
    aversive conditioning against, 173
    binge drinking, 149–150, 150*f*
    birth defects from, 285
    effects of, 147–149, 149*f*, 156*f*
    operant conditioning and, 187
Alcoholics Anonymous (AA), 151, 503
alcoholism, **150**–151
algorithms, **247**
all-or-nothing principle, **51**
alpha waves, 137, 137*f*
altered states of consciousness, 130
altruism (prosocial behavior), 10, 316–317, **410**–412
Alzheimer disease
    acetylcholine and, 53
    neurogenesis and, 75
    sleep and, 141
    working memory and, 210, 238
Ambien, 142
amenorrhea, 462
American Indians/Alaska Natives (AI/AN), 461, 461*f*
American Psychological Association (APA)
    on abnormal behavior, 441–442
    *DSM-IV* classification system of, 444–448, 445*f*
    on eating disorders, 464
    ethics guidelines of, 33–35
    on gay marriage, 339
Americans with Disabilities Act (ADA) of 1990, 478
Amish people, 5, 5*f*, 20
amnesia, **234**
    anterograde and retrograde, 234
    dissociative, 466
    in dissociative identity disorder, 466–467
    episodic and semantic memory in, 213
amphetamines, 54, 153, 156*f*
amplitude, 96, 97*f*, 109, 110*f*

amputees, phantom limb pain in, 88
amygdala, **61**
    in adolescence, 289, 290*f*
    emotion and, 348–349, 348*f*
    location and function of, 60*f*, 61–62
    memory and, 465
    personality and, 388, 389
anal retentive individuals, 367
anal sex, 336
anal stage, 366, 367*f*
androgens, 312, **331.** *See also* testosterone
anima/animus, 368
animals. *See also specific animals*
    aggression in, 412–413
    altruism in, 410, 410*f*
    big five personality traits in, 377
    brain in different species of, 62*f*, 65
    ethics of research on, 36
    instinctive drift in, 194–195, 195*f*
    sleep needs of, 135*f*
    taste aversion learning in, 175*f*
anorexia nervosa, **462**, 463–464, 503
ANS (autonomic nervous system), **45**–46, 45*f*, 346, 346*f*
Antabuse, 173
antagonists, **55**
anterior cingulate, 127, 161, 389
anterior pituitary gland, 72. *See also* pituitary gland
anterograde amnesia, **234**
antianxiety drugs, 151, **483**–484
antidepressant drugs, **484**–485, 484*f*
antipsychotic drugs, **485**–487, 487*f*
antisocial personality disorder (ASPD), **473**–475, 473*f*
anvil, 110*f*, 111, 111*f*
anxiety, 161
anxiety disorders, **448**
    cognitive therapy for, 499
    drug therapies for, 483–485, 487*f*
    generalized anxiety disorder, 448–449
    obsessive-compulsive disorder, 451–452
    panic disorder, 449–450, 487*f*, 499
    phobic disorder, 450–451, 451*f*, 487*f*
    post-traumatic stress disorder, 452–454
    suicide and, 459–461, 460*f*, 461*f*
anxious attachment style, 304, **435**–436
APA. *See* American Psychological Association
aphasia, 67
apparent movement, **106**
applied behavior analysis, **187**–188
archetypes, **368**
Area 17, 57
arousal
    in consciousness, 126, 127
    in emotions, 346, 346*f*, 349
    levels of, 354, 354*f*
    measuring, 346–347
    misinterpreted, 349
    performance and, 327
artificial intelligence (AI), **244**–245, 244*f*
Asch's conformity experiment, 418–419, 419*f*
Asian Americans, 307, 461*f*, 504
*As Nature Made Him* (Colapinto), 314
ASPD (antisocial personality disorder), **473**–475, 473*f*
aspirin, 117

assimilation, **294**, 321
association cortex, 64*f*, **67**, 127
associative learning, **167.** *See also* conditioning
asthma, sleep and, 141
athletes, brain injuries in, 74
Atkinson-Shiffrin theory, **207**, 207*f*, 209
attachment, 303–305, 303*f*, 317, 435–436
attention
    divided *vs.* sustained, 203–204
    in observational learning, 188–189
    selective, 93, 203
attention deficit hyperactivity disorder (ADHD), **446**, 447
attitudes, **406**–409, 408*f*
attraction, 120, 401–402, 434–435
attribution theory, **403**, 403*f*, 456
atypical antipsychotic medications, 486–487
audiology, 85
auditory illusions, 113
auditory nerve, 110*f*, 111*f*, **113**
auditory system, 109–114
    absolute threshold in, 89–90, 89*f*
    brain processing and, 64*f*, 89, 113
    cochlear implants, 112
    ear structure, 109–112, 110*f*, 111*f*
    experience of sound, 109, 110*f*
    hearing theories, 112–113
    localizing sound, 113–114, 114*f*
authoritarian parenting, **306**–307
authoritative parenting, **306**
autism, 48, 129, 188
autobiographical memories, **223**
    genetics and, 390
    life story and, 237, 238
    retrieval of, 223–224, 224*f*
automatic processes, 129*f*, **130**
autonomic nervous system (ANS), **45**–46, 45*f*, 346, 346*f*
autonomy, as need, 342–343
autonomy support, 365
autonomy *vs.* shame and doubt, 304*f*, 306
availability heuristic, 251*f*, **252**
aversive conditioning, **173**, 494–495, 495*f*
avoidance learning, **182**, 389
avoidant attachment style, 304, **435**–436
awareness, 126, 127, 130–132. *See also* consciousness
axons, **49**, 49*f*

## B

babbling, 273
babies. *See* infants
bacteria, resistance in, 8
bankruptcy, racial prejudice and, 430–431
barbiturates, **151**, 156*f*
BAS (behavioral activation system), 389, 389*f*
basal ganglia, **62**–63, 148, 161
base rate fallacy, 251*f*, **252**
basilar membrane, 111–112, 111*f*
"beautiful is good" stereotype, 401–402*f*
Beck's cognitive therapy, 496–499, 498*f*
BED (binge eating disorder), **464**–465
bedwetting, 138

behavior, 2
  abnormal, 441–442
  altruism, 10, 410–412
  attitudes and, 406–409, 408f
  behavior genetics, 78–79, 79f
  cognitive dissonance and, 406–407, 408f
  cross-situational consistency in, 385
  internal vs. external locus of
    control in, 384
  prosocial, 10, 316–317, 410–412
  purposive, 190–191
  selective breeding and, 78
  social, 409–418
  Type A vs. Type B, 529
  Type D, 529
behavioral activation system (BAS),
  389, 389f
behavioral approach, 9, 11
behavioral inhibition system (BIS),
  389, 389f
behavioral medicine, 514
behavior genetics, 78–79, 79f, 390–391
behaviorism, 9, 167. See also classical
    conditioning; operant conditioning
behavior modification, 187–188. See also
    classical conditioning; operant
    conditioning
behavior therapies, 494–495, 494f,
    495f, 500f
bell-shaped curve, 257–258, 258f
benzodiazepines, 151, 483
beta waves, 136–137, 137f
bias
  attributional, 403, 403f
  availability heuristic, 251f, 252
  base rate fallacy, 251f, 252
  confirmation, 251f, 252
  decision making and, 426–427
  experimenter, 25–26
  faulty memory and, 228
  hindsight, 251f, 252
  in intelligence tests, 258–259
  representativeness heuristic, 251f,
    252–253
  research participant, 26–27
  sample selection and, 30
  self-serving, 405
  in survey results, 18
biculturalism, 308
big five factors of personality, 374
  assessment of, 393
  evaluation of, 378
  model overview, 374–378, 375f
  obesity and, 379
binding, 101
Binet intelligence test, 257–258,
    257f, 258f
binge drinking, 149–150, 150f
binge eating disorder (BED), 464–465
binocular cues, 104–105
biofeedback, 36
biological approach, 8–9, 387–391,
    388f, 389f
biological clock, 133–135
biological rhythms, sleep and,
    133–135, 134f
biological (biomedical) therapies,
    483–489, 484f, 487f
biopsychosocial model, 444, 501,
    514–515
bipolar cells, 99
bipolar disorder, 457, 459, 459f, 487f
birth control, 333
birth defects, 285
birth order, 369
BIS (behavioral inhibition system),
    389, 389f
bisexuality, 335, 338
black widow spiders, 53, 53f
blastocyst stage, 76
blindness, sleep problems and, 133–134
blind spot, 99, 99f, 100f
blinking effect illusion, 108f
blood chemistry, hunger and, 328–329, 329f

blood clotting, stress and, 529
Bobo doll study, 189, 414–415
body image, 298, 462–463, 534
body temperature, hypothalamus and, 63
body weight. See obesity; weight loss
bogus pipeline, 337
borderline personality disorder (BPD),
    475–476, 500
bottom-up processing, 86
box problem, 191–192, 192f
brain, 42–81. See also brain damage;
    hemispheres; nervous system;
    specific brain areas
  in adolescence, 289–290, 290f
  aggression and, 413–414
  aging and, 292–293, 293f
  association areas, 64f, 89
  auditory processing in, 64f, 89, 113
  in bipolar disorder, 459, 459f
  cerebral cortex (See cerebral cortex)
  computers compared with,
    243–245, 244f
  conformity and, 419–420
  connectionism and, 216–217
  consciousness and, 127
  in depression therapy, 488, 488f
  development of, 59, 60f, 287–289, 288f
  in different species, 62f
  in dissociative disorders, 465
  eating disorders and, 464
  emotions and, 69–70, 347–349, 348f
  facial recognition and, 58, 69
  hunger and, 329
  in hypnosis, 158
  integration of function in, 43, 70–71
  language and, 69–70, 69f, 271
  meditation and, 292
  memory locations in, 212,
    218–219, 219f
  methods for study of, 56–59, 57f, 59f
  obsessive-compulsive disorder and, 452
  pain perception and, 88–89, 117
  personality and, 58, 388–390,
    388f, 389f
  phantom limb pain and, 88
  plasticity and capacity for repair, 44,
    73, 75, 135
  psychoactive drugs and, 147, 147f
  psychosurgery on, 488–489
  in schizophrenia, 471
  sensory receptors and, 65–67, 66f,
    87–89, 87f, 88f
  sexual behavior and, 330–331
  sleep and, 138–139
  split-brain research, 67–70, 69f
  structure and regions of, 59–66, 60f,
    62f–66f
  touch and, 115
  vestibular sense and, 122
  visual cortex, 64, 64f, 100–101, 101f
  visual processing in, 100–101, 101f
brain damage
  amnesia and, 234
  association cortex and, 67
  behavioral effects of, 42, 65, 65f
  brain lesioning, 56
  brain tissue implants, 75–76
  plasticity and capacity for repair, 73,
    75, 135
  traumatic brain injury, 42, 65, 65f,
    73–75
brain grafts, 75
brain imaging, 57–59, 59f
brain lesioning, 56
brain stem, 61
brainstorming, 254
brain tissue implants, 75–76
Breaking Free: My Life with Dissociative
    Identity Disorder (Walker), 467
broaden-and-build model, 355
Broca's area, 67–68, 67f, 271
Buddhism, cognitive-behavior therapy
    and, 505
bulimia nervosa, 463–464

buspirone, 483
bystander effect, 412

C

caffeine, 151–152, 156f
caffeinism, 151
cancer, 141, 530
candle problem, 249f, 275f
Cannabis sativa, 154–155
Cannon-Bard theory, 347
CAPS (cognitive affective processing
    systems), 386–387
cardiovascular disease, stress and, 529
care perspective, 316
Caroline Islands, intelligence in, 256, 256f
case studies (case histories), 18–19, 27f
castration anxiety, 366
CAT (computerized axial tomography), 57
catatonia, 469
catharsis, 491
causal relationships, 20–22, 23, 28, 38
CBT (cognitive-behavior therapy),
    499, 505
CCK (cholecystokinin), 328
cell body, neuron, 49, 49f
cellular-clock theory of aging,
    291–292, 292f
centenarians, 291
central executive, 210f, 211
central nervous system (CNS), 45, 45f
cerebellum
  in different species, 62f
  location and function of, 60f, 61
  memory and, 219, 219f
cerebral cortex, 64–67
  association cortex in, 64f, 67, 127
  in different species, 62f
  in evolution, 64
  fear and, 348, 348f
  in hypnosis, 160
  integration of function in, 70–71
  lobes of, 64–65, 64f
  location of, 60f, 61
  motor cortex in, 64f, 65–67, 66f
  neocortex in, 64
  sexual behavior and, 330–331
  somatosensory cortex in, 64f, 65–67, 66f
  in split-brain research, 67–70, 69f
cervical cancer, 540
change blindness, 94
Chantix (varenicline), 539
cheating, research on, 34–35, 317
chemical senses, 117–120, 120f
chemoreception, 87f, 88
children. See also child sexual abuse
  aggression in, 413, 415–416
  attention deficit hyperactivity disorder
    in, 446, 447
  birth order of, 369
  brain development in, 287–289, 288f
  brought up by same-sex parents, 339
  brought up in isolation, 271–272
  cognitive development in, 294–297,
    294f, 295f, 296f
  Erickson's childhood stages, 304f,
    306–307
  as eyewitnesses to their abuse,
    226–227
  Freud's personality development in,
    366–367, 367f
  gender development in, 312–314
  gifted, 261–263
  intellectual disability in, 263–264
  intelligence in, 260
  language learning by, 271–274, 273f
  mental age of, 257
  moral development in, 315–317
  nightmares and night terrors in, 142
  parent divorce and, 310
  physical development in, 286–289,
    286f, 287f, 288f
  in psychoanalytic theory, 366–367, 367f
  resilience in, 281

  sleep in, 139, 140f
  of smokers, 538
  suicide by, 460
  temperament development in,
    302–303, 304
  theory of mind in, 127–129
  toy design and, 298
child sexual abuse
  borderline personality disorder
    and, 475
  dissociative identity disorder and, 467
  eating disorders and, 463
  repressed memories of, 226–227
  suicide and, 461
chlamydia, 540
cholecystokinin (CCK), 328
chromosomes, 76
  aging and, 292, 292f
  gender and, 312
  number in human cells, 312
  structure of, 76–77, 77f
chronic stress, 46, 527
chunking, 209
cigarettes. See tobacco
cilia, in ears, 111f, 112
circadian rhythms, 133–134
circumcision, 19
circumplex model of mood, 354, 354f
classical conditioning, 169–177
  acquisition in, 170–171, 172f
  aversive conditioning in, 173
  counterconditioning in, 173
  definition of, 168, 169
  drug habituation and, 175–177, 177f
  embedded marketing and, 176
  extinction and spontaneous recovery
    in, 172–173, 172f, 183
  fears and, 173, 173f, 450
  generalization and discrimination in,
    171–172, 172f
  immune and endocrine systems and, 174
  marketing and, 92, 176
  operant conditioning compared with,
    168f, 177
  Pavlov's studies in, 169–170,
    170f, 171f
  placebo effect and, 173–174
  pleasant emotions and, 63, 63f
  role of information in, 190–191
  "scapegoat" conditioned stimulus
    in, 175
  systematic desensitization in, 494, 494f
  taste aversion learning as, 174–175,
    175f, 195
  as therapy, 494–495, 494f, 495f
client-centered therapy, 493–494
closure, gestalt principle of, 104f
Clozaril (clozapine), 486–487
cocaine
  effects of, 153–154, 154f, 156f
  hypothalamus and, 63
  neurotransmitters and, 54, 153, 154f
cochlea, 111–112, 111f
cochlear implants, 112
cocktail party effect, 93
cognition, 243. See also cognitive
    development; thinking
  in adulthood, 299–302, 301f
  artificial intelligence and, 244–245, 244f
  behaviorism and, 9
  computers and, 243–245, 244f
  concepts and, 245–246
  decision making and, 250–253, 251f
  intelligence and, 255–256
  language and, 267–270
  in learning, 190–193, 192f, 193f
  prejudice and, 262–263
  problem solving and, 246–248, 248f,
    249f, 253
  reasoning and, 249–250
  sexuality and, 332
  wisdom, 301
cognitive affective processing systems
    (CAPS), 386–387

cognitive appraisal, **530**–531
cognitive approach, **10,** 11
cognitive assessment, 397
cognitive-behavior therapy (CBT), **499,** 505
cognitive development
  in adolescence, 295f, 297, 299–300
  in adulthood, 299–302, 301f
  cultural complexity and, 299
  evaluating and expanding Piaget's theory, 297–300
  gender development and, 313
  Piaget's theory of, 294–297, 294f, 295f, 296f
  scaffolding in, 299
cognitive dissonance, **406**–407, 408f
cognitive psychology, 245. *See also* cognition; thinking
cognitive restructuring, 495
cognitive theory of dreaming, **144**–145
cognitive therapies, **495**–499, 498f, 500f
cohort effects, 279
collateral sprouting, 73
collective unconscious, **368**
collectivist cultures
  characteristics of, 28
  conformity and, 420–421
  measures of success in, 28
  parenting styles in, 307
  self-determination theory in, 343
  theory of mind in, 128
college students. *See also* adolescents
  cultural diversity among, 193, 193f
  sexual behavior of, 337
color blindness, 102, 102f
color constancy, 107
color tree, 96, 97f
color vision, 99, 102–103, 102f, 103f
communication. *See* language
community mental health, 504
companionate love, 436
compensation, 368–369
competence, as need, 342
complementary colors, 103f
complex sounds, 109, 110f
compulsions, 452
computerized axial tomography (CAT or CT scan), 57
computers
  cognition and, 243–245, 244f
  cybertherapy, 497
  emoticons and, 353
conception, 284
concepts, **245**–246
conclusions, in scientific method, 14f, 16
concrete operational stage, 295f, **297**
concussion, 74
conditioned response (CR), **170,** 177f
conditioned stimulus (CS), **170,** 171–172, 172f, 175, 177f, 191
conditioning
  aversive, 173, 494–495, 495f
  classical (*See* classical conditioning)
  counterconditioning, 173
  definition of, 167
  endocrine system and, 174
  operant (*See* operant conditioning)
conditions of worth, **371**–372
condoms, 540
conduct disorder, 416
cones, in eyes, **99,** 99f, 100f
confederates, **24**
confidentiality, in research, 34
confirmation bias, 251f, **252**
conformity, **418**–421, 419f, 422f, 423f
confounds, 22, 26
connectionism, **216**–217
conscience development, 317
conscientiousness, 375f, 376, 523
consciousness, 125–163, **126.** *See also* psychoactive drugs
  altered states of, 130
  automatic processes in, 130
  brain and, 127

controlled processes in, 129–130, 129f
daydreaming, 130
developmental psychology and, 127–128
hypnosis and, 157–160, 159f
levels of awareness, 129–132, 129f
meditation and, 160–163
purpose of, 132
stream of, 7, 126
subconscious awareness, 130–131
theory of mind and, 127–129
unconscious thought, 131–132
consensual validation, 434
consequences, in operant conditioning, 178, 179–180
conservation, 296, 296f
consistency, Mischel's critique of, 385
contagion, of depression, 457, 458
contamination stories, 237
contemplation stage, 517, 517f
content analysis, 381
context-dependent memory, 222–223
contiguity, in conditioning, 171
contingency, in conditioning, 171, 178
continuous reinforcement, 183
contraception, 333
control group, **24**
controlled processes, **129**–130, 129f
convergence, **105**
convergent thinking, **254**
*Convicting the Innocent* (Garrett), 229
coping, **530**–533, 532f
cornea, 98, 98f
corpus callosum, **68,** 68f
correlational coefficient, 20
correlational research, **20**
  application of, 27, 27f
  causal relationships and, 20–22, 59, 263
  correlations in, 20, 21f
  longitudinal designs in, 22–23
corticosteroids, 46
corticotropin-releasing hormone (CRH), 527, 528
cortisol
  binge eating and, 464
  DNA damage and, 80
  jet lag and, 134
  stress and, 527
co-rumination, 458
counterconditioning, **173**
couples therapy, **502**–503
CPAP (continuous positive airway pressure), 143
crack, 154
creativity, **254**
  insight learning and, 192
  intelligence and, 262, 265
  moods and, 355
  personality and, 375
  in problem-solving, 246, 254, 255
CRH (corticotropin-releasing hormone), 527, 528
criterion validity, 256
critical thinking, **3,** 253–254
cross-cultural competence, **505**
cross-cultural psychology
  cognitive-behavioral therapy and, 505
  conformity and, 421
  education and, 193, 193f
  episodic memory and, 214
  social psychology and, 28
  social support and, 522
cross-sectional design, **279**
cross-situational consistency, 385
crowdfunding, 242
crystallized intelligence, 300
crystal methamphetamine (crystal meth), 153
CT scans, 57
cultural-familial intellectual disability, 264
culture. *See also* collectivist cultures; ethnicity; individualistic cultures
  abnormal behavior, 442, 443
  aggression and, 415

attribution and, 403
biases on intelligence tests from, 258–259
big five factors of personality and, 376–377
cognitive development and, 299
conformity and, 420–421
as correlational variable, 28
definition of, 11
depression and, 455, 457f
dissociative disorder and, 467–468
emoticons and, 353
episodic memory and, 214
ethnic identity, 308
expression of emotions and, 351–352, 352f
gender roles and, 314
of honor, 415, 461
individualistic *vs.* collectivist, 28
infant attachment and, 304
influence on learning, 193, 193f
intelligence and, 255–256, 256f
language and, 269
moral development and, 316
pain and, 117
parenting and, 307
perception and, 94
psychotherapy and, 504–506
self-determination theory and, 343
sexual motivation and, 332–333
social support and, 522
taste and, 118, 119
terror management theory and, 319
theory of mind development and, 128
culture-fair tests, **258**–259
culture of honor, 415, 461
curiosity, in psychology, 3
cutaneous senses, 114–117, 115f
cybertherapy, 497
cytokines, 141
Cytoxan, 174

**D**

"The Dark Side of the American Dream" (Kasser and Ryan), 16
data, definition of, 16
data analysis, 16
daydreaming, 129f, 130
DBT (dialectical behavior therapy), 500
DD (dysthymic disorder), **455**
death
  Bonanno's theory of grieving, 320
  Kübler-Ross's stages of dying, 319
  meaning from reality of, 320
  terror management theory, 318–319
debriefing, 34–35
decay theory, **233**
deception, in research, 34–35
decibels (dB), 109
decision making, **250**–253, 251f, 426–427
declarative memory. *See* explicit memory
deductive reasoning, **249**–250, 249f
deep brain stimulation, 488
deep processing, 204, 204f
default network, 144–145
defense mechanisms, **364**–365, 364f, 367f
deindividuation, **425**
deinstitutionalization, 504
delayed punishment, 186–187
delayed reinforcement, 185–187
delay of gratification, 386
delta sleep, 137f, 138
delta waves, 137f, 138
delusions, **469**
demand characteristics, **26**
dendrites, **49,** 49f, 52f, 287–288, 288f
denial, 319, 364–365, 531
deoxyribonucleic acid (DNA), 76–77, 77f
dependent variables, **24**
depressants, **147**–151, 149f, 150f, 156f. *See also* psychoactive drugs

depression. *See also* depressive disorders
  from benzodiazepines, 483
  cognitive therapy for, 496, 499
  co-rumination and, 458
  drug treatment for, 54, **484**–485, 484f, 486
  in dying, 319
  electroconvulsive therapy for, 488, 488f
  meditation and, 161
  neurotransmitters and, 54, 456
  sleep and, 141
depressive disorders, **454**
  biological factors in, 456
  bipolar disorder, 457, 459, 459f
  cognitive therapy for, 496, 499
  drug therapies for, 54, 484–485, 484f, 486
  dysthymic disorder, 455
  electroconvulsive therapy for, 488, 488f
  major depressive disorder, 455
  psychological factors in, 456–457
  sociocultural factors in, 455, 457
  suicide and, 459–461, 460f, 461f
depth perception, **104**–106, 105f, 106f
descriptive research, 17–20, 27f
desensitization hierarchy, 494, 494f
desensitization therapies, 494, 494f
desynchronous waves, 137
detriangulation, 502
development, 278–322, **279**
  active, in aging, 321–322
  of the brain, 59, 60f
  cognitive, in adolescence, 295f, 297
  cognitive, in adulthood, 299–302, 301f
  cognitive, in childhood, 294–297, 295f, 296f
  divorce and, 310
  domains of, 282–283
  early experiences and, 280–281
  emerging adulthood, 309
  Erikson's theory of socioemotional, 304f–305f, 305–311, 307f
  gender, 312–314
  infant attachment in, 303–305, 303f
  of language, 272–274, 273f
  Marcia's theory of identity status, 307–308, 307f
  moral, 315–317
  nature and nurture in, 280, 281, 282
  parents and, 281
  of personality, 366–367, 367f
  physical, in adolescence, 289–290, 289f, 290f
  physical, in adulthood, 290–293, 292f, 293f
  physical, in infancy and childhood, 286–289, 286f, 287f, 288f
  prenatal, 284–285, 284f
  of preterm infants, 285
  resilience and, 281
  socioemotional, in adolescence, 289
  socioemotional, in adulthood, 309–311
  socioemotional, in infancy and childhood, 302–305, 303f, 304f
  of temperament, 302–303
  of visual system, 101
developmental psychology, 127–128, 279
  research methods in, 279
deviant behavior, 441–442
dialectical behavior therapy (DBT), 500
diathesis-stress model, **472**
DID (dissociative identity disorder), **466**–468, 467f
diet, 330, 536–537
difference threshold, **91**–92
disabilities, intellectual, 263–264
discovered memories, 226–227
discrimination, **432**
  Civil Rights Act of 1964 and, 432
  in conditioning, 171–**172,** 172f, **183**
  psychological disorders and, 477–478
  sexual harassment as, 432
  sexual orientation and, 339
dismissive attachment style, 304

displacement, 364
display rules, **352**
dissociation, 465
dissociative amnesia, **466**
dissociative disorders, 443, **465**–468
dissociative fugue, **466**
dissociative identity disorder (DID), **466**–468, 467f
divergent thinking, **254**
diversity. *See* culture; ethnicity
divided attention, **203**–204
divided consciousness view of hypnosis, **158**–159, 159f
divorce, development and, 310
DNA (deoxyribonucleic acid), **76**–77, 77f
Dodo bird hypothesis, 507
dogs
  conditioning studies in, 166, 180, 182
  personality in, 377
  sense of smell in, 118–119, 166
dominant-recessive genes principle, **78**
door-in-the-face technique, 409
dopamine
  aggression and, 81
  antipsychotic drugs and, 485
  binge eating and, 464
  in drug addiction, 147, 150
  emotions and, 349
  functions of, 54
  orgasm and, 331
  personality and, 389
  psychoactive drugs and, 152, 153, 154f, 155
  schizophrenia and, 471
double-blind experiments, **26**–27
Down syndrome, 264, 264f
dream analysis, **492**
dreams
  activation-synthesis theory of, 145
  artists' portrayals of, 143–144, 144f
  cognitive theory of, 144–145
  content of, 143–144
  nightmares and night terrors, 142
  REM sleep and, 138
  subconscious awareness during, 131
drinking. *See* alcohol
drive reduction theory, 326
drives, **326**
drug addiction, 63
drug habituation, 175–177, 177f
drugs. *See* psychoactive drugs
drug therapies, 483–487, 484f, 487f, 500
*DSM-IV* classification system, **444**–448, 445f, 473
dual-code hypothesis of memory, 206
Duchenne smiling, 15, 15f
dying
  cultural beliefs and, 318–319
  grieving and, 320
  Kübler-Ross's stages of, 319
  meaning from reality of, 320
dysthymic disorder (DD), **455**

**E**

ear, 109–112, 110f, 111f
eating, healthy, 536–537
eating disorders, 462–465
echoic memory, 208, 208f
Ecstasy, 154, 156f
ECT (electroconvulsive therapy), **487**–488
education. *See also* learning
  Alzheimer's disease and, 238
  gifted children and, 262–263
  influence on intelligence, 260, 260f
  intellectual disabilities and, 264
  self-fulfilling prophecies and, 402
  sex, 333
  starting time in schools, 139–140
EEG (electroencephalograph), 56–57, 57f
efferent nerves, **44**
effortful control, 302
effort justification, 407
ego, 363f, **364**, 367
egocentrism, adolescent, 299

egoism, **410**
elaboration, **204**–205, 205f
elaboration likelihood model, **408**
electrochemical transmissions, 44
electroconvulsive therapy (ECT), **487**–488
electroencephalographs (EEG), 56–57, 57f
electromagnetic spectrum, 96, 97f
embedded marketing, 176
embryonic period, 284–285, 284f
embryonic stem cells, 75–76
emergent properties, 280
emerging adulthood, **309**
emoticons, 353
emotional intelligence, 265, 355
emotion-focused coping, **531**
emotions, **345**–355. *See also* happiness
  adaptive functions of, 355
  arousal level of, 346–347, 346f, 354, 354f
  biological factors in, 345–347, 346f
  in borderline personality disorder, 475
  brain hemispheres and, 69–70, 349
  classical conditioning and, 172
  culture and expression of, 351–352, 352f
  emoticons and, 353
  facial feedback hypothesis, 350, 351f
  flat affect, 469
  gender and, 352–354
  hypothalamus and, 63, 63f
  memory retrieval and, 224–225
  neurotransmitters and, 347–349, 348f
  physiological theories of, 347
  primacy of cognition vs., 349–350
  resilience and, 355
  retrieval of emotional memories, 224–225
  temperament development, 302–303, 304
  two-factor theory of, 349
  valence of, 354, 354f
empathy, 48, 372, **411**, 493–494
empirically keyed tests, **392**
empirical method, **4**
Employee Polygraph Protection Act, 347
encoding, **203**
  attention in, 203–204
  context and, 222–223
  elaboration in, 204–205, 205f
  encoding specificity principle, 222
  failure of, 231–232, 231f
  imagery in, 205–206, 206f
  levels of processing, 204, 204f
  serial position effect and, 221
  in studying, 235–236
  of traumatic events, 225
encoding specificity principle, 222
endocrine system, **71**–72, 72f, 174
endorphins, 54, 117, 349
environment
  aggression and, 415–416
  in Bandura's social cognitive theory, 383–384, 383f
  gender development and, 314
  genetics and, 7, 79–81
  height and, 80
  intelligence and, 259–261, 260f
  language and, 271–272, 272f
  obesogenic, 536
  sensory receptors and, 101
epilepsy, 56, 66, 211–212
epinephrine (adrenaline), 72, 349
episodic memory, **213**–214, 213f
Erikson's theory of socioemotional development
  in adolescence, 307–309, 307f
  in adulthood, 309–311
  in childhood, 304f, 306–307
  evaluation of, 311
  stages of, 304f–305f
erogenous zones, 366
ESM (experience sampling method), 22
ESP (extrasensory perception), 89, 90–91
estradiol, 289
estrogens, 289, 291, **331**
e-therapy, 497

ethics
  in animal research, 36
  in conditioning studies, 173, 173f
  deception in research, 34–35
  in Milgram experiments, 35, 423
  research guidelines, 33–36
  in Stanford prison experiment, 424
ethnic identity, 308, 430f
ethnicity. *See also* culture
  diversity and education, 193, 193f
  eyewitness testimony and, 228
  obesity and, 536
  pain and, 117
  prejudice and, 430–431
  research bias from exclusion of, 30
  stereotypes and perception of, 405
  suicide and, 461, 461f
  therapies and, 504–506
ethnocentrism, **429**
ethology, 325
etiology, 448
event-specific knowledge, 224, 224f
evidence-based practice, **507**
evolution
  aggression and, 412–414
  altruism and, 410
  attraction and, 435
  of the brain, 61, 64
  functionalism and, 7–8
  homosexuality and, 338–339
  motivation and, 325–326
  natural selection and, 7–8
  sleep and, 135
evolutionary approach, **10**–11
executive control, 65
exercise, 291, 301, **534**–535, 535f
expectancy learning, 190–191
experience sampling method (ESM), 22
experiment, **23**
experimental group, **24**–25
experimental research, 23–27, 27f. *See also* research
experimenter bias, 25–26
explicit memory, **212**
  brain and, 212, 219, 219f
  episodic and semantic memory in, 213–214, 213f
  retention of, 212–213, 213f
explicit racism, 431
*The Expression of the Emotions in Man and Animals* (Darwin), 351
externalizing symptoms, 458
external locus of control, 384
external validity, **25**
extinction, in conditioning, **172**–173, 172f, **183**
extrasensory perception (ESP), 89, 90–91
extraversion
  brain and, 388
  genetics and, 390
  neurotransmitters and, 54, 389
  in reinforcement sensitivity theory, 389
  in reticular activation system theory, 388–389, 388f
  subjective well-being and, 377–378
  in trait theories, 375, 375f, 377–378
extrinsic motivation, 16, **343**–344, 520
eye, structure of, 96, 98–99, 98f, 99f, 100f. *See also* visual system
eye color, 78
eyewitness testimony, 226–227, 228–230, 228f

**F**

face, person perception and, 401
face validity, **393**
facial attractiveness, 401–402
facial expressions
  display rules in, 352
  Duchenne smiling, 15, 15f
  emotions and, 350, 351f
  universality of, 351–352, 352f

facial feedback hypothesis, **350**, 351f
facial recognition, 58, 69, 222, 222f
factor analysis, 374
false belief task, 127–129
false consensus effect, **404**
false memories, 227, 230
familial intellectual disability, 264
families. *See* parents
family therapy, **502**, 504
FASD (fetal alcohol spectrum disorders), 285
fast pathway, for pain perception, 117
fears
  brain and, 348, 348f
  classical conditioning and, 173, 173f, 450
  of gaining weight, 462
  panic attacks and, 449–450
  phobias, 450–451, 451f
  of snakes, 195
  stereotype threat, 405
feature detectors, **100**–101
Federal Office for Protection from Research Risks, 35–36
feminist therapists, 506
fetal alcohol spectrum disorders (FASD), 285
fetal period, 284f, 285
"fighting spirit," health outcomes and, 524–525
"fight or flight" reaction, 46
figure-ground relationship, **104**, 104f
first impressions, 402–403
five-factor model of personality. *See* big five factors of personality
fixation
  problem solving and, **248**, 248f, 249f
  in psychoanalytic theory, 367, 367f
fixed-interval schedules, 183–184, 185f
fixed mindset, 196, 198
fixed-ratio schedules, 183–184, 185f
flashbacks, 452
flashbulb memory, **224**–225
flat affect, **469**
flexibility, creative thinking and, 254
fluid intelligence, 300
Flynn effect, 260, 260f
fMRI (functional magnetic resonance imaging), 58–59, 59f
folic acid, 285
foot-in-the-door technique, 409
forebrain, **61**–63, 63f, 145
Fore tribe, 352, 352f
forgetting, 230–234
  amnesia and, 234
  decay and, 233
  electroconvulsive therapy and, 488
  encoding failure in, 231–232, 231f
  interference and, 232–233, 232f
  motivated, 226
  prospective memory and, 233–234
  tip-of-the-tongue phenomenon, 233
forgiveness, 5
formal operational stage, 295f, **297**, 299–300
fovea, 98f, 99
fraternal twins, 78
free association, **491**
free-radical theory of aging, 292
frequency, 109–110, 110f, 112
frequency theory of hearing, **112**
Freud's psychoanalytic theory
  critics and revisionists of, 367–369, 368f
  defense mechanisms in, 364–365, 364f
  dreams in, 143
  evaluating, 369–370
  hysteria in, 362–363
  influence of, 5
  personality development stages in, 366–367, 367f
  personality structures in, 363–364, 363f
  psychoanalysis, 10, 362, 491–492
  unconscious in, 131

frontal lobes, **65.** *See also* prefrontal cortex
 aggression and, 413
 alcohol and, 148
 association cortex in, 64*f,* 67, 127
 in different animals, 65
 location of, 64*f,* 65
 memory and, 218–219, 219*f*
 personality and, 388
frustration-aggression hypothesis, 414
functional fixedness, **248,** 248*f,* 249*f*
functionalism, 7–8
functional magnetic resonance imaging
 (fMRI), 58–59, 59*f*
fundamental attribution error, **403,** 403*f,* 404
fusiform face area (FFA), 58

**G**

GABA (gamma aminobutyric acid),
 53–54, 148
Gage, Phineas T., brain injury of, 65,
 65*f,* 388
galant reflex, 286*f*
Gallup World Poll (GWP), 31
ganglion cells, 100
Gardner's multiple intelligences, 265–266
GAS (general adaptation syndrome),
 **527,** 527*f*
gastric signals, 328, 328*f*
gays, 336, 338–339, 365
gender, definition of, **312**
gender development, 312–314
gender differences
 in aggression, 416
 in alcohol effects, 148
 in altruism, 411–412
 in attraction, 435
 in color perception, 102, 268
 in depression, 457, 457*f*
 in emotional experiences, 352–354
 in Freud's psychoanalytic theory, 363,
  366, 368
 in growth, 289
 in panic attacks, 450
 in same-sex partners, 336
 in sexual behavior, 336, 337
 in sexual motivation, 337
 in suicide, 461, 461*f*
gender roles, **313**–314
gender schemas, 313
gender similarities hypothesis, **314**
gene x environment (g x e) interaction, **81**
general adaptation syndrome (GAS),
 **527,** 527*f*
generalization
 in classical conditioning, 171–**172,** 450
 in operant conditioning, **182,** 183*f*
 panic attacks and, 450
generalized anxiety disorder,
 **448**–449, 487*f*
Generation Me, 4
generative people, 237
generativity *vs.* stagnation, 305*f,* 310
genes, **77**
 chromosomes, DNA, and, 77, 77*f*
 dominant and recessive, 78
 environment and, 7, 79–81
 in gender development, 312–313
 number of, in humans, 77
genetic disorders
 Down syndrome, 264, 264*f*
 in ob mice, 330
 phenylketonuria, 380
 Williams syndrome, 270
genetic expression, 80
genetic influences
 on aggression, 413
 on anxiety disorders, 448, 449, 452
 on bipolar disease, 459, 459*f*
 on depression, 456
 on eating disorders, 463
 on happiness, 356
 on intelligence, 259–261, 260*f*
 on obesity, 330
 on personality, 390–391, 474

on schizophrenia, 470–471, 470*f*
 on sexual orientation, 338–339
 on suicide, 460
genetics
 behavior genetics, 78–79, 79*f,* 390–391
 chromosomes, genes, and DNA in,
  76–77, 77*f*
 dominant-recessive genes principle, 78
 environment and, 7–8, 79–81
 evolution and, 7–8
 genotypes and phenotypes, 80
 intelligence and, 259–261, 260*f*
 Mendel's early discoveries in, 77–78
 molecular, 78
 selective breeding, 78
genital stage, 366
genome, 77
genotype, **80,** 280
genuineness, 372, 494
germinal period, 284
gestalt psychology, **104,** 104*f*
gifted, **261**–263
girls. *See* women and girls
glands, 71
glaucoma, marijuana and, 155
glial cells, **47**
global brain workspace, 127
glucose, 328
glutamate, bipolar disorder and, 459
goals
 of evolution, 435
 happiness and, 357–358
 in life, 521, 522, 526
 role in behavior, 520
 self-regulation and, 344–345
 subgoaling, 247
gonorrhea, 540
Google, as a workplace, 255
gratitude journals, 357
Greek philosophy, ancient, 6
grieving, 320
gripping reflex, 286*f*
group identity, 428–429, 429*f*
group influence, 425–427
group performance, 425–426
group polarization effect, **426**–427
group results, individual needs and, 38
group therapy, **501**–502
groupthink, **427**
growth hormone, sleep and, 139
growth mindset, 198
GWP (Gallup World Poll), 31

**H**

HAART (highly active antiretroviral
 therapy), 539
habituation, drug, **175**–177, 177*f*
hair cells, 111*f,* 112
hallucinations, in schizophrenia, **469**
hallucinogens, **154**–156, 156*f*
hammer, 110*f,* 111, 111*f*
happiness
 activities for, 357–358
 aging and, 311
 altruistic behavior and, 357
 biological factors in, 356
 brain hemispheres and, 57, 349
 explaining unhappiness, 371–372
 in the Gallup World Poll, 31
 goals and, 357–358
 hedonic treadmill and, 357–358
 intimacy motivation and, 381
 life events and, 377
 longevity and, 22–23
 meaningfulness and, 23–24
 neuroticism and extraversion and,
  377–378
 neurotransmitters and, 349
 in nonindustrial societies, 19–20
 operational definitions for, 15
 personality traits and, 377–378
 Satisfaction with Life Scale, 15, 19
 well-being therapy, 509
hardiness, **532**

hashish, 154
health behaviors, **515**–516
health promotion, 514
health psychology, 513–541, **514**
 biopsychosocial model in, 444, 501,
  514–515
 cognitive appraisal and, 530–531
 coping strategies in, 531–532, 532*f*
 diet and, 536–537
 mind and body relationship in, 515
 motivation in, 520
 personality characteristics and, 523–526
 physical activity and, 534–535,
  535*f,* 536
 positive thinking and, 524–525
 religious faith and, 523
 safe sex and, 539–540
 smoking cessation and, 538–539, 538*f*
 social support and, 520–522
 stages of change model in,
  516–519, 517*f*
 stress and, 526–533, 527*f,* 528*f,* 532*f*
 stress management programs, 532–533
 supportive environments and, 536
 theoretical models of change, 516
 weight loss and, 513, 535–537
hearing. *See* auditory system
heart disease, 141, 529
hedonic treadmill, 357–358
Heinz dilemma, 315–316
hemispheres
 association cortex in, 64*f,* **67,** 127
 Broca's and Wernicke's areas,
  67–68, 67*f*
 corpus callosum and, 68, 68*f*
 emotion and, 57, 349
 integration of function, 70
 lateralization in, 68–70, 69*f,* 293
 left hemisphere function, 68–70, 69*f*
 lobes in, 64–65, 64*f*
 location of, 64*f*
 right hemisphere function, 68–70, 69*f*
 split-brain research, 67–70, 69*f*
 visual processing in, 69–70, 69*f,* 89,
  100–101, 101*f*
heritability, **259.** *See also* genetic
 influences
heroin, 151, 176, 285
herpes infections, 540
heterosexual people, same-sex partners
 and, 336
heuristics
 decision making and, 251–253, 251*f*
 problem solving and, **247**
 in social information processing, 404
hierarchy of needs, **340,** 340*f,* 342
highly active antiretroviral therapy
 (HAART), 539
hindbrain, **60**–61, 60*f*
hindsight bias, 251*f,* **252**
hippocampus, **62**
 exercise and, 291
 location and function of, 60*f,* 62
 memory and, 219, 219*f,* 465
 neurogenesis in, 75
history of psychology, 6–8, 6*f,* 7*f*
Hitler, Adolf, profile of, 380, 380*f*
HIV (human immunodeficiency virus),
 151, 285, 539–540
Hodgkin lymphoma, 160
homeostasis, **326**
homophobia, 365
homosexuality, 336, 338–339, 365
honesty, attachment and, 317
honor, culture of, 415, 461
hormonal stress theory of aging, 292
hormones, **71.** *See also specific hormones*
 aggression and, 413–414
 hypothalamus and, 72, 72*f*
 puberty and, 289
 sex, 331
 stress, 46, 225, 292
Horney's sociocultural approach,
 **11,** 368, 368*f*
hostility, cardiovascular disease and, 529

hot flashes, 291
HPA axis (hypothalamic-pituitary-
 adrenal axis), **527**
hue, 97*f*
human development. *See* development
human embryonic stem cells, 75–76
Human Genome Project, 77
human immunodeficiency virus (HIV),
 151, 285, 539–540
humanistic approach, **10,** 11
humanistic perspectives, **370**–373
humanistic therapies, **493**–494, 500*f*
human nature, Freud's view of, 5
human papilloma virus (HPV), 540
human sexual response pattern, **331**
humor, 70, 355
hunger, 328–330, 328*f,* 329*f*
Huntington disease, 75
hypervigilance, 476
hypnagogic reverie, 161
hypnosis, **157**–160, 159*f*
hypocrisy, 365
hypothalamic-pituitary-adrenal axis
 (HPA axis), **527**
hypothalamus, **63**
 daily rhythms and, 133, 134*f*
 endocrine system and, 72, 72*f*
 hunger and, 329
 location and function of, 60*f,* 63, 72*f*
 pleasure and, 63, 63*f*
 sexual behavior and, 331
 stress and, 527, 528
hypothesis, **14**–15, 14*f,* 16
hypothetical-deductive reasoning, 297
hysteria, 362–363

**I**

Iatmul people, 256, 256*f*
iceberg analogy, 363, 363*f*
iconic memory, 208, 208*f*
id, **363**–364, 363*f*
idealistic thinking, 297
identical twins, 78–79, 79*f. See also* twin
 studies
identity
 in adolescence, 307–309
 in emerging adulthood, 309
 ethnic, 308, 430*f*
 group, 428–429, 429*f*
 identity confusion *vs.,* 305*f,* 307
 life story approach to, 237, 238,
  381–382
 Marcia's theory of identity status,
  307–309, 307*f*
identity status, 307–309, 307*f*
identity *vs.* identity confusion, 305*f,* 307
illusions, 107, 108*f,* 113
imagery, in encoding, **205**–206, 206*f*
imitation, 48, 168. *See also* observational
 learning
immediate punishment, 186–187
immediate reinforcement, 185–187
immune system
 classical conditioning and, 174
 sleep and, 141
 stress and, 527–528, 528*f,* 530
immunosuppression, 174
implementation intentions, **520**
implicit learning, **191**
implicit memory, **214**–216, 219, 219*f*
implicit racism, 431
impulsivity, 379
inattentional blindness, 93–94
incubation, 131
independent variables, **24**
Indian culture, cognitive-behavior
 therapy and, 505
individualistic cultures
 characteristics of, 28
 conformity and, 420–421
 measures of success in, 28
 self-determination theory and, 343
 social support and, 522
 theory of mind in, 128

individual psychology, **368**–369
induction illusion, 108*f*
inductive reasoning, **249**, 249*f*
industry *vs.* inferiority, 304*f*, 306
infant attachment, **303**–305, 303*f*
infants
　attachment in, 303–305, 303*f*
　attractive faces and, 401
　brain development in, 59, 60*f*,
　　287–289, 288*f*
　brain plasticity in, 73, 75
　importance of early experiences, 280
　language development in, 272–274, 273*f*
　massage of, 285
　motor and perceptual skills in,
　　286–287, 287*f*
　object permanence and, 295–296, 296*f*,
　　297–299
　observational learning by, 168
　oral stage in, 366, 367*f*
　preferential looking in, 287, 401
　preterm, 285
　reflexes in, 286, 286*f*
　sleep in, 139, 140*f*, 143
　socioemotional development in,
　　304*f*, 306
　sudden infant death syndrome, 143
　temperament in, 302–303, 304
　touch perception in, 272*f*
　trust *vs.* mistrust in, 304*f*, 306
infinite generativity, **266**
information, in learning, 190–191
informational social influence, **419**
informed consent, 34, 35–36
in-group, 429
inhibition, 302–303
Inis Beag culture, 332
initiative *vs.* guilt, 304*f*, 306
inner ear, 110*f*, **111**–112, 111*f*
inoculation, against persuasion, 409
insight learning, 191–**192**, 192*f*
insight therapies, 494
insomnia, 141
instant messaging, 204, 353
instinct, **325**
instinctive drift, 194–**195**, 195*f*
institutional review board (IRB), 33–34
instrumental conditioning. *See* operant
　conditioning
insulin, 72, 328
integration, by the brain, 43, 70–71
integrative therapies, **500**–501
integrity *vs.* despair, 305*f*, 310–311
intellectual disability, **263**–264
intelligence, 255–266, **256**. *See also*
　　IQ tests
　artificial, 244–245, 244*f*
　bias in testing of, 258–259
　crystallized *vs.* fluid, 300
　cultural differences in, 255–256, 256*f*
　Flynn effect on, 260, 260*f*
　genetic and environmental influences
　　on, 259–261, 260*f*
　giftedness, 261–263
　intellectual disability, 263–264
　in late adulthood, 301
　measuring, 256–259, 257*f*, 258*f*
　multiple intelligences, 264–266
　prejudice and, 262
　social conservatism and, 262–263
　working memory capacity and, 210
intelligence quotient (IQ), **257**. *See also*
　　IQ tests
interference theory, **232**–233, 232*f*
intergroup relations, 428–433
internalizing symptoms, 458
internal locus of control, 384, 523–524
internal validity, **25**
interpretation, in psychoanalysis, **492**
interval schedules, 183
interviews, 18, 27*f*
intimacy motive, 381
intimacy *vs.* isolation, 305*f*, 309–310
intrinsic motivation, 16, **343**–344, 520

introspection, 6
introversion, 388*f*. *See also* extraversion
intuitive decision making, 250–251
Inuit tribe (Inughuits), 19, 268
investment model, **437**
invincibility, in adolescents, 299
in vitro fertilization, stem cells from, 76
ion channels, 50–51, 51*f*, 52*f*
IQ tests, 257–259, 258*f*, 260*f*. *See also*
　　intelligence
Iraq and Afghanistan War veterans, 88,
　　453, 454
IRB (institutional review board), 33–34
iris, 96, 98*f*
*Iron Chef*, 118
Islets of Langerhans, 72

**J**

Jamaican culture, cognitive-behavior
　　therapy and, 505
James, William, American psychology
　　and, 7, 7*f*
James-Lange theory, **347**, 350
Japanese culture, social support in, 522
jet lag, 134–135
Jim twins, 79, 79*f*
"John/Joan" case, 314
Jung's analytical theory, 368, 368*f*
justice perspective, 316
just noticeable difference, 91–92

**K**

Katrina, Hurricane, 403
kindness. *See* altruism
kinesthetic senses, **121**–122
Kohlberg's theory of moral development,
　　315–316
koro, 451
Ku Klux Klan, 425*f*

**L**

laboratory research, 30
lactate, panic disorder and, 449
language, **266**–274. *See also* speech
　biological influences on, 270–271
　cognition and, 267–270
　computer-mediated communication, 353
　development of, 272–274, 273*f*
　environmental influences on,
　　271–272, 272*f*
　evolution of, 270
　intelligence tests and, 258
　left hemisphere and, 69–70, 69*f*
　people-first, 446, 477
　properties of, 266–267
　universals in, 271
latency period, 366
latent content, **143**–144, 492
latent learning, **191**
lateral hypothalamus, 329
lateralization, 68–70, 69*f*, 293
Latinos, 461, 461*f*, 465, 504, 536
law of effect, **178**–179, 179*f*
learned helplessness, **182**, 456
learning, 166–198, **167**. *See also*
　　education
　associative, 167
　avoidance, 182, 389
　biological constraints in, 194–195, 195*f*
　classical conditioning (*See* classical
　　conditioning)
　cognitive factors in, 190–193, 192*f*, 193*f*
　cultural influences in, 193, 193*f*,
　　196, 196*f*
　expectancy, 190–191
　insight, 191–192, 192*f*
　latent, 191
　learned helplessness, 182
　learning styles, 197
　observational, 168, 188–189, 190*f*, 384
　operant conditioning (*See* operant
　　conditioning)
　overlearning, 327

psychological constraints in, 196, 198
　taste aversion, 174–175, 175*f*, 195
　types of, 167–168, 168*f*
left-brained people, 70
left hemisphere functions, 68–70, 69*f*.
　　*See also* hemispheres
lens, 98, 98*f*
leptin, 328–329, 329*f*
lesbians, 336, 338–339, 365
levels of processing, **204**, 204*f*
lexical approach, 374
L-glutamate, 118
Librium, 483
lie detectors, 347
life changes. *See* health psychology
life expectancy, 291
life satisfaction, Gallup World Poll on, 31
life story approach, 237, 238, 381–382
lifestyles, healthy. *See* health psychology
life tasks, 344
life themes, 282
life time periods, 223–224, 224*f*
light, 96, 97*f*
limbic system, **61**
　aggression and, 413
　emotion and, 348–349, 348*f*
　memory and, 219, 219*f*
　pain and, 117
　sexual behavior and, 331
　smell perception and, 120
　structures in, 61–62, 65
linear perspective, 105, 105*f*
linguistic relativity hypothesis, 268–270
lithium, **485**
lobotomy, 489
locked-in syndrome, 125
logic, 249–250, 249*f*
longevity, happiness and, 22–23
longitudinal designs, **22**–23
long-term memory, **211**–219
　brain and, 211–212
　connectionism and, 216–217
　explicit memory and, 212–214, 213*f*
　implicit memory and, 214–216
　location of memories, 217–219, 219*f*
　schemas in, 216
　systems of, 211–212, 212*f*
long-term potentiation, 218
loudness, 109, 110*f*
love, 54, 436
LSD (lysergic acid diethylamide),
　　155–156, 156*f*
lying, in research, 34–35

**M**

"The Magical Number Seven, Plus or
　　Minus Two" (Miller), 208–209
magnetic resonance imaging (MRI),
　　57–59, 59*f*
Maier string problem, 248, 248*f*
maintenance stage, 517*f*, 518
major depressive disorder (MDD),
　　**455**, 456
major histocompatibility complex
　　(MHC), 120
majority influence, 427
maladaptive behavior, 442
Mangaian culture, 332
mania, 54, 457, 459
manifest content, **143**, 492
Mankato Nun Study, 293, 293*f*
MAO (monoamine oxidase) inhibitors, 484
Marcia's theory of identity status,
　　307–308, 307*f*
marijuana, 154–156, 156*f*
market economy, reciprocity in, 411
marketing, 92, 176
marriage
　couples therapy and, 502–503
　divorce and, 310
　same-sex, 339
　success of, 310
Masai people, happiness in, 19–20

Maslow's hierarchy of needs, **340**, 340*f*,
　　342, 370–371
massage of preterm infants, 285
master gland (anterior pituitary), 72. *See
　　also* pituitary gland
mastery, 342
masturbation, 336
maturation. *See* development
maze-running ability, selective breeding
　　and, 78
MDD (major depressive disorder),
　　**455**, 456
MDMA (Ecstasy), 154, 156*f*
mechanoreception, 87*f*, 88
media
　altruism and, 412
　body image of women and, 298, 463
　evaluating reports in, 38–39
　reality TV, 1
　violence in, 415–416, 417
medical marijuana, 156
medical model, **443**
meditation, **160**–163, 292
medulla, 60–61, 60*f*
melanin, 291
melatonin, 135, 139, 141
memory, **202**–238. *See also* long-term
　　memory; memory retrieval;
　　memory storage
　autobiographical, 223–224, 224*f*, 237,
　　238, 390
　dual-code hypothesis, 206
　echoic, 208, 208*f*
　electroconvulsive therapy and, 488
　encoding, 203–206, 204*f*, 205*f*, 206*f*
　episodic, 213–214, 213*f*
　exercise and, 291, 301
　explicit, 212–214, 213*f*
　false memories, 227, 230
　flashbulb, 224–225
　hippocampus and, 62
　iconic, 208, 208*f*
　implicit, 214–216, 219, 219*f*
　Internet and, 211
　kinesthesis and, 121
　location of, 217–219, 219*f*
　neurogenesis and, 75
　permastore, 213
　preserving, 201, 237–238
　priming, 215–216
　procedural, 215
　product marketing and, 176
　prospective, 219, 233–234
　reasoning and, 274
　REM sleep and, 135, 138
　repressed, 225–227
　retrospective, 219, 233
　schemas, 216
　semantic, 213–214, 213*f*
　sensory, 207–208, 207*f*, 208*f*
　short-term, 208–211, 210*f*
　studying and, 235–237
　temporal lobe and, 65
　working, 209–211, 210*f*, 221
　world champions of, 206*f*
memory retrieval, **220**–230. *See also*
　　forgetting
　aging and, 301
　of autobiographical memories,
　　223–224, 224*f*, 237
　discovered memories, 226–227
　effortful, 213*f*, 233–234
　of emotional memories, 224–225
　in eyewitness testimony, 226–227,
　　228–230, 228*f*
　failure of, 232–234, 232*f*
　false memories, 227, 230
　repressed memories, 225–227
　retrieval cues and the retrieval task,
　　221–223, 222*f*
　serial position effect in, 220–221, 221*f*
　in studying, 236–237
　of traumatic events, 225
memory socialization, 214

memory span, 209
memory storage, **207**–219
  Atkinson-Shiffrin theory, 207, 207*f*, 209
  explicit memory and, 212–214, 213*f*
  location of memories, 217–219, 219*f*
  in long-term memory (*See* long-term memory)
  sensory memory and, 207–208, 207*f*, 208*f*
  short-term memory and, 208–211, 210*f*
  working memory and, 209–211, 210*f*
men. *See* gender differences; gender roles
menarche, 289
Mendel's genetics studies, 77–78
menopause, 291
mental age (MA), **257**
mental illnesses. *See* psychological disorders
mental imagery, 205–206, 206*f*
mental processes, **2**
mental retardation, 263–264
mere exposure effect, **434**
meta-analysis, 507
metacognition, 126. *See also* consciousness
meth, 153
Mexican Americans, binge eating disorder in, 465
MHC (major histocompatibility complex), 120
midbrain, **61**
middle ear, 110*f*, **111**, 111*f*
mild traumatic brain injury (MTBI), 74
Milgram's obedience experiments, 422–423, 422*f*, 423*f*
mind–body link, 515
mindfulness, **253**
mindfulness meditation, 160–161
mindset, 196, 198
mind wandering, 130
Minnesota Multiphasic Personality Inventory (MMPI), **393**
Minnesota Study of Twins Reared Apart, 79, 79*f*
minority influence, 427
mirror neurons, 47, 48
modeling. *See* observational learning
molecular genetics, 78
*Monitoring the Future,* 146, 149, 153
monkeys, attachment in infant, 303, 303*f*
monoamine oxidase (MAO) inhibitors, 484
monocular cues, **105**–106, 105*f*
mood disorders, **454**–461, 457*f*, 459*f*, 460*f*, 461*f*, 487*f*
moods, 354, 354*f*, 411. *See also* emotions
moral development, 315–317
moral judgment, sleep deprivation and, 136
Moro reflex, 286*f*
morphemes, 267
morphine, 54
morphology, in language, **267**
motion perception, 106
motivated forgetting, **226**
motivation, **325**–345. *See also* emotions
  Adler on, 368
  delay of gratification and, 386
  drive reduction theory and, 326
  evolutionary approach to, 325–326
  Freud on, 362, 366–367
  hierarchy of needs and, 340, 340*f*, 342
  Horney on, 368
  in hunger, 328–330, 328*f*, 329*f*
  intimacy and, 381
  intrinsic *vs.* extrinsic, 16, 343–344
  Jung on, 368
  Murray on, 381
  optimum arousal theory and, 326–327
  for positive life changes, 520
  self-determination theory and, 342–343
  self-regulation and, 302, 344–345
  in sex, 330–339, 334*f*, 335*f*
  of suicide bombers, 341
motor cortex, 64*f*, **65**–67, 66*f*

motor reproduction, 189
motor skills, development of, 286–287, 287*f*
movement disorders, 469
MRI (magnetic resonance imaging), 57–59, 59*f*
multiple intelligences, 264–266
multiple personality disorder, 466–468, 467*f*
multiple sclerosis (MS), 49
multitasking, 203–204
Murray's personological approach, 380–381
musterbating, 496
myelin sheath, **49**, 49*f*
myoclonic jerks, 137
*The Myth of Mental Illness* (Szasz), 446

## N

NAc. *See* nucleus accumbens
narcissism, 4
narcolepsy, 142
narcotics (opiates), **151**, 156*f*
narratives, 381–382
National Suicide Prevention Lifeline, 482
National Weight Control Registry, 537
Native Americans, 461, 461*f*
naturalistic observation, **32**
natural selection, **7**–8
nature, in development, **280**. *See also* genetic influences
Nazi prisoner experiments, 33
needs, **326**
negative affect, 303, **354**
negative correlations, 20, 21*f*
negative punishment, **185**, 186*f*
negative reinforcement, **181**–182, 181*f*, 186*f*
neglectful parenting, **306**
Nembutal, 151
neocortex, **64**
nervous system, **43**–46. *See also* brain; neurons
  characteristics of, 43–44
  divisions of, 45–46, 45*f*
  embryological development of, 59, 60*f*
  glial cells, 47
  neural impulse, 50–51, 50*f*, 51*f*
  neural networks, 44–45, 55, 55*f*, 145, 216–217
  neurogenesis, 75
  neuron structure, 47, 49, 49*f*
  pathways in, 44–45
  synapses and neurotransmitters in, 51–55, 52*f*, 54*f*
neural impulse, 50–51, 50*f*, 51*f*
neural networks, **44**
  dreaming and, 145
  example of, 44–45, 55, 55*f*
  long-term memory and, 216–217
neural tube development, 284–285
neurogenesis, 75
neuroleptics, 485
neurology, 85
neuronal membranes, 49
neurons, **47**–55
  binding by, 101
  cell structure of, 49, 49*f*
  collateral sprouting, 73
  in ganglia, 100
  glial cells and, 47
  graded currents from sensory receptors, 87
  memory and, 218
  mirror, 47, 48
  neural impulse, 50–51, 50*f*, 51*f*
  in neural networks, 44–45
  neurogenesis, 75
  neurotransmitters secreted by, 53–55
  pain and, 116–117
  in visual processing, 100–101, 101*f*
neuroscience, **9**

neuroticism
  assessment of, 394–395
  genetics and, 79
  obesity and, 379
  serotonin and, 389–390
  subjective well-being and, 377
  in trait theories, 374–375, 375*f*, 377–378, 393
Neuroticism Extraversion Openness Personality Inventory–Revised (NEO-PI-R), 393
neurotransmitters, **52**. *See also specific neurotransmitters*
  action of, 52–53, 52*f*
  aggression and, 413
  bipolar disorder and, 459
  depression and, 54, 456
  drugs and, 55, 154, 154*f*
  emotions and, 347–349, 348*f*
  examples of, 53–55
  excitatory *vs.* inhibitory, 53
  hunger and, 329
  midbrain and, 61
  panic attacks, 449
  personality and, 389–390
  reuptake of, 53
  schizophrenia and, 471
  sexual behavior and, 331
  sleep and, 139, 145
"niceness," 58
nicotine, 152–153, 152*f*, 153*f*, 156*f*, 538. *See also* tobacco
nicotine gum, 538
nicotine patch, 538
nicotine spray, 538
nightmares, 142
night terrors, 142
nine-dot problem, 249*f*, 275*f*
9/11 terrorist attacks, 224, 355, 427
NK cells, 530, 530*f*
noise, in sensory perception, **91**
nonconscious thought, 131–132
nondeclarative memory, **214**–216
nondirective therapy, 493–494
noradrenergic and specific serotonergic antidepressants (NaSSAs), 484
norepinephrine (noradrenaline)
  adrenal glands and, 72
  bipolar disorder and, 459
  cocaine and, 153, 156*f*
  depression and, 54, 456, 484, 485
  Ecstasy and, 154
  functions of, 54, 72
  panic disorder and, 449
  psychoactive drugs and, 153, 154*f*
  sleep and, 139
normal distribution, **257**–258, 258*f*
normative social influence, **419**
nucleus accumbens (NAc)
  addiction and, 147
  alcohol and, 148
  cocaine and, 154*f*
  conformity and, 420
  in reward pathway, 147, 488
Nun Study, 22
nurture, in development, **280**. *See also* environment
*The Nurture Assumption* (Harris), 281

## O

obedience, **422**–425, 422*f*, 423*f*
obesity. *See also* weight loss
  biology of, 330
  community support for weight loss, 513
  diet and, 330, 536–537
  hypothalamus and, 329
  leptin and, 329, 329*f*
  personality traits and, 379
  prevalence of, 329, 535–536, 537*f*
  psychological factors in, 330
  sleep and, 141, 143
obesogenic environments, 536

objectivity, 4, 254
object permanence, **295**–296, 296*f*, 297–299
ob mice, 330
observational learning, **168**
  aggression and, 414–415
  Bandura's model of, 188–189, 190*f*, 384
observations
  in descriptive research, 17–18, 27*f*
  naturalistic, 32
  in the scientific method, 13–14, 13*f*
obsessive-compulsive disorder (OCD), 451–**452**
occipital lobes, **64**, 64*f*, 89
Oedipus complex, **366**, 367
olfactory bulb, 75
olfactory epithelium, **119**, 120*f*
olfactory sense, 90*f*, 118–120, 120*f*
*On Death and Dying* (Kübler-Ross), 319
*One Flew Over the Cuckoo's Nest* (film), 488
one-third rule for alcoholism, 150–151
online support groups, 503
*On the Origin of Species* (Darwin), 7
open-mindedness, **254**
openness, 375, 375*f*
operant conditioning, 177–188, **178**
  applied behavior analysis, 187–188
  classical conditioning *vs.,* 168*f*, 177
  definition of, 168, 178
  generalization, discrimination, and extinction in, 182–183, 183*f*
  positive and negative reinforcement in, 181–182, 181*f*
  primary and secondary reinforcers in, 182
  punishment in, 185
  reinforcement definition, 180–181
  schedules of reinforcement, 183–184
  shaping in, 180, 180*f*
  Skinner's approach to, 179–180, 180*f*
  as therapy, 495
  Thorndike's law of effect, 178–179, 179*f*
  timing of reinforcement and punishment, 185–187
operational definitions, **15**–16
operations, in Piaget's theory, 295
ophthalmology, 85
opiates, **151**, 156*f*
opium, addictive action of, 54
opponent-process theory, **102**–103, 103*f*
optic chiasm, 100, 101*f*
optic nerve, 98*f*, **99**, 99*f*
optimism, 525–526, 532
optimistic attributional style, 456
optimum arousal theory, 326–327
oral sex, 334, 335*f*, 336
oral stage, 366, 367*f*
organic intellectual disability, 263–264
orgasm, 55, 331
outer ear, **110**, 110*f*
out-group, 429, 433*f*
oval window, 111, 111*f*
ovaries, **72**, 72*f*
overdetermined symptoms, 363
overgeneralizing, 38, 497
overlearning, 327
overt aggression, **416**
overweight, 536, 537*f*. *See also* obesity
oxytocin, 54–55, 331

## P

pain, **115**
  expectation and, 191
  hypnosis and, 158–160, 159*f*
  meditation and, 160–161
  perception of, 84, 88, 115–117
  phantom limb, 88
  substance P and, 456
  treatment of, 151

Pakistani culture, cognitive-behavior therapy and, 505
pancreas, **72**, 72*f*
panic attacks, 161, 449–450
panic disorder, **449**–450, 487*f*, 499
papillae, **118**
parallel distributed processing (PDP), **216**–217
parallel processing, **101**
Paralympics, 342*f*
paraprofessionals, 503
parasympathetic nervous system, 45*f*, **46**, 346, 346*f*
parathyroid gland, 72*f*
parents
    adolescent development and, 308–309
    culture and, 307
    divorce of, 310
    generativity and, 310
    nature *vs.* nurture and, 281
    obese, 330
    oxytocin and, 55
    parenting styles, 306–307
    prosocial behavior in children and, 317
    same-sex, 339
    sexual orientation of children and, 365
    teenagers as, 333, 334*f*
parietal lobes, 64*f*, **65**, 88, 89
Parkinson disease, 54, 63, 75
partial reinforcement, 183
passionate love, 436
pathogens, cultural differences and, 421
*The Path to Purpose* (Damon), 344–345
pattern recognition, 108*f*
Pavlov's studies, 169–170, 170*f*, 171*f*
Paxil, 484
PDP (parallel distributed processing), **216**–217
peer review, 38–39
peers, 308–309, 416, 458
penis envy, 366, 368
penny exercise, 231–232, 231*f*
people-first language, 446, 477
perception, **85**. *See also* sensation
    auditory (*See* auditory system)
    binding, 101
    bottom-up and top-down processing, 86, 99
    culture and, 94
    of depth, 104–106, 105*f*, 106*f*
    expectations and, 191
    extrasensory, 89, 90–91
    illusions, 107, 108*f*
    by infants, 286–287, 287*f*
    kinesthetic senses, 121–122
    of motion, 106
    of pain, 84, 88, 115–117
    parallel processing, 101
    perceptual constancy, 106–107, 107*f*, 108*f*
    perceptual set, 94–95
    person, 401–403
    purposes of, 86–87
    role of language in, 267–270
    selective attention and, 93–94, 94*f*
    sensory adaptation, 95
    sexual activity and, 332
    of shape, 103–104, 104*f*
    skin senses, 114–117, 115*f*
    of smell, 118–120, 120*f*
    social experiences and, 116
    subliminal, 92–93, 93*f*
    synaesthesia and, 88
    of taste, 90*f*, 118, 119
    thresholds in, 51, 89–93, 89*f*, 90*f*
    vestibular sense, 121–122, 121*f*
    visual (*See* visual system)
perceptual constancy, 106–**107**, 107*f*, 108*f*
perceptual set, 94–**95**
peripheral nervous system (PNS), **45**–46, 45*f*

permastore memory, 213
permissive parenting, **306**
persona, 368
personal ads, gender differences in, 435
personal control, 424–425, 523–524
personality, 361–397, **362**
    accuracy of judgments of, 394–395
    Adler's individual psychology, 368–369
    Allport's and Odbert's traits in, 373–374
    Bandura's social cognitive theory, 383–384, 383*f*
    behavioral genetics and, 79, 390–391
    big five factors of, 374–378, 375*f*, 379, 393
    biological perspectives on, 387–391, 388*f*, 389*f*
    birth order and, 369
    brain and, 58, 388–390, 388*f*, 389*f*
    brain damage and, 65, 65*f*
    CAPS theory, 386–387
    defense mechanisms in, 364–365, 364*f*, 367*f*
    disorders of, 473–476, 473*f*, 499
    Eysenck's reticular activation system theory, 388–389, 388*f*
    Freud's psychoanalytic theory, 10, 363–364, 363*f*
    frontal lobes and, 388
    Gray's reinforcement sensitivity theory, 389, 389*f*
    Hippocrates on, 387
    Horney's sociocultural approach, 11, 368, 368*f*
    humanistic perspectives, 370–373
    iceberg analogy of, 363, 363*f*
    Jung's analytical theory, 368, 368*f*
    life story approach to identity, 237, 238, 381–382
    Maslow's approach, 340, 340*f*, 342, 370–371
    Mischel's contributions, 384–387
    Murray's personological approach, 380–381
    neurotransmitters and, 389–390
    obesity and, 379
    online *vs.* real, 361
    positive life changes and, 523–526
    projective tests of, 393–395, 394*f*, 396*f*, 397
    psychodynamic perspectives on, 362–370
    psychosexual development stages, 366–367, 367*f*
    Roger's approach, 371–372, 371*f*
    self-report tests of, 392–393
    social cognitive perspectives, 383–387, 383*f*
    subjective well-being and, 377–378
    summary of approaches, 396*f*
    trait theories of, 373–379, 375*f*
*Personality and Assessment* (Mischel), 385
personality disorders, **473**–476, 473*f*, 499
personological and life story perspectives, **380**–381
person perception, 401–403
persuasion, 407–409
pessimistic attributional style, 456
PET scans, 57–58
phallic stage, 366, 367*f*
phantom limb pain, 88
phenotype, **80**, 280
phenylketonuria (PKU), 280
philosophy, Western, 6
phobias (phobic disorder), **450**–451, 451*f*, 487*f*
phonemes, 266–267
phonological loop, 210*f*, 211
phonology, **266**–267
photoreception, 87*f*, 88

physical activity, 534–535, 534*f*, 535*f*, 536
physical dependence, **147**
physical development
    in adolescence, 289–290, 289*f*, 290*f*
    in early adulthood, 290
    in infancy and childhood, 286–289, 286*f*, 287*f*, 288*f*
    in late adulthood, 291–293, 292*f*, 293*f*
    in middle adulthood, 290–291
    prenatal, 284–285, 284*f*
Piaget's theory of cognitive development, 294–297, 294*f*, 295*f*, 296*f*
pigeon-guided missiles, 179, 179*f*
pinna (plural, *pinnae*), 110, 110*f*
pitch, 109, 110*f*
pituitary gland, **72**
    hypothalamus and, 63
    location and function of, 60*f*, 72, 72*f*
    stress and, 527
PKU (phenylketonuria), 280
placebo, **26**
placebo effect, **26**, 173–174, 191
place theory of hearing, **112**
plasticity, **44**, 73, 75, 135
playful thinking, 254
pleasure, hypothalamus and, 63, 63*f*
PNS (peripheral nervous system), **45**–46, 45*f*
polarized neurons, 50
police lineups, 229
political beliefs, intelligence and, 262–263
polygenic inheritance, 78
polygraphs, **347**
Ponzo illusion, 108*f*
population, **29**–30
pornography, violence in, 416
positive affect, **354**
positive correlations, 20, 21*f*
positive illusions, **404**–405
positive punishment, **185**, 186*f*
positive reinforcement, **181**–182, 181*f*, 186*f*
positive thinking, power of, 524–525
positron-emission tomography (PET scan), 57–58
posterior cingulate cortex, 58
postsynaptic neurons, 52*f*
post-traumatic stress disorder (PTSD), **452**–454
pot (marijuana), 154–156, 156*f*
potassium ions, 50–51, 51*f*
poverty, 457
pragmatics, in language, **267**
precognition, 89, 90–91
precontemplation stage, 516–517, 517*f*
predictions, 14*f*, 15
preferential looking, **287**
prefrontal asymmetry, 57
prefrontal cortex, **65**
    in adolescence, 289–290, 290*f*
    consciousness and, 127, 161
    hypnosis and, 158
    location and function of, 64*f*, 65
    memory and, 219
    peer pressure and, 290
    personality and, 389
    psychoactive drugs and, 147, 147*f*
    sleep deprivation and, 136
prefrontal lobotomy, 489
pregnancy, 333, 334*f*
prejudice, **430**
    factors in, 431–432
    intelligence and, 262–263
    psychological disorders and, 477–478
    racial, 430–431
    stereotyping and, 423
prenatal development, 284–285, 284*f*

preoccupied attachment style, 304
preoperational stage, **295**–296, 295*f*
preparation/determination stage, 517–518, 517*f*
preparedness, **195**
presynaptic neurons, 52*f*
preterm infants, 285
primacy effect, 220–221, 221*f*, 349–350
primary appraisal, 530–531
primary reinforcers, **182**
priming, **215**–216, 217, 219, 317
proactive interference, **232**–233, 232*f*
pro-anorexia websites, 503
problem-focused coping, **531**
problem solving, 246
    coping as, 530–531
    critical thinking in, 253
    fixation and, 248, 248*f*, 249*f*
    steps in, 246–248
    strategies in, 247
procedural memory, **215**
projection, 364
projective tests, 393–395, 394*f*, 397
proprioceptive feedback, 121
prosocial behavior, **316**–317, 410–412
prospective memory, 219, **233**–234
prostaglandins, 116–117
prototype model, **246**
proximity, 104*f*, 434
Prozac, 54, 484, 484*f*
psychoactive drugs, **146**–156
    alcohol (*See* alcohol)
    amphetamines, 153, 156*f*
    barbiturates, 151, 156*f*
    caffeine, 151–152, 156*f*
    cocaine, 54, 63, 153–154, 154*f*, 156*f*
    consciousness and, 130
    habituation to, 175–177, 177*f*
    LSD, 155–156, 156*f*
    marijuana, 154–156, 156*f*
    MDMA (Ecstasy), 154, 156*f*
    medical uses of psychedelic drugs, 155–156
    neurotransmitters and, 55
    nicotine, 152–153, 152*f*, 153*f*, 156*f*
    opiates, 151, 156*f*
    prevalence of use, 146, 146*f*
    self-assessment on use of, 148*f*
    tolerance, dependence, and addiction in, 63, 146–147
    tranquilizers, 151, 156*f*
psychoanalysis, 10, 362–363, **491**–492
psychoanalytic theory
    Adler and, 368–369
    evaluation of, 369–370
    Freud and, 362–367, 362*f*, 363*f*, 367*f*
    Horney and, 368, 368*f*
    Jung and, 368, 368*f*
psychobiography, 382
psychodynamic approach, **9**–10, 11
psychodynamic perspectives, **362**–370. *See also* psychoanalytic theory
psychodynamic therapies, **491**–493, 500*f*
psychological dependence, **147**
psychological disorders, 440–478. *See also* therapies
    abnormal behavior definition, 441–442
    anxiety disorders, 448–454
    attention deficit hyperactivity disorder, 446, 447
    classifying abnormal behavior, 444–448, 445*f*
    dissociative disorders, 443, 465–468
    eating disorders, 462–465
    mood disorders, 454–461, 457*f*, 459*f*, 460*f*, 461*f*
    personality disorders, 473–476, 473*f*
    prevalence of, 476, 477*t*
    schizophrenia (*See* schizophrenia)
    stigma in, 476–479
    suicide and, 459–461, 460*f*, 461*f*
    theoretical approaches to, 443–444

psychological research. *See* research
psychologists, types and training of, 490*f*
psychology, 2. *See also* research
approaches to, 8–13
cognitive, 245
developmental, 127–128, 279
evaluating media reports of, 37–39
frame of mind in, 3–4
gestalt, 104, 104*f*
health, 513–541
in historical perspective, 6–8, 6*f*, 7*f*
individual, 368–369
mind–body link, 39–40
research types in, 17–27, 21*f*
as the science of all human behavior, 4–6
scientific method in, 13–16, 14*f*
settings for psychologists, 4*f*
social (*See* social psychology)
specialization summary, 12*f*
psychoneuroimmunology, **527**–528, 528*f*
psychopaths, 474–475
psychosurgery, **488**–489
psychotherapy, **490**–501
behavior therapies, 494–495, 494*f*, 495*f*, 500*f*
cognitive therapies, 495–499, 498*f*, 500*f*
effectiveness of, 506–509, 507*f*, 508*f*
humanistic therapies, 493–494, 500*f*
integrative therapies, 500–501
mental health professionals using, 490–491, 490*f*
psychoanalysis, 10, 362–363, **491**–492
PTSD (post-traumatic stress disorder), **452**–454
puberty, **289**, 289*f*
public health, 514
punishment, **185**–187, 186*f*, 189
pupil, 98, 98*f*
purity, of wavelengths, 96
purposive behavior, 190–191
puzzle boxes, 179*f*

**Q**

quasi-experimental design, 22, 25

**R**

racism, 262, 430–431
random assignment, **23**
random sample, **30**
rape myth, 416
RAS (reticular activation system) theory, 388–389, 388*f*
rational-emotive behavior therapy (REBT), **496**, 498
ratio schedules, 183
Raven Progressive Matrices, 258, 258*f*
reaction formation, 365, 367*f*
reality principle, 364
reality TV, 1
reasoning, **249**
inductive and deductive, 249–250, 249*f*
memory and, 274
moral, 315–317
spatial, 269
REBT (rational-emotive behavior therapy), **496**, 498
recall, 222. *See also* memory retrieval
recency effect, 220–221, 221*f*
reciprocal determinism, 383–384
reciprocity, altruism and, 410
recognition, 222
redemptive stories, 237
referential thinking, **469**
reflective speech, **493**
reflexes, 169–170, 286, 286*f*
refractory period, 331
rehearsal, in memory storage, 209, 236

reinforcement, **180**
definition of, 180–181
immediate and delayed, 185–187
in observational learning, 189
positive and negative, 181–182, 181*f*, 186*f*
punishment and, 185–187
reinforcer types, 182
schedules of, 183–184, 185*f*
timing of, 185–187
vicarious, 189
reinforcement sensitivity theory, 389, 389*f*
reinforcers, 180, 182
relapse, **518**
relatedness, as need, 342
relational aggression, **416**
relationships, close. *See also* marriage
attachment and, 435–436
attraction in, 434–435
benefits of, 520–522
couples therapy, 502–503
love in, 436
models of, 436–437
reliability, of tests, 16, **257**, 257*f*
religions, altruism and, 411, 411*f*
religious faith, 523
Remeron (mertazapine), 484
reminiscence bump, 223
REM (rapid eye movement) sleep, 137*f*, **138**, 138*f*
representativeness heuristic, 251*f*, **252**–253
repressed memories, 225–227
repression, 364
rescue dogs, 166
research
animal, 36
applications of, 27, 27*f*
correlational, 20–23, 21*f*, 27*f*
cross-cultural, 11
cross-sectional design, 279
descriptive, 17–20, 27*f*
empirical, 14*f*, 15–16
ethics guidelines for, 33–36
experimental, 23–27, 27*f*
interpreting media reports on, 37–39
longitudinal designs, 22–23
random assignment in, 23
sample in, 29–30
setting for, 30, 32
split-brain, 67–70, 69*f*
third variable problem, 21–23
values and, 36–37
research participant bias, 26–27
resilience, **281**, 320, 355
resistance, **492**
respondent behavior, 177
resting potential, **50**, 50*f*
retention, in observational learning, 189
reticular activation system (RAS) theory, 388–389, 388*f*
reticular formation, **61**
daily rhythms and, 133, 134*f*
location and function of, 60*f*, 61, 134*f*
personality and, 388–389, 388*f*
sleep stages and, 138–139
retina, **98**–99, 98*f*, 99*f*
retrieval. *See* memory retrieval
retrieval cues, 221–223, 222*f*, 233
retroactive interference, **232**–233, 232*f*
retrograde amnesia, **234**
retrospective memory, 219, **233**
reuptake, of neurotransmitters, 53
reward pathway, 147, 147*f*, 464, 488
right-brained people, 70
right hemisphere functions, 68–70, 69*f*. *See also* hemispheres
risks, 254
risky shift, **426**–427
Risperdal (risperidone), 486–487
rods, 98–**99**, 99*f*, 100*f*
Rogerian therapy, 371–372, 371*f*, 493–494

role models, 189
romantic love, **436**
rooting reflex, 286*f*
Rorschach inkblot test, **394**–395
rotational illusion, 108*f*
rumination, 458

**S**

safe sex, 149, 539–540
salt, 119
Samburu people, 411*f*
same-sex marriage, 339
sample, in research, **29**–30
satiety, 328
Satisfaction with Life Scale (SWLS), 15, 19, 321
saturation, of visual stimulus, 96, 97*f*
scaffolding, 299
scapegoat conditioned stimulus, 175
scatter plots, 20, 21*f*
schedules of reinforcement, 183–184, 185*f*
schemas, **216**
in cognitive development, 294
in gender roles, 313
memory and, 216
schizophrenia, **468**
causes of, 470–472, 470*f*
dopamine in, 54
experiences in, 440
stigma of, 476–477
suicide and, 468
symptoms of, 468–470
treatment of, 485, 487*f*
schools. *See* education
science, **2**
scientific method, 13–16, 14*f*
scientific theory, **14**
sclera, 96, 98*f*
SCN (suprachiasmatic nucleus), **133**, 134*f*
scripts, **216**, 217*f*, 332
sea slugs, memory in, 218
sea urchins, 118
Seconal, 151
secondary appraisal, 531
secondary reinforcers, **182**
secondhand smoke, 538
second impact syndrome, 74
secure attachment, **303**–304, **435**–436
seeing. *See* visual system
seizures, anticipated by service dogs, 194
selective attention, **93**, 203
selective breeding, 78
selective disobedience, 183
selective optimization with compensation, 291
selective serotonin reuptake inhibitors (SSRIs), 484, 484*f*
self-actualization, **340**, 340*f*, 370–371
self-awareness, 132
self-concept, Rogers on, 372
self-determination theory, 16, **342**–343, 372–373, 520
self-efficacy, **384**
Bandura on, 384
in cognitive-behavior therapy, 499
control and, 384
eating disorders and, 463
positive life changes and, 524–525
in self-determination theory, 342
self-esteem, 404–405
self-fulfilling prophecies, 402
self-help support groups, 503
self-instructional methods, 499
self-perception theory, **407**, 408*f*
self-reference, 205, 205*f*
self-regulation, 302, **344**–345
self-report tests, 263, **392**–393
self-serving bias, **405**
semantic memory, **213**–214, 213*f*
semantics, **267**
semicircular canals, 110*f*, **121**, 121*f*
semipermeable membranes, 50

sensation, **85**. *See also* perception
bottom-up and top-down processing, 86
brain and, 65–67, 66*f*, 87–89, 87*f*, 88*f*
hypnosis and, 158–159
information flow in, 87–89, 88*f*
kinesthetic senses, 121–122
memory and, 121
noise in, 91
in phantom limb pain, 88
purposes of, 84, 85, 86–87
sensory adaptation, 95
thresholds in, 51, 89–93, 89*f*, 90*f*
vestibular sense, 121–122, 121*f*
sensorimotor stage, **295**, 295*f*
sensory adaptation, **95**
sensory memory, **207**–208, 207*f*, 208*f*
sensory receptors, 65–67, 66*f*, **87**–89, 87*f*, 88*f*
September 11, 2001 terrorist attacks, 224, 355, 427
serial position effect, **220**–221, 221*f*
serotonin
aggression and, 413
bipolar disorder and, 459
depression and, 456, 484, 484*f*, 485
eating disorders and, 463
functions and pathways of, 54, 54*f*
hunger and, 329
memory and, 218
neuroticism and, 389–390
psychoactive drugs and, 153, 154, 154*f*, 155
sleep and, 139
social phobia and, 451
suicide and, 460
service dogs, 194
set point, **330**, 356
sex and sexuality
alcohol and, 149
attitudes and practices, 333–336, 335*f*
biology of, 330–331
cognitive and sensory/perceptual factors in, 332
cultural factors in, 332–333
education, 333
Freud on, 363
gender differences in attitudes, 336, 337
genetic influences in, 338–339
human sexual response pattern, 331
oral, 334, 335*f*, 336
preventing unwanted pregnancies, 333
same-sex attraction, 365
sexually transmitted infections and, 285, 333
sexual orientation, 336, 338–339
sex hormones. *See also* estrogens
estrogens, 289, 291, 331
sex drive and, 331
testosterone, 285, 289, 331, 413–414, 474
sexual abuse. *See* child sexual abuse
sexual harassment, **432**
sexually transmitted infections (STIs), 285, 333, **539**–540
sexual orientation, **336**, 338–339, 365
sexual scripts, 332
shape constancy, 107, 107*f*
shape perception, 103–104, 104*f*
shaping, **180**, 180*f*
shift work, sleep and, 134
shock therapy, 487–488
short-term memory, **208**–211, 210*f*
SIDS (sudden infant death syndrome), 143
signal detection theory, **92**–93, 93*f*
similarity, 104*f*, 434
single research studies, 38
situationism, 385
six-matchstick problem, 249*f*, 275*f*
size constancy, 107, 107*f*
skepticism, in psychology, 3
skin conductance level (SCL), 346–347
Skinner box, 179–180, 180*f*

skin senses, 114–117, 115*f*
sleep, **133**. *See also* dreams
  amount needed by animals, 135*f*
  biological rhythms and, 133–135, 134*f*
  brain and, 138–139
  cycling, 138, 139*f*
  deprivation of, 136
  disease and, 141
  disorders, 141–143
  functions of, 135, 135*f*
  neurotransmitters and, 54
  REM, 137*f*, 138, 138*f*
  stages of, 137–139, 137*f*, 139*f*
  subconscious awareness during, 131
  throughout the life span, 139–140, 140*f*
  wakefulness stages and, 136–137
sleep apnea, 143
sleep driving, 142
sleep eating, 142
sleep spindles, 137*f*, 138
sleep talking, 138, 142
sleepwalking, 138, 141–142
slow pathway, for pain perception, 117
smell, 90*f*, 118–120, 120*f*
"smelly T-shirt" paradigm, 120
smiling, 272*f*
smoking. *See* tobacco
snakes, fear of, 450
social behavior, 409–418
social bonding, memory and, 237
social cognition, 401–409, 408*f*. *See also*
  social psychology
social cognitive perspectives, **383**
  Bandura's social cognitive theory,
    383–384, 383*f*
  evaluation of, 387
  on hypnosis, **159**
  on personality, 383–387
social comparison, **405**–406
social conservatism, intelligence and,
  262–263
social construction, dissociative identity
  as, 467
social contagion, **425**
social desirability, 392
social exchange theory, **436**–437
social facilitation, **426**
social identity, **428**–429, 429*f*
social identity theory, **429**
social loafing, **426**
social media, cries for help in, 482
social movements, 400
social phobia, 451
social psychology, 400–437, **401**
  aggression and, 412–418
  altruism and, 10, 410–412
  attachment and, 317, 435–436
  attitudes and, 406–409, 408*f*
  attraction and, 434–435
  attribution theory and, 403, 403*f*
  bystander effect and, 412
  close relationships and, 434–437
  cognitive dissonance theory and,
    406–407, 408*f*
  conformity and, 418–425, 419*f*,
    422*f*, 423*f*
  culture and, 28
  first impressions and, 402–403
  group identity and, 428–429, 429*f*
  group influence and, 425–427
  heuristics in social information
    processing, 404
  intergroup relations and, 428–433
  love and, 436
  obedience and, 422–425, 422*f*, 423*f*
  perception and, 116
  personal control and, 424–425
  person perception and, 401–403
  persuasion and, 407–409
  prejudice and, 430–432
  relationship models in, 436–437
  self as a social object and, 404–406
  self-perception theory and, 407, 408*f*
  social behavior and, 409–418

social influence and, 418–427, 419*f*,
  422*f*, 423*f*
suicide bombers and, 341
social role view of gender, 435
social support, 520–522, **521**
sociocultural approach, **11**, 368, 368*f*, 443
socioeconomic status, 457
socioemotional development
  in adolescence, 289
  in adulthood, 309–311
  divorce and, 310
  Erikson's theory of, 304*f*–305*f*,
    305–311, 307*f*
  gender development and, 313–314
  infant attachment in, 303–305, 303*f*
  moral, 316–317
  parenting styles and, 306–307
  prosocial behavior, 316–317
  temperament in, 302–303, 304
socioemotional selectivity theory, 311
sodium ions, 50, 51*f*
soldiers, PTSD in, 453–454
somatic nervous system, **45**, 45*f*
somatosensory cortex, 64*f*, **65**–67, 66*f*
somnambulism, 141–142
somniloquy, 142
sound, 109, 110*f*. *See also* auditory
  system
sound shadow, 113–114, 114*f*
spatial relationships, culture and, 269
speech, 67–69, 67*f*, 69*f*, 271
spina bifida, 285
split-brain research, 67–70, 69*f*. *See also*
  hemispheres
splitting, 475
spontaneous recovery, **172**–173, 172*f*
SSRIs (selective serotonin reuptake
  inhibitors), 484, 484*f*
stages of change model, **516**–519, 517*f*
stages of sleep, 137–139, 137*f*, 139*f*
standardization of tests, **257**, 257*f*
Stanford-Binet intelligence test,
  258, 258*f*
Stanford prison experiment, 423–424
startle reflex, 286*f*
statistics, in data analysis, 16, 91
stem cells, **75**–76
stereotypes, **402**, 404, 432
stereotype threat, **405**
Sternberg's triarchic theory, 265–266
stick problem, 191–192
"sticky mittens," 287, 287*f*
stigma of psychological disorders,
  476–479
stimulants, **151**–154, 152*f*, 154*f*, 156*f*.
  *See also* psychoactive drugs
stirrup, 110*f*, 111, 111*f*
STIs (sexually transmitted infections),
  285, 333, **539**–540
storage. *See* memory storage
strange situation test, 303–304
stream of consciousness, 7, **126**
stress, **46**
  acute *vs.* chronic, 46, 527, 528, 528*f*
  aging and, 292
  cancer and, 530
  cardiovascular disease and, 529
  cognitive appraisal and, 530–531
  coping strategies for, 531–532, 532*f*
  corticosteroid release and, 46
  disease and, 529, 530, 532, 532*f*
  dissociative disorders and, 465
  general adaptation syndrome and,
    527, 527*f*
  hypothalamus and, 527, 528
  immune system and, 527–528,
    528*f*, 530
  meditation and, 161
  oxytocin and, 55
  physiological reaction to, 527
  schizophrenia and, 472
  sympathetic nervous system and, 46
  traumatic memories and, 225
stress hormones, 46, 225, 292

stress management programs, **532**–533
stressors, 46
stress response, 46
strip malls, conformity in, 420
stroke, 64, 141
structuralism, **6**–7, 8
  studying, 235–237
Study of Mathematically Precocious
  Youth (SMPY), 262
subconscious awareness, 130–131
subgoaling, 247
subjective well-being, **377**–378
sublimation, 364–365, 367*f*
subliminal perception, **92**–93, 93*f*
substance abuse. *See* psychoactive
  drugs
substance P, 456
substitution of function, 73
success, explaining reasons for, 28
sudden infant death syndrome
  (SIDS), 143
suicide
  antidepressants and, 486
  borderline personality disorder
    and, 475
  by children and adolescents,
    460–461, 461*f*
  factors in, 460–461
  prevention of, 482
  schizophrenia and, 468
  statistics on, 460
  what to do, 460*f*
suicide bombers, 341
superego, 363*f*, **364**
*Super Size Me*, 517
support groups, 503
suprachiasmatic nucleus (SCN), **133**, 134*f*
surveys, 18
sustained attention, 203
SWLS (Satisfaction with Life Scale),
  15, 19, 321
sympathetic nervous system (SNS), **46**
  arousal and, 46, 346, 346*f*
  learned associations and, 184
  structure of, 45*f*, 46
synaesthesia, 88
synapses, **51**
  development of, 288, 288*f*
  structure of, 51–53, 52*f*
synaptic density, 288, 288*f*
synaptic gap, 51–52, 52*f*
synaptic vesicle, 52*f*
synchronous waves, 137
syntax, 267
syphilis, 285, 540
systematic desensitization, **494**, 494*f*

**T**

tardive dyskinesia, 485–486
task-oriented cooperation, 433
taste
  absolute threshold in, 90*f*
  age and, 291
  salt and, 119
  tongue and, 118
taste aversion learning, 174–175,
  175*f*, 195
TAT (Thematic Apperception Test), 381,
  **395**–396
TBI (traumatic brain injury), 42, 65, 65*f*,
  73–75
tectorial membrane, 111*f*, 112
telepathy, 89
television, 1, 415–416
telomerase, 292
telomeres, 292, 292*f*
temperament, development of,
  **302**–303, 304
temperature, perception of, 115,
  115*f*, 116
temporal lobes, **65**
  auditory processing in, 89
  fusiform face area in, 58

location and function of, 64*f*, 65
  memory and, 219, 219*f*
  sexual behavior and, 331
"tend and befriend" response, 55
teratogens, 285
terminal buttons, 52, 52*f*
"Termites," 261–262
terrorists, 341
terror management theory (TMT),
  318–319, 341
testes, **72**, 72*f*
testosterone
  in adolescence, 289
  aggression and, 413–414
  antisocial personality disorder
    and, 474
  sexual response and, 331
tetracyclic antidepressants, 484
texting, 94, 497
texture gradient, 106, 106*f*
thalamus, **62**
  emotion and, 348, 348*f*
  location and function of, 60*f*, 62
  pain and, 88, 117
  sensory signals and, 88, 101*f*
  sleep deprivation and, 136
  touch and, 115
THC, 154
Thematic Apperception Test (TAT),
  381, **395**–396
theory, **14**
theory of mind, 127–129
theory of mind mechanism (TOMM),
  128–129
theory of planned behavior, **516**
theory of reasoned action, **516**
therapeutic alliance, **509**
therapies, 482–509
  behavior, 494–495, 494*f*, 495*f*, 500*f*
  client factors in, 509
  cognitive, 495–499, 498*f*, 500*f*
  cognitive-behavior therapy, 499, 505
  community mental health and, 504
  comparison of, 500*f*
  couples, 502–503
  cultural perspectives on, 504–506
  cybertherapy, 497
  dialectical behavior, 500
  drug, 483–487, 484*f*, 487*f*, 500
  effectiveness of psychotherapy,
    506–509, 507*f*, 508*f*
  electroconvulsive, 487–488
  ethnicity and, 505, 506
  family, 502, 504
  gender and, 506
  group, 501–502
  humanistic, 493–494, 500*f*
  integrative, 500–501
  psychodynamic, 491–493, 500*f*
  psychosurgery, 488–489
  for quitting smoking, 538
  self-help support groups, 503
  therapeutic alliance, 509
  well-being, 508–509
thermoreceptors, **115**, 115*f*
theta waves, 137, 138
thinking, **245**. *See also* cognition
  biases and heuristics, 251–253, 251*f*
  concepts, 245–246
  creative, 254–255
  critical, 3, 253–254, 255
  decision making, 250–253, 251*f*
  divergent *vs.* convergent, 254
  fixation and, 248, 248*f*, 249*f*
  intuitive *vs.* analytical, 250–251
  moods and, 456
  primacy of emotion *vs.*, 349–350
  problem solving, 246–248, 248*f*, 249*f*
  reasoning, 249–250, 249*f*
third variable problem, **21**–23
Thorndike's law of effect, 178–179, 179*f*
thought disorder, 469
*The Three Faces of Eve*, 467, 467*f*
thresholds, 51, 89–93, 89*f*, 90*f*

thyroid gland, 72f
timbre, 109–110, 110f
tip-of-the-tongue (TOT) phenomenon, 233
TMT (terror management theory), 318–319, 341
tobacco
    deaths from, 538
    nicotine in, 152–153, 152f, 153f, 156f
    operant conditioning and, 187
    smoking cessation, 538–539, 538f
toe curling reflex, 286f
token economy, 182
tolerance, for drugs, 147
TOMM (theory of mind mechanism), 128–129
tongue, 118
top-down processing, 86, 99
TOT (tip-of-the-tongue) phenomenon, 233
touch, 90f, 115, 116, 272f
toy design, 298
trait theories, 373
    Allport and Odbert on, 373–374
    big five factors of personality, 374–378, 375f, 379, 393
    CAPS theory, 386–387
    evaluation of, 378
    Mischel's critique of consistency in, 385
    obesity and, 379
    subjective well-being and, 377–378
    traits vs. states, 378
tranquilizers, 151, 156f, 483–484
transcendence, 518
transcranial magnetic stimulation (TMS), 59
transference, 492
traumatic brain injury (TBI), 42, 65, 65f, 73–75
traumatic events, memory for, 225–227
triarchic theory of intelligence, 265–266
trichromatic theory, 102–103, 103f
tricyclic drugs, 484
trust vs. mistrust, 304f, 306
twin studies
    behavioral genetics and, 78–79, 79f
    on bipolar disease, 459, 459f
    identical vs. fraternal twins in, 78–79

on personality, 390
on sexual orientation, 339
two-factor theory of emotion, 349
tympanic membrane (eardrum), 110f, 111
Type A behavior pattern, 529
Type B behavior pattern, 529
Type D behavior pattern, 529

U

umami, 118, 127
unconditional positive regard, 371–372, 493
unconditioned response (UCR), 170, 177f
unconditioned stimulus (UCS), 170, 171–172, 172f, 191
unconscious, 131–132
unconscious thought, 131
United Nations, resolution on happiness, 31
Utku culture, 352

V

valence of emotion, 354, 354f
validity, 25, 256
    criterion, 256
    external, 25
    face, 393
    internal, 25
    of tests, 256, 257f
Valium, 151, 483
values, in psychological research, 36–37
variable-interval schedules, 183–184, 185f
variable-ratio schedules, 183–184, 185f
variables, 13–14, 24
ventral tegmental area (VTA), 147, 148, 154f, 420
ventromedial hypothalamus, 329
vestibular sense, 121–122, 121f
veterans, 88, 453, 454
vicarious punishment, 189
vicarious reinforcement, 189
video games, violence in, 417
vigilance, 203
violence, 415–416, 417. See also aggression

virtual lesions, 59
vision. See visual system
visual cortex, 100
    emotion and, 348, 348f
    location and function of, 64, 64f
    visual processing and, 100–101, 101f
visual system, 96–108
    absolute threshold in, 90f
    age changes in, 291
    binding, 101
    blind spot, 99, 99f, 100f
    brain processing and, 69–70, 69f, 89, 100–101, 101f
    color vision, 99, 102–103, 102f, 103f
    depth perception, 104–106, 105f, 106f
    eye structure, 96, 98–99, 98f, 99f, 100f
    light, 96, 97f
    motion perception, 106
    parallel processing, 101
    perceptual constancy, 106–107, 107f, 108f
    in predators vs. prey, 86f, 87
    shape perception, 103–104, 104f
visuo-spatial working memory, 210f, 211
volley principle, 113
VTA (ventral tegmental area), 147, 148, 154f, 420
vulnerable populations, ethical research on, 36

W

wakefulness stages, 136–137. See also sleep
waking subconscious awareness, 131
war, wounds of, 88, 453, 454
wavelength, 96, 97f, 109
Weber's law, 92
weight loss. See also obesity
    community support for, 513
    diet and, 536–537
    physical activity and, 535, 536
    stages of change model and, 516–518, 517f
well-being, 57, 377–378, 508–509
well-being therapy (WBT), 509

wellness programs, meditation in, 160–163
Wernicke's area, 67–68, 67f, 271
White Americans, 461, 461f, 462
Whorf's linguistic relativity hypothesis, 268–270
Williams syndrome, 270
windigo, 443
wisdom, 301
withdrawal symptoms, 147, 151–152
within-participant design, 24–25
women and girls. See also gender differences
    co-rumination by girls, 458
    depression in, 457
    eating disorders in, 462–463
    gender roles of, 313–314
    menarche in, 289
    menopause in, 291
    pregnancy in, 333, 334f
    relational aggression and, 416
    sexual behavior, 336, 337
    stress and, 55
    testosterone in, 331
word salad, 469
working memory, 209–211, 210f, 221
workplaces, 134, 162, 255
writing about trauma, 521, 521f
Wundt, Wilhelm, founding of psychology by, 6–7, 6f

X

X (Ecstasy), 154, 156f
Xanax, 151, 483
X rays, 57
XTC, 154, 156f

Y

Y chromosome, 312
Yerkes-Dodson law, 327

Z

Zoloft, 484
Zyban, 538–539
zygotes, 284